The Management of the National Debt of the United Kingdom, 1900–1932

I0894811

This is a most impressive piece of work. The research has clearly been exemplary, both wide and deep, and the prose is lucid... this is a book which will immediately establish itself as indispensible.

Kathleen Burk
Professor of Modern and Contemporary History
University College London

This pioneering work describes and analyses how the National Debt of the United Kingdom was managed between the Boer War (1899–1902) and the Great Depression at the beginning of the 1930s. It traces how the Debt's managers in the Treasury and Bank of England adapted their techniques to make possible the tenfold expansion o the Debt during during the Great War of 1914–18. The domestic developments are explained alongside those in external finance: British borrowing in the US, Canada, Japan and the markets of neutral countries.

Part I looks at the Victorian and Edwardian background to the National Debt. Jeremy Wormell outlines the legal structures and institutional arrangements of nineteenth-century debt management: the nature of the securities, the role of the savings banks, the method of issuing and the Byzantine arrangements for the sinking funds. The book goes on to examine borrowing for the Boer War and how the legacy was brought under control in the following ten years.

Part II shows how the terms of the Treasury's borrowing changed during the Great War and describes how the securities were sold and distributed. Once the US had become a belligerent, the UK became a debtor to the US Treasury, and the author describes the legal, political and personal constraints which produced the Anglo-American contribution to the inter-allied debt problem.

Part III shows how the debt to the US Treasury was funded into long-term bonds and discusses the terms in the context of the reparations crisis of 1922 and 1923. Internally, the author discusses the relationship of debt management to monetary control and how the short-term and expensive debt inherited from the war was repaid, converted, refinanced and refunded in the decade following the Armistice.

The Management of the National Debt of the United Kingdom is the first definitive work on the subject. Using an impressive array of research, from archives and unpublished material. Jeremy Wormell has brought together material that is unavailable in any other form. It will be an invaluable resource for political and economic historians, as well as economists in general, civil servants, bankers and financial journalists.

Jeremy Wormell worked in the gilt-edged market in London. His previous publications on the fixed-interest markets have been *The Gilt-edged Market* (1985), *The Gilt-edged Market Compendium* (1989) and *National Debt in Britain 1850–1930* (1999).

Routledge Explorations in Economic History

1 **Economic Ideas and Government Policy**
Contributions to contemporary economic history
Sir Alec Cairncross

2 **The Organization of Labour Markets**
Modernity, culture and governance in Germany, Sweden, Britain and Japan
Bo Stråth

3 **Currency Convertibility**
The gold standard and beyond
Edited by Jorge Braga de Macedo, Barry Eichengreen and Jaime Reis

4 **Britain's Place in the World**
A historical enquiry into import controls 1945–1960
Alan S. Milward and George Brennan

5 **France and the International Economy**
From Vichy to the Treaty of Rome
Frances M. B. Lynch

6 **Monetary Standards and Exchange Rates**
M. C. Marcuzzo, L. Officer and A. Rosselli

7 **Production Efficiency in Domesday England, 1086**
John McDonald

8 **Free Trade and its Reception 1815–1960**
Freedom and trade: Volume I
Edited by Andrew Marrison

9 **Conceiving Companies**
Joint-stock politics in Victorian England
Timothy L. Alborn

10 The British Industrial Decline Reconsidered
Edited by Jean-Pierre Dormois and Michael Dintenfass

11 The Conservatives and Industrial Efficiency 1951–1964
Thirteen Wasted Years?
Nick Tiratsoo and Jim Tomlinson

12 Pacific Centuries
Pacific and Pacific Rim economic history since the 16th century
Edited by Dennis O. Flynn, Lionel Frost and A. J. H. Latham

13 The Premodern Chinese Economy
Structural equilibrium and capitalist sterility
Gang Deng

14 The Role of Banks in Monitoring Firms
The case of the Crédit Mobilier
Elisabeth Paulet

15 The Management of the National Debt of the United Kingdom 1900–1932
Jeremy Wormell

16 An Economic History of Sweden
Lars Magnusson

The Management of the National Debt of the United Kingdom, 1900–1932

Jeremy Wormell

Routledge
Taylor & Francis Group
LONDON AND NEW YORK

First published 2000
by Routledge
2 Park Square, Milton Park, Abingdon, Oxfordshire OX14 4RN

Simultaneously published in the USA and Canada
by Routledge
711 Third Avenue, New York, NY 10017

First issued in paperback 2016

Routledge is an imprint of the Taylor and Francis Group, an informa business

Typeset in Times by
Prepress Projects, Perth, Scotland

British Library Cataloguing in Publication Data
A catalogue record for this book is available
from the British Library

Library of Congress Cataloging in Publication Data
Wormell, Jeremy.
The management of the national debt in the United Kingdom, 1930–1932 / Jeremy Wormell.
p. cm. – (Routledge explorations in economic history)
Includes bibliographical references and index.
1. Debts, Public – Great Britain – History. 2. Debts, Public – Great Britain – History – Sources. I. Title. II. Series.
HJ8627.W63 1999
336.3'43341–dc21 99-31077
CIP

ISBN 13: 978-1-138-99555-0 (pbk)
ISBN 13: 978-0-415-21724-8 (hbk)

Contents

Illustrations

Tables

Figures

Glossary

These explanations relate to the meaning of terms between 1900 and 1932. They are described in the past tense, even if their meanings have not changed. Terms which are explained in the text or notes are not included.

acceptance A **bill of exchange** signed with a promise to pay on maturity by the bank or acceptance house on whom it was drawn.[a]

Account The period during which transactions were not settled, but carried forward to be settled on a single day, known as the Account Day.

accrued interest The amount that would have been paid if interest were payable daily. It was included in the price of the security except in the case of **shorts**, in which it was accounted for separately. It was calculated (even in a leap year) on the basis of a 365-day year.

assented, non-assented Securities in which their holders have accepted/not accepted an option to convert into another security. The securities were traded assented and non-assented.

authorities Used anachronistically. The Treasury, Bank of England and relevant ministers who were responsible for the conduct of monetary policy and managing the Debt.

bear Used of someone who had sold. Used by investors when they had sold securities they owned; in this case, they were 'covered bears'. Also used when someone had sold securities they did not own ('uncovered bears') or someone who believed that the price of a security, or securities generally, was going to fall.

bill of exchange This was an unconditional order in writing, addressed by one person to another, signed by the person giving it, requiring the person to whom it was addressed to pay, on demand or at a fixed or determinable future time, a sum of money to, or to the order of, a specified person or to bearer.[b]

Bonds See Appendix I.

book A jobber's, issuer's, trader's or investor's inventory of marketable assets and liabilities.

a Gillett Brothers Discount Company Ltd (1976), p. 22.

b Ibid., p. 15.

broker An intermediary, or agent, who acts for a buyer or a seller of securities.

call (1) The capital sum, payable on a day specified in the prospectus, **on a partly paid** issue; (2) the right, provided for in the prospectus, for the Treasury to buy (repay) the securities at a predetermined price, on a specified day or days, or between two dates.

clean The price of a medium-, long-dated or **perpetual gilt-edged** security after deducting the **accrued interest**.

Committee of Treasury The senior Committee of the Court of Directors of the Bank of England.[c]

Consolidated Fund Under the Exchequer and Audit Departments Act 1866, the revenues of the government were paid into the Exchequer account at the Banks of England and Ireland. The monies standing to the credit of the account were the Consolidated Fund.

coupon A piece of paper attached to the back of a **Bond** which had to be presented to the paying agent when the holder demanded payment of interest. Hence, it was used as shorthand for the nominal rate of interest on a security. The sheet of paper comprising the coupons was known as a talon.

Court of the Bank of England The Governor, Deputy Governor and twenty-four directors of the Bank of England, a privately owned joint stock company operating under Royal Charter.[d]

discount The amount by which a security stood beneath its **par** value. It could also mean the amount by which it stood beneath its issue price.

double-dated A security where the borrower had the right to repay, or **call,** it between two dates. The borrower could not call for repayment before the first date, and was compelled to repay at the last date. See **maturity**.

flat yield See **running yield**.

floating debt In the late nineteenth century, sometimes used to describe all the Debt which was not **funded**. By the 1920s, it was used to describe Ways and Means Advances and Treasury Bills.

funding (1) To replace shorter-dated debt with longer-dated debt, with the implication, in the 1920s, that the shorter debt is **floating debt** or debt nearing **maturity**; (2) during the debt negotiations with the US Treasury and Funding Commission: to convert the British demand obligations into longer-term **Notes** or **Bonds**.

funded debt See **perpetual debt**.

gilt-edged market The **secondary market** in British government sterling securities. The term excluded Treasury Bills, which were not quoted on the London Stock Exchange.

gilt-edged security/issue Marketable British government sterling security. The term excluded Treasury Bills.

gross Before tax had been paid or deducted.

Gross Redemption Yield (GRY) The standard method of calculating the value

c Sayers (1976), I, p. xxii.

d Sayers (1976), I, p. xxi.

of a dated fixed-interest security. It was 'the rate of interest at which the value of the interest payments discounted to the present time plus the value of the redemption proceeds discounted to the present time equal the price.'[e] If the security was **double-dated**, the GRY was calculated on the first date if the price stood at a **premium**, and to the last date if it stood at a **discount**. **Perpetual** issues standing at a **premium** were valued by calculating the GRY to the first date on which the Treasury could **call** the issue.

income yield See **running yield**.

jobber An individual or partnership which stood ready to buy and sell securities on a Stock Exchange.

lists close The date and time when the Bank(s) of England (and Ireland) ceased to accept applications for a new issue. The latest time was specified in the prospectus, but the Bank(s) could close the list earlier if the issue had been fully subscribed.

lists open The date and time, specified in the prospectus, when the Bank(s) of England (and Ireland) began to receive applications for a new issue.

liquid market A market was said to be liquid, or 'good', when large amounts could be bought or sold on narrow differences (or spreads) between the buying and selling prices. The opposites were illiquid, narrow, thin.

long Used generally to describe dated **gilt-edged** securities with a remaining life to maturity, or first **redemption** date, of many, but an unspecified number of years. Later, more precisely, a **gilt-edged security** with a remaining life to its **redemption** date (if the price was above **par**) or to **maturity** (if its price was beneath **par**), of more than ten, or more than fifteen, years from the date of dealing.

maturity The date on which a borrower was contracted to repay a security. The price was usually **par**, but in the case of National War Bonds it was at a premium.

medium Used anachronistically. Gilt-edged securities with a remaining life of more than five, and less than ten or fifteen, years to maturity, or to final redemption date, from the date of dealing.

net After tax had been paid or deducted.

Net Redemption Yield The **GRY** after the relevant amounts of tax had been deducted.

nominal (1) The nominal value of the National Debt was the sum of the nominal values of the individual securities which comprised the liabilities of the **Consolidated Fund**; (2) the nominal value of a holding fixed an investor's share in an issue and was the unit on which the **redemption** and interest payments were based.

paid up A security on which the **calls** had been paid.

paper A general term for marketable financial assets.

par The **nominal** or face value. Normally £100, but with new issues it could refer to the issue price.

e Day and Jamieson (1980), II, p. 28.

partly-paid Securities on which there is a liability to pay a **call**, or **calls**, of a specified amount on a specified day.

perpetual debt Also known as perpetual annuities, permanent debt, funded debt or, incorrectly, irredeemable **Stock** or **Bonds**. Debt for which the **Consolidated Fund** had the liability to pay the interest, but no liability to repay the capital. The Treasury always retained the option to **call** the issue for repayment after a protected period. Hence, the securities were neither 'irredeemable' nor 'undated'.

place/pre-place Selling securities before offering them to the public.

premium The amount by which a security stood above its **par** value. It could also refer to the amount by which it stood above its issue price.

primary market The original sale by a borrower or his/her agent.

prospectus The document, published at the time of an issue of securities, which contained the terms and conditions governing the contractual relationship between the borrower and the lender.

put The right to sell securities at a predetermined price.

redemption The act of repaying a security, with the implication that it had been **called** before the last date on which the borrower was contracted to repay. See **maturity**.

running yield The income provided by the interest payment or **coupon** payable each year stated as a percentage return on the price paid per £100 nominal. In the case of **perpetual** securities and dated securities with remaining lives of more than five years, the **clean** price was used. Also known as flat yield or income yield. See **yield**.

secondary market The market in existing securities.

shorts Issues with remaining lives of five years or less from the date of dealing.

Stock see Appendix I.

tender A sale of securities where the price was not fixed by the borrower, but determined by the prices bid by investors. It could mean the Treasury asked for bids for a pre-announced volume of securities or, on occasions, for an unstated volume.

turn The profit or margin on a transaction.

unfunded debt Debt for which the government had the liability to repay the capital on a definite date, or the right to repay between two definite dates, on the last of which repayment was mandatory.

volatility The change in the price of a security in response to a change in its **Gross Redemption Yield**. Volatility depended on the remaining life to **maturity** and the **coupon** or interest payment.

Votes The monies voted each year by Parliament to meet the expenditure of government departments. Also known as 'Supply Charges'.

xd Ex-dividend, or the date after which a buyer did not benefit from the payment of the interest although the payment date was still in the future. The period allowed preparation of the list of holders and the sums due to each

yield Shorthand for **running yield** in the case of **perpetual securities** and for the **Gross Redemption Yield** in the case of dated securities.

Abbreviations

AA	Automobile Association
ABI	Association of British Insurers: Minutes of the Life Offices' Association
AC	Austen Chamberlain papers
AFSC	American Foreign Securities Corporation
MS Asquith	Asquith Manuscripts
ARSF	US Department of the Treasury: *Annual Reports of the Secretary of the Treasury on the State of the Finances*
BGS	Pember & Boyle (1950)
BIS	Bank for International Settlements
BLP	Bonar Law papers
BoE	Bank of England archives
Bt.	Baronet
C$	Canadian dollar
C., Cd. and Cmd.	Command papers
Cab.	Cabinet Office papers in the PRO
CB	Companion of the Order of the Bath
CBA	The Canadian Bankers' Association
CLCB	Committee of the London Clearing Banks
CLCBm	Committee of London Clearing Banks minutes
CLCBt	Committee of London Clearing Banks, minutes of the Treasury sub-committee
CNRA	Currency Note Redemption Account
CNRIA	Currency Note Investments Reserve Account
CNRA ledgers	See Chapter 13, endnote 72
CO	Colonial Office papers in the PRO
Col(s).	Column(s)
Court Minutes	Bank of England archives, Minutes of the Bank's Court
CPR	Canadian Pacific Railway
CTM	Bank of England archives, Committee of Treasury Minutes
DBFP	Documents on British Foreign Policy
Dkr.	Danish krone
DNB	*Dictionary of National Biography*

DORA	Defence of the Realm Act
EcHR	*Economic History Review*
EEA	Exchange Equalisation Account
EHR	*English Historical Review*
E. in C.	Evidence in Chief
EJ	*The Economic Journal*
EPD	Excess Profits Duty
fl.	Dutch florin
FO	Foreign Office, and Foreign Office papers in the PRO
FOTRA	Free of Tax to Residents Abroad
FRBNY	Federal Reserve Bank of New York
FRUS	Department of State (1932): *Papers Relating to the Foreign Relations of the United States*
GCB	Knight Grand Cross of the Order of the Bath
GCMG	Knight Grand Cross of the Order of St. Michael and St. George
GNP	Gross National Product
GPO	General Post Office
Grenfell	Eddie Grenfell, Senior Resident Partner of Morgan Grenfell in London
GRO	Gloucestershire Record Office
GRY	Gross Redemption Yield
HBP	Hicks-Beach Papers
HCP	House of Commons Paper
HMG	His/Her Majesty's Government
HMSO	His/Her Majesty's Stationery Office
HR	House of Representatives
IAC	Inter-Allied Council
IMB	Imperial Munitions Board
IR	Inland Revenue papers in the PRO
IOL	India Office Library
IOU	I owe you
Issue	The Issue Department of the Bank of England
JPM	J. P. Morgan & Co., New York
KBE	Knight Commander of the Order of the British Empire
KCB	Knight Commander of the Order of the Bath
KCIE	Knight Commander of the Order of the Indian Empire
KCMG	Knight Commander of the Order of St. Michael and St. George
KG	Knight of the Order of the Garter
Kt.	Knight
LCC	London County Council
LEC	London Exchange Committee
LGP	Lloyd George Papers
MBa	HSBC group archives (including Midland Bank archives)
MG	Morgan Grenfell
MGP	Morgan Grenfell Papers, Morgan Grenfell, London

MGP/GH	Morgan Grenfell Papers, Guildhall, London
MI6	Military Intelligence
MND	Montagu Norman Diaries
MP	Member of Parliament
MWB	Metropolitan Water Board
n/a	Not available
NAC	National Archives of Canada
NDO	National Debt Office
NHI	National Health Insurance
Nkr.	Norwegian krone
NRY	Net Redemption Yield
OMIC	Open Market Investment Committee of the Federal Reserve.
Osborne	Bank of England archives; Osborne (1926)
PDO	Principal of the Discount Office Diary in BoE, C55/99
PML	Archives of the Pierpont Morgan Library
POa	Post Office archives
POR	Post Office Register
POSB	Post Office Savings Bank
PoW	Prisoner of War
PPS	Parliamentary Private Secretary
PRO	Public Record Office
pta.	Spanish peseta
RAC	Royal Automobile Club
RESD	Restriction of Enemy Supplies Department
s.	Succeeded
Skr.	Swedish krona
T	Treasury papers in the PRO
TM	Treasury Minute
TSBA	Trustee Savings Banks Association
TSBs	Trustee Savings Banks
TUC	Trades Union Congress
UK	United Kingdom of Great Britain and Ireland until 1922. Thereafter, United Kingdom of Great Britain and Northern Ireland
USA	United States of America

Issues of British government marketable sterling debt: 1900–32 (excluding Treasury Bills and War Expenditure Certificates)

Date of prospectus	*Nominal rate (per cent)*	*Security*	*Maturity/redemption*
9 March 1900	$2^3/_4$	National War Loan	5 April 1910
3 August	3	Exchequer Bonds	3 August 1903
23 November	3	Exchequer Bonds	7 December 1905
8 February 1901	3	Exchequer Bonds	7 December 1905
20 April	$2^3/_4$	Consols*	On or after 5 April 1923
16 April 1902	$2^3/_4$	Consols*	On or after 5 April 1923
24 July 1903	3	Exchequer Bonds	7 August 1904
23 July 1904	3	Exchequer Bonds	6 August 1907
30 September	3	Exchequer Bonds	14 October 1909†
12 April 1905	$2^3/_4$	Exchequer Bonds	18 April 1906–15
8 October 1909	3	Exchequer Bonds	14 October 1912†
18 March 1910	3	Exchequer Bonds	5 April 1915
1 January 1912	3	Exchequer Bonds	1 January 1930
8 October	3	Exchequer Bonds	14 October 1916†
17 November 1914	$3^1/_2$	War Loan	1 March 1925–8
5 March 1915	3	Exchequer Bonds	24 March 1920
21 June	$4^1/_2$	War Loan*	1 December 1925–45
16 December	5	Exchequer Bonds*	1 December 1920
27 May 1916	5	Exchequer Bonds	5 October 1919
	5	Exchequer Bonds*	5 October 1921
29 September	6	Exchequer Bonds*	16 February 1920
8 October	$5^1/_2$	Exchequer Bonds	14 October 1922†
11 January 1917	4	War Loan	15 October 1929–42
	5	War Loan*	1 June 1929–47
12 April	5	Exchequer Bonds*	1 October 1919/1 April 1922
1 October	4	National War Bonds	1 October 1927
	5	National War Bonds*	1 October 1922
	5	National War Bonds*	1 October 1924
	5	National War Bonds*	1 October 1927
28 January 1918	3	Exchequer Bonds	28 January 1930
28 March	4	National War Bonds	1 April 1928
	5	National War Bonds*	1 April 1923
	5	National War Bonds*	1 April 1925
	5	National War Bonds*	1 April 1928
30 September	4	National War Bonds	1 September 1928
	5	National War Bonds*	1 September 1923
	5	National War Bonds*	1 September 1925
	5	National War Bonds*	1 September 1928

31 January 1919	4	National War Bonds	1 February 1929
	5	National War Bonds*	1 February 1924
	5	National War Bonds*	1 February 1929
12 June	4	Victory Bonds*	
	4	Funding Loan*	1 May 1960–90
19 January 1920	5$^{3}/_{4}$	Exchequer Bonds*	1 February 1925
30 April	5	5–15 Year Treasury* (variable) Bonds	1 May 1925–35
26 April 1921	3$^{1}/_{2}$	Conversion Loan*	On or after 1 April 1961
11 July	5$^{1}/_{2}$	Treasury Bonds*	1 April 1929
30 November	5$^{1}/_{2}$	Treasury Bonds*	15 May 1930
21 January 1922	5	Treasury Bonds*	1 February 1927
18 February	3$^{1}/_{2}$	Conversion Loan*	On or after 1 April 1961
21 April	4$^{1}/_{2}$	Treasury Bonds*	15 April 1930–32
21 April	3$^{1}/_{2}$	Conversion Loan*	On or after 1 April 1961
8 October	4$^{3}/_{4}$	Exchequer Bonds	14 October 1926†
22 February 1923	4$^{1}/_{2}$	Treasury Bonds*	15 April 1930–32
23 March 1923	4	Treasury Bonds*	15 April 1931–3
1 April 1924	4$^{1}/_{2}$	Conversion Loan*	1 July 1940–4
15 November	4$^{1}/_{2}$	Treasury Bonds*	1 February 1934
1 January 1925	3$^{1}/_{2}$	Conversion Loan*	On or after 1 April 1961
25 March	3$^{1}/_{2}$	Conversion Loan*	On or after 1 April 1961
23 September	3$^{1}/_{2}$	Conversion Loan*	On or after 1 April 1961
29 September 1926	4$^{1}/_{2}$	Treasury Bonds*	1 February 1934
8 October	4$^{3}/_{4}$	Exchequer Bonds	4 October 1930†
29 December	4	Consolidated Loan*	On or after 1 February 1957
6 September 1927	4$^{1}/_{2}$	Treasury Bonds*	1 February 1934
15 September	3$^{1}/_{2}$	Conversion Loan*	On or after 1 April 1961
22 December	5	Treasury Bonds*	1 February 1933–5
16 August 1928	5	Treasury Bonds*	1 February 1933–5
28 November	4$^{1}/_{2}$	Treasury Bonds*	1 February 1932–4
2 November 1929	5	Conversion Loan*	1 May 1944–64
22 February 1930	4$^{1}/_{2}$	Conversion Loan*	1 July 1940–4
2 October	4	Treasury Bonds*	15 April 1934–6
8 October	4$^{3}/_{4}$	Exchequer Bonds	14 October 1934†
16 March 1932	4$^{1}/_{2}$	Conversion Loan*	1 July 1940–4
	4	Consolidated Loan*	On or after 1 February 1957
29 April	3	Treasury Bonds	15 April 1933–42
30 June	3$^{1}/_{2}$	War Loan*	On or after 1 December 1952
10 October	2	Treasury Bonds*	15 April 1935–8
3 November	3	Conversion Loan*	1 March 1948–53

Notes

The table does not include securities created to satisfy options written into the original prospectuses. Thus, it does not include 5 per cent War Loan created to satisfy those converting from National War Bonds or 3$^{1}/_{2}$ per cent Conversion and 4 per cent Consols created to satisfy those converting from shorter securities during the 1920s.

Excludes £2.6m. Exchequer Bonds issued under the Cunard Agreement (Money) Act 1904, for which no prospectuses have been found.

*Also available on the Government Stock Register or the Post Office Register.

†Issued under the Capital Expenditure (Money) Act 1904.

Notes

Pounds sterling

Prior to decimalisation in February 1971, the British currency was based on pounds (£), shillings (s) and pence (d):

£0.00417 equalled one penny
£0.05 equalled 12d, or one shilling
£0.125 equalled 30d, or half a crown
£1 equalled 240d
£1 1s 0d, or 252d, equalled one guinea.

Thus, for example, £1.625 was stated as £1 12s 6d.
$^{1}/_{4}$ d was referred to as a farthing, $^{1}/_{2}$ d as a half-penny, $^{3}/_{4}$ d as three-farthings, 6d as a tanner and 2s (24d) as a florin.

Dollars

$ refers to the US currency and C$ to the Canadian. Sometimes US$ has been used where it improves clarity.

Gross Redemption Yields

Calculation of GRYs requires that assumptions be made about the period between coupon or divident payment dates and the treatment of holidays. For this reason, those presented by the author may differ by a few pennies from those quoted from contemporary sources.

Introduction

The National Debt of the United Kingdom is unusual in combining great age with continuity. With a single exception, for 300 years it has not experienced a default, nor has it been destroyed by political upheaval or an inflation so great that it has lost all value. At the end of the twentieth century, the UK Treasury still pays £6.9m each year for the interest on 2½ per cent Consols, a marketable security that has been in existence since 1888 and is the direct and traceable descendant of debt sold to finance the European and North American wars of the eighteenth and early nineteenth centuries. Despite the damage wrought by the price inflation of two world wars and the second half of the twentieth century, Consols stands out starkly against the political disturbances and the budgetary and monetary excesses that have totally destroyed the debts of so many nations.

What do Consols teach us about British society and politics and the state whose liability they have been for nearly 250 years? Perhaps at its most banal, Consols say that the UK is a group of islands that has not been invaded or had its government overthrown and replaced by another – foreign or home-grown – with no reason to recognise its defeated predecessor's debts. At this level, the Debt's survival is explained by power – geography and natural resources, the technology to produce goods, organise people, and build and maintain defence forces – and the statesmanship and diplomacy which have ensured that the resources have been used for clear and attainable purposes; and that, when there have been lapses, they have not been mortal.

On another level, the Debt's continuity and age reflect the legitimacy that British governments have enjoyed in the eyes of their citizens: the population's willingness to offer the state service, accept the monetary and fiscal disciplines that give value to the money in which the obligations have been denominated and tolerate the extraction of the taxes that have enabled the securities to be serviced. It also shows that the distribution of the burden has been considered fair, so that the coercion and dislocation that are inseparable from all tax raising have not created such resentment that the stability of the state has been threatened and default or monetisation has become the preferred or necessary option.

When J. P. Morgan, the Treasury's American bankers, were issuing the Anglo-French Loan in New York in 1915, they coupled the citizens' willingness to recognise and pay for the Debt with their income and wealth:

> the ultimate security behind a national loan lies in the taxing power of the Government, which in turn is limited by the national wealth and the 'financial morality' of the governed; that is, the ability and willingness of the people to contribute from their private resources to sustain the nation's honour and credit. The steady accumulation of national wealth in Great Britain and France, and these nations' long record of scrupulous fidelity to their financial obligations have ranked their credit in the very forefront of the nations of the world.[1]

That was a rosy view, intended to persuade reluctant investors to subscribe to the obligations of a Britain and France at war, and, like all sales literature, it simplifies. Measuring the level of acceptable tax extraction was, and is, not just a matter of comparing the size of the Debt with some measure of income and wealth – government revenues, a nation's capital stock or Gross National Product – although historians, bankers and civil servants seeking to compare debt burdens over time or between nations have frequently done so.

The acceptable level of taxation in Britain has grown as the responsibilities British society has placed on its governments have grown. At many points in the nineteenth century, taxes were felt to be very heavy, although by any measure they were low compared with those imposed in the second half of the twentieth. Tolerance of higher taxes in general might have been expected to raise the tolerance of the taxation needed to service the Debt, except that the priorities attached to government spending have changed: in 1931, the proper service of the Debt was in danger of succumbing to the maintenance of expenditure on unemployment relief and the wages of public sector workers, a possibility that would have been unthinkable in 1831 or 1900. Sometimes, the immediate circumstances have determined attitudes. Losing income and wealth to the Debt has been less painful during periods of economic growth, when only part of an increment was being extracted. It has been more painful during price deflations, when taxpayers have resented unplanned increases in the Debt holders' purchasing power which has made them reluctant to contribute. This has been most noticeable after wars, when interest has absorbed a large part of government revenues, social and political tensions have been high and the distribution of the tax burden has been questioned. In short, the tolerable level of service is a moveable feast. The circumstances of each period of the Debt's growth and the shape of financial, political and social forces when it has been at its most costly have to be examined in order to understand why the Debt has continued to be recognised.

The long record of correct debt servicing is also to be explained by the predominance of sterling indebtedness, which, in its turn, has reflected the capacity of the UK in the eighteenth and nineteenth centuries to satisfy its wartime needs from domestic production and earn the wherewithal to buy, and then safely import, the balance from overseas. Servicing overseas debt requires a second extraction as output is diverted from domestic uses to increasing exports or replacing imports. This is often accompanied by dislocation and unemployment, whose extent depends on the economy's structure and suppleness. Monetary and fiscal policy, perhaps already tight to curb wartime inflation, have to be kept even tighter to create room for new industries. Other countries have to keep their markets open to imported goods and accept a deterioration in their payments balances, with implications for their growth, employment and public finances. Adjustment may be refused, protection for domestic producers introduced, or exchange rates devalued. The process is the more disruptive if the creditor adopts policies to protect its economy from increased imports, so that the debtor has to earn the surpluses from elsewhere.

This book is about the management of the Debt between 1900 and 1932, one of the most difficult periods in its history, when most of these aspects of national indebtedness were on display. Between 1914 and 1918, the UK's survival as an independent nation was challenged, the size of the Debt rose tenfold and, for the first time since the early seventeenth century, foreign currencies were borrowed as the Treasury drew into the fray resources from other countries. After the war, the increased Debt had to be serviced from an economy undergoing severe structural strains as it struggled to adapt its production to changed markets. An expanded electorate, with new expectations, looked for increased government spending when there was little buoyancy in tax revenues. The legitimacy of the newly incurred Debt and the distribution of the servicing cost came into question, stretching the nation's willingness to pay for its service almost to breaking point.

The story falls into three periods. It begins with the foundations on which the twentieth-century debt was built: the characteristics of the late nineteenth-century obligations; the statutory arrangements; the part played by the savings banks; and the Byzantine arrangements for debt reduction from sinking funds. The war in South Africa between 1899 and 1902 was the first since 1815 to entail substantial borrowing. It was met by successfully exploiting the instruments the Treasury had inherited, but with some changes in the way in which they were sold. It left a legacy of short-term debt, large enough for officials to feel disturbed, but not so large as to require radical departures.

The second period, the years of the Great War of 1914-18, was very different. Domestically, there was innovation in the design of securities, in the way they were sold and the machinery for receiving subscriptions and recording ownership. Externally, the Treasury borrowed from neutral and allied governments, banks and the public. By the beginning of 1920, it was clear that its indebtedness to the US Treasury was of such a size, and on such terms, that it could not be treated as a technical matter, the repayments to be settled between Treasury officials in strict accordance with the terms of the advances when they were made.

The third period shows how the authorities brought order to the Debt. For four years, their operations centred on changing the structure of the obligations. Internally, within the limitations imposed by the politicians on higher interest rates, they sought to reduce the volume of very short-term debt so that the Bank of England could recover control of the money markets. Externally, they used fiscal and balance of payments surpluses to repay foreign currency debt, while, after much prevarication, they converted the obligations held by the US Treasury into stable, long-dated Bonds. This period of fire-fighting ended with the funding of the US Treasury debt, and after the recession which followed the post-war boom had diverted money from the private economy to the purchase of longer-dated government securities. The pace, which had more in common with the wartime debt operations than with that of peace, then changed.

All the internal securities issued between 1914 and the Armistice had to be refinanced, or could be refinanced, in the following eleven years; for all but the great War Loans, the exact dates were known in the spring of 1919. Plans could be made a year or two ahead and there was considerable freedom in the choice of the moment to refinance or convert. The Treasury felt it could have a programme, with definite dates studding the calendar for years ahead, with each conversion giving greater confidence and a cheaper Debt. Moreover, there was a focal point which lay (with proper dramatic perspective) at the end of the programme – the promise of budgetary savings after June 1929 if the Treasury was able to convert the large and expensive 5 per cent War Loan to a lower nominal rate.

For each of these periods, the book describes how officials and politicians determined the terms of the obligations on which the Treasury borrowed, the method of sale; and the lenders they should attract. Throughout, there recur themes that are common to any sales process. What securities should be sold, and at what price? Who were the investors being sought? How should the terms be adapted to suit potential subscribers and changing circumstances? Once the securities had been designed, how should the potential investors be persuaded to become subscribers? And how did the Treasury ensure that it was selling at the most favourable price?

The book has been shaped by the lack of previous histories of the Debt and the nature of securities markets. Two official histories were prepared by the National Debt Office in the 1890s, the first a history of the National Debt Commissioners since their establishment in 1786, the second of the funded debt between 1694 and 1786.[2] Both stressed the form of the securities, and the legal and institutional arrangements that underpinned them, giving little explanation of how their issue related to events. The origins of the Debt and its history during the first half of the eighteenth century is well served by Peter Dickson's *The Financial Revolution in England*.[3] Eric Hargreaves's *The National Debt* also covers the early Debt, carrying the story forward to the 1920s, but he did not have access to the archival material used in this volume.[4] Pember & Boyle's *British Government Securities in the Twentieth Century* is an invaluable record of the composition of the Debt, the terms of the securities, and the issues, conversions and refinancings which created them. However, it is not widely available, the coverage is severely factual and the data are confined to that available in published accounts. Its focus is the quoted sterling debt, and it does not extend far into the UK's overseas borrowing.[5] Some British borrowing in the USA is treated in Kathleen Burk's *Britain, America and the Sinews of War 1914-1918*, but her primary interest is in the effects of British spending and borrowing on intergovernmental relations.[6] Similarly, Susan Howson in *Domestic Monetary Management in Britain 1919-38* limits her treatment to the part the Debt played in the formation of monetary policy.[7] Thus, even basic information about the obligations is not easily available. The very existence, let alone the terms, of some overseas borrowing between 1915 and 1919 is virtually unknown and the story of other debts has sometimes been inaccurately or partially recorded, especially when they have been peripheral to an historian's main theme. The book, therefore, seeks to provide a comprehensive record of the securities and explain how they were designed and sold. At the other end of the securities' lives, it shows how they were refinanced, converted, funded or paid off for cash. In each case, the transaction is explained in terms of the financial and political conditions at the time.

It is a truism, oft repeated, that there is no event, anywhere, which does not affect the government debt market. Anything that alters the demand for capital, the level of savings, the price of imports, the demand for exports, economic activity (whether at home or abroad), the cost of labour, the price and availability of raw materials, the security of asset holdings, the return on alternative investments and the technology of production and communication will influence the yields on government securities. Markets fluctuate as they receive and absorb into prices new information and the changed perspectives that come with the interplay of news and the lapse of time. When investors buy, they can reverse themselves by selling in the secondary market, even if it means a less than satisfactory price. When a borrower, the Treasury, sells a new issue it is an irreversible act, for it has bound itself into a contract involving (among other terms) the rate of interest and the date and conditions for repayment of the capital. Events, sometimes following closely on the borrowing, may prove the contract to have been most onerous, but the Treasury has to live with the decision made in the few days, or even hours, when it was deciding the terms. For this reason. the book lays stress on the circumstances surrounding each debt operation, using contemporary records, in the knowledge that even a few hours can change perspectives, add to information which was only partial, or clarify incoherent or poorly deciphered cables. Sometimes, it is not possible to meet this ideal. Tired and busy officials or bankers reacting to market changes tend to write sparingly, leaving little to explain how a decision was made. In wartime, manpower shortages can lead to poor record keeping or mistaken destruction. It is only when there is little or no contemporary evidence that this story uses later accounts or speculates from first principles.

One development, and one episode, provide continuity through the many events that determined the terms and prices of the government's borrowing between 1900 and 1932. The twentieth century has seen increased fluctuations in the supply of debt in peacetime as the government has become more involved in its citizens' lives. This has been most marked since 1945, when the financial authorities began adjusting their spending to mitigate the low points in the economic cycle, with the consequential borrowing seen not just as acceptable, but as a duty. The provision and maintenance of a wide range of publicly provided social services and infrastructure are now seen as the duty of the state and have become tests of whether governments are deserving of an electorate's support. As a consequence, the government debt market has become sensitive to any event that might lead to state intervention, with increases in its expenditure unmatched by revenues. The first effects of these changes were felt in the last quarter of the nineteenth century in the origins of Treasury Bills and Local Loans Stock and, later, in 1911–12, in the diversion of the budget surplus from debt repayment to building sanatoria. At different points in the 1920s, housing finance, the cost and method of supporting the unemployed, local taxation and publicly provided pensions play their part in the Debt's story. In 1922–3, the Treasury broke with tradition, curtailed the refinancing of the wartime floating debt, and relinquished the opportunity of fixing the cost of that part of the Debt represented by Treasury Bills in order to protect the banking system's ability to finance economic activity. In the second half of the decade and the first two years of the 1930s, the interest rates required to support the overvalued exchange rate clashed with the political and social objectives of stimulating economic activity and reducing unemployment.

Debt markets have traditionally been most sensitive to any event that changes the relationships between states, for the great expansions in national debts have come from wars: budget deficits have been incurred; the increased supply of debt has pushed down prices; pressure on resources has produced inflation, either as a by-product of government spending or, in the twentieth century, as a deliberate, acceptable, if regretted, means of extracting resources from the economy; often wars have produced such tensions between the privations necessary for victory and citizens' tolerance that there has been radical political and social change and, in extreme cases, destruction of the value of debts denominated in money or, even, default. The pivot of the book, therefore, is a particular episode – the fiscal and monetary strains of a Great War.

Endnotes

1 PML, Archives, Horn Box 4, 'From Recognised Authorities Figures have been Compiled Showing some of the Essential Facts About Great Britain and France', October 1915.
2 *History of the Earlier Years of the Funded Debt from 1694 to 1786* (C. 9010), 1898; *National Debt: Report by the Secretary and Comptroller General of the Proceedings of the Commissioners for the Reduction of the National Debt, From 1786 to 31st March 1890* (C. 6539), 1891.
3 Dickson (1967).
4 Hargreaves (1930).
5 Pember & Boyle (1950).
6 Burk (1985).
7 Howson (1975).

Acknowledgements

The gilt-edged market has many participants drawn from many disciplines and with many roles. It is a community of actuaries, economists, mathematicians, accountants and academics; of those who can analyse, quantify and compute; and those who are just attracted by honeypots. Connected by telephones and screens, and in the past by the floor of the Stock Exchange, they have a characteristic in common. They talk. My thanks go to all those who, consciously or unconsciously, aroused my interest in government debt markets and taught me that mixture of weary cynicism and never satisfied hope that is the hallmark of its participants. Of these, I send special thanks to the partners and staff of Pember & Boyle, who will stand aghast at the time spent on such an unremunerative enterprise as this.

Over thirty years, I have accumulated debts to many individuals, most of whom will be unaware that they have made a contribution to this book. My colleagues and partners during my time in the market: Bill Allen, Nigel Althaus, Robin Bevan, Brian Griffiths, James Hamilton, George Nissen, Bob Pearce, Robin Porteous, Jonathan Quirk, John Scrope and John Yarde-Buller. From the wider City, past and present, I would like to thank the community of fixed-interest managers; those responsible for official operations in the gilt-edged market; and the officers of the National Investment and Loans Office.

My gratitude goes to Roger Brown and Ian Spreadbury, who spent many hours compensating for the poverty of my mathematics. Andrew Wilson took me deeper into the mysteries of Terminable Annuities and calculated the yields on Consols before 1903.

The book could not have been written in its present form without the great generosity and encouragement of two friends. Kathleen Burk read the script in draft, gave me the freedom of her library and has lent me the notes and photocopies arising from her history of Morgan Grenfell and her archival work in the USA. Without the latter, the book would have taken several additional years and, perhaps, been beyond my financial resources. Susan Howson read the script and commented in great detail from her knowledge of inter-war monetary policy. She also lent me her notes and photocopies of the ledgers of the Currency Note Redemption Account and the Issue Department between 1919 and 1931.

I am grateful to Leslie Pressnell, who read and commented on the draft, making many invaluable suggestions, and to Donald Moggridge who lent me his notes of the Issue Department ledgers between 1931 and 1938. The original ledgers for 1919 to 1938 have been lost and if they had not been made available I would have been partially blind as I traced the evolution of the authorities' market management.

R. J. Q. Adams, Daniel P. Davison and Robert Rhodes James answered specific questions, and John Caldwell acted for me in the Canadian National Archives. Dennis Flynn drew the charts – many times. My thanks also go to Andy Barnett, Alex Duncan, Perry Gauci, Richard King, John Martin and Claire Preston.

Errors that remain are all my own.

I am indebted to many archivists and librarians. In particular, I would like to thank Henry Gillett of the Bank of England Archives for the patience displayed in the face of continuous importunity. Also in the Bank, Charlie Turpie, Elizabeth Ogborn, Sarah Millard (in the Archives) and Sarah Flew (Research and Special Operations Group) came readily to my aid. I have greatly appreciated the tolerance of the staff of the Bodleian Library and its dependent library at Rhodes House. Martin Carmel of the Committee of London and Scottish Bankers (British Bankers' Association) lent me the Minutes of the Committee of London Clearing Banks and its Treasury subcommittee.

I gratefully acknowledge the following for permission to examine and refer to material in their care or to which they hold the copyright: Association of British Insurers; Bank of England; Birmingham University Library; Bodleian Library, Oxford; British Bankers' Association; British Library; Cambridge University Library; Churchill College, Cambridge; Federal Reserve Bank of New York; Gloucestershire County Council; Harvard Business School; House of Lords Record Office; HSBC Group Archives (including Midland Bank Archives); the India Office Library; the Labour Party; Library of Congress, Washington DC; Lloyds TSB Group; Morgan Grenfell & Co. Ltd; Pierpont Morgan Library Archives, New York; National Archives of Canada; the Post Office Archives; The Rothschild Archive; Trinity College, Cambridge; US National Archives, Washington DC; and Yale University Library. I am grateful to the Warden and Fellows of New College, Oxford, for their permission to refer to the Milner Papers. Unpublished Crown-Copyright material in the Public Records Office is reproduced by kind permission of the Controller of Her Majesty's Stationery Office.

Finally, I have to acknowledge the unhelpful presence of Rowley, Percy and Jester, and the help and forbearance of my wife, Susan.

Jeremy Wormell
Wotton Underwood
October 1999

Part I

The foundations of the twentieth-century debt

1 Sinking funds, annuities and savings banks

> The present Parliament cannot of course bind the next Parliament...But what this Parliament can do is, to make things easier for those who hereafter desire to conserve the Sinking Fund, and to place difficulties in the way of those who may desire to make an onslaught on it. The Sinking Fund, no doubt, requires to be handled at all times with great care and delicacy. If it is overdone it may be undone. To ask taxpayers to make an undue sacrifice is to endanger its existence.
>
> Sir Edward Hamilton, 'The Sinking Fund', 30 September 1897, T 168/86

The British government borrowed little in the forty-three years that lay between the end of the Crimean War in the spring of 1856 and the start of the South African War in the autumn of 1899. Although the Treasury was squeezed by social and military spending in the final two decades, budgets habitually produced surpluses and, without undue exaggeration, the administration of the National Debt was, as in Sir Edward Hamilton's story of the origins of George Goschen's 2½–2¾ per cent Consols, a question of 'conversion and redemption':[1] conversion to lower interest rates and repayment. Mingled with the repayments came temporary borrowings to pay for colonial and imperial wars, but these were not so great as to demand innovation. When new instruments came, it was advances for capital investment by local bodies and central government departments that gave the stimulus: Exchequer Bonds, Treasury Bills and advances from the savings banks to pay for military works, telephones and government buildings.

Much of the administrative machinery, the system of repayment, the securities and the attitudes of officials passed unchanged into the twentieth century and, indeed, in some cases, into the present day. This chapter sets the scene by describing the Victorian institutions and orthodoxies: the arrangements for managing the Debt; the sinking funds and the statutory structures which protected them from political interference; the role of the National Debt Commissioners (the Commissioners) and the savings bank funds; and the characteristics of the securities. The next chapter chronicles the borrowing that accompanied the South African War and then shows where the Edwardian Treasury departed from the arrangements of the previous century to lengthen or repay the new debt which had been incurred.

Debt repayment: sinking funds and annuities

The Treasury had no general borrowing powers until 1914, and legislation was required each time a new issue or conversion offer was contemplated. Two marketable instruments – Exchequer Bonds and Treasury Bills – were governed by statute and Treasury Minutes (TMs), but these did not give the Treasury the power to borrow: they merely prescribed the methods of issue and administration. Legislation enabling the Treasury to make advances for public works might give it power to borrow on Exchequer Bonds, Treasury Bills or Exchequer Bills. Legislation sanctioning expenditure on naval or military works might specify the same instruments, although latterly it became usual for this kind of spending to be met from annuities sold to the funds administered by the Commissioners. The approval of expenditure on wars would be accompanied by the power to borrow, and the legislation sanctioning Goschen's conversion included authority to borrow to pay off dissentients. The discretion given to the Treasury varied. Legislation always specified the maximum amount that could be borrowed and the duration of the authority. If it specified Exchequer Bonds, it would usually prescribe the length and the maximum rate of interest. After 1875, the legislation would also state whether the interest was to be met from the Permanent Charge.

The Permanent Charge, Sir Stafford Northcote's machinery for repaying debt, was introduced to supplement a system of repayment by annuities, which were included in the budget as expenditure, and the application of unforecast, or 'casual', budget surpluses. The annuities were administered by the Commissioners, or the Commissioners for the Reduction of the National Debt, to give them their full title. This body had been established in 1786[a] to receive and apply sinking fund monies. In the late nineteenth century, it administered the assets of nineteen other funds, of which the most important were those of the Post Office Savings Bank (POSB) and Trustee Savings Banks (TSBs). The Commissioners were the Speaker, the Chancellor of the Exchequer, the Master of the Rolls, the Accountant-General of the Court of Chancery and the Governor and Deputy-Governor of the Bank of England. The Chief Baron of the Exchequer was added in 1808.[b] The Lord Chief Justice replaced the Chief Baron in 1880, when his office was abolished. The office of Accountant-General was abolished in 1872, and the Paymaster-General of the Court of Chancery became a Commissioner.[c] Although three Commissioners were needed to form a quorum, in practice day-to-day business was performed by the Comptroller-General under the direction of the Chancellor and his Treasury officials.[2] In 1899, the Comptroller-General was George Hervey.

Repayment of debt by means of annuities took two forms. The general public could buy annuities from the Commissioners, using either securities, or money, which was used to buy securities. The arrangements had altered over the years,

a The National Debt Reduction Act 1786.

b The Life Annuities Act 1808.

c 35 & 36 Vict. c. 44

but by the end of the century they were mainly regulated by the Government Annuities Act 1829 and the National Debt (Supplemental) Act 1888. These gave the Commissioners the power to sell annuities for a term of years, or on single lives, two lives and the life of the survivor, or on the joint continuance of two lives. The annuities could be either immediate or deferred. As with all annuities, the value was determined by the yield on securities and the mortality tables, with the Treasury having powers to adjust the rates. When investors purchased annuities, the securities that were surrendered, or bought with their money, were cancelled and the annuity became a liability of the Consolidated Fund. Because the capital, as well as the interest, was being paid to the annuitant, the annual cost to the Consolidated Fund was greater than the annual interest on the securities that had been cancelled. On the other hand, when the annuity ceased, the debt had been written off and the National Debt reduced. Annuities were thus a disguised sinking fund.[3]

As well as being a method of repaying debt, annuities were intended to be a service to the public, enabling a secure pension to be bought with a capital sum. Despite the intention, they were not popular. They were not marketable: the return of capital over a period meant that annuitants had the problem of continuously receiving principal and finding a suitable new investment; they were unsuitable for trustees; and the entire annuity was at that time treated by the Inland Revenue as income and liable to tax, despite a proportion being a return of capital.[4]

More important than the annuities sold to the public were Terminable Annuities, or 'departmental' annuities, which were held by the funds under the control of the Treasury. The largest were those of the savings banks, whose deposits were invested by the Commissioners in Parliamentary Securities once a balance had been put aside to ensure that sufficient funds were kept liquid to meet withdrawals.[d] As the Consolidated Fund was the ultimate guarantor of the interest and capital, the Treasury felt justified in investing part of the funds in illiquid securities. It was this combination of the State as borrower and lender which was used by William Gladstone in 1863, when Chancellor of the Exchequer, to extend the principle of annuities,[e] which were proving difficult to sell to the general investor.[5]

As with annuities bought by the public, Gladstone's system required the surrender of securities for cancellation. In return, the Consolidated Fund paid the Commissioners an annual sum for a specified number of years. This was calculated

d There was no statutory definition of a Parliamentary Security. In 1860, Gladstone described such securities as those 'issued by the authority of Parliament, and charged directly on the revenues of the country, whether by supply services or on the Consolidated Fund', distinguishing them from securities carrying a British government guarantee. 'Parliamentary stocks or public funds or Government securities of the United Kingdom' used in the Acts regulating Trustee investments implied that the interest and principal were a charge on the revenues of the British government or were guaranteed by it. *Hansard* (Commons), 5 March 1960, col. 2278; T 160/688/F14984, answer of the Office of Parliamentary Counsel to letter from Akroyd & Smithers, 10 March 1937.

e The Post Office Savings Bank Act 1863.

to produce an amount equal to the interest the Commissioners would have received on the cancelled securities, together with enough money to replace them, or to provide their equivalent in other government securities or in cash. The calculations were periodically tested to ensure that the securities would be exactly replaced, despite movements in market prices, and, if necessary, adjustments were made to the annual payments. The funds were thus left in an unchanged position when the annuity expired.

Until 1883, the system had only been applied to the funds of the savings banks, but the Court of Chancery (Funds) Act 1872 also made the Consolidated Fund responsible to the suitors of the Court of Chancery for all monies and securities held in Court. This allowed the principle to be extended. In 1884, the Chancery Funds Annuity was set up, £40m of Consols being cancelled in return for an annuity of twenty years. Because the cancelled securities actually belonged to the suitors, rather than being assets held as machinery against a liability, the securities to be replaced had to be Consols.[6]

There were two minor annuities that were payable to funds under government control, but differing from other Terminable Annuities by being wholly a return of capital. They were the Trustee Savings Bank Deficiency Annuity, set up in 1881 to make good a deficiency in the capital of the TSBs, and the Sinking Fund Annuity, set up in 1884 to extinguish an increase in the nominal value of the Debt arising from a conversion scheme. Finally, there was an annuity which fell into neither category. The Red Sea and Telegraph Annuity resulted from a government guarantee given to a company which was to lay a telegraph line between Britain and India. When the company went bankrupt, the Treasury met its guarantee by setting up an annuity in favour of the shareholders. It was due to expire in 1908.

Northcote's mechanism for repaying debt was called the 'New Sinking Fund', to contrast it with the 'Old Sinking Fund' that came from casual surpluses. The principle of the New Sinking Fund was that a specific sum of money – known variously as the Permanent Annual Charge, Fixed Debt Charge, Fixed Charge or just 'the Charge' – was made available each year to service the Debt. To give protection against encroachments by needy Chancellors, it was included in the budget as an item of expenditure, that is the casual surpluses (or deficits) were struck after the Fixed Charge had been met. From the Charge was met the expenses of management, the interest on both the funded and unfunded debt and the capital and interest on annuities. The balance between the Fixed Charge and the cost of interest and management, the New Sinking Fund, was used to repay debt, the monies growing each year as the interest saved on repaid debt was used to repay more debt. Cash was issued to the Commissioners, who had to spend it within six months on buying in, paying off or redeeming debt, other than Ways and Means or Deficiency Advances (see pp. 20–1). If this last condition had not been included, the sinking fund monies could have been used to repay temporary borrowing, which, when repaid, would have left Exchequer balances at a higher level. They would then have been available to meet expenditure. The same Act directed that the casual surpluses, the Old Sinking Fund, should be issued to the Commissioners during the year after the end of the year in which they had accrued, and that they should be spent within six months. In this case, they could be applied to annuities, funded or unfunded debt and to redeeming Deficiency, but not Ways and Means, Advances (see pp. 20–1). The securities bought by both sinking funds were cancelled. To provide further protection for the New Sinking Fund, the Fixed Charge could only be used to pay the interest on securities issued after 1875 if the legislation sanctioning the new borrowing specifically so directed. The exceptions were Ways and Means and Deficiency Advances. The Charge also excluded the interest on any debt issued to make advances for local works. Thus, in principle, the total amount of interest paid on the Debt could exceed the interest paid out of the Fixed Charge. At a later date, new debt was often absorbed into the main body of the debt serviced by the Fixed Charge, usually, but not invariably, with an increase in the Charge to keep the sinking fund element intact. The most notable example of this was the decision to include the Boer War debt in the Fixed Charge, while increasing the Charge's size. If the Fixed Charge was not increased when such a transfer was made, or not increased sufficiently, the sinking fund was said to have been 'raided': the sinking fund element had been reduced.

The 1875 Act prescribed a Fixed Charge of £27.4m in 1875–6, £27.7m in 1876–7 and £28m thereafter. In the first year, this covered the capital repayment within the annuities of £5.4m, with £0.3m left over for repayment of other debt.[7] It actually remained at £28m for only two years before being raided in 1880–1;[8] in 1881–2, it was increased to meet the cost of various new debts, including the annuity set up to meet the deficiency on the TSB funds;[f] in 1885–6 and 1886–7, the sinking fund element was suspended, that is, not paid; in 1887–8, the Charge was reduced from £28m to £26m; in 1889–90, it was further reduced to £25m to reflect the reduction in interest after Goschen's conversion. It remained at this level until 1899–1900, when it was reduced to £23m. The capital repayments within the annuities payable to the Commissioners were suspended only once, in 1885–6, to help meet military expenditure in the Sudan and Afghanistan.[9]

Northcote had three reasons for establishing the Permanent Charge: annuities periodically fell in, subjecting the Chancellor of the day to the temptation of using the windfall to reduce taxation; it was difficult to find enough securities in the government portfolios to cancel when setting up new annuities; and the annuities were created on a basis that the general public found unattractive – indeed, this was why they were being sold to government accounts. Thus, by implication, the portfolios were making expensive investments.[10] Writing in 1888, Buxton saw the machinery as 'simple and intelligible'. The sum voted would remain the same each year, instead of varying as annuities fell in, money was borrowed or interest rates varied. Compound interest would be able to do its work, the amount of the sinking fund rising automatically as interest was saved on the repaid debt.[11] Almost a decade later, Hamilton, Assistant Financial Secretary to the Treasury, called it '...one of our great national strengths. It is one of the primary causes of our extraordinary credit' and drew attention to five advantages. Three were technical:

f The Post Office Savings Bank Acts 1861–93.

it provided an automatically increasing sinking fund; it simplified the forecasting of expenditure; and it permitted variations in the size of the annuities, without the need to raise taxes, when the original calculations had been upset by the rise in the price of Consols. Two were political: it presented an obstacle to a Chancellor tempted to cut taxes when annuities fell in; and the public became accustomed to paying a fixed sum for debt, which it regarded as a national obligation, in the same way as it thought of the interest.[12]

A system of annuities contained within a Fixed Charge was a circuitous way of reducing debt. Admittedly, it had the advantage of securing an even payment from the Treasury, but then so did the Fixed Charge itself. For officials, the real advantage lay in the complexity of the whole process. In 1896, Hamilton wrote:

> the apparent complication and consequent mystification [of annuities]...constitute a material safeguard against their being tampered with in slight or temporary exigencies. The general belief is that such securities cannot be touched without a breach of faith; and, fortified by this belief, successive Governments and Parliaments have (with one exception in 1885) declined to interfere with arrangements for reducing the National Debt when they have taken the form of Terminable Annuities. On the other hand, experience shows that Sinking Funds, not wrapped up in Terminable Annuities, do not elicit equal virtue in Government or Parliament...[but] notwithstanding that the sanctity of Terminable Annuities granted in exchange for perpetual annuities, which are being held on account of Funds under the practical control of the State, has been so uniformly respected, such annuities do not in reality tie the hands of Governments and Parliaments more tightly than Sinking Funds consisting of specific sums appropriated out of revenue for redemption of debt. For, if a real emergency arises, the Government at any time can propose, and Parliament can empower, either the suspension of so much of the Terminable Annuities as represents repayment of capital...or the prolongation of the Terminable Annuities and the consequent diminution of the Annual Charge on the taxpayer, or their re-conversion into perpetual annuities.[13]

In other words, the lack of public understanding meant that they could continue as long as the Treasury thought it wise, while they could be suspended when it was convenient. A precondition for this flexibility was that, with the exception of those sold to the public, annuities were not a contract with the lender. Thus, in contrast to the sinking funds of Stanley Baldwin and Winston Churchill, in which most of the available monies were earmarked for payments on specific securities held by private investors, repayment could be diverted or suspended. Again, as Hamilton put it:

> Such a latitude...is a reserved power of immense value...an amount which last year reached £6,331,000 could not only itself be made available for extraordinary supplies, but could be made to constitute the security on which we could raise (say) £200,000,000 in a short space of time, without imposing any additional taxation.[14]

Table 1.1 Securities (other than advances for capital works) held by government departments: 31 March 1899

£m nominal	*$2^3/_4$ per cent Consols*	*$2^3/_4$ per cent Annuities*	*$2^1/_2$ per cent Annuities*	*Book Debt*	*Treasury Bills*	*Estimated capital value of Annuities*	*Total Government Securities*	*3 per cent Local Loans*	*Local Loans Bonds*	*Guaranteed Land Stock*	*Total*
Trustee Savings Banks (ordinary departments)	25.0	–	0.1	2.8	–	6.4	34.3	6.4	0.6	2.0	43.2
Post Office Savings Bank	77.9	0.2	9.0	10.2	0.2	3.4	100.8	11.0	2.1	0.8	114.8
Savings Banks investment account	6.6	0.1	0.7	–	–	–	7.4	1.4	–	–	8.8
Supreme Court of Judicature	20.0*	0.1	0.8	–	–	13.8	34.7	0.1	–	–	34.8
Trustee of Charitable Funds	15.0	–	0.4	–	–	–	15.5	–	–	–	15.5
Other	16.2	–	1.5	–	0.4	–	18.1	2.9	–	2.1	23.1
Total	160.7	0.5	12.4	13.0	0.6	23.6	210.8	21.8	2.7	4.9	240.2

Notes

– denotes less than £49,000.

*£6.2m held in their own name and £13.8m held on their account by the Commissioners who had purchased it as replacement Stock with the annuity (46 & 47 Vict. c. 54 and 51 & 52 Vict. c. 15) expiring in 1904. It excludes the Supreme Court of Judicature (Deposit and Exchange Account), administered by the Commissioners, which held £1.3m on 31 March 1899.

Columns may not sum because of rounding.

Source: *Government Departments Securities* (HCP 147), 11 April 1899 .

A free, but wrapped, sinking fund was one of the great national strengths: 'it is one of the primary causes of our extraordinary credit…the country's reserve fund, or a war chest', providing financial flexibility in case of emergency.[15]

The departmental portfolios

The government's own departments were the most important administrators of investments in the Debt. On 31 March 1899, eighty accounts held £210.8m nominal of marketable central government debt, Book Debt[g] and Terminable Annuities, £29.4m of other public sector securities and had made £7.5m of advances for capital expenditure. Most of the accounts were small – the Science and Art Department's Murchison Prize Fund had assets of just £540 8s 9d, all invested in 2¾ per cent Consols – and over 90 per cent by value belonged to only five funds. Two-thirds belonged to the main funds of the POSB and the TSB, making the Commissioners the most important of the departmental managers. Of the other sizeable portfolios, those of the Official Trustee of Charitable Funds and the Supreme Court of Judicature (England) had investments in public securities of £15.5m and £34.8m apiece. These were not the responsibility of the Commissioners.[16] On 31 March 1899, the government departments' holdings represented 33.2 per cent of the total Debt and 31.2 per cent of the marketable funded debt. The most important single holding was Consols, of which the government portfolios held £160.7m, or nearly 31 per cent of those in issue. They also held £12.4m of the 2½ per cent Annuities (39 per cent of the issue), Terminable Annuities with an estimated capital value of £23.6m and £13m Book Debt (Table 1.1).[h]

In addition to central government debt, the departments held two government-guaranteed issues. Local Loans Stock, additional tranches of which were to continue to be issued to the public and the Commissioners until April 1931, originated with accounting reforms introduced by Goschen in the National Debt and Local Loans Act 1887. Until then, advances to local bodies had come from a mixture of Exchequer balances, issues of Exchequer Bonds, Exchequer and Treasury Bills and the Commissioners' savings bank monies. Goschen took the advances out of the budget, setting up a separate Local Loans Fund with its own liabilities. Thereafter, 3 per cent Local Loans Stock, irredeemable until 1912, was created and issued to the Commissioners and, a little later, to the general public. In exchange, the savings bank funds surrendered debt of the central government

g Under the National Debt (Conversion of Exchequer Bonds) Act 1892, a 'Book Debt' was created in favour of the savings banks in return for the cancellation of £13m Exchequer Bonds and other unfunded debt, which had been issued under the National Debt Redemption Act 1889 in consideration for money advanced to pay off dissentients to the Goschen conversion. A Book Debt was a charge on the Consolidated Fund represented by a credit, in favour of the savings banks, written in the books of the Treasury. It was unmarketable. T 168/21, Hamilton, 'Book Debt', 11 March 1892.

h Annuities could only be 'estimated' because the liability was for annual payments whose capital element had to be calculated making assumptions about future interest rates.

and Public Works Loan Board for cancellation.[17] The 2¾ per cent Guaranteed Stock was the first of three issues to raise money for buying out Irish landowners.[i]

The government departments' portfolio of marketable debt and Terminable Annuities expanded from £198.4m in 1890 to £240.2m in 1899, while its holdings of central government debt (excluding advances for capital works) rose from £179.2m to £210.8m. As the capital element within the savings bank and Chancery Fund Annuities had been reduced (from £60.9m to £23.6m) and replaced by Stock, the departments' holdings of marketable funded debt had risen more sharply – from £104.6m to £173.6m.[j] These almost entirely comprised Consols, in which its holdings rose from £91.7m to £160.7m.[18]

While demand from the departments expanded in the 1890s, the National Debt contracted, with central government obligations falling from £688.9m to £635m. However, because so much of the fall came from the reduced value of the departmental annuities, the volume of marketable funded debt outstanding contracted by only 2 per cent, from £567.5m to £556.5m. The consequence of the twofold changes – the marketable debt falling slightly and the departments' holdings expanding sharply – was a contraction in the volume available to outside investors, so that, during the decade, the central government's marketable funded debt held in the private sector fell from £462.9m to £382.9m, or from 81.6 per cent to 68.8 per cent of the total (Table 1.2 and Appendix 3).[19]

The role of the savings banks: deposits and the Stock purchase facility

The expansion in the departments' holdings came from the investment of savings bank deposits, which had grown in response to legislation that raised their maximum permitted size, and the low level of competing interest rates (Figure 1.1). Until the Savings Bank Act 1893, the maximum that could be deposited by any one person in any one year was restricted to £30, and the total that could be held by any one person to £150. The Savings Bank Act 1891 raised the total limit to £200 and the Savings Bank Act 1893 raised the annual limit to £50.[k] The reasons

i 2¾ per cent Guaranteed Stock was created under the Purchase of Land (Ireland) Act 1891 and the Irish Land Acts 1903 and 1909. 3 per cent Guaranteed Stock was created under the Irish Land Acts 1903 and 1909. The Stocks were not redeemable for thirty years from the dates of the relevant Acts. The Treasury was authorised to create the Stocks to raise money for the Irish Land Purchase Fund, which was responsible for advances to enable Irish tenants to buy land. The Acts of 1891 and 1909, but not that of 1903, authorised Stock to be issued to vendors instead of cash. The Stock, other than that issued to vendors, was sold either to the public or to the Commissioners. The Stocks were often called 'Irish Land Stocks', and the term is used here interchangeably with 'Guaranteed Stocks'.

j The accounting system of the Supreme Court of Judicature was unified in 1883 (46 & 47 Vict. c. 29). Thereafter, the Chancery Funds Annuity appeared in the annual returns of securities held by government departments under 'Court of Judicature, Supreme'.

k There were higher limits for deposits by charities and deposits awaiting investment in government issues or destined to pay for life assurance policies or annuities. Savings Bank Acts 1880, 1882, 1887 and 1893.

Table 1.2 Holdings of central government debt by the departments and the general public: 31 March 1890 and 1899

£m nominal (per cent)	*1890*	*1899*
Total National Debt		
Departments:		
Marketable debt and Terminable Annuities	179.2 (26.0)	210.8 (33.2)
Advances for capital works	– –	7.5 (1.2)
General public	509.7 (74.0)	416.7 (65.6)
Total	688.9 (100.0)	635.0 (100.0)
Marketable Funded Debt		
Departments	104.6 (18.4)	173.6 (31.2)
General public	462.9 (81.6)	382.9 (68.8)
Total	567.5 (100.0)	556.5 (100.0)

Sources: *National Debt: annual returns; National Debt (Conversion and Redemption Operations)* (HCP 153), 29 April 1890; *Government Departments Securities* (HCP 263), 27 June 1890, and (HCP 147), 11 April 1899.

for the restrictions were, in part, historical. The rate allowed on deposits with the TSBs had for many years been set at a level that produced a deficit on the fund, which ultimately needed to be met by a reluctant Treasury. Legislators saw little justification in subsidising any but the smallest savers. It was, in part, politics: the banking interests wanted to limit competition. And it was in part prudence: the deposits were a large potential liability, payable on demand, for which the Consolidated Fund was the guarantor.

In 1890, the POSB had 4.8m accounts and £67.6m in deposits. The TSBs had 1.5m depositors providing £43.6m to their General or Government ('Ordinary') Departments and £4.4m to their Special Investment Departments.[1] At the end of 1899, deposits in the POSB had nearly doubled to £130.1m, while those in the TSBs had risen to £51.4m (Figure 1.1).[20]

As well as collecting deposits, the banks provided facilities for small investors to buy government securities on their own account. The 'Stock purchase facility' was introduced by the Savings Banks Act 1880. Paying with a savings bank deposit, investors were credited with a holding of their chosen Stock at the market price of the day within seven days of giving their order. A certificate was issued and a small commission charged. The holding was not actually purchased. Instead, the Commissioners made a transfer of part of their existing holding to an account

1 Special Investment Departments were established by the TSBs from the 1870s, when the banks' trustees began taking advantage of their freedom to invest depositors' money other than with the Commissioners. The Departments enabled the TSBs both to circumvent the limit on the size of deposits and to offer a higher rate by investing in securities other than those of the central government. Horne (1947) pp. 221–5.

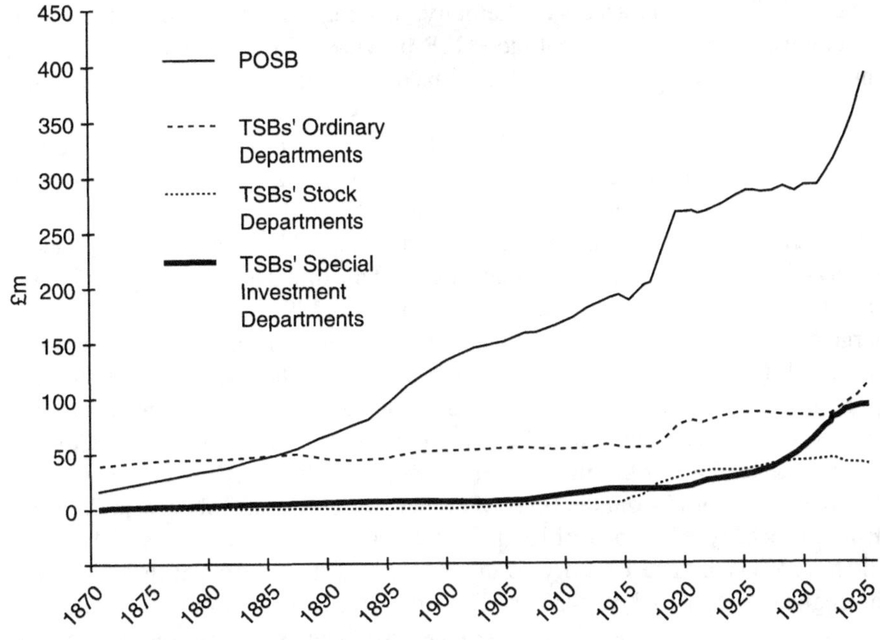

Figure 1.1 Deposits of the POSB and TSBs, 1870–1935. Source: Horne (1947), Appendices II and III.

held at the Bank of England called the 'Savings Bank Investment Account'. Like deposits, the amount that could be invested was restricted. Under the 1880 Act, the maximum that a depositor could buy in any one year was £100, and the maximum that could be held was £300. The 1893 Act raised the limits on purchases in any one year to £200, the limit on total holdings to £500 and, with some exceptions, made automatic the investment in Stock of any deposits in excess of the limits.

Little advantage was taken of the Stock purchase facility. Sir George Murray, then Secretary of the Post Office, in anticipation of official opinion in the first year of the 1914–18 War, wrote:

> The average depositor is such a queer creature. There is, no doubt, something of the speculator in him; but this element is rarely developed; and he is certainly not an investor. What he cares about apparently is to keep his capital *safe* and easily *accessible*. If he can get these two considerations he will be content with a very moderate rate of interest.

The number of investors had never been greater than 1.2 per cent of the number of depositors and the amount invested had never been greater than 7.8 per cent of the sums deposited.[21]

The savings bank funds had one other role. When Gladstone established the POSB he intended that it should reduce the City's influence on government finance by giving the Treasury access to alternative sources of money. In this he believed that he was successful and that the POSB provided 'the finance minister...with an instrument sufficiently powerful to make him independent of the Bank and City power when he has occasion for sums in seven figures.' The funds' capacity to purchase Exchequer Bonds and Local Loans, and provide capital advances, gave support to his confidence (see pp. 9, 19, 23–4).[22] As well as providing new money, the two portfolios – those of the older TSBs and the new POSB – made an important contribution to conversions. They accepted offers and lent spare balances to pay off dissentients, while the knowledge that the offers had their support helped persuade other investors to accept the terms. The 1890s was a decade with no large conversions, but the habit of using the portfolios to aid Treasury operations persisted. The Consolidated Fund guarantee meant that the assets could be shuffled to make cash or securities available to the outside market when there was a need for speed or secrecy. One example was an exchange of Treasury Bills for Consols during the Barings crises in November 1890. The Bank of England needed to borrow £2m of gold from the Bank of France, which would only accept Treasury Bills as security. The Bank of England did not have sufficient Bills, although it did have Consols. The Treasury arranged to issue £3m Treasury Bills to the Bank of England and pay off Ways and Means Advances from the Commissioners with the proceeds. The Commissioners used the cash to buy Consols from the Bank of England. The Bank had Treasury Bills, the Commissioners had some cheap Consols and the Treasury had a liability on Bills, instead of on Advances.[23] A second example came during 1897 and 1898 when the Cabinet were considering making a loan to China with which she could pay part of her war indemnity to Japan. The scheme came to nothing, but it showed how officials viewed the savings banks' portfolios. The sum needed would have been £12m, which was larger than the savings banks' immediate cash resources. Hamilton thought that Japan could not want the whole indemnity in cash and devised a scheme whereby the savings banks would provide Japan with Consols, as well as cash. In return, the savings banks would be given an annuity charged on the Consolidated Fund, which would receive the annual payments from the Chinese. The exchange of Consols for an annuity was an operation with which the public and Parliament were familiar, the rate on the annuity would be better than that on Consols, a scarcity of Consols in the market would be reduced as the Japanese sold and the money market would be undisturbed because cash would pass through gradually. The project was dropped when it was found that the Chinese wanted additional money, unattached to debt repayments, for general purposes.[24]

The nature of the securities

The pre-1914 annual debt returns divided the liabilities of the central government into four parts: 'the funded debt'; 'Terminable Annuities'; 'the unfunded debt'; and 'other capital liabilities' (Table 1.3). The first three were also referred to as the 'dead-weight debt' to signify that no assets had resulted from the expenditure. The unfunded debt was also referred to as 'the floating debt' or 'temporary debt'.

Table 1.3 The National Debt: 31 March 1899, 1903 and 1914

£m nominal (per cent)	*1899*		*1903*		*1914*	
$2^{3}/_{4}$ per cent/$2^{1}/_{2}$ per cent Consols	520.2	(81.9)	590.6	(74.0)	539.4	(76.4)
$2^{3}/_{4}$ per cent Annuities	4.6	(0.7)	4.5	(0.6)	3.8	(0.5)
$2^{1}/_{2}$ per cent Annuities	31.8	(5.0)	31.3	(3.9)	29.8	(4.2)
Debts to the Banks of England and Ireland	13.6	(2.1)	13.6	(1.7)	13.6	(1.9)
1892 Book Debt	13.0	(2.0)	–	–	–	–
Total funded debt	583.2	(91.8)	640.1	(80.2)	586.7	(83.1)
Annuities: estimated capital value	36.2	(5.7)	55.6	(7.0)	29.6	(4.2)
Treasury Bills	8.1	(1.3)	21.1	(2.6)	13.0	(1.8)
Exchequer Bonds	–	–	24.0	(3.0)	32.8*	(4.6)
$2^{3}/_{4}$ per cent National War Loan 1910	–	–	30.0	(3.8)	–	–
Total unfunded debt	8.1	(1.3)	75.1	(9.4)	45.8	(6.5)
Other capital liabilities	7.5	(1.2)	27.6	(3.5)	44.1	(6.2)
Total debt	635.0	(100)	798.3	(100)	706.2	(100)

Notes
*Includes £12.3m Exchequer Bonds issued under the Capital Expenditure (Money) Act 1904, the Cunard Agreement (Money) Act 1904 and the Telephone Transfer Act 1911.
Percentages may not sum because of rounding.

Source: *National Debt: annual returns.*

In some years, the Debt had to be further divided according to its statutory origins. Thus, having distinguished each type of debt, the returns were divided into securities in which the interest was included in the Permanent Charge and securities in which it was excluded. In March 1903, before the interest on the South African War debt had been absorbed into the Charge, Consols could be found both inside and, for the newly created debt, outside. At times during the 1890s, a note subdivided the unfunded debt by the powers which sanctioned its creation and continuation. Thus, in the returns for 1895, 'for supply' was broken down into £6.5m Treasury Bills and £3.1m Exchequer Bills: 'Under the National Debt Redemption Act 1889', £3.4m Treasury Bills and £1.9m Exchequer Bonds; and 'Under the Imperial Defence Act 1888', £2.5m Treasury Bills.[25]

The funded debt

Funded debt had a precise meaning: it was debt for which the Treasury had the liability to pay the interest, but no liability to repay the capital. Investors in such issues, which were also referred to as 'perpetual annuities' and 'permanent debt', had only one right in addition to the interest: there was a period during which they were protected from a reduction in the interest rate, the borrower having no option to call, or redeem, the issue. This put the Treasury in an astoundingly strong position, for it could never be forced to reborrow on worse terms. Perpetual annuities were a ratchet, enabling the Treasury to ignore yields when they rose and, once the period of protection had ended, to convert the debt to lower interest rates when they fell. This characteristic accounted for the dominance of a single issue after 1888. The authorities had no need to consider one of the rules that was later to become basic – breaking up the Debt so that maturities were spread and the Treasury could not be embarrassed by having to find a large sum in cash within a short period – and were able to live contentedly with one marketable issue, which represented over 80 per cent of the whole Debt. That investors were prepared to buy securities with such an asymmetrical risk reflected a long period of political stability, with economic growth that was accompanied by only cyclical price inflation. Of course there were setbacks, but the central characteristic of the security meant that these could be ignored. The bias seemed little appreciated until yields rose in the twenty years before 1914. Until then, investors had treated Consols as a dated security, concerned that, if the price were to rise above par, the rate would be reduced at the first opportunity, which would be in 1923. As the price fell below par, they started worrying about the effect on their balance sheets, but only slowly seemed to appreciate that there was no support to the price from a redemption date.

At the end of the century, the funded debt comprised five securities – 2¾ per cent Consols, 2½ per cent Annuities, 2¾ per cent Annuities and the unmarketable debts to the Banks of England and Ireland. The last were the least important. They represented the ancient debts of the Treasury to the two banks – £11,015,100 and £2,630,769 respectively. In 1892, it was arranged that the interest rate on these debts would be brought into line with the new, lower rate on Consols; this meant a cut to 2¾ per cent immediately and a further cut to 2½ per cent after 5 April 1903.[26]

The origins of both Annuities and Consols are to be found in conversions earlier in the century.[27] The 2½ per cent Annuities came out of five conversions: £3.0m were created by Gladstone in 1853 as a result of an offer to convert the rump of the South Sea Annuities and a range of other 3 per cent Stocks;[m] £1m were created under an Act passed in 1863 which permitted the Treasury to convert 3 per cent Stock held by the Commissioners on behalf of the POSB into 2½ per cent Stock;[n] a further £4m were created in 1883–4 from conversion of 3 per cent Consols, also held on behalf of the POSB; £5.8m came from the funding in 1881–2 and 1882–3 of Exchequer Bonds issued for local loans purposes; and £19.2m came in 1884 from Hugh Childers's unsuccessful scheme to convert the 3 per cents.[o] Two-thirds of the 2½ per cents created on this last occasion were on account of the government portfolios.

All £4.6m of the 2¾ per cent Annuities were created on account of the general public to satisfy Childers's conversion offer.[28]

m 16 & 17 Vict. c. 23.

n The Post Office Savings Bank Act 1863.

o National Debt (Conversion of Stock) Act 1884.

Both issues paid interest quarterly on the same dates as 2¾ per cent Consols and were redeemable at the Treasury's option on or after 5 January 1905.

On 31 March 1899, £31.8m of the 2½ per cent Annuities and £4.6m of the 2¾ per cents were outstanding. Together, they represented 5.7 per cent of the Debt (Table 1.3).

After Childers's failure, George Goschen tried again in 1888.[p] Three issues were attacked. First, Consolidated 3 per cent Annuities, dating from 1752 when several small issues were consolidated;[q] they paid interest twice yearly, on 5 January and 5 July. About £322m were outstanding in March 1888. Second, Reduced 3 per cent Annuities, which were a group of issues, the first dating from 1746, that had borne interest at 4 per cent. From 1750, this rate had been 'reduced' to 3½ per cent and then, seven years later, to 3 per cent. It was probably the first reduction that gave the issue its name. It paid interest twice yearly on 5 April and 5 October. About £69m were outstanding in March 1888. Last, New 3 per cent Annuities, dating from Henry Goulburn's conversion in 1844.[r] They had borne a rate of 3¼ per cent for ten years and 3 per cent thereafter. The interest dates were the same as those of the Reduced Threes. About £160m were outstanding in March 1888.[29]

As would happen again in 1932, the Chancellor took advantage of the low interest rates on alternative investments and his option to call the issues and offered to exchange the securities into a new issue: Consols, bearing a 2¾ per cent interest rate until 1903, 2½ per cent thereafter and irredeemable until 5 April 1923. The interest was payable four times a year, on 5 January, April, July and October, thus ensuring that holders of all three existing issues continued to receive income on the customary dates. While this enhanced the attractions of the conversion offer and simplified administration, it ensured the continued large use of Deficiency Advances (see pp. 20–1) because the payments fell at the beginning of each quarter, before revenue had been collected.

Faced with unattractive returns elsewhere, holders responded enthusiastically. The total of the securities Goschen attacked was £592.6m, or 80 per cent of the nominal value of the Debt.[s] Of this, £549.1m was converted and £1.2m paid off. The remaining £42.3m was dealt with under the National Debt Redemption Act 1889.

On 31 March 1899, £520.2m Consols (as they will henceforth be called until 4 per cent Consols were created in 1927) were outstanding, representing 81.9 per cent of the Debt (Table 1.3).

p National Debt (Conversion) Act 1888.

q 25 Geo. II. c. 27.

r 7 & 8 Vict. c. 4 and 5.

s Including £34.6m 3 per cent Consols created on account of the Chancery Funds Annuity set up under the National Debt Act 1883. The capital part of the annuity had to be reconverted temporarily into Stock to allow suitors to convert into the new 2¾ per cent Consols and to receive the bonus payable on the exchange. An equivalent amount of the new Consols were then cancelled in return for a Terminable Annuity, which would expire in 1904 in accordance with the intentions of the 1883 Act. Hamilton (1889) p. 26.

The unfunded debt

The annual accounts treated Exchequer Bills, Exchequer Bonds, Ways and Means Advances and Treasury Bills as unfunded debt. The category would also have included Deficiency Advances, except that they had to be paid off within the quarter in which they were taken and therefore never appeared in the annual returns.

Exchequer Bills had been first issued in 1696,[t] but in their later form were regulated by the Exchequer Bills and Bond Act 1866 and the Treasury Minute, which arose from it.[30] By then, they were already in decline. In the 1830s and 1840s, their marketability suffered from the competition of new high yielding railway debentures and the Bank of England (the Bank) ceased using them as its prime liquid holding. In 1841, serious frauds by officials administering the issue were discovered, with a loss of liquidity while Bills were examined. The Bills were issued with an original life of five years, with the interest rate reset every six months by the Chancellor after consultation with the Comptroller-General of the National Debt Office (NDO) and the broker who transacted the Commissioners' business in the gilt-edged market (the Government Broker). The rate needed to be kept competitive with money market rates because holders had the option of surrendering the Bills for cash on each anniversary of their issue and of using them during the preceding six months to make tax payments .

The last £1.5m of Exchequer Bills were extinguished by the New Sinking Fund in 1896–7 (after which date 'Bills' will refer to Treasury Bills). They had become increasingly unpopular with the Treasury as it became accustomed to the greater flexibility of Treasury Bills and the simplicity of Exchequer Bonds. The Treasury regarded Exchequer Bills as antiquated; the half-yearly setting of the interest rate was a chore and investors were prone to grumble at the decision. Their unpopularity with the money market could make the interest rate expensive compared with that on commercial bills or short-dated French Treasury debt, such as *Bons du Trésor*. They were unmanageable – if the rate was set too low they ran off and, in any case, the option of surrendering, or putting, them lay with the investor. As Sir William Harcourt wrote when he was Chancellor:

> We have no facility for dropping them at short notice when we have funds in hand as we can in the case of Treasury Bills. This is of the very essence of Floating Debt and the difficulty we have of getting rid of these securities is in itself a condemnation of them.[31]

Thus, whereas at mid-century sometimes as many as £20m or £30m were outstanding, in the final years of their existence there were only a few millions.[32]

The term 'Exchequer Bond' was introduced by Gladstone in 1853 to describe a security transferable by simple delivery, in contrast to the funded debt which was transferable in the Banks' transfer books (Appendix I).[u] Gladstone, who wished

t 7 & 8 Will. III. c. 31.

u The Bank of England and the Bank of Ireland kept separate books recording the ownership of securities. Reference to registration and transfer is, therefore, to 'Banks'.

to issue the new Bonds to help pay off dissentients from a conversion scheme, saw in them a range of advantages compared with Exchequer Bills. They would enable the government to lock in an interest rate: settlement by simple delivery would increase demand as the Bonds were traded and settled in the provinces away from the centralising influence of the Banks of England and Ireland; lower settlement costs would make them more attractive, raising their price and reducing the cost of borrowing; ease of deposit would appeal to those wishing to borrow on security; and, as Bonds, they would be attractive to foreigners.[33]

In other respects, the first issue was similar to funded debt.[v] Indeed, they were included as such in the annual returns. They carried an interest rate of 2¾ per cent from the date of issue (the beginning of 1854) until September 1864, and thereafter 2½ per cent until 1894. They were then redeemable at the option of the Treasury.

In 1866, the Exchequer Bills and Bond Act gave the Treasury powers to record the transfer of ownership on a register, while fixing the original life of the Bonds at a maximum of six years. In practice, this was not restrictive because the Act only regulated issuing, without empowering the Treasury to make an issue, so that the legislation authorising the Treasury to borrow could specify a longer term. One of the best known pieces of legislation, the Exchequer Bonds Act 1876, which provided for the sale of Bonds to pay for the purchase of shares in the Suez Canal, authorised a term of not more than 36 years, or any shorter period specified by the Treasury on the Bond.

The Bonds could be sold direct to the Commissioners when they were in funds and the size of the issue moderate. Thus, the £6m issued in 1854–5 to help provide for the Crimean War went to the public, but the £7.8m three-year Bonds issued between 1874–5 and 1879–80 to finance public works were taken by the Commissioners, as were the £4m issued to finance the Suez Canal purchase. Of the £6m Bonds issued to pay off the dissentients to the 1888 conversion scheme, only £1m were placed with the Commissioners.[34] The Commissioners took the much smaller issue made under the Cape of Good Hope (Advance) Act 1885.[35]

The Bonds taken by the public were normally sold by tender. A variation was used at the end of June 1891 when bidding for £3m was poor and felt to be providing expensive money; the Bonds were bought by the Banking Department of the Bank, advertised and 'by letting them out by degrees [the Bank] secured par terms for us.'[w] Later that summer, a further issue of £2m Exchequer Bonds was made by tender, only part being allotted. The remainder were sold differently. Instead of

v 16 & 17 Vict. c. 23.

w Tenders were invited for £3m one-, two- and three-year 2¾ per cent Exchequer Bonds. £1.625m were allotted and the remaining £1.375m were taken by the Bank. The notice read 'Applications for the unallotted balance...will be received, until further notice, at the Chief Cashier's Office...for payment on the 4th July, or after that date, at par, with accrued interest.' The Banking Department ledgers show that £600,000 were taken on 4 July. It is not known where the balance of £775,000 was held since the Issue Department balance sheet for 31 August shows no holding. BoE, AC 30/106, ADM 19/7 and ADM 7/54.

buying them, the Bank received applications for newly created Bonds, the interest running from the first day of the month of the application. They therefore matured at different dates, a 'considerable inconvenience', as Hamilton commented.[36] Thus were introduced the first recorded tap issues.

On 31 March 1899, there were no Exchequer Bonds outstanding.

Ways and Means Advances was the name given to temporary advances which might be made to the government on the credit of 'Ways and Means', i.e. the cash provided by Parliament to meet the expenditure sanctioned by the Votes. The purpose of the Advances was limited to preventing a stoppage of the government service in the event of a sudden reduction in revenue or some other emergency. If the reduction in revenue was more than temporary, it was assumed that the Chancellor would go to Parliament for longer-term finance. The total of Advances could not exceed the total of Ways and Means voted, and they had to be repaid not later than the end of the quarter after that in which the Advances were taken. The powers were given to the Treasury each year in the Consolidated Fund Acts, the last of which was called the Appropriation Act.

Until 1866, the Advances could be taken from anyone on the security of Exchequer Bills although, in practice, they came from the Bank of England, with a special clause exempting them from the provision of an Act of 1819[x] which forbade the Bank from lending to the government without the authority of Parliament. In 1866, the Exchequer Bills and Bond Act made the new form of Exchequer Bill unsuitable as security for Advances that might be paid off at any time and, in any case, could never be longer than six months. Instead, a new security, a simple IOU of a few lines, was introduced.[37] A further alteration was made in the same year so that Advances could only be taken from the Bank. The Appropriation Act 1869 made a further change, which allowed Advances to be taken from anyone. This was directed at the Commissioners, from whom an Advance was taken in October of that year. By an oversight, the need to exempt the Bank's Advances from the restrictions of the 1819 Act was omitted when the new clauses were being drafted and the Advances made by the Bank were *ultra vires* for more than twenty years. The position was corrected in the Fourth Consolidated Fund Act 1893 so that at the end of the century the Treasury had powers to take them from any source, including the Bank.[38]

Although the Treasury could take Advances from anywhere, there were advantages in limiting itself to the Bank and the Commissioners. Repayment was flexible, both in timing and amount, and the IOU sanctioned in 1867 was considered to be unsuitable as a negotiable instrument for the money market.[39]

Heavy disbursements were made by the Treasury at the beginning of each quarter, mainly because of the incidence of the payment dates on Consols and Annuities. These payments could have been met by holding Exchequer balances at a higher level, but the Treasury usually preferred to borrow because it would

x The Bank of England Act 1819.

otherwise have to hold large amounts of cash idle through much of the year. The Exchequer and Audit Departments Act 1866 gave the Treasury power to take Deficiency Advances from the Bank, as long as they were repaid in the same quarter. The Advances were restricted to the deficit on the Consolidated Fund for the previous quarter, together with the debt charges to be paid at the beginning of the following quarter.

The amount of these Advances depended on the size of the Exchequer balances and the pattern of revenue receipts. Repayment was flexible, both in size and amount, provided that the Advances were cleared by the end of the quarter.[40]

Treasury Bills originated in the 1870s when loans to local bodies for public works were straining Treasury resources and Exchequer Bills' design was deterring money market buyers, making temporary borrowing more expensive than the private sector's bank bills. The Chancellor, Northcote, asked Reginald Welby, at that time a Treasury junior and later its permanent secretary, to consult Walter Bagehot, editor of *The Economist*, about an alternative to Exchequer Bonds.[41] Bagehot suggested an instrument that was widely described, not least by himself and Welby, as being similar to a bill of exchange. This description was misleading, except that it was short-dated and appealed to the same type of investor, the banks and discount houses. In other respects, the new Bills were a form of certificate issued by the Treasury stating that the bearer was entitled to a specified sum out of public funds on a specified day; in contrast, a bill of exchange was an order signed by one person to another instructing a certain sum of money to be paid to the bearer or a specified third person.[42]

The Treasury Bills Act 1877 gave the Treasury powers to issue the new security, and a Treasury Minute of 16 March of the same year established the machinery: the Act did not provide any borrowing powers. The temporary nature of the finance was emphasised in the Act. The Bills could be issued with lives of up to twelve months. They could be renewed in the same financial year as they were paid off – that is they could be renewed, or dropped temporarily and renewed, up to 31 March of the year in which they were issued. If they were not renewed within this period, the power to borrow on them was permanently lost. The power for renewal provided in the 1877 Act also applied to Exchequer Bills and it was provided that one could replace the other. A Treasury Minute of 31 May 1889 added that Bills could be issued either by tender, for which it provided the regulations, or at a fixed rate to the Commissioners or 'such other person or persons as may be willing to buy' – wording which was to prove useful in 1928 when Currency Notes and Bank of England notes were being amalgamated. The 1877 Act and the Treasury Minutes of that year and of 1889 did not specify any denomination: £1,000, £5,000 and £10,000 were normal.

Every Treasury Bill was issued under some statutory borrowing authority. In 1876–7 and 1877–8, three- and six-months' Bills were issued to enable the Exchequer to make advances for public works; because the Bills were issued for this purpose, the interest was not met from the Fixed Charge. The issues reached £5.8m before the Public Works Loans Act 1879 authorised the Commissioners to make such advances from savings bank money. In 1885, Supply Bills were introduced as a convenient way of carrying part of the dead-weight debt, the interest being included in the Fixed Charge. They could be renewed indefinitely so long as the power to renew was exercised in the same financial year or, after a change incorporated in the Revenue Act 1906, in the first quarter of the following financial year. In 1887, when the separate Local Loans Fund was established, the Bills which had been issued for local loans purposes were merged into Supply Bills and the interest on these was then met from the Permanent Charge. Further Bills were issued under the National Debt Conversion Act 1888 and the National Debt Redemption Act 1889 to help meet expenses and pay off dissentients. Between 1890–1 and 1893–4, £2.6m were issued under the Imperial Defence Act 1888 and £2.6m in 1891–2 and 1892–3 under the Naval Defence Act 1889. More were issued during the Boer War. These were absorbed into the Permanent Charge in 1903 with the other war securities, so that they became indistinguishable from ordinary Supply Bills. During the following three years, the volume of Supply Bills was reduced to £14.5m by sinking fund purchases. After the outbreak of the Great War, these Bills were kept distinct in the annual accounts, from 1916 being firmly distinguished as 'Pre-War Treasury Bills', with the interest paid from the Permanent Charge. They were reduced by tenders for the two War Loans and National War Bonds in 1917 and 1918 until, at 31 March 1919, those remaining were treated as paid off and no longer appeared separately in the Finance Accounts.[43]

In 1902, Ways and Means Bills were added to Supply Bills and Bills issued for specific purposes. Between 1867 and 1902, the Consolidated Fund and Appropriation Acts had not provided for the issue of any marketable security, and fluctuations on the government account were financed by taking or repaying Ways and Means Advances. The money markets had become accustomed to an influx of liquidity at the beginning of each quarter as the Treasury took Deficiency Advances with which to pay the interest on Consols and tightness in the final financial quarter, when tax revenue was paid. The temporary borrowing in the first three quarters increased with the reliance on income tax. These flows on account of the Bank's largest customer were additional to its long-standing difficulty when money was easy of keeping rates up near its own rate, or 'making Bank rate effective'.[44] In 1902, when income tax had been raised to help pay for the Boer War, the Treasury took powers in the Appropriation Act to borrow on Bills from the public in the place of the customary Ways and Means Advances. These Ways and Means Bills differed from Supply Bills by being issued only for such periods as would permit them to be paid off in the financial year in which they were issued and, once paid off, they could not be renewed. The interest was paid from the Fixed Charge. The powers to borrow for the current year were renewed in each subsequent Appropriation Act and issues became frequent, averaging about fifteen a year and reaching a maximum of twenty-two in 1910 when the House of Lords rejected the 1909 Finance Bill and the collection of revenue was delayed. At one point in that year, the volume of tender Bills outstanding reached £36.7m. Despite the increase in the size and frequency of issue, Bills remained an instrument of temporary finance until 1914.[45] It was not until the Great War, when Bills were issued under the various War Loan Acts, that they became 'a means of carrying permanent or semi-permanent debt in short-dated form.'[46]

On 31 March 1899, there were £8.1m Treasury Bills outstanding.

Annuities due to the public and to other investors, including the Commissioners, appeared in the annual accounts as separate items. At 31 March 1899, the estimated capital value of the annuities for life and terms of years (the annuities outstanding to the public) was £12.4m and the total £36.2m (Table 1.3).

'Other capital liabilities' comprised borrowing by spending departments to pay for specific and tangible assets, mainly dockyards, telephones and government offices, whose nature was thought to justify treatment as capital expenditure spread over several years. Interest and repayment of principal were a charge on the Departmental Vote. Contemporaries contrasted the item with the dead-weight debt, in which the expenditure, in the oft-used phrase, 'had gone in powder and shot', leaving nothing behind. Three conditions had to be fulfilled before expenditure could be met by loan, although, the Treasury admitted in 1903, 'their hand has occasionally been forced': the item had to be above a certain limit (say £50,000) because the Vote prima facie was the source from which all administrative expenditure was expected to be met; the item had to be extraordinary, not resulting from wear and tear or the gradual growth of the service, but from new policies or an unforeseen increase in the establishment; and the work had to have a life which justified it being spread over years, perhaps as many as thirty. In principle, the Treasury resisted any suggestion that Advances could grow as *matériel* employed or personnel grew, but it agreed that this was academic because, if the number of men increased, so would the need for barracks, dockyards and hospitals.[47]

The borrowing was sanctioned under a wide range of Acts. Those appearing in the 31 March 1899 accounts give the flavour of the expenditure covered: the Imperial Defence Act 1888, the Russian–Dutch Loan Act 1891, the Barracks Act 1890, the Telegraph Acts 1892–8, the Uganda Railway Act 1896, the Naval Works Acts 1895 and 1899, the Royal Niger Company Act 1899, the Public Offices (Acquisition of Site) Act 1895, and the Public Offices (Whitehall) Site Act 1897.

The money was usually borrowed from the Commissioners on annuities and, less often, from the market on Treasury Bills or Exchequer Bonds. For the savings banks, there were both advantages and disadvantages in the arrangement. It reduced their demand for Consols, an increasingly important consideration as the price rose in the 1890s, and they gave a somewhat higher yield than that on Consols since the annuities were unmarketable and the capital was repaid over a period. On occasions, such as during the Boer War, it meant that they were not buying Consols at the same time as the Treasury was issuing them, a combination which would have been difficult to explain to the public. The major drawback was that the yield on Consols might have fallen before the returned capital could be reinvested.

In all cases, the interest and repayment of capital were met from the borrowing Departments' Votes. The rationale for this treatment was twofold. It further protected the Permanent Charge, ensuring that a separate and additional sinking fund was provided when new debt was created, and it was thought that Departments would be more careful in their spending if they were responsible for the debt throughout its life.[48]

On 31 March 1899, the total of other capital liabilities outstanding was £7.5m (Table 1.3).

Rearranging the sinking funds

Nine months before the nineteenth century went out and six months before the outbreak of war in South Africa, the Chancellor proposed an extension of some of the departmental annuities and a reduction in the Fixed Charge. Hamilton's advice came straight out of the Treasury's experience of the previous thirty years, scepticism about the strength of politicians' commitment to the virtuous path of debt reduction, and awareness that paying off the Debt too rapidly was to risk a public revolt, which could put an end to all debt repayment. The measures were immediately overtaken by the financing of the first expensive war since the beginning of the century and by the world-wide rise in interest rates.

The occasion for the changes was the need to plan for the expiry of three large departmental annuities and the reduction of the interest rate on Consols from 2¾ per cent to 2½ per cent in 1903 (see p.17). The changes would release £2.2m in 1902–3, a further £1m in 1903–4, £2.5m in 1904–5, and £1.5m in 1905–6; a total of £7.1m a year by 1905–6. Within this, the saving on Consols, on the assumption that £520m would be outstanding, was £1m in 1903–4, and £1.3m in a full year.[49]

The falling in of the annuities would have no effect on the size of the capital repayments within the Fixed Charge; less capital would be repaid through the annuities, but more would be available for repayment elsewhere. The drop in the rate on Consols, in contrast, would pass straight through into a larger repayment. The problem, thought Hamilton, was that the repayment would be seen to increase:

> Nobody, however, will imagine that that fund, which is not specifically appropriated, could be retained at so vastly an increased amount. The taxpayers have an unanswerable claim to the relief (or greater part of it) afforded by the reduction of interest on Consols, and their claim to a large portion of the diminished payments in respect of the service of the Debt, by reason of the termination of the annuities, would be by no means easy to resist.
>
> The Chancellor of the Exchequer of the day would, accordingly, be exposed to a series of temptations in quick succession, and to great pressure for sweeping reductions in taxation. For this reason, and for the reasons that the taxpayers of the four years ending 1905–6 have no special title to an abnormal relief, it seems to be highly desirable to bespeak part of the windfalls.

He then recalled a step proposed by Gladstone in 1881, and taken by Childers in 1883. Various annuities, amounting to £5m, had been due to expire in 1885. By prolonging their lives before they had actually expired, Childers had removed temptation from the path of a future Chancellor:

> By taking a somewhat similar step now, we shall be strengthening the hands of the Chancellor of the Exchequer in the early years of [the] next century, and thus working in the interests of the future of the Sinking Fund.

The present Parliament could not bind the hand of the next, but it could strengthen the hand of those who wanted to protect the sinking fund. To have an excessive debt repayment was making the whole process vulnerable.[50]

To these arguments for reducing the size of the sinking fund in the short term, so that it would be maximised in the long term, Hamilton added three others. First, both Northcote and Childers had had in mind the possibility of conversion and the support of gilt-edged prices when they determined the size of the Fixed Charge. The Treasury now had less interest in market prices: it could not foresee returning to the markets as a borrower and Consols could not be redeemed or converted until 1923. Second, the size of the sinking fund should bear some relation to the amount of debt. Until recently, the high point for debt reduction had been 1884–5, when the sinking fund represented 0.95 per cent of the Debt. It seemed that this would rise to 1.18 per cent in 1898–9. A reduction of £1½m would bring the proportion back to the 1884–5 level. Third, the unfunded debt had been reduced to only £8m and the market was so thin that there could be only minimal dealings in 2½ per cent and 2¾ per cent Annuities; in practice, buying government securities for the sinking fund meant buying Consols. Of the £520m of this issue outstanding, the Commissioners already owned £131.5m and other departments £30.5m. Of the remaining £358m, an unknown proportion was held by banks, insurance companies, trustees and foreigners, who would be difficult to dislodge. In 1884–5, the New Sinking Fund had represented 1.3 per cent of the £530m of the Consols in public hands. By 1899–1900, it was estimated to have risen to 2.2 per cent. This was reflected in the difficulties the savings banks had experienced in investing their deposits:

> 8 or 9 millions per annum represent a formidable sum for which the Government have to find employment; and though every opportunity is taken to invest money in other Parliamentary securities than Consols (such as loans to the Local Loans Fund, the Irish Guaranteed Land Stock, and the recently guaranteed Greek Bonds), yet the residue which has to be invested in Consols cannot be otherwise than very large. In short, the Savings Banks Funds are most formidable competitors with the Sinking Fund for Consols…[51]

The point was being reached when public opinion would no longer tolerate buying Consols at a premium as the government would soon be able to redeem them at par.[52]

Following the precedent of 1883, the Chancellor decided to prolong the £2.2m Savings Bank Annuities to 1911–12, converting them into smaller £0.6m annuities.

With the money saved, he set up two new annuities to run to 1923: an annuity of £0.7m in exchange for the cancellation of the Book Debt of £13m and another of £0.9m in exchange for £15m Consols. The other two annuities were left to run; their falling in in 1906 was to provide a useful flexibility to the sinking fund in the very different circumstances after the Boer War.

These terms reflected the experience of the 1890s in two ways. First, the Book Debt was selected because it would not affect the supply of Consols, while it avoided the cancellation of a security which stood at a premium. Second, the year chosen for expiry coincided with the option to redeem Consols, so that the Treasury could be sure that its price would have fallen back towards par when the largest purchases were being carried out.[53]

✣ ✣ ✣

The structure of the Debt, the characteristics of the securities and the arrangements for repayment described in this chapter survived the challenges of financing the War of 1914–18 and of the refinancings of the 1920s with only technical adjustments. Internal borrowing for the Great War was primarily on Exchequer Bonds, or on National War Bonds and War Loans with very similar features. Funded issues, similar to Consols, returned between 1921 and 1932 as the vehicle for the Treasury's long-term – permanent – borrowing. Very short-dated borrowing during the Great War took the form of Ways and Means Advances, Deficiency Advances and Treasury Bills. After the War, capital advances from the savings banks grew as they provided the credit for supporting the unemployed. Even the floating rate on Exchequer Bills returned for a short, abortive, innings. The emphasis on the disciplines of debt repayment continued to hold the Treasury in their thrall. The Fixed Charge lingered on during the War, was replaced by a fixed sinking fund, and then returned in 1928, inadequate, its funds earmarked to the repayment of specific marketable issues, but recognisably the same. Innovation lay in two areas. Borrowing in foreign currencies and designing new instruments suitable for sale to a mass market. It was in the method of selling to the general investor and in placing paper overseas that the first, tentative changes were seen during the war in South Africa.

Endnotes

1 Hamilton (1889).
2 *National Debt: Report by the Secretary and Comptroller General of the Proceedings of the Commissioners for the Reduction of the National Debt, from 1786 to 31st March 1890* (C. 6539), 1891, p. 3; Higgs (1914) pp. 89–91. The most recent formal meeting of the Commissioners was held in 1861.
3 *BGS*, pp. 320–1; T 168/11, Hamilton, 'Memorandum on the Sinking Funds', 16 October 1896, pp. 2–4; Hargreaves (1930), pp. 158–60.
4 Royal Commission on Income Tax (1920), Appendix 7(j); Buxton (1888), II, pp. 29–30; Horne (1947) p. 234; T 168/61, Hamilton, 'The Financial Outlook vis à vis the City', 9 October 1903.
5 *Hansard* (Commons), 13 February 1863, cols 322–3.

6 T 168/11, Hamilton, 'Memorandum on the Sinking Funds', 16 October 1896, p. 9.
7 Buxton (1888), II, p. 351.
8 Hargreaves (1930) p. 190. £6m Exchequer Bonds were replaced by a Terminable Annuity expiring in 1885. The annuity cost £1.4m a year, but the Permanent Charge was only raised by £0.8m, to £28.8m.
9 T 168/86, Hamilton, 'The Sinking Fund', 30 September 1897; Mallet (1913) pp. 4–6, 352–3; *National Debt: Report by the Secretary and Comptroller General of the Proceedings of the Commissioners for the Reduction of the National Debt, from 1786 to 31st March 1890* (C. 6539), 1891, pp. 48–9.
10 *Hansard* (Commons), 15 April 1875, cols 1039–41; T 168/11, Hamilton, 'Memorandum on the Sinking Funds', 16 October 1896, p. 10.
11 Buxton (1888), II, p. 218.
12 T 168/11, Hamilton, 'Memorandum on the Sinking Funds', 16 October 1896; T 168/86, Hamilton, 'Sinking Fund', 30 September 1897.
13 T 168/11, Hamilton, 'Memorandum on the Sinking Funds', 16 October 1896, pp. 7–8.
14 Ibid.
15 T 168/86, Hamilton, 'The Sinking Funds', 30 September 1897. In referring to a 'war chest' and the capital sum of £200m, which could be supported by the Charge if the New Sinking Fund were suspended, Hamilton was following comments made by Harcourt two years earlier. GRO/HBP/D 2455/PCC 18, Harcourt to Hicks-Beach, 18 November 1895.
16 *Government Departments Securities* (HCP 147), 11 April 1899 .
17 Hargreaves (1930) pp. 206–9; *BGS*, pp. 212–3.
18 *Government Departments Securities* (HCP 263), 27 June 1890, and (HCP 147), 11 April 1899 .
19 Ibid. (HCP 263), 27 June 1890, and (HCP 147), 11 April 1899; *National Debt: annual returns*. For a contemporary discussion of these trends and their effects on the prices of government securities, see the *Bankers' Magazine*, March 1899.
20 Horne (1947), Appendices II and III.
21 *National Debt: Report by the Secretary and Comptroller General of the Proceedings of the Commissioners for the Reduction of the National Debt, from 1786 to 31st March 1890* (C. 6539), 1891, p. 275; T 168/87, Murray to Hamilton, 10 January 1900.
22 Morley (1903), I, pp. 650–1, and II, p. 52. The quotation comes from an 'Undated fragment.' I would like to thank Professor Pressnell for drawing my attention to this reference.
23 Clapham (1944), II, p. 330; Bahlman (1993), pp. 126–7; BoE, C40/399, 'Treasury Bills'. Hamilton refers to £2m gold, and Clapham and the Bank memorandum to £3m.
24 GRO/HBP/PCC 72/1, Hamilton to Hicks-Beach, 2 and 4 January 1898; Bahlman (1993), pp. 345–50. GRO/HBP/PCC/34 contains Hicks-Beach's correspondence with Salisbury.
25 *National Debt: annual returns*, 1895 and 1903.
26 Clapham (1944), II, pp. 340–1.
27 Hamilton's *An Account of the Operations under the National Debt Conversion Act, 1888, and the National Debt Redemption Act, 1889* (Hamilton, 1889), published in the same year, is the classic record of Goschen's great conversion. He provides an account of previous conversions in pp. 11–14.
28 *BGS*, pp. 130–3; *National Debt: annual returns*; Hargreaves (1930), pp. 162–4, 207, 209–10.
29 Hamilton (1889), pp. 1–2; Hargreaves (1930), pp. 53–4 and 161–2.
30 The Minute was dated 9 March 1867.
31 T 168/32, Chancellor to Hamilton, 1 December 1894. Underlining in the original.

32 *Exchequer Bills Forgery: Report of the Commissioners*, BPP, Session 1842, vol. XVIII; T 168/5, Welby, 'Floating Debt of the United Kingdom: Memorandum drawn to give information requested by the Netherlands Government', 23 January 1878; T 168/12, Hamilton to Chancellor, 2 September 1886; T 168/23, Memorandum, Hamilton, 8 May 1891; T 168/32, Hamilton to Chancellor, 28 November, and Chancellor to Hamilton, 1 December 1894; T 168/76A, Hamilton, 'Our Unfunded Debt Liabilities', January 1887; T 168/38, Hamilton to Chancellor, 9 May, and Hamilton to Chancellor, 12 May 1896; *National Debt: annual returns*; Palgrave (1894) pp. 784–5; King (1936) pp. 115–7; Bagehot (1978) XI, pp. 410–1.

33 *Hansard* (Commons) 8 April 1853, cols 815–28; Northcote (1862), pp. 225–6.

34 Hargreaves (1930), p. 169; Northcote (1862), pp. 251–4; Hamilton (1889), p. 52.

35 T 168/76A, Hamilton, 'Our Unfunded Debt Liabilities', January 1887; Hamilton (1889), p. 63.

36 T 168/27, Hamilton to Chancellor, 24 August 1892; T 170/31, Hamilton, 'Conversion Exchequer Bonds', 21 January 1900. Tenders were invited for £2m one-, two- and three-year $2^3/_4$ per cent Exchequer Bonds and applications for £1.149m were allotted at par. The balance of £851,000 was offered on the same terms. BoE, AC 30/109.

37 The IOU is reproduced in BoE, G15/103, Hamilton, 'Ways and Means Advances', 30 August 1893.

38 Ibid.; T 168/30, Hamilton to Chancellor, 30 August 1893.

39 T 168/76A, Hamilton, 'Our Unfunded Debt Liabilities', January 1887; T 168/5, Welby, 'Floating Debt of the United Kingdom: Memorandum drawn to give information requested by the Netherlands Government', 23 January 1878; Higgs (1914) p. 94; BoE, G15/103, Hamilton, 'Ways and Means Advances', 30 August 1893.

40 T 168/76A, Hamilton, 'Our Unfunded Debt Liabilities', January 1887; T 168/35, Hamilton to Chancellor, 13 September 1895; T 168/5, Welby, 'Floating Debt of the United Kingdom: Memorandum drawn to give information requested by the Netherlands Government', 23 January 1878; Higgs (1914), pp. 22–3.

41 *The Economist*, letter from Welby, 20 November 1909, p. 1045; Bagehot (1978), XI, pp. 405–11.

42 BoE, C40/399, 'Treasury Bills'.

43 Ibid; *National Debt: annual returns*.

44 Sayers (1976), I, pp. 37–43; King (1936), pp. 311–15: BoE, C40/399, 'Treasury Bills'.

45 King (1936) p. 277; BoE, C40/399, 'Treasury Bills'.

46 The words are from King (1936), p. 277.

47 GRO/HBP/D 2455/PCC 83, Memorandum on Capital Advances, 14 March 1903, probably Hamilton or Mowatt.

48 T 168/38, Hamilton to Chancellor, 16 June 1896; T 168/11, Hamilton, 'Memorandum on the Sinking Funds', 16 October 1896.

49 *National Debt Charges* (HCP 154), 13 April 1899.

50 T 168/86, Hamilton, 'The Sinking Fund', 30 September 1897.

51 *National Debt Charges* (HCP 154), 13 April 1899 .

52 T 168/86, Hamilton, 'The Sinking Fund', 30 September 1897; *National Debt Charges* (HCP 154), 13 April 1899.

53 T 168/86, Hamilton, 'The Sinking Fund', 30 September 1897; *National Debt Charges* (HCP 154), 13 April 1899; *Hansard* (Commons), 13 April 1899, cols 1002–16.

2 An Edwardian debt

> Our unfunded debt is much too big. It is very inconvenient and might be a great danger. It is bad enough to run the risk of war with an impaired field gun. It is almost worse to run the risk of war with an impaired credit; and there [is] nothing [more] calculated to have a bad effect upon it than an unmanageable floating debt.
>
> Sir Edward Hamilton,
> January 1905 (Bahlman, 1993), p. 454

> [we]...are never out of the money market. Our repeated borrowings are a source of disquietude in the City and of constant anxiety to those who are charged with the care of the National Finances. A situation is thus created which is precarious even in time of peace, and might become most serious if we were engaged in war...My colleagues will understand with what feelings I watched the development of the North Sea incident and contemplated the possibility that we might at any moment be called upon to finance another great national struggle.[a]
>
> Austen Chamberlain, February 1905,
> 'The Unfunded Debt', 14 February 1905, T 168/94[a]

The South African War was financed by a mixture of old and new techniques and instruments. It began with Treasury Bills and continued with a War Loan sold direct to the public, a revolution in British debt management and the precursor of the Exchequer Bonds and War Bonds of the Great War. There followed more Exchequer Bonds and Treasury Bills: a reversion to instruments suited to the large professional investor and the money market. The reliance on short-dated paper produced indigestion in the markets and, when peace negotiations failed and continued conflict was promised, there came two issues of permanent debt:

a The reference is to an incident in October 1904 when Russian naval vessels passing through the North Sea on their way to the Far East and the Russo–Japanese War fired on British fishing boats.

Consols, partly pre-placed with City and overseas syndicates and partly sold direct to the general investor; a mixture of the traditional and new methods of issue.

After the war, the Treasury's priority was to lengthen or pay off the new short-term debt. Its efforts were hampered by a rise in the yield on Consols and the growth of other government demands on savings: a government-guaranteed loan for the Transvaal, Local Loans, Irish Land Stock and capital advances. It was feared that borrowing by colonial governments and local authorities in their own names would add to the Treasury's problems. By the time the floating debt had been tamed and the Treasury was able to turn its thoughts to reducing the size of the funded debt, the sinking fund was seen as a way of supporting Consols, whose weak price was causing the government embarrassment, rather than of retiring debt *per se*.

The challenge was met without a funding operation. Two changes helped to bring the short-term debt under control: the Commissioners' Terminable Annuities were not replaced as they fell in and capital expenditure for military works was met from current revenue, freeing the savings banks to take up other debt. The most important contribution, however, came from handsome revenue surpluses and increases in the New Sinking Fund – a decision taken by both Conservative and Liberal governments to increase the tax revenues applied to debt repayment. The Fixed Charge reached a peak under Henry Asquith in 1907–8, before the volume of short-term debt was reduced and the demands of social welfare and the Navy grew; a weaker approach was signalled by Lloyd George's diversions of Old Sinking Fund to capital works. By 1914, the overall Debt, although still above that of 1899, had been reduced by £92.2m, or 11.5 per cent, from its level in 1903.

Borrowing for the South African War

The war that broke out in South Africa in October 1899 was the first since the Crimean War to require borrowing on a large scale. As would happen in 1914 and 1939, the Treasury looked to the financing of previous wars for guidance, and in particular for the balance between borrowing and taxation.[b] Hamilton's paper, prepared in February 1900 shortly before the first loan was issued, was based on a brief from John Bradbury, who was to be a Joint Permanent Secretary during the Great War. Recent wars had been colonial or imperial expeditions, whose cost was relatively small and spread over several years.[c] However, the major conflicts were more costly. After allowing for normal peacetime expenditure on the armed

b I would like to thank Professor Howson for drawing my attention to the 1939 memoranda.

c The Abyssinian expedition of 1867–9 cost £8.3m and was wholly met from revenue; precautions taken during the Franco–Prussian War of 1870 cost £1.5m, all of which was met from revenue; military and naval operations between 1877 and 1881 in Afghanistan, Zululand and precautions during the Russo–Turkish War cost £12m, of which two-thirds was borrowed; in 1881–6, military and naval operations in Afghanistan, South Africa, Egypt, the Sudan and precautions in central Asia cost £21m, of which 42 per cent was borrowed. T 170/31, Bradbury, 'The Financing of Naval and Military Operations', 12 February 1900, and Hamilton, 'Taxation versus Loans', 20 February 1900.

Table 2.1 Borrowing for the South African War and Boxer rebellion

Date of prospectus	*Security*	*Nominal issued (£m)*	*Price (yield)*	*Cash proceeds (£m)*
1899 and 1900				
	Treasury Bills	8		8
1900				
9 March	2¾ per cent National War Loan 5/4/10	30	£98 10s 0d (£2 18s 1d)	29.5
July–December	Treasury Bills	5	–	5
3 August	3 per cent Exchequer Bonds 7/8/03	10	£98 0s 0d (£3 17s 9d)	9.8
23 November	3 per cent Exchequer Bonds 7/12/05	3	£98 2s 10d* (£3 8s 2d)	2.9
1901				
8 February	3 per cent Exchequer Bonds 7/12/05	11	£97 5s 4d* (£3 13s 5d)	10.7
20 April	2¾ per cent Consols	60	£94 10s 0d (£2 13s 2d)	56.6
1902				
16 April	2¾ per cent Consols	32	£93 10s 0d (£2 13s 7d)	29.9
Totals		159		152.4*

Notes
*Average price at tender.
Cash proceeds is the sum raised after expenses, including the cost of discount on payments made in full.

Sources: *BGS*, pp. 144-5, 166-7, 170-1, 240-1; T 170/31, Turpin, 'War Loans', 30 August 1914; *Wars in South Africa and China (Cost and Expenditure)* (HCP 130), 29 April 1903.

forces, the French wars at the beginning of the century were estimated to have cost £831m over twenty-three years, financed by £440m of borrowing (53 per cent) and £391m of taxation. The cost of the Crimean War, spread over three financial years, was found to be about £67.5m, of which 47 per cent was borrowed.[1]

The Boer War together with the British contingent that helped suppress the Boxer rebellion in China, which broke out at the same time, were to cost £217.2m spread over thirty-two months. Of this, £149.5m (69 per cent) was to come from borrowing. Actual borrowings during the period were £152.4m of cash from £159m nominal of debt (Table 2.1).[2] In addition, the Debt was increased by £9.2m over the level it would have reached in 1900–1 and 1901–2 by the suspension of the New Sinking Fund, including the Terminable Annuities 'wrapped' in it.

The Treasury also looked to the Crimean War for guidance on the procedures and methods when borrowing was large and a deliberate pace not possible. The first loan had been announced on 13 April 1855 when the Stock Exchange was told that the Bank had been informed of the Government's intention to make an issue and contractors – financial houses that would purchase the entire issue for sale to investors – were invited to attend a meeting at the Treasury. The proposal was to raise £16m by means of the contractor paying £100 for each £100 nominal of 3 per cent Consols plus a thirty-year annuity: a principle similar to Goschen's Consols, which could be regarded (and are so treated in this book) as 2½ per cent with a £0 5s 0d annuity for fifteen years.[d] The bids were in terms of the price to be paid for the annuity. The best bid, £0 14s 6d for each £100 of Consols, came from Rothschilds, with whom a provisional contract was made on 20 April.[e] Later the same day, the Chancellor announced the terms in his budget speech and embodied them in a series of detailed Resolutions.[3] The same procedure was followed with the second and third loans, except that the price was in terms of the amount of Consols which the contractor would accept for £100 cash. That of February 1856 found Rothschilds the only bidder.[f] Once again, the Chancellor made a provisional agreement and the details were announced later in a supplementary financial statement. It received Parliamentary sanction and the Royal Assent during the following three weeks. Rothschilds were also the contractors for the final borrowing taken in May 1856 at the same time as the budget.[4]

2¾ per cent National War Loan 1910 (9 March 1900)[g]

As always, the war was expected to be short and the first borrowing was on Bills.[h] By the middle of January 1900, £8.1m had been sold and the Treasury had the power to issue a further £8m. Hamilton was feeling uncomfortable; only once had this amount been exceeded, after Goschen's conversion, when £17.5m was outstanding for a short period.[5] Soundings about a longer-term loan were started at the beginning of that month and proceeded at an unhurried pace, covering the

d As we have seen, between 1888 and April 1903 Consols carried a nominal rate of 2¾ per cent. Thereafter, they carried a rate of 2½ per cent. They could be called by the Treasury after 5 April 1923. Following contemporary methodology, the additional ¼ per cent paid until 1903 is treated as a Terminable Annuity expiring on 5 April 1903. The value of this annuity is added to the running yield to give the yields quoted in this book before 1903. Because Consols were callable after 5 April 1923, they are valued as a perpetual issue if their price was beneath par, and as a dated issue redeemable on 5 April 1923 if their price was above par. Before 1903, this rule is complicated by the additional ¼ per cent annuity. The solution has been to ignore the *price* and treat the issue as redeemable in 1923 if the *yield* (including the annuity) is less than 2½ per cent.

e The cost to the government was therefore £3 14s 6d per cent for thirty years and 3 per cent thereafter. This was calculated to be the same as issuing 3 per cent Consols at 87⅝ to yield £3 8s 6d per cent as a perpetual annuity. T 170/31, Bradbury, 'The Financing of Naval and Military Operations', 12 February 1900. Bradbury's source was Northcote (1862), p. 278.

f Rothschilds offered £100 for each £112 5s 0d of Consols. The Treasury rejected this and Rothschilds agreed to pay £100 for each £111 2s 2d, the equivalent of buying Consols at 90. T 170/31, Bradbury, 'The Financing of Naval and Military Operations', 12 February 1900. Bradbury's source was Northcote (1862), p. 278.

g The dates included in the subheadings for each issue refer to the day on which the prospectuses were published.

h Treasury Bills Act 1899.

type of security, the terms and the method of issue – whether by public subscription or, in the Crimean fashion, by direct sale to contractors or perhaps with some kind of guarantee or pre-placing.

Because the Treasury had so little experience of borrowing, the Chancellor, Sir Michael Hicks-Beach, and Hamilton consulted widely: from within the government, Hervey, the Comptroller-General, and Murray, from the POSB; from the City, the Bank of England, the Government Broker, Barings, Morgans (both the New York and London houses), Rothschilds, several stockbrokers and a private financier, Sir Ernest Cassel. The notable absences were the joint stock bankers, with a single exception – Felix Schuster, the Governor of the Union Bank of London, who Hamilton called 'probably the highest banking authority in London'.[6]

A scheme to attract small investors by selling unmarketable five- or seven-year securities to savings bank depositors was considered and rejected during January, but not before it had drawn attention to the advantages of borrowing directly from the 'genuine' investor, throwing subscriptions open to the public and favouring small applicants. Small investors, advised the officials, disliked fluctuations in the price of their securities and were content with a low rate of interest providing they had easy access to their capital. As we have seen, there had been little use made of the savings bank Stock-dealing facility since its introduction almost twenty years earlier. To be successful, an issue would require a rate of 3½ or 3¾ per cent, compared with 3 per cent in the open market. This would not only be expensive, but also hard to justify to other investors. Echoing comments made by Gladstone in 1859, Hamilton pointed out that selling such securities to depositors would be a new departure which might draw attention to the underlying security held by the savings banks and the use the Treasury made of the funds. It would need expensive advertising and many circulars would not reach depositors as they constantly changed addresses. Finally, it might appear that the government was turning to the small investor because its credit in the money market had deteriorated.[7] It was left to Schuster to warn that the response of existing depositors could be such that the savings banks would have to sell Consols and that this would be compounded if they were also required to make advances for capital works. Schuster described this possibility as 'serious'.[8] The methods of pricing used during the Crimean War – Consols plus an annuity or an amount of Consols for £100 of cash – were not even mentioned; it seems to have been assumed from the start that there would be a simple price per £100 nominal. Three types of security were considered: Exchequer Bonds, with the implication that they would be short- or medium-dated; a further tranche of Consols; and a special dated issue to be called 'National War Loan', to distinguish it from Exchequer Bonds, which, said Schuster, had the reputation among the investing public of not being a 'very convenient or negotiable security' and were 'almost extinct & never much appreciated'.[9]

From the start, the City advised against permanent debt, with two powerful exceptions. The Bank of England throughout the war urged reliance on Consols, which it believed could always be sold on the finest terms because bankers needed them for liquidity and because they bore 'a special air of sanctity.'[10] The other was Rothschilds, who were regarded by the Treasury as essential, whether it was to be a sale or a guaranteed subscription. They thought Consols would ensure success and that 'the whole amount could be guaranteed in an afternoon by the Bankers and large financial institutions.'[11]

Schuster showed the greatest capacity to approach the subject with a fresh mind. In common with Hamilton and many in the City, he thought Consols would prove expensive because interest rates would fall after the war: although it would not be popular with investors, borrowing should be kept as short as possible, and he urged a security of the type ultimately issued. He floated the possibility of underwriting, a 'Guarantee Syndicate', to take any of the issue not subscribed by the public, and made two suggestions that would be adopted after 1914. With the US Treasury's 5–20 year Bonds in mind, he proposed a double-dated maturity and, to add to the attractions of a ten-year issue, he thought holders should be given the right to convert into a replacement at par.[12] Cassel, although agreeing that Consols could be sold on fine terms, warned that there were bear positions in the market and that the opportunity would be taken to drive down the price.[13] The Treasury itself thought that Consols' protection from redemption until 1923 was an additional reason for expecting them to recover strongly after the war as interest rates fell, so that the sinking funds would end up buying them back at a higher price. Finally, neither the Chancellor nor his officials wanted to add to the permanent debt, but intended leaving the obligation as an incubus to encourage future governments to pursue a 'virtuous' sinking fund policy – an objective that fitted with the expectation that the rebellious, but gold rich, Transvaal would in due course pay an indemnity, enabling a short maturity to be paid off from the proceeds.[14] The choice came down to Exchequer Bonds or a special War Loan. Exchequer Bonds were rejected because, as well as having little appeal to the general investor, the Treasury were told they could sell only a few millions.[15]

The decision to issue at a fixed price was made without difficulty; there was universal agreement that private investors would have difficulty with the process of tendering and be shy of selecting prices for themselves.[16] Indeed, some of the professionals felt the same, having recently suffered losses when jobbers had worked the price lower of Local Loans in front of a new issue, tendered successfully, and then worked the price up by some five points.[17]

The question of a guarantee, or underwriting, was not so easily decided. The most recent large borrowing, for the Crimean War, had been by sale of the entire issue to a contractor. Since then, the Treasury's experience had been limited to issuing Treasury Bills by tender and Exchequer Bonds, both by tenders and at fixed prices. This was its first experience of large, uncovered, borrowing by means of a public issue. Schuster's suggestion that the 'Continental and American custom' of forming a guaranteeing syndicate of 'Banks & financial firms & Institutions' to contract to subscribe any part not taken by investors was barely discussed.[18] Instead, the sale of part before the public issue was canvassed, although not in the cosy terms proposed by Cassel:

> Guarantee should be worked quietly among few big City houses & Banks – no need for commission, merely 1/8% brokerage. The inducement to guarantors

> to cover Stock should be promise [*sic*] that not less than one third of Stock should be allotted to them.
>
> ...that at instance of Rothschilds & himself an offer or offers should be made to C. of E. by limited numbers of guarantors who would be privately apprised of his views.[19]

The question of a pre-placement was tied to the possibility of selling part in the USA through J. P. Morgan & Co., thus helping to restore the Bank of England's gold holdings, which had fallen to a low level, and gaining a demonstration of American support for the war. By the beginning of March, however, Hamilton was treating the decision as a choice between issuing at a higher price with a guaranteed subscription or at a lower price with a pure public subscription.[20] With enthusiasm in the City mounting, taking with it the proposed price, the Chancellor decided to appeal directly to the investor for the whole amount. J. S. Morgan & Co. in London reported to J. P. Morgan & Co. in New York that the decision reflected the Chancellor's fear of a public reaction if part was sold in the USA, but it seems to have been settled by two developments:[21] by 7 March, two days before the prospectus was published, the Loan was being quoted 'blind' (priced in the market before the Loan had been issued) at one point premium and Hamilton had lined up £10m of firm subscriptions from only six investors 'without any formal guarantee'.[i]

The issue that came from these deliberations was in most ways a long-dated 2¾ per cent Exchequer Bond, the precursor of those which were to become common fifteen years later. It was not sold to a contractor or syndicate, nor was it underwritten. Instead, it was offered directly to the investor; the name itself was meant to attract the patriot in the street. This was reflected in the wide distribution of prospectuses and the means of evidencing ownership.[j] There was some debate about the latter. Some thought Bonds could deter the small investor, who wanted to be able to invest in smaller round amounts than £100, whereas inscribed Stock (see Appendix I) was neither understood by, nor convenient for, the foreigner, especially the Americans. At Schuster's suggestion, therefore, ownership was recorded in both forms and the issue became the first 'Loan'.[22] There was a single fixed maturity date, 5 April 1910, and it was issued at a fixed price: 98½ to give a Gross Redemption Yield (GRY) of £2 18s 1d per cent. To simplify calculations and to attract long-term holders, the first three dividends were payable on the whole nominal amount, although the issue was partly paid. Officials calculated the value of the interest earned on the money waiting to be paid over on the call

i Bank of England £4m, Bank of Ireland £0.5m, Commissioners £3m, Rothschilds £3m, Cassel £1m and Glyn Mills £0.5m. T 168/87, Hamilton, note for the Chancellor, 3 March 1900. The letter from Hervey describing the considerations lying behind the Commissioners' application is in T 168/87, Hervey to Hamilton, 22 February 1900.

j Prospectuses were available from London banks and the principal stockbrokers, unlike those for issues of Exchequer Bonds, which could be obtained only at the Banks of England and Ireland and the Government Broker, Mullens, Marshall & Co.

dates to be worth £0 14s 5d, which reduced the issue price to £97 15s 7d and raised the yield to £2 19s 10d per cent.[23] In one respect, the Loan differed from most of the Exchequer Bonds and all of the War Bonds issued in the Great War. Because the Chancellor was advised that a single large loan was preferable to a series of smaller issues, it was made payable in ten instalments spread over eight months. Short-dated borrowing after December 1915 was always fully paid as the Bonds were on tap and it was never possible to envisage demand being in excess of the Treasury's needs.

When asking for borrowing powers, the Chancellor rejected the procedure used at the time of the Crimean War. He needed £35m, of which £30m should come from the Loan and the rest from Bills. He asked for a Resolution that limited him to that amount and a maximum length of ten years, but left him free to select the other terms. He would insert the other details in the Bill that was to become the War Loan Act 1900 at a later stage.[24]

The terms were well received, with 39,000 applications for £335m (of which 30,800 were for between £100 and £1,000) and the issue promptly rose to a premium of two points.[k] None was pre-placed, so little was sold in the USA. Morgans had been authorised to receive and forward subscriptions and applied for £12m, including £5m for themselves and £2m for Mutual Life Insurance Co. They agreed that they would be prepared to ship gold to meet the payments and the Bank agreed to meet any loss from shipping metal, rather than remitting by bills. They were allotted only £755,500 and, because of the insignificant size, they had to offer to take over any which their clients did not want.[25]

3 per cent Exchequer Bonds 1903 (3 August 1900)

Hamilton described the decision taken during the summer of 1900 to issue Exchequer Bonds as 'almost Hobson's choice'. He felt that the Treasury 'had got out perhaps a sufficient amount of Treasury Bills' and the Chancellor still wanted to avoid Consols. A further issue of the War Loan would have been unpopular because selling by small investors had taken its price to a two point discount and the City was 'overloaded with it'. Leaving themselves with plenty of discretion, the Treasury took powers in the Supplemental War Loan Act 1900 to borrow £13m by Bills, Exchequer Bonds or a War Loan.[26]

Once more, the Chancellor saw advantages in placing part of the issue in the USA to attract gold to the Bank, whose reserve was at its lowest for the time of year for seven years, as well as on this occasion to 'relieve the [London] market.'[27] Again, the Treasury consulted widely – except with the joint stock bankers. A coupon of 3 per cent and a price of 98 (£3 17s 9d per cent) on a three-year Bond suited both London and New York and half the £10m was pre-placed with Morgans,

k Applications for £400 or less were allotted in full and those for £5,000 and more were allotted 6 per cent. The Chief Cashier reported the number of applications at between 40,000 and 45,000. T 170/31, 'The War Loans', unsigned, June 1905.

who also put in an application in the ordinary way for a further £1m. As a condition of the £5m pre-placement, they agreed to ship gold.[l]

The sale at a fixed price, rather than by tender, was unusual for Exchequer Bonds and was probably intended to make possible the placing in the USA. They were payable in four instalments and, in common with the War Loan, there was a full coupon on the first interest payment date. This reduced the price by £0 7s 3d per cent, raising the yield by £0 2s 7d per cent. It was an unfortunate issue because there was an additional cost. Morgans insisted on 1/4 per cent commission, which the Treasury felt unable to pay as London was receiving only 1/8 per cent. Instead, the Treasury paid the Bank 1/8 per cent for its services, which it passed to Morgans, together with the standard 1/8 per cent disclosed in the prospectus. This was legitimised by the Bank regarding it as 'fair consideration for the chance of receiving gold'.[28]

This unfortunate issue was marked by City rivalries and official error. Competition between Barings and Morgans over distribution in the USA soured their relations.[29] The Bank withdrew the notice in the prospectus that stated that half had been pre-placed, and, unsurprisingly, was accused of withholding material information. Many, including Rothschilds, were angered when the Bank shut them out by closing lists as soon as it was clear that the balance had been subscribed.[30] The lesson, said Hamilton, was to state 'boldly' in the prospectus when there was a pre-placing and to keep the lists open all day, even if it meant that allotments had to be scaled down drastically.[31]

3 per cent Exchequer Bonds 1905 (23 November 1900 and 8 February 1901)

The remaining £3m authorised by the Supplemental War Loan Act 1900 was raised during November by means of five-year 3 per cent Exchequer Bonds.[m] Another tranche of £11m of the same issue, authorised by the Supplemental War Loan (No. 2) Act 1900, was issued in February 1901. Once again, there were negotiations with Morgans about a placing in New York, but the City, although feeling that it had absorbed more short government paper than was comfortable, also complained that the profits on the issues were accruing to foreigners.[32] The Chancellor, no doubt influenced by the earlier problems with the New York tranche, decided to make the entire issue in London by tender. He was proved right; the issue was covered more than twice and sold at an average price of £97 5s 4d (£3 3s 5d per cent).

l Morgans tried to put in an application for a further £1m, but were shut out by the early closing of the lists. The initial application for £1m was scaled down pro rata with other applicants so that the House ended up with £5.6m. MGP/GH, MS 21802/8 and MS 21802/9: T 168/89, Chancellor to Hamilton, 4 August 1900; PML, Archives, Syndicates No. 2, ff. 147–8; Burk (1985), p. 118.

m Unlike the August issue, the Bonds were sold by tender in the normal way. The issue was of 3 per cent Exchequer Bonds maturing on 7 December 1905. They were sold at an average price of £98 2s 10d (£3 8s 2d per cent). They were fully paid. Applications covered the issue more than three times.

Between July and December 1900, the Exchequer Bonds were followed by the sale of a further £5m Bills, which was the balance of the £35m authorised by the War Loan Act 1900. Three million pounds of Ways and Means Advances were also taken from the Bank, and repaid in the first quarter of 1901–2.

First Tranche of $2\frac{3}{4}$–$\frac{1}{2}$ per cent Consols (20 April 1901)

The failure of peace negotiations in South Africa at the end of February 1901 meant that financial planning had to assume that the war would continue for some time. By the middle of that month, short- and medium-term borrowing had reached £67m. The Chancellor felt that it had reached, or even exceeded, the maximum that it would be possible to pay off over the following ten years out of sinking funds and any contribution from the Transvaal.[33] The market was 'stuffed' with Bills and Exchequer Bonds. At the beginning of January, with the Bank's reserve at a low level, Bank rate had been raised briefly to 5 per cent.

Added to this, the speculative interest, and therefore turnover and liquidity, had been diverted from Consols to the new and shorter issues. Yet Consols still formed the largest and most important issue. Thus, in April 1901, when the government needed to borrow on a larger scale, the City agreed with the Bank that it should be Consols.[34] The tranche was of £60m, a size that made the Chancellor feel he should rely on the public subscription for only half. The rest was pre-placed with a Rothschild syndicate taking £20m, of which £9m was for the Bank of England,[n] and Morgans in New York taking £10m for themselves and their associates as well as receiving and forwarding £11.8m of applications for clients.[35] The price was $94\frac{1}{2}$ (£2 13s 2d per cent) to the public, with $\frac{1}{8}$ commission being paid to Rothschilds and $\frac{1}{4}$ to Morgans. In addition, the full 5 July, 5 October and 5 January dividends were paid, although lists closed on 25 April and the calls were spread over eight months. This was equivalent to reducing the price by £1 4s 0d to £93 6s 0d (£2 13s 10d per cent).

The sale was another success. The £30m offered to the public saw 17,409 applications for £217m. 'Applications for small amounts' said the Chancellor 'were favourably treated'.[36]

Second Tranche of $2\frac{3}{4}$–$\frac{1}{2}$ per cent Consols (16 April 1902)

The final borrowing for the war came in April 1902 and coincided with the opening stages of the negotiations that were to lead to the Boers' surrender on 31 May. Hamilton described the choice of security as presenting much difficulty and the decision as 'awkward'. The decision lay between a Transvaal Loan guaranteed by

n Of this, the Secretary of State for India took £0.5m and the Commissioners £2m. The Banking Department retained the whole amount, its holding rising by £6.7m between end-February and end-August 1901. That of the Issue Department was little changed. *Hansard* (Commons), 2 May 1901, col. 412; BoE, ADM 19/8 and 19/9.

the Treasury and more Consols. The City, long of unabsorbed Consols from the earlier sale and scenting both a higher yield and higher fees, pressed for the former: Lord Rothschild was reported to have been 'violent' for a Transvaal issue when he saw the Chancellor on 18 March, advice which Morgans in London thought was influenced by his House being long of the previous tranche.[37] Joseph Chamberlain, the Colonial Secretary, also wanted a guaranteed issue, feeling that a definite obligation to contribute to the cost of the war should be placed on the new colony before it could assert itself. The Chancellor disagreed. He doubted both the wisdom and legality of saddling the colony with a debt when it did not yet have a settled government and there was no local legislature to sanction revenue collection. Controversy promised debate and delay. A guaranteed issue would be expensive, need a 3 per cent interest rate and be priced at par to yield some £0 6s 0d per cent more than Consols, which were about to become a 2½ per cent issue. He decided on Consols.[38]

Again, the Chancellor decided to pre-place half the £32m issue;[o] Morgans, heavily involved elsewhere and with money in New York tight, took only £5m.[p] The Treasury requested Rothschilds to organise a syndicate to take the other £11m, stipulating that £2m each should be earmarked for the Bank of England[q] and Cassel.[39] Morgans were also allotted £125,500 from an application of £2.5m. They placed £1m with the New York Life Insurance Co., £0.2m with John D. Rockefeller and £0.5m with National City Bank. The previous issue of Consols had been accompanied by allegations that foreigners and Jews had kept the placing to themselves and that the joint stock banks had been excluded. On this occasion, the Bank, at the Treasury's behest, prodded the syndicate into opening up and the joint stock banks were given part of the business.[40]

The prospect of peace was strong. There were 21,625 applications, amounting to over £302m, for the £16m available to the public, and no less than seventy-five were for over £1m. Once more, it was decided that the allotments should favour the small investor, but that larger applications should receive allotments pro rata. The 2,540 applying for £100, the minimum, were allotted in full; those applying for over £100 and up to £3,000 received allotments of £100; and the remainder received about 4.8 per cent.[41] By the end of May 1902, the price had risen by three points.

o The issue was of £32m at 93½ (£2 13s 7d per cent). As with the earlier issue, the full dividend was payable on 5 July, 5 October and 5 January, although lists closed on 18 April and the last call was on 9 October. This was worth £0 19s 11d, so that the price can be taken as £92 10s 1d (£2 14s 2d per cent). As had now become standard practice, Morgans in New York were paid ¼ per cent and London ⅛ per cent.

p Morgans headed the group, taking 45 per cent for themselves, 5 per cent for Hambros and 50 per cent for Baring, Magoun, Barings themselves and Kidder Peabody. PML, Archives, Syndicates No. 3, ff. 75–6.

q It is not recorded whether the Bank took these £2m for itself. If it did so, it held them for a short time, as the Banking Department's holding fell by £2.9m between the end of February and the end of August 1902. The Issue Department's holding rose by £0.4m. BoE, ADM 19/9.

Stabilising the South African war debt

The South African War Consols were issued when prices had already fallen some twenty points from the peak of 113½ reached in the summer of 1896, a year when Bank rate averaged £2 9s 0d per cent and the rate of discount on three-months' bills of exchange £1 9s 5d per cent (Figure 2.1).[42] After the war, the widely expected recovery lasted only a few months, and by the end of 1902 Consols were trading at under 93; by the summer of 1914, they had fallen to 75¼ (£3 7s 0d per cent). The rise in yields on long-dated and perpetual fixed-interest securities was world-wide. The value of gold production had been £223m in the ten years between 1882 and 1891, and with new output from South Africa, Australia and North America it was £823m in the period 1902–11.[43] This increase met the depressed conditions of the first half of the 1890s and pushed down interest rates before activity was stimulated and the cycle pulled them up once more. Hamilton described it in 1901 as:

> a low value of money, which was being aggravated by the rapid output of gold in South Africa, invariably means Consols at a high price... By 1896–7 the reverse movement began to take place. The Barings fright was over. The ordinary public were tempted to obtain new and more remunerative investments...Trade became very active all over the world, and money was wanted to meet the requirements of such activity.[44]

Growth in the UK was slower than in the USA or Germany, but Gross Domestic Product (GDP) still grew by 53 per cent between 1893 and 1913. The volume of domestic investment, having doubled in the 1890s, rose to a peak in 1903, from which it quickly subsided.[45] The volume of exports doubled in the twenty years up to and including 1913. Growth was accompanied by inflation, wholesale prices rising by 32 per cent between 1896, their low point, and 1913.[46]

The rise in yields had particularly powerful institutional effects in the UK, where Consols were, until the Boer War, virtually the only security available to those seeking the safety of British government paper. In 1890, the banking system treated bills of exchange as relatively risky assets, machinery for extending advances to customers, and rarely rediscounted them. Instead, it regarded its second reserve as Consols: paper that had a stable price and was easily 'melted' into cash. They had replaced Exchequer Bills in the Bank of England's portfolio in the 1830s and 1840s (see p. 18) and their liquidity had been improved by the Bank's custom of making its rate effective by 'borrowing on Consols', or selling them spot and repurchasing them forward, so that the market was temporally deprived of cash. Their importance in bank balance sheets was reduced in the five years of cheap money that followed the Barings collapse. The crisis itself, when Consols became difficult to sell, may have helped to change attitudes and, as yields fell, banks sought higher returns in other securities, such as the obligations of colonies and railways. Changes in the way the Bank maintained the effectiveness of Bank rate also made Consols less important. Searching for income from commercial

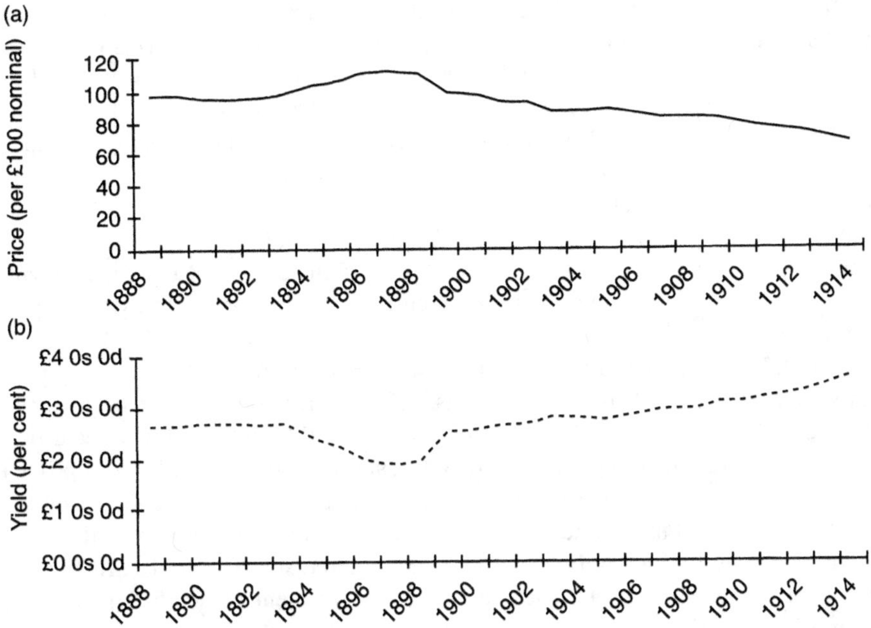

Figure 2.1 (a) The price and (b) the yield on 2¾ per cent, later 2½ per cent, Consols, 1923 or after. Sources: *The Economist*, 1888–99; *BGS*, p. 145, 1900–14. Yields for 1888–1902 by Andrew Wilson FIA.

lending, it increased its Stock Exchange business, lending to jobbers against their long positions in Stock. Because, in the first instance, 'borrowing on Consols' involved selling Consols to the self-same jobbers, the Bank found itself adding cash to the system as fast as it withdrew it. Partly as a result, it started to borrow directly from its customers, a technique which was to be central to the Bank's control of the money market between 1915 and 1919. In 1902, when Ways and Means Treasury Bills were introduced, there was a reduction in both the Treasury's reliance on Bank Ways and Means and the seasonal volatility in market liquidity. Thus, Consols' diminished role as a reserve asset was already a well-established trend by the time of the South African War.[47]

Consols might have become less attractive as a reserve, but the *Bankers' Magazine* of March 1899 did not disagree with reports that the banks held £150m in funded debt.[48] As the price of Consols fell further, the profits of joint stock banks were badly damaged as they wrote down the value of investments.[r] Some weaker deposit takers, especially if they had an abnormal proportion of their assets

r The *Bankers' Magazine* estimated the cost of depreciating investments in the fourteen years 1902–15 to have been £23m. It commented that the published figures were an understatement and suggested that the actual figure was 'more than' £27m. *Bankers' Magazine*, February 1916, pp. 175–6.

in fixed-interest securities, failed or needed help. As early as 1902, two small banks – the Bucks and Oxon Union Banking Co. Ltd and the Cornish Banking Co. Ltd – were so weakened by the need to write down their holdings that they had to be absorbed by large joint stock banks. During the summer of 1911, the Birkbeck Permanent Benefit Building Society (popularly known as the Birkbeck Bank, under which name it traded) was suspended with deposits of over £7m, having failed to depreciate its securities: depositors recovered only part of their money and the goodwill was absorbed by the London County and Westminster Bank.[s] Also in 1911, the Yorkshire Penny Bank, with deposits of £18.5m and with insufficient reserves to cover losses on securities, had to be rescued by a group of joint stock banks.[49]

The fall in Consols, 'our National Stock', as Hamilton called it, excited the City, investors, journalists and politicians.[50] The public may have been accustomed to bank failures, but not to failures caused by holding British government securities. Suggestions were made in the press that the 'national credit' should be improved by altering the terms of the issue: income tax should no longer be levied on the interest, or at least should be compounded at a fixed rate; all or part of the issue should be given a redemption date; the nominal interest rate should be raised to 3 per cent; or they should be accepted at par in payment of death duties.[51] The proposals resurfaced during the Great War in the decisions to offer inflated conversion terms to holders of Consols and to attach tax privileges to new issues. There is little evidence, however, that officials gave them serious consideration at this time, although some sections of the press thought them worthy of a reasoned reply.

Chancellors of both parties – Ritchie in 1903, Asquith in 1907 and Lloyd George on numerous occasions – were pressed for explanations.[52] While pointing in general terms to the influence on interest rates of the expansionary phases of the cycle and the increase in gold production, they added a range of factors, peculiar to the UK, which had exaggerated both the fall in yields in the years to 1896, and the subsequent rise. Thus, it was said, the demand for liquidity that accompanied the Barings crisis in 1890 had helped weaken Consols just after Goschen had converted them to a lower rate. The low short-term interest rates in the first part of the 1890s had supported long-dated paper (the process of borrowing at low rates to invest in higher-yielding Consols was known as 'sweating Consols').[53] Once the loans made by the Commissioners to help pay off the dissentients to Goschen's conversion had been absorbed, the official portfolios had bought increasing amounts of Consols and helped create a dearth; between 31 March 1890 and 31 March 1899, the government portfolios increased their holdings of Consols from £91.7m to £160.7m and the proportion available to the public fell from 83 per cent to 71 per cent.

s On March 1910, the deposits of the Birkbeck Bank were stated to be £11.8m. There was a run in November 1910 and by June 1911 they had fallen to some £7m. Gregory (1936), II, pp. 5–8; MS Asquith, 24, ff. 21–2, Speyer to Asquith, 7 June 1911. Treasury briefing papers and press cuttings are in T 171/12.

Despite the departments' buying, yields rose after 1896 as economic activity revived, pulling with it short-term rates. During the South African War, the New Sinking Fund was suspended and the supply of debt increased; Bills and Exchequer Bonds were issued on yields above those on Consols. After the war, the supply of government-guaranteed debt increased. Comparisons were drawn to show that the rise in yields on foreign government debt and other sterling-denominated fixed-interest issues was similar to that on Consols.[54]

Some of this was just politics, the Conservative opposition trying to show that social spending and the higher taxation imposed in 1909–10 were scaring away capital. In the summer of 1911, after the closure of the Birkbeck Bank, the opposition were presented with the opportunity of attacking Lloyd George when an official of Birkbeck claimed that the collapse was caused by 'the effect of Lloyd George finance' on the value of the bank's portfolio.[55] In the spring and summer of 1912, the political skirmishing linked the failure to Lloyd George's attempt to divert the £6.5m surplus of 1911–12 to Exchequer balances, keeping the money temporarily in suspense rather than applying it to debt repayment. The Opposition tried to couple the fall in the price of Consols with the reduction in the sinking funds; the rises in taxation with the insecurity of capital; the insecurity of capital with the fall in Consols; and the reduction of the sinking funds with rising government spending. Lloyd George was accused of irresponsible finance, an accusation no doubt fed by the stories of his personal dealings in the Stock of the Port of London Authority and Marconi. The government defended itself by focusing on its record of debt repayment, making comparisons with the Unionists' period of office, and the fall in Consols, which had already taken place before it

Table 2.2 Monies applied to debt reduction in times of peace by successive governments: 1861–7 to 1907–14

Financial years	*Chancellor*	*Money applied (£m)*
1861–7	Gladstone	3.2
1868–9	Disraeli and Hunt	1.7
1870–74	Lowe	5.5
1875–80	Northcote	2.5
1880–1	Northcote	4.6
1882–5	Gladstone and Childers	5.7
1886–7	Harcourt	6.3
1888–93	Goschen	6.4
1894–6	Harcourt	6.3
1897–9	Hicks-Beach	5.6
1903–6	Ritchie and Chamberlain	3.1
1907–14	Asquith and Lloyd George	10.2

Notes
Including net capital advances.

Source: T 171/56, f. 14, 'Debt Reduction under Successive Administrations'.

had come into power, while seeking to widen the argument by putting the rise in interest rates into a cyclical and international context (Table 2.2).[56]

The government placed much emphasis on extensions of the list of securities in which trustees were permitted to invest, the largest of which conveniently occurred when the Conservatives were in office. Until the Trust Investment Act 1889, trustees were only allowed to invest in British government issues, the Stock of the Banks of England and Ireland and mortgages on freehold property, unless the trust deed specified otherwise. In that year, the list was extended to include British government-guaranteed issues, some Indian government Stocks, some UK and Indian railway debentures, and certain municipal and water company debt. Minor additions were made in the Trustee Act 1893. The Colonial Stock Act 1900 added Colonial issues registered in the UK to the list. In 1912, Lloyd George claimed that the effect was an expansion from £300m in 1888 to £1,800m in the value of securities other than gilt-edged Stocks in which trustees could invest and a diversion of investment from Consols.[57]

Capital Advances

If the weakness in Consols ruled out funding into permanent debt, the unfunded debt held by the public could only be reduced by repayment from revenue, refinancing with more Exchequer Bonds or application of the Commissioners' funds. The Treasury had both technical and political reasons for placing a high priority on repayment and, especially, repayment of short-dated debt. Most generally, and universally, rolling over oft-maturing debt might coincide with political, financial or military events that would make the refinancing either impossible or expensive. The international scene was becoming more tense, with a series of wars and diplomatic crises; the war in South Africa and the Boxer rebellion were followed by the Russo–Japanese War (1904–5), the Dogger Bank incident (1904), the Kaiser's first challenge to French claims in Morocco (1905) and the Austrian annexation of Bosnia, which infuriated Russia (1908). The German Navy Law of 1898 was followed by a series of shipbuilding challenges to British naval supremacy. To the Treasury, the capital repayment within the Fixed Charge was, in Hamilton's words in October 1896, a 'reserved power of immense value': the larger the amount of the Fixed Charge devoted to sinking funds which were not part of the bargain with the holder, the larger was the amount which could be diverted in an emergency either to new expenditure or to meeting the interest on new debt. Although the importance of the Fixed Charge was common to both parties – Balfour said it was 'worth many battleships' – it was of greater importance to a Liberal government wedded to free trade than to the Conservatives: suspension would allow increased expenditure without new or higher taxes, taxes which might have to include tariffs.[58] The Treasury also believed that its borrowing was curtailing access to the markets for savings: it was, as Asquith said, 'competing and locking up funds that might otherwise be available for commercial and industrial purposes' and denying local authorities and others the loans they needed at a reasonable cost.[59]

Although there is no evidence that officials foresaw the severity of the fall in Consols in the years after the South African War, they felt a general concern about the demands being made on the markets. In October 1903, Hamilton described 'the outlook of the capital account as very disquieting'. As well as the lengthening of the Treasury's own debt, advances from the Local Loans Fund were running at about £5m a year, with municipalities borrowing another £15m in their own names; Guaranteed Stock, issued to compensate the Irish landlords, would be at a rate of £5m to £6m a year, but could well be exceeded; there was borrowing by the colonies of perhaps £19m a year; and money would be needed for the purchase of the London Water Companies and improvements to the Port of London.[60] There were also isolated demands, such as the £30m for the Transvaal. This, which Hamilton at one time had hoped would be available to pay an indemnity to the British and enable the Treasury to retire debt, was largely spent in South Africa.[t]

In December 1904, the unfunded debt totalled £88.1m – the £30m National War Loan 1910, £26.5m Exchequer Bonds, and £31.6m Bills.[u] Hamilton advised the Chancellor that it was not necessary to refinance the £10.5m Bills issued for Ways and Means or the £8m pre-war Supply Bills, which could be kept to maintain a secondary market. The 2¾ per cent National War Loan could not be touched until 1910. Help might be expected from the Transvaal and an indemnity from the Chinese agreed after the Boxer rebellion.[v] Thus, he thought, the debt needing to be refinanced was about £30m.[61]

The 'simplest' method of funding was for the savings banks to buy the short-dated debt in the market and convert it into new issues of Consols. This was the Treasury's preference, but the savings banks did not have the resources: deposits were being absorbed by Advances for capital works and their growth was being reduced by the rise in competing interest rates.[62] If the money market was to be relieved, the security would have to have characteristics which would make it

t Transvaal Government £3 per cent Guaranteed was raised under the South African Loan and War Contribution Act 1903 and the Transvaal Guaranteed Ordinance 1903 (5 May 1903). The first issue in May 1903 was for £30m; there was a second tranche of £5m in June 1904. The proceeds were used by the Transvaal government to repay debt, to compensate loyalists, to acquire and build railways and to finance land settlement. In 1903–4, £3m was used to repay a loan made by the British government, who used it to repay Exchequer Bonds. A further £1.2m was used by Transvaal to buy stores taken over from the British. This was also used to pay off Exchequer Bonds. BoE, AC 19/650; *Hansard* (Commons), 30 April 1906, col. 293.

u These excluded £6m 3 per cent Exchequer Bonds 14 October 1909, which were issued in September 1904 to finance Capital Advances to the Departments (Table 2.3).

v By the terms of a protocol dated 7 September 1901, China agreed to pay an indemnity to the 'aggrieved powers'. The British share was 11¼ per cent of the total, or £7.6m. Payment was to be spread over 39 years from 1902 and 4 per cent interest was to be charged on the balance. One and a half million pounds was earmarked to settle private claims for compensation, mainly those of the North China Railway Administration, and the remainder was available to the Treasury. *Hansard* (Commons), 30 April 1906, col. 296; T 168/94, Hamilton, 'The National Debt and Sinking Fund', 1 January 1906.

attractive to the long-term saver.[63] Consideration was given – indeed, at one time the decision seemed taken – to an issue of £25m for twenty years: a long-dated Exchequer Bond. A proposal to attach to the Bonds a sinking fund so that they would be repaid by means of drawings at par or by market purchases seems to have come from Lord Revelstoke of Barings, who advised that it would produce demand from professional investors, provide price stability, compel the 'present generation' to contribute to reversing the recent increase in the Debt and show that the Treasury was in earnest in wanting to reduce the unfunded debt, which 'constitutes a grave menace to our well-being'.[64] Initially, the advice was rejected and it was proposed that there should be a simple increase in the Fixed Charge, which should be available for repayment of any part of the Debt.[65] The officials' lack of enthusiasm for Revelstoke's idea was for the traditional reasons: the inflexibility of a sinking fund which was part of the bargain with the lender, the advantages of being able to apply monies where it was most convenient or the securities were cheapest, possessing the spending or borrowing power which came from suspending the sinking fund in case of emergency, and fear that a specific sinking fund could entail the government borrowing at a higher rate to pay off debt at a lower. The next two decades were to show that these apprehensions had a real basis. Other disadvantages were more technical. It would mean that the issue had to be of Bonds, as it would not be possible to have drawings of inscribed Stock (Appendix I). In turn, this meant that the minimum holding would need to be £100, thus excluding the small investor.[w] More important, although drawings were well known overseas and occasionally had been attached to foreign issues with a British government guarantee, it would be a departure in the mainstream gilt-edged market.[66] Finally, introducing chance into State finance could alienate the non-conformists, as the prospect of premium bonds threatened to do in the Great War.

In the event, 2¾ per cent Exchequer Bonds 1906–15, announced in the 1905 budget, did have an attached sinking fund. As in similar circumstances in June 1919, when the Treasury had to offer the gorged investor a change in fare, the repayment depended on chance, hence 'Lottery Bonds'. Also, as in 1919, the result was afterwards considered disappointing. The Chancellor on both occasions was Austen Chamberlain, himself a Unitarian.

The 1905 issue took the form of drawings at par of £1m a year between 1906 and 1915, with the Fixed Charge increased by a similar amount. It was of only £10m, and had the limited purpose of refinancing part of the £14m Exchequer Bonds maturing on 12 December 1905; the other £4m was to be repaid from the New Sinking Funds of 1904–5 and 1905–6 and the receipt of £1.1m from the Transvaal in payment for stores (Table 2.3). Despite the attractions of the drawings, the Bonds were sold by tender at an average price of only £98 13s 10d (£3 0s 9d

w A system of drawings required that investors have a chance of being drawn that was in proportion to the size of their holding. Registered holdings could be in odd sizes. It was, therefore, necessary to use Bonds, in which holdings came in units.

Table 2.3 Issues of marketable government debt (excluding Treasury Bills), 1903–4 to 1913–14

Date of prospectus	*Security*	*Nominal issued (£m)*	*Price (yield)*	*Purpose*
1903				
24 July	3 per cent Exchequer Bonds 7/8/04	7	£99 9s 2d* (£3 11s 1d)	Refinance part of 3 per cent Exchequer Bonds 7/8/03
1904				
23 July	3 per cent Exchequer Bonds 6/8/07	6.5	£98 13s 6d* (£3 9s 4d)	Refinance part of 3 per cent Exchequer Bonds 7/8/04
30 September	3 per cent Exchequer Bonds 14/10/09	6	£98 16s 0d* (£3 7s 2d)	Capital works of Army and Navy
1905				
12 April	$2^3/_4$ per cent Exchequer Bonds 1906/15	10	£98 13s 10d* (£3 0s 9d)	Refinance part of 3 per cent Exchequer Bonds 7/12/05
1909				
8 October	3 per cent Exchequer Bonds 14/10/12	4.8†	£100 9s 0.3d* (£2 16s 10d)	Refinance part of 3 per cent Exchequer Bonds 14/10/09
1910				
18 March	3 per cent Exchequer Bonds 5/4/15	21	£99 10s 0d (£3 2s 2d)	Refinance part of $2^3/_4$ per cent War Loan 1910
1912				
1 January	3 per cent Exchequer Bonds 1/1/30	4‡	£93 10s 0d (£3 10s 9d)	Acquisition of National Telephone Co. Ltd
14 October	3 per cent Exchequer Bonds 14/10/16	4.1§	£100 0s 0d (£3 0s 0d)	Refinance part of 3 per cent Exchequer Bonds 14/10/12
1913				
Further tranche of 1 January 1912	3 per cent Exchequer Bonds 1/1/30	3¶	£94 0s 0d (£3 10s 1d)	Acquisition of National Telephone Co. Ltd
Further tranche of 1 January 1912	3 per cent Exchequer Bonds 1/1/30	0.4**	††	Acquisition of National Telephone Co. Ltd

Notes

*Average accepted price at tender

†£3.5m were issued to the public, £0.6m to the Secretary of State for India and £0.7m to the Commissioners.

notes are continued on the next page

Notes to Table 2.3 (continued)

‡Of which £3.8m were bought by Rothschilds on 17 July 1912 and placed at £93 10s 0d plus interest on 17 July 1912, the balance of £200,000 being retained by the Liquidator as an investment for surplus assets.
§£4m were issued to the Secretary of State for India and £0.1m to the Commissioners.
¶Bought by Rothschilds at 94 plus interest on 10 February 1913 and sold to market on 3 March 1913 at the same price.
**No record of the date of issue or price have been found.
††No record of the price has been found.

Exchequer Bonds were issued under the Cunard Agreement (Money) Act 1904 as to £1m in 1905–6, £1.2 m in 1906–7 and £0.4m in 1907–8. No prospectus has been found and it may be assumed that the Bonds were bought by the Commissioners. The Bonds, less the amount paid off by the sinking fund, were rolled forward on maturity until they were paid off in 1927/8. *BGS*, p. 349.

Sources: *BGS*; *National Debt: annual returns*; BoE, relevant Loan Wallets and Stock Jackets; Rothschild Archive, London, XI/III/56; T 133/1, Ramsay to Commissioners, 2 November 1917.

per cent). Asquith, who became Chancellor in the new Liberal government that December, called it a 'disappointing operation', Hamilton having been expecting that the attached Sinking Fund would attract a price near to par.[67]

The reason for shelving the grander £25m or £30m scheme was a change in policy on the financing of capital works and a decision not to replace two large Terminable Annuities, which expired in 1906. By 31 March 1905, other capital liabilities, advances by the Commissioners to the spending departments, had grown into a major part of the Debt, with further commitments outstanding. The largest Advances were for the building of dockyards, coastguard stations and barracks, but there were also considerable sums for public buildings, a railway in Uganda and telephones. On 31 March 1899, advances stood at £7.5m (1.2 per cent of the Debt); six years later they had risen to £41.7m (5.2 per cent) and there was a further £26m committed (Figure 2.2).[68] Advances in 1904–5 were particularly heavy, exceeding repayments of the dead-weight debt from the New Sinking Fund and foreshadowing the early 1930s when new borrowing by the Unemployment Fund threatened to exceed the annual sinking fund. To make the resemblance complete, for three years the savings banks were only able to meet their commitments by selling Consols, albeit on a minor scale.[69] In September 1904, when the Treasury feared that the savings banks would not be able to find all the money needed, £6m Exchequer Bonds[x] had been issued to help pay for capital works, the interest and sinking fund taking the standard form of annuities payable from Departmental Votes, in this case those of the Army and Navy (Table 2.3).

At the end of 1904, Hamilton drew attention to the size and outlook for capital advances. Having surveyed the size of the commitments under existing legislation, he warned that it was unlikely that the savings banks would be able to go on finding the money unless deposits started to grow more quickly; he was doubtful about this because of the competition from the higher rates being paid by local

x The Capital Expenditure (Money) Act 1904 authorised the Treasury to borrow by Exchequer Bonds when it was authorised to borrow on Terminable Annuities.

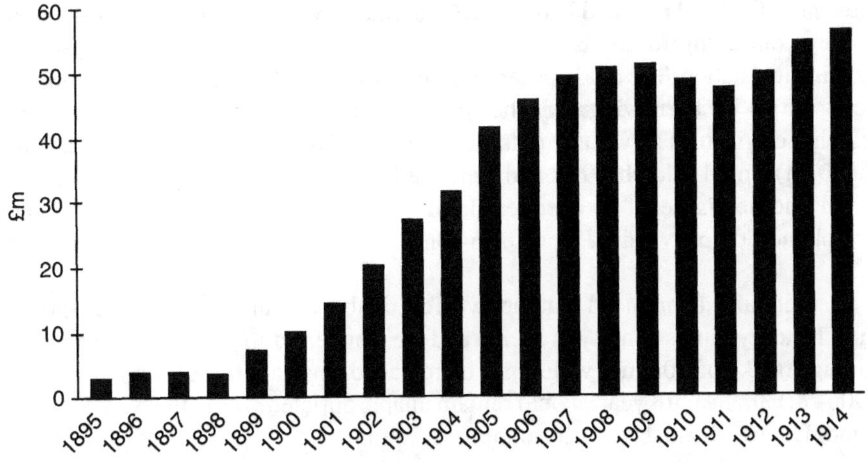

Figure 2.2 Other capital liabilities outstanding, as at end-March 1895–1914. Source: *National Debt: annual returns.*

authorities. The alternative was for the Treasury to borrow in the open market; yet the City was overfull with short-term debt, and it was Treasury policy to fund it. Consols were weak. Moreover, it would be difficult to defend the issue of Consols to pay for capital works when the sinking fund was simultaneously buying them for cancellation. The answer, Hamilton said, was for finance in excess of the Commissioners' resources to go on the Votes – that is, be paid out of revenue.[70]

Adoption of the new policy bridged the change of government at the end of 1905. In the budget of that April, Chamberlain had said that he did not believe that borrowing for capital works should form part of the 'permanent financial system', although it might be necessary to meet 'exceptional and extraordinary' circumstances, and that he hoped that Parliament would not sanction advances beyond the existing programmes.[71] The actual decision to wind up borrowing, at least for military purposes, had to wait for the Liberal government and Asquith the following year:

> There must undoubtedly arise from time to time cases of Charges which properly fall under the head of capital expenditure for which temporary borrowing is legitimate: but in the main I regard this as a most unhappy chapter in the history of our national finance; and so far as the Army and the Navy are concerned my intention is at the earliest possible moment to bring it to a close. The system, as it has been developed of recent years has, in my opinion, three fundamental vices. In the first place it tends to confuse the distinction between capital and revenue Charges. In the next place it inevitably encourages in the spending departments crude, precipitate, and wasteful experiments. And in the third place...it draws large items of annual expenditure from any effective Parliamentary supervision.[72]

Advances for the Army and Navy were phased out with effect from 1907–8, with money continuing to be made available where there were commitments under existing legislation. The total outstanding tailed off, with repayments by the military being offset by borrowing for other purposes, especially for investment in the telephone system. The volume outstanding reached about £49.7m (6.4 per cent of the Debt) on 31 March 1907 and remained at about that level until 1912–13, when another issue of Exchequer Bonds, this time to purchase the National Telephone Company, raised them to £54.8m (7.7 per cent of a smaller debt) (Figure 2.2).

Asquith also announced that the two Terminable Annuities expiring in 1906 – the Chancery Funds annuity of £2.3m and the Converted Annuities payable to the savings banks of £0.7m – would not be replaced. Instead, the £1.8m released in 1906–7 (£3m in a full year) would remain unappropriated within the New Sinking Fund. He was dismissive of the annuity system:

> Terminable annuities are in many ways a convenient and useful instrument of Debt reduction. They wrap and disguise the process of repayment and they are supposed – though recent experience has shown that that is not always the case – to be safe from temporary suspension or reduction at the hands of a hardly-pressed Chancellor of the Exchequer...[it makes no difference to the amount repaid] whether it passes through the devious channel of terminable annuities or whether it goes straight and direct into the new Sinking Fund. In determining which method you ought to adopt, you must determine what part of the capital you are most anxious to attack.[73]

This followed Hamilton's brief, in which he had provided a range of reasons for changing the advice he had given Hicks-Beach in 1897. He now judged the public to be so concerned about the Debt that the sinking fund was safe for the foreseeable future; public anxiety about Consols made it advantageous to have the sinking fund appear as large as possible and to apply it to the purchase of securities in the open market. The annuities were no longer sacrosanct, having been suspended as easily as the unappropriated sinking fund during the South African War. The payments exacerbated the Treasury's seasonal borrowing, which had become more marked since 1897 with the rise in income tax rates, because they were spread over quarters or half-years, whereas the sinking fund was paid to the Commissioners in the final, revenue-rich, financial quarter. The only argument for fresh annuities was that the payments to the Commissioners could be reborrowed for capital works – the repayments and new borrowing would remain 'domestic' – but this would become less important as departmental borrowing was phased out.[74]

Repayment

Between the end of March 1903 and 1914 the nominal value of the dead-weight debt was reduced by £121m and that of the National Debt (including capital advances) by £92.2m. Within this, the funded debt fell by £53.4m, the unfunded debt by £41.6m and the capital value of annuities by £26m; capital advances rose by £28.8m. The reduction was a result of policy, rather than cautious budgetary forecasting and casual surpluses. Of the £116.2m cash applied to the dead-weight debt, £85.4m was provided by the New Sinking Fund and £18.9m by the Old.[y] The balance of £11.9m came from miscellaneous receipts: changes in Exchequer balances, the Transvaal contribution, the Chinese indemnity and sums provided by Land Tax Redemption and the Composition of Stamp Duty.[75]

This was an unprecedented rate of repayment, averaging £10.2m a year over the eight years of the peacetime Liberal government, at a time when central government revenue was £155m (1906–7) rising to £198.2m (1913–14). As Lloyd George, assailed by those who sought to hold him responsible for the misfortunes of Consols, repeatedly stated, it was almost twice the highest rate of repayment achieved by earlier administrations (Table 2.2).

The pace was not maintained as the unfunded debt came under control and military and welfare expenditure rose. The Permanent Charge had been £27m in 1903–4, when for the first time it included the South African War debt. In 1905–6, Balfour wanted to increase it by more than the £1m needed to cover the annual drawings on the Lottery Bonds, but was dissuaded: it would, recorded Hamilton, 'be an invitation to cut it down next year; and what is most wanted is continuity. To overdo it, is to undo it.'[76] Instead, the duty on tea was reduced and the sinking fund became £28m. Come the new Liberal government, it was raised to £28.5m in 1906–7 and to £29.5m in 1907–8. In that year, the capital repayment within the Charge was almost £11m. With a further £5.2m from the Old Sinking Fund, miscellaneous receipts and net advances for capital works, the total applied was £15.5m, or 9.9 per cent of gross revenue (Table 2.4).[77] This was the peak, being the almost incidental effect of the decision not to remit £1.5m of taxation because increases in social spending planned for the following year would consume the surplus.[78]

The change began as Asquith was leaving the Treasury. Presenting the 1908 budget in place of Lloyd George, who had been appointed but only a month earlier, he reported a large repayment during the previous year, and pointed to the forecast of a further £15m in 1908–9. If he were the Chancellor, he said, he would not feel:

> justified in asking the taxpayers of the country to continue to pay £14,000,000 or £15,000,000 a year for further reductions of Debt. I think the efforts we have made, unprecedented in their character, will justify a review of the situation and the setting free of some substantial part of the revenue which in the last three years we have applied to that purpose.[79]

The review duly followed, but in conditions of political turmoil. In 1909, Lloyd

y Cash applied of £116.2m was not equal to the reduction of £121m in the dead-weight debt because the cash extinguished more or less of the Debt depending on whether the price of securities bought and cancelled was below or above par.

Table 2.4 Repayment of debt: 1903–4 to 1913–14

	£m (per cent of gross revenue)								
	Permanent Charge	*New Sinking Fund*		*Old Sinking Fund*	*Other**	*Total of columns 2–4*	*Other capital liabilities (net increase+)*	*Total of columns 5 and 6*	
	(1)	(2)		(3)	(4)	(5)	(6)	(7)	
1903–4	27.000	6.5	(4.3)	–	3.4	9.9	+4.3	5.6	(3.7)
1904–5	27.000	7.4	(4.8)	–	2.3	9.7	+9.8	–0.1	(–)
1905–6	28.025	8.8	(5.7)	†	1.5	10.3	+4.1	6.2	(4.0)
1906–7	28.500	9.6	(6.2)	3.5	0.8	13.8	+3.9	10.0	(6.4)
1907–8	29.500	10.9	(7.0)	5.3‡	0.5	16.7	+1.2	15.5	(9.9)
1908–9	28.000	10.0	(6.6)	2.6§	0.6	13.2	+0.6	12.6	(8.3)
1909–10	21.758	3.5	(2.7)	–	0.6	4.1	2.2	6.3	(4.8)
1910–11	24.554	6.6	(3.2)	–	0.6	7.3	1.4	8.7	(4.3)
1911–12	24.500	7.0	(3.8)	2.4¶	0.4	9.8	+2.2	7.6	(4.1)
1912–13	24.500	7.3	(3.9)	5.0**	0.4	12.7	+4.8	8.0	(4.2)
1913–14	24.500	7.6	(3.8)	0.2	0.9	8.7	+1.6	7.1	(3.6)

Notes
*Miscellaneous receipts and sums taken from Exchequer balances applied to the reduction of debt.
†Applied to the repayment of temporary advances.
‡A further £100,000 was diverted to the cash balance of the Supreme Court of Judicature Suitors' Funds.
§A further £1.5m was diverted to the payment of deficiency advances and £600,000 to the erection of public buildings.
¶A further £1.5m was diverted to the Development Fund, £1.5m to sanatoriums and £250,000 for a loan to Uganda.
**A further £1.5m was retained in Exchequer balances, earmarked as to £1m for claims created by the new German Navy Bill and £0.5m for Uganda.
Rows may not sum because of rounding.

Sources: *National Debt* (HCP 219), 29 April 1915: Mallet (1913), Table XVI; Mallet and George (1929), Table II.

George faced a deficit of £16.5m. The Conservative House of Lords had been throwing out or emasculating legislation, and the inability of the government to introduce social reform was damaging its standing in the country. The Cabinet decided to introduce far-reaching rises in expenditure, and the taxation to pay for them, in a money Bill which, by tradition, the Lords would not touch. The most expensive measure was the introduction of non-contributory old age pensions, but there was also a new Board to finance road improvements, a system of national unemployment exchanges, a Development Commission to finance and promote schemes to restore the countryside, valuation staffs for a new capital tax on land, and child allowances for income tax payers. More acceptable for the Conservatives was the laying down of additional Dreadnoughts for the Navy. As well as steep increases in taxation on the wealthier sections of the community, the Chancellor proposed to find £3m by reducing the Fixed Charge, from £28m to £25m: a reduction which showed the potential of the sinking fund as a reserve which could be used to finance increases in expenditure and which would not have been possible (or at least more difficult) if repayments had been attached to specific issues, as they were during the Great War.

Controversial and heavy taxation meant that the Finance Bill was subjected to lengthy debate in the Commons, and it was in Committee until 6 October 1909. It was then sent to the Lords and rejected on 30 November. Parliament was prorogued on 2 December and dissolved on 10 January 1910. The election over, and the Liberals still in power, Lloyd George introduced the Finance (1909–10) Bill on 19 April; it received the Royal Assent on 29 April. The resolutions following the presentation of the 1909 budget, which authorised the collection of customs and excise duties, income tax and the new scale of death duties, lapsed when Parliament was prorogued and a large amount of revenue was not collected until the following year; 1909–10 showed an abnormal deficit and 1910–11 an abnormal surplus. This fracas required three measures affecting the Debt; £17m of Ways and Means Bills and £4m of Ways and Means Advances were used to cover the shortfall in revenue in 1909–10, but could not, under existing legislation, run beyond 31 March 1910. The Treasury (Temporary Borrowing) Act 1910 authorised Ways and Means Bills issued in 1909–10 to be renewed up to 30 September 1910 and the Ways and Means Advances to run to 30 June 1910. Adjustment of the sinking fund arrangements was also required. Under the 1875 Act, the surplus of 1910–11 would have been Old Sinking Fund and, therefore, unavailable to repay Ways and Means Advances resulting from the deficit of 1909–10: new borrowing would have been needed to repay the Ways and Means taken in 1909–10 and the surplus of 1910–11 would have been used to repay other debt. This would have been hard to defend. It was avoided by a provision in the Revenue Act 1911 that, for the purposes of calculating the Old Sinking Fund for 1910–11, the two years 1909–10 and 1910–11 should be combined. The Treasury (Temporary Borrowing) Act also limited the New Sinking Fund for 1909–10 to the amount needed for annuities and the £1m to meet the drawings on Chamberlain's Lottery Bonds, an exception which provided an early example of one of the disadvantages of a sinking fund attached to a specific issue.[80]

The Fixed Charge was reduced by a further £0.5m in 1910–11 to £24.5m. Thanks to buoyant revenue after the recession, which had contributed to the problems of 1909–10, debt repayment did not fall as far as Lloyd George had intended, and repayment in 1911–12 and 1912–13 still absorbed over 4 per cent of gross central government revenues. It was not until the Old Sinking Fund practically disappeared in 1913–14 that repayment fell under 4 per cent of gross revenues (Table 2.4). In the budget of 1914, Lloyd George, proposing a further reduction of £0.5m, pointed to the record of repayment over the whole life of the Liberal government and, echoing his Prime Minister's comments of 1908, said 'We are not justified in imposing fresh taxation to keep up this unprecedented rate of liquidating our debts.'[81]

Because the reductions in the New Sinking Fund reflected the intention of policy and repayment was being maintained by casual surpluses – forecasting errors – there was justification for appropriating the Old Sinking Fund for capital expenditure, especially if the alternative would have been borrowing. The precedents were three occasions in the second half of the 1890s when the Unionists had diverted the surpluses of the previous year to capital spending. This had been much frowned on by the previous Chancellor, the Liberal Harcourt, who had advised Hicks-Beach when the possibility was being mooted of using Old Sinking Fund to fund a deficit in the Indian Army Pension Fund to 'keep up the established principle and tradition that old Sinking Fund shall go to the redemption of the Permanent Debt and to no other purpose whatever. It would accustom people to play tricks with it and use it for all sorts of occasional necessities'.[82] The amounts that had been appropriated had been large: between 1895–6 and 1905–6, 74 per cent of the surpluses had been diverted.[z] Now, ten years later, the Liberals themselves followed suit, albeit on a smaller scale. Between 1906–7 and 1909–10, there were three diversions, equal to 21 per cent of the surpluses (Table 2.4).[aa]

There was also an attempt to divert the whole of the £6.5m surplus of 1911–12 to strengthening Exchequer balances. Lloyd George defended this proposal on the grounds that resources were needed in case revenue was damaged by a miners' strike which had begun on 1 March, for meeting Admiralty expenditure transferred from the previous year (when delays in its building programme had caused it to underspend) and for meeting the threat of a new German naval building programme.[bb] The Unionists were incensed, and in the course of the following three months were partially successful in their opposition: £5m went to the Sinking Fund, £1m to meeting the claims of the Navy and £0.5m to the development of Uganda.[83]

Departmental buying

Despite Hamilton's forebodings, the departmental portfolios were able to support the Treasury, buying government-guaranteed issues, unfunded debt and Consols. Between 1903 and 1914, the assets administered by the departments grew by a third, from £283.4m to £383.3m (Table 2.5); even the deposits in the POSB rose by £44.4m, although those of the TSBs' Ordinary Departments grew little.[84] Two

z Surpluses were diverted in three years: £4.2m of that of 1895–6 was appropriated under the Naval Works Act 1896; £2.5m of that of 1896–7 under the Military Works Act 1897; and £2.6m of that of 1897–8 under the Public Buildings Expenses Act 1898.

aa Of the surplus of 1906–7, £0.1m was diverted to make good a deficiency in the Suitors' Fund of the Supreme Court of Judicature; £0.6m of the surplus of 1907–8 was appropriated under the Finance Act 1908 to help pay for the erection of public offices; £3.3m of the surpluses of the two years ending 31 March 1911 were appropriated under the Finance Act 1911 to the Development Fund, the building of sanatoriums and a loan to the government of the East Africa Protectorate.

bb For two years, between the autumns of 1910 and 1912, the UK suffered from an outbreak of severe industrial unrest. The dispute between the colliery owners and the labour force in 1912 was about a minimum wage. On 1 March, some 850,000 miners struck, and within ten days another 1.3m workers had been made idle. The sting was drawn from the strike when the government brought in a Bill to establish minimum wage machinery.

new portfolios were particularly important contributors. The holdings of the India Office rose fourfold to £16.8m, with the bulk being on account of the gold standard reserve: on 31 March 1914, the Office held nearly 30 per cent of the Treasury Bills and Exchequer Bonds in issue. The funds established under the National Insurance Act 1911 grew to become £22.3m nominal. They held almost 20 per cent of the Bills and Exchequer Bonds.[85]

The pattern of investment was as Hamilton envisaged when the capital expenditure of the Army and Navy were put on the Votes and the two sets of Terminable Annuities were not renewed. Capital advances grew by only £16.5m, mainly before 1907, and the value of Terminable Annuities fell by £27.4m (Tables 2.5 and 2.6). The money thus released, together with the growth in resources, was used to buy Local Loans and Irish Land Stock, which absorbed £61.4m or 60 per cent of the new money becoming available, and to support the gilt-edged market, which absorbed £49.4m. Of this £49.4m, £30.3m were Consols and £3m the quoted 2½ and 2¾ per cent Annuities. The purchases of funded debt were heavily weighted towards the four years after 31 March 1910 when the Birkbeck and Yorkshire Penny Banks collapsed and the Chancellor was being stridently criticised for the weakness in the price of Consols. The savings banks themselves took only £7.8m: although there was only one issue of Local Loans to the Commissioners during

Table 2.5 Holdings of individual obligations by government departments: 31 March 1903 and 1914

	£m nominal (per cent)			
	1903		*1914*	
2¾ (2½) per cent Consols	150.2		180.6	
Other marketable funded debt*	14.0		17.0	
Unfunded debt†	5.6		21.6	
Total marketable central Government debt	169.8		219.2	
Terminable Annuities	42.2		14.8	
Capital Advances	27.6		44.1	
Total central Government securities	239.6	(84.5)	278.1	(72.6)
Other securities§	43.8	(15.5)	105.2	(27.4)
Total securities	283.4	(100.0)	383.3	(100.0)

Notes
*2½ per cent and 2¾ per cent Annuities.
†2¾ per cent War Loan 1910, Exchequer Bonds and Treasury Bills.
‡3 per cent Local Loans Stock, Local Loans Bonds and 2¾ per cent Guaranteed Loan Stocks issued under the Acts of 1891, 1903 and 1909.
§Excluding £12.3m Exchequer Bonds issued to finance capital works under the Capital Expenditure (Money) Act 1904, the Cunard Agreement (Money) Act 1904 and the Telephone Transfer Act 1911.
Columns may not sum because of rounding.

Sources: *Government Departments Securities* (HCP 160), 1 May 1903, and (HCP 291), 23 June 1914; *National Debt: annual returns.*

Table 2.6 Holdings of central government debt by government departments and the general public: 31 March 1903 and 1914

	£m nominal (per cent)			
	1903		*1914*	
Departments				
Marketable securities	169.8	(21.3)	219.2	(31.0)
Capital advances	27.6	(3.5)	44.1	(6.2)*
Terminable Annuities	42.2	(5.3)	14.8	(2.1)
Total	239.6	(30.0)	278.1	(39.4)
Debts to the Banks of England and Ireland	13.6	(1.7)	13.6	(1.9)
General public (residual)	545.1	(68.3)	414.5	(58.7)
Total	798.3	(100.0)	706.2	(100.00)

Notes
*Excluding £12.3m Exchequer Bonds issued to finance capital works under the Capital Expenditure (Money) Act 1904, the Cunard Agreement (Money) Act 1904 and the Telephone Transfer Act 1911.
Columns may not sum because of rounding.

Sources: *Government Departments Securities* (HCP 160), 1 May 1903, and (HCP 291), 23 June 1914; *National Debt: annual returns.*

this period (£1.5m in February 1913), they bought others, and they had to absorb £18m Irish Land Stocks.[86] The purchases by the Commissioners coincided with increased buying by the sinking funds, so that between 1903 and 1914 the government portfolios and the sinking funds together supported the market in funded debt to the extent of £86.7m nominal (Figure 2.3).[87] As the portfolio of central government debt expanded and the size of the Debt contracted, the proportion owned by the general public fell from 68.3 per cent to 58.7 per cent (Tables 2.5 and 2.6).

3 per cent Exchequer Bonds 1915 (18 March 1910) and issues to finance Advances to the Cunard Steamship Company and the purchase of the National Telephone Company

The last set of accounts published before the Great War, those for 31 March 1914, showed the National Debt to have been £706.2m. Of this, the unfunded Debt was £45.8m, comprising £13m Bills, £18.5m 3 per cent Exchequer Bonds 1915, the £2m balance of Chamberlain's Lottery Bonds and the £12.3m Exchequer Bonds issued to finance capital advances. This was a strong position, especially as £21.6m of the unfunded debt was in the hands of the Departments with £9.3m in a single India Office account.[88] Except for the Lottery Bonds, the refinancing of maturing debt since 1902 had been largely routine. The sinking funds bought what they could afford as the Bonds approached maturity. Part of the replacement issue was placed directly with the Commissioners and the India Office and the balance was

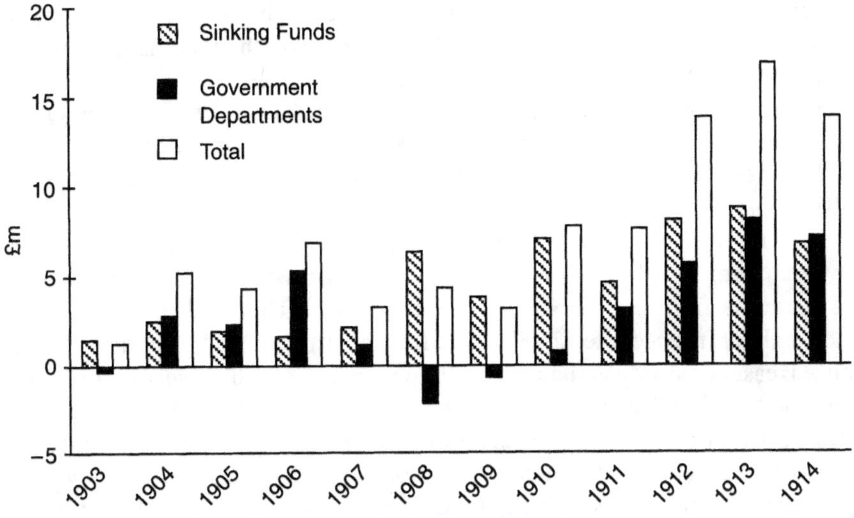

Figure 2.3 Purchases of funded British government marketable debt by the government Departments and the sinking funds, years ending 31 March 1903–14. Sources: *Sinking Fund* [annual accounts], 1903–14; *Government Departments Securities,* 1903–14.

sold by tender to the professional market, with the applications sometimes coming from only half a dozen investors (Table 2.3; Notes).[89]

Just three transactions stand out. Between 1907–8 and 1909–10, the £30m of 2¾ per cent National War Loan 1910 was reduced to £21m by sinking fund purchases.[90] The powers provided in the War Loan (Redemption) Act 1910 in preparation for the maturity reflected the wide distribution of the securities when they were issued in 1900. In addition to the standard authorisation to borrow new money up to a specified sum, the Act included a schedule describing the manner in which the maturity should be administered: technical matters such as the closing of the books, the machinery for making the payments, and the provision that maturity proceeds not claimed should be reinvested by the Bank in Consols in the names of the holders on the War Loan register. Applications for the £21m 3 per cent Exchequer Bonds 1915 at a fixed price of £99 10s 0d (£3 2s 2d per cent) were £48.3m, but it was a narrow shave.[91] All was going well until 21 March when the government published its proposals to curb the power of the Lords, short rates firmed, news arrived of a deterioration in the labour situation in the South Wales coal field and rumours about the King's health intensified.[92] Before this, applications had reached £74.5m, but investors started to withdraw them and the Bank closed the list on 22 March, two days early.[93] One of the applications that was not withdrawn showed the advantages of being a valued Bank client. The Secretary of State for India wanted £1.5m of the issue, but as the India Office feared that it would be over-subscribed it asked the Bank to apply for whatever it judged would be needed to ensure that the £1.5m was obtained. The Bank put in an application for £3.5m and the Secretary of State was allotted £1.523m.[94]

There were two special issues for capital advances. The £6m issue made under the Capital Expenditure (Money) Act 1904, when it was thought that the savings banks would not be able to provide all the advances needed for capital works, was followed by £2.6m Exchequer Bonds under the Cunard Agreement (Money) Act 1904. These came in three tranches in 1905–6, 1906–7 and 1907–8, and the proceeds were lent to the Cunard Steamship Company.[cc] The issue was a response to the announcement by J. P. Morgan & Co. in April 1902 that they had formed a syndicate to finance a consolidation of the North Atlantic shipping business. This provoked fears that shipping was passing out of British control and there were noisy protests from the press and some politicians. This, and the Admiralty's concern about its access to fast liners in time of war, enabled Cunard to extract both a Treasury subsidy and a loan at 2½ per cent, repayable over twenty years, with which to build two new ships, the *Lusitania* and the *Mauretania*.[95] The Treasury borrowed the money on the Exchequer Bonds and Cunard reimbursed it with the interest and sinking fund at a rate of £130,000 a year for twenty years.

There was another issue for capital expenditure in 1912 and 1913. Although advances for telephone investment had hitherto come from the Commissioners, the Treasury decided to finance part of the Post Office's acquisition of the bankrupt National Telephone Company by issuing to the receivers £7.4m 3 per cent Exchequer Bonds 1930. This, it can be assumed, was to retain savings bank monies to support the Consols market. The Bonds, dated 1 January 1912, were handed to the Liquidator in three tranches as the Railway and Canal Commission made its awards and, in his turn, the Liquidator sold them so that creditors might be paid. The first tranche was of £4m, of which £3.8m was sold to Rothschilds on 17 July, who started selling them to investors and brokers the same day. Rothschilds were also the buyers of the second tranche, this time of £3m; they bought it on 10 February 1913 and held the Bonds for three weeks before selling on 3 March. There is no record of the sale of the third tranche.[96] Strictly, the sale was by the Liquidator and not the Treasury, but the issue can claim to be the last occasion on which a contractor bought an entire issue and sold it to the market and investors in the traditional manner (Table 2.3).

✣ ✣ ✣

Borrowing for the South African War and the measures taken to subdue the floating debt inspired changes in the way the Debt was managed, many of which were to reappear during the Great War and in the inter-war years, in both benign and malignant forms. The issue of 2¾ per cent War Loan was by far the most important departure, the whole being sold to the general public with an emphasis on the small saver. It was considered that the small investor was uncomfortable with the risks of keeping bearer Bonds and, with this sale, inscription as a method of

cc Unusually, there is no record of, or prospectus for, the issue in the Bank of England archives, so the issues are not included in Table 2.3.

recording ownership was introduced, an alternative that had previously only been available for permanent debt. There followed issues which were partly pre-placed with syndicates of professional risk takers, a method which was both a partial return to selling a whole issue to a single contractor and a forerunner of the pre-placements with the banks of the War Loans of the Great War. After 1902, the Conservative government's policy of paying for departmental capital expenditure by taking advances from the Commissioners reached a scale where the savings banks had to sell Consols: in one year, borrowing by the Departments exceeded the sinking fund (Table 2.4). Finally, the Treasury, seeking price stability and applications from the general investor, produced an issue redeemable by annual drawings. This introduced in a single issue both an attached sinking fund and a yield (to the investor), which was determined by chance; the first, repeated with several later issues, was to be the bane of the Treasury's debt repayment policy between 1919 and 1932, and the second was to be a lively source of political controversy during the Great War.

Endnotes

1 T 170/31, Bradbury, 'The Financing of Naval and Military Operations', 12 February 1900, and Hamilton, 'Taxation versus Loans', 20 February 1900.

2 *Wars in South Africa and China (Cost and Expenditure)* (HCP 130), 29 April 1903; *Hansard* (Commons), 23 April 1903, cols 234–5; Mallet (1913), pp. 199–202.

3 *Hansard* (Commons), 20 April 1855, cols 1575–7.

4 T 168/87, Hamilton, 'Crimean War Loans', 15 February 1900, and 'Crimean War Finance', undated; Northcote (1862), pp. 264–6; T 170/31, Bradbury, 'The Financing of Naval and Military Operations', 12 February 1900. On this occasion, Rothschilds paid £100 for each £108 of Consols.

5 T 170/31, 'Methods of Borrowing', 12 January 1900.

6 T 170/31, Hamilton, note for the Chancellor, 22 January 1900. Hamilton kept records of his conversations. These, together with correspondence from those he consulted, are in T 168/87 and T 170/31.

7 T 168/87, Murray to Hamilton, 10 January 1900; T 170/31, Hamilton, 'Methods of Borrowing', 12 January 1900.

8 T 170/31, note from Schuster, 20 January 1900, Hamilton to Chancellor, 22 January 1900, and Schuster, 'The Term Exchequer Bond', 25 January 1900.

9 T 170/31, note from Schuster, 20 January 1900, and Schuster, 'The Term Exchequer Bond', 25 January 1900.

10 Sayers (1976), I, p. 15. The only reference to this view in the Hamilton papers is in T 168/87, Samuel Gladstone (Governor of the Bank) to Hamilton, 6 February 1900.

11 T 168/87, Hamilton, 'The Opinion of Rothschilds', 7 February 1900.

12 T 170/31, note from Schuster, 20 January 1900, and Schuster, 'The Term Exchequer Bond', 25 January 1900.

13 T 168/87, Hamilton, 'Opinion of Sir E. Cassel', 7 February 1900, and 'Note of further talk with Sir E. Cassel on 12 Feb 1900', 13 February 1900; Burk (1989), p. 114. Those with bear positions were rumoured to include Jefferson, the largest jobber in Consols. T 168/87, Revelstoke to Hamilton, 19 February 1900; T 170/31, note from Schuster, 20 January 1900.

14 T 168/87, Hamilton, 'Taxation versus Loans', 20 February 1900; T 170/31, 'The War Loans', unsigned, June 1905; *Hansard* (Commons), 5 March 1900, cols 75–8.

15 T 170/31, Hamilton, 'Methods of Borrowing', 12 January, and Hamilton to Chancellor, 19 January 1900; T 168/87, Hamilton, 'The Opinion of Rothschilds', 7 February 1900; T 170/31, Schuster, 'The Term Exchequer Bond', 25 January 1900.

16 For example T 170/31, Hamilton, 'Methods of Borrowing', 12 January 1900; T 170/31, Hamilton, Note of Conversation with Mr Arthur Hill of Panmure Gordon & Co., 30 January 1900, and notes from Schuster, 20 and 25 January 1900; ibid., Hamilton, 'Opinion of Mr Hichens, Stockbroker', 25 January 1900; T 168/87, 'Opinion of Rothschilds' and 'Opinion of Sir E. Cassel', 7 February 1900.
17 T 170/31, note from Schuster, 20 January 1900; T 170/31, Hamilton, Note of Conversation with Mr Arthur Hill of Panmure Gordon & Co., 30 January 1900; T 168/87, Revelstoke to Hamilton, 19 February 1900; *BGS*, p. 212.
18 T 170/31, Schuster, 'The Term Exchequer Bond', 25 January 1900.
19 T 168/87, Hamilton, 'Note of further talk with Sir E. Cassel on 12 February 1900', 13 February 1900.
20 T 168/87, Hamilton, note for the Chancellor, 3 March 1900.
21 Burk (1989), p. 114; Carosso (1987), p. 510.
22 T 170/31, Note from Schuster, 20 January, and Schuster, 'The Term Exchequer Bond', 25 January 1900.
23 T 168/87, NDO, 'National War Loan', 12 March 1900. The calculation assumed that the money would earn the same as the nominal rate on the Loan.
24 *Hansard* (Commons), 5 March 1900, cols 76–7.
25 PML, Archives, Syndicates No. 2, ff. 121–2.
26 *Hansard* (Commons), 30 July 1900, col. 56; T 168/89, Hamilton, 'Supplemental War Loan August 1900', 3 August 1900.
27 T 168/89, Hamilton, 'Supplemental War Loan August 1900', 3 August 1900; *Hansard* (Commons), 7 August 1900, col. 910.
28 T 168/89, Hamilton, 'Supplemental War Loan August 1900', 3 August 1900.
29 PML, Archives, Syndicates No. 2, ff. 147–8. Burk (1989), pp. 115–8, describes the manoeuvrings between Morgans and Barings, and within Morgans, to win the business.
30 T 168/89, Hamilton, 'Closing of the Lists', 7 August, 'Draft explanation for C. of E. to make in H. of C.', 7 August, and Rothschild to Hamilton, 7 August 1900; MGP/GH, MS 21802/9; *Hansard* (Commons), 7 August, cols 909–10.
31 T 168/89, Hamilton, 'Supplemental War Loan August 1900: The Closing of the Lists', 7 August 1900.
32 Burk (1989), pp. 119–20; T 168/89, Hamilton, note for the Chancellor, [end-January] and Daniell to Hamilton, 25 and 30 January 1901; ibid., Steer, Lawford & Co. to Hamilton, 31 January 1901.
33 Mallet (1913), pp. 171–2; *Hansard* (Commons), 18 April 1901, cols 647–50.
34 T 168/89, Daniell to Hamilton, 25 January 1901; T 170/31, 'The War Loans', unsigned, June 1905; T 168/89, Hamilton, note for the Chancellor, end-January 1901, and Steer, Lawford & Co. to Hamilton, 31 January 1901
35 PML, Archives, Syndicates No. 2, ff. 217–8; Carosso (1987), p. 513. Copies of the agreements with the placees are in T 168/89. Morgans sold £5.1m to New York Life, Mutual Life, National City Bank and other miscellaneous clients.
36 *Hansard* (Commons), 2 May 1901, col. 412.
37 Milner Papers, Box 215, f. 40, Dawkins to Milner, 21 March 1902.
38 T 168/89, 'Loan of 1902', Hamilton, [end-April 1902]. Some of the uncertainties are described in GRO/HBP/D 2455/PCC 28, Hicks-Beach to Ritchie, 28 August 1902.
39 T 168/89, 'Loan of 1902', Hamilton [end-April 1902]; Carosso (1987), p. 513; PML, Archives, Syndicates No. 3, ff. 75–6.
40 T 168/89, Hamilton, 'Loan of 1902' [end-April 1902], and Hamilton to Chancellor, 12 April 1902; PML, Archives, Syndicates No. 3, ff. 75–6; GRO/HBP/D 2455/PCC 96, Rothschild to Chancellor, 16 April 1902. A list of the principal brokers and banks in the Rothschild syndicate is in T 168/89.
41 T 168/89, Hamilton, 'Consols Loan £32,000,000', 14 May 1902; GRO/HBP/D 2455/PCC/96, Hamilton, 'Consol Loan 1902', undated.
42 Morgan (1943), p. 208. The data are taken from the *Bankers' Magazine*.

43 *Hansard* (Commons), 18 July 1912, col. 568. The data for gold production are taken from *The Statist*, 10 February 1912, p. 285, which, in its turn, takes it from US Mint Estimates.
44 T 168/47, Hamilton, 'The Fall in Consols', 29 October 1901.
45 Feinstein, T 19 and T 94.
46 Imlah (1958) and Board of Trade Wholesale Price Indices in Mitchell and Deane (1962), pp. 329 and 476.
47 Goodhart (1972), pp. 127–41; King (1936), pp. 116, 296 and 315; Sayers (1976), I, pp. 38–43; Clapham (1944), II, pp. 251–2, 295–7.
48 *Bankers' Magazine*, March 1899, p. 5.
49 Gregory (1936), II, pp. 4–9: Holmes and Green (1986), pp. 143–7; Sayers (1957), pp. 188–9, 256–7; *Hansard* (Commons), 18 July 1912, cols 558–62.
50 T 168/94, Hamilton, 'Proposal to fund certain Exchequer Bonds: Brief for the Budget', 30 March 1905.
51 Report of Lord St. Aldwyn's comments at the AGM of the London Joint Stock Bank, *Morning Post*, 26 January 1912, and report of Sir Edward Holden's comments at AGM of the London City and Midland Bank, *The Times*, 27 January 1912, p. 19; *The Economist*, 13 January 1912, p. 64, and 27 January 1912, p. 165; *The Times*, 9 November 1911, p. 18. During a speech at the City Liberal Club on 3 February 1912, Lloyd George asked for suggestions to improve the price. The speech is reported in *The Times*, 5 February 1912, p. 6. The replies are in T 172/92.
52 For example *Hansard* (Commons), 23 April 1903, cols 240–4, 18 April 1907, cols 1186–8, 9 August 1911, cols 1174–81, 13 December 1911, cols 2443–4, and 18 July 1912, cols 557–72.
53 T 168/53, Turpin, 'Consols', 23 October 1901.
54 As well as the debating points made in the Commons, see briefing papers such as: T 168/53, Turpin, 'Consols', 23 October 1901; T 168/47, Hamilton, 'The Fall in Consols', 29 October 1901; T 171/56, various papers comparing debt reduction under different governments; T 171/14, Blackett, Memorandum, 12 December 1911, 'Price of Consols', undated and unsigned, and 'Reduction of Debt', also undated and unsigned, with comments by Chalmers.
55 *Hansard* (Commons), 15 June 1911, cols 1680–3, and 19 June 1911, cols 27–31. In T 171/12, there are clippings from *Hansard*, briefing papers, and the calculations which argued that the major damage was done during the Boer War under the Unionists.
56 *Hansard* (Commons), 2 April 1912, cols 1064–7; ibid., 29 April 1912, cols 1523–1636; ibid., 24 June 1912, cols 48–58; ibid., 18 July 1912, cols 557–583. The briefs for the debates on the Birkbeck failure are in T 171/12. *The Statist* slavishly supported Lloyd George, reiterating the arguments of the previous ten years; 3 February 1912, pp. 237–8, and 13 April 1912, pp. 69–71.
57 *The Statist*, 10 February 1912, pp. 295–7, and 13 April 1912, pp. 69–71; *The Economist*, 10 February 1912, p. 276; *The Times*, 5 February 1912, p. 6.
58 GRO/HBP/D 2455/PCC 18, Harcourt to Hicks-Beach, 18 November 1895. On this occasion, Harcourt pointed out that the capital repayment within the Charge, if applied to interest, would pay for the amount of the French indemnity to Germany after the Franco–Prussian war, without any additional taxation.
59 *Hansard* (Commons), 30 April 1906, col. 294, and 18 April 1907, col. 1188; T 168/94, Turpin, 'Unfunded Debt', 4 January 1905.
60 T 168/61, Hamilton, 'The Financial Outlook *vis à vis* the City', 9 October 1903.
61 Ibid.; T 168/61, Hamilton, 'Our Capital Account', 2 November 1904, and 'The Unfunded Debt', 21 December 1904; ibid., Turpin, 'Unfunded Debt', 4 January 1905; ibid., Revelstoke to Hamilton, 6 January 1905; ibid., 'The Unfunded Debt', draft of paper for the Cabinet, 14 February 1905.

62 T 168/94, Chancellor of the Exchequer, 'The Unfunded Debt', draft of paper for the Cabinet, 16 February 1905; ibid., Turpin, 'Unfunded Debt', 4 January 1905.
63 Ibid.
64 Ibid., Revelstoke to Hamilton, 6 January 1905; Bahlman (1993), p. 455.
65 T 168/94, Chancellor of the Exchequer, 'The Unfunded Debt', draft of paper for the Cabinet, 16 February 1905.
66 Ibid.
67 *Hansard* (Commons), 30 April 1906, col. 293; Bahlman (1993), p. 455.
68 T 168/94, Hamilton, 'Our Capital Account', 2 November 1904; *BGS*, pp. 343–51.
69 *BGS*, pp. 466–9.
70 T 168/94, Hamilton, 'Our Capital Account', 2 November 1904, and 'The National Debt and Sinking fund', 1 January 1906.
71 *Hansard* (Commons), 10 April 1905, col. 1058.
72 Ibid., 30 April 1906, col. 290.
73 Ibid., 30 April 1906, cols 294–5.
74 T 168/94, Hamilton, 'Sinking Fund', 25 September 1905, and 'The National Debt and Sinking Fund', 1 January 1906.
75 *National Debt: annual returns.*
76 Bahlman (1993), p. 456.
77 Mallet (1913), Table XVI; HCP 219, 29 April 1915. Old Sinking Fund in 1907–8 was actually £5.3m, but £100,000 was appropriated to the aid of the cash balance of the Supreme Court of Judicature Suitors' Funds. *National Debt: annual returns.*
78 Mallet (1913), pp. 275–7.
79 *Hansard* (Commons), 7 May 1908, cols 458–9.
80 Mallet (1913), pp. 307–13; *National Debt: annual returns*; BoE, C40/399, 'Treasury Bills'.
81 *Hansard* (Commons), 4 May 1914, col. 93.
82 GRO/HBP/D 2455/PCC 18, Harcourt to Hicks-Beach, 18 November 1895.
83 Mallet (1913), pp. 336–9. The major debates are reported in *Hansard* (Commons), 2 April 1912, cols 1055–1130, and 29 April 1912, cols 1523–1636. Lloyd George's change of mind is reported on 24 June 1912, cols 48–58.
84 Horne (1947), Appendices II and III.
85 *Government Departments Securities* (HCP 291), 23 June 1914.
86 *BGS*, pp. 208–13; *Government Departments Securities* (HCP 165), 18 May 1911, and (HCP 291), 23 June 1914.
87 *Government Departments Securities* (HCP 160), 1 May 1903, and (HCP 291), 23 June 1914.
88 *Government Departments Securities* (HCP 291), 23 June 1914.
89 *Sinking Funds* [annual accounts], 1904–14.
90 *BGS*, p. 241; *National Debt: annual returns*; *Sinking Funds* [annual accounts] (HCP 158), 2 June 1908; (HCP 169), 17 May 1909; and (HCP 143), 8 June 1910.
91 *Government Departments Securities* (HCP 155), 8 June 1910. The discussions on the legislation are in BoE, AC 30/302.
92 *The Times*, 22 March 1910, pp. 10, 11 and 15. The King was to die six weeks later, on 6 May.
93 BoE, AC 30/302, Bank to Murray, 22 March 1910.
94 BoE, AC 30/302, Sir James Mackay to Nairne, 17 March 1910, and Nairne to Mackay, 21 March 1910.
95 Carosso (1987), pp. 481–6; Burk (1989), pp. 105–11; Vale (1984) tells the story.
96 BoE, AC30/316, George Franklin (Liquidator) to Nairne, 11 February 1913; The Rothschild Archive, London, XI/III/56.

Part II

The Great War

3 Lloyd George's Loan

The whole loan was very quickly over-subscribed

David Lloyd George (1933), p. 121

The Edwardian debt structure survived only four months of the Great War. 3½ per cent War Loan 1925–8, issued in November 1914, acted like a sledgehammer. The Boer War National War Loan was small, equivalent to under 5 per cent of the existing Debt, whereas the 1914 Loan represented nearly 45 per cent. At a stroke, one of the principal characteristics of the nineteenth-century Debt was blown away for, even if there were no further borrowing of the same kind, a future Chancellor was to face not just the payment of the interest on the increased debt, but the repayment of a substantial amount of capital by, or on, a specified date (Appendix IV). There was no alternative. In 1900, Consols had been considered and rejected, and a temporary issue was chosen so that future Chancellors would feel under pressure to repay. Since then, there had been a rise in yields, reflecting a fall of some twenty-five points in the price of Consols and, as a direct result, balance sheet problems in the financial sector. It was only left for the Treasury to retain some of the benefits of perpetual debt by giving itself an option over the date of repayment, an innovation which was to be repeated with the 1915, 1917 and 1919 Loans.

In other ways, the 1914 Loan was the last of an older method of borrowing. Part was pre-placed with the banks or, as it might be, sold to contractors. This done, the Treasury seemed unconcerned about who applied, whether they be foreigners, domestic institutions or individuals. It did not aim to encourage saving, curb consumption or attract capital from industry or from overseas. Unlike the 1900 National War Loan, it was not aimed at the personal sector, although it carried, as if without purpose, the same registration and distribution facilities that had been introduced with that issue. Advertising was rudimentary, grassroots collection of contributions unknown. It was assumed that the Loan would sell on its attractions: its yield.

The return of capital to London and advances by the Bank of England to the banks and money market during the three months which followed the outbreak of war had produced plentiful liquidity, low short-term interest rates and a steep yield curve. This did not help in the selection of a suitable price for longer-term paper, for there was no effective secondary market in gilt-edged securities. The London Stock Exchange had been closed since the outbreak of war and a system of minimum prices kept yields at artificially low levels. In this vacuum, the senior joint stock bankers, with narrow perspectives and little experience of government borrowing, were the primary non-official influence on the terms. As throughout the war, their advice was notably unhelpful.

The poor response, carefully hidden from the public, affected borrowing for the rest of the war. The terms of the second War Loan, issued in the summer of 1915, had to be designed so that the first was absorbed and the banking system's balance sheet protected. Fearing a repetition of the failure of the first Loan, holders of the second were given options to convert into future Loans issued during the war, options which, in due course, produced the towering mass of 5 per cent War Loan 1929–47. After the 1914 Loan, issues were open-ended, sold by increasingly sophisticated propaganda, and spiced with attractive conversion options, tax privileges and attached sinking funds.

The credit system at the outbreak of war

The prospect of hostilities dislocated the financial markets throughout the world.[1] The Archduke Francis Ferdinand was assassinated in Sarajevo on 28 June 1914, Austria declared war on Serbia on 28 July, Germany on Russia on 2 August and on France on 3 August. During July, prices of equities and fixed-interest securities fell sharply: there was panic in Vienna on 25 July and, by the end of the month, all the main stock exchanges had closed. On 31 July, settlement of bargains on the Paris exchange was postponed for a month. The closure in London on the same day had a twofold effect on the banks: they could neither sell their own securities nor those pledged by customers. With no market, the banks could not even determine the value of securities held as collateral. They also experienced large movements of deposits. Some overseas centres and, especially, Paris were selling their London balances. Others were trying to buy sterling because London houses were demanding repayment of acceptances in cash as they matured, while refusing new accommodation.

A breakdown of the foreign exchange markets meant that customers could not repay in sterling, even if they had balances in foreign currencies. The major financial institutions were threatened: the discount houses and bill brokers, who had their names on acceptances as guarantors if the borrower and acceptor could not pay; the banks, who were both holders and acceptors of bills, as well as being owners of securities which had become unsaleable; and the stock exchanges,[a] where both brokers and jobbers were owed money by foreigners and had borrowed from the banks on the security of depreciated securities.

a The London Stock Exchange was the dominant exchange, but there were eighteen provincial exchanges.

As was customary, the Bank stepped in as lender of last resort and bought bills: between 22 July and 1 August 'other securities' (its assets other than government debt) rose from £33.6m to £65.4m. In such uncertain times, the public increased its demand for cash, which the Bank met by passing notes and gold into circulation. Bank rate was raised from 3 per cent to 4 per cent on 30 July, to 8 per cent on 31 July and to 10 per cent on 1 August. On the same day, the Bank was given permission, in the manner of previous crises, to exceed the maximum fiduciary issue. By good fortune, Monday 3 August (the day before Britain declared war on Germany) was a Bank Holiday. Over that long weekend, a royal proclamation allowed any maturing bill to be reaccepted for a date one month ahead; the Bank Holiday was extended for three days; a moratorium was declared on all but the smallest debts, on wages, and tax payments; and the Treasury was given power to issue an emergency currency, 'Currency Notes', of which much more later. The banks reopened on Friday 7 August. The tension was subsiding and Bank rate, which had already been cut to 6 per cent on the Thursday, was cut to 5 per cent, where it was to stay until July 1916.

The financial crisis had been controlled, but the credit machinery was jammed. The acceptance houses remained liable for the acceptances which their customers could not meet at maturity, and the banks and discount houses had money frozen in bills, which were both unsaleable and of uncertain value. Several moves were made to ease the position. On 13 August, the Chancellor published a letter with the terms on which the Bank would rediscount bills accepted before the moratorium (4 August): there was to be no recourse to the holders and the Treasury was to reimburse the Bank for any losses that it might incur. Not surprisingly, the facility was used freely and the Bank bought some £120m before the offer was withdrawn at the end of November. Although the scheme protected the holders of the bills, which were usually a bank or a discount house, the acceptance houses still had a contingent liability, as had discount houses and bill brokers, for bills they had endorsed. The acceptance houses did not know the extent of their bad debts, had a reduced credit rating and were unwilling to assume new risks.

From 5 September, the facility was gradually replaced by a scheme whereby the Bank made advances to acceptors to enable them to pay off pre-moratorium bills as they matured, repayment to the Bank being delayed until one year after the war. The liability for these advances ranked as a second charge after that for new, post-moratorium acceptances. This improved the acceptance houses' credit, allowing them to resume business, while the discount houses and bill brokers were relieved of all liability on bills they had endorsed. Over £60m was advanced under the scheme. This, together with normal repayments by borrowers, enabled all but £12½m of the bills discounted by the Bank to be repaid by the end of November. On 3 September, the moratorium was extended for one month and applied to debts falling due until 4 October. With a further two weeks' grace, the first acceptances fell due for repayment on 19 October and, for other debts, on 4 November.

The closure of the stock exchanges

The London Stock Exchange remained closed until 4 January 1915.[2] This was not to avert selling diverted to London by the closure of continental bourses, for jobbers could always move prices sufficiently fast to deter sellers, but because bargains could not be settled. Moratoriums in other countries, postponement of settlement in Paris and the seizure of the foreign exchanges made debts owed by foreign clients temporarily irrecoverable. Those in London who had bought from overseas clients were left with depreciating securities, but retained the money they could not remit to the sellers. Those who had sold to foreigners were unable to receive payment and could only resell at a loss the securities of which they unexpectedly found themselves long. At least one important firm with German business was hammered for this reason. However, the problem appears to have been short-lived, affecting only a few firms and lasting only as long as the foreign exchange and overseas stock markets were closed.[3]

There were other reasons for the length of the closure. Nearly £81m of advances were outstanding to members of the London Stock Exchange, and another £11m to those in the provinces, secured on securities held by the lenders. There was £37.1m owing to the joint stock banks, £23.6m to other banks and £20m to other lenders. The bulk of the borrowings from the banks were on margin – the market value of the securities pledged was agreed to exceed the value of the advance by a stipulated percentage – and were repayable at the end of the Account. If the lenders called in the advances, the borrowers would need to sell and prices would weaken, and perhaps collapse. If the lenders themselves sold the collateral, prices would also fall, further damaging the borrower's position. The borrowers would have to find more securities to make good the value of their collateral and, with lower prices, it would become more difficult to raise the money with which to make repayments. The general moratorium meant that there was no immediate problem, but it could not be ended without forcing the sale of securities, with a general fall in prices, which would affect the banks and insurance companies, as well as the members of the stock exchanges.

On 23 October, the Chancellor agreed to a scheme based on proposals put to him by the Committee of the London Stock Exchange and the Committee of London Clearing Banks (CLCB).[b] The markets' debts were smaller than the Chancellor had expected and most were due to the bankers, who would be amenable to pressure. Those banks in receipt of Currency Note facilities agreed not to call in loans or demand extra margin until twelve months after the end of the war. Other lenders, the remaining £20m, could be repaid with advances from the Bank of England. In the event, the Bank needed to advance only £2.1m. The last debt was repaid in May 1919.[4]

b The Treasury's memorandum incorporating the scheme was dated 31 October 1914. The proposals on which it was based and the memorandum are reproduced in Osborne (1926), IV, pp. 190–3.

These measures allowed settlement to proceed during November, the first and largest being on 18 November as applications for the War Loan began flowing in.[5] By this time, however, there was another reason, more important for the story of the Debt in 1914 and 1915, for keeping the market closed. Jobbers in the Consols market had been refusing to deal at prices lower than those of 27 July in order that there might be no official record of transactions at a level which would compel them to write down their holdings and increase their margin calls. In defiance of this, jobbers outside the Consols market were negotiating marriages – transactions which did not involve taking positions – at lower prices. The Consols jobbers petitioned the Committee to introduce minimum transaction prices, which would be binding on all members, and suggested that a new official list of prices should be published. On 14 September, the Committee published a new list, together with a rule that members were not to transact business at prices lower than those it carried. This move appears to have had the Chancellor's blessing.[6]

As the stock exchanges settled down, the Chancellor's attention shifted to the protection of the banks' balance sheets. In September, the Chancellor told a subcommittee of the London Stock Exchange that most members of a delegation of bankers had been unconcerned about the problems of the exchanges and the level of security prices. By December, the CLCB was asking that any reopening should be delayed until the end of January so that the bankers would not have to write down their securities when drawing up their end-year accounts or answer questions at their annual meetings. They were promised that the minimum price regime would continue until the end of January and would not be altered except with the agreement of the Treasury. Although reassuring to the bankers, this did little to help the exchanges resume their role. A minimum price of 68½ in Consols (irrespective of the amount of the accrued interest) produced no more buyers after 4 January, when the London Stock Exchange reopened, than it had before. The queue of would-be sellers continued to lengthen. Consols, whose liquidity had once made them a second line of banking defence, continued to have no market except for a few banks and other non-members, who negotiated transactions outside the stock exchanges.

Currency Notes and the Currency Note Redemption Account

The issue of Currency Notes was to lead to one of the most important developments in debt management. Until 1914, the Bank of England issued Notes backed by gold, with a further amount – the fiduciary issue – backed by securities. Originally limited to £14m, by the outbreak of war the fiduciary issue had risen to a maximum of £18.5m, of which £11m was covered by the Book Debt of the government to the Bank. Thus, the marketable securities held against the fiduciary issue were only a few millions and the volume was inelastic. In contrast, Currency Notes were a Treasury responsibility and, from their introduction, the volume rose steeply as inflation took hold in the war economy.

Although issued by the Treasury, Currency Notes were distributed through the Bank, which was required to establish an account to hold the securities bought with the proceeds of their sale. At first, this account – the Currency Note Redemption Account (CNRA) – acquired gold, invested in Treasury Bills and made advances on Ways and Means.[7] As the portfolio grew further, it bought longer-dated securities, providing the Treasury with a *masse de manoeuvre* with which to operate in the gilt-edged and Treasury Bill markets. As interest rates rose, it became clear that this could involve selling securities at a loss, and in May 1915 the Treasury established a Currency Note Investments Reserve Account (CNIRA) as a liability of the CNRA.[8] The CNIRA was to be credited with the interest which accrued from the advances of Notes and the securities held by the CNRA. Securities were to be shown in the accounts at cost price, but any profit or loss on realisation or repayment would be credited or debited to the CNIRA. Interest on the portfolio would, therefore, be available to cover any capital losses which might be incurred. If the cover fell beneath the stipulated amount, interest was to accrue until the cover had been rebuilt. There was no requirement for the Treasury to make good any shortfall, the deficit disappearing when sufficient income had accrued. The Treasury was given discretion to determine the size of the CNIRA in the light of the character of the securities it held. Initially, it was fixed at 5 per cent of 'total securities held and advances outstanding' and any amounts in the Account above £0.1m were to be transferred to the Exchequer.

Lloyd George's first war budget

The creation of credits at the Bank and the reduced supply of acceptances pushed down short-term interest rates, while the demand for sterling to repay debts in London kept the exchange rate strong and led to an influx of gold. The government was able to issue Treasury Bills and take Ways and Means Advances on terms which gave no budgetary incentive to borrow longer, even if the state of the financial markets had made it possible. Between 7 August and 30 November, £20m Ways and Means Advances were taken from the Bank at 3 per cent and £15m at 2½ per cent; £82.5m six-months' Bills were sold at average discount rates of between £2 18s 6d and £3 15s 6d per cent; and a further £7.5m twelve-months' Bills were sold in mid-September at an average discount rate of £3 8s 3d per cent.[9]

Although journalists and the City began speculating on the size and terms of a loan almost as soon as war broke out, no issue was announced until Lloyd George presented his first war budget on 17 November. The previous May he had budgeted for peacetime expenditure of £206.9m. To this he now added war expenditure of £328.4m.[10] With revenue expected to fall short of its pre-war estimate by £11.4m, the Chancellor faced a deficit of £339.6m. Towards meeting this, he doubled income and super taxes, but only for the final four months of the year, so that those who had already made their financial arrangements, or whose incomes had disappeared altogether, would not be disturbed. The only indirect taxes of note to be raised were the duties on beer and tea.

The measures were estimated to contribute £15.5m in the current year, which increased to £18.3m when a partial suspension of the New Sinking Fund was included. Of the £23.5m originally voted for the Fixed Charge in 1914–15, £16.7m was to have been applied to interest and management and £6.8m to the repayment of capital. Borrowings for the war on the credit of Ways and Means had already increased the interest payable from the Charge, reducing the balance available for sinking fund to £5.9m. This became £2.8m after the partial suspension. Thus, although not fully exploited, Hamilton's 'reserved power' provided 15 per cent of the new resources for 1914–15, paying the interest on £76m new War Loan.

There were two reasons for continuing some repayment from the Charge. First, as it was a contract with the lender, £1m had to be found to meet the final instalment of the Lottery Bonds: as the Chancellor said, 'To interfere with this...would be very undesirable and might be regarded, perhaps, as a breach of faith towards the holders'.[11] He was undoubtedly correct. The terms of the sinking fund were unambiguous, although meeting the commitment flew in the face of the principle of suspending the whole sinking fund when the budget was in deficit so that the absurdity might be avoided of borrowing with one hand (the new War Loan, costing about 4 per cent) to repay debt with the other (the Exchequer Bonds, costing 2¾ per cent). However, it was not necessary for the £1m to pass through the Permanent Charge, for the payment could equally well have come directly from the Consolidated Fund. The Chancellor's explanation, and the routing of the £1m, showed that the Treasury felt it had to retain the form of the sinking fund, irrespective of the substance. This was to become of importance in the 1920s, when the Treasury was to argue that the revenue surplus and, by implication, the Fixed Charge had to be sufficient to meet all attached sinking funds if a breach of contract was to be avoided. The payment of Terminable Annuities and the repayments from the departmental Votes for capital advances were also to continue because three-quarters of the money for 1914–15 had already been issued and the Commissioners could apply additional sums to advances for new capital works, Local Loans and Irish land purchase.[12] Behind this, it may be surmised, lay the assumption that normal spending would continue and, if money for these purposes was not found from the Annuities, it would have to be found from elsewhere, thus leaving total borrowing unchanged.[13]

3½ per cent War Loan 1925–8 (17 November 1914)

The Chancellor followed custom by announcing the terms of a new issue alongside his revenue measures. The War Loan Act 1914, which received Royal Assent on 28 August, could have been used as authority since it provided the Treasury with general borrowing powers, permitting the money to be raised 'in such manner as the Treasury think fit' with securities 'bearing such rate of interest and subject to such conditions as to repayment, redemption, or otherwise as they think fit.' However, the power to borrow was limited to the supply granted for the period up to 31 March 1915. Thus, when the Chancellor announced that he would borrow an amount that would carry him through to July in the following financial year, he had to seek additional powers. These were included in the Finance Act 1914 (Session 2).

The issue was simple compared with those that came later: there were no conversion options; no exemptions from withholding tax, whether for residents or non-residents; and no special terms for the small investor. Despite this, there were aspects that would have been difficult to price, even if the markets had been open; £350m was an unprecedented sum. It was the first British government double-dated issue. It towered above any other issue requiring repayment on, or by, a specific date. The price of 95 could be considered a deep discount compared with previous dated borrowing – the Boer War issue of 2¾ per cent National War Loan 1910 and Exchequer Bonds – and investorswere unaccutomed to calculating its value.

The interest payment was 3½ per cent and the latest redemption date 1 March 1928, but the Treasury retained the option of calling it at any time after 1 March 1925 by giving at least three calendar months' notice in *The London Gazette*. The GRY at 95 was £4 2s 0d per cent to 1925 and £3 19s 9d per cent to 1928. It was stated boldly at the top of the prospectus that £100m had been placed, for the authorities were still scarred by the issue of the Exchequer Bonds in August 1900. It was partly paid, with £2 per cent due on application and the balance payable in ten instalments stretching into the 1915–16 financial year. Unlike most of the issues during the South African War, the first two interest payments were broken: interest was paid on the actual money received by the Treasury so there was no hidden discount in the price.[14] The National War Loan had extended the distribution of prospectuses and this was now taken further: application forms could be obtained from the General Post Office's (GPO) Money Order Offices and all banks in the UK,[c] in addition to the Banks of England and Ireland, their branches, the London banks and the principal stockbrokers that had received subscriptions in 1900.[15]

Holders enjoyed one further privilege, which was not part of the prospectus. A notice was issued at the same time that the Loan was launched, stating that 'The Bank of England will be prepared for a period of three years, say until 1st March, 1918, to lend on War Loan, at 1 per cent under Bank Rate.'[16] This was generous for a normally cautious Bank. It was made to all holders and the price was to be taken as that of issue, with no margin. Thus, the Bank was laying itself open to exploitation by all investors, irrespective of their creditworthiness. It was especially vulnerable if the price fell, since it was bound to continue making advances as if the paper was still worth 95. It is not surprising that in 1916 the Bank started to examine applications with a critical eye, despite the promise.[d] Advances under the scheme reached a maximum of £40.7m in 1917.[17]

c The earlier prospectuses excluded banks outside London and Money Order Offices. The availability was widened at the suggestion of the CLCB. MBa, 158/6, Murray and Hyde to Holden, 12 November 1914.

d The Bank had to write off £0.4m of its advances, mostly in 1920, when it was forced to sell the collateral at prices of between 80½ and 83½. It was not until 1922 that the Loan rose above its issue price. Osborne (1926), I, p. 305.

Designing the terms

When announcing the issue, the Chancellor emphasised that the terms had been the subject of prolonged discussion and uncertainty.[18] The interest payment, price, date and even the size were undecided right up to the evening before the budget. However, it was a comment on the experience of the fixed-interest markets since the Boer War that the most basic question – whether the Loan should be a permanent annuity such as Consols or a dated issue such as National War Loan – was rarely discussed. On the few occasions it was considered, opinion was unanimously against.

After a month of war, Sir William Turpin, Comptroller-General of the NDO, summed up prevailing sentiment:

> The heavy and continuous drop in the price of securities during recent years has led to so much loss on realisation or to writing down in the valuations, that the tendency now is for lenders to prefer investments which will return the capital at some definite date.

Bankers would be most tempted by Exchequer Bonds; otherwise, he said, the Japanese method of financing their war with Russia should be adopted: dated issues with long option periods so that they could be refinanced if yields fell.[19] In October, Maynard Keynes, who was not to receive a formal Treasury appointment until the following January, gave Bradbury the same advice: the banks, 'after their recent experiences, are likely to attach much importance to a due date [a single redemption date].' He suggested that they should be tapped by an issue of £50m or £60m five- to ten-year Exchequer Bonds, an amount which would not be unmanageable when they matured on a single day. The general public would prefer a single date, but would be unlikely to pay sufficient for the preference to compensate the government for its disadvantages.[20] Bradbury's memorandum, written on budget day, gave the same advice:

> The great War Loans of the past have been raised in the form of permanent annuities. In return for the payment of a capital sum the state has undertaken to pay a fixed amount year by year until such time as it is convenient to repay the capital debt. This arrangement has great advantages from the point of view of the Treasury. The obligation to make a payment of hundreds of millions at a particular future date is one which no Chancellor of the Exchequer can impose on his successor with equanimity. On the other hand it has serious disadvantages from the point of view of the investor. The market value of a perpetual annuity which the State is under no obligation to redeem necessarily fluctuates with the ruling rate of interest. Consols, which in the time of very cheap money seventeen years ago stood as high as 114 fell as low as 70 even before the War. The security which is redeemable at par at a comparatively early date is much less liable to market fluctuations, and is therefore much more attractive to the investor who desires to keep his capital intact. We therefore come to the conclusion that in the case of the present Loan the

> Exchequer must take responsibility not only for the payment of interest but also for the repayment of capital.[21]

Reflecting the prevailing sentiment, there is no record of an undated issue being discussed during the bankers' conversations with the Chancellor in the days immediately before the issue: they pressed for ten-year paper, whereas the Chancellor was wanting something five years longer.[22]

Having accepted that it would have to be dated, the Treasury adopted the suggestion first made by Schuster in January 1900 and now, in 1914, by Turpin and Keynes of giving itself a period during which it had the option, but not the obligation, to redeem. The benefits were spelt out by the Chancellor in the Commons:

> The loan will...be redeemed by the Government at par on the 1st March 1928, or, subject to three months' notice, at any time between 1st March, 1925, and 1st March, 1928...The point of our securing an option to redeem three years before the termination of the full period is there may be – no one can tell – a period of cheap money...and the State ought then to be in a position immediately to take advantage of it and redeem at par, so as to reduce the percentage of the security.[23]

The Treasury did not try to calculate the value (to the investor) or cost (to itself) of the double-dates when issuing this loan or, indeed, of those of 1915 and 1917: it was merely seeking the flexibility of a long option. It was, however, very aware that double-dates made issues less attractive to investors, who were sensitive to the closeness of the first optional repayment date and the length of the option period.

The cost of dated borrowing has two components: the cost of the initial security and a judgement, some might say a guess, of the cost of refinancing at maturity. A double-date gives borrowers the option of two dates or, depending on the terms of the prospectus, any time between two dates, on which to repay. The longer the period of the option, the lower the assessed cost, as there is a greater probability that the option will coincide with a period of lower interest rates. The closer the first date, the sooner borrowers will have the opportunity of exercising their option and the shorter is the period for which they are contracted to continue paying the initial interest rate. Clearly, borrowers will only exercise their options if interest rates have fallen, enabling the debt to be refinanced more cheaply. For these reasons, the dates of surviving draft prospectuses show anxious debate about how long an option the government could retain and for how long it had to give protection from conversion: 1925–30, 1930–45, 1925–8 or 1925–35.[24]

The value of an option to the borrower is greater the nearer the price of issue is to par; the GRYs on issues made at 95 with a $3^1/_2$ per cent interest payment or at 100 with a 4 per cent payment might be the same, but the refinancing cost on the former has to fall below $3^1/_2$ per cent and on the latter below 4 per cent before it becomes worthwhile for borrowers to exercise their option and call the loan. For these reasons, the 1915 War Loan, made at 100 with a twenty-year option beginning in 1925, was a better bargain for the government than the 1914 issue made at 95 with a three-year option, also beginning in 1925. It was also the point, in relation to the 3½ per cent Conversion Loan after the war, that Sir Otto Niemeyer was so slow to grasp.

Although there is no record of debate within the Treasury about how the option period would affect the decision whether a yield of 4 per cent should be provided by a 3½ per cent issue at 95 or by a 4 per cent issue at par, officials must have been aware of the implications, even if Bradbury had not seen Keynes's letter in October:

> An issue in the neighbourhood of par must not be redeemable at the sole option for [*sic*] Government for a considerable period, if it is to be popular. Consols at 62 (e.g.), whatever the date of optional redemption, give a certainty of an annual income of £4 until the rate of interest has fallen below 2½ per cent; and in that event there is a large increase in capital value. 4% Consols at 100 do not carry any part of this advantage, unless the date of the optional redemption is very remote.

There was a balance between an early first date, a long option period and a high nominal interest rate allowing issue near par:

> it would be unsafe to issue a loan in the neighbourhood of par with optional redemption earlier than 1945 at the earliest, and a much longer run than this might be desirable. If the government, in issuing a 4 per cent loan, attaches great importance to the possibility of early conversion, they must, I believe, fall back on a due date (with all its risks). Redeemability, both early and optional, is giving the investor, as distinguished from the patriotic citizen, too little.[25]

In the event, the interest payment and issue price seem to have been mainly determined by the City. The Chancellor said in his budget speech that he would have preferred a 4 per cent issue at par: 'a simple and direct method intelligible to everybody.' But, although admitting some differences of opinion among the financial interests he had consulted, he said that he had found 'an overwhelming' opinion in favour of a 3½ per cent issue at 95.[26]

Negotiations with the CLCB

By 'financial interests' Lloyd George meant the bankers: the joint stock bankers, the members of the CLCB, who had conspicuously increased their influence since the South African War. At the beginning of the century, it was the merchant bankers who were consulted and took the pre-placed paper, with the joint stock banks only admitted to the business in 1902 after persuasion by the Bank, pushed by the Treasury. In 1914, the position was reversed. Despite their experience of public issues, the merchant bankers were not consulted and, to drive home the point, the bankers were represented by the Committee of London Clearing Bankers and its Treasury subcommittee. Until 1 July 1915, its chairman was Schuster and then, until his death in April 1916, Lord St Aldwyn, previously Michael Hicks-Beach, who had been Chancellor during the Boer War. The change produced no improvement in the quality of the advice offered; throughout the war, the members of both committees were jealous of each other, unimaginative, intemperate, showing little grasp of markets and providing counsel which suited their own banks rather than the Treasury.

On 13 November, four days before the budget, the CLCB formally recommended an issue of 3½ per cent War Loan at 95, redeemable within fifteen years: in fact, given the juxtaposition of resolutions, it might be said to have made the size of its support largely dependent on the acceptance of its advice.[27] As would have been expected, it reflected a preference for stability of capital value over income. A dated 3½ per cent security issued at 95 would have the pull of redemption at par to offset the effect of any rise in interest rates: a yield of 4 per cent would be maintained by the price rising in a straight line over its life. A 4 per cent issue would yield 4 per cent at par throughout its life, so that a rise in interest rates at any time would send it to a discount.[28] In addition, bankers, caught in the years before the war by having lent on the security of depreciating fixed-interest securities, believed that the greater stability provided by a 3½ per cent stock 'gradually appreciating in capital value until the date of redemption' would lend 'itself more readily to the purposes of credit facilities, which are likely to be increasingly important not only during the duration of the war, but during the period of reconstruction after it'.[29] Finally, it was argued that a 4 per cent issue with its higher running yield would appeal to trustees and the general public and thus have had a greater effect on the prices of other fixed-interest issues.[30]

The banks appear to have won their case on the terms of the issue without difficulty, mainly, as we have seen, because the Treasury was already more than half convinced. Instead, negotiations centred on the amount for which they would subscribe and the terms for advances of Currency Notes and cash from the Bank against the security of their holdings. The budget speech was to be on Tuesday 17 November. On the previous Thursday (12 November), the Treasury subcommittee of the CLCB had met the Chancellor, who asked it to consider the size of its members' subscriptions on the assumption that arrangements were made with the Bank for making cash advances against the Loan, as of right. He asked the Committee to return the following afternoon and give him definite commitments. According to Henry Bell, the General Manager of Lloyds Bank, the Chancellor was uncertain of what he was offering:

> [he] did not express his plans definitely but showed that his mind was running on 250 millions at 4 per cent at 99 and a 15 years Bond. He said he did not like 10 years as he thought it was putting too much on the next Chancellor and he would much prefer 15 years...he was not at all definite but that was the general drift...[Lloyd] George seemed rather depressed...was very indefinite and did not define any clear programme.[31]

St Aldwyn, who was a member of the Treasury subcommittee, realising that the Chancellor needed to show a steadier hand, suggested that he address a meeting of the CLCB and representatives of the Scottish and Irish banks that had been called for the following Monday (16 November). At the same time, he encouraged the Chancellor to make a 'personal appeal' to Sir Edward Holden, *quondam* Liberal MP, Chairman of the London City and Midland Bank and one of the Liberal Government's most influential City supporters. He had failed to attend the recent meetings about the Loan. In fact, Holden had influenza, but the advice was sound. Of the bankers, Holden, together with Bell, felt most strongly about the terms for Currency Note advances.[32] It is not recorded whether a meeting took place, but Holden's bank – the largest in the country – subscribed and underwrote on the proposed scale.

Bell's report of the meeting of the CLCB on Friday morning was explicit about the connection in the bankers' minds between the availability of Currency Notes at Bank rate, with a maximum of 4 per cent, and their willingness to subscribe.[33] The resolutions passed to the Treasury were only a shade less crude:

> That it be a recommendation of this Committee that the issue of the Loan be on the following terms viz. 3½ to yield 4% per annum, redeemable within 15 years.
>
> That the facilities either in currency notes or at the Bank of England should be available at [a rate] not exceeding 4%. That the Committee finds a difficulty in stating the probable amount of Banks' subscriptions, but an opinion is expressed that probably 5% of their deposit and current accounts might be subscribed 'Firm'.
>
> That meetings of the Boards of the Banks, where necessary, should be called for Monday next to decide the point.[34]

The part of the resolution referring to the terms for obtaining Currency Notes was stressed by the CLCB's subcommittee when the resolution was passed on to the Chancellor. Lloyd George's initial reaction was that 'he could see the point which did not appear unreasonable.' Second thoughts followed within minutes: after conferring with Lord Cunliffe, the Governor of the Bank, the Chancellor refused, explaining that it would mean that 'the Bank of England would lose control over the rate.' Instead, he suggested that the Bank should lend to 'anybody and everybody' for three years at 1 per cent under Bank rate against the deposit of the new issue when fully paid. The bankers accepted this with little argument.[35]

The Chancellor also pointed out that subscriptions equivalent to 5 per cent of deposits would amount to only £50m, and that he was expecting them to find at least £100m. He suggested that they make a firm subscription equivalent to 5 per cent, with another 5 per cent as an underwriting commitment and, with normal Treasury parsimony, insisted that there be no underwriting commission.[36] Although he had no firm promise from the bankers and the budget was the following day, the Chancellor failed to attend the meeting on the Monday. The depression noted by Bell had given way, according to Asquith, to 'one of those psychological 'chills' which always precede his budgets, when he does not feel altogether certain of his ground', and he remained at home at Walton Heath.[37] Instead, he wrote a letter to St Aldwyn, for use at the meeting, calling on the bankers' patriotism and pointing to the efforts made by German bankers when the first German war loan had been issued in September: 'I hope the Bkrs of the U.K. can see their way to give a patriotic lead by undertaking a substantial portion of the loan.'[38]

On the Monday, there were two meetings of bankers. The first was of the CLCB and the second of the CLCB together with representatives of the provincial, Scottish and Irish banks. The approximately one hundred representatives at the second meeting passed a threefold resolution, which was delivered in the Chancellor's absence to Lord Reading, who, although Lord Chief Justice, was to play a crucial role in British finance throughout the war:

> That this Meeting of Bankers is most anxious to assist His Majesty's Government in any way in its power in the issue of the proposed War Loan, and recommends that the Banks should subscribe, firm or underwritten, an amount equal to 10% of their Current and Deposit Accounts in the United Kingdom to the Loan.
> That in particular they will place the whole machinery of their Head Offices and Branches free of charge at the service of the Government.
> That strong representations be made to the Chancellor of the Exchequer that the charge on Currency Notes should not exceed 4%.[39]

Thus, twenty-four hours before he was to deliver his budget, the Chancellor had the recommendation of the bankers that they should subscribe or underwrite, in an unspecified combination, the equivalent of 10 per cent of their deposits. This would amount to some £70m for the members of CLCB and perhaps £110m for the banking system as a whole. The arrangement was made more specific in a letter from the Secretary of the CLCB to the Chancellor the following day:

> I now beg to inform you that the London Clearing Bankers will undertake to subscribe about £70,000,000 of the new War Loan of which half is firm; and we are confident that when the decision of the various Boards of Directors in the country, still to be taken, are known, a further amount of at least £20,000,000 to £25,000,000 will be similarly subscribed.[40]

As well as providing comfort for the Treasury and encouraging the investing public, the pre-placing of £100m reduced a potentially massive underwriting commitment for the Bank. Cunliffe, apparently on his own responsibility and without consulting his Committee of Treasury, had not only promised to provide the cheap and automatic borrowing facilities for all holders of the Loan, but had agreed to subscribe for any part of the issue that the public did not want and that had not been pre-placed with the banks.[41] His original proposition was that the Bank would subscribe

> for any portion which may not be applied for by the public, and of financing holders during the next three years on specially favourable terms...
>
> the Bank will be prepared to bring out the loan, to subscribe for any portion which may not be applied for by the public, to defray all costs of printing Prospectuses, Allotment Letters, and scrip, also all costs of postages and advertizing, besides taking the obligation of financing all holders during the next three years...in consideration of a charge of 1/8 th per cent. over the whole issue of £350,000,000.[42]

A memorandum written by Bradbury shortly afterwards showed that the Governor's attempt to extract a commission on the whole Loan in return for this spacious promise had been rebuffed, but that the 'guarantee' had become something less than the certainty of an underwriting:

> There will be no underwriting in the ordinary sense. Such underwriting has never been a feature of State loans in this country; nor would the great houses, which usually undertake such operations, desire to secure a condition for bringing about the success of the loan. We shall rely as heretofore on the patriotism of the community for an adequate response...But if it should happen that the enormous total for which we are asking is beyond the resources of the ordinary subscriber, the great banks have assured me that they will be prepared to make yet a further effort, and to increase their subscriptions beyond what they have already promised by a very substantial amount. Nothing will be paid by the Exchequer in respect of this guarantee beyond the ordinary commission of one-eighth of 1% on the amount of Stock and Bonds actually subscribed. We have thus through the patriotism of the banks secured the advantages of underwriting without the cost to the Exchequer of the underwriters' commission.[43]

Apparently, the Bank had agreed to an increased subscription, should it be necessary, and it might have agreed to a subscription sufficient to cover the issue.

The process by which the pre-placement of the £100m was achieved is fogged by the way that 'subscribe' was used by the banks to mean both a 'firm' application and an 'underwriting' commitment. The CLCB had said that its members would subscribe for 'about £70m' of the Loan, of which half was 'firm'. The meeting of the CLCB and other bankers in London on the day before the budget recommended that the banks should subscribe for the equivalent of 10 per cent 'firm or underwritten'. Thus, the only definite subscriptions in the banks' resolutions were the CLCB's £35m, as the other £35m was only underwritten. The other banks' 10 per cent of deposits was firm or underwritten in unspecified proportions and they could have met the terms of their resolution with no 'firm' applications at all. The uncertainty is reflected in the way that the bankers described their commitment. Lloyds saw it as 'the amount of the War Loan which this Bank would have been glad to take if necessary'. The investments committee of the same bank saw it as 'an undertaking'. The London City and Midland saw it as a 'conditional application' and the London Joint Stock Bank as 'contingent'.[44]

The prospectus, however, stated that £100m had been 'placed in the terms of this Prospectus': in other words, that it had been pre-placed – subscribed firm – before the issue was made. The Governor may have agreed that the Bank would make up the difference between whatever the banks subscribed and £100m, or the Treasury may have been viewing the amount underwritten as a subscription, either being unaware of the precise meaning of the terms being used or treating the announcement in the prospectus with a degree of cynicism. There are two other possibilities. The Bank of England's contribution was a peculiarly exact £39,498,200. The remaining £60,501,800 pre-placed with the remaining banks was not £35m (the amount which the CLCB undertook to subscribe), nor £70m (the amount the CLCB undertook to subscribe and underwrite), nor £55m (the CLCB subscription of £35m plus the equivalent of 5 per cent of the deposits of the rest of the banks). It was close enough to 5 per cent of the banking system's deposits to arouse the suspicion that the Bank was simply assuming that that would be the amount of the application.[e] This is borne out by Osborne's account, which describes the recommendation of the Monday meeting as 'an undertaking to apply' (the resolution actually said 'recommends that the Banks subscribe, firm or underwritten') for an amount equivalent to 5 per cent of deposits and to 'take a further 5% if required'.[45] The other possibility is that the Bank monitored the amounts that each bank promised as it made its decision and then made up the total to £100m in the light of the subscriptions that had reached it by the time lists closed.[f]

Choice of size

The issue was increased to £350m at the last moment, having been fixed at £250m as early as the end of October: 'I lunched at the Assyrian's [Edwin Montagu] with a lot of colleagues' Asquith wrote on 27 October. 'We talked financial shop: at what price and on what terms the War Loan of 250 millions is to be issued.' On 6 November, he repeated the amount, as did the Chancellor on 12 November when he opened negotiations with the CLCB.[46] Explaining in his budget speech how the size had been selected, Lloyd George did not mention the change and moved straight from forecasting his £321m deficit for 1914–15 to the question of how it was to be financed. The Loan would raise £332.5m, or more than was required in the current year, because £90m had already been raised on Bills since the outbreak of war. This might have implied a decision to lengthen the Debt, an admission

e In part, the size of the commitments was imprecise because the date to be taken as the base for applications was rarely made clear. The London City and Midland Bank, one of the few to have been specific, took 30 June 1914. MBGa, Board Minutes, 20 November 1914.

f This interpretation is supported by BoE, Loan Wallet 226, which contains reports from the CLCB of banks' firm applications and guarantees, 16 and 17 November 1914.

that, in the uncertainties of war, it might be difficult to refinance Bills when they matured and that it would be dangerous to place too much reliance on them. However, this would have been a warning to investors and might be used by critics if the Bill issue climbed further in the future. Instead, Lloyd George said that renewal must depend on financial conditions when the Bills matured and that it would be a 'mistake' to make the decision 'so many months in advance'. Closely following Bradbury's brief,[47] he emphasised two other reasons for borrowing more than £231m:

> The instalments must be spread over four or five months, and it is undesirable to have recourse to borrowing on Treasury Bills while the instalments upon the great loans [*sic*] are in process of being paid. The other [reason] is, that it is desirable to raise an amount that will carry the War forward ...not merely to the end of the financial year, but for some weeks beyond that, because at that time we shall certainly, I think, be in a better position to form an estimate as to the prospects of the War... [by the summer] there will have been great decisions taken. Therefore we have decided... to raise a sum of money which will enable us to carry the War through without a further appeal to the public up to the month of July next year.[48]

No doubt the Treasury was trying to reassure investors that no further issue was in immediate prospect although, if this was the explanation, the words would have meant little beside finding an extra £100m. It is more likely that the Treasury was trying to have it both ways – keeping open the option of renewing Bills, having the resources to repay the Bills if it were found necessary or convenient, and giving itself finance into July 1915, if all went well.

The small saver

'Mr Lloyd George's huge loan was intended to appeal to rich men and bankers' stated *The Economist* at the beginning of December.[49] The comment required no great insight for, when it was launched, the Chancellor had explained that the £100 minimum was being retained to exclude small investors who might apply by withdrawing their POSB deposits, which were only costing 2½ per cent.[50] Raising money was a commercial question, he said, and there was nothing to be gained by involving the entire community:

> We considered very carefully the question whether investors could apply for smaller amounts than £100, but the advice we received on that point was against the experiment. It has been tried repeatedly, not merely in this country, but abroad. The result has not been satisfactory as far as the aggregate is concerned. The effect is very largely to deplete the Savings Bank. That does not help the Government at the present moment...It is something which rather appeals to the public, but does not mean very much in the cash that comes into the State...when you are raising money for the purpose of carrying on a

> war, you are not raising money for the purpose of benefiting the investor, you are raising money for the purpose of carrying on war.[51]

The Germans might be driven to borrowing from small investors but, Lloyd George said, the British could raise the money without. This changed once the government knew the results of the issue:

> What was the result of our appeal to the public, and to the great financial interests of the country? We have not only raised the whole of the loan, but it has been over-subscribed, and the most remarkable thing about it is not merely that the great financial interests came in...the feature of the loan is the enormous number of small applicants. On the occasion of the last loan for the Boer War, these small applicants numbered about 21,000. Now, in this case, they number nearly 100,000, and we have been glad to give the first chance of co-operation to the small capitalist. The first allotments will be made to the small applicants who came forward.[52]

No doubt the Chancellor had seen the opportunity to make a propaganda point. More important for immediate purposes was to avoid scaling down subscriptions equally for all, for this would have shown the true size of the applications. Giving preference to the small investor had an additional advantage, amounting to a necessity. Of the commitment recommended by the CLCB, only half was to be taken 'firm'. On the other underwritten half, a bank only had a liability to take its share of the undersubscription pro rata with the other banks. If any subscriber had been scaled down, the banks would have had to take more than their commitment. Evidence of the importance of this consideration is to be found in the basis of allotment actually adopted: 'small applications' turned out to mean all applications by members of the general public, irrespective of size.[53]

Failure

For the offer had been a disaster, the general public applying for only £91.1m of the £250m not pre-placed. The Bank took £113.5m to ensure that it was fully subscribed, in addition to the £39.5m that it had taken of the £100m pre-placing. The other banks took £105.9m: £60.5m as their share of the pre-placing and £45.4m that they had underwritten. The Bank's subscription was for slightly more than was necessary to cover the issue, presumably so that it could be reported, not as fully subscribed, but as over-subscribed, so that total applications (including the £100m pre-placing) were £352m. The banks were asked to take up 96 per cent of their commitments (Table 3.1).[54]

The manoeuvre could not be admitted without also admitting failure. The £113.5m was therefore not acquired directly by the Bank. Instead, it was taken by the Chief Cashier and his Deputy in their own names, with the Bank making advances to the two officials to finance their subscriptions. Because these were included in 'Other Securities', an increase in 'Government Securities' in the weekly

Table 3.1 $3^{1}/_{2}$ per cent War Loan 1925–8: distribution of applications and underwriting

	£m nominal	*Per cent of issue*	
General Public*	91.1	26	On 24 November
Bank of England†	39.5	11	Part of the bankers' £100m on 24 November
Bank of England†	113.5	32	On 25 November
Remainder of the banks‡	105.9	30	
Total	350.0	100	

Notes
*Osborne (1926), I, pp. 252 and 386. Also, see Sayers (1976), I, p. 81.
†BoE, C40/729, undated.
‡Residual. McKenna said £197m was the amount of 'the old War Loan which was subscribed without the assistance of the Bank of England'. BoE, C40/729, McKenna to Cunliffe, 31 July 1915.
Percentages may not sum because of rounding.

Bank Return was avoided, and with it public admission of failure. Camouflage was further improved as the securities were not subscribed fully paid and some calls were not made on the due date, although this was primarily to fit in with the pattern of normal government disbursements.[55]

Cancellation

The Bank supported the issue during December and January, with purchases of £1.6m, so that by 12 January 1915 its holding had crept up to £154.6m. This was the high point. Four sales, amounting to £5.8m, were made to the Commissioners during February and March, reducing the holding to £148.8m, where it remained, with one trifling exception,[g] until cancelled in July 1915 using powers provided in the War Loan Act 1915 and funds raised from the issue of $4^{1}/_{2}$ per cent War Loan 1925–45.[56]

The Governor had failed to obtain the Court's consent to the subscription and was pressed to ensure that the Bank did not make a loss, especially as the Court must have suspected that the promise to make advances against the Loan would turn out to be costly.[57] The Cabinet does not appear to have been informed of the Bank's subscription: McKenna, who was Home Secretary at the time of the issue, knew nothing about it until he became Chancellor.[58] There was an 'informal letter of assurance' signed in November by the Prime Minister and Chancellor, and a general, but unwritten, understanding between the Chancellor and the Governor

g A purchase of £69,000 was made with the Chancellor's agreement at the end of that month. This was overlooked at the final accounting and was sold to the Commissioners under a separate arrangement later in the summer. Sayers (1976), I, p. 81; BoE, C40/729; Osborne (1926), I, p. 256; T 133/1, Bradbury to Commissioners, 26 August 1915.

that the Treasury should 'take over' the holding at the earliest possible moment.[59] The Governor believed that the verbal agreements 'admitted of no ambiguity', while conceding that there was 'no definite understanding or arrangement'.[60] As the Bank had not underwritten the issue and had borne no risk, it could not expect to receive the interest on the War Loan or the 1/8 per cent commission. Negotiations with the Treasury on the terms of cancellation therefore centred on a suitable short-term interest rate to be charged by the Bank. At times, the correspondence between McKenna and Cunliffe was bad tempered.[61] Without doubt, the Bank was acting *ultra vires* in its subscription to both the War Loan and some Exchequer Bonds, which were taken later in the spring in similar circumstances (see p. 96). The Bank of England Act of 1819 regulated the Bank's power to make advances to the government and to purchase government securities, requiring that advances and purchases have 'the express and distinct authority of Parliament for that Purpose first obtained': that applications by the Treasury be in writing; and that the applications and answers, together with an annual return, be laid before Parliament. The Bank's action contravened all three. Section III, however, permitted the Bank to buy securities, which 'by Law they are now authorized to purchase'. These ambiguous words were interpreted to mean that it could make purchases in the course of its normal business as a commercial concern.[h]

There were several precedents for the Bank's actions, although the scale of the subscriptions, if nothing else, lifted them unambiguously beyond purchases of securities in the course of the Bank's normal business. Advances on Ways and Means had been *ultra vires* between 1869 and 1893 (see p. 20). In 1901, the Bank took for itself £6.5m of the £60m 2 3/4 per cent Consols. The Bank may also have taken £2m of the £16m pre-placement of the 1902 issue. The public did not become aware of the slip over Ways and Means, which was technical. The Boer War placings were known immediately and caused little stir. The present case was different: the intention from the start was to mislead the public.

The Bank's actions continued *ultra vires* until the War Loan Act 1916. This lifted, retrospectively, any statutory limitations on the purchase of government securities by anyone, including the Bank. It did not affect the need to make the annual return to Parliament, which in the past had included every transaction on behalf of the Treasury except those made in 1901 and 1902.[62] It was a belated desire for written assurance of a Parliamentary indemnity for the failure to make full returns that led to an exchange of letters with the Treasury in the last days of

h This interpretation was confirmed and clarified when the power of the Bank to lend to the Treasury, and the 1914 and 1915 subscriptions, came under examination in 1939. The Bank was advised that (1) Section III of the 1819 Act was ambiguous (2) a subscription for government securities was not *per se* an advance to the government and that (3) the test lay in the motive for the subscription. If a subscription by the Bank was for its own purposes, and on its own initiative, it would not contravene the intention of the Act. If the application was for the convenience of the government, it would be contrary to the spirit of the Act. The correspondence is in BoE, G15/103.

Cunliffe's governorship in February and March 1918. Bonar Law gave the necessary reassurance:

> Whatever may be the precise position as regards the legality of these subscriptions there is no doubt in the opinion of His Majesty's Government that in the circumstances of the time the making of them was essential in the national interest...I am satisfied that in the event of the action of the Bank being challenged whoever might be Chancellor of the Exchequer when the question arose would feel it to be his duty to recommend to Parliament that the Bank should be indemnified.[63]

Reasons for the failure

Presenting the issue as a success to the Commons, Lloyd George pointed to the difficulties that the issue had encountered:

> It was the largest loan ever raised. We had already raised £90,000,000 [Treasury Bills] for the same purpose and under the same conditions. We had just got through the most serious financial crisis that the country had ever seen. A moratorium in which we protected debtors against their debts, if called upon, had only just come to an end...the Stock Exchange was closed.

Then he described the role of the speculator in taking a new issue and holding it while investors decided whether to buy:

> The absence of machinery of that kind at this moment was a serious detriment. If the Stock Exchange had been open we would have had the loan applied for several times over. They would have made enormous applications, and taken time [*sic*] for the distribution of the allotment.[64]

Viewed as reasons for failure, they have a characteristic in common: they were all known to the authorities before they decided to launch the issue. The comments were valid, but the terms should have reflected the financial conditions and the investors' states of mind that Lloyd George described.

The Loan was, indeed, very large, in comparison with both earlier issues for the British government and the size of the economy. During the thirty-two months of the South African War, £152m had been borrowed. The largest single sale had been of £60m Consols in April 1901, from which £56.6m was raised. The £350m War Loan would have raised £332.5m. This was equal to almost half of the nominal value of the National Debt at the end of March 1914, 14 per cent of GNP, two years' Gross Domestic Capital Formation or nearly one-third of bank deposits.[65]

Apart from the negotiations with the CLCB, there is no record of officials trying to identify the sources of demand, or trying to assess the size and flow of savings and the amounts of cash and bank deposits held by investors. Instead, they looked in the other direction, at the level of incurred or estimated government spending and the budget deficit which it was throwing up. Once a deficit was forecast, it was customary to announce plans for borrowing: Treasury Bills, the alternative had no plans been announced, would have been unacceptable to public opinion and to a Treasury that had yet to become accustomed to the shifts to which a great war would bring government finance. Thus, the decision was taken to make the issue before the stock markets were open and when the financial crisis was still fresh; it also explains the readiness to increase the size of the Loan by £100m at the last minute.

The Loan was priced in a vacuum. Normally, the yield would be selected with the help of those on existing issues in the secondary market. Indeed, market prices on comparable issues would be the single most important factor in that nice balancing of price and nominal interest payment, of the gauging of investors' appetite for term and credit risk, that makes a successful issue. The handicap was greater because the range of government issues was so limited; with only a couple of very short-dated Exchequer Bonds (one of only £1m) and Consols, which could be viewed as either a 1923 maturity or permanent debt, identification of a relationship between yield and term meant making comparisons with lesser credit risks: guaranteed loans, colonials and municipals. With the stock exchanges closed, realistic prices for these issues did not exist, any more than they did for Consols.

Such comparisons became more important with the decision to issue at a discount and with a double-date. The investor in gilt-edged securities was accustomed to Consols and to measuring yield in terms of the annual income received on the price paid per £100 nominal. Exchequer Bonds were bought by institutional or banking investors and were generally issued at discounts of only a point or two. The only dated government issue to have been taken up by a wider investing public was 2¾ per cent National War Loan 1910, issued on a wave of enthusiasm fourteen years earlier at the relatively small discount of one and a half points. A dated government issue, in which the discount was to be eliminated and the issue redeemed at par in a period so short as to open a gap of over six shillings per cent between the running yield and the GRY, was new to the investing public. The lack of familiarity with GRYs was reflected in the fumbling manner in which the newspapers discussed the value of the five points of discount; a discount sometimes referred to as a 'bonus'.

The Treasury, therefore, did not obtain full value for the £0 6s 1d per cent a year that those five points cost and the issue sold largely on its income yield. This was £3 13s 8d per cent compared with £3 13s 0d per cent on Consols at their minimum (clean) price of 68½. Consols were seeing no demand at this level: at a price at which there might have been buyers, say 66 (clean), they yielded £3 15s 9d per cent. This comparison should not have been relevant because the two issues were not comparable. War Loan would be liable to repayment in 1925 if its price rose more than five points, where it yielded 3½ per cent; Consols would be liable to repayment after 1923 if their price rose thirty-two points, reducing their yield to 2½ per cent.[66] In contrast, War Loan had to be paid off at par by 1928; Consols need never be repaid. War Loan was for pessimists and Consols for optimists. Yet the comparison had to be made because there were no comparable securities in the gilt-edged market. Thus, when commentators compared the two, they tended to pay ritual homage to the greater price stability to be expected from War Loan and pass on to compare its yield with that of Consols, as if they had similar characteristics.

A new issue cannot be priced successfully unless the investors it is expected to attract have been identified, so that their appetites and needs can be met. Later in the war, the investing public was to be separated into categories and instruments were to be tailored to meet the needs of each.[67] As the need for this was not yet understood, and officials had not identified any other group on whom to focus, the banks found the way open to ensuring that the terms suited them.

There were also errors of timing and presentation. The coincidence of the first day for applications with the first stock exchange settlement since the beginning of the war – a settlement covering three months and accompanied by concern that there would be failures – could have been easily avoided.[68] It may have been necessary to announce the Loan in the budget, but it cannot have encouraged a healthy response when it was coupled with a doubling of income tax rates. Surely, investors in any age would wish to assess the implications for their portfolios of such extreme tax changes before making large investments? Austen Chamberlain advised Lloyd George that new taxation should be postponed because it would adversely affect any loan he might be considering and, six months later, Robert Horne, a future Chancellor, ascribed part of the reason for the failure to the same cause.[69] It is not reassuring for potential investors to hear the Chancellor spell out the advantages to the borrower of double-dated securities or to hear an MP being told that he was 'very sanguine if he expects a lower Bank Rate than 5 per cent. during the currency of the War, or even immediately after the War.'[70]

The newspapers gave the Loan patriotic support with extensive coverage of both a technical and generally exhortatory nature. A sense of short supply was created: even the most sober reported that it would be over-subscribed; the more excitable reported that it could be over-subscribed anything up to twelve times.[71] Its good points were emphasised, with particular weight put on the stability given to its price by the redemption date and the Bank's commitment to lend against it. The banks, fired by patriotism and the commission payable on applications bearing their stamp, instructed their branches to draw it to customers' attention. Yet the impression is given that the issue was produced and then left dangling for investors to take or leave as they thought fit; there was little sense of urgency. A City observer may have said, 'you could no more rush a loan of this amount than you could rush the German Army', but it was a mixture of *élan* and organisation that carried the great loans and made a success of continuous borrowing in the final two years of the war.[72]

✣ ✣ ✣

By the spring, it would be clear that it was not possible to avoid a depreciation in existing securities when borrowing on the scale needed to finance a great war whose costs, risks and outcome was uncertain. It was necessary to make a new issue attractive to the marginal saver, not to make it unattractive to protect prices in the secondary market. Short rates would need to be held at historically high levels if they were to play their part in sustaining sterling. The closure of the stock exchanges and the artificialities of the minimum price regime could not continue forever. When these protective devices disappeared, investors would have to face the effect of the war on their holdings of fixed-interest securities.

Endnotes

1 The story of the financial seizure that followed the outbreak of war has often been told. These three paragraphs are based on Morgan (1952), pp. 3–32; Sayers (1976), I, pp. 66–78, and III, pp. 31–45; Withers (1915).
2 Unless otherwise specified, the following three paragraphs are based on transcripts of meetings between the Chancellor and his advisers (including Reading, Montagu, Bradbury and Cunliffe) and delegations of bankers and the London and provincial Stock Exchanges. These are T 172/125, 11 September 1914; T 170/59, 23 October 1914; T 172/139, 12 November 1914; T 172/140, 10 December 1914; T 172/153, 21 December 1914; T 172/175, 30 December 1914; and T 172/155, 31 December 1914. Drafts and correspondence concerning the reopening of the Exchanges are in T 170/29, Parts I and II.
3 Morgan (1952), pp. 24–5; JMK, XI, pp. 240–1.
4 Osborne (1926), I, pp. 303–4.
5 The details of the settlement arrangements are provided in *The Economist*, 3 October 1914, p. 558.
6 Morgan (1952), p. 25. He cites *The Economist*, 12 September 1914, pp. 445–6, and 19 September 1914, pp. 485–7.
7 Currency Notes were issued under the Currency and Bank Notes Act 1914 and the Currency and Bank Notes (Amendment) Act 1914. The TMs setting up the machinery for the issues were dated 6 August, 20 August and 22 October 1914, and 19 January 1915. They were published as Cd. 7836.
8 The TM, dated 3 May 1915, was published as Cd. 7918.
9 Morgan (1952), p. 106; *The Economist*, 12 September 1914, p. 442, and 19 September 1914, p. 492.
10 This and the following paragraph are based on Mallet and George (1929), pp. 34–48, and Hirst and Allen (1926), pp. 21–35.
11 *Hansard* (Commons), 17 November 1914, col. 370.
12 Ibid., 17 November 1914, cols 369–70.
13 T 171/110, Ramsay, 'Suspension of Annuites included in the Fixed Debt Charge', 1 May 1915.
14 Some of the draft prospectuses in T 170/32 included a full half-year's interest payment in the manner of the Boer War issues.
15 In common with the National War Loan, holdings could either be in the form of Bonds to bearer or of inscribed stock. Lists were to remain open for a maximum of six working days, the minimum subscription was the conventional £100 nominal and trustees were empowered to invest in the Loan even if the price at the time of the purchase was above 100.
16 *Hansard* (Commons), 17 November 1914, col. 376.
17 Sayers (1976), I, p. 79: Osborne (1926), I, pp. 304–7.
18 *Hansard* (Commons), 17 November 1914, cols 371–2.
19 T 170/31, Turpin, 'War Loans', 31 August 1914.
20 'Note on Government Loans', 23 October 1914, Keynes (1971–89), XVI, p. 40.
21 T 171/106, Bradbury, 'War Loan', 17 November 1914.

22 MBa, 158/6, Murray and Hyde to Holden, 12 November 1914.
23 *Hansard* (Commons), 17 November 1914, col. 373.
24 T 170/32, copies of draft prospectuses.
25 Keynes, 'Note on Government Loans', 23 October 1914, Keynes (1971–89), XVI, pp. 40–1.
26 *Hansard* (Commons), 17 November 1914, col. 372.
27 T 170/32, 'Copy of Resolution passed by the Committee of Clearing Bankers' [*sic*] at a meeting held on 13th November 1914.'
28 *Hansard* (Commons), 17 November 1914, cols 372–3.
29 *Hansard* (Commons), 17 November 1914, col. 373. Clapham says that the advances from 'banks' secured by stock exchange securities were £250m at the outbreak of war. He does not provide a source. 'Clapham on August 1914', reproduced in Sayers (1976), III, p. 43.
30 T 171/106, Bradbury, 'War Loan', 17 November 1914; *The Times*, 17 November 1914, p. 14.
31 MBa, 158/6, Murray and Hyde to Holden, 12 November 1914.
32 Lloyd George papers, C/7/7/2, St Aldwyn to Lloyd George, 13 November 1914; Sayers (1976), I, p. 75n; MBa, 158/6, Murray, Madden and Hyde to Holden, 13 November 1914, second letter.
33 MBa, 158/6, Murray, Hyde and Woolley to Holden, 13 November 1914.
34 T 170/32, 'Copy of Resolution passed by the Committee of Clearing Bankers' [*sic*] at a meeting held on 13th November 1914'.
35 MBa, 158/6, Murray, Madden and Hyde to Holden, 13 November 1914, second letter.
36 Ibid., Murray, Hyde and Woolley to Holden, 13 November 1914, second letter.
37 Brock and Brock (1982), Asquith to Venetia Stanley, 16 November 1914, p. 316.
38 Lloyd George papers, C/7/7/3, draft of letter from Lloyd George to St Aldwyn, undated.
39 T 170/32, J. Herbert Tritton (temporary Honorary Secretary to the Bankers' Clearing House) to Lloyd George, 16 November 1914.
40 Ibid., Tritton to Lloyd George, 17 November 1914.
41 Sayers (1976), I, pp. 79–81; Court Minutes and CTM, October and November 1914.
42 BoE, Loan Wallet 226, Cunliffe to Bradbury, 16 November 1914.
43 T 170/32, Bradbury, memorandum for the Chancellor, 16 November 1914.
44 Lloyd George papers, C/11/2/74, Vassar Smith to Lloyd George, 26 November 1914; Lloyds Bank Archives, 498/166, Investments Committee, 27 November 1914; MBa, Board Minutes of The London City and Midland Bank, vol. 28, 20 November 1914, and Board Minutes of the London Joint Stock Bank, 19 November 1914.
45 Osborne (1926), I, p. 386.
46 Brock and Brock (1982), Asquith to Venetia Stanley, 27 October and 6 November 1914, pp. 288 and 312; MBa, 158/6, Murray and Hyde to Holden, 12 November 1914.
47 T 171/106, Bradbury, 'War Loan', 17 November 1914.
48 *Hansard* (Commons), 17 November 1914, cols 370–1.
49 *The Economist*, 5 December 1914, p. 993.
50 *Hansard* (Commons), 17 November 1914, col. 374, and 19 November 1914, col. 623.
51 Ibid.
52 *Ibid.*, 27 November 1914, col. 1554.
53 Osborne (1926), I, p. 387.
54 MBa, Board Minutes of London City and Midland Bank, vol. 28, 20 and 27 November 1914, and Board Minutes of the London Joint Stock Bank, 19 and 26 November 1914; Lloyd George papers, C/11/2/74, Vassar-Smith to Lloyd George, 26 November 1914.
55 Sayers (1976), I, p. 81; BoE, G15/111 and G15/103; Osborne (1926), I, pp. 252–4 and 386.

56 T 170/82, Turpin to Chancellor, 18 May 1915; BoE, C 40/729; NDO 15/9, ff. 103–4, Turpin to Bradbury, 20 and 25 February 1915. There is an unexplained discrepancy of some £9,800 between the amount given in the Bank's account rendered to the Treasury (£148,763,430) and the amount actually cancelled (£148,773,228).
57 BoE, C40/729, especially Bradbury to Governor, 26 July 1915, Nairne to Bradbury, 28 July 1915, Cunliffe to Chancellor, 29 July 1915, Chancellor to Cunliffe, 31 July 1915, and Cunliffe to Chancellor, 3 August 1915.
58 BoE, C40/729, McKenna to Cunliffe, 31 July 1915.
59 Sayers (1976), I, p. 81. Sayers describes the agreement as explicit. It may have been explicit, but it was verbal. BoE, C40/729, Nairne to Bradbury, 28 July 1915. Also, see BoE, G15/111, Chief Cashier's evidence in front of the Special Committee, 12 November 1917.
60 BoE, C 40/729, Nairn to Bradbury, 28 July 1915.
61 The correspondence and accounts are in BoE, C40/729.
62 BoE, G15/103, Cunliffe to Bradbury, 19 February 1918.
63 BoE, G15/103, Bonar Law to Governor, 12 March 1918. Other correspondence and memoranda concerning the legality of the subscription are in G15/111.
64 *Hansard* (Commons), 27 November 1914, cols 1553–4.
65 Feinstein (1972), T 1 and T 86; *National Debt: annual returns*; Morgan (1952), p. 228.
66 For example, *The Economist*, 19 December 1914, p. 1067.
67 Keynes was an early advocate of breaking up lenders into categories and treating them separately. 'Note on Government Loans', 23 October 1914, Keynes (1971–89), XVI, pp. 39–42.
68 *Financial News*, 19 November 1914, p. 3; *The Economist*, 21 November 1914, p. 915.
69 *Hansard* (Commons), 21 June 1915, cols 983–4; *The Times*, 28 November 1914, p. 9; Lloyd George papers, C/3/14/5, Chamberlain to Lloyd George, 9 November 1914; *The Times*, 12 November 1914, p. 9. *The Economist*, 21 November 1914, p. 915, dismissed the influence 'as a consideration which applies to other securities as well, and therefore carries no especial weight'.
70 *Hansard* (Commons), 17 November 1914, cols 373 and 390.
71 For example, *The Economist*, 21 November 1914, p. 907; *The Times*, 18 November 1914, p. 9, and 20 November 1914, p. 5; *The Financial News*, 19 November 1914, p. 3.
72 *The Economist*, 21 November 1914, p. 907.

4 McKenna's conversion

> As a means of getting money out of all classes they [the terms] could not possibly be improved upon. The only question is whether they will not in this respect be too successful. This criticism applies especially to the terms under which holders of other forms of British debt are invited, or in some cases in fact compelled, to convert... If they do not convert, they will face a heavy capital depreciation. If they do, in most cases they will have to put up, in order to buy the necessary amount of new War Loan, more cash than they have got, or can accumulate within a reasonable time.
>
> Hartley Withers, 'The Financial Position', June 1915, T 170/67

Issued in the summer of 1915, 4½ per cent War Loan 1925–45 was dated, with an option period, and large. The similarities with Lloyd George's Loan went no further. McKenna's Loan was open-ended, the first such issued by the British Treasury. The purpose was to repay monies the Treasury had borrowed from the Bank of England, curb consumption and increase saving. The smallest investor was courted with tailor-made issues. Advertising was professional. Most importantly, the Loan carried two conversion privileges: an option to convert into it from existing issues and an option to convert out of it into any long- or medium-dated loan which might be sold later in the war. Thus, if yields rose and the government found it necessary to produce another loan, an issue would be created that was at the same time expensive to service, probably dated, and potentially as large as its own new money subscription and the 1915 Loan combined. The Loan was clever, technically innovative, and the most clumsy debt management episode of the war.

3 per cent Exchequer Bonds 1920 (5 March 1915)

The November 1914 War Loan had been intended to carry hostilities a few weeks into the new financial year, by which time, Lloyd George had thought, the prospect for the war would be clearer, 'assuming that it has not come to an end.'[1] Even as he spoke, governments and General Staffs were grasping that the armies on the western front were deadlocked. Winter attacks by the French were costly and showed the Germans' skill in trench fighting. Further attacks in the first half of

1915 were equally expensive and gained little. Seeking a way round the trench system, on 25 April British and Empire troops landed on the Gallipoli peninsula where, as on the western front, they were pinned down, absorbing ever more men and ships, until they were withdrawn in December 1915 and January 1916. This right hook to the control of the Black Sea was in part intended to relieve the Russians. After a winter attempting to clear the Carpathians and the way into Hungary, on 2 May they found themselves vigorously attacked, and during the summer were in full retreat: by mid-August they had lost 750,000 troops and Poland had been occupied. On 24 May, Italy declared war on Austria–Hungary, her hereditary enemy, and became an immediate burden on British finance. Seeking to aid Serbia, in October 1914 allied troops were landed in Salonica where, having arrived too late to help, they remained, stranded, in what the Germans called their 'largest internment camp'.[2] In the UK, dissatisfaction with the progress of the war, reports of shortages of munitions and the resignation of the First Sea Lord (the professional head of the Admiralty) led during May to the fall of the last Liberal government and a coalition. Asquith remained Prime Minister, Lloyd George went to the newly created Ministry of Munitions and Reginald McKenna, moving over from the Home Office, replaced him at the Treasury.

McKenna took up his post at a time when these events were producing a rapid change in the public's understanding of war finance.[3] Manpower shortages had appeared as the labour force lost members to the armed forces and industry scrambled for resources with which to meet government orders. Prices rose abruptly. Underlying these symptoms was an increase in government spending far in excess of the new taxation imposed the previous November and an expansion of credit at the Bank of England. The deterioration was reflected in the foreign exchange markets. The repayment of debts in London at the outbreak of war had strengthened sterling, at one point taking the rate as high as \$7.[a] A depot was set up in Ottawa so that the USA could export gold to buy sterling without the risk of loss from German surface raiders and submarines. By mid-November, business was becoming more normal and the rate against the dollar had returned to par (\$4.86½). The demand for sterling with which to settle debts had run its course and government departments were buying in the open market the foreign currencies with which to pay for munitions and food. The purchases were predominantly from the USA and the strain was felt mainly against the dollar and the currencies of the neutral European countries, sterling remaining firm against the currencies of the combatants. This was the beginning of the problem of finding finance for American supplies which was to dog the Treasury for the remainder of the war.

In the New Year, sterling weakened further, and on 18 February the Bank's agents in New York were given instructions to support the rate (see p. 162). Short rates reached their low point the same month, three-months' Bank bills falling briefly to 1¼ per cent. Although it had been the intention not to issue Treasury

a '\$' will in future refer to the American currency, although 'US\$' is used if the context demands greater clarity (see p. xxii).

Bills so long as calls on the November Loan were outstanding, tenders were resumed on 23 February 1915, not with the purpose of making 'disbursements' but of 'taking money off the market and keeping it in the Exchequer.'[4] On 14 April, a system of tap sales, imposing on the market a minimum level of rates, was introduced.[b] Three-months' Bills were made available at a rate of discount of 2¾ per cent, six months' at 3⅝ per cent and nine months' at 3¾ per cent. To these were added, on 8 May, twelve-months' Bills at a rate of 3¾ per cent. The rates were all raised to 4½ per cent on 9 August, with a further rise on 27 October (Table 4.1).

Also in February, the Bank started taking deposits directly from lenders, a technique that grew so that in February 1916 the Report of the Committee on the Co-ordination of Military and Financial Effort felt able to say that it enabled the Treasury to obtain 'practically the *whole* of the available funds within the country.'[5] The device was not new, having been used at least as early as 1890, when money was taken from the India Office. Other pre-war lenders had been official or semi-official bodies such as the Crown Agents, the Ecclesiastical Commissioners and the Bank of Japan. The Bank began borrowing from the banking system in 1905–6.[6] Now, in the first instance, it took deposits from only a few lenders: from the India Office and, shortly afterwards, from Barings, who had received on deposit the proceeds of Russian Sterling Treasury Bills discounted with the Bank. Further large amounts of sterling were provided from the sale of dollars in New York. Finally, and most long-lasting, from the beginning of March the Bank began borrowing directly from the clearing banks, initially paying 1½ per cent for money at seven days' notice (Table 4.2).

These began modestly, with £5.6m in mid-February 1915, but rose sharply to £48.9m at the end of March. They reached £76.2m in the middle of July, before falling as the subscriptions and calls on the new Loan were settled. They did not exceed £17m until October, when they again grew rapidly as other banks were allowed to participate: they were £56.9m in December, before the end-year window dressing (Table 4.3 provides data for end-quarters).[7] The special deposits, as they were called after the pre-war borrowings, were concealed in the weekly Bank Return by deducting them from Government Securities, or partly from Government Securities and partly from Other Securities. Until 1917, the Bank lent the proceeds to the Treasury by purchasing Treasury Bills.[8]

The Bank engineered a rise of nearly a point in March, shortly after it had taken another failed issue. The £21m 3 per cent Exchequer Bonds 1915 issued in 1910 to help refinance the Boer War National War Loan had been reduced by sinking fund purchases to £16.4m and were due to mature on 5 April. The Commissioners held only £0.4m.[9] The authorities decided to take advantage of

b The system was introduced under a TM dated 13 April 1915. It was published as HCP 199 of 15 April 1915. Sales at a fixed price were one of the alternatives provided for in the TM of 31 May 1889, but it had hitherto only been used to provide Bills for the Commissioners and public departments (see p. 21).

Table 4.1 Rates of discount (yields) (per cent) on tap Treasury Bills: 14 April 1915 to 4 January 1917

	Three-months'	*Six-months'*	*Nine-months'*	*Twelve-months'*
14 April to 7 May 1915	$2^3/_4$ (£2 15 3)	$3^5/_8$ (£3 13 10)	$3^3/_4$ (£3 17 2)	–
8 May to 8 August 1915	$2^3/_4$ (£2 15 3)	$3^5/_8$ (£3 13 10)	$3^3/_4$ (£3 17 2)	$3^3/_4$ (£3 17 11)
9 August to 26 October 1915	$4^1/_2$ (£4 10 9)	$4^1/_2$ (£4 12 1)	$4^1/_2$ (£4 13 2)	$4^1/_2$ (£4 14 3)
27 October to 11 November 1915	$4^3/_4$ (£4 15 11)	$4^7/_8$ (£4 19 11)	5 (£5 3 11)	5 (£5 5 3)
12 November 1915 to 23 March 1916	5 (£5 1 0)	5 (£5 2 7)	5 (£5 3 11)	5 (£5 5 3)
24 March to 15 June 1916	$4^1/_2$ (£4 10 9)	$4^3/_4$ (£4 17 4)	$4^3/_4$ (£4 18 6)	5 (£5 5 3)
16 June to 13 July 1916	5 (£5 1 0)	5 (£5 2 7)	5 (£5 3 11)	5 (£5 5 3)
14 July to 26 September 1916	$5^1/_2$ (£5 11 3)	$5^3/_4$ (£5 18 5)	–	6 (£6 7 8)
27 September 1916 to 4 January 1917	$5^1/_2$ (£5 11 3)	$5^1/_2$ (£5 13 1)	–	$5^1/_2$ (£5 16 5)

Notes

Until May 1950, Bills were issued for calendar months so that the actual number of days for which Bills were outstanding could change according to the month and the day of the week on which they were issued. To avoid this problem, these yields are calculated on 91, $182^1/_2$, $273^3/_4$ and 365 days. BoE, C40/399, 400 and 401.

One-month Bills were issued to government departments and to Bank of England accounts, but not made available to the public.

A special issue was made to the Prudential Assurance Co. on 31 July 1915 of three-, six-, nine- and twelve-months' Bills at a rate of discount of $4^1/_2$ per cent.

I would like to thank Professor Howson for the reference to the change from a calendar month basis in May 1950.

Sources: T 171/129, 'Treasury Bills': Osborne (1926), I, p. 487.

Table 4.2 Interest rates on special deposits with the Bank of England (per cent)

	Domestic				
	From Clearing Banks		*From other banks*		*Foreign*
	Three days	*One month*	*Three days*	*One month*	*Three days*
1915					
4 March	1½ (7 days)				
6 April	2 (7 days)				
22 July	3 (7 days)				
2 September	3½ (7 days)				
27 October	3½	4½		4½	
23 November	4½	4½		4½	
1916					
24 March	4	4½		4	
16 June	4½	4½		4½	
13 July	5	4½		5	
1917					
4 January	5	4½	4½	5	
19 February		4½		4¾	
26 February	4½	4½	4	4½	
20 June	4	4½	3½	4	
12 November	4	4½	3½	4	4½
28 December	3½	4½	3	3½	4½
1918					
2 January	3½	4	3	3½	4½
15 February	3	3½	2½	3	4½
1919					
8 January	Special rate ceased for French, Belgian and Italian deposits.				
23 July	The Bank ceased taking fresh deposits from the Clearing Banks.				
18 October	All foreign money withdrawn from the Bank.				

Source: Osborne (1926), I, pp. 287-8.

easy money and refinance the maturity, with something left over, by issuing £50m 3 per cent Exchequer Bonds 1920.[c]

The press treated the Bonds as money market instruments to be bought by the banks and discount market. Emphasis was placed on the cash that was being made available from maturing Exchequer Bonds and Treasury Bills and the relatively

c The tender was held on 10 March and the initial payment was £2 per cent. A call of the amount that would leave £50 per cent was payable on 19 March, the day £7.5m Treasury Bills matured, and the remaining £50 per cent ten days later. The Bonds were the last issue made without the privileges relating to taxation at source and exemption from tax for non-residents. The description in Committee on National Debt and Taxation (Colwyn Committee), *Appendices*, V, p. 20, is erroneous.

Table 4.3 Domestic and foreign special deposits at the Bank of England: 1915–19 (£m)

End-quarter	*Total*	*End-quarter*	*Total (of which foreign)*	
31 December 1914	4.9	30 March 1918	137.4	(96.5)
31 March 1915	49.3	29 June 1918	195.6	(130.4)
30 June 1915	57.6	25 September 1918	n/a	(151.4)
30 September 1915	7.3	24 December 1918	n/a	(163.8)
30 December 1915	39.1	26 March 1919	n/a	(153.4)
31 March 1916	29.0	25 June 1919	n/a	(151.1)
30 June 1916	50.9	24 September 1919	n/a	(149.0)
30 September 1916	66.8			
30 December 1916	103.8			
31 March 1917	91.1			
29 June 1917	64.6			
29 September 1917	70.1			
31 December 1917	94.0			

Notes
Balances cease to be provided after the middle of July 1918. The accounts for January–October 1919 (BoE, C58/40) are missing.
'Total' relates to the last working day of the quarter. 'Foreign' are the figures reported to the Committee of Treasury meeting held nearest to the end of the quarter. It is not clear to which day of the month they refer. Until October 1915, the data are entered under 'Special', and thereafter under 'Market'.

Sources: BoE, C58/38 and C58/39; CTM, relevant dates.

small proportion that represented new money. The authorities made no attempt to interest a wider public, nor, it seems, did anyone expect them so to do. A yield of $3^{1}/_{4}$ per cent had been mooted when the tender was announced the previous week, but sentiment deteriorated as the suspicion grew that cheap money was coming to an end.[10] The market was right. Two days after the tender, the Bank tightened: the rate on three-months' Bank bills climbed, rising from around $1^{5}/_{16}$ per cent to about 3 per cent, where it stayed before rising further, to 5 per cent, during the summer.[11] The result of the sale was considered disappointing.[12] Tenders amounted to £72.8m. Applications at £95 10s 6d received about 19 per cent, with those bidding higher being allotted in full. The average price was £95 18s 1d and the average yield £3 18s 2d per cent.

The market would have been more depressed had it known of the Bank's subscription to enable all tenders at yields of 4 per cent and above to be rejected.[13] On 10 March, at the tender, the Bank subscribed for £10m. By the time the first instalment was due nine days later, the holding had risen to £37.9m.[14] The Bank reduced this by selling to the India Office, the Commissioners and the CNRA, so that its holding was £18.3m at the beginning of August when it was cancelled.

The episode was notable for being the first occasion that the CNRA was used as the receptacle for unwanted paper, with the important difference from post-war practice that the Bonds were cancelled, rather than being held and then sold into the market. Although the CNRA's assets, other than gold, were still modest, it bought £10m of the Bank's holding; at the end of March, the Account held £9m 'Exchequer Bonds and Treasury Bills', valued at £8.6m.[15] These were almost certainly £9m of the Exchequer Bonds taken at a price of about £95 16s 3d.[d] More of the issue was acquired during the summer, and the holding was £10m when it was cancelled at the beginning of September.[16] In the meantime, interest rates had risen and the Account would have displayed a loss on its investments if it had been unable to value them at cost; the timing of the May Treasury Minute establishing a reserve fund was not fortuitous.

Understanding resource limitation and Lloyd George's last budget

At the beginning of June, Bradbury stated the case for a new loan:

> The economic education of all belligerent countries has made great progress during the past nine months, and it is now almost universally recognised that the creation of huge credits by a State bank for the purpose of meeting public expenditure has almost precisely the same effect on money and prices, and consequently upon the foreign exchanges, as an indiscriminate issue of paper money.
>
> It is not, however, yet so generally understood that similar results tend to follow the use of ordinary 'bankers' money' for the same purpose. The underlying principle is that, if the aggregate purchasing power of a community is increased while its powers of production remain stationary or are diminished, the inevitable result is a general rise in prices. This stimulates imports and discourages exports, and the exchanges move against the country in which the inflation has taken place…
>
> The moral is that, if it is necessary – as I believe it is – in times of national emergency to inflate currency or credit to provide for Government expenditure, the process must not be repeated *ad libitum*, but future expenditure must be met by reabsorbing the currency or credits originally created…
>
> The conclusion is that any further call upon (which means also creation of) 'bankers' money' is highly dangerous, and that a new loan, which will be as unattractive as possible to the money market for its own purposes and as attractive as possible to the private investor, should be issued without delay.[17]

Several papers and a budget had paved the way to the recommendation. In the middle of March, Bradbury had warned that, with consumption of the ordinary family growing, output dislocated by recruitment and rising war demand, it was necessary to husband resources. Consumption had to be reduced by permitting the rise in prices to have its effect on real incomes. However, allowing inflation to

d Evidence for this is to be found in a scribbled note in T170/71 listing purchases of unspecified securities during March and April 1915. One item reads 'Currency Note Account £9,000,000…' and 'Sale to tsy to be at av. price of Bank's successful tender (£95 – 17 – 1).'

transfer resources to war purposes was only a temporary answer: the UK was an open economy and 'The maintenance of the Exchanges is absolutely vital to us and the loss of the gold standard would produce economic consequences of a disastrous character.' Unlike Germany, Britain was dependent on foreign supplies of food and raw materials and on world markets to absorb the exports with which to pay for them.[18] In April, a comprehensive survey of the war and its financing came from Sir George Paish, Lloyd George's special adviser. This long paper, comparing expenditure on the war with the size of the economy and quantifying the resources that might be released by selling overseas assets, borrowing in the USA and increasing taxation and saving, joined Bradbury's in shaping the comments on the limits of British resources made in the budget statement on 4 May.[19]

The budget was peculiar for combining tax increases which were widely regarded as inadequate with a powerful statement of the stretched state of British resources. In a much-quoted passage, Lloyd George listed three roles for the UK: controlling the seas; furnishing a continental army; and supplying and financing her allies, both from her own output and by exporting to pay for their imports. But, he said, 'Britain can do the first, she can do the third, but she can only do the second within limits, if she is to do the first and the last.'[20] The gap between spending and output could be bridged in three ways, two of which were unacceptable or impracticable. First, by inflation, or disguised taxation, 'levying taxes on the income of the people'. This would lead to a collapse of the exchange rate and higher import prices. Second, by increasing imports, paying by borrowing foreign currencies and selling overseas assets: 'both of them perfectly legitimate but only helpful within limits'. The money that could be raised was limited by the capacity of overseas investors to lend or buy: prices of securities would be driven down and interest rates up; the country would be impoverished by the time the war ended. Third, by saving more and making the proceeds available to the government. Only this alternative was sustainable:

> The State, in carrying through a great War like this, must primarily depend on the savings of the community…it is vital … if we are to take our part not merely in financing our own share but in helping our Allies to finance theirs, that the national savings should be increased.

Following Paish, he estimated saving before the war to have been between £300m and £400m a year, and suggested that it could be doubled out of the increased incomes currently being enjoyed.[21]

In the middle of May, Keynes pointed to the necessity of refinancing earlier borrowing from the Bank of England. The message for the new loan was the same as Bradbury's was to be in June:

> *we do not want the bankers' money*. They should not be encouraged to make applications. Their spare funds can be obtained more safely and conveniently from Treasury bills, and they have no business to be putting large sums into

> funded debt. On the other hand there should be an advertising campaign on a very splendid scale to induce the public to come in.[22]

A month later, with the First Coalition and the new Chancellor in place, the savings theme was taken up by a letter from 'A Banker' to *The Times*. This began a campaign by that newspaper for increased economy in both the public and private sectors. Besides stressing the general need to save, buy government securities and reduce consumption to improve the balance of payments, the newspaper pointed to a redistribution of income to manual workers being produced by government spending, a widely held belief at the time:

> The problem of securing economy among these [prospering] workers will not be solved merely by asking the men to save. They must be shown how to save, and methods of saving money must be made easy for them.

Organisation, it said, was required to explain the need for thrift and to influence public opinion.[23]

Choosing the size: the first open-ended issue

Savings needed to be borrowed for two purposes: to finance current or envisaged expenditure; and to refinance earlier borrowing from the banks and, especially, from the Bank of England. In his Financial Statement, Lloyd George had made the public aware of the scale of government spending, estimating expenditure from Votes of Credit (the armed services, advances to allies, compensation for damage and other expenditure relating to the war) as £2.1m per day. Borrowing, on the assumption that the war would last for the full financial year, would be £862m. When the Prime Minister moved a new Vote of Credit in the middle of June, he revised expenditure to £3m per day.[24] He did not refer to the deficit but, as there had been no tax increases since the revenue estimates published in May, the public could infer that the whole increase was to be borrowed.

Although the borrowing required to meet current expenditure was in the public domain, the extent of the government's reliance on the Bank of England and the banking system to cover previous borrowing was known to few. Since the war began, the Treasury had borrowed £697.4m, of which, perhaps, £616.3m had come from the Bank and the banking system.[25] The £616.3m took two forms: purchases of securities, and advances made by the Bank to third parties at the request of the Treasury. The prospectus for the November Loan stated that £100m had been pre-placed and it was widely known that this involved the banks. That all but £91m of the £350m had been subscribed by the Bank and the banking system was not known. Of the 3 per cent Exchequer Bonds 1920, £37.9m were held at one time by the Bank and most of the remainder, the authorities assumed, had been bought by the banks or discount market. By 5 June, the government's liability on Treasury Bills had reached £225.3m and, once again, it was assumed that the banks were the takers (Tables 4.4 and 4.5).[26]

Table 4.4 Government borrowing in the public market from the outbreak of war to 5 June 1915 (£m nominal)

	Issued	*Taken by Bank of England and banks*
3½ per cent War Loan 1925–8 (as at 31 March 1915)	349.1	258.1
3 per cent Exchequer Bonds*	50.0	50.0
Treasury Bills	225.3	225.3
Total	624.4	533.4

Notes
*£17.4m was used to refinance maturities.
'Taken by the Bank of England and banks' is estimated and includes War Loan and Exchequer Bonds passed on to government accounts.

Source: T 170/71, 'National Debt: Liabilities maturing at fixed dates. Outstanding 5th June', 7 June 1915.

Table 4.5 Bills discounted, advances made and securities taken by the Bank of England by arrangement with the Treasury: amounts outstanding 8 June 1915

	£m cost in books
Discounted bills unpaid	0.1
Advances against premoratorium bills	42.3
Advances against post-moratorium bills	–
Advances to members of the Stock Exchange under the Treasury scheme	0.2
Advance to the Belgian government	1.2
Greek government Treasury Bills	0.5
Roumanian government Treasury Bills	4.0
Russian government Treasury Bills	24.7
Subtotal	73.0
3½ per cent War Loan (£148.8m nominal)	141.4
3 per cent Exchequer Bonds 1920 (£18.3m nominal)	17.6
Total	232.0

Note
– denotes less than £50,000.

Source: T 170/71, 'Particulars of Bills Discounted, Advances made and Securities Taken by Arrangement with H. M. Government', Chief Cashier's Office, 9 June 1915.

In addition to the £159m (at cost) 3½ per cent War Loan and 3 per cent Exchequer Bonds 1920 held at the beginning of June, the Bank had made advances under the various schemes to relieve the financial crisis and, also by arrangement with the Treasury, to the allies. These amounted to £73m, the major items being the discounting of the pre-moratorium acceptances (£42.3m) and Russian, Greek and Roumanian Treasury Bills (£29.2m) (Table 4.5).

Repaying the £232m advanced by the Bank and financing current expenditure from outside the banking system implied an unrealistic demand on savings. Bradbury estimated the requirement for 'new money' to be £450m. This would provide £350m to cover war expenditure and advances to the Allies for four months and £200m to repay the Bank's advances, enough, he thought, to restore the 'credit position'. Against this, £100m would be released from Exchequer balances, which had been held at high levels, to the puzzlement of contemporary observers, to help the Bank finance its holdings of government securities and its other advances on behalf of the Treasury. Throughout the war, officials and journalists were equivocal about whether sales of long-term securities against Bills counted as 'new money'. They often seemed to think of Bills as money which had – in some sense – already been secured, although they included those 'converted' (used for applications) when a dramatic total for a new loan was being sought. On this occasion, Bradbury was no exception. He thought that £200m of the outstanding £230m Bills should be refinanced, excluded them from 'new money', and included them below the line when stating the securities needing to be issued to satisfy conversions from existing securities. These – 3½ per cent War Loan and 3 per cent Exchequer Bonds held outside the Bank of England – he estimated to need a further £200m of new loan (Table 4.6).

There was, he thought, 'little prospect' that £450m could be raised and, in any case, no figure should be mentioned:

> It will, however, be undesirable to invite subscriptions for any specified amount. There is, I fear, little prospect that even the most attractive terms

Table 4.6 4½ per cent War Loan 1925–45: 'amount of the loan'

	£m
To repay the Bank of England so much of their advances made to the Treasury and to others on the Treasury's account as 'is necessary to restore the credit position (say)'	200
To provide for war expenditure, advances to allies, etc., for four months (say)	350
Subtotal	550
Deduct surplus Exchequer balance, which can be released when the credit position has been adjusted as above	100
Total new money needed	450
To repay excess of outstanding Treasury Bills over £30m	200
To convert War Loan Stock and Bonds held by the public	200
Total	850

Source: T 170/71, Bradbury, 'War Loan', 7 June 1915.

> which we can offer will bring out as much as 450,000,000l. new money. If we offer 450,000,000l. we shall probably alarm the public, and in the event of a part of the loan offered not being subscribed, the whole transaction will be regarded as a failure.
>
> On the other hand, if we offer a comparatively small amount, we may have to reject subscriptions of which we are in urgent need.[27]

These arguments, which were so persuasive that open-ended issues were to be the rule for the remainder of the war, were repeated when McKenna was pressed in the Commons about the novelty of omitting the size of the offer. Unsurprisingly, he did not mention the desire to avoid a repetition of 1914.[28]

The legislation, the War Loan Act 1915, gave the Treasury general borrowing powers similar to those contained in the 1914 War Loan Act, together with specific powers to offer conversion options on existing issues, and to cancel converted securities, Treasury Bills and any securities issued under the War Loan Act 1914. The only limits were on the amount of borrowing: the expenditure of £660m voted for 1915–16, plus a margin of £250m, plus amounts required to convert existing issues.

4½ War Loan 1925–45: the terms[e]

Although the ostensible and published price of the Loan was 100, it was actually issued at a discount, which comprised two parts. As with the National War Loan and Consols at the beginning of the century, those paying by instalments received full dividends: in this case, the half-year's £2 5s 0d per cent on 1 December. Because the calculated interest on the money actually paid on the eight instalment dates was £1 2s 5d per cent, the issue in its partly paid form can be regarded as having been made at £98 17s 7d, to give a running yield of £4 11s 0d per cent and GRYs of £4 14s 1d per cent to 1925 and £4 12s 0d per cent to 1945. The GRY to 1 December 1932, when the issue was actually redeemed, was £4 12s 11d per cent.[f] To put them on an equal footing, those subscribing fully paid had to be paid extra interest. This presented a dilemma. Should it be the rate which investors would have received if they had subscribed partly paid and left the call money on deposit, or should it be the running yield or one of the GRYs on the security? The

e 4½ per cent War Loan matured on 1 December 1945, but was redeemable at any time after 1 December 1925 on the Treasury's giving at least three months' notice. Lists were to close at the latest on 10 July. Applications had to be accompanied by a deposit of £5 per cent. Subscriptions could either be paid in full on or after 20 July, or in eight instalments stretching from 20 July to 26 October. The minimum application at the Bank of England was £100 and registration and distribution were the same as those for the November Loan.

f Contemporaries differed in their calculations. The *Bankers' Magazine* said the price was £98 16s 0d, while the Treasury and the Committee of the Stock Exchange agreed it was £98 17s 6d. *Bankers' Magazine*, October 1915, p. 476; T 172/228, Conference with the Stock Exchange Committee, 22 June 1915.

early prospectuses offered the first, a discount at a rate of 3 per cent, when the tap rate on three-months' Treasury Bills was 2¾ per cent. The final version offered the second, 4½ per cent, so that, as the Chancellor said, 'whether you take it in the form of discount at once or get the dividend on the 1st December, the bonus is precisely the same.' This late change was, perhaps, a reaction to the weak sterling rate and accelerating war spending. Whichever, the ploy worked. About £300m was paid up in full on 20 July: the transfers of cash to the Bank tightened monetary conditions, pushed up money market rates, making the Bill tap inoperative, strengthened the exchange rate, albeit for only a few days, and allowed the Bank's advances to the government to be repaid earlier than otherwise.[29]

The conversion options were of two kinds. The first was bald, and was to be repeated often in the prospectuses for Exchequer Bonds and National War Bonds later in the war. It read:

> In the event of future issues (other than issues made abroad or issues of Exchequer Bonds, Treasury Bills, or similar short-dated Securities) being made by His Majesty's Government, for the purpose of carrying on the War, Stock and Bonds of this issue will be accepted at par, plus accrued interest, as the equivalent of cash for the purpose of subscriptions to such issues.

The other option provided the second part of the discount in the price.[g] By subscribing, investors could surrender their 3½ per cent War Loan at 95, when its price in the market before the announcement was some two points lower: Consols at 66⅔, when they were unsaleable at the minimum price of 66½; 2¾ per cent Annuities at 74⅝ (minimum price 74½); and 2½ per cent Annuities at 64⅛ (minimum price 63½).[h] The terms gave handsome yields on new money subscribed. To take the example of Consols: the investor subscribed for £100 of new Loan, so gaining £4 10s 0d per cent; converted from £75 of Consols, so losing £1 17s 6d per cent; and converted into £50 of new Loan, so gaining £2 5s 0d per cent. A yield of £4 17s 6d per cent was, therefore, obtained from a subscription of £100 (Table 4.7).[30] Contemporaries frequently referred to these options uncovenanted benefits given to the holders of existing issues.[i] In fact, they were covenanted rights, included in the terms of the new Loan and only available to those who held it. Holders of older issues would have been more

g The prospectus is unclear on the details of the conversion terms. It needs to be read in conjunction with two memoranda issued by the Bank on 21 June and 28 June 1915.

h This took the form of an option, in respect of each £100 of new War Loan Stock or Bonds subscribed for cash, to convert: £100 of 3½ per cent War Loan 1925–8 plus a cash payment of £5, into £100 of new War Loan; £75 of Consols into £50 of new War Loan; £67 of 2¾ per cent Annuities into £50 of new War Loan; and £78 of 2½ per cent Annuities into £50 of new War Loan.

i McKenna himself misled the Commons in his original statement. *Hansard* (Commons), 21 June 1915, cols 954–6; *The Times*, 28 June 1915, p. 13.

Table 4.7 $4^{1}/_{2}$ per cent War Loan 1925–45: return on new money to the investor

	Income (£ per cent pa)
Converting from $3^{1}/_{2}$ per cent War Loan	
Subscribe for £100 $4^{1}/_{2}$ per cent War Loan 1925–45	4 10s 0d
Convert £100 $3^{1}/_{2}$ per cent War Loan 1925–8	−3 10s 0d
Into £100 $4^{1}/_{2}$ per cent War Loan 1925–45 (plus £5 cash on conversion)	4 10s 0d
Less present value of £5 in 1928	9s 7d
Equals	5 0s 5d
Percentage return on new money	4 15s 8d
Converting from $2^{1}/_{2}$ per cent Consols	
Subscribe for £100 $4^{1}/_{2}$ per cent War Loan 1925–45	4 10s 0d
Convert £75 $2^{1}/_{2}$ per cent Consols	−1 17s 6d
Into £50 $4^{1}/_{2}$ per cent War Loan 1925–45	2 5s 0d
Equals	4 17s 6d
Percentage return on new money	4 17s 6d
Converting from $2^{3}/_{4}$ per cent Annuities	
Subscribe for £100 $4^{1}/_{2}$ per cent War Loan 1925–45	4 10s 0d
Convert £67 $2^{3}/_{4}$ per cent Annuities	−1 16s 10d
Into £50 $4^{1}/_{2}$ per cent War Loan 1925–45	2 5s 0d
Equals	4 18s 2d
Percentage return on new money	4 18s 2d
Converting from $2^{1}/_{2}$ per cent Annuities	
Subscribe £100 for $4^{1}/_{2}$ per cent War Loan 1925–45	4 10s 0d
Convert £78 $2^{1}/_{2}$ per cent Annuities	−1 19s 0d
Into £50 $4^{1}/_{2}$ per cent War Loan 1925–45	2 5s 0d
Equals	4 16s 0d
Percentage return on new money	4 16s 0d

accurately described as having the opportunity to convert into the new Loan, rather than having the right to do so.

The precedent was a French issue made immediately before the war. Launched in July 1914, it had been badly placed, with instalments still due after the outbreak of hostilities. The price had fallen very sharply. The French authorities had responded by giving holders the right to convert it, at its original price, into future issues. It thus bridged the two options attached to the new British Loan: it was a retrospective gift to the holders of an existing issue, but it applied to issues yet to be sold. The move was described with approval by Keynes in January 1915:

> Until this loan could be cleared out of the way it was obviously difficult to issue a new one, and it was, therefore, one of the preoccupations of the Minister of Finance to find some settlement of the problem. He began in September by offering a new advantage to all holders of the scrip who had paid up the remaining instalments within a certain period; this concession was that the

scrip of the July loan would be accepted at its issue price of 91 in payment for any new loans to be issued by Government...since the French government in issuing its eventual loan must issue it at terms satisfactory to the public, the scrip of the July loan is bound to be worth approximately 91 in cash. This concession seems to me to be an ingenious and sound device. It amounts to a guarantee that investors coming forward during the progress of war shall be at least as well off as those who delay their subscriptions until the war is over.[31]

Four months later, talk of conversions of both kinds was in the air. At the end of April, Turpin discussed the possibility of reliquefying the market in Consols by offering conversion to those subscribing for a new loan, but made no mention of extending the option to the November Loan or of offering conversion options into future issues.[32] Two weeks later, Hartley Withers, who had recently been appointed to the new post of Director of Financial Enquiries in the Treasury, reported after a meeting with Keynes that the new Loan should have an option to convert into future issues and another to permit holders of old Loan to subscribe for it at the issue price. He did not agree that Consols should be taken against new Loan because, unlike old War Loan, they had been bought for commercial reasons, it would narrow the market for what remained of the issue and the removal of the minimum price would lead to a fall in values at an inconvenient moment.

Perhaps unaware of the full problems of the banking system, ten days later Keynes confirmed his opinion that the option should not be extended to Consols when he concluded an analysis of government borrowing by recommending that:

while Consols, etc., may be left to look after themselves, it would be disastrous to leave the recent War Loan to look after itself. It would be inequitable to recent subscribers and might by its effect on sentiment, which counts for a very great deal, much injure the new loan. The first War Loan, therefore, must be accepted at the value of £95 for subscriptions to the new loan.[33]

On 7 June, when recommending that an issue should proceed, Bradbury agreed that it was necessary to 'take a leaf out of the French book' and give subscribers the right to convert into future loans. As he also believed that the Treasury would be paying 5 per cent on its borrowing before the war ended, it would mean eventually paying 5 per cent on the money about to be raised, whatever was paid in the meantime. He did not accept that pausing at 4½ per cent would present any greater problems for balance sheets than moving straight to 5 per cent: 4½ per cent would be enough to freeze all marketable issues at their minimum prices, where they would stay until the banks and insurance companies were in a position to write them down. This argued against cutting the terms too fine. Additional considerations were that 5 per cent at par would sell successfully in the USA and that it would appeal to the general public at home, which would easily understand interest of 1d per month per £1 subscribed, making a scheme for small savers easier to design.

Both on 'sentimental and political grounds', Bradbury thought it was necessary to accept the November Loan at its issue price in subscription for the new Loan. It might be considered to be unfair to the general taxpayer and would have to include subscribers who had been motivated by profit, as well as those who had been driven by patriotism: 'But, be that as it may, public opinion would not support an effort to make them abide by their bargains.'[j] The 3 per cent Exchequer Bonds 1920 could be ignored, but Consols should be included because some were subscribed in an outburst of patriotism during the Boer War and it would be unfair to tax holders of Consols to provide a benefit to holders of the November Loan. Bradbury then turned to some 'much more important', and hard-headed, arguments:

> we are in grave danger of the Consols-holder subjecting us to the Chinese form of blackmail – the threat to commit suicide on our doorstep.
>
> When the new loan is issued, the intrinsic value of Consols will not be above 60 [£4 3s 4d per cent]…They cannot, however, be sold below 66½ [£3 16s 2d per cent], and the bankers are very unlikely to consent to the reduction of the minimum price to any figure at which dealings would be possible, more particularly as the immense volume of stock awaiting a market would be certain for the time being to force the price even below the true value.
>
> The difficulties arising from the unmarketability of Consols (even in the event of the holder's bankruptcy) are daily becoming more formidable. They will become still more acute when the rest of the gilt-edged list freezes at the minima.
>
> There is no doubt that before long something will have to be done, and I am disposed to think that the simplest and best course would be to accept Consols at 60 in exchange for the new loan…
>
> This is of course no very great boon to the Consols-holders not in actual difficulties, but it does enable the holder who is in difficulties to get a marketable security in exchange for his holding at a price, and so creates an emergency method of realisation while maintaining the fiction, regarded as essential from the point of view of bankers' balance sheets, that (at any rate apart from exceptional cases of forced realisation) Consols are worth 66½.[34]

It can be surmised that there were other arguments difficult to commit to paper for circulation to a relatively wide audience which was not aware of the results of the 1914 Loan. Officials may have felt uncomfortable at having misled the public when it was announced that the Loan had been oversubscribed. If the story became

j Not everyone agreed with this. Investors, of course, were delighted, but other outsiders, unaware of the state of public finances and the size of the Bank's holdings of government paper, were uncomprehending. Many would have agreed with *The Economist*'s comment: 'it is to us an entirely new idea that when the State after borrowing on good terms, is forced by market conditions to borrow on bad terms, it should pay a contribution to all those with whom in the past it made a better bargain.' *The Economist*, 26 June 1915, p. 1287.

public, investors would have good grounds for complaint, which would be particularly difficult to answer after the war when arguments of expediency might be less easily accepted and when tongues would be less inhibited by patriotism. It was necessary to buy back the Bank's holding on terms which would leave it without a loss and officials may have felt that equity required that other investors be given equivalent treatment. Finally, there was a practical point. If the legislation authorising the Loan included the power to apply the proceeds to the cancellation of earlier issues, public admission of the Bank's holding could be avoided: 3½ per cent War Loan could be cancelled and, when the *annual returns* were published, the public left to assume that it was paper that had been converted by the public.

While the principle of offering conversion opportunities to holders of existing issues was gaining acceptance during April and May, the idea of pricing the options so generously that they would attract subscriptions came later. At the end of April, Turpin had suggested that offering a price higher than the minimum might be 'good finance' if it created a demand for Consols and made them saleable. There was no mention of this part of the scheme in Bradbury's recommendation on 7 June, which only envisaged a safety net for Consols' holders. Indeed, his recommendation that a yield of 5 per cent should be offered strongly implies that he only came to accept 4½ per cent because of the strength and generosity of the options. Where, then, did the idea originate? The nub was included in a wider scheme put to the Treasury subcommittee of the CLCB a week before the issue by Frederick Goodenough, a director of Barclays Bank. Taking Consols at 66 against a new issue, he said, would secure a greater response than a simple offer of new paper and increase the demand for existing issues. If the minimum price of Consols was reduced to 65, holders would:

> realise a portion of their holding in order to provide funds for taking up…[new Loan], thus securing conversion of a further part of their holding: at the same time buyers will be forthcoming for Consols at 65, as there will be a profit in buying Consols at that price for conversion into…[new Loan], and this will produce further applications for the [new Loan].[35]

It is not recorded whether Goodenough's paper was ever passed to the Treasury or, if it was, whether the point was extracted from others in a two-page document. The timing was exactly right, and the connection between the rate finally chosen and the conversion options is confirmed by a draft prospectus for a 4½ per cent issue at a lower price than that chosen (98) with conversion opportunities for old War Loan, and no other issue.[36]

On the day after the prospectus was published, the Chancellor made no secret of his intention: 'we are not converting for the sake of converting. We are converting because we want to make the person who converts subscribe.'[37] It was both the strength and weakness of the scheme. By giving holders of older issues the opportunity to dispose of their securities, in large amounts, at attractive prices, it turned an ostensible yield of 4½ per cent into nearly 5 per cent through a process whose complications may have been, in part, deliberate; the rate at which the belligerents could borrow was being treated as a measure of financial strength and propaganda could trumpet a successful loan at 'only 4½ per cent' (Table 4.7).[38] However, by making it so attractive, it practically guaranteed that holders of existing issues would apply for more than they would want to hold and that the price in the secondary market would be weak.

The City, as reflected in Withers's monthly reports, 'The Financial Position', knew that the terms were a trap into which it was bound to walk:

> Critics in the City, who admit the great ingenuity and cleverness of the loan arrangements, are inclined to fear that the Stock is likely to be what they call a 'bad market' for some time to come owing to this reason: that a large number of people have been practically forced to buy it, and will await the first opportunity of turning it into cash.[39]

The Treasury's analysis was different, but the conclusion was the same: a weak market. It started from the premise that the banks could not lend all that would be needed by the holders of existing issues who wanted to subscribe so that they could convert. If these holders were to subscribe, they would have to finance themselves by selling part of their holding of existing securities. It followed that if holders of existing issues were to convert, and without the carrot of conversion subscriptions to the new Loan would not be maximised, there had to be buyers for their existing holdings. The problem was that Consols and Annuities were being held at unrealistically high levels by the system of minimum prices.

The previous February and March the Treasury had discussed changes to the system with representatives of the CLCB and the London Stock Exchange. The latter wanted to retain minimum prices, but at reduced levels, and suggested that the minima should be lowered by the amount of the accrued interest each time the securities went ex-dividend. Fearing that reductions would be seen as the first of many and that buyers would hold off in anticipation, the Chancellor preferred to wait for the appropriate moment to end the regime altogether. The bankers agreed, preferring to keep the minima unchanged until there was good news from the war, so that prices might remain stable. The Treasury compromised, and on 19 March minimum prices on a range of securities were cut, in the case of Consols from 68½ to 66½.[40] This was still too high and did little to free the market.

The problem was not only a question of finding a level at which there would be buyers who would enable sellers to raise the money with which to subscribe. Investors with cash would only buy Consols with part of their money, using the remainder to subscribe for new Loan to give them conversion rights, if this enabled them to obtain new Loan by conversion at a lower price than by straight subscription. In other words, buyers had to obtain some of the advantage of the conversion offer and a price had to be found which would share the profits of conversion between buyers and sellers. In old War Loan, there was no problem: there was no minimum price and it soon settled at around 93, two points discount to the conversion price of 95, and three and a half points premium to what Bradbury called its 'intrinsic value' of 89½ (providing a GRY equal to that on the new

Loan).[41] Consols had a minimum price of 66½, near to the conversion price of £66 13s 8d, and presented a problem which the Chancellor put clearly to the Stock Exchange Committee:

> you cannot leave the minimum price of Consols at practically the same price of [*sic*] the conversion, otherwise you may not get buyers. You see, it does not pay anybody to buy Consols at 66 and 2/3rds., because, putting it another way, the holder of the war loan and Consols has got rights. If the holder of Consols is not strong enough to take up all the amount of war loan, he ought really to give up some of his rights to the other holder…You must allow the buyer to get some advantage in the rights.[42]

It might have been logical, once the bankers were able to convert their Consols into new Loan, to have removed the minimum price altogether. There were both advantages and disadvantages to a lower price. The incentive to subscribe and then convert would be increased, enabling sales to be made by those holders of Consols who had no money. In their turn, they would be able to subscribe and, therefore, convert. But, if Consols were bought at a price lower than 66⅔, those converting would be obtaining their new Loan at a discount. There seemed to be no avoiding this: if Consols were to be bought in the market, the price had to be less than 66⅔. Despite this, the Stock Exchange Committee dissuaded the Chancellor from removing the minimum by forecasting a very steep, but temporary, fall in prices as pent-up selling was released, which would be avoided if investors were given time to react to the buying opportunity.[43] He compromised again, keeping the system, but reducing the prices. That of Consols became 65.

The bankers had not been consulted and were furious. Although the offer justified them in valuing Consols at 66⅔ and 3½ per cent War Loan at 95 for their end-June balance sheets, they were so scarred by the capital losses incurred over almost twenty years that they continued to fear both reductions and the complete abolition of the minima.[44] They were also left exposed to their other fixed-interest holdings, Holden muttering darkly of falls of ten and twenty points if the minima were removed.[45] The CLCB Treasury subcommittee minuted that:

> in [the] case of the new War Loan no minimum should be imposed, but should a serious fall in prices occur, the Committee should…ask the Chancellor of the Exchequer to fix a minimum.

The Economist reported that the story was circulating that a minimum price had been fixed and the Chancellor had to deny the story, although he refused to rule out the possibility for the future.[46]

The reduction in the minimum price of Consols to 65 on 23 June was ineffective. Shortly afterwards, *The Economist* reported that no fresh buyers had appeared, although:

> it is a little less difficult to sell Consols now than it was a week ago, because

> buyers can see their way to making a turn by the process of taking Consols in order to convert them into the new War Loan.

In the same edition, it reported that Consols continued illiquid as:

> a flood of selling began, mainly by trustees who wanted either to clear up deceased estates or to realise part of their holding in order to convert the remainder into the 4½ loan.[47]

At the end of July, there was an opportunity to limit the damage caused by the decision to maintain a minima. Members of the Stock Exchange were permitted to carry out 'conversion bargains', whereby an investor sold Consols at the minimum price and bought new War Loan at a price above that in the market. At the same time, banks were permitted to carry out the same bargains for their customers for a fee, using their new War Loan holdings.[48] As lists had closed, the transactions could not have increased cash subscriptions, so it can be assumed that the Treasury was taking advantage of the banks' reduced sensitivity to minimum prices to provide aid for Consol holders in the interests of equity.

The banks' special subscription

The wounds left by Lloyd George's Loan were seen in the contrast between the failure to consult the CLCB before the issue and the bankers' later extensive involvement. The conversion opportunities for Consols and old War Loan were aimed in part at their holdings, and ensured that they were substantial subscribers; their branches played an important role in the Loan's distribution; and, as the means of settlement with the Bank of England, they had to manage the transfer of the subscription money.[k] Finally, whatever the original intention, they were recruited to ensure that an impressive subscription was achieved.

The CLCB was only consulted on a single occasion before the publication of the prospectus. On 11 June, the bankers visited the Treasury, several of the delegation advising that a yield of 4½ per cent would be necessary for a large loan while recoiling from the effect on prices and calling for the retention of the minima at their existing levels.[49] Possibly at this meeting, and certainly at another held on 1 July, after the prospectus had been published, the problem of the money market shortages, which would be thrown up by the transfer of the proceeds to the Bank, was discussed. Concern within the banking system about its ability to find enough cash had grown alongside the recognition that the terms of the issue made early payment in full very attractive. There was agreement that the banks would need exceptional help and that it could be provided by cash advances from the Bank of England against the banks' holdings of the new Loan and, under the terms of Cunliffe's promise, of the old Loan, which need not be surrendered for

k There was one report that the banks may have seen some £200m of the subscriptions, that is half of the total excluding those they made on their own account. *The Times*, 12 July 1915, p. 13.

conversion until the end of October. The banks also pressed for advances of Currency Notes against the new Loan.

The discussions centred on the terms, with the bankers aware of British payments difficulties in the USA and of the threat that interest rates might be raised in the traditional manner to attract gold to London. A scribbled conversation in the Bradbury Papers records how the Treasury team saw the bankers' position:

> They are afraid of a high bank rate – They want protection against it – The method of protecting them is to make a high bank rate impossible whatever our gold position. How? Because the amount they have to find to pay to the Exchequer on behalf of their depositors + themselves may exceed the amount of their reserves. Yes, but how can I secure a steady bank rate [?]. You cannot. They must take the risk. They can maintain their reserve at a price.[50]

The Chancellor, on behalf of the Bank, offered to make cash available for six months from the date of the advance against new War Loan at 1/2 per cent under current Bank rate with a 5 per cent margin on the market price. The bankers countered with a margin of 1 per cent under current Bank rate, with the arrangement to continue until one year after the end of the war.[51] The Chancellor compromised:

> The Bank of England will agree as a temporary measure and to facilitate transactions in connection with the subscription of the loan for a period of twelve months from the 10th instant to make advances to Bankers against War Stock and Bonds up to an amount not exceeding 95 per cent. of the par value of the Stock or Bonds deposited at 1/2 per cent. below Bank Rate varying. I understand that Bankers will make similar advances to their customers at a rate not exceeding Bank Rate varying.
>
> We have thus been able to meet the bankers' wishes as to the method of calculating the margin and to allow a substantial prolongation of the period we originally contemplated. I do not, however, feel justified in asking the Bank of England to reduce the rate to 1 per cent. below Bank Rate, since the result of such reduction might be to necessitate a higher Bank Rate than would otherwise be required, with prejudicial results to commerce and industry.[52]

At the same time, the Chancellor refused the banks' request for advances of Currency Notes against the new Loan on the same terms. The proposal had been strongly opposed by the Governor.[53] Whether because of his opposition or on the merits of the case, the Chancellor said that he could see no advantage to the banks of such a scheme because they could always obtain Notes with the cash released under the scheme of advances against Loan, and:

> It would certainly create the impression abroad that the British Government was following in the footsteps of Germany in financing the subscription for its own loans, and, by linking on to the currency a purely credit operation, it might give rise – at any rate in the minds of the uninstructed – to the notion that we were pursuing a policy of inflation.[54]

The failure to bring the banks into closer consultation when designing the new Loan, the reduction without warning in the minimum prices of Consols and the disagreement about the terms for cash advances strained relations between Chancellor and bankers. On 1 July, the Chancellor apologised to the CLCB for the lack of consultation about the design of the Loan.[55] On 5 July, the Treasury subcommittee of the CLCB saw the Chancellor to discuss the banks' subscriptions. When these were considered by the full Committee the following day, several members proposed doubling those made the previous November. On 8 July, the Committee duly recommended this to its members, and the following day the entire banking community agreed to a similar resolution.[56]

This 'special subscription', as it came to be known, was planned to be £200m. It is unclear, however, why the Chancellor should have wanted it. The banks would have found the conversion terms – promising reliquefaction of their Consols and a reduced need artificially to bolster balance sheets with minimum prices – hard to resist; they would have wanted £106m new War Loan to convert their November Loan and, perhaps, a further £130m to convert their Consols. It is possible that the Chancellor was looking for propaganda with which to support the exchange rate and impress neutrals and enemy with British financial strength. Perhaps he wanted to shore up his political position by raising an amount far in excess of that borrowed by Lloyd George at a time when the two ministers were in conflict. Or perhaps, although aware that the banks would be large applicants, he wanted to be certain of their size. Most plausibly, it was because an expectation had developed that the Treasury was looking for £600m of new money.[57]

The scheme for small savers

When issuing the 3½ per cent Loan, the Chancellor had been pressed by backbenchers and newspapers to lower the minimum subscription. Critics had pointed to the large number of small applicants for the war loans in France and Germany and it was not only Labour members who pressed for small savers to be put on the same footing as the better off. In May, the Chancellor promised to give the position of the small investor further consideration when the terms of the next issue were being prepared.[58]

When recommending the Loan to the Chancellor, Bradbury departed from the advice traditionally given by officials, notably in 1900 and 1914. Although doubting whether the amount that could be collected would 'reach any very large total as Exchequer figures run nowadays', he pointed to the increased prosperity of the working classes and the rise in savings bank deposits. There would, he said, be great value in reducing consumption and creating a mass appetite for government paper. He thought that the most important arguments were those of morale and publicity: an appeal on a broad front, to include those on low incomes, would influence the rich. A switch into the new Loan from savings bank deposits paying 2½ per cent would be expensive, but there would be advantages. At a time of rising interest rates, savings bank deposits might be withdrawn, forcing the government to refund them on worse terms than those currently being contemplated. There was likely to be acute industrial distress after the war and a consequent withdrawal of deposits; the difficulties would be eased if savers held marketable loans, rather than deposits, so that the cost of depreciating assets would fall on them, rather than the Treasury.

The design of the security and its method of distribution were at the centre of the Treasury's planning. Bradbury placed much emphasis on giving the small saver the same terms as those available to the large. A separate instrument with a lower yield, but superior facilities for capital repayment, would be open to the misinterpretation that the small investor was being offered worse terms than those available to the large, creating 'such prejudice and recrimination as will be fatal to the "atmosphere" of a national loan.'[59] From this premise followed the features that were to contribute to the scheme's failure: a marketable security with a fluctuating price; cumbersome procedures for selling on the Stock Exchange, using the Post Office and the Commissioners; an unknown realisation price when a sale order was given; and the charging of a commission, albeit small.

There were two methods of subscribing, their terms being incorporated in a separate Post Office prospectus, the first of many. Investors could subscribe in cash, paying in full, for up to £200 of the Loan in multiples of £5 at any Money Order Office. The Offices could accept subscriptions for more than £200, but would pass them on to the Bank of England for processing and registration in its books. Investors were given a receipt, or scrip certificate (bearing Bradbury's increasingly well-known signature), which was later exchangeable for the definitive Stock. Sales were to be made, as with the existing Stock purchase facility, by giving an order to a Money Order Office, which would pass it to the Commissioners. Closing of the lists was left to the discretion of the Treasury, unlike that for the Bank issue, which could not remain open after 10 July. To ensure parity with the 4½ per cent rate of discount on fully paid subscriptions made through the Bank, the price was £4 19s 4d for each £5 of Stock, or a discount of 0.67 per cent. On 10 July, when the Bank issue closed, the subscription period was extended to 31 July, but with an increase in price to £4 19s 8d. No reason for this is recorded, but it can be surmised that it followed the decision taken four days earlier to postpone first Stock Exchange dealings in the new Loan from 10 July, when lists closed, to some date after allotment letters had been posted. This meant that there would be several weeks when there would be no secondary market and, therefore, no danger of the Post Office selling Loan at a different price from that available elsewhere.[60] Subscriptions by employers for sale to their employees continued until the end of August.

The second scheme was designed for investors of smaller amounts. 'Scrip vouchers', in denominations of 5s, 10s and £1, were put on sale at Money Order Offices and, by arrangements which had not been discussed with participants by the time the Loan was launched, through trade unions, friendly societies and employers. The vouchers could be taken to Money Order Offices between 1 December and 15 December and used at par to subscribe for the Loan. If the vouchers did not amount to the £5 minimum subscription on the Post Office prospectus, or were not an even multiple of £5, the excess would be returned to the investor, without interest, or retained for further investment on terms that the government had not yet determined when the scheme was launched. Investors would forfeit their interest if they changed their minds and surrendered the vouchers before 1 December; in this case, they would be credited with the principal by means of a POSB account.

When the vouchers were used to subscribe, interest was payable at a rate of 1d per month for each £1 (5 per cent a year) , starting from the first day of the first complete month after the date of purchase. In addition, the investor received a bonus of 1s for each £5 of vouchers used for subscriptions. The combination of the 1/2 per cent higher yield, the loss of interest on the broken month and the 1s bonus was calculated to provide equality with the 4 1/2 per cent rate of discount on fully-paid applications at the Bank.[61]

An interdepartmental committee (the 'War Loan Committee') was hurriedly appointed on 5 July, two weeks after the Loan was launched.[1] The short time it had for discussions meant that some aspects of the scheme were badly handled. The Post Office prospectus and its accompanying explanatory literature emphasised that subscribers were entitled to the same conversion privileges as those subscribing through the Bank, an equality which was similarly stressed by the Chancellor when launching the main Loan in the Commons.[62] However, under the Bank prospectus, the minimum that carried conversion rights was £100. It must have been felt that withholding conversion opportunities from subscriptions for less than £100 was carrying equality too far because, on 7 July, the Chancellor told the Commons that arrangements were 'under consideration' for allowing subscribers for less than £100 of new Loan to convert in proportion to their holdings and, sometime in mid-July, a circular was published in which it was made clear that subscriptions down to £5 would carry the rights.[63]

A further problem came to light when it was realised that vouchers would be on sale until 1 December and could be used to subscribe for the Loan for the following two weeks, whereas subscribers through the Bank had to exercise their rights by 30 October. Denying very small savers the right to convert would be difficult to present, even if it was giving equal treatment. It was therefore decided to attach conversion rights to all vouchers purchased before the end of November as long as they were used to convert Stock held by the applicant on 30 October, but with the various rights coming into effect six months later.[64]

Although the main points of distribution for both applications and vouchers were the Money Order Offices, explanatory literature was available from all Post Offices. This seems to have worked smoothly, despite complaints, which were to

1 The War Loans (Supplementary Provisions) Committee was established by a TM dated 5 July 1915 and consisted of Turpin, Blackett, Bunbury (from the National Health Insurance Commission), Murray, Davies and a secretary. It appears that Montagu was chairman. It was reconstituted by another Minute, dated 7 September 1915, but with Bradbury replacing Blackett, who had accompanied Reading to the USA. The report was not formally printed until 6 November. A copy is in POa, 30/3979.

surface at intervals throughout the war, that the Post Office was failing to advertise vigorously and instruct staff how to answer the public's enquiries. At their meeting with the Chancellor on 1 July, the banks offered to imitate the Post Office and distribute literature and receive applications. The offer was taken up, although it appears some banks, and perhaps all, failed at first to extend this to vouchers.[65]

Shortly after the Loan was launched, the Chancellor saw representatives of large employers, trade unions and friendly societies to ask for their co-operation. He emphasised that the government was not offering a blueprint for distribution, but would try to adapt to the needs and customs of each organisation. One point of principle had always to be met: no pressure should be put on employees to buy that was not being put on the rest of the community. Consistent with this, the organisations were asked to sell the vouchers and urge on their members the need for thrift. Employers could set up collecting centres near the pay offices in their works or, with the agreement of the employee, deduct a regular sum from wages.[66]

In the following weeks, many company schemes were established: some employers bought blocks of Loan or vouchers and distributed them to their employees when regular deductions from pay had reached the necessary amount; others offered discounts or interest-free loans to subscribers; in other cases, the money or vouchers were held by trustees until a sum had been accumulated which would buy the minimum £5 of Stock.

The scheme could not be called straightforward. The accounting and control might be standard for a large organisation, but they must have been daunting for the unsophisticated, and it was in the nature of selling on the scale envisaged that the unsophisticated had to be involved. The selling organisation was required to find the money to pay the Money Order Office at the time the securities were bought. The money would come back to the organisations immediately if they sold them immediately, but even in these cases a float was needed, even if only for the inside of a day. The Treasury offered to find a banker's guarantee for purchases, or a straight cheque if the organisation was deemed financially sound. There was the further problem that the $^1/_8$ per cent commission was insufficient to cover the cost of printing, postage and incidental expenses, let alone salaries or overheads.[67]

Publicity

Responsibility for the cost of distribution and publicity quickly became part of the wider organisation of the 'patriotic boom' for the Loan. This, in its turn, was part of the new drive for private and public economy which had grown naturally from the awareness of resource limitation. High points in this process were a meeting to publicise the Loan, and saving generally, addressed by the Prime Minister and Bonar Law, the Unionist Leader, at the Guildhall at the end of June: a speech in the Lords by Viscount Midleton a few days later, calling for economy in civilian and non-military government spending;[68] a meeting called by the CLCB in the middle of July, which appointed a deputation to see the Chancellor and request reduced civil spending and increased taxation;[69] and the appointment of a retrenchment committee of MPs to report on the prospects for making savings in non-military spending.[70]

The day after the Loan was announced, McKenna asked Lord Northcliffe's advice about publicity. The newspaper proprietor recommended a businessman, a professional agent, Hedley Le Bas. He was already well known to McKenna and was promptly appointed.[71] At the same time, at the Chancellor's request, a cross-party Parliamentary War Savings Committee was formed, with the Prime Minister, Bonar Law and Arthur Henderson as presidents. Its purpose was to encourage thrift in general, and support the Loan in particular, by preparing advertisements, leaflets and booklets, organising meetings and supplying speakers. The Committee thus became responsible for many of the expensive items of publicity that the trade unions, friendly societies and insurance companies were unable to afford. In the middle of July, the Committee circulated a letter to 400,000 employers, signed by the three presidents, asking for co-operation in encouraging thrift and showing how to collect contributions. At the same time, it printed eleven million leaflets for distribution in offices and factories and for inclusion in pay packets.[72] Full-page advertisements began to appear in the newspapers, with a prospectus, application form and hard-hitting copy: encouraging quotations from the Chancellor's speeches, together with exhortations that went straight to the heart, sometimes mixing the call of sentiment with that of the pocket:

> Use your money to save the lives of the men who are fighting your battle. Every penny of it is safely secured in [*sic*] the Consolidated Fund of the United Kingdom…It is not a favour that is being asked of you, but a privilege which you are offered – the privilege of helping our Sailors and Soldiers with the munitions and equipment needed to save their lives…If you cannot use the sword for your country, you can use your pen by filling up the form…Our Sailors and Soldiers are sacrificing life and limb for the sake of their King and Country – do *your* part today.[73]

The results

In June, Bradbury had said that there was 'little prospect' that 'even the most attractive terms' would produce £450m of new money, even apart from the additional £200m wanted to reduce the Bill issue to a few tens of millions.[74] He must have deemed the Loan a success, with the pattern of subscriptions for both the Bank and Post Office issues encouraging belief in the existence of a mass savings market.[m] Cash subscriptions were £587.2m, within which the banks'

m Forty-five applications, each of more than £1m, totalled £86m. The largest individual subscriptions were from the clearing banks, five applications of more than £10m apiece totalling £98m. The London City & Midland and Lloyds each applied for £21m and the London County & Westminster for £20m. Forty-five thousand applications for between £1,000 and £5,000 produced £69m, 184,000 for between £200 and £500 produced £46m, and 259,000 for between £100 and £200 'special subscription of £200m' turned out to have been £183.1m, some of which, Osborne suggests, may have been on behalf of customers. Of the £183.1m, £14m came from the Bank of England. A further £289.8m was created to satisfy those converting from existing issues (Tables 4.8 and 4.9).[75] This used about £442m, or about three-quarters, of the cash subscriptions at the Bank.

There are three reasons why it would be unsafe to treat this as the measure of the impact of the conversion option. First, with patriotic sentiment running high, some investors may have been prepared to subscribe for non-commercial reasons, even if they subsequently used the options. Second, investors may not have subscribed with conversion in mind, even if someone to whom they later sold used the rights for that purpose. Third, the Loan was issued at several GRYs: £4 12s 0d per cent (to 1945) for cash and between £4 15s 8d per cent and £4 18s 2d per cent if used for conversion. It is not possible to judge the response if it had only been available at the lower yield.

The cash application was overstated by manoeuvres performed by the savings bank portfolios. At their 1914 year ends, the banks held £86.4m 2½ per cent Consols. Instead of subscribing for new Loan and converting in the normal fashion, £35.8m of the Consols were cancelled outside the main public offer and the banks then subscribed for £23.9m of Loan.[76] It is tempting to view this as a means of artificially inflating cash subscriptions but, while the Treasury would have been unaware of this happy effect, there were two, less cynical, explanations. First, the Treasury feared that applications by customers might be so large that the savings banks would be forced to sell securities, dislocating the market. The banks, therefore, were issued with Loan against their Consols on the understanding that, if applications threatened an embarrassing reduction in deposits, they would utilise their holding of the Loan to satisfy the applications. The fall in liabilities would match the fall in assets, without any further transaction.[77] Second, to do this, the CNRA advanced £25.7m to the Commissioners to enable them to apply for the War Loan. The alternative, selling Consols in the market, would have been impossible in the size, the attempt would have driven down prices, and it would have been contrary to the Commissioners' traditional practice.[78]

The total subscribed through the small savings schemes was £39.9m, net of £91,000 of vouchers which were encashed in the first four months of 1916.

produced £26m. The 508,000 subscribers for amounts up to £1,000, who applied for £109m, represented 28 per cent of the non-bank subscriptions on the Bank prospectus. The Post Office scheme produced 9 per cent of the applications taken from outside the special subscription (Table 4.9). 886,000 applicants for amounts between £5 and £50 subscribed for £15.7m and 76,500 applicants who applied for amounts between £55 and £100 subscribed for £6.7m. Even if the results from the voucher scheme had suggested there was little to be borrowed from very small savers, there were clearly useful sums to be found in the somewhat larger mass market. *The Times*, 10 July 1915, p. 10; T 170/88, '4½ per cent War Loan: number of applications'; T 170/70, 'Reports from the Comptroller of the Post Office Savings Bank', 4 August 1915.

Table 4.8 Cash subscriptions and conversions: 4½ per cent War Loan 1925–45 (£m nominal)

	Stock converted or cancelled	*4½ per cent War Loan created*
By conversion		
2½ per cent Consols	219.4	
3½ per cent War Loan 1925–8	137.5*	
2½ per cent Annuities	8.2	
2¾ per cent Annuities	1.1	
Total by conversion		289.8
Savings Bank Funds	35.8	23.9
For cash		587.2
Total		900.9

Note
*Excluding cancellation of the Bank of England's holding of £148.8m 3½ per cent War Loan 1925–8.

Source: *National Debt: annual returns*, 1916, p. 34.

Table 4.9 Results of the small savings scheme for 4½ per cent War Loan 1925–45

	Value (£)	*Number*
Subscriptions for the Post Office issue		
Post Office Savings Bank	30.6	
Trustee Savings Banks (in round numbers)	3.8	
Total on the Post Office prospectus	34.5	
Sales of vouchers and scrip certificates		
5s vouchers		1,501,000
10s vouchers		421,000
£1 vouchers		827,000
Total vouchers	1,413,000	
£5 scrip certificates	3,991,100	798,220
Total	5,404,100	

Note
The total on the Post Office prospectus does not sum because of rounding.

Sources: *Hansard* (Commons), 20 January 1916, col. 612, and 22 August 1916, cols 2485–8: T 170/97, 'Subscriptions to the 4½ per cent War Loan through the Post Office', 31 December 1915.

Subscriptions on the Post Office prospectus totalled £34.5m, of which £3.8m were through the TSBs; the banking system handled about £3.6m. Vouchers were sold to the value of £1.4m (net) and scrip certificates to the value of £4m (Table 4.9).[79] The Treasury considered this disappointing.[80] It was the more disappointing

Table 4.10 Securities cancelled and converted between 31 March 1915 and 31 March 1916 (£m nominal)

	Outstanding on 31 March			*Of which*	
	1915	*1916*	*Change**	*Converted*	*Cancelled†*
$2^1/_2$ per cent Consols	536	280.5	–255.6	255.2‡	–
$3^1/_2$ per cent War Loan 1925–8	349.1	62.8	–286.3	137.5	148.8†
$2^1/_2$ per cent Annuities	29.8	21.6	–8.2	8.1	–
$2^3/_4$ per cent Annuities	3.8	2.7	–1.1	1	–
3 per cent Exchequer 1920	50	21.7	–28.3	–	28.3

Notes
*The change during the year may not be equal to the amount of Stock converted, or the amount converted and cancelled, because small amounts were cancelled under arrangements other than the $4^1/_2$ per cent War Loan scheme.
†Under the War Loan Act 1915, e.g. the holdings of the Bank of England and government departments.
‡Including £35.8m held by the savings banks.
Columns may not sum because of rounding.

Sources: *National Debt: annual returns*: *BGS*, pp. 131, 133, 145, 181 and 291.

in that £23.7m had been withdrawn from the savings banks to subscribe.[n] Thus, well over half of the sales to the smallest investors represented the refunding of existing borrowing, justifying the warnings of officials in 1900 and November 1914.

✤ ✤ ✤

The Loan was successful in its immediate objectives. It raised some £400m from outside the banking system, the equivalent of about one year's pre-war savings. The first steps were taken to persuade those on small incomes to consume less, save more and buy government debt. Issues which were unmarketable because there were no buyers at their minimum prices were absorbed into a single liquid issue, a free market revived, death duties and legacies paid, estates wound up and bank advances made against realistically valued collateral. In due course, balance sheets were freed from the scaffolding of minimum prices: 'If the result of this is that the bankers are freed from the incubus of carrying Consols, I think you will have no more trouble' was the Chancellor's forecast when a stockbroker asked about the bankers' attitude to a reduction in minimum prices.[81] Indeed, the minima on Consols, Annuities and various overseas loans were removed with little fuss

n Estimates differed, in part because of the difficulty of allowing for the effect on the growth in new deposits. The POSB lost £18.5m and the TSBs £5.2m in the three months June–August. *Hansard* (Commons), 22 August 1916, cols 2485–6.

on 24 November 1915, some three weeks after applications for conversions had closed.[82]

The price was high and was to be felt for the next seventeen years. The new borrowing, conversions and cancellations transformed the structure of the Debt. The size of old War Loan fell from £349.1m to £62.8m between end-March 1915 and end-March 1916. The volume of Consols almost halved, falling from £536m to £280.5m. In their place was created a single issue of £900.9m with options to convert into any medium- or long-dated loan issued during the remainder of the war, bearing interest at 4½ per cent and needing to be redeemed or converted during a twenty-year period beginning in only ten years (Table 4.10). In 1916, the administrative problems of fulfilling the conversion options contributed to the Treasury's failure to make a new long-dated issue. In 1917, most of the 1915 Loan was to be converted into a new security with a historically high nominal rate, whose servicing cost was to keep the public attention continually on the Debt until it was converted in 1932.

Endnotes

1 *Hansard* (Commons), 17 November 1914, col. 371.
2 Liddell Hart (1970), pp. 179–268.
3 This paragraph is based on Osborne (1926), II, pp. 1–11; Morgan (1952), pp. 344–5 and 356; Sayers (1976), I, pp. 85–9.
4 T 170/71, Bradbury, 'War Loan', 7 June 1915.
5 The words are those of Keynes. The italics are in the original. Keynes (1971–89), XVI, pp. 163–4, 'The Financial Problem', 1 February 1916. Unless otherwise specified, this and the following paragraph are based on Sayers (1976), I, pp. 82–3; Osborne (1926), I, pp. 263–65 and 275–99; CLCBm, 27 October 1915, and CLCBt, 18, 22, 25 and 26 October 1915.
6 Sayers (1976), I, pp. 39–41; CTM, 18 June 1890; BoE, C40/736.
7 Osborne (1926), I, pp. 100 and 275–6; BoE, C58/38. The accounts and portfolios of 'Investments o/a Bank Borrowings' have been lost but Osborne provides glimpses of the latter, and a record of its liabilities, but not its assets, are recorded in BoE, C58/38 and 39, and are the source for Table 4.3.
8 BoE, C58/38; Osborne (1926), I, pp. 263 and 286. An early instruction is pasted into the front of the ledger: 'Each day the money is to be invested in the purchase of Treasury Bills of such currency as the Governor may direct.' The note is initialled by Cokayne, 23 October 1915. Osborne (1926), I, p. 263, says that the separate account 'Investments o/a Bank Borrowings' was opened on 27 October 1915 with £4m of one- and three-months' Bills. He also says that 'Subsequently 6, 9 and 12 months' Bills were also held (but no other security)'.
9 *BGS*, pp. 179 and 479; *National Debt: annual returns*, 1916.
10 *The Times*, 6 March 1915, p. 12.
11 *Bankers' Magazine*, April 1915, p. 617; Morgan (1952), pp. 174 and 176.
12 For example *The Economist*, 13 March 1915, p. 518, and *The Times*, 11 March 1915, p. 13.
13 Osborne (1926), I, pp. 255–6; Sayers (1976), I, p. 82.
14 BoE, C40/729, '£3 per cent Exchequer Bonds 1920', 5 August 1915.
15 *Government Departments Securities* (HCP 247), 3 June 1915 .
16 BoE, C98/6937, entry for 3 September 1915; *The London Gazette*, weekly accounts of the CNRA; T 170/82, Turpin to Chancellor, 18 May 1915; BoE, C40/729, '£3 per

cent Exchequer Bonds 1920', 5 August 1915; Osborne (1926), I, pp. 255–6; T 133/1, Bradbury to Commissioners, 17 August 1915.

17 T 170/71, Bradbury, 'War Loan', 7 June 1915.

18 T 171/110, Bradbury, 'The War and Finance', 17 March 1915.

19 Ibid., Paish, 'The Finances of Great Britain', second half of April. He suggested that savings had increased during the war and were running at between £400m and £500m per year. As private sector loans to colonies and allies were £100m a year and domestic investment was £75m, savings available for war loans were 'about' £300m.

20 *Hansard* (Commons), 4 May 1915, col. 1014.

21 Ibid., cols 1015–18.

22 'The Bank of England in relation to Government Borrowing and the Necessity of a Public Loan', 14 May 1915, Keynes (1971–89), XVI, p. 105.

23 *The Times*, 9 June 1915, pp. 9–10, and 11 June 1915, p. 5. A copy of the letter is in T 170/82. Bradbury and Keynes also believed that the living standards of working people had risen. T 171/110, 'The War and Finance', 17 March 1915; T 170/71, 'War Loan', 7 June 1915; Keynes (1971–89), XVI, p. 118.

24 *Hansard* (Commons), 4 May 1915, cols 1008–9, and 15 June 1915, col. 556.

25 T 170/71, 'National Debt: Liabilities maturing at fixed dates. Outstanding 5th June,' 7 June 1915.

26 T 170/71, Bradbury, 'War Loan', 7 June 1915.

27 Ibid.

28 *Hansard* (Commons), 21 June 1915, cols 956–7 and 998–9.

29 T 172/228, 'Conference between the Chancellor of the Exchequer and the Stock Exchange Committee', 22 June 1915, p. 5; *Bankers' Magazine*, September 1915, p. 36. *The Times* points to a large proportion being paid in full. *The Times*, 21 July 1915, p. 11.

30 T 170/76, Bradbury, memorandum, second half of June; *The Economist*, 26 June 1915, p. 1303, letter from G. P. Collins; *Hansard* (Commons), 22 June 1915, col. 1084. Collins failed to take account of the discounted value of the £5 cash payment required to convert old War Loan. McKenna, having been asked about the relative rate of return on 3½ per cent War Loan 1925–8 and Consols, couched his answer only in terms of those two issues.

31 'Notes on French Finance', 6 January 1915, Keynes (1971–89), XVI, pp. 51–2.

32 T 170/72, Turpin, 'War Finance', 27 April 1915.

33 'The Bank of England in Relation to Government Borrowing and the necessity of a Public Loan', 14 May 1915, Keynes (1971–89), XVI, p. 105; T 170/71, Withers to Bradbury, covering note 4 May 1915.

34 T 170/71, Bradbury, 'War Loan', 7 June 1915.

35 CLCBt, 15 June 1915, Frederick Goodenough, 'Memorandum re New War Loan'.

36 T 170/71, ff. 17–39. The draft is typed, suggesting that it came early in the design process. It, and another with a rate of 4 per cent and a price of 93, are dated 'June 1915'.

37 *Hansard* (Commons), 22 June 1915, col. 1086.

38 For example, see 'Speech of the Financial Secretary, Dr. Helfferich, in the Reichstag, August 20, 1915', pp. 6–7, in LGP, D/24/6/1.

39 T 170/67, Withers, 'The Financial Position', June 1915.

40 T 172/216, 'Conference between the Chancellor of the Exchequer and the Committee of the Stock Exchange', 17 February 1915; T 172/218, 'Conference between the Chancellor of the Exchequer and the Bankers' Clearing House Committee', 22 February 1915; T 172/217, 'Conference between the Cabinet Committee and the Stock Exchange Committee', 5 March 1915; T 172/219, 'Conference between The Cabinet Committee, Representatives of the Bankers and Committee of the Stock Exchange', 10 March 1915.

41 T 170/76, Bradbury, untitled Memorandum, June 1915. The announcement of the conversion terms produced a classic reaction in old War Loan. The price rose from 93⅝ to 95¾ and then sank back to its previous level as the market absorbed the implications. *The Economist*, 26 June 1915, p. 1319.
42 T 170/228, 'Conference between the Chancellor of the Exchequer and the Stock Exchange Committee', 22 June 1915, p. 18.
43 Ibid., pp. 8–25.
44 CLCBt, 24 June 1915. The CLCB passed a resolution demanding that it should be consulted before any further changes were made to minimum prices.
45 CLCBm, 2 July 1915; CLCBt, 24 June and 15 July 1915.
46 CLCBm and CLCBt, 15 July 1915; *The Economist*, 17 July 1915, p. 91; *Hansard* (Commons), 19 July 1915, col. 1158. A resolution from the CLCB is in T 170/78.
47 *The Economist*, 26 June 1915, pp. 1292 and 1319.
48 Lloyds TSB Group Archives, Waley to Martin-Holland, 30 July 1915; *The Economist*, 21 August 1915, p. 287.
49 T 170/78, note in Bradbury's hand and Walter Leaf to Chancellor, 14 June 1915.
50 Ibid., unsigned and undated note. Underlining in the original.
51 CLCBm, 1 July 1915.
52 T 170/78, Chancellor to Martin-Holland, 2 July 1915. The Governor did not approve of the extension to one year. BoE, G30/2, Governor to Pallain (Governor of the Banque de France), 19 October 1915.
53 T 170/78, Cunliffe, note of telephone message taken by Waley, 1 July 1915.
54 Ibid., Chancellor to Martin-Holland, 2 July 1915.
55 CLCBm, 1 July 1915. An emotional view of the bankers was taken by Montagu, whose judgement had no doubt suffered from the strain of his campaign to win Venetia Stanley. T 170/78, Montagu to Chancellor, 30 June 1915; MS Asquith, 14, f. 91–2, Montagu to Asquith, 3 July 1915.
56 CLCBm, 6 July 1915, and 8 July 1915; T 170/93, Martin-Holland to Chancellor, 9 July 1915.
57 *The Times*, 22 June 1915, p. 9, 26 June 1915, p. 9, and 28 June 1915, p. 9.
58 *Hansard* (Commons), 19 November 1914, cols 612–13, 623 and 647–9, and 12 May 1915, cols 1631–2. Also, see 15 March 1915, cols 1745–6.
59 T 170/71, Bradbury, 'War Loan', 7 June 1915.
60 T 170/78, Turpin, Report of the War Loan (Supplementary Provisions) Committee, 8 July 1915, and Waley to Samuel, 19 July 1915; POa, 30/3979, Turpin, 'War Loan Committee', 9 July 1915; *The Times*, 7 July 1915, p. 15.
61 *Hansard* (Commons), 21 June 1915, cols 958–9 and 980–1.
62 Ibid., cols 958 and 980.
63 Ibid., 7 July 1915, col. 358. *The Times*, 21 July 1915, p. 8, mentions the circular. A copy is in T 170/34, but is dated 'August 1915'.
64 T 170/78, Turpin, 'Report of the War Loan (Supplementary Provisions) Committee', 8 July 1915; POa, 30/3979, 'Report of the War Loan (Supplementary Provisions) Committee', 6 November 1915, and Turpin, 'War Loan Committee', 9 July 1915; Lloyds Bank Group Archives, Circular to Branch Managers, 9 July 1915.
65 CLCBm, 1 July 1915; T 170/78, Chancellor to Martin-Holland, 2 July 1915; Lloyds Bank Group Archives, Circular to Branch Managers, 9 July 1915.
66 T 172/229, Transcript of a 'Conference between the Chancellor and Representatives of the Trade Unions and Friendly and Approved Societies', 24 June 1915; T 172/230, Transcript of a 'Conference between the Chancellor and Representatives of Large Employers', 24 June 1915.
67 T 172/229, Transcript of a 'Conference between the Chancellor and Representatives of the Trade Unions and Friendly and Approved Societies', 24 June 1915; T 172/230, Transcript of a 'Conference between the Chancellor and Representatives of Large Employers', 24 June 1915.

68 *Hansard* (Lords), 6 July 1915, cols 248–63.
69 *The Times*, 17 July 1915, p. 7, and 23 July 1915, pp. 9–10.
70 Ibid., 15 July 1915, p. 8.
71 Northcliffe Papers, Add. 62157/189, McKenna to Northcliffe, 22 June 1915, Add. 62157/190, Northcliffe to McKenna, 24 June 1915, and Add. 62157/191, McKenna to Northcliffe, 25 June 1915; Beaverbrook (1928), I, pp. 150–1; McEwen (1986), pp. 10–11.
72 *The Times*, 9 July 1915, p. 5. A copy of the circular is in the Bodleian Library, Oxford, 'Papers on National War Savings'.
73 *The Times*, 7 July, 8 July and 9 July 1915.
74 T 170/71, Bradbury, 'War Loan', 7 June 1915.
75 £146.3m were created on account of Consols, £137.5m on account of the old War Loan and £6m on account of 2½ and 2¾ per cent Annuities. *Hansard* (Commons), 15 May 1916, col. 1121; *'National Debt: annual returns'*; Osborne (1926), I, pp. 269 and 400–1.
76 *Hansard* (Commons), 15 May 1916, col. 1121; *National Debt: annual returns*; *Government Departments Securities* (HCP 247), 3 June 1915; T 133/1, Ramsay to Commissioners, 30 July 1915. The original amounts were £33.8m into £22.5m. These were subsequently increased. See T 133/1, Ramsay to Commissioners, 27 October 1915.
77 T 133/1, TMs, 29 July 1915.
78 Ibid., Ramsay to Commissioners, 22 November 1915.
79 *Hansard* (Commons), 20 January 1916, col. 612, and 22 August 1916, cols 2485–8; T 170/70, 'Reports from the Comptroller of the Post Office Savings Bank'.
80 *Hansard* (Commons), 22 November 1915, col. 28. Montagu called it a 'failure', T 170/97, Committee on War Loan for Small Investors, Minutes of First Meeting, 13 December 1915.
81 T 172/228, Conference between the Chancellor of the Exchequer and the Stock Exchange Committee, 22 June 1915.
82 CLCBt, 12 and 15 November 1915. Consols immediately fell to 57, before recovering to 60. *The Economist*, 27 November 1915, pp. 884–5.

5 The small saver and continuous borrowing

> The weapons of finance are the Government securities which are open to subscription by all classes. The larger Exchequer Bonds are our heavy artillery. Post Office Exchequer Bonds and War Savings Certificates are our rifles and hand-grenades. The Central Committees for War Savings and the War Savings Associations are the staff of the financial army.
>
> McKenna to Kindersley at the beginning of War Savings Week, T 172/299, 11 July 1916

It might have been expected that initiatives to increase lending by the small investor would have followed immediately it was recognised that the voucher scheme attached to the main issue of 4½ per cent War Loan had been a failure. There was a growing understanding in the country that resources were not limitless and that consumption and imports had to be reduced. There was a large and expanding budget deficit, price inflation and a weak exchange rate. It was recognised that one of the answers was to raise the level of personal savings. Yet it was not until December that the members of the Committee on War Loans for the Small Investor, the Montagu Committee, were appointed.[1] Once in place, the Committee took only seven weeks to recommend the introduction of fractional Exchequer Bonds and War Savings Certificates, together with an organisation to distribute them and encourage saving. The savings movement was to be permanent, its propaganda continuous and the securities it sold constantly on tap. This, and the need to have Exchequer Bonds constantly available to pay for foreign securities as they were sold to the Treasury by British investors, was the beginning of 'day-by-day', or 'continuous', borrowing, a term not used by the Montagu Committee, although the concept was implicit in its recommendations. Thus, continuous borrowing came in by the back door, unheralded by publicity or name, as the converse of the Treasury's declared policy of borrowing from the banking system and then absorbing the deposits by occasional 'spectacular' war loans.

The origins of the Post Office Register

During the summer and autumn of 1915, the Treasury's preparations for expanding sales of securities to the small saver were limited to determining the administrative machinery which would record ownership by a mass investing public. Responsibility lay with the same interdepartmental War Loan Committee which had been charged with advising on the conversion rights to be given to subscribers for the Post Office issue of 4½ per cent War Loan (see p. 114). As well as representatives of the Treasury and the NDO, the Committee included officials from the National Health Insurance Commission, the Post Office and the POSB: the departments which had experience of keeping records on a large scale and administering millions of small receipts and payments from all over the country.

As has been indicated, the existing Stock purchase facility for the small investor, the Savings Bank Investment Account, with its machinery, the 'Government Stock Register', had never been popular; on 31 March 1914, it held only £20.1m Consols, £7.2m Local Loans and a handful of 2½ and 2¾ per cent Annuities and Irish Land Stocks (see pp. 12–13).[2] Yet, the obvious move was to extend the machinery to the new war issues. Neither the Commissioners nor the Banks of England and Ireland could handle the accounts of the millions of small savers which it was hoped to introduce to government securities. Only the Post Office had the network of offices with which to distribute the securities and the experience of collecting and disbursing monies, documenting transactions and issuing records of deposits: it could make interest payments, record the transfer of holdings, issue receipts and administer the new issues.[3]

This was, indeed, the decision made in July 1915. Then a delay in introducing legislation until the following session gave time for second thoughts. At the end of July, Basil Blackett, the Treasury's representative on the Committee, pointed out that the 'very striking innovation' of selling the 4½ per cent War Loan through Post Offices all over the country could be whittled down to 'an almost imperceptible extension of the old system of purchase and sale of limited amounts of Government Stock through the Savings Banks.' Any new system would involve duplication of administrative machinery, but simplification was needed if adequate facilities were to be provided for meeting the demands of 'a working class clientele of rentiers'. To the argument that the enthusiasm of new investors would be best kept alive if the new Loan assumed 'a special character of its own in the eyes of the class to whom the special appeals have been made' was added a practical, and legal, problem.[4] The Government Stock Register required that those carrying out transactions be savings bank depositors so that, if the system was to be extended to war securities, the new army of holders would have to open accounts; such a condition had not been mentioned in the prospectus for 4½ per cent War Loan.

Thus was born the Post Office Register (POR), into which the old Government Stock Register was merged in 1929.[a] It was established in accordance with the War Loan (Supplemental Provisions) Act 1915, which received the Royal Assent at the end of December. In accordance with the Act, and regulations made under it, the Register recorded individual holdings, the corpus of each issue being inscribed in the name of the Commissioners in the books of the Bank of England

a The Savings Banks Act 1929. The papers covering the merger are in T 160/263/F10669.

(there was no provision for registration at the Bank of Ireland). Orders to buy and sell were in the first instance used to offset each other: only the balance between the totals were bought or sold in the open market. In this way, the Bank was relieved of registering changes other than differences. Because holding the same issue on both systems would lead to confusion, all of the 4½ per cent War Loan held on the Government Stock Register was transferred to the POR. The POR was also made responsible for all the other securities which would be issued for the purpose of the war, while pre-war issues – Consols, Annuities, Local Loans and Irish Land Stocks – remained with the Government Stock Register. As the principle was simplicity and cheapness, a limit on holdings was imposed, the rationale being that the incentive for fraud would rise with the size of holdings and, in guarding against it, simplicity would be lost. Moreover, if there was no limit, the Register would merely duplicate the main registers of the Banks of England and Ireland. A limit of £200 nominal was placed on the amount of Stock on which interest could be paid without suffering withholding tax.[5]

The Committee on War Loans for the Small Investor

Although the machinery for registering the holdings and transactions of the small saver was established, the Treasury was slow to design new securities or reorganise the methods of distribution and sale. This lack of immediacy reflected the administrative difficulties of making further issues until the last was seen of the summer's Loan: the calls paid, the ownership inscribed and the vouchers exchanged for Stock. Nor, it may be surmised, could there be any public hint that new schemes were under discussion because it would undermine demand for the vouchers that were still on sale and give grounds for complaint from those who had already bought them. But there was nothing to delay departmental consideration of new schemes as soon as it had become clear that the vouchers were a failure. Despite this, a memorandum from Bradbury calling attention to the need for a decision on the voucher scheme and the facilities needed to replace it was not circulated until the middle of November, only two weeks before the scheme was due to end.[6]

Six days later, on 22 November, the Chancellor announced the establishment of the Committee on War Loans for the Small Investor, with Montagu as Chairman: the membership was not announced until 7 December.[7] The Chancellor drew two lessons from the failure of the voucher scheme. The security was wrong – 'the working classes' did not like their savings to fluctuate in value – and the sales organisation was wrong: 'we require to organise the assistance of those with influence in inducing the people to take advantage of our proposals.' He outlined a new scheme, involving the issue of securities in units of £1, bearing interest at 5 per cent per year, encashable at their face value at any time, but paying no interest for the first six months. The last provision would reduce the rate of interest to 2½ per cent after one year, 3¾ per cent after two years, 4$^{1}/_{16}$ per cent after three years and so on. As well as providing a disincentive to early withdrawal, this structure had the advantage of reducing competition with the banks for short-term deposits and making the new security unattractive, compared with the 2½ per cent offered by the POSB, for any period of less than one year. The Chancellor emphasised that the scheme was only tentative, and opened the subject to public debate.[8]

The Montagu Committee included representatives of all political parties, the Treasury, the banks, the TSBs, insurance companies and trade unions. Besides Montagu himself, the politicians included Stanley Baldwin; Frank Goldstone, a Labour backbencher and an official of the National Union of Teachers; Cecil Harmsworth, McKenna's Parliamentary Private Secretary and a brother of Northcliffe; and Halford Mackinder, a Liberal Unionist backbencher and a former Director of the London School of Economics. From outside the Commons, there was Cunliffe, who was ill for much of the time the Committee was sitting; Bradbury; Bell; Joseph Burn, the Prudential Assurance Company's actuary; Alexander Cargill, actuary (secretary) of the Edinburgh Savings Bank (a TSB); and Le Bas. Because time was short, and members themselves had wide experience, the Committee heard only eight witnesses, although they received several hundred communications in response to the Chancellor's appeal for ideas.[9] These ranged from printed submissions by TSBs to barely literate, if sometimes lively, scrawls from working men.

At its first meeting, Montagu proposed that the Committee's investigations should be divided into the two parts identified by the Chancellor: the design of the new security and the organisation needed for its sale.[10] For a time, attention was focused on premium bonds, then known as bonus bonds, and a compulsory loan.[11] These, however, did not flow naturally from the four principles that seem to have become common ground at an early stage and were to be included in the introductory passages of the *Final Report*: the system should be simple to use and understand; the securities should not fluctuate in price; they must be quickly and easily saleable; and they should pay a return similar to that on the large loans.

The logical starting place was the existing facilities provided by the savings banks and the Committee felt that a decision on whether these could, or should, be extended was necessary before it could make recommendations about new securities and organisation. Two aspects of the restrictions on the banks demanded consideration: the limit on the size of deposits, £200 for each individual and £50 each year, which had been unchanged since the early 1890s, and the 2½ per cent deposit rate. The TSBs, seeing an opportunity to place themselves at the centre of the war savings movement, made proposals which included both. However, if the savings banks were to be used, budgetary and monetary considerations required that a scheme be devised which would confine any higher rate to new or increased deposits and at the same time limit their liquidity. Since the beginning of the war, there had been several attempts by backbenchers to have the limits on deposits increased.[12] The previous May the savings banks, excited by the stress Lloyd George laid in his budget statement on saving and the growing public awareness of its importance, had tried to have both the total and annual limits lifted. On 10 May, the actuary of the Sheffield Savings Bank had written to the Chancellor with the support of the TSB Association (TSBA), arguing that the government was failing to exploit the savings banks' potential: the average wage earner preferred a liquid deposit paying 2½ per cent to a marketable security paying 3½ per cent. The removal of the limits would produce an immediate increase in the flow of savings into government paper.[13]

Recognising that limitations on lending to the government had been outdated by the war, both Turpin and Henry Davies, Controller of the Savings Bank Department of the Post Office, supported legislation to lift the limits on the size of deposits, or vest the Treasury with powers to determine any limit for the period of the war.[14] By June, Montagu had agreed to a rise and the discussion had reached the point where the Postmaster-General was preparing to write formally to the Chancellor.[15] The decision was then postponed at the Chancellor's request because it was thought that change would conflict with the new schemes for small savings that were being attached to 4½ per cent War Loan.[16]

In December 1915, the Treasury provided itself with powers to lift the deposit limits for the period of the war and six months thereafter. This enabled it to move at once when the Montagu Committee recommended, in the *Interim Report* published on 28 December, that, as a wartime measure, the limits should be abolished.[17] The recommendation was duly accepted and the change became effective from the end of the year.[18] The other restriction, the 2½ per cent interest rate on deposits, stayed. Early drafts of the *Final Report* show that the Committee (or at least Bradbury, who drafted it) had already made its decision when the *Interim Report* was published. The sentiments were to be frequently repeated by the Treasury during the ensuing twenty years:

> We have considered whether any fresh limits [on deposits] should be imposed, but I [*sic*] think this unnecessary, provided the rate of interest is not disturbed...We are convinced that the interest earned is not the primary consideration with those whose earnings we wish to attract; it is very doubtful if any large amount of new money would be attracted by anything less than a steep rise in the rate, while any rise in the rate involves a heavy extra charge on the taxpayer to provide the extra interest on the 200,000,000l. odd which is already left contentedly lying in the Post Office Savings Bank at 2½ per cent...there is nothing to show that 2½ per cent is on the low side for money which can be withdrawn practically at call...it is quite clear that the offer of a high rate for such money would cause the joint stock banks, building societies, penny banks, and similar institutions serious and even critical difficulties...[19]

Various proposals were devised to meet these arguments. Turpin suggested offering higher rates on new deposits. However, this would have been simple for existing depositors to exploit because accounts were classified according to the branch in which deposits were first made. Depositors would merely have to close their accounts with one branch and transfer the proceeds to another in order to enjoy the increased rate. Similarly, depositors with one TSB could transfer their accounts to another TSB or to the POSB. There were, therefore, suggestions that a higher rate should be paid only on additional deposits, those above the previous minimum.[20] Understandably, the TSBs' solutions assumed there would be no new organisation or security. Instead, they proposed new types of account, to run alongside the old ordinary departments, so avoiding a higher rate of interest on existing deposits. The suggestions differed in details, but included a higher rate than the standard 2½ per cent deposit rate, the lifting of limits on deposits and a loss of interest for early withdrawal.[21]

In the end, several considerations contributed to the Committee's recommendation. There was Bradbury's feeling that a small rise would have little effect in attracting new deposits and be expensive, while a large rise would have adverse effects on other institutions. Additionally, if the Committee were mistaken, and deposits at the new level of rates proved attractive, there would be a rise in liquid assets in the hands of the public which might embarrass the government after the war; a new instrument, tailored to prevent early withdrawal, was safer. Savings banks could not change their deposit rates quickly or easily and needed a rate that was sustainable over a long period. Introducing a separate account with higher rates for large deposits would be difficult in practice and a problem to present: the smaller saver would resent being paid a lower rate and it would be contrary to one of the Committee's basic principles if the small was seen to earn less than the large.[22] Amid the smoke, one is left feeling that the Treasury believed that it would be giving too much away if it lifted the interest rate, lifted the deposit limit, saw deposits expand and was then liable to pay them on demand.

The *Interim Report*'s second recommendation was for the issue of fractional Exchequer Bonds of £5, £20 and £50 on the same terms as the 5 per cent Exchequer Bonds 1920 issued on tap by the Bank of England some two weeks earlier, on 16 December (see pp. 193–4). It recommended that the fractional Bonds should be available through all Post Offices, not just Money Order Offices, with facilities available for holders to deposit Bonds with the Post Office and a record being provided for the investor in 'Exchequer Bond Deposit Books'. These proposals were accepted by the Treasury the same day.[23]

The Committee considered the savings banks adequate for those who could accumulate between £1 and £5. Smaller savers, however, required a new scheme. This would be provided by War Savings Deposits (renamed War Savings Certificates before their introduction on 19 February 1916). Either by depositing with the savings banks or by filling in cards which had spaces for 31 sixpenny stamps, 15s 6d would be accumulated, enabling a Certificate to be bought. Ownership would be registered at the Post Office and recorded in a passbook. The 15s 6d would accumulate to become £1 at the end of five years, 15s 6d being the value of £1 five years' hence at an interest rate of £5 4s 7d per cent a year.[b] The deposits would be encashable at 15s 6d at any time within the first year, and

b Although the Treasury was usually scrupulous in its calculation of yields, on this occasion it was slapdash. The *Final Report* spoke of 15s 6d as being 'approximately the present value of £1 five years hence at 5 per cent compound interest'. This was the yield that entered the public's consciousness and was generally quoted.

at 15s 9d at the end of the year; thereafter, 1d was added for each complete month in excess of twelve since the date of issue. It was recommended that the interest be free of income tax: the Certificates should therefore be confined to those with incomes of £300 or less (reduced from £500 during discussions).[24]

The proposal for issuing a security at a discount was submitted by Bradbury.[c] Until the Committee's third meeting on 20 December, the proposed schemes were couched in terms of a sum of money on which interest was payable, either by warrant or by directly crediting the depositor's account. Indeed, the first draft of the *Report*, dated 22 December, still included a scheme for War Deposit Accounts as well as War Savings Deposits. The former was very similar to that outlined by the Chancellor the previous month when announcing the appointment of the Committee.[25] Compared with this, which was a conventional Bond except for the disincentive to early encashment, issue at a discount in the manner of Treasury Bills had overwhelming advantages: it avoided a large number of small and expensive quarterly or half-yearly dividend payments; the idea of a sum of money becoming a larger sum which was also a round number could be easily presented and understood; it was thought that the small saver would more easily understand 'profit' than 'interest'; and the return of 1d a month on each Bond was simple to calculate. Unfortunately, the Treasury were in such a hurry to issue the new security that administrative preparations were inadequate: identifying surrenders and accounting for the accrual of interest was to be a major problem for budgets in the second half of the 1920s.

Bonus bonds and compulsory loans

The Montagu Committee gave serious consideration to two unconventional forms of borrowing: bonus bonds and a compulsory loan. Proposals for the former kept reappearing during the war, pressed with remarkable passion by some newspapers and a group of backbenchers, and opposed only slightly less noisily by non-

c After the war, there was a skirmish between Bradbury and Sir Laming Worthington-Evans, at that time the Secretary for War, when the latter laid claim to the Certificates' parentage. Bradbury asked the surviving members of the Montagu Committee for their recollections. All those who could remember the events said that Bradbury was the author. The minutes of the third meeting of the Committee merely record that he submitted the scheme. The secretary of the Committee wrote later that Bradbury 'if not the sole begetter of a solution which crystallised after discussion, was its substantive discoverer.' Later memories also ascribed the Certificates to him. Hawtrey, in his contribution on Bradbury in the *DNB*, wrote that 'to him more than to anyone is due the credit for devising in the war savings certificate a type of security which has gained a permanent footing in the structure of government finance.' Ernest Harvey, writing thirty years later, said, 'At the time…Cunliffe was Governor & he was not always very communicative about what went on behind the scenes but I always understood that the Certificates were originally suggested by Bradbury & that the scheme was hammered out between him & Cunliffe'. T 170/97, Committee on War Loans for the Small Investor, Minutes of Third Meeting, 20 December 1915; McFadyean (1964), pp. 63–4; *DNB*, 1941–50, Hawtrey; BoE, G15/572, Harvey to Clapham, 12 October 1944. The correspondence with Worthington-Evans is in T 172/1479.

conformists, the churches and welfare workers. These groups were able to give their views formally later in the war, when the issue was investigated by a Select Committee, which reported adversely in January 1918.[26]

The early drafts of the *Final Report* of the Montagu Committee placed bonus bonds squarely at the centre of the drive for small savings. It pointed, like the final version, to the small investor's need for simplicity, capital stability, easy withdrawal and a rate of interest similar to that on the large loans. However, the conflict between the last two needs was made explicit and linked with protecting the deposits of existing financial institutions and the short time available for 'educational propaganda'. The difficulty of selecting a rate of interest that met all these requirements was such that the Committee felt

> very strongly that...the course which offers by far the most considerable chance of success is frankly to fix a rate of interest, which is less than we can afford to offer, and to utilise the money thus saved in offering to certain investors chosen by chance substantial but not extravagant prizes or premiums.

The capital would remain intact, a submarket rate of interest paid, and the difference between this and the market rate would be distributed as prizes. It was admitted that the solution would be considered by many as 'a lottery and gambling transaction', but it was stressed that the whole capital would be returnable and that it would attract money that would otherwise be spent: it had been used in 'thrifty' France and, the Committee understood, would not be contrary to the Lotteries Act of 1823.[d] The scheme would be based on the widespread desire to speculate. A purist might think that 'once a man tastes the subtle excitement of such speculation he may be led insensibly to other less reputable operations where the whole stake might be lost', but this was a prejudice, so many of which had already been sacrificed to the war.[27] The recommendation was dropped in the *Final Report*, which cautiously commented that the bonds 'would probably be a very attractive form of investment and very considerable sums might be obtained by an issue of this character.' However, because many would object to any scheme which involved 'an element of chance' and the Committee was 'somewhat sharply divided', it was unable to recommend them.[28]

McKenna himself was an opponent, with his Commons defence of the decision not to make an issue ringing with conviction.[29] Two years later, when giving evidence to the Select Committee on Premium Bonds, he gave his reasons for having opposed their introduction in 1916 and said that his views had remained unchanged:

d The Law Offices later gave a contrary opinion, although it did not blunt the supporters' enthusiasm. They argued that the legality of bonus bonds was irrelevant because legislation was required to sanction the issue and any clause later found to be necessary could be tacked onto it.

> I base my objection to such an issue primarily on the ground that it would be contrary to the settled policy of this country as defined in between twenty and thirty Statutes, covering a period of 400 years. Those Statutes were all framed with a view – mistaken or otherwise – that it was not in the public interest to encourage or even to allow lotteries…I do not see any ground for a variation of the view.

He said that he had consulted his officials about the size of subscriptions which might be expected (assuming that the interest rate, that is the value of the prizes, was the same as that on conventional issues) and had been informed that there was not the 'remotest chance' of raising £50m, let alone £100m. He did not approve of gambling and would have found it impossible as a constituency MP to recommend such a security to those seeking security while helping the government's finances. He had suspected that agitation had been drummed up by newspapers wanting to change the climate of opinion so that the law could be amended, enabling them to continue to hold prize competitions, which had been a valuable aid to their circulation. In the end, McKenna said, he had taken the question to the Cabinet and it had been rejected.[30]

At the time, there was little to suggest that the Committee's change of view had been engineered from above. The witnesses who represented women's causes and the Workers Educational Association, reflecting the conscience of the educated social reformer, considered such schemes undesirable although, perhaps, effective.[31] *The Times*, a month later, reported that a banker, who was a non-conformist and a member of the Committee, had presented a scheme that was turned down by the political members. This was almost certainly Bell, a Congregationalist.[32] By this time, however, debating points were being made, or perhaps manufactured, amid a storm that had blown up around the bonds. At its centre were the two bodies recently appointed on the recommendation of the Montagu Committee to oversee the war savings movement – the National Organising Committee for War Savings and the Central Advisory Committee for War Savings – and the Northcliffe press.

Northcliffe had shown an interest in bonus bonds at the time of the issue of the $4^1/_2$ per cent War Loan the previous summer.[33] He had let it lie while the Committee was sitting and when the *Final Report* was published, but at the beginning of March 1916 *The Times* City pages had used the occasion of a request by McKenna for new ideas for attracting savings to state that many 'bankers and merchants' believed that bonus bonds would be very successful.[34] Two days later, the Central Advisory Committee wrote to the Chancellor that it had received:

> numerous proposals for the establishment of War Savings Associations to issue premium bonds, or work schemes with prize drawings. In view of the opinion of the Law Offices of the Crown [that an issue would be contrary to the Lotteries Act] the Committee are unable to sanction the adoption of any such scheme. The Committee, however, are strongly of the opinion that:

> (1) In order to induce individuals to save who would otherwise never save
> (2) In order to assist the Treasury in the economical raising of money for financing the War, and
> (3) With a view to favourably influencing the foreign exchanges
>
> the issue of a National loan based on the lottery principle, is urgently desirable.[35]

An amendment to the resolution some days later showed that the Committee was alive to the political difficulties of their proposal: the words 'principle of premium bonds' replaced 'the lottery principle'.[36] The National Organising Committee wrote in similar vein that:

> its efforts to promote saving by the wage earning classes will be seriously weakened unless the Government takes the necessary steps to make an issue of bonus bonds, securing to investors the return in full of their capital subscribed, together with a fixed rate of interest and the chance of a bonus…[37]

A head of steam now developed. A group of bankers and financiers, including two members of the Montagu Committee, Bell and Baldwin, as well as Sir William Plender (senior partner of the accountants Deloitte, Plender, Griffiths & Co.) and Richard Vassar-Smith (Chairman of Lloyds Bank) met on 9 March:[38] they urged an issue of bonds on the Chancellor and asked him to receive a deputation to discuss it. They believed an issue:

> would not only be successful in its immediate object of securing large sums of money; but would also indirectly lead to more thrifty conditions of life and a stoppage to a large extent of useless and unproductive expenditure, which is so prevalent.[39]

Despite its weight, the Chancellor refused to see the deputation, telling Plender that the government had already made a decision against an issue.[40]

The press had adopted party positions: the Northcliffe Papers, together with the *Globe*, *Pall Mall Gazette* and the *Daily Express*, urged an issue; the Liberal papers scarcely mentioned it. The stance of the advocates was to be expected: an unwillingness to allow the 'nonconformist conscience' to impede the war effort; the necessity of subordinating prejudice to the raising of money; the effectiveness of the appeal to the newly affluent working class; the precedent of those thrifty French; and the effect on the imagination of the opportunity of becoming rich. The difference from gambling, in which the entire stake was at risk, was hammered home.

The government's decision against an issue was greeted with ritual outrage, but drew the sting of the campaign. Attempts to revive it in the Commons later in the month carried no conviction.[41] At the beginning of April, a number of MPs, including Baldwin, formed a committee to press for an issue, and at the beginning of May they circulated a specific proposal, several speaking at length during the reading of the Finance Bill in the middle of the month. The campaign had little of the previous co-ordinated violence, with the Northcliffe press showing none of its earlier venom. The Chancellor pointed out that, although there was no gamble with the principal, there was 'a gamble in interest'. If bonus bonds were immoral, but justified in time of war, the decision became one of weighing the degree of immorality against the extent of the benefit. Members had suggested a yield of £150m or £200m over an unspecified period; he doubted whether it would be greater than an additional £10m or £15m per year, taking transfers from existing savings deposits into account.

> I do not think gambling is a good thing, and I do not think it is wise of the state to encourage people to look for making a living without working for it...Is it the duty of the Government to encourage people in that line of thought?[42]

The second form of unconventional borrowing, a compulsory loan, was debated alongside bonus bonds. Whereas support for the latter was found mainly in the Conservative Party, that for a compulsory loan was found on the left, although it was, by no means, confined to Liberal radicals or the Labour party. In April 1915, Paish advised Lloyd George to introduce a compulsory loan from income as the only way of reducing consumption and ensuring that Britain had resources available for the war equal to its commitments.[43] That summer, Bonar Law aired the possibility in a speech at the Guildhall during the War Loan campaign, although, as in 1917 when issuing 5 per cent War Loan, it appeared more an encouragement to subscribers than a real possibility.[44] At the end of November 1915, *The Economist* reported that the idea was only being 'tentatively put forward here and there'. It saw it as an effective way of curbing extravagance, although it was 'repugnant to every economic principle that this country has established in times of peace and liberty.'[45] A discussion held by the Treasury subcommittee of the CLCB on 18 February 1916 showed that there were advocates even among the bankers, with support coming from Walter Leaf, who feared that each successive loan would have to offer a higher rate and that a new loan might be accompanied by hints that, should it not be fully subscribed, compulsion would follow. Holden and Schuster opposed the proposal, the former saying that: 'A compulsory loan would have the effect of causing a run on the deposits of the Banks, the more so as the Chancellor had said that the government was not going to seize the deposits of the banks. Further a compulsory loan would persuade the Americans that we were rapidly verging on bankruptcy.'[46]

The day the Montagu Committee had its first sitting and discussed both compulsion and bonus bonds, the Chancellor, replying in the Commons to a Member who had drawn his attention to rumours that a compulsory loan might become necessary, kept his options open, stating his confidence that voluntary methods would provide the necessary resources.[47] The scheme which was put before the Committee has not survived in the minutes, but a suggestion, sent to Lloyd George by Chiozza Money, a Liberal MP who was later to join the Labour

Party, advocated a compulsory levy to cover eighteen million people. Those with incomes of more than £250 a year, about one million people, would be asked to pay quarterly on their own assessment, as with income tax. The remainder would have the deduction made by means of stamps from wages and salaries by the employer. The system would be designed to emphasise that the money was borrowed: a passbook would be issued and exchanged each year for inscribed Stock. To avoid the Stock being used as currency, it would be illegal to transfer it or advance money on its security. There could be early repayment, however, in cases of hardship, death or unemployment, provided it was sanctioned by a local tribunal.[48]

The section of the Montagu *Report* that rejected compulsion was written by Bradbury and used the same arguments as those in the Treasury evidence to the Committee on Co-ordination of Military and Financial Effort, although with more detail (see p. 192). Deduction from wages at source, and the various allowances that would be necessary, would reduce the yield to 'insignificance'. A loan of 5s in the £ on incomes of over £130 a year (the existing income tax threshold), with the same allowances as those in force for income tax, would yield about £200m, of which 75 per cent might be at the expense of voluntary loans. Even if the loan were extended to incomes of between £1 and £2 10s 0d a week, it would be 'very improbable' that the additional yield would justify the hardship and administrative cost involved. If the securities representing the loan were negotiable, they would pass into circulation at a discount to legal tender. Wage earners would view their incomes as being reduced by the amount of the discount. The securities would discredit and drive out of circulation the existing paper currency, costing the government the interest on the £70m of Currency Notes outstanding. If the securities were non-negotiable, they would be regarded as additional income tax, requiring exemptions and allowances which would make the scheme 'administratively impossible.' Future voluntary loans would be jeopardised. Finally, it would be unwise to attempt compulsion until voluntary means had failed.[49]

Organisation: voluntary savings associations

The suggestion for achieving flexibility by introducing agencies between the Treasury and the saver came from Mackinder, perhaps building on the experience of savings collected by organisations set up by companies in their works during the campaign to sell the 4½ per cent War Loan. He thought there would be no need for a new security as the agencies could invest in a mixture of Treasury Bills, Exchequer Bonds and deposits in joint stock and savings banks. The organisations would be free to choose their own constitutions and they could be either local or national. They would decide for themselves how to organise collection, whether door-to-door, by stamps or with a deposit book, making use of organisations, not necessarily financial, which already existed, such as schools, churches and local authorities. As they would be handling money, they would need to be subject to some kind of supervision.[50]

In its *Final Report,* the Committee envisaged the intermediaries, or War Savings

Associations, being in close touch with the saver, providing the facilities to make saving easy and, having persuaded someone to save, ensuring that it became a habit. Associations would be cheap to run and, being near the saver, would be able to tap the flow of income rather than receive transfers of existing deposits. Organisation would come from employers, trade unions, committees of workmen, local authority officials and co-operative and friendly societies, which would form associations of two types: agencies which would collect contributions for investment in government securities, merely acting as a conduit; and investment societies which would collect contributions and invest them in their own names so that the saver would be a fractional owner of a society's assets. The securities in which societies might invest should be determined by the Treasury, but should include Treasury Bills, available only to them, of denominations smaller than £1,000.[e] The Montagu Committee recommended the appointment of two permanent committees at a national level. The first would be responsible for propaganda and encouraging the formation of the collecting agencies and investment societies. The second would be a body to which societies would be affiliated, providing advice and approving and supervising their working. In addition, there would be a department which would recognise collecting agencies, ensuring the proper payment of sums subscribed, and preparing and distributing the securities. Co-ordination would be ensured by the two committees having members in common and by the administrative department being represented on both.[51]

Continuous borrowing

Two of the Committee's recommendations ran contrary to the way securities were sold in 1914 and 1915: the organisations were to be permanent and the securities they were to distribute would be continuously available or 'on tap'. The sale of the two War Loans in November 1914 and June 1915 showed that the system of borrowing by occasional large issues had notable disadvantages. There were only a few weeks in which to persuade potential investors to save and then buy government paper. Yet, by their nature, savings were generated throughout the year as incomes were received. As a result, subscriptions had to come from existing savings, investors being asked to make important decisions and rearrange their portfolios with unnatural speed. This must have added to the yield that had to be offered. The short period for which the Loans were on sale was partially addressed by making issues partly paid, with calls stretching over some months, and by encouraging investors to borrow from their banks and repay as savings accrued. However, the urgency of the need for funds did not always permit this, as in the summer of 1915 when an incentive was given to pay up early in full. The difficulties

e The Act of 1877 and the TMs of 1887 and 1889 did not restrict Bills to any particular denominations (see p. 21): the TMs of April 1915, and March and June 1917, which regulated the issue of tap Bills, specified a minimum of £1,000. There is no record of Treasury Bills of denominations of less than £1,000 having been issued. BoE, C 40/399, 'Treasury Bills'.

of selling to the general investor on the necessary scale, the temptation to show a large total for propaganda purposes, and the relative ease with which they could be influenced meant that both the 1914 and 1915 Loans relied heavily on the banks for direct subscriptions. There were strains in the money market as the banks ran down their deposits at the Bank of England and then reduced their Treasury Bill holdings to settle the subscriptions made by both themselves and their customers. Such a system was cumbersome, expensive and inefficient: the advertising campaigns had to be quickly mounted and then dismantled, and the staff at the banks, savings banks and Bank of England experienced brief periods of intense activity. Finally, it meant the loss of the sales momentum that had been built up with expense and effort. All this pointed to continuous advertising and social pressure to make people save from an income flow that was also continuous, and to a permanent war savings structure, employing enthusiastic volunteers, kept in existence by continuous campaigning.

There is nothing in the records to suggest that there were critics of the system of large and occasional loans within the Bank or the Treasury, although Osborne says that the idea of the '"tap" Loan system' was incorporated into a Bank paper on Exchequer Bonds in October 1915.[52] The two most important critics were external: provincial bankers, fertile with ideas for change. They were Drummond Drummond Fraser, the Managing Director of the Manchester and Liverpool District Bank, and Alfred Gibson, Northern District Manager of the Anglo-South American Bank in Bradford. Most of their proposals were widely known by the autumn of 1915, and those concerning the small investor were available to the Montagu Committee in the winter. Unfortunately, their views were expressed incoherently and sporadically, Fraser's publications being interrupted by the death of his two sons in action. Gibson's published contributions[53] were mainly of detailed schemes for collecting and recording small savings by passbooks and his claims to seeing the need for continuous borrowing were mainly made later.[f]

Fraser had experience of the working-class savings movement in Lancashire, as well as of joint stock banking. He had been a part-time lecturer at the University of Manchester and was active in professional bodies, such as the Institute of

f An exception to this generalisation was an article published in the *Bankers' Magazine*, August 1915, pp. 146–7, although the need for continuous availability is not spelt out. Gibson suggests that, if short-dated paper had been offered in June, the government would have been able to borrow at 4 per cent: 'The reason why the Government decided to offer so high a rate of interest as $4^1/_2$ per cent was because it desired to raise as large an amount as possible in a relatively short time, and an occasional loan of large amount lends itself more to exceptional Press advertisements than lesser loans issued at more frequent intervals as required, though in the aggregate to the same amount. The art of loan raising is to substitute scrip for goods and services with as little financial disturbance as possible'. Osborne says that Gibson 'asserts' that he wrote to the Treasury on the 5 July and 4 November 1915 and that Fraser, 'it is said', wrote in August. The letters have not been found. Osborne also says that 'The plan may very likely have occurred to several persons, and it is not possible to say whether or no [*sic*] the Bank or the Treasury arrived at it independently of outside suggestion.' Osborne (1926) I, p. 406n.

Bankers, the Royal Statistical Society, the British Association and the Manchester Statistical Society. The suggestions he made, mainly through the press and in lectures, went so much with the grain of events that by the end of the war they had been adopted, even with his terminology, as the main approach to internal borrowing.[54] He was knighted in 1920 and committed suicide in 1929.

There were three distinct aspects to his scheme: the continuous availability of government securities; selling direct to individuals as their savings accrued from income; and the organisation required to persuade people to buy and to distribute the securities. Central to his plan was the belief, derived from pre-war experience in the northern industrial savings market, that millions of families had the capacity to make a contribution to the financing of the war, provided they were approached in the right way. The later emphasis of Fraser's own articles and the adoption, at the end of 1917, of continuous availability as the sole form of borrowing sometimes led to the propaganda and organisational aspects being ignored. Thus, some, including Fraser himself on one occasion, could treat Treasury Bills as a form of continuous borrowing, merely because they were continuously available.[55] Such was Professor Herbert Foxwell, who wrote in March 1916 that continuous borrowing on Treasury Bills and Exchequer Bonds had 'largely superseded the old methods of borrowing by large loans at long intervals' and that 'it is hardly too much to claim that it is the most successful financial device yet adopted.'[56] Ten years later, Osborne described the issue of 5 per cent Exchequer Bonds in December 1915 as the first trial of the 'day-to-day system of borrowing from the public', although this was not the Treasury's intention – certainly not its primary intention – when adopting the method of issue (see pp. 193–4).[57]

Fraser's earliest suggestion was for the government to borrow directly from the general public and, in particular, from the small investor. Before the war, local authorities had raised large sums by borrowing individually small amounts from the public at various, relatively short, terms and at fixed rates of interest. Industrial insurance companies, savings banks, friendly societies, penny banks, trade union funds and building societies testified to the willingness of those on small incomes to save.[58] In September 1915, Fraser carried this further, advocating 'continuous day-by-day borrowing' from the general public. Savings accrued 'day-by-day' and were best tapped by the continuous issue of securities, of maturities to suit all needs, direct to the investor. The banks should only provide temporary finance, by means of Treasury Bills, and not by buying longer-dated paper:

> it is notorious that the antiquated system of the other two loans [the 3½ per cent and 4½ per cent War Loans], with their 'short-time' limit for application and payment, has not attracted the bulk of the people; and, in consequence, the banks have subscribed for a considerable portion of the two War Loans.[59]

The Bonds would be issued in units of £5, with scrip vouchers for smaller amounts, and cards would be provided into which stamps would be pasted until the minimum subscription for a Bond had been accumulated.

In November 1915, when the Chancellor threw open the question of small savings to public debate, Fraser saw Bradbury and then some London bankers. Having failed to make any headway, he was invited by the editor of *The Economist* to set out his ideas in a letter.[60] In this, he said that borrowing should be governed by the working family's needs: an investment into which it could pay week by week; stable capital values; ease of access; and a form of security or record of ownership, which could not be lost. He suggested £1 Bonds should be put on permanent tap with purchases recorded in a passbook: the subscription money would be accumulated in weekly 1s instalments by means of stamps; interest of 5 per cent would be paid half-yearly on the Bonds; early withdrawal would incur a sacrifice of interest, otherwise repayment would take place one year after the war in cash or by means of a funding exercise. The advantages to the government were a steady inflow, as savers would contract to contribute weekly and lose interest if they failed to keep up subscriptions; a steady outflow of interest payments; a steady repayment of principal, mirroring the previous steady inflow of subscriptions; and, most importantly, a tapping of accruing savings rather than a transfer of existing deposits. Propaganda should be aimed at wives, who controlled the savings, and emphasise patriotism as well as self-interest. The machinery would be the existing philanthropic, religious and savings bank institutions co-ordinated by 'local central committees'. Volunteers would collect contributions, buying stamps from the Post Office against some suitable guarantee. For the better off, there would be £50 Bonds bought in £5 instalments. The Bonds would be issued for three, five, seven or ten years at the interest rate ruling at the time of purchase. For the wealthier, there would be similar Bonds in units of £500, available at the banks, with a rate of interest announced in the press from time to time:

> I am convinced, then, that this scheme...will raise, if it is properly worked, two or three million pounds a week from the working classes alone. The amounts paid by each individual each week may be small, but there are 52 weeks in the year, and the possible contributors are to be numbered by many millions...an immense pressure of public opinion must be awakened to effect the necessary economy. For the Government's day-to-day borrowing can only be successful if the people are really made to see the necessity for economy.[61]

Establishing the mass savings movement

The Chancellor accepted the recommendations of the Montagu Committee, and by a Treasury Minute of 8 February 1916 there were established the National Organising Committee for War Savings, under the chairmanship of George Barnes, a Labour MP and trade unionist, and the Central Advisory Committee for War Savings, under the chairmanship of Robert Kindersley, a banker. The function of the first was 'to undertake propagandist work and to promote the formation of agencies and investment societies', and that of the second 'to advise upon and approve the financial details of schemes for investment societies and to supervise their working.' In April 1916, it was found, in the words of the Savings Committee's

First Annual Report, that 'in practice the work of the two Committees was inseparable and they were amalgamated under the title of the National War Savings Committee'. At the end of March 1917, it had sixteen members, in addition to the chairman. Six were MPs and two were from government departments (the Treasury and the Registrar of Friendly Societies). Two had been members of the Montagu Committee (Burn and Le Bas). The remaining six included Beatrice Chamberlain (half-sister of Neville and, therefore, close to the Birmingham Municipal Savings Bank) and Withers, who had moved to *The Economist* after his spell at the Treasury.

The organisation that was developed, although recognisable from the blueprint in the Montagu Report, differed in important respects. Before its amalgamation with the Central Advisory Committee in April, the National Organising Committee had recommended that a separate committee for Scotland should be set up; this began work in May. The distinction between investment societies and collecting agencies disappeared: in their place, 'War Savings Associations', working within a structure of organising 'War Savings Committees', became responsible for the collection of savings and the distribution of securities.

The vehicle for establishing War Savings Committees was normally local authorities and, initially, their Mayors or Chairmen. They would call a meeting of prominent local people and form a Committee, which they often chaired. Every County Borough, Borough and Urban District in England and Wales with a population of more than 20,000 had a War Savings Committee, known as a Local Central Committee, which reported directly to the National War Savings Committee in London. The rest of a county was covered by County Committees, which became responsible for establishing Local Committees in Rural Districts and those Urban Districts with populations of less than 20,000. The Rural Districts might also be amalgamated with neighbouring Urban Districts. At the end of June 1916, there were 157 such committees in England and Wales; they had risen to 1,147 by the end of March 1917. These committees performed both of the roles envisaged by Montagu: propaganda and the formation and affiliation of the War Savings Associations. A committee might have anything between a dozen and a couple of hundred members. A Treasurer in each Local Central and County Committee, helped by local volunteers with accountancy experience, was responsible for auditing the associations, and a secretary in each committee was responsible for administration. Members specialised in different types of association and it was considered that the larger the Local Central and County Committees the more effectively they could find specialists.

Each War Savings Association was an independent, self-governing investing society, with its own chairman, treasurer, secretary and committee. They were formed in existing social groups such as schools, churches, shops, mines and factories. The intention was to supplement the savings banks, aiming at the very smallest saver, and the means was the purchase of government securities by co-operative effort. A condition of affiliation was that members' contributions would be amalgamated and immediately used to make a purchase. When individuals had accumulated sufficient to buy a whole War Savings Certificate, they received ownership from the supply that had been bought out of the float which had accumulated from individual subscriptions. The interest on the securities which had not yet been transferred to individual owners could be used either to pay the expenses of the association or to allow subscribers to start earning interest before the full 15s 6d had been paid. Some 1,287 associations had been formed by the end of June 1916 and about 16,000 by the end of the year. The number expanded rapidly during the War Loan campaign at the beginning of 1917, reaching 26,584 by the end of March; of these, 31 per cent were in 'business firms', 6 per cent in munitions works, 10 per cent in churches and Sunday Schools and 30 per cent in other schools. The number of members in each association varied from ten to 10,000; in March 1917, the total membership was between two and three millions.[62]

The first War Savings Association was formed in Scotland in July 1916. Little happened in the summer, but a War Savings Week in December and the War Loan Campaign (the difference in name from the Victory Campaign in England and Wales reflected the desire to be independent from the National Committee in London that was to recur often) in January and March 1917 stimulated activity so that at the end of the first year there were 170 Local Central Committees and 3,190 Associations. In May 1917, the Scottish Committee was asked by the Treasury to help the savings movement and advertising drive in Ulster.

The Birmingham Municipal Savings Bank

One of the best-known War Savings Associations was a savings bank established in Birmingham by its City Council in September 1916 as a result of the influence and enthusiasm of the Lord Mayor, Neville Chamberlain, a future Chancellor. Birmingham had neither a TSB nor a Penny Bank and its citizens relied on the POSB and the joint stock banks. These, Chamberlain felt, failed to cater for those who had never saved before and, especially, artisans; McKenna, he believed, should have been trying to increase savings, rather than sell more securities.[63] After a lengthy struggle with a powerful combination of Treasury officials and the joint stock banks, Chamberlain had to accept a complete change in his bank's purpose and, instead of being a source of municipal finance, it became a collector of small savings for investment in government securities.

The rise in interest rates in 1915 and 1916 produced casualties among those who had borrowed short-term money to make long-term investments, or who had bought long-term securities with short-term deposits. An example of the former were some local authorities, notably Halifax in Yorkshire, which the Treasury rescued, and, of the latter, some of the special investment departments of the TSBs. Several of these had become insolvent at the outbreak of war, and some of the TSBs had proposed that the government take over the departments or guarantee their deposits.[64] The Treasury thus had reason for being unsympathetic when Chamberlain suggested that his savings bank would encourage thrift, appeal to local patriotism and enable the Corporation to raise the money to meet its maturing obligations without competing with the government's war borrowing. Montagu's reply, drafted by Blackett, confessed that the Treasury had for:

> a long time felt some alarm at the widespread system by which local authorities have financed their capital expenditure by means of money borrowed at call or short notice. The experience gained since the war began has shown that this alarm was well-grounded, and all the local authorities are now feeling the difficulty of replacing the moneys called in or not renewed by the holders of short-dated mortgages.

The new War Savings Committee would be enlisting the local authorities in its propaganda work, and the envisaged municipal banks would divert their energy as well as the flow of savings. Easy access to finance might lead to increased local expenditure at a time when the government was seeking economy.[65]

As this went to Chamberlain in February 1916, the Treasury learnt that some local authorities feared that their borrowing would be further damaged by the competition from government securities. The threat to national war savings led the Treasury to consider advancing them the money to meet their maturing debts up to the value of the government securities sold in their districts.[66] This was probably the origin of the scheme introduced in 1920 to attract local authority support for national savings by giving them access to up to one-half of the proceeds of Certificates sold in their areas for housing purposes (see pp. 631–4).

In the middle of March, Chamberlain realised that he would not win approval for a bank unless the deposits were lent to the Treasury, and he offered to invest a minimum of 80 per cent in war securities and to keep the remainder as till money or as a balance with the Corporation. The Central Advisory Committee was prepared to approve the scheme, provided the bank's life was limited to the duration of the war, the bank's deposits were kept separate from the City's own balances and it was run in accordance with regulations agreed with the Treasury. Blackett also advised approval because the Treasury would be able to write the rules so they would protect existing savings banks. Bradbury remained opposed, but was overruled by Montagu and the Chancellor.[67] A Bill was introduced in the Commons on 11 April 1916, but was promptly condemned by the CLCB:

> it will not have the desired effect of providing or stimulating the collection of funds for carrying on the war, but would probably involve grave risk to the Government's own Savings Banks and might, should withdrawals become numerous, seriously affect the financial stability of the Councils, Boroughs and Urban Districts establishing such Banks.[68]

With this opposition, the Chancellor withdrew the Bill.[69]

Over the following week, the bankers filled out their reasons for opposing the bank. They would have no objection if Birmingham were to provide facilities to enable savers to accumulate small sums, so that they could invest directly in government securities; they had every objection to the City accepting deposits itself, guaranteeing them, investing them in government securities and paying a rate of interest which could only be earned by holding long-dated securities liable to depreciation. It would merely be 'doing under better auspices, but with no better banking principles, what was done by the Birkbeck Bank, the Charing Cross

Bank, and the Civil Service Bank.'[70] They expected that, if a run on a municipal bank did take place, the sponsoring local authority would ask its bankers to advance it the necessary cash; the bankers would, therefore, be expected to keep reserves to help the savings banks which were competing with them.[71]

Chamberlain then lobbied the chairman, Vassar-Smith of Lloyds (a Birmingham bank, which was also the City's bankers), and other members of the CLCB. They were not convinced.[72] On 10 May, the Committee passed another resolution that, while it was 'anxious to assist War Savings [it] is of [the] opinion that the proposed scheme is unsound inasmuch as the distinction between Banking and Investment has not been observed.'[73] At the end of May, the Chancellor and Montagu saw the CLCB after Birmingham had made changes which Austen Chamberlain, Neville's half-brother, thought would meet the bankers' objections. The bankers, in any case, were wilting under their customers' displeasure; Vassar-Smith and Holden were prepared to withdraw their objections, provided the new institutions were confined to Birmingham, as was the Bank of Liverpool, provided the banks were confined to cities such as Liverpool. The Chancellor suggested that the CLCB and Neville Chamberlain should negotiate directly and, once Neville Chamberlain had seen the Chancellor the following day, an outline Bill was sent for drafting. At the end of June, the CLCB grudgingly agreed to drop its opposition.[74]

The result of this tacking was that the freedom of municipally owned savings banks was severely limited. The Municipal Savings Banks (War Loan Investment) Act 1916 restricted the banks to authorities with populations of more than 250,000 and limited their customers to employed people. Other restrictions included deposit solely by deduction from wages; a maximum deposit of £200; 80 per cent of the funds to be remitted to the Commissioners; investments limited to Treasury Bills and Ways and Means Advances; approval by the Treasury of the interest that could be paid to the savings banks and of the rate they could pay to depositors; limitation of withdrawals to £1 unless seven days' notice was given; and the winding up of the banks within three months of the end of the war. Regulations for running the banks were to be agreed with the Treasury in consultation with the Local Government Board or, in the case of Scotland, with the Secretary of State for Scotland.[75]

Thus, only large cities could have the banks. The limit on withdrawals and the method of deposit meant that they could not be used by businesses. Keeping the entire portfolio very short, instead of allowing a proportion to be invested longer, as would be customary, meant they could not offer a generous interest rate. Deposits had to come from savings flow, not from a transfer from existing savings.[g] The banks were strictly a war measure, to be wound up when hostilities ceased. In sum, the Treasury's control meant that they had little commercial flexibility. It is hardly surprising that only one bank was established and that, despite the

g Depositing did not involve the employee providing cash. Instead, an employer would buy stamps issued by the bank and pay the employee partly in these. The employee would stick the stamps on a card until £1 had been collected. It would then be taken to a branch of the bank, where it would be exchanged for a deposit.

propaganda of local publicists arguing its success, it grew slowly. At end-December 1916, the Commissioners had received £18,000; at end-December 1917, £173,000.[76]

The problem was a real one, and not a fabrication of a CLCB seeking to curb potential competition. The POSB and TSBs were only able to offer immediate withdrawal while investing in long-dated issues or Consols because the Treasury was guarantor. The Treasury's concern at this potential liability had long been one reason for limiting the size of deposits. In the years before the war, several banks and savings banks had been bankrupted by holding Consols as interest rates rose. In 1911, the joint stock banks rescued the Yorkshire Penny Bank. The POSB and TSBs ordinary departments would also have been bankrupted, invested heavily in Consols as they were, if they had stood alone. In January 1917, a Treasury Committee was to take evidence from some of the worst-affected TSBs with special investment departments, after which arrangements were made for the CNRA to make them loans, a temporary expedient before the Savings Banks Act 1918 put them under the control of the Commissioners and established a mutual guarantee fund.[77]

There was the inconsistency, well-recognised, in the new savings schemes, in that they provided both immediate withdrawal and a yield that was similar to that on the issues made through the Bank,that is on Exchequer Bonds and War Loans which could depreciate. The pressures of war had made the Treasury accept the abolition of the limits on the deposits of the POSB and the TSBs, but it had refused a rise in interest rates and it had limited the number of Certificates individuals could hold. Otherwise, the investor took the risk when buying any of the issues on the Post Office Register or the Savings Bank Investment Account. Yet, here was a local authority wanting to offer a generous rate of interest, immediate withdrawal and the guarantee of its own credit.

Propaganda

The 1916 savings campaign lacked the stimulus of a great war loan and was unsophisticated compared with those that came later. The newspapers were fed suitable pieces, posters and handbills distributed, a monthly journal called 'War Savings' produced. A single film was made. Lectures were given in theatres and picture palaces. In July, a War Savings Week was held, by chance as the Somme battle opened. This had the threefold aim of explaining the reason for saving, selling Certificates and giving momentum to the formation and affiliation of associations. Under the unexciting motto of 'Save and help win victory and peace', speakers addressed meetings in factories, offices and shops: the Anglican clergy, on the instructions of the Archbishop of Canterbury, encouraged thrift from the pulpit; volunteers distributed pamphlets; and advertising increased. It was claimed that 798 associations were formed during the week.[78]

Results

'During the first six months of the Committee's existence both apathy and hostility were met with', reported the National War Savings Committee in March 1917.[79] If newspapers and politicians' speeches are a guide, there was a widely held view that real incomes among manual workers had risen strongly. However, witnesses had warned the Montagu Committee that there was little margin for saving: workers, and especially women, were working harder and needed better nourishment and clothing; more was being spent on children; debts were being paid off; and the man of a household was often with the forces earning less than usual.[80] The Montagu Committee took the point:

> The desire for a better standard of life, especially amongst those who are working harder and feel entitled to enjoy the fruits of their labour, commands universal sympathy.[81]

The savings movement met other problems, in addition to the natural desire to spend. The war did not command universal support. Many saw saving and government borrowing as a way of avoiding an increase in taxes on the better off: the Montagu Committee had commented that a higher proportion of the cost of the war should be met from taxation, especially on the 'wealthier portion of the community'.[82]

Assessing the impact of the movement on the small saver was made difficult by two changes introduced in the first half of 1916. It had been found that the machinery for declaring income at the time of purchase was cumbersome, that many wage earners were drawing pay in excess of the limit and that the exclusion of those with higher incomes from savings associations, who were holding and then selling Certificates to their members, introduced a class distinction into the system. On 10 June, the £300 income limit for those eligible to purchase Certificates was removed and replaced by a limit of 500 on the number of £1 units that could be held by any one person.[83] Interpreting the effect of this change on the sales statistics was to be the subject of some debate later in the war. Second, at the end of May, the Post Office issue of Exchequer Bonds was given a valuable tax privilege. It was originally intended that coupons should suffer withholding tax in the normal way. After some public pressure, it was announced that there would be no withholding tax as long as they were deposited with the Post Office.[84] Thus, under pressure of war, there appeared the first crack in a rigid policy.

The Certificates proved more popular, or suitable, than fractional Exchequer Bonds for those saving through associations, so that by the end of 1916 associations were selling little else.[85] Certificates represented 43 per cent of the small savers' contribution during the year: if purchases of single 500 Certificates, assumed to be bought by those on high incomes for tax reasons, were excluded, they were still 33 per cent.[h] In the five war months of 1914, the small investor had contributed

h Certificates for £500 to the value of £14.3m were bought in 1916, with the number purchased being particularly strong in the summer when the income restriction was removed. The purchases were: June, £1.2m; July, £4.3m; August, £3m; September, £2.1m; October, £1.6m; November, £1.2m; and December, £0.9m. National War Savings Committee, *First Annual Report*, Table 1.

£1.2m to the Treasury, all in the form of savings bank deposits: this implied net withdrawals because interest of £4.5m had been credited. In 1915, small investors contributed £33.5m. They subscribed to £40m of the Post Office issue of 4½ per cent War Loan, but much of this was financed by withdrawing savings from elsewhere; over the year, savings bank deposits fell by £6.5m, even after the crediting of the same £4.5m interest. In 1916, the Post Office issues of 5 per cent Exchequer Bonds 1920 were on offer from 10 January to 14 October (the prospectus was dated 4 January), 6 per cent Exchequer Bonds 1920 from 16 October to 30 December, and Certificates from 19 February 1916. The total contributed was £97.8m: of this, £11.9m came from increased savings bank deposits; £43.9m from the Post Office issues of Exchequer Bonds; £27.8m from Certificates of less than £500; and £14.3m from Certificates of £500. Of vouchers bought under the 4½ per cent War Loan scheme, £0.1m were surrendered for cash.[86]

Endnotes

1 Committee on War Loans for the Small Investor (Cd. 8146), *Interim Report*, 28 December 1915, and *Report* (Cd. 8179), 26 January 1916, .
2 *Government Departments Securities* (HCP 291), 23 June 1914.
3 POa, Post 30/3979, Turpin, 'Post Office Register', 11 August 1915, and 'Report of the War Loan (Supplemental Provisions) Committee', 6 November 1915.
4 Ibid., Blackett, Memorandum, undated, with covering letter, Sydney-Turner to Murray, 30 July 1915.
5 Ibid., War Loan (Supplemental Provisions) Committee, *Report*, 6 November 1915.
6 T 170/97, Bradbury, 'War Loans for the Working Classes', 16 November 1915.
7 *Hansard* (Commons), 7 December 1915, cols 1178–9.
8 Ibid., 22 November 1915, cols 28–9. The Chancellor's scheme was based on Bradbury's memorandum, 'War Loans for the Working Classes', 16 November 1915, in T 170/97.
9 Committee on War Loans for the Small Investor, *Report*.
10 T 170/97, Committee on War Loans for the Small Investor, Minutes of First Meeting, 13 December 1915.
11 Ibid., Minutes of First and Second Meeting, 13 and 16 December 1915.
12 The questions and the ministerial answers are in POa, Post 30/3172.
13 Horne (1947), pp. 305–6; POa, Post 30/3979, Davies, 'Savings Bank Limits: Proposed Extension or Removal for the Period of the War', 8 June 1915; Lloyds TSB Group Archives, TSBA Minutes, 13 and 20 May 1915.
14 T 170/82, Turpin to Davies, 12 May 1915, Davies to Turpin, 17 May 1915, and Turpin to Chancellor, 18 May 1915; POa, Post 30/3979, Davies, 'Savings Bank Limits: Proposed Extension or Removal for the Period of the War', 8 June 1915.
15 POa, Post 30/3979, Montagu to Postmaster-General, 9 June 1915.
16 Ibid., Postmaster-General to Chancellor, undated, but probably November or December 1915.
17 Committe on War Loans for the Small Investor, *Interim Report*.
18 POa, Post 30/3172, 'Removal of Limits for Savings Bank Deposits', notice issued to the press, 31 December 1915.
19 T 170/97, Bradbury, 'Rough Draft Report', 23 December 1915.
20 Ibid., Turpin, 'Interest payable on Savings Bank Deposits,' 9 December 1915.

21 Lloyds TSB Group Archives, TSBA, Minutes, 4 January 1916; T 170/97, Alexander Cargill, 'The War Loan and the Working Classes', undated; Thomas Jaffrey, Actuary of the Aberdeen Savings Bank, 'War Loans for Small Investors', 10 January 1916; John Mallaband, Sheffield Savings Bank, 'Scheme for Raising Money for War Purposes', 5 January 1916; W. Louis Lawton, York County Savings Bank, 31 December 1915.
22 T 170/97, Bradbury, 'Rough Draft Report', 23 December 1915; Committee on War Loans for the Small Investor, *Final Report.*
23 Committee on War Loans for the Small Investor, *Interim Report.*
24 Committee on War Loans for the Small Investor, *Final Report.*
25 T 170/97, Bradbury, 'Rough Draft Report', 23 December 1915.
26 Select Committee on Premium Bonds, *Report* (HCP 168), 16 January 1918.
27 T 170/97, Bradbury, 'Rough Draft Report', 23 December 1915.
28 Committee on War Loans for the Small Investor, *Final Report.*
29 *Hansard* (Commons), 18 May 1916, cols 1764–7.
30 Select Committee on Premium Bonds, *Report*, 16 January 1918, McKenna's evidence, paras 1231, 1232 and 1431–6; Cab. 41/37/10, 10 March 1916.
31 T 170/97, Committee on War Loans for the Small Investor, Minutes of Fifth Meeting, 22 December 1915, evidence of Albert Mansbridge; ibid., Seventh Meeting, 4 January 1916, evidence of Marion Phillips; ibid., Eighth Meeting, 12 January 1916, evidence of Margaret Bondfield.
32 *The Times*, 7 March 1916, p. 11; Sayers (1957), p. 60.
33 McKenna Papers, MCKW 5/10, Northcliffe to McKenna, 4 July 1915; Northcliffe Papers, Add 62157/193, McKenna to Northcliffe, 5 July 1915.
34 *The Times*, 2 March 1916, p. 13. See also *The Daily Mail*, 7 March 1916, p. 3.
35 T 172/285, Secretary of the Central Advisory Committee to Chancellor, 4 March 1916.
36 Ibid., 10 March 1916.
37 T 172/285, Secretary of the National Organising Committee for War Savings to Chancellor, 7 March 1916.
38 Ibid., note of 'The "City People"', undated, unsigned.
39 Ibid., Plender to Chancellor, 10 March 1916.
40 Ibid., Chancellor to Plender, 11 March 1916.
41 *Hansard* (Commons), 28 March 1916, cols 556–9, and 30 March 1916, cols 912–13.
42 Ibid., 18 May 1916, col. 1764.
43 T 171/110, Paish, 'The Finances of Great Britain', second half of April 1915.
44 The speech is reported in *The Times*, 30 June 1915, p. 10.
45 *The Economist*, 27 November 1915, p. 887.
46 CLCBt, 18 February 1916.
47 *Hansard* (Commons), 13 November 1915, col. 1754: T 170/97, Committee on War Loans for the Small Investor, Minutes of First Meeting, 13 December 1915.
48 LGP, D/13/1/1, Chiozza Money, 'Note on Practical Methods to be Adopted in Carrying out the Levy scheme', 13 December 1915.
49 Committee on War Loans for the Small Investor, *Final Report.*
50 T 170/97, 'Committee on War Loans for Small Investors [*sic*]: Memorandum Submitted by Mr. Mackinder M.P.', December 1915.
51 Committee on War Loans for the Small Investor, *Final Report.*
52 Osborne (1926), I, p. 406n. The paper has not been found.
53 *The Economist*, 11 November 1916, p. 913; *Bankers' Magazine*, August 1915, pp. 146–7; Ibid., September 1916, 'War Loans and the Passbook System', pp. 299–307; Ibid., January 1916, 'War Finance', pp. 50–1. His suggestions to the Montagu Committee are in T 170/97, 'War Finance', 14 December 1915.

54 See Fraser's articles, letters and the reports of his speeches and lectures: *The Manchester Guardian*, 8 September 1914, 14 March 1916, and 25 July 1917; *Daily Dispatch*, 25 July 1917; *The Economist*, 4 December 1915, p. 943; ibid., 13 May 1916, pp. 862–3; ibid., 2 March 1918, pp. 390–1; ibid., 10 August 1918, pp. 181–2; and ibid., 5 October 1918, p. 424; *Manchester Statistical Society*, 8 December 1915, 'Treasury War Bonds', pp. 25–39; Kirkaldy (1915), Appendix, pp. 251–3. Parts of some articles are reproduced in Fraser (1917). A suggestion sent to the Montagu Committee is in T 170/97, 'The Wage Earner and £1 War Bonds', 18 December 1915.
55 *Manchester Chamber of Commerce Journal*, August 1917, reproduced in Fraser (1917).
56 *EJ*, December 1915, pp. 560–1, 'British War Finance'; ibid., March 1916, pp. 1–19, 'Ways and Means', both reprinted in Foxwell (1919).
57 Osborne (1926), I, pp. 405–6.
58 *The Manchester Guardian*, 8 September 1914.
59 Kirkaldy (1915), Appendix, p. 252. Extracts were sent to Bradbury and are in T 170/97; *The Economist*, 25 September 1915, pp. 471–2.
60 T 170/97, Fraser to Bradbury, 29 November 1915; Fraser, *The Manchester Chamber of Commerce Journal*, August 1917. This is reproduced in Fraser (1917).
61 *The Economist*, 4 December 1915, p. 943. A draft, with a covering letter dated 29 November, was sent to Bradbury and, with other submissions by Fraser to the Montagu Committee, is in T 170/97.
62 National War Savings Committee, *First Annual Report*.
63 Neville Chamberlain Papers, 18/1/33, Neville Chamberlain to Hilda Chamberlain, 28 November 1915; Dilks (1984), p. 157.
64 Lloyds TSB Group Archives, Trustee Savings Banks Association, TSBA 1/1, Minutes of Meeting of Savings Banks having Special Investment Departments, 29 September 1914, and Minutes of the Committee appointed by Savings Banks having Special Investment Departments, 6 November 1914; T 133/1, Ramsay to Commissioners, 28 May 1915; T 160/714, Note of meeting between deputation from City Governments of Liverpool and Birmingham and Kershaw of the Local Government Board, 18 March 1916; T 160/1170/F4850/1, Blackett for McKenna and Montagu, 7 February 1916, and Bradbury to McKenna and Montagu, 14 March 1916.
65 T 160/1170/F4850/1, Blackett to Montagu, 7 February 1916, and Montagu to Chamberlain, 8 February 1916; T 160/714, Blackett, 'Proposed establishment of Savings Banks by municipalities for the promotion of War Savings', 23 March 1916. Horne (1947), p. 320, says that the provision of finance to Birmingham was not part of Chamberlain's scheme until after the war.
66 T 160/1170/F4850/1, Bradbury to Montagu, 29 February 1916, Bradbury to Chancellor and Montagu, 14 March 1916, and Montagu to Chamberlain, 21 March 1916.
67 T 160/714, Blackett, 'Proposed establishment of Savings Banks by municipalities for the promotion of War Savings', 23 March 1916, with comments by Bradbury, Montagu and the Chancellor.
68 CLCBm, 17 April 1916.
69 T 160/714, Montagu to Neville Chamberlain, 18 April 1916.
70 Ibid., Bell to Montagu, 17 April 1916.
71 Ibid., Bell to Montagu, 17 April 1916, Note by Hamilton of meeting with Vassar-Smith and Martin-Holland, 17 April 1916, and Montagu to Chamberlain, 18 April 1916; T 170/93, Martin-Holland to Chancellor, 18 April 1916; CLCBm, 28 April 1916.
72 Neville Chamberlain Papers, 18/1/58, Neville Chamberlain to Hilda Chamberlain, 29 April 1916.
73 CLCBm, 10 May 1916.

74 CLCBm, 28 June 1916; Dilks (1984), p. 169; Neville Chamberlain Papers, 18/1/58, Neville Chamberlain to Hilda Chamberlain, 29 April 1916; T 160/714, Note of meeting between the bankers, the Chancellor, Montagu and Bradbury, 31 May 1916, with note by Hamilton, 1 June 1916, and Martin-Holland to Bradbury, 29 June 1916. Dilks (1984), p. 170, writes that the change of mind 'probably owed much' to Austen's intervention and this is implied by the latter note. Also Dilks's view is borne out by a note in T 160/714 from Austen pressing the bank's case. The letter is on 10 Downing Street notepaper.
75 A briefing paper for the Chancellor on the first attempt to introduce the Bill in April is in T 171/134, 'Municipal Savings Banks (War Loan Investment) Bill'.
76 National War Savings Committee, *First* and *Second Annual Reports*.
77 Lloyds TSB Group Archives, TC/65/a/8.0, Leeds Skyrac and Morley TSB, Minute Book of the Committee of Management: Finance Sub-Committee and Property Sub-committee, 18 December 1916, 1 and 8 January and 26 February 1917; T 172/601, NDO to TSBs, February 1917. The version provided in Horne (1947), pp. 316–18, is imaginative. The TM establishing the Treasury Committee was dated 21 December 1916.
78 *The Times*, 24 July 1916, p. 5.
79 National War Savings Committee, *First Annual Report*.
80 T 170/97, Committee on War Loans for the Small Investor, Minutes of Sixth, Seventh and Eighth Meetings held on 23 December 1915 and 4 January and 12 January 1916.
81 Committee on War Loans for the Small Investor, *Final Report*.
82 Ibid. There are records in T 172/342 of the kind of problems met by the campaign. These describe the hostility found by the organisers in South Wales in June and July 1916 and the methods used to persuade local authority leaders to help.
83 National War Savings Committee, *First Annual Report*; *Hansard* (Commons), 21 June 1916, cols 281–2.
84 *The Times*, 29 May 1916, p. 8.
85 National War Savings Committee, *First Annual Report*.
86 Ibid., Table 1.

6 The beginning of overseas borrowing and the Anglo-French Loan

> It must be remembered that America is unaccustomed to lend money except upon collateral security and for its own internal and domestic purposes and in comparatively small sums. The banking and financial system in America is not adapted to transactions of such magnitude as a large external loan.
>
> 'Statement by Lord Reading', 29 October 1915, Cab. 37/136/39

When the war began, foreigners owned small amounts of Treasury Bills and gilt-edged securities, but there was no British government debt denominated in currencies other than sterling. On 31 March 1919, the foreign-currency debt had a nominal value of £1,292.8m (see Appendix III).[a] The debt returns identified only one security, the Anglo-French Loan issued in the autumn of 1915, of which the British moiety was £51.4m. The remainder was hidden, as it had been since the returns of 1916, in the anonymity of 'other debt' created under the War Loan Acts. It was not until 31 March 1920, by which time the total had fallen to £1,189.9m, that the individual components were published.[1] The debt was incurred in over a dozen countries, Dominions and colonies, and for a range of purposes: to support the sterling exchange rate; for raw materials and munitions of war; for produce from border neutrals, which would otherwise have been sold to the Central Powers; for sugar bought in the Dutch East Indies and grain bought in South America; and to finance the coupons on Russian external debt payable in Amsterdam. Borrowing from European neutrals started in 1916, beginning in the Netherlands, and expanding to include Denmark, Norway, Sweden, Switzerland and Spain. Japan, as well as making advances to Russia, lent to the UK. Later in the war, loans were taken, with American encouragement, from the Argentine and Uruguay. Within the Empire, Canada was Britain's largest creditor, but small loans were taken from Fiji, the Straits Settlements and Mauritius.

The largest lender was the USA, first its private capital markets, and then its Treasury. It had a large industrial base able to manufacture weapons of war and was endowed with the natural resources with which to supply raw materials and food. In 1914, it was in recession with the spare capacity to meet a sudden increase

a Unless otherwise specified, the rates used in the remainder of the book are pre-war par of exchange.

in allied buying. It was physically close, so minimising the use of scarce shipping space and the resources needed to protect vessels from attack. As the world's second largest economy, it supported a capital market which, although it sometimes groaned under the burden, was deep enough to absorb both the UK's holdings of American securities and its new debt issues. Finally, when it became a belligerent, its Treasury was able to tap an economy whose industrial plant and labour force were undamaged by war and thus lend to others on a scale which dwarfed that of any of the other allies except the UK itself. In the five years ending 31 March 1920, the British Government disbursed a net $10,384m in US dollars (Table 6.1). Nearly two-thirds, or $6,211m, went on supplies: food, raw materials and munitions. $642m was advanced directly to the allies in dollars and $3,056m was spent buying sterling. The dollars came from the sale of assets and gold, and from borrowing. $1,248m was raised from the sale of securities bought by the Bank in the London market during 1915 or acquired by the Treasury under purchase schemes introduced at the end of 1915; $1,208m came from gold shipments, much of the metal being acquired from the French and Russians in return for British advances, mostly in sterling, but also in dollars. $7,026m was borrowed, $4,277m from the US Treasury, and the remainder from the private sector: public loans, dollar Treasury Bills, credits extended by munitions contractors, Japanese

Table 6.1 British government transactions in the USA: 1915–16 to 1919–20 [years ending 31 March (US$m)]

	1916	*1917*	*1918*	*1919*	*1920*	*Total*
Receipts						
Exchange	26	31	8	411	185	663
Securities	271	564	173	88	152	1,248
Loans	427	1,358	2,828	1,740	673	7,026
Gold	48	878	254	–	28	1,208
Interest	–	2	6	5	5	18
US Shipping Board	–	–	82	–	–	82
Reimbursements	–	–	704	1,150	57	1,911
Other	1	–	21	28	1	51
Total	773	2,834	4,076	3,422	1,101	12,207
Expenditure						
Exchange	–	930	1,488	603	35	3,056
Supplies	435	1,373	1,843	2,281	279	6,211
Advances to Allies	163	474	5	–	–	642
Repayment of loans	143	102	529	436	569	1,779
Interest	–	27	96	183	139	445
Other	–	–	–	5	25	30
Total	741	2,906	3,961	3,508	1,047	12,163
Change in balances	+32	–72	+115	–86	+54	+43
Total	773	2,834	4,076	3,422	1,101	12,206

Source: T 170/134, ff. 3, 5, 7, 10 and 13, Chadwick, 'British Government Transactions in America', 1922.

Table 6.2 British government public issues in the US: 1915–19

$500m Anglo-French Five-Year 5% External Loan

Issued 15 October 1915 at 98 ($5.46 per cent). Price to underwriting syndicate 96 ($5.94 per cent). Selling commission: 3/4 per cent. Partly paid: calls 25 per cent on 15 October, 25 per cent on 15 November, and the balance on 15 December. Maturity 15 October 1920. Coupons 15 April/15 October. Convertible at par at holder's option into 4 1/2 per cent Bonds 1930–40, also at par. 'The Joint and several obligation of the Governments of the United Kingdom of Great Britain and Ireland and the French Republic'. Britain's half share $250m.

Members of the underwriting syndicate who were National Banks, together with some other institutions, were permitted to retain on deposit at 2 per cent the proceeds of their own participation.

Repaid: Converted $14,000. Balance paid off for cash on 15 October 1920.

$250m 5 per cent United Kingdom of Great Britain and Ireland Secured Gold Notes 1 September 1918

Issued 1 September 1916. Sold to underwriters at 98 ($6.06 per cent) and to public at 99 ($5.55 per cent). Commissions: 1/2 per cent to JPM.

Coupons 1 March/1 September. Redeemable prior to maturity: until 31 August 1917 at 101 and until 31 August 1918 at 100 1/2.

Repaid	*$m*
1916–17	54.8
1917–18	2.3
1918–19	192.9

Collateral. Group 1 $300m of not less than $100m stocks and Bonds and/or other securities of corporations organised in the USA; Group 2 of not less than $100m of Bonds and/or other obligations of the Dominion of Canada, either as maker or guarantor, and stocks and Bonds and/or other securities of the CPR; Group 3 of not less than $100m of Bonds and/or other obligations of the governments of Argentina, Chile, Norway, Sweden, Denmark, Switzerland and Holland, either as maker or guarantor.

$150m 5 1/2 per cent United Kingdom of Great Britain and Ireland Gold Notes 1 November 1919 and $150m 5 1/2 per cent United Kingdom of Great Britain and Ireland Gold Notes 1 November 1921

Issued 1 November 1916. Prices: three-year Notes at 97 3/4 ($6.34 per cent) to underwriters and 99 1/4 (5.79 per cent) to public; five-year Notes at 97 ($6.21 per cent) to underwriters and 98 1/2 (5.85 per cent) to public. Principal and interest payable, at the option of the holder, in either US dollars or sterling at a rate of $4.86 1/2.

Commissions. JPM 1/2 per cent. Allowance to offering group of 1/4 per cent at Morgans' discretion to meet expenses plus 1/8 per cent on sales.

Coupons 1 May/1 November. Principal and interest payable in dollars or, at holder's option, in sterling at $4.86 1/2.

Redeemable prior to maturity:

Three-year Notes	– until 31 October 1917 at 103
	– until 31 October 1918 at 102
	– until 31 October 1919 at 101
Five-year Notes	– until 31 October 1917 at 105
	– until 31 October 1918 at 104
	– until 31 October 1919 at 103
	– until 31 October 1920 at 102
	– until 31 October 1921 at 101

Table 6.2 continued.

Repaid	*Three-year ($m)*	*Five-year ($m)*
1916–17	18.7	18.1
1917–18	0.8	2.9
1918–19	–	–
1919–20	130.5	–
1920–21	–	17.6
1921–22	–	111.5

Collateral: Group 1 $360m of not less than $100m of US corporation Stocks, Bonds and/or other securities, including obligations of the CPR, plus not less than $80m of Bonds and/or other obligations, either as maker or guarantor, of the Dominion of Canada, the Colony of Newfoundland and/or Provinces of the Dominion of Canada and/or Canadian municipalities; Group 2 of $180m of Bonds and/or other obligations, either as maker or guarantor, of the governments of Argentina, Chile, Australia, South Africa, New Zealand, Japan, Egypt, Cuba and/or approximately $25m in Bonds or other obligations of dividend-paying British domestic railway companies.

$100m 5$^1/_2$ per cent United Kingdom of Great Britain and Ireland Gold Notes 1 February 1918 and $150m United Kingdom of Great Britain and Ireland Gold Notes 1 February 1919

Issued 1 February 1917. Sold to underwriters: one-year at 98.02 ($7.56 per cent) and two-year at 97.57 ($6.84 per cent). Sold to public: one-year Notes at 99.52 ($6.02 per cent) and two-year Notes at 99.07 ($6.01 per cent). Principal and interest on the Notes and Bonds, and the Bonds into which they might be converted, payable, at the option of the holder, in either US dollars or sterling at a rate of 4.86^1/_2$.

Commissions: JPM $^3/_8$ per cent. Allowance to offering group for expenses $^1/_4$ per cent, to be paid at Morgans' discretion.

Coupons 1 February/1 August. Convertible at par before maturity at holder's option into unsecured 5$^1/_2$ Treasury Bonds 1 February 1937, also at par.

Redeemable before maturity:

One-year Notes	– up to 31 January 1918 at 101
Two-year Notes	– up to 31 January 1918 at 102
	– up to 31 January 1919 at 101

Repaid	*One-year ($m)*	*Two-year ($m)*
1916–17	5.1	6.3
1917–18	94.2	0.5
1918–19	–	0.2
Converted		
1917–18	0.7	0.3
1918–19	–	142.9

Collateral. Group 1 $300m of not less than $150m of specified amounts of US Corporation Stocks, Bonds and other securities, securities of the CPR, the Dominion of Canada, Canadian provinces and municipalities and Newfoundland; Group 2 of not less than specified amounts of securities of the Argentinian Railways, the Grand Trunk Railway of Canada, the Argentine, Chile, Australia, New Zealand, South Africa, Egypt and Japan.

$250m United Kingdom of Great Britain and Ireland 5$^1/_2$ per cent Convertible Gold Notes 1 November 1922 and Convertible Gold Bonds 1 August 1929

Issued 1 November 1919. $101.621m three-year Notes sold to underwriters at 96$^1/_2$ ($6.83 per cent) and offered to the public at 98 ($6.26 per cent) and $148.379m ten-year Bonds sold to underwriters at 94 ($6.33 per cent) and sold to public at 96$^1/_4$ ($6.02 per cent).

Table 6.2 continued.

Commissions: Morgans 1/2 per cent plus 1/4 per cent to Managing Group, to be disbursed at Morgan's discretion.
Coupons 1 February and 1 August.
Convertible at holder's option into 5 per cent National War Bonds (Fourth Series), 1 February 1929, at fixed exchange rate of $4.30, e.g. $1000 Notes or Bonds for £232.12 National War Bonds, with the accrued interest adjustment paid in cash.
Repaid: $244.8m Notes and Bonds converted into £56.9m 5 per cent National War Bonds; $3.2m Notes and $2m Bonds were paid off at maturity.

British Government Dollar Treasury Bills
Ninety-day Bills placed from 24 August 1917 and the proceeds applied to the Morgan call loan. Instructions were given on 9 November 1921 to cease issuing and to repay maturities as they fell due. The last Bills were repaid at the end of January 1922.

Outstanding on selected dates ($m):

1917	
31 August	30.0
30 September	71.5
31 October	97.8
30 November	92.6
31 December	92.8
1918	
31 January	97.6
28 February	94.4
31 March	88.8
30 June	87.2
30 September	87.8
31 December	82.3
1919	
31 March	93.3
30 June	97.7
30 September	98.0
31 December	67.3
1920	
31 March	45.2
30 June	28.6
30 September	36.6
31 December	16.7
1921	
31 March	16.7
30 June	14.6
30 September	10.7
31 December	4.9

Sources: T 170/134, f. 29, Chadwick, 'British Government Transactions in America, 1922'; PML, Syndicate Books nos. 8 and 9; MGP, Brit. Gov. Loan 1, File 2; ibid., BG Loan 7, F. 6/3; ibid., BG Loan 1, File 3/2; ibid., BG Loan 2, File 4; ibid., B. Hist. 3, F. 26, no. 90782, MG to JPM, 9 November 1921; *BGS*, p. 226; *National Debt: annual returns;* prospectuses.

Table 6.3 UK Treasury borrowing in foreign currencies, or with foreign currency options, other than Canada: 1915–19

$50m Exchange Loan with New York Banks
Borrowed by a Committee of London Bankers from a Committee of American Bankers. 17 November 1915 at 4½ per cent for six months. Renewed 17 June 1916 at 5 per cent for one year.
Collateral: 4½ per cent War Loan 1925–45.
Proceeds held by LEC in New York and paid to UK Treasury on 13 July 1916.
Repaid: 17 June 1917.

E. J. du Pont de Nemours Powder Co.
$15.95m borrowed 2 October 1916 and repaid 2 October 1917.
$13m borrowed 15 December 1916 and repaid 15 December 1917.
$17.8m borrowed 15 March 1917 for one year, but repaid 28 February 1918.
Secured by 5 per cent one-year Treasury Notes. Interest paid half-yearly.

$6.5m borrowed 15 December 1917 and repaid 28 February 1918.
Secured by Treasury Bills under discount at 6 per cent.

Maitland Coppell and Co.
$4m advanced on 21 June 1916 to Messrs Robert Fleming and re-lent to the British government on the security of one-year sterling Treasury Bills. Against collateral of US securities owned by Robert Fleming. Interest 5 per cent.
Repaid: 21 June 1917.

Metropolitan Water Board (MWB)
$6.4m one-year Bills on 18 September 1916 placed through Guaranty Trust at discount rate of 6⅛ per cent. Dollars paid to Treasury in New York against sterling used to repay MWB Bills in London. At maturity, MWB would pay sterling to Treasury and Treasury repay the dollars. Both transactions at fixed rate of $4.76½; $6.3m renewed for twelve months on 18 September 1917 at discount rate of 7½ per cent.

English Sewing Cotton Ltd
$4.9m advanced on 1 December 1916 by JPM on security of $6m Common Stock of American Thread Co., which English Sewing Cotton had declined to deposit under Scheme B for fear of losing control of the company. Re-lent to the British government on the security of £1m twelve-months' Treasury Bills. Renewed 1 December 1917 and paid off on 1 December 1918.

6 per cent Yen Exchequer Bonds
¥100m issued 15 December 1916. Maturity 15 December 1919. Coupons 15 December/15 June. Bought by a syndicate of Japanese banks and resold to public at par. Proceeds remitted to New York and realised $49.5m.
Calls: 30 per cent on 15 December 1916 and 70 per cent on 15 January 1917.
Repaid: 15 December 1919.

Asiatic Petroleum Company (Royal Dutch Petroleum Company)
$14.209m in the form of purchases of one-year US dollar Treasury Bills dated 17 January 1917. Collateral of securities of Argentinian and Canadian railway companies. Repayable on six months' notice on either side. Rate of discount of 5 per cent. Renewed twice. Repaid: 17 January 1920.

Table 6.3 *continued.*

Central Argentine Railway
$15m 6 per cent ten-year Convertible Bonds issued at par in New York. The proceeds were advanced to the British government on 1 February 1917. The British government bought and cancelled the company's sterling debt and undertook to repay $15m at 102. Redeemable at option of the company on any interest date after five years. Repayable 1 February 1927 in dollars or sterling at $4.85 at option of holder. Interest 1 February/1 August.
Repaid: in 1926–7 financial year.

E. W. Bliss and Co.
$2.325m two-year Notes dated 2 April 1917. Interest 5 per cent payable 2 October and 2 April.
Repaid: 2 April 1919.

Rifle Contracts
$27.4m three-year Notes. Dated 21 October 1916, but issued between March 1917 and February 1918. Interest 5 per cent.
Repaid: $0.3m on 7 June 1918.
$27.1m on 21 October 1919.

Bethlehem Steel Co.
$37.3m two-year Notes. Dated 1 February 1917, but issued in 1917 and 1918. Interest 5 per cent payable 1 February and 1 August.
Repaid: 1 February 1919.

Marlin Arms Co.
$2m two-year Notes. Dated 30 April 1917, but issued 10 August 1917. Interest 5 per cent payable 30 April and 30 August.
Repaid: $0.6m on 27 January 1919.
$1.4m on 30 April 1919.

American Locomotive Co.
$2m two-year Notes in part payment for Russian shell contract. Dated 14 July 1917, but issued August and September 1917. Interest 5 per cent
Repaid: 14 July 1919.

British Government Yen Treasury Bills
¥80m one-year Yen Treasury Bills, with option of two renewals, sold to Japanese government and placed on market. Part of arrangement included the sale to the Japanese by the India Office of 30m rupees against another £2m of British gold. Issued 21 January 1918. Rate of discount 5½ per cent. Proceeds remitted to New York. On maturity, the proceeds were reinvested in ¥85.8m one-year Treasury Bills issued on 18 January 1919, also at a rate of discount of 6 per cent. Although the UK Treasury had the necessary dollars, the US Treasury advised against buying gold for shipment to Japan and on maturity ¥70m were reinvested in ¥20m Bills due 15 July 1920 and ¥50m due 14 January 1921.

$25m Danish Government Loan (Virgin Islands)
Loaned in US dollars via Hambros and British Bank of Northern Commerce. Secured on £5.5m Sterling Treasury Bills. None repayable before 1 January 1919, but from 1 July 1918 the loan could be called or repaid on six months' notice. In the event of peace, 20% repayable in one month, 40% in two months and the balance in three months. Interest 5 per cent calculated in US dollars, but payable in sterling.

Table 6.2 continued.

Received between 1 December 1917 and 3 April 1918.
Repaid: $12.5m in sterling 31 December 1919.
$12.5m in sterling 31 March 1920.

5 per cent Guilder Exchequer Bonds 7 November 1920 (Java sugar)
fl.23.4m (£2m). Issued 7 November 1917 at 97½. Interest 5 per cent. Principal and interest payable in sterling or guilders at fl.12. They could be repaid at any time if the rate of exchange for cable transfers was over fl.12.15. If thus repaid the price would be 98 in 1918, 99 in 1919 and 100 in 1920. Due date 7 November 1920.

Repaid	*fl.m*
1919–20	9.57
1919–20	4.92
1920–21	8.91

Dutch Government Loan (PoW) (advances for maintenance of British prisoners interned in Holland)
fl.8.1m advances by Dutch government starting at 4½ per cent and then at such rate as may be paid on new public loans raised in Holland: 5 per cent from 15 February 1919.

Advanced to 31 March 1919	fl.7.9m
1919–20	fl.0.2m

Repaid: 27 January 1920.

Guilder Exchequer Bonds 31 December 1923
fl.175m (£14.5m) loan from the Dutch government negotiated by Treasuries of USA, UK, France and Italy in December 1918. British share fl.75m (£6.2m) in form of 5 per cent Exchequer Bonds.
fl.50m (£4.1m) issued.
Purchased by the Dutch government at par between January and May 1919.
Option of repayment in sterling at fl.12 or, at any time, when the rate was fl.12.15 or above.
Maturity: any time on three months' notice from the borrower, but not later than 31 December 1923.
Repaid: 31 December 1919.

Norway
Nkr.40m (£2.2m) in June 1916 in the form of 90-day bills drawn half by Hambros and half by British Bank of Northern Commerce.
Collateral: Sterling Treasury Bills.
Term: renewable for up to two years.
Interest: ½ per cent over Norwegian Bank rate with a minimum of 5½ per cent.

Nkr.140m (£7.7m) in September 1916 from Norges Bank (the 'Leverton Harris' loan).
Collateral: Sterling Treasury Bills.
Term: one-half for one year (31 August 1917) and one-half for two years. That for one year extended to two years.
In July 1918 25 per cent repaid and remainder due 31 July 1919 or six months after the end of the war, whichever was the earlier. In July 1919 NKr.57m renewed for one year.
Interest: 1 per cent over Norges Bank [Bank rate] except that, when Bank rate was above 6 per cent, the margin became ½ per cent.

Nkr.51.5m (£2.8m) in May 1917 from the Central Bank of Norway in form of bills drawn one-half by Hambros and one-half by British Bank of Northern Commerce. Conditions: relaxation of British coal exports to Norway.

Table 6.2 continued.

Collateral: Sterling Treasury Bills.
Term: renewable for up to two years.
Interest: 1/2 per cent over Norwegian Bank rate with a minimum of 5 1/2 per cent.

Denmark
Dkr.20m (£1.1m) in June 1916 in the form of 90-day bills drawn half by Hambros and half by British Bank of Northern Commerce and a further Dkr.10m (£0.6m) in cash.
Term: renewable for up to two years. In November 1917, extended until declaration of peace by UK.
Collateral: Sterling Treasury Bills.
Interest: 1/2 per cent above Danish Bank rate with a minimum of 5 per cent.

Dkr.24m (£1.3m) in December 1917 in form of 90-day bills and a further Dkr.6m (£0.3m) in cash.
Term: renewable until declaration of peace by UK.
Collateral: Sterling Treasury Bills.
Interest: 1/2 per cent above Danish Bank rate with a minimum of 5 per cent.

Sweden
Skr.10m (£0.6m) overdraft arranged in July 1916 at 6 per cent.
Activated: December 1916.
Term: one months' notice.
Repaid: February 1917.

Skr.6.25m (£0.3m) monthly credit negotiated by Treasuries of USA, UK and France to be used for purchases in Sweden.
Signed 29 May 1918.
Terms for UK share:
Exchange on London above Skr.17.50.
Secured against Hambros three-year Promissory Notes, in its turn secured against British government 6 per cent three-year Swedish kronor Notes equal to 120 per cent of the loan outstanding.
Interest: cash credit rate of Swedish Central Bank for preceding half-year with a minimum of 5 1/2 per cent and a maximum of 7 1/2 per cent.
Repayable in Swedish kronor or sterling.
Outstanding: Skr.31.25m on 31 March 1919.
Repaid: Skr.18.75m in 1919–20 and the balance in 1921–2.
Under the same agreement, one-half of payments for iron ore could be made in one-year 6 per cent sterling Notes, with UK option to extend to 1 August 1920. Notes non-negotiable, nor usable as collateral, outside Sweden unless exchange rate reached Skr.17.50.

A similar arrangement for pulp and paper, except that Swedish exporters had option of depositing sterling with a UK bank for one year, renewable at UK Treasury's option for a further year.

A similar arrangement for one-half of the monies paid on account of losses of Swedish ships.

£2.7m outstanding on 31 March 1919 and none a year later. It is not clear to which of the three agreements this related.

Rio Tinto Co. (Spain)
Rio Tinto Co. issued a Spanish pta.50m (£2m) mortgage debenture secured on its Spanish mines and plant. The proceeds were advanced to the British government on 25 October 1918 on the security of £2.5m sterling Treasury Bills.

Table 6.2 continued.

Term: ten years with an option to repay at par at any time on three months' notice.
Interest: 6 per cent payable 1 January and 1 July.
Repaid: 31 December 1920.

Government of Argentina
Argentinian gold dollars 200m (US$193m) borrowed for two years from the Argentinian government at 5 per cent by the British and French governments on 15 January 1918. British share one-half (US$96.5m).
Repayment: on 15 May 1920, an Argentinian government loan for US$50m matured in New York. The Argentinians were unable to renew and the British arranged to pay it off, in effect repaying early $50m of the British debt to the Argentinians due 15 January 1921. The balance was repaid over three years by means of the British government paying the interest and sinking fund on Argentinian government debt held in the UK.
Terms: the Argentinians could draw on the French and British governments up to the amount of the loan when the rate of exchange on London did not exceed 50d and on Paris Ffr.5.60, subject to an undertaking that the proceeds would not be remitted to the USA.
Repaid: 15 January 1921.

Government of Uruguay
Arranged with the British and French governments. The UK had borrowed 19m Uruguayan pesos (£3.8m or US$18.4m) by 31 March 1919, rising to 24.6m (£4.9m or US$23.8m) by 31 March 1920. Fixed at 5 per cent. Due 6 December 1920.

Switzerland
Three-months' bills for Swfr.100m (£4m) drawn by four joint stock banks in London, renewable for up to a maximum of three years. First drawing 20 March 1918 and the last was paid off 20 March 1920.
UK Treasury indemnity to the banks.

Notes
$ denotes US currency unless otherwise specified.
Sterling and dollar equivalents are calculated at par of exchange.
In some cases, the date of the advance or loan was different from the date of issue of the securities. Interest accrued from the date of the advance or loan, but the debt was only taken into the accounts from the date of the issue of the securities. In only some cases have the differences been noted.
In some cases, it is not clear whether the interest is in the form of a discount in the price or interest on the principal. 'Interest' is used where there is an ambiguity.

Sources: PML, Syndicate Books Nos. 8 and 9; T 170/134, ff. 2-49, Chadwick, 'British Government Transactions in America'; FO 371/3118, no. 594, Treasury to FO, 24 February 1917; T 171/235, Blackett to Chancellor and Fisher, 17 April 1920; T 172/453, Bradbury to Blackett, 3 July 1919; FO 371/3115, no. 2689, Treasury to Spring-Rice, 10 July 1917; BoE, C91/1–20, LEC, Papers and Minutes, various dates; Osborne (1926), II, pp. 29-69; T 172/429, Lever's Diary, 18 June 1917; MGP, B. Hist. 2, F. 12, no. 22937, MG to JPM, 20 September 1916; ibid., F. 14, no. 33931, JPM to MG, 1 January 1917; ibid., F. 22, no. 70699, MG to JPM (Copy to Blackett), 29 November 1919 and no. 89314, JPM to MG (Copy to Blackett), 2 December 1919; ibid., no. 72053, MG to JPM, 24 December 1919; ibid., F. 24, no. 78235, MG to JPM, 7 May 1920; *The Economist*, 9 November 1918, p. 657; BoE, C98/6938; *External Debt as on 31 March 1919, 31 March 1920, 31 March 1921 and 31 March 1922* (Cmd. 1648), 1922; *National Debt: annual returns*.

Table 6.4 The Morgan call loans, 1916–19: amounts outstanding on selected dates ($m)

	No. 1 loan	*No. 2 loan*	*Total*
1916			
31 May	20	60	80
30 June	12	117	129
31 July	–	72	72
31 August	14	87	100
30 September	–	–	–
31 October	33	112	145
30 November	84	17	101
31 December	86	146	232
1917			
31 January	79	186	265
28 February	63	136	199
6 March	55	212	266
31 March	48	310	358
25 April	92	345	437
26 April	42	298	341
30 April	42	298	341
15 May	85	314	399
31 May	71	314	384
30 June	71	314	384
31 July	71	314	384
18 August	Merged		381
28 August			346
30 September			287
31 October			250
30 November			238
28 December			225
1918			
31 January			217
1 February			136
31 March			135
30 September			113
31 December			89
1919			
31 March			73
August			–

Note
Lines may not sum because of rounding.

Source: T 170/134, f. 28, Chadwick, 'British Government Transactions in America', 1922.

purchases of British dollar obligations and a call loan provided by a syndicate organised by the Treasury's American bankers, Messrs J. P. Morgan & Co. (Tables 6.2, 6.3 and 6.4).[2]

This chapter shows how the Anglo-French Loan issued in New York in the autumn of 1915 grew out of the mixture of neglect and indifference which characterised the Treasury's attitude to the exchange rate in the first year of the war. It then describes the negotiations over the Loan's terms and explains why it was so difficult to sell, why it was so weak in the secondary market, and the limiting effect it had on subsequent British borrowing. The reasons for borrowing in European neutral countries is discussed, and a brief outline provided of the more important operations. After the Anglo-French Loan had been issued, the British had no alternative but to borrow on collateral, both in the public markets and from the Morgan banking syndicate. A description of the terms of the mobilisation schemes which made British-owned foreign securities available to the Treasury ends the chapter.

Sterling: January to September 1915

On 15 January 1915, the Admiralty and the War Office appointed J. P. Morgan in New York as their Financial Agents, with responsibility for purchasing the departments' supplies in the USA.[b] In May, the French followed suit. There was no central account from which funds could be provided for departmental payments until August 1915, when the British Treasury Account was established, also with Morgans.[c] Until then the spending departments bought their dollars in the open market, finding it increasingly difficult to satisfy their needs, even when they had driven sterling to cheaper levels. The J. P. Morgan partnership, whose senior was Jack Morgan, was the half-owner of the London merchant bank, Morgan Grenfell, whose resident senior partner was Edward Grenfell, a director of the Bank of England and one of the few bankers to enjoy a close personal relationship with

b For brevity, it is assumed that instructions were given direct to J. P. Morgan in New York. In fact, neither the Bank nor the Treasury spoke or cabled to them directly. Morgan Grenfell in London, with their own code free from the censor's interference, sent and received messages, passed on market and political news, and relayed enquiries and purchasing orders for government departments. Grenfell interpreted and advised the Bank and Treasury on policy in the light of information from New York, showing ministers and officials a judicious selection of the telegrams, which were sometimes sent at his request to make a point.

c The Treasury Account was established to hold its dollar balances. Into it were paid the proceeds of debt issues, gold shipments, the sale of British-owned American securities and, in due course, advances from the US Treasury. From it were paid loan charges, dollar advances to the allies and sums to support the exchange rate. From it also came expenditure on supplies: when the Commercial Agency Account was in deficit, it was replenished from the Treasury Account. When the Treasury Account was insufficient, and provided there were securities available to act as collateral, Morgans were to make an advance. T 170/62, Treasury to MG, 30 August 1915.

Cunliffe.[d] With their purchasing contracts for the allies and the connection with their sister business in Paris, Morgan Harjes & Cie, the Morgan Houses had a full picture of allied ordering and the demand for dollars that was being unleashed. Between February and August 1915, the partners in London and New York experienced growing alarm at the exchange position, but were unable to induce a similar anxiety in the Treasury in Whitehall:

> Chancellor of Exchequer and colleagues so fully occupied other matters that cannot give proper attention to this matter and we think exchange position may have to become worse before proper remedies taken. This may appear to you very foolish procedure but from your own experience dealing with Government Officials you will understand it is often impossible to make them appreciate a difficult situation especially on such complicated matter as exchange[3]

was Grenfell's description of the Treasury's state of mind in February 1915, an attitude that was maintained until, as he foretold, the position worsened and events forced a change.

The first dollars were borrowed for the support of the exchange rate and were organised by, and in the name of, the Bank of England. Morgans believed that a long-term loan – securities issued in the public market – would be necessary but, until this could be arranged, they proposed a temporary expedient: a 'Trio' of themselves, First National Bank and National City Bank, acting as fiscal agents of either the government or the Bank, would advance dollars in the form of a demand loan and buy sterling bills offered in New York. On 18 February, without being able to speak to the Chancellor, the Governor gave Morgans instructions to spend up to $10m buying sterling at rates beneath $4.82. This was quickly exhausted and the Bank sanctioned further amounts at lower levels so that, by 14 August, Morgans had sold some $154m. On 11 May, the Bank gave instructions for the first shipment of gold from the depot in Ottawa and by 21 June these had reached $47.5m.[4] The gold, the sale of US securities by British investors to apply for 4¹/2 per cent War Loan and the general tightening of the London markets it produced relieved the pressure for a few days and Morgans' advance was cleared on 26 July by a purchase of $12.2m against sterling.[5]

At the end of that month, sellers once more appeared and in the first half of July Morgans became increasingly anxious, especially as they had instructions from the Treasury to sell £12m, despite a thin market, to meet a down payment on a munitions contract for the Russians.[6] On 21 July, fearing the rate was about to break, Grenfell by-passed the Governor and saw the Prime Minister and Chancellor. The following day, having arranged for Henry Davison, one of Morgans' most senior partners, to send a suitably depressing cable on conditions in the New York

d Florence Grenfell, Edward's wife, was the niece of Cunliffe's first wife, Mary Henderson, who died in 1893.

market, he again saw the Chancellor, and was able to report that 'I have at last got a move on here and have I hope thoroughly alarmed the authorities'. A month later, he added 'They were rather outraged and considered me an alarmist, but I woke them up for a time, and only for a time.' It was only when the exchange broke that they 'came thoroughly to heel.'[7]

That July Morgans offered to advance \$50m, but conditions had changed. Hitherto, the advances had been secured by part of the Bank's holding of 3½ per cent War Loan 1925–8 – the British government's own sterling debt – with an understanding that there was gold cover in Ottawa. Most of the gold having been sold, Morgans now asked for American securities. In a well-known episode, \$40m was provided by the Prudential Assurance Company after a meeting between its senior officers and the Chancellor,[e] the balance coming from £5m of the Bank's gold.[8]

In the middle of August, sterling was approaching \$4.70 and Morgan's loan to the Bank had been resurrected, reaching \$42.4m. Against this, Morgans held securities with a loanable value of \$26m, there was \$5m of gold in transit and the Commercial Agency Account (the operating account for British munitions purchases) had a balance of only \$3.9m. Payments for the week beginning 16 August were forecast to be \$17m. On 14 August, Davison asked for more collateral and Grenfell warned Lloyd George, now Minister of Munitions, that the Morgan loan facility was almost exhausted.[9] On the same day, Cunliffe, having failed to persuade the Chancellor to assume responsibility for the Bank's losses on its sterling purchases, promised Morgans that the Bank would ship gold or securities to make good the collateral and asked Grenfell to instruct Morgans not to advance more than \$50m. In other words, they were to cease buying sterling when the credit had risen by another \$7.6m. Grenfell added the advice, apparently on his own initiative, that 'If you have not already expended whole \$50m loan I think you had better retain some unexpended balance for Commercial Agency payments'.[10] Without support from the Bank, sterling fell further, briefly reaching a low point on 2 September of \$4.53, before improving as McKenna, pressed hard by the bankers, at last took action and the newly established Treasury Account began supplying the dollars to meet some of the major departmental purchases.[11]

On 18 August, following advice from Morgans, the Cabinet had agreed that American securities should be purchased from their British owners for use in New York and that £100m in gold should be shipped. The British contribution would be £40m, raised equally from the Bank of England and the joint stock banks. It was hoped that the remainder would be contributed by the allies.[12] The following day, the Chancellor went to Boulogne to meet the French, where it was agreed that each should hold \$200m of gold for shipment when the Bank of England, in consultation with the Banque de France, judged it necessary, and that

e The Company agreed to sell \$38.9m and £0.7m securities for a cash sum of £8.4m. The valuation was not based on market prices, but on their value at a running yield of 4½ per cent. Payment was made in a special issue of sterling Treasury Bills. BoE, C40/729, Bradbury to Governor, 26 July 1915, and Nairne to Bradbury, 28 July 1915.

the Russians should be asked to do the same. It was also agreed to send an Anglo-French mission to New York to negotiate a loan, whose proceeds would be shared between the British, French and Russians in proportion to the amount of gold each supplied.[13] On 30 September, the Anglo-Russian Financial Agreement (the 'Treasury Agreement') was signed, by which the British agreed to lend Russia £25m a month against the deposit of one-year Russian sterling Treasury bills. The arrangement was to run for twelve months, but for the second six months it would depend on the British financial position in the USA. Russia would hold £40m of gold for export to the USA, of which £20m would be available before 31 March 1916. The transaction took the form of a purchase of British Exchequer Bonds repayable in gold after three years, which permitted the gold to be treated as a loan, to be unwound as the Bonds matured, and an unchanged holding to be shown in the Russian central bank's published balance sheet.[14]

The Anglo-French External Loan (1 November 1915)

From the start, it had been understood that the Morgan loan was a stopgap, to be repaid from the public issue of longer-dated debt as soon as markets allowed.[15] For six months, as conditions deteriorated, Morgans took the initiative. As with the exchange position, they found it impossible to make the Chancellor understand that a decision was necessary. Morgans' proposals always seemed either too expensive, or too small, or too short, or coincided with a temporary recovery in the exchange rate.

In February, Morgans reported that they could sell between $100m and $200m unsecured Notes, with maturities of between six months and two years, at yields of between 4¼ per cent and 5¼ per cent. This was not only short but, to those raised in a world of fixed exchange rates, expensive; on 23 February, six-months' sterling Treasury Bills were sold at a rate of discount of £1 12s 3d per cent and twelve months' at £2 17s 1d per cent.[16] Instead of a New York issue, the Bank tightened the sterling money markets (see pp. 93 and 96). At the beginning of April, the Chancellor, urged by Jack Morgan, asked for a proposition. The French and, especially, the Russians had been damaging allied credit in New York by seeking loans from all and sundry: the latter had been borrowing small amounts at very high rates and offering to settle purchases with Treasury Bills. Morgans were trying to issue $50m one-year 5 per cent Notes for the French and were about to admit that they could only sell $26.5m, and that at a higher yield than originally envisaged.[17] The indication given to the British was for an unsecured $50m ten-year Bond taken firm by a syndicate, with an option to take a further $100m. The yield would need to be about 5 per cent to the public and the cost to the borrower 5.38 per cent after commissions of 3 per cent. Coupled with this would be a firm offer to take $50m one-year Notes at 5 per cent. Thus, there would be a certain $100m and a possible $200m. Jack Morgan urged acceptance, emphasising that the pool of money for lending to belligerents was limited and that there was competition from other governments. The Treasury hesitated. The New York market had strengthened, enabling more British-owned securities to be sold, and the proposition was not obviously attractive. It would cost 1 per cent more than borrowing in sterling and this, said the Governor, was hard to justify and might antagonise British lenders. Half was for a very short period. Moreover, even \$150m (£31m) did not look large to a Treasury spending £2½m per day.[18] Jack Morgan's diagnosis was that the Treasury:

> would prefer take the chance of somewhat less favourable rate in America later on, should it at that time become desirable to get help there...Russia paying such very high rates, and France paying substantially more than normal, it is very possible American public will be educated on wrong lines and feel that all belligerent credit should be at considerably higher rates...Believe, however, they will face this chance rather than do now what they think would be a mistaken operation.[19]

The new Chancellor, McKenna, settled in, the question was resurrected by the Governor and Grenfell in the middle of June. Confidence had deteriorated further: sterling continued to weaken and it was widely known on Wall Street that the allies were spending dollars freely. There were reports of disagreements between British politicians, military leaders and newspaper proprietors, the Germans were rolling the Russians back from Poland and sales of securities by British investors, which Morgans thought might be running at between \$3m and \$5m a day, were producing indigestion in New York.[20] With both the risk and the size of the financing becoming greater, thoughts were turning to collateral: a 5 per cent one-year Note secured on US railway Bonds was being sold by Rothschild Freres for the account of the French Treasury and meeting an enthusiastic response: it was increased from \$30m to \$40m on 15 June.[21] Enquiries did, indeed, show a waning appetite for unsecured paper and the Trio proposed a \$75m ten-year 5 per cent issue, to be sold to a syndicate at 97 and to the public at par. The cost to the British would be 5.35 per cent: if it was a combined Franco-British loan, the size might be expanded to \$100m. With sterling strengthening as British investors sold US securities to buy the new War Loan, the Treasury once again balked.[22] By 9 July, after a New York partner, Thomas Lamont, had returned from Chicago to report that there was no interest in British paper in the mid-west, Morgans were beginning to think that even these terms were too optimistic.[23] On 17 August, in the same cable which forced the Cabinet to take its first measures to support the exchange rate, they advised abandoning any idea of an unsecured Loan and starting the collection of securities for a secured issue. In the meantime, their own advance should be expanded to \$100m, against collateral. The only feasible unsecured public borrowing would be for only one year, and even that would cost the Treasury 6½ per cent.[24]

A weak sterling exchange rate, difficulties finding the dollars with which to pay on contracts, issuing terms which had steadily deteriorated during the previous seven months and a clear need to borrow did not augur well for the Anglo-French Mission, which arrived in New York on 10 September. The British members were Reading, Blackett, Holden and Sir Henry Babington Smith; the French were represented by Octave Homberg from the Quai d'Orsay and Ernest Mallet, a banker. Holden was not a happy choice. The obvious banker would have been the Governor, but he enjoyed the worst of relations with McKenna and could not easily be described as diplomatic: his behaviour on missions later in the war confirms that his exclusion was a sound decision. Grenfell could not have been selected: the City was jealous of Morgans, they had many enemies, and their purchasing contract had been under political attack. Later, McKenna told Grenfell that the jealousy of both Cunliffe and Morgans in the City had led him to ask the other bankers to select a candidate and that they had nominated Holden. The CLCB's minutes confirm Holden's jealousy of Morgans, that its members had endorsed him in the warmest terms and that they had suggested Babington Smith. The minutes also show that the bankers juxtaposed Holden's appointment with their agreement to contribute £20m of their gold for export to the USA.[25]

Holden and the French appear to have been caught up in the anti-German fever. Holden began by insulting Cassel, who was not a member of the Mission, but was travelling on the same boat. Cassel was a German Jew who had been naturalised in 1878, a prominent financier, and a friend of Reading. He was also a long-standing friend of Jacob Schiff, the senior partner of Kuhn, Loeb & Co., who was a powerful influence in the New York Jewish banking community. Holden continued to behave badly when he arrived in New York. No doubt the introductions were not helped when Morgan's American partners received hostile briefings from Grenfell, who clearly loathed him. Reports soon came back both to the City and the Treasury that Holden had insulted Jack Morgan, his partners, Babington Smith and Blackett. At one point, Jack Morgan reported that he had wanted to 'punch his head' and that he (Holden) had behaved so rudely that Reading had taken him to one side and given him a dressing-down. More than one member of the Mission would agree, wrote Blackett, that his behaviour had cost a point in the price.[26]

Schiff's unwillingness to participate[f] reflected the fierce rivalry between Morgans and those banks on Wall Street who were not their associates and anxiety that the Loan would be used to aid Russia, with its history of pogroms.[27] This was just one of several ethnic problems facing the Mission: the issue was opposed both by the politically powerful Catholic Irish and the Germans, many of whom had settled in the mid-west and would help ensure that little of the Loan was underwritten, let alone sold, outside the east coast. Also affecting attitudes in the mid-west was the hostility of the Chicago meat packers, who had had cargoes confiscated by the British Prize Court when they had tried to run meat products through Copenhagen into Northern Germany.[28] A campaign against the Loan was waged by the German-language press, banks being threatened with the withdrawal

f Schiff's hagiographer says that Schiff was sympathetic, but would not help unless the French and British guaranteed that no part would be made available to the Russians. He also says that Morgans advised that it would not be possible, even with collateral, to raise more than $250m. When Reading talked to other banks to check this advice, Schiff's junior partners said that $500m was possible without collateral. The date of this advice is not given. Adler (1929), II, pp. 249–53.

of deposits if they participated. There was other opposition from isolationists, the Hearst Press and pacifists, such as Henry Ford. More parochially, there was resistance from oil companies, which had had their London company's tankers requisitioned. The decision to use Morgans carried its own risks. They were the most successful and powerful bank on Wall Street and had won many enemies in the course of their rise. They were Republicans, political enemies of the Democratic Wilson administration. To it, and to those in the mid-west, the west and the south who traditionally mistrusted east coast bankers, Morgans epitomised the power of Wall Street. Then there were the financial and legal problems, some of which the Treasury had experienced earlier in the year. Morgans had repeatedly told the British authorities that Americans were not accustomed to overseas investments and expected much higher returns than those customary in the sterling markets. The structure of the investing and risk-taking institutions was different. Deposits were widely dispersed in over 25,000 banks. The National Bank Act was believed to forbid national banks from lending more than 10 per cent of their capital and surplus to any one person, company, firm or corporation and the same rule was applied 'with some elasticity' to state banks and trust banks. It was not until the end of September that the Comptroller of the Currency ruled that a government was not to be considered as falling within the limitation.[29] Until then, if every bank in the country took up to its legal limit, it would only amount to $350m.[g] Unlike the sterling markets, Bond issues were generally made on collateral. Finally, the Mission was wanting an unprecedented sum.[30]

Unless the private cables from Morgan Grenfell in London to their partners in J. P. Morgan in New York were designed to mislead, the Chancellor and Governor directed Reading before he sailed not to approach other banks, but to open negotiations immediately with Morgans and the Trio.[31] Otherwise, the instructions given to Reading by the Treasury have left no trace. Perhaps there were none. The Mission thought that £200m (say $1,000m) was necessary to restore the exchange rate and meet immediate commitments, but, at an early stage of the negotiations, Reading cabled the Chancellor that it was too large to be raised by public issue and additional forms of credit might have to be used.[32] The Chancellor agreed, but pointed out that the amount might be found in instalments rather than in a single issue:

> After consultation with Montagu and Bradbury I think that it is so important to establish the fact that a loan can be raised in America that the opportunity should not be lost even if only £100,000,000 can be obtained at the present time. It is moreover very important both for France and ourselves that the nominal rate of interest should if possible not exceed five per cent.[33]

Such points of principle might have been expected to have been part of the

g Reading told the Cabinet in October that the maximum capacity of New York City under this rule was less than $150m. Cab. 37/136/39, 'Statement by Lord Reading', 29 October 1915.

Mission's briefings before it left London. If there had been such, it would also have covered the various propositions produced by Morgans since February. As it was, it took several days for the Mission to realise that £200m was completely beyond the capacity of the market and that any coupon under 5 per cent was unrealistic.[34]

The negotiations started immediately the Mission arrived on 10 September and lasted for a fortnight. A suggestion being bandied in the press, that the issue was to be secured, was the first condition to be dealt with: Reading just told Morgans that collateral was 'impossible'.[35] The Mission also successfully resisted an option to convert into any subsequent obligation issued in the USA with a life beyond 1920 and priority over internal borrowing of both countries. A conversion option into a longer, pre-determined, issue seems to have been agreed without argument. Nor, once the Mission had rejected Morgan's initial suggestion of a three-year life, did the date seem to have been in dispute: the Chancellor believed that five or ten years should be selected according to cost.[36]

It was around the size and the price, with a 5 per cent coupon, that the negotiations revolved. Morgans judged that $250m would be sufficient to control the exchanges for a time and might allow the price to rise to a small premium, thus leaving the door open to further borrowing. They also believed that $500m was beyond the capacity of the banks and the placing power of any issuing House. It would be necessary to attract the general public in competition with high-grade domestic Bonds yielding 5 per cent. This would need education – an expensive sales campaign – and a low price, perhaps as low as 96. The Mission thought $250m to be far too small and that the yield would spoil the credit of their respective Treasuries when raising money on their own markets: the French members of the Mission put greater emphasis on the size than the cost. [37]

Jack Morgan later described the discussions as 'interminable'.[38] Morgans' first suggestion had been for a 5 per cent three-year Note with an option to convert at maturity into ten-year Bonds at 5 per cent or fifteen-year Bonds at 4½ per cent. The Mission countered with half the issue for five years and half for ten.[39] The following day, Morgans came back with 5 per cent for five years with an option to convert into 4½ per cent Bonds 1930–40. The price to the purchasing syndicate and, therefore, to the borrower, would be 97½ and they thought they might be able to handle $500m.[h] The Chancellor considered this acceptable, but on further investigation Morgans found they had been too optimistic and that the market would only take $250m at the price. They said they would be prepared to try $500m if the price was made 96 to the syndicate, who would then sell to the public at 97½. The Mission countered with 97½ to the syndicate and 99 to the public and there was deadlock.[40]

By this time, the initial enthusiasm had evaporated and the momentum was

h This is consistent, except in its size, with a cable from J. P. Morgan to Morgan Grenfell on 23 September, which refers to $250m 5 per cent five-year Notes at 97½ to the syndicate and, perhaps, around par to the public, convertible into 4½ per cent Bonds 1930–40. MGP, B. Hist. 1, F. 7, JPM to Grenfell, 23 September 1915.

draining away. Morgans' group of bankers feared that, unless a decision was made at once, the project would have to be called off. On 23 September, Jack Morgan saw Reading alone and put three propositions to him. These so shocked Reading that, at first, he was not even prepared to communicate them to the British and French governments. The following day Jack Morgan put the offers into writing.[41] First, Morgans would try to form a syndicate to buy $500m at a price of 96, which would then offer that amount to the public at 98 – a plan, he wrote, 'best calculated to fulfil your desires'. Second, they would try to form a syndicate to buy $250m at 96½, which would then offer $500m to the public at 98½. The second $250m would not be taken firm, but, if sold, would be bought by the syndicate at 97; sales to the public would be divided equally between the half bought outright and the second $250m. Thus, if all $500m of the issue was sold, the average price would be 96¾. Third, they would try to form a syndicate to buy $250m at 97½ for resale at 99 or 99½. He also warned that 'the situation is daily looking less favourable...failure on your part to reach a speedy decision will...lead to a situation so difficult as to make a successful operation of such a magnitude for this country almost impossible'.[42]

Even after reflection, Reading did not consider it worthwhile to pass the last two proposals to the Chancellor, cabling on 24 September of the first proposal,

> Position becomes more imperative. Have we your authority to accept these terms if we find that no better terms are obtainable. We cannot get immediate contract as already explained even (? at these) figures and may have difficulty to complete amount but it is the best chance.[43]

The same day, the Chancellor agreed to the first alternative, $500m 5 per cent five-year Bonds at 96 ($5.94 per cent) to the syndicate and 98 ($5.46 per cent) to the public, and on Saturday, 25 September, Reading told Morgans to proceed. A week later, the Cabinet endorsed the decision, although with 'some reluctance'.[44]

The standard practice in New York was for the bank or banks to buy an issue outright – underwrite it, in the local parlance – for resale to the investor.[i] If the issue was large or particularly risky, a bank might bring in others as underwriters and become a manager of a syndicate of underwriters. The underwriters received

i The issuing terminology was used loosely. Morgans and their Management Syndicate would contact their associates and persuade them to purchase part of the Loan. The Syndicate and their associates, having bought the Loan, could either sell it to the investing public or withdraw it – either because they wanted to hold it as an investment or because they were unable to find buyers. Although it was buying the Loan outright, and not just agreeing to take it should it fail to find buyers among the investing public, the formation of the Syndicate was called 'underwriting'. For stylistic reasons, 'buying syndicate' and 'underwriting' will be used in the same sense both in this chapter and in Chapter 8. The terms were used with precision in the written agreements and press release. Examples of correct, or explicit, use are to be found in FO 371/2589, no. 1495, Reading to Chancellor, 27 September 1915, and no. 1511, Babington Smith to Chancellor, 29 September 1915.

payment for their services in assuming the risk and finding buyers by taking the difference between the price they paid the borrower when purchasing the securities and the price they charged investors: an organising, managing or initiating bank might take an additional payment in the form of the difference between the price it paid the borrower and the price paid by its syndicate, or as a straight commission. In addition, a 'selling' commission might be charged when a borrower was unknown, or an issue particularly difficult and expensive to retail. These differences were called 'compensation'. They were taken when the securities were issued and represented a reduction in the price and a commensurate increase in the GRY being paid by the borrower. Because UK borrowing in 1915 and 1916 was short-dated, the effect was to open up very large differences between the GRY being bought by the investor and the GRY being sold by the UK Treasury (Table 6.2).

As the Anglo-French Loan was both large and risky, Morgans acted as agents for a Syndicate of Managers, which they expected to form once they had negotiated terms with the Mission. It was envisaged that the Syndicate, in its turn, would form a larger underwriting syndicate drawn from all over the USA to buy the issue: until this wider syndicate had contracted to purchase the securities, the risk of not obtaining the money lay with the British and French governments.

Formation of the underwriting syndicate began on 30 September and was completed, to Morgans' relief, on 5 October.[45] It comprised 1,570 individuals, banks and companies managed by sixty-one banks, trust companies and investment houses in New York City.[46] In creating the Managing Syndicate and the buying syndicate, Morgans were using knowledge, goodwill and skills acquired over many years. It involved discovering from potential members of the Managing Syndicate the terms on which they would buy the Loan themselves and find others who would do the same. Clearly, this exercise involved divulging the terms which were being discussed with the borrowers. Testing ideas was dangerous, but necessary if the demand at various combinations of coupon, price and maturity was to be gauged. One of the skills was judging how much each bank could be told: in the wrong hands, news of terms being mooted would quickly spread, giving a handle to criticism from traditional competitors, German sympathisers, isolationists and pacifists. This could break the momentum of the publicity campaign and damage the chances of another approach on different terms. Another skill lay in judging the reliability of the information being offered. Potential underwriters were always trying to work up the terms. Morgans were always trying to assess how much was bluff, how reliable were those whose views they were canvassing, whether they could really vouch for the sale of the amount of the Bonds they were promising or whether, having taken their compensation, they would throw them back onto the secondary market. Even if he was to be judged a man of straw on this occasion, was the underwriter so large, or so important, or so powerful, that he had to be given some of the Anglo-French business because he would be vital to underwriting other issues in the future? In the background was a relationship with Morgans and the managing banks: the profits which Morgans had given them, and they had given Morgans, on past business; the hope of profits on future business; the threat that attractive opportunities would be denied them in the future, and the judgement of whether the threat was real. The size and the risks meant that Morgans and their associates were calling in the capital, the goodwill, accumulated over the years. Despite this, and their difficult relations with the Anglo-French Mission, Morgans regarded the issue to be so important that they waived the traditional management commission.

The underwriting syndicate had two characteristics: it came overwhelmingly from the east coast and it was composed of large individual commitments. One hundred and two underwriters took $404m. New York banks and Trust companies underwriting $1m or more were responsible for $191m. Those with whom Morgans had close associations behaved handsomely: the other members of the Trio – the National City Bank and First National Bank – took $32m and $15m. Chase National Bank took $17m, Bankers Trust $10m and Guaranty Trust $15m. There was only one large Chicago bank on the list, the Central Trust Co. of Illinois, for $0.9m. Morgans started by putting themselves down for $10m, while agreeing to hold themselves in reserve for $25m. These, however, were no more than the normal capacity of the market and the issue's size meant that Morgans had to reach further, especially as banks in so much of the country refused to participate. As would have been customary, a week before terms had been agreed, they had compiled a list of potential underwriters, and made a judgement, based on experience, of the amount for which each might be responsible. As well as traditional participants, the list included companies with allied contracts. In the long run, this could turn out to be costly because the contractors would expect wider profit margins on future allied business to compensate them for taking securities with both a credit and a price risk, in the place of cash; but needs must. At first, Morgans had hopes that the manufacturers would underwrite $150m, about 15 per cent of the value of their contracts. Not all would or could contribute: some were only being kept afloat by their bankers, and others, such as the Chicago meat packers, were unfriendly, although enjoying the business the allies brought. To Morgans' disappointment, the contractors took only $90m, of which the Du Pont interests were responsible for $42.5m and Bethlehem Steel (after pressure from Morgans) $20m.[47] Morgans also approached rich individuals, at one time considering pressing the British members of wealthy American families into the syndicate; of the larger participants, Cassel took $5m, John D. Rockefeller $10m, Daniel Guggenheim $5m and Henry Frick $1m.

Underwriters were found for just $512.3m, a total which fully justified both Morgans' anxiety and their advice that the issue was beyond the capacity of the market. Anxiety continued after the formation of the underwriting syndicate on 5 October for, in London, the autumn budget measures were being carried through the Commons and enabling legislation could not be introduced until 12 October: it received the Royal Assent the following day.[j] Later, Morgans had to step into

j The American Loan Act 1915.

the breach when the contract was actually signed on 14 October. They had not yet received all the signed Syndicate Agreements, but were relying on assurances given over the telephone or by cable. This was necessary, but risky, when adverse war news could break at any time, and when there were many participants with whom Morgans had not worked before; strictly, it left that amount of the Loan unbought. To avoid delay, Morgans took responsibility for the missing Agreements, amounting to $162.4m. That the risk was real is confirmed by a discrepancy between the total underwritten when the lists closed and the final figures. On 5 October, underwriting was $508m, but included nothing from Morgans. The final list totalled $512.3m, including $30.2m from Morgans, its partners and clients. About $25m appears not to have been confirmed.[48]

The underwriters offered the Loan to the public for three months, between 14 October and the dissolution of the syndicate on 14 December. The tone of the offer was set in the announcement that the underwriting syndicate was to be formed:

> The proceeds of the loan will be employed exclusively in America for the purpose of making the exchange rate more stable, thereby helping to maintain the volume of American exports.[49]

The issue, it was stressed, was a matter of business, with sentiment playing no part. It was not a loan to finance a war, but a commercial necessity to finance America's best customers, who were playing such an important part in pulling the economy out of recession. The USA was running an enormous current account surplus and capital had to flow the other way to balance the account. Every penny would be spent in the USA.[50]

Although Morgans' immediate circle of bankers believed the Loan was cheap, the approach did not work.[51] Of the $512.3m agreements to underwrite, $296.4m was withdrawn from sale by members of the syndicate who had decided to hold the securities as an investment. Du Pont retained $28m (some of which was later paid to shareholders in lieu of dividends), but Bethlehem threw back all its $20m. Frick kept his $1m and Guggenheim and Cassel half of their $5m. Morgans and their clients kept $13.6m, National City Bank $17.6m and First National Bank $11.6m. Sales to the public of the $215.9m not withdrawn was miserably slow. At the beginning of November, Morgans predicted that between $150m and $200m would come back to them for disposal: on 4 November, sales were only $10m and on 15 December $12m. The excess underwriting of $12.3m was treated as if it had been an application from the public and was added to the $12m actually subscribed, so that the subscription became $24.3m.[k] It was the problem Morgans had predicted: the net had been spread so wide that most potential investors had already received as underwriters any of the securities they wanted.[52]

At the end of November, Homberg prompted Sir Paul Harvey, who had been sent from London at the end of October to operate on the Treasury Account and

k In addition, before the syndicate closed, Morgans bought back $1.5m at prices of between 97½ and 98¼. The net sales were, therefore, $22.8m.

supervise the details of the Loan, to suggest to Morgans that the most important underwriters might find it in their interests, as large holders, to support the price when the syndicate was dissolved on 15 December. Davison dismissed the idea, pointing out that the syndicate had been 'crowded to the limit' and that he would not think of asking it to support the market. It was a matter for the British and French governments.[53] When Davison met the Special Committee of the Syndicate Managers on 1 December, he found some members predicting prices as low as 90 when the market opened. Davison clearly agreed with the tone, if not the price: the few investors wanting Bonds had already been absorbed; pro-German interests (and, it can be assumed, the usual commercial competition) were trying to talk the price down; and a break in the price would make holders all the more nervous, precluding future borrowing. The market clearly needed support, but, if it became known, it would make matters worse. In the light of this, Morgans proposed that they should be authorised to intervene. Most of the large subscribers and, especially, the banks would hesitate to sell at a loss. If Morgans could buy out small offerings, never giving the market a chance to break unless an overwhelming volume was offered, they could establish a price at which there was two-way trade and give an impression that investor demand was absorbing selling by the underwriters. Panic might be averted. At the same time, Morgans would talk to the largest holders and persuade them that it was in their interests to retain their Bonds.[54] In the utmost secrecy, although the Trio knew something would be going on because Harvey had consulted Frank Vanderlip, of National City Bank, about the terms, Morgans were authorised to spend up to $25m in the first instance, with the same amount in reserve, to buy in the secondary market. They were to advance the money and take the Bonds as collateral, with a 5 per cent margin. Only the manager on the spot would be able to judge the relationship between price and volume, choose the most effective moment to intervene, and Morgans were duly given discretion. Starting at a price not higher than 95, so that underwriters were not able to sell at a level where they would break even, Morgans steadied the price as it fell, selling back as the market recovered.[55] Relatively small intervention had the desired result. By 15 May 1916, Morgans had bought $18.8m and sold $15.9m, having held the price at between 94 and 95 for the greater part of December 1915 and the first three months of 1916, after which it rose above 95 for the summer.[56]

The London Exchange Committee and the bankers' loan

In 1915, one other credit was arranged in the US. On 12 August, two days before he told Morgans to cease buying sterling when their advance reached $50m, Cunliffe asked the Treasury subcommittee of the CLCB to consider how it could help support sterling, perhaps with a dollar credit.[57] Although fearful that a drawing on New York banks in dollars would facilitate the transfer of the sterling-based acceptance business from London to the USA, while in New York Holden approached his associates and, especially, Vanderlip.[58] In London, the Treasury was preparing a scheme to use British-owned securities as collateral for borrowing in the USA. This, and the bankers' loan, were organised together.

In the middle of October, the bankers suggested to the Governor that a committee, led by the Bank, should administer both the proceeds of New York drawings and the envisaged scheme for borrowing securities, and on 25 October the Chancellor agreed to the establishment of the American Exchange Committee.[59] Three days later, Holden reported to the Treasury subcommittee of the CLCB that:

> both the Governor & Deputy Governor were agreed that the scheme could not be worked satisfactorily unless everything was to go through the hands of the Ctee. and that he had told Sir John Bradbury this, and that the Treasury should hand over the gold, the proceeds of the [Anglo-French] loan and the proceeds of the securities and inform the Ctee of the full extent of their [the Treasury's] liabilities.[60]

Which, translated, meant that Holden had refused to serve on any other terms. The Committee's powers were, indeed, sweeping. It was charged with the 'regulation of the foreign exchanges', with control of all the gold which was in the Treasury's ownership, the British share of the Anglo-French Loan, and the proceeds of further borrowing and from the sale of securities. On 18 November 1915, the Committee's appointment was confirmed in writing.[61]

'Further borrowing' included a $50m loan from a committee of New York banks, the 'Vanderlip Committee', to a committee of London joint stock banks. Vanderlip had established his committee when he found that London banks, stimulated by Cunliffe's request for help, were seeking dollars by independently cabling their correspondent banks in New York and that the uncoordinated requests and reactions were producing different terms and a limited response. It had also been discovered that finance bills – acceptances unrelated to the movement of goods – would be difficult to arrange because they could not be discounted with the Federal Reserve Banks. The members of the Vanderlip Committee provided a straight loan against the deposit of 4½ per cent War Loan, with a margin of 10 per cent, with the Bank of England in London. The rate was 4½ per cent and the term six months. The collateral was provided by twenty-six banks, including some from Scotland and the provinces, although the loan was in the name of the eight largest London banks.[62] The money remained unused, kept on deposit in a range of banks as an 'extra reserve for moral effect', until 13 July 1916, when it was paid to Morgans for the account of the Treasury.[63]

The American Exchange Committee, later renamed the London Exchange Committee (LEC), had four members: Cunliffe, his Deputy (Brien Cullen, later Lord Cokayne), Holden and Schuster. Holden ceased to attend after January 1916, and Gaspard Farrer from Barings, who had been an original choice but had declined to serve, joined in May 1916. Baldwin, as Financial Secretary, joined in August 1917 to provide better co-ordination with the Treasury after Cunliffe had quarrelled with the Chancellor. A representative from the Foreign Office joined in November 1917 and, in April 1918, a Treasury official replaced Baldwin. The Committee met frequently, having held 706 meetings when it was dissolved at the end of 1919.[64]

The business conducted by the Committee is not easy to describe. Its minutes show it to have been mainly an advisory body, but with operating responsibilities in some of the European neutral currencies.[65] Despite its origins, it had least power in dollar exchange. The importance of American finance, its close connection to politics and diplomacy and the presence of responsible Treasury officials and missions on the spot meant that decisions passed to Whitehall and, in particular, to Sir Robert Chalmers and Keynes. Although the Committee established a foreign exchange dealing room in London, the centre of activity was in New York and it was necessary to give Morgans wide discretion. The Committee received daily reports of transactions, sent instructions on the rate to be maintained and the amount of sterling that could be bought. Until responsibility drifted away to the Treasury, it arranged the sales of British securities in New York and negotiated Morgans' remuneration. Between January 1916 and the removal of the peg in March 1919, it bought £556m sterling and sold £47m.[66] However, as long as the rate was pegged at \$4.76½, these responsibilities meant little: Morgans bought whatever was offered at \$4.76 7/16. The problem was to find the dollars, and this was a matter for Morgans as the Treasury's agent and, later, for the Treasury operating officer in New York in cable correspondence with Whitehall and for the British government in conjunction with the US Treasury. The dealing instructions were cabled by the Bank and the Treasury guaranteed advances.

The transactions were settled through the LEC's account with Morgans, known to them as the 'Client No. 1 account', or 'Special Loan account No. 1', when it was overdrawn. The Treasury's own account was the 'Client No. 2 account'. Although it was the LEC's account, the No. 1 account was in the name of the Bank of England because it was mostly in overdraft and the LEC was not an acceptable obligor in New York.

The Special Loan account No. 1 probably originated in October 1915, when the Governor arranged a \$50m facility with Morgans as a stopgap until the LEC was established. In the middle of November, the facility was used, on the Governor's instructions, in secret, and as a separate operation from the LEC, to support sterling, which had wilted to \$4.66. While the Governor was ill with jaundice in the second half of December and January (incidentally taking him away from his duties on the Montagu Committee on small savings), the proceeds of the British share of the Anglo-French Loan came under the control of the LEC, which also started to issue instructions on intervention levels and volume.[67] On 17 January 1916, it gave instructions to hold the rate at \$4.76½.[68] The parallel accounts, Bank and Treasury, were retained until the summer of 1917, when they were amalgamated: they helped circumvent the US banking laws regulating the amount banks could lend to one name.

The LEC had more responsibility in European neutral exchanges, where, in varying degrees, it remained the operating body until the end of the war. It organised exchange intervention, selected agent banks, determined buying and selling levels, advised (on occasions, upbraided) government departments spending without prior thought for finance, and negotiated – with more or less Treasury supervision – the terms of the welter of acceptances, Treasury Bills and Exchequer Bonds with various currency options and guarantees that were issued to lenders in the Netherlands, Spain, Norway, Denmark, Sweden, Switzerland, Java and the Argentine. As such, it was responsible for some of the most obscure issues of British government debt (Table 6.3).

Borrowing in neutral Europe

By the end of 1915, it was known that border neutrals (the Netherlands, Denmark, Norway, Sweden and Switzerland) were deflecting supplies to the Central Powers, often replacing the goods they were selling with imports, which were being allowed through the allied blockade because they were for neutral consumption. Such, it will be recalled, was the problem with the Chicago meat packers. The potential for reversing this depended on a range of influences, including the political inclination of the neutral government, the ability of its armed forces to withstand a German invasion and the authority and stability of the government itself. Thus, coercion, whether by rationing, blockade or the withholding of vital supplies, such as coal, was not always the wisest course. Instead, the produce was often bought, sometimes on credit. The Foreign Office was concerned with the wider question of mixing coercion with politics, the Board of Agriculture with identifying and advising on the size of normal trade flows: other Ministries were concerned inasmuch as supplies bought from the border neutrals could be used to meet the needs of the UK or its allies. Otherwise, responsibility lay with the Ministry of Blockade, which was created on 23 February 1916, and with the Restriction of Enemy Supplies Department (RESD).[69]

Sterling had been weak against the Dutch guilder in the autumn and winter of 1915 and the problem was one of the first to be tackled by the LEC. The Committee began supporting the rate in January 1916, at first using a London bank and, after April 1916, Hopes in Amsterdam.[70] The LEC's next move was to take existing Dutch sterling balances off the market. In April 1916, it arranged for £7m to be absorbed by permitting the export of £1.8m in gold (mainly on account of the Java Bank, the Central Bank of the Dutch East Indies) and the issue of twelve-months' sterling Treasury Bills. These bills were unusual on two counts. They bore an option for repayment at fl.12 and, to make them eligible for rediscount at the Dutch Central Bank, which required two signatures, they were endorsed by the Bank of England.[71] The Committee also negotiated an arrangement with Royal Dutch Petroleum and its subsidiaries by which the companies took Treasury Bills with a guaranteed rate of exchange for part of their sterling balances and agreed not to sell sterling for a year. This was to become the first of many such transactions with those companies.[72] The flow of sterling into Dutch hands was coming from two sources. The Treasury Agreement at the end of September 1915 had permitted the Russians to use British advances to meet the interest on Russian external debt. As a result, Barings were sellers of sterling to pay the coupons being presented in Amsterdam. The LEC arranged that these should be met, in the main, from gold shipments.[73] Second, before the war, two-thirds of the UK's sugar was supplied by Germany and Austria. On the outbreak of war, there was panic buying and on 20 August the Royal Commission on Sugar Supply was established. It became a buyer of cane sugar from new suppliers Cuba, Mauritius, the Philippines and Java. The latter required settlement in guilders. To this was later added purchases of Dutch agricultural and fish produce by the RESD. A series of issues of sterling Treasury Bills and Exchequer Bonds with guilder options were used to finance both the sugar and the produce. By the end of 1916, over £15m Treasury Bills with exchange options or guarantees had been issued, mostly maturing in the first half of 1917.[74]

From the early spring of 1916, sterling was weak against the Scandinavian currencies. Exchange was needed to buy timber and iron ore (from Norway and Sweden), fish products and other food (Norway and Denmark), to acquire and insure ships, and for munitions (Norway and Sweden).[75] In June 1916, Nkr.40m (£2.2m) was borrowed in Norway by means of two-year bills drawn on Hambros and the British Bank of Northern Commerce, with Sterling Treasury Bills as collateral, and another Dkr.30m (£1.7m) was borrowed in Denmark. In July, a loan of Nkr.140m (£7.7m), secured against the deposit of sterling Treasury Bills, was arranged with the Norges Bank, specifically to help purchase £8m of Norwegian and Icelandic fish, which would otherwise have been sold to Germany. One half of the loan was for one year and one half for two years. An overdraft for Skr.10m (£0.6m) was arranged in Sweden in July to finance purchases of timber for pit props. In July, Hambros were given discretion to intervene, within limits specified by the LEC, and by the autumn the exchanges were stabilising (Table 6.3).[76]

The American Dollar Securities Committee

The securities bought by the Treasury from the Prudential in the summer of 1915 to provide collateral for Morgans' advance were lodged at the Bank for sorting and recording, before being shipped in cruisers. The first batch of about $28.5m arrived in New York on 12 August 1915 and two days later the Bank ordered sales to begin.[77] Following the Cabinet decision of 18 August, the Bank began buying American securities in the open market in London, holding them for its own account until the Treasury was ready to pay for them; later, when the amounts became too large for the Bank to handle, they were bought directly for Treasury account.[78] By the end of the year, $233m nominal had been acquired, including the Prudential's $40m and part of a block of $28m US Steel Corporation Bonds belonging to Scottish Carnegie Trusts.[79] These *ad hoc* arrangements can be assumed to have been the origin of the later, more formal, scheme to purchase securities.

The scheme to borrow securities had less obvious origins. The sales of US securities, both by the Treasury and private investors, were rapidly depleting British holdings. Stocks of gold were limited and, indeed, small by continental standards. Dollar acceptances would be short and relatively small, even had they not been opposed by the British banking community fearing for post-war business. It was widely agreed after the near-failure of the Anglo-French Loan that unsecured public issues would provide little more money. There was only one option: find collateral, and borrow on its security.[80] For McKenna, this had the advantage that, as the securities were to be pledged, they need only be borrowed from their owners, and not bought outright. This was an important consideration for a Liberal Chancellor dealing with investors who had not yet understood the encroachments on individuals' rights which would result from total war.[1] In December 1915, when negotiating with the insurance and trust companies, the Chancellor promised that the companies would be able to repurchase dollars should the Treasury sell their securities, with the effect that the drain of exchange would exactly absorb the proceeds of securities sales. In August 1916, at the instigation of the LEC, which had advised that investors would be deterred from lending securities if the Treasury was free to sell them at low prices, the Chancellor promised that borrowed securities would only be sold if Britain faced default on its collateralised loans. That many securities were only borrowed, with conditions surrounding their sale and the way the proceeds could be used, was to impose a rigidity on British borrowing in the USA for the remainder of the war.

After possibilities had been explored by Reading over the previous month, on 13 December 1915 the Chancellor announced a scheme to mobilise British holdings, and two days later he sent the life and accident companies and the investment trusts a circular asking them to submit lists of American dollar securities that they were willing to sell or lend to the Treasury. On 31 December, a similar circular was published for the general public and the American Dollar Securities Committee was established by Treasury Minute.[81] The scheme, which became known as 'Scheme A', provided for the purchase of securities named by the Treasury, at current New York prices, with payment being made in sterling at the exchange rate of the day either in cash or, at the option of the seller, in 5 per cent Exchequer Bonds 1920 (see pp. 193–4). The alternative was for securities to be deposited with the Treasury for two years. The depositor would receive the dividends or interest payments, together with an additional 1/2 per cent per year; the securities would be transferred to a Treasury Register and certificates negotiable on the Stock Exchange issued. Depositors could have their securities released by paying the dollar value to the Treasury in New York or the Treasury could sell them against a sterling payment in London. In the latter case, the transaction was deemed to have taken place at the closing New York quotation on the day the

1 The contemporary attitude is shown by a story recorded by Grenfell after an interview with the Chancellor in July 1915: 'I told them if they could not get them [US securities] voluntarily they would have to do so by force. Barings, Sir Everard Hambro, the Governor and the Chancellor were much shocked and told me that this was rank confiscation. My answer was that if they could buy 300 guinea hunters at a uniform price of £50 they could buy American securities from English holders by paying full price, or full price plus 10% in English money or Treasury Bonds. As usual, politics came in and they were afraid of the House of Commons.' MGP, Grenfell's Letter Book, Grenfell to Jack Morgan, 24 August 1915.

Table 6.5 Securities bought and borrowed by the American Dollar Securities Committee (millions)

	Bought	*Borrowed*	*Total*	*Number of Different Securities*
Dollar Bonds	$680	$198	$878	1,421
Dollar shares	$241	$304	$545	389
Sterling Bonds	£28	£115	£143	123
Registered Stocks	£4	£172	£176	40
British railways	–	£17	£17	43
Franc Bonds	–	Ffr8	Ffr8	2
Krone Bonds	–	kr8	kr8	3
Guilder Bonds	–	fl4	fl4	4
Guilder shares	fl5	–	fl5	1

Notes
The data include securities bought by the Bank of England before the establishment of the Committee.
It is not stated whether the data are for nominal or market values, although it is likely to be the former.
As they are not included in any other category, it can be assumed that 'dollar' securities includes Canadians.
The data do not include C$40m CPR 4 per cent Debentures deposited by the CPR.

Source: T 170/130, Report of the American Dollar Securities Committee, 4 June 1919.

holder was notified of the Treasury's intent, and the holder was paid the sterling plus 2½ per cent at the exchange rate of the day.

The Treasury preferred to buy outright, and at first the Committee confined itself to purchases. It sent out its first list of 54 securities and started operations on 1 January 1916. By 17 March, the list had grown to 256 and the value of acquisitions to £40.5m. Accepting securities on loan began on 27 March, when the Committee issued a list of 778. The response was insufficient to meet the Treasury's rising American expenditure. On 19 May, McKenna warned the Cabinet that the UK was 'likely' to enter the final calendar quarter with 'no further [dollar] resources in sight', and on 29 May, by resolution of the House of Commons, an additional 2s 0d in the £ income tax was imposed on those securities, designated by the Treasury, which were not put at its absolute disposal either by sale or deposit.[82] The effect was immediate, with sales and deposits rising from £4.4m in the last week of May to between £16m and £20m per week in June. On 12 August, as the first collateral loan in New York was being planned, a new scheme for borrowing securities – 'Scheme B' – was announced (see pp. 219 and 221). This was different from Scheme A in two respects. The securities were to be deposited for five years from 31 March 1917, with an option to the Treasury to return them at any time after 31 March 1919, and the Treasury retained the right to sell them, continuing the payment of the interest or dividends, and the ½ per cent, for the period of the deposit, when it would either return similar securities, or the value of the securities when they were deposited plus 5 per cent, or the price realised, whichever was the greatest. Depositors under Scheme A were given the option to transfer to Scheme B and £57.5m of the £82.5m deposited under the earlier scheme took advantage of the offer before it was withdrawn on 4 September 1916. The third stage came on 17 February 1917, shortly after Bonar Law became Chancellor. An order was issued under the Defence of the Realm (Securities) Regulations requiring the owners of securities specified by the Treasury to deliver them to the Committee. The effect was to make such securities the property of the government. In view of this, on 11 May 1917, the acceptance of securities on deposit was discontinued.[83]

The selection of the securities, often in response to requests from Morgans for specific collateral for forthcoming public issues, was the responsibility of George May of the Prudential, who was also responsible for dealing with the investor, helped by clerical staff seconded from his own company and the Settlement Department of the London Stock Exchange. The National Debt Commissioners administered the Treasury Register, which recorded the transactions and paid the interest and additional allowances. The Bank took the securities from the Commissioners and shipped them to New York.

During the life of the schemes, the Committee purchased or borrowed 2,027 different securities: \$680m dollar Bonds and \$241m dollar shares were bought and \$198m Bonds and \$304m shares were borrowed. It also borrowed sterling-denominated shares and Bonds of overseas entities, British railway debentures and small amounts of securities denominated in French francs, florins and the Scandinavian currencies (Table 6.5).[84]

✤ ✤ ✤

Until the summer of 1915, the government treated the exchange rate as if there were no war expenditure: if there was a problem, it was one for the Bank. The spending departments in Whitehall sold sterling and bought dollars. The Bank in the City bought sterling and sold dollars. Between them came sales of securities by their British owners, the return of short-term capital to London, the Bank's gold and Morgans' intervention. The Treasury's inaction can be explained by personalities and poor communication: Lloyd George was happy to leave matters to Cunliffe and, later, Cunliffe's dislike of McKenna was fully reciprocated. More importantly, it reflected pre-war roles and assumptions about the way the fiscal and monetary system worked: Whitehall was politics and government finance, the Bank was the gold standard and interest rates. Inactivity was permitted, even sanctioned, by the ignorance of war finance, of resource limitations, among both politicians and public. As this changed, and the pressure on the exchange rate intensified, so did the Treasury's attitude. The internal waymarks were the Financial Statement in May 1915, the emphasis on selling 4½ per cent War Loan outside the banking system and the moves to tap the small saver.

One way of escaping from the necessity of tailoring demand to domestic output – and a very tempting way, enabling hard decisions to be avoided – was to buy overseas, selling assets or borrowing: 'both of them perfectly legitimate but only helpful within limits', as Lloyd George said (see p. 98). The proposals for public issues in New York made by Morgans in the first six months of 1915 should have shown the Treasury that unsecured borrowing in the USA would do little to fill the gap. As it was, the Anglo-French Loan became the external waymark, driving home the lesson that the New York capital market was not going to allow the allies to take from the American economy whatever they needed to fight their war: it was too small, too domestic and, unsurprisingly, it had only a limited appetite for unsecured lending to governments the other side of the Atlantic fighting a war whose outcome was far from certain. It would not be possible, as Keynes optimistically wrote in September 1915, 'to obtain by negotiation the greater part of the floating funds of Wall Street,' let alone 'some' of the savings of the interior.[85] Instead, external spending had to be tailored to the supply of external assets, whether sold or pledged. The principle was well understood in the Treasury: as long as the UK could borrow in the USA at the same interest rate as it could sell its American securities, it made no difference which route was used to raise funds.[86] Thanks to the skills of the Treasury's New York bankers, the supply of securities turned out to be sufficient – by a hair's breadth – to carry the allies to the time when the US Treasury provided alternative finance.

Morgans' understanding of markets, and the British authorities' ignorance of them, was the second lesson of the Anglo-French Loan. The Mission went to New York knowing what it needed to borrow, rather than planning to borrow what the market could make available, an approach parallel to that taken when deciding on the size of 3½ per cent War Loan in November 1915.[87] The Mission forced the market to take more than it could digest, with the inevitable result. At the end of October, Reading was speculating that two further unsecured Anglo-French Loans, each of $250m, might be possible in 1916. There were provisos: an improved military and political position, investment demand appearing for the recent Loan, so that the underwriting syndicate made a profit, and a premium in the price. Far from appetites being whetted for another issue, there was a weak price, a demoralised market and, for nearly a year, reliance on sales of securities and advances from Morgans. The following eighteen months were to show that the Treasury had learnt its lesson. In future, with a few exceptions, the design, size and timing of issues was to be left to the specialists.

Endnotes

1 *National Debt: annual returns*, 31 March 1919 and 1920.

2 T 170/134, Chadwick, 'British Government Transactions in America', 1922; Weems (1923), p. 66.

3 MGP, B. Hist. 1, F. 5, no. 2276, Grenfell to Jack Morgan and Davison, 19 February 1915.

4 MGP, B. Hist. 1, F. 5, nos 1226 and 1235, Jack Morgan and Davison to Grenfell, 17 February 1915 (Copy left with Governor), and 18 February 1915; ibid., nos 2249 and 2263, Grenfell to Jack Morgan and Davison, 17 and 18 February 1915; ibid., F. 6, nos 2564 and 4290, MG to JPM, 23 March, and 11 May 1915; ibid., no. 3899, JPM to MG, 21 June 1915; US Senate (1937), XXVI, pp. 7826–7. Osborne (1926), II, p. 1, says that the Bank began to make arrangements to ship gold on 10 May 1915. For the origins of the relationship between Morgans and National City Bank, see Cleveland and Huertas (1985), pp. 56–7.

5 Osborne (1926), II, p. 2.

6 T 170/62, ff. 8–11, Grenfell, 'Memorandum – Exchange', 20 July 1915; MGP, B. Hist. 1, F. 6, no. 4958, Davison to JPM, 25 June 1915; ibid., no. 5035, Jack Morgan to MG, 28 June 1915; ibid., no. 5078, Jack Morgan to Davison, 30 June 1915; ibid., no. 5291, JPM to MG, 12 July 1915; ibid., no. 6364, MG to JPM, 17 July 1915; ibid., B. Hist. 11 Letters, F. 13, Whigram to Davison, 4 June 1915; Neilson (1984), pp. 102–5.

7 MGP, Grenfell's Letter Book, Grenfell to Jack Morgan, 24 August 1915.

8 T 170/62, Grenfell, 'Memorandum – Exchange', 20 July 1915; MGP, B, Hist. 1, F. 6, no. 5035, Jack Morgan to MG, 28 June 1915; ibid., nos 6364 and 6410, Grenfell to JPM, 17 and 20 July 1915; ibid., no. 5490, Davison to Grenfell (Copy left with PM and Lloyd George. Copy sent to McKenna), no. 6437, Grenfell to Davison; ibid., no. 5524, Davison to Grenfell, 22 July 1915, and nos 6457 and 6460, Grenfell to JPM, 22 and 23 July 1915. For a lively account of this episode, see Beaverbrook (1928), pp. 153–5.

9 MGP, B. Hist. 1, F. 7, no. 5923, JPM to MG, 13 August 1915, and no. 5927, Davison to MG (Copy to Governor), 14 August 1915; ibid., B. Hist. 11 – Letters, F. 13, Morgan Grenfell to Lloyd George, 14 August 1915; Burk (1985), p. 64.

10 MGP, B. Hist. 1, F. 7, no. 6820, 14 August 1915, MG to JPM, and no. 6821, Grenfell to JPM; Sayers (1976), I, p. 89; Osborne (1926), II, pp. 2–4. The Bank knew the importance of what it was doing for, unusually, its instructions were confirmed in a letter signed by the Chief Cashier.

11 MGP, B. Hist. 1, F. 7, no. 7269, JPM to MG, 2 September 1915; CLCBt, 12, 17 and 18 August 1915; CLCBm, 19 August 1915; US Senate (1937), XXVI, p. 7886.

12 MGP, B. Hist. 1, F. 7, no. 5955, Jack Morgan to Grenfell (Copy to Governor. Read by Grenfell to Chancellor), 17 August 1915; T 170/62, Martin-Holland to Treasury, 19 August 1915; CLCBm, 19 August 1915; CLCBt, 17 and 18 August 1915; Cab. 41/36/39, 19 August 1915. Osborne (1926), I, p. 256, says that the government realised in July that that it should increase its US resources by acquiring and shipping securities. He says that the first purchases were made on 22 July, with the Bank acting as principal. The Bank had spent £3.4m when the Treasury established its own account and began to pay for them as they were bought.

13 FO 371/2589, no. 133322, Chancellor to Reading, 16 September 1915; T 172/256, Keynes, 'Protocol – Boulogne, August 22, 1915'; Burk (1985) p. 64; Cab. 41/36/41, 27 August 1915.

14 Neilson (1984), pp. 112–13. Also see Keynes (1971–89), XVI, pp. 67–71.

15 MGP, B. Hist. 1, F. 5, no. 1226, Jack Morgan and Davison to Grenfell (copy left with Governor), 17 February 1915, and F. 6, no. 4925, Davison to Jack Morgan, 23 June 1915; US Senate (1937), XXVI, p. 7834.

16 MGP, B. Hist. 1, F. 5, no. 1226, Jack Morgan and Davison to Grenfell (Copy left with Governor), 17 February, and no. 1287, 24 February 1915; ibid., no. 2285, Grenfell to Jack Morgan and Davison, 20 February 1915.

17 US Senate (1937), XXVII, pp. 8341–6; MGP, B Hist 1, F. 6, no. 1924, Davison to Grenfell, 17 April 1915, and no. 4129, Jack Morgan to Davison, 30 April 1915. The issue was of a French Republic one-year 5% Note due 1 April 1916 at a price of $98^3/_4$ ($6.29 per cent) to the syndicate and $99^1/_2$ ($5.51 per cent) to the public. Morgans bought $10m firm and a selling syndicate was formed for the balance, but with no commitment. The proposition put to the French on 23 March had been that that the securities would be sold on a $5^1/_2$ per cent basis. The syndicate was successful for a week and then made few sales. PML, Archives, Syndicates No. 8, ff. 115–16.

18 MGP, B. Hist. 1, F. 6, nos 2686 and 2763, Jack Morgan to Davison, 1 and 8 April 1915; ibid., no. 1763, Davison to Jack Morgan, 7 April 1915; FO 371/2589, no. 293, Spring-Rice to Grey, 10 June 1915; PML, Archives, Box 11, Jack Morgan to Spring-Rice, 8 June 1915; Lamont (1933), p. 192.

19 MGP, B. Hist. 1, F. 6, no. 2916, Jack Morgan to Davison, 19 April 1915.

20 MGP, B. Hist. 1, F. 6, no. 5292, JPM to MG, 12 July 1915.

21 US Senate (1937), XXVII, pp. 8207 and 8347–54. The comment from Spring-Rice was 'strength of loan…is the collateral rather than the obligors.' FO 371/2589, no. 1040, Spring-Rice to Grey, 21 June 1915. Further tranches were issued until it reached $44.4m on 15 October 1915. US Senate (1937), XVII, p. 8347.

22 MGP, B. Hist. 1, F. 6, nos 4925 and 6033, Davison to Jack Morgan, 23 and 29 June 1915; ibid., no. 3993, JPM to Davison, 25 June 1915; ibid., no. 5035, Jack Morgan to MG, 26 June 1915; ibid., nos 5048 and 5078, Jack Morgan to Davison, 29 and 30 June 1915; Lamont (1933), p. 192; FO 371/2589, no. 293, Spring-Rice to Grey, 10 June 1915.

23 MGP, B. Hist. 1, F. 6, no. 5249, JPM to Davison, 9 July 1915.

24 MGP, B. Hist. 1, F. 7, no. 6795, Grenfell to Davison (Excerpt shown to Governor), 13 August 1915; ibid., no. 5955, Jack Morgan to Grenfell (Copy to Governor. Read to Chancellor), 17 August 1915; ibid., no. 5991, JPM to MG (part shown to Governor and Deputy), 19 August 1915; US Senate (1937), XXV, pp. 7854–5 and 7886. An almost simultaneous despatch from Spring-Rice on opinion in New York confirms that Morgan's judgement was widely shared. T 170/62, Spring-Rice to Grey, 17 August 1915.

25 CLCBt, 17 and 18 August 1915; CLCBm, 19 August 1915; MGP, Grenfell's Letter Book, Grenfell to Jack Morgan, 24 August and 26 November 1915, Grenfell to Lamont, 25 November 1915, and Grenfell to Jack Morgan, 14 January 1916.

26 T 170/62, Blackett to Bradbury, 2 October 1915; MGP, B. Hist. 1, F. 7, no. 6933, Grenfell to Jack Morgan, 21 August 1915; ibid., no. 8465, Grenfell to Jack Morgan and Davison, 23 September 1915; ibid., no. 10255, Grenfell to Lamont, 2 November 1915; ibid., no. 7722, JPM to Grenfell (Shown to Governor), 23 September 1915; Carosso (1987), pp. 204–5; Burk (1985), pp. 67–8. Two Morgan partners wrote to Grenfell with accounts of the negotiations. Lamont's has not been found. Jack Morgan's is in PML, Archives, Box 12, 16 November 1915.

27 Adler (1929), II, pp. 249–53; Carosso (1987), pp. 204–5.

28 Bell (1961), pp. 273 and 289–98. An illuminating report on the difficulties of selling to the mid-west and the attitude of the meat packers was provided by Lamont after he returned from a trip to Chicago with Reading to drum up support for the Loan. It is in Thomas Lamont Papers, II, 81-15, 'Memo. of Chicago Trip,' November 1915.

29 PML, Archives, Memorandum on newspaper treatment of the Anglo-French Loan, unsigned, 4 June 1935; Cab. 37/136/39, 'Statement by Lord Reading', 29 October 1915.

30 FO 371/2589, nos 1394, 1473 and 1487, Reading to Chancellor, 15, 23 and 25 September 1915; ibid., no. 1845, Spring-Rice to Grey, 16 September 1915; ibid., no. 1500, Babington Smith to Chancellor, 28 September 1915; ibid., no. 1561, Reading to Asquith, 3 October 1915; MGP, B. Hist. 1, F. 7, no. 7722, JPM to Grenfell (Shown to Governor), 23 September 1915; Burk (1985), pp. 68–71.

31 MGP, B. Hist. 11 – Letters, F. 13, Grenfell to Davison, 30 August 1915; ibid., B. Hist. 1, F. 7, no. 8115, Grenfell to JPM, and no. 8116, Grenfell to Jack Morgan, 2 September 1915; ibid., no. 8142, MG to Jack Morgan, 3 September 1915. Evidence that, despite Grenfell's assurances, Morgans were uncertain of their ground can be found in an incident as the Mission reached the USA. Despite a cable from Reading stating that he would not make any arrangements until he had heard from the British Embassy, Morgans boarded his liner from Jack Morgan's yacht before it docked. PML, Archives, Box 116, Reading to Jack Morgan, 9 September 1915.

32 FO 371/2589, no. 1420, Reading to Chancellor, 17 September 1915; Cab. 37/136/39, 'Statement by Lord Reading', 29 October 1915.

33 FO 371/2589, no. 487, Chancellor to Reading, 18 September 1915.

34 FO 371/2589, no. 1373, Reading to Chancellor, 14 September 1915; T 170/62, Blackett to Bradbury, 2 October 1915; US Senate (1937), XXV, pp. 7909.
35 FO 371/2589, no. 1371, Reading to Chancellor, 12 September 1915.
36 FO 371/2589, nos 1420, 1423 and 1495, Reading to Chancellor, 17, 18 and 27 September 1915; no. 487, Chancellor to Reading, 18 September 1915.
37 FO 371/2589, no. 1473, Reading to Chancellor, 23 September 1915; MGP, B. Hist. 1, F. 7, no. 7722, JPM to Grenfell (Shown to Governor), 23 September 1915.
38 PML, Archives, Box 12, Jack Morgan to Grenfell, 16 November 1915.
39 FO 371/2589, no. 1420, Reading to Chancellor, 17 September 1915.
40 FO 371/2589, nos 1423 and 1473, Reading to Chancellor, 18 and 23 September; ibid., no. 490, Chancellor to Reading, 20 September 1915.
41 PML, Archives, Box 12, Jack Morgan to Grenfell, 16 November 1915. This letter refers to the meeting having been held on 23 September and the letter to Reading having been sent on 24 September. However, Morgan's letter, which is in PML, Archives, Box 116, is dated 23 September.
42 PML, Archives, Box 116, Jack Morgan to Reading, 23 September 1915; FO 371/2589, no. 1482, Reading to Chancellor, 24 September 1915; MGP, B. Hist. 1, F. 7, no. 7772, JPM to Grenfell (Copy left with Governor), 24 September 1915.
43 FO 371/2589, no. 1482, Reading to Chancellor, 24 September 1915.
44 FO 371/2589, no. 507, Chancellor to Reading, 24 September 1915; Cab. 41/36/46, 2 October 1915.
45 MGP, B. Hist. 1, F. 7, no. 7972, Jack Morgan to Grenfell, 4 October 1915; FO 371/2589, no. 1578, Babington Smith to Chancellor, 29 September 1915, and nos 1540 and 1578 Reading to Chancellor, 3 and 5 October 1915. A copy of the Syndicate Agreement is in PML, Archives, Horn Box 4.
46 PML, Archives, Syndicates No. 8, ff. 141–2.
47 FO 371/2589, no. 1469, Reading to Chancellor, 22 September 1915, and no. 511, 25 September 1915; T 170/102, Blackett, untitled memorandum, 9 June 1916; Lamont (1933), pp. 195–7; T 160/66/F2114, Appendix 1, 'Final List of participants in Anglo-French loan 1915 syndicate'.
48 PML, Archives, Syndicates No. 8, ff. 141–2; T 170/102, Blackett, untitled memorandum, 9 June 1916; MGP, B. Hist. 1, F. 7, no. 9202, JPM to Grenfell, 14 October, and no. 9334, 19 October 1915; Lamont (1933), pp. 195–7; T 160/66/F2114, Appendix 1, 'Final List of participants in Anglo-French loan 1915 syndicate'.
49 FO 371/2589, no. 1511, Babington Smith to Chancellor, 29 September 1915.
50 Carosso (1987), p. 205; CLCBt, 18 October 1915; T 170/62, Blackett to Bradbury, 2 October 1915; FO 371/2589, no. 1495, Reading to Chancellor, 27 September 1915; Thomas Lamont Papers, II, 81-15, Lamont, 'Memo. of Chicago Trip'; ibid., 113-13, 'Address Delivered to the Representatives of Bond Houses Assembled in the Astor Gallery of the Waldorf Astoria', 8 October 1915. In his hagiography of Davison written seventeen years later, Lamont was still emphasising that the loan was to help US exports. Lamont (1933), pp. 187, 192–3. Copies of the circulars are in PML, Archives, Horn Box 4.
51 PML, Archives, Box 12, Jack Morgan to Grenfell, 16 November 1915.
52 Burk (1985), p. 75; MGP, B. Hist. 1, F. 7, no. 9658, Lamont to Grenfell, 4 November 1915; T 170/102, Blackett, untitled memorandum 9 June 1916; T 160/66/F2114, Appendix 1, 'Final List of participants in Anglo-French loan 1915 syndicate'; PML, Archives, Syndicates No. 8, ff. 141–2. Different figures for the selling syndicate and for Notes withdrawn from sale are given in US Senate (1937), XXVII, pp. 8303–18.
53 T 170/63, unnumbered, Spring-Rice to FO, 29 November 1915; MGP, B. Hist. 1, F. 8, no. 11171, Davison to Grenfell (Shown to Governor), 30 November 1915; Burk (1985), pp. 74–5.
54 MGP, B. Hist. 1, F. 8, no. 11199, JPM to MG (Copy to Governor and Harvey), 1 December 1915.

55 MGP, B. Hist. 1, F. 8, no. 10680, Grenfell to Davison, 30 November 1915; ibid., nos 11199 and 11204, JPM to Grenfell (Copy to Governor) and Davison to Grenfell (Copy left with Governor and shown to Reading), 1 December 1915; ibid., no. 10716, Grenfell to Davison, 2 December 1915; ibid., no. 11240, JPM to MG (Copy to Governor), 3 December 1915; ibid., no. 10789, Grenfell to JPM, 6 December 1915; ibid., no. 11553, JPM to MG, 18 December 1915; FO 371/2590, no. 1930, Harvey to Bradbury, 1 December 1915.
56 Daily reports of activity are recorded in cables in MGP, B. Hist. 1, F. 8 and 9 and B. Hist. 2, F. 10; US Senate (1937), XXVII, pp. 8171 and 8321–9.
57 CLCBt, 12 August 1915.
58 CLCBt, 4 October, and 13 October 1915; ibid., Holden to CLCB, 12 October 1915; FO 371/2589, nos 1394, 1420, 1578 and 1613, Reading to Chancellor, 15 and 17 September, 5 and 9 October 1915; MGP, B. Hist. 1, F. 7, no. 9452, JPM to MG, 23 October 1915.
59 CLCBt, 18, 19 and 26 October 1915; Osborne (1926), II, pp. 11–13.
60 CLCBt, 28 October 1915.
61 BoE, C91/1, McKenna to Cunliffe, Cokayne, Holden and Schuster, 18 November 1915; Sayers (1976), I, p. 90; Osborne (1926), II, p. 13. The letter of appointment is reproduced in Sayers (1976), III, pp. 49–50.
62 BoE, C91/1, TM, 17 November, and McKenna to Cunliffe, Holden, Schuster and Cokayne, 18 November 1915; MGP, B. Hist. 1, F. 7, nos 9583, 9638 and 9777, JPM to MG, 30 October, 2 and 9 November 1915; ibid., no. 9823, JPM to MG (Copy left with Governor), 11 November 1915; CLCBt, 26, 27 and 28 October, and 5 and 11 November 1915; T 170/63, Harvey to Bradbury, 2 November 1915. The TM is reproduced in Sayers (1976), III, pp. 46–9.
63 MGP, B. Hist. 2, F. 11, no. 18625, Grenfell to JPM, 12 June 1916; ibid., no. 21966, JPM to MG (Copy to Governor), 11 July, and no. 23052, JPM to MG, 13 July 1916.
64 CLCBt, 2 November 1915; Osborne (1926), II, pp. 14–15; Sayers (1976), I, p. 90n; BoE, C91/4, TM, 27 May 1916.
65 The Committee's papers are in BoE, C91/1-20. C91/16-20 are the Minutes.
66 BoE, C91/15, 'London Exchange Committee: Purchases and Sales of American Exchange,' 25 March 1919.
67 MGP, B. Hist. 1, F. 7, no. 10017, Grenfell to JPM, 20 October 1915, and no. 9375, JPM to MG (Copy to Governor), 21 October 1915; ibid., no. 10453, MG to JPM, 13 November 1915; BoE, C91/16, LEC, Minutes.
68 MGP, B. Hist. 1, F. 8, no. 12492, Grenfell to JPM, 17 January 1916.
69 Bell (1961), pp. 467–89.
70 Osborne (1926), II, p. 32; BoE, C91/16, LEC, Minutes, 14 April 1916; Morgan (1952), pp. 345, 357–8.
71 Osborne, II, pp. 32–3; BoE, C 91/16, LEC, Minutes, 24 January to 3 March 1916.
72 Osborne, II, p. 33; BoE, C 91/16, LEC, Minutes, 14 December 1915 and onwards.
73 Osborne, II, pp. 33–4; BoE, C 91/16, LEC, Minutes, 6 January 1916 and onwards.
74 Osborne, II, pp. 33–4; BoE, C91/16, LEC, Minutes; ibid., C91/1-4: Beveridge (1928), pp. 6–7, 122 and 125; Barnett (1985), p. 31.
75 There is a survey of food buying in neutral European countries in BoE, C 91/4. The LEC Minutes 11 April, 23 June and 7 July 1916 report the discussions. There is a breakdown of British expenditure and its method of finance in Osborne, II, p. 60.
76 Morgan (1952), p. 346; Osborne, II, pp. 45–8; BoE, C 91/16, LEC Minutes, 12 April 1916 and onwards.
77 MGP, B. Hist. 1, F. 7, JPM to MG, no. 5873, 12 August 1915 and no. 6820, MG to JPM, 14 August 1915; Osborne, II, p. 5.
78 Cab. 41/36/39, 19 August 1915; Osborne, II, p. 6.

79 Osborne, I, p. 257, and II, p. 6; MGP, B. Hist. 1, F. 8, no. 11380, JPM to MG, 10 December 1915, no. 11497, 15 December 1915 and no. 12377, MG to JPM, 10 January 1916; ibid., F. 9, no. 15040, JPM to MG (Shown to Governor), 18 February 1916; T 170/130, Report of the American Dollar Securities Committee, 4 June 1919.
80 T 170/62, Memorandum by Strauss, with covering letter, Strauss to Blackett, 25 October 1915, and Blackett to Bradbury, 27 October 1915; CLCBt, 19 October 1915.
81 *Hansard* (Commons), 13 December 1915, cols 1793–1802, and 23 August 1916, cols 2673–5; *The London Gazette*, 17 December 1917; T 170/130, Report of the American Dollar Securities Committee, 4 June 1919; T 172/437, no. 4353, Chancellor to Reading, 17 October 1917; BoE, C91/17, LEC Minutes, 14 August 1916, and C91/5, Cunliffe to Chancellor, 15 August 1916; T 172/221, 'Conference between the Chancellor of the Exchequer and Representatives of British Life, Fire and Marine Insurance Companies and Societies and Representatives of Trust Companies', 11 December 1915. A copy of the circular to the Life and Trust companies is in BoE, C91/1.
82 LGP, D/24/6/1, McKenna, 19 May 1916; *Hansard* (Commons), 29 May 1916, cols 2426–76. The provision was included in the Finance Act 1916.
83 T 170/130, Report of the American Dollar Securities Committee, 4 June 1919.
84 *Hansard* (Commons), 29 May 1916, cols 2426–31; T 170/130, Report of the American Dollar Securities Committee, 4 June 1919.
85 Keynes (1971–89), XVI, 'The Financial Prospects of This Financial Year', p. 120.
86 T 170/84, Bradbury, 'Limits of Borrowing Abroad and At Home', 9 September 1915; T 170/85, Keynes, 'The Financial Prospects of the Financial Year', 9 September 1915, reproduced in Keynes (1971–89), XVI, pp. 119–20.
87 Cab. 37/136/39, 'Statement by Lord Reading', 29 October 1915.

7 The year of drift

Internal borrowing in 1916

> I am sorry not to be able to tell you of a reduction in our unfunded debt…All I can say is that it must long since have passed any danger-point that exists. The Government is now selling Securities in one form or another to run from three months to 5 years, for the immediate needs of the War, but I have no idea when it may be possible to introduce any general funding scheme.
>
> Thus, both for domestic and foreign expenditure we are perhaps living from hand to mouth, hoping as it seems that the double effects of armies and blockade may bring us soon into a position of clearer vision.
>
> Norman to Strong, 21 June 1916, BoE, G1/420.

The offensives in France, Russia and Italy agreed at Chantilly in December 1915 were pre-empted by a German attack at Verdun. This assault, aiming to dislocate the allied plan and destroy French manpower, started in February 1916 and, after initial success, came slowly to a halt: by the end of the year, the French were able to counterattack. To relieve them, in the spring and summer the Russians launched a series of attacks, which drew German reserves, but powerfully contributed to the final destruction of the Russian Armies. That summer, the British took heavy losses on the Somme, as did the Italians in a series of actions against Austria–Hungary. Both failed to attain any useful strategic object, although they diverted pressure from the French. The only allied success on land was in Mesopotamia. At sea, the main battle fleets of the British and Germans met in the North Sea off Jutland at the end of May: the British took the heavier losses, but the German surface fleet withdrew, not to re-emerge. The blockade continued and the Germans relied on submarines: in July, one of these sank several neutral ships off the American coast.

Attrition applied to finance, as well as manpower. Supplying herself and the allies with food, munitions, transport and foreign currency stretched the UK to the uttermost. The government, unable to choose between manufacturing *matériel* and reducing the size of her Armies, was forced to fill the gap by buying from overseas and, in particular, from the USA. By the end of the year, her financial resources in the USA were sufficient to cover only a few months' supplies. All borrowing other than the Anglo-French Loan was secured, so there was no question that the UK could repay the debts she had incurred, but by April 1917 her ability to continue to keep supplies flowing was in doubt.

There was no great loan between the summer of 1915 and January 1917. Domestic borrowing, reflecting the lack of purpose of the first coalition, drifted. The Treasury's plan was to borrow from the banking system, allowing deposits to rise, and periodically reduce them by issuing loans to tap the savings that had been accumulated. In the meantime, open-ended issues of Treasury Bills and Exchequer Bonds were to be on permanent sale, a system that some commentators prematurely described as continuous borrowing. The plan foundered on the Bank's inability to process a great conversion, and conversion of the 4½ per cents was necessary before the Treasury could again borrow in the longer end of the market. In the autumn of 1916, a scheme was prepared for two long-dated loans, such as were finally launched at the beginning of the following year. These failed to materialise because the political will was lacking to overcome disagreements between the Treasury and the Bank about the design of an issue which the Bank would be able to execute. The Treasury schemes tended to be elaborate, with a multiplicity of conversion options. The Bank, emphasising its inability to process even a small issue for cash if it were to be accompanied by a complex conversion offer, preferred straightforward loans.

The government thus found itself issuing an unprecedented volume of short-dated securities. Treasury Bills ceased being a residual source of finance, to be refinanced at the first opportunity, and for fourteen months became the most important instrument of internal borrowing. Investors from outside the banking system – commercial and industrial concerns and wealthy individuals – bought Bills for the first time. The Treasury welcomed the new holders, and especially the foreign currency provided by those from overseas, tolerating the threat to monetary control and the exchange rate from the growth of short-term liabilities. The Bills were supplemented by four issues of Exchequer Bonds and two new instruments: War Savings Certificates and War Expenditure Certificates. However, for most of the period, the Treasury priced Exchequer Bonds to yield less than Bills and they sold poorly, especially during the summer, until a three-year Bond with a 6 per cent coupon was issued at the beginning of October. Although the general public had never previously bought such short-dated securities, and the Treasury believed that the needs of war finance were both immediate and massive, the Exchequer Bonds and War Expenditure Certificates were largely left to sell themselves, while Savings Certificates provided only a dribble of money. In the background, the war savings movement steadily grew and it mounted its first campaigns, but altering attitudes towards savings and familiarising the small investor with these new instruments were lengthy processes.

The pressure on the Treasury was reflected in a series of technical changes in the terms on which the government borrowed. These cumulatively amounted to a revolution. Open-ended issues were introduced. To attract overseas capital, investors who were able to satisfy the authorities that they were non-resident could receive dividend payments and cash coupons without deduction of withholding tax and, if also domiciled overseas, were no longer liable to British taxation of any kind on their holdings of the relevant issues. Later, all interest payments on registered Bonds, whether inscribed or transferable by Deed, whether or not owned by British residents, became payable without deduction of withholding tax. The suggestions that continuous small offerings from deceased estates had a disproportionate effect on prices when taps were absorbing most of the newly generated savings was accepted and the securities could be tendered at their issue prices in settlement of death duties. While retaining inscription, facilities to register Bonds and make transfers by Deed from the first day of sale were introduced (Appendix I). The minimum unit for transfers was reduced to £5. Finally, there was retrospective legislation, altering prospectuses to bring them into line with the terms of the most recent issues.

This chapter explains how the Treasury's internal borrowing drifted into reliance on Exchequer Bonds and Treasury Bills during 1916. It stresses the technical and administrative complexities which made the Bank reluctant simultaneously to convert earlier issues and make an issue for cash. The decision, or lack of decision, which led to the reliance on Bills is poorly documented, but the chapter tries to explain why sales of Exchequer Bonds were so meagre and speculates on how officials assessed the risks they were taking.

The Treasury's borrowing policy

On 21 September 1915, the British artillery bombardment began in preparation for the assault on Loos, the first action in which the territorials and the new armies of volunteer citizens were to play a prominent part. On the same day, McKenna delivered the third budget of the war, which in contrast with Lloyd George's spring measures raised taxes sharply.[1] Revenue for 1915–16 was now forecast to be £272m (a small rise from the £267m estimated in May) and expenditure, assuming that the war continued for the remainder of the financial year, £1,590m (a large rise from May's £1,133m). Of this, £423m was for advances to the Dominions and allies. After the tax changes, the Chancellor estimated revenue for the current year to have increased to £305m so that, with expenditure remaining at £1,590m, the deficit became £1,285m. The tax changes were sweeping. Income tax rates were raised by 40 per cent, to produce £11.3m in 1915–16 and £44.4m in a full year. Customs and excise duties were increased on luxury foods, sugar, tobacco, tea and petrol to provide £21.8m in 1915–16 and £47.7m in a full year. Postal charges were raised. In the guise of saving foreign currency and shipping space, the Free Trade Chancellor imposed duties on a range of imported luxury goods, the 'McKenna Duties'.

Most importantly for future revenue, for the terms of future gilt-edged issues and for the post-war sinking fund, an Excess Profits Duty (EPD) was introduced. As part of a settlement with the labour force working in munitions factories, the Munitions of War Act, which had become effective on 2 July 1915, empowered the Ministry of Munitions to declare any plant in which munitions were manufactured to be a 'controlled establishment'. Once so designated, the right to strike was curtailed, but profits were limited, all those in excess of 120 per cent of the average of the two immediate pre-war years being paid to the Ministry as Munitions Exchequer Payments. McKenna now extended the concept, without the strike agreement, to all trading and manufacturing concerns. With various allowances, they became liable to a duty equal to 50 per cent of the profits earned in excess of those assessed for income tax in 1914–15. With no precedents, he guessed that this would provide £6m in 1915–16 and £30m in a full year.

McKenna again raised taxes in his second budget on 4 April 1916. Revenue in 1915–16 had exceeded the September estimate by £32m, although practically nothing had been collected in EPD. Expenditure was £31m less than forecast, mainly because advances had been reduced as France raised a loan in her own name in the London market and Canada borrowed domestically and in the USA. The deficit was £1,222m. Expenditure in 1916–17 was estimated to be £1,825m, revenue £502m and the deficit £1,323m. Further increases in taxation were estimated to yield £63m. Once again, income tax was raised, to produce £43.5m. Indirect taxes were both extended in scope and increased, to yield £21.8m. EPD became 60 per cent and, with Munitions Exchequer Payments, was forecast to produce £86m.

Inadequate as they may seem, these steep increases in taxation were an acknowledgement by the Chancellor and the Treasury that consumption had to be cut to release resources for government spending. This was not universally recognised. McKenna and his officials fought a series of battles with those in the Cabinet who were either prepared to take risks with the country's financial stability to deliver a swift and decisive military blow or were unprepared to accept that resources were limited or, at least, inelastic. The Treasury formally presented its views to Cabinet committees on two occasions: in the late summer of 1915 and in January 1916. Although the committees had been appointed as a result of the debate about conscription and evidence was couched primarily in terms of manpower use, the size of government spending in comparison with the supply of internally generated savings and the potential for borrowing overseas or selling overseas assets was an integral part of the Treasury's argument against an expansion of the army.

The first submission was to a Cabinet Committee on War Policy, which sat during August and September 1915.[2] In July, when McKenna had reported his difficulties with the down payment for Russian munitions in New York, he had stressed that the problem came from the diversion of manpower from production and had questioned the country's ability to provide both an army of seventy divisions and financial support for the allies.[3] The Treasury now elaborated this, arguing that British spending on the war, whether directly on its own armed forces or indirectly by making advances to its allies, had to be met by a supply of goods and services: these could either come from Britain's own production or from overseas, which meant, in practice, the USA. Any supply from overseas meant a call on British output inasmuch as goods had to be produced and exported to pay for them: the only alternative was to borrow in foreign currencies or sell assets for foreign currencies. Yet Britain's capacity to produce, whether it be for export, military supplies or consumer goods, had been reduced by the loss of manpower to the armed forces. If, as the Treasury argued, the capacity of the USA to lend to Britain or buy assets from her was limited and British consumption could not be reduced, there was only one alternative: to recall men from the forces to increase production. Put in financial terms, the Treasury foresaw a budget deficit of some £800m in the second half of 1915–16, of which all but £100m would have to be met from internal borrowing. Although it was unrealistic to suppose that such a sum could be made available from domestic savings, it would, McKenna said in his introductory comments, cause no 'grave anxiety' if the war was guaranteed to end on the 31 March 1916:

> Familiar expedients could be adopted – issue of Treasury Bills, and loans from the Bank of England – to eke out the probable deficiency on a new permanent loan; and no great harm would be done provided the advent of peace rendered the subsequent absorption of the floating debt a comparatively easy task.[4]

On one level, this approach made the decision on the shape of borrowing dependent on the expected length of the war. On another, it was the exact opposite of the continuous borrowing being advocated by Fraser. Instead of borrowing day-by-day from the general public as it saved, the government should borrow temporarily from the banking system, tolerating the resulting rise in deposits. These would then be eliminated by draining off accumulated savings by periodic loans. This would do no harm, said that part of the report written by Keynes:

> so long as the persons, into whose hands the increased stock of money comes, make no attempt to spend it. There is likely to be an appreciable interval between the creation of this money and the spending of it...Cautiously used...inflationism [adding to the stock of potentially spendable money] may be a useful temporary measure in anticipation of a loan. If when the money comes to be spent it is spent on a government loan, the proceeds of the loan can be used to cancel the inflationism and so regularise the situation.[5]

The second committee, the Committee on Co-ordination of Military and Financial Effort, held its first meeting on New Year's Day 1916 and delivered two reports on 4 February and 13 April. Only the first dealt with borrowing. The Committee had been set up by Asquith as part of another exercise to hold the coalition together during a ministerial crisis over conscription. Once again, the concern was manpower distribution and the size and structure of the British contribution to the war effort. Those parts of the Treasury's submission covering borrowing were drafted by Keynes and rewritten by Bradbury.[6]

At this point, the Treasury saw the need to raise £2,000m, including the refinancing of £400m Bills and £70m 'other short-term' loans, in the fifteen months from end-December 1915 to end-March 1917. It expected 'only a comparatively small amount' to be raised overseas. Little extra could come from taxation and, if income taxes were increased, it would reduce the amount raised from voluntary loans 'to an almost equal extent'. It followed that:

> the minimum required in the shape of permanent loans from genuine subscribers [the general public using their savings] in the fifteen

months...is...not far short of 1,500,000l., a sum very greatly in excess of any savings which the community is likely to be able to make within this period.

A forced loan from the banks:

> ...would shake the very foundations of credit and disorganise commerce and industry....It would lead to an almost immediate withdrawal of foreign deposits...and forced suspension of specie payments.

The loss of producers' working balances would lead to increased borrowing from the banks on the security of the loans themselves. A compulsory levy on incomes would be a sounder approach, but a levy of 5s in the pound on taxable income (with the normal income tax allowances) would raise only £195m, 75 per cent of which would be at the expense of voluntary loans (see p. 135).[7]

The Treasury's arguments appear persuasive, pointing to the need to accept a reduction in Britain's contribution to the war, whether in the form of financial support for the allies, of supplies or of its own military forces. Political considerations were paramount, however, and, having stated its case, the Treasury drew back, merely concluding that total expenditure should not be increased and that any increases in one area should be offset by reductions elsewhere. The conclusion for domestic borrowing was equally lame:

> After an exhaustive examination of the whole subject, the Treasury have come to the conclusion that the plan of raising the money by big loans interspersed with short-term borrowing, is the one open to the least objection.[8]

The meaning was clear: it was not possible to cover the deficit from domestic savings and the government would have to continue its inflationary reliance on the banks. The implication for borrowing policy must have seemed equally clear: the greater the amount that could be borrowed from the general public the less would be the inevitable inflation.

The ideal at which the Treasury should aim was spelt out in an internal estimate made by Keynes when the first report was presented on 4 February. Borrowing between the beginning of the war and the end of January 1916 had been £1,408m. Of this, £484m had been met from the Bank of England, the CNRA and the joint stock banks 'in replacement of American Securities, Bills of Exchange, and loans to the SE [Stock Exchange] and the Money Market', which could 'only be used once, and are not available in any appreciable degree for the future'. The remaining £924m represented a weekly rate of £12m. If it was assumed that spending was to be £35m per week and tax revenues £10m, the rate of borrowing would need to double, to £25m per week.[9]

5 per cent Exchequer Bonds of 1919, 1920 and 1921 (16 December 1915 and 27 May 1916)

The last call on the 4½ per cent Loan was paid on the 26 October and the last date for receiving applications to convert was four days later. According to Osborne, the preparation of the warrants for the first dividend on 1 December 'taxed the Bank to the utmost'.[10] Until this work was completed, there could be no further issues. Shortly afterwards, on 11 December, the Chancellor proposed that payment for the acquisition by the Treasury of insurance companies' and investment trusts' foreign currency securities should be made in five-year 5 per cent Exchequer Bonds, and five days later the prospectus was published.[11]

The first tap, in the sense of a nominal amount created on a specific day in which some, or all, was subscribed by the authorities and then sold into the market, had come in June 1891. The first, in the sense of an announced nominal amount, but with no securities being created until they had been sold, came later the same summer. The December 1915 issue was the first tap in which the size was open-ended, no securities were issued and held by the authorities, but paper was created to meet sales as they were made. It was an innovation which, in view of the Treasury's evidence to the Committee on Co-ordination of Military and Financial Effort, must have been dictated by the need to have securities permanently available to pay for overseas securities as their holders sold them to the Treasury, rather than any conversion to the merits of continuous borrowing.[a]

Reflecting the widening of the target market to include non-professional investors who might have difficulty keeping bearer documents secure, once the Bonds had been prepared and issued, they could be converted into registered form.[b] 'Registered Bonds' could either be inscribed or held on the Deed Register, although the latter option was not mentioned in the prospectus. This, which to all intents and purposes made the Bonds identical to inscribed or Deed Stock, was the first blurring of the hitherto clear distinction between Bonds, Stock Certificates to bearer (Consols) and inscribed or registered Stock (Appendix I).[12] Other changes were designed to save clerical labour. Because it could be assumed that large blocks would not be sold at any one time, the whole subscription was made payable on application and the complexities of administering several, or many, instalments were avoided.[c] It also meant that the receipts could be exchanged into the definitive Bonds, without the intermediate stage of issuing scrip certificates. In the case of Deed holdings, a Register Certificate was issued. Continuous sale meant that the first coupon had to be broken, so that it represented the interest from the date of receipt by the Bank of the subscription monies to the first payment date on 1 June 1916.[d] Also new was the exemption from:

a Osborne (1926), I, pp. 405–6, describes the issue as the first experiment in day-to-day borrowing.

b Not all the prospectuses have been found, but those examined show that the power to register Exchequer Bonds provided by the Exchequer Bills and Bond Act 1866 (see p. 19) had not previously been used.

c The issue at par also reduced the labour required, although there is no record of this having influenced the pricing.

d Osborne comments that 'This caused many disputes in the case of Scotch [*sic*] and Irish applicants.' Osborne (1926), I, p. 406. The day from which interest started to accrue was to be changed later in the war to satisfy investors outside London.

> all British taxation, present or future, if it is shown in the manner directed by the Treasury that they [the Bonds] are in the beneficial ownership of a person who is neither domiciled, nor ordinarily resident, in the United Kingdom of Great Britain and Northern Ireland...the relative Coupons will be paid without deduction for Income Tax, or other taxes, if accompanied by a declaration of ownership in such form as may be required by the Treasury.[e]

So ended the century-old principle that income tax was payable on income arising in the UK irrespective of the country of residence of the asset's owner, and that payment would be ensured by withholding the basic rate of tax at the income's source.

The minimum Bond was £100 thus, initially, continuing the policy of excluding the small investor. Two weeks later, the Treasury accepted one of the recommendations of the *Interim Report* of the Montagu Committee that £5 Bonds be made available to the small investor through the Post Office and then, on 25 May 1916, a Treasury Minute permitted transfers in multiples of £5 on the Bank Register (see p. 129).

The issue followed the 1915 War Loan by carrying the option, which was to become standard in 1916 and, again, in late 1917 and 1918, of conversion into future loans raised for the purposes of the war unless the securities were Exchequer Bonds, Treasury Bills or such 'similar short-dated securities'.

The issue produced a strong reaction from the members of the CLCB, who had just borrowed $50m on their own credit from the Vanderlip Committee and were holding it available for the Treasury (see p. 174). The CLCB feared that the new high rate would weaken gilt-edged prices immediately before the banks' end-years:

> It was essential that the English Banks Balance sheets should be as strong as possible, for on the strength of those balance sheets depended our retention of the foreign money and our credit in the eyes of the neutrals, and yet not one word had been said as to this new issue being imminent.[13]

A letter was sent to the Chancellor, signed by the seventeen members of the CLCB,

e On 22 December, Bradbury sent a definition of 'domiciled' and 'ordinarily resident' to Holden, who had been told that US investors would be encouraged to buy Exchequer Bonds provided they were sure of the meaning of the terms. After some discussion, the draft read: 'A person is domiciled in the United Kingdom if he has his permanent home there or if, having had his home there, he has taken up his residence elsewhere, but has not abandoned all intention of returning to this country; he is ordinarily resident in the United Kingdom if as a matter of habit he spends the greater part of his time there.' From January 1916, this definition formed the basis of a sidenote to the declaration required from those claiming exemption from income tax. The definition needed considerable reworking after the war, by which time the problem was no longer one of reassuring foreigners, but of limiting tax avoidance. T 160/165/F6446, Hopkins to Niemeyer, 20 July 1923, and 'Correspondence regarding definitions of "domicile" and "ordinary residence" cabled to America'.

including St. Aldwyn, Holden, Schuster, Sir Frederick Banbury and Vassar-Smith. They drew attention to the failure of the Chancellor to consult them before the issue of 4½ per cent War Loan and deplored the lack of co-operation between the banks and the Treasury: unless greater confidence was shown in them, and they were called into consultation with regard to the government's financial policy, they would be unable to give the country and government the 'effectual' help that they sought. A meeting of a group of the bankers was arranged with the Chancellor, although it appears that it was cancelled and replaced by a smaller session with St. Aldwyn and Holden.[14]

The Bank issue of the 1920 Exchequer Bonds remained on tap until 1 June, by which time 272,140 applications had been received for £205.4m.[15] It was replaced by two new open-ended taps: 5 per cent Exchequer Bonds 1919 and 5 per cent Exchequer Bonds 1921. The terms were the same as those on the 1920 Bonds, except that for the first time registered holdings transferable by Deed were offered in the prospectus and, to save labour, the actual Bonds were not prepared for those wishing to hold the securities in registered form. Instead, subscribers requested registration when they purchased the securities.

The reasons for introducing the two new issues are not recorded, but were probably twofold. The 1914 and 1915 War Loan Acts had given the Treasury general borrowing powers, whereas those in the 1916 Finance Act were for a maturity of only five years. It can be surmised that the Treasury wanted to exploit its limited freedom to the full and so replaced the 1920 issue, which by the summer had a life of only four and a half years. Also, the Bank may have wanted to spread the preparation of dividend warrants: 1 June/1 December were the payment dates for the 4½ per cent Loan, as well as for the 1920 Exchequer Bonds.

It can be assumed that the opportunity was then taken to make further changes, including changes to the terms of the earlier issue. Thus, the new registered Bonds, whether inscribed or transferable by Deed, were transferable from the outset in units of £5. Another breach of long-standing British tax policy was promised in the prospectus. Subject to Parliamentary sanction, registered Bonds of both the new issues and the previous 1920 Bonds would have their coupons paid, even to British residents, without deduction of withholding tax. It would then be the responsibility of the taxpayer, if a British resident, to declare the income.[f] Finally, using powers added as an afterthought at the Committee stage of the Finance Bill, the Bonds were to be accepted at par (together with their accrued interest) in settlement of death duties. This clause was also applied retrospectively to the 1920 issue.[16]

After the 1916 Finance Act had been passed, it was found that the 1921 Exchequer Bonds were *ultra vires*. The Treasury had been overenthusiastic in its desire for length and the Bonds had been issued on 1 June 1916 to mature on 5

f The power to issue Exchequer Bonds (and it excluded any other type of security) with this condition was included in the Finance Act 1916 and the terms of the prospectuses were duly altered in July. *The London Gazette*, 21 July 1916, p. 7210.

October 1921. The position was corrected by a further piece of retrospective legislation, the Finance (Exchequer Bonds) Amendment Act 1916.

The Post Office's pioneering issue of 1920 Exchequer Bonds remained on sale until 14 October 1916, although a replacement was discussed during the summer after the introduction by the Bank of the 1919 and 1921 Bonds. Davies' argument was that there was no public demand for the Post Office to offer a choice of maturity, and that two simultaneous issues would confuse counter clerks and investors. Thus, there would be no reason to replace the 1920s if it were not for a problem with the dividend payments. The Post Office's capacity was fully stretched by the preparation of over two million warrants for the 4½ per cent War Loan and the 1920 Exchequer Bonds payable on 1 June. A new issue with different dividend dates was required and the opportunity should be taken to make other technical improvements. Ninety per cent of the applicants through the Post Office had taken registered Bonds and it was thought that the proportion would be even larger once the prospectus actually stated that the dividends were to be paid without deduction of withholding tax. The new system would be simpler. A 'Bond purchase book', in which each transaction would be recorded, would be handed to the investor at the time of application and a confirmation sent by post. There would be no further formality. Those wanting Bonds would be handed the securities in return for the book a few days after purchase. The new issue should be introduced in September because the holiday month of August was always a bad period for savings.[17] These suggestions were adopted in October with the aborted 1921 issue (see pp. 209n).

War Expenditure Certificates

War Expenditure Certificates were on tap between 3 June 1916 and 1 January 1917. They had a life of two years from the date of issue and were, in effect, long-dated Treasury Bills: they bore no interest, but were sold at a discount; they were only available from the Bank of England; and their accounting treatment in the Bank's books was the same as that of Bills, with pre-paid interest debited when they were sold.[18] Initially, they were aimed at the wholesale market, being sold in units of £1,000, £5,000 and £10,000, but three weeks after they were introduced, without explanation and with no change in the arrangements for distribution, units of £100 and £500 were added. The price was subject to change without notice. Until 13 July 1916, they were sold at 90 (£5 8s 2d per cent) and then, when Bank rate was raised, at 89 (£6 0s 0d per cent). On 12 August, the tax privileges for those living overseas which were already attached to Exchequer Bonds were extended to the Certificates.

The Certificates were not popular, with only £29.9m nominal sold in the seven months they were on tap.[g] From 16 February 1917, they were given uncovenanted

g Sales were: June £10.2m; July £6.4m; August £3.3m; September £3.6m; October £3.4m; November £2.0m; December £1m. T 172/776, 'War Expenditure Certificates', covering letter Hamilton to Sutton, 30 May 1918.

conversion rights into both 5 per cent War Loan 1929–47 and 4 per cent War Loan 1929–42: holders of £6.3m took advantage of the offer. A similar option, into National War Bonds, was given in January 1918 to holders of Certificates with remaining lives of less than six months: only £0.6m took advantage of the offer in 1917–18 and £38,000 in 1918–19.[19] The remaining £23m were paid off for cash, the Treasury believing that the bulk was in the hands of the money market.[20]

The banks' investments

A scheme to relieve the banks of some of their 4½ per cent War Loan was responsible for the creation of additional Exchequer Bonds during 1916. The context was the presumed need for banking subscriptions when another loan was issued, the threat to the banks' capacity to make advances posed by their existing investments, and the losses that they would suffer if taxes were raised on the income. Although not mentioned, the furore over the issue of the Exchequer Bonds the previous December must have reminded the bankers of how vulnerable they were to a rise in yields, even if the pre-war fall in Consols and the minimum price regime had faded from memory.

The subscriptions to the 1914 War Loan and the further 'special subscription of £200m' to the 4½s the previous summer had almost doubled investments as a proportion of the CLCB's members' assets: a rise from around 19 per cent before the war to 33.9 per cent at the end of 1915.[21] While discussing a tax-free loan with the Chancellor in February 1916, Holden drew attention to the vulnerable position in which the banks found themselves, stressing that there were political and industrial reasons to offer assistance:

> There is a contraction of 40 millions in the Deposits of these Banks [on account of tax payments] during the month of January, and if that contraction continues, I am afraid the industries will be asked to pay off some of their advances. These investments, as I have told you before, are frozen, and for the protection of the industries and of the Banks, every effort ought now to be made to thaw them.[22]

Holden enclosed a statement of the member banks' investments. This showed that Holden's own bank, The London City & Midland, had the lowest percentage of investments to deposit and current accounts, namely 26.2 per cent. The highest was the National Provincial with 38.0 per cent. 'Sir E. Holden is quite right,' scribbled Keynes on the scrap of paper circulated with the list to Montagu, Bradbury, Chalmers and Ramsay, 'The Banks have taken up more War Loan than they carry [*sic*] except with the aid of inflation.'[23]

Cunliffe proposed that, instead of receiving the normal ⅛ per cent commission on Exchequer Bonds sold through their branches or taken by them as principals, the banks should be allowed to convert their 4½ per cent Loan at par into Exchequer Bonds, also at par. The basis suggested was £15,000 or £20,000 of the 4½s for every £100,000 of the Exchequer Bond applications for which banks were responsible.[24] The Treasury accepted the proposal in principle, without agreeing the terms, because it regarded the issue price of the 4½s as 98⅞ (see p. 102). The banks must have accepted this for, by a Treasury Minute of 11 April, they could elect, in lieu of commission, to convert £20,227 11s 2d of the 4½s into £20,000 5 per cent Exchequer Bonds 1920 on account of each £80,000 of the Exchequer Bonds handled, subject to adjustment for accrued interest. In the event, no conversions were made into the 1920s, and the scheme had to be extended to include the 1919s and the 1921s.[25] Enabling powers were included in the 1916 Finance Act. Under the arrangement, £17.1m 4½s were cancelled and £4m 5 per cents of 1919 and £12.9m 5 per cents of 1921 created before a more radical measure was adopted at the beginning of 1917.[26]

The Treasury Bill issue: 1916 and 1916–17

The two War Loans enabled much of the Treasury Bill issue to be paid off during February and March 1917, making the picture for the financial year 1916–17 very different from that for the calendar year 1916 and diverting attention from the reliance on short-dated borrowing which characterised McKenna's later finance. The volume of Exchequer Bonds outstanding on 31 March 1917 also understates the part they played in calendar 1916 because all those sold between December 1915 and December 1916 enjoyed conversion options into future loans, many of which had been exercised by the time of the annual returns. Furthermore, the uncovenanted conversion rights into Exchequer Bonds given to the banks on part of their holdings of the 4½ per cent Loan opened a difference of £75.7m between the cash raised from sales and the amount of Bonds created (Table 7.1).

During 1916, with no great loan and desultory sales of Exchequer Bonds, Savings Certificates and War Expenditure Certificates, the full effect of the fiscal deficit was felt on Treasury Bills as the residual source of finance: constantly rolled over, they became, in effect, medium-dated debt carried by means of short-term paper. Even in the third quarter of 1915, the calls on the 4½ per cent War Loan did little more than hold the volume of Bills static, and in November the issue rose briskly. By the end of December, the volume was £395.6m. The amount in issue then rose every month until December 1916, when sales of 6 per cent Exchequer Bonds and the receipt of the proceeds from borrowing in the USA held it steady. It was £566.8m at the end of March 1916, £1,115.8m at the end of December 1916, and £463.7m at the end of March 1917 (Table 7.2).[27]

It might have been assumed that officials, brought up in a tradition of perpetual debt, would have looked on such finance – not just dated, but short dated – with nothing but disquiet. The unexpected must be assumed, especially in time of war, and adverse news would have caused the Bills to run off, with their renewal demanding an immediate and steep rise in interest rates. It was also a period when the coalition was under extreme political strain and relief from any direction would have been welcome, especially if the price was no more than tinkering with the yield curve at the short end of the government debt market. Yet, at no time between the introduction of 5 per cent Exchequer Bonds 1920 in December 1915 and the

Table 7.1 Sales of Exchequer Bonds, War Expenditure Certificates, War Savings Certificates and Treasury Bills: calendar year 1916 and financial year ending 31 March 1917 (£m nominal)

	Calendar year 1916	*Financial year 1916–17*
5 per cent Exchequer Bonds 1919	34.2	18.5
5 per cent Exchequer Bonds 1920*	237.8	55.2
5 per cent Exchequer Bonds 1921	62.5	83.2
5 per cent Exchequer Bonds 1919, 1920 and 1921 including £75.7m issued to the banking system against the surrender of 4½ per cent War Loan 1925–45†	*411.2*	*156.9*
6 per cent Exchequer Bonds 1920	160.8	141.7
War Expenditure Certificates	29.9	23.6
War Savings Certificates	40.3	74.5
Treasury Bills (change in issue during period)	720.3	103.1
Total	1,285.8	499.8

Notes
*From their issue on 16 December 1915.
†The *Annual Return* for 31 March 1917 shows £256,563,610 as the combined total of 5 per cent Exchequer Bonds 1919, 1920 and 1921 created in 1916–17. *The London Gazette* shows a total of £180,826,000. The difference of £75,737,000 represents Exchequer Bonds issued to the banks under the two schemes by which they surrendered 4½ per cent War Loan 1925–45 against Exchequer Bonds. Bonds issued under these schemes did not appear in *The London Gazette* because they did not provide the Treasury with cash. The *annual return* does not distinguish the issue of the Exchequer Bonds for this purpose, but does show £77,254,211 4½ per cent War Loan 1925–45 as cancelled under Section 60 of the Finance Act 1916. The difference between the Exchequer Bonds created and the War Loan cancelled of £1,517,211 reflects the price of 98⅞ at which the 4½ per cents were taken and the different amounts of accrued interest in the Bonds and War Loan at the time of each transaction.
The Stock Exchange Year Book records the original issue of the 1920 Bonds as £238,015,000. Morgan (1952), p. 110, states that 5 per cent Exchequer Bonds 1920 'raised' £107m in 1915–16 and £155m in total. The amount sold for cash in 1915–16 was £155.4m and the amount issued in total was £237.8m.

Sources: *The London Gazette*; *National Debt: annual returns*; Osborne (1926), II, pp. 409-10.

issue of 6 per cent Exchequer Bonds in September 1916 was it possible to sell twelve-months' Bills and buy Exchequer Bonds without sacrificing at least 5s per cent in yield. Even after October 1916, when Exchequer Bonds were being sold to yield 6 per cent and Bill rates had been reduced to 5½ per cent for all dates, the incentive to buy the Exchequer Bonds was only £0 3s 7d per cent. Curiously, Bills were at their most attractive relative to Exchequer Bonds between 14 July and 26 September, when the Chancellor was under intense political pressure to reduce his reliance on Bill finance. During this period, twelve-months' Bills yielded £6 7s 8d per cent and 5 per cent Exchequer Bonds were on tap at par. In contrast, it was attractive to switch longer within the Bill market. This, at times, was considerable: in March 1916, the reductions in the rates at which the shorter

Table 7.2 Treasury Bills outstanding: August 1914 to March 1917 (£m)

1914			
25 July	16	31 October	87
29 August	43	28 November	100
30 September	50	31 December	98
1915			
30 January	96	31 July	246
27 February	87	28 August	233
31 March	77	30 September	254
24 April	125	30 October	237
29 May	205	27 November	294
30 June	251	31 December	396
1916			
29 January	418	29 July	842
26 February	428	26 August	909
31 March	567	30 September	1,041
29 April	606	28 October	1,083
27 May	668	25 November	1,124
30 June	761	31 December	1,116
1917			
27 January	991		
24 February	718		
31 March	464		

Source: *The London Gazette*.

maturities were being sold widened the yield difference between three-months' and twelve-months' Bills to £0 14s 6d per cent. This was once more reduced to £0 4s 3d per cent in June, when the rates for all maturities were moved to 5 per cent. After July, when rates on twelve-months' Bills were raised by 1 per cent and those on three-months' Bills by only 1/2 per cent, there was an incentive of £0 16s 5d per cent to sell three-months' and buy twelve-months' Bills (Table 4.1).

There is little to show why the authorities chose these rates. We can only speculate. Was it fear of the reaction of the City, or the banks, if investment values were attacked as they had been at the end of 1915? Were the authorities only prepared to act, as they did in the autumn, when the initiative came from the bankers themselves? Or was it that they felt that investors in the two markets were so different that it would be pointless to offer a yield advantage to those buying longer Bills? This last might have been true, in particular, with foreign holders: the times were uncertain and overseas investors might be expected to want short-dated Bills and be unresponsive to rewards for moving longer. If a higher yield would not persuade them to lengthen, why offer more to domestic investors who might, anyway, be attracted by longer securities? The argument would have been strengthened by the authorities' belief that wartime interest rates were temporarily high and that longer securities could be sold on lower yields than those on short: provided investors shared this view, they would invest longer, even at some sacrifice.

The risks depended on the nature of the holders. In principle, if the Treasury believed that the Bills were held by stable investors who would automatically reinvest at maturity, there was nothing to be gained by paying them to lengthen. In reality, few reinvest irrespective of the circumstances and the characteristics of the holders are all important. Unfortunately, there is little to show how the authorities saw the distribution of the Bill issue between the general public, companies, overseas investors and the banking system, or how they assessed the risks they were running. There are not even data on the size of official holdings.[h] In a letter to Benjamin Strong, Governor of the Federal Reserve Bank of New York, in September 1916, Norman emphasised the importance of 'stable' investors, but did not quantify them:

> A large amount of these Bills are intended (and must be used) for the payment of accruing taxation; another large amount belongs to Government Departments, or to Indian or such Governments, and yet another to Bankers or to Discount Houses. So that the proportion which counts effectively, and which is in the hands of foreigners or people here who can really use it as they please, is far from the total.[28]

As new holders – industrial and commercial concerns, financial institutions and wealthy individuals – bought, there was discussion outside the Treasury and the Bank about their importance. Like Norman's comments, these were couched in impressionistic terms.

In the last resort, the Treasury would, presumably, have called into play tax incentives, a forced loan or other coercion. But these would have only been effective with the domestic investor. It was the overseas holdings that made the government most vulnerable. By encouraging the purchases, the Treasury showed itself willing to accept the risk.[i] In May 1916, the Chancellor warned of the danger of default on his North American payments.[29] He repeated the warning at the end of October, declaring that from the end of the year only a public loan in the USA would enable the country to meet its American obligations and, by the middle of

h There are, fortuitously, weekly data between 27 November 1915 and 29 January 1916 for holdings of Bills. On the latter date, the total was £418.1m distributed as to: Bank of England (£40.8m); CNRA (£15m); Bank of England, as collateral for advances to foreign governments (£73.8m); held otherwise (£288.4m). Thus 'held otherwise' was 69 per cent of the issue. There are no data for holdings by other departments and it is not clear whether the Bank's holdings included 'investments o/a bank borrowings'. There are other, unsystematic, pieces of data: on 27 December 1916, investments o/a bank borrowing held the maximum amount for the year (£137.6m) and on 21 February 1917 the account held £97.3m. Osborne (1926), I, pp. 263–4; *The London Gazette*; BoE, C58/38; T 171/129, 'Treasury Bills'.

i Notices bringing the tax treatment of Bills held by non-residents into line with that on the newly issued Exchequer Bonds were published on 10 March 1916 and 14 August 1916. They are reproduced in the *Bankers' Magazine*, April 1916, p. 600, and September 1916, p. 311.

1917, the direction of British policy would have passed into American hands. Sales of sterling Bills to foreigners delayed this prospect as much as borrowing in foreign currencies. However, given the problems of issuing in New York, selling Bills was not a question of balancing risk against cost and financial orthodoxy. The alternative was not a longer piece of sterling paper on the right terms, but of not being able to borrow from foreigners in sterling at all, of obtaining fewer supplies from overseas and of scaling down the allied war effort. In August 1916, when criticised for paying high rates of interest free of tax to overseas residents and accumulating dangerous short-term claims, McKenna pointed to the difficulties of finding foreign currency. Foreigners would not lend if they had to pay British tax, and its absence was 'one of the merits of the Treasury Bills instead of being a defect.'[30]

The sale of short paper to foreigners may have been a way of easing the foreign currency shortage, but it does not explain why domestic holders were not offered a longer loan. In part, it was because official attitudes were ambiguous. Traditionally, the Treasury, like any borrower, was sensitive both to the cost of the debt and to its length. The two traditions met in the view that interest rates were temporarily high and that cheaper borrowing would be possible after the war. The reliance on short- and medium-dated paper – Exchequer Bonds, National War Bonds, War Expenditure Certificates, War Savings Certificates and Treasury Bills – may not have been what the Treasury would have chosen in an ideal world, but at least it had the advantage of leaving the way open to a reduction of the interest burden.

The relation between the cost of the Debt and the level of taxation was given formal expression in the 'McKenna principle', the nearest the Treasury approached to a framework within which to view the desirable balance between taxation and borrowing. The origins of the principle lay in a riposte – seemingly unprepared – made by McKenna during the debate on the War Loan Bill in June 1915. Denying that taxation was currently not playing its full part,, the Chancellor promised that there would be further rises if the war continued. The size and timing were easy to calculate: when interest had reached the point where it cost the equivalent of the Treasury's 'surplus revenue [that being absorbed by the war]', taxes would have to be raised for, surely, 'there is nobody who would suggest that we should borrow in order to pay the interest.'[31] In the budget of April 1916, the comment was developed and became a claim to fiscal conservatism, reassuring to holders of the Debt. The claim fell into two parts: that, excluding 'temporary' revenue such as EPD and making an assumption for normal peacetime expenditure, there should be a balance sufficient to pay the interest on the Debt and provide an 'ample' sinking fund, while also permitting some reduction in taxation; and that taxation had been raised by enough, in September 1915 and in the current budget, to service new borrowing incurred in the current financial year, that is to 31 March 1917. The annual interest was assumed to be 5 per cent and the sinking fund 1 per cent of the Debt, after netting out loans to allies and Dominions.[32]

Evidence that the authorities believed holders of Treasury Bills to be inert and that it was pointless to load the budget with the extra costs of persuading them to move longer when interest rates were temporarily high is to be found in two

Commons debates in August and October 1916.[33] With little internal Treasury or Bank documentation surviving, it is not possible to assess the importance of each argument in determining the authorities' decisions. Inevitably, McKenna's comments have the ring of a brief putting a case. In the first debate, he presented data to show that the Treasury had repaid three-months' Bills in the first four months of the financial year and relied more heavily on six-, nine- and twelve-months' Bills, which:

> appeal to a different class of investor. Yearly [*sic*] bills are regarded, and fairly regarded, with the great bulk of those who invest, as truly invested, and not intended to be drawn in the course of the year for the discounting of bills, and probably intended to be reinvested. The point at issue is that when any war continues, as this war is continuing, the investor prefers to have his money in a form of security in which his capital is guaranteed. If the war goes on long enough there is a time when all loans depreciate in value, the consequence being that the genuine investor likes yearly Treasury Bills.[34]

These were comments from a politician justifying inaction, but the financial press agreed that the new investors were unlikely to buy longer instruments because they were accumulating liquid capital to spend after the war. Such holders were encouraged by what they thought was the tax treatment of Bills: there was a commonly held, but erroneous, view that the Inland Revenue would treat the discount as capital gain rather than income or that, at the least, some taxation would escape the net.[35]

The Chancellor put the non-bank investor in the longer Bills at the centre of his defence. The main consideration in deciding whether to issue a loan was that described by Bradbury in June 1915 and by Keynes to the Cabinet Committee on War Policy the following September:

> whether or not the state of the Money Market at any given moment discloses a condition of inflation, and if credits are being heaped up which do not really and truly represent real money. If we got a condition of inflation, and if these yearly Treasury Bills were in truth not invested money, but were going to be discounted and made the basis of new credit, we should have to issue a loan, it would not matter what the price. It would not be the price that would determine our judgement: it would be the whole condition of trade and the state of the country.[36]

By October, the Chancellor had been pushed into agreeing that a new loan would be issued when conditions were right.

In the meantime, there was an issue of 6 per cent Exchequer Bonds to defend, an issue aimed at reducing the reliance on Bills. On this occasion, the Chancellor emphasised the cost:

> We had no alternative except either to issue a long loan, or to issue Exchequer Bonds at 6 per cent. We naturally took these Exchequer Bonds at a high rate

> of interest for the shortest period possible, three years only, in order to issue a security which would cost the least to the taxpayer...We ought not, in the interest of the taxpayer, to be pushed into issuing a Loan against our own judgement, a Loan which for fifteen, twenty or twenty-five years might throw an additional charge upon the taxpayer.[37]

In none of this could he mention a second reason for not issuing a loan: the inability of the Bank and Treasury to agree on how to overcome the problems of meeting the conversion pledges.

Long-dated loans: February, May and August 1916

There were frequent rumours of long-dated loans during the second half of 1915 and in 1916. One such was in October 1915 as the last of the calls on the summer's Loan was paid.[38] The story was improbable: it would have produced an impossible administrative strain, with the final date for conversions into the Bank issue of the 4½ per cents falling on 30 October, the 1 December interest payments approaching and the tendering of vouchers as subscriptions at the Post Office and the conversion of the newly created Stock beginning on the same day. There followed, during the first quarter of 1916, further persistent reports. This time the stories had an identifiable source: the bankers, and Holden in particular, seeking to influence the government in favour of a tax-free loan.

Both Holden and Schuster discussed a loan at the annual general meetings of their banks at the end of January, the former openly advocating that it should be tax-free, or at least that it should be liable to a maximum rate. In the middle of February it was the subject of a session of the Treasury subcommittee of the CLCB:

> the time had come when it was evident that the govt must ask for a new loan at no distant date, it was therefore incumbent on the Bankers to suggest on what lines and for what amount such a loan should be made. It had been suggested that the next loan should be if not tax free, then with the maximum income tax limited say to 3/6 in the £.[39]

The subcommittee decided that its discussions could go no further without knowing how the Chancellor would react to the principle of a tax-free issue.[40] In the meantime, Holden spoke to the insurance companies with a view to co-operation in an approach to the Treasury about the terms and, in particular, the tax treatment.[41] The Chancellor's answer, given to St Aldwyn and Holden, put the matter temporarily to rest:

> it appeared that the Chancellor thought that a loan entirely free of tax would not pass the House of Commons, and was repugnant to him, that he thought patriotic motives were sufficient to secure adequate subscriptions. He was further of opinion that the Banks had done enough.[42]

In May 1916, as McKenna warned of the possibility of default on American payments (see p. 218) and commentators voiced the suspicion that the government was relying on short-dated paper to avoid giving investors the opportunity of exercising their conversion rights, the Treasury and Bank were debating how to make a long-dated issue. Norman, who, at this stage, had only partial access to the Treasury, recorded that the Chancellor had given 'vague agreement…to various terms, nothing is done & opportunity will pass. Ch wants the biggest loan on earth – a spectacle – & the issues on tap prevent that.'[43] However, the Treasury's attention was not so much directed at raising new money or at the cost of the higher interest rate, as at ensuring the successful conversion of the 4½ per cent War Loan and the removal of 'the horrible incubus to future operations created by the conversion rights attaching to that stock'. The problem was how to handle the paperwork and, especially, issue at a discount with broken dividends when the Bank had lost much of its skilled labour to the forces.

The Governor took the unhelpful view that a conversion was 'physically impossible'. Only slightly more helpfully, at the end of May, his officials advised that:

> As regards the Bank's ability to conduct simultaneously an issue of a new Loan to cash subscribers and a conversion of existing holdings, it may be stated at once that such an undertaking would be quite beyond the powers of the present available staff, unless the operation were conducted on very much simpler lines than that of last year.[44]

The Treasury tended to defer to the Bank's expertise in the more technical aspects of issuing and accepted this, but warned that 'however difficult' conversion might be:

> the contingency may arise in which we shall have to face it. And if a conversion has to be made it is, of course, easier to convert an old stock into a new stock £ for £. than to accept an old stock at par plus accrued dividend as the equivalent of cash for new issue of a different denomination at a different price.[45]

The conversion schemes designed to meet this need for administrative simplicity were so intricate that it is difficult to see how they could have been sold to the investing public on a wave of patriotism. Bradbury, hitherto as hostile to tax-free borrowing as the Chancellor,[46] although for different reasons, even proposed a scheme granting protection against tax rises. It involved a new loan with the same interest rate, and dividend and redemption dates, as the old, but with the gross interest payment being adjusted to produce a net yield of £3 15s 0d per cent at the highest rate of income tax. Thus, whenever the rate of income tax was greater than 3s 4d (the rate of tax that reduced 4½ per cent gross to £3 15s 0d per cent net), the gross dividend would be greater than 4½ per cent. The cost to the government would be the difference between 3s 4d and the prevailing rate of tax whenever it was above 3s 4d. On conversion, investors would obtain, under existing tax rates, an increase from 4½ per cent to 5 per cent in their gross dividend (as the current income tax rate was 5s in the £) and from 3⅜ per cent to 3¾ per cent in their net dividend. Holders would continue to benefit from having converted as long as the rate of income tax remained above 3s 4d: if it fell beneath 3s 4d, they would not be worse off. Bradbury admitted that the cost to the Treasury was high, but he could not see investors surrendering their conversion rights for less.[47]

The proposal was ingenious: at a blow it disposed of all the problems of broken dividends and odd amounts of converted Stock. In these respects, it was a similar scheme to that used in 1932 when 5 per cent War Loan was 'continued' into 3½ per cent War Loan (see pp. 614–15). In other respects, it would have been more complex. The Bank warned that inscribing the new issue and carrying out the actual conversion before the shutting for the December dividend on the existing 4½s would be 'a stupendous work' because there were 'probably' more than one million holders of the 4½s and 5 per cent Exchequer Bonds. The scheme for adjusting the gross interest payment:

> would throw upon the Bank a task so large and complicated as to render impracticable the work of preparing the dividends, which already taxes to the utmost the entire clerical resources on which the Bank in existing circumstances are able to rely.

In any case, there would have to be changes to the system of issuing if the Treasury wanted to raise new money at the same time as a conversion. Offering a discount diminishing day-by-day when payments were made in full would have to be replaced by a single amount of discount for each of the instalment dates: this would also need to apply to payments in full made between instalment dates. The number of scrip certificates and the amount of correspondence would be reduced if investors could be persuaded by the offer of a discount to pay in full on application. The intervals between instalments would need to be lengthened from two to three weeks and the size of each instalment increased.

The Bank also pointed out how adjustment to the gross dividend would always leave some holders aggrieved. About £90m of the 4½s were held by investors who were not assessed to income tax: among these were a large number, perhaps one-third of the total number of accounts, who were not assessed because their half-yearly dividend was less than £2 10s 0d. If the gross dividend were raised, these investors would be worse off because their dividends would be increased and become a taxable amount. One solution would be to permit all holdings of less than £111 6s 0d of the new Loan to be unassessed. This, however, was inequitable as these small investors would then find themselves better off when the gross dividend was raised, whereas other investors would find their incomes unchanged. An alternative scheme would be to leave the gross interest payment at 4½ per cent, but introduce a provision that the rate of tax on holdings of the new loan would never be assessed above the 3s 4d required to give a net yield of 3¾ per cent. But, in this case, a rise in tax would benefit larger holders who were exempt from its effects and provide no benefit to the non-assessed holders.[48] It was all very technical: an effort of will was required to cut the Gordian knot and this was not available to the First Coalition.

Nothing more was done until the end of August. The Treasury was about to sell its first secured issue in New York and was scrambling to assemble the collateral. At home, the Bill issue continued to rise. Bank rate moved from 5 per cent to 6 per cent on the 13 July and a day later Bill rates were increased. Norman reported to Strong:

> Here things have not changed much since your visit, beyond the advance in the Bank Rate a couple of weeks ago. There was at that time a flurry in your [New York] market which gave us a good reason for doing what must have been done sooner or later…The effect has been satisfactory: the exchanges have been steadier and we have the feeling of being in an improved position.[49]

The rise in the rates may have steadied the exchanges, but it also made the 5 per cent Exchequer Bonds less attractive. Bond sales fell sharply and the volume of Bills grew further. On 28 August, the Bank proposed an issue of a new 4½ per cent War Loan 1925–45 at 91. It would be callable at 95 in either 1925 or 1926, or at par between 1927 and 1945. To meet the terms of their options, holders of the existing 4½ per cent War Loan and 5 per cent Exchequer Bonds would be able to convert into the new Loan on the basis of £100 of their existing holding for £100 of the new, together with an allocation of £10 of new Loan for each £100 they held of the old issues. The advantages were that the nominal amounts would be the same, plus a round addition: the dividends would be unchanged; it gave the government 'the short-term Loan it desires', while providing for a further nineteen years if rates rose; and it would rise in price as its redemption dates approached.[50] The Chancellor rejected the scheme and countered with a main issue of a 4 per cent taxable Loan at 82 (a running yield of £4 17s 7d per cent), irredeemable for twenty years, and thereafter only at the government's option – a true funding loan – and an issue to the bankers, as a replacement for their 4½s, of a five-year 5 per cent Exchequer Bond at par, subject to tax, with a holder's option to roll it over for a further ten years;[j] and a ten-year 4 per cent Exchequer Bond at par, free of income tax. Holders of the 4½ per cents and the 5 per cent Exchequer Bonds would have the option of converting into the two shorter issues on the basis of nominal for nominal and into the funding issue at the rate of £100 for £122 (that is, slightly better than the proper conversion rate of £121 19s 2d, taking the issue price of the 4½s as 98⅞). Those making cash subscriptions would be able to

j The Treasury's original suggestion did not make it clear that this was to allow the bankers to convert their 4½ per cent Loan. The Governor made some sharp criticisms, to which the Treasury replied as if their letter had been wilfully misunderstood. It was a petty storm that only showed how poor had become the relations between Chancellor and Governor. BoE, Loan Wallet 230 A & B, 'War Loan', 8 September 1916, Governor to Chancellor, 12 September 1916, and Chancellor to Governor, 13 September 1916.

rediscount Bills at the Bank at the rate at which they were originally issued, thus protecting investors who had bought Bills before the rise in Bill rates from loss.[51]

There followed a replay of the May discussions, with the Bank pointing to administrative difficulties and the Treasury suggesting complex designs. The Bank rejected the 4 per cent funding issue on the grounds that:

> Having regard to the huge total of the 4½% War Loan, and to the serious inroads that have been made upon our staff...it would be a physical impossibility for the Bank to undertake to convert that Loan into any new Loan issued at a discount.

The five-year Exchequer Bond was seen as an 'unfunding' of the 4½s: if interest rates rose, the whole £1,000m would need to be refinanced on more expensive terms; if interest rates fell, the whole would be rolled over by the investor, so that the Treasury would not enjoy the benefit of the lower rates. The Bank saw no problem with the ten-year tax-free Bond, except that it would prefer it to be 10–25 years. Rediscounting Bills at their original prices, with separate calculations for each, would be impossible to administer at the same time as a conversion. In any case, a given packet of Bills could be made up of various original maturities, issued at different rates, even if they were due to be repaid on the same day. Finally,

> it would be quite impossible to undertake a conversion involving more than two options, and [we] are confident that to attempt to offer three options would end in failure.

The Governor reminded the Chancellor that at a recent meeting with the Prime Minister, Reading and McKinnon Wood he had been promised a conversion into either a 4 per cent tax-free loan or a taxable 5 per cent loan, 'without any complications.'[52]

The Chancellor thought that neither a conversion nor an issue for cash would be a success unless investors were able to acquire paper at a heavy discount. On the 13 September, he therefore asked for the Bank's views on a 5 per cent loan, subject to tax, and a 4 per cent loan, tax-free at par (as the Bank wanted) with the option to convert either issue into a 4 per cent loan at £83 6s 8d at some later date.[53]

The planned issue date of 25 September,[k] for which the Bank had prepared prospectuses for a 5 per cent Loan 1935–50 and a 4 per cent Loan 1930–48, was no longer possible and the date was moved to the middle of October.[54] Disagreement continued. The Governor said that the Bank could not convert Bills, Exchequer Bonds and the 4½ per cent Loan at the same time as making an issue

k There is a note in Norman's diary on 26 September that 'Funding Loan has been definitely recommended for issue during past few weeks. Today as definitely refused by Ch – ? presumably because of promise to issue French Loan this month'. MND, 26 September 1916.

for cash that was any larger than £60m or £70m. He did not believe that a perpetual annuity would be popular, or that the Treasury's suggestion of a 4 per cent thirty-year issue at a deep discount could be considered as attractive to the government as a 5 per cent issue at par with a nearby optional redemption date. He advised against another Treasury scheme which would suspend sales of all other instruments for cash in May, June and July of the following year, leaving the Treasury to rely on tax revenues, and freeing the Bank to convert new 4 per cent and 5 per cent Loans into a 4 per cent issue at 85. He again pointed the Treasury towards simple cash and conversion issues of 5 and 4 per cents.[55]

The failure to agree by the end of September was pushing the earliest possible date towards the end of October. The Treasury was thrashing around, presenting unrealistic schemes that reflected a loss of judgement under the demands of the war and the Chancellor's inability to provide direction as the storms broke around the Coalition. Irritation is scarcely suppressed in the correspondence between Governor and Chancellor. Failure was signalled at the beginning of October when an issue of three-year Exchequer Bonds with a 6 per cent coupon was announced. To the public, it marked another rise in interest rates and escape from the conversion options on existing issues. To the authorities, they were a stopgap until a long-dated loan could be agreed.[l]

6 per cent Exchequer Bonds 1920 (29 September 1916)

The six per cent Bonds were intended to attract both domestic and foreign money, deflecting investors from Bills.[m] To encourage this, the issue was accompanied

l The damage wrought to decision-making was shown by the clumsy handling of the replacement of the 5 per cent Exchequer Bonds. The Bank issue of 1919s was withdrawn from sale on 27 September 1916, but the Bank 1921s continued to be available. On 1 October, it was announced that the Post Office issue of 1920s was to be withdrawn from 14 October and be replaced by an issue of the 1921s, similar to that of the Bank. On 2 October, the Bank started receiving subscriptions for the new 6 per cent Exchequer Bonds and the following day the Post Office announced that from 16 October it would be receiving applications for its own issue of the 6 per cents. Both the Bank and Post Office issues of the 5 per cents of 1921 were to continue alongside the shorter 6 per cents, an example of the authorities' belief that they could sell longer paper on a lower yield than shorter. Without explanation, it was announced on 20 October that sales of both the Bank and Post Office issues of the 5 per cents of 1921 were to be suspended, the Post Office issue having been on sale for only five days. No Post Office 1921s are recorded as having been sold. POa Post 30/3980, PO circulars 3 October and 24 October 1916; ibid., Davies, '6% Exchequer Bonds – Post Office Issue', 2 October 1916; ibid., Treasury to Postmaster-General, 21 October 1916; ibid., 'Post Office Issue of Exchequer Bonds', draft notice for press, 29 September 1916; *The Times*, 28 September 1916, p. 13, 2 October 1916, p. 9, and 21 October 1916, p. 12.

m Osborne (1926), I, p. 412. There was one change relating to overseas residents. The clause still spoke of the Bonds being free of tax (i.e. taxes on both income and capital) for those who were 'neither domiciled nor ordinarily resident' in the UK, but the exemption from all taxes was to be applied specifically to interest payments made to those who were 'not ordinarily resident' in the UK 'without regard to the question of domicile.' This change was necessary because withholding tax was being levied on those living overseas ('not ordinarily resident') unless they could show that they had given up all intention of returning to the UK (no longer 'domiciled in the UK').

by a reduction in the rates on six- and twelve-months' Bills, the Chancellor making it clear that he was aiming to encourage sales of the Bonds at the expense of Bills (Table 4.1).[56] The ploy was effective: in the thirteen weeks they were on tap sales were £161m, or over £12m a week, whereas those of the 1919 and 1920 issues had been at a rate of only £5.8m a week and, after the July rise in Bill rates, under £2.8m a week.

For the new Exchequer Bonds to do their work, there had to be a rise in the yields on existing securities. In the two months after the issue, the *Bankers' Magazine* valuation of Stock Exchange securities recorded a fall of 3.3 per cent, with that of British and Indian funds down 5.8 per cent.[57] This was accompanied by a violent reaction in the press, although there had been widespread criticism of the size of the Bill issue.[58] In contrast, there was silence from the CLCB, for its members, in cahoots with Cunliffe, had participated in the decision. The CLCB may have even proposed the issue, although it was certain to further damage its members' balance sheets. The change in the bankers' attitude took place between 13 July, when the CLCB minuted that a rise in Bank rate would be premature, and 9 August when its Treasury subcommittee recorded the opinion 'that the present system of finance by short dated securities was one that might be attended by grave dangers to the state, unless farsighted arrangements were made for funding the debt' and that it was 'impossible' for a Loan to be issued before October.[59] These, without doubt, were the reasons for the change: the acceleration in the rate of expansion of the Bill issue as sales of Exchequer Bonds faltered, which was itself a reaction to July's rise in the Bank and Bill rates,[n] and the authorities' failure to agree on how to fulfil the conversion options at the same time as making an offer for cash.

During September, the CLCB's Treasury subcommittee held a series of meetings on a subject ambiguously described in the minutes as the 'war finance of the country'. The discussion on 13 September was followed by a meeting with the Chancellor. The subcommittee then held three further meetings on 'national finance', with the Governor being asked to join that on 20 September so that he could 'be informed of the views of the Ctee. prior to their being laid before the Chancellor.' We are told that the Governor participated in the discussion and, afterwards, he and the subcommittee again visited the Treasury. Six days later, the subcommittee's minutes blandly state that 'the matters discussed at the Treasury were again debated', and record without comment that the new Bonds and reduction in Bill rates would be announced the following evening.[60] The behaviour of the life companies confirms the CLCB's involvement: they were preparing to protest to the Chancellor about the lack of consultation but abandoned the idea after speaking to Martin-Holland, the Committee's Honorary Secretary.[61]

n This rise was to continue into the autumn, so that between 8 July and 30 September the issue expanded from £797m to £1,041.5m.

We know from elsewhere that Cunliffe was prepared to accept an issue at 6 per cent, although the advice was tendered, in his usual style, without consulting or informing his Committee of Treasury, which strongly criticised the issue.[62] On 25 September, he referred to the most recent meeting between the Treasury and the CLCB's subcommittee (that on 20 September) in the context of the 'physical impossibility' of simultaneously handling a conversion and an offer for cash, and advocated a simple conversion offer followed, if necessary, by a 6 per cent five-year Exchequer Bond to mop up further Treasury Bills once the offer had closed. From this to accepting Clay's account that he 'virtually approved' the issue is but a step.[o]

The heat generated in the Commons, City and newspapers by an issue at 6 per cent was partly caused by the losses on holdings of the 4½ per cents, which sank beneath 93½ when the new issue was made. Critics, as so often during the war, seemed to have the interests of investors, rather than taxpayers, at heart: they again accused the government of issuing Exchequer Bonds to avoid triggering the conversion rights on the 4½s. In August, the Chancellor had had to deny any such consideration affected borrowing decisions: although unable to provide a date for a new issue, whether to refinance Bills or to raise new money, he promised that:

> whenever the opportunity is favourable, and whenever the general conditions of our finance not only warrant it, but indicate that it ought to be done, we shall do it without hesitation.[63]

On 10 October, the Chancellor gave his hostage to fortune: the 6 per cent Exchequer Bonds had been issued because the moment was not favourable for a long loan, but whereas he could not 'give any definite pledge to issue such a loan at any particular date', it was his 'intention to recommend such an issue to Parliament at the first suitable opportunity.' On 20 November, he lunched with Jack Morgan, who reported that the Chancellor intended to issue in the new year and that he was confident that it would be a success.[64] It was not to be McKenna's responsibility. On 10 December, Bonar Law became Chancellor and Leader of the House in a new coalition led by Lloyd George.

o BoE, Loan Wallet 230 A & B, Governor to Chancellor, 25 September 1916. Clay records that 'The Governor confided to Norman afterwards [the meeting of the Committee of Treasury] that he had virtually approved it.' Clay (1957), p. 100. His source is MND, 27 October 1916. Others disagree. Sayers says that 'At the Bank itself there was a revulsion against the issue of bonds yielding as much as 6 per cent; when Exchequer Bonds were issued at this rate in October 1916, it was at the insistence, oddly enough, of the joint stock banks and against the advice of the Bank of England.' He gives his source as Lord Cullen (the Deputy Governor at the time of the issue) eight years later. Cullen was also responsible for Osborne's version: 'The introduction of a 6% security was largely due to Sir Edward Holden, who was at this time maintaining that the public required a yield of 4½% free of tax and who apparently convinced the other bankers.' Sayers (1976), I, p. 96; Osborne (1926), I, p. 412.

Endnotes

1 These two paragraphs are based on Mallet and George (1929), pp. 68–119; Hirst and Allen (1926), pp. 73–165; *Financial Statements (1915–16)* (HCP 344), 21 September 1915, and *(1916–17)*, (HCP 50), 4 April 1916.

2 McKenna gave evidence on 23 August and it is recorded in Cab. 37/133/9. The Committee's Report is Cab. 37/134/9, 8 September 1915. The Treasury's submissions are: McKenna, untitled, 13 September 1915; Bradbury, 'Limits of Borrowing at Home and Abroad', 9 September 1915; and Keynes 'The Financial Prospects of this Financial Year', 9 September 1915. Copies are Cab. 37/134/11, Cab. 37/134/12 and Cab. 37/34/17. Keynes's contributions are reproduced in Keynes (1971–89), XVI, pp. 110–15 and 117–25.

3 Cab. 37/131/37, 22 July 1915.

4 Cab. 37/34/17, untitled, 13 September 1915.

5 Cab. 37/34/12, Keynes, 'The Financial Prospects of this Financial Year', 9 September 1915. Reproduced in Keynes (1971–89), XVI, pp. 117–25.

6 The Report is in Cab. 37/142/11. The original draft of Keynes's contribution is in Keynes (1971–89), XVI, pp. 162–7. T 170/74, Bradbury to Hankey and Hankey to Bradbury, 6 January 1916. There are several drafts of the evidence written during January by Bradbury and Hankey and two drafts of the report printed on 4 February in MS Asquith, 123 and 124, and T 170/84.

7 Cab. 37/142/11, 'Cabinet Committee on the Co-ordination of Military and Financial Effort', 4 February 1916. The part written by Keynes is reproduced in Keynes (1971–89), XVI, pp. 162–77.

8 Ibid.

9 T 171/129, Keynes to Hamilton, 4 February 1916; Keynes (1971–89), XVI, pp. 162–77.

10 Osborne (1926), I, p. 404.

11 T 172/221, 'Conference between the Chancellor of the Exchequer and Representatives of British Life, Fire and Marine Insurance Companies and Societies and Representatives of Trust Companies', 11 December 1915.

12 *Hansard* (Commons) 6 January 1916, col. 1106.

13 CLCBt, 20 December 1915.

14 T 170/93, seventeen bankers to Chancellor, 22 December 1915, and Hamilton to Martin-Holland, 28 December 1915.

15 Osborne, I, p. 407.

16 *Hansard* (Commons), 26 June 1916, col. 691.

17 POa Post 30/3980, Davies, 'Exchequer Bonds (Post Office Issue)', 6 July 1916, and 'Exchequer Bonds. Post Office Issue', 28 July 1916; ibid., Murray to the Secretary of the Treasury, 11 July 1916; ibid., 'Exchequer Bonds. Post Office Issue. Notes of a Discussion at the Treasury, 28th July 1916.'

18 BoE, Loan Wallet 252, TM, 26 May 1916.

19 *National Debt: annual returns*.

20 T 172/776, Sutton to Hamilton 14 May and 30 May 1918, Ramsay to Bradbury, 17 May 1918, and Hamilton to Sutton 30 May 1918.

21 Goodhart (1972), pp. 127–41, and Morgan (1952), p. 228. Morgan draws his data from *The Economist*. The ratios for the earlier years were 18.5 per cent (end-1913), 19.8 per cent (1914) and 33.9 per cent (1915).

22 T 170/93, Holden to McKenna, 21 February 1916.

23 CLCBt, 24 February 1916; T 170/93, 29 February 1916. The scrap is about one by two inches and loose in the file. It will be a miracle if it is not already lost.

24 CLCBm, 26 January 1916; CLCBt, 14 March 1916.

25 The TMs extending the scheme were dated 10 June and 18 August 1916. Copies are in BoE, Loan Wallet 238.

26 Osborne (1926), I, pp. 409–10.
27 *The London Gazette*, relevant dates. The rates and amounts of Bills sold at tender are recorded in Osborne (1926), I, pp. 485–7.
28 BoE, G1/420, Norman to Strong, 22 September 1916.
29 Cab. 42/13/4, 4 May 1916; LGP, D/24/6/1, 17 May 1916, McKenna, Memorandum for Cabinet Finance Committee.
30 *Hansard* (Commons), 10 August 1916, col. 1286.
31 Ibid., 21 June 1915, col. 1000.
32 Ibid., 4 April 1916, cols 1052, 1054–5 and 1064–5. See Morgan (1952), pp. 92–3.
33 Ibid., 10 August 1916, cols 1265–1325, and 19 October 1916, cols 771–802.
34 Ibid.,10 August 1916, cols 1282–3. The analysis of the Bill maturities and the briefing papers for the debate are in T 171/129. The Chancellor, and the briefing papers, do not distinguish departmental from market holdings. It is not impossible that official holdings of shorter Bills had been run off and invested in longer Bills, leaving the length of market holdings unchanged.
35 Osborne (1926), I, pp. 478–9; BLP, 52/1/63, James Gardiner (shipowners and brokers) to Bonar Law, 29 December 1915; *Hansard* (Commons), 14 December 1916, cols 850–1.
36 *Hansard* (Commons), 10 August 1916, col. 1285.
37 Ibid., 19 October 1916, cols 787–8.
38 *The Times*, 21 October 1915, p. 7. This may have been a late report of discussions between the clearing bankers in the early part of September. CLCBt, 8 and 16 September 1915.
39 CLCBt, 16 February 1916.
40 T 170/93, St Aldwyn to Hamilton, 25 February 1916; CLCBt, 24 February 1916 and 1 March 1916.
41 ABI, The Life Offices' Association, Minutes of the Association, 3 March 1916.
42 CLCBt, 2 March 1916.
43 MND, 26 May 1916.
44 BoE, Loan Wallet 237(1), Bradbury, 'Conversion of 4½% War Loan', May 1916, and Loan Wallet 230 A & B, Bank of England, 'Memorandum', 27 May 1916.
45 BoE, Loan Wallet 237 (1), 'Conversion of 4½% War Loan', May 1916, and Bradbury to Governor, 31 May 1916.
46 T 170/71, Bradbury, 'War Loan', 7 June 1915.
47 BoE, Loan Wallet 237(1), 'Conversion of 4½% War Loan', Bradbury, May 1916.
48 BoE, Loan Wallet 230 A & B, Bank of England, 'Memorandum', 27 May 1916, and Loan Wallet 237 (1), Bradbury to Governor, 31 May 1916.
49 BoE, G3/174, Norman to Strong, 24 July 1916. Quoted in Sayers (1976), I, p. 95.
50 BoE, Loan Wallet 237 (1), '4½% War Loan 1925–45', 28 August 1916.
51 BoE, Loan Wallet 230 A & B, 'War Loan', 8 September 1916.
52 BoE, Loan Wallet 230 A & B, Cunliffe to Chancellor, 12 September 1916, and Chancellor to Cunliffe, 13 September 1916. No other reference to this meeting has been found. The Chancellor denied that any such promise had been made.
53 BoE, Loan Wallet 230 A & B, Chancellor to Governor, 13 September 1916.
54 BoE, Loan Wallet 237(2), Governor to Chancellor, 7 September 1916, and draft prospectuses; Loan Wallet 230 A & B, Governor to Chancellor, 14 September 1916.
55 BoE, Loan Wallet 230 A & B, Governor to Chancellor, 14 September 1916 and 25 September 1916.
56 *Hansard* (Commons), 11 October 1916, col. 92; BoE, Loan Wallet 230 A & B, Governor to Chancellor, 25 September 1916.
57 *Bankers' Magazine*, November and December 1916, Stock Exchange Values.
58 Morgan (1952), p. 111. For examples of comment, see *The Economist*, 30 September 1916, p. 555; *The Financial News*, 29 September 1916, p. 2; *Bankers' Magazine*, November 1916, pp. 548–52.

59 CLCBm, 13 July 1916; CLCBt, 9 August 1916.
60 CLCBt, 11, 13, 18, 19, 20 and 26 September 1916.
61 ABI, Life Offices' Association, Minutes of the Association, 2 October and 5 October 1916. The Finance Committee was preparing a memorial to the Chancellor on the issue, but decided that the Chairman should first see Martin-Holland to find out whether the banks were going to take any action and whether they had been consulted. The result of the meeting is not recorded, but there is no suggestion in either The Life Offices' Association Minutes or the Treasury files of a memorial having been written or received.
62 MND, 4 October 1916. No discussion is recorded in CTM.
63 *Hansard* (Commons), 10 August 1916, cols 1280 and 1288.
64 Ibid., 10 October 1916, cols 17–18; MGP, B. Hist. 2, F 13, no. 26519, Jack Morgan to Davison, 20 November 1916.

8 The year of drift

External borrowing in 1916

As we know they want all the money that they can get when and as we can get it.

Henry Davison, 12 September 1916,
MGP, Box History 2, F12

Any feeling of irritation or lack of sympathy with this country or with its policy in the minds of the American public...would render it exceedingly difficult, if not impossible, to carry through financial operations on a scale adequate to our needs. The sums which this country will require to borrow in the United States of America in the next six or nine months are so enormous, amounting to several times the entire national debt of that country, that it will be necessary to appeal to every class and section of the investing public.

John Maynard Keynes, 10 October 1916,
Keynes (1971–89), XVI, pp. 197–8

If things go on as at present, I venture to say with certainty that by next June or earlier the President of the American Republic will be in a position, if he wishes, to dictate his own terms to us.

John Maynard Keynes, 18 October 1916,
Keynes (1971–89), XVI, p. 201

During 1916, the Morgan partners in New York and London ran British finance in the USA. Their success in raising $500m with the Anglo-French Loan played some part in this, but it was more important that they had shown that exploiting the American capital market required experience, flair and placing power: the connections, both business and personal, to enable the securities to be underwritten; knowledge of the pipelines down which securities flowed to investors, and of how the distribution system should be remunerated; the ability to judge investors' capacity to buy, and how it might be stimulated; the skill which maximised sales, while creating a sense of scarcity. Besides showing the Treasury in London that it should leave the issuing decisions to Morgans, the Anglo-French Loan had two lasting effects: it ensured that nothing could be done in the public markets until its sour taste had been washed away; and it drove home the message that little could be borrowed except against collateral.

In the seven months before the USA became a belligerent, Morgans used their skills on behalf of the Treasury on three occasions. The issues, documented in the cables passing to London, provide a fascinating picture of market judgement and manipulation in which – adjusted for British legal and institutional arrangements – can be clearly discerned the origins of the post-war operations of the CNRA in the gilt-edged market. In November, with the market sated with allied paper and the British pressing for yet more credit, Morgans' mastery was shown wanting, not in their judgement of the market's willingness to take unsecured allied dollar Treasury Bills, but in their grasp of politics and their assessment of the Federal Reserve Board's preparedness to regulate and guide the banking system. The episode made little difference to the volume of credit flowing to the allies, but it ended Morgan's dominance of British finance in New York, a change which was marked by the despatch of a resident Treasury Mission to New York, headed by S. Hardman Lever, Financial Secretary to the Treasury.

Secured issues in the public markets fitted conveniently with the Treasury's schemes for mobilising securities, many of which were only borrowed from their owners. The securities also made it possible for the British to borrow from the American banking system on call. From September 1915, Morgans and a group of banks provided the Treasury with occasional advances collateralised by British securities deposited with Morgans in New York. This call loan, the 'Morgan overdraft', was put on a formal footing in February 1916. Intended as a temporary bridge if markets were unable to absorb sales of the Treasury's securities, it was used intensively after May 1916 when the Treasury's stream of wholly owned American securities ran less strongly: in combination with the existing facility for the Bank, it became a permanent source of finance, only occasionally paid off by public issues. At the end of the year, as the Treasury's warnings of a stop in the USA came near to being justified, the overdraft became the mainstay of British finance.

This chapter shows how the call loan originated in the arrangement between the Treasury and Morgans for the sale of British-owned US securities. It then describes the issue of the British secured loans of September and November 1916 and February 1917, laying particular emphasis on the techniques Morgans used during the sales process. The Federal Reserve's intervention to forestall the issue of British dollar Treasury Bills is shown to be of political, rather than financial, importance.

The origins of the Morgan call loans

The need for the Treasury to have its own account in New York became clear during July and August 1915, when it bought, and the Bank sorted, shipped and sold, the Prudential's securities. The accounting and legal relationship was in disorder. The Treasury owned the securities, the Bank was the obligor for Morgans' advance, the securities were the collateral and the proceeds of sales were credited to the Bank. There must have been some formal agreement between the Treasury and the Bank, the details of which have been lost, but the position could only have been unsatisfactory and, on 26 August, two weeks after the Prudential's securities began to arrive in New York and twelve days after the Bank gave instructions for their sale to begin, the Treasury opened its own account into which was paid the proceeds of the securities' sale 'effected both before and after' the account was opened.[1]

The instructions for the Account's establishment included provision for advances against securities on the same terms as those being made to the Bank. The first advance was recorded on 4 September. This was soon paid off, the proceeds from securities maintaining the Account in balance until the end of October.[2] *Ad hoc* advances were made to the Treasury at the end of that month, and in November in expectation of the receipt of the calls on the Anglo-French Loan.[3] Terms for the call loan, the Client No. 2 account, were formally negotiated in January 1916.[4]

The provision of loan facilities against collateral grew naturally out of Morgan's business of selling the securities. At the beginning of January 1916, as the peg was inserted, Reading asked Grenfell whether Morgans would act as agent for the disposal of the paper being collected by the newly created American Dollar Securities Committee and what commission they would charge. He then left the negotiations to the LEC and Grenfell, the latter equipped with cabled arguments from New York.[5] On 11 January, the LEC said that it could not negotiate the level of commissions unless it knew whether Morgans would be prepared to make advances against the securities. Behind this lay two considerations. It was thought that any bank providing advances would want to see the securities and have the business of selling them: then, as now, much paperwork would be saved if the same bank provided the loan, held the securities as collateral, sold the securities and credited the overdrawn account. More importantly, sales would take place when money was needed and when market conditions permitted: if the market dried up, the Treasury would want to borrow against the securities until sales again became possible. For banks in New York, there was the convenience that loans secured against stock exchange collateral and repayable at call at the demand of the lender was a standard procedure, the traditional method of employing temporary funds.[6]

Two days after the LEC asked its question, Morgans proposed commissions of 1/4 per cent on all transactions and a loan facility of up to $250m, provided by themselves and their associates against 'acceptable' American securities, with the 'standard' 20 per cent margin, or lower, if the collateral were high-grade Bonds. The advance would be a mixture of a term and call loan and, in current conditions, the former would cost 4 per cent. Morgans proposed handling the advance as they had that to the Bank. Up to a level they did not specify, Morgans, or Morgans and the other members of the Trio, would be solely responsible and the expectation would be that the facility's existence would be kept secret. Beyond that level, the circle of banks would be progressively widened, starting with 'friends' such as Bankers Trust and Chase National. The loan would not be made to Morgans, but each bank would own part, and this would be evidenced by participation receipts.[7]

In February 1916, Morgans reported that the New York market was becoming tired from absorbing $2.5m of British-owned Bonds each day and suggested that the Treasury should consider withdrawing and, if necessary, making use of the loan facility. The Treasury agreed in principle, but that spring it was in no position to reduce sales for long.[8] On 2 May, it took $12m from Morgans, its first advance under February's agreement, and two days later the Governor asked Morgans to advance $50m to the Bank (that is, the LEC) against gold in transit or awaiting shipment. On the same day, McKenna issued dire warnings to the Cabinet War Committee. France, he said, had joined Russia and Italy as a major drain on British financial resources. Russian spending was out of control and

> Our own liabilities are constantly increasing as it is, especially in the United States of America. We cannot pay off our debts, and we are only piling up new ones. Another year of war, if we go on at the present rate, will find us absolutely bankrupt…The time will come when I shall have to state to this Committee that in three or four months' time we must make peace.[9]

By the end of the third week in May, the No. 1 account (the Bank) was overdrawn by $24.8m and the No. 2 (the Treasury) by $45.5m. On 1 June, Morgans began to distribute between $15m and $20m of the No. 1 account's loan outside the Trio. On 12 June, the No. 2 loan reached $124m and Morgans informed the Treasury that the 20 per cent margin was impaired, that the advance was about to exceed the available collateral and that they were having to provide $56.5m themselves to avoid embarrassing their client.[10]

As in 1915, the short-term arrangements were intended to provide temporary accommodation. If sales of securities were insufficient, public loans had to be issued. On 24 May, with the approval of the Governor and the Chancellor, Grenfell asked Morgans to advise on public issues totalling $1,000m, not necessarily to be taken simultaneously, secured against the debentures of British and colonial railways.[11] Grenfell arranged that Morgans give a strong answer: securities should be conscripted and the size of British holdings of neutral paper ascertained. Issues in units of $250m would be no problem, provided the collateral was of the customary type. If it were the suggested railway paper, 'we should have to plan for a great deal of education' over several months.[12] Two days later, the additional £0 2s 0d tax on the income from designated overseas securities was imposed, and securities for a time flowed more easily (see p. 179).

The first collateral loan (22 August 1916)

During June and July, Morgans and Brown Brothers were preparing to borrow for the French by means of a financing vehicle, the American Foreign Securities Corporation (AFSC).[13] This was a device. The company was chartered in New York State with a capital of $10m and a host of directors from banks around the country. It was to issue debentures secured by a mixed bag of the securities of neutral governments, the Province of Quebec and US corporations provided by

French investors. The proceeds, together with as much of the capital as would produce \$100m, were to be used to buy a three-year French Government Note with a coupon of 7¼ per cent. Although Morgans were nervous about the reception of the neutral government securities, an unknown risk to American investors, the sale of \$94.5m 5 per cent three-year Notes at 96 (\$6.48 per cent) to a syndicate was completed without difficulty on 18 July. Morgans suggested that the British should consider the same method, except that the proceeds should be borrowed for up to a year.[14] The contrivance was thought to have several advantages. Morgans believed that British credit would suffer if they were seen to be borrowing small sums because there was the implication that they had tried to borrow large and had failed. Although it was artificial, Morgans advised that this would be avoided if the liability was indirect. For the same reason, British credit would not suffer from the high rate being paid, although it would be a less direct comparison with the Anglo-French Loan, and so help protect its price. Finally, as with the two Morgan loans, it would be a separate obligor for the purposes of the National Bank and state regulations.[15]

The French issue was oversubscribed, applications from the public at 98 being \$111.4m. Despite the success, sellers appeared when the market opened and Morgans and Brown Brothers had to buy \$10.7m to prevent the price collapsing. Not surprisingly, Morgans had second thoughts about a similar vehicle for the British and instead recommended an issue of a direct liability: \$250m two-year Notes secured by US corporate, Canadian government and South American government securities in equal amounts. The coupon would be 5 per cent, the price to the buying syndicate 98 (\$6.06 per cent) and to the investor 99 (\$5.55 per cent): Morgans would be paid an additional ½ per cent, so the price to the Treasury would be 97½ (\$6.34 per cent). In case the Treasury was unable to extend its borrowing of securities under Scheme A, the option was taken of calling the loan at 101 in the first year and at 100½ in the second; the prospect of being bought out at a premium adding to the issue's speculative attractions (Table 6.2). The Treasury quickly agreed, except for the composition of the collateral.[16]

The term was selected – the maturity date was 1 September 1918 – so that it would not bear direct comparison with the four years remaining of the Anglo-French Loan or the three years of the AFSC issue. It would also match the two years for which securities were being borrowed under Scheme A. This limitation led straight to Scheme B, with the lengthening of the period for which securities were borrowed (see p. 221).[17]

Morgans believed that the issue would have to be treated 'in a strong and aggressive manner.' Aggression had two constituents. Terms were included which permitted the Treasury to withdraw part of the collateral, sell it, and apply the proceeds to buying Notes in the market at prices lower than the relevant call prices or, by lot, at the call prices.[18] This was intended to support the price and improve liquidity, but only when it was convenient to the Treasury. It was envisaged that only the American securities would be sold, perhaps because the others enjoyed a poor market. Although it was not divulged in the prospectus, half of the Americans were wholly owned by the Treasury and the other half were borrowed. This, in conjunction with an option to substitute one security for another as long as it did not disturb the three broad categories into which the collateral was divided, ensured that if sales were such that all the wholly owned securities were used the Treasury would be able to replace borrowed securities with those wholly owned and continue to make sales.[19]

The other part of Morgans' aggression was kept very quiet. They arranged that the Bank of England and themselves would underwrite up to $50m apiece, with the other two members of the Trio underwriting a further $25m each.[a] Thus, only $100m would be available for the market. If Morgans and the Bank had to take any of the first $100m, Morgans intended to trade back and forth, keeping the market active, intimating investor buying and, finally, selling out the whole position.[20]

As the issue unfolded, two further twists were added. Having ensured that they had firm commitments from the largest underwriters, Morgans overallotted the remainder by $60m. Provided that most was accepted, this would enable them to cut the underwriting allotted to each participant, so that the market would believe that the issue had been enthusiastically received. It turned out as Morgans envisaged; nearly all the extra underwriting was accepted and their friends' commitments were reduced. The incidental effect was to relieve the Bank of England of its $50m, but it was asked, and it agreed, to subscribe for that amount when it came to the public offering, or in the secondary market, should Morgans deem it helpful.[21] A second ruse was adopted just before the period for sales to the public ended. Morgans, finding that subscriptions were only $164m and surmising that some banks had not subscribed because they believed that they would be left with the Notes in the underwriting, announced that the lists for subscriptions would close early. The implication that the issue had been fully subscribed brought in more applications, taking the total to $211m. The balance of $39m was taken equally by the Bank and Morgans, with Morgans immediately taking over the Bank's share. This was not the whole story, which turned out very well for the New York partners. Both the underwriting and syndication (sales to the public) lists for this issue have survived. They show that Morgans as a partnership did, indeed, underwrite $50m, Davison as an individual underwriting an additional $4.8m. The syndication list shows that they sold all their underwriting, so earning the underwriters' 1 per cent on $50m, in addition to their ½ per cent on $250m. Morgans' profit was $1.1m.

The underwriting list also shows important differences from the Anglo-French Loan. As would be expected, there were fewer names – 487, about one-third of those conscripted in September 1915 – with many for as little as $25,000. As well as large commitments from Morgans' usual associates in New York, there were many from the west and mid-west, notably from Chicago. Once again, the names of Rockefeller ($5m), Guggenheim ($1m) and Frick ($1m) appear. Noticeably

a This division between the three New York banks had been a regular practice since at least 1907. Cleveland and Huertas (1985), p. 56.

more contractors subscribed than underwrote. Of the munitions manufacturers, Du Pont underwrote $5m, which it kept. Bethlehem Steel, in contrast with its reluctance to underwrite the Anglo-French Loan, actually subscribed for $5m.[22]

The limitation on the Notes' length and the call option showed the necessity for a scheme which would give the Treasury longer use of borrowed securities, while preparation of the collateral, and the prospect of further loans, showed that the Treasury list should be extended. Once a collateral loan had been issued, it was unlikely that unsecured issues could be made again and, with British holdings of American securities dwindling, the obligations of neutral countries, the Dominions and colonies would have to be used more extensively. Further, the use of collateral should be carefully planned, for it would be dangerous not to secure later issues with much the same mixture of paper: lower quality securities would imply that the bottom of the barrel was being scraped.

The first collateral issue showed the potential for using the securities of neutral countries (henceforth called 'neutrals'), as had that for the AFSC, an experiment that came at a useful moment. Thus, Scheme B was accompanied by an extension of the list to include the securities of neutral governments, of the Dominion of Canada and of the Canadian Pacific Railway (CPR). A further list, published on 24 August, included more debt of neutral governments and their railways.[23] On 12 September, the sale of American securities was suspended, and in October the Treasury reported to the Cabinet that the remainder needed to be 'employed to render palatable to the American investor a much larger proportion of non-American securities, as our collateral for ensuing loans'.[24]

None of this came in time to contribute to the 1 September deadline. Canadian securities presented no difficulty: the Dominion government had recently agreed to issue to the UK Treasury $107m of its Bonds in respect of Canada's war indebtedness to Britain and these would be in New York by the issue date.[25] Neutrals were more difficult. The Treasury pointed out that it took about four weeks for securities to be processed and despatched, so that those on the extended list would not be available in New York by 1 September and that, anyway, it was too early to estimate the size of British holdings. Morgans wanted Argentinians to the value of US$75m and Chileans to the value of US$25m because the former were well-known to American investors and they had started their negotiations with members of the syndicate on the basis of that mixture. An additional difficulty was that the LEC wanted the government securities of neutral Europe, and especially those of Holland and Scandinavia, for their own exchange operations. The compromise was one that left the collateral strong, but the Treasury and Morgans with the flexibility to exchange securities within each group for other securities according to the appetite of the New York market for particular issues and the supply available from the UK. The Canadians were to comprise debt of, or debt guaranteed by, the Dominion government, together with issues of the CPR; the former was to come from the $107m of the newly issued Bonds, which would be replaced by Canadian government sterling securities when they had been collected. The neutrals were to be those of Argentina, Chile, Norway, Sweden, Denmark, Holland and Switzerland (Table 6.2). All the securities, other than the $100m of Americans and those of the CPR, were to be government, or government-guaranteed. American securities quoted in New York or cash could be deposited until the neutrals had arrived in New York.[26]

The second collateral loan (30 October 1916)

During the autumn of 1916, allied spending in North America was assessed by two committees in London. Relations with the USA had deteriorated during the late spring and summer. The execution of the leaders of the Easter Rebellion in Dublin had inflamed Irish–American opinion. Britain had tightened the blockade on the Central Powers: cables and mail were being censored and shipping intercepted. In July, she published a blacklist of American and Latin American firms suspected or accused of trading with the enemy. The USA had emerged from recession and was no longer in such need of allied markets. Relations between the USA and Germany had improved when Germany abandoned her first unrestricted submarine campaign in April. On 5 September, Congress approved legislation giving the President power to retaliate against interference, that is British interference, with its vessels. In an interview with the United Press on 26 September, Lloyd George sought to pre-empt American mediation by warning Wilson not to meddle. On 30 September, the Foreign Office called together an interdepartmental committee to assess allied dependence on the USA.

While Morgans were preparing during August to sell the first British collateral loan, they found themselves being pressed by the French for a further issue and to join a group of banks led by National City Bank, which was preparing a $50m issue for the Russians.[27] The French had become suspicious that UK borrowing in New York was receiving priority and its loans were being issued on superior terms, while Morgans felt that allied finances in the USA needed planning. Between 3 and 10 October, at Morgans' request, a Joint Anglo-French Financial Committee, with Jack Morgan and Davison attending some sessions, examined spending and resources for the six months to March 1917.

The reports and papers that came out of these committees made sombre reading.[28] Although there was little hope of acquiring any more gold from the allies beyond that already promised, they would require continued 'lavish and increasing financial assistance'. Daily expenditure on the war by the UK was about £5m, of which £2m was being incurred in North America. Expenditure between May and September 1916 had been at a rate of $208m a month. Between August and March 1917 it was expected to rise to $250m a month, providing no more orders were placed, exchange intervention was no greater than forecast and the UK maintained its industrial output. In recent months, about 60 per cent of the sums required had come from the sale of securities and gold, with the remainder being borrowed. In the next six months, it was possible that $250m could be met from gold sales, so that $1,250m would need to be borrowed: $200m a month, compared with $80m a month. The UK would need to borrow in the USA sums equal to between 20 and 40 per cent of its entire war expenditure.[29] Morgans were appalled: 'All devices must be used' was Jack Morgan's comment; 'Your confidential information as to requirements of Allied Governments is staggering' was that of the partners in New York.[30]

For the French, 'devices', or more bluntly scraping the bottom of the barrel, were to include a \$25m one-year Commercial Export Credit (12 September);[b] \$10m loaned by Morgans and Brown Brothers on a 60-day collateralised French Government Note (15 September); a \$12m 6 per cent one-year issue, secured on St Louis and San Francisco Railway Bonds, through Seligman (15 October); an issue of \$50m five-year 6 per cent gold Bonds for the City of Paris through Kuhn, Loeb (to be used, said the circular, for 'the alleviation of suffering') (15 October); issues of 6 per cent three-year gold Bonds totalling \$36m for the Cities of Bordeaux, Marseilles and Lyons, for the same purpose as the Paris Bonds (1 November); a loan of \$4m from du Pont Nemours (2 November); and a \$50m industrial credit (11 November).[31] For the British, devices had started the previous June when Robert Fleming had arranged to borrow \$4m from its New York correspondents, Maitland Coppell, using as collateral some unmarketable American securities and lending the proceeds to the British government against one-year sterling Treasury Bills.[32] In the middle of September, the Metropolitan Water Board had issued \$6.4m one-year bills at a discount rate of 6¹/₈ per cent through the Guaranty Trust Co. and there was much discussion of issues by British cities, Morgans hoping that up to \$100m might be obtained in total.[33] They were postponed several times, first for the enabling legislation,[c] and then to keep the way free for the Treasury's own issues and those of the French. With the delays, none had been issued before the USA became a belligerent and US Treasury advances replaced private credits.[34] On 2 October, the Treasury issued \$16m Notes in lieu of cash to du Pont Nemours, a major supplier of explosives. This was followed by another \$13m in the middle of December. Also in December, English Sewing Cotton Co. borrowed \$4.9m from Morgans on the security of its holding in the American Thread Co. and lent the proceeds to the Treasury against one-year Treasury Bills deposited in London, and a syndicate of Japanese banks bought ¥100m 6 per cent three-year Yen Exchequer Bonds and remitted the \$49.5m proceeds to New York (Table 6.3).[35]

These, in aggregate, were important, but the main source had to be public issues by the Treasury: more collateral loans. The proceeds of the 1 September issue lasted four weeks, the Treasury Account being exhausted on 4 October, and the No. 2 facility being reactivated the same day (Table 6.4). On 12 October, heavy disbursements took the advance on the No. 2 account to \$67m, of which Morgans were responsible for \$57m and the First National and National City Banks the balance. The No. 1 facility was reopened on 14 October. The pace continued, and on 17 October the No. 2 account was overdrawn by \$125.5m, Morgans supplying \$98m.[36] Raising it above this level was presenting difficulties.

b This credit was on the same terms as those arranged on 21 August 1915 by Brown Brothers. French banks drew ninety-day bills on US banks, who accepted them. They were then discounted and the proceeds passed to the Banque de France. Three renewals were provided for. PML, Archives, Syndicates No. 8, f. 179.

c Public Authorities and Bodies (Loan) Act 1916.

The maximum that had been supplied from outside the Trio the previous summer was $35m. Caution and regulation were making banks in New York City loath to lend more, and it was feared that if borrowing was extended further afield it would affect the demand for a new British issue. On 17 October, the New York partners asked the Treasury to postpone payments when possible and renewed their calls for gold from Ottawa.[37] Fortunately, the markets were strengthening and Morgans were able to sell their accumulated holdings of the first collateral loan and the AFSC. An issue, which they had hitherto pencilled in for January, began to look feasible for November.

However, British ministers first had to deal with a problem that was both delicate and expensive. The partners in New York cabled that negotiations were being held up by the imminent bankruptcy of two munitions contractors, the Winchester Repeating Arms Co. and the Remington Arms–Union Metallic Cartridge Co., which had British contracts for ammunition and rifles. The companies were late with their deliveries and the rifles were failing their inspections: on 21 September, the British gave formal notice of cancellation. The high level of rejection was, the companies claimed, not the result of poor manufacture, but of a new design of what was anyway a difficult specification. The creditors most closely involved were National City Bank and Guaranty Trust Co. from New York and Kidder Peabody and Lee Higginson & Co. from Boston, all of central importance in underwriting and distributing British securities. Important shareholders included William Rockefeller, a director of National City Bank, and his son-in-law Hartley Dodge. Both companies were well-known to Morgans: they had originally financed Winchester, later turning the business over to Kidders.[d] The total bank advances amounted to $76m. Morgans still held $2.4m of Winchester Notes, as well as $1m of those of Remington, and had guaranteed other debts. The bankers threatened to withhold support for the new loans, pressing Morgans to ensure that the contracts were renegotiated on terms which would keep the companies in business.

Jack Morgan and Davison, who were still in London after the meetings of the Joint Anglo-French Financial Committee, negotiated with Ministers. They presented the problem, not as a question of whether the companies had fulfilled their contracts, but as a matter which could call into question the value of the British government's business, alienate industrial and commercial America and dry up the enthusiasm of investors. Most importantly, it would make new issues through the banks well nigh impossible. The Chancellor had no doubt that he was being blackmailed, but had no trouble persuading other ministers of the seriousness of the position. The lenders, however, would not be fobbed off with vague expressions of goodwill and the intention to be helpful. After stormy meetings,

d In November 1914, Jack Morgan wrote to Grenfell 'Our relations with both the Remington and Winchester people are so close that we have been able to discuss these matters [rifles] without standing at arm's length. The Winchester people have been customers of J. P. Morgan & Co. and their predecessors for almost fifty years and the Remington people have been intimately known to William Porter for a great many years.' PML, Archives, Box 11, Jack Morgan to Grenfell, 27 November 1914.

the Treasury had to authorise Morgans to adjust the differences with the companies by offering payments in the form of not more than $30m UK three-year 5 per cent Notes, with the condition that they could not be sold into the market. The old contracts were to be cancelled and replaced with new ones for a total of two million rifles on which the companies would make no profit, but which the British could cancel at any time (Table 6.3; 'Rifle Contracts').[38]

The French thought that the UK's 1 September loan should have been a joint issue, like that of autumn 1915, and there had been tension before the meetings of the Joint Anglo-French Financial Committee.[39] In the interests of harmony, early in the conference Reading had asked Morgans to advise on another combined $500m unsecured loan, perhaps with the two governments quietly taking a quarter to ensure that it did not exceed the market's capacity and appeared to be a success. Not surprisingly, Morgans had firmly rejected the possibility: it was too large, the market had become accustomed to secured borrowing and the Anglo-French Loan was trading at a discount of 2½ points.[40] Instead, the second British collateral loan, dated 1 November 1916, was offered to the public on 30 October, shortly before the Presidential election.

The partners in New York originally recommended equal amounts of one-year, three-year and five-year Notes. They envisaged that the ease in the money market would allow the shortest to be sold 'with a rush' and that the enthusiasm would carry the longer issues. As there was no two-year maturity, there could be no direct comparison with the September issue, while the five-year was longer than the Anglo-French Loan, which was now four years and, in any case, unsecured. At the insistence of the Treasury, the one-year was dropped and the issue was divided between three years and five years. The coupons on both were 5½ per cent (Table 6.2).

Morgans attacked the sale with aggression, as they had two months earlier. Following the Treasury's policy of shipping gold to the USA to help keep money cheap, they wanted to import gold 'to load up the Banks…getting them to groan in spirit with the burden, making them more ready to take on good commitments', keeping the 'money market very easy but not so much as to induce a highly speculative market.'[41] They attempted, but failed because of a lack of interest from other banks, to form a consortium to buy the Anglo-French Loan, in hopes that the munitions contractors would be released to take the new issue.[42] They supported the September loan, selling collateral and buying the Notes in the market, so that when the time came to sign the pledges at the beginning of November there were only $210m outstanding. They arranged for the Bank to join them in the underwriting and the public sale, each agreeing to take up to $60m. They again included in the prospectus the provision enabling collateral to be sold and the proceeds used to support the Notes in the market. Two carrots were provided for the speculative: the Treasury retained an annual option to call the issues at premiums which, if exercised, would have the effect of raising the GRYs by almost one per cent and the Notes were repayable in dollars or sterling at par of exchange, as were the coupons, if presented in London (Table 6.2).[43]

The issues were not fully subscribed, although Morgans considered the results to be satisfactory, a comment that may have been influenced by their profit of $3.6m on the transaction. Sales to the public were $272.1m. Once again, Morgans relieved the Bank and took the entire balance of $27.9m.[44]

Again, there was lengthy negotiation about collateral. The ideal would have been a mixture similar to that for the September issue, Morgans suggesting 30 per cent Americans with equal amounts of Canadians and miscellaneous neutrals, colonies and Dominions making up the balance. The Treasury, watching its store rapidly disappearing, pressed hard for the Americans to be reduced to 25 per cent. Morgans responded by fudging the categories, dividing the securities into two groups; $100m Americans (including the CPR), with another $80m Canadians and $180m mixed colonies and neutrals. The latter group included $25m domestic British railway sterling debentures borrowed from British institutions and, after the LEC had overcome the doubts of a reluctant Chancellor, special issues of Australian, New Zealand and Union of South Africa Bonds representing their war debts to the UK (Table 6.2).[45]

Allied dollar Treasury Bills and the Federal Reserve warning

The device which had the most far-reaching political and diplomatic consequences was a scheme to sell British and French dollar Treasury Bills. The idea was first mooted by Jack Morgan and Lamont in September – when it had seemed that the market would be unable to take another British issue until the New Year – and Davison discussed it with the Chancellor in the second half of October, even as the issue of the 1 November Notes was being prepared.[46] By the middle of November, Morgans thought it had become the obvious next move. The Treasury's supply of wholly owned American securities was running low and, although the imports of gold were making American banks liquid, Morgans judged a new public issue to be impossible until the underwriters had sold the British Notes and France's American Foreign Securities and their prices had strengthened so that holders had a profit.

While Davison was on the steamer, he had sketched out an optimistic statement of the allied position and, by the time he had arrived, Lamont had introduced into the press the possibility of a Bill issue. In the first week of November, Davison saw bankers in New York, Chicago and Boston. He stressed the increase in munitions output in Britain and France, an improved military position, the commercial necessity of giving credit to customers and the inflation being produced by the influx of gold: it was time, he said, for the banks to consider buying unsecured obligations, including those which were very short-dated. After visiting Chicago, he cabled to Jack Morgan, who was still in London, that when he had introduced the topic bankers had given him 'much encouragement'. Because they were a new instrument, he advised that the first should be issued for only thirty days, so that they would run off quickly, showing investors how the machinery worked as they were quietly issued and repaid. He 'hesitated' to express an opinion on the volume which might be issued, 'but would hope that after lapse of some months it might reach say $500m.'[47]

The British disliked the Bills on principle. Short-term foreign currency debt of a country at war held by investors in neutral countries could only be unstable. They were short and a 'last resort'. The Chancellor had refused to offer sterling Treasury Bills for less than ninety days to the domestic market, despite encouragement from the bankers. It was possible that dollar Bills would provide no new money, but merely attract funds from London and replace sterling acceptances in American banks' portfolios. Because regulation limited exposure to a single obligor, purchases by American banks would be at the expense of their holdings of other, longer-term, British debt.[48] Chalmers, Joint Permanent Secretary of the Treasury, showed 'considerable hesitation' and, said Grenfell, 'encouraged the Chancellor to take a small view.'[49] The LEC looked on the 'project with much uneasiness…as contrary to sound policy', which would place the country 'very much in the hands of the United States.'[50] The Governor told Jack Morgan that 'he did not like the whole idea' and that if an issue was necessary it should be a tap, as in London: a supply would be kept on hand and sold if there was demand. If there was no demand, 'no harm is done'.[51]

However, the money was needed. On 8 November, Grenfell cabled that the Chancellor wanted the issue to proceed. The next day there was an instruction to delay: the Treasury had recalled the difficulties with the French over the 1 September Notes and wanted time to consult them. On 9 November, Jack Morgan reported that the French were prepared to issue, only to cable the following day that the instruction was being postponed. There was then a further hold-up because relations between Morgans and the French had become tense as Kuhn, Loeb & Co., who had issued the Paris loan, won the business of issuing loans for three French cities.[52] Finally, on 16 November, the Chancellor reluctantly agreed to an issue of not more than $10m per week of thirty- and sixty-day Bills.[53]

Davison's first move was correct, if naive: he gave time for opposition to be drummed up by briefing Paul Warburg, the New York representative on the Federal Reserve Board, about the plans. Warburg was notoriously pro-German and, until 1914, had been a partner of the Hamburg bank of the same name. Whether at Warburg's instigation or because, as Davison explained to Jack Morgan, he was anxious as a result of the Federal Reserve Board's recent warning that it might discriminate against an issue of French commercial acceptances, Davison went to Washington on 18 November and saw both the Board and Wilson.[e] Davison told the former that further gold imports would be inflationary, that they should be replaced by credits and that Morgans proposed to issue an 'indefinite' volume of British and French Bills to both banks and private investors.[54] He was also brusque, sought no ruling, saying that he was just keeping the Board informed. Irrespective

e The French Industrial credit was being arranged by Bankers Trust, Guaranty Trust and Bonbrights for a maximum of $100m. It was intended that the acceptances would be drawn on the US banks for an initial ninety days, but would be renewable for five more ninety-day periods. PML, Archives, Syndicates No. 9, f. 61; FO 371/2800, no. 986, Spring-Rice to Grey, Enclosure 1, 5 December 1916, and no. 240887, Crawford to FO, 28 November 1916; Harding (1925), pp. 63–5.

of what Warburg might have been saying, the attitude could only provoke the fledgling central bank. He was warned by its Governor, William Harding, that, although the Board would say nothing about private investors buying the Bills, it might warn the banking system that they were an undesirable investment. Davison replied that there were no immediate plans to issue.[55]

Davison's own version, written two days later, was consistent with this. The meeting was:

> not satisfactory. Their attitude towards Treasury Bills not encouraging. However, they gave me to understand they would take no steps at this time and would confer with me before doing so should they desire to make statement afterwards. Had an interview with Woodrow Wilson, which was altogether cordial and rather more encouraging, but on the whole my trip to Washington does not increase my hopes for easy future financing. However no use speculating this subject. Only thing we can do is to continue to do our best.[56]

By the time of this interview, Jack Morgan in London was being pushed hard. The proceeds of the 1 November Notes were evaporating and would be exhausted on 24 November, when the call loan would be reactivated. When the time came, Morgans planned to provide as much as possible themselves so that the market would not become aware of the rate of British spending.[57] With the government falling to pieces around him, McKenna was losing touch with reality. The day after the meeting in Washington, he told Jack Morgan that equal amounts of gold and securities, totalling $1,000m, would become available by the end of February. He did not want to use the gold and, in any case, Jack Morgan subsequently found that there was only $100m actually in Ottawa, enough to cover spending for about ten days. The remaining $418m was on its way from San Francisco, Vladivostok and France. The Chancellor pressed Morgan for further public loans, both secured and unsecured: he even proposed that holders of the Anglo-French Loan be offered conversion, a condition being that new money be subscribed, in the manner of the domestic issue of 4½ per cent War Loan in 1915. The New York partners advised that there was no possibility of an unsecured issue, and that a secured issue would have to wait until January at the earliest: all the British issues were at a discount, they needed time to be absorbed and the public was becoming aware that issue would succeed issue, so great were the allies' requirements. More gold was needed to increase the banks' liquidity.

In his turn, Jack Morgan warned that the Chancellor doubted whether he should exhaust his available gold and remaining American securities and was wondering whether, in the absence of a public loan, he should not take the problem to the Cabinet, or to the allies, or adopt a different policy, including the cancellation of contracts. In contrast, if he could cover expenditure until the end of December by borrowing 'a reasonable amount' on his non-American securities, he would have some assets in hand and feel more confident. Although sympathising with their irritation with the French, Morgan pressed his partners hard: 'if there is any way in which it can be forced between now and 1st January I believe it is essential it should be done.'[58] To the exasperated Davison and Lamont, it looked as if the options were Bills or the Morgan overdraft.

On 24 November, a report of the intention to sell Bills appeared in the press. At ten in the morning, Morgans in New York cabled Jack Morgan to warn that, although 'proceeding as rapidly as possible' with the issue of Bills, few would be sold during the following three months. 'This fear' was strengthened by rising money rates and:

> much more important, by the distinctly antagonistic attitude of the Federal Reserve Board which met with the Advisory Council in Washington yesterday and let it clearly be known that it did not look with favour upon member banks investing in these bills. It seems hardly probable that Federal Reserve Board will issue any statement on this point, but its views as thus privately expressed are already becoming widely disseminated.

The Chancellor might not want to sell gold and American securities but, with expenditure of $450m forecast for the seven weeks to 15 January, there was no alternative. In addition, 'serious as such a step must be', there should be 'rigid economy' (that is, cancellation of contracts) and utilisation of the call loans. Municipal borrowing should be hastened, the possibility of commercial dollar drawings to finance British trade with the USA re-examined and a refinancing of CPR sterling debt held in London investigated. They would even look at raising dollars on British-owned colonial and Dominion war debt. Any balance not met by Bills would then have to be covered by the call loans, which would 'undoubtedly result in utilizing more of our own balances than we and the Chancellor desire, but see no other way out of it.'[59]

Later that day, Harding, having seen the press reports, rang from Washington to point out that Davison had said that there were no plans for an immediate issue and, following the promise the Board had given, to warn that it might make its views known. Lamont replied for Morgans that the article exaggerated, the issue was intended to be small, it would not be made before 1 December and that, if the Board issued a warning, the Bills might have to be withdrawn.[60] Morgans' next move was not designed to placate. The following morning another article appeared with a short statement from Morgans, reiterating that they had authority to sell 'a limited' amount of British and French Bills, starting on about 1 December. The headline in *The New York Times* was 'gold paves way for British Loan' and it was coupled with a report of further large shipments, which, it was said, were intended to ease interest rates and help support foreign loans. The latter story was not attributed to Morgans, but it was made clear that they were the source.[61] On the same day, there was a meeting between the partners and Harding, at which the Governor again warned that the Board might have to issue a caution. 'We are trying to point out the unwisdom of such a step from point of view American commerce, but as you can understand the situation is difficult one,' the New York partners told Morgan Grenfell. [62]

The Board did, indeed, draft a warning. It contained judicious advice, well within its remit, even if it was unhelpful to the allies. It began by 'disclaiming any intention of discussing the finances or of reflecting upon the financial stability of any nation.' It was only concerned with general principles. It denied that gold imports were an inflationary threat because they could be absorbed by bringing forward the transfer of reserves to the Federal Reserve Banks, as envisaged under the Federal Reserve Act. Member banks should, therefore, remain liquid and not lock up their funds in long-dated securities, which must happen if foreign issues exceeded the absorptive power of the general investor. Recent borrowing was very attractive as a banking investment. However,

> banks should proceed with much caution in locking up their funds in long-term obligations, or in investments which are short-term in form or name, but which, either by contract or through force of circumstances, may in the aggregate have to be renewed until normal conditions return…liquid funds of our banks, which should be available for short credit facilities [domestically]…would be exposed to the danger of being absorbed for other purposes to a disproportionate degree, especially in view of the fact that many of our banks and trust companies are already carrying substantial amounts of foreign obligations, and of acceptances which they are under agreement to renew.

A draft was shown to the President, who authorised its publication and made two additions. Banks were told explicitly that the Board did 'not regard it in the interest of the country at this time that they invest in foreign Treasury Bills of this character' and general investors were encouraged to investigate fully the risks, especially if the loans were unsecured.[63] The Board's notice, with the President's additions, was sent to member banks on 27 November and appeared in the press the following day. The market in foreign Bonds promptly collapsed.[64]

The shock to allied credit at this critical moment was subjected to intense scrutiny by British diplomats in Washington. They found Morgans, American politics, the President, the pro-German press and German Jews to blame.[f] Only the allies and the risks to which they were subjecting the American financial system escaped responsibility. The diplomats reported that Morgans and, in particular, Davison had exposed themselves and the allies shortly after an election and its accompanying high feelings. They stressed that the partners, together with much of Wall Street, had supported and financed the Republicans and that only Schiff and some of his connections had supported Wilson. Moreover, Wilson had won with the votes of the west and mid-west. In the words of Sir Cecil Spring-Rice, the British Ambassador, 'Wilson having won, there is a natural tendency [for the

f Montagu Norman's diary entry for the day of the announcement covers the possibilities 'due to? Peace movements or ?Politics in US or ?German ?Warburg ?anti-Davison.' MND, 28 November 1916.

Jewish financiers] to avenge themselves on his antagonist and support the interests of those who have supported him'.[65]

The débâcle came from British need, Jack Morgan's absence in London and the New York partners' failure to understand that times had changed. There were good reasons for the American partners to favour Bills. They could see the rate at which the British were spending and the rapid disappearance of the cash raised on 1 November. They were being pressed by their senior partner in London to make a public issue before the New Year, but knew it to be impossible. The Treasury was an important, prestigious and lucrative client. There was sentimental attachment to the allied cause. The UK's financial position described in the cables from London was the context for Morgans' actions, contributing to the willingness to take the plunge and discover if the Board was bluffing.

By advocating unsecured loans, Davison allowed the hostile press and supporters of the Central Powers to claim that the British were running out of resources. By talking to Warburg before he spoke to the Board, he gave time for opposition to Bills to be worked up. By pursuing the proposal, despite several cautions and the Board's hostility to the French acceptance credit, he gave Morgans' enemies an opening. These actions need to be explained by something more than avoiding activating the call loan, for it would be fully collateralised, as it always had been, and the cables show a preparedness – albeit reluctant – to see it used. An explanation is needed for the disproportion between the relatively small sums which the Bill issue was to raise and the risk being taken by ignoring the Federal Reserve Board.

Davison's attitude when he first saw the Board in Washington was a leftover from the buccaneering pre-war days when there was no Federal Reserve and the firm was headed by Pierpont Morgan. Morgan partners were in a risk business – buying bond issues, bluffing investors and markets, throwing their fortunes on the green baize table – and they had to have the temperament which went with it. That Davison could make ill-judged and sudden decisions, especially when there was no steadying hand from his senior partner, was to be shown in May 1917 when he told Oscar Crosby that Morgans would withdraw support from sterling unless cash was in hand and, again in the summer, when he demanded the immediate repayment of the overdraft (see pp. 250–1, 256–7). Spring-Rice, a friend of Jack Morgan, said Davison had 'all the aggressiveness of the older Morgan without his genius and that he was always inclined to slop over,' and that he had no judgement.[66]

Whatever may have been Warburg's part, the Board's warning to banks was consistent with its earlier attitudes and actions. Its members shared the standard bankers' suspicion of finance bills. Although the Federal Reserve Act did not forbid their creation, by limiting the right to rediscount bills with Federal Reserve Banks to those of ninety days 'arising out of actual commercial transactions', it showed that legislators shared the bankers' prejudice. As it was clear that British resources were fully stretched, it could be assumed that Morgans intended to roll the Bills over, making them long-term debt carried in a short-term form. The warning was in conformity with the Board's attitude to the French commercial credit. When stories had appeared in the press that this would be eligible for rediscount at Federal Reserve Banks, it had warned that the paper could not be regarded as self-liquidating within a period of ninety days and that, 'if offered in excessive amounts, Federal Reserve Banks may be obliged to discriminate against or to exclude entirely acceptances of this character.'[67] In addition, the Board was sensitive after a week of heavy issuance for overseas borrowers and it had every right to assume that the securities were still held in the banking system: credits for Montreal, the Republic of China and the Imperial Russian Government, as well as the three French cities, had been reported in the press that week. It was said that a total of $118.8m (an exaggeration, as it happened) had been raised for foreigners.[68]

The President's decision to extend the warning to the individual investor and the failure to give timely, and private, warning to the British and French governments is to be explained by the wider context. Relations with the allies, and with the British in particular, were strained. On 15 November, Wilson had commented to Colonel House that if the Allies wanted war the USA would not 'shrink from it'.[69] The President wanted to be the mediator, for both humane and political reasons. He was fresh from an election victory and the proposal came from his political enemies on Wall Street. In September, Lloyd George had peremptorily warned him not to interfere. In late November, Wilson drafted a note, which he contemplated sending to all the belligerents, calling on them to state their peace terms and to attend a peace conference. It was to be pre-empted by the Central Powers who, on 12 December, issued a call for a peace conference with the intention of provoking a divided allied response. Although it was not mentioned by the diplomats, applying pressure by directly threatening war supplies would have offended many interests, such as those of the farmers of the west and mid-west, that had supported him. An indirect attack by means of credit would appear to be vengeance limited to his enemies and provide some camouflage for the hurt to other interest groups. Finally, the economy was booming and did not need allied orders, as it had in 1914 and 1915.

Morgans, as financial agents of the Treasury reporting directly to London, had never liaised with the British Embassy. Once the practical meaning of neutrality in finance and supply had been worked out, contracts had been let, securities sold, gold shipped and dollars borrowed with little discussion between governments and with the minimum of interference from Washington. The Board's warning and, especially, Wilson's additions signalled a change. The Secretary of the Treasury and the Comptroller of the Currency were members of the Board and the banking members were political appointees. The Foreign Office immediately assumed that the warning had come from the Administration.[70]

The Treasury in London decided on 29 November to drop the project and, with the agreement of the French, on 1 December Morgans announced its withdrawal.[71] Spring-Rice and Sir Richard Crawford, the Commercial Adviser at the Embassy, had already begun to investigate the reasons for the action – with the results already described – and to limit the damage. They found some members of the Administration to be remarkably willing to make amends. Their efforts were helped by the furore which followed the warning and the fall, albeit short-lived, in prices on Wall Street, where it was believed that the Board was justified in issuing a private warning to the banks, but that it was trespassing in publicly offering wider advice. Harding, who had a warm personal relationship with the British diplomats and was distinctly pro-allied in his sympathies, claimed that he had not liked the caution given to the general investor and that if the Secretary of State, Robert Lansing, agreed the Board would clarify its statement. On 2 December, the Board announced that 'they did not want to reflect on the credit of any Government but only wished to warn persons in small communities who did not understand "real values"'.[72] In the middle of December, Harding went further. Speaking in Boston, he repeated that he had not intended to attack the credit of any government or to reflect on the worth of any particular security. Privately, he told Crawford that the Board would not again interfere 'with matters of this kind' and would raise no objection to the floating of a further loan, although it is unclear whether this self-denial applied only to unsecured issues.[73]

The effect of the warning on the flow of credit to the British in the four months until the USA entered the war has been much exaggerated.[74] The Treasury and the LEC disliked the Bills and wanted to minimise the volume. A maximum of $40m ($10m thirty-day Bills each week) would have been issued initially. There was the risk emphasised by the LEC that US banks would have withdrawn funds from London to buy the Bills: there was the more definite problem that friendly banks, already carrying the maximum exposure to the UK allowed by regulation, would have been unable to buy them. It is clear from the advice crossing the Atlantic during November, before the warning, that market conditions precluded a public loan until January, when money was duly raised. Gold and the call loan were expected to carry the British until then, as they did.

Arguably, the warning's importance lay in persuading Morgans that there was no alternative to increasing the call loans and merely raised the loans' size by the amount of Bills not issued. The warning may have contributed to the run on sterling, but the level of intervention had been rising through the autumn and was already heavy in November before the Board issued its warning: £13m bought in August and September had risen to £18m in October, to £25m in November and to £44m in December. In the first quarter of 1917, purchases averaged £18m per month.[75] Clearly, there were other influences at work. From the end of November, money rates were very firm in New York and American banks were withdrawing funds from London; their balances fell from £50m on 25 November to £38m on 16 December, representing $57m of the intervention. The allies were no doubt continuing to sell sterling advanced to them by the UK Treasury. At the beginning of December, news of a Cabinet crisis became public, and it was not until 7 December that the newspapers carried the news that Lloyd George was forming a new government.[76]

The third collateral loan (22 January 1917)

The two Morgan call loans rose from $101m to $232m during December, despite the shipment of $179m in gold and the receipt of $33m from miscellaneous loans (Table 6.4).[77] At the first Cabinet of the new government on 9 December, Chalmers, having described the British financial position in the USA in anodyne terms, reported that Morgans 'advised that nothing could be raised in the form of a straight loan in January, or until the effect of the Federal Reserve Board's announcement had worn off.'[78] Two days earlier, on 7 December, already looking ahead to January, Morgans had cabled with suggestions for the collateral which should be assembled (Table 6.2).[79] The mixture was agreed and all the securities were in New York by 20 December, except for $25m domestic railway debentures and Bonds of the Dominions of Australia, New Zealand and the Union of South Africa.[80]

To groom the market, Morgans wanted to sell the collateral attached to earlier loans and use the proceeds to support prices. The aim would be to raise the prices of the British issues to their original levels, the Anglo-French Loan being so large that it was thought that nothing could be done. The results of support had so far been encouraging. At the end of December, the yield on the UK two-year Notes (1 September 1918) was 6.20 per cent, on the UK three-year Notes (1 November 1919) 6.10 per cent, and on the UK five-year Notes (1 November 1921) 6.00 per cent. In contrast, the unsupported, but unsecured, Anglo-French Loan (15 October 1920) yielded 7.25 per cent, although it was a joint and several obligation.[81] There was already $12m of cash attaching to the 1 September and 1 November loans deposited with the trustees, and the Treasury agreed that it should be used when the time came to make the new issue. Morgans feared that this would be insufficient and wanted to rearrange the earlier collateral, swapping wholly owned securities for those borrowed, so that more could be sold to 'take care' of the market position in the old loans and to protect the new one. However, although there were plenty of borrowed securities in New York, there were few which were wholly owned by the Treasury. Morgans suggested selling securities borrowed under Scheme A, paying the holders sterling as the rules demanded, or selling the more marketable securities borrowed under Scheme B and replacing them later with similar paper bought in the market. The Treasury refused both proposals because they would violate McKenna's pledge not to sell and the effect would be neutralised by the agreement with the insurance and trust companies that they could reinvest the proceeds in the USA. It did warn that it was considering 'drastic action' to acquire the remaining British holdings of dollar securities, a warning of the requisition order that was to be announced in February (see p. 180).[82]

From the start, Morgans intended that the loan should be so attractive that it would rise to a premium, thus helping banks which were holding earlier issues at a loss and enabling a French issue to follow. It was given the same exchange rate option as the November loan, but the main attractions were a combination of maturity, collateral and conversion option: it was short-dated to attract the banks, secured so that the banks could treat it as a first-class asset and convertible so that it would attract the investing public. Thus, it was the first of the British issues to be both secured and convertible.[83] It was agreed that the Bank of England and Morgans together should be prepared to underwrite, or apply for, up to $150m.[84]

If Morgans had won all the arguments with the Treasury, it would have been even more attractive. Pressed for three- and five-year issues, such as those of 1 November, they pointed out that there were already two-, three-, four- and five-year British maturities outstanding. The Federal Reserve Board's warning was still echoing around Wall Street. The banks most closely associated with Morgans, those with the largest participations, had not been able to find buyers for the November issues and still held them at a loss, as did the munitions contractors. If the usual participants were gorged, buyers would need to be found among individual investors. It was to tempt these that Morgans proposed an option to convert into any subsequent issue. This the Treasury refused. The prospectuses for the 4 and 5 per cent sterling War Loans were published in the UK on 11 January, and the Treasury felt unable to give the American investor a conversion privilege which it was newly withholding from its own investors. Although disliking the principle, it was prepared to offer conversion into a named new issue, provided it was not as long as the ten or fifteen years suggested by Morgans. Morgans pointed out that there was no encouragement in offering conversion into an unsecured 5½ per cent five-year security at par when the British five-year collateral loan was yielding about 6 per cent and the Anglo-French Loan about 7 per cent.

In the end, a compromise was reached embracing the two conversion rights: there would be no blanket conversion into future issues, but there would be an option to convert into an unsecured 5½ per cent Loan maturing in fifteen years.[85] Then, in the middle of January, market conditions deteriorated and Morgans had to ask the Treasury to be more generous. A call envisaged at ten years was abandoned, the spread between the underwriters' buying price and the price to the public was raised from 1¼ per cent to 1½ per cent and, as with the previous loan, an expenses allowance for the management group of ¼ per cent, payable at Morgans' discretion, was added. Fifteen years for the conversion issue became twenty, this length being, it was said, both popular and customary in the USA. The pain of these changes, which on such a short loan entailed a large increase in the annual cost, was reduced by giving part of the issue a two-year maturity (Table 6.2).[86]

Morgans started to work on the issue immediately after the New Year and, said Lamont, 'at the start it was very discouraging...Money had not begun to flow back much from the interior...the Group didn't feel like taking hold at all. We moved along steadily, but didn't try to force things, for it would have been useless.' After the middle of the month, the money market turned favourable and, on 19 January, Morgans began forming their underwriting syndicate for $100m one-year and $150m two-year Notes.

When the issues were offered to the public on 22 January 1917, applications were $292.2m. The Bank was promptly released from its commitments and Morgans opted to demonstrate that there had been an enthusiastic response by cutting by half the amounts allotted to the larger subscribers, who were their own associates with the large holdings in earlier loans. US Steel had already been promised $20m, and Rockefeller and the Equitable $5m apiece. They were allotted in full. Morgans subscribed for $10m, and would have liked 'many more because they were so attractive', but they already held $15m of the previous issue. Playing fair, they cut themselves by half, in line with the other large subscribers.[87] In market trading, the issues immediately met the news that Germany had declared unlimited submarine warfare and the price moved from a small premium to a small discount, despite Morgans purchases of $6m.[88]

Inexplicably, after the experience with the dollar Treasury Bills, neither Morgans nor the British told the US Treasury or Federal Reserve Board about the new issues. On 25 January, a week after they had been announced, Crawford was invited to visit Harding and the Secretary of the Treasury, William Gibbs McAdoo. McAdoo pointed out that he had to make heavy demands on the banking system to cover his budget deficit and that he needed to ensure that it did not become over-exposed to illiquid foreign obligations. Hitherto, he had learnt of British borrowing from the press. He reminded Crawford that the Federal Reserve Board had not been told about the plan to issue Treasury Bills and that it had been forced to intervene. He wanted to avoid similar intervention in, for example, the case of the new Notes, but feared misunderstandings unless the US Treasury was advised of the 'character and extent' of such operations before the arrangements had been completed. He also would like to be given some indications of British plans for financing future purchases in the USA. The following day, Crawford saw Harding and was told that the interview was 'most satisfactory' and that no difficulties need 'now' be feared with the issue.[89] In two months, British borrowing had completed a rapid journey from the private market place to the political and diplomatic arena.

Endnotes

1 T 170/62, ff. 39–40, Treasury to MG, August 1915; MGP, B. Hist. 1 , F. 6, nos 6477 and 6460, Grenfell to JPM, 22 and 23 July 1915; Osborne (1926), II, pp. 4–5.

2 T 170/62, ff. 39–40, Treasury to MG, August 1915; MGP, B. Hist. 1, F. 7, nos 6996, 6998 and 8042, MG to JPM, 26 August and 30 August 1915; ibid., nos 7150 and 7328, JPM to MG, 27 August 1915 and 4 September 1915; ibid., no. 9646, JPM to MG, 2 November 1915.

3 T 170/63, Blackett to Bradbury, 22 October 1915; ibid., Harvey to Bradbury, 31 October, 2 and 7 November 1915; T 170/62, Bradbury to Cunliffe, 8 November 1915.

4 T 170/134, Chadwick, 'British Government Borrowing in America', 1922; US Senate (1937), XXVIII, pp. 8752–79; MGP, B. Hist. 2, F. 10, no. 17963, JPM to MG, 3 May 1916.

5 BoE, C91/16, LEC Minutes, 7 and 11 January 1916; MGP, B. Hist. 1, F. 8, nos 12276 and 12363, Grenfell to JPM, 4 and 8 January 1916: ibid., JPM to MG, nos 11920, 11977 and 13007, 6, 8 and 10 January 1916. The peg was put in place on 6 January 1916.

6 Myers (1931), I, Chapters VII and XIII.

7 BoE, C91/16, LEC, Minutes, 11 January 1916; MGP, B. Hist. 1, F. 8, nos 12392, 12429 and 12451, Grenfell to JPM, 11, 13 and 14 January 1916; ibid., nos 13089, 13143 and 13152, JPM to Grenfell, 13, 14 and 15 January 1916; Cleveland and Huertas (1985), p. 26.

8 MGP, B. Hist. 1, F. 9, no. 15063, JPM to MG (Copy to Chalmers), 19 February 1916, and no. 14207, MG to JPM (Copy to Governor), 21 February 1916.

9 Cab. 42/13/4, 4 May 1916. Also see Cab. 37/147/5, 2 May 1916.

10 BoE, C91/16, LEC, Minutes, 5 May 1916; MGP, B. Hist. 2, F. 10, no. 17906, JPM to MG, 2 May 1916; ibid., no. 16740, MG to JPM, 4 May 1916, and no. 16776, 5 May 1916; ibid., no. 19469, JPM to MG (Copy left with Bradbury and shown to Governor), 22 May 1916; ibid., no. 19760, JPM to MG, 2 June 1916; ibid., F. 11, nos 21104 and 21105, JPM to Grenfell, 12 June 1916; T 170/122, MG to McKenna, 13 June 1916.

11 MGP, B. Hist. 1, F. 10, no. 18191, Grenfell to Jack Morgan and Davison, and no. 18196, Grenfell to Jack Morgan, 24 May 1916.

12 MGP, B. Hist. 1, F. 10, no. 18191, Grenfell to Jack Morgan or Davison, 24 May 1916, and no. 18196, Grenfell to Jack Morgan, 24 May 1916; ibid., no. 19627, JPM to MG (shown to Chancellor, Montagu and Bradbury), 27 May 1916; ibid., no. 18347, Grenfell to Jack Morgan and Davison, 31 May 1916; ibid., no. 19767, JPM to Grenfell (Taken to Treasury. Copy left with Chancellor. Read by Montagu, Deputy Governor and Norman), 2 June 1916.

13 A copy of the prospectus for this issue is in PML, Archives, Horn Box 4.

14 MGP, B. Hist. 2, F. 10, no. 19767, JPM to Grenfell (Taken to Treasury. Copy left with Chancellor. Read by Montagu, Deputy Governor and Norman), 2 June 1916, and no. 18431, Grenfell to JPM, 3 June 1916; ibid., no. 19881, JPM to Grenfell (Copy given to Deputy Governor and Norman and submitted by them to Chancellor), 6 June 1916; ibid., no. 18516, Grenfell to JPM (Shown to Deputy Governor and Norman), 7 June 1916; ibid., no. 19992, Jack Morgan and Davison to Grenfell (Copy given to Deputy Governor and shown to Chancellor; copy sent to Deputy Governor), 9 June 1916; ibid., F. 11, no. 21303, JPM to MG, 17 June 1916, and no. 21457 (Copy shown to Deputy Governor and Bradbury), 22 June 1916; Carosso (1970), pp. 206–7. Carosso lists the directors.

15 MGP, B. Hist. 1, F. 11, no. 21371, JPM to MG (Copy handed to Deputy Governor and Norman. Shown to Chancellor and Montagu), 20 June 1916, and no. 18827, 22 June 1916 (Copy shown to Deputy Governor and Bradbury); ibid., nos 23206 (Copy sent to Deputy Governor) and 23324 (Shewn to Deputy Governor), JPM to Grenfell, 18 and 22 July 1916; ibid., no. 23509, JPM to MG (Copy to Deputy Governor), 29 July 1916; ibid., no. 23656, Davison to Grenfell, 3 August 1916; ibid., no. 23860, Davison to MG, 9 August 1916.

16 PML, Archives, Syndicates No. 8, ff. 207–8; MGP, B. Hist. 1, F. 11, no. 23656, JPM to Grenfell, 3 August 1916.

17 MGP, B. Hist. 1, F. 11, no. 23656, Davison to Grenfell, 3 August 1916, and no. 23860, Davison to MG, 9 August 1916.

18 MGP, B. Hist. 1, F. 11, no. 23656, Davison to Grenfell, 3 August 1916.

19 MGP, B. Hist. 1, F. 11, no. 23860, Davison to MG, 9 August 1916.

20 MGP, B. Hist. 2, F. 11, no. 23656, Davison to Grenfell, 3 August 1916; ibid., no. 20816, MG to JPM, 4 August 1916; ibid., no. 23860, Davison to MG, 9 August 1916; ibid., no. 23863, Davison to Grenfell, 10 August 1916; ibid., no. 20947, MG to JPM, 10 August 1916.

21 MGP, B. Hist. 2, F. 11, no. 25199, Davison to Grenfell, and no. 22158, MG to JPM, 18 August 1916; ibid., no. 25212, Davison to Grenfell, 19 August 1916.

22 MGP, B. Hist. 2, F. 11, no. 25415, JPM to Grenfell (Copy to Bradbury), 25 August 1916, and no. 25488, Jack Morgan and Davison to MG, 28 August 1916; ibid., no. 25542, Jack Morgan and Davison to Grenfell (Copy handed to Governor) and no. 22463, MG to JPM, 30 August 1916; PML, Archives, Syndicates No. 8, ff. 211–12.

23 MGP, B. Hist. 2, F. 11, no. 20985, MG to Davison, 11 August 1916, and no. 25027, Davison to MG, 14 August 1916; T 170/130, Report of the American Dollar Securities Committee, 4 June 1919.

24 Cab. 37/157/40, 24 October 1916; BoE, C91/17, LEC, Minutes, 13 September 1916; ibid., C91/6, Bradbury to MG, 15 September 1916. The Cabinet report is reproduced in Keynes (1971–89), XVI, pp. 201–9.

25 MGP, B. Hist. 2, F. 11, no. 20654, MG to JPM, 28 July 1916.

26 MGP, B. Hist. 2, F. 11, no. 23656, JPM to Grenfell, and no. 20788, Grenfell to Davison, 3 August 1916; ibid., no. 23860, Davison to MG, 9 August 1916; ibid., no. 20925, MG to JPM, 9 August 1916; ibid., no. 23897, Davison to MG, 10 August 1916; ibid., no. 20985, MG to Davison, 11 August 1916; ibid., no. 25057, Davison to Grenfell, 15 August 1916; ibid., no. 22102, MG to JPM, 16 August 1916; ibid., no. 25166, Davison to Grenfell, 18 August 1916.

27 MGP, B. Hist. 2, F. 11, no. 23860, Davison to MG, 9 August 1916; ibid., no. 25120, Davison to Grenfell, 17 August 1916; ibid., no. 25301, Jack Morgan and Davison to Grenfell, 22 August 1916; ibid., F. 12, no. 25775, JPM to MG, 7 September 1916; ibid., no. 21347, JPM to MG (shown to Deputy Governor and Norman), 19 June 1916; PML, Archives, Horn Box 3, no. 17,802, Harjes to Jack Morgan, 18 August 1916. A copy of the prospectus for the Russian loan, finally issued on 26 November 1916, is in PML, Archives, Horn Box 4.

28 PML, Archives, Horn Box 3, no. 17,802, Harjes to Jack Morgan, 18 August 1916, and Harjes to Davison, 4 September 1916; Burk (1985), pp. 80–2.

29 T 170/95, 'Report of the Inter-Departmental Committee to consider Dependence of the British Empire on the United States', 13 October 1916; Cab. 42/22/4, 'Our Financial Position in America', 24 October 1916.

30 Cab. 24/2, G 87, 24 October 1916, and Cab. 37/157/40, 24 October 1916; Keynes (1971–89), XVI, pp. 196–209; MGP, B. Hist. 2, F. 12, no. 27834, JPM to Davison, 10 October 1916. The papers and the report of the committee are in T 170/95.

31 PML, Archives, Syndicates No. 8, f. 213; US Senate (1937), XXVIII, pp. 8708, 8956–70. The dates are those on which the underwriters made their purchases. The issues for the three French cities, for example, were signed on 1 November, but were offered to the public a few days before the Federal Reserve Board's warning on 28 November. There is a table of foreign government issues in ARSF (1920), pp. 350–4, which in places is inconsistent with the data provided in this paragraph. The US Treasury warned that it could not vouch for the data, which was received principally from unofficial sources. If there is an inconsistency, it is assumed that Morgans, as the issuer or participant, had the better information.

32 BoE, C91/16, LEC, Minutes, 14 January to 26 June 1916. C90/1–4 contains correspondence.

33 MGP, B. Hist. 2, F. 12, no. 27885, JPM to Davison, 11 October 1916; BoE, C91/17, LEC, Minutes, 31 July 1916. C91/4–5 contains correspondence leading up to the Metropolitan Water Board issue. The cables covering the negotiations for municipal borrowing are in MGP, B. Hist. 2, F. 12, 6 October 1916 onwards.

34 Morgan (1952), p. 323, says that there was one small issue, of $1.5m, for Dublin. Morgan cites Brown (1940), p. 61. There is no mention of the issue on this page of Brown nor, indeed, anywhere in his two volumes. No confirmation that this borrowing took place has been found in official sources. For evidence that there was such an issue, see MGP, B. Hist. 2, F. 14, no. 28495, MG to JPM, 22 December 1916. This cable says the issue was for ten years at 6¹/₄ per cent through Lee, Higginson.

35 MGP, B. Hist. 2, F. 12, nos 24326, 24532 and 24654, MG to JPM, 6 October, 16 October, and 20 October 1916; BoE, C90/16–20, LEC, Minutes, various dates.

36 MGP, B. Hist. 2, F. 12, no. 27634, Lamont to Davison, 4 October 1916, no. 27931, Lamont and Morrow to Davison, 12 October 1916, and no. 29065, JPM to Jack Morgan and Davison, 17 October 1916.

37 MGP, B. Hist. 2, F. 12, no. 24464, Jack Morgan to JPM, 13 October 1916; ibid., no. 29065, JPM to Jack Morgan and Davison, 17 October 1916; ibid., no. 29171, JPM to MG, 19 October 1916.

38 Cab. 42/22/1, 17 October 1916, and Cab. 42/22/2, 18 October 1916; Carosso (1970), pp. 208–9; MGP, B. Hist. 2, F. 12, no. 29013, JPM to Jack Morgan and Davison, 14 October 1916; ibid., no. 29045, Lamont and Morrow to Davison, 16 October 1916; ibid., no. 29013, Lamont to Jack Morgan and Davison, 17 October 1916; ibid., no. 24611, Jack Morgan and Davison to JPM, 18 October 1916; ibid., no. 29238, Lamont and Morrow to Davison, 20 October 1916; ibid., 24664, MG to JPM, 20 October 1916; Williamson (1961), pp. 217–35; US Senate (1937), XXV, pp. 7575–643; Weems (1923), pp. 194–202; Thomas Lamont Papers, II, 91–2, Lamont to Davison, 29 September 1916. Chandler and Salsbury (1971), pp. 360–3, draws general lessons for US business seeking to make profits from allied war contracts.

39 MGP, BG Loan 1, note by Grenfell of interview with the Chancellor on 22 August 1916.

40 MGP, B. Hist. 2, F. 12, no. 22758, Davison to Jack Morgan, 12 September 1916, no. 24324, Davison to Lamont, 6 October 1916, and no. 27834, JPM to Davison, 10 October 1916.

41 BoE, C91/7, Nairne to Treasury, 23 November 1916; MGP, B. Hist. 2, F. 12, no. 27616, JPM to Davison (Shown to Governor and Deputy Governor), 3 October 1916, and no. 27634, Lamont to Davison (Copy left with Governor and Deputy Governor), 4 October 1916.

42 MGP, B. Hist. 2, F. 12, no. 27634, Lamont to Davison (Left with Governor and Deputy Governor), 4 October 1916, and no. 27749, 7 October 1916; ibid., no. 27980, JPM to Davison, 14 October 1916; Thomas Lamont Papers, II, 91–2, Lamont to Davison, 27 September 1916.

43 MGP, B. Hist. 2, F. 12, no. 27616, JPM to Davison (Copy left with Governor and Deputy Governor), 3 October 1916; ibid., no. 27884, JPM to MG, 11 October 1916; ibid., no. 24465, Davison to Lamont (Read aloud by Chancellor to Governor, Chalmers and Bradbury on 19 October), 13 October 1916; ibid., nos 29013, 29154 and 29170, JPM to Jack Morgan and Davison, 14 October, 18 October, and 19 October 1916; ibid., no. 24617, JPM and Davison to JPM, 19 October 1916; ibid., no. 29242, JPM to MG, 21 October 1916, and no. 29330, JPM to Jack Morgan, 24 October 1917, and no. 24747, MG to JPM, 24 October 1916.

44 MGP, B. Hist. 12, no. 29444, JPM to MG, 27 October 1916; ibid., no. 29577, Davison to Jack Morgan, 31 October 1916; ibid., no. 24859, Grenfell to MG, 28 October 1916; ibid., F. 13, no. 29897, JPM to MG, 7 November 1916; PML Archives, Syndicates No. 9, ff. 5–6.

45 T 170/130, Report of the American Dollar Securities Committee, 4 June 1919; MGP, B. Hist. 2, F. 12, no. 27616, JPM to Governor and Deputy Governor, 3 October 1916; ibid., no. 27893, JPM to Anderson, 11 October 1916; ibid., no. 24465, Davison to Lamont (Read aloud by Chancellor to Governor, Chalmers and Bradbury at meeting at the Treasury, 19 October 1916), 13 October 1916; ibid., no. 27834, JPM to Davison, 10 October 1916; ibid., no. 29154, JPM to Jack Morgan and Davison, 18 October 1916; ibid., no. 24617, Jack Morgan and Davison to JPM, 19 October 1916; ibid., no. 24747, MG to JPM, 24 October 1916; ibid., no. 29493, JPM to MG, 28 October 1916; BoE, C91/17, LEC, Minutes, 27 and 29 September 1916.

46 MGP, B. Hist. 2, F. 12, no. 27028, Jack Morgan and Lamont to MG, 15 September 1916; ibid., no. 29260, Lamont and Morrow to Jack Morgan (To Governor), 21 October 1916, and no. 26142, Grenfell to Davison, 8 November 1916.

47 MGP, B. Hist. 2, F. 13, no. 29868, Davison to Grenfell, 7 November 1916; PML, Box 35, no. 14,683, Harjes cable, Davison to Jack Morgan, 7 November 1916.

48 BoE, C91/7, Cunliffe to Treasury, 28 November 1916, and Chalmers to Cunliffe, 1 December 1916; MGP, B. Hist. 2, F. 13, no. 26693, Jack Morgan to Davison, 27 November 1916. The arguments are those of the LEC, but Chalmers's answer was that they 'weighed no less forcibly' with the Treasury.

49 MGP, Box British Government Loan 3, File November–December 1916, Grenfell to Davison, 20 November 1916.

50 BoE, C91/7, Cunliffe to Treasury, 28 November 1916.
51 MGP, B. Hist. 2, F. 12, no. 24877, Jack Morgan to JPM, 30 October 1916. For a different version, see Burk (1985), p. 240, note 26.
52 PML, Archives, Box 35, no. 14,684, Harjes cable, Davison and Lamont to Jack Morgan, 7 November 1916, and no. 14,706, Davison to Jack Morgan, 10 November 1916; ibid., Box 118, no. 502, Harjes to Jack Morgan, 18 November 1916; ibid., Horn Box 3, nos 18,298 and 18,302, Jack Morgan to Davison, 9 and 10 November 1916; MGP, B. Hist. 2, F. 13, no. 31011, JPM to Jack Morgan, 11 November 1916; ibid., no. 31152, Davison to Jack Morgan, 15 November 1916; ibid., no. 352, Jack Morgan to Herman Harjes, 15 November 1916; ibid., no. 506, Herman Harjes to Jack Morgan, 23 November.
53 MGP, B. Hist. 2, F. 13, no. 26428, Grenfell to JPM, 16 November 1916; PML, Archives, Horn Box 3, no. 14,781, JPM to Morgan Harjes, 16 November 1916.
54 Harding (1925), p. 65.
55 Burk (1985), pp. 83–4; Ferguson (1995), pp. 141–2; FO 371/2800, no. 3581, Crawford to FO, 28 November 1916. Burk cites Charles S. Hamlin Papers, Diary, vol. 4, 19 November 1916, and US Senate (1937), V, pp. 204–5. Some versions give the date of Davison's interviews as 19 November. That was a Sunday and, in any case, the interview was reported in *The New York Times* on the 19th. *The New York Times*, 19 November 1916, p. 5. See also, ibid., 21 November 1916, p. 14.
56 MGP, B. Hist. 2, F. 13, no. 31415, Davison to Jack Morgan, 21 November 1916.
57 MGP, B. Hist. 2, F. 13, nos 31499 and 31592, JPM to MG, 23 and 24 November 1916.
58 MGP, B. Hist. 2, F. 13, nos 26519 and 26591, Jack Morgan to Davison, 20 and 23 November 1916; ibid., no. 31458, Davison and Lamont to Jack Morgan (Copy left with Chancellor), 22 November 1916; ibid., no. 26592, Jack Morgan to Davison, 23 November 1916; ibid., nos 31592 and 26659, JPM to Jack Morgan and Jack Morgan to JPM, 24 November 1916.
59 MGP, B. Hist. 2, F. 13, no. 31592, JPM to Jack Morgan, 24 November 1916. *The New York Times*, 25 November 1916, p. 4, carries a report of the Advisory Council's views.
60 Burk (1985), p. 84. She cites Charles S. Hamlin Papers, Diary, V, 24 November 1916.
61 *The New York Times*, 25 November 1916, p. 14.
62 MGP, B. Hist. 2, F. 13, no. 31646, JPM to MG, 25 November 1916.
63 Harding (1925), pp. 66–9; Burk (1985), p. 84. Burk cites Charles S. Hamlin Papers, Diaries, V, 25 and 27 November 1916.
64 MGP, B. Hist. 2, F. 13, no. 31646, JPM to MG, 25 November 1916; Burk (1985), p. 84; FO 371/2800, no. 986, Spring-Rice to Grey, 5 December 1916; US Senate (1937), XXVIII, pp. 8517–69 and 8714–47; *The New York Times*, 28 November 1916, p. 1.
65 FO 371/2800, no. 986, Spring-Rice to Grey, 5 December 1916; FO 371/2800, no. 3581, Crawford to FO, and no. 3582, Spring-Rice to FO, 28 November 1916; ibid., no. 3606, Crawford to FO, and no. 3607, Spring-Rice to FO, 30 November 1916; ibid., no. 963, Spring-Rice to FO, 1 December 1916; ibid., no. 3613, Crawford to FO, 2 December 1916; ibid., no. 986, Spring-Rice to Grey, 5 December 1916; T 172/429, Lever's Diary, 23 March 1917.
66 Quoted in Burk (1985), p. 89. She cites Charles S. Hamlin Papers, Diary, IV, 30 December 1916, and US Senate (1937), V, pp. 204–5.
67 Harding (1925), pp. 63–5.
68 *The New York Times*, various dates.
69 Edward M. House Papers, Diary, IX, 15 November 1916.
70 Cab. 42/26/2, 28 November 1916.
71 BoE, C91/7, Chalmers to Cunliffe, 1 December 1916; MGP, B. Hist. 2, F. 13, nos 26788 and 26810, Grenfell to JPM, 29 November 1916; ibid., no. 31864, Davison and Lamont to Grenfell, 2 December 1916.

72 Harding (1925), pp. 42–4; FO 371/2800, nos 3606 and 3613, Crawford to FO, 30 November, and 2 December 1916; ibid., no. 3619, Spring-Rice to FO, 2 December 1916.
73 FO 371/2800, no. 255116, Crawford to FO, 16 December 1916.
74 Sayers (1976), I, p. 92; French (1995), p. 42; Burk (1982), p. 92.
75 BoE, C91/15, f. 40, 'Purchases and Sales of American Exchange', 25 March 1919.
76 MGP, B. Hist. 2, F. 13, no. 31780, JPM to Grenfell, 29 November 1916; ibid., no. 31844, JPM to Grenfell (Shown to Governor, Deputy Governor and Chancellor), 1 December 1916; BoE, C 91/17 and 18, LEC, Minutes, 28 November 1916, and 11 January 1917; ibid., C91/7, f. 56, Treasury to LEC, 1 December 1916; T 170/122, no. 33061, Davison to Grenfell, 7 December 1916; T 160/18/F557/015/1, no. 33707, JPM to MG, 23 December 1916; T 172/421, Chalmers, 1 March 1917; US Senate (1937), XXVIII, pp. 8587–8, 8591–2 and 8783; MND, 27 November 1916; FO 371/3114, no. 1265, Chalmers to Lever, 11 May 1917.
77 US Senate (1937), XXVIII, pp. 8606.
78 Cab. 23/1, Cabinet 1 (16) 5, 9 December 1916.
79 T 170/122, no. 33077, JPM to MG, 7 December 1916.
80 T 160/18/F557/015/1, Leith-Ross to Lever, 20 December 1916, and no. 28556, MG to JPM, 27 December 1916.
81 T 160/18/F557/015/1, no. 33836, JPM to MG, 29 December 1916. The yields are for the morning of the cable.
82 T 160/18/F557/015/1, no. 33836, JPM to MG, and no. 28673, Grenfell to JPM, 30 December 1916.
83 PML, Archives, Horn Box 3, no. 30,290, JPM to Morgan Harjes, 19 January 1916; ibid., no. 30.353, JPM to Morgan Harjes, 27 January 1916; ibid., no. 30,428, JPM to Morgan Harjes, 3 February 1916; ibid., no. 30,451, JPM to Morgan Harjes, 5 February 1916.
84 T 160/18/F557/015/1, no. 35177, JPM to MG, 8 January 1917; ibid., no. 28945, MG to JPM, 10 January 1917; ibid., nos 35661 and 35784, JPM to MG, 19 and 23 January 1917; PML, Archives, Syndicates No. 9, ff. 31–2.
85 T 160/18/F557/015/1, no. 33945, JPM to MG, 1 January 1917; ibid., no. 28768, MG to JPM, 3 January 1917; ibid., no. 35165, JPM to MG, 6 January 1917; ibid., no. 35445, JPM to MG, 13 January 1917; ibid., no. 30074, MG to JPM, 13 January 1917; ibid., no. 35525, JPM to MG, 16 January 1917.
86 T 160/18/F557/015/1, no. 35445, JPM to MG, 13 January 1917, and no. 35525, JPM to MG, 16 January 1917.
87 T 160/18/F557/015/1, no. 37032, JPM to MG, 30 January 1917; MGP, B. Hist. 2, F. 14, no. 35177, JPM to MG (To Governor and Lever), 8 January 1917, and no. 37076, JPM to MG (To Treasury), 31 January 1917; PML, Syndicates No. 9, ff. 31–2; Thomas Lamont Papers, II, 91–2, Lamont to Davison, 31 January 1917.
88 MGP, B. Hist. 2, F. 14, no. 37245, JPM to MG (Copy to Treasury and Governor), 5 February 1917.
89 MGP, B. Hist. 2, F. 14, no. 35628, JPM to MG (Copy to Lever and Governor), 18 January 1917; FO 371/3070, no. 215, Crawford to FO, 27 January 1917; T 172/429, Lever's Diary, 19 February 1917. For a different interpretation of Crawford's cable see Burk (1982), pp. 91–2.

9 External borrowing 1917–18

(I) The United States of America

> I think that the pressure of this approaching crisis has gone beyond the ability of the Morgan Financial Agency for the British and French Governments.
>
> The US Ambassador in London, 5 March 1917, *Foreign Relations of the United States* (Department of State, 1932, supplement 2, I, p. 518)

> He [Crosby] stated in confidence that the President and other members of the Administration were more hostile to Morgans than words could express.
>
> Lever's Diary, 19 April 1917, T 172/429.

For the allies, the only relief from the gloom of the first half of 1917 was provided by the American entry into the war. In February, revolution broke out in Russia, threatening her continued participation and enabling German troops to be transferred to the western front. The spring offensive in France, opened by the British at Arras on 9 April, was costly and continued too long as it sought to relieve the French, who were attacking further south. The French assaults finally broke the spirit of her already weakened army and, starting on 3 May, there were widespread mutinies. At sea, allied shipping losses from German submarines, which had been running at around 300,000 tons per month, rose to 540,000 tons in February and 881,000 tons in April: 60 per cent were British. In the latter month, one in four ships leaving the British Isles did not return. Food stocks in the UK fell to six weeks' consumption.[1] It was the submarines that finally turned American public opinion and persuaded Wilson that war was inevitable. On 1 February, the Germans informed the US Administration that, with the exception of a single marked weekly liner in each direction, all vessels found in the approaches to Europe and the eastern Mediterranean would be attacked and, on 3 February, the USA broke off diplomatic relations with Germany. Three weeks earlier, Germany's Foreign Minister Artur Zimmerman had proposed to Mexico that, if the USA declared war on Germany, Mexico should become an ally, with the expectation of regaining the territories in the American south-west, which she had lost in the previous century. The telegram had been intercepted and decoded by British intelligence which, on 24 February, selflessly passed it to the US

Administration. Wilson delayed publication in the hope that war might still be averted, only releasing it to the press on 1 March. That month, US merchant ships were sunk and, finally, on 6 April Congress recognised a state of war between the two countries.

The US declaration of war was heartening, but brought little immediate relief. The exception was in finance, where the UK was within four weeks of exhausting her ability to pay for the American spending of herself and her allies. The new financial relationship between the UK and the USA did not prove easy. Congress was shocked, and the US Treasury frightened, by the size of the allies' demands. Suspicion of the British, in particular, lingered and pro-German and isolationist sentiment did not die with the declaration of war. Many thought that the British were using American advances to sustain themselves as a commercial and banking rival and, until the British learnt the necessity of divulging their full financial position, there was scepticism that their resources were as depleted as they claimed. There was little disagreement, or even negotiation, about the terms for the advances, which were to provide such fertile soil for misunderstanding and acrimony when it came to the terms for their funding: winning the war was uppermost in the British mind, the need was too pressing and the terms and amounts were obviously superior to anything available in the private markets. Instead, strains in the relationship centred on the use of the advances for three purposes: the maintenance of the sterling exchange rate; the repayment of British debts to the American private sector incurred before 1 April; and their use for expenditure outside the USA.

This chapter describes how the British debt to the US Treasury was created amid the tensions that came from national rivalry, Congressional sensitivities, ignorance, inexperience, misunderstandings and personal animosities. Canadian, Indian and neutral finance and its relation with borrowing in the USA is discussed in Chapter 10.

On the cliff edge: January to April 1917

In the first quarter of 1917, the UK Treasury sold $55m securities and $300m gold, increased its call loans with Morgans by $125m and borrowed $340m elsewhere. It spent $265m on buying sterling, the Commercial Agency Account absorbed $350m and munitions another $40m. Dollar advances to the French and Russians took $105m.[2] On 16 March, Keynes estimated that only $251.5m remained available in the USA, of which $66m was gold and $185.5m borrowed securities, which were subject to McKenna's pledges. There was another $100m gold *en route* from Russia, and $130m belonging to the CNRA coming from South Africa and the UK: $132.5m might be won by taking gold from the Bank of England and the CNRA and by acquiring the remaining British-owned American securities. With dollar expenditure, excluding that in Canada, running at $65m per week, the position could only be described as dire.[3]

As relations with Germany deteriorated, the Administration softened its attitude towards allied borrowing. Starting the day the USA broke off diplomatic relations with Germany, Crawford had conversations with Harding about the Federal Reserve Board's policy and a British issue guaranteed by the US Treasury. Held with the knowledge of Lansing and McAdoo, the talks seem to have continued in a desultory fashion for two weeks.[4] In the middle of February, after seeing McAdoo and Harding, Davison told Grenfell that the Administration was seeking 'a bridge' to enable it to change its public attitude to Bills.[5] On 19 February, Crawford told London that the Administration had agreed to encourage the banks to participate in an issue of $250m British Exchequer Bonds, the proceeds to be used to finance American exports. The proposal should be seen to come from Morgans and would be the opportunity for the Board to withdraw from the position it had taken in November. The interest rate should be a maximum of 6 per cent and, after one year, holders would be able to put the Bonds on thirty days' notice. They would be unsecured, but gold equivalent to 20 per cent of the issue would be kept in Ottawa to provide for redemptions.[6] The terms were described by Bradbury as, prima facie, 'attractive' and by Keynes as being 'supportable', but not 'brilliant'. More important than the length or cost was whether the proposal would enable an issue to be made earlier than the alternatives: the money would be of most assistance if it was available by mid-March. On this, the cables were silent.[7]

Morgans warned that investors would not find the Bonds attractive. Since the breaking of diplomatic relations with Germany, with the prospect of war and massive US Treasury borrowing, bankers and investors had become unwilling to take decisions: the markets had seized up. At the beginning of March, Morgans were finding it difficult to increase the call loans, despite a rise in the rate, and on 6 March Lever, who had arrived in New York on 11 February, sanctioned the sale of securities borrowed under Scheme B.[a] On 2 March, the Chancellor agreed, with great reluctance, against the advice of Chalmers and with caveats from the LEC, to Morgan's renewed proposal for an issue of Treasury Bills. He stipulated a maximum of $250m.[8]

There was no issue of Bills or Exchequer Bonds, although on 9 March the Board published a statement modifying its advice on allied credits. Foreign lending, it said, was a 'very important natural and proper means' of settling the US current account surplus. The Board's warning had not been aimed at any particular country, but had dealt with banking principles and the excessive investment by banks in foreign obligations; it did not address their merits as investments. The Board still felt that the banks should not impair their liquidity and that the securities should be bought by the general public. However, since November, gold reserves had expanded further and provided a solid base from which to increase credit, so that the banks 'may perform a useful service in facilitating the distribution of

a Morgans hoped that sales would grow to $4m per day. They would be sold at the same time as the Treasury's wholly-owned securities and be concentrated on marketable issues, so facilitating repurchase when the time came for the Treasury to return them to their owners. T 172/421, ff. 73, Chancellor to Lever, 2 March 1917; ibid., no. 360, Chancellor to Lever, 7 March 1917; T 172/429, Lever's Diary, 28 February 1917; FO 371/3114, no. 1394, Lever to Chancellor, 20 May 1917; MGP, B. Hist. 2, F. 14, no. 39085, Davison to Grenfell, 28 February 1917.

investments and in carrying out this process may with advantage invest a reasonable amount of their resources in foreign securities.'[9] Faint ripples had been felt in the markets before the announcement and as they settled down Morgans found it easier to syndicate the call loans and started to plan for a $100m issue for the French Treasury, to be followed by a smaller one for the London County Council (LCC).[10] The French loan, although Morgans ensured that it appeared oversubscribed, was not a success.[b] That for the LCC had already been delayed by the UK Treasury's 1 February issues and the break in US–German relations. Now it was postponed once more, first in favour of the French, then because the French issue was selling poorly and, again, as political events overtook the markets.[11]

The origins of US Treasury advances

On 19 March, the day after three American merchant ships had been sunk without warning, Harding told the French that the Administration was studying ways of providing financial help to the allies and asked them to make suggestions. He, himself, made two: either the USA should guarantee 'certain future Allied loans' or allied loans should be given the same tax and regulatory privileges as US Treasury issues. The French preferred the second as they thought that it would cause least damage to the prices of existing allied issues and best protect their independence.[12]The British, in both London and Washington, preferred the first. Keynes minuted that loans with an American guarantee could be floated on better terms than those with tax privileges and would enable countries to make their own issues, so that the British, as the best allied credit, would not find themselves acting as intermediaries and bearing the cost of defaults.[13] It was Crawford who suggested that the US Treasury should do the borrowing and make advances to the allies at the same rate of interest as it itself paid. He thought the advantages would be a lower rate of interest, a longer term, avoidance of competition with the US Treasury and a signal to the country that financial aid was of more immediate help than the 'dissipation of funds in military preparations'. It would also indicate to a lukewarm west and mid-west that the Administration was committed to the allied cause. To these arguments Bradbury added that of avoiding difficult questions of apportioning access to the market between the allies. The Administration was already thinking on the same lines, persuaded by the need to avoid disturbing its

b The issue was of $100m secured $5^1/_2$ per cent two-year Notes convertible into a $5^1/_2$ per cent twenty-year Bond. For the speculative, it was repayable at maturity in either dollars or French francs at a fixed rate of Ffr. 5.75. The Notes were underwritten at 97 and sold to the public at 99. There was a management fee of $^1/_2$ per cent and an allowance of $^3/_8$ per cent, payable at Morgans' discretion, available to the management group. The collateral was a mixture of the securities of the US ($20m) and neutral countries ($100m). MGP, B. Hist. 2, F. 15, no. 39884, JPM to MG (Copy to Governor), 19 March 1917, and no. 41287, JPM to MG (sent to Deputy Governor), 29 March 1917; T 172/429, Lever's Diary, 22 March 1917; PML, Archives, Syndicates No. 9, ff. 45–6.

own borrowing and giving discriminatory approval of issues by different countries. On 27 March, McAdoo told Crawford that the plan had his personal support.[14]

The same day, Lever and Jack Morgan saw McAdoo and Harding. They were told that, if there was war, legislation enabling the US Treasury to make advances to the allies would take some three to four weeks to pass Congress and, in the meantime, the British should avoid new borrowing, including, presumably, the $250m Exchequer Bonds suggested in February.[15] 'The prospect of obtaining no further funds for three to four weeks is certainly serious' was Keynes's reaction.[16] More gold was ordered from Ottawa and further sales of Scheme B securities authorised. Between the end of March and 25 April, the call loans expanded by another $79m (Table 6.4). Earlier in the year, the UK had received several credits, among them an instalment of $34.7m from the Japanese 6 per cent Exchequer Bonds (on 15 January), $14.2m from Royal Dutch Petroleum (17 January) and $15m from the Central Argentine Railway (1 February) (Table 6.3). Then came the break in relations and the markets' seizure. Bethlehem Steel had been late with a contract to deliver shells to the Russians. Morgans and the Ministry of Munitions had negotiated an extension in the delivery time, a reduction in price and payment in $37.3m UK Treasury two-year Notes. However, Bethlehem needed cash, and in the second half of February it issued $50m of its own Notes partly secured on those of the UK Treasury. It was, in effect, borrowing on the Treasury's behalf.[c] Although the prospectus concealed that the issue was being made because the British were paying in paper, Morgans found the response unenthusiastic.[17] On 15 March, another munitions contractor, du Pont, took a further $17.8m One-Year Treasury Notes (Table 6.3).

Now, during April, after the request from McAdoo to postpone public issues, a large, but ultimately unsuccessful, manoeuvre was attempted. Under its mobilisation schemes, the UK Treasury had collected nearly $200m of Canadian railway sterling debentures, mostly of the CPR. A plan, hatched the previous autumn and developed in January, involved depositing the debentures with the CPR, which would use them as the collateral with which to borrow in New York. The effect would be to replace the CPR's sterling debt with US dollar debt, with the dollars being advanced to the UK Treasury.

The scheme ran into problems from the start. Legislation in Canada was needed

c Morgans bought $50m Bethlehem Steel Co. two-year 5% Notes dated 15 February 1917 at $95^3/_8$ and sold them to Bankers Trust and Guaranty Trust at $96^3/_8$. The Notes were secured by $25m Bethlehem Steel Co. First Lien and Refunding Mortgage 5% Bonds and $37.6m British Government two-year Notes. The records of the UK Treasury and Morgans' syndicate books show a discrepancy of $0.3m in the value of the UK Notes issued. PML, Archives, Syndicates No. 9, f. 1; T 170/134, f. 43, Chadwick, 'British Government Transactions in America', 1922; T 171/149, f. 14, Ramsay, 'Memorandum by the Treasury as to the Financial Effort of Great Britain and the Cost of the War', 2 December 1918.

to amend the CPR's borrowing powers and this was not possible before the second half of April. Also, Morgans had difficulty forming a syndicate. The markets in New York were fearful of the US Treasury's own borrowing, whose expected size grew from $1,000m to $5,000m while Morgans were making their preparations. They wanted the UK Treasury to underwrite up to $100m, without Morgans' usual help, because they were already overexposed to British securities and the call loans. The threatened rise in Federal income taxes reduced the prospective net yield to American investors and, hardly surprisingly, the British were unwilling to create a precedent and offer holders compensation, making the securities, in effect, protected from tax for American residents. The British also thought the terms unattractive.

The Administration delivered the *coup de grâce*. On 9 April, Jack Morgan, Crawford and Lever discussed the allies' financial requirements with Harding and warned that the British would need $500m 'as quickly as possible: in view of the overdraft this could not be expected to last more than thirty days, but a second and third instalment of the same amount would last sixty days apiece'.[18] Lever also told him about the CPR refinancing, indicating that the UK preferred a temporary advance from the US Treasury. When Harding consulted McAdoo, he was told that, as legislation to permit advances to the allies would be delayed, the British should proceed. A week later, on 16 April, with the prospects for speedy legislation improving, McAdoo asked the British to cancel the issue and to finance themselves from their own resources for the following two months. The scheme was then dropped.[19]

Summer 1917: US Treasury advances and the peg

The first Liberty Bond Act was approved by the President on 24 April 1917. It authorised the Secretary of the Treasury, with the approval of the President, to issue Bonds for up to $5,000m and to use a maximum of $3,000m to establish credits for foreign governments by buying their obligations. In addition, the Act provided for borrowing on certificates of indebtedness with a term of not more than one year, as long as the amount outstanding at any one time did not exceed $2,000m. The Act tied the Secretary's hands by specifying the purpose of advances to the allies as 'more effectually providing for the national security and defense and prosecuting the war' and authorised him to 'enter into such arrangements as may be necessary or desirable for establishing such credits and for purchasing such obligations' (see Chapter 16).

On 17 April, McAdoo agreed to lend $150m or $200m to the British as soon as legislation was passed and on 25 April, the day after the Bill was approved by the President, the US Treasury made its first advance to the UK from part of the proceeds of $268m sixty-day certificates; $200m was paid to Morgans via the Federal Reserve Bank of New York (as were all future advances), McAdoo being unprepared to make a payment directly to the Administration's enemies; $50m was applied to the No. 1 Loan account; $46.3m to the No. 2 Loan account; and $100m credited to the Treasury Account. The balance was used to pay interest.[20]

This was the only occasion that a US Treasury advance was used to repay Morgans' loans and over the years it was to cause the British embarrassment.

The restrictions placed by the Liberty Loan Acts on the use of advances was the most important problem encountered by the British when negotiating with the US Treasury for dollars with which to support the sterling exchange rate. In the two years 1 April 1917 to 31 March 1919, the British sold $1,727m to peg sterling at $4.76½. The sales were predominantly at the start of the period: $1,476m in the year ending 31 March 1918, of which $515m was in the quarter ending 30 June 1917, when the US Treasury was feeling its way towards a new role.[21] Explaining why the exchange rate should be supported, and at $4.76½, was the responsibility of the UK Treasury's 'A' Division, or the external finance Division carved out of the Finance Division by Bonar Law in January 1917. It was headed by Keynes. The recipients of his expositions were McAdoo and Crosby (the Assistant Secretary) with interpretation provided by American bankers: Benjamin Strong, Jack Morgan, Vanderlip and Fred Kent.

When the USA entered the war, sterling was coming onto the New York market from five sources. First, there was the bilateral balance of payments deficit with the USA on civilian account. Second, and most observable because it was easily identified and understood, was the movement of American banking balances. These tended to come in surges, such as that experienced in November and December 1916, around the time when the Federal Reserve Board issued its warning, and were usually a reaction to specific events, such as war news or changing conditions in the New York money market. The amounts could be considerable: American banks' balances and bills held in London fell by £31m ($147.7m) between 14 April and 23 June 1917.[22] Third, although some of the advances made to the allies by the UK Treasury were in dollars, the greater part were in sterling. The agreements with each ally differed, and changed over time. By 1917, sterling advances fell into three categories: those to be used for purchases of goods and services; those to be used for the support of the recipient's exchange rate; and those which could be used freely, at the discretion of the borrowing ally. Within the constraints of each agreement, the advances could be sold by the ally to make dollar payments in the USA, or arbitraged over New York to settle expenditure in neutral countries, or used to enable holders of the recipients' currencies to buy dollars arbitraged over sterling.[d] Even if the sterling was spent in the UK, it had an effect on the exchange rate because the UK economy had no spare industrial capacity and additional spending passed straight through into higher imports or lower exports. That spending of advances directly in the USA was an alternative

d An example was provided by the French Treasury in April 1917. Monthly payments in New York were stated to be $110m, with a further $22.9m described as 'Payments actually made in London in pounds but finally settled in dollars'. The items purchased included frozen meats, oats, nitrates, timber and wool. The timber was Canadian, the nitrates (probably) Chilean and the wool (probably) Argentinian. *FRUS* (1917, 2, I), pp. 520–2, Sharp to Lansing, 11 April 1917. That the French had been converting about £5m per month into dollars out of the £25m per month advanced to them under the Calais Agreement was confirmed by Keynes. T 170/124, ff. 70–4, Keynes, 'Advances to Allies', end-October 1917.

to finding dollars to finance an increased current account deficit was recognised by the UK Treasury at an early stage of the war.[23] Fourth, even after the Treasury Account with Morgans had been opened in August 1915, some British government departments and agencies continued to buy dollars in the open market. It was not until mid-June 1917 that the decision was made to pay for all government purchases from the Account and, until July 1917, payments for wheat purchased by the British Wheat Export Company on behalf of all the allies were made by means of sterling bills sold in the New York market.[24] Other sterling bills were also easily identified as drawn to meet purchases of American produce, such as cotton and tobacco, and produce from third parties, such as grain from Canada and Argentina. Finally, until the USA introduced licensing of gold exports in September 1917, neutrals and allies earning surpluses in sterling, or currencies saleable into sterling, could always obtain ultimate settlement in their own currencies by selling sterling into dollars and dollars into gold.

Summer 1917: 'negotiating' for advances to support the sterling peg

Problems with using advances to support sterling began a month after the USA declared war as growing British demands for credit, American inexperience and uncertainty about the US Treasury's ability to raise sufficient funds to meet its commitments coincided. On 2 May, McAdoo announced that the first issue of Liberty Bonds would be $2,000m and appealed to investors for subscriptions. Seven days later, the terms were published, including a coupon of 3 1/2 per cent, a rate lower than many in the financial community recommended. The Bonds were offered on 14 May and they were to remain on sale until 15 June. Sales were slow until the last week of the campaign and the prospect of failure was very real.[25] The alternative was short-term debt, certificates, which were limited under the Act to $2,000m. Understandably, the US Treasury doubted whether it could meet the allies' demands in full: even if all the money was raised, the British, Italian and French estimates would have absorbed the $3,000m allocated to the allies in less than six months. It was inevitable that the USA should seek economies in the advances being used to support sterling, whose role in allied finance it did not understand and which were suspected by some in Congress of being the means by which dollars were being spent outside America.

Sterling wheat bills came onto the market in the final week of April, to which were added £20.8m ($99.2m) withdrawals of American banking funds from London in the first half of May and, Strong reported, sales of cotton bills: at one stage, £9.1m ($44.3m) was bought in two and a half days' trading. The US Treasury established a credit of $50m in favour of the British on 5 May, half of which was drawn down that day and half on 7 May (Table 9.1). Despite this, the call loans rose from $341m to $398.5m in the first seven days of the month. On 6 May, Morgans warned that they would purchase no more sterling unless they had cash in hand, explaining that they were unable to arrange further borrowing from their syndicate: just as the banks were withdrawing sterling from London in preparation for the Liberty Loan, so they were calling in their dollar advances (Table 6.4).[26]

Table 9.1 Credits established and cash advanced by the US Treasury to the UK Treasury: April–August 1917 ($m)

	Credits established	*Cash advanced*
25 April 1917	200	200
5 May	50	25
7 May		25
14 May	75	75
25 May	75	75
9 June	75	75
14 June	25	25
19 June	35	35
26 June	15	15
30 June	35	10
2 July		25
5 July	100	100
17 July	85	
20 July		85
25 July	185	
1 August		50
9 August		50
16 August		50
21 August	50	
23 August		50
30 August		35

Source: *ARSF* (1920), pp. 325 and 330–1.

The next day, the UK Treasury decided to make the use of US Treasury advances easier to identify and ordered wheat payments to be transferred from the market to the Treasury Account once the existing contracts began expiring in July. Lever was finding clear signs that such a step was needed. US Treasury officials, he told the Chancellor, were having 'difficulty in persuading themselves' that advances for exchange intervention came within the scope of the Liberty Loan Act. On 11 May, he recorded in his diary that the USA might curtail the next advance so that the UK would have to ship more gold, and a fortnight later he warned the Chancellor that some part of the money to support the exchange and make Canadian payments would have to come from other sources.[27]

The selling coincided with two incidents, which could not have helped to persuade the US Treasury to be generous. Both involved bankers. Immediately the USA declared war, the British had sent a mission, headed by Arthur Balfour, the Foreign Secretary, to the USA to investigate, encourage, cajole and liaise with the new ally. It comprised seven departmental missions, including one from the Treasury. A member of the latter was Cunliffe, who, in the first half of May, showed himself to be a loose cannon by continually advocating different policies from those of the UK Treasury and, in particular, in the presence of American officials, recommending that the British continue to rely on sales of securities and gold and that the US Treasury delay making advances.[28] The second incident was the manner in which Morgans let it be known that they would extend no more credit on the call loans. Without the client having been informed, the decision was given in a blunt and offensive fashion by Davison to Crosby on a Sunday in a club. It was only later the same day that Crosby asked Lever to call on him and the British heard of Morgans' decision.[29]

With the prospect for June already black, on 25 May Lever learnt that the money required for British food purchases had unexpectedly grown. At the end of March, the Cabinet had decided to raise stocks of wheat in the UK to thirteen weeks' consumption by the end of August. The additional demand had to be met almost exclusively from the USA and Canada because India was suffering from a poor harvest, the Wheat Commission had ceased shipping from Australia to save transport and, almost simultaneously with the Cabinet's decision, Argentina banned grain exports to the UK. The sum was £27m ($128.7m) and the bills would be coming onto the market over the following thirty days. Lever's reaction was that he was 'very apprehensive' whether the money could be found. Keynes's estimates for June confirmed the fear. Expenses for the month would be $300m, including the wheat. 'We ought just to get through the month,' on condition that the US Treasury provided $200m, that there was no run on exchange and that Morgans were prepared to maintain the overdraft.[30] In the event, the US Treasury provided only $175m and it was to prove the costliest month of the war for sterling support, with purchases of £55.1m ($262.5m).[31]

Not unexpected were two debt repayments. On 1 June, a $20m wheat loan from Canadian banks came due: the Chancellor accepted Lever's advice that it would be impolitic to use US Treasury funds, even if they had been available, and instead applied $18m received from Japan in payment for a shipment of Russian gold (Table 10.1).[32] On 17 June, the $50m bankers' loan, which had been renewed for a year in June 1916, matured. For reasons which are not recorded, but may have been influenced by Cunliffe in one of his difficult moods, the committee of joint stock bankers was reluctant to renew, while the Vanderlip Committee found it impossible to organise the 300 lending banks when they were losing deposits to the Liberty Bonds. The Chancellor said that he would prefer renewal, but, on condition that the suggestion was not seen to have come from him, he was prepared to have it repaid with gold provided by the British bankers. At maturity, the Federal Reserve Bank of New York sold dollars against the earmarking of the gold in London, thus avoiding the risk of shipment.[33]

The UK had applied for $185m for June, asking that $100m be paid on the 10 June and the balance on 25 June. No written reply was received and no credits were established.[34] Instead, Crosby questioned the size of the application and the use of advances for intervention: only $75m was received on 9 June, and by 13 June the other $25m had still not materialised, despite another meeting between McAdoo and Crawford (Table 9.1).[35] On 11 June, the day that Lord Northcliffe arrived as Head of the British War Mission, Lever ordered £10m ($47.6m) gold from Ottawa, cabling that he feared that if the remaining $25m of the 10 June application was not received, he would be short by the time of the next requested advance on 25 June. He would try to persuade the US Treasury to anticipate part of this and, in the meanwhile, he warned that the Liberty Loan was faring badly and that the UK might be asked to raise money in the markets on its own account.[36] The $25m was obtained but 'with considerable difficulty' after Lever had met Crosby, who again objected to the exchange purchases and seemed 'overwrought', McAdoo having retired exhausted after a trip to the west selling Liberty Bonds. Lever provided data to show that in April and May the UK had spent upwards of $180m more in the USA than the US Treasury had advanced and explained that the exchange purchases included settling sterling bills for cotton, grain and other food. Crosby said that he was being asked why the UK was receiving such a large proportion of the total advances: he was not going to allow McAdoo to be 'crucified', but the information he had received 'threw a good deal of light on the situation'. In view of Crosby's anxiety, Lever decided to delay mentioning early payment of the 25 June advance.[37]

With high call money rates and no let up in sales of sterling, on 16 June Lever asked the Chancellor for confirmation that he should continue to peg the rate 'by all means at [his] disposal' and suggested that, in future, all government purchases should be settled through the Treasury Account, as had been arranged for wheat. Both moves were confirmed.[38] After another long meeting on 18 June, during which McAdoo argued that under the terms of the Liberty Loan Act he was not justified in making advances for exchange support and queried British spending in Argentina, Japan and Spain, Crawford succeeded in persuading him to anticipate the 25 June advance by making an 'emergency' loan of $75m the following day. Only $35m was paid (Table 9.1).[39] Crawford and Lever saw Crosby two days later to emphasise the difficulties caused by not knowing when funds would become available and to point out that they did not even know the size of advances they would receive over the remainder of the month. The reply showed that Crosby still did not recognise the seriousness of the position: 'he would discuss matter with McAdoo, that it was impossible for them to meet demands of Allies, that they were subject of criticism by politicians and particularly for large (group omitted – advances?) they were making to us and that while he could make no promise now he hoped to let me have a reply this week.'[40]

By this time, Crawford and Lever thought they had identified the reasons for the Americans' behaviour. McAdoo was tired, and often away ill, while Crosby was strained. McAdoo resented what he took to be British importunity. Although the British had financed all their own US expenditure during April and May, passing the US advances on to the allies, American officials were suspicious that their credits were being used to buy goods outside the USA. This centred on purchases of sterling, much of which came from unidentified sources: by the end of June, the US Treasury had compiled data for the surplus on trade account and the movement of bankers' balances and found that there were sales of sterling for which they could not account. Finally, with the British unwilling to provide hard information to support their arguments, there was suspicion that they were exaggerating their weakness and that, if pressed, they could find more dollars.[41] The cables did not mention the most important problem, perhaps because it was too obvious. At the beginning of May, the British had asked for $1,500m over six months, $400m to repay the call loans, a figure so large that McAdoo had said at once that he doubted his ability to find it. By 5 July, the USA would have advanced $1,095m to the allies, of which $685m was to the UK. The British were, therefore, asking for $815m of the remaining $1,905m authorised by the Liberty Loan Act (see p. 247).[42] The advance due on 25 June (Monday) was not paid, Lever reporting that McAdoo was conferring with the President about the policy on advances in general.[43] McAdoo then left Washington for the remainder of the week, having authorised only $15m of the $50m balance outstanding for the month and wanting time to consider the position. Crawford warned Crosby that unless the UK received further advances there would be a stop on Thursday, 28 June. To the argument that it was unreasonable to withhold advances at such short notice, Crosby replied that the British had no right to assume that $185m would be loaned in June merely because the US Treasury had not replied to their application, that McAdoo felt the UK's demands to be 'too insistent' and that he was being deprived of his discretion under the Liberty Bond Act. When Crosby telephoned McAdoo, he refused to reconsider the matter until he returned to Washington.

Lever then changed tack. He asked Crawford to approach the State Department and, with only $22m gold in Ottawa and a handful of securities, which could only be sold with difficulty in a thin market, he cabled the Chancellor to urge that approaches be made through diplomatic channels, to ask whether he should ship the remaining gold and for instructions on which payments should take precedence should he be forced to declare a stop.[44] He also approached Strong, who had long been an influential advocate of maintaining the sterling rate, and arranged for him to see the President's confidant, Colonel House.[45] In Washington, Crawford, having once more failed to move Crosby, talked to Frank Polk, Counselor of the State Department, who in turn spoke to Lansing.[e] When Lansing intervened with McAdoo, the Secretary promised to pay the $35m on 28 June on the understanding that it did not commit him 'any further'.[46] Before hearing this, Lever, feeling that even a few hours might save the position, ordered the sale of $10m Scheme B securities and shipped the remaining gold from Ottawa.[47]

The cable with news that McAdoo had agreed to advance the balance of the June application was sent on 27 June (Wednesday), but was not recorded as arriving in London until the Friday.[48] On Thursday evening, Balfour and the Chancellor saw the American Ambassador Walter Hines Page, who told Lansing that:

> Bonar Law reports that only half enough has been advanced for June and that the British agents in the United States now have enough money to keep the exchange up for only one day more. If exchange with London fall, exchange with all European Allies also will immediately fall and there will be a general collapse. Balfour understood [when on his mission] that in addition to our other loans and our loans to France and Italy, we would advance to England enough to pay for all purchases by the British Government made in the United

e The Counselor was the second most senior post in the State Department.

> States. He authorizes me to say that they are now on a brink of a precipice and unless immediate help be given financial collapse will follow.[49]

The same day, Balfour cabled House, urging him to use his influence with the President.[50] On investigation, House concluded that:

> There seems to have been bad judgement on both sides. Sir Wm [Wiseman] Lever and Sir R. Crawford do not work closely together. Crawford works with our people and Lever has a tendency to work with J. P. Morgan & Co., and it is not certain that Morgan does not want such a crisis as has arisen in order to force themselves again into the situation from which they have been ejected by the Government.[51]

Another Note from Balfour, drafted by Keynes and toned down by the Chancellor, followed on 1 July. This asserted that a collapse in sterling would have an effect 'no less disastrous than a great military reverse': trade between the USA and the UK, including that in cotton, would be 'thrown into complete disorder' and the 'basis of financial relations of all the Allies with the rest of the world will be removed.' Balfour had understood that all the other allied financial requirements in the USA would be met by the US Treasury, beginning when war was declared, but those of Russia had continued to be borne by the UK. The Treasury had been assured that the USA would meet British needs and it had ceased market borrowing so that the way be left free for the Liberty Bonds. Yet, during June, American advances of $150m had had to be supplemented by shipping $125m gold and sales of $10m securities: a further $25m gold had been authorised for shipment. The increase in expenditure during June arose 'largely' from the withdrawal of $100m of American banking funds from London, which was 'in effect a diminution of the amount loaned by the United States'. The Note then made formal requests for repayment of sums paid in the USA on behalf of the Russians, a firm commitment for advances for July and August, including $100m by 4 July, and assistance in repaying the Morgan call loans.[52] The part of the Note listing the remaining British resources was not handed over, but given verbally: $166m securities (other than those pledged as collateral) in the USA, at sea or in London; $30m of gold, apart from that already authorised for shipment from Ottawa, with another $15m due to arrive shortly. The only other gold was £84m in the CNRA and Bank of England, which was the published gold reserves of the UK and could not be reduced without a loss of confidence. The joint stock banks might have reserves of £50m, which could only be obtained with difficulty and after delay.[53]

Northcliffe saw the President on either 30 June or 1 July and found him well briefed, but vague on specifics.[54] Wilson was also sympathetic when he met Spring-Rice, but made clear that McAdoo enjoyed his confidence and suggested that the British should ask him what information he needed and provide it freely; once the USA had the data, it would better know how to use its financial resources. He wanted to ensure that advances produced military results, and this also meant the provision of the fullest information.[55] When McAdoo saw Northcliffe and

Crawford, the emphasis was only slightly different. He said that he was bound to satisfy himself that funds were allotted in the 'spirit' of the legislation and used to bring the war to a speedy and successful conclusion. He needed to know the connection between advances and military goals and illustrated this by asking for a reasoned statement of the importance of maintaining sterling at $4.76^{1}/_{2}$. In the meanwhile, the flurry of diplomatic activity had eased the position: $10m was advanced on 30 June, $25m on 2 July, and $100m on 5 July (Table 9.1).[56]

McAdoo's formal reply to the British Note of 1 July said that he had never been given the information which would have enabled him to know that the UK's ability to meet its commitments was in jeopardy: that, although he was aware in general terms that the British had lent about $5,000m to the allies, he had not received any details of the advances; that the Note did not show why the exchange rate needed to be maintained at any particular level; that the British should not mistake general expressions of goodwill and discussions as a commitment to make specific advances; that, however dissatisfied the British might be with the extent of the advances, they were greater than anything which would be available from elsewhere; and that it required the agreement of the Russian and Belgian governments before the USA could agree to make repayments to the British a first charge on the US advances to them. Finally, he had the repayment of the call loan 'under consideration', but could offer no assurance that he would help with debts incurred before the USA entered the war.[57]

Summer 1917: Morgans call their loans

At this most sensitive moment in the relations between the British and American Treasuries, Morgans had announced that they were expecting the immediate repayment of the call loans: debts incurred before April. The loans had fallen from $437m to $341m when the first US advance was received on 26 April (Table 6.4). With no market borrowing, normal expenditure and abnormal purchases of sterling, they had been rapidly restored, so that by the end of the first week in May, when Morgans told Crosby that they would cease buying exchange unless they had money in hand, they stood at $398.5m. At the end of June, Morgans' deposits contracted as their customers made their semi-annual debt payments and paid for the first instalment of their Liberty Bonds. For the same reasons, other members of the syndicate were calling in their participations. To replace lost deposits, and maintain the call loans, the partners had been borrowing on their own account and, to placate participating banks, they had been promising repayment on 2 July out of US Treasury advances.[58] McAdoo's reluctance to provide funds to peg sterling, with the implication that there would, at best, be a delay in paying off the loans, thus came at an unfortunate moment.

Receiving an advance from the US Treasury for application to the call loans had been a concern of the British Treasury from the day the USA declared war and the attention of the Administration had been repeatedly drawn to its importance. At different times Balfour, Lever, Cunliffe, Spring-Rice and Morgan partners had been given the impression that repayment would be favourably considered once the Liberty Bonds had been issued. However, the only unequivocal promises were made to Crawford, a relatively junior diplomat. On 10 April, he reported that McAdoo had 'agreed that repayment of overdraft of some $400 millions should be first call on the [Liberty] loan' and that, on the following day, Harding had called, at the Secretary's request, 'and confirmed the views expressed by latter.' That evening, Crawford had gone 'over the matter again with the Counselor of the State Department [Polk] who fully concurred that our overdraft should be a first charge.' In the same cable he said that he was planning to discuss the details, and other matters covered in his conversations, with Lever and Davison, although it was not reported whether the meeting took place.[59]

Other conversations were less specific. At the end of April, Balfour discussed the allies' financial needs with McAdoo and asked whether it would be permissible to include the call loans on the list of uses to which advances could be applied. Without suggesting that he would pay them off, McAdoo said that he did, indeed, want a complete statement of British debts, together with details of the attached collateral.[60] Later, after Morgans had called the loans, Balfour told Grenfell that he was not at all clear 'in reference to the arrangements' as his attention was focused elsewhere.[61] There are inconsistencies in Cunliffe's recollections. One unsigned report says that the Governor had understood that the loans would be regarded as a first call on the Liberty Loan, but that there had been no formal agreement. On 4 July, the Governor said that on 9 April McAdoo had promised him that the US Treasury would make an advance to repay the loans. Unfortunately, as McAdoo later pointed out, Cunliffe had not arrived in Washington until 22 April. Grenfell reported that the Governor had 'distinctly understood from McAdoo that you [Morgans] were to be repaid $400m or thereabouts out of the first proceeds of the Liberty Loan' and that he had pressed for the arrangement to be written down.[62] On 3 May, when applying for the advance of $200m for that month, Spring-Rice stated the UK's requirement for the following half-year. This was divided into two sums, $1,100m for current expenditure and $400m for the call loans which it was 'hoped…may be regarded as a first charge on the credits to be advanced by the United States Government'.[63] There is no record of a response.

So matters stood until 28 June, the day that the British appealed for advances through diplomatic channels. Crawford was talking to Crosby in the Treasury Department when Davison entered and asked whether arrangements were in place to cover the call loans, which were due to be repaid on 1 July. His manner, said Crawford, was 'very aggressive, and the result upon the Treasury Department was very disastrous.' Crosby denied knowledge of an advance for such a purpose, whereupon Davison claimed that there had been a formal exchange of notes between Balfour and Lansing in which the USA had agreed to furnish the money on that date. He also said that Cunliffe and Lever had assured him that the agreement was in place and that Lansing would confirm it. Crawford then telephoned Lever, who said that there must have been a misunderstanding and that he had no recollection of ever having given the impression that there was any formal engagement with the USA to cover the debts. On 3 July, Davison saw Northcliffe, and repeated his story.[64]

Morgans' reaction was to call the loans. On the day Davison saw Northcliffe, Morgans, which presumably means Davison, told the Treasury in London that 'all plans and movements during the past two months have been predicated on our definite understanding that No. 1 and No. 2 would be liquidated on 2nd July' from US Treasury advances. Relying on this understanding, Morgans had told many of the sixty participating banks that they would be repaid:

> It is a cause of great regret that conditions here make it clear that this Loan payable on demand cannot be continued longer, and unless some other solution can be arranged for immediately, we feel we must proceed to sell collateral and apply proceeds toward reduction of Loan…We are greatly distressed at the position we now necessarily take, but as we were informed and confidently expected the Loan to be paid to-day, all the arrangements of ourselves and associates have been made accordingly, and we are consequently left no alternative.[65]

As was customary, Grenfell left a copy of the cable with Cunliffe. The Governor had been boiling with resentment for some time and his personal relations with Bonar Law were poor. The politicians were taking risks with financial stability which increasingly worried conservative finance, both in the City and in some parts of Whitehall. The Bank, with its statutory responsibility under the 1844 Act for the gold standard and the maintenance of the gold cover for its Note Issue, was anxious about the size and structure of the Treasury's overseas borrowing. While in the USA, Cunliffe had behaved in an erratic, independent and ill-judged fashion, all of which had been reported to London. He returned from the USA on 11 June to find that Keynes and Chalmers had absorbed many of the responsibilities of the LEC in dollar finance and, in the heat of the financial battle, were failing to keep the members of the Committee briefed.[66] On seeing Davison's letter, Cunliffe protested to the Prime Minister, demanding Keynes's and Chalmers's dismissal.[f] This was refused. On the same day, Cunliffe ordered £17.5m of the Bank's gold held in Ottawa to be placed at Morgans' disposal to close the No. 1 loan account, which, it will be recalled, stood in the Bank's name.[67] Over the following two days, the Governor learnt that Lever was also ordering shipments, which would have had the effect of reducing the gold that could be shown in the Bank's weekly return. Without referring to the Bank's Committee of Treasury, the politicians or Treasury officials, he cabled the Canadian government with instructions to ignore further orders from Lever if it precluded the earmarking of the £17.5m.[68] He thus directly provoked a confrontation with the Treasury, as Lever was its representative with powers to order shipments. A month later, Bonar Law forced an apology, together with a promise to work with the Treasury and obey its instructions.[69] In the meantime, it was another complication to add to Morgans' demand for repayment.

f See Sayers (1976), I, p. 103n, as to whether the demand was made in writing.

Although Morgans' action came as a complete surprise to the Treasury in London, and there was no correspondence to give substance to Morgans' story, on 4 July Lloyd George, Bonar Law, Balfour, Cunliffe and their advisers saw Page. They told him that both Spring-Rice and Cunliffe had received definite assurances that monies to repay the loans were to be advanced by the US Treasury from the proceeds of the Liberty Loan and that they hoped that they would now be paid. On being questioned, the British were unable to explain why they expected the advance on 2 July, except that the money from the Liberty Loan was to have been received on 1 July.[70] This was strange. The first call, of only 18 per cent, or $360m, was actually paid on Thursday, 28 June, and 1 July was a Sunday.

McAdoo's emotional reaction was that he did not propose 'to allow New York bankers and their allies to use the British government as a club to beat the United States Treasury with' and he rejected any suggestion that he had promised an advance:[71] nothing had been written down, there had been discussions with Balfour, but no commitment; no one could have promised anything in the first half of April because the Liberty Loan was not introduced to Congress until 11 April, the form in which it would emerge from its deliberations was not known, and it did not receive Presidential approval until 24 April: 'At no time, directly or indirectly, has the Secretary of the Treasury, or any one connected with the Treasury Department, promised to pay the Morgan overdraft'. The loans should be capable of renewal and, in any case, he had no information about them and asked for a list of participants and the details of collateral.[72] Later, in conversation with Northcliffe, McAdoo gave other reasons for refusing to help. Morgans were Republicans, the impression was widespread that they had made large profits from floating allied credits, acting as purchasing agents, and investing in industries which had benefited from the war. He did not feel that he should use US Treasury funds to help them.[73]

The episode showed that the judgement of British ministers was buckling under the strain of finding the dollars to meet their expenditure and policies. They saw Page without first enquiring into Morgans' story or the strength of the commitments given to British representatives. They did not understand the nature of the call loans or, therefore, their exposure to Davison's move. In short, the Treasury – Keynes, Bradbury and Chalmers – had failed to keep ministers briefed. What were the realities? Nothing has been found in the records to suggest that the loans were other than traditional New York advances against stock exchange securities callable at the lender's option at any time, with the right for the lender to sell the collateral if the borrower was unable to make repayment.[74] This seems to have been understood in London, for there is no suggestion in the Treasury records that Morgans were not acting properly, however ill-advised or embarrassing their behaviour was thought to be. When the British ministers saw Page, they did not suggest that Morgans were breaking the terms of an agreement: they were asking for US Treasury funds to make repayment. On the other side of the hill, McAdoo had correctly judged the commercial reality. As a New York financier, he would have known that the call loans were collateralised with the customary 20 per cent margin so the banks would get their money. He would also have known that Morgans had no reason, or right, to declare the British in default: their remedy lay in the sale of the collateral. Then, there were practical reasons for Morgans to show forbearance. The sum was so large that it would have gravely embarrassed both themselves and their associates, whereas a demand for repayment was pointless because, as they well knew, the UK's only resources were the US Treasury and the collateral. Sale of collateral on such a scale would have driven the market lower, with adverse effects on the collateral held throughout the US banking system. It would have been disastrous for Morgans standing in the country and their relations with the US Administration to declare an allied power in default in the middle of a war.

No doubt these considerations influenced Jack Morgan. More immediately, Morgans themselves quickly realised that they had no reason for expecting repayment on 2 July other than it having been the first working day after the receipts from the first call on the Liberty Loan had reached the US Treasury, while their enquiries in London showed that they could expect no support from Balfour, who was unable to recall a definite agreement with McAdoo.[75] It can also be surmised that they quickly realised that Cunliffe was overreaching himself.

On 3 July, the day that Cunliffe cabled Ottawa to release the gold, Grenfell told Morgans that the transfer would have a 'bad effect' and that if Washington did meet all, or part, of the No. 1 loan they should use as little as possible of the gold. The New York partners promised to bear this in mind, to co-operate 'in every possible way' and only use the gold to the extent they judged 'absolutely necessary.'[76] On 6 July, Jack Morgan returned from holiday:

> We shall be entirely satisfied to know Gold is in Ottawa and available if we need it, and trust that we shall not be forced to call for actual shipment, which we would regret from many points of view. Should American Government now make up its mind that it will not help in paying off this Loan [*sic*], we believe there are various methods which can be applied which will provide enough money, and at the same time there is no pressing need for the payment here. Even if it should be necessary later to sell part of the Collateral, we will not sell it in a hurry nor in such a way as to get less for it than we ought, and of course nothing will be done except in consultation with British Treasury Agents here.[77]

Northcliffe confirmed that Morgans were not anxious to bring down the gold and added that it could be avoided if Cunliffe approached Jack Morgan direct.[78]

Opening the books: the British Notes of July 1917

Although purchases of sterling fell from £55.1m ($262.5m) in June to £20.3m ($96.7m) in July, the paucity of its resources meant that there was no lessening of the UK Treasury's need for advances. The British requests were received by an American Treasury which was itself hard pressed for cash: the two earlier calls ($360m and $400m) on the First Liberty Bonds had been paid largely in certificates and the ordinary deficit in July and August was $466m. On 31 July, $300m certificates were sold followed by a further $250m on 18 August. On 14 August, McAdoo told the Chairman of the Ways and Means Committee of the House that it was necessary for Congress to authorise another $9,000m for the war, of which $4,000m would be for the allies. Three days later, he asked for authority to issue $7,500m in Bonds, $2,000m in certificates and the same amount in war savings certificates.[79]

In the middle of July, Spring-Rice had warned that the US Treasury had found the demands of the allies much greater than expected and that it was approaching the point where it would either have to ask Congress for additional borrowing powers or refuse further advances.[80] The Treasury in London described this as 'in the highest degree alarming'. Allied demands on the UK for funds, notably from a financially exhausted France, which was costing £1m per day, had not been reduced by the advances now being made directly to them by the Americans. Spring-Rice was instructed to say that:

> His Majesty's Government now possess no further means wherewith to pay for their purchases in the United States, and in consequence the whole financial system of the alliance will break down unless the United States Government is able to meet the payment due on this [Russian and Belgian] account.
>
> Such an eventuality would be disastrous, and not improbably fatal, to the cause for which the Allies are fighting.[81]

There followed on 20 July, three days later, the survey of British expenditure and borrowing which McAdoo had requested. This, the first time the British had provided the Americans with a comprehensive picture of their financial contribution, denied that the US Treasury was assuming the 'entire burden of financing the war', as McAdoo had suggested; between 1 April and 14 July, the British had advanced over twice as much to the allies as had the USA and this assistance exceeded that provided by the USA to the UK. Moreover, whereas the US Treasury insisted that advances be spent in its own country, the British were financing the allies' expenditure throughout the world. The Note gave details of British spending between August 1914 and April 1917, and showed how the money had been raised, before listing the assets which remained. Finally, it reiterated that the UK's dollar resources were exhausted and that 'Unless the United States Government can meet our expenses in America, including exchange, the whole financial fabric of the alliance will collapse. This conclusion will be a matter not of months but of days.'[82]

A second Note followed at the end of the month, defending the policy of maintaining the exchange rate by showing its importance to the USA and the allies and warning that the removal of the peg was imminent. It pointed out that fixing sterling at $4.76½ was the means by which the allies could turn their sterling advances into dollars to meet their payments in both the USA and neutral countries. Not all purchases had come under government control and the peg facilitated American exports on private account to the UK, its Empire and the allies. If sterling was left unsupported, allied exchange rates would collapse against both the dollar and other currencies. US export trade would seize up and American banks' sterling assets would be frozen. Countries selling to the UK and the allies would no longer be prepared to build up balances in sterling, so that an important source of credit would be cut off. The move would be seen as indicating 'a deep-seated distress', bringing comfort to the Central Powers:

> We must therefore know if possible immediately whether the Government can give us the financial assistance we need.
>
> In asking this we do not overlook that we are asking [the US Treasury] to moderate two conditions which they have hitherto considered essential
>
> ...to provide funds for the exchange is to defray uncontrolled expenditure for undefined purposes
>
> ...[and it] involves in part the employment of American funds to finance the purchases of the Allies outside America.

The support given to sterling over the previous three months had been inflated by the withdrawal of American banks' London balances and included the cost of allied wheat purchases, which were now to be met from the Treasury Account. The average cost of buying exchange in the future, assuming bankers' balances remained stationary, 'is not likely to be less than' $100m per month. It was necessary to know the US attitude within a few days because the exchange could only be maintained with American assistance and at any moment it might be necessary to withdraw support.[83]

Lever and the British diplomats had been telling London since the early summer that the huge scale of war-related expenditure in general, and advances to the allies in particular, was causing McAdoo difficulties with Congress. At the beginning of August, the Secretary was preparing for appearances in front of Congressional committees to explain his use of the first loan and request further borrowing powers. The committees included some very hostile members. A defence against allegations that money was being wasted or misallocated was the establishment of an Inter-Allied Council (IAC), with authority to determine allied needs and priorities before passing on the requests to a purchasing body in Washington, but it did not provide a defence against those challenging the size of the advances made to the UK or their use to support sterling. The questions McAdoo feared most, Northcliffe and Spring-Rice explained, were: did he use advances specifically for war purposes? was there proof of this? did he have guarantees that prices paid for supplies were fair? had he shown a preference for one ally over another? had capitalists and trusts benefited unfairly? and had the expenditure contributed to price inflation? Clearly, he would have difficulty explaining that he had used advances to repay a loan to Morgans, allowed the withdrawal of Wall Street money from London without loss and maintained sterling's value throughout the world for the 'general purposes of trade'. McAdoo appreciated that a break in the rate 'would be an Austerlitz for Germany' with a moral effect which might prolong the war but, for him, the question was whether Congress would appreciate this. The present moment, as he prepared to approach Congress, was critical, and he asked the British how long the rate could be maintained as the situation would be very different in one or two months' time.[84]

Balfour soothingly replied that his government understood from its own experience with the Commons the problems faced in obtaining supplies and that it would help by providing all the information it had at its disposal: 'The exchanges of the Allies are entirely dependent on the maintenance of sterling exchange…we are supporting exchange only by means of dollars supplied by the United States Government.' Could a temporary solution be found in reimbursing British expenditure in the USA on behalf of Russia? If this $100m was made available, together with the $185m already promised, 'we ought to get through August, unless there is an exceptional run in exchange'.[85]

The next day, Northcliffe cabled that he 'was better pleased with the atmosphere in Washington' and that, although it would require a monthly struggle, he believed that the British would 'get what was required'. This was followed by news that the $185m already promised for August was to be increased by $50m to assist in exchange support and to carry the UK over until McAdoo was able to form a more permanent policy (Table 9.1). McAdoo asked that the British state that the advance was for 'general purposes'.[86] Anxiety was never at an end, but greater information, Reading's diplomacy, and, as Wiseman commented towards the end of September, McAdoo's realisation of the 'very serious responsibility which he would assume if Allied finance collapsed through any petty action of his' transformed the US Treasury's attitude, even before the establishment of the IAC in Europe in November.[87] Purchases of sterling on the scale required during June were never again necessary during the war, although they still averaged over £26.6m ($126.7m) per month in the second half of the year. Measures to take sterling bills off the market, the raising of loans in neutral currencies and the introduction of exchange controls in the UK on 21 December produced a dramatic improvement in the first half of 1918. Purchases were £17.4m ($83.1m) in January and £13.4m ($64m) in February. On 21 March 1918, the long-awaited German offensive in France began and, although it was not turned until the second half of July, by April purchases were down to only £3.1m ($15m); they averaged £5.2m ($24.8m) per month in the second quarter. With the scent of victory, sales of sterling were necessary in August, September and October.[88]

Dollar Treasury Bills: the taming of the call loans

During July and August, with McAdoo in his new more helpful mode, the UK Treasury repaired some of the damage done by Cunliffe's earmarking of the Ottawa gold and, with the help of a Treasury Bill issue and sales of collateral, reduced the call loans to a level at which Morgans felt comfortable. Once again, the episode began with a tantrum.

The Bank did not think it could properly ask Morgans to release the gold which Cunliffe had placed at their disposal as long as it was the obligor for the No. 1 account. To side-step this, in the second half of July the Treasury persuaded Morgans to merge the two accounts. Both became the Treasury's direct obligation and Morgans was able to treat the gold as tendered against a consolidated loan of \$384m (Table 6.4). Morgans themselves were carrying \$58m of the No. 1 loan and were prepared to substitute the No. 2. The only problem was that two trust companies, responsible for \$14.75m of the No. 1 loan, would have exceeded their legal limits for lending to any one name if they transferred their advances. It was arranged that they be paid off in cash by the withdrawal of part of the Bank's gold earmarked in Ottawa.[89]

The details were still being worked out when, on 27 July (Friday), Morgans warned Blackett that, if prospects had not 'materially altered' by 10 August, they would have 'seriously to consider' the sale of collateral.[90] The reason for this can only be surmised. In the middle of the month, Morgans had provided a list of the participants in the call loans and details of the collateral, together with a written note on British finance, for Northcliffe to pass to McAdoo. Morgans had hoped that this would encourage McAdoo to act, but there had been no response.[91] Hitherto, in bankerly fashion, they had kept the size of the loans, and the names of the participating banks, a strict secret. The details may have leaked from the US Treasury and aroused the concern of some participants, who had demanded repayment. Whatever the reason, the following Monday, 30 July, when 'it was 100 in the shade in New York and Washington and a very damp heat', Lamont saw McAdoo and heard for himself that the US Treasury would not make advances to clear the loans because Congress would not tolerate taxpayers' money being used to repay debts incurred before 1 April. This unnerved the bankers, Lamont being 'much exercised', although McAdoo had been helpful and had made two suggestions: a British loan might be floated in the market and savings might be made from the US Treasury's monthly advances and applied to the overdraft. On the Tuesday after the interview, Lamont gave Lever formal notice of the intention to start selling collateral and the outline of a scheme for a 5½ per cent one-year secured Note convertible into a 6 per cent twenty-year Bond. The collateral would have come from the securities released by repaying the call loans, but the overall cost to the UK would have been 8 per cent, which, said Lever, 'was clearly not much more than a scheme for compensating participants in overdraft for converting their participation into time loan'.[92]

Jack Morgan insisted that the matter be shelved for a few days and, on his return, cooled the partners' anxieties. Writing to Grenfell on 9 August, he described the episode as a 'silly mix-up' and was, unusually, angry:

> Unfortunately, I was away at the time it [the 'mix-up'] developed that there had been a misunderstanding, and my partners had become more disturbed than was, I think, necessary over the matter, and had begun to stir around in too active a way. This could not produce any result except that of irritating all parties concerned; so I managed to calm things down, and we are now all co-operating in a most friendly spirit.

He added in a back-handed defence of the Administration:

> I must say that there is something to be said on their side since they are entirely inexpert business men and did not realize how much the other parties to the conversations would count on rather careless expressions on their part.[93]

An earlier, intemperate, cable had not been despatched and Jack Morgan was able to apologise to the British for his partners' hasty action. A second, more considered, message suggested that, because it was clear there would be no advance from McAdoo, collateral should be slowly and carefully sold, avoiding disturbing the markets either for further sales or for the next Liberty Loan, and that a public issue should be made of either Notes or Bills.[94] This became the centrepiece of the UK Treasury's response. The aim should be 'to induce Morgans to give long enough time to avoid necessity of making unsatisfactory arrangements': sales of collateral should be 'pushed'; if necessary, a maximum of £10m of the gold earmarked to Morgans could be shipped – any larger amount would show in the published figures – and money should be raised in the markets.

Although the Chancellor did not like Treasury Bills, he could not rule them out as Morgans did not consider a longer maturity feasible.[95] McAdoo, perhaps influenced by Strong, who believed that British Bills would damage the market for the US Treasury's own certificates of indebtedness, agreed with the Chancellor: he told Crawford that he would consider allowing an issue of $200m Notes, provided that they were for at least two years and, shades of January, the US Treasury was given the details first.[96]

On 10 August, Lever authorised Morgans to sell up to $11m of collateral when conditions were favourable. He also promised, and the Chancellor agreed, that the compensation, or 'ship money', which was to be paid by the USA when it acquired vessels being built to the order of the UK in American yards, would be applied to the call loans (see p. 267).[97]

The failure of the Canadian $100m issue (see pp. 301–2) convinced Morgans and McAdoo that the outside money would have to come from Treasury Bills. After discussions with Morgans, Lever suggested that the maximum should be $150m at any one time and $15m per week, at a market rate of discount not exceeding 5¾ per cent. The first issue should be placed at 5 per cent discount, mainly with the banks who were providing the call loans, thus ensuring the minimum of publicity. They would be a straight refinancing, the entire proceeds being applied to the loans. The commission would be ½ per cent a year and if, at any time, sales did not match maturities the difference would come from the Treasury Account.

The advantages were as Lever saw them when cabling his recommendation. Whereas the Notes would have been secured, the Bills would release collateral as the call loans were repaid. There was little danger of a withdrawal of sterling balances because the Bills were refunding existing borrowing, with no public subscription: at worst, they converted a call liability into a 90-day liability. The expenses were moderate, certainly well beneath those being mooted the previous November.[98] There was one other advantage. A condition of the Chancellor's agreement was that Cunliffe's gold was no longer to be earmarked to Morgans, but would remain available in Ottawa against 'the general situation' in the USA, not being used for new purchases or to meet expenditure elsewhere.[99]

Morgans were careful to obtain McAdoo's agreement to the issue in writing and then, to make doubly sure, they finessed him into a public declaration. The Bills met strong demand, and a good deal of publicity, so the first could be sold earlier than intended, on 22 August, for issue two days' later at a discount rate of 5¼ per cent.[100] On the same day, the two call loans were amalgamated.[g]

Over the remainder of the year, various schemes were mooted to help the British to repay the balance of the call loan without attracting the attention of Congress. The US Treasury never accepted the British suggestion that it should reimburse the UK for advances made to Russia to meet its dollar expenditure and allow the proceeds to be applied to the call loan, but the prospect helped keep Morgans happy and was a kite which was frequently flown. At the end of August, House proposed a different ploy, namely that the French apply to the US Treasury for $100m to $200m more than they needed, hand the dollars over to the British, and be reimbursed by the UK in sterling. This would avoid making a repayment to Morgans, and the Chancellor and the French approved. However, McAdoo disliked the subterfuge, fearing the reaction if Congress learnt about it, and even Reading's persuasive powers were unable to make any impression on him.[101] Morgans were relaxed: by November, the British were keeping a 'very satisfactory' balance with them and there was the promise of ship money.[102]

Subrogation, ship money and the 1 February 1918 maturity

The Second Liberty Bond Act was approved on 24 September 1917 and the sales campaign began on 1 October.[h] Once again, investors were slow to respond and, once again, the US Treasury became anxious. Reading, who had arrived in New York on 11 September as special envoy to the USA and had gone straight to Washington, reported that the US Treasury was spending $600m a month and that, from October, this was expected to rise to $1,000m, in addition to $500m a

g The volume of Bills in issue rose rapidly to about $100m and remained between $80m and $100m until September 1919. The general market for which Morgans looked did not develop, however, and buyers were limited to banks switching from the call loan (Table 6.2). PML, Archives, Horn Box 3, no. 31,964, JPM to Morgan Harjes, 13 October 1917; Weems (1923), Appendix XXI.

h The Act authorised the issue of a maximum of $7,539m Bonds (including the $3,000m sanctioned by the first Act, which had not been offered for subscription), with a coupon of not more than 4 per cent and a price of not less than par. An additional $2,000m certificates could be issued, together with $2,000m War Savings Certificates. $4,000m was appropriated for advances to the allies in addition to any amount still not used from the first Act. $3,000m were offered, but additional Bonds could be allotted up to one-half of any over-subscription. They were dated 1927–42. Two per cent was payable on application and 18 per cent on 15 November, 40 per cent on 15 December and 40 per cent on 15 January 1918. The lists opened on 1 October and closed on 27 October. Subscriptions were $4,618m and, in accordance with the prospectus, $3,809m were allotted. Gilbert (1970), pp. 124–8.

month earmarked for advances.[103] Receipts from new war taxes would not reach the Treasury in any size until the following year and, in the meantime, they added only $50m a month to the existing revenue of $100m a month. The Treasury was facing the prospect of borrowing at least $1,250m a month. Reading reported that he did not:

> believe these estimates can be realised. But even with liberal deduction for the exaggeration of inexperience the figures are still such as naturally appal the United States Treasury Authorities...I am not surprised that Vanderlip, on whose advice they rely, advised them that they are faced with the impossible...
>
> Officials of United States Treasury are nervous and oppressed. Pending result of forthcoming Liberty Loan and even thereafter they will hesitate to commit themselves. I believe that for the present we shall always get our money in the end but it will probably be at the expense of constant importunity and some anxiety.[104]

Two weeks later, he reported that the US Treasury had resorted to Ways and Means Advances – it had borrowed a 'large' sum from the Federal Reserve Banks on the security of certificates of indebtedness, 'an expedient hitherto unknown in United States Government.'[105] A week afterwards the position was unchanged:

> Treasury and their advisers are seriously alarmed at the present financial position and do not see their way to raise the enormous sums required...This general apprehensiveness is much accentuated by the outlook for the second Liberty Loan, which is at present poor...Rate at which various Departments of State are spending their appropriations is at present alarming, and the aggregate demands of the Allies for Advances threatens to use up available total before the end of the current United States Financial Year. Cumulative strain upon actual cash resources as well as upon nerves of the United States Treasury Authorities is very severe.[106]

Reading had noted that the big subscriptions might flow in late, as they had with the first Loan. This was, indeed, the case: it was oversubscribed, but the pressure on the US Treasury remained intense.[107]

Reading left for the UK on 3 November and returned to replace Spring-Rice as Ambassador on 9 February 1918. In his absence, Lever resumed control of the Treasury Mission and relations with the US Treasury. Shortly after Reading left for Europe he was followed by the House Mission to the Inter-Allied Conference in Paris, called at Lloyd George's instigation with a view to establishing a more co-ordinated direction of the war. The Mission included Crosby, who resigned as Assistant Secretary to the Treasury and became Special Finance Commissioner of the United States in Europe and president of the IAC. Thus, during November,

December and January, Reading and Crosby were on one side of the Atlantic and McAdoo and Lever on the other.

Before leaving the USA, Reading had seen McAdoo who, probably because he now knew that the Liberty Loan was a success, had agreed to advance $200m for November and $235m for December, although he had refused to promise more than $185m for January; $235m had been requested. In explanation, Reading cabled that US expenditure had risen to a monthly rate of $1,500m in the second half of October, in addition to the advances of $500m.[108] Reading and McAdoo also discussed the $81.8m due from the Shipping Board, which the US Treasury wanted to see used for current expenditure in order that its own advances might be reduced. Reading firmly rejected this and McAdoo agreed that it should be spent as the UK wished.[109] The payment had always been considered apart from the standard Treasury advances because it was compensation for down payments made by the British on contracts signed before 1 April and the money was to come from the Shipping Board's budget. As Jack Morgan said, some part of the call loans had been 'made to enable the Government to make those very payments [for the ships].'[110]

During November, Crosby, in London, was reported to be 'apprehensive lest the whole burden of Allied financing would prove too heavy for his resources' and as worrying 'that any break in America would be so serious that it must at all hazards be prevented', a nervousness that Morgans judged to be considerably greater than that of McAdoo in Washington. In the middle of the month, Crosby asked Lamont, who was also in London, to explore the possibility of refinancing in the private sector the $94.2m one-year British Notes issued just before the USA entered the war, which came due on 1 February 1918. The markets having been weak through the autumn, Morgans unhesitatingly advised that this would be impossible.[111] Crosby also suggested that the ship money should be held in reserve to pay off the 1 February Notes and another $17.8m Notes held by du Pont, due on 28 February. Although no other funds were available to meet these liabilities, both Reading and Chalmers repeated their promise to apply the ship money to the call loan.[112] In Washington, McAdoo also stood by his promise, calculating that the British might be able to arrange refinancing of the 1 February maturity in the markets if the banks were relieved of part of the call loan, an illiquid asset until the collateral was sold. If this were done, the ship money could simultaneously be made to strengthen the banks, bolster the markets, help prepare the way for the next Liberty Loan and enable the British to arrange new financing. What was more, it would do this while protecting the principle of not using advances to repay pre-April 1917 debt.[113]

The last consideration lay behind one of the conditions McAdoo wanted to impose. When the First Liberty Loan Bill was passing through Congress, there had been reports in some newspapers that the USA had been pushed into the war by bankers seeking to protect their lending to the allies. The Act did not forbid the US Treasury from using Liberty Bond funds to repay allied debts incurred before April 1917, but McAdoo was sensitive about reports that he had told a Congressional committee that they would not be thus used. To provide himself with a defence in the event of attack, he sought to mark off the advances made to repay the debts by having investors' rights in the securities held as collateral transferred to the US Treasury. This was known as 'subrogation.' At first, the UK Treasury accepted it.[114]

The background to the other condition was the weakness of the US financial markets and a desire to make British securities available for general allied use. The dollar exchange rate had fallen against neutral currencies as the allies sold their US Treasury advances to buy goods in third countries; the securities market was weak, and it was suspected that British selling was making an important contribution; the US Treasury was negotiating for a credit in Argentina, for which British-owned Argentinian securities could be used as the collateral; and there had been a recent incident when the British had refused to lend securities to France for use in Spain until the French had first mobilised their own holdings, which included more Spanish paper than was held by British investors (see pp. 285). If British-owned securities could be brought under US Treasury control, it would both protect the US markets from their sale and facilitate secured allied borrowing in neutral countries, so relieving the dollar.[115]

In pursuit of his plan, at the beginning of December, McAdoo, having agreed that the ship money should be applied to the overdraft, tried to wash his hands of the 1 February maturity, 'which should be taken care of by the British Government and their bankers independently'.[116] It was not realistic. In the middle of December, Morgans were unequivocal about the connection between repaying the call loan and refinancing the maturity: the call loan stood at about $225m and at least $200m would have to be repaid in the early part of January if the maturity was to be refinanced in the market.[117] In other words, the same banks provided the call loan as held the Notes. Repayment could only come from US advances. Both Americans and British thought these might be made in the guise of the reimbursement of between $140m and $160m of Russian expenditure previously met by the UK in the USA. This had the same advantage as the ship money: it would help clear the call loan, but keep intact the principle of not using advances.[118] It was also a lot of money, even if spread over some months.

The strain being placed on the US Treasury became clear around Christmas as the allied applications for January were collated. There were differences in the calculations made in Washington and London, but it was agreed that they amounted to over $500m for the month, excluding any reimbursement to the British on Russian account. Thus, Crosby reported that the French and British applications would be $440m and that, in addition, the:

> British Government will undoubtedly ask funds to meet $94,000,000 maturing 1 February. Although I have expressed your attitude on this subject apparently no way now known to Treasury here of meeting this debt, ship money having been promised for overdraft.[119]

McAdoo called the size of the British January application 'extraordinary' and pointed out that he had agreed to the use of ship money for the call loan on the assumption that the 1 February maturity would be looked after by the British and Morgans. Whatever, it would not be possible to make advances of more than $500m in the month: the needs of the USA were increasing, the last call on the second Liberty Loan would be received on 15 January and a third Liberty Loan campaign that winter would be a failure.[120] In contrast, he was considering a plan

> for taking up overdraft and collateral behind it and issuing in exchange United States Treasury certificates of indebtedness or Liberty loan Bonds with restriction upon sale...Steady liquidation collateral behind overdraft presents grave impediment to our own finance measures and leads me to reconsider position heretofore taken in this respect...In my judgement an attempt to increase loans beyond that amount [$500m per month] would involve risk of financial disaster as gravely injurious to Allied cause as military defeat.[121]

The financing, or refinancing, of the ship money was arranged by 21 January. On 1 February, the banks participating in the call loan purchased $150m 4 per cent US Treasury certificates and McAdoo arranged to place 'substantial' deposits in the buying banks. $80.8m was paid to the British and applied to the call loan, reducing it to $135.7m. All the outside participations were cut by 40 per cent and that of Morgans by slightly less, to $49.8m: 'We feel that the loan is now down within limits where it can be handled', Lamont told Davison.[122]

The other half of the arrangement – placing the British-owned securities under the control of the US Treasury – was only negotiated after misunderstanding and acrimony. The ingredients were two parallel sets of negotiations – between the Treasury in London and Crosby in Paris, and between Lever and McAdoo in Washington – enriched by Lever's poor relations with McAdoo, time differences, encoding and decoding inaccuracies and delays, poor lines and unclear drafting. It started simply. In the middle of January, Lever held semi-official talks with Russell Leffingwell, the Assistant Secretary, who advised that McAdoo might provide the ship money and $100m towards the maturity and the call loan. In the background, reported Lever, was an understanding that ultimately the whole overdraft, 'including ripe bills might possibly be paid off.' Both the $100m and the later advances would take the form of a US Treasury security bought by the banks participating in the call loan and, again, would be in the guise of the reimbursement of British spending on Russian account. The conditions would be a 'special' rate of interest and the ceding of control over 'such amount of our American and other securities as it [the US Treasury] may wish.'[123] It soon became clear that this was an extreme view held only by some officials. Leffingwell himself was prepared to accept a general statement that the UK would 'refrain', inasmuch as was consistent with existing commitments (securities deposited as collateral), from selling or pledging both borrowed and wholly owned securities in the USA except with the approval of the US Treasury, while wanting the British to co-operate in placing their securities at the disposal of the USA and the allies for loan operations. On 19 January, Lever recommended agreement to the first condition, but not the second. The Chancellor accepted this advice with minor adjustments to the wording.[124]

As Lever was drafting his recommendation, McAdoo telephoned to tell him that he wanted to add a further condition: the collateral lying behind the maturity and such of the call loan as was paid off with the ship money should be subrogated to the US Treasury. On this, concerned that Congress would attack him for helping Wall Street by repaying pre-April 1917 debt, McAdoo refused to be moved.[125] On 25 January, he instructed Crosby, in an incoherent message, to tell the Chancellor that advances to repay 'old indebtedness' would only be made if the securities were subrogated: he would ensure that the British did not actually default on their 1 February Notes, but advances for their repayment would be deducted from other advances for current spending. This, said McAdoo, would force the UK to make a secured public issue 'under conditions most unfavourable' to it, always assuming he was prepared to authorise an issue at all. Subrogation should apply to the securities released by the repayment of the call loan since the ship money should have been spent on the support of sterling made necessary by British expenditure in neutral countries.[126]

The same day, Lever told the Chancellor that McAdoo's demand for the subrogation of the collateral backing the Notes had to be accepted. If this was agreed, he thought he could persuade him to drop subrogation as far as it applied to the ship money and adjust, or remove, the condition that the UK securities be made available for allied use. Lever followed this three hours later with another cable suggesting that the Chancellor should himself cable McAdoo and agree in general terms to the use of British securities for the war effort, emphasise the prospect of criticisms from the Commons if the Chancellor agreed to something which the British had never demanded when they made advances, and refuse subrogation of the securities released by ship money, but accept it for those released by the Notes.[127]

The Chancellor's message adopted Lever's suggestion:

> I so much appreciate the assistance you are offering us in dealing with great anxiety of February 1st maturity that I feel difficulty in objecting to above condition [subrogation of the collateral lying behind the Notes] if you think it will help you in meeting your political difficulties...But I am afraid that the pledging of British-owned securities to United States Treasury is bound to cause unfavourable comment in this country and I shall have to face British Parliamentary criticism for consenting to a precedent for which...there is no parallel in our own dealings with Allies. I trust, therefore, that this aspect of the matter will be borne in mind before a final decision is made.

He was careful to place this request solely in the context of the maturing Notes, not even mentioning the possibility of subrogation of the collateral held against the call loan. He thus threw back onto McAdoo the onus of renewing the request for subrogation of the securities released by the ship money, a request which would look the more unreasonable if he had already ignored the Chancellor's political difficulties and taken the securities backing the Notes. In his instructions to Lever, Bonar Law authorised him 'in case of extreme necessity' to agree to the subrogation of the securities lying behind the 1 February Notes, but not those securing the call loan. If this was offered, he hoped that the clause pledging British-owned securities for allied borrowing would be dropped.[128]

McAdoo was always sensitive to political arguments. In a disjointed reply, despatched on the evening of 29 January, he agreed to drop his demand for subrogation, without making it clear to what collateral he was referring:

> I have received your personal message with respect to the February first maturity and the *money*...in view of what you say as to the situation which would be created in Great Britain if you should assent to my desire to be subrogated to the position of pledges in respect to collateral of these *loans* and in view of your statement that there is no parralel [*sic*] for such an arrangement in your own dealings with the Allies I am constrained though with great reluctance to defer to your wishes...I have received from the British representatives here certain assurances in respect to the securities owned or controlled by the British Government. These assurances are more restricted in form than I expected. I am confident that your Government will co-operate with me to the full extent in your power...both here and elsewhere in meeting the financial burden in the aid of the common cause, however and whenever those burdens may have their inception and thereby facilitated [*sic*] the financing of the requirements of Great Britain and assisting in lightening the almost intolerable burden which the war is placing on the Treasury of the United States [italics added].[129]

Obscured by coding or decoding, or his own lack of clarity, we can only assume that 'money' meant 'ship money' and 'loans' – in the plural – meant both the 1 February maturity and the call loan. How the Treasury in London interpreted the two words is not known.

The tenor of McAdoo's message was confirmed by Lever late the following day when he triumphantly reported a successful conclusion to his negotiations:

> Final settlement has been reached. U.S. Treasury will make an advance 95 millions on February 1st and on same day ship money approximately 81 millions will be paid. Latter will be applied to Call Loan and former to February 1st maturity. Subrogation is dropped.

Lever had accepted that his government would not carry out transactions in the securities held in the USA except with the approval of the US Treasury and the clause promising their use for allied transactions was emasculated.[130]

The story thereafter becomes confused, as McAdoo's agreement twisted itself into reverse. Although despatched on 29 January, the Secretary's cable did not arrive at the Treasury in London until 31 January (indeed, the formal Note from the Embassy did not arrive until 1 February).[131] Lever's message had been despatched on 30 January, but only arrived on the evening of the 1 February. In the meantime, Crosby, having received the cable McAdoo had despatched on 25 January, had urged the Chancellor to accept McAdoo's original terms, specifically referring to the securities lying behind both the maturity and the call loan, but in such a way that there must have been a coding or typing problem. From London, Paul Cravath had cabled McAdoo, warning that the Chancellor's cable had been misunderstood and that he intended to leave McAdoo 'free to deal with matter as you think best.' He did not mention the securities released by the ship money, but emphasised that the Chancellor wanted any announcement to make it clear that the transaction was a 'special one' and that the US Treasury was not changing its policy of unsecured advances.[132]

Inexplicably, Crosby also told the British that McAdoo 'had it in mind' to repay the balance of the call loan: he had, as he later told McAdoo, 'presumed matter included February first maturities and Morgan overdraft'. The Chancellor, therefore, cabled McAdoo that he had been in communication with US Treasury representatives in Europe and that:

> judging from the impressions they have formed from your cable to Mr. Crosby, there must be some misunderstanding. Position as I understood it was explained in my previous message which I did not intend to be a refusal of any arrangement you might press for…
>
> Mr. Crosby, however, believes that proposed arrangements cover a much wider field than I had understood and that you had it in mind to provide not only for the February 1st maturity but for the entire balance of Morgan's overdraft after application of ship money…
>
> we greatly appreciate what you are doing to meet our old obligations and that I am ready to agree to any arrangement respecting our American securities which you may think necessary either for the protection of your market or to assist you in future market operations.[133]

Thus, the first part of the Chancellor's message agreed to subrogation, without making it clear whether this included the collateral released by the ship money, and the second part, agreeing to the use of British-owned securities in its market operations by the US Treasury (but not the other allies), assumed that the call loan had been repaid.

Leffingwell immediately cabled to the Chancellor that McAdoo had not intended that 'the arrangements should cover a much wider field' and that McAdoo considered the matter closed in terms of Lever's cable of 30 January, with subrogation dropped.[134]

On 5 February, Crosby told McAdoo that he was 'convinced' that the Chancellor had 'all along' intended to leave him 'free' to deal with the securities as he thought fit. The failure to make this clear had resulted from the pressure of the Chancellor's Parliamentary duties and the inadequacy of British officials in London and, 'especially', in Washington: in other words, the blame was to be fixed on Lever.[135] The next day, Lever cabled the Chancellor that the 'misunderstandings' had arisen from the difficulty of finding out precisely what McAdoo wanted and that the 'only proper course' was to 'place ourselves entirely in McAdoo's hands'. Lever hoped that the Chancellor did not feel that this was inconsistent with the negotiations that he had carried out during January, but McAdoo 'must not be left by us with any feeling of grievance even though it may be ill-founded.'[136] The Chancellor then told McAdoo that he suspected that his message of 30 January had been misunderstood and accepted subrogation of all the securities released at the beginning of February. At last, a message became specific:

> I intended last paragraph to mean that I left myself entirely in your hands. The last thing I should have thought of would have been that I should make conditions as to financial assistance accorded by United States Government...I am giving instructions that you are to be subrogated to lien of former lenders upon securities previously pledged to holders of one year notes and that these securities as well as other securities pledged to secure overdraft be dealt with according to your instructions.[137]

He did not mention that when he had agreed to the arrangement he had been under the impression that the entire call loan was to be repaid from US Treasury advances.

Reading returns as Ambassador: the Danish and Japanese loans

By the end of the contretemps, the US Treasury had advanced funds to meet UK expenditure incurred before April 1917. The price, subrogation of the collateral and the sole example of secured British borrowing from the US Treasury, was mainly paid because the borrower judged it politic to give the lender the benefit of the doubt in a misunderstanding. In small part it was because the Chancellor wanted McAdoo to drop a request that the UK use loans from Japan and Denmark, together with the proceeds of gold shipments, to meet current expenditure, rather than to repay market debt. McAdoo's request, which would have enabled US advances to be reduced, had been in the air since the beginning of January and was formally requested on 5 February. On 21 January, ¥80m ($38.2m) had been borrowed from Japan. Because a surge in British food buying threatened to exceed US advances, it had been decided to keep this, and a further $10.2m paid for Indian rupees sold to the Japanese under the same agreement, on deposit. The loan from Denmark grew out of the sale of the Danish West Indies to the USA in 1917. The British had arranged to borrow the $25m proceeds as the bank deposits matured between 1 December 1917 and 3 April 1918 (Table 6.3).[138] The Chancellor, rather hopefully, thought that McAdoo's demand that these be used for current spending was 'probably made in a fit of annoyance' and that his agreement to subrogation 'may have modified his attitude.' If he persisted:

> he necessarily makes himself entirely responsible for meeting our capital

> liabilities as they mature. If he cuts us off from every opportunity of meeting them by our own efforts the responsibility for them becomes his. Indeed I cannot believe that his words were meant seriously. If the above demand is withdrawn as I have little doubt it will be I suggest that Japanese money and balance of Danish money be applied first to Dupont March 15th. maturities and second to paying off Treasury Bills.[139]

Once the refinancing of the 1 February Notes had been determined, the heat went out of the exchanges between London and Washington, and it was not until the end of April that Reading took up with Leffingwell the matter of the Japanese and Danish loans. By then, the British had used two-thirds of the money as they had originally intended: on 28 February, half of the Japanese money had been used to buy back the $24.3m Notes held by du Pont and all the Danish money had been used to repay Treasury Bills (Tables 6.2 and 6.3).[140] Thus, there was only the $24m remaining from Japan. Reading's hand was not strong. Since the autumn, the Americans had been pressing the British (and French) to take credits from allies and neutrals, specifically to relieve the US Treasury, and here he was actually repaying such loans (see pp. 282–8). He must have felt some embarrassment as the new borrowings had apparently been spent without discussion with McAdoo. His case was also weakened by the unusually high level of British dollar balances. As well as the Japanese $24m, they had deposits of some $81m and were due to receive an advance of $45m from the US Treasury to last only a week. As Leffingwell pointed out, it was difficult to justify advances if they were not required. Moreover, the USA had made advances at the beginning of February to repay British debts and the Japanese loan had been held in reserve in case the food situation demanded more cash for current spending. There was a feeling that it should now be used, so US Treasury advances could be reduced. Reading judged that relations with the Americans required that he agree to their request. The Chancellor was prepared to accept this advice, provided there was agreement in writing that the US would meet maturing UK capital liabilities.

Reading felt that he could not ask for this without damaging relations: he was not Lever, and he proceeded to give in gracefully to Leffingwell's demand.[141] There was outrage in some parts of the Treasury in London. Keynes's draft for the Chancellor read:

> I cannot but acquiesce in the course you have taken…the action of the U.S. Treasury has been in my opinion small-minded and unreasonable. Coupled with their action earlier in the year over subrogation and paying off our maturing obligations it almost looks as if they took a satisfaction in reducing us to a position of complete financial helplessness and dependence in which the call loan is round our necks like a noose and whenever obligations of ours mature in future we shall have to submit to any conditions they may choose to impose.

'Small-minded' was deleted and the final sentence was not sent.[142]

Endnotes

1 Liddell Hart (917), pp. 400–2; Roskill (1970–4), pp. 355–75; Beveridge (1928), pp. 91–2.
2 T 170/134, f. 24, Chadwick, 'British Government Transactions in America', 1922.
3 T 172/422, ff. 3–4, Keynes, 'Statement of Resources and Liabilities in America', 16 March 1917.
4 FO 371/3114, nos 303 and 391, Spring-Rice to FO, 7 and 13 February 1917.
5 T 172/420, ff. 17–18, Davison to Grenfell, 22 February 1917.
6 FO 321/3114, no. 466, Crawford to Chancellor, 19 February 1917; T 172/429, Lever's Diary, 19 February 1917.
7 T 172/420, f. 12, Bradbury to Hamilton, ff. 14–15, Keynes to Chalmers and Bradbury, and f. 11, Chancellor to Lever, all 22 February 1917.
8 Ibid., ff. 7–8, Lever to Chancellor, 25 February 1917; T 172/421, ff. 80–1, Chalmers, 1 March 1917, and ff. 76–7, Mahon to Treasury, 2 March 1917; ibid., ff. 73–4, Chancellor to Lever, 2 March 1917, and f. 65, Lever to Chancellor, 6 March 1917; MGP, B. Hist. 2, F. 14, no. 39124, Davison to Grenfell, 1 March 1917; T 172/429, Lever's Diary, 19, 27 and 28 February, and 1 and 5 March 1917; BoE, C91/9, f. 101, Mahon to Treasury, 2 March 1917.
9 T 172/421, ff. 59–60, Crawford to FO, 8 March 1917. The statement was cabled to London and is in T 172/421, ff. 57–8.
10 T 172/429, Lever's Diary, 7 and 8 March 1917, and f. 55, Lever to Chancellor, 13 March 1917; MGP, B. Hist. 2, F. 15, no. 39631, JPM to MG, 13 March 1917.
11 T 172/429, Lever's Diary, 12 and 22 March 1917; T 172/421, f. 37, Lever to Chancellor, 23 March 1917; T 172/638, no. 805, Lever to Chancellor, 23 March 1917; MGP, B. Hist. 2, F. 14, no. 30213, MG to JPM, 17 January 1917, and F. 15, no. 41287, JPM to MG, 29 March 1917.
12 T 172/421, ff. 44–5, Chancellor to Crawford, 19 March 1917.
13 Ibid., f. 42, Keynes to Chalmers, 22 March 1917.
14 Ibid., ff. 38–41, Crawford to Chancellor, 22 March 1917, and ff. 18–19, Crawford to Chancellor, 27 March 1917.
15 Ibid., f. 35, Crawford to Chancellor, 23 March 1917, and ff. 27–8 and 14–15, Lever to Chancellor, 25 and 29 March 1917; ibid., ff. 18–19, Crawford to Chancellor, 27 March 1917.
16 Ibid., ff. 10–13, Chancellor to Lever, 30 March 1917.
17 T 172/429, Lever's Diary, 12, 16, 19, 21 and 26 February, and 2 March 1917; FO 371/3118, no. 594, Treasury to Spring-Rice, 24 February 1917; Thomas Lamont Papers, II, 91–2, Lamont to Davison, 31 January 1917. The Treasury correspondence is in T 1/12114/43703.
18 T 172/429, Lever's Diary, 9 April 1917.
19 BoE, C91/6, 'Memorandum', 4 October 1916. Papers covering the CPR refinancing are in T 172/638, and MGP, B. Hist. 2, F. 14 and 15, January–April 1917. Other papers are in T 172/420 and T 172/423 and there are entries in Lever's Diary in T 172/429. Also see Burk (1985), p. 128.
20 MGP, B. Hist. 2, F. 15, nos 43248 and 43279, JPM to MG, 26 and 27 April 1917; FO 371/3113, no. 1105, Spring-Rice to FO, 26 April 1917; T 172/429, Lever's Diary, 17 and 19 April 1917; Gilbert (1970), p. 149.
21 T 170/134, ff. 7, 10, 24, Chadwick, 'British Government Transactions in America', 1922.
22 T 172/443, Chancellor to McAdoo, 30 July 1917.
23 T 171/107, Keynes, early January 1915; Keynes (1971–89), XVI, pp. 135–7, 'Expenditure of Advances to Allies Within and Without the United Kingdom', 15 October 1915; Cab. 27/136/39, Reading, 'Finance Committee: Interim Report', 29 October 1915.

24 FO 371/3115, no. 897, Chancellor to Lever, 21 June 1917.
25 Gilbert (1970), pp. 120–3.
26 BoE, C91/18, LEC, Minutes, 4 and 7 May 1917; FO 371/3114, nos 1619 and 1765, Chalmers to Lever, 11 and 17 May 1917; MGP, B. Hist. 2, no. 43679, JPM to MG, 9 May 1917; T 172/429, Lever's Diary, 7 May 1917. The half-day's trading was Saturday, 5 May.
27 T 172/429, Lever's Diary, 11 May and 4 June 1917; FO 371/3114, nos 1222 and 1229, Lever to Chancellor, 7 May 1917; ibid., no. 1352, Lever to Chancellor, 25 May 1917; *FRUS* (1917, Supplement 2, The World War, Volume I. Henceforth cited as 1917, 2, I), pp. 527–8, McAdoo to Lansing, 9 May 1917; Keynes (1971–89), XVI, p. 240–2, Keynes to Chalmers, 30 May 1917; T 170/134, f. 25, 'British Government Transactions in America', Chadwick, 1922.
28 Burk (1985), pp. 129–30. The most important source is T 172/429, Lever's Diary, for the relevant dates.
29 FO 371/3114, nos 1222 and 1229, Lever to Chancellor, 6 and 7 May 1917; T 172/ 429, f. 112, Lever's Diary, 6 [?] May 1917. The entry is undated, and 6 May was a Sunday. The entry is on the only page which is not dated; 6 May is the only day for which there is no dated entry and is the date of the cable which informed London of Morgans' decision.
30 French (1995), pp. 80–1; Barnett (1985), p. 101–4; FO 371/3114, no. 1353, Lever to Chancellor, 25 May 1917; Keynes (1971–89), XVI, pp. 240–2, Keynes to Chalmers, 30 May 1917; Beveridge (1928), pp. 91–2. Payment was only made when the wheat was actually loaded onto the ships.
31 BoE, C91/15, Bank of England, 'Purchases and Sales of American Exchange', 25 March 1919.
32 MGP, B. Hist. Box 2, no. 36752, MG to JPM, 24 May 1917; FO 371/3114, nos 1306 and 1377, Lever to Chancellor, 11 and 18 May 1917; ibid., nos 1737 and 1377, Chancellor to Lever, 16 and 22 May 1917.
33 BoE, C91/18, LEC, Minutes, 31 May and 13 June 1917; T 172/429, Lever's Diary, 28 May 1917; FO 371/3114, no. 1361, Lever to Chancellor, 17 May 1917, and no. 767, Chancellor to Lever, 26 May 1917.
34 T 172/429, Lever's Diary, 31 May 1917; *FRUS* (1917, 2, I), pp. 530–1, Crawford to McAdoo, 29 May 1917.
35 T 172/429, Lever's Diary, 5, 6, 8, 11 and 13 June 1917.
36 FO 371/3114, no. 1549, Lever to Chancellor, 13 June 1917.
37 T 172/429, Lever's Diary, 14 June 1917; FO 371/3114, no. 1571, Lever to Chancellor, 16 June 1917.
38 FO 371/3114, no. 1572, Lever to Chancellor, 16 June 1917, and no. 897, Chancellor to Lever, 21 June 1917.
39 T 172/429, Lever's Diary, 18 and 19 June 1917.
40 FO 371/3115, no. 1627A, Northcliffe and Lever to Chancellor, 22 June 1917; T 172/ 429, Lever's Diary, 20 June 1917.
41 FO 371/3114, no. 1697, Spring-Rice to FO, 17 June 1917, and FO 371/3115, no. 2415, Treasury to Spring-Rice, 23 June 1917; ibid., no. 1627A, Northcliffe and Lever to Chancellor, 22 June 1917; ibid., no, 1777, Crawford to FO, 26 June 1917; ibid., no. 1705, Lever to Chancellor, 29 June 1917; Burk (1985), pp. 195–7.
42 *FRUS* (1917, 2, I), pp. 525–6, Spring-Rice to Lansing, 3 May 1917; Burk (1985) p. 201. T 172/429, Lever's Diary, 2 May 1917, reports a discussion with Balfour and Cunliffe during which the British needs for six months were estimated to be $1,100m *plus* $400m for the overdraft *plus* the $200m already granted.
43 FO 371/3115, no. 1651, Lever to Chancellor, 26 June 1917.
44 Ibid., no. 1777, Crawford to FO, 26 June 1917; ibid., no. 1662, Lever to Chancellor, 27 June 1917; ibid., no. 1807, Crawford to FO, 27 June 1917; ibid., no. 1665, Lever to Chancellor, 28 June 1917; T 172/429, Lever's Diary, 25 and 26 June 1917; Burk (1985), pp. 198–9.

45 T 172/429, Lever's Diary, 29 June 1917. Fowler writes that it was Wiseman who called in Strong, who then contacted House and McAdoo. Fowler (1969), pp. 48–9.
46 FO 371/3115, no. 1807, Crawford to FO, 27 June 1917; Burk (1985), pp. 198–9.
47 FO 371/3115, no. 1705, Lever to Chancellor, 29 June 1917; T 172/429, Lever's Diary, 28 June 1917.
48 FO 371/3115, no. 1807, Crawford to FO, 27 June 1917.
49 *FRUS* (1917, 2, I), pp. 532–3, Page to Lansing, 28 June 1917; FO 371/3115, no. 952, Chancellor to Lever, 28 June 1917.
50 FO 800/209, f. 174, Balfour to House via Wiseman, 28 June 1917.
51 Edward M. House Papers, Diary, vol. 11, 29 June 1929, quoted in Burk (1985), p. 200.
52 *FRUS* (1917, 2, I), pp. 533–5, Spring-Rice to Lansing, 1 July 1917.
53 FO 371/3115, no. 2500, FO to Spring-Rice, 29 June 1917.
54 T 172/428, ff. 149–50, Northcliffe to Prime Minister and Balfour, 1 July 1917.
55 FO 371/3115, nos 1858 and 1867, Spring-Rice to FO, 2 July and 3/4 July 1917.
56 Ibid., no. 1872, Crawford to FO, 3/4 July 1917; T 172/429, Lever's Diary, 30 June, 2 July, and 5 July 1917.
57 *FRUS* (1917, 2, I), pp. 539–43, McAdoo to Spring-Rice, 9 July 1917.
58 MGP, B. Hist. 2, F. 16, no. 47446, JPM to MG (Shown to Governor & Chancellor. Discussed fully at Cabinet:– present Mr Page, Mr Balfour, Sir R. Chalmers), 4 July 1917.
59 FO 371/3112, no. 911, Crawford to Chancellor, 10 April 1917.
60 *FRUS* (1917, 2, I), pp. 533–6, Spring-Rice to Lansing, 1 July 1917; FO 371/3115, no. 1969, Northcliffe to Prime Minister, Chancellor and Balfour, 11/12 July 1917.
61 MGP, B. Hist. 2, F. 16, no. 38709, Grenfell to JPM, 4 July 1917.
62 *FRUS* (1917, 2, I), pp. 535–6, Page to Lansing, 5 July 1917, and pp. 543–5, 12 July 1917; MGP, B. Hist. 2, F. 16, no. 38709, Grenfell to JPM, 4 July 1917; T 170/124, ff. 19–25, Blackett, undated record of call loan problem.
63 *FRUS* (1917, 2, I), pp. 525–6, Spring-Rice to McAdoo, 3 May 1917.
64 T 172/429, Lever's Diary, 28 June 1917; FO 371/3115, no. 1873, Crawford to FO, 4/5 July 1917.
65 MGP, B. Hist 2, F. 16, no. 47404, JPM to MG (copy left with Chancellor, Governor and Deputy-Governor), 3 July 1917, copied to Northcliffe; FO 371/3115, no. 2552, Chancellor to Northcliffe, 3 July 1917.
66 BoE, C91/11, f. 96A, Cunliffe to Lloyd George, 3 July 1917.
67 BoE, C91/11, f. 98, Nairne to Treasury, 3 July 1917, and f. 99, note of instructions, 3 July 1917.
68 Sayers (1976), I, p. 104; BoE, C91/11, f. 135, Nairne to Canadian High Commission, 5 July 1917, and ff. 136, 147 and 156, Nairne to Treasury, 5, 6 and 10 July 1917.
69 Sayers (1976), I, pp. 99–109; MGP, B. Hist. 2, F. 16, no. 38681, Grenfell to Jack Morgan, 3 July 1917; FO 371/3115, no. 2611, Chancellor to Northcliffe, 6 July 1917.
70 *FRUS* (1917, 2, I), pp. 535–6, Page to Lansing, 5 July 1917; FO 371/3115, no. 1873, Chancellor to Northcliffe, 6 July 1917.
71 Quoted in Keynes (1971–89), XVI, p. 244. The reference is Wiseman Papers, 91/91, Northcliffe to Chancellor, 5 July 1917. See Burk (1985), p. 207.
72 *FRUS* (1917, 2, I), pp. 543–5, McAdoo to Balfour, 12 July 1917; FO 371/3115, no. 1873, Crawford to FO, 4/5 July 1917.
73 FO 371/3115, no. 1969, Northcliffe to Lloyd George, Bonar Law and Balfour, 11/12 July 1917.
74 Myers (1931), I, chapters VII and XIII; MGP, B. Hist. 2, F. 16, no. 47404, JPM to MG (Copy left with Chancellor, Governor & Deputy-Governor), 3 July 1917.
75 MGP, B. Hist. 2, F. 16, no. 38709, Grenfell to JPM, 4 July 1917, and no. 47472, JPM to Grenfell, 6 July 1917.

76 MGP, B. Hist. 2, F. 16, no. 38690, Grenfell to JPM, and no. 38691, Grenfell to Jack Morgan, 3 July 1917; ibid., no. 47446, JPM to Grenfell (To Governor and Chancellor. Discussed fully at Cabinet – Ambassador Page, Balfour, Chalmers), 4 July 1917.
77 MGP, B. Hist. 2, F. 16, no. 47482, Jack Morgan to Grenfell (extract to Cunliffe), 6 July 1917, and no. 38795, Grenfell to Jack Morgan, 6 July 1917.
78 FO 371/3115, no. 1911, Northcliffe to Chancellor, 6/8 July 1917, and no. 1807, Lever to Chancellor, 9/10 July 1917.
79 Gilbert (1970), pp. 124 and 150–1.
80 FO 371/3120, Spring-Rice to FO, 14 July 1917.
81 *FRUS* (1917, 2, I), p. 545, British Embassy to Department of State, 17 July 1917; FO 371/3115, no. 2776, Chancellor to Northcliffe, 17 July 1917.
82 *FRUS* (1917, 2, I), pp. 549–54, Chancellor to Lansing, 20 July 1917. The Note was drafted by Keynes from an outline provided by Bonar Law. Keynes (1971–89), XVI, pp. 244–52.
83 T 172/443, f. 47–58, Chancellor to McAdoo, 30 July 1917. The Note is reproduced in Keynes (1971–89), XVI, pp. 255–63.
84 FO 371/3120, no. 147270, Spring-Rice to FO, 26 July 1917; FO 371/3116, no. 2224, Spring-Rice to FO, 31 July/1 August 1917, no. 2227, Northcliffe and Spring-Rice to FO, 1/2 August 1917 and unnumbered, Spring-Rice to FO, 2 August 1917.
85 *FRUS* (1917, 2, I), pp. 558–60, Balfour to Lansing, 2 August 1917, and Chancellor to McAdoo, 2 August 1917.
86 FO 371/3115, no. 148490, Northcliffe to Chancellor, 26/27 July 1917; FO 371/3116, no. 2081, Northcliffe to FO, 3 August 1917; ibid., no. 2259, Spring-Rice to FO, 4/5 August 1917; FO 371/3120, no. 2080, Northcliffe to Chancellor, 2/3 August 1917; Burk (1985) pp. 205–6.
87 T 172/446, f. 186, Wiseman, 'Situation in America', 21 September 1917.
88 BoE, C91/15, Bank of England,'Purchases and Sales of American Exchange', 25 March 1919.
89 FO 371/3115, nos 1872, 1928 and 1969, Lever to Chancellor, 16/17, 19/20 and 23/24 July 1917; ibid., nos 1074 and 1116, Chancellor to Lever, 18 and 21 July 1917; MGP, B. Hist. 2, F. 16, nos 40134 and 40294, MG to JPM, 21 and 30 July 1917, and no. 47952, JPM to MG, 24 July 1917.
90 T 172/430, Lever's Diary, 27 July 1917. From 14 July 1917, the diary was written by Blackett.
91 MGP, B. Hist. 2, F. 16, no. 47701, Jack Morgan to Grenfell, 14 July 1917, and no. 47888, JPM to MG (Shown to Deputy-Governor and Norman), 21 July 1917.
92 FO 371/3116, no. 2069, Lever to Chancellor, 1 August 1917; T 160/580/F14218, Blackett to Waley, 28 May 1935.
93 PML, Archives, Box 14, ff. 242–4, Jack Morgan to Grenfell, 9 August 1917; T 160/580/F14218, Blackett to Waley, 28 May 1935.
94 FO 371/3116, nos 2054 and 2069, Lever to Chancellor, 31 July/2 August and 1 August 1917; MGP, B. Hist. 2, F. 16, no. 49272, JPM to Grenfell, 3 August 1917; T 172/430, Lever's Diary, 31 July and 1 August 1917.
95 FO 371/3116, no. 1196, Chancellor to Lever, 4 August 1917.
96 Ibid., no. 2251, 3/4 August 1917; T 172/439, no. 3104, Lever to Chancellor, 3 December 1917.
97 FO 371/3116, no. 2146, Lever to Chancellor, 10/11 August 1917; T 172/431, f. 89, Chalmers to Lever, 14 August 1914.
98 FO 371/3116, no. 2211, Lever to Chancellor, 15/16 August 1917; MGP, B. Hist. 2, F. 16, no. 49662, Jack Morgan to Grenfell (Copy left with Chancellor), 17 August 1917; T 172/430, Lever's Diary, 14 August 1917; PML, Archives, Box 14, ff. 243–4, Jack Morgan to Grenfell, 9 August 1917, and ff. 278–9, Jack Morgan to McAdoo, 16 August 1917.

99 MGP, B. Hist. 2, F. 16, no. 40742, MG to JPM, 20 August 1917; ibid., no. 40743, Grenfell to Jack Morgan, 20 August 1917; ibid., no. 49765, JPM to MG, and no. 49766, Jack Morgan to Grenfell, 21 August 1917.

100 PML, Archives, Box 14, ff. 278–9, 295–6 and 302, Jack Morgan to McAdoo, 16, 21 and 24 August 1917; ibid., Horn Box 3, no. 31,964, JPM to Morgan Harjes, 13 October 1917; *The New York Times*, 24 August 1917, p. 14.

101 T 172/430, Lever's Diary, 27 and 30 August 1917; Burk (1985), p. 207; FO 371/3116, no. 1388, Chancellor to Lever, 4 September 1918; T 172/431, f. 32, House to Chancellor, 25 August 1917; T 172/434, f. 42, Northcliffe to Chancellor and Balfour, 27 August 1917; T 172/435, f. 133, Lever to Chancellor, 31 August 1917.

102 PML, Archives, Box 14, ff. 4–6, Jack Morgan to Grenfell, 2 November 1917.

103 *Second Emergency Bond Issue*, House Committee on Ways and Means, on HR 5901, 28 August 1917, pp. 3–14, and 29 August 1917, pp. 58–9. $500m did not have statutory authority. In front of the House Ways and Means Committee, McAdoo started by saying that experience suggested that advances would run at about $500m per month and then, under questioning, found himself backed into a statement that they would be a maximum of $500m per month. He gave himself room for escape, but he would have to explain himself.

104 T 172/446, ff. 189–93, Reading to Prime Minister, Chancellor and Balfour, 29 September 1917.

105 T 172/437, f. 87, Reading to Chancellor, 12 October 1917. Gilbert (1970), p. 152, says that after 9 August the 'Treasury adopted the device of permissive payment by credit, whereby the subscribing depository banks made payment merely by crediting the account of the Treasurer of the United States. Since the reserve requirements did not apply to government deposits, the transaction was no different in its effects from that of printing money.' The device was introduced without a public announcement or Congressional discussion.

106 T 172/437, ff. 69–73, Reading to Chancellor, 17 October 1917.

107 Gilbert (1970), p. 127–8.

108 T 172/444, ff. 83–6, Reading to Chancellor, 27 October 1917; T 172/437, f. 61–2, Reading to Chancellor, 21 October 1917.

109 Burk (1985), pp. 178, 207–8.

110 PML, Archives, Box 14, Jack Morgan to Grenfell, 9 August 1917.

111 MGP, B. Hist. 2, F. 16, nos 44748, 44774 and 44839, Lamont to JPM, 15, 16 and 19 November 1917; ibid., no. 55633, JPM to Lamont, 17 November 1917; ibid., no. 55811, Jack Morgan to Lamont, 22 November 1917; T 172/439, no. 3104, Lever to Chancellor, 3 December 1917.

112 *FRUS* (1917, 2, I), pp. 579–80 and 587, McAdoo to Crosby, 15 November and 4 December 1917, and pp. 582 and 584, Crosby to McAdoo (two cables), 21 November 1917; MGP, B. Hist. 3, F. 17, nos 44975 and 44986, Lamont to Jack Morgan (two cables), 22 November 1917.

113 T 172/439, ff. 141–3, Lever to Chancellor, 3 December 1917; T 172/439, ff. 127–9, Lever to Chancellor, 6 December 1917. That the US Treasury appreciated the call loan was damaging the markets was confirmed by Lamont in January. MGP, B. Hist. 3, F. 17, no. 61200, Lamont to Grenfell (to Chancellor), 21 January 1918.

114 US National Archives, RG 39, Box 116, GB 132.5/19–1, Davis, 'Memorandum for the Secretary', 21 November 1919; Leffingwell Papers, Box 13, LB 1, ff. 253–6 and 261, Leffingwell, two memoranda for Secretary of the Treasury, 24 November 1919; *FRUS* (1917, 2, I), pp. 581–3 and 589–90, Crosby to McAdoo, 21 November and 16 December 1917.

115 T 172/439, ff. 127–9 and 66, Lever to Chancellor, 6 and 15 December 1917, and ff. 102–3, Chancellor to Lever, 12 December 1917; T 172/448, f. 42, Chancellor to Lever, 23 January 1918.

116 *FRUS* (1917, 2, I), p. 587, McAdoo to Crosby, 4 December 1917.
117 T 172/439, f. 52, Lever to Chancellor, 18 December 1917.
118 Ibid., ff. 127–9, Lever to Chancellor, 6 December 1917; *FRUS* (1917, 2, I), p. 590–2, McAdoo to Crosby, 24 December 1917.
119 *FRUS* (1917, 2, I), pp. 589–90, Crosby to McAdoo, 16 December 1917.
120 T 172/439, ff. 7–8, Crawford to FO, 29 December 1917.
121 *FRUS* (1917, 2, I), pp. 590–2, McAdoo to Crosby, 24 December 1917.
122 MGP, B. Hist. 3, F. 17, no. 61200, Lamont to Grenfell, 21 January 1918; T 172/448, ff. 56–7, Lever to Chancellor, 20 January 1918; US National Archives, RG 39, Box 115, GB 132.5/17–11, Lamont to Leffingwell, 19 February 1918; Thomas Lamont Papers II, 91–3, Lamont to Davison, 13 February 1918.
123 T 172/444, ff. 16–18, Lever to Chancellor, received in London 10 January 1917, and f. 13, Lever to Chancellor, received in London 12 January 1917. The reason given for charging a special rate of interest was that it was being used to repay debt. Although not mentioned, we can assume that an equally important reason was to differentiate them, providing a defence against Congressional attack.
124 T 172/448, ff. 56–7 and 58–60, Lever to Chancellor, 19 January 1918 (two cables), and f. 42, Chancellor to Lever, 23 January 1918.
125 T 172/448, f. 55, Lever to Chancellor, 19 January 1918, and, ibid., ff. 56–7, 20 January 1918.
126 US National Archives, RG 39, Box 115, GB 132.5/17–11, McAdoo to Crosby, 25 January 1918.
127 T 172/448, ff. 23–6, Lever to Chancellor (two cables), received in London 27 January 1918. The second cable refers to the first cable having been sent the previous day.
128 Ibid., ff. 17–18, Chancellor to Lever for McAdoo, received in London, 28 January 1918, and ibid., f. 5, 28 January 1918.
129 Ibid., ff. 201–5, McAdoo to Chancellor via Lansing and the US Embassy, 29 January 1918.
130 Ibid., f. 200, Lever to Chancellor, 30 January 1918, received in London 8 p.m., 1 February 1918.
131 Ibid., f. 206–7, Hamilton to Chancellor, 31 January 1918, f. 208, Hamilton to Keynes, 31 January 1918, and f. 201, frontispiece of message from McAdoo to Chancellor via Lansing and US Embassy, 1 February 1918.
132 Ibid., f. 213, Crosby to Reading, 30 January 1918, and f. 212, 'Memorandum for Lord Reading' Cravath to McAdoo, 30 January 1918; ibid., f. 206, Hamilton to Chancellor, 31 January 1918.
133 T 172/448, ff. 6–7, Chancellor to McAdoo (copy to Crosby), 30 January 1918; US National Archives, RG 39, Box 115, GB 132.5/17–11, Crosby to McAdoo, 31 January 1918.
134 T 172/449, f. 197, Lever to Chalmers, 1 February 1918; ibid., ff. 92–3, Chancellor to Reading, 16 February 1918.
135 US National Archives, RG 39, Box 39, GB 132.5/17–11, Crosby to McAdoo via Page, 5 February 1918.
136 T 172/449, f. 160, Lever to Chancellor, 6 February 1918.
137 Ibid., f. 161, Chancellor to McAdoo, 6 February 1918.
138 T 172/448, ff. 102–3, Bertie to Chancellor, 11 January 1918; T 172/449, no. 271, Lever to Chancellor, 6 February 1918.
139 T 172/449, f. 92–3, Chancellor to Reading, 16 February 1918.
140 T 172/448, Lever to Chancellor, 5 January 1919; T 172/449, f. 54, Lever to Chalmers, 21 February 1918.
141 T 172/445, ff. 24–6 and ff. 16–17, Reading to Chancellor, 24 and 30 April 1918; ibid., f. 22, Chancellor to Reading, 28 April 1918. For a different interpretation, see Burk (1985), pp. 214–16.

142 T 172/445, ff. 11–14, two drafts of cable, 6 and 7 May 1918; T 172/445, ff. 18–19, McFadyean to Chalmers and Keynes, with note by Keynes, 1 May 1918; Keynes (1971–89), XVI, pp. 286–8.

10 External borrowing 1917–18

(II) The neutrals, Canada and silver

> The [US] Treasury has urged upon the Governments of the Allies the necessity of their obtaining neutral currencies through loans or credits or the sale of foreign securities which they hold. The [US] Treasury also itself effected arrangements for stabilizing exchange in a number of neutral countries.
>
> US Secretary of the Treasury,
> *Annual Report on the State of the Finances* (1918), p. 39

Just as sterling had weakened against the currencies of neutral countries in 1915, so the dollar was to weaken after America entered the war. By November 1917, it had reached massive discounts against a range of currencies, including those of Norway, Denmark, Argentina and India; that on the Swedish krona had reached 70 per cent. The discounts against other currencies, those of Spain, Holland, Switzerland, Japan, Chile and Peru, fell to their lowest points in the late spring or summer of 1918.[1] With neutral currencies convertible into sterling, and sterling pegged to the dollar, the UK Treasury's exchange rate policy clearly played some part in this weakness. The explanation and defence of British policy given to McAdoo on 30 July 1917 drew attention to the advances which were being used to buy sterling against sales of neutral currencies. The sterling might either come from existing balances or from new deposits created by current transactions between a neutral and the UK, or between a neutral and an ally with the payment coming from sterling advanced to the ally by the UK. It was not possible to trace the transactions which provided the neutrals with the sterling, but the British Note acknowledged that some of the dollars being lent by the US Treasury were being used 'to defray uncontrolled expenditure for undefined purposes' and 'to finance the purchases of the Allies outside America.' (see p. 261).[2]

Although McAdoo never admitted that spending his advances in this way was justified, by continuing to lend for the support of sterling he tacitly accepted the necessity of helping to finance allied purchases in neutral countries, although seeking ways of reducing their size. During August 1917, spurred by the prospect of asking Congress for further borrowing authority and answering questions on the use of advances for exchange support, the US Treasury sought to identify the intervention which represented purchases of sterling bills drawn to finance American exports. It was most interested in large and easily identified categories

– cotton, cereals, meat and tobacco – in part because behind them lay powerful Congressional interests which would defend the advances.[3] As we have seen, the UK had already decided to pay for American grain directly from its account with Morgans. Bills for bacon, ham and lard were removed from the market in September. Difficulties were met in taking cotton bills off the market – they had to wait until the beginning of 1918 – as did the expenditure of the Army and Navy Canteen Board.[4]

A related aspect of neutral finance came to the fore during the first half of September 1917. At the beginning of August, the US Treasury had become concerned that its support for sterling might be contributing to the outflow of gold, an anxiety heightened by the need to keep reserves ample and money easy in preparation for its next loan campaign. Although it would have been clear to the UK Treasury that using dollars to buy sterling sold by neutrals was tantamount to permitting them to demand settlement in American gold, when asked it cheerfully denied that there could be any implication for US gold exports.[5] By the beginning of September, the US Treasury thought otherwise and was considering an embargo.[6] The dollar had turned weak against neutral currencies and there had been heavy shipments to Japan, Mexico and Spain. Strong pointed out that this was closely related to the pegging of sterling against the dollar; if sterling was allowed to depreciate in New York, the dollar would strengthen.[7] The peg remained, but on 10 September licenses for gold exports were introduced, and it was reported that they would only be issued for shipments to countries where the USA was running a bilateral trade deficit. Neutral countries responded by accumulating claims on New York, but this was not a permanent solution: the US Treasury still needed to provide the dollars and there would come a point when they would no longer be prepared to continue adding to their balances.

Several measures for relieving the position were considered. Forbidding the sale in New York of sterling bills, which were traceable to transactions between neutrals and the European allies, would have been difficult to enforce. More importantly, it would have deprived the allies of goods from neutral suppliers where settlement was in dollars acquired by selling their sterling credits. It was thought that the allies' financial difficulties were already forcing them to substitute American for neutral produce and that most of what they were still buying from elsewhere was not available from the USA. Thus, unless the allies were to be deprived, American advances to enable allies to buy in neutral countries would rise by as much as their advances to the UK as the support of sterling fell.

There were more attractive alternatives: persuading neutral countries to accept payment in sterling or French francs, retaining the balances as post-war claims; and borrowing from neutrals in their own currencies to pay local producers.[a] In both cases, important governments would be susceptible to persuasion. The British had long used their blockade to ration supplies to neutral countries, applying

a Cash and bills held by neutral countries in sterling on 13 October 1917 were £78.1m ($380m). The largest were Brazil (£7.5m), Denmark (£14.2m), Holland (£8.9m), Norway (£30.5m) and Spain (£6.8m). T 172/437, ff. 42, Chancellor to Reading, 25 October 1917.

pressure on them to follow more friendly policies. In addition, as we have seen, the RESD bought produce in border neutrals to deny the Central Powers. Inevitably, with such countries as Holland and Norway, control of trade had become entangled with the provision of credits. The entry of the USA into the war increased the scope for persuasion. On 15 June 1917, Congress legislated for export control; the first proclamation was issued on 9 July. Despite its protests when similar measures had been applied to its own trade before April, the USA used these powers vigorously to ration supplies to the neutral nations. There were incidental financial effects. Some produce had no other markets and the neutrals had no alternative but to provide credit in order to sell their output; some European neutrals were desperate to buy coal and oil, while the available shipping was owned or controlled by the allies, who could refuse to move the goods unless they were given time to pay.[8]

The first part of this chapter describes the credits arranged by the UK in neutral Europe and South America, and in Japan. The second follows UK borrowing in Canada and shows how British expenditure and the Dominion's lending responded to the US Treasury's policy of confining its advances to expenditure within America's borders. Last, the chapter chronicles the strangest episode in Anglo-American financial relations of the war, the arrangement whereby the British bought US Treasury silver with US Treasury advances so that the Indian rupee could remain convertible, the dollar–rupee rate stable and US importers able to pay for Indian produce.

Borrowing from Japan and the Neutrals outside North America

Between autumn 1917 and the Armistice, the British took loans from nine neutral or allied countries outside the USA and Canada. The records of these transactions are sketchy, even as to amounts, interest rates, maturity and dates of issue. Data are notably lacking for loans taken in South America.

In October 1917, Barings proposed a six-month credit of between £10m and £20m in Argentina with Argentinian securities as collateral. This came to nothing, both the LEC and the Treasury believing that it was too short to be useful. However, the British and French needed grain and the Argentinians were vulnerable to persuasion because they could not move their crop without shipping, shipping which was only available to the allies. Crosby's original blueprint for allied borrowing from such countries was to encourage them to expand their note issues against securities provided by the borrowing allies. This was suggested to the Argentinian government and incorporated into a Convention with the French and British governments, signed in January 1918. The loan to the UK was for 200m Argentinian dollars (£39.7m or US$193m) with interest at 5 per cent (Table 6.3).[9] Another $100m in pesos was taken by the US Treasury against a deposit of dollars in New York. A further loan for a similar amount, mooted in the summer of 1918 to finance an abundant wheat crop, came to nothing.[10]

Across the River Plate, and for the same purpose, the Government of Uruguay agreed to lend the French 15m pesos (£3.2m or $15.5m) at 5 per cent until 1927. On 6 December 1918, the British arranged to borrow for two years, also at 5 per cent: on 31 March 1919, 19m pesos (£3.8m or $18.4m) was outstanding and on 31 March 1920, 24.6m pesos (£4.9m or $23.8m). The British duly made repayment on 6 December 1920.[11]

Until 1916, the Bank reluctantly shipped gold to settle the UK's current account deficit with Spain. As the shipments tailed off in 1916, the peseta gently appreciated, before rising sharply in 1917 as British buying of agricultural produce was added to long-standing purchases of ores and French buying of pack animals and timber. No measures were taken that summer as the LEC judged that effective support would entail shipping more gold than could be justified by the UK's resources. Sterling reached a low point of pta.16.8 in April 1918, although Spanish banks had been behaving as the US Treasury had hoped and envisaged: over the war years, they had been accumulating balances in dollars and sterling, which by August 1918 had reached $110m (£22.6m). In the final quarter of 1917, the US embargo on gold exports, and consequent French difficulties in paying for Spanish produce, and the Spanish need to buy coal, petroleum products and raw cotton combined to force negotiations for a loan. Cunliffe headed a Financial Mission to Madrid to negotiate an advance, but without success: the Spanish banks were unable to buy foreign securities without government approval and the Spanish government wanted credits to be part of a more general Commercial Agreement to include iron ore and coal.[12] Earlier, in the second half of 1917, French negotiations had envisaged the use of British securities as collateral.[13] As we have seen, this was successfully resisted by the UK Treasury, and in March 1918 a Franco-Spanish Commercial and Financial Agreement was signed, giving the French credits of pta.5m (£0.2m or $1m) per month for ten months.[b] In April, it was agreed that the French and British should each provide pta.50m (£2m or $10m) to support their currencies, the British share to come from a peseta loan to be floated by the mining company Rio Tinto in Spain (Table 6.3). In the meantime, gold was shipped.

In August, the US Ambassador in Madrid cabled that the British and French Treasuries had won 'firm control of exchanges after two months of work' and in October the rate reached pta.23.37.[14] At the end of August 1918, the US Treasury signed a Financial Agreement, negotiated by Norman Davis, for an advance of up to pta.250m (£10m or $48m) with a group of Spanish banks, and in October Rio Tinto issued its debenture.[c] The UK Treasury repaid the loan to Rio Tinto at the end of 1920 (Table 6.3).

b The maximum charge was to be 7½ per cent, including commissions, and the credits 90-day bills drawn by French banks on Spanish banks renewable for two years. French Treasury Bills were deposited as security. BoE, C91/20, LEC Minutes, 22 March 1918.

c The Agreement involved US banks having the option of drawing 90-day bills, renewable for three periods, on Spanish banks. It was secured on a special issue of US Treasury Bonds, repayable in pesetas or gold. *FRUS* (1918), pp. 1708–11, 'Spanish–American Financial Agreement of August 29, 1918'; *The Economist*, 28 September 1918, pp. 397–8.

British expenditure in Switzerland was mainly for munitions, in part to keep them from the Central Powers, and for the maintenance of British prisoners of war. The first orders were placed in the summer of 1915, for fuses to be supplied to the Russians, and soon extended to gauges, optical munitions and machine tools. Remittances were telegraphed to Switzerland by the Bank of England: in other words, sterling was sold against Swiss francs in the open market. Several attempts to create credits during 1917 came to nothing and when sterling (and the dollar) weakened in the final quarter of 1917 the Treasury urged that purchases should be reduced. The Foreign Office and the Ministry of Munitions disagreed and buying continued, although at a reduced rate. Here was an obvious example of the need to create credits in neutral currencies, to support both sterling and the dollar. Negotiations were delayed to leave the ground free for the French but, in March 1918, it was arranged that four London joint stock banks should draw three-months' bills for Swfr.100m (£4m or $19m) (Table 6.3). These funds were transferred to the purchasing agent of the Ministry of Munitions by a special arrangement between the Bank and the Swiss Federal government.[15]

With two exceptions, credit arrangements in Holland and Scandinavia followed the pattern of earlier borrowing: *ad hoc* issues of Exchequer Bonds and Treasury Bills, often with exchange rate options or guarantees, and bank acceptances. They were mainly the result of initiatives from the LEC, which regarded them as a means of paying for specific items and strengthening the exchange rate, rather than as a means of supplementing British and American financial resources. The minutes suggest the credits would have been taken even if there had been no American encouragement.

The greater part of the £15m Treasury Bills with Dutch guilder exchange rate guarantees or options outstanding at the end of 1916 were due to mature in the first half of 1917. At the request of the Dutch central bank, the options were changed to give holders liquidity, but only when sterling was strong. Holders could be repaid only in guilders at maturity but could receive repayment in sterling at any time, under discount at 5 per cent, provided the exchange rate was fl.12.15 or above. After much negotiation, arrangements were made to renew the larger holdings. Large gold shipments were also made so that by the end of 1917 issues had been reduced to £9.7m and by the end of 1918 to below £5m. The balance was repaid in 1920.

At the end of 1918, two issues of Exchequer Bonds were made. In November, £2m 5 per cent three-year Exchequer Bonds were issued to pay for sugar from Java. The next month, the British, French, Italian and US Treasuries agreed to borrow fl.175m (£14.5m or $70.4m) from the Dutch government, of which the British share was to be fl.75m (£6.2m or $30.2m), evidenced by 5 per cent guilder Exchequer Bonds with a sterling option and a final date of 31 December 1923. The intention was to use the proceeds to repay Treasury Bills, but only fl.50m (£4.1m or $20.1m) were issued: the arrangement was overtaken by the post-Armistice recovery in sterling against the neutral currencies and sizeable guilder receipts from sales of coal, disposals of British-owned Royal Dutch shares and payments for food sold to the Germans. By May 1919, the position had so improved that Morgans were investigating the sale of UK Treasury-owned florins into dollars to help repay the call loan.[16]

Two Scandinavian loans stand out from the many arrangements for the discounting of acceptances and the provision of bank loans in the final two years of the war. On 29 May 1918, the UK, the USA and France signed a commercial agreement with the government of Sweden which involved allied chartering of ships, rationing of Swedish exports and imports and the only joint allied loan arranged in Scandinavia. The loan was a monthly credit of Skr.6.25m (£0.3m) for expenditure in Sweden. On 31 March 1919, Skr.31.25m was outstanding, and Skr.12.5m a year later; the balance was repaid on 1 August 1921. The agreement also provided for half of the payments for iron ore, paper and pulp to take the form of UK Treasury 6 per cent one-year sterling Notes, with an option to renew until 1 August 1920. On 31 March 1919, £2.7m was outstanding, and none a year later (Table 6.3).[17]

The other loan was more esoteric. The sale of the Danish West Indies to the USA had been first negotiated in 1867, but the agreement was not ratified by the US Senate. Another attempt was made at the beginning of the century after the USA acquired nearby Puerto Rico, but it was narrowly rejected by the Danish Rigsdag. With Denmark in need of funds, half-hearted and inconclusive negotiations were held between 1909 and 1911. The sale became imperative with the threat of an invasion of Denmark and the acquisition by Germany of a base off the US coast.[18] The sale was signed on 4 August 1916 and the islands were transferred on 31 March 1917. The Danes received $25m, which to avoid the risk of shipping gold, was paid in dollars deposited in four New York banks.[19] The LEC approached the Danes through Hambros with a view to borrowing the funds, but they were unsuccessful until November 1917. It was then arranged that Hambros and the British Bank of Northern Commerce should borrow the money on behalf of the Treasury as the deposits matured. The first $1m, which was at call, was borrowed on 1 December 1917 and applied to the repayment of UK dollar Treasury Bills – as were the remainder – until the last was paid over on 3 April 1918 (Table 6.3).[20]

Negotiations for the Japanese advance which was used in February 1918 to purchase the Notes held by du Pont began in the summer of 1917. In August, the Diet authorised the government to give financial assistance to its allies up to a maximum of ¥200m (£20.5m or $100m). The same month, ¥100m (£10.2m or $49.8m) 5 per cent Exchequer Bonds were issued by the Japanese government to enable Russian Yen Treasury Bills held by Japanese investors to be converted and to raise additional cash. The government lent the proceeds to the Russians against Treasury Bills. In October, the government issued ¥50m (£5.1m or $24.9m) of the same Bonds, again lending the proceeds to the Russians against Bills; another ¥16m (£1.6m or $8m) was lent by the Japanese Savings Bank on Russian Yen Treasury Bills.[21] It was not until Christmas that the skeleton of a loan for the UK was agreed. The British wanted dollars, the Japanese wanted rupees, the Indians wanted gold and the US Treasury did not want to issue a licence to the Japanese for the export of gold to India. It was arranged that the Japanese government would buy ¥80m (£8.2m or $39.9m) British one-year Yen Treasury Bills, sell them to investors and remit the proceeds to New York in dollars. In a parallel transaction, the British would sell £2m gold held in India to the India Office. The India Office would credit the Japanese with 30m rupees, and they in turn would credit the British with $10.2m in New York. The two transactions raised $48.2m for the British (Table 6.3).[22]

Canada: 1915 and 1916

As part of the Empire, the Dominion of Canada entered the war in August 1914, her first troops arriving in Europe in October. Geographically close to Europe compared with Australia, New Zealand and India, Canada could supply food and some manufactured products. Europe needed wheat, oats, bacon, cheese and munitions and Canada needed sterling for her expeditionary force. She was also a large debtor to London, the Dominion government, provinces, cities and railways traditionally having raised much of their long-term capital in sterling. This combination made financial relations between Britain and Canada unique. After April 1917, however, many of the constraints on British financial relations with neutral countries also applied to Canada. With only one or two exceptions, the US Treasury refused to countenance the use of its advances to buy products from its northern neighbour, sought to reduce the sterling thrown on the New York market by British and allied transactions with Canada and pressed the British to meet their Canadian expenditure from local borrowing. Adjustment to these restrictions was painful for both Britain and Canada. The late spring and early summer of 1917, when the British could remit little from New York for munitions and were learning that the Canadian Department of Finance was unprepared to increase its advances to the UK, were chaotic: bills piled up, the subventions from the Dominion were forestalled and very short-term loans taken from the Canadian banks. By mid-summer, the Treasury had accepted that the united financial resources of the UK and Canada were inadequate for the purchases of the food and munitions which the Dominion could have supplied, and the British government cut its buying programme.

Throughout the war there were heavy flows of credit in both directions. The accounts are ambiguous and need to be treated with caution, but by 31 March 1919 the Canadian chartered banks had lent the Imperial Treasury C$200m to buy munitions and wheat, while the Dominion government had lent the UK C$859.2m and the UK had lent the Dominion C$714.4m (Tables 10.1 and 10.2). From the start, the UK Treasury financed Canadian capital spending and maturing liabilities that could not be handled in the London market, together with the cost of Canadian forces in Europe. From the beginning of 1916, the Dominion government and the Canadian chartered banks financed an increasingly large share of British spending. These transactions at first left the UK a net creditor. Until the end of 1915, the UK paid for all its munitions in cash.[23] The balance rapidly changed as increased British spending coincided with the need to replace remittances from the Treasury account in New York with local credits (Table 10.2).

Table 10.1 Terms of UK Treasury market borrowing in Canada: 1914–19 (C$)

Chartered Banks (Munitions)

Banks' First Munitions Loan. $50m under an agreement dated 31 March 1916 between the Minister of Finance and the CBA on behalf of twenty-one banks. A further $26m, divided equally between 1 May and 1 June. The Finance Department issued one-year 'Imperial Treasury Bill Certificates' to the banks against the deposit at the Bank of England of £10.3m one-year British sterling Treasury Bills. The latter were held to the order of the Minister of Finance, acting as trustee for the banks. Interest rate 5 per cent, payable quarterly by means of coupons attached to the Certificates. Commission 1/2 per cent. Renewable after one year, at the option of the Treasury, at the same rate or lower, with commission of 1/2 per cent payable on each occasion.

1 April 1916	50
1 May	13
1 June	13

The arrangement was extended for one year on 1 April of 1917, 1918, 1919 and 1920. Interest rate continued at 5 per cent throughout. By an agreement dated 31 October 1920, the loan was merged on 1 April 1921 into the General Scheme of Repayment.

Banks' Second Munitions Loan. $24m, 3 July 1916. Terms and arrangements as for the First Loan.

1 July 1916	12
1 August	12

The arrangement was extended for one year on 3 July 1917, 1918, 1919 and 1920. Interest rate continued at 5 per cent throughout. By an agreement dated 31 October 1920, the loan was merged on 1 July 1921 into the General Scheme of Repayment.

Banks' Third (Earmarked) Munitions Loan. $50m (originally planned to be $75m) under an agreement in either December 1916 or January 1917 between the Minister of Finance and the CBA on behalf of twenty chartered banks. The banks having opted to take Canadian securities, the Finance Department issued tailor-made one-year Dominion Treasury Bills payable in gold in Ottawa. The Bills could not be sold and, if pledged, they had first to be offered to the Department of Finance. Rate of discount 5 1/2 per cent. Commission 1/2 per cent.

15 January 1917	19.0
15 February	18.9
15 March	12.1

Banks Fourth (Earmarked) Munitions Loan. $75m advanced by eighteen banks. Rate of discount 5 1/2 per cent. The Bills issued on 15 June and 16 July (15 July was a Sunday) were for four months and those issued on 15 August were for three months. Thus, $25m matured in October and $50m in November. Other terms as for the Third Loan.

15 June 1917	25
16 July	*25
15 August	*25

*$16.5m of the July issue and $11.8m of the August issue were sold early at various dates during the previous month.

Table 10.1 continued.

Bank 'overdrafts' arranged by the IMB
Bank of Montreal.
US$5m in New York, arranged sometime in April 1917 for repayment on 25 April.

$10m in June 1917, in conjunction with the CPR and the Royal Trust Co., against sterling Treasury Bills in London. Due 15 June 1917. Rolled over each month and repaid on 15 September 1917.

Canadian Bank of Commerce. $5m arranged in May 1917 [?]. Due 5 June. Rolled over each month and repaid on 5 September 1917.

Banks (Wheat)
$20m advanced on 1 June 1916 for one year. Repaid on 1 June 1917 by shipping a consignment of $18m in Russian gold (originally destined for Ottawa for the account of the British under the Anglo-Russian Financial Agreement of September 1915) to Japan for sale against dollars.

The Royal Wheat Loan. $100m under an agreement dated 1 November 1917 between the Minister of Finance and the CBA representing twenty-one banks. The Finance Department issued one-year 'Imperial Treasury Bill Certificates' to the banks against the deposit at the Bank of England of £22.2m ($108.2m) one-year British sterling Treasury Bills, representing the principal and a year's interest. The latter were held to the order of the Minister of Finance, acting as trustee for the banks. Interest 6 per cent, payable quarterly by means of coupons attached to the Certificates. No commission. Renewable after one year, at the option of the Treasury, at the same rate of interest.

1 November 1917	50
1 January 1918	10
1 February	10
1 March	10
1 April	10
1 May	10

The arrangement was extended for one year on 1 November 1918 and on the first day of January, February, March, April and May 1919. $50m was repaid in instalments of $10m on maturity on the first day of January, February, March, April and May 1920. The other $50m was extended for one year by an agreement dated 1 November 1919.
By an agreement dated 31 October 1920, the loan was extended and merged into a General Scheme of Repayment.

The General Scheme Of Repayment
Under an agreement dated 31 October 1920, the $150m balance of the Banks' First and Second Munitions Loans and the Royal Wheat Loan were extended and merged (on their respective maturity dates of 1 November 1920, 1 April 1921 and 3 July 1921) into a General Scheme of Repayment. Interest 6 per cent payable from the loans respective maturity dates. Other terms unchanged.
Repayment:
$5m each month from 1 November 1920 to 1 April 1921.
$10m each month from 1 May 1921 to 1 April 1922.

Miscellaneous

National Trust Co.
$1m on 25 January 1917. In the form of the purchase of £0.2m one-year sterling Treasury Bills. Interest [discount?] 5¼ per cent.
Repaid: $0.15m on 1 July 1917 and monthly thereafter until 1 January 1918.

Table 10.1 continued.

Canadian Pacific Railway
$10m advanced to the IMB via the Bank of Montreal on 5 July 1917. Interest [discount?] 6 per cent. Secured on one-year Canadian Dollar Treasury Bills deposited with Bank of Montreal in London.
Repaid: $5.7m. on 5 July 1918, with balance renewed. $4.3m renewed on 5 July 1919 and paid off on 16 October 1919 from proceeds of gold shipments.

Sources: T 170/134, ff. 40–2, Chadwick, 'British Government Transactions in America', 1922; Ministry of Munitions (1921), II, Part IV, pp. 56–73; *Canada, Public Accounts for the Fiscal Year ended March 31 1915 to 1922*; Knox (1940); NAC, RG19/595/155-35-3, 4 and 5, RG19/596/155-35-13 and 16.

Until the end of 1915, British purchases in Canada were channelled through the Shell Committee (for munitions) and the Militia Department (saddlery, harnesses, horse blankets and so forth). The Shell Committee, by far the largest spender, indented the Militia Department, which forwarded the requisitions to the Department of Finance. Until August 1915, the War Office paid sterling to the Canadian High Commissioner in London for the account of the Department of Finance, and the sterling was sold for Canadian dollars on the open market. For the rest of the year, the Canadian dollars were obtained by taking gold from the British stock in Ottawa or by making transfers from the Treasury Account with Morgans to the New York branch of the Bank of Montreal, the Dominion's bankers. Until February 1916, the Canadian Finance Department bought US dollars, if and when they were needed by the Imperial Munitions Board (IMB), in the open market. Thereafter, it drew on its own account in New York, debiting them to the IMB as advances to the UK Treasury.[24]

All the Shell Committee's expenditure was met in cash from British resources but the payments were often late, in part because of the difficulties of selling sterling into Canadian dollars during the late summer of 1915, difficulties which no doubt led to the payments being re-routed via New York. Neither the Finance nor Militia Departments recognised financial responsibility for the Shell Committee and if there were no funds they left requisitions unpaid. Sometimes, the Department of Finance would step in, apparently without formal prior arrangement, and make payment, advancing the money to the Imperial Government. Matters came to a head in the autumn of 1915. On 26 October, advances to the Shell Committee, Militia and Agriculture had risen to some C$10.6m and Finance told the Treasury in London that it was facing large cash outflows on other accounts and could lend no more. In November, the Shell Committee's unpaid bills again reached C$10m. On both occasions the position was only corrected by transfers from Morgans and the Ottawa gold stock.[25]

The Shell Committee, inefficient and corrupt, was replaced by the IMB in November 1915. Believing that one of the main reasons for the Shell Committee's embarrassing lack of funds was a failure to keep London informed of its needs, the Canadian Finance Minister, Thomas White, proposed that his Department

Table 10.2 Transactions between the UK Treasury and the Canadian Department of Finance: years ending 31 March 1915 to 1924 (C$m)

	UK borrowing	*Canadian borrowing*	*Net*
1915			
New borrowing		61.5*	61.5*
1916			
New borrowing	45	76.5*	31.5*
Cumulative to 31 March 1916	45	138*	93*
1917			
New borrowing	124.6	150.5*	25.9*
Cumulative to 31 March 1917	171.8	288.5*(1)	116.7*
Adjustments	2.3(2)		
Debt outstanding on 31 March	169.6	288.5*(1)	118.9*
1918			
New borrowing	335.0	211.7*	123.3*
Cumulative to 31 March 1918	504.6(3)	500.2*(4)	–4.4*
Cancelled	384.5(5)	384.5(5)	
Other cancellations	8.2	8.2	
Other adjustments	0.2(2)		
Debt outstanding on 31 March	111.7	107.6*	–4.1*
1919			
New borrowing	354.6	214.1*	–140.5*
Cumulative to 31 March 1919	859.2	714.4*	–144.8*
US dollar advance in New York	30.6(6)		
Cancelled in 1918–19	392.7	392.7	
Other adjustments	0.4(2)		
Debt outstanding on 31 March 1919	435.6(7)	321.7(8)	–113.9*
1920			
Cancellations	403.0(9)	403	
Reduction in 1919–20	58.5(10)		
Outstanding on 31 March 1920	181.5(11)		
Balance at end-year			–171.2*(10)
1921			
Reduction in 1920–1	29.8(10)		
Outstanding on 31 March 1921	132.3(11)		
Balance at end-year			–141.4*(10)
1922			
Reduction in 1921–2	18.7(10)		
Outstanding on 31 March 1922	127.4(11)		
Balance at end-year			–122.7*(10)
1923			
Reduction in 1922–3	56.2(10)		
Outstanding on 31 March 1923	69.7(11,12)		
Balance at end-year			–66.5*(10)

Table 10.2 continued.

1924			
Cancellations	58.9(13)	58.9(13)	
Repayment in cash 8.7(13)			
Outstanding on 31 March 1924	0	0	0

Notes
(1) Shown as $289.6m in text of *Canada, Public Accounts for the Fiscal Year ended March 31*, 1917, p. x.
(2) Sale of Imperial Government Property, Remittances for Flour, Bullion Special Account, Flaxseed Account etc.
(3) Shown as $506.1m in *Canadian Government (Advances)* (Cd. 9234), TM, 14 November 1918.
(4) Shown as $512.9m ($405.3m plus $107.6m Bonds) in *Canadian Government (Advances)* (Cd. 9234), TM, 14 November 1918.
(5) Shown as cancellation of $384.5m of principal and $20.9m of interest in *Canadian Government (Advances)* (Cd. 9234), TM, 14 November 1918.
(6) Shown as US$30.6m of principal and $1m of interest in *Canadian Government (Advances)* (Cmd. 583), TM, 1 January 1920.
(7) Shown as $446.8m in *External Debt as on 31 March 1919, 1920 etc.* (Cmd. 1648), as $444.8m plus interest on the sterling debt in CO 42/1014, f. 468, Blackett, April 1919, and $466.7m in *Canadian Government (Advances)* (Cmd. 583), TM, 1 January 1920. The Canadian accounts treat the $30.6m advanced to Canada in New York and the $0.2m raised from the sale of Imperial property in Canada as amounts to be deducted from Canadian advances to the UK, whereas in *Canadian Government (Advances)*, 1 January 1920, they are treated as amounts to be added to British advances to Canada. Deducting $30.8m from the $466.7m shown in the Canadian accounts gives $435.9m.
(8) Shown as C$252m in *Canadian Government (Advances)* (Cmd. 583), TM, 1 January 1920, . This needs to be adjusted by adding indebtedness represented by Bonds ($107.6m) and deducting the US dollars advanced in New York (US$30.6m). The remaining difference of $7.3m cannot be explained and emerges in the debt outstanding on 31 March 1919, which is shown as $107.1m in the Treasury Minute.
(9) *Canadian Government (Advances)* (Cmd. 583), 1 January 1920, (Cmd. 616), 1 March 1920, and (Cmd. 651), 29 March 1920.
(10) *Canada, Public Accounts for the Fiscal Years ended March 31, 1920–24.*
(11) *National Debt: annual returns.*
(12) Shown as $66.8m in *Canadian Government (Advances)* (Cmd. 2181), TM, 27 May 1924.
(13) *Canadian Government (Advances)* (Cmd. 2181), TM, 27 May 1924.
*Capitalised value.
– denotes balance in favour of Canada.
Rows and columns may not sum because of rounding.

Sources: *Canada, Public Accounts for the Fiscal Year ended March 31 1915–23*, except where otherwise stated.

take the pivotal role in paying the IMB's bills, in effect placing the machinery of the Department at the disposal of the Imperial Government and becoming its paying agent. At the beginning of each month, the IMB was to state its requirements to the Ministry of Munitions in London and the Department of Finance in Ottawa. The last would pass the statement to the UK Treasury. Payments would be made from the Department of Finance to the credit of the IMB at the Bank of Montreal.[26] Opportunities for corruption would be reduced. Importantly for the story of the Debt, the change coincided with Canada issuing her first domestic war loan. This was such a success that, instead of C$50m that had been expected, White was able to allot C$100m. Lists closed on 30 November, and on 4 December he offered to lend the British between C$40m and C$50m for munitions. The loan would be in instalments, spread over the three months to March, with the same interest rate as the Dominion was itself paying.[27] Apart from the *ad hoc* advances to the Shell Committee and Department of Agriculture the previous autumn, this was the first Dominion credit for the Imperial Government.

Although White was careful to disclaim any responsibility for Imperial debts, it was, perhaps, inevitable that a system evolved whereby his Department sent the monthly statement of the IMB's needs to the Treasury in London with the amount that Canada would pay, using its recent war loan, together with the balance to be met by London. As early as January 1916, there were premonitions of where this would lead. The monthly statement showed a requirement of C$35m. The prompt query from London read 'Understood you would be able to finance at least part of Munitions requirements...Can you do this in January or do you make estimate thirty five millions as required after deducting amount which you can provide.' The answer was Ottawa C$18m and London C$17m.[28]

During the first quarter of 1916, the UK transferred C$27m from Morgans and drew heavily on the Department of Finance to meet IMB spending of between C$25m and C$35m per month. By the end of March, Canadian advances had risen to C$45m, absorbing nearly all the funds allocated from the war loan. The balance of C$5m was held over until July (Table 10.3).[29] With a growing shortage of US dollars, the Treasury in London was reluctant to place further orders unless they were partly financed in Canada. The Department of Finance was also feeling financial pressure and was unprepared to give further help. Instead, on 1 March, White met a small group of the major Canadian banks, who agreed to recommend that members of the Canadian Bankers' Association (CBA) should be asked to lend C$50m, perhaps C$75m, to the IMB. On 31 March, twenty-one banks agreed to lend the smaller sum against Canadian one-year Treasury Bill Certificates, representing participation in the ultimate security: British sterling Treasury Bills. These, at the insistence of the British, were deposited in London to the order of the Minister of Finance so that they could not be discounted in New York at an inconvenient moment. As the C$50m ran out, another C$26m was extended. A Second Munitions Loan of C$24m, dated 3 July, followed on the same terms (Tables 10.1 and 10.3).[30]

The arrangement was unusual, probably unique, in British borrowing. The Minister of Finance approached the banks and the advances were made at his initiative as substitutes for Dominion advances. The Memorandum of Agreement was between the Minister and the President of the CBA, 'representing the banks'. The Imperial Treasury Bills were held by the Bank of England 'for account of the Minister as Trustee for the banks.' In due course, the Department of Finance was to administer the issue of the securities, the receipt of the monies, the payments of interest, repayments of principal and the surrender of its own Certificates in Canada and the underlying Treasury Bills in London. The interest and the banks' ½ per cent commission was paid by the Department of Finance and charged as an advance to the UK Treasury, later to form part of the settlement between the two governments.[31]

Table 10.3 UK Treasury borrowing from the Canadian Department of Finance and the Canadian private sector (excluding loans repaid in the same year in which they were incurred): 1915 to 1919 (C$m)

Years ending 31 March	
1915	
None	
1916	
Finance Department advance for munitions from the proceeds of Canada's first war loan	45
Banks' Wheat Loan of 1 June 1916	20
1917	
Banks' First Munitions Loan	76
Banks' Second Munitions Loan	24
Finance Department advance for munitions from the proceeds of Canada's first war loan	5
Finance Department advance for munitions from the proceeds of Canada's second war loan	50
Banks' Third (Earmarked) Munitions Loan	50
Finance Department advance for munitions, January–February 1917	20
National Trust Co.	1
Total (official)	124.6
Total (private)	101
Total	225.6
1918	
Balance from January–February 1917 of the Finance Department advance for munitions	5
Banks' Royal Wheat Loan	80
National Trust Co.	–1
Loan from the CPR	10
Other Finance Department advances	330
Total (official)	335
Total (private)	89
1919	
Banks' Royal Wheat Loan	20
Finance Department advances	354.6
CPR	–5.7
Total (official)	354.6
Total (private)	14.3

Note
– denotes repayment

Sources: As in text of Chapter 10; *Canada, Public Accounts for the Fiscal Year ended 31 March 1915–19*; *Canadian Government (Advances)* (Cd. 9234) and (Cd. 583), TMs, 14 November 1918 and 1 January 1920.

The Second Munitions Loan was not easy to arrange. White, wanting to keep the banks liquid before his postponed second internal war loan, had proposed that the British ship gold, increasing the Canadian banks' reserves. The Treasury's financial position ruled this out. The Canadians also sought to impose a condition that the money should be used to finance new orders but, after McKenna's dire warnings to the Cabinet in May and June about dollar expenditure, the Treasury was aiming to dispense with all external supplies unless they were accompanied by credits.[32] In any case, C$24m would have lasted less than a month, even if it had not been spread over both July and August. The Treasury found the balance needed for the last week in July from New York, but on 4 August the Chancellor asked White to meet all the IMB's bills, starting the following day. White refused the request, which would have almost doubled the Dominion's war spending. As he pointed out, he could hardly be expected to provide an open-ended commitment to cover expenditure authorised by the London government without consultation with the Dominion: he had frequently told the IMB – a British government agency – that with Canadian war expenditure rapidly increasing he could not provide more help, while the banks had to be kept liquid for the new war loan and to finance the harvest. If the position of the banks justified further loans, he would try to make arrangements, but he would make no promises and the Treasury should expect to find all the money for the orders the IMB was placing. The Chancellor climbed down and during August, September and October supplied US$80.5m from New York, heavily trenching on the proceeds of the two collateral issues.[33]

After the second domestic war loan in September, White advanced a further C$50m to the IMB in two equal instalments, in November and December. The Treasury met the balance from New York, the IMB's expenditure alone being C$62m for the two months.[34]

On 1 June 1916, C$20m was advanced to the UK by the chartered banks for wheat purchases (Tables 10.1 and 10.3).[35]

Canada: spring and summer 1917

The failure to break out of the Somme in the summer of 1916 prompted another large munitions programme, for which there was insufficient capacity in the UK. In the first half of 1917, the IMB placed orders in Canada for C$244m of *matériel* for delivery between January and June: C$41m per month, to which was added, in due course, orders for ships. Although the programme was subsequently reduced, in May the IMB's expenditure reached C$50m, excluding the cost of shipping. In 1917, nearly twenty-four million shells, equivalent at times to between one-quarter and one-third of the ammunition used by the British artillery, came from Canada.[36] Treasury sanction for contracts was forthcoming only if local credits were arranged to cover most of their value.

A Third Munitions Loan was provided by the chartered banks during the first quarter of 1917. Differing from the First and Second, it can be best viewed as the means by which White met his share of the IMB's expenditure. His Department had insufficient funds from revenues and previous borrowings to make an advance and it again approached the CBA, proposing that the banks discount $50m or $75m one-year Bills, with the option of Dominion or Imperial Treasury obligations. The banks opted for the former and the lesser amount, which they provided by buying gold-backed Dominion Treasury Bills at a discount of 5½ per cent, the Department of Finance onlending the proceeds to the IMB (Table 10.1). As a loan to the Dominion government, whoever might be the ultimate debtor and however earmarked, the Bills were Canadian debt and appeared in the Bank Statements as 'Balance due to the Dominion Government.'[37] White had to find the missing $25m from his own resources (of which $5m fell into April and the 1917–18 financial year), so that Department of Finance lending to the IMB in the year to 31 March 1917 became C$125m. Canadian lending rose to C$225m when the Banks' First and Second Munitions Loans were included (Tables 10.1 and 10.3).[38]

On 21 May 1917, Chalmers warned the Chancellor that the 'Canadian position will become awkward if not dealt with forthwith.' It was already becoming awkward. White had found some money for advances from the third Canadian internal war loan (for C$150m) issued in March, and this enabled him to promise C$25m for each of April and May, with the possibility of a similar sum in June, but this was well short of the IMB's expenditure. It was left living from hand to mouth, delaying payments and borrowing from the chartered banks for short periods.[39] Payments in April had been heavy, Lever in New York was waiting for Congress to pass the First Liberty Bond Act, and the British had raised C$55m in Canada in a single month: the C$25m White had promised from the third war loan; the C$5m not used in March; a supplement of C$10m from the Department of Finance, with another C$10m from the same source for shipbuilding; and C$5m arranged by the IMB from the Bank of Montreal.

It was the beginning of a summer of anxiety, part of the crisis in British finance in North America. The Imperial Government had few US dollars of its own in New York and US Treasury advances could not be used to meet Canadian payments, even if the British could spare them: only $10m to $15m per month, representing US components of Canadian munitions, could be remitted. Increasingly overt threats were used by both sides. By the British: if no credit was supplied, orders would have to be cancelled and bills left unpaid. By the Canadians: if orders were cancelled, or bills left unpaid, the supply of munitions would cease. Always in the background was the danger to the British and Canadian Armies if munitions' supply failed. To add colour to the implications for employment, the banks and the war effort, White had to react at a moment of great uncertainty in Canadian politics: in May, the Prime Minister, Sir Robert Borden, had returned to Canada from Europe believing that conscription was necessary, together with a coalition government to carry it. During the summer, the government pushed through Parliament a Military Service Bill, at the same time manoeuvring to form a coalition with the Liberals. This was not agreed until the middle of October: on 17 December, an election was held at which the Union Government was returned with a large majority.

In May, as Borden announced that conscription would be introduced (the Bill was to be given its first reading on 11 June), White told the British that the Liberty

Bond issue was damaging his ability to continue lending for munitions. He was unable to issue another domestic war loan until the autumn: the market in existing issues was weak as American investors switched from Canadian securities to the new Liberty Bonds and White was unable to borrow in New York because of US Treasury restrictions on new allied issues. He was arranging a Fourth Munitions Loan with the chartered banks, which would enable him to continue providing some help, but he would not be able to maintain his advances at $25m per month after June. Moreover, the political situation in Canada, and the demands being made on the banks to finance output at inflated prices, meant that he could play no part in persuading the banks to roll over the $20m wheat loan, due on 1 June (Table 10.1). He would consider inflating the note issue, but only against gold or Bank of England notes.[40]

The Fourth Munitions Loan, of C$75m, was negotiated during May and taken from the banks in three equal tranches. As in the first quarter, the security was Dominion Treasury Bills so, although earmarked to the IMB, the debt was once again a liability of Canada. The first tranche in June was allotted without difficulty, but the later tranches were, initially, uncovered. Because the money was urgently needed, the Department let it be known that it was prepared to allot the 16 July and 15 August Bills early. The accounts are not wholly clear, but it seems that the early bids arrived at the Department piecemeal, and that Bills were allotted as they arrived, leaving a balance to be issued on the planned dates. As it turned out, the bids on the planned dates were insufficient to cover the remaining Bills, but they were sold within a few days, with the Bank of Montreal ready to mop up at least part of any remaining. The term was never used, but it seems that some sort of tap was running (Table 10.1).[41]

The policy that the Treasury was to pursue in Canada until the autumn was drafted by Keynes. White's C$25m per month, far from being cut, must be increased. Otherwise, the IMB would have to cancel orders. If White claimed he could not find funds, he should be told that:

> (1) Canada has not restricted unessential [*sic*] imports from the United States and elsewhere.
> (2) Heavy expenditure railway development referred to by him capable of postponement.
> (3) Still open to him to obtain large credits by expansion note issue. Policy so conservative hitherto that probably room considerable expansion without inflation. This course by easing monetary position banks would greatly facilitate further loans from them.

Canada could only pull her full weight by putting her finances on a war footing.[42]

As well as the regular expenditure for munitions and food, June and early July saw several bank loans coming due: the C$20m Wheat Loan, taken the previous summer, was due on 1 June; C$1m borrowed from White's own National Trust Co. was due on 1 July; and the banks' Second Munitions Loan, of C$24m, came up on 3 July. In addition, there were bank credits arranged directly by the IMB:

C$5m taken from the Canadian Bank of Commerce due on 5 June and C$10m borrowed from the Bank of Montreal due on 15 June.[43]

The British just squeezed through June: C$18m to repay the wheat loan was found from Russian gold; the Munitions Loan was rolled over for one year; repayment of the National Trust's C$1m was spread over six months; the C$5m owed to the Canadian Bank of Commerce was extended until 5 September; and the C$10m due to the Bank of Montreal was extended to 15 July and then to 15 August (Table 10.1). For current spending, C$10m came from the Treasury Account in New York and White provided his usual C$25m. The remainder was scraped together by the IMB from the banking system, or just not paid: by the end of the month, the IMB held C$19m of cheques awaiting despatch and unpaid bills.[44] The position was clearly unsustainable and on 8 June the Chancellor cabled:

> We require our gold, the amount of which as you know is now very limited, for payments external to the Empire. We can continue to finance such part of Munitions Board expenditure as is incurred in the US. But Canadian expenditure can only be met from Canadian sources. I fear that it will be necessary to take immediate steps to reduce total expenditure in Canada including shipbuilding through Munitions Board to amount of advances forthcoming through White.[45]

At the end of June, as the British sought more US Treasury advances to support sterling and the Morgan overdraft was called, a further argument was added: if Canada did not pay, there would be a stop. The IMB's July requirement was C$69m, the War Office needed C$6m, and cheese contracts C$8m immediately and C$40m by the end of September. The Department of Finance would only provide its usual C$25m. The British were blunt. Only C$12m each month of the US advances could be remitted from New York and there was no other means of paying except in gold, which had to be kept for payments outside the Empire: 'there is thus no alternative to provision of above balance from Canada's own resources.' The Bank of Montreal's C$10m might be rolled over and C$5m of interest deferred or set off against sterling advances in London. Despite White's reluctance, the Dominion note issue, according to the Chancellor, had to be expanded:

> a stage of the war has been reached, when, however regrettably, it is necessary to take risks. It is for the Dominion Government to weigh the disadvantages of the course of action we now urge upon them with the effect on the supply of munitions of the British Army and the loss and confusion in which Canadian manufacturers would be involved if the Imperial Munitions Board was not in a position to meet its liabilities.
>
> The above applies equally to funds required to finance purchases of cheese and other commodities.[46]

This was gentler than the IMB, which warned of 'financial panic' and the cessation of Canadian munitions supplies.[47]

The money for July was found after ten days of negotiations, which included a personal message from Lloyd George to Borden. A loan of $10m came from the CPR, the proceeds of land sales which would normally have been used to repay its market debt (Table 10.1). White promised $25m for each of July, August and September, with $10m of that due in August brought forward to cover July's deficit. Loan repayments would be delayed, interest postponed and contracts extended.

The British had already helped several allies inflate their currencies, opening book credits to back note issues by Russia, Roumania and Greece.[d] Although the Canadians warned that unsecured currency notes would reduce the appetite for Dominion securities and reduce the amount that could be borrowed, on 4 July White retreated from his demand that an expanded note issue was only acceptable against gold and Bank of England notes and agreed to an increase of between C$50m and C$100m over the following three months against the deposit in London of British-owned Canadian municipal, provincial or provincial-guaranteed securities. The proceeds were to be earmarked for cheese purchases, with the balance of C$10m to be used to repay debts to his Department. He would also approach McAdoo for authority to issue a loan in New York – a project planned since February – and, meanwhile, he asked the British to press the Secretary to allow more than US$10m to US$15m each month to be remitted from New York: the exchange rate was in New York's favour and he should allow US$25m to US$50m to be used each month in Canada. This would cover the balance of British expenditure. Finally, White asked for longer notice of requests for advances.[48] The British once more stressed that no funds, other than those which could be justified by US sales to Canada for munitions production, could be remitted from New York so that the proceeds of the note issue would have to be pooled to meet the most pressing needs.[49]

White refused to give way any further. On 7 July, he had warned that he could not pay for War Office purchases of oats, forage and flour, and two weeks later he cabled the precise understanding reached with London, making it clear that his advance of C$25m for October was contingent on US$15m per month being remitted from the USA, the note issue being used for cheese and debt repayment, and the UK finding from its own resources the $15m to repay the Bank of Montreal on 15 August and the Canadian Bank of Commerce on 5 September.[50] Four days after the latter cable was received, the Treasury ordered the War Office to start selling flour, oats and hay and the spending departments to cancel orders up to the end of September 'to the utmost extent possible' and not to agree new commitments until 'we have ascertained for them that Canadian Government can supply funds.'[51]

Once the British accepted that orders had to be made to fit financial resources, rather than financial resources expanded to fit the orders, their policy became

d The credits had been opened in the books of the Commissioners. They were: Russia £200m, Roumania £8m and Greece £2.4m. T 172/437, f. 18, Chalmers to Lever, 30 October 1917. The instructions are in T 133/1.

more coherent and they concentrated on bridging the gap until the cuts became effective. The IMB's August requirement was C$50m, including US$10m to repay the Bank of Montreal; C$15m, US$10m having been brought forward into July, would come from White and C$15m from New York. The balance of C$20m, together with payments for cheese, oats and hay, if the latter payments could not be cancelled, would have to come from expanding the note issue or by anticipating the September advance. White, said the Chancellor, should not be misled about British resources by the gold lying in Ottawa: the Canadians presumably did not know of the Cunliffe storm and White was merely told that it was part of the Bank of England's published reserve or earmarked against the call loans in New York.[52]

At first, White treated these proposals with suspicion, believing that the demand for a forestalment would be repeated the following month and that there was no reason for the Dominion government to pay IMB debts which had been contracted without its knowledge. Lever was instructed to assure him that the British were doing their best to 'curtail commitments as drastically as we can' and, although an advance out of the October instalment could be necessary in September, it was thought that 'we might get clear' by then:

> We are only asking White to anticipate by a few weeks advances which he has promised to make in any case...We are in real need of his assistance and ask him to believe that if we had any alternative we would not press him further.[53]

White accepted the British plan and increased his August contribution from C$15m to C$35m. In return, the British promised to repay the C$5m due to the Canadian Bank of Commerce on 5 September from their own resources and the $10m Bank of Montreal loan on 15 September from White's advances.[54]

In August 1917, the Canadian issue in New York failed spectacularly, contributing to the decision that the British should use Treasury Bills rather than Notes to reduce the call loan.[e] White had cash in New York to repay on 1 August $20m 5 per cent Notes issued as two-year paper in 1915, but the Canadian dollar was weak and the demands in the coming autumn were forecast to be heavy. In June, White had refused an advance from McAdoo because he preferred to raise money in the market and did not want to add to the demands being made on the US Treasury; in the middle of July, he asked McAdoo to authorise and then support a public issue. McAdoo had encouraged the Canadians to issue 'upwards of $50m', as usual asking that his political problems be remembered.[55] Instructed by the US Treasury to ensure that the issue did not interfere with its own certificates of indebtedness or with Liberty Bonds, Morgans decided to offer $100m 5 per cent two-year Notes.[56]

e The issue was of $100m two-year 5 per cent Notes due 1 August 1919. They were sold to the underwriters at 96 for sale to the public at 98. If conditions so justified, it was agreed that 1/4 per cent of the spread between the price paid by the underwriters and that paid by the public should be returned to the Dominion government.

Morgans ran into problems from the start. Markets were dull. On 25 July, newspapers carried reports that McAdoo had requested a further $5,000m for the war, most of which was expected to be borrowed, and as Morgans formed their syndicate the headlines continued to be of estimates, taxation and borrowing.[57] Morgans' Canadian Group, their usual associates, agreed to underwrite $100m, but could pass on only $51.7m of the risk to the 541 banks and brokers who they approached to be sub-underwriters. The sales campaign began on 30 July; when lists closed on 2 August, investors had subscribed for only $50.2m. Morgans and their syndicate were left holding securities almost certain to depreciate. Morgans advised the British that a public admission of failure would damage confidence, make future Canadian borrowing more expensive, and affect the banks' willingness to carry the British call loans, whose future was then being negotiated. Moreover, Morgans' immediate associates, the members of the Canadian Group and the participants in the call loans, were often the same banks.

Morgans 'had to make some pretty strong plays to enable [them] to say it had all gone', Grenfell was told.[58] Following the practice when issuing British secured loans before the USA entered the war, Morgans suggested that the Finance Department should subscribe for $25m. This, White said, could not be concealed and, in any case, would be beyond his powers. Morgans then suggested, and it was agreed, that the British should subscribe for $25m, using money borrowed from White.[59] Morgans' Canadian Group took the balance of $24.8m, so that the selling syndicate were entirely relieved and could not know whether the issue was succeeding. On 10 August, White placed $20m on deposit with Morgans for thirty days at 2½ per cent to help carry some of the unsold securities. He was thus taking, or was financing, nearly half the issue. Hardly surprisingly, when the Notes started to trade in the secondary market, the price collapsed. In December, Morgans were still selling their holding at prices as low as 93⅝, a GRY of nearly 10½ per cent, and they were unable to sell the balance until February 1919.[60]

Canada: autumn 1917

In August, the Anglo-Canadian debate had moved from the size of the Canadian financial contribution to how it should be spent. The British continued to press White to place the proceeds of the note issue in a pool for general use and White continued to hold it against purchases of cheese.[61] The British also wanted to reduce munitions expenditure and use part of the Canadians' monthly C$25m to pay for food. But agricultural produce had a wide market, munitions had only one buyer. Fearful of cancelled orders and lay-offs in the munitions industry at a time when Borden was manoeuvring towards a coalition, White wanted all his advances spent by the IMB. The British tried to exploit this. They agreed that the C$25m should be spent on munitions, but argued that the US$15m from New York would have to be used for food 'unless you are in a position to provide further funds in Canada for purchases of essential foodstuffs after the $50m note issue is exhausted.'[62]

One way of maintaining orders would be further to inflate the currency:

> May I take the liberty of urging you to go further in the direction of creating currency against Canadian collateral. It is what we have done in this direction which has enabled us to so far finance the war and I cannot help thinking that you could do much more without serious danger to your American exchange. Though there would undoubtedly be grave disadvantages later the immediate effect would be to increase the volume of Canadian trade and to stimulate general prosperity.[63]

White was unconvinced. He had already delayed issuing the original C$50m of notes, instead using the proceeds of the New York loan and other monies, and he feared criticism and damage to the prospects for the next internal war loan in November. There was to be no further inflation of the issue.[64] At the end of August, White said, and the British accepted, that only his own C$25m would be spent by the IMB and that he would provide no more money for food after the proceeds of the C$50m note issue had been spent.[65] After talks in September between Reading, White and Flavelle, overall Canadian spending – other than for bacon, butter, wheat and oats – was limited to C$40m and the IMB programme was tailored to expenditure of some C$30m per month.[66]

The Royal Wheat Loan

Lever rarely reminded White of the US dollars which the British were spending on other products in Canada, one result of which was to greatly strengthen the Canadian banks' financial position in the USA.[67] Until the summer of 1917, the UK Treasury had been using the proceeds of the securities sold in New York, gold shipments, its American loans and US Treasury advances to support sterling, buying bills on the open market in New York. Besides munitions and War Office supplies, these bills represented a large part of Canadian agricultural sales to the allies: the Canadians may have been lending for munitions, but for most other goods they were receiving US dollars, or sterling bills good for immediate sale into dollars. During the summer of 1917, as other payments were taken off the commercial exchange and settled directly from the UK Treasury account at Morgans, these payments became exposed. In future, if the UK, or the allies, wanted to buy in Canada, using US advances, they would need the explicit agreement of the US Treasury.

The 1916 and 1917 American grain crops were poor, the latter barely sufficing for domestic consumption, and Herbert Hoover, the US Food Administrator, restricted US exports during August and September.[68] The Canadian government was anxious that, if it did not sell, its export trade would suffer permanent damage. The Western grain producing provinces waited anxiously for news that finance was available and shipments could begin.[69] The allies were to buy the Argentinian and Uruguayan crops (see pp. 284–5), but the British were fearful that they themselves, the Italians and the French would be short if the Canadian crop was not bought and shipped.[70] The Canadian crop could start moving in the last week of September and shipping allocations were needed by the middle of that month.[71]

Although the Wheat Commission, the British body responsible for British wheat imports, was prepared to buy the entire Canadian crop, on 10 September its representative in New York, the Wheat Export Company, was told to stop all buying until finance had been arranged.[72] With the Canadians wanting to sell, the allies needing to buy and the USA unable to supply, Reading arrived in the USA on 12 September 1917. White, suffering from a breakdown, was happy to leave matters in Reading's hands. The US Administration was still reluctant to have its advances applied outside the USA, but six days after he arrived Reading persuaded McAdoo that the shipping situation was so urgent that he should advance US$50m in October for Canadian purchases by the UK, France and Italy.[73] There remained a further C$300m to be found. The US Administration, reported Reading,

> never lose opportunity of emphasising dissatisfaction with Canadian financial effort. They will not help Canada until it is much plainer than at present that Canada is prepared to help herself.[74]

Reading met the Canadian Cabinet and bankers at the beginning of October. He told them it would be 'practically impossible' to persuade the US Treasury to provide further help unless the Canadians themselves made a greater effort. If the banks would lend C$100m for at least two years, he had hopes that he could persuade the US Treasury to find the balance of US$200m. The banks and White rose to the bait and they agreed to provide C$100m, one-half in 1917 and one-half in the spring of 1918, when the Great Lakes and St. Lawrence reopened to shipping. The money would be paid direct to the Canadian Wheat Export Company in Winnipeg, acting as agent for London (Table 10.1).[75]

As in 1916, with the Munitions Loans, the agreement was between the Minister of Finance and the President of the CBA 'representing the banks making advances.' Contingent on the Imperial Treasury obtaining C$250m 'from sources outside of Canada for the purchase of Canadian wheat and oats, 1917 crop', the chartered banks agreed to lend C$50m on 1 November and C$10m on 1 January and each of the following four months. The term was one year and, to satisfy the US Treasury, it was renewable at the UK's option for a further year at the same interest rate. The terms were the same as for the Munitions Loans. The security was again Imperial Treasury sterling Bills deposited with the Bank of England for the account of the Minister of Finance as trustee for the banks, with the participation evidenced by (Imperial) Treasury Bill Certificates. The interest rate was 6 per cent, payable by coupon attached to the Certificates. Unlike the Munitions Loans, the banks received no commission and the British met the interest in cash by remittance from Morgans.[76]

Reading appears to have had considerable difficulty persuading the US Treasury to lend the balance of $200m. Crosby was, as usual, concerned at the size of his spending, objected to the use of advances outside the USA and did not want to commit himself more than a week or two ahead. Reading pointed out that, although the UK could supply itself from elsewhere in the Empire, albeit at a cost in shipping space, Italy and France could not. Eventually, Crosby advanced the money, with the request that his assistance be kept secret. A month later the US Treasury agreed that payments for Canadian meat and bacon, and other foodstuffs of which the USA was short and unable to satisfy export demand, could be met from its advances; the British accounts show that during July, August and October they lent $30.6m to Canada in New York for food purchases, presumably against the Canadian dollars which were actually disbursed.[77] The advances were cancelled on 1 April 1919 against sums owed by the UK to the Dominion (see p. 469).[78]

The Canadian Department of Finance continued to place C$25m per month at the disposal of the IMB until the Armistice, and the IMB's expenditure continued to be limited to C$30m. Having almost breached its budget during November 1917, by the end of January 1918 the IMB had accumulated $20m from White's monthly credit. By then, the change in priorities had become overt. In November, there was a threat to transfer part of White's C$25m to food purchases. In March, the Board released C$5m of its credit to the purchase of food. Another C$10m followed in June.[79] By the end of September, the British had built up surpluses of C$60m in Ottawa, which White agreed should be earmarked to the purchases of the new wheat crop. In the year ending 31 March 1919, for the first time, advances for 'Cereals' (C$68.5m) appear in the Dominion Accounts, together with 'foodstuffs (some $18.5m) and dairy produce (C$34.8m)'.[80]

The Pittman Silver Act

Overseas buyers of Indian produce were provided with rupees by the Secretary of State for India selling rupee bills of exchange and telegraphic transfers for sterling in London: that is, selling merchants and bankers the right to draw rupees from the Indian government treasuries in India. This gave the Secretary of State the sterling to meet charges, such as interest on sterling debt, pensions and government purchases. It also provided him with the sterling with which to buy silver for rupee coinage, with the effect that the traditional Indian external payments surplus was settled in bullion. By selling Council Bills for rupees and standing ready to buy rupees for sterling, the Secretary of State held the value of the rupee closely to 1s 4d. If it moved more than about $^1/_8$d above this level, it became cheaper for merchants and bankers to ship gold sovereigns to India, where they would be sold to the government at a fixed price of 15 rupees, or 1s 4d per rupee.

The Indian currency was a mixture of silver rupees, gold sovereigns and currency notes, against which were held sterling and rupee securities, sovereigns, bullion and rupees. The proportion of securities in the paper currency reserve held against notes was limited by law. Before the war, the Indian government had found the coinage of rupees profitable, the value of the silver in a rupee and the cost of manufacture being less than 1s 4d. With war and inflation, there was an increased demand for subsidiary silver coins in Europe, while the silver-based currency systems of India, Japan and China absorbed more of the metal as their economies prospered. This demand met inelastic supply: low prices before the war had closed most of the 'straight' silver mines (mines producing only silver) in the USA, and Mexican output had been reduced by revolution. The price of silver shot up: in 1911, it averaged $24^{19}/_{32}$d an ounce; in 1915, $23^{21}/_{32}$d; in 1916, $31^{5}/_{16}$d; in 1917, $40^{7}/_{8}$d; and in 1918, $47^{9}/_{16}$d. Between 11 and 27 September 1917, it was over 50d an ounce. At the same time, war put strains on Indian finance. The demand for Indian produce – jute, burlap, hides and grain – rose and the current account of its balance of payments moved further into surplus. The British paid for Indian forces in Mesopotamia and East Africa in sterling, while the troops were paid in rupees. The rise in the silver price also threatened to move the bullion value of the rupee above its face value, providing an incentive to melt the coin. Clearly, the Government of India had either to increase the supply of rupees, or raise their price, that is revalue. An increase in supply was limited by a shortage of rupees in the government treasuries in India: the Government of India had sterling in London, but could not convert it into bullion, nor risk shipping it. If more paper rupees were paid out in India without the paper currency reserve acquiring more gold or silver, convertibility would be threatened.

Supplying India with silver to maintain convertibility, while providing US importers with rupees to strengthen the dollar, became the most complex of the allies' credit operations.

On 14 December 1916, the Secretary of State imposed a limit on remittances to India in the form of Council Bills and transfers, at the same time raising the price of rupees to 1s $4^{1}/_{8}$d.[81] When the rate rose to 1s 6d in January 1917, the Secretary of State and the banks came to an agreement to observe rates based on 1s $4^{7}/_{32}$d for transfers and to ensure that such rupees as were available were used for priority war supplies.[82] This provided stability until 28 August 1917 when continued demand for rupees and a further jump in silver prices to 44d forced a rise in the official rate to 1s 5d.[83]

These events affected the USA as a silver producer, as a buyer of Indian produce and as the source of the advances with which the British were buying sterling, including the sterling being sold by the Government of India as it scrambled for the silver output of US mines. The US Treasury first raised the possibility of rupee credits at the end of May 1917.[84] The India Office was prepared to help, but only against bullion because 'India is in acute currency difficulties through shortage both of gold and of silver in hands of Government.'[85] This was not acceptable: the US Treasury was not prepared to make dollar advances to the UK at the same time as it was selling gold against rupees from British India.

The question was one of the first which Reading took up when he arrived in Washington in September 1917. He found the US Treasury sympathetic to India's problems and in a position to help, for it had large holdings of silver acquired under the Bland-Allison Silver Act of 1878 and the Sherman Silver Purchase Act 1890. The latter had been repealed in 1893, but the silver could not be sold without legislation. Several interests would have to be satisfied before this could be passed. The bimetallic controversies of the previous century lay only just beneath the surface and could easily reappear if the US Treasury sold silver without replacing it with new purchases. Agreement would be needed from the senators from the western silver-producing states, who would only agree if it was clearly in the interests of the producers: the price had to rise.[86]

During the autumn and winter of 1917, American importers had an urgent need for rupees and the US Treasury came to see their provision against payment in dollars as a valuable precedent to quote when negotiating for credits in South America against balances held in the USA, France and the UK.[87] The India Office was reluctant:

> India is faced with double danger:– First, of metallic portion of Paper Currency Reserve falling below what is needed to secure convertibility. Second, of Treasury balances falling below what is needed for disbursements of primary importance owing to enormous war payments in India for which return is received only in credits in Europe.[88]

On 26 October, at Keynes's urging, the Secretary of State made an emergency arrangement, opening a credit of 30m rupees ($10.1m) in favour of the New York Federal Reserve Bank for resale to American importers against dollars. In return, export licenses had been issued for silver bought by the Government of India. These purchases led to the suggestion that India and, indeed, all the allies, should allow the US Treasury to become the monopoly buyer of American silver, so placating those silver interests which feared that the US Treasury could offer them a lower price than those being offered elsewhere.[89] To avoid sudden pressure on the Government of India's balances, the rupees were to be released slowly and the dollars paid to India would be used to buy silver: the arrangement, therefore, would settle the Indian payments surplus in bullion and be only a temporary drain on the Government of India's silver rupee balances.[90]

The India Office's forecast for silver demand in 1918–19 was bleak: India would need 200m ounces, an increase from 136m in 1916–17 and about 80m in 1917–18; the US mint was a large buyer for subsidiary coinage and shipments to China and Japan were growing.[91] Shortly before Christmas 1917 there was a meeting between the US Treasury, the silver producers and the western senators. The result was described by Lever on 9 January 1918. US importers needed about 25m rupees each month and 'practically no rupees are available except by arrangement with Government of India'; the US Treasury were convinced that unless something was done the price of silver would rise above $1 an ounce; the only large stock of silver was held by the US Treasury against Silver Certificates and this could not be released without legislation. The silver interests would not give their support unless the US Treasury purchased newly mined silver at $1 an ounce (or 50d in London, including costs) to replace each ounce borrowed from the reserve. Legislation on these lines would enable the USA to meet the demand for silver, but would not of itself provide rupees.[92]

By 16 May, the Government of India's credits at the Federal Reserve Bank of New York had grown to 60.2m rupees ($20m).[93] Bullion holdings were drawn down and during April the Government of India came near to declaring the rupee inconvertible.[94] India needed silver, the USA needed rupees, and neither would be forthcoming unless there was a rise in the price. The Pittman Bill, named after its sponsor, a Senator from silver-producing Nevada, was introduced on 8 April.

It came under threat from sectional interests even as the absorption of rupee coinage was pushing India towards inconvertibility. The US Treasury, in the shape of Leffingwell, responded to Reading's appeal for help and pushed the Bill vigorously. After a message from the President that the Bill should be treated as a war measure of national importance, it passed through Congress in under a week and was approved on 23 April 1918.[95]

The preamble stated that the intention was 'to conserve the gold supply of the United States; to permit the settlement in silver of trade balances adverse to the United States; to provide silver for subsidiary coinage and for commercial use; to assist foreign governments at war with the United States; and for the above purposes to stabilise the price and encourage the production of silver.' It authorised the Secretary of the Treasury to melt and sell as bullion up to 350m silver dollars, the equivalent of about two years' world mining output. The sale price of the bullion was to be a minimum of $1 an ounce and be replaced from the output of US mines, also at $1 an ounce.

On 28 May, Reading reached agreement with the US Treasury on the details of sales to India.[96] The British government would buy 200m of silver at $1 an ounce plus expenses. A quarter of the purchases ($50m) would be settled in gold supplied by India, but this would be deferred until the metallic proportion of the Indian Currency Paper Reserve reached 40 per cent. At that point, gold would begin to be transferred to the USA, but only in such quantities as would leave India's proportion above 40 per cent. In the meantime, India would pay a preliminary $10m in gold as soon as shipment was safe. She would also sell the US telegraphic rupee credits at 42.7 US cents. Until the US Treasury had replaced all the silver it was selling, the British and the Secretary of State for India would not buy at a lower price. In the unlikely event that more dollars were earned through the provision of rupee credits than were needed to settle silver purchases, they would be spent as if they were US Treasury advances to the British: they had to be spent within the US, in a manner satisfactory to the US and, by implication, would reduce the volume of the other advances. In the more likely event that the dollars generated by the sale of rupee credits and the shipment of Indian gold failed to cover the cost of the silver, payment would be made by drawing dollars from the UK Treasury Account with Morgans. Thus, although the US Treasury was careful not to make the connection explicit, the purchases not covered by rupees or gold would be settled from US advances. Reading's last word was to pledge the British and Indian governments to the maintenance of the dollar's parity against the rupee and to assure Leffingwell of the Government of India's 'sympathetic support in maintaining the credit of the dollar in India'.[97]

In principle, if India bought more silver than she sold rupees she could herself have borrowed dollars from the US Treasury. The arrangement whereby the UK borrowed the dollars was to protect India from an exchange loss should the rupee weaken against the dollar, as seems to have been widely predicted, and because of legal difficulties with India assuming a dollar liability.[98] The arrangement, therefore, became a sale of silver by the USA to the UK in return for either Indian rupees or gold, with the balance being met in dollars; an advance of dollars by the

USA to the UK to buy the silver, inasmuch as payment could not be met from gold or rupees; and a purchase of silver by India from the UK settled in sterling.

Under the 'Pittman Silver Act', the Government of India was supplied with 200m ounces of silver, $122m of which was settled by means of advances from the US to the UK Treasury. The advances were made under the Liberty Bond Acts on the same terms as those for current spending on US products, and were evidenced by identical certificates of indebtedness. To the US Treasury, which had made such efforts to make the silver available, they were different and in the summer of 1920, despite British efforts to have them treated like the other debt, it was agreed that obligations to the value of the silver advances should be repaid in annual instalments between 1920 and 1924. The last were repaid early, in 1923–4. As such, they were the only UK Treasury debt to the US government incurred under the Liberty Bond Acts to be repaid in full and thus, bar Cuba, the only allied debt to be so paid.[f]

✤ ✤ ✤

A note on the British and Canadian Accounts

Between 31 March 1915 and 31 March 1919, the UK borrowed some C$859m from the Canadian Department of Finance and the Department of Finance borrowed C$714m from the UK: C$107.6m in the form of dollar Bonds (C$12.4m 3½ per cent War Loan 1925–8 and C$95.2m 4½ per cent War Loan 1925–45); US$30.6m in New York; and the balance in sterling book debt. Between 31 March 1919 and the end of the calendar year, the British made further advances of £22m (C$107.1m, or C$110.4m including interest), mainly, it can be surmised, to finance the repatriation of the Canadian Expeditionary Force, and the Canadians made advances for commercial purchases, such as C$25m for timber, which were drawn when the sterling rate was particularly weak.[99] In addition, the sums owed – on both sides – were adjusted from time to time as bills were presented or expenditure identified and its size determined.

Tables 10.1, 10.2, 10.3 and 15.1 show UK Treasury borrowing from the Finance Department, Finance Department borrowing from the UK Treasury, and UK borrowing from the Canadian private sector between 1914–15 and 1923–4. The general magnitude of the flows, and the size of the outstanding debts, are clear, but the exact figures are not: the Tables' precision is not justified and the data should be treated with caution. Until 1920, the British debt returns did not identify borrowing from the Dominion's Finance Department, instead including it within 'other debt created under the War Loan Acts, 1914–18'. British borrowing from the Canadian banks was never separately identified; since sterling Treasury Bills

f Finland repaid her advances in full, but these had been taken under the Act of 25 February 1919 establishing the American Relief Administration. *ARSF* (1921), pp. 32–5, and (1923), p. 26. I would like to thank Professor Burk for drawing my attention to Finland's virtue.

were deposited as security, the debt was included within the overall Bill issue, with a footnote drawing attention to the amount of Bills 'issued as collateral for sundry loans payable abroad,' only some of which were Canadian.

From 1920 until the debt was paid off in the 1923–4 financial year, the British returns showed gross debt to the Dominion government, but the Dominion accounts only showed the UK's net debt, together with the amount by which it had been reduced during the year, without specifying whether the reduction was produced by cancellation, cash payment or expenditure newly identified. The British and Canadian figures for the UK debt do not agree, but it is unclear whether the reason was, indeed, lack of agreement, or whether there was a residual, offsetting, debt due by Canada to the UK. A separate British publication presenting annual data for gross British external debt agrees with the British Debt returns for the years from 1920 to 1922.[100] To add to the confusion, or explain the confusion, in 1920 the Canadian accounts warn that the amount of the debt was subject to 'final adjustments on the basis of exchange rates' and in 1921, 1922 and 1923 that there were 'further amounts to be determined by agreement when final adjustments' had been made.[101] In the UK, a Treasury Minute in 1920 merely speaks of a 'small account still under consideration.'[102] As these were adjusted, it can be assumed that the amount owing was also adjusted. When, at what stage, of which year, is unknown. In view of the uncertainties, some parts of this text departs from standard practice and refers to round millions of dollars.

There are three other complications. The Canadian accounts treat the $107.6m Bonds issued to the Imperial government in 1916 as funded – debt other than 'temporary' – and, in places, these have to be added back to the data given in the text of the Canadian public accounts. The tables in the Canadian accounts make the position clear. Second, the British lent to their allies, Dominions and colonies on the same terms as they themselves were borrowing, including any discount in the price of issues from which the advance was deemed to have been financed. It started simply. For example, the £2.4m lent from the proceeds of 3½ per cent War Loan 1925–8 (issued at 95) was represented by £2.5m, or C$12.4m, Canadian debt. It ended less simply, with the discount changing as the securities on which the British borrowed changed and then becoming an amalgam of issue prices. Advances were assumed to have been financed rateably from each of the tax-paying issues in each series of War Bonds. Worse, when War Bonds were issued with conversion options, the terms became provisional, to be determined only when it was known how many were converted into which new securities.[103] A further complication was that the Bonds represented sterling advances in London, but were denominated in Canadian dollars. The equivalent of the sterling in Canadian dollars was calculated by taking the rate of exchange ruling on the day of the original advances. These were deemed to have been made on twenty-four occasions between 30 September 1914 and 30 September 1915, at rates between $4.64 and $4.922. The effect of the two adjustments was to open a gap between the cash advanced and its 'capitalised' value. The latter has been used here.[104] Third, once sterling had been unpegged in the first quarter of 1919, it becomes impossible to state how much Canadian dollar debt was repaid by the sterling the

UK Treasury reported it had spent. Some of the Canadian dollars came from US dollar deposits with Morgans, and sterling was weaker against the US dollar than the Canadian dollar. Some were purchased in the commercial market. Some came from the Exchange Account, in which the price paid for a particular dollar cannot be identified.

Thus, the only sources for debt transactions between 1915 and 1919 are the Canadian accounts, and the British and Canadian sources for 1920, 1921, 1922 and 1923 cannot be reconciled. Tables 10.2 and 10.3, until 1919, are based on the Canadian accounts, with notes calling attention to where they disagree with the British versions, where one exists. From 1920, Table 10.2 records both Canadian and British versions. The differences are never more than C$10.3m (31 March 1920) and then fall away steadily as the sums involved are reduced. By the final year, 1924, the difference is only C$3.2m.

Endnotes

1 *ARSF* (1918), pp. 38–9; *A Bill to Supplement the Second Liberty Bond Act*, Hearings before the Committee of Ways and Means, US House of Representatives, 12 September 1918, pp. 29–33.
2 T 172/443, ff. 7–20, Chancellor to McAdoo, 30 July 1917. Reproduced in Keynes (1971–89), XVI, pp. 255–63.
3 FO 371/3116, no. 2167, Lever to Chancellor, 10/11 August 1917; T 172/433, ff. 6–9, Reading to Chancellor, 29 September 1917; PML, Archives, Box 14, ff. 227–8, Jack Morgan to McAdoo, 7 August 1917.
4 FO 371/3116, nos 2279 and 2370, Lever to Chancellor, 21/23 and 29/30 August 1917; ibid., no. 2382, Lever to Chancellor, 30/31 August 1917; T 172/431, ff. 67–8, Lever to Chancellor, 20 August 1917, and f. 55, Lever to Chancellor, 21 August 1917; T 172/435, ff. 106–7, Chancellor to Lever, 4 September 1917; T 172/449, f. 148, Chalmers to Lever, 8 February 1918.
5 FO 371/3116, unnumbered, Spring-Rice to FO, 3/4 August 1917, and no. 3069, Chancellor to Spring-Rice, 4 August 1917.
6 Ibid., no. 2523, Spring-Rice to FO, 31 August/2 September 1917.
7 Ibid., no. 2578, Spring-Rice to FO, 5 September 1917; BoE, C91/12, f. 50, 'American Gold Export Prohibition', 8 September 1917.
8 T 172/433, ff. 6–9, Reading to Chancellor, 29 September 1917; T 172/437, ff. 69–73, Reading to Chancellor, 17 October 1917, and ff. 43–7, Chancellor to Reading, 25 October 1917; T 170/124, ff. 49–53, Crosby to Lansing (copy), 18 October 1917, and ff. 4–7 and 54, undated and unsigned notes; MGP, B. Hist. 2, F. 16, no. 44839, Lamont to JPM, 19 November 1917, and no. 55812, Jack Morgan to Lamont, 22 November 1917; Keynes (1971–89), XVI, pp. 291–3.
9 T 170/124, ff. 49–53, Crosby to Lansing (copy), 18 October 1917; T 172/439, f. 127–9, Lever to Chancellor, 6 December 1917, and f. 102, Chancellor to Lever, 12 December 1917, and f. 66, Lever to Chancellor, 15 December 1917; BoE, C91/20, LEC, Minutes, 14 November 1917 and 6 December 1917; Osborne (1926), II, pp. 29–31; Haig (1929), Tables 30, 31 and 32.
10 *A Bill to Supplement the Second Liberty Bond Act*, Hearings before the Committee of Ways and Means, US House of Representatives, 12 September 1918, p. 31.
11 *External Debt as on 31 March 1919, 31 March 1920, 31 March 1921 and 31 March 1922* (Cmd. 1648), 1922; Haig (1929), Tables 30, 31 and 32.

12 BoE, OV61/25, 'Relations with the Bank of Spain', January 1927, and C91/19, LEC, Minutes, 20 August 1917, and C91/20, 5 February 1918. Morgan (1952), pp. 345–8; *FRUS* (1917, Supplement 2, The World War, Volume II), pp. 1199–1230, gives the trade background to the agreement of December 1917; ibid., (1918, Supplement I, The World War, Volume II), pp. 1697–1702, Davis to Leffingwell, 11 and 16 August 1918; T 172/437, ff. 164, Reading to Chancellor, 8 October 1917. A draft of the abortive agreement of 6 December 1917 is in T 1/12121/44247.

13 T 172/448, ff. 58–60, Lever to Chancellor, 19 January 1917.

14 Morgan (1952), pp. 345–8; *FRUS* (1918, Supplement I, The World War, Volume II), pp. 1697–9, Davis to Leffingwell, 11 August 1918; Osborne (1926), II, pp. 62–6; BoE, C91/20, LEC, Minutes, 23 November 1917, 22 March and 16, 23 and 30 April 1918.

15 Osborne (1926), II, pp. 67–9; BoE, C91/19, LEC, Minutes, 17 July, and 20 and 21 August, and 9 and 19 October 1917; T 172/433, f. 12, Bradbury to Reading, 29 September 1917; *The Economist*, 28 September 1918, pp. 397–8; Ministry of Munitions (1921), II, Part VII, pp. 1–8.

16 Osborne (1926), II, pp. 35–42; *The Economist*, 19 June 1920, p. 1343; MGP, B. Hist. 3, F. 20, no. 66412, Grenfell to JPM, 7 May 1919.

17 Osborne (1926), II, pp. 55–7; BoE, C98/6937; *External Debt as on 31 March 1919, 31 March 1920, 31 March 1921 and 31 March 1922* (Cmd. 1648), 1922. The latter source gives the due date of the UK share of the joint allied loan as 31 July and of the forest products, iron ore and shipping loans as 30 June.

18 Tansill (1932), especially Chapters II, V, VI and VIII.

19 *FRUS* (1917), pp. 457–706; *ARSF* (1917), p. 34.

20 BoE, C91/12, f. 182, Mahon to Treasury, 16 November 1917, and draft of letter from representative of Danish government, f. 183, November 1917; MGP, B. Hist. 3, F. 17, no. 57194, JPM to MG, 4 December 1917.

21 BoE, C91/12, ff. 14–15 and 23, Kengo Mori (Financial Commissioner of the Imperial Japanese Government in London) to Cunliffe, 17 and 22 August 1917; *The Economist*, 13 October 1917, p. 530.

22 BoE, C91/12, f. 227, Cunliffe to Kengo Mori, and f. 226, Bank of England to Chancellor, 3 December 1917; ibid., C91/13, ff. 17–20, Kengo Mori to Cunliffe, 17 December 1917, and f. 16, Cunliffe to Bradbury, 18 December 1917.

23 Ministry of Munitions (1921), II, Part IV, p. 56.

24 NAC, RG 19/763/304–5, IMB to Finance Department, 23 February 1916, and Finance Department to IMB, 24 February 1916; Ministry of Munitions (1921) II, Part IV, pp. 56–7.

25 NAC, RG 19/763/304–5, Ross, 'Memorandum re advances on Imperial Government account', and White to Perley, both 26 October 1915; ibid., Borden to Perley, 15 November 1915; Bliss (1992), pp. 269–70; Ministry of Munitions (1921) II, Part IV, p. 56. Difficulties with selling sterling in a thin foreign exchange market are documented in T 170/62.

26 NAC, RG 19/763/304–5, White to Boville (Deputy Minister of Finance), 10 December 1915, and Boville to Flavelle (Chairman of the IMB), 15 December 1915.

27 NAC, RG 19/763/304–5, White to Perley, 4 December 1915, and Perley to White, 13 December 1915.

28 NAC, RG 19/763/304–5, Perley to White, 1 January 1916, and White to Perley, 5 and 7 January 1916. The system was made formal at the end of February 1916. See NAC, RG 19/763/304–5, Bradbury to Perley, 24 February 1916.

29 NAC, RG 19/763/304–5, Ross to Perley, 20 April 1916; Ministry of Munitions (1921), II, Part IV, p. 57.

30 Bliss (1992), pp. 269–70 and 285; Knox (1940), Table III; T 170/134, f. 40, Chadwick, 'British Government Transactions in America', 1922; BoE, C91/10, f. 6, 'Dollar Obligations in Canada and U.S.A.', no date; Ministry of Munitions (1921), II, Part IV, pp. 58–9.

31 NAC, RG19/596/155–35–13, 'Memo re loan by Canadian Chartered Banks to Imperial Treasury', end-1920.
32 Burk (1985), pp. 77–8; Ministry of Munitions (1921), II, Part IV, pp. 59–60.
33 Ministry of Munitions (1921), II, Part IV, pp. 61–2.
34 *Canada, Public Accounts for the Fiscal Year ended March 31 1917*, p. XI; Ministry of Munitions (1921), II, Part IV, p. 62.
35 Knox (1940), Tables I and IX.
36 Carnegie (1925), pp. 127 and 133, and Appendix III; Ministry of Munitions (1921), II, Part IV, pp. 2, 35 and 64–5.
37 NAC, RG 19/596/155–38–3, Report of the Committee of the Privy Council, 15 January 1917; ibid., Union Bank of Canada to Boville, 26 December 1916, and Boville to Sterling Bank of Canada, 19 January 1917; Bliss (1992), pp. 315–16. The Finance Department wrote, very firmly, at the top of its letters 'Re Imperial Munitions Loan' and the proceeds were paid into a special account.
38 *Canada, Public Accounts for the Fiscal Year ended March 31 1917*, p. X.
39 Ibid., p. XI; Bliss (1992) pp. 315–16.
40 T 172/432, ff. 128–30, Chancellor to Lever, 21 May 1917.
41 NAC, RG 19/596/155–38–2, CBA to Assistant Deputy Minister of Finance, 12 June 1917, and the Dominion Bank to Boville, 5 July 1917. The records of the allotments are scattered throughout this file.
42 T 172/432, ff. 128–30, Chancellor to Lever (draft by Keynes), 21 May 1917; T 172/429, Lever's Diary, 10 May 1917.
43 T 172/432, ff. 128–30, Chancellor to Lever (draft by Keynes), 21 May 1917.
44 T 172/432, ff. 128–30, Chancellor to Lever (draft by Keynes), 21 May 1917; ibid., f. 114, Lever to Chancellor, 10 June 1917, and f. 109, Chancellor to Lever, 26 June 1917; ibid., ff. 95–6, Flavelle to Minister of Munitions, 2 July 1917.
45 Ibid., f. 115, Chancellor to Lever, 8 June 1917.
46 Ibid., ff. 101–3, Chancellor to Canadian government, 30 June 1917; ibid., ff. 80–1, Keynes to Davidson, 4 July 1917.
47 Ibid., ff. 95–6, Brand to Ministry of Munitions, 2 July 1917; ff. 85–94, Addison, 'The Financial Position in Canada', 3 July 1917.
48 Ibid., ff. 83–4, Lever to Chancellor, 4 July 1917; ibid., f. 76, Lever to Chancellor, 5 July 1917; ibid., ff. 74–5, Borden to Lloyd George, 7 July 1917; ibid., f. 73, Chancellor to White, 9 July 1917.
49 Ibid., f. 73, Chancellor to White, 9 July 1917.
50 Ibid., ff. 74–5, Borden to Lloyd George, 7 July 1917, and f. 64, Lever to Chancellor, 20 July 1917; ibid., ff. 62–3, White to Chancellor, 21 July 1917, and ff. 57–9, Chancellor to Lever, 26 July 1917.
51 Ibid., ff. 57–9, Chancellor to Lever, 26 July 1917.
52 Ibid., ff. 52–4, Chancellor to Lever, copy of cable to Governor General of Canada for White, 1 August 1917.
53 Ibid., f. 51, Governor General to Chancellor, 7 August 1917, and ff. 46–7, Chancellor to White, 9 August 1917.
54 Ibid., ff. 44–5, Lever to Chancellor, 9 August 1917, and f. 37, Chancellor to White, 18 August 1917; T 172/431, ff. 74–5, Chancellor to Lever, 18 August 1917.
55 *The New York Times*, 26 July 1917, p. 16.
56 MGP, B. Hist. 2, F. 16, no. 47895, JPM to Grenfell, 21 July 1917.
57 *The New York Times*, 25 November 1917, pp. 1 and 15, and 26 November 1917, pp. 1 and 10, and onwards.
58 PML, Archives, Box 14, f. 243, Jack Morgan to Grenfell, 9 August 1917.
59 T 172/432, ff. 46–7, Lever to Chancellor, 9 August 1917.
60 PML, Archives, Syndicates No. 9, ff. 49–51.
61 T 172/432, f. 69, Lever to Chancellor, 17 July 1917, and f. 51, Governor General to Chancellor, 7 August 1917; ibid., f. 27, Lever to Chancellor, 29 August 1917, and f. 26, Chancellor to Lever and Blackett, 30 August 1917; T 171/431, f. 58, Chancellor to Lever, 21 August 1917.

62 Ibid., ff. 44–5, Lever to Chancellor, 9 August 1917, and f. 33, Chancellor to White, 23 August 1917.
63 Ibid., ff. 17–18, Chancellor to White, 1 September 1917.
64 Ibid., f. 15, White to Chancellor, 6 September 1917, and ff. 4–5, Lever to Chancellor, 11 September 1917.
65 Ibid., f. 43, Lever to Chancellor, 13 August 1917, and f. 26, Chancellor to Lever and Blackett, 30 August 1917.
66 Ibid., ff. 23 and 23A, Ministry of Munitions to Flavelle, 1 September 1917, and ff. 17–18, Chancellor to White, 1 September 1917; T 172/433, ff. 91–3, Chancellor to Reading, 17 September 1917, ff. 73–4, Reading to Chancellor, 19 September 1917, and ff. 68–70, Reading to Chancellor, 19 September 1917.
67 Such an occasion is recorded in T 172/432, ff. 44–5, Lever to Chancellor, 9 August 1917. For the strength of the Canadian banks' finances, see T 172/432, ff. 80–1, Keynes to Davidson, 4 July 1917. The Canadians' position in New York can be traced through the reports on the Canadian banks in the *Bankers' Magazine* for 1916–18.
68 Livermore (1966), pp. 48–9; T 172/437, f. 125, Chancellor to Reading, 5 October 1917.
69 T 172/432, ff. 2–3, Northcliffe to Long, Chancellor and Phillips, 11 September 1917.
70 T 172/435, ff. 80–1, Chancellor to Lever, 7 September 1917; T 172/432, f. 1, Chancellor to Lever, 13 September 1917; French (1995), pp. 194 and 209; Harris, 'Bureaucrats and Businessmen in British Food Control, 1916–19,' in Burk (1982), pp. 143–4.
71 T 172/432, f. 1, Chancellor to Lever, 13 September 1917.
72 Ibid., ff. 11–12, Colonial Office to Governor General, 10 September 1917. The Wheat Export Company also had authority to buy for the French and Italians.
73 T 172/433, ff. 68–70, Reading to Chancellor, 19 September 1917.
74 Ibid., f. 8–9, Reading to Chancellor, 29 September 1917.
75 T 172/437, ff. 109–10, Reading to Chancellor, 6 October 1917; NAC, RG19/595/155–35–4, 'Memorandum of Agreement', 31 October 1917.
76 NAC, RG19/596/155–35–13, 'Memo re loan by Canadian Chartered Banks to Imperial Treasury', end-1920. The papers for the initial transaction, including a copy of the 'Memorandum of Agreement', are in NAC, RG 19/595/155–35–4.
77 T 172/433, ff. 73–4, Reading to Chancellor, 20 September 1917; T 172/437, ff. 91–3 and 100, Reading to Chancellor, 12 October 1917, and f. 132, Reading to Chancellor, 3 October 1917 (two cables); CO 42/1014, ff. 347, Blackett, April 1919, and ff. 470–1, 'Dominion of Canada', statement of capital book debt outstanding, 31 March 1919; Ministry of Munitions (1921) II, Part IV, p. 72. The $30.6m is entered in the Canadian accounts as 'Credit Account.'
78 *Canadian Government (Advances)* (Cmd. 583), TM, 1 January 1920.
79 Ministry of Munitions (1921), II, Part IV, pp. 72–3 and Appendix III.
80 T 172/446, ff. 34–5, Chancellor to Reading, 20 July 1918, and ff. 32–3, Lever to Chancellor, 2 August 1918; *Canada, Public Accounts for the Fiscal Year ended 31 March 1918*, p. XII, and *1919*, p. XII; Ministry of Munitions (1921), II, Part IV, p. 73; CO 42/1029, Blackett, April 1919. There is also an item, 'Salmon Pack', of Can$8.8m. The Canadian Public Accounts change their food categories between 1918 and 1919, and the comparisons made here are not exact.
81 IOL, L/F/5/35, f. 6, Secretary of State to Viceroy, 14 December 1916.
82 IOL, L/F/5/35, ff. 21–2, Viceroy to Secretary of State, 6 January 1917; ibid., ff. 24–5, 10 January 1917; ibid., ff. 29–30, India Office to Chartered Bank of India, Australia and China, 18 January 1917.
83 Keynes (1971–89), I and XV; Spalding (1924), pp. 40–69 and 328–45; IOL, L/F/5/33, f. 474, India Office to Colonial Office, 6 September 1917; ibid., L/F/5/100, f. 75, 'Monthly Absorption of Rupees', 1905–6 to 1922–3; ibid., f. 199, 'Net Increase or Decrease in Circulation of Rupee Notes and Coin in India'; ibid., f. 180, 'Silver received for coinage into rupees and amount of rupees coined, 1899–1900 to 1918–19'; ibid., L/F/5/33, ff. 413–14, Secretary of State to Viceroy, 16 August 1917.

84 T 172/427, f. 132, Crawford to FO, 8 June 1917, and ff. 102–3, Chancellor to Lever, 20 June 1917; T 172/429, Lever's Diary, 21 June 1917; IOL, L/F/5/36, f. 1, 'Note by American Ambassador', 31 May 1917.

85 IOL, L/F/5/36, f. 4, Chancellor to Lever, 20 June 1917.

86 T 172/433, ff. 39–41, Reading to Chancellor and Montagu, 25 September 1917; T 172/438, ff. 10–13; Lever to Chancellor and Montagu, 27 November 1917; T 172/439, f. 26, Lever to Montagu, 24 December 1917; Spalding (1924), pp. 44–50.

87 IOL, L/F/5/36, f. 13, Telegram drafted by US authorities and handed by Keynes to Abrahams, October 1917.

88 T 172/437, ff. 122–3, Phillips to Reading, 6 October 1917.

89 IOL, L/F/5/36, ff. 15–16, Reading to Chancellor, 2 November 1917, and f. 16, India Office to Treasury, 8 November 1917; ibid., f. 17, Secretary of State to Viceroy, 15 November 1917; ibid., f. 18–19, Lever to Chancellor, 13 November 1917, and ff. 24–5, Lever to Chancellor and Secretary of State, 27 November 1917.

90 T 172/437, f. 36, note in Keynes's hand, 27 October 1917, ff. 37–9, Montagu to Reading, 26 October 1917 (two cables), and ff. 11–12, Reading to Chancellor and Montagu, 30 October 1917; Keynes (1971–89), XVI, p. 265. Keynes was certainly the 'well-informed member' of Reading's mission who was quoted by the Secretary of State as urging rupee credits 'in view of the large credits which are being opened on behalf of the Allies in the States.' IOL, L/F/5/36, f. 14, Secretary of State to Viceroy, 25 October 1917.

91 IOL, L/F/5/36, f. 45, Note for Lord Reading, 21 January 1918.

92 IOL, L/F/5/36, f. 31, Lever to Chancellor and Secretary of State, 18 December 1917, and ff. 35–6, Memorandum of an interview between Kent, Lever and Blackett, 18 December 1917.

93 IOL, L/F/5/36, f. 155, Appendix.

94 LGP, F/40/1/10, Islington to Lloyd George, 15 April 1918.

95 A detailed and fascinating account of the events surrounding the passage of the Bill is provided by Reading in IOL, L/F/5/36, ff. 279–85, Reading to FO, 22 July 1918.

96 The text of the letter from Reading to Leffingwell, which constitutes the agreement, is in IOL, L/F/5/34, pp. 1015–17.

97 The agreements are reprinted in IOL, L/F/5/36, ff. 288–91, Reading to Leffingwell, 28 May 1918, and Leffingwell to Reading, 4 June 1918. Also see ibid., L/F/5/34, ff. 1013–15, Reading to FO, 7 June 1918.

98 IOL, L/F/5/35, p. 246, India Office to Blackett, 27 February 1920, and p. 266, Viceroy to Secretary of State for India, 17 April 1920.

99 *Canadian Government (Advances)* (Cmd. 651), TM, 29 March 1920; CO 42/1014, ff. 495–6, Heath to High Commissioner for Canada, 25 March 1919. There is other correspondence on the timber advance in the same file. The credit was originally arranged for $50m.

100 *External Debt as on 31 March 1919, 31 March 1920, 31 March 1921 and 31 March 1922* (Cmd. 1648), 1922.

101 *Canada, Public Accounts for the Fiscal Year ending March 31 1920*, p. xi, *1921*, p. xii, *1922*, p. xiii, and *1923*, p. xii.

102 *Canadian Government (Advances)* (Cmd. 583), TM, 1920.

103 NAC, RG 19/2670, Treasury to the Under-Secretary of State, the CO, 22 April 1919.

104 For the calculations, see NAC, RG19/596/155–35–13, unsigned and undated. A copy of the Report of the Committee of the Privy Council, 28 August 1916, which authorised the arrangement, is in the same file. An example of the effect is to be found in *Canada, Public Accounts for the Fiscal Year ended March 31 1916*, p. xiii.

11 Bonar Law's Loans

> Dear Sir, It is heartbreaking to read in the The Daily Mail everyday, a request for money for the War Loan when one has not any to give, as I have no money I am hoping you can turn this bracelet into a Bullet, appreciating your efforts with Mr. Lloyd George.
> Believe me, Yours Sincerely, A. Mother, Essex.
>
> An anonymous letter to the Chancellor, 15 February 1917, T 172/696. Quoted by Bonar Law in *Hansard* (Commons), col. 1701, 26 February 1917.

At the end of March 1917, 5 per cent War Loan 1929–47 represented half of the nominal value of the Debt. It thus maintained the tradition of a single dominating issue: 2½ per cent Consols, then 3½ per cent War Loan 1925–8 and 4½ per cent War Loan 1925–45. The comfort to be derived from precedent went no further. Consols bore a low nominal interest rate and redemption was only at the Treasury's option. In 1888, they were created from a position of strength. The War Loans came out of weakness. They bore a high interest rate and were dated. To sell the 1915 Loan and the Exchequer Bonds, the Treasury had offered conversion privileges. These, accumulating over five issues during 1915 and 1916, meant that earlier issues with lower interest rates would dissolve into one long security if it bore a higher interest rate. The reliance on occasional open-ended war loans added to this loss of control over the structure. 'Spectacular' loans were long anticipated and, when they came, were sold on a wave of patriotism, compared with those in Germany, and treated as symbols of financial power and resilience. To the propaganda advantages of a large total was added the need for a method of continuously tapping the public's savings as incomes flowed. Thus, there was a financial justification for techniques that artificially inflated subscriptions: partly paid issues and advances from the banks, with payment or repayment out of their depositors' future savings. It was, perhaps, inevitable that this produced subscriptions which were out of proportion to many investors' ability to repay.

The decision to launch a new internal loan was made within days of Bonar Law's appointment as Chancellor on 10 December 1916. On 23 December, he told the Treasury subcommittee of the CLCB that:

> for the time being the credit of the Government in the City of London stood higher than the credit of the late Government had been for the past few months, and that the German peace note was taken by the ordinary investor to mean not only that Germany was suing for peace but that she needed it. These two considerations...made the present moment a very favourable one for bringing out a new loan...In his [Bonar Law's] view it was essential that the new loan should be primarily one for converting the 4½% and funding the short loans and that the amount of new money to be obtained was a secondary consideration.[1]

That day the Treasury Bill issue had reached a peak of £1,149m and officials and bankers had no doubt that it should be reduced: its growth and size had been widely criticised during McKenna's Chancellorship and a reduction would help mark off the new regime and improve financial confidence. The apparently eccentric emphasis on converting the 4½ per cent War Loan reflected the Treasury's inability to raise new money in the long end of the gilt-edged market unless conversion was offered to holders of earlier issues, a task which the Bank had advised would be complex, labour intensive and time-consuming. The sooner investors used their options, even at a cost to the Exchequer, the sooner the government would once more have access to long-dated money. Conversion would also encourage investors. A suspicion had developed during the previous year that the Treasury had been relying on Exchequer Bonds and Treasury Bills, primarily, or even solely, to evade paying the higher rate on the converted debt, and that the government was reneging on its contracts. Part of the improved credit of which Bonar Law spoke depended on the Treasury giving investors an opportunity to exercise their rights.

Bonar Law had two advantages not available to his predecessor in 1915. The war savings movement provided him with an organisation which was in touch with individual investors and experienced in selling and distributing fractional Exchequer Bonds and Savings Certificates. For the first time, it was possible to sell securities at a local level, exploiting patriotism and self-interest to present a message that coupled saving to release resources for the war with lending the proceeds to the nation. In a very different sector of the economy, industrial and commercial concerns had accumulated balances from profits and depreciation which they were unable to distribute or spend in wartime. A long-dated issue was not such companies' natural investment, as contemporaries appreciated, but some might be persuaded to subscribe.[2] After the war, the authorities would find sales by businesses – or their unwillingness to reinvest the proceeds of maturing issues – a recurring problem.

The new savings organisation was an advantage in tapping the very small saver and creating the right 'atmosphere', but the most important institutional lever over millions of savers remained the banks and their branches. Once again, the CLCB wielded great influence although, on this occasion, its members did not themselves subscribe for large amounts for cash. Learning from 1915, the Treasury consulted the banks on the terms. Later, their branch networks sold and administered the issues. Encouraging investors to borrow and apply for more than they could currently afford meant lengthy negotiations on the terms that the banks should offer customers, and that the Bank of England should offer the banks if they subsequently wanted cash. The authorities, who had been concerned for a year about the proportion of the banks' assets tied up in long-dated paper, introduced a scheme which enabled them to convert their holdings of the 4½ per cents into Exchequer Bonds. In the same breath, however, the need for a spectacular result made the Chancellor propose that they convert their Bill holdings into the new Loan.[3] Later, the banks underwrote sufficient to ensure that applications would exceed those for McKenna's Loan.

A departure was the organisation of subscriptions by institutional investors other than the banks, notably the insurance companies, investment trusts and local authorities. They lacked liquid resources and strong savings inflows such as the Chancellor was seeking, so that the financing of their subscriptions – which in the case of the investment trust scheme never materialised – depended on advances from the banks that could only be repaid over the very long term.

It was the patriotic drum which enabled the Chancellor to overcome the problem of pricing. He had inherited from McKenna plans for two issues – 4 per cent tax-compounded[a] and 5 per cent subject to tax – and, although there were notable differences of opinion among those in the City whom the Chancellor consulted, by the end of December officials had selected the approximate yields. The City's lack of agreement was mainly the fault of the bankers and, in particular, of Holden, mesmerised by the attractions of a tax-free issue. The differences also reflected the lack of issues trading in the secondary market able to indicate investors' preferences on term and yield and ignorance, notably among some bankers, of the effect that length could, or should, have on yield.

The 1917 War Loans

Cost, date, tax privileges and price support

Besides its sheer size, five features of the 5 per cent Loan were to be of importance after the war: the nominal interest rate, the first optional redemption date, the Depreciation Fund, the Death Duty clause and the payment of interest to all holders without deduction of withholding tax.

The most important influence in the selection of the yield on a new issue was, and is, those available on similar issues in the secondary market: this, after all, shows how the investor is thinking and behaving. In 1917, there were no government securities comparable to the issues the Treasury was envisaging. There were Bills with lives of up to one year: Exchequer Bonds, with those marketable maturing in between thirty-two and fifty-six months; some £60m 3½ per cent War Loan, an eight- to eleven-year issue with the unique attraction of automatic borrowing facilities at the Bank; the rump of Consols, redeemable after 1923,

a For the meaning of tax-compounded, see p. 713.

with a low nominal interest rate and increasingly unmarketable; and the bulky 4½ per cent War Loan, with a twenty-year option and the right to convert into any medium- or long-dated wartime issue, so that the price rose with the imminence of a new loan. There were no tax-free securities with which to compare the 4 per cent tax-compounded Loan. Restricted as it was, the Treasury selected as indicators Consols and the long-dated debt of entities enjoying a government guarantee and of other high-class borrowers. Consols yielded £4 10s 6d per cent; 3 per cent Irish Land Stock, redeemable after 1939, yielded £5 6s 2d per cent; 3 per cent Local Loans, redeemable since 1912, yielded £5 0s 0d per cent; three colonial issues yielded between £5 3s 9d per cent and £5 6s 3d per cent; three local authority issues yielded between £4 17s 3d per cent (a perpetual Liverpool loan) and £5 11s 10d per cent; and three railway debentures gave between £4 16s 9d per cent and £5 2s 7d per cent.[4]

Such a pricing exercise had its dangers: the latter issues were of lower quality and judgement of relative credit risk was subjective; the price for a normal-sized issue would be higher than that for a large; the value of liquidity in an issue which would tower above all others was difficult to evaluate; selling the whole, all at once, meant that pricing would have to be generous. The discount and the long option period opened up a large difference between the GRY calculated to 1929, when the issue could be called, and 1947, when repayment was mandatory. The comparisons of term and nominal interest rate were particularly inexact: in this case the nominal interest rate would be 1½ or 2 per cent higher than those on the pre-war issues being used for comparison. This said, to the historian, the approximate basis for the new taxable Loan was clear: 5 per cent would be too low; 6 per cent absurdly high; 5½ per cent would be generous. In short, the yield of £5 6s 8d per cent (to 1947) actually selected was sufficiently close to that dictated by existing market levels as to make it likely that it was the major influence on the choice.

That officials identified the approximate yield without difficulty is suggested by the early agreement that the nominal rate should be 5 per cent on the taxable issue, with the precise yield, determined by moving the price, not being selected until the last moment. On 27 December, Norman recorded that the price seemed certain to be 96. Two days later, before meeting the Treasury subcommittee of the CLCB, the Chancellor was told by Horace Hamilton, his private secretary, that Lever, Chalmers and Bradbury preferred 95, rather than 96, which 'would imperil the success of the Loan'.[5] The first item in a briefing paper for the bankers' meeting was the price at which a 5 per cent Loan with a life of thirty years yielded 5¼ per cent. It was 96¼. The same paper suggested (although still with a question mark) a 5 per cent thirty-year issue, subject to tax, at 95 and gives the GRY as £5 6s 9d

b Schuster reported that Sir Robert Nivison believed that 90 per cent of the members of the London Stock Exchange favoured a taxable 5 per cent Loan at par, or 'possibly' 97 or 98 and a yield of 5 per cent was endorsed by at least one of those present at a meeting between the Chancellor and the Stock Exchange Committee on 2 January. CLCBm, 29 December 1916; T 172/746, 2 January 1917.

per cent gross, and £4 0s 6d per cent after tax at £0 5s 0d. A nominal rate of 4 per cent was proposed for the tax-compounded issue.[6]

Although the advice from members of the Stock Exchange was close to that of the officials, the bankers' ideas were very different.[b] They were also far from unanimous and, thanks to disagreements between Schuster and Holden, chaotically presented. On 22 December, Holden, in the absence of Schuster, persuaded a reluctant meeting of the full CLCB that 'the only possible terms' were 4½ per cent tax free (6 per cent gross with income tax taken as 5s), with 'possibly an equivalent for the non-income tax payer.' He pointed out that 4 per cent tax-free at 89, 5½ per cent at 91½ subject to tax at 5s and 4½ per cent tax-free at par all gave net yields of 4½ per cent. He thus ignored the discount, valuing the Loans only on their running yield.[7] Later the same day, Schuster, like the Chancellor, gave priority to the conversion of the 4½s when telling the Treasury subcommittee of the CLCB (with Holden absent) that he did not, 'like Sir Edward Holden', favour 'a spectacular war loan'. The subcommittee decided that there would be a successful conversion if two issues were offered: 4 per cent tax-free and 5 per cent taxable, both at 95, to yield £4 4s 2d per cent net with tax at 4s. Thus, once again, the value of the discount was ignored. There would be a sinking fund and a term of 25–50 years. If the Chancellor wanted to raise a 'large' amount of new money and reduce the floating debt, the price of both Loans should be reduced to 'about 90.'[8] This lightly given advice would have added £0 5s 10d per cent to the running yield of the taxable Loan and £0 4s 8d per cent to that on the tax-compounded, while giving grotesque GRYs of £4 12s 4d per cent and £5 13s 11d per cent (to 1947). The following day, Vassar-Smith admitted to the Chancellor that there was disagreement between the two bankers and Schuster stressed that he had been looking at the question from the point of view of conversion: he did not think more favourable terms would make 'much difference to the amount of new money' that would be raised, which both he and Vassar-Smith agreed would be no more than £50m to £80m.[9]

The bankers took three formal resolutions to a meeting with the Chancellor on the 29 December. Two were unanimous: that 4 per cent tax-compounded at par would 'not even ensure conversion of the 4½% War Loan, and would fail entirely to obtain either new money or conversion of Treasury Bills' and that an 'effective Sinking Fund' was necessary. The third, proposed by Holden and opposed by Schuster, split the CLCB ten to four, and was carried: the Loan must be tax-free and yield 4½ per cent net. It 'might be accompanied', if the Chancellor thought it 'necessary', by a parallel Loan subject to tax. Vassar-Smith explained that the first resolution was the Committee's opinion on a suggestion made by the Chancellor at the meeting on 23 December of a tax-free 4 per cent loan and that the disagreement on the third resolution came from a large minority, led by Schuster, believing that 4½ per cent net was too liberal and 4¼ per cent sufficient.[10]

The assumption in the CLCB's discussions was that the yield on a tax-free Loan, re-christened 'tax-compounded' at Schuster's request, should be the same as the net yield on a Loan liable to tax: the investor would pay nothing for insurance against higher taxes.[11] Ignoring this, the Treasury priced it to give a lower yield than the net return on the taxable issue. In other words, it was to be a speculation on a further rise in the rate of income tax and the investor had to pay for the protection. The Chancellor himself disliked the tax-compounded Loan on principle: *The Economist* reported that he had called it an 'excrescence'. Like McKenna in 1915, he thought it would be unpopular in the Commons and would appear to favour the rich. The day before lists closed in the middle of February, Bonar Law received a deputation from the Trades Union Congress:

> I very carefully considered that [the tax-compounded loan] before I agreed to do it, and neither Sir Edward Holden nor anyone else influenced me…They [investors] are not getting any benefit unless income tax goes above 5/s., not merely at a particular time but over an average of the whole 25 years. I have only put that in because I thought that the people who own money are a very timid race and they might think that gentlemen like you might be in power some time soon and they would like to be sure of something. (Laughter.)

Not only was it a speculation, but the timid would have to pay for the luxury of sleeping well.[12] There is no record to confirm the supposition, but, as at the end of the year when issuing a tax-compounded National War Bond, it was probably the prospect of raising a substantial sum and pressure from the bankers which led the Chancellor to ignore his instincts.

The bankers' discussions show them to have been both ignorant of traded debt and content to subordinate their advice to the parochial needs of their own banks. Holden and Schuster, although both members of the LEC and aware of the crisis facing the country in its New York payments and the circumstances surrounding the withdrawal of the dollar Bill issue, were at loggerheads and unable to present their best and agreed advice to the Chancellor. Holden is shown as having been only interested in a tax-compounded issue and as being able to impose his views on the other bankers. The impression is given that he did not appreciate, he is certainly not recorded as discussing, the wider effects of an issue on such a yield, whether on taxation, public sentiment, the demand for sterling or, even, on balance sheets, including that of his own bank. Yet, as Cunliffe pointed out, 6 per cent before tax, 4½ per cent tax-compounded at 5s, repeated the 6 per cent Exchequer Bonds issued the previous October amid so much criticism.[13]

All whose views are recorded ignored the discount in the price and valued the paper on its running yield – the concept of GRY, relevant in a market of dated obligations, apparently was not yet understood in the higher reaches of the banking system. Holden, carrying most of the other bankers, could see no difference between a long security and a short security, an ignorance that term could make a difference to yield shared by other contemporaries: they just noted the 4½ per cent net yield on 6 per cent Exchequer Bonds. It was consistent with this that Holden could ignore the normal method of valuing a new issue – looking at the yield on existing securities – whether gross or net of tax. In comparison, Schuster's pricing seems about right, but was marred by his advice on the yield needed if substantial amounts of new money were to be subscribed.

In choosing the first optional redemption date, the Treasury made the same assumption about interest rates as it had made in 1915: they were at an unsustainable level. In principle, therefore, officials looked for the longest acceptable repayment option, the nearest first optional redemption date and, it can be assumed, the lowest possible sinking fund (that is, refinancing) in the early years when rates were expected to be high and fiscal problems at their most intense. 'Acceptable' and 'nearest' were clearly a matter of judgement, and the discussions which resulted in their meaning 1929–47 and 1929–42 have left little mark in the records. This is more the pity as the first optional redemption date turned out to be pregnant with social and political implications in the fifteen years after the war and, unlike the yield, which was effectively chosen by the market, within the discretion of the Treasury.

Officials advised against a very early first date with, once again, the bankers giving divided advice. The CLCB suggested an option beginning in 1925 – a lack of protection which both Cunliffe and Schuster felt would deter trustees – or 1942.[14] Lever, Chalmers and Bradbury preferred:

> 15 to 20 [years] for the cum tax loan, again on the ground that they think 10 years would be cutting matters too fine for the success of the loan.[15]

On 27 December, Norman recorded the term as almost certain to be 15–30 years.[16] The date actually selected, 1929, therefore erred strongly towards the earlier dates being canvassed. The same first date was selected for the tax-compounded Loan, although officials, following the principle of making the tax-compounded loan less attractive than the taxed loan, had recommended that it should be shorter.[17]

Despite these discussions and officials' belief that interest rates would fall after the war, there is no record of the yields to 1929 having been discussed. It was assumed that the taxable Loan had a life of thirty years and the yield to any other date was irrelevant. Nor are there records of officials choosing the GRY to 1929 to reflect a relationship with the returns on the shorter, most recent, Exchequer Bonds: those with 5 and 6 per cent coupons running for three or five years. The failure to consider GRYs, other than those to maturity, was of no importance in the case of the tax-compounded Loan; it was issued at par, with redemption at par. However, the price of 95 on the taxable Loan meant that differing redemption dates produced very different GRYs. That to 1 June 1947 may have been £5 6s 8d per cent, but that to 1 June 1929 was £5 11s 5d per cent. In due course, called for 1 December 1932, the GRY turned out to have been £5 9s 7d per cent.

It was widely believed that the weakness displayed by the Lloyd George and McKenna War Loans in the secondary market could have been reduced if there had been some form of official support, or sinking fund, attached to the Loans. Traditionally, the Treasury did not like tying budget surpluses to particular issues, preferring to be free to buy the cheapest in the market or pay off maturities for cash. Its experience in 1910 and 1914 with Asquith's Lottery Bonds, whose annual drawings were a contract with the holder, must have strengthened this prejudice.

A purchase fund was not, therefore, envisaged as a mechanism for repayment, although clearly this was involved, but as a device for persuading investors that the Loans would show greater price stability than their predecessors. Indeed, at one time the Chancellor thought an alternative might be to allow trustees to buy the Loans in the market and tender them at par in payment of estate duty.[18] Thus, although 'sinking fund' was used in discussion, it was more appropriately described by its official name – Depreciation Fund – and the prospectus stated that the purchases were to provide 'against depreciation in the market prices of the Loans'.[c]

The Chancellor, although conceding that a sinking fund might be necessary to make the Loans attractive, saw it as 'bad finance'. Using the orthodox arguments, he said that it could entail raising taxation to pay off long debt at a time, such as the end of the war, when the Treasury might be wanting to pay off short, and, 'if the war continued for a long time', the Treasury might find itself borrowing at a higher rate to buy back an issue bearing a lower rate.[19] The latter fear clearly needed presenting with care when launching loans with no conversion option into future loans.

The Chancellor's briefing paper for his second meeting with the CLCB's subcommittee described two types of sinking fund. First, cash equal to 1/2 per cent per year of the nominal value of the Loans would be issued for the currency of the Loans' lives and applied to purchases in the market when prices fell below their issue prices: the fund would either be suspended or invested in other government securities when market prices rose above these levels. Second, a fund to which the Treasury would only issue cash when the Loans fell below their issue prices. The briefing paper suggested that one per mille per month of the securities currently outstanding, or 1.2 per cent per annum, might be made available. It was Cunliffe who suggested 1 1/2 per cent per annum, to be applied only when the Loans were beneath their issue prices.[20] The source of the proposal that the fund should be based on the original nominal created – a proviso that smacks of a sinking fund, rather than a stabilisation fund – is not recorded. The wording in the prospectus is imprecise, speaking of 'one-eighth of one per cent of the amount of each loan', and arouses the suspicion that bad drafting required later interpretation.

The mechanism adopted, that of accumulating unused monthly payments until they reached a maximum of £10m, was therefore a compromise. It avoided the danger of an unlimited fund investing in other securities when the market was strong or stable and selling them when the market was weak, while it ensured that there would usually be some money immediately available. No scheme avoided the problem that a prolonged period of weakness would leave the fund with nothing but its monthly receipts with which to make purchases.

c Seven years later, Niemeyer claimed the Depreciation Fund was 'in effect practically a Sinking Fund'. Committee on National Debt and Taxation (Colwyn Committee) *Minutes of Evidence*, 2 May 1924, para 80.

d In the period to 31 March 1918, thirteen monthly payments of £2.7m, totalling £34.7m (including £26,979 interest on balances), were received for the Fund by the Commissioners. Purchases of the 5 per cent Loan were heavy: the Fund bought £34.0m nominal in the year ending 31 March 1918 at a cost of £32.1m. Purchases of the 4 per cents were only £10,000.

The Depreciation Fund became operative on 16 February 1917 under a temporary arrangement, which enabled the Government Broker to make purchases on behalf of the Treasury, with the Stock or Bonds passing straight through to that increasingly useful reservoir whose activities were so free from Parliamentary scrutiny or control, the CNRA.[21] A few months later, the Finance Act 1917 established an account under the management of the Commissioners.[d]

Officials were split over whether tax should be deducted at source, as had been standard practice until the issues of the Exchequer Bonds in 1916. Hamilton's report of their rather subjective views read:

> If 95 is agreed to, Sir R. Chalmers is strongly of opinion that taxation at the source should be retained; otherwise he fears a considerable leakage. Mr. Lever & Sir J. Bradbury lean to the other view – but not so strongly – on the ground that it would attract subscriptions that would not otherwise be obtainable. They admit that leakage would take place but do not think it would be very serious.[22]

The Inland Revenue agreed with Chalmers, an ex-chairman. The current chairman Sir Edmund Nott Bower, learning that the bankers were urging that an arrangement which had applied to temporary borrowings – Exchequer Bonds – should be applied to a 'regular long-term investment', emphasised the importance of taxation at source to the efficiency of the tax system. The dividends, he said, were only chargeable to tax in the year after the year in which they were paid: the Exchequer would therefore suffer from delayed receipts at a time when revenue was badly needed. It would also suffer the loss of the interest on the revenue for one year. The Inland Revenue regarded 'with some scepticism' the prospects of receiving any revenue in the year in which the Loan was paid off, so there would be a permanent loss of one year's receipts. The Inspectors would be unable to catch every 'delinquent', if for no other reason than they would be very busy after the war and would be concentrating on the big taxpayers. If a holder died or transferred the securities there would be 'a tendency for a year to be dropped out altogether as the new owner won't return the interest for assessment till the year following its receipt and the previous owner won't declare it at all.' Finally, the foreigner would pay no tax. The plea came too late.[23] The Chancellor had already decided to allow payment of dividends without deduction.

The terms

The result of these deliberations were two issues covered by a single prospectus published on 11 January 1917. First, 5 per cent War Loan was dated 1 June 1929–47 and issued at 95 to give a running yield of £5 5s 3d per cent and a GRY of £5 11s 5d per cent to 1929 and £5 6s 8d per cent to 1947. Interest was payable on 1 June and 1 December. These dates were the same as those on 4½ per cent War Loan, thus adopting Bradbury's suggestion that conversion would be simplified if the same dividend dates were used for the new issue. The first dividend was broken, calculated (unlike that on the $4^1/_2$ per cents in 1915) according to the amount of money actually paid at any one time by the investor.[e] The dividends on both inscribed and Deed Stock were payable without deduction of tax while, as usual, the coupons on the Bonds were paid net.

Second, 4 per cent War Loan ('income tax-compounded') was dated 15 October 1929–42 and issued at 100.[f] Dividends were exempt from British income tax, but not supertax. The Treasury was not liable to make any repayment in respect of untaxed dividends to those who paid no income tax, or who paid less than the standard rate of tax.

The rest of the prospectus was common to both Loans and included features which were entirely new, or new to long-dated issues, although they had been introduced into Exchequer Bonds over the previous year to save labour.[g] The Loans could take the form of Bonds or inscribed Stock and, for the first time, the prospectus for a long-dated issue permitted registration as Deed Stock from the outset. Some of the much-resented fees for transfer were also abolished (Appendix I). Treasury Bills were accepted in lieu of cash under discount at 5 per cent per annum, and War Expenditure Certificates at $5^1/_2$ per cent per annum, as from 16 February, provided the entire proceeds were used to subscribe for fully paid allotments; there was to be no leakage, even if temporary.

As soon as the relevant legislation had been enacted, the Inland Revenue would accept the Loans at their issue prices in payment of estate duty, provided they had been in the continuous ownership of the deceased for at least six months. The arrangements for taxation of overseas holders, who were unlikely to subscribe for the tax-compounded issue, were the same as those for 6 per cent Exchequer Bonds 1920.

The Treasury was to pay the equivalent of $^1/_8$ of 1 per cent per month of the original nominal value of each Loan into a Depreciation Fund. This would be used to buy in the market whenever the price fell beneath its issue price, this being taken to include accrued interest.[h] Payments into the Fund were to cease whenever the unexpended balance reached £10m and resume as soon as the balance

e Thus, on 1 June 1917, £1 8s 9d per cent was payable on fully paid allotments and £0 11s 10d per cent on instalment allotments. In the latter case, £5 was payable on application and £90 in five further instalments at intervals of about three weeks.

f Interest was payable on 15 April and 15 October. A broken dividend of £0 12s 8d per cent was payable on 15 April 1917 on fully paid allotments and a full half-year's dividend (by chance, this was the calculated amount due on the money paid) was payable on 15 October 1917 on instalment allotments.

g Applications could be fully paid or partly paid. Instead of making a down payment and then paying the balance at a later date, those subscribing fully paid paid the whole amount on application. Hitherto, the system had allowed subscribers to pay the calls under discount on any day between the instalment dates. This facility was now dropped. Investors could still pay the balance at any time, but the discount was calculated from the following call date. Thus, the complex system of calculating an amount of discount day-by-day ceased. The minimum size of applications on the Bank register was reduced to £50.

h This was not made clear in the prospectus, but was clarified in an answer to a broker's question. T 172/686, Hamilton to Pember & Boyle, 16 February 1917.

dropped beneath £10m. The prospectuses did not make it clear, and there seems to have been some doubt in the minds of Bank officials, but the intention seems to have been that the whole fund would be available to buy either Loan.[24]

In accordance with the terms of their prospectuses, holders of the 4½ per cent War Loan and the Exchequer Bonds could exchange into either of the two new Loans, or into a combination, with their holdings taken at par. Thus, in the case of the 4½ per cents, the actual issue price of £98 17s 6d had to be ignored and the transaction was based on the published price, so that £100 nominal was convertible into £105 5s 3d of 5 per cent War Loan or £100 of 4 per cent War Loan. Application to convert had to be made by 16 February, but would not take effect on the Banks' books until 2 July.[i]

There were no options to convert into subsequent issues.

It was found necessary to make four additions to the terms after the prospectus was published. First, as interest on the Loans only began to accrue when lists closed on 16 February, investors were tempted to delay applications until the last moment. This would have bunched the processing of the issues and, perhaps, misled commentators when small receipts were published in the weekly Exchequer returns. The Treasury suggested to the Bank that some kind of advantage, a discount in the price or an interest payment, should be given to applicants to reflect the loss of interest. The Bank considered it impossible to make daily calculations for odd values when it might be handling 50,000 applications each day.[25] The Chancellor then asked the CLCB if its members would pay interest to customers making early applications: in its turn, the CLCB decided that this was not possible.[26] Rebuffed, the Treasury won the Bank's agreement for a single uniform payment,[j] involving little administrative effort, to those who lodged their applications before the close of business on the last day of January.[27]

Second, at the same time that the incentive for early applications was announced, the six months' condition in the death duty clause was altered so that the Loans could be tendered provided holdings had been continuously in the possession of the deceased since subscription or conversion.

Third, on 21 January, it was announced that those borrowing from their banks to apply for inscribed or registered Stock of the 5 per cent issue could, when making their income and supertax returns, set off the dividends against the interest

i The holdings would not change until 2 July, except that those which were destined for conversion into the 5 per cent Loan would be designated 'B' and those destined for the 4 per cent loan 'C'. It followed that each holding would contain two sources of accrued interest: that relating to the original holding for the period up to 16 February and that relating to one of the two new Loans for the period between 17 February and 15 April (in the case of the 4 per cents), or 1 June (5 per cents). Eight broken dividends were involved.

j The payment was equivalent to 3.8 per cent per annum, or £0 3s 4d cash per £100 nominal, on fully paid, and £0 0s 2d per £100 nominal, on partly paid, applications. The payments did not apply to subscriptions using Bills or War Expenditure Certificates because they could only be used for applications made after 16 February, when interest had anyway begun to accrue on the Loans.

due to the bank.[28] Tax was then chargeable on the difference at the tax payer's marginal rate. Finally, it was decided to allow applications of up to £50 by those who, having converted into odd amounts of the new Loans, wanted to round up their holdings.[k]

The Post Office issue

Reflecting the long period available for preparation, the Post Office issue was more comprehensive than that for the 1915 Loan and was presented in a more formal manner. Thus, instead of a blanket statement that applicants would receive as favourable treatment as subscribers through the Bank, it recited the rights of holders in full. The only exceptions to this were the taxation of non-residents and the terms of the Depreciation Fund, in which holders were referred to the Bank prospectus. From the start, banks joined Money Order Offices in receiving applications; in 1915, they had only begun to distribute the Post Office issue half way through the campaign. The minimum subscription was for £5 nominal and applications had to be in units of £5. In common with the 1915 Loan, there was no facility for part payment.

There was no Post Office issue of the tax-compounded Loan but, to fulfil the terms of earlier issues, holders could convert into it on the Bank prospectus on application through the Post Office. Holdings of less than £100 nominal of 4½ per cent War Loan and 5 per cent Exchequer Bonds 1920 of the Post Office issue were automatically converted into the taxable Loan, unless holders signified dissent by the time lists closed on 16 February. Holders of more than £100 nominal of the two issues and all holders of the Post Office issues of the 5 per cent Exchequer Bonds 1921 and the 6 per cent Exchequer Bonds 1920, irrespective of size, had to apply for conversion by 16 February.

The role of the banks

At the same time as the CLCB was advising the Chancellor on the terms for the new Loans, it was negotiating the conversion into Exchequer Bonds of part of its members' holdings of the 1915 War Loan and securing the Treasury's agreement to the payment for customers' applications in fifteen-day bills.[29] The beginning of January also saw negotiations on the terms on which the banks would make advances to their customers to finance applications. Further negotiations took place at the end of the month and into the first half of February when the Chancellor

k In providing this facility, the authorities planned to avoid a clash with the work on the main cash applications, while avoiding giving investors the option which would have resulted if applications had been delayed until dealings had begun. It was decided that such subscriptions should be made at the same time as the applications for conversion, but payment would be delayed until between 21 May and 31 May. In these cases, the first dividend was to be paid on 1 December 1917. *The Times*, 22 January 1917, p. 12, 25 January, p. 13, and 27 January, p. 10; BoE, Loan Wallet 237A, '5% War Loan', 22 January 1917.

arranged underwriting to ensure that subscriptions at least equalled those for the 1915 issue.

The scheme to enable the banks to convert 4½ per cent Loan was intended to provide them with a shorter-dated security with less price volatility and remove the threat of sales, which might disrupt the secondary market and drive up yields. Some relief had already been provided by the scheme, put into effect the previous spring, which enabled the banks to convert the Loan into Exchequer Bonds in lieu of commission on applications for Exchequer Bonds bearing their stamp (see pp. 197–8). Now, a more extensive arrangement was agreed. The 'memorandum of 4 January' authorised the Bank of England to exchange 4½ per cent War Loan acquired as part of the 'special subscription of £200m' for 5 per cent Exchequer Bonds 1921. The terms of the exchange were nominal for nominal, with adjustment for accrued interest. There were three conditions. First, banks were to place additional 4½ per cent War Loan with the Bank of England equal to three times the amount they exchanged into Exchequer Bonds. The War Loan was frozen, Bonds being deposited and Stock being inscribed into a separate account. Second, to ensure that the securities exchanged were part of the original special subscription, applications had to be accompanied by a declaration that the securities had been held continuously since issue and that they were in a bank's absolute ownership. Third, banks had to undertake not to sell the Exchequer Bonds until one year after the war unless the price was above par and not sell any of their 4½ per cent War Loan, or any Loan into which it might be converted, at a price lower than one point (excluding accrued interest) above the issue price, unless it had first received the Treasury's authorisation. Conversion of the frozen 4½ per cents into the new 4 and 5 per cent Loans was permitted under the scheme, as were further conversions into Exchequer Bonds in lieu of commission.[30] The CLCB accepted the terms once the Bank had agreed that in an emergency members would be able to borrow on the security of the new Loans or the Exchequer Bonds at a rate not exceeding Bank rate. It was expected that the clearing banks' entire holdings would be included if this assurance was forthcoming.[31]

Fifty-three banks took advantage of the offer when conversion took place on 11 January; £60.2m 5 per cent Exchequer Bonds were created and £240.8m 4½ per cent War Loan was converted or frozen. There were few requests for permission to sell, and none were granted, before the Treasury released the banks from their agreement on 14 April 1920.[32]

The Chancellor had hoped to announce that the banks had agreed to give liberal terms to customers borrowing to apply when he launched the sales campaign. However, his initial proposal that advances should be at Bank rate, with a maximum of 6 per cent, met no agreement. Cunliffe feared that 'it was dangerous from the point of view of the exchanges'. The CLCB were unhappy, presumably because it would mean a cap on their lending rates when there was no theoretical limit on their borrowing rates, and instead proposed advances at a maximum of Bank rate to 'approved customers'. The Chancellor then suggested that the Treasury might guarantee the banks against loss and left the Governor and the CLCB to negotiate further about his original request for advances at a maximum of 6 per cent.

There was common ground that the Bank of England should stand behind the banks if the illiquidity of their advances endangered them.[33] By the time the Chancellor saw the representatives of the insurance companies on 5 January, the arrangement had been agreed. Provided he could say in public that the banks would make 'reasonable' advances at a rate not exceeding Bank rate, he would instruct the Bank to make similar advances at the same maximum rate on the security of the Loans taken by the banks as collateral for their advances. In addition, the Bank would accept payment of subscription money in fifteen-day bills, thus making it less likely the banks would have recourse to the central bank facility.[34] The CLCB Minutes make the intention clear:

> the latter [the Chancellor] had definitely stated that the Bank of England would make to the Banks all such loans as might be necessary to enable the Banks to lend freely to their customers for the purpose of the new loan.[35]

A neater, and more generous, solution was adopted by the Governor three days later: the Bank would lend to approved borrowers at 1 per cent under Bank rate, with a minimum of 5 per cent, for periods of three months. He hoped that the banks would follow suit.[36] With a running yield of £5 5s 3d per cent on the 5 per cent Loan, the Governor was saying that he was prepared to underwrite a small profit for those borrowing, but not an excessive profit should Bank rate fall, and that he was not prepared to give protection against a steep rise in rates; an unsurprising decision in view of the state of British finance in New York and the possibility that sterling would be unpegged.

The Chancellor wanted the banks to provide one other privilege. Many potential subscribers were uncomfortable borrowing on terms that were fixed for only three months, when they could only repay over a longer period. On this, he was prepared to press hard. He asked the CLCB to extend the currency of its members' advances to cover the whole period of the war, while warning that, if the banks failed 'to raise very large subscriptions from the public', it was very probable that they would have to make a further subscription themselves; by cash or conversion of short paper, either temporary, 'to make this loan up to a given amount', or 'more permanent', if the issues had to be followed by a forced loan. The CLCB ignored the threat and passed a resolution refusing to pledge its members to an extension of the term, but reiterating that they were prepared to be generous.[37]

After lists had closed, the banks claimed to have handled about three-quarters of the subscriptions by value: £655m of the 5 per cent Loan; £17m of the 4 per cent Loan; £69m of the Bills converted; and £5m of the Post Office applications.[38] There is only sporadic evidence for the amount that was financed from the advances – monetary contraction being offset by monetary expansion – and the pace at which the advances were repaid. In the summer, the *Bankers' Magazine* reported that only two banks identified lending to finance applications in their loan portfolios. The London City & Midland, with deposits of £175m at the end of December 1916, had made advances of £26.8m; these had been reduced to £22m by the end of June 1917. The Bank of Liverpool, with deposits of £38m, made advances of £9m; some £6½m were still outstanding at the end of 1917. Privately, the National Bank of Scotland reported that, with deposits of £24m, it had advanced about £7m. Some £2½m was still outstanding in August.[39] In April 1918, Grenfell reported to his New York partners that the 'Principal Clearing banks' had lent about £70m, of which approximately 40 per cent had been paid off by September and about 70 per cent by the following spring.[40] It seems that the pace of repayment was, indeed, slow. The report in the *Bankers' Magazine* in August that 'it is generally understood that some 25 to 40 per cent of the amounts originally borrowed have been repaid' probably stemmed from the CLCB itself, which, at the beginning of September, reported to the Chancellor that 62 per cent of the advances made by the joint stock banks were still outstanding.[41]

It is all very nebulous, but it can be hazarded that advances may have represented about one-fifth of deposits and financed about one-third of the cash subscriptions for the two issues (excluding those made with Bills and Expenditure Certificates). Perhaps 50–60 per cent of the issues were still outstanding at the end of the year, by which time it may be safe to assume that, even if they had been the subject of separate agreements when the money was borrowed, they were being absorbed into customers' overall indebtedness.

In the final week of January, the Loans appeared to falter and a subscription from the banks, instead of being a threat aimed at extracting more generous financing terms and stimulating the enthusiasm of bank staff, became a subject for detailed negotiations. On 2 February, Bonar Law told the CLCB that he had discussed the target for subscriptions of new money with the Prime Minister. They had agreed that:

> it was of the utmost importance in the national interest that the total obtained should exceed that of the 4½% Loan. Germany was watching the financial situation of this country and would welcome any sign that our staying power was beginning to fail, and it appeared to them [the Prime Minister and Chancellor] that the total amount of new money, including Treasury Bills…must reach at least £620,000,000.

There was a possibility, he added, that an arrangement could be made which involved short-dated rather than long-dated securities.[42]

On 8 February, the CLCB agreed to authorise Cunliffe to put in an application on behalf of the banks if the total subscriptions of cash and Bills fell beneath this £620m. The application would be for the amount required to take the total to £620m, but would not be greater than £150m. There was an important condition: the banks should have the right to exchange the securities resulting from the subscription, at the issue price, for Currency Notes, at a maximum interest rate of 5 per cent, for the entire life of the Loans. The CLCB also asked its Treasury subcommittee to negotiate facilities for the conversion of its members' other holdings of the Loan into Exchequer Bonds up to the amount of Stock or Bonds that they might acquire as a result of the underwriting.[43]

Neither Cunliffe nor Bradbury were prepared to accept these proposals.[44]

Currency Note facilities were designed to meet a run on the banks, wrote Bradbury, whereas:

> The situation for which the banks wish to provide is a shortage of their reserves, which may be caused by quite normal currency movements either internal or external or by restriction of credit by the Bank of England.

Such a shortage should be reflected in a restriction of credit by the banks until gold was attracted from abroad. Restriction of the supply of gold or fiduciary paper, 'the only known remedy for an adverse trade balance and falling exchanges', would become impossible if the banks could acquire reserves at a comparatively low interest rate as fast as gold or fiduciary paper were withdrawn. Central control of the money market would disappear. The authorities would anyway face a difficult period after the war when the export of gold was no longer threatened by submarines: it would be more difficult if their hands were tied by the proposed agreement. Additionally, the arrangement was 'grotesquely favourable to the banks.' They would be lending to the government at £5 6s 9d per cent (the GRY to 1947 on 5 per cent War Loan) with freedom to hand it back, continuing to earn £0 6s 9d per cent until such time as they chose to take it back, when they would again obtain £5 6s 9d per cent.[45]

The terms that were sent back to the CLCB were therefore very different. The 5 per cent War Loan from the subscription would be converted immediately after the war into equal amounts of three- and five-year 5 per cent Exchequer Bonds at the rate of £95 for every £100 of Stock. The Treasury would make cash advances at Bank rate up to the value of the Stock or Bonds at any time between the subscription and the maturity of the Exchequer Bonds. These terms were agreed by the CLCB with a small amendment.[46]

The CLCB wanted each bank's participation in the £150m underwriting to be proportionate to its deposits.[47] Holden, however, had not attended the meetings and the Treasury was warned at an early stage that it might be difficult to get the banks to act on the CLCB's resolution if the London City & Midland failed to participate.[48] The CLCB's suspicion proved well-founded, and, when Holden refused to join in, the subscription was agreed for £124.5m, the reduction reflecting the commitment that the London City & Midland would have taken in accordance with its share of deposits.[49] Although the other members of the CLCB were prepared to assume the entire £124.5m themselves, they 'thought it only right' that all the banks that had participated in the special subscription of £200m for the 1915 Loan should be included. Thus, forty-four banks were involved, underwriting amounts that ranged from £15.6m (Lloyds) to £70,000 (Gillett & Co.).[50]

By 16 February, when the Secretary of the CLCB was finally instructed to write to the Governor authorising him to put in the application, the results were looking more promising. The daily report from Cunliffe that morning showed that nearly £550m of applications in cash, Treasury Bills and War Expenditure Certificates had been counted: the next day, it was almost £600m, with more to be processed.[51] The Chancellor, looking for a yet more spectacular result, asked the

CLCB if the bankers would be prepared to subscribe to bring the loan up to £700m. He met a flat refusal and, with subscriptions still being counted, pressed them no further.[52]

Grooming the markets

The authorities made maximum use of their limited freedom to set the scene for the issues. The 6 per cent Exchequer Bond 1920 and War Expenditure Certificate taps were closed on 30 December and the Treasury Bill tap on 4 January. The closures were dictated by the Bank's inability to process other tenders or applications at the same time as it was issuing two new Loans, but the absence of alternative investments was expected to sharpen investors' appetites. As the cash from the Loans did not start coming in for some weeks it was necessary for the Treasury to borrow from the Bank: its Ways and Means Advances rose sharply, reaching nearly £300m in the middle of February, when the calls permitted a rapid reduction.[53] The increase in liquidity pushed down rates, those on three-month bank bills falling during the first week in January from 5½ to 5 per cent. A reduction in Bank rate had been in McKenna's mind the previous November and was one reason why he wanted a public issue in New York around the turn in the year: as Grenfell told Davison, once McKenna was 'fairly free of anxiety for a certain time as regards exchange…he would drop Bank rate here and cheapen money with a view to his domestic Loan'.[54] Bonar Law had clearly been given similar advice and asked the bankers for their views when he met the CLCB for the first time on 23 December. On 18 January, when money market rates had eased in New York and Morgans became confident that they could form their underwriting syndicate for $250m of loans, the rate was cut from 6 per cent to 5½ per cent.[55]

Persuasion

The general public

Contemporaries believed that the Chancellor rejected the advice offered by the professionals in the City and relied on a wave of patriotism to sell his issues. The Chancellor certainly beat the big drum, and with great success, but the story that he ignored the experts' views largely depended on his rejection of the advice given by Holden and some members of the CLCB that a tax-free yield of 4½ per cent would have to be offered, irrespective of the maturity. The Chancellor did nothing to discourage the myth, whether in the Commons or in interviews with the press: it flattered his judgement and was good for national morale.[56]

He described the campaign in a permissibly upbeat fashion to one American journalist:

> I organised individual effort. I think I may almost say that the War Loan was the biggest effort to organise individualism that has ever been carried out in

> this country…I called upon the Local Authorities to help me…I knew that if I called on them to assist in a financial operation I should have agents in every part of the country…Then I had the War Savings Committees…The members of these Committees were representative of every group in the country, clergy and ministers of all denominations, school teachers, social workers, officials of trade unions and friendly societies and the leaders of all sorts of social and industrial groups…Having got my machinery I tried to give it a suitable atmosphere in which to get to work…I took the advice of those who best knew how to attract the public and I called in the aid of the Press. The publicity campaign was most carefully worked and most far-reaching. The newspaper editors responded splendidly and within a week or two the whole country was talking War Loan, thinking War Loan, almost dreaming War Loan. The combination of the local machinery and the universal sentiment carried the country. No one could take up his paper without reading about War Loan and no one could go out of doors in any town or village throughout the length and breadth of the country without having War Loan thrust on his attention.[57]

The campaign was inaugurated by the Prime Minister and Chancellor at a meeting at the Guildhall on 11 January. The latter singled out small savers and businesses for special attention, while appealing to all investors to borrow from their banks to apply for more than they could currently afford, repaying the debt out of future savings. Then, using a stick which would not have been acceptable to an American public, he gave a warning that:

> so long as there is money in this country the war will not be stopped, the progress of the war will not be hampered for the want of money. The conditions of this country make it necessary to buy abroad; the result is that the rate of interest for home money is much higher than it would have been but for the necessity of keeping up our exchange. There is a limit to the price which those who are responsible for the government of this country are justified in paying for money having regard to the whole obligations of the State. That limit has been reached in the issue which we are now making public. So far as I can judge the future, and so far as, if I continue to be Chancellor of the Exchequer, I can control the future…a higher rate of interest will not be paid. If I should fail…the resources of civilization are not exhausted. There are other methods – and if other methods are applied the rate will not be $5^1/_4$ per cent. If there is anyone who is inclined to hold back, with the idea he would get better terms in the future, then I think he will be mistaken.[58]

The Chancellor gave a similar warning a week later in Glasgow: he preferred the voluntary approach, whether it be in conscription or finance, as long as it provided the necessary resources. If compulsion was necessary:

> it would be bad for the country, but it would be worst of all for those who

> have money and have not given it freely in the service of the country. I do not believe that any such steps will be necessary, and I need not say that if they ever were, in considering the amount of the levy to be made either upon individuals or institutions an account would be taken of the contributions which had already been made voluntarily.[59]

Afterwards, he admitted that he had no idea how he would have carried out the threat.[60]

The day after the campaign was launched, he addressed 1,500 of those on whom it would depend: the Chairmen of the Local War Savings Committees, the Lord Mayors, Mayors and Chairmen of the Urban District Councils. The National War Savings Committee directed its efforts to stimulating the Local Authorities and Local Committees, suggesting methods of conducting the campaign and publicising the Loans. In the following five weeks, 1,300 public meetings were addressed by ministers and MPs and 5,000 private meetings were held under the guidance of Local Committees. Nearly eleven million leaflets were produced (300,000 in Welsh), including 14,000 'Notes for War Loan Sermons' for the clergy and 10,000 'Points for Speakers'. A letter with a facsimile of the Chancellor's signature covering a copy of the prospectuses was sent to 650,000 households. Slides were shown in over 2,000 cinemas. Articles were written and news items collected and distributed for publication in the newspapers. Up to sixty journalists were interviewed each day. A central information bureau and 1,100 local bureaux were set up. Half of the Local Committees carried out house-to-house distributions of literature and a quarter carried out a complete canvass of the houses in their area.[61] A special circular and questionnaire were sent to some 42,000 wealthy individuals by the Inland Revenue and to companies by His Majesty's Stationery Office (HMSO).[62] The Bank distributed eight and a half million prospectuses, twenty million application forms and three million conversion forms.[63]

Once again, newspaper advertising had been put in the hands of Le Bas and his Caxton Advertising Agency, with an Advertising Advisory Committee of four other agencies. General publicity was the responsibility of a separate Treasury committee. At the end of January, the Chancellor decided that the advertising was unsatisfactory, although Le Bas claimed he had been caught between the Bank's desire to advertise the prospectuses widely and a mean Treasury budget. In his stead, the Chancellor appointed Kennedy Jones, a henchman of Northcliffe's, a Unionist MP and an abrasive businessman, widening his responsibilities to cover all publicity.[64] Jones moved into the headquarters of the National War Savings Committee and acquired the use of the movement's publicity machine. 'I got Kennedy Jones to take the press in hand, both advertizing and news columns, and the change produced by him was wonderful' the Chancellor wrote at the end of the year, a view confirmed by Reading: 'The publicity campaign in the last two or three weeks was a whirlwind.'[65]

Jones's appointment reflected concern that the Loans were selling poorly. Uncertainty was fed by the decision, apparently made by the Bank, and initially accepted by the Treasury, to ensure secrecy by not totalling subscriptions each day.[66] This changed at the end of the month when, at the request of the Chancellor, daily returns of the applications processed, but not of those received, were made: the first return was made on 31 January and showed subscriptions up to the previous day of only £151m for the 5 per cent Loan, £6m for the 4 per cent loan and, surprisingly, £23m on account of conversions from Bills.[67]

The Treasury, perhaps also hoping to spur on the banks, asked the CLCB to organise a return of cash subscriptions and conversions of Bills that had been submitted through them in the period to the end of January and the applications which had been definitely arranged to be made through them during the two remaining weeks of the campaign. The results, in common with the first return from the Bank, were not encouraging. The thirteen banks with deposits of some £650m whose replies were available by 2 February reported only £111m cash subscriptions and conversions of Bills, equivalent to 17 per cent of deposits: they knew of a further £34m which was to be subscribed during the following sixteen days.[68] If these banks proved typical of the banking system, applications would be only £325m.

The large investor

While the campaign, using the tools of mass persuasion, was working on the enthusiasm of the individual saver and small business concern, the Chancellor was orchestrating subscriptions by large investors. In his address at the Guildhall, the Chancellor singled out industrial and commercial enterprises for particular mention. One of the most powerful, and one that felt most vulnerable, was the shipping industry, which the public saw as among the greatest of the war profiteers. They had benefited as freight rates rose on that part of their fleets not chartered to the government at the fixed 'blue book rates' established early in the war and had accumulated liquid resources from the compensation paid by government and insurers for lost and damaged vessels. These, together with normal retentions for depreciation, were in excess of the amounts that they were able to spend on new building.

The initiative came in the middle of January from Lord Inchcape, who himself controlled a fleet of over 1.5m tons. He wrote to Bonar Law:

> I wonder whether you have considered the advisability of suggesting to the shipowners of this country that they might help your war loan by something like a uniform contribution of £3 or £4 a ton? – This would give you something like fifty or sixty millions.[69]

Bonar Law agreed that Inchcape should sound out Sir John Ellerman and Sir Owen Philipps, who together controlled a further 2.4m tons. They reacted favourably, Philipps suggesting that a company should be formed with £10m capital provided by three or four of the largest owners and the facility to borrow a further £40m from the banks. It would then apply for £50m.[70] Nothing came of this scheme, no doubt because of the owners' stipulation that the banks' advance should be fixed at 5 per cent for ten or twelve years. However, after encouraging discussions with two additional owners, Inchcape addressed a meeting of the Executive Council of the Chamber of Shipping, which recommended that shipowners should subscribe new money on the basis of £4 for each gross ton in their fleets, 'new money' to be construed to include Treasury Bills and Exchequer Bonds, as well as cash. With the British fleet estimated to be twenty million gross tons, the Chamber could 'confidently' hope for a contribution of 'at least one hundred millions'.[71] A fortnight later the Chamber's General Manager told Bonar Law that this would be exceeded.[72]

Local authorities, encouraged by the Local Government Board and the connection between local politicians and the local war savings movement, were responsible for some of the largest applications. On 1 February, the attitude of the Local Government Board was spelt out in a circular, approving the use in the Loans of any money that local authorities had available for investment.[73] Included were balances held in pension and sinking funds, cash being accumulated for the repayment of maturing loans, and reserve and depreciation funds. In addition, they could use revenue balances which would not be needed 'in the near future' – balances that had been swollen by the postponement of work on repair and maintenance – and subscribe for further amounts if the money was to become available 'within a reasonable time'. The policy of the Board when it was asked to give authority for subscriptions which were *ultra vires* was explained to the bankers as 'while they [the Board] were unable to authorise such borrowing, they will not object to it.'[74] The greatest number of Local Authority applications which were given publicity were between £100,000 and £1m, although the distribution between new money and conversions was not always made clear. Among subscribers for over £1m were: the London County Council, £7m (of which 'about half' was 'new'); Cardiff, £6m (£0.2m being new); Swansea, £3.1m; the Corporation of the City of London £2m; Glasgow, after intervention by the Chancellor over the terms of the advance from its bank, £2m; and Liverpool, £1m.[75]

A scheme proposed by Kindersley for investment trusts to form a company which would borrow from the banks and subscribe to the Loans was opposed by the CLCB and came to nothing once the Chancellor was sure that the Loans were a success.[76] More successful was marshalling the insurance companies so that they would apply on a large and uniform scale. Bonar Law saw the Chairman of the Prudential at the beginning of January and received a promise that the Company would contribute £20m, provided that the Board of Trade would allow it to publish accounts valuing dated British Government Securities at their redemption prices. Unsurprisingly, this was refused, but authority was given for their inclusion at the lower of redemption value or cost. The Prudential accepted this, allowed the Chancellor to use its subscription for publicity purposes, and later borrowed to increase its application to £25m. Of this, £12m was fully paid, £7.6m partly paid and £5.3m came from conversions.[77] Alongside this, the Chancellor called a meeting of representatives of six other large insurers. He told them that he hoped that the industry's holding of British Government securities would be £100m, or 20 per cent of their £500m assets, once the Loans had been issued. To reach this total, he expected them to have to contribute £50m of new money.[78] There followed a letter to ninety-five offices asking them to support the Loans by using all their cash resources, converting Bills and War Expenditure Certificates and 'by anticipating their future surplus revenue by borrowing substantially from their Bankers.' The cash subscriptions for each fund, the letter said, should be equivalent to 10 per cent of assets and total holdings of the new Loans, including conversions, 20 per cent. To aid their enthusiasm, the Chancellor enclosed a questionnaire so that the Offices could report their existing holdings of British Government securities and the amounts they planned to convert or subscribe to meet the envisaged 10 and 20 per cent levels.[79]

The Offices responded by stressing the differences in their financial positions and the small size of the surpluses that were accruing each year, especially with the rise in income tax and increase in claims as a result of the war. Several pointed to the assets held overseas to meet claims made overseas – assets which were effectively unavailable for remittance to the UK: the Pearl pointed to the reduction in its staff, and hence its earning and collecting capacity; the Commercial Union to the possibility of a sudden call on its general funds caused by claims such as those that followed the San Francisco earthquake in 1906; the Scottish Amicable to the need to take account of contributions to previous Loans; the National Provident Institution to its unwillingness to invest more than the surplus for the current year because of the banks' unwillingness to fix terms for advances for longer than three months; Standard Life to the need to clarify its tax position (a wish granted by the Inland Revenue after intervention by the Treasury); and the Scottish Provident Institution to the need to take account of the age of the fund, earlier contributions to allied loans and the size of the industry's surpluses. There was also anxiety that the amount that Offices could afford to subscribe was being reduced as policyholders borrowed from the offices on the security of their policies to apply in their own names, a transaction that did not increase the amount subscribed but did create more work for the Bank.[80]

Four concerns were taken up formally by The Life Offices' Association: the dangers posed for slow growing funds of borrowing sums which would take many years to repay although the terms were fixed for only three months; the restrictions on borrowing placed on some Offices by their constitutions; the inclusion of holdings of allied governments' securities in the 20 per cent of assets specified by the Chancellor; and the effect on Offices' tax position of the 4 per cent tax-compounded Loan.[81] The Chancellor, who was being briefed by Sir Gerald Ryan of the Phoenix Assurance Co., said that he was aware of the difference between old and new funds and did not expect the former to contribute as generously as the latter. He also agreed that the securities of allied governments – by which he meant holdings of the 5 per cent French National Defence Loan sold in London in December 1915 – should be included in the 20 per cent, to introduce legislation to indemnify companies which exceeded their borrowing powers and to speak to those who were encouraging policyholders to borrow. He also stressed that the credit ratings enjoyed by the Offices 'ought to insure them against any risk of their loans being called in at an early date' and that 'it was inconceivable that the Government could allow Insurance Companies to get into difficulties owing to their patriotic action in contributing to the loan'. Clarification of the effect of the tax-compounded Loan was held over for later discussion with Bradbury.[82] This ended unsatisfactorily for the Offices, which no doubt helped ensure that Loan's failure.[83]

Although the life and composite offices may have shown little interest in the tax-compounded Loan, their applications for the taxable Loan made their contribution larger than the Chancellor had hoped. They took some £107m of the two Loans: of this, about £72m represented cash or the conversion of Treasury Bills and War Expenditure Certificates.[l]

Results

£836.5m of the 5 per cent Loan (including £38.4m of the Post Office issue) and £22m of the 4 per cent Loan were created to meet cash applications. Conversions of Bills and War Expenditure Certificates required the creation of £130.2m of the 5 per cent Loan and £0.6m of the 4 per cents (Tables 11.1 and 11.2). The total for both Loans was, therefore, £989.4m. When announcing the preliminary results in the Commons, the Chancellor, wishing to magnify the success, used these nominal values and included £22m Savings Certificates sold during the period of the campaign.[84] This permitted reference to a figure in excess of £1,000m. More accurately, including conversions of the Bills and War Expenditure Certificates, £941m new money was raised in the gilt-edged market from the issue of £989.3m nominal of paper: the amount raised, including the £22m from Savings Certificates, was £963m – equivalent to about one-quarter of GNP or two-thirds of end-December 1916 bank deposits.

Almost the same amount was created on account of conversions: £1,100.5m of the 5 per cent Loan and £29.8m of the 4 per cent Loan were created by the conversion of £779.1m 4½ per cent War Loan 1925–45 and £266.4m 5 per cent and 6 per cent Exchequer Bonds (Table 11.3).[m] Although this represented 98 per

l Because it is often unclear whether nominal or money values were being used, the values used here are those found in the sources. Sixty-four Offices with £408m of assets completed the Chancellor's questionnaire and had their returns collated. Two (the Sun and the London & Lancashire) made returns, but were not included in the totals. The Commercial Union wrote a letter giving a global figure, but with less detail than that requested. The sixty-four planned to convert £20.6m 4½ per cent War Loan 1925–45: £9.1m 5 per cent Exchequer Bonds 1919, 1920 and 1921; £0.5m 6 per cent Exchequer Bonds 1920; £19.1m Bills and War Expenditure Certificates; and use £26.7m cash. The conversions and cash applications represented £76m of the new issues. The totals given in the text are for the sixty-four, together with the Prudential, which was not asked to complete the questionnaire, and the Sun, London & Lancashire and the Commercial Union. It is assumed that the whole of the Commercial Union's £5m subscription was new money, Bills and War Expenditure Certificates.

m The London City & Midland Bank was responsible for one-third of the conversions into the tax-compounded Loan. The bank's end-June 1917 balance sheet shows that it had converted £10m 4½ per cent War Loan into the tax-compounded Loan, and that it held only £10.092m of the 5 per cent Loan. MBa, Midland Bank Balance Sheets.

Table 11.1 Creations of 5 per cent War Loan 1929–47

On account of	*£m nominal created*
Cash subscriptions – Bank of England issue	798.1
– Post Office issue	38.4
Conversions from Treasury Bills and War Expenditure Certificates	130.2
Total	966.7
Conversions from:	
4½ per cent War Loan 1925–45	820.1
5 per cent Exchequer Bonds 1919, 1920 and 1921 and 6 per cent Exchequer Bonds 1920	280.4
Total	2,067.2

Note
Columns may not sum because of rounding.

Sources: *National Debt: annual returns*; Osborne (1926), I, pp. 425–7.

Table 11.2 Creations of 4 per cent War Loan 1929–42

On account of	*£m nominal created*
Cash subscriptions	22
Conversions from Treasury Bills and War Expenditure Certificates	0.6
Total	22.7
Conversions from:	
4½ per cent War Loan 1925–45	23.2
5 per cent Exchequer Bonds 1919, 1920 and 1921 and 6 per cent Exchequer Bonds 1920	6.6
Total	52.4

Note
Columns may not sum because of rounding.

Sources: *National Debt: annual returns*; Osborne (1926), I, pp. 425–7.

Table 11.3 Conversions of 4½ per cent War Loan 1925–45, 5 per cent Exchequer Bonds 1919, 1920 and 1921 and 6 per cent Exchequer Bonds 1920 into 5 per cent War Loan 1929–47 and 4 per cent War Loan 1929–42

	£m nominal converted into	
	5 per cent War Loan 1929–47	*4 per cent War Loan 1929–42*
4½ per cent War Loan 1925–45	779.1	23.2
5 per cent Exchequer Bonds 1919, 1920 and 1921	247.7	6.1
6 per cent Exchequer Bonds 1920	18.7	0.5
War Expenditure Certificates	---- 6.3 ----	

Sources: *National Debt: annual returns*; Osborne (1926), I, pp. 425–7.

Table 11.4 Number of subscribers and amounts subscribed fully-paid and partly-paid: 5 per cent War Loan 1929–45 and 4 per cent War Loan 1929–42

	Number of subscribers	*Nominal of securities*
5 per cent War Loan 1929–47		
Bank of England issue		
Fully-paid	958,023	720.4
Partly-paid	108,088	207.9
Post Office issue		
Fully-paid	1,060,516	38.4
Total	2,126,627	966.7
4 per cent War Loan 1929–42		
Fully-paid	22,655	19.6
Partly-paid	2,116	3.1
Total	24,771	22.7

Sources: BoE, Loan Wallet 237 (1): Osborne (1926), I, p. 426; T 172/696, 'War Loan 1917', Bank of England, 24 February 1917.

cent of the 4½ per cents outstanding, it was only 61 per cent of the 5 per cent Bonds and 12 per cent of the 6 per cent Bonds. The low figure for the 6 per cents may be assumed to have reflected the high coupon: after coming off tap at the end of December, the price had risen to 101¼.[85]

There had been 98,000 subscribers for the 1914 Loan. In 1915, there had been 1.1m, of which 560,000 were for the Bank issue, and a further 200,000 had bought vouchers. In 1917, the 5 per cent Loan saw 1.07m subscribers for the Bank issue and 1.06m for the Post Office issue: the 4 per cent tax-compounded issue saw 25,000.[n] The total, including those applying for Savings Certificates, was a matter for surmise and propaganda. The Chancellor, in presenting the provisional data to the Commons, made flattering comparisons with the German loans, claiming that the number of applicants was 'an indication of the spirit of the peoples where the loans are raised'. He stressed that the data were an understatement because many applications were made on behalf of several investors. As they could not be estimated, he had to ignore them, but he went on to estimate the number of buyers

n The pattern reflected the growth of the war savings movement and the character of the campaign, as well as the absence of large cash applications by the banks. Whereas applications of over £100,000 represented 48 per cent of the total subscribed for the 1915 Loan, they represented only 18 per cent of those for the 5 per cent Loan in 1917. Subscriptions for between £25,000 and £100,000 represented 11 per cent of the 1917 Loan (7 per cent of the 1915 Loan) of the total; those for between £5,000 and £25,000, 16 per cent (10 per cent); those for between £1,000 and £5,000, 18 per cent (11 per cent); those for between £500 and £1,000, 9 per cent (6 per cent); and those for between £100 and £500, 20 per cent (12 per cent). T 170/88, '4½ per cent War Loan, number of applications', undated; Osborne (1926), I, p. 426.

of Savings Certificates. He included 400,000 investors, representing the number of purchases of Certificates of £12 and above, each of which was assumed to be one individual, and a further 2.8m, representing the 5.6m £1 Certificates sold, each person being assumed to have bought two Certificates. Thus, a total of 5.29m subscribers was claimed. This he compared with 3.81m for the fifth German loan and 5.28m for the fourth. If every small subscriber for Certificates were included, the number of participants rose, he said, to at least 8m.[86]

The subscriptions were mainly for the fully paid Loans. Excluding those made to round up converted holdings, 78 per cent by value of the applications for the 5 per cent Loan and 86 per cent of those for the 4 per cent tax-compounded issue on the Bank register were fully paid (Table 11.4). This was easily explained. Deposit rates paid by the banks were 4 per cent (both before and after Bank rate was cut on 18 January), the banks charged 5 per cent to finance applications and the 5 per cent Loan gave a running yield of £5 5s 3d per cent.

✣ ✣ ✣

As the failure of the 4 per cent issue became clear, it was lost to sight, and 'Loans' became 'Loan'. For Austen Chamberlain, it was an 'amazing success', which had exceeded Bonar Law's 'wildest dreams'.[87] Chamberlain had been Chancellor, and was to be Chancellor again, but Reading was nearer to current finance:

> I must congratulate you on the magnificent success of the Loan. The figures are really quite extraordinary – my own impression from the first was any sum over £300 millions 'new money' (apart from Treasuries [Bills]) would be a triumph…I am surprised, however, that more Treasury Bills were not converted.[88]

In 1917, politicians had reason to applaud the amount of money which had been raised and present it to the world as evidence of the nation's resources and stamina. After the war, the size and interest cost of 5 per cent War Loan drew the public's attention, while the tax-compounded Loan, whose privileges had caused Bonar Law such disquiet, remained in its obscurity. Did the taxable Loan, its interest rate and size deserve such notoriety? As a thirty-year issue, it was correctly priced to a market which was reflecting great uncertainty: about the outcome of the war, unrestricted submarine warfare (declared in the middle of the loan campaign), the financial problems in North America (known to the bankers on the LEC), the pressure being put on the economy by government spending, price inflation and the mass of Bills to be refinanced. The size came from technical debt management decisions; the reliance on open-ended spectacular loans, with the loss of control over when to close the issue, and the conversion options. One-half of the issue came from cash and Bills, an outcome which both Treasury and politicians welcomed unreservedly. After 5 per cent War Loan, spectacular loans gave way to continuous borrowing and an attempt was made to break with the policy of offering conversion options into future issues.

The low figure for conversions of Bills to which Reading alluded may be explained by the type of holders being drawn into short-dated government securities. The shipping industry was the exception, being under heavy public pressure, and enjoying strong leadership. It was widely reported in the press that industrial and commercial firms were investing in Bills and, to a lesser extent, Exchequer Bonds, until the money could be used in their businesses after the war. Schuster had noted a segmentation in the market the previous December:

> [He] did not think the Treasury could hope to get many of the outstanding Treasury bills converted into a long dated issue as they represented for the most part liquid assets not suitable for permanent investment. Treasury bills, it was stated, were held by three classes, bankers, commercial firms (Treasury Bills having largely replaced commercial bills) and the timid investor. None of these classes would be willing to part with their Bills in return for a long dated investment. On the other hand Sir Felix thought that many holders of Treasury Bills would probably be willing to put their money into short dated Exchequer Bonds for 3, 4 or 5 years, and suggested that after the issue now in contemplation an issue of Exchequer Bonds should be made with this object.[89]

Attracting such money, and the belief that interest rates would fall after the war, pointed the authorities to offering a range of short- and medium-dated securities. With one exception, the compensation paid to the banks for losses on Czarist credits, there were to be no more public issues longer than ten years until after the Armistice.

Endnotes

1 T 172/746, First Conference with the Treasury subcommittee of the CLCB, 23 December 1916.

2 See Bonar Law's speech launching his Loans at the Guildhall, reported in *The Times*, 12 January 1917, p. 8, 15 January 1917, p. 14, 17 January, p. 12, and 20 January, p. 10.

3 T 172/746, Third Conference with the Treasury subcommittee of the CLCB, 3 January 1917.

4 T 172/741, unsigned and undated briefing paper for the Chancellor, 28 or 29 December 1916. Also see Schuster's comments in First Conference with the Treasury subcommittee of the CLCB, 23 December 1916 in T 172/746.

5 MND, 27 December 1916; T 172/741, Hamilton to Chancellor, 30 December 1916.

6 T 172/741, undated and unsigned briefing paper for the Chancellor, 28 or 29 December 1916. On 27 December, Norman recorded that the tax-compounded issue would come at par. This seems to have been taken for granted and was not mentioned in the briefing paper.

7 CLCBm, 22 December 1916; T 172/746, First and Second Conferences with the Treasury subcommittee of the CLCB, 23 and 29 December 1916.

8 CLCBt, 22 December 1916; T 172/746, First Conference with the Treasury subcommittee of the CLCB, 23 December 1916.

9 T 172/746, First and Second Conferences with the Treasury subcommittee of the CLCB, 23 and 29 December 1916; CLCBm, 22 December 1916, and CLCBt, 22 December 1916.

10 T 172/746, Second Conference with the Treasury subcommittee of the CLCB, 29 December 1916.
11 Ibid., Second Conference with the Treasury subcommittee of the CLCB, 29 December 1916.
12 *The Economist*, 20 January 1917, p. 88; T 171/167, Deputation from The TUC to the Chancellor, 15 February 1917; T 172/746, First and Second Conferences with the Treasury subcommittee of the CLCB, 23 and 29 December 1916, and Conference with the Stock Exchange Committee, 2 January 1917.
13 T 172/746, Second Conference with the Treasury subcommittee of the CLCB, 29 December 1916.
14 CLCBt, 22 December 1916; T 172/746, Second Conference with the Treasury subcommittee of the CLCB, 29 December 1916.
15 T 172/741, Hamilton to Chancellor, 30 December 1916.
16 MND, 27 December 1916.
17 T 172/746, Second Conference with the Treasury subcommittee of the CLCB, 29 December 1916; CLCBt, 22 December 1916; T 172/741, Hamilton to Chancellor, 30 December 1916.
18 T 172/746, Second Conference with the Treasury subcommittee of the CLCB, 29 December 1916.
19 Ibid.
20 Ibid.; T 172/741, briefing paper for the Chancellor, 29 December 1916.
21 T 111/I, Bradbury to Bank of England, 5 March 1917. The correspondence setting up the arrangement is in T 133/1.
22 T 172/741, Hamilton to Chancellor, 30 December 1916.
23 Ibid., two letters from Nott Bower to the Chancellor, 1 January 1917.
24 BoE, Loan Wallet 237(2), Harvey to Messel, 20 January 1917. The correspondence does not make clear how the money was to be distributed if both Loans were beneath their issue prices simultaneously. The implication is that it would be spent in proportion to the amount of the Loans outstanding at the time of purchase.
25 BoE, Loan Wallet 237A, Cunliffe to Bonar Law, 9 January 1917.
26 CLCBm, 10 January 1917.
27 *The Times,* 16 January 1917, p. 14, and 18 January, p. 5; *Financial News*, 18 January 1917, p. 3.
28 *The Times*, 22 January 1917, p. 9.
29 CLCBm, 22 December 1916 and 4 January 1917, and Governor to Vassar-Smith, 5 January 1917; T 172/746, First, Second and Third Conferences with the Treasury subcommittee of the CLCB, 23 and 29 December 1916 and 3 January 1917. The CLCB was concerned to protect the banks against a sudden loss of deposits, which were anyway expected to contract during the tax-gathering season in the first quarter. It had originally wanted the money to remain on deposit in a Treasury account in the subscriber's bank until drawn down. The system of delayed payment was negotiated between Vassar-Smith and the Governor.
30 T 172/746, Second and Third Conferences with the Treasury subcommittee of the CLCB, 29 December 1916 and 3 January 1917, and Third Conference with the bankers, 3 January 1917; CLCBm, 4 January and 5 January 1917. A copy of the agreement is pasted in the CLCB Minute Book.
31 CLCBm, 5 January 1917; Cunliffe to Vassar-Smith, 5 January 1917. A copy of the letter is pasted in the CLCB Minute Book.
32 Osborne (1926), I, pp. 410–11 and 411n.
33 T 172/746, Third Conference with the Treasury Subcommittee of the CLCB, 3 January 1917; CLCBm, 4 January 1917.
34 CLCBm, Cunliffe to Vassar-Smith, 4 January 1917. The original letter said 'at Bank Rate or under'. This was altered at the request of the CLCB. CLCBm, 5 January 1917.

35 CLCBm, 5 January 1917.
36 Ibid., 8 January 1917.
37 T 172/746, 'Resolution – Clearing House, 10th January 1917'; CLCBm, 10 January 1917.
38 T 172/745, 'Analysis of War Loan Applications', covering letter Martin-Holland to Hamilton, 16 October 1917.
39 *Bankers' Magazine*, August 1917, p. 116, and September 1917, p. 314; Holden, address to shareholders, 29 January 1918, reproduced in *The Economist*, 2 February 1918, pp. 166–74; BLP, 82/3/23, Younger to Bonar Law, 23 August 1917.
40 MGP, B. Hist. 3, F 17, Grenfell to JPM & Co., 3 April 1918.
41 *Bankers' Magazine*, August 1917, p. 116; T 172/555, Chancellor to Inchcape, 6 September 1917.
42 T 172/746, Conference with the Treasury subcommittee of the CLCB, 2 February 1917; CLCBt, 2 February 1917.
43 T 172/746, Conference with the Treasury subcommittee of the CLCB, 8 February 1917, and Martin-Holland to Hamilton, 9 February 1917; CLCBm, 8 February 1917; CLCBt, 7 February 1917.
44 T 172/746, Conference with the Treasury subcommittee of the CLCB, 8 February 1917; CLCBm, 9 February 1917.
45 T 172/741, Bradbury, 'Currency Note Facilities at a Fixed Rate of Interest', covering letter Hamilton to Chancellor, 10 February 1917. It will be noted that Bradbury's GRY differs by 1d from that calculated by the author.
46 T 172/746, Conference with the Treasury subcommittee of the CLCB, 8 February 1917; CLCBm, 9 and 12 February 1917.
47 CLCBm, 12 February 1917.
48 T 172/746, Conference with the Treasury subcommittee of the CLCB, 8 February 1917.
49 CLCBm, 16 February 1917; T 172/746, Meeting with the Bankers, 16 February 1917.
50 T 172/745, correspondence between Martin-Holland and the Chancellor. The file contains a complete list of the underwriting banks and their commitments.
51 T 172/685, Cunliffe to Chancellor, 'War Loan Results', daily.
52 CLCBm, 16 February 1917.
53 Osborne (1926), I, p. 291.
54 MGP, Box British Government Loan 3, File November–December 1916, Grenfell to Davison, 20 November 1916.
55 T 172/746, Meeting with the Treasury subcommittee of the CLCB, 23 December 1916.
56 *Hansard* (Commons), 26 February 1917, cols 1696–7.
57 T 172/731, Interview with a journalist from United Press, March 1917.
58 *The Times*, 12 January 1917, p. 8.
59 Ibid., 19 January 1917, p. 34.
60 T 171/167, Deputation from the TUC to the Chancellor, 15 February 1917.
61 National War Savings Committee, *Second Annual Report*, p. 3; T 172/696, Kindersley, 'War Loan Campaign', undated.
62 Copies of the questionnaires and the replies are in T 172/701.
63 Osborne (1926), I, p. 419.
64 BLP, 65/3/15, Bonar Law to Northcliffe, 20 February 1917; Northcliffe Papers, Add. 62170/196–8, Le Bas to Northcliffe, undated, covering letter 7 February 1917. It appears that Le Bas had a breakdown. Add. 62170/200, Northcliffe to Le Bas's secretary, 12 February 1917.
65 T 172/623, Bonar Law to Strathclyde, 17 December 1917; BLP, 65/2/19, Reading to Bonar Law, 27 February 1917.
66 BoE, Loan Wallet 237(1), Bonar Law to Cunliffe, 16 January 1917.

67 T 172/685, Chancellor to Governor, 26 January 1917, and 'War Loan Results', 30 January 1917.
68 T 172/745, 'War Loan Subscriptions and Bank Deposits', 2 February 1917. There is an analysis of results for the whole banking system in the same file. Although it is undated, it was clearly produced after lists closed.
69 T 172/762, Inchcape to Chancellor, 15 January 1917.
70 Ibid., Philipps to Chancellor, 21 January 1917.
71 Ibid., H. M. Cleminson (General Manager of the Chamber of Shipping) to affiliated Associations of the Chamber of Shipping, 1 February 1917.
72 Ibid., W. H. Raeburn (President of the Chamber of Shipping) to Chancellor, 12 February 1917.
73 T 172/725, Local Government Board, 'Circular to County Councils, Town Councils and Metropolitan Borough Councils, Urban and Rural District Councils, and Boards of Guardians', 1 February 1917.
74 Lloyds Bank archives (Lloyds TSB Group Archives), circular from Ernest Sykes (Secretary of the Institute of Bankers), 7 February 1917.
75 Extracted from the subscriptions listed in *The Times*, 13 January to 20 February 1917.
76 The documents are in T 172/707, T 172/742 and T 172/746. See also CLCBm and CLCBt.
77 Chairman's Report for 1916, *The Economist*, 3 March 1917, pp. 437–8. The correspondence on the Prudential's subscription is in T 172/747.
78 T 172/746, Conference with certain Insurance Companies, 5 January 1917.
79 T 172/747, Chancellor to Insurance Companies and enclosed questionnaire, 22 January 1917.
80 The correspondence with the Life Offices is in T 172/712.
81 ABI, Life Offices' Association, Minutes of the Finance Committee, 30 January and 2 February 1917: T 172/746, W. P. Phelps (Chairman of The Life Offices' Association) to Bonar Law, 31 January 1917.
82 T 172/746, Meeting between the Chancellor and a deputation from The Life Offices' Association, 2 February 1917. For the French Loan, see *Bankers' Magazine*, January 1916, pp. 37–8, and February 1916, p. 292, and *The Economist*, 4 December 1915, p. 967.
83 ABI, Life Offices' Association, Minutes of the Taxation Committee, 15 February 1917, and Minutes of the Association, 12 March 1917.
84 Osborne (1926), I, p. 425; *Hansard* (Commons), 26 February 1917, cols 1695–1701.
85 Osborne (1926), I, p. 425.
86 *Hansard* (Commons), 27 November 1914, col. 1554, and 26 February 1917, col. 1698; T 172/696, 'War Loan: Post Office Issue', undated, and 'Comparison with Previous War Loans', unsigned and undated briefing paper for Commons statement, end-February 1917, and 'War Loan 1917', Bank of England, 24 February 1917; T 170/88, '£4:10/-% War Loan 1925–45', undated; Osborne (1926), I, p. 387. Strictly, the data for the Bank were not the number of subscribers, but the number of allotments.
87 Self (1995), Austen Chamberlain to Ida Chamberlain, 23 and 25 February 1917.
88 BLP, 65/2/19, Reading to Bonar Law, 27 February 1917.
89 T 172/746, First Conference with the Treasury subcommittee of the CLCB, 23 December 1916.

12 National War Bonds and continuous borrowing

> When I started this system a year ago I was doubtful whether it could be made to succeed. But we were so certain that it was the best method that I was determined to leave no effort undone to make it a success. After a year of trial, I am prepared to say not only that it has succeeded in the past, but that it is as certain as anything in the future can be that it will succeed until the end of the war.
>
> Andrew Bonar Law, 31 September 1918,
> *The Silver Bullet*,[a] 16 October 1918.

> There are two methods by which the money we need can be obtained. One is by periodical loan. The other is by a system of obtaining money week by week, or, as it is called, of continuous borrowing. The second method is admitted by every one to be the best. It disturbs to the smallest possible extent the general financial arrangements of the country. It is best, too, because it is in itself an indication of that constant staying power on which the issue of the war depends. It is best while the war is going on, but from the point of view of financial stability it will be found to be by far the best when the war is over.
>
> Andrew Bonar Law launching the 'Feed the Guns' campaign,
> *The Silver Bullet*, 16 October 1918.

The authorities were unwilling to press new paper on the investor immediately after the 1917 War Loans; in addition to the calls stretching to the end of May, they were well aware that many subscribers were carrying the Loans with borrowed money and that time was required if it was to be repaid from savings. A further issue of Exchequer Bonds was announced in April, but it sold poorly through the summer. Thus the reduction in the Bill issue was short-lived. The amount outstanding reached its low point for 1917 in April, sales were resumed the same month and by the end of the year the volume had returned to the levels of the

a The first edition of *The Silver Bullet*, a fortnightly journal, was published on 15 May 1918. Sutton claimed that 'They used to publish a *War Savings Journal*, very dull and most uninteresting, so I changed it into a live sheet of news to the various secretaries.' T 172/771, Sutton to Hamilton, 23 September 1918.

previous December. To this was added for the first time a substantial volume of Ways and Means Advances from the Bank. By the autumn it was clear that a new approach was required. The Bank proposed a medium-dated tap but, after testing outside opinion, both this and a long-dated loan were rejected, and four open-ended issues of short- and medium-dated Bonds with yields 7s to 8s per cent higher than those on the earlier Exchequer Bonds were introduced. They were to be sold in conjunction with the banks' branches and be the subject of intense publicity. To help the sales campaign, they were named National War Bonds, but they were Exchequer Bonds with technical improvements. There was one retrograde step: in the hope of selling sufficient to avoid another spectacular loan, holders were once more given the option to convert into future long-dated issues. With War Bonds, the authorities began consciously to practise a system of day-to-day borrowing.

To the general public, the most noticeable changes were the advertising campaigns calling for continuous saving and investment organised by the National and Scottish War Savings Committees. Bonar Law, at least in retrospect, was uncertain whether it was possible for advertising to maintain the pressure on the saver and recalled that he was only persuaded by the disadvantages of great loans. The record justified his decision: in May 1918, he was worrying about whether the system was workable; at mid-summer, he was persuaded it was a success; by the autumn, he was promising that War Bonds and continuous borrowing would be used until the war ended.

US Treasury advances gave the authorities more flexibility in setting interest rates and, for the first time, short-term rates were reduced to make longer-dated issues more attractive. At the end of 1917, two administrative measures gave further confidence. In November, the Bank started discriminating in favour of foreign balances when taking deposits from the banking system, and the following month controls on the export of capital were introduced.[1] At the end of December, the effectiveness of the new arrangements was put to the test: the rates on Bills and special deposits from domestic sources were reduced, while those on foreign-owned balances were left unchanged.

This chapter describes the growth of the Treasury's borrowing from the Departments, the Bank of England and, indirectly, the money market on Ways and Means. It then shows how the decision was made in the autumn of 1917 to rely on the continuous sale of War Bonds, in place of another great loan. Continuous availability meant little without equally continuous sales propaganda; the campaigns are described, together with moves to stimulate demand by reducing the return on very short-dated assets.

Fiscal policy

The budget presented on 2 May 1917 was prepared as the USA became a belligerent and shortly before the summer's exchange crisis. It was noteworthy for the paucity of its revenue-raising measures.[2] McKenna had forecast £1,825m of spending and £502m of revenue for 1916–17; borrowing of £1,323m would cover 72.5 per cent of expenditure. In the event, spending was £2,198m and revenue £573m, so that borrowing of £1,625m met 73.9 per cent of expenditure. Even with such a deficit, the Chancellor was reluctant to raise taxes, stressing that although a large debt would be 'a burden upon our trade and industry' taxes were already 'extremely heavy' and were reducing the capital which would be available after the war. In making his decision in favour of some increase, Bonar Law cited McKenna's dictum:

> that at the end of each financial year we should be able to show a surplus of revenue, not including the duties which will come to an end when the War closes, which will provide us with the amount necessary to carry on the service of the country, including a reasonable provision for paying off the debt which has been incurred.[3]

On this basis, and allowing a charge for interest and sinking fund equivalent to 5½ per cent of the Debt less advances to allies and the Empire, he estimated the previous year to have produced a surplus of £59m. In the current year, the standard would not be met unless taxes were raised. Nor would revenue cover as much expenditure as in the past. Thus he proposed increases in tobacco duty, entertainment tax and EPD. The rise in the latter, from 60 per cent to 80 per cent, was accompanied by the winding up of the Munitions Levy, which was absorbed into it, and – despite their endeavours when the War Loans were being issued – the loss by the shipowners of the right to claw back Duty paid in previous years. With the changes, revenue of £639m in 1917–18 would meet expenditure of £2,290m, so that borrowing of £1,652m would cover 72.1 per cent of spending. On McKenna's basis there would be a surplus of £2m.

Bonar Law's second budget was very different. On 3 March 1918, the Central Powers and the new Soviet government signed the Treaty of Brest-Litovsk. With their eastern border secure, the Germans transferred troops to the west and, knowing that the US army was fast expanding, on 21 March they launched their final great offensive. By the end of the month, they seemed on the point of a breakthrough. On 10 April, Lloyd George introduced another Man Power Bill, raising the age for conscription, and twelve days later Bonar Law presented his budget. With the newspapers filled with stories of military reverses, he felt able to impose sharp rises in taxation, including all the major revenues except death duties and EPD.[4] Income tax, supertax, postal charges, cheque stamps, excise duties and taxes on farmers were increased.[b] Despite the severity of the measures, they passed quietly through Parliament with little alteration. The only major exception to this was a proposal for a tax on luxuries, which was dropped.

With revenue in 1917–18 of £707m and expenditure of £2,696m, borrowing had turned out to be £1,989m instead of the £1,652m forecast in May 1917.

b The normal rate of income tax was raised from 5s to 6s, the starting point for supertax was reduced from £3,000 to £2,500 per year, and the maximum rate was raised from 3/6d to 4/6d.

Revenue in 1918–19 was forecast to be £842m, to which the tax increases were expected to contribute £68m. Spending was expected to be £2,972m. Of this, £2,130m, or 71.7 per cent of expenditure, was to be met from borrowing. Although these forecasts could have been used to justify the rise in taxation, the Chancellor chose instead to make propaganda, showing satisfaction at the part played by revenue in financing the war and contrasting it with Germany's greater reliance on borrowing. He dwelt once more on meeting the McKenna standard

> which I adopted and tried to carry out last year...the Chancellor of the Exchequer should aim to produce such a result that, on the assumption that the War came to an end at the close of the year for which the financial statement was made, there would be a sufficient revenue without new borrowing or new taxation to make sure that not only the expenditure left after the War, but the Debt charge could be met. My budget last year was designed to obtain that result...I venture to say that, whatever difference of opinion there may be on other aspects of finance, no one will doubt that, as long as it is humanly possible for the country to live up to that standard, it is our absolute duty to see that it is carried out.[5]

Spelling out how it dictated the rises, the Chancellor estimated peacetime expenditure to be £650m: £380m for interest and sinking fund and £270m for other expenditure. Peacetime revenues at existing tax rates, excluding items to be regarded as temporary, such as EPD, were estimated to be only £540m. Thus, observing the rule meant raising revenue by at least £110m in a full year. The Chancellor's measures, excluding the luxury taxes, aimed to raise £114m.

The Chancellor was on uncertain ground when estimating the debt charge. In previous budgets, all the allied and Dominion debts had been treated as good. After the events in Russia this was no longer tenable and some write-off had become necessary. Bonar Law now assumed that one-half of the £1,632m forecast to have been advanced to the allies by the end of 1918–19 would not be repaid, and that all the Dominions' debts of £244m and the remaining £64m of India's 1917 gift of £100m were good (Appendix VI); £380m was 5½ per cent of a net Debt calculated on these assumptions to be £6,856m at the end of March 1919.

The argument was wholly artificial. It is not recorded why exactly 50 per cent was selected; the previous year, the Chancellor had met the standard with only £2m to spare, the equivalent of the interest and sinking fund on just £36m of securities, or about ½ per cent of the Debt. The 5½ per cent was inherited and the sinking fund component was becoming rapidly less, and the interest cost more, as securities were issued bearing high wartime interest rates. Other reasons have to be found for the write-down. Most importantly, as in the previous year, Bonar Law saw himself as treading a path between increasing the contribution to war expenditure from revenue and damaging the economy, threatening support for the war by imposing an excessive tax burden; although it is supposition, the precise level of the write-off was surely determined by the size of the tax increases that the Chancellor judged to be acceptable. Then there was the need to show public creditors that their security was safe, especially after the Russian default and the rumbles about a capital levy in the UK. Least important, there may have been the tactical argument that McKenna's attack would be blunted if the rise in taxation was justified by his own dictum.

5 per cent Exchequer Bonds 1922 (12 April 1917)

Only £131m Treasury Bills were tendered as subscriptions for the Loans in January and February 1917, but the volume in issue fell rapidly as the maturities ran off and were not renewed: on 2 April, the amount outstanding dropped to £452m, the low point for the year. The following day sales were resumed, the volume in issue again breaking through £1,000m in November and reaching £1,139m on 7 December.[c] This proved to be a peak, not to be exceeded until 1920. Until then, £1,000m became a permanent level and, except in the summer of 1919 when sales were suspended for the sale of the Victory Bonds and Funding Loan, the issue only occasionally moved outside a range of £950m to £1,050m. (Table 12.1).

When the issue of Bills was resumed, it was on an experimental basis with £50m three, six and twelve months' maturities being sold by tender. This method was chosen to provide a guide to the appropriate price if it became necessary to resume sales by tap and to reward the banks for their support during the issue of the War Loans. However, it was found that there were considerable drawbacks: tendering excluded non-professional investors, who lacked the expertise to price their bids; the size was too large for the money market to handle by itself; the banks and discount market were able to work the price against the government; and the concentration of settlements upset the banks.[6] From 28 April, at the Bank's suggestion, the offers at the regular tenders were reduced and applications were received, between the tenders, for smaller amounts of the same maturities at fixed rates of discount. The rates on these 'intermediate' or 'additional' Bills were lower than the average for the same maturity sold at tender during the previous seven days. The initial rate was fixed at 4⁵/₈ per cent for three and six months' maturities and 4⁷/₈ per cent for twelve months' maturities (Table 12.2). In order not to divert purchasers from longer paper, they were issued in minimum amounts of £25,000 and tenders were confined to banks and discount houses.[7]

The Treasury returned to the market on 12 April with a further issue of Exchequer Bonds. The earlier 5 per cent Bonds stood at a discount; in the middle of March, those maturing in 1919 and 1921 were changing hands at about 99½. Despite this, with the memory of the problems produced by the conversion options on the 4½ per cent Loan and the Exchequer Bonds still fresh, the authorities decided not to offer conversion into future long-dated issues.[8] Thus, if a 5 per cent interest rate at par was to be retained, privileges had to be given which were unavailable on the previous issues.[9]

c Although tenders for Bills were not renewed until 3 April 1917, the announcement was made on 23 March.

Table 12.1 The floating debt: September 1914 to March 1920 [£m (end-quarters)]

	Treasury Bills	Ways and Means			Total
		Departmental	[of which CNRA]	Bank	
September 1914	50	9	[7]	–	59
December	98	7	[6]	–	105
March 1915	77	–	–	–	77
June	251	–	–	–	251
September	254	1	–	–	255
December	396	70	[25]	–	466
March 1916	567	20	[16]	–	587
June	761	42	[42]	9	812
September	1,041	36	[19]	–	1,077
December	1,116	95	[40]	46	1,257
March 1917	464	153	[81]	65	682
June	652	136	[57]	79	867
September	949	130	[83]	91	1,170
December	1,058	122	[99]	157	1,337
March 1918	974	124	[99]	69	1,167
June	1,060	155	[127]	160	1,375
September	1,109	187	[142]	158	1,454
December	1,092	222	[169]	233	1,547
March 1919	957	227	[168]	229	1,413
June	796	45	[184]	529	1,370
September	851	190	[105]	203	1,244
December	1,106	187	[93]	56	1,349
March 1920	1,107	205	[47]	–	1,312

Notes

Ways and Means exclude those made on account of special deposits from overseas customers of the banks.

The data for Departmental and CNRA Ways and Means at end-June 1919 are unexplained, but may be produced by inflows from the sale of Victory Bonds and Funding Loan.

Sources: *The London Gazette*; BoE, C98/6937 and C98/6938; *National Debt: annual returns*; CNRA Ledgers; Morgan (1952), p. 170.

The early drafts gave holders the option to demand repayment at par half-way through the issue's life and on every subsequent six-monthly interest payment date. Cunliffe considered this to be too generous, indeed, any such right to be too generous:

> I cannot recommend repayment after 2½ years at the option of the holder, because it gives away too much. If money should become dear, all holders would demand early repayment and vice versa if it should become cheap.

Table 12.2 Treasury Bill rates: 1917–21

By tender from 3 April to 19 June 1917 (average rates of discount)

	High	Low
Three months'	£4 16s 3d	£4 11s 10d
Six months'	£4 17s 10d	£4 14s 5d
Twelve months'	£4 19s 11d	£4 17s 2d

Intermediates from 28 April to 19 June 1917 (rates of discount)

	Bills dated: 30 April*	7 May
Three months'	4 5/8	4 5/8
Six months'	4 5/8	4 5/8
Twelve months'	4 7/8	4 13/16

Bills issued by tap from 20 June 1917 to 2 June 1919, reintroduced 15 July 1919 and continued until April 1921 (rates of discount)

	Two months'	Three months'	Six months'	Twelve months'
20 June 1917	–	4 1/2	4 1/2	–
4 July	–	4 3/4	4 3/4	–
28 December	–	4	4	–
15 February 1918	–	3 1/2	3 1/2	–
2 June 1919		Sales suspended		
15 July	3 3/8	3 1/2	4	–
16 August	–	3 1/2	4	–
7 October	–	4 1/2	5	–
8 November	–	5 1/2	5 1/2	–
20 March 1920	–	5 1/2	–	5 1/2
15 April	–	6 1/2	–	6 1/2
30 April	–	6 1/2	–	–
12 March 1921	–	6	–	6
23 April	–	5 5/8†	–	6
27 April	–	5 5/8†	–	5 3/4
30 April	–	5 3/8†	–	5 3/4
14 May	–	5 1/4†	–	5 3/4
23 May	–	5 3/8†	–	5 3/4
6 June	–	5 1/4†	–	5 3/4
24 June	–	5†	–	5 1/2
1 July	–	5†	5 1/2	–
8 July	–	5†	–	–
11 July	–	4 7/8†	–	–
18 July	–	4 5/8†	–	–
25 July	–	4 1/8†	–	–
8 August	–	4 1/4†	–	–
15 August	–	4 1/2†	–	–
22 August	–	4 3/8†	–	–

Table 12.2 continued.

By tender from 25 April 1921 (average rates of discount)

	Three months' only:	
	High	Low
April/May	£5 19s 4d	£5 11s 3d
June	£5 12s 2d	£5 6s 9d
July	£5 7s 3d	£4 8s 3d
August	£4 15s 4d	£4 8s 8d

Notes
*Application on Saturday 28 April for payment Monday 30 April.
†Additional Bills, issued in parallel with three-months' tender Bills at advertised rates.

Sources: Osborne (1926), I, pp. 485–88: *The Economist*, various dates.

Despite the common sense of this, the Governor won only part of his case, presumably because, without a conversion option, the new Bonds were so much less attractive than the old. In their final form, they matured on 1 April 1922 with a put on 1 October 1919, but on no other date until maturity. It was probably this that made the Treasury decide to extend further the use of the Bonds for the payment of taxes. The Governor had hoped that the Bonds could be made sufficiently attractive, even without the puts, if holders could use them to pay all taxes, but, once again, his advice was only partially taken.[10] An option to use the Bonds to pay EPD, as well as the usual death duties, had been included in the first drafts. To these were now added Munitions Exchequer Payments, a minor concession, it might be thought, to put in the balance against the less generous put. In all cases, acceptance of the Bonds by the Inland Revenue, following the precedent of the War Loans, was conditional on their having been held since subscription or for at least six months.

The issue was withdrawn on 24 September 1917. It had sold poorly, with the total reaching only £82.3m, or £3m per week.[d] Many reasons were advanced to account for this: the absence of conversion rights, the increase in EPD announced in the budget, the reduction in British sales of American securities, the strain on savers of their subscriptions for the War Loans, the need to repay bank advances and the attractions of the 5 per cent Loan in the secondary market at a discount to its issue price. In June, Bradbury had pinned the blame on the last three, disagreeing with Blackett, who had stressed the absence of the conversion option:

> I do not attach much importance to the comparison…between the sales of 5% Exchequer Bonds in 1916/17 and 1917/18. Last year they had not to compete with a 5% Government Stock [5 per cent War Loan] at 94½ nor was the average investor then carrying his subscription to a previous loan with the aid of a banker's advance.
>
> Sir Felix Schuster estimates that at least 25% of the subscriptions of private [personal sector] investors to the 5% Loan are still owing to the banks and if

d Even this included £7.9m (11 per cent of the amount outstanding at 31 March 1918) sold to the Commissioners. *BGS*, p. 482.

> this is so we cannot expect the Exchequer Bonds to go very well with this class.
>
> ...the average daily sales are higher than either the Governor of the Bank or I contemplated when the issue was brought out, but I am afraid that the bulk of them are being taken as a merely temporary investment of Excess Profits Duty awaiting payment and are therefore substantially merely Treasury Bills.

In any case, he said, because the rump of the 4½ per cent War Loan was being quoted at only 91½, the investor could not value conversion options highly.

However, although he did not agree that the terms should be altered and conversion rights included, Bradbury did think that some stimulus to sales was required.[11] This was provided on 19 June by measures to reduce the return on short-term assets. The combination of weekly tenders for three-, six- and twelve-months' Bills and intermediates was replaced with tap sales of three and six months' maturities; the absence of longer Bills was widely interpreted as an encouragement to sales of Exchequer Bonds.[12] Simultaneously, the rate offered on special deposits from the banks was reduced by ½ per cent (Table 4.2). Although Bill rates were raised on 4 July when sterling was suffering its greatest strain in New York and it was uncertain whether US Treasury advances could be used to maintain the peg, the moves were the first to take advantage of US Treasury support to make longer-dated sterling securities more attractive.

Bill rates were cut twice during the winter. When differential rates on foreign-owned deposits were being discussed in November, consideration was given to a reduction, specifically to increase the attractions of War Bonds. The cut was postponed; the Chancellor wanted Reading, who did not leave the USA until 3 November, to advise on its effects, while the CLCB decided against cutting deposit rates because sterling (and the US dollar) were weak against the Scandinavian currencies and the seriousness of the Italian defeat at Caporetto was becoming clear.[13] The reduction came at the end of December, and was followed by another in February 1918, contributing to the improvement in War Bond sales seen in the new year (Table 12.2).

Ways and Means Advances

Until the beginning of 1917, Ways and Means Advances were taken from the Bank of England on a minor scale and retained their pre-war character of temporary help in anticipation of revenue.[e] In April and September 1916, the Bank expressed its concern at the Advances it was making to enable the Treasury to make its

e Osborne's comment was that 'Until the close of the year 1916 Advances by the Bank to H. M. Exchequer on the credit of Ways & Means retained their pre-War character of purely temporary Advances in anticipation of Revenue...Early in 1917 [Advances] gradually assumed a much more permanent character.' Osborne (1926), I, p. 291. The entries in BoE, C74/1, 'Ways & Means & Deficiency Advances. 1871–1921' illustrate the change.

interest payments but, although large, these were akin to Deficiency Advances and were repaid by the end of the month. That summer, Advances were £5m at the end of May and £9m at the end of June, July and August.[f] The first substantial Advances were taken in January 1917 when Bill sales were suspended for the War Loans campaign and, for the following five years, they were to be a permanent feature. They reached nearly £300m in the middle of February 1917, before the proceeds of the Loans permitted a rapid repayment. They drifted up to about £90m in the summer, and to above £100m at the beginning of July, leading the Court on 5 July to signal their anxiety to the Chancellor.[14] Despite this plea, and the introduction of War Bonds on 1 October, Advances continued to expand and by the end of December they were £157m. Business Men's Week and tax-gathering then produced a rapid reduction and they stood at £69m on 31 March 1918, only £3.5m above their level of a year earlier. This did not last. At the beginning of April, they were once more over £100m, and by the beginning of June only just short of £200m. They then fluctuated between about £140m and £200m until the Armistice (see Table 12.1 for end-quarter data).[15]

Outside the Bank, there were three sources of Ways and Means. The Exchequer Accounts in the books of the Bank of England show that the traditional pre-war providers – the Commissioners, the Secretary of State for India, the Road Improvement Fund and the Paymaster-General – continued to make Advances, those from the latter growing particularly strongly, both during and after the war; in March 1920, they amounted to over £130m.[16] To these were added in 1916 and 1917 Advances from new departments conducting government trading activities. Overshadowing both traditional and new providers were two accounts which played a central role in the wartime monetary system: the CNRA and 'investments o/a Bank Borrowing', whose liability was the special deposits lodged with the Bank of England (Tables 4.3 and 12.1).

The CNRA made Advances from its inception, its first (of £7m) being on 1 September 1914.[17] As the security for the Currency Note issue and the Treasury's *masse de manoeuvre*, its holdings would have been expected to be fluid and, indeed, it moved freely between Bills and Advances, as it came to do later between securities in the longer part of the market. It made no Advances during much of 1915, its cash being used to absorb 3 per cent Exchequer Bonds 1920, help finance the savings banks' applications for 4½ per cent War Loan and buy the £28.5m of gold transferred to it during 1914 and 1915 (see pp. 96–7 and 117). The Account's Advances became permanent from the last quarter of 1915, after which they moved

f BoE, ADM 33/1, 'Annotated Sayers'; CTM, 6 September, 13 September and 20 September 1916; the correspondence is recorded in CTM, 20 September 1916. Sayers (1976), I, pp. 95–6, has a different emphasis: 'The government had relied also on large advances from the Bank; these had been allowed to run on, for all the world as if they were no different from the marginal borrowings of peacetime. In 1916 the Bank formally represented to the Treasury its view that the creation of credit by the Bank at such a rate was increasing the difficulties of the Bank in its efforts to uphold the value of money and maintain the foreign exchanges.' See also Osborne (1926), I, pp. 300–1.

erratically, but generally upward, to reach £169m at the end of December 1918 (see Table 12.1 for end-quarter data).

When the Account 'investments o/a Bank Borrowing' was established in the autumn of 1915, the money was invested entirely in Treasury Bills (see p. 93). This continued until November 1917, when it was decided that higher rates should be offered on foreign-owned deposits than on domestic.

This measure had been suggested during the controversy surrounding the rise in interest rates in the second half of 1916.[18] Advocates had included the Chancellor and Norman, but the Governor opposed it, believing that it would be impossible to police.[19] The weak exchange rate in the autumn of 1917 gave the case renewed impetus and a scheme was introduced on 12 November. Concern about the potential for abuse led the Bank initially to confine it to the clearing banks, but on 2 January 1918 it was extended to cover any bank having an account with the Bank of England and other firms and companies approved by the Governor.[g]

Foreign deposits with the Bank rose rapidly from the moment the scheme was introduced, the expansion coming from deposits identifying themselves, and not from the attraction of new money into sterling.[h] The higher rates meant that a new vehicle had to be found for onlending them to the Treasury. The Bills in which the Account had been investing since October 1915 normally earned 1/2 per cent more than was paid by the Bank to the clearing banks. The rate paid by the clearing banks on interest-bearing deposits from the public was normally the rate they were paid by the Bank of England on the special deposits: an exception was the fourteen months from 23 November 1915 to 2 January 1917 (Table 4.2). However, Bills would not yield sufficient to cover the higher rate paid by the Bank on overseas deposits, nor could it be assumed that the rate on Bills would move in parallel with that paid to foreigners. It was decided that the domestic special deposits should continue to be invested in Bills, but overseas deposits should be lent to the Treasury on Ways and Means at an artificially high rate (Table 12.3). This procedure was not always followed slavishly. Ways and Means shown by the annual returns are too small to include all the overseas deposits taken under the Bank's scheme; either some of the deposits were, like their domestic brethren, invested in Treasury Bills in the normal course of events or the window was dressed by switching into Bills over make-up days.[20]

g 'Foreign balances' were defined as those held in sterling in the UK by a firm or bank for a non-British Empire client (whose name needed to be disclosed) or for a non-British Empire bank or firm which did not have a office in the UK. The depositor had to declare that the money was freely available for sale into other currencies. It excluded money held for a foreign branch of the bank or firm by whom the money was being lent to the Bank.

h Within two days foreign deposits were £24m. By the first week of January 1918, they had risen to £59m; they broke through £100m in April. The maximum on foreign account in 1918 was £166m and in 1919 £172m (see Table 4.3 for end-quarter data). Osborne (1926), I, pp. 283–5; BoE, C58/38 and C58/39; CTM, weekly.

Table 12.3 Interest rates paid on Ways and Means Advances

7 August 1914	Bank rate with a maximum of 5 per cent*
8 August 1914	Bank rate with a maximum of 5 per cent*
9 August to end-August 1914	4 per cent
October 1914	3 per cent
November 1914	2½ per cent
31 May to 27 September 1916	4½ per cent
27 December 1916 to 18 June 1917	5 per cent
19 June 1917 to December 1917	4½ per cent
31 December 1917 to 14 February 1918	4 per cent (plus 1 per cent on foreign money from end-December)
15 February 1918 to end-May 1919	3½ per cent

Notes

*Bank rate: 30 July, 4 per cent; 31 July, 8 per cent; 1 August, 10 per cent; 6 August, 6 per cent; 8 August, 5 per cent.

Source: Osborne (1926), I, p. 297.

When the scheme was abolished in October 1919 it was accompanied by a steep rise in Bill rates, the intention being to attract the deposits into marketable debt; the effect on government borrowing was to deflate Ways and Means and to inflate the Bill issue (see p. 411).

National War Bonds: the beginning of day-to-day borrowing

By the beginning of September 1917, the Bill issue had reached £846m. Reflecting this, and the Advances from the Bank of England, bank deposits had risen steeply.[i] Later that month, after consultation with a group from the City which included Harry Goschen (the new chairman of the CLCB), Inchcape and Sir Robert Nivison, a stockbroker, the decision was made to postpone a long-dated loan[j] and rely on redesigned short- and medium-dated Bonds.[21]

i Net bank deposits were £1,451m at end-December 1916, £1,431m at end-June 1917, and £1,706m at end-December 1917: Capie and Webber (1985), Table 11.(1). Although contemporaries accepted that deposits had expanded rapidly, not all agreed that they were available to buy government securities. For example, Rupert Beckett, a partner in a Leeds bank, agreed that customers' balances in the north were 'very high' but emphasised that they were awaiting the determination and payment of EPD. Arthur Kiddy, City Editor of the *Morning Post*, wrote to the Chancellor that he 'was impressed by the almost unanimous opinion amongst bankers that while the unemployed funds in the hands of manufacturers, profiteers etc are great, smaller individuals have little spare margin at the moment.' T 172/555, Beckett to Chancellor, 8 September 1917 and Kiddy to Chancellor, 24 September 1917.

j The Governor was reported as saying, slightly petulantly, that 'The Chancellor seemed to be in favour of piling up Treasury Bills and Ways and Means Advances until early next year, when he felt he could bring out another funding loan, but the bankers were not in agreement with him.' The Committee of Treasury hoped that the Chancellor would issue short-term Bonds 'in order that without further delay, the way might be open for a rise in the rate for Treasury Bills and in the Bank Rate'. Apparently, the view continued to be held that the level of three and six months' rates did not affect the attractions of longer securities. CTM, 19 September 1917.

The initial advice from the Governor and Goschen had been to have an immediate loan limited to about £350m, followed in February by another of a similar size.[k] This had not appealed to the Chancellor. The momentum of the publicity campaign would be lost, only to need restarting a few months later, while Goschen himself had told him that the banks were unwilling to commit themselves to further underwriting when so many of the advances made to help investors subscribe for the two earlier loans had yet to be repaid. Also, it was 'psychologically' a bad moment for a loan. The situation in Russia was confused and, in common with many of his Cabinet colleagues, the Chancellor believed that nothing would come of the offensive launched in Flanders on 31 July.[22] Through August and September, the Committee of Treasury at the Bank was debating a rise in Bank rate. Although US Treasury advances were flowing more easily, McAdoo was anxious about his ability to meet the demands being placed on him by the allies and was about to launch the Second Liberty Loan campaign. Short-term rates in New York were hardening and the problems caused by US banks' sales of sterling when the First Liberty Loan was producing tight conditions must have been fresh in officials' minds.[23] On 18 September, a few days after the decision against a spectacular loan had been made, Bonar Law wrote to Lloyd George that 'The financial situation is getting increasingly difficult and the bankers are not much help.'[24] There were also personal reasons for avoiding the strain of a campaign: the Chancellor was finding it difficult to run both the Treasury and lead the Commons and, in addition, at the end of September his eldest son was reported missing in France.[25]

An increase in the coupon on the new Bonds to 5½ per cent was considered, but dismissed, the CLCB advising that the rise in the rate would not by itself ensure success. Instead, the Committee suggested that the Bonds should be redeemed at a premium and include the option to convert into future long-dated loans, the ghost that the Treasury thought had been laid that spring with the 5 per cent Exchequer Bonds 1922.[26] The reason for this advice, which was echoed by Inchcape, is not recorded. There was opposition from the Chancellor and Nivison, who claimed to have foreseen the problems which would result from the conversion options on the 4½ per cent War Loan in 1915. He had advised then and would repeat now that:

> it would be a halter round the Chancellor's neck, would put him at the mercy of holders whose personal interest would be served by the price going down just before a new issue, enabling them to use that fact as an argument for more attractive terms – that while it was going to be called a 4½% loan it

k There seems to have been disagreement within the Bank. Clay says that during the summer Norman urged a ten-year 'tap bond' on the Committee of Treasury and HM Treasury. He also puts the Chancellor's testing of outside opinion in the context of his lack of confidence in Cunliffe. Clay (1957), p. 105. Also see CTM, 5 September 1917. The Bank's inability to handle a large loan may have been partly responsible for the Governor's advice. CTM, 12 September 1917, and Clay (1957), p. 105.

> might be a 5% – 5½% or even 6% before he was done with it...I could see no justification for it unless he [the Chancellor] was satisfied that he would be able to go on financing the war without the option coming into operation.

In the present case:

> You must not be surprised if conceding the option gives rise to a good deal of private, if not of public criticism, especially from the holders of the 5% when they see a very valuable privilege given to subscribers of the new loan which was withheld from them.[27]

Although the Chancellor agreed, he was persuaded that if there were to be a new issue it must be capable of raising a really large sum, so making it possible to avoid a conventional long-dated loan whose sale might coincide with a military setback.[28] The same argument – as usual, favoured by the bankers – persuaded him to accept a ten-year, 4 per cent tax-compounded issue, although he still feared it would be criticised as favouring the wealthy.[29] In the event, the tax-compounded War Bonds met some demand, in contrast with the similar War Loan in January and February 1917. The success was confined to the First Series and it is probable that the sales preceded the budget of 1918, when there were strong expectations that income tax rates would be raised (Table 12.4).

Four series of the War Bonds were issued: in October 1917, April 1918, October 1918 and February 1919. Each series included three or four separate issues, so that investors could select maturities according to their needs. The issues in each series were similar, but with slightly later maturity dates. The eleven taxable issues had 5 per cent coupons with maturity at a premium. The four tax-compounded issues had 4 per cent coupons with maturity at par. The yields on the taxable Bonds ranged from £5 7s 1d per cent on the shortest to £5 7s 8d per cent on the longest (Table 12.5).

There is a hint in the records, and it is only a hint, that the new series were introduced to spread the number and size of coupon payments.[30] Otherwise, we are left with surmising from first principles. Limiting the size of individual issues, especially as they were single-dated, can be assumed to have been the most important. Putting short-dated Bonds with redemption at a premium to their issue levels on sale at a fixed price meant that the GRYs rose noticeably over quite short periods: that on the shortest War Bond of the First Series, the 5 per cents of 1 October 1922, rose by nearly 10d per cent over the first six months and that on the 5 per cents of 1924 by 7d per cent. This made leaving a series on tap for a long period bad debt management; War Bonds of the same series sold later were more expensive for the Treasury than those sold earlier and it paid investors to delay purchases. As the shortest issues were the most successful, it also meant that the Treasury was selling securities with rapidly shortening maturities. Finally, if the GRYs had been allowed to continue to rise, it might have embarrassed the Chancellor, who had promised at the beginning of 1917, when launching the 4 and 5 per cent Loans, that there would be no borrowing at a higher rate. This

Table 12.4 National War Bonds outstanding: 31 March 1918 and 1919 (£m nominal)

	31 March 1918	*31 March 1919*
First Series		
5 per cent of 1 October 1922	237.9	217.8
5 per cent of 1 October 1924	28.7	28.3
5 per cent of 1 October 1927	263.2	251.9
4 per cent (tax-compounded) of 1 October 1927	119.5	113.0
Second Series		
5 per cent of 1 April 1923		229.9
5 per cent of 1 April 1925		13.6
5 per cent of 1 April 1928		186.5
4 per cent (tax-compounded) of 1 April 1928		51.4
Third Series		
5 per cent of 1 September 1923		172.8
5 per cent of 1 September 1925		20.9
5 per cent of 1 September 1928		286.0
4 per cent (tax-compounded) of 1 April 1928		28.6
Fourth Series		
5 per cent of 1 February 1924		12.3
5 per cent of 1 February 1929		20.9
4 per cent (tax-compounded) of 1 February 1929		2.3

Note
The total amount of each issue sold is not recorded.

Source: *National Debt: annual returns*.

promise may also have contributed to the decision to adopt the bankers' proposal of maturity at a premium as the means of increasing the 5 per cent yields that had been offered on Exchequer Bonds since December 1915; retaining 5 per cent coupons provided camouflage, ostensibly flimsy but, because of the conversion options, actually very powerful.

There were a welter of these. Holders of the first three series had the same option as the holders of the 4½ per cent War Loan 1925–45 and the earlier 5 per cent and 6 per cent Exchequer Bonds to tender their holdings at par (thus forfeiting the premium at maturity) as the equivalent of cash for subscriptions into future long-dated securities issued during the war. The holders of the three taxable issues of the first three series also had the option on any coupon payment date to convert at par (also forfeiting the premium) into 5 per cent War Loan 1929–47 at the issue price, that is, to obtain £105 5s 3d of Loan for £100 of War Bonds. Holders of the 4 per cent tax-compounded Bonds had a similar option to convert into 4 per cent War Loan 1929–42, in this case converting £100 into £100.

Thus, if the GRYs on the taxable War Bonds were questioned, it could be answered that the cost of the premiums was indeterminate until it was known how many War Bonds had been converted into 5 per cent War Loan and when 5 per cent War Loan was going to be redeemed. Both would only be known a safe

Table 12.5 The four series of National War Bonds

	Price at issue	*Price at maturity*	*GRY (per cent)*
First Series			
(in issue from 2 October 1917 to 31 March 1918)			
5 per cent of 1 October 1922	100	102	£5 7s 1d
5 per cent of 1 October 1924	100	103	£5 7s 2d
5 per cent of 1 October 1927	100	105	£5 7s 8d
4 per cent (tax-compounded) of 1 October 1927	100	100	£5 6s 8d*
Second Series			
(in issue from 2 April to 1 October 1918)			
5 per cent of 1 April 1923	100	102	£5 7s 1d
5 per cent of 1 April 1925	100	103	£5 7s 2d
5 per cent of 1 April 1928	100	105	£5 7s 8d
4 per cent (tax-compounded) of 1 April 1928	100†	100	£5 6s 8d*
	101½	100	£5 9s 1d‡
Third Series			
(in issue from 1 October 1918 to 18 January 1919)			
5 per cent of 1 September 1923	100	102	£5 7s 2d
5 per cent of 1 September 1925	100	103	£5 7s 4d
5 per cent of 1 September 1928	100	105	£5 7s 10d
4 per cent (tax-compounded) of 1 September 1928	101½	100	£5 9s 1d‡
Fourth Series			
(in issue from 1 February to 31 May 1919)			
5 per cent of 1 February 1924	100	102	£5 7s 1d
5 per cent of 1 February 1929	100	105	£5 7s 8d
4 per cent (tax-compounded) of 1 February 1929	101½	100	£5 9s 1d‡

Notes
*Grossed-up net redemption yield with income tax at 5s in the £.
†Until 22 April 1918, thereafter 101½.
‡Grossed-up net redemption yield with income tax at 6s. in the £.
Yields are calculated from the first day on which the Bonds were in issue.

number of years away. The yield on the War Bonds would have been £5 0s 0d per cent until converted at 100 into 5 per cent War Loan; £5⅜ per cent, if held to maturity as War Bonds; or about £5 7s 0d per cent if converted into 5 per cent War Loan and held to maturity in 1947 (the precise GRY depended on when the option was exercised). For the purposes of the defence, the £5 13s 0d per cent yield given by War Loan if it was redeemed at its earliest date in 1929 could be legitimately ignored.

Holders of the rump of the 4½ per cent War Loan 1925–45, the 5 per cent Exchequer Bonds 1919, 1920 and 1921 and the 6 per cent Exchequer Bonds 1920, with their options of being used as the equivalent of cash to subscribe for new long-dated loans at par, were given the right to convert into either the 1924 or the

1927 5 per cent War Bonds or the tax-compounded 4 per cents for as long as they were on tap. This last clause was necessary because it was thought that the Bonds were being 'subscribed' as long as they were on 'tap'.

There was some debate about whether the latter privilege was necessary. The prospectuses spoke of the acceptance of the securities 'as the equivalent of cash for the purposes of subscription' to new loans. Excluded were loans raised abroad, Exchequer Bonds, Bills and other short-dated securities. As Bradbury put it:

> The 5 year National War Bond though not in terms an Exchequer Bond is undoubtedly a similar short-dated security. The 7 year and 10 year Bonds might, I think, reasonably be regarded as falling within the same category, but the Government is most anxious, in any case of doubt, to place on its pledges the interpretation most favourable to those to whom they were given.[31]

This was no doubt true, but the option was also good debt management. Giving Exchequer Bonds dated 1919, 1920 and 1921 costing 5 per cent the option to convert into 1924 and 1927 War Bonds costing £5$^3/_8$ per cent was a justifiable price to pay for lengthening the Debt: giving them the option to convert into a 1922 Bond, also costing 5$^3/_8$ per cent, was not. Equally, giving an Exchequer Bond dated 1920 costing 6 per cent the right to convert into 1924 and 1927 War Bonds costing 5$^3/_8$ per cent could only have the effect of lengthening the Debt while reducing its cost.

There were also good reasons for offering conversion into the two War Loans. As was to be shown in the 1920s, it could suit the Treasury if holders of the 5 per cent and the 4 per cent War Bonds converted. The War Bonds matured on specific dates. If holders converted they would be moving a minimum of two years longer, as well as giving the government a thirteen- and an eighteen-year option. Moreover, the option would cost nothing unless 5 per cent War Loan was called well before 1947. In the case of the tax-compounded issues, the cost was 4 per cent on both the War Bonds and the War Loan. In the case of the 5 per cent War Bonds, the GRY, when the premium on redemption was included, was almost the same as that on the 5 per cent War Loan at the exercise price of 95 if held to 1947. If the War Bonds were converted, the government would not have to pay the premium, the yield that investors had enjoyed until they converted was 5 per cent and the GRY (to 1947) that they obtained on the War Loan into which they were converting was the same that they would have enjoyed on their War Bonds had they held them until maturity.

The bankers had suggested more generous terms. They had wanted the tax-compounded issue to be convertible into either the tax-compounded 4 per cent War Loan 1929–42 or the 5 per cent taxable War Loan 1929–47. The Chancellor himself pointed out that this would mean that the investor could hold the tax-compounded War Bond when tax rates were high and convert into the taxable Loan with its higher gross yield when taxes fell. It would also mean that the Treasury would not know how much interest was potentially untaxable. Thus, both symmetry and caution demanded that the tax-compounded War Bond should only be convertible into a tax-compounded Loan.[32] Oddly, although the Chancellor was sensitive to the charge that tax-compounded securities favoured the wealthy, symmetry did not extend to the conversion terms, those attached to the tax-compounded Bonds being more generous than those attached to the taxable. Holders of the 4 per cents could exercise their options on the same terms (£100 nominal for £100) each half-year throughout their lives, but the tax-paying Bonds lost their redemption premiums when they were converted. Because the premiums could be regarded as accumulating in a straight line over the life of the Bonds, the longer conversion was delayed the greater was the amount of premium forfeited. It is plausible that the Bank won the Treasury's agreement because converting nominal for nominal was straightforward and reduced administration. It might also have judged that the high rates of income tax being levied in 1917 would not last into the peace. In this case, tax-compounded borrowing would represent cheap finance, which could be contemplated with equanimity.

Except for the maturity, the terms of the First and Second Series were the same. The interest payment dates on the Third were moved, 1 April/1 October being crowded with 5 per cent Exchequer Bonds 1922 as well as the two series of War Bonds. There were two other adjustments to the Third Series. In order to keep the net yield unchanged, the price of the tax-compounded War Bond of the Second Series was increased from 100 to 101½ when the normal rate of income tax was raised from 5s to 6s in April 1918.[33] This presented difficulties for those investors in earlier issues with unused conversion rights holding their securities in the form of Bonds to bearer because, when converting, they would need to be issued with an odd value of Bonds, although the War Bond prospectus only authorised bearer holdings in round values.[34] The new prospectus was changed so that holdings of the converting issues could be used as the 'equivalent of cash' in payment for applications. The other change, justifiably described by Ernest Harvey, the Deputy Chief Cashier, as 'a little complicated', was to the method of lodging applications to convert from War Bonds into the 5 per cent and 4 per cent War Loans.

The Fourth Series was on sale between 1 February and 31 May 1919. On this occasion, there were only three issues: two were taxable, dated 1 February 1924 and 1 February 1929, and one tax-compounded, as usual with a maturity date coinciding with the longest taxable issue. The Armistice signed, the terms were markedly tighter. There were no options to convert into either future loans or the two existing War Loans. In contrast, there was no tightening of the tax privileges such as had been advocated by Bradbury when designing the funding loan in 1918 (see p. 388).

The lack of a middle-dated issue reflected the lack of demand for that maturity in the first three series (Table 12.4). There is only anecdotal evidence to explain their unpopularity. It seems that they fell between the banks, foreigners and industrial and commercial enterprises, who took the shorter issues, and individuals, trustees and life funds, who were reported to be buying the War Loans and 2½ per cent Consols during the summer of 1918. It was also believed that there was demand for the shorter-dated War Bonds, and for Bills, from investors who had cash which was destined either for the Inland Revenue or for financing business after the war – balances derived from depreciation and retained profits, such as those of the shipping industry tapped by Inchcape in January and February 1917. In December 1918, Bradbury described the amount of the War Bonds taken with a view to using them to pay EPD as 'very large', hazarding that at any one time £100m (he crossed out £200m) was held for the purpose.[35] The revenue from death duties, EPD and Munitions Exchequer Payments in 1918–19 was £315m. Of this, over one-fifth was paid in government debt: £58m in War Bonds and £9m in the two War Loans and 5 and 6 per cent Exchequer Bonds.[36]

Several additional facilities were introduced while the War Bonds were on tap. On 29 December 1917, the Bank announced that it would accept Treasury Bills under discount at 4 per cent in payment for Bonds, as long as the Bills had a remaining life of six months or less. The following month it was announced that War Expenditure Certificates would be similarly accepted. After the cut in Bill rates in mid-February 1918, the rate for both Bills and Certificates was reduced to 3½ per cent; £17m Bills and £0.7m Certificates were tendered under the scheme, mainly for the First Series.[1]

Other novelties failed to attract investors. It was thought in 1917 that investors would be tempted by being able to purchase a War Bond, with its coupons, by simply walking into the branch of a bank. The system would have been complex to administer. Each branch would have needed a stock of Bonds, which, being bearer instruments, would have been expensive to produce and safeguard. In addition, it was unclear how the first coupon would have been provided. The existing procedure involved printing a separate coupon for each Bond, the amount depending on the day on which the Exchequer received the funds and interest started to accrue. This was expensive and cumbersome, with a delay before the physical Bond could be handed to the investor. Asking the issuing bank to fill in blank coupons with the amount of the first payment was considered to be open to error and fraud. Requiring investors to pay for the interest that had accrued from the date of the last coupon, or from the date of the prospectus, to the date on which they bought the Bond would entail tax being withheld on interest not actually received. The idea was dropped after Cunliffe pointed out that investors increasingly wanted their Bonds in registered form and it tended to be the large and sophisticated who wanted bearer: these understood the system and would be

1 £13.7m Bills and £0.6m Certificates were used to apply for the First Series. The use in applications for the remaining series were: Second Series £0.7m and £36,600; Third Series £2.6m and £1,000; none were used for the Fourth Series. Osborne (1926), I, p. 439–40.

prepared to wait for physical delivery and the specially printed first coupon.[m] It was his suggestion that the interest should accrue from the date on which payment was received by the bank.[37]

Continuous borrowing

In May 1918, when being questioned about a fall in War Bond sales and the problems of continuous borrowing, the Chancellor was carefully open-minded about the possibility of success, pointing to the advantages but hardly sanguine. By 1 August, he was speaking of the system with confidence and, on 15 August, he laid the 'War Bond Triumph' firmly at its door in words which might have been written by Drummond Fraser in 1915:

> this great result has been achieved by regular, continuous, week-by-week investment. There has been no sudden huge transfer of capital, such as is inevitable when hundreds of millions are borrowed in a short time. Consequently we have avoided the dislocation of the money market and the upheaval of credit which after a great loan renders it impossible for the Government to issue another loan for many months. In the case of National War Bonds the money flows in as it is required in a steady stream. This it is which makes the success of National War Bonds a unique achievement.[38]

Yet, as we have seen, the decision to introduce War Bonds was as much a decision against another Loan as it was a decision in favour of continuous borrowing. Moreover, there was little to distinguish the new system from the method of issuing Exchequer Bonds introduced at Christmas 1915. The distinction was clear between spectacular loans and the way the various issues of Exchequer Bonds, Savings Certificates, Treasury Bills and War Expenditure Certificates were sold: War Loans were only available for subscription for a limited period whereas the other securities were continuously available. There was no such distinction between Exchequer Bonds continuously on offer in 1916 and 1917 and the 'continuous borrowing' on War Bonds after the autumn of 1917. Both streamed

m The proposal reappeared a couple of months later with a 'Nominative' issue of the 1927 War Bonds. These were issued in units of £5 and were only available from banks, presumably to minimise the risks of loss and fraud that had worried Cunliffe. They were bearer instruments with a counterfoil containing a request for registration in place of the coupons. The Bonds were supplied undated to the banks. When the Bond was sold, the bank filled in the date, from which interest started to accrue. The counterfoil, with the name of the owner, was forwarded to the Controller of the POSB, who supplied the Bonds and administered the issue. The Bond was, in effect, a bearer instrument until the name of an owner had been entered on the counterfoil. Once it had been registered, it was little different from the ordinary registered Post Office issue, except that it could not be bought through the Post Office. Such a peculiar hybrid proved unpopular. BoE, Loan Wallet 239, circular in the form of a letter from Kindersley to the banks, 1 January 1918; Lloyds Bank archives (Lloyds TSB Group archives), 'Memorandum to Bankers' from the GPO, December 1917.

from an open-ended tap. Both were sold through the branch bank network. Both benefited from the general savings campaigns of the war savings movement, as well as from their own special publicity, which could increasingly be called 'continuous'. The improvements in the issue terms for War Bonds were part of a trend.

The difference lay not in the system, but in the authorities' awareness of the system they were using, the conscious combining of continuous propaganda, continuous supply and convenience of purchase. Surprisingly, when so much publicity was given to the idea, there is no hint before the autumn of 1917 that the authorities were considering alternatives to occasional long-dated loans or debating the merits of continuous borrowing.[n] The strands seemed to have come together naturally, appeared almost fully developed, once the decision had been made against issuing a new spectacular loan.

Since the system had been used for two years, this is hardly surprising. Although in his briefing paper Bradbury described the decision to issue War Bonds as continuing:

> for the time being at any rate, the plan of day to day borrowing, but to introduce in the place of the Exchequer Bond, which makes a somewhat limited appeal, a more popular form of what I may call middle-dated securities which it is hoped and believed will bring in much larger amounts from a wider circle of investors...,

he thought it so unfamiliar that he had to spell out how the new system would work:

> we must look for success not merely to the attractive character of the investment; indeed I am not sure that a quarter per cent interest more or less is, in the case of a War Loan, a very vital influence in determining the success or failure of an appeal...The investor is entitled to a fair return...But given this return his willingness to subscribe will be determined by the clearness with which it is brought home to him that his subscription is necessary to help his country and to win the war...Even more important, therefore, than the precise terms of the issue is the machinery for bringing this home to the subscriber, and when it has been brought home to him, making it easy for him to subscribe. For the former, we rely greatly on the National War Savings Committees and the Press...and for both, and more particularly for the latter,

n This did not preclude officials, after the event, using the term 'continuous borrowing' or 'day-to-day' borrowing to describe the method used to issue Bills from the spring of 1915 and Exchequer Bonds from Christmas 1915. An example is a passage from Bradbury, T 170/114, 'New Issue of National War Bonds', marked 'Proof for PM', end-September 1917. Another is Osborne (1926), I, p. 405.

> we rely very greatly on the banking community...With this help we are satisfied that such a response will be forthcoming that we shall be able to finance the expenditure of the country for some time to come without any dangerous increase in the amount of the floating debt, and be able to avoid the disturbance of financial conditions which must inevitably accompany the subscription of a great popular loan within a limited period, if not until the war is over, at any rate until the end is in sight.[39]

Improved distribution was to come from involving the banks more closely in the application and payment process. The prospectus carried a list of banks which were authorised to receive subscriptions. Instead of merely having application forms available, which either they or the investor could forward to the Bank of England with payment, the sixty-six banks actually received the subscriptions and payment. They were awarded 1/8 per cent commission on applications bearing their stamp and were authorised to retain the application money for fifteen days, making payment to the Bank with post-dated cheques. The interest on the War Bonds accrued from the date on which payment was made to the branch.

There was little that was radical or, indeed, new about these arrangements. They continued the pattern of the previous two years: piecemeal improvements in design, nothing too extreme. The banks had always enjoyed 1/8 per cent commission on applications bearing their stamp. Retention of the application monies for fifteen days had been introduced with the War Loans in 1917, although on that occasion the aim was to reduce dislocation in the money market rather than compensate the banks for their work. The banks had always been prepared to forward applications to the Bank and handle the paperwork. The inclusion of the banks by name was new, although hardly to be described as revolutionary.

Publicity

At the beginning of March 1917, the war savings movement was diverted to joining the Ministry of Food in organising propaganda for economy in food use. This absorbed much of its attention until August. The Savings Committee had then planned a savings drive for the autumn but, instead, was asked to mount a special campaign to sell the War Bonds. This was launched by the Prime Minister and the Chancellor at a rally in the Albert Hall on 22 October.

The start of the campaign was unfortunately timed. Money held up by large investors in expectation of a new loan ensured that sales started well, but during November 1917 subscriptions were disappointing. The public, seeing Soviet Russia default and the steep rise in the British Treasury's interest payments, had become concerned about the government's credit, while the small investor anticipated an issue of premium bonds.[40] The rumours intensified with the furore which followed the Chancellor's comments on the desirability of a post-war capital levy (see p. 665). At the beginning of December, the Chancellor offered reassurance:

> in my opinion no British Government, present and future, will seek to break

> faith with those who have placed their financial resources at the disposal of the State in this crisis of its history. Such a policy would not only mean that the Government...was in the hands of men who were blind to all considerations of national honour, but would, to my mind, involve the overthrow of any Government that adopted it. The repudiation of the State's liabilities would, in my judgement, be as disastrous as it would be dishonourable. Nothing after the war will be more important than to preserve and buttress the fabric of national credit, and nothing would so easily undermine it as the refusal of the Government to honour its debts. It would be...impossible for a Government which had destroyed its credit by repudiating its liabilities ever to borrow again.[41]

These comforting words, the savings campaign and the reductions in Bill rates in December and February had their effect. In December, aided by the reinvestment of the interest payment on 5 per cent War Loan, sales of War Bonds were between £20m and £30m per week, a rate that was maintained in the new year.[42]

Also responsible for the improvement was a new approach to the sales campaign. In the first two weeks of November, sales had averaged no more than £10m. On 18 November, a newspaperman, George Sutton, chairman of the Amalgamated Press, was appointed Director of Publicity. Energetic and aggressive, Sutton saw no difference between selling War Bonds and selling anything else; it was his job to persuade the public that the goods had value and to make them ask after them. There was then the need to have effective and enthusiastic selling at the point of distribution, in this case the branch banks.[o] Sutton did not confine himself to advertising, although he brought to it professionalism and drive. He moved freely anywhere in the pursuit of sales. Why not reduce Bill rates? Can the Bishop of London be harnessed to the campaign? What is to be done about maturing War Expenditure Certificates? Can the publication of transactions in War Bonds in the secondary market be banned if they take place under par? What is the policy on encouraging banks to promise advances on the security of War Bonds? How can the campaign in Scotland be enlivened?

Sutton took over and developed a War Bond campaign whose plans were already well advanced.[43]A target of £25m per week for sales was being turned into a quota of 10s per person and each area was being encouraged to compete in meeting its target.[44] To stimulate competition, statistics of local sales were published each week. The Local Savings Committees and Local Authorities were encouraged to organise meetings, distribute literature and place advertisements. Dividend warrants included an application form and a letter from the Governor encouraging reinvestment in War Bonds or Savings Certificates.[45] The banks distributed letters, signed by the Chancellor, asking for support and were encouraged to persuade

o The part branch banks might play in selling War Bonds is described in a paper in T 172/771. It is unsigned and undated, but is almost certainly written by Sutton on or about 23 September 1917.

customers of the securities' merits. Booklets aimed at specific professions and advertisements with suitable messages from public figures were published. Most effectively, starting in Trafalgar Square in December, the month after their first use at Cambrai, tanks began to be used to draw attention to the campaign, with clerks from the Bank of England sitting inside to collect money and issue receipts. Between 4 and 11 March 1918, the first special weekly campaign was held in England and Wales – 'Business Men's Week' – when £114m War Bonds were sold.

Business Men's Week produced the most spectacular results, but was confined to England and Wales. In Scotland, the Scottish War Savings Committee, jealous of its independence from the National War Savings Committee in London, held its own autumn War Bond campaign. A 'Tank Campaign', the use of tanks as 'Tank Banks' in which money was subscribed, was held for five weeks in January and February 1918, a spillover from the first use of tanks in London. There was no Business Men's Week, but a 'War Weapons Week' was held between 8 and 13 April 1918. This involved each city, town and village endeavouring to subscribe for sufficient War Bonds and Savings Certificates, on the basis of £2 10s 0d per head, to buy a chosen weapon – anything from aeroplanes for the smaller communities to super-dreadnoughts for the larger. Posters of the selected weapon were distributed in each area, films of tanks in action shown, the churches encouraged to devote sermons to war savings, advertisements and stories placed in the newspapers, meetings held and speeches made.

The campaigns also helped sales of Savings Certificates. The twelve months January–December 1917 saw subscriptions for 86.5m Certificates (£67m in cash) or 1.7m (£1.3m) Certificates per week. In the first quarter of 1918, they doubled to 3.5m (£2.7m) per week. The picture for the small savings movement as a whole was similar. The total (including savings bank deposits, Certificates and the Post Office issues of the War Loans, fractional Exchequer Bonds and War Bonds) were £2.3m per week in the twelve months January–December 1917. In the first quarter of 1918, they doubled to £4m. These comparisons are the more impressive in that 1917 included the exceptional first quarter when the two War Loans were being sold and sales of Certificates were benefiting from the accompanying publicity.[46]

Steepening the yield curve: spring 1918

The authorities were aware that maintaining the momentum of War Bond sales would require strenuous efforts and that there would be some poor weeks, especially during the holiday seasons; between the adoption of continuous borrowing in the autumn of 1917 and 30 March 1918 sales averaged £25m per week, fluctuating between £10m (over the Christmas period) and £114m (in Business Men's Week). At the beginning of April, as the Second Series was introduced, sales began to fall. The authorities were prepared for some reduction, but the drop from a weekly £15m in April to some £9m in the first two weeks of May seems to have taken them by surprise. Various explanations were offered.

Kindersley stressed the Man Power Bill, extending conscription, which he thought was particularly affecting the income expectations of the better off, and a continued reaction after the special efforts of Business Men's Week.[47] Sutton agreed that the Bill was taking its toll, but also pointed to the increase in income tax in the budget and competition from 5 per cent War Loan (available at a discount to its issue price) and 3½ per cent War Loan which, at a price of 85, had a high net yield.[48] The Chancellor put a brave face on the figures. It was difficult, he said, 'to keep the steam constantly on'. The January Loans had raised about £1,000m, partly because investors had borrowed from their banks to apply, and this had made another money-raising operation impossible for nine months: 'it was not too much to hope' that, having raised £719m on War Bonds in the eight months since October 1917, 'not far short' of £1,000m would be raised in the complete nine months.[49]

Since the USA entered the war, the authorities had on three occasions sought to stimulate sales by cutting short-term interest rates. In June 1917, the Bank had cut the rate on Bills and special deposits. Rates on both Bills and domestic special deposits were reduced at the end of December, and again in February 1918 (Tables 4.2 and 12.2 and p. 354). On these occasions, as was customary, the CLCB had agreed its members' deposit rates. The bankers' resolutions, however, only applied to published rates and were so worded that they permitted higher rates to be paid to customers 'who kicked', as *The Economist* put it in May 1918.[50] The resolution passed on 15 November 1917 – at a time when the banks were being pressed to help divert deposits into Bonds, but a reduction in the deposit rate from the 4 per cent set on 13 July 1916 was being rejected – displayed a tough intention but left at least four loopholes:

> that the deposit rate at 7 days' notice shall remain at 4% and that *subject to any already arranged rates* no Bank will after today allow at the outside more than 4¼% for any new deposits, or for any renewal of existing deposits, for any period, & will wherever a higher rate exists *endeavour* to reduce the rate to 4% or 4¼% *exceptionally*. No manager to be allowed to give more than 4% *without reference* to his General Manager.[51]

The resolution passed at the beginning of January, when bank deposit rates were cut from 4 per cent to 3½ per cent, was similar, but presented another opening for demanding customers by specifying a higher limit of 4¼ per cent on 'fresh deposits'. The February 1918 resolution was bald, setting the seven-day rate at 3 per cent and rescinding the tougher and more detailed wording adopted in November.[52] The result was that banks continued to bid for deposits 'at variable but higher rates'.[53]

The authorities' approach to the drop in sales in the spring was tempered by the Chancellor's unwillingness to see any general reduction in rates, probably because sales of sterling in New York were tending upwards.[54] First, he asked the banks to ensure that no higher rate than the published 3 per cent was actually paid on deposits. The CLCB's resolution on 23 May was unambiguous:

> That at the urgent request of the Chancellor of the Exchequer, who wishes every possible inducement given to the public to invest in War Bonds,...no higher rate than 3% shall be given by them either in London or the Country for any monies at whatever notice on deposit or current account, excepting for foreign monies entitled to the special rate given by the Bank of England.[55]

Second, a special effort was made to ensure that the dividends on 5 per cent War Loan payable on 1 June were reinvested in War Bonds. The Chancellor made an appeal through the press and warrants were accompanied by another signed by the Governor: those paid to large companies included a letter from Sutton, addressed to the chairmen.[56] As one result, the banks agreed to reinvest all their dividends.[57] Third, the banks' staff were encouraged to see themselves as agents of the government and the banks were asked to pay them a commission when they made a sale. The banks were reluctant but, with the Chancellor pressing, they agreed to credit branches with one-half of the commission earned on securities sold through them and distribute it to the staff in proportion to their salaries.[58]

The result of the three measures was to double sales: they averaged £23.3m in each of the following four weeks and fell beneath £20m on only six occasions during the rest of the year.[59]

Publicity: summer and autumn 1918

War Weapons Week in Scotland in April 1918 was followed during the summer by a more prolonged campaign with the same name in England and Wales. Each town with a population of over 30,000 was assigned a weapon whose cost would be appropriate to the subscriptions the town should produce. Communities whose populations were less than 30,000 were asked to provide aeroplanes. Tanks, guns and aeroplanes (but not ships) were provided with the names of the places raising money. To this general propaganda was added the various specific measures aimed at reversing the weakness in sales experienced during May – the agreement of the CLCB to a maximum level of deposit rates, the reinvestment of the 1 June 5 per cent War Loan dividend by the banks and an appeal from the Chancellor at the end of May to save and invest. New ration books began to include an appeal from the Chancellor to live more simply, cut household expenses, invest savings each week in government paper and reduce balances in the banks to a minimum.[60] Sutton, in his element, organised enthusiastic news coverage when sales of War Bonds reached £1,000m on 15 August.[61]

The autumn campaign and the Third Series of War Bonds were launched by the Chancellor on 30 September. On this occasion, as well as stressing the advantages and success of the continuous system, he predicted that its success would continue for the remainder of the war.[62] The slogan of the campaign was 'Feed the guns with war bonds and help to win the war', shortened for general use to 'Feed the Guns'. The campaign was the most sophisticated yet. It was planned to last for about eight months, beginning in the first week in October. Guns – Howitzers, 60-Pounders and anti-aircraft guns drawn by caterpillars – were placed at the centre of the stage; a machine for stamping receipts was placed in the breeches of the guns so that subscribers could see them being 'fed'. They were accompanied by crew, bands and military guards. The provincial campaign was launched three weeks after that in London, where a reproduction ruined village from the western front had been erected in Trafalgar Square: a damaged church, farmhouse and mill, camouflaged hut, trenches, observation post and splintered tree trunk.[p] There was the usual press coverage, speeches and meetings, advertising, posters, cinema films and slides. 'Egbert', a battle-scarred tank, was to be presented to the city or town which subscribed for the largest amount per head of its population. There were to be four guns for runners-up and inscribed shells for the most successful smaller communities.[63]

The opening of the campaign, even with the special effort in the opening 'Gun Week' in Trafalgar Square, was disappointing by the standard the Chancellor had set himself. The successes in France and the smell of peace were too strong. On Armistice Day, the Chancellor called for continued effort, pointing to the need for savers to continue to buy War Bonds to help pay for the armed services and demobilisation, to 'smooth over the inevitable dislocation of our industries' as soldiers returned to civilian work, and to improve health and housing. Peace, he said, made no difference to the weekly target of £25m.[64]

The results over the life of the Third Series were a tribute to continuous borrowing. Sales averaged almost £33m during the sixteen weeks that the Series was on tap, including £150m sold in a single week in the middle of January when it became known that the existing Series was to be withdrawn. As important, sales were remarkably steady. For only two weeks did they fall beneath £20m and, excluding the exceptional sales in the middle of January, for only two weeks did they rise above £30m.

The small savings movement

During 1917, the number of Local War Savings Committees increased by 746 to 1,619. By the end of 1918 there were 1,840. In 1917, 20,929 War Savings Associations were affiliated, bringing the total to 37,840 with a membership of about four million; a further 3,461 were affiliated in 1918.[65] By the end of 1917, a quarter of Certificate sales came directly through the Associations and the remainder through the banks, Post Offices and 'Official Agents'.

'Official Agents' were first appointed in 1917 when the War Savings Committee thought that the number of War Savings Associations, at one per thousand people in England and Wales, was reaching saturation. At the same time, the Committee thought that it had not reached, nor was likely to reach through the Associations, some sections of the working population, especially the better-off artisan. It therefore arranged to license tradesmen and firms to sell Certificates and War

p A picture of the battlefield in Trafalgar Square is in *The Silver Bullet*, 18 October 1918. Plans for the campaign are in T 172/771.

Bonds to their customers. The Agents bought the securities outright with their own funds and received them dated, but not registered, for sale. By the end of 1918, the number of Agents had risen to 6,000 and the number of points of sale to 14,000. The Committee was unable to provide data for Agents' sales, but said that the evidence pointed to 'considerable sums' having been invested through them and that a 'class of individual has been reached…who would probably not have been influenced by any other means'.[66]

In June 1917, after consulting the Reconstruction Committee, a subcommittee of the National War Savings Committee was appointed to report on the facilities that should be made available to the small saver after the war. The subcommittee, which included Kindersley and Bradbury, delivered a report in December, and another the following year.[67] The first recommended that the state should continue to encourage the small saver, the existing savings machinery should be retained and a security similar to War Savings Certificates continue to be sold. The new National Savings Certificates should be introduced six months after the end of the war and carry a return and intermediate encashment value determined by the market rate of interest at the time of sale. They would not be encashable for one month from the date of purchase. Otherwise, the terms should be the same as those borne by War Savings Certificates. The subcommittee also recommended that savers who owned Certificates bought at different times should not be required to cash them separately, but should be able to hold them until the most recently purchased Certificate matured. This, it was hoped, would reduce administration, meet the convenience of investors and retain the savings of those who might feel the temptation to spend small sums, but not large. Interest on Certificates during this period should be paid at a rate of 1d per month, equivalent to about 5 per cent in the first year, 4¾ per cent in the second and 4½ per cent in the third. Finally, the subcommittee was concerned about maintaining the momentum generated by wartime patriotism and suggested that local loyalties might replace national if the savings movement was linked to the financing of local improvements including, perhaps, housing.

The second report recommended that holders, while retaining the option to cash their Certificates at £1 after five years, should be able to continue their investment for a further five years. The Certificates would increase in value at a rate of 1d per month and a bonus of 1s would be paid at the end of the period. This would increase the value of a Certificate from 15s 6d to 26s over the ten years.[68]

The Treasury's borrowing and maturity challenges and the composition of the subcommittee ensured that most of the recommendations were adopted as soon as the Armistice was signed on 11 November. A circular from Kindersley announced that the organisation would become permanent and pointed to the expansion during the war from 345,000 to over 17 million in the number of people holding government securities, the social benefits of savings and the need for capital. He also announced the terms for prolonging Certificates in accordance with the recommendations of the second report. They would be encashable at any time and the extension would apply to future as well as past purchases, thus further underwriting the movement's prospects.[69]

Table 12.6 Creations and reductions of National War Bonds (£m nominal) (years ending 31 March)

	Amount outstanding	*Creations*					*Reductions*	
		1	*2*	*3*	*4*	*5*	*6*	*7*
1918	649.4	641.3	3.6	14.0	0.4	–	–	10.0
1919	1,636.2	1,045.8	1.8	2.8	0.2	–	–	58.3
1920	1,475.8	44.6	0.2	–	–	–	0.8	60.1
1921	1,412.8	–	–	–	–	6.7	–	66.5
1922	1,200.6	–	–	–	–	12.0	–	22.1
1923	953.1	–	–	–	–	21.3	–	0.3
1924	820.1	–	–	–	–	2.6	–	–
1925	777.8	–	–	–	–	3.6	–	–
1926	705.7	–	–	–	–	6.7	5.7	0.1
1927	555.3	–	–	–	–	1.2	1.4	0.2
1928	193.8	–	–	–	–	1.2	0.4	0.2
1929	Nil	–	–	–	–	1.6	0.6	–
Total		1,731.7	5.6	16.8	0.7	56.9	9.0	217.7

Notes

Column headings:

1 For cash.
2 For conversion of 4½ War Loan 1925–45.
3 For conversion of 5 per cent Exchequer Bonds 1919,1920 and 1921.
4 For conversion of 6 per cent Exchequer Bonds 1920.
5 For conversion of 5½ US three- and ten-year Notes and Bonds.
6 Transferred or purchased for cancellation.
7 Surrendered against death duties etc.
8 Converted into 5 per cent War Loan 1929–47.
9 Converted into 4 per cent War Loan 1929–42.
10 Converted into 4 per cent Funding 1960–90.
11 Converted into 4 per cent Victory Bonds.
12 Converted into 5½ per cent Treasury 1929.
13 Converted into 3½ per cent Conversion Loan.
14 Converted into 4½ per cent Treasury 1930–2.
15 Converted into 4 per cent Consols.
16 Converted into 5 per cent Treasury 1933–5.
17 Converted into 4½ per cent Treasury 1932–4.
18 Repaid.

– denotes less than £50,000.

Columns and rows may not sum because of rounding.

Source: *BGS*, pp. 226–7.

✣ ✣ ✣

The decision to rely on the continuous issue of short- and medium-dated securities determined the shape of internal borrowing until the Armistice. Over the following twenty months, the fifteen new War Bonds changed the structure of the Debt, which had previously always been dominated by a single great issue. On 31 March 1917, the unfunded debt comprised nine issues. A year later, there were fifteen, and on 31 March 1919 twenty-six. In 1917–18, £641.3m War Bonds were created

8	*9*	*10*	*11*	*12*	*13*	*14*	*15*	*16*	*17*	*18*
–	–	–	–	–	–	–	–	–	–	–
1.5	4.0	–	–	–	–	–	–	–	–	–
3.9	7.9	80.2	52.4	–	–	–	–	–	–	–
–	3.2	–	–	–	–	–	–	–	–	–
–	–	–	–	37.9	164.1	–	–	–	–	–
139.7	0.6	–	–	–	70.5	13.8	–	–	–	43.8
70.5	0.9	–	–	–	–	11.5	–	–	–	52.7
38.3	1.1	–	–	–	–	–	–	–	–	6.4
57.6	7.2	–	–	–	–	–	–	–	–	8.2
45.6	3.8	–	–	–	–	–	100.8	–	–	–
84.7	16.3	–	–	–	59.4	–	–	125.1	–	76.6
12.3	1.0	–	–	–	–	–	–	–	53.3	128.3
454.1	46.1	80.2	52.4	37.9	294.0	25.3	100.8	125.1	53.3	315.9

for cash, £1,045.8m in 1918–19 and £44.6m in 1919–20, a total of £1,731.7m. In addition, there was the tangle of creations and reductions resulting from the host of rights and options either given in the original prospectuses or offered later to lengthen the issues. The options attached to the five older issues (the 4½ per cent War Loan 1925–45, and the 5 per cent and 6 per cent Exchequer Bonds) permitted conversion into the eleven longer War Bond issues of each of the four Series as long as they remained on tap; there were fifty-five different ways in which War Bonds could be created. Further amounts came from satisfying conversions from the 5½ per cent three- and ten-year US$ Notes and Bonds (see pp. 458–62). Reductions resulted from conversions into the 4 per cent and 5 per cent War Loans in accordance with the prospectuses for the first three series, and the use of the War Bonds for the payment of death duties, EPD and Munitions Exchequer Payments. In addition, between 1919 and 1928 no fewer than eight new issues gave options to holders of the War Bonds to convert (Table 12.6).

Although the maturities of the War Bonds were well spread, and with the help of conversions were to become more so, the longest issue was about ten years and they were all single-dated. The options on which the authorities had hitherto insisted on all but its five-year Exchequer Bonds were forgone. For ten years after the Armistice, the Treasury was to face maturity after maturity, refinancing after refinancing. Not only were officials assuming that rates would fall from wartime levels, but – given the single dates and the constant stream of maturities – that they would be continually lower. They were mistaken. The War Bonds made Debt management and, in particular, the cost of servicing the Debt, vulnerable in a way which would not have been possible had the securities been perpetual or double-dated, or had they been spread further out into the longer part of the market. It was not until the early 1930s that depression was to deliver the easier money and lower interest rates which would enable the cost and maturity problem to be finally overcome.

Endnotes

1 DORA, Regulation 41 D, 21 December 1917.
2 This paragraph is based on *Hansard* (Commons), 2 May 1917, cols 371–91; Mallet and George (1929), pp. 120–43, and Hirst and Allen (1926), pp. 166–99.
3 *Hansard* (Commons), 2 May 1917, col. 376.
4 The remainder of this section is based on *Hansard*, 22 April 1918, cols 691–720, Mallet and George (1929), pp. 143–74, and Hirst and Allen (1926), pp. 200–41.
5 *Hansard* (Commons), 22 April 1918, cols 695 and 698.
6 *The Times*, 7 April 1917, p. 10, and 25 April 1917, p. 12; BoE, Loan Wallet 272, Norman, 'Funding', 2 March 1921, and CO/399, 'Treasury Bills', p. 8; *Bankers' Magazine*, May 1917, p. 697, and June 1917, p. 811; *The Economist*, 7 April 1917, p. 618.
7 Osborne (1926), I, p. 479; *The Economist*, 28 April 1917, pp. 725–6.
8 T 170/121, Bradbury to Hamilton, 6 June 1917.
9 BoE, Loan Wallet 238, Memorandum, 'Exchequer Bonds', undated and unsigned.
10 Ibid., Cunliffe to Bradbury, 31 March 1917.
11 T 170/121, F. Franklin to Chancellor, 5 June 1917, Blackett to Ramsay, 5 June 1917, and Bradbury to Hamilton, 6 June 1917. Ramsay's comment scribbled on Blackett's Memorandum was 'Surely we have had enough of conversion rights?'.
12 For example, see *The Economist*, 23 June 1917, p. 1143; *The Times*, 20 June 1917, p. 12, and *The Financial News*, 20 June 1917, pp. 1 and 2.
13 T 172/610, Chancellor to Drummond Fraser, 7 November 1917; CLCBt, 6 and 14 November 1917.
14 CTM, 20 September 1916; Morgan (1952), p. 170; BoE, Court Minutes, 5 July 1917; Osborne (1926), I, p. 291; BoE, C98/6937. The letter is reproduced in the Court Minutes, 12 July.
15 Osborne (1926), I, pp. 291–2; BoE, C98/6937 and ADM 19/10 and 19/11; Morgan (1952), p. 170.
16 BoE, C98/6937; Morgan (1952), p. 125. Morgan cites 'information supplied by the Treasury' as the source for the importance and size of the Paymaster-General's Advances.
17 BoE, C98/6937.
18 *The Economist* was an early and continuous proponent of the measure. See, for example, 30 December 1916, p. 1211, 20 January 1917, pp. 78 and 80, and 17 February 1917, p. 290. Also, see BoE, G 30/2, Drummond Fraser to Governor, 22 September 1917, and Governor to Drummond Fraser, 24 September 1917.
19 CTM, 5 December 1917; Osborne (1926), I, p. 282n; Clay (1957), p. 105; Sayers (1976), I, p. 97.
20 CTM, 31 December 1917; BoE, G 15/103, Cunliffe to Bradbury, 29 December 1917; Osborne (1926), I, p. 283; T 172/1384, f. 21, Blackett, 'Dear Money', 19 February 1920. The Bills included a special issue of one-month maturities. Window-dressing would be consistent with the data for foreign deposits in Table 4.3 because these are for an unspecified date near the end of the quarter.
21 T 172/555, Inchcape to Chancellor, 14 September 1917, and enclosed cutting from the *Glasgow Herald*, 14 September 1917, p. 8; Chancellor to Inchcape, 17 September 1917.
22 T 172/555, Chancellor to Inchcape, 6 September 1917; Blake (1955), p. 362; French (1995), pp. 124–47.

23 The Governor reported to the Committee of Treasury at the end of August that Strong was warning that 'he was anticipating great stringency in the autumn'. CTM, 29 August 1917. Also see CTM, 15 August, 5 September, 12 September and 19 September for the Bank's concern about the trend of rates in New York, the effect on sterling and the possibility of a rise in Bank and Bill rates. On 17 September, the Chancellor told Nivison that he was 'rather alarmed by the position of money in America'. T 172/555, Bonar Law to Nivison, 17 September 1917. Also see Sayers (1976), I, p. 97.

24 Quoted in Blake (1955), p. 362.

25 Blake (1955), p. 362; T 172/445, f. 89, Davidson to Standing, 25 September 1917. Davidson wrote that 'I have grave apprehension that if son proves to be dead complete collapse Chancellor of Exchequer.'

26 T 172/555, Chancellor to Inchcape, 17 September 1917, and Chancellor to Nivison, 19 September 1917; CLCBt, 14 and 17 September 1917.

27 T 172/555, Nivison to Chancellor, 22 September 1917.

28 Ibid., Chancellor to Nivison, 24 September 1917.

29 Ibid., Bonar Law to Chisholm, 24 September 1917.

30 BoE, Loan Wallet 244, Harvey to Deverell, 23 September 1918.

31 T 170/114, 'New issue of National War Bonds', marked 'Proof for PM', Bradbury, end-September 1917; BoE, Loan Wallet 239, Bradbury's comments on the first draft of the prospectus, 21 September 1917.

32 T 172/555, Chancellor to Nivison, 19 September 1917, Chancellor to Chisholm and Kiddy, 24 September 1917, and Hamilton to Chisholm and Kiddy, 25 September 1917; BoE, Loan Wallet 239, Bradbury's comments on the first draft of the prospectus, 21 September 1917.

33 BoE, Loan Wallet 242, 23 April 1918, supplementary leaflet altering the price and conversion terms for the tax-compounded War Bond of the Second Series.

34 BoE, Loan Wallet 244, Price to Harvey, 17 August 1918, and Harvey to Price, 18 August 1918.

35 BoE, C40/397, 'The Funding Loan and Income Tax', Bradbury's comment on the 'abortive January 1919' Funding Loan, December 1918.

36 *National Debt: annual returns*, 1919. Strictly speaking, this was the amount cancelled having been used to pay taxes, rather than the amount paid in the different forms of debt.

37 BoE, Loan Wallet 239, Cunliffe to Chancellor, 8 September 1917; T 170/114, Memorandum, 'Proposal', 8 September 1917. At the time of the Governor's letter, £73m of the 5 per cent Exchequer Bonds 1922 had been sold, of which £38m were Bonds to bearer and £35m were registered.

38 *Hansard* (Commons), 14 May 1918, cols 236–8, and 1 August 1918, cols 673–4; T 172/775, 'War Bond Triumph: Chancellor of the Exchequer's Statement', released 15 August 1918.

39 T 170/114, 'New Issue of National War Bonds', marked 'Proof for PM', Bradbury, end-September 1917.

40 For example, see Kindersley's evidence to the Select Committee on Premium Bonds. Select Committee on Premium Bonds (1918), *Report* (HCP 168), pp. 13–23.

41 Letter from the Chancellor published in the daily newspapers, 6 December 1917, reproduced in *The Economist*, 8 December 1917, p. 908. Also see letters from the Chancellor to a meeting of representatives of the Scottish War Savings Associations, Glasgow, 1 December 1917, reported in the *Bankers' Magazine*, January 1918, p. 93, and another from Barnes to the South Wales newspapers. Drafts of these and other papers concerning the scare are in T 172/763. There is a survey of sovereign defaults 'Some recent instances of the Repudiation by Countries of their National Debt', 11 December 1917, in T 171/144.

42 Weekly sales are recorded in 'Sales of 5 per cent National War Bonds', BoE, Loan Wallet 230 A & B.

43 See, for example, Chambers to Hamilton, 8 November 1917, in T 172/623. The papers covering the organisation of the campaign from 6 November 1917 to the end of the year are in the same file. Papers for January 1918 to June 1918 are in T 172/776.
44 T 172/776, Sutton to Hamilton, 14 February 1918.
45 BoE, C40/615, Bonar Law to Governor, 8 August 1918.
46 National War Savings Committee, *Second* and *Third Annual Reports*.
47 T 172/776, Kindersley to Chancellor, 17 May 1918.
48 Ibid., Sutton to Hamilton, 10 May 1918.
49 *Hansard* (Commons), 14 May 1918, cols 236–8.
50 *The Economist*, 25 May 1918, p. 905.
51 CLCBm, 15 November 1917. Italics added.
52 CLCBm, 19 and 21 June, 15 November, and 27 December 1917, 2 January and 14 February 1918; CLCBt, 5 and 14 November 1917.
53 *Bankers' Magazine*, July 1918, p. 16.
54 CTM, 15 May 1918; BoE, C91/20, LEC Minutes and C91/15, f. 40, 'Purchases and Sales of American Exchange', 25 March 1919.
55 CLCBm, 23 May 1918.
56 A copy of the Chancellor's interview with the Press Association is in T 172/776, dated 25 May 1918, for publication 29 May 1918. T 172/776, Ramsay to Bradbury, 17 May 1918, and Sutton to Hamilton, 10 May 1918. *The Economist*, 1 June 1918, p. 939. Copies of the letters from the Governor and Sutton, dated 31 May 1918, are in T 172/907.
57 CLCBm, 23 May 1918.
58 Ibid., 23 May 1918. The role of the managers in selling War Bonds as seen by the War Savings Committee is to be found in T 172/776, Kindersley to Chancellor, 17 May 1918.
59 BoE, Loan Wallet 230 A & B, 'Sales of 5 per cent National War Bonds'.
60 A copy of the appeal is in T 172/775. The idea came from the Rev. J.F. Stern of the East London Synagogue and was agreed by the Ministry of Food on 27 July 1918. T 172/775, Stern to Bonar Law, 22 July 1918, and Sutton to Gower, 25 July 1918.
61 T 172/775 contains the correspondence between Sutton and the Treasury and copies of the Chancellor's statement for the press, an advance statement to allow the press to prepare their comments and an interview with Sutton on 'The Second Thousand Million'.
62 The speech is reproduced in *The Financial News*, 1 October 1918, p. 3.
63 The papers covering the Feed the Guns campaign are in T 172/771.
64 *The Silver Bullet*, 20 November 1918.
65 National War Savings Committee, *Second* and *Third Annual Reports*.
66 National War Savings Committee, *Second Annual Report*.
67 A copy of the first report is in T 170/116. No copy of the second report has been found.
68 National War Savings Committee, *Third Annual Report*.
69 *The Economist*, 16 November 1918, p. 678; *The Silver Bullet*, 5 March 1919, open letters from Kindersley to War Savings workers and from the Chancellor to Kindersley.

Part III

Repayment, refinancing, conversion and funding

13 Victory and Funding

> To regard the adverse exchanges as a necessary result of the large Government purchases abroad is a grave misconception. To regard them as a necessary result of the spending abroad of the money lent to Allied Powers in the United Kingdom is only less fallaceous. So long as an adverse trade balance is settled in gold and the country from which the gold is drawn pursues a sound currency policy the Exchanges are safe. The withdrawal of the gold will lead to a restriction of credit and a fall in prices, civil imports will be curtailed and exports stimulated. High money rates and falling prices will reduce the profits of industry and 'bad trade' will make the workman content to take lower wages when he sees his employer suffering with him.
>
> Sir John Bradbury, autumn 1915, T 170/20.

> Such a vast amount of short-dated securities spread an atmosphere of insecurity over the business world, and is an undoubted obstacle to the revival of trade and industry...It prevents our restricting the continued issue of currency notes, or doing anything to reduce the inflation of the currency, and it prevents our taking any steps to stabilise our foreign exchange. Accordingly, it is not merely financial interests, it is not merely the Treasury that are concerned. It is each and every person of this realm who has an interest in the prosperity and well-being of the country, and the need for support to this loan...is as great and the claim on the patriotism of the citizen is as strong, as were that need and those claims during the progress of active operations.
>
> Austen Chamberlain, 2 June 1919, *Hansard* (Commons), col. 1729.

Between 1919 and 1932, the Treasury managed the greatly expanded Debt in a world which was scarcely recognisable to the eyes of the Edwardian. By the time the peace treaty was signed in the summer of 1919, three empires – those of the Habsburgs, the Romanovs and the Ottomans – had collapsed, fragmenting into numerous unstable successor states. A Bolshevik regime had won power in Russia, intent on exporting its revolutionary anticapitalist doctrines. Expectations among ordinary citizens, whether for employment, living standards, social welfare, or political freedom, had grown. In over four years of war much of the fixed investment in the main battle areas of France, Belgium, Italy and Poland had been destroyed. Wealth had been transferred to the USA as the investments built up over a century were sold and debts, to both the private and public sectors, incurred. In the allied economies, industrial capacity had been expanded where it was needed for the war, but had otherwise contracted and deteriorated. European exporters had lost markets as their output was diverted to military uses. In many neutral countries indigenous industries had been established, while the USA and Japan had invaded Europe's traditional markets. To a greater or lesser extent, all the combatants had relied on inflationary finance, their governments borrowing from their central and commercial banks and expanding their fiduciary issues.

The fiscal and monetary dislocation was felt throughout Europe, among both neutrals and combatants. For Austria, Hungary, Poland, Russia and Germany, the challenge was too great, and they relapsed into hyperinflation. For France, the UK and Germany, the most important, and enduring, external problem came directly from one of the terms of the peace treaty. Reparations, the condition that Germany should pay in money, goods or services for all or part of the damage caused by hostilities, remained a source of instability until they were buried in the summer of 1932. Reparations were resented by the Germans, who believed them to be unjust, and relied on by the French, who abstained from taking corrective fiscal and monetary actions until 1926, in part because they had expectations of being paid. Until their extent had been credibly determined, the Germans could not settle their fiscal policy and their currency could not find a sustainable level. Reparations bedevilled British relations with the French, whose reactions to any German failure in meeting the payments were more severe. They were also an important source of friction with the USA, which after 1919 quickly withdrew into isolationism. Her Congress refused ratification of the peace treaties, of participation in a security guarantee to France or membership of the League of Nations. In 1922, the Fordney–McCumber Act established the highest tariffs in US history. Congress dictated that Administrations take an unforgiving line on the debts incurred to the US Treasury; it insisted that each had to be treated as a bilateral matter, that there was no connection between a debtor's payments to the USA and others' payments to that debtor, and that reparations received from Germany had no bearing on the ability of America's debtors to fulfil their contracts.

In some measure, the UK shared the problems of the other European combatants. Her empire was strained by the same nationalism as that which affected Europe. Much of Ireland, which had been an unreliable western flank during the war, wanted the autonomy of which it had been thwarted in 1914. Outside her merchant marine, the UK had suffered little material damage, but she had lost wealth to the USA and neutrals: her citizens had sold foreign securities, many of them American; at the end of November 1918, her Treasury had borrowed £1,345m ($6,546m) in foreign currencies: £196m ($956m) from the US private sector, £780m ($3,796m) from the US Treasury and £369m ($1,796m) from elsewhere.[1] A fluctuating exchange rate and diminished resilience in her industry and finance reduced her ability to export capital and remain the banker and clearing house for the world. As a great exporter of manufactured goods, she had been a notable loser in overseas markets, especially those of South America and Asia. In the following twenty years, the problems of her pre-war staple industries – cotton fabrics, coal extraction, steel, shipbuilding and heavy engineering – were to come to dominate the public mind and damage the public purse via the highly visible, if localised, unemployment that they caused. She was exceptional in Europe for having raised taxes steeply during the war and in having borrowed largely on medium- and long-dated securities from the saver. Although the Treasury was much criticised both by contemporaries and later for the inadequacy of her tax measures, she had met almost 30 per cent of government expenditure from revenue. This still left a daunting debt. At the end of November 1918, the sterling debt was £5,826m and the total Debt £7,171m, the equivalent of some 150 per cent of GNP. Within this, the floating debt was £1,420m. In common with the other European combatants, but on a smaller scale, she had borrowed from the central bank and, at the end of November, Ways and Means Advances from the Bank of England were £182m. Assuming interest cost 5 per cent, the Treasury could look forward to finding some £360m each year for debt service, £65m for overseas.[2]

Even if there had been no increase in other demands on the Exchequer, the cost of servicing this debt would have strained the political consensus. But new expectations demanded new expenditure without any obvious increase in the willingness, or ability, to pay taxes: the prospect for each budget was of a grim struggle. The Reform Act of 1918 more than doubled the electorate. The number of people paying income tax had risen from 1.2m in 1913–14 to 5.7m in 1918–19.[3] At the end of the war there was a pent-up anger and a refusal among manual workers to return to pre-war conditions. Shared experience in the military services and in industry had democratised attitudes, while centralised control in the war economy had drawn the trades unions into management decisions. In 1922, the Labour Party, conservative in practice but with some members using rhetoric which frightened the established order, replaced the Liberals as the main alternative party of government. In 1924, the first Labour government was formed. Seeking to maintain labour morale and discipline, the wartime government had promised an extension of social spending: the infamous 'Land Fit for Heroes' promised by Lloyd George. Although post-war reconstruction was to end with the cry for lower taxes and smaller, less wasteful, government, the Treasury was to find politicians seeking electoral advantage and social stability by widening the role of government.

The gold standard, Free Trade, balanced budgets, debt repayment and minimal State intervention were the foundations, learnt by both Treasury and Bank officials in their careers before 1914, on which policies in the 1920s were based. They believed their function to be one of finance, which meant the finance of the central government: in 1926, Sir Thomas Heath, who had been a joint Permanent Secretary between 1913 and 1919, described the Treasury as 'responsible for the administration of the public finances…the one permanent institution which stands between the country and national bankruptcy'.[4] In this conception, the functioning and control of the economy played no part. A flexible market in labour and goods would adjust to changes in the supply of money as the gold stock fluctuated and the Bank of England moved interest rates to protect its holdings: there was no place for the Treasury or politicians. As late as 1951, Horace Hamilton felt able to write a biographical note on Warren Fisher which made no reference to the economic problems of the inter-war years.[5]

The agenda for monetary, debt and exchange rate policy was set during 1918 and 1919, with the acceptance by the government in December 1919 of the recommendations of the Committee on Currency and Foreign Exchanges after the War.[6] The Committee had been appointed by the Treasury and the Ministry of Reconstruction in January 1918 as a contribution to government planning for post-war reconstruction: its *Interim Report* was signed on 15 August 1918.[7] After Austen Chamberlain had refused the position, Cunliffe was appointed Chairman. Most of its other members were also bankers, the notable exceptions being Bradbury, who was responsible for much of the drafting, and A. C. Pigou, an academic economist.[a]

At the end of the war, sterling was pegged at $4.76½ with the help of US Treasury credits and formal and informal controls on movements of gold and exports of capital. Throughout the Committee's discussions, it was assumed that sterling would return to an effective gold standard (the UK had never left it legally) at the pre-war rate. With British prices above foreign prices, the Committee accepted that some deflation would be necessary and that the transition to normality would take ten years. It expected that this process would be difficult, especially in the early years during demobilisation and when social discontent would be at its greatest. There was some disagreement about the pace at which the deflation should take place and this, together with uncertainty about post-war developments, accounts for the *Interim Report* being pitched in general terms.[8]

Both members of the Committee and witnesses reflected the general consensus and supported a return to gold.[9] The recommendation, and the manner of achieving it, was unequivocal:

> In our opinion it is imperative that after the war the conditions necessary to the maintenance of an effective gold standard should be restored without delay. Unless the machinery which long experience has shown to be the only effective remedy for an adverse balance of trade and an undue growth of credit is once more brought into play, there will be grave danger of a progressive credit expansion which will result in a foreign drain of gold menacing the convertibility of our note issue and so jeopardising the international trade position.[10]

The preconditions were the cessation of government borrowing, the 'raising and making effective of Bank rate' and the limitation of the fiduciary issue. The first

a In addition to Cunliffe, who was still Governor at the time, the Committee was appointed, the fourteen members included Bradbury, Inchcape, Goschen, Farrer, seven other bankers and Pigou. Between the Committee on Currency and Foreign Exchanges after the War (Cunliffe Committee) *First Interim Report* (August 1918) and the *Final Report* (December 1919), Bradbury was replaced by Blackett. The other member was a secretary from the Ministry of Reconstruction. Sayers (1976), III, p. 57.

recommendation embraced the balancing of the budget, the immediate refinancing of the floating debt and the longer-term objective of reducing the size of the overall Debt:

> If a sound monetary position is to be re-established and the gold standard to be effectively maintained...Government borrowing should cease at the earliest possible moment after the war...A primary condition of the restoration of a sound credit position is the repayment of a large portion of the enormous amount of Government securities now held by the Banks. It is essential that as soon as possible the State should not only live within its income but should begin to reduce its indebtedness. We accordingly recommend that at the earliest possible moment an adequate sinking fund should be provided out of revenue, so that there may be a regular annual reduction of capital liabilities, more especially those which constitute the floating debt.[11]

The Cunliffe recommendations met little criticism in Parliament, the City or the press and were supported by the scenes of fiscal and monetary chaos in some Continental economies.

in operational terms, at the time of the Armisticezzzzx§§ officials saw two challenges: to increase government borrowing from the banking system or the public, so that the Bank's Ways and Means could be repaid, and to increase borrowing from the general public, so that Treasury Bills held by the banking system could be repaid. In seeking to change the source of the government's borrowing, the Bank found itself constrained by ministerial indecision in a way which was outside its experience. A reluctance to issue a loan, the most straightforward method of meeting both challenges, was nothing new. Having to cajole the Chancellor, the Prime Minister and the entire Cabinet into raising short rates to restore the Bank's control over the markets was new.

Bank rate had become ineffective by reason of the banking system's holdings of Treasury Bills. If the Bank sold securities, squeezing money and raising interest rates, Bills would not be renewed and the government would have to borrow from the Bank on Ways and Means. As these were paid out, the banking system would replace the cash it had lost in the Bank's restrictive moves. In short, a higher Bank rate could not be made effective unless Bill rates were also raised and the power to set interest rates had passed out of the Bank's hands. Moreover, it had passed not just to Treasury officials, such as Bradbury, who shared the view that the pre-war gold standard protected by changes in Bank rate remained the best monetary system, but to politicians.

The amount of Ways and Means and Bills to be refinanced with longer, more permanent, debt would have been daunting at any time. As it was, the challenge had to be met as the world economy passed through a violent and unstable boom. For about six months after the Armistice, trade was at a standstill and unemployment rose. Then, in the spring of 1919, conditions changed abruptly. There was a pent-up demand for consumer goods and strong demand from overseas markets. Industry had to adapt to a new pattern of demand, worn-out capital equipment had to be replaced, and stocks rebuilt. Growth was fed by the budget deficit and ample credit, the legacy of the government's wartime borrowing from the banks, and Treasury Bills. Retail and wholesale prices rose abruptly and there was speculation in securities and commodities. By the end of 1919, there was full employment, while industrial production had risen by 10 per cent and, in 1920, was to recover further, almost reaching its 1913 level.

Shortly after the Armistice, the US Treasury ceased making advances to the UK and, with the current account in deficit and gold shipments again possible, in March 1919 sterling went off gold: by the end of August, the rate against the US dollar had fallen to $4.20, and by the end of December to $3.77. Without the traditional chart and rudder, officials had to persuade politicians to curb the boom by discretionary monetary restriction. Their efforts failed until the autumn of 1919: an army was being demobilised, unemployment was feared, social and industrial tensions were at dangerous levels, investment in housing was a priority and the budget was sensitive to the cost of the floating debt. It was only when the economy was showing clear signs of rapid and inflationary growth that officials prevailed.

A long-dated loan was prepared in the autumn of 1918, and postponed by Bonar Law in December. In the first quarter of 1919, the Governor frequently appealed to Austen Chamberlain, Bonar Law's successor in Lloyd George's new coalition government, for a rise in Bill rates. An issue was delayed through the first half of the year. In June, pressed hard by the Bank and CLCB, and much against his own judgement, Chamberlain issued two loans. Although afterwards the results were commonly viewed as disappointing, the new money raised met expectations at the time.[12]

This chapter describes the Bank's efforts to persuade the Chancellor to issue long-dated loans as part of the more general measures it was advocating to restore control over the monetary system. It then examines the design and sale of Chamberlain's two Loans, Victory and Funding.

The abortive funding of January 1919

During the war, the Bank subordinated its views to the needs of the Treasury, providing Ways and Means to cover whatever part of the budget deficit was not being financed by War Bonds and Treasury Bills. 'In 1918–19', writes Sayers, 'the Chancellor hardly went through the motions of consultation with the Bank when fixing the Treasury Bill rates.'[13] An initiative for an issue came shortly before the Armistice from Sir Brien Cokayne, who had succeeded Cunliffe as Governor in March 1918. Cokayne made no effort to moderate anxieties, reckoning the debt to be refinanced as some £3,200m, including, in the pre-war manner, all Exchequer Bonds, War Bonds and Savings Certificates, as well as Treasury Bills and Ways and Means. He advised that the anticipation of peace might create a more favourable climate than its realisation and that 'if the foreign exchanges are to be controlled at all, money rates will be very stiff', especially as the controls on capital exports would probably be lifted:

> although it was not inconceivable that a longish loan should be taken at a

> fairly low rate (say perhaps 4½) while even Treasury Bills were selling at, say, 7%, yet it is evident that tight money rates must militate against the success of any such issue...Would it therefore be well to attempt the issue of a funding loan or loans before the end of the war while the artificially cheap rates for money still obtain, and remittances abroad are still prohibited? And if so, would it not be well to take advantage of the present optimistic tone of the stock markets?

He doubted whether the holders of short-dated securities could be 'induced to fund into a long loan on any terms', so it would be necessary to repay them by borrowing from others. This, together with covering the accruing budget deficit and paying off the Bills which matured during the period of the offer, meant that the issue would have to be for cash and, therefore, provision would have to be made for meeting the conversion options on 4½ per cent War Loan and the Exchequer and War Bonds. Although this would represent a valuable lengthening, the administration would involve the usual manpower problems and it would be necessary to arrange an early release of the Bank's staff from the army. There was no point in tarrying: holders of short-dated securities would be no more willing to convert after the Armistice and, although the operation might be 'very far from complete', the funding of 'even a few hundred millions would be a great gain'.

Cokayne felt that in principle the best results could be achieved by offering a wide range of securities, 'catering for all tastes'. This, however, would involve more work for the short-staffed Bank, 'use up' a large number of the privileges which were available to attract investors, and carry the danger that the least successful issue would be so small that it would be illiquid. For these reasons, the Governor thought that there should be a maximum of two issues. As to the terms, no perpetual issue should be made until well after the war when the country had had time to make some recovery. He doubted:

> ...whether it would be advisable to offer a really long funding loan to yield much more than 4½%...it would probably be well to offer one loan with a good income yield, say, perhaps 4½% @ 98, and another with an equivalent yield at a smart discount.

An unknown hand has scribbled alongside the prices on the Governor's draft 'too low' and Cokayne had second thoughts before he wrote to the Chancellor; avoiding being specific, he pointed out that it would require a 'handsome rate' to persuade holders to lengthen because most existing short-dated securities already had the option of converting into 5 per cent War Loan at a yield of '5¼%'. No rate 'within reason' would enable a great part of the floating debt to be refinanced and, in any case, the lack of staff would preclude anything but the registration of consents to conversion; issue of the actual securities would have to wait. The Chancellor agreed that preliminary discussions should be held and ideas submitted.[14]

The draft prospectuses offered conversion to holders of 4½ per cent War Loan 1925–45, all of the 5 per cent Exchequer Bonds, all of the 5 per cent War Bonds and Treasury Bills issued before 14 January 1919.[15] As there was no provision for cash subscriptions, it has to be assumed that the Treasury was relying on the tax-gathering season to carry it through the period when no Bills would be on sale, a plan which had already been aired in 1916. The other terms were drawn from recommendations made at a meeting on 22 November attended by the Chancellor, Treasury officials, Cokayne, Norman, Inchcape and representatives of the CLCB.[16] The bankers, including the Governor, advised that funding should not be attempted unless food rationing, and the restrictions on capital issues and foreign exchange transactions, were retained. With these, a sinking fund to redeem the issue in fifty years and the same privileges as War Bonds enjoyed in the payment of taxes, a 'fair amount' might be funded on the basis of £130 nominal of a new 4 per cent Funding Loan for each £100 nominal of short debt, a price of 77 and a running yield of about £5 4s 0d per cent. When the Loan was announced, the Third Series of War Bonds should be withdrawn and be replaced by a tap issue of ten-year Bonds carrying no conversion options.[17]

Bradbury was particularly concerned to withdraw the wartime tax privileges – non-deduction at source, the exemptions for non-residents and the option to tender securities in settlement of EPD and Munitions Exchequer Payments (see Chapter 22). On reflection, he must have felt such tightening to be premature, for the draft of the planned Loan provided for non-deduction of tax and the option to use the securities to pay death duties, but not EPD or Munitions Exchequer Payments, while the Fourth Series of War Bonds, on tap from the beginning of February, included the same tax privileges as the earlier Series. The reimposition of withholding tax and the withdrawal of the EPD and Munitions Exchequer Payments privilege had to wait for Victory and Funding in the summer. Those were also the last issues to include the death duty clause. The 5¾ per cent Exchequer Bonds 1925, the issue which followed Victory and Funding in January 1920, was to be the last to provide freedom from taxation for non-residents.

From the first, drafts for 4 per cent Funding Loan 1969, or 4 per cent Consolidated Stock 1969–79 as it was later called, included a provision for interest and sinking fund equal to 2¼ per cent each half year of the nominal originally created less surrenders in settlement of taxation. The Treasury accepted the sinking fund with reluctance and only on the advice of the bankers, maintaining its opposition on the traditional ground of its potential for causing budgetary difficulties. It also drew attention to a new danger. The drafts had a single date, providing that any securities remaining in 1969 would be redeemed in full. Hardly surprisingly, in view of the importance attached to long option periods on previous loans, this attracted Bradbury's fire; if interest rates rose after a period of cheap money, so that the money being applied had bought less of the Loans than had been assumed, there would be a large balance to be repaid on a single date with money borrowed at the higher rate of interest. He saw this obligation to redeem at a fixed date as:

> objectionable in principle…the public creditor ought to be satisfied with the undertaking to maintain the fixed annuity of 4½% per annum until the whole loan has in fact been actually redeemed.[18]

If this plan were adopted, the issue would take on more of the aspect of a funding loan in the pre-war sense of the term. The result was a compromise: a period of ten years, 1969–79, in which to repay any rump. The following summer, 4 per cent Funding would have a thirty-year option period and Victory Bonds would have no final date.

The issue was cancelled after a meeting between the Chancellor and the bankers on 17 December. The timing was unfortunate. The general election had been on 14 December, but the results were being delayed for a fortnight to allow military votes to be counted. Bonar Law must have known that his future at the Treasury was in doubt. He could hardly have wanted either to become entangled in another time-consuming and exhausting campaign at the end of his term of office, selling the issue and facing the possibility that it would be a failure, or make a decision which would become the responsibility of his successor to implement. Norman's diary tells the story of the discord which gave the Chancellor the chance to bow out gracefully:

> Treasy. at 11. Gov. Goschen. Leaf. Inchcape. Holden. Discussion as to issue of 4% Cons Stk – c130% for funding all possible short indebtedness: not to be for cash. C of E. said at once he was wobbly. Holden gave details for believing £1000 millions would fund: ie about 1/3d. of short indebtedness: but was against doing anything. Inchcape agreed to arguments on both sides. Leaf was uncertain. Goschen strong for doing something but preferred <u>cash</u> <u>&</u> conversion. Gov. strong for conversion only – on lines of draft prospectus.

The Chancellor eventually said that he needed unanimity and that they should wait and see. The entry finishes with the prediction 'Probably Cash & Conversion Loan early next summer, wh wd. perhaps be final demand for fresh borrowing.'[19]

Restriction: autumn 1918 and spring 1919

After the election, fears of unemployment and the necessity of absorbing demobilised servicemen into the economy overshadowed the Cabinet's decisions on fiscal and monetary policy. During January and February 1919, there was widespread industrial unrest: in the London docks, the coal mines, the Underground, the engineering and shipbuilding industries, electricity generation and the railways. At the beginning of February, a violent forty-hour strike in Glasgow ended in riots. In France, there was an attempt on the life of Georges Clemenceau, the Prime Minister, and at the beginning of March violence in Berlin.

A clash between the Bank and the Chancellor had been presaged in September 1918, a month before the Governor had proposed his Loan. Sales of War Bonds had weakened in the middle two weeks of September. They recovered without any stimulus except from the 'Feed the Guns' campaign, but not before Sutton had suggested to the Chancellor that a further cut in Bill rates would help sales.[20] The Governor was unenthusiastic. Although unable to prove it, he did not believe a reduction in rates would increase subscriptions to War Bonds and:

> I am convinced that the temptation to employ money abroad is already too great and that there are innumerable ways of doing it without risking prosecution. I also feel very strongly that it will be impossible to preserve our international credit unless we have comparatively dear money after the War and that the more we artificially cheapen it now, the more difficult it will be to revert to normal conditions. In fact, as you know my own feeling is that money is too cheap here already [21]

After the election, the Bank's first move was to take advantage of a strengthening of sterling against continental currencies to withdraw the special deposit facility for French, Italian and Belgian funds. The Bank thought the deposits were a threat to sterling: they were at only three days' notice and it could not be sure that the Treasury would be able repay them without using the Bank's own Ways and Means.[22] It also urged increased rates on Bills and a reduction in its existing Advances, repeatedly pressing the new Chancellor for action. On 30 January, the Governor argued for a rise to strengthen sterling before peace was signed and the restrictions on the export of gold were lifted:

> unfortunately in the present abnormal circumstances the Bank of England will be unable, without the co-operation of H. M. Government, to raise the level of money rates. The Government has created such a volume of short debt that were the Bank to endeavour to make even their present moderate rate of 5% really effective they would, for instance, have to borrow the greater part of the more than £1,000,000,000 at present employed in 3½% Treasury Bills, which would obviously be impossible.
>
> It is very important, not only from the international point of view which I am here considering, but also from the domestic point of view, that the earliest possible steps should be taken to reduce by some funding operation the present enormous amount of Government floating debt. Until that is done it will not be possible for the Bank to control the exchanges and protect the gold standard by raising money rates before Peace is declared unless the Government will also raise the rate for Treasury Bills.[23]

An expansion in the Bank's Advances, despite it being the revenue-collecting season, produced another letter in a similar vein on 12 February.[24] Bradbury explained to the Chancellor that the rise in Advances was a result of lower War Bond sales, a natural reaction after the large issues made in January, and pointed out that the Bank's Advances had previously fallen by £95m. The rise in the first week in February came from the non-renewal of Bills by those who had bought War Bonds before the Third Series came off tap and, 'perhaps more probably', from banks topping up cash holdings after they had been depleted by the settlement of their customers' Bond purchases: 'There is therefore nothing really disquieting in this rebound…and the Governor himself quite recognises this.' The Chancellor sent a soothing reply based on Bradbury's draft.[25]

On 28 February, a formal letter protesting at the continued expansion in

Advances, which was being used to repay Bills, was withdrawn on Bradbury's advice; in the words of Norman's diary, 'it is no good crying for the moon.'[26] A week later, on the insistence of the Committee of Treasury, a letter did go to the Chancellor on behalf of the Court. It urged the restoration of the Bank's power over the market before the restrictions on gold movements were lifted, and advocated early gradual rises in rates instead of later more violent moves.[27]

The Bank's advice went to a Cabinet fearful of the effect of restriction on activity, employment and social stability.[28] In March, policy on sterling showed where ministers' priorities lay. If sterling was sold, and foreign currency resources were insufficient to continue its support, there would have to be either greater monetary restriction or removal of the peg. During the first three weeks of the month, Morgans bought £16.9m in New York. Since the middle of February, some ministers had been using the forum of ministerial conferences on Unemployment and the State of Trade to press for sterling to be unpegged as a means of stimulating economic activity. In his absence, this view was urged on the Chancellor on 17 March.[29] The following day the Chancellor and Bradbury had a long meeting with three members of the LEC – the Governor, Schuster and Farrer. The Chancellor described his position in the USA as 'comfortable' for the following few months, as long as he did not have to support sterling. He did not tell the bankers that the US Treasury had refused further advances the previous December, merely warning that his position *vis-à-vis* the US Administration would 'become increasingly difficult' if he had to ask for fresh credits with which to support the rate. What, he asked, should he do? The Governor favoured removing the peg, provided it was accompanied by higher interest rates; indeed, it should still be removed, even if rates were not raised. Although the other bankers agreed that rates should go up, their emphasis was different. Schuster, concerned about the effect on inflation, advised retaining the peg until the treaties were signed, and then accompanying its withdrawal with controls on gold shipments, that is, abandoning the gold standard. Farrer advised immediate withdrawal. The Chancellor replied that it was 'politically impossible…to raise money rates against himself' and that the date of the peace treaty was too uncertain to be the basis of a decision.[30] On 20 March, the peg was removed and on 1 April an Order in Council made the export of gold subject to license. There was no rise in rates.

To drive home his message, on 21 March, the day after intervention ceased, the Governor sent a more detailed letter to the Chancellor:

> The Bank are powerless to control the rate of money while Treasury Bills renewable at 3½% are constantly maturing in enormous quantities, and they therefore recommend that the Government's promised co-operation should take the form of at once releasing the Bankers' Deposit Rate and promptly but gradually raising the rate for 3 Months' Treasury Bills and offering 6 Months' and 12 Months' Bills at sufficiently higher rates to effect some spreading of the maturities…
>
> The Court also view with grave apprehension the rapid growth of their Ways and Means Advances to the Government at a period of the maximum revenue collection…

> The Directors therefore feel bound respectfully but earnestly to suggest that for this reason also, unless prompt steps are taken to repay or, at any rate, largely reduce their said advances by a long funding loan or by other methods, the Government should tempt the public to renew Treasury Bills, by offering these at more attractive rates.[31]

All that spring the Chancellor remained unwilling either to raise rates or make an issue. To the industrial troubles was added uncertainty about whether the negotiations in Paris between the allies and the Central Powers could turn the Armistice into a peace, and on what terms. Ireland was in turmoil, and there were disturbances in India and Egypt. The Commons debate on the budget proposals repeatedly turned to a levy on capital to repay debt. The problems posed by the poor state of national morale were described by Kindersley in a memorandum handed to the Chancellor at the end of March as the Governor was pressing for an issue:

> 1 The new issue should coincide with the signing of the Peace.
> 2 A Loan before Peace is signed will possibly go flat. The campaign will not be wholeheartedly undertaken. The present atmosphere is a bad one. There is the cry of Government Departments' extravagance. There is the unemployment benefit and there is general lassitude.
> 3 A fundamental change of atmosphere is necessary before a Loan can be issued with prospects of success.
> 4 This will most likely be effected by peace being signed.[32]

The debate continued. On 30 April, in the budget, the Chancellor explained why he was unwilling to follow a restrictive policy. It was obvious that the expansion of the Currency Note issue could not be allowed to continue indefinitely, but deflation would require a 'violent' rise in interest rates and contraction of credit which would:

> have the most serious effect on the prices of securities, on wages, and on the rates charged on Government borrowing, but also on the revival of trade and industry at a critical moment when the revival of trade and industry is the most important object we have in hand.

Even the Cunliffe Committee – which could not be criticised as 'erring on the side of heterodoxy' – had recognised that discipline would be most difficult to impose during demobilisation and the adjustment to peace. A new international price level had not yet been established and restriction might turn out to be unnecessarily harsh. In contrast, it was practicable and desirable to tackle the underlying causes of inflation; reduce expenditure; meet that expenditure from revenue; borrow, if borrowing were necessary, from the saver; repay Ways and Means; and fund the Bill issue.[33]

Revenue in the previous year had again exceeded estimates while expenditure, thanks to the Armistice, had been nearly £400m under the forecast; borrowing was £1,690m, not £2,130m. For 1919–20, Votes of Credit were to be replaced by normal departmental estimating, but the forecasts for both revenue and expenditure were very uncertain.[34] Expenditure on advances to allies, the armed services, demobilisation and subsidies to the coal industry and the railways were continuing, albeit at reduced rates. War revenues – EPD and 'miscellaneous' items[b] – were difficult to gauge. With these uncertainties in mind, expenditure in 1919–20 was estimated to be £1,435m, of which £360m was for debt service, and revenues £1,201m. Borrowing, therefore, was £234m or, in deference to the difficulties of estimating, £250m.[c]

The previous year, Bonar Law had justified a rise in taxation by pointing to a shortfall from the McKenna standard, the centre of the estimate being an assumption about the cost of servicing the Debt after deducting as potential bad debts one-half of the sums owed by allies. This year, Chamberlain repeated the exercise in a different guise, forecasting 'normal' post-war revenue and expenditure in pursuit of the outlines of a permanent budget. Once EPD had been abolished and asset sales had been completed, revenue might be £652m. Expenditure might be £766m after ending subsidies to industry and advances to the allies, reducing the armed forces and civil service and assuming the debt charge (including ½ per cent sinking fund) was £400m. This gave a normal year's deficit of £114m. Although the Chancellor repeatedly stressed the tentative nature of the exercise, he raised £109m in a full year by increasing death duties and excise duties on spirits and beer and by halving, rather than abolishing, EPD. The assumptions differed from those used the previous year in one crucial respect. With widespread agitation for some kind of capital levy, the service of the Debt was neither used to justify the tax rises nor placed at the centre of the estimates of normal expenditure; it became one of several items contributing to the total. Moreover, without stressing the change, the Chancellor allowed for the service of the entire Debt, ignoring sums owed or reparations except to promise that, if any were paid, capital would be applied to capital and interest to interest.[35]

Victory and Funding (12 June 1919)

The Chancellor did not refer directly to a loan in his budget, although his meaning was clear when he drew attention to the floating debt and said that proposals for dealing with it occupied his 'grave' attention.[36] Two weeks later, he discussed the terms of an issue with the Bank and the CLCB. On 23 May, Norman recorded that the Chancellor was still undecided, but prices had been fixed and printing of the prospectuses authorised.[37] On 27 May, the Governor saw the Chancellor. This meeting went unrecorded, but the Chancellor's views can be seen from the minutes

b Receipts from the sale of assets bought with Votes of Credit, repayments of advances to allies and the Empire, and reductions in balances.

c Expenditure of £1,435m was shown in the *Financial Statement*. To this was added £16m for contingencies.

of another held the following day, this time with the CLCB, with the Governor present. The Chancellor said bluntly that he was against an issue. If it were not for the approach of the summer holidays, he would postpone it for a month:

> the circumstances...were not favourable...The preliminaries of Peace had not yet been signed and his private opinion was that there would be a prolonged period of negotiation and passive resistance on the part of Germany...The foreign situation was disquieting...Home affairs were equally unsettled. There was serious agitation in the Police Force which might result in a partial strike of the Police within a week...on June 28th the Coal Commission[d] had to present their report. If on the one hand it decided upon the nationalisation of coal mines this might have a prejudicial effect on the loan: if on the other hand it decided against the policy of nationalisation the result would probably be a strike...

As it was, any delay would mean putting the issue off until the autumn. The Governor reacted strongly:

> I am perturbed by what you said to me yesterday evening. I am afraid that you will greatly regret it if you do not attempt a funding operation now. The country is ready for it and expecting it. We shall be so near the holiday season by the 12th June that any postponement will mean waiting for the autumn by which time the signature of Peace will perhaps have ceased to be a novelty, and though I would like the signature to take place while the loan is open I would sooner have it in prospect than a matter of past history. I know the 'atmosphere' is not good now, but I fear it will get worse rather than better and may well become impossible by the autumn, indeed I am not sure that the present is not your last chance of a big voluntary funding loan.
>
> I am sure that the loan which we have ready will bring in a large amount of money in spite of the atmosphere and in spite of the Sankey Report (if that cannot be postponed) and I think it would be great pity not to take the money when you can get it, while I dread the effect on British credit of continuing to finance by increasing the floating debt...
>
> I earnestly beg therefore that you will not allow another opportunity to be missed of grappling with the incubus of floating debt.[38]

Similar advice was given by the CLCB. The bankers' predictions of the disastrous effect of 'further postponement of an issue which the public are expecting' carried the day and on 29 May the Chancellor told the Prime Minister that, despite the difficulties, he was going ahead.[39]

Without promising an immediate issue, on 2 June the Chancellor obtained from

d The Sankey Commission was established to make recommendations on the future of the coal industry. In the event, the report was in the government's hands on Friday 20 June, and in the press the following Monday.

the Commons power to issue.[40] The Resolution became the basis of the War Loan Act 1919, which, in due course, gave the sinking funds attached to the Loans statutory authority and, importantly for the following decade, was so drawn that the Treasury was given powers to make practically any issue it chose for whatever purpose. Thus, the Act not only gave discretion over the terms, as was first authorised by the War Loan Act 1914, but also authority to borrow to repay maturing securities issued under the War Loan Acts, Ways and Means Advances and Treasury Bills. Because most new issues would be to refinance war debt, and any deficits on post-war budgets could be expected, in the first instance, to be financed by Bills or Ways and Means, the Commons effectively delegated power over all borrowing to the Treasury. The powers were not changed until Snowden's 1930 Finance Act.

The Treasury did not intend this.[41] The primary purpose of the new Loans and, it was thought, of issues in the future was the lengthening of short-term debt. It followed that wider powers were needed than those already provided by the Finance Act 1916, which limited the Treasury's authority to issues of less than five years, and the War Loan Act, 1918, which, although authorising longer-dated issues, limited the size to the sums voted for supply plus £250m. Of this, some £60m had already been absorbed in seven- and ten-year War Bonds and American borrowing.[42] From technical need, the gaze directed by public and Parliament to funding, and inadvertence, came the powers under which the Treasury carried out most of its borrowing in the 1920s.

There were two simultaneous issues at heavy discounts: 4 per cent Funding Loan 1960–90 was issued at 80 to give a running yield of £5 0s 0d per cent and a GRY of £5 3s 7d per cent to 1960, and £5 0s 9d per cent to 1990; 4 per cent Victory Bonds were issued at 85 to give a running yield of £4 14s 1d per cent. The prospectuses were dated 12 June and lists closed on 12 July. The issues included most of the innovations to save labour which had been introduced during hostilities.[e]

e The Funding Loan could be inscribed, registered as transferable by Deed or held as bearer. The Victory Bonds could be registered and were then transferable by Deed. Applications could be for either fully paid or instalment allotments. If fully paid, the whole amount was payable on application and there were no receipts. Instead, in the case of the Funding Loan, Stock was inscribed or registered at once; Bond certificates were issued until the definitive Bonds had been prepared. In the case of the Victory Bonds, Bonds were issued immediately. If the Loans were partly paid, the first instalment of £5 was payable on application and allotment letters were issued. When all the instalments had been paid, the letters were inscribed, registered or exchanged for Bonds.

The calls on both issues stretched away to 8 January 1920. If payment was made in full between instalments, the discount for early payment was calculated from the following instalment date and not from the actual date of payment. The minimum application was for £50 in both cases, although there were also Post Office issues. The interest on the Funding Loan was paid on 1 May/1 November and the coupons on the Victory Bonds on 1 March/1 September. The first payments were broken, representing the calculated interest accruing from the date of payment of application money and calls.

In accordance with the terms of their prospectuses, conversion was offered to holders of 4½ per cent War Loan 1925–45, 5 per cent Exchequer Bonds 1919, 1920 and 1921, 6 per cent Exchequer Bonds 1920 and the 4 and 5 per cent War Bonds of the first three series. A similar offer was made to 5 per cent Exchequer 1922, the first uncovenanted conversion offer since 1915, and the first of many. So there would be no loss of running yield and, no doubt, because of their approaching maturity, holders of the 6 per cent Exchequer Bonds 1920 who converted were offered a bonus of 1 per cent at an annual rate for the period between 21 June 1919 and the maturity date. The converting issues were accepted at par as equivalent of cash for applications and (remembering that the new issues were not being sold at 100 and the changes needed to the Third Series of National War Bonds), if they failed to represent an exact £50, cash had to be paid to make up a round amount (see p. 363).

Unlike the funding loan designed the previous year, the two issues were for cash, as well as conversion.[f]

The tax clauses reflected the comments made by Bradbury the previous autumn during the preparations for that abortive loan: withholding tax was reimposed on any holding yielding more than £5 per year, investors wishing to receive interest without deduction of tax had to satisfy the Treasury that they were non-resident and the issues could not be tendered in payment of EPD. In contrast, the use of securities in payment of death duties was an intrinsic part of the sinking fund attached to the Victory Bonds.

The Victory Bonds provided two gambles, intended to attract those investors who yearned for a premium bond. First, there was the option, in return for the lower running yield, to pay death duties in the Bonds at par; the cost of this fifteen points to the Treasury was unknowable because it depended on how long holders lived. Second, 2¼ per cent of the original nominal value of the issue was to be made available each half-year to meet interest and sinking fund. After paying interest, the balance was to be used to redeem Bonds by lot in an annual drawing, also at par. This gave the Loan an estimated life of about 56 years.[43]

2¼ per cent of the original nominal value was also paid each half year on the Funding Loan. After meeting the interest, the balance was to be used in the following half-year to purchase the Loan in the market for cancellation as long as the price was under par. Thus, the saving on interest as the principal contracted was to be applied to pay off the Loan. If the price rose above par, the Treasury could either continue buying or invest the monies in other securities. The length depended on the pattern of prices at which the sinking fund operated; the lower the prices, the more the sinking fund could buy and cancel, the shorter would be the life, and the higher would be the yield to the investor holding to the end. This effect would be most powerful in the early years. It followed that the maturity dates did not have their usual significance: 1960 was a precaution lest prices had

f Bills issued before 1 June were to be accepted under discount at 3½ per cent in lieu of cash for subscriptions to both issues in their fully paid form.

been high over the previous 41 years, were still high, and it was profitable to call the issue; 1990 was to reassure the investor, but was of doubtful – certainly incalculable – relevance. The prospectus merely stated that the Loan was 'redeemable within 71 years.'

It was found impossible to design a system which enabled Victory Bonds tendered for death duties to be cancelled. The only practical scheme for the drawings involved grouping Bonds of different values into batches so that each batch would be of the same value. If Bonds were extracted at random, as would happen if tendered Bonds were cancelled, the odds on being drawn would become different in each batch. This could only be avoided if the batches were rearranged each year to restore them to their original value, an impossible task.[44] The Treasury therefore opened an account with the Commissioners to hold surrendered Bonds until they were drawn. Any sums received on these Bonds by way of repayment of principal or interest were used to buy Bonds that had been surrendered to the Inland Revenue in payment of death duty; inasmuch as this was insufficient to meet the value of the surrenders, funds were advanced by the Treasury. In this roundabout way, the Inland Revenue received cash for the value of Bonds tendered and the Commissioners found the cash out of the income from the surrendered holdings or from the Consolidated Fund. The system was used for both the Funding Loan and the Victory Bonds and had statutory authority under the War Loan Act 1919.[45]

The arrangement was to be the source of one of Winston Churchill's lesser known raids as Chancellor. When the New Sinking Fund (1923) had been established, it became the source of the balance of the funds needed by the Commissioners to buy the Bonds tendered for death duties. Because Victory Bonds were accepted at par and the Funding Loan at its issue price of 80, little of the Funding Loan was surrendered for death duties; on 31 March 1928, £81.6m Victory Bonds, but only £1.5m of the Funding Loan, were held by the Commissioners in the Account. As the Commissioners' holdings grew, so did the interest. It was Frederick Phillips who suggested that expenditure could be reduced by ceasing to pay interest on these holdings, although it would mean that the Commissioners would have to draw more heavily on the sinking fund, leaving less available for other purposes. The ploy was incorporated in the Finance Act 1928 (see p. 686).[46]

It can be surmised that the authorities had three objects in mind when designing the issues. If the Loans were to be well subscribed, they had to give the promise of price stability. The 1917 War Loans had introduced a Depreciation Fund to make purchases if prices fell beneath issue levels. A sinking fund, working either by purchase or drawings, was very similar in the way it worked, except that it operated even if prices rose, and there was a cumulative increase in its resources. The right to tender the issues for death duties had the same purpose: it supported prices by attracting buyers wishing to minimise their tax liabilities, while reducing forced realisations from deceased estates. Second, the Loans had to appear different; investors, overfull with government securities, had to be tempted by new fare. Hence, issue at a smart discount and the gamble in the Victory Bonds. Hence also, the need for two issues. Victory Bonds, although tempting to those who had been agitating for premium bonds, had disadvantages. As they attracted one kind of investor, so they repelled another. Trustees did not like drawings, which entailed the reinvestment of small amounts of cash and a clash between the interests of those beneficiaries enjoying income for life and those looking forward to the inheritance of capital. Small investors, including trustees, liked to be able to invest broken sums and no system of drawing had been devised which did not require uniform minimum sizes of bearer Bonds. And third, the issues had to be long-dated, while not being redeemable solely at the government's option. Unless a long period without the Treasury being obliged to redeem was balanced by giving investors a long period without the threat of being called, they would buy 5 per cent War Loan at 93⅞ (to yield £5 16s 2d per cent to 1929 and £5 8s 5d per cent to 1947). The result of the longer dates was that 4 per cent Funding could be sold on a £5 0s 0d per cent running yield and a £5 3s 7d per cent GRY (to 1960) despite the competition.

The five point difference in the prices of the two new issues seems to have been a matter of instinct. The Victory Bonds had two advantages over the Funding Loan: they could be tendered at par for death duties and the sinking fund operated by drawings at par instead of by purchase at market prices. As Bradbury pointed out, the value of the advantages was not capable of calculation because it depended on the course of market prices. If prices fell or remained stable, the advantage of being drawn at par was clearly great. As prices rose, the advantage diminished and, if they rose above par, it became a disadvantage. The value of the option to tender the Victory Bonds at par depended on the life expectancy of the holder and the demand the market expected from potential payers of death duties:

> Taking the price of 80 as the value of a 5% Stock without this privilege, the value of the privilege would vary from nearly 20 points to a subscriber who is at death's door, down to very little in the case of the juvenile who may not only live for a long time, but may live to see the Stock itself rise to par and destroy the value of the privilege altogether.

The Chancellor's advisers from the City valued the drawing at par as being worth two points, the death duty privilege as the same and the 'attraction of the gamble' as one point.[47]

Negotiations with the bankers

The wartime habit of consulting the CLCB on the terms and canvassing its members' support persisted. The CLCB had been among the advisers from the City who had met the Chancellor the previous November and helped to design the broad shape of the loan then being contemplated. There was another meeting on 15 May 1919. The terms that were in official minds beforehand and the extent that officials led the bankers is not recorded, but the discussions were closely reflected in the prospectuses.[48] Negotiations followed the usual path; first, the terms on which the Bank would finance the commercial banks on the security of the issues and on which the banks would finance their customers' applications; and, second, the size of the banks' subscriptions and the possibility of underwriting.

On 4 June, the Governor described the terms on which the Bank would be 'instructed' by the Chancellor to make advances to the banking system on the security of the allotment letters. If the CLCB agreed to the Chancellor announcing that the bankers would make 'reasonable' advances to approved customers at a rate not exceeding Bank rate, the Bank would be prepared to make advances to the bankers, at the same rate, on the security of the allotments. The period would be a minimum of one month and a maximum of three. As was by now customary, payment for subscriptions would be accepted by the Bank in fifteen-day bills. These terms were agreed by the CLCB the following day.[49]

When the Governor made this proposal, he did not mention any margin on the security for the advances, although Cunliffe's promise to lend against 3½ per cent War Loan was generating considerable losses for the Bank as the price of the issue fell, impairing the value of the collateral. Some debts had been proving hard to collect.[50] It was probably a belated desire to protect the Bank from further losses which led the Governor on 10 June to tell the CLCB that he was prepared to offer more generous terms as to rate – Bank rate less ½ per cent, with a minimum of 4½ per cent, for a minimum of one month and a maximum of three – but with a margin of 5 per cent.[51] After some debate, the CLCB agreed to match the Bank's terms, but asked for the facility to be lengthened to the six months that its members had agreed for their own customers.[52] Cokayne refused, pointing to the Bank's 'special responsibilities', which precluded it from committing itself for longer.[53]

The CLCB's concern with its members' access to cash and the Bank's determination to ensure that its hands were tied as little as possible was not just bankers' caution. The economy was some months into the boom and the Governor was looking forward to the more restrictive policies, involving higher short-term rates, which he had been advocating since the Armistice. Equally, the commercial banks' wanted to retain the freedom to finance their customers' fast-expanding demands. This concern for liquidity was seen in the banks' negotiations with the Treasury on subscriptions and underwriting.

Neither the Chancellor and Treasury officials, nor those advising him from the banks, expected the Loans to raise as much new money as those issued in 1915 or 1917. In the middle of May, Holden told the Governor that the maximum he should expect was £300m.[54] At the end of the month, the CLCB, warning of the weight of new issues, the demands from industry and the absence of wartime spirit, showed an unusual unanimity; £400m might be raised, with a somewhat larger amount if the securities were to be accepted at par for death duties. At the same meeting, the Chancellor said that if he could be sure of raising £500m of new money he would immediately have an issue. A month later, he was privately optimistic, writing to his sister:

> But the Loan [*sic*] begins well. Experts foretold to me 250–350 millions *new* money (*new* money includes Treasury Bills & early maturing Exchequer Bonds *but* not conversions of early longer dated issues) I said that nothing

> less than 500 millions was worth having. I believe that we shall get 600 to 700 millions certain. I wonder whether we *can* get more. In my bones I feel that we shall.[55]

His advisers' moderate ambitions and his own optimism did not prevent the Chancellor from being nervous about the outcome, as had his predecessors in similar circumstances. At the end of May, he had asked the CLCB whether its members would consider guaranteeing that the Loans would raise £500m of new money. The bankers had pointed out that their ratio of investments to deposits was already 'formidable' and that fulfilling the pledge might impair their ability to finance reconstruction. Besides, Holden's London Joint City & Midland Bank, which was to be troublesome over the terms for advances, would be unlikely to join such an agreement.[g] The most that the CLCB would promise was its members' 'utmost support' and that they would come to the Chancellor's assistance to the 'utmost of their power' if the Loans fell short of expectations.[56]

By the end of the first week in July, subscriptions were disappointing and the Chancellor asked the banks named in the prospectuses to guarantee a maximum of £150m, to bring subscriptions up to £600m. As expected, the London Joint City & Midland refused to join the other banks, instead promising a subscription of £12m nominal, the equivalent of only 3¼ or 3½ per cent of deposits.[57] The remaining members of the CLCB agreed, together with the other banks on the prospectuses, to underwrite their share of £150m if the authorities met certain conditions: no liability to income tax on the premiums on Victory Bonds taken under the guarantee and drawn; lists to be extended to 17 July, presumably to reduce the risk of having to meet the underwriting commitment; the London Joint City & Midland's failure to participate to be made known, so that the reason for its relatively low exposure to gilt-edged investments would be explained to the public; the banks to be able to borrow, as of right, from the Bank on any of the securities taken under the guarantee at a maximum rate of 5 per cent; and the guarantees to be for nominal values and not cash. Hardly surprisingly, the Chancellor refused. The CLCB withdrew its offer and instead promised, again with the exception of the London Joint City & Midland, that its members would subscribe the equivalent of 5 per cent of their end-December 1918 deposits in cash and Treasury Bills and recommend that the other banks should do the same.[58] The result was bank subscriptions (in their own names) for £37.7m nominal of the Funding Loan and £73.4m nominal of the Victory Bonds.[59]

Publicity: the last of the big drum

After Sutton had refused an invitation to return to government service, the Chancellor appointed Sydney Walton, another newspaperman and a friend of

g In October 1918, the London City & Midland Bank Ltd had absorbed the London Joint Stock Bank Ltd to form the London Joint City & Midland Bank Ltd. It was renamed the Midland Bank in 1923. Holden died on 23 July 1919 and was succeeded as chairman by McKenna.

Kennedy Jones, as Director of Press Publicity for the campaign.[60] Walton had a difficult task. As well as the social and industrial turmoil and the uncertainties about the peace which had led the Chancellor to delay issuing, it was difficult to arouse the enthusiasm of a tired country. Many considered the government extravagant and thought it pointless to raise money which would be wasted. The War Savings Committee reported Local Committees hesitating to help the government and, indeed, only half of them participated in the campaign.[61] Walton's professional challenge, however, was to persuade investors that reducing the Treasury's short-term debt was reason for a subscription. The campaign had to speak of Ways and Means, the effect of credit creation on prices, of unemployment, the foreign exchanges and exports. The Chancellor had to point to the reduction in government expenditure since the Armistice and promise an end to extravagance. In one form or another, the words reproduced at the beginning of this chapter were repeated again and again in the propaganda. The advertising agents did their best, but a full-page advertisement of a damsel bound with ropes called 'short-dated loans' being rescued by the knight 'Victory Loan' could not equal the big drum and hostilities.[62]

The issues came as no surprise to the investing public, for the necessity of funding the floating debt had been widely discussed. Although they were not announced until 12 June, Kindersley had written to nearly two thousand War Savings Committees on 31 May warning of the difficult task ahead.[63] The campaign was launched, in the usual manner, by Lloyd George and Bonar Law at the Guildhall on 16 June. This was followed by a meeting with 1,200 secretaries of Local Committees (only two-thirds of the total) at the Queen's Hall to discuss practical details. The suggested keynote for the campaign was 'organised personal influence'. As a new initiative, imported from Liberty Bond campaigns, specific sums were suggested to individuals as appropriate subscriptions.[64] As usual, the local authorities were asked to support the local savings committees.[65] Eight hundred information bureaux and 750 temporary selling banks were set up. The press was fed stories. Armoured cars, films, leaflets, boy scouts and posters were drafted. The dirigible R 33 dropped leaflets over London advertising the 'Joy Loan' and illuminated aeroplanes performed stunts spelling 'VL' over Trafalgar Square. Letters from the Archbishop of Canterbury, the Archbishop of Westminster, the National Council of Evangelical Free Churches and the Chief Rabbi urged the support of clergy and laity.[66] Sir Douglas Haig added his weight. Harrods were entrusted with the manufacture of a Victory Flag for presentation to the city or town which subscribed the most.[67] To his horror, the Chancellor found himself delivering a speech to cameras in the Downing Street garden, his children being filmed buying Bonds at the local Post Office and his wife giving a personal message to women for the Sunday newspapers.[68] As in 1917, the CLCB agreed to circularise its customers with a facsimile letter from the Chancellor; 1,885,000 copies were sent accompanied by 1,169,000 letters from the banks' chairmen.[69]

Results

The two Loans raised £475.9m of cash, including £18.7m Treasury Bills tendered as subscriptions, from the sale of £576.9m nominal of securities (Table 13.1).[70] Although this made Chamberlain's campaign the least successful since that of Lloyd George in 1914, the result exceeded by a good margin all expectations other than those the Chancellor had voiced privately to his sister at the end of June and was within a few millions of the level at which he had said that he would consider an issue to be worthwhile. 'I have got more money by the Loan [*sic*] than anyone, who knew anything about it, expected but less than I hoped' was his own description of the result.[71] The exact margin by which the sum raised exceeded the advisers' forecasts is fogged because they, unlike the Chancellor, failed to specify what constituted new money.

Almost equal amounts of cash were contributed by the two issues: £244.7m came from Victory Bonds and £231.2m from the Funding Loan. However, this was distorted by the Commissioners' portfolios, which at the end of their 1919 years included £35.6m Funding Loan but only £1.5m Victory Bonds, of which all, or most, was taken on subscription. Neither the CNRA nor the Banking Department of the Bank of England subscribed for the issues.[72] A further £191.8m was created to meet conversions (Table 13.1). There was a disappointing response to the offer to convert the 5 and 6 per cent Exchequer Bonds, whose near maturity made them the most pressing targets. Of the £205.3m 5 per cent Exchequer Bonds 1919, 1920, 1921 and 1922 which had been outstanding on 31 March 1919, four months earlier, only £12m were converted; of the £141m 6 per cent Exchequer Bonds, only £11.1m were converted. The bulk of the creations, £161.9m, satisfied conversions from War Bonds.[73] The explanation for the failure to convert Exchequer Bonds was probably their relatively short dates: they were held overwhelmingly by temporary investors, such as industrial and commercial companies, which would be difficult to tempt into long-dated securities, especially when a growing economy promised more profitable uses for money. The maturities

Table 13.1 Subscriptions for 4 per cent Funding Loan 1960–90 and 4 per cent Victory Bonds (£m nominal)

Created for	*4 per cent Victory Bonds*	*4 per cent Funding Loan*	*Total*
Cash	287.6	270.5	558.1
Treasury Bills	0.3	18.4	18.7
Total	287.9	289.0	576.9
Total cash value	*244.7*	*231.2*	*475.9*
Conversions	71.6	120.1	191.8
Total created	359.5	409.1	768.6

Note
Columns may not sum because of rounding.

Sources: *National Debt: annual returns*; *BGS*, pp. 207, 226–7 and 285; Osborne (1926), I, p. 450.

of the War Bonds that were converted are not identified but it is probable that they were the longer dates, whose volume in issue showed substantial reductions between 31 March 1919 and 31 March 1920.[74]

✤ ✤ ✤

Victory Bonds and Funding Loan were designed for jaded palates. The proportion of private sector wealth held in government securities had risen sharply and investors had to be offered a very different kind of asset if they were to be tempted to buy more.[75] As well as attracting an unbalanced share of long-term savings, money had come from places for which the government market was not a natural home. The reserves of industrial and commercial enterprises were destined for productive use and it would be difficult to retain them in short-dated securities, let alone attract them into Victory Bonds and Funding Loan. The banks were overfull with government paper, whether Treasury Bills, War Bonds or War Loans, and were seeing profitable opportunities to lend to their customers. Yet, if Victory and Funding were to pay off Ways and Means or Treasury Bills, it would require either that these unnatural and overburdened holders switch longer or that newly generated savings flow into the new issues. The size of the refinancing relative to savings generation would have made the latter unrealistic, even if returns in the booming private economy had not been so attractive.

The next great refinancing was to be 3½ per cent Conversion Loan. Issued in 1921, it was to be the most controversial of the inter-war securities; it carried an attached sinking fund, it was perpetual and it was priced at a heavy discount. The origins of the terms can be traced to Victory and Funding. All the gilt-edged securities issued since 1915 had had provisions intended to support their prices: Victory, Funding and Conversion were no exception. Investors, including the banks which were advising the Chancellor, had suffered heavily from the depreciation of their fixed-interest holdings and since 1914 all Treasury borrowing had been due-dated. It is a measure of the force of tradition within the Treasury that, despite this, in September 1918 Bradbury could say that the public creditor 'ought' to be satisfied with a fixed annuity until the whole of a loan had been redeemed: that, in the event of a sinking fund not being able to repay within a specified period, the risk should be borne by investors finding themselves with a longer-dated security than they had expected, and not by the Treasury. Nine months later the authorities did not dare return all the way to perpetual borrowing, but they did move their redemption dates longer than anything seen since they adopted dated borrowing.[76] The 1919 issues also had their effect on the pricing of Conversion. The issues in 1919 were made at 80 and 85, yet there was no criticism of the effect on the nominal value of the Debt. The silence was nothing new. In 1914, the bankers had pressed for an issue at 95. There had been no criticism of the issue of 5 per cent War Loan at the same price. A price of 77 for a funding loan had been mooted by the Bank in November 1918 without apparent fear of public criticism. The storm over Conversion's discount was to come without warning.

Endnotes

1 T 171/149, Ramsay, 'Memorandum by the Treasury as to the Financial Effort of Great Britain and the Cost of the War', 2 December 1918.
2 Ibid.; Morgan (1952), p. 170; Feinstein (1972), T 4.
3 Mallet and George (1929), Table VIII.
4 Heath (1927), p. 1. Quoted in Newman (1972), p. 18.
5 This point is made in Newman (1972), p. 18. She refers to Hamilton, 'Sir Warren Fisher and the Public Service', *Public Administration*, XXLX, (1951).
6 *Hansard* (Commons), 15 December 1919, cols 43–5.
7 Committee on Currency and Foreign Exchanges after the War (Cunliffe Committee), *First Interim Report* (Cd. 9182), 1918. There was also a *Final Report* (Cmd. 464) signed on 3 December 1919. It added little to the *Interim Report*.
8 Moggridge (1972), pp. 18–21.
9 Clay (1957), p. 112.
10 Committee on Currency and Foreign Exchanges after the War (Cunliffe Committee), *Interim Report*, para. 47. The summary of the Committee's conclusions is reproduced in Sayers (1976), III, pp. 58–60.
11 Ibid., paras 16–17.
12 For example, Morgan (1952), p. 116; Howson (1975), p. 14; Clay (1957), p. 119. It was only some months later that officials started to think that the issues had been unsuccessful. See T 172/1384, Blackett, 'Dear Money', 4 March 1920, p. 20, and Hawtrey, 'Cheap or Dear Money', 4 February 1920.
13 Sayers (1976), I, p. 112; Clay (1957), p. 110; Osborne (1926), I, p. 129.
14 The 'Memorandum on Funding', 10 October 1918, is reproduced in Osborne (1926), IV, Appendices. The draft in the Governor's handwriting is in BoE, C40/397. Correspondence is in T 172/895.
15 A copy of the printed draft, together with several earlier typewritten versions, is in BoE, C40/397.
16 The full list was Bonar Law, Baldwin, Bradbury, Cokayne, Norman, Goschen, Leaf and Inchcape. Holden excused himself, but had agreed to the recommendations. BoE, C40/397, 'Memorandum', 22 November 1918.
17 BoE, C40/397, 'Memorandum', 22 November 1918. Ceasing to issue all but ten-year War Bonds was a Bank objective. MND, 1 January 1919.
18 BoE, C40/397, 'The Funding Loan and Income Tax', Bradbury's comments on the 'abortive January 1919' Funding Loan, December 1918.
19 MND, 17 December 1918. Also, see the entry for 1 January 1919, which lists tasks for 1919, including 'Announce issue of Funding Loan next summer.'
20 T 172/771, Sutton to Hamilton, 13 September 1918.
21 BoE, G30/1, Cokayne to Chancellor, 18 September 1918. CTM, 18 September and 25 September 1918; Osborne (1926), I, p. 124–6.
22 Clay (1957), pp. 110–11; Osborne (1926), I, p. 284.
23 BoE, G3/175, Governor to Chancellor, 30 January 1919; Clay (1957), p. 116. The letter is quoted in Osborne (1926), I, pp. 129–30.
24 T 172/1020, Cokayne to Chancellor, 12 February 1919; Clay (1957), p. 116. The letter is quoted in Osborne (1926), I, pp. 131–2.
25 T 172/1020, Bradbury to Chancellor, 13 February 1919, schedule of borrowing from the Bank, 13 February 1919, and Chancellor to Governor, 15 February 1919.
26 MND, 28 February 1919; Osborne (1926), I, p. 132.
27 BoE, G3/175, Cokayne and Norman to Chancellor, 6 March 1919; Clay (1957), p. 116; Sayers (1976), I, p. 112; CTM, 5 March 1919; Court Minutes, 6 March 1919.
28 Johnson (1968), pp. 358–74; Howson (1975), pp. 11–12.
29 Howson (1975), pp. 11–12.

30 BoE, C91/15, 'Purchases and Sales of American Exchange', 25 March 1919, and C91/20, 'Minutes of a Meeting on the 18th March 1919 between the London Exchange Committee, The Chancellor of the Exchequer, Sir John Bradbury and Sir Auckland Geddes'.
31 Governor to Chancellor, 21 March 1919. Quoted in Osborne, I, pp. 133–4: Clay, p. 116.
32 T 172/1081, 'New Loan', Kindersley, 31 March 1919.
33 *Hansard* (Commons), 30 April 1919, cols 184–6.
34 The estimating problems particularly applied to expenditure. For example, see T 171/157, Ramsay, 'A Note on the Commitments of the Exchequer for the year 1919/20 and subsequently', 10 February 1919, and Chancellor to Stamfordham, 29 April 1919.
35 *Hansard* (Commons), 30 April 1919, cols 187–90 and 211–12.
36 Ibid., 30 April 1919, col. 184.
37 T 172/1080, Conference between the CLCB and the Chancellor, 15 May 1919; MND, 15 and 23 May 1919.
38 T172/1080, Conference between the CLCB and the Chancellor, 28 May 1919; BoE, C40/397, Governor to Chancellor, 28 May 1919.
39 T 172/1080, Conference between the CLCB and the Chancellor, 28 May 1919; MND, 29 May 1919; T 172/1079, Chancellor to Prime Minister, 29 May 1919.
40 *Hansard* (Commons), 2 June 1919, cols 1727–31.
41 Although it did not intend it, it appreciated the advantages. See T 188/14, Niemeyer, Finance Bill 1927, 'Note on New Clause (Exchange and Issues of Securities)', June 1927.
42 T 171/169, Niemeyer, 'War Loan Resolution', 30 May 1919; T 176/21, Phillips to Niemeyer, 18 February 1927.
43 *Hansard* (Commons), 7 July 1919, col. 1404.
44 T 176/39 'The National Debt'; T 160/503/F1102/2, Chamberlain to Croom-Johnson, 23 April 1934; BoE, EID 4/140, 'National Debt', 28 July 1930.
45 'The Victory Loan (Transfer to National Debt Commissioners) Regulations, 1919' were dated 16 December 1919.
46 T 177/5, Phillips, 'Notes on Debt Interest Estimates 1927', 11 February 1926.
47 T 172/1079, Bradbury to Bonar Law, 10 June 1919.
48 T 172/1080, Conference between the CLCB and the Chancellor, 15 May 1919.
49 BoE, G3/175, Governor to Leaf, 4 June 1919; CLCBm, 5 June 1919.
50 Sayers (1976), I, p. 80; Osborne (1926), I, pp. 306–7.
51 CLCBm, 10 June 1919.
52 Ibid., BoE, G3/175, Cokayne to Leaf, 11 June 1919.
53 BoE, Cokayne to Leaf, 11 June 1919; CTM, 11 June 1919.
54 BoE, G30/3, Holden to Governor, 15 May 1919.
55 T 172/1080, Conference between the CLCB and the Chancellor, 28 May 1919; Self (1995), p. 116, Austen Chamberlain to Ida Chamberlain, 13 June 1919. Italics in the original.
56 T 172/1080, Conference between the CLCB and the Chancellor, 28 May 1919; MND, 29 May 1919; T172/1078, Holden to Chancellor, 17 June 1919, and Chancellor to Holden, 18 June 1919.
57 MND, 11 July 1919. The Provincial Bank of Ireland also refused to join the other bankers.
58 CLCBm, 8 July and 10 July 1919; *Hansard* (Commons), 8 July 1919, col. 1615.
59 *Hansard* (Commons), 30 July 1919, col. 2118. Osborne (1926), I, p. 451, gives £43.3m and £74.5m, but comments that they were approximate figures which 'doubtless' included applications on behalf of clients.
60 T 172/1079, Sutton to Chancellor, 29 May 1919; T 172/1077, Sutton to Gower, 1 June 1919, and Gower to Sutton, 4 June 1919.

61 T 172/1082, 'Interim Report of Victory Loan Campaign', 28 June 1919; National Savings Committee, *Fourth Annual Report.*

62 *The Times*, 8 July 1919, p. 16.

63 T 172/1082, Kindersley to Secretaries of the Local War Savings Committees, 31 May 1919.

64 T 172/997, War Savings Committee, 'Memorandum on the Policy to be Adopted in connection with the forthcoming Victory Loan', May 1919.

65 T 172/997 and T 172/1079 contain copies of correspondence and printed circulars.

66 National Savings Committee, *Fourth Annual Report*; *Financial News*, 5 July 1919, p. 3, and 8 July, p. 6. T 172/1077 contains correspondence with the local authorities, Scottish Office, Board of Education and various professional bodies. The correspondence with church leaders is in T 172/1046.

67 *The Times*, 2 July 1919, p. 14, and 14 July 1919, p. 12.

68 Self (1995), pp. 115–16, Austen Chamberlain to Ida Chamberlain, 13 June 1919.

69 CLCBm, 5 June 1919; T 172/1082, 'Interim Report of Victory Loan Campaign', 28 June 1919.

70 Osborne (1926), I, p. 450 and 450n. Included in these totals are applications on the Post Office Prospectuses, which were £17.1m in cash. Excluded is £12.1m that the POSB estimated to have been raised from sales of Savings Certificates during the period of the campaign. *Hansard* (Commons), 9 December 1919, col. 1147. The briefing paper is in T 172/1083.

71 Self (1995), p. 117, Chamberlain to Ida Chamberlain, 19 July 1919.

72 *National Debt: annual returns*; *BGS*, p. 484. The records of the CNRA were in the Departmental Records Office of the Treasury in the early 1970s, but have subsequently disappeared. The portfolios for each quarter from the end of March 1919 to 21 November 1928 were transcribed by Professor Howson in the late 1960s. Photocopies of the portfolios for each month between 31 January 1924 and 21 November 1928 were made by Professor Moggridge. Both sets of records have generously been made available to me. They will henceforth be referred to as 'CNRA ledgers'.

73 Osborne (1926), I, p. 450; *BGS*, pp. 206, 227 and 284; BoE, OV 31/2, Bank to Federal Reserve Bank of New York, 16 July 1919; *National Debt: annual returns.*

74 *National Debt: annual returns*, 1919 and 1920. It can be surmised that the reduction of £60.1m on account of tenders to meet taxes was of the shorter dates.

75 Morgan (1952), p. 122.

76 BoE, C40/397, 'The Funding Loan and Income Tax', Bradbury's comments on the 'abortive January 1919' Funding Loan, December 1918.

14 The struggle for internal control, 1919–23

> There are two possible ways of dealing with the floating debt. One is to fund it, and the other to pay it off out of revenue. At the present moment it would be impossible to fund the floating debt, I should say, almost at any figure. If the Government were to offer a bond at such an attractive rate that people tumbled over one another to subscribe, there would be such an immediate contraction of credit that you might have a financial crisis, and it could only be done, at any rate, at a very high rate of interest. Indeed, it is quite doubtful whether the public would subscribe at all to a funding loan at the present time, unless you had, first of all, taken steps to effect a very considerable reduction in the floating debt.
>
> Basil Blackett, 11 March 1920,
> Select Committee on Increases of Wealth (War),
> *Evidence*, para. 1535.

It took three years and a recession to reduce the floating debt to a level at which the authorities felt comfortable. Until the autumn of 1920, officials were preoccupied with trying to fight inflation when ministers were reluctant to raise Bill rates. Another funding loan was impossible as long as the private sector's demand for credit was so strong and the prices of fixed-interest securities so weak. In 1920, the only issues were of two short Bonds. Both, in different ways, were designed to provide the price stability of long-dated Treasury Bills. Since the only other method of repaying debt was a fiscal surplus, in the first half of 1920 the Chancellor considered a tax on wealth accumulated during the war. After a Select Committee report and warnings of financial panic, he was persuaded that the revenue would not justify the dislocation and damage to confidence; after some debate, the Cabinet agreed. In April 1920, higher conventional taxation was imposed with the purpose of increasing an already substantial surplus to permit a reduction in the floating debt.

In April 1921, as short rates began a delayed descent into recession, the authorities issued $3^1/_2$ per cent Conversion Loan ('Conversion'). The intention was not to pay off the floating debt, but to change investors' expectations. Blackett calculated that, if the shortest War Bonds could be refinanced before they reached maturity, the market would no longer be able to assume that maturities would continually feed the floating debt, the threat of continuous official sales would be lifted, and investors might be inveigled into buying at higher prices. It was an adventurous sally into market psychology, and it failed. Henceforth, the authorities were to rely on short- and medium-dated Treasury Bonds, sometimes with options to convert into tranches of Conversion. They continued to sell aggressively into the bull market until the spring of 1922 when, the floating debt beaten into submission, policy changed amid concern that bank deposits were being contracted so fast that industry was being deprived of credit.

After the South African War, the authorities had been able to handle maturities from revenue surpluses, an expanded New Sinking Fund, and the release of monies from Terminable Annuities and military capital spending. With only one exception – Austen Chamberlain's Lottery Bonds – refinancings were both short and conventional. After 1919, with a greater number and size of individual maturities, there was a need for innovation in design and in market management. In 1921, drawing on their New York experience and Morgans' wartime tuition in the art of market manipulation, the authorities began using the portfolio of the CNRA as an instrument of continuous market intervention: buying maturing issues, accepting conversion offers and selling when demand was seen, always lengthening the debt held in the private sector.

This chapter records how the Governor of the Bank and Treasury officials persuaded the politicians to raise Treasury Bill rates so that they could regain monetary control. In addition to Conversion, two issues are discussed in the context of the policy of reducing the floating debt and, within it, the Bank's Ways and Means Advances: 5¾ per cent Exchequer Bonds 1925 was successfully tailored to attract the banks and discount houses. It was the first of the string of conversion offers which would refinance the single-dated wartime issues and the only operation which did not enjoy the support of the CNRA portfolio; 5–15 Year Treasury Bonds, with a variable coupon, were an unsuccessful attempt to reduce the floating debt when it was thought that conventional issues would fail at any yield the Treasury could tolerate. Finally, the chapter describes the subsequent conversion and refinancing issues which brought the floating debt under control and refinanced the maturities of the first half of the 1920s.

Lifting the wartime restrictions and the first moves to control the floating debt: summer and winter 1919

The peace treaty with Germany was signed on 28 June 1919, leaving the government more free to attend to domestic policy. With the economy growing strongly, price levels were rising and the Commons and public were becoming alarmed at the level and waste of government spending. On 10 July, two days before lists closed for the Victory Bonds and Funding Loan, the Governor returned to the attack, urging the Chancellor to raise Bill rates and repay the Bank's Ways and Means by the end of September. He suggested that, as a first step, the limit of 3 per cent on the rate that banks could offer for domestic deposits should be abolished.[1]

As usual, Bill sales had been suspended during the sale of the Loans. When the taps were reopened on 15 July, the three months' rate remained at 3½ per cent, the six months' rate was increased to 4 per cent and, with the intention of filling the gap in portfolios caused by the suspension, a two-months' Bill was added at 3⅜ per cent. The sale of this maturity ceased after a month (Table 12.2).[2]

Lifting the restrictions on the export of capital and the bankers' deposit rate was discussed on 24 July at the first meeting of the Cabinet's new Finance Committee. Bradbury advised that the abolition of cable and postal censorship had made the restrictions on the export of capital ineffective and he recommended that they should be abolished. Whether or not the controls were removed, 'immediate steps should be taken to erect the proper economic barrier against the outflow of capital': if interest rates were left unchanged, the exchange rate would find its equilibrium at a level which would 'dislocate our whole national economy and jeopardise our Food Supply'. Public opinion was 'ripe' for the first steps towards the sound currency recommended by the Cunliffe Committee, although it would make the floating debt more expensive and drive down the prices of securities, including those of Victory and Funding. If, at the same time as the restrictions were abolished, the earmarking of Bank notes against increases in the Currency Note issue were introduced, the depletion of the Banking Department's reserve would force the Treasury to raise the rates on Bills and enable the Bank to make its rate effective; the government would have placed itself in the position where it would have no alternative but to raise Bill rates. The lifting of the restrictions was agreed, but nothing was said about Bills.[3]

The 3 per cent limit on bank deposit interest was abolished from 1 August, although its continuation was supported by the banks, who had found it profitable.[4] In July, notice had been given that the Bank would cease paying interest on domestic special deposits and the last were repaid on 18 August. At the same time the Bank ceased to use its customers' money in the scheme. From 6 August, the Bank unofficially, but publicly, began earmarking Bank notes against increases in the Currency Note issue. On 18 August, controls on capital exports were abolished, with the exception of the licensing system for public issues in which the proceeds were to be used outside the UK, which remained until 11 November.[5] Concerned that foreigners could borrow at a lower rate than they could lend to the Bank, and hoping to divert the money from Ways and Means to Bills, on 7 October 1919 the Bank gave notice that the scheme for foreign deposits was to end; the last were repaid on 18 October (Table 4.2).[6] An already weak exchange rate fell further.

The earmarking led directly to the higher rates of the autumn and the following spring.[7] They took place against forecasts that both income and expenditure were failing to meet the budget estimates. At the Prime Minister's behest, a few days before the Financial Committee of the Cabinet discussed lifting the restrictions, the Chancellor produced a statement on the government's finances. It reflected his mood. He was suffering from 'fatigue of body & mind', and had even been tempted by the offer of the Washington Embassy:[8]

> I need make no comment on the extreme gravity of the position.
>
> The Victory Loan has just closed. It was required to meet the deficit on the

> year [£250m], but its main object was to fund the Floating Debt. By an immense effort we have succeeded in raising £450,000,000 in cash. Of this £250,000,000 is required to meet the deficit disclosed in the budget statement. It is now apparent that the whole proceeds of the issue may be swallowed up by the excess of expenditure over the estimates for the current year.
>
> This is the road to ruin. In the present temper of the public, whether richer or poorer, no further issue would have the least chance of success. Every effort to secure support for the Loan [*sic*] was met by the cry of 'Government extravagance'. The big money came in fairly well in spite of this. The small man no longer subscribes, and the big man will not subscribe again if he sees his effort to restore sound finance stultified by new expenditure.[9]

On 7 August, the Chancellor warned the Commons that the April budget forecasts would not be met.[10]

Bank Ways and Means rose steeply in the second half of August. In the middle of September, Strong, on a visit to London, wrote in his journal that the Bank was 'getting ready to put the limit of pressure upon the Treasury to get money rates up to reduce their short borrowings and to put the Bank in a position to control the market.'[11] The Governor was, indeed, calling for higher Bill rates. There was encouragement from Strong and the Chancellor was sympathetic, but he was unable to carry his colleagues and, in particular, Bonar Law and Milner. At the Chancellor's invitation, on 25 September, the Governor wrote a paper for circulation to the Cabinet, pointing to the internal excesses and stressing sterling's vulnerability since the restrictions on the export of capital had been abolished:

> The Court fully understand that a Chancellor of the Exchequer should hesitate to raise the rate at which he is borrowing. Yet this is what the Bank have habitually done, often at great expense to themselves, when the good of the State appeared to demand higher rates for money: and I submit with all deference that, so long as Treasury operations prevent the Bank from performing this duty to the State, the Treasury becomes responsible for its performance and is justified in incurring expense to enable it to be performed.

The 'best solution' would be to reduce the floating debt with a 'huge' funding operation, but this was impracticable in the near future. Giving an early hint of why the Treasury would consider a levy on war wealth and the judgement which was to lie behind the 1920 budget, the Governor warned that it was probable that the Bank would not regain complete control of the market until part of the floating debt had been absorbed by a fiscal surplus.[12] On 6 October, it was announced that Bill rates were to be raised (Table 12.2).

Although he was calling for higher rates, by the middle of September 1919, the Chancellor was more sanguine about the fiscal position. His pessimism in July had been exaggerated by exhaustion after selling Victory and Funding. Perhaps he had been deliberately exaggerating: 'it is very difficult to find the juste milieu of statement which does not lead to childish pessimism on the one hand or to foolish & reckless optimism on the other' he was to say a month later.[13] Now, as he reported to the Commons at the end of October, he had good reason to seek an optimistic gloss. Morgans were making two new issues of $250m, finding investors' response cool, and were nervous about the effect of the announcement of the greater than forecast deficit.[14] The Chancellor estimated this to be £473.6m, but emphasised that normal revenues (with the exception of EPD) were coming in well and much of the shortfall came from delays in the sale of assets, the winding up of the food accounts and the repayments of advances to allies. These, and revenues from EPD, would now fall into the following year. A substantial surplus was in prospect in 1920–1; it was open to Parliament to seek a more rapid reduction in debt and a levy on wealth accumulated during the war would be explored by a Select Committee (see Chapter 21). There had been a reduction in the floating debt from £1,412m at the beginning of the financial year to £1,286m. Within this, Ways and Means had been reduced and the Bill issue increased. The Chancellor did not point out that much of this resulted from the ending of the special deposits scheme for foreigners and the absorption of their deposits into Treasury Bills.[15]

The October rise in interest rates was inadequate. Price inflation, speculation, strikes and a weak exchange rate continued. There were further increases in the Currency Note circulation and, therefore, under the earmarking procedure, reductions in the Bank's Reserve. The USA was also suffering from speculation and a severe bout of labour unrest; on 3 November, the Federal Reserve Board raised its rate to member banks and on 6 November some Federal Reserve Banks raised their discount rates. On 6 November, the Bank raised its rate to 6 per cent and the following day announced that the rates for three- and six-months' Bills were to be increased to 5½ per cent (Table 12.2).

Since August, monetary policy had felt the earmarking of Bank notes, but the government had not acknowledged that it intended to re-establish the gold standard. On 15 December this changed with the Chancellor's announcement that, with minor reservations, he accepted the Cunliffe recommendations. He agreed that a free gold market should be re-established 'at the earliest possible moment', together with the pre-war credit control mechanism to maintain it. Earmarking would be continued, the arrangement whereby the banks could obtain Currency Notes from the Bank would be discontinued and the actual maximum fiduciary issue for each year would be fixed as the maximum legal fiduciary issue for the following year. He also accepted the Committee's recommendations that government borrowing should cease and that 'every effort' would be made to pay off Bank Ways and Means and confine future borrowing to Deficiency Advances. As far as he could foresee, the Debt would reach its highest point during the following few weeks and thereafter show a 'gradual but steady' reduction.[16]

5¾ per cent Exchequer 1925 (19 January 1920)

This was scarcely conducive to raising new money or refinancing maturities. The prices of the Victory Bonds and the Funding Loan had fallen immediately dealings began. Victory (issued at 85) ended the year 1919 at 81, having been as low as

79 3/8. Funding (issued at 80) also finished four points lower, having been as low as 74. Some investors who had paid the minimum deposit, finding their securities had no value, limited their losses by failing to pay the instalments, forfeiting their £5 deposits.[17]

Fortunately, the first post-war maturity, 5 per cent Exchequer 1919 due on 5 October, had never been large. Only £16.9m was outstanding on 31 March, of which the CNRA and the Commissioners held £2.7m. The funds for repayment were found by adding to the floating debt and, in the first place, from taking Bank Ways and Means.[18] The next maturity, 6 per cent Exchequer 1920, was due on 16 February. This was the issue whose high coupon caused such upset in both the markets and the Bank itself in the autumn of 1916. Because of its coupon, holders had not been tempted into using their conversion options and on 31 March 1919 there was still £141m outstanding. Only £6m were owned by the Departments, about half each by the Commissioners and the CNRA. Half of the latter's holding had been bought in the fourth quarter of 1919 as the issue approached maturity.[19] There were also the 3 per cent Exchequer Bonds 1920, the issue which the Bank had rescued for the Treasury in 1915. These matured on 24 March. Over half of the original £50m had been cancelled with the proceeds of McKenna's 1915 War Loan, since when £21.7m had been outstanding. Nearly one-third, £6.5m, was held by the Commissioners, and none by the CNRA. Further ahead, there were the 5 per cent Exchequer Bonds 1920, maturing on 1 December. £49.1m were in issue, with £3.8m owned by the Commissioners and £2.4m by the CNRA.[20]

The Governor was anxious lest the repayment of the 6 per cents increase the floating debt and, in particular, the Bank's Ways and Means. On Christmas Eve, he wrote to the Chancellor urging that a conversion issue should be made during January. He could see the case for temporary financing if it was judged that better terms would be available shortly after:

> But even if this were certain I believe that the impression created by an apparent policy of drift and further expansion of the floating debt would create such a bad moral effect that it would be worth paying more in January to avoid it.

He agreed with the Chancellor that revenue collection in the first quarter, with consequent repayment of debt, would improve government credit, but thought that the effect on the markets 'would be enormously greater' if floating debt was repaid rather than 'if the net result [after paying off the Exchequer Bonds] is merely that the floating debt has not increased so much as might have been expected.' It was therefore, 'well worth making some small sacrifice in rate for a few years' to ensure that the revenue surplus reduced floating debt and other means were found to refinance the maturity:

> Probably if any such repayment of debt out of revenue is accomplished it will be possible to do some real funding of short debt on more favourable terms than would otherwise be possible, as the public will be more inclined

> to believe that the funding will be permanent and will take a more hopeful view of the future of the country's finances.[21]

The Governor's letter is a rare glimpse of the Bank's reading of market sentiment, whose importance would be so great as refinancing followed refinancing. It describes how investors might react to financial news, how the authorities might shape data so that it would produce reactions helpful to their market operations and how a virtuous circle might work: if once the process of repayment could be started it would create confidence, permit more debt sales, leading to greater confidence and more debt sales, and at lower rates. The hope of triggering this sequence was the major argument for issuing 3½ per cent Conversion Loan in 1921.

The Chancellor agreed that an issue should be made and, in January 1920, an offer was made of an unlimited amount of 5¾ per cent Exchequer Bonds of 1 February 1925 at par. Lists opened on 20 January and closed for conversion applications on 14 February and for cash applications on 28 February. Conversion was offered to all the 1920 maturities: the 6 per cent, the 3 per cent and the 5 per cent Exchequer Bonds. The issue was the last until 1940[a] to be tax-free to residents abroad; the Royal Commission on Income Tax was to report in March and recommend the end of the practice.[22] Otherwise, the issue returned to the pre-war norm. Tax was deducted at source and there were no privileges to tender holdings in payment of taxes. The forms of ownership settled down to a standard three alternatives; Bonds to bearer and inscribed or Deed Stock.

The most important term, which probably ensured the issue's success, was new to the gilt-edged market and was to be seen again later in the decade. Holders could give notice each January in 1921, 1922 and 1923 for repayment on 1 February of the following year. Thus, the new Bonds were either a five-year 5¾ per cent issue or (at the beginning and end of their lives) a twenty-four months' issue, or (in middle age) a twelve-months' Bill, at the option of the holder. The option, aimed at the professional short-term market, was a measure of the authorities' anxiety to ensure that the floating debt was not seen to expand. If they had issued twelve-months' Bills, they would have been classified as floating debt. By issuing a security with an option, even if it could mean payment in cash at the end of twelve months, it was classified as a five-year Bond until any part was put. The authorities felt they had no alternative. They did not believe they could sell longer paper to the general public, so they had to reborrow from the banks and money market, who were the holders of the maturing 6 per cents. This entailed giving protection against a rise in yields, spiced by the potential for profit if yields fell. Potential profit to the investor meant potential loss to the Treasury: refinancing for a period that could be as short as two years if interest rates rose or be expensive to service if interest rates fell. It was of unknown cost because nobody could

a 3 per cent War Loan 1955–9, issued 5 March 1940.

foretell the level of the refinancing yield in 1922, 1923 and 1924. It was, in fact, similar to the option that Cunliffe had disliked so strongly when it was suggested in March 1917 and it was to prove an inconvenience at the first put (see pp. 351 and 353).

Two terms were introduced which were often to be repeated. The interest accruing on the securities being converted overlapped for about two weeks with that accruing on the new Bonds. This bonus, offered at the suggestion of the Bank, may be regarded as a discount in the price and was worth about £0 5s 3d per cent in the case of those converting from 6 per cent Exchequer Bonds.[23] It had the advantage of avoiding broken coupon payments, so saving on clerical costs. Second, for the first time, 1/8 per cent commission was paid to agents handling conversion applications. This became the norm for those handling conversions, 1/8 per cent as a minimum and 1/4 per cent when a maturity was pressing. Alongside this generosity, the opportunity was taken to reduce from fifteen to seven days the period for which the banks could post-date cheques: the period was to be reduced further to five days with the next issue, the 5–15 year Treasury Bonds.

The offer was made for £211.8m of Exchequer Bonds: £99.5m were converted. More importantly, this included about £73m, or nearly half, of the 3 per cent and 6 per cent Exchequer Bonds. There was also £67.2m subscribed in cash (Table 14.1). Official accounts played a useful, but not a crucial, part, contributing £17.8m to the conversion result. With a large holding of the 3 per cents, the Commissioners were responsible for some two-thirds of this; the CNRA converted £5.5m and by 31 March 1920 owned £6.8m of the new issue.[24] Thus, about £140m of the £162.7m immediate maturities had been converted or refinanced.[25]

At first sight, the success of the offer is surprising. At the end of January, three-months' Treasury Bills at a discount rate of 5 1/2 per cent yielded £5 11s 3d per cent. War Bonds and Exchequer Bonds maturing in 1921, 1922 and 1923 were yielding nearly 6 1/2 per cent. At the end of November, the Federal Reserve Board had refused a request from the FRBNY for a further rise in rates. Although this was not known to the market, it was widely believed that the direction of US rates was still upward and, indeed, an increase came on 22 January.[26] During January, the sterling rate in New York fell from $3.77 to $3.51.

The explanation lies with one of those transitory improvements in confidence to which markets are prone, the realisation that government borrowing was coming under control and the put on the new Bond. Although the attitude of organised labour remained ominous, in the middle of January a railway strike had been avoided. The cost of living had been expected to rise sharply but, in the event, it remained static in November, December and January.[27] Sterling may have fallen against the US dollar, but the market had not become demoralised. The cash part of the issue was deliberately timed so that it would precede the tax-gathering season and coincide with the unwinding of the banks' end-year window-dressing. At the same time, the equity market improved, no doubt for the same reasons which enabled the Exchequer Bonds to be sold. Shortly before the Treasury's issue, three new loans for colonial governments had been successfully subscribed and had presented investors with immediate profits. Above all, the National Debt

Table 14.1 New issues and conversions of British Government sterling securities: 1919–32 (£m nominal)

Security	*Date of prospectus*	*Created for* *Cash**	*Created for* *Conversion*
1919–20			
4 per cent Funding 1960–90	12/6/19	289.0	120.1
4 per cent Victory Bonds	12/6/19	287.9	71.6
5¾ per cent Exchequer 1925	19/1/20	67.2	99.5
National War Bonds	31/1/19	44.6	0.3
5 per cent War Loan created by conversion from 5 per cent National War Bonds of the First, Second and Third Series			4.1
4 per cent War Loan created by conversion from 4 per cent National War Bonds of the First, Second and Third Series			7.9
Treasury Bills (net)		150.3	
War Savings Certificates (net)		46.6	
1920–1			
5–15 Year Treasury	30/4/20	20.8	2.8
4 per cent War Loan created by conversion from 4 per cent National War Bonds of the First, Second and Third Series			3.2
US$ 5 per cent three-year and ten-year Notes and Bonds into National War Bonds			6.7
Treasury Bills (net)		20.9	
National Savings Certificates (net)		11.5	
1921–2			
3½ per cent Conversion Loan	26/4/21		266.1
5½ per cent Treasury 1929	11/7/21	154.3	90.8
5½ per cent Treasury 1930	30/11/21	134.7	
5 per cent Treasury 1927	21/1/22	41.1	
3½ per cent Conversion Loan	18/2/22		19.7
5 per cent Treasury 1927	10/3/22†	69.0	
US$ 5 per cent three-year and ten-year Notes and Bonds into National War Bonds			12.0
National Savings Certificates (net)		57.0	
1922–3			
3½ per cent Conversion Loan	21/4/22		94.5
4½ per cent Treasury 1930–2	21/4/22		14.2
4½ per cent Treasury 1930–2	26/5/22‡	95.6	

Table 14.1 continued.

3½ per cent Conversion Loan created by conversion from 5½ per cent Treasury 1929 on 1/4/22 and 1/10/22 under the terms of the prospectus for that security published on	11/7/21		313.2
4½ per cent Treasury 1930–2	22/2/23		11.5
4 per cent Treasury 1931–3	23/3/23	15.0	
4 per cent Treasury 1931–3	29/3/23§	49.6	
5 per cent War Loan created by conversion from 5 per cent National War Bonds of the First, Second and Third Series			147.0
4 per cent War Loan created by conversion from 4 per cent National War Bonds of the First, Second and Third Series			0.6
US$ 5 per cent three-year and ten-year Notes and Bonds into National War Bonds			21.3
National Savings Certificates (net)		11.9	
Ways and Means Advances (net)		46.6	
1923–4			
5 per cent War Loan created by conversion from 5 per cent National War Bonds of the First, Second and Third Series			74.2
4 per cent War Loan created by conversion from 4 per cent National War Bonds of the First, Second and Third Series			0.9
US$ 5 per cent ten-year Bonds into National War Bonds			2.6
National Savings Certificates (net)		12.3	
1924–5			
4½ per cent Conversion 1940–4 created from 5 per cent War Loan	1/4/24		152.9
4½ per cent Treasury 1934	15/11/24		24.3
4½ per cent Conversion 1940–4	15/11/24		57.7
3½ per cent Conversion Loan	1/1/25	59.7	
3½ per cent Conversion Loan	25/3/25	30.0	
5 per cent War Loan created by conversion from 5 per cent National War Bonds of the First, Second and Third Series			40.4
4 per cent War Loan created by conversion from 4 per cent National War Bonds of the First, Second and Third Series			1.1
US$ 5 per cent ten-year Bonds into National War Bonds			3.6
National Savings Certificates (net)		2.7	

Table 14.1 continued.

1925–6			
$3^{1}/_{2}$ per cent Conversion Loan	23/9/25	40.0	
5 per cent War Loan created by conversion from 5 per cent National War Bonds of the First, Second and Third Series			60.6
4 per cent War Loan created by conversion from 4 per cent National War Bonds of the First, Second and Third Series			7.2
US$ 5 per cent ten-year Bonds into National War Bonds			6.7
National Savings Certificates (net)		6.7	
1926–7			
$4^{1}/_{2}$ per cent Treasury 1934	29/9/26		83.8
4 per cent Consols	29/12/26	32.6	133.8
$4^{1}/_{2}$ per cent Conversion Loan created by conversion from National Savings Certificates under prospectuses of	25/6/26 10/10/27 2/4/28 29/12/31		30.4
National Savings Bonds by conversion under the prospectuses of	25/6/26 10/10/27 2/4/28 29/12/31		4.7
5 per cent War Loan created by conversion from 5 per cent National War Bonds of the First, Second and Third Series			48.0
4 per cent War Loan created by conversion from 4 per cent National War Bonds of the First, Second and Third Series			3.8
US$ 5 per cent ten-year Bonds into National War Bonds			1.2
National Savings Certificates, cash (net) and conversion		—— 31.9 ——	
Treasury Bills (net)		34.3	
1927–8			
$4^{1}/_{2}$ per cent Treasury 1934	6/9/27	65.0	
$3^{1}/_{2}$ per cent Conversion Loan	15/9/27	–	111.7
5 per cent Treasury 1933–5	22/12/27	86.1	131.2
5 per cent War Loan created by conversion from 5 per cent National War Bonds of the First, Second and Third Series			89.1
4 per cent War Loan created by conversion from 4 per cent National War Bonds of the First, Second and Third Series			16.3
US$ 5 per cent ten-year Bonds into National War Bonds			1.2

Table 14.1 continued.

National Savings Certificates, cash (net) and conversion		37.4	
Ways and Means Advances (net)		45.2	
1928–9			
5 per cent Treasury 1933–5	16/8/28	35.0	
4 per cent Consols created by conversion from 5 per cent Treasury 1933–5 in July 1928 and January 1929 under the terms of the prospectuses for that security published on	22/12/27, 16/8/28		161.0
4½ per cent Treasury 1932–4	28/11/28	46.2	104.0
5 per cent War Loan created by conversion from 5 per cent National War Bonds of the First, Second and Third Series			12.9
4 per cent War Loan created by conversion from 4 per cent National War Bonds of the First, Second and Third Series			1.0
US$ 5 per cent ten-year Bonds into National War Bonds			1.6
National savings certificates, cash (net) and conversion		—— 41.9 ——	
Treasury Bills (net)		173.4	
1929–30			
5 per cent Conversion 1944–64	2/11/29	155.3	88.3
5 per cent Conversion 1944–64	6/11/29		79.4
4½ per cent Conversion 1940–4	22/2/30	60.8	32.0
4 per cent Consols created by conversion from 4½ per cent Treasury 1932–4 in July 1929 under the terms of the prospectus for that security published on	28/11/28		10.9
National Savings Certificates, cash (net) and conversion		—— 42.1 ——	
1930–1			
4 per cent Treasury 1934–6	2/10/30	105.0	
National Savings Certificates, cash (net) and conversion		—— 50.5 ——	
1931–2			
4½ per cent Conversion 1940–4	16/3/32		41.7
4 per cent Consols	16/3/32		73
National Savings Certificates, cash (net) and conversion		—— 85.5 ——	

Table 14.1 continued.

1932–3			
3 per cent Treasury 1933–42	29/4/32	110.0	
3½ per cent War Loan	30/6/32		1920.8
2 per cent Treasury 1935–8	10/10/32	76.8	73.2
3 per cent Conversion 1948–53	3/11/32	301.8	
2½ per cent Conversion 1944–9		5.0	
National Savings Certificates, cash (net) and conversions		—— 53.0 ——	

Notes
*Including Treasury Bills.
†Notice of tender for Bonds and Bills.
‡Beginning of sales by tender.
§By notice in *The London Gazette*. Sales by tender began 6 April 1923 and probably ended in April 1927.
In some cases, prospectuses were published in one financial year and the securities were created or sold in later years.
Amounts of less than £100,000 are ignored.

Sources: *BGS*; *National Debt: annual returns*; BoE, Loan Wallets 279 and 294.

was near its peak; it was the eve of the 1919–20 tax-gathering season and a surplus was expected in 1920–1.[28]

The newspapers gave encouragement, stressing the price stability provided by the puts, the contrast with the long-dated Victory and Funding issues and the improved control over government expenditure; typical was the *Morning Post*, which called the issue 'a clean one': refinancing, not new borrowing.[29] As Norman told Strong on 15 January, 'on the whole things look rather better than they did a couple of months ago.'[30] It was temporary. By the time lists closed, money had tightened, the exchange rate was more volatile, there was talk of a 7 per cent Bank rate and the gilt-edged market was weak. Consols had fallen under 50 and 5 per cent War Loan under 90. National War Bonds of early date were yielding nearly 7 per cent to buyers.[31]

Controlling the floating debt: spring and summer 1920

While lists were open for the 5¾ per cent Bonds, opposition to restricting credit intensified with the Prime Minister, Bonar Law and the bankers pressing for a cut in rates to help the sale of Housing Bonds, reduce the cost of the floating debt and enable the banks to sell their gilt-edged holdings.[32] The banks' balance sheets were showing the effect of the continued rise in their advances and the repayment of Ways and Means. They had been hoping to replenish their cash from the maturity of the 6 per cent Exchequer Bonds, but that was being taken by the 5¾ per cent Exchequer Bonds. They began to run off their Bills.[33] Additional pressure came from plans to ship £5m gold from the Bank's Reserve to help repay the UK's moiety of the Anglo-French Loan, due on 15 October. In March, Blackett was to acknowledge in public that funding would be impossible 'almost at any figure' and that, in any case, a reduction in the floating debt would be a precondition for success. He simultaneously cautioned that if the Treasury issued at a very high rate there could be such a response that the contraction in credit would provoke a financial crisis.[34] As an alternative to higher rates, the Chancellor was considering a capital tax on wealth accumulated during the war as a more direct method of paying off floating debt (see Chapter 21).

Seeking to strengthen his position, during February the Chancellor sought advice from the Bank, Blackett, Niemeyer, Ralph Hawtrey and Keynes on the effect of higher rates. The Bank defended the rises of the previous year as having had 'all the advantages which long experience has rightly attached to a rise in rates.' In his covering letter, the Governor said that had it not been for the issue of the 5³/₄ per cent Exchequer Bonds he would have been asking for an immediate increase in Bill rates to support a rise in Bank rate: the Bank's advances to customers ('other securities' in the Bank Return) were expanding, the market was expecting a rise and the direction in the USA was also upward.[35]

Although not opposing higher rates, the Chancellor feared the reactions of the Cabinet, press and bankers. On 9 March, he sought the bankers' agreement to a rise and, failing, asked for a voluntary reduction in their advances and investment of cash in Bills. Although the bankers were unable to agree specific proposals, on 16 March the Chancellor refused the Governor's request for increased Bill rates.[36] At the end of March, Norman replaced Cokayne as Governor and, twelve days later, he pointed out to the Chancellor that all the indicators were demanding greater restriction. The volume of Bills in issue had fallen; both Bank and Departmental Ways and Means had increased, as had outstanding Currency Notes; and the Bank's Reserve had fallen (Figure 14.1). On 8 April, the Bank of France raised its discount rate. In London, on 15 April, Bill rates were raised to 6¹/₂ per cent and the next day Bank rate went to 7 per cent.[b] In his budget statement four days later, the Chancellor explained the rise as a response to the non-renewal of Bills and the consequent need to borrow from the Bank.[c] This accords with Norman's recollection that it was the rise in the Ways and Means that finally persuaded the Chancellor to act.[37]

In a year of rapid and inflationary growth, both revenue and expenditure had exceeded forecasts.[38] In April 1919, revenue had been estimated at £1,201m; in October, it was forecast to be £1,169m and the outcome was £1,340m. In April, expenditure had been estimated to be £1,435m; in October £1,642m and the outcome was £1,666m. Thus, actual borrowing of £326m was well short of the £474m feared in October, although above the £250m forecast in April.

b On 14 April, another wartime restriction on the banks was removed. The Treasury released from their commitment the banks who had exchanged 4¹/₂ per cent War Loan into 5 per cent Exchequer Bonds 1921 under the terms of the Memorandum of 4 January 1917 (see pp. 327–8). MND, 30 March 1920; CLCBm, Blackett to Secretary of the Clearing House Bankers Committee, 14 April 1920.

c The Chancellor also pointed out that returns had begun to distinguish between Bank and Departmental Ways and Means Advances. These were provided with comparisons for a year earlier, so that a published series is available from 31 March 1919. *Hansard* (Commons), 19 April 1920, cols 73–4; CTM, 31 March 1920.

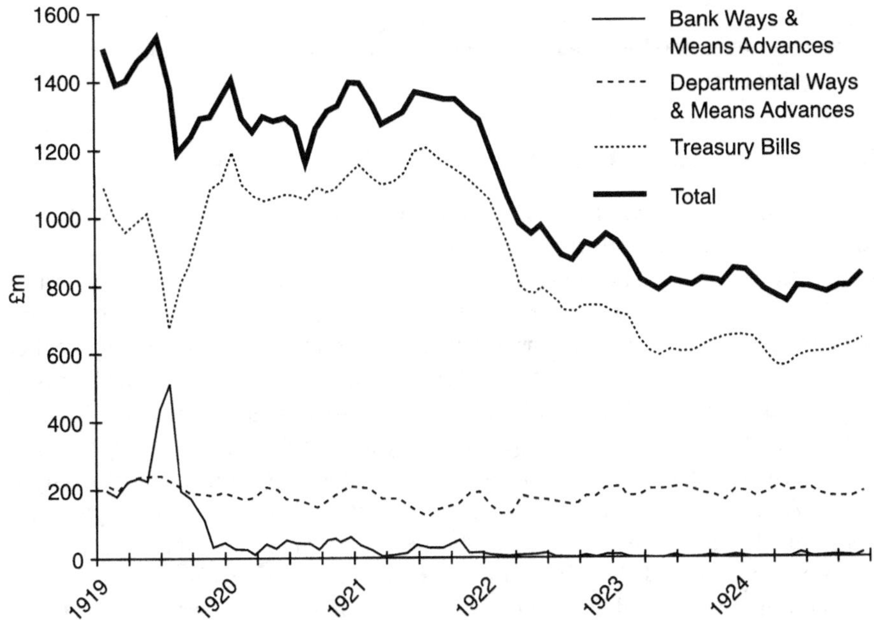

Figure 14.1 Components of the floating debt: January 1919 to December 1924. Source: *Statistical Abstract: BoE, C98/6937.*

With no changes in taxation, the estimates for 1920–1 showed revenue of £1,342m, expenditure of £1,177m and £164m for the reduction of debt. Within these totals, Special Miscellaneous Revenue was estimated to be £302m, almost exactly equalling extraordinary war-related spending. Pointing to expenditure of £160m on specific sinking funds and overseas debt, which had to be met before the floating debt could be touched, the Chancellor announced: a rise in postal charges; increased taxation on motor cars, beer, wine, spirits and tobacco; higher stamp duties; and a return of EPD to 60 per cent, together with a new Corporation Profits Tax. The changes were estimated to produce £77m in 1920–1 and £198m in a full year. The revenue estimate for 1920–1 became £1,418m, expenditure £1,184m, and the surplus about £234m. He expected that this would enable over £70m to be applied to the floating debt.

On 1 June, rates were raised in New York.[39] In London, the Currency Note issue was again pressing against its limit. A breach was only avoided by the Treasury declaring the withdrawal from circulation of the first two series of notes, a rump which had been destroyed, damaged or lost by the public. In August, Norman urged the Chancellor to raise Bill rates to support an 8 per cent Bank rate; the exchange rate was weak, prices rising and Ways and Means and the note circulation again increasing. Treasury officials supported the Bank, but the Chancellor 'was from the outset determined to make no change in rates and said in effect that it was politically impossible for him to do so.'[40] By the end of

September, Bank Ways and Means had been paid off, but they were needed once more in October and by the end of the year were £87m.[41] By this time, the boom was clearly over.

5–15 Year Treasury Bonds (30 April 1920)

For more than a year after the issue of 5³/₄ per cent Exchequer Bonds 1925, the authorities made little effort to refinance the floating debt or to convert issues approaching maturity. For most of this period, in a desultory fashion, Treasury Bonds with a partially variable interest rate were on tap.[d] The adjustable coupon had three purposes. By moving the nominal interest rate in line with money market rates, the authorities were, as with the Depreciation Fund and the attached sinking funds, seeking to provide the investor with an assurance of price stability. An annual put after 1925 was intended to have the same effect. Second, by providing a new instrument they hoped to minimise the impact on the price of existing issues. And, third, they were seeking to protect the taxpayer against paying a costly fixed rate for the whole life of the issue.[42] To provide further reassurance, the prospectus stated that 'The proceeds of this issue will be applied to the redemption of Unfunded Debt of early maturity', the first and last occasion that a prospectus bound the Treasury to use general borrowing for a specific purpose.

The Bonds were invented by the Bank.[43] Learning from its experience with Exchequer Bills, the interest payment was determined by formula, judgement playing no part, so that the 'grumbling' to which holders of Exchequer Bills had been prone was avoided. The coupon was a minimum of 5 per cent and a maximum of 7 per cent. Until May 1925, 'additional interest' would be added to the minimum 5 per cent at the rate of 1 per cent per annum if, in the half-year preceding a coupon date, the average discount rate on Treasury Bills sold to the public was greater than 5¹/₂ per cent and less than 6¹/₂ per cent and at a rate of 2 per cent per annum if the average were over 6¹/₂ per cent. Thus, whereas, in principle, holders of the 5³/₄ per cent Exchequer Bonds were protected from depreciation by a put, holders of the new Bonds were protected until 1925 by the coupon adjustment and from 1925 to 1935 by a put. To facilitate price-making in the market, the additional interest was payable on the following interest date, so that the rate of accrual would be known for the previous six months.[e] They were dated 1925 to

d There were two series, amalgamated after the books had closed for the preparation of the first interest payment on the Second Series. The first was in issue from 3 May to 30 October 1920, and the second, 'Series B', from 2 November 1920 to 30 April 1921. 'Series B' was offered in conversion at par to holders of 5 per cent Exchequer 1920, £25.2m of which matured on 1 December. This was unsuccessful, although, as with the 5³/₄ per cent Exchequer Bonds, the interest on the two issues overlapped, this time for thirteen days, to provide a bonus of exactly £0 5s 0d per cent. BoE, Loan Wallet 265, Harvey to Niemeyer, 26 October 1920: *BGS*, p. 189.

e The interest paid was at a rate of 7 per cent in both November 1920 and May 1921, 6 per cent in November 1921, and 5 per cent thereafter until the issue was called by the Treasury on 1 May 1925, the earliest date allowed by the prospectus. *BGS*, pp. 278–9.

1934 because the Treasury could call, and the investor put, the Bonds at par each year between 1 May 1925 and 1934 by giving notice in the April of the previous year.

Norman was more ambitious, and hopeful, than Blackett about the prospect of reducing the floating debt with such an issue. In April, when choosing the terms, Norman said he wanted 'a big sum of money' to refinance debt maturing 'within a year or two', even if it were only for five years; in other words, he was not seeking to sell the Bonds to the general investor, but to persuade the banks and money market to move longer. This entailed providing an instrument with money market characteristics. Hence, the variable rate in the early years and the put in the later:

> if this [short debt]...could all be postponed for 5 years how much easier would our position be; this is a proposal to postpone a part of it for at least 5 years, at a cost which may be below the cost of the remaining Floating Debt but which can hardly be above it...we may hope to be beyond our acute troubles in 5 years: if we are not beyond them such extra maturities as may be added by the optional repayment...cannot alter, to any great extent, the incubus of then maturing debt.[44]

Blackett had been pessimistic about selling debt when he gave his evidence to the Select Committee on War Wealth the previous February and he had not changed his mind come July:

> funding is really not possible now. It will only begin to be possible when the demand for banking accommodation for commerce and industry has become less insistent & money has begun to be released from such demands & to seek an outlet in long-term investments. All we can hope to do at present is to wring a small surplus out of the taxpayers' pocket for reduction of Floating Debt & by keeping an offer of a new Govt. issue of some kind – Treasury Bonds or something of the kind – continually on tap to pick up small sums for funding as the public is willing to offer us.
>
> We could no doubt do more in the way of Funding by offering a very high rate for a reasonably long-term. But this would not only be very expensive in the charges for interest it would involve: but would also stop completely the finance of housing, cause a very heavy (temporary) further depreciation in the value of existing Govt. & other issues, & if it were successful would probably bring on a financial crisis by causing too sharp a deflation of credit.

The only sound policy until January 1921 was to wait for the rise in rates to work, tightening when the opportunity offered and easing 'the pressure if it threatens to be too strong for people's nerves.' Tax collection in January would add to deflation and a funding Loan might be possible in the 'early summer [of 1921].'

> But I see no reason to hope that it will be possible to do anything in the autumn as regards funding more effective (if indeed as effective) than Treasury Bonds have proved, & we shall still be up against the necessity of not smashing Housing finance.[45]

Blackett was right. The Treasury was only able to 'pick up small sums'. The variable coupon, like Exchequer Bills in the final sixty years of their lives and Variable Rate Treasury issues in the 1970s and 1980s, were not popular, and only £20.8m were sold for cash and £2.8m for conversions (Table 14.1). The design had to meet inconsistent needs and, as a consequence, it fell between two stools. After the collapse in the prices of the Victory Bonds and Funding Loan and with the refundings to come, Blackett wanted to minimise pressure on the market, although clearly pressure was unavoidable if substantial volumes of paper were to be sold. He also wanted to avoid paying high rates for a lengthy period, although such would be needed if the investor was to be tempted.[46] Most importantly, a government priority was to keep its promise to increase house building. Part of the finance was to come from the public sale of Housing Bonds by local authorities and the Treasury wanted to avoid competing directly with them, to avoid 'smashing housing finance'. Underlining this, the first day for subscriptions to the new Treasury Bonds coincided with the launch of the Housing Bond campaign when Bonar Law stressed the distinction between the floating rate on the Treasury's paper and the 6 per cent fixed rate on the Housing Bonds and pointed out, yet again, that the Treasury was replacing debt, not increasing its borrowing.[47]

Enthusiasm in the market was lacking from the start. *The Economist* called attention to the Treasury's right to call the Bonds: the limitation of the additional interest to 2 per cent, which might, 'under quite possible circumstances, be an inadequate protection against depreciation'; the catch that if the issue were a success Bills would be in shorter supply, pushing down rates and the return on the Bonds; and – displaying the contemporary preoccupation with the level of public spending – misgivings when the Chancellor said that the proceeds would be used to pay off floating debt, while the prospectus spoke of redemption of 'Unfunded Debt of early maturity'.[48]

3½ per cent Conversion Loan (26 April 1921)

In April 1921, the Treasury borrowed on a perpetual annuity for the first time since it sold Consols during the South African War. It was the most controversial of the inter-war issues. Contemporary criticisms of 3½ per cent Conversion Loan 1961 or after, known simply as 'Conversion', were fourfold: it was issued at an unnecessarily high yield, it was badly timed, it bound the Treasury to a high rate for a long period and it made an unjustified addition to the nominal value of the Debt. Not altogether consistently, it was also attacked as a failure.[49]

The reason for the offer was the failure to reduce the floating debt and the Bank's conviction that investors had little money available for a new issue. Bank Ways and Means had fallen sharply when the foreign deposit scheme ended in

October 1919; at the end of March 1920, they were £8.9m and a year later £4.8m. Bar these window-dressed levels, they fluctuated between £20.7m and £63.1m. Once Treasury Bills had expanded to absorb the foreign deposits, the issue had remained steady, fluctuating between a low of £1,055.7m and a high of £1,152m. With Departmental Advances showing little change, the Floating Debt had fallen, but marginally (Figure 14.1).[50] Additions were threatened if maturities were not refinanced. On 5 October 1921, £72m 5 per cent Exchequer Bonds fell due, and holders of £32m 5¾ per cent Exchequer Bonds 1925 had exercised their option for repayment on 1 February 1922. Officials believed that most of this paper was held by the banks and money market and, as such, 'particularly troublesome'. On the first day of the new financial year, £35m 5 per cent Exchequer 1922 matured. The floating debt, said Blackett in March 1921, was 'for practical purposes' £1,400m, or the same as two years previously. Matters looked no better thereafter. Between 1 April 1922 and 31 March 1930, £1,680m (excluding foreign currency debt) was due; £800m matured before 31 March 1926.[51]

The limited role fiscal surpluses could be expected to play in repaying floating debt and the need for a borrowing initiative were shown by the results of the financial year drawing to a close.[52] The budget was on 25 April. On 21 March, when the resignation of Bonar Law on account of ill-health had forced Lloyd George to reshuffle his Cabinet, Austen Chamberlain had been elected Chairman of the Party, and was appointed Lord Privy Seal and Leader of the House. At the beginning of April, Sir Robert Horne succeeded Chamberlain as Chancellor, but he was still engaged in leading the government's efforts to settle a coal strike. On budget day, therefore, following the precedent of 1908 when Asquith had delivered Lloyd George's speech shortly after a reshuffle, Chamberlain spoke in Horne's place.

The 1920–1 forecasts had proved accurate, despite the collapse of the boom: expenditure £1,195m against the estimate of £1,184m, and revenue £1,426m (£1,418m). The surplus was £231m, close to the estimated £234m, 'a very remarkable result considering the summer coal strike, the trade slump & other adverse factors, as well as the immense figures with which we were dealing', thought Chamberlain.[53] Exchequer balances and the New Sinking Fund raised the sum applied to debt repayment to £259.5m, or between 5 and 6 per cent of GNP. Despite this, the surplus applied to the floating debt had not been the intended £70m, but £37m. The rest had gone to repaying foreign debt and maturing Exchequer Bonds and the purchase from the Inland Revenue of securities tendered for the payment of death duties and EPD.

For 1921–2, a distinction was introduced between ordinary and extraordinary receipts and expenditure. Ordinary expenditure was estimated to be £974m (debt charge £345m) and ordinary revenue £1,058m. Although this gave a balance of £84m, the Commons were warned that the coal strike would seriously affect both sides of the accounts. The estimate for extraordinary revenue and expenditure gave a balance of £92.8m, but there were war-related liabilities, especially to the railway companies, yet to be determined. Although the apparent surplus was £176.8m, the Chancellor hazarded that the amount available for debt redemption would be about £80m. With sinking funds already included in ordinary expenditure – Terminable Annuities (£2m), the New Sinking Fund (£7.5m), the Victory Bonds and Funding Loan sinking funds and their surrender for the payment of death duties (£14m) – there might be a debt repayment of £103.5m. This was

> very substantially below the contribution of £259,500,000 made in the year which has just closed, but circumstances have changed. Depression has succeeded to a boom in trade, and the very fact that we did so much last year, when things were going well, may be reasonably pleaded as a justification for moving more slowly in our present temporary difficulty.

The outlook beyond the current year was not strong and there was, he said, no room for lower taxes. In 1922–3, Special Revenue would be 'comparatively small' and EPD, whose abolition had been announced in February, would be reduced to the collection of arrears. Interest on the US Treasury debt would cost £40m a year if sterling returned to par, more if there was no rise. In sum, both revenue and expenditure might be £950m and there was a clear necessity to cut spending.

The Chancellor described the Debt in sombre terms. Statutory and contractual repayments of internal debt were estimated to absorb £113m in 1921–2, with a further £80m needed to repay overseas debt, mainly on account of the Canadian banks and the 1 November 1921 Notes in New York. With maturities of sterling Exchequer Bonds, the total required was almost £300m (Table 14.2). The picture year-by-year for the decade was almost as bleak . The Chancellor then turned to Conversion:

> The existence of our present huge Floating Debt is a grave inconvenience. Further large additions to it will be a standing menace to our credit, our security and our prosperity. I had hoped we should be able to reduce the Floating Debt before these earlier maturities began to threaten, but…the Sinking Fund has been largely earmarked for other purposes and largely required for foreign debt. All the authorities whom my right hon. Friend [Horne] has been able to consult, official and unofficial, agree that the present time is not suitable for attempting to fund the Floating Debt. But as these short-dated maturities approach their date of maturity they tend to pass out of the hands of the investor into the hands of the money market…They become to all intents and purposes an addition to Treasury Bills; so that if we waited till the date of maturity before we offered the holders anything in return…we would find that the holders…required cash…and that the former holders have already re-invested the money they had previously lent to the State.[54]

Conversion was designed by the Bank on Blackett's initiative and had been put to Chamberlain a week before he moved to his new appointments. Blackett said that he had been unanimously advised that there was 'practically' no money available for an issue for cash. He agreed with this, and thought a better opportunity might come in June or July. In the meantime, it was not the size of the floating

Table 14.2 Internal debt maturing in the two financial years following the beginning of each financial year: 1920 to 1923 (£m nominal)

	Ways and Means	*Treasury Bills*	*Securities*	*Total*
As at 31 March 1920				
1920–1	205	1107	25	1337
1921–2	205	1107	72	1384
As at 31 March 1921				
1921–2	154	1121	103	1378
1922–3	154	1121	233	1508
As at 31 March 1922				
1922–3	147	877	169	1193
1923–4	147	877	245	1269
As at 31 March 1923				
1923–4	194	616	113	923
1924–5	194	616	157	967

Source: *National Debt: annual returns.*

debt which was the 'biggest stumbling block', but the maturities. As long as investors knew that the Treasury had to reborrow large sums year by year to meet these, they would hesitate to subscribe for a loan to reduce the floating debt 'unless the terms are impossibly attractive'. Rolling over the floating debt and refinancing the maturities meant that the Treasury would not be able 'to relax its control of money rates' and would always be borrowing expensively: '"Funding is impossible till rates go down, and rates won't go down till funding has been accomplished". This seems to be the dilemma.' Because experience suggested that investors could be most easily tempted to convert if the offer was made before maturity,

> we are driven to the conclusion that the first step is not to fund Floating Debt but to attempt to convert the National War Bonds maturing in 1922 and later years…If a moderately successful issue on these lines could be made…a sensible inroad would have been made upon the National War Bonds of earlier maturity, and a gleam of daylight begin to be visible through the dark shadows of the next few years.[55]

The Bank decided on a traditional funded issue, offering a forty-year run before it could be called so that conversion could coincide with the earliest date on the 4 per cent Funding Loan 1960–90, and a depreciation fund to try, once again, to persuade investors that the price would be stable. It suggested a 3½ per cent nominal rate to avoid 'direct comparison' with other issues, in particular with 5 per cent War Loan, 4 per cent Funding Loan, 3 per cent Local Loans, 2½ per cent

Consols and (shades of $3^1/_2$ per cent War Loan in 1914) to give the investor the 'prospect' of capital appreciation.[56] Although the authorities were offering this bait, there is no evidence that they were hoping to avoid the 'psychological drag on Government interest rates generally', which later came from issues such as 5 per cent War Loan that were unable to appreciate because of their high nominal rate and uncertain redemption date.[57] Nor is there contemporary evidence to support Niemeyer's claim, made some years later when providing his Minister with debating points, that the rate was chosen to indicate a downward trend in interest rates.[58]

The offer was limited to the conversion of the shorter-dated 5 per cent National War Bonds, the seven issues maturing up to and including 1 September 1925.[f] Blackett thought the absence of a cash offer had three advantages. Any issue for cash would appear 'ridiculously small' in comparison with the wartime loans, whereas a conversion could be expected to produce more 'imposing' results. As the prospectus would only state the terms for the exchanges, there would be no acknowledged price for Conversion, and more than one implied price, so 'No one in the future would be able to say, as he has done in respect of all British Government War issues, that his stock had gone to a discount'. The government could also not be accused of raising new money for 'extravagances'.[59]

Was the issue expensive to the Treasury? The Bank selected the terms by valuing the War Bonds to give a GRY of 6 per cent, including their premiums on redemption. This was generous; on 22 April 1921, the GRYs in the market ranged from £6 7s 0d per cent to £6 11s 0d per cent. It also priced Conversion to give the same GRY of 6 per cent[g] to a redemption assumed to take place in 1961.[60] This is inexplicable, for using a GRY to determine the price of a perpetual annuity is, of course, to misunderstand the meaning of the term. The government had the right,

f The sinking (or depreciation) fund, equal to 'not less' than 1 per cent of the nominal amount in issue at the end of any half-year whenever the average daily price had been beneath 90 in that half-year, was to be applied to purchases in the market for cancellation in the succeeding half-year. The interest payments were 1 April/1 October and the date from which conversion was effective, 1 April 1921. These coincided with those on five of the War Bond issues, with broken payments necessary for the other two. In this, economy, rather than the shortage of labour, had become the driving force. Generous commissions to agents gave for the first time an incentive to make an early decision. Commissions on conversion applications had been paid for the first time with $5^3/_4$ per cent Exchequer Bonds 1925. On this occasion, the rate was increased to $^1/_4$ per cent for applications to convert lodged not later than 18 May, after which it reverted to $^1/_8$ per cent. After the issue had been announced, the Treasury responded to fears that businesses would be unwilling to convert their War Bonds and exempted the issue from the new Corporation Tax. BoE, Loan Wallet 272, TM, 14 May 1921; *Hansard* (Commons), 4 May 1921, col. 1059.

g The Bank calculated the GRY on a forty-year, $3^1/_2$ per cent security, to be £6 0s 0d per cent at a price of $62^1/_4$. BoE, Loan Wallet 272, '$3^1/_2$ Conversion Loan', 2 March 1921. The author agrees this. Morgan says that 'On the terms offered to the 1922 bond-holders, the new stock gave approximately 5.6 per cent in interest alone, while its true yield to the earliest redemption date was 6.8 per cent.' His calculation of the running yield can be agreed, but he was in error if by 'true yield' he means the GRY. Morgan (1952), p. 118.

but not the obligation, to redeem 3½ per cent Conversion after 1961. The GRY was only of relevance to those eccentrics wanting to know the annual yield in the event that interest rates were beneath the nominal rate on 1 April 1961 and the government called the issue. Such a calculation was not made when tranches of Consols were sold at a discount during the South African War.

On closer examination, the Bank's method of selecting the conversion terms was irrelevant to the question of whether the issue was expensive for the taxpayer. Only two first-class perpetual annuities traded in the secondary market. The first of these, 2½ per cent Consols, gave a running yield of £5 3s 0d per cent. But, as officials pointed out, this was a small issue (£276.9m), nearly 20 per cent owned by the Commissioners and increasingly unmarketable.[61] If yields should fall, Consols' lower nominal rate would give it greater protection from being called than Conversion. However, Consols were callable any time after 1923, whereas Conversion's protection extended to 1961. Thus, in principle, Consols should be relatively cheap when yields were high and become steadily more expensive as yields fell. That they were expensive when yields were high supports the argument that they were a poor market. The second, 3 per cent Local Loans (callable after 1912), gave a running yield of £5 13s 0d per cent, but with a higher nominal interest rate they gave less protection against being called than Consols. Additional comparisons could be made with long-dated Loans with free markets. The running yield on 5 per cent War Loan was £5 15s 0d per cent and the GRY £6 0s 0d per cent (to 1947).[h] The running yield on the very long 4 per cent Funding Loan was £5 12s 6d per cent and the GRY £5 13s 6d per cent (to 1990), but the Loan had features which made it expensive to the market, even when it was issued (see pp. 396 and 398). Using the prices implied by the conversion terms, the running yields on Conversion were between £5 12s 0d per cent (at a price of £62 10s 0d) and £5 14s 0d per cent (£61 8s 0d), depending on the War Bond being converted (Table 14.3). Thus, the running yield was in line with those on Local Loans and the very long 4 per cent Funding, and above that on Consols. As a perpetual annuity, its value lay somewhere between being cheap to the Treasury and being correctly priced; as Norman said to Strong, and Niemeyer said to the Chancellor, the Treasury paid no more than the market rate.[62]

Did it add unnecessarily to the nominal value of the Debt? Officials argued (and they would have to argue it many times in the following half decade) that it was the annual interest cost which mattered to taxpayers, not the nominal value, especially as the issue was only callable at the government's option. Any securities issued at a discount increased the nominal Debt, notable examples being Victory and Funding.[63] Neither the Treasury nor the Bank mentioned the most powerful argument, which only surfaced later in the decade: the lower the nominal rate borne by a perpetual annuity, the greater had to be a fall in yields before it was

h The author calculates that the price at which the running yield was £5 15s 0d per cent was 86.93 (clean), which on 21 April gave a GRY of £6 3s 9d per cent to 1947.

Table 14.3 Rates of conversion of National War Bonds into 3½ per cent Conversion Loan 1961 or after: offer of April 1921

	Nominal of 3½ per cent Conversion Loan per £100 of War Bonds	*Implied price*	*Running yield (per cent)*	*GRY to 1961 (per cent)*
1 October 1922	163	£61 8s 0d	£5 14s 0d	£6 1s 7d
1 April 1923	162	£61 14s 7d	£5 13s 5d	£6 1s 0d
1 September 1923	162	£61 14s 7d	£5 13s 5d	£6 1s 0d
1 February 1924	161	£62 2s 3d	£5 12s 8d	£6 0s 3d
1 October 1924	161	£62 2s 3d	£5 12s 8d	£6 0s 3d
1 April 1925	160	£62 10s 0d	£5 12s 0d	£5 19s 6d
1 September 1925	160	£62 10s 0d	£5 12s 0d	£5 19s 6d

profitable for the Treasury to call it. Assigning a price to this, and the justification of issuing at such a discount, is discussed in Chapter 22.

Was it badly timed? If the Treasury had waited even six months it would have been able to take advantage of the lower rates that came with deepening recession. However, officials thought they could not delay. What they believed when they selected the terms has become clouded by the accretion of later arguments made to repel political attack. Norman, in May, when lists were still open but there was no going back, stressed the advantages of 'getting rid of' the 1922–5 War Bond maturities: the floating debt was as large as the authorities could handle or 'ought to allow' and 'under present conditions' it was 'unfundable'. It would not be wise to add the cash from maturities to the floating debt and the whole outlook would be changed if the authorities had no maturities for five years.[64] Some part of Niemeyer's much later defence can be accepted, although (perhaps because) he did not participate in the decision. The cost was justified by the need to start funding immediately. The Treasury had only just ceased borrowing to meet budget deficits and it had a string of maturities to refinance; if it could sell this loan, the market would be encouraged, enabling later issues to be sold on lower yields; and time was pressing, as the shortest War Bonds had already passed into the hands of the banks and money market and investors' money absorbed elsewhere. To use Niemeyer's own words: 'It follows we could not wait. We had to act at once.'[65]

By not waiting, the authorities ran into some very heavy weather and lost the advantage of markedly easier money. When the Loan was being designed, there had been no change in administered interest rates for nearly a year: Bank rate had not moved from the 7 per cent and three-months' Treasury Bill rate from the 6½ per cent where they had stood since 15 April 1920. Recession had come sometime in the spring or early summer of 1920, but the central bankers were cautious. In both the UK and USA, they feared a resurgence of inflation and sought deflated, not just stabilised, prices.[66] Wholesale prices reached their peak in May 1920, but the fall was slow until the autumn, while retail prices continued to rise until November. Weekly wage rates continued to rise until January 1921 and then fell slowly until the summer. Unemployment rose slowly until December 1920.[67] After hesitation at the turn of the year, both Norman in the UK and Strong in the USA were disinclined to make monetary policy less restrictive.[68] With retail prices and wage inflation falling only slowly, and security prices recovering, Norman told Strong on 3 February that he would like to maintain Bank rate 'for an indefinite period', even if Bill rates could not be held.[69] It was political pressure, both in the UK and USA, which forced the central bankers to ease.

The Bank's expectation that any reduction in rates would, at best, be slow can be assumed to have made it unwilling to delay issuing Conversion, while the first changes in policy were used to prepare the markets. The Treasury led the Bank, actuated by now rapidly rising unemployment and the prospect of savings on the floating debt. On 12 March, it reduced the three-months' Bill rate to 6 per cent and added a twelve months' maturity. On 21 April, it announced a return to the method of selling Bills used in May and June 1917 – withdrawing the tap system for three-months' Bills and returning to the traditional system of sale of fixed amounts by weekly tender. In parallel, applications were invited for 'additional' Bills, between tenders, at advertised rates, based on the previous week's rates, but lower by £0 5s 0d per cent, rounded down to the nearest £0 2s 6d per cent. A few twelve-months' Bills were kept on offer at advertised rates, but from 8 July all Bills sold to the public were for three months. On 23 April, two days before the budget and the announcement of the Conversion Loan, the rate for the three-months' additional Bills was reduced from 6 per cent to $5^5/_8$ per cent and on 27 April that on twelve-months' Bills was reduced to $5^3/_4$ per cent. On 28 April, Bank rate was cut to 6 per cent (Table 12.2).[70]

The ending of the tap system returned power over the market to the Bank. In future, rates would depend on the market's resources and the supply of Bills; the primary object, Norman told Strong, was to remove from the Treasury the 'need' to fix money rates.[71] The change also contributed to the authorities' funding plans. A memorandum, written at the beginning of March and corrected in Norman's hand, described the effects of limiting the volume of Bills on offer to be the removal of an easy investment, a reduction in short-term rates, and pushing investors into lengthening: the banks and the money market into short bonds and private investors into the longs.[72]

While the Bank was lowering rates, with the incidental effect of setting the scene for Conversion, there were wider developments whose adverse impact on investors should have been foreseen. During the time the offer was open – 25 April to 28 May – the markets were living with the allies' attempts to make Germany accept the bill determined by the Reparation Commission and, at home, with a coal strike.

The Reparation Chapter of the Versailles Treaty provided for a German payment of 20,000m gold marks (£1,000m) by 1 May 1921, otherwise leaving the determination of Germany's liability to a Reparation Commission. At the end of January 1921, the allies adopted a scheme of annuities with a levy on German exports by which payment was to be made. On 1 March, Germany made a counter offer, which Lloyd George rejected, and the allies occupied three Rhine ports. In the middle of the month, the Commission demanded the balance of the original 20,000m marks owed under the Treaty and, when it was ignored, declared Germany in limited default. On the day that the Conversion offer was announced, the Commission demanded a 1,000m mark payment before 30 April. The French government was convinced that the Ruhr should be occupied and on 2 May ordered mobilisation. The following day, the Commission declared Germany in default. On 10 May, a new German government was formed and the next day it accepted the allies' terms. These included the payment of £50m within three months in gold or US dollars. German sales of European currencies strengthened the dollar, helping to drive sterling down from $3.96 at the end of April to $3.88 at the end of May.[73]

The number of days lost in labour disputes in 1921 was the highest in any inter-war year except 1926.[74] The trouble centred, as it had so often since 1919, on the coal mines. In October 1920, a strike had been settled, largely on the miners' terms. As long as the UK economy was buoyant and war-damaged continental pits crippled, export profits were sufficient to subsidise both lower prices in the home market and uneconomic pits. This was changing as the owners resumed control on 1 April 1921. They had already given notice of reductions in wages and a return to the pre-1914 practice of setting local pay rates and, when the miners rejected both, a three-month lockout began on 31 March. Until 15 April, there was a threat that the Railway and Transport Workers would support the miners in the so-called 'Triple Alliance'; because this combination would have approached a general strike, there had been precautionary movements of troops. The coal strike continued until 4 July, exports collapsed, unemployment shot up to over 20 per cent, tax revenues and investment suffered. Thus, although the worst of the threat to the economy had been lifted by the time Conversion was issued and, in retrospect, the government had isolated the miners, a major industry remained stopped.[75] Had they known how long the strike was going to continue, Norman told Strong in the middle of May, 'I doubt if…we should have attempted to carry out our plans as we have done. But that is merely "jobbing backwards"'.[76]

Was the offer a failure? If the holders of all the securities for which the offer was made had accepted, the Treasury would have replaced a liability of £632m nominal of War Bonds with £1,012m Conversion. As it was, only £164.1m War Bonds, one-quarter of those to which the offer applied, were converted into £266.1m Conversion.[77] This would have been disappointing, even if official portfolios had not been responsible for nearly 40 per cent; the CNRA converted about £56.3m into £90.4m, the Commissioners may have taken £2.1m Conversion and the Banking Department certainly took £10.9m, partly financed by switching 5 per cent War Loan into War Bonds, which it then converted. The CNRA's conversion was not only of the £25.9m 1 April 1923 War Bonds it held at the end of March, but also of a further £12.7m it had bought in the market. Similarly, it added £13.4m of the 1 October 1922s to a small existing holding and converted them. The same switches were made, on a much smaller scale, from acquisitions of the 1 September 1923s and the 1 February 1924s. By the end of December 1921, the CNRA had sold £51.8m of the Conversion it had acquired.

The use of the portfolio in this fashion to buy maturing issues, tentatively pioneered when the Treasury offered to convert 6 per cent Exchequer Bonds 1920 into 5¾ per cent Exchequer Bonds 1925, had been extended.[78] The part played by the CNRA remained a close secret, so that the poor public response which it camouflaged could not be used as a defence against accusations of generosity in the terms.

As the failure of the issue cannot be ascribed to its pricing, it is tempting to emphasise the tensions surrounding reparations, the coal strike and the exchange rate. However, even without these, the offer's ambition, or its lack of focus, would have ensured failure; 5¾ per cent Exchequer 1925 succeeded partly because of luck, and partly because it was a money market security designed to attract holders of another money market security, 6 per cent Exchequer Bonds 1920. Conversion was a perpetual annuity which was intended to attract holders of short-dated securities, mainly with remaining lives of up to thirty-odd months. It was simply the wrong obligation. The Treasury had not borrowed on a perpetual annuity since the South African War. Investors were still suffering from Consols, which had recently plunged under 50. The international and social background was unstable, short-term money was neither cheap nor plentiful. Yet holders, many of them banks and money market funds, were being invited to move from short-dated paper into a perpetual annuity, for a drop in yield and with no more support for their new holding than an attached sinking fund.

Other reasons contributed to the failure. The issue was the first since 1914 to be designed by the Bank without the advice of the private sector. There was no co-ordinated response from the members of the CLCB. Because they were not consulted, their members felt no obligation to show confidence in their advice by participating generously. It was also the first issue since 1914 not to be sold vigorously. Perhaps because it fell between the Chamberlain and Horne regimes, there was no organised City subscriptions, no ministerial speeches, no great advertising campaigns, no Kennedy Jones or George Sutton, no razzmatazz and no surges of enthusiasm from the savings movement. There is no mention of the issue in the annual *Report* of the National Savings Committee.

Recession: Conversion Loan, Treasury Bonds and the CNRA

Since the Armistice, the authorities had never felt free of the menace of the floating debt and maturing issues. Within a few months of the issue of Conversion in the late spring of 1921 their problems dissolved. On 23 June, Bank rate was reduced to 6 per cent, on 21 July to 5½ per cent and on the 3 November to 5 per cent. There were three further cuts in 1922, taking the rate to 3 per cent, where it remained for a year. The average rate of discount at the first tender for three-months' Bills at the end of April 1921 had been £5 19s 4d per cent. By the end of July 1922, it was £1 13s 6d per cent (Figure 14.2). Over the same period, the yield on the longest War Bond (5 per cent of 1 February 1929) fell from £5 16s 7d per cent to £4 16s 1d per cent and that on Consols from £5 5s 1d per cent to £4 6s 7d per cent. The yield curve steepened, with the incentive to move from Bills into perpetuals

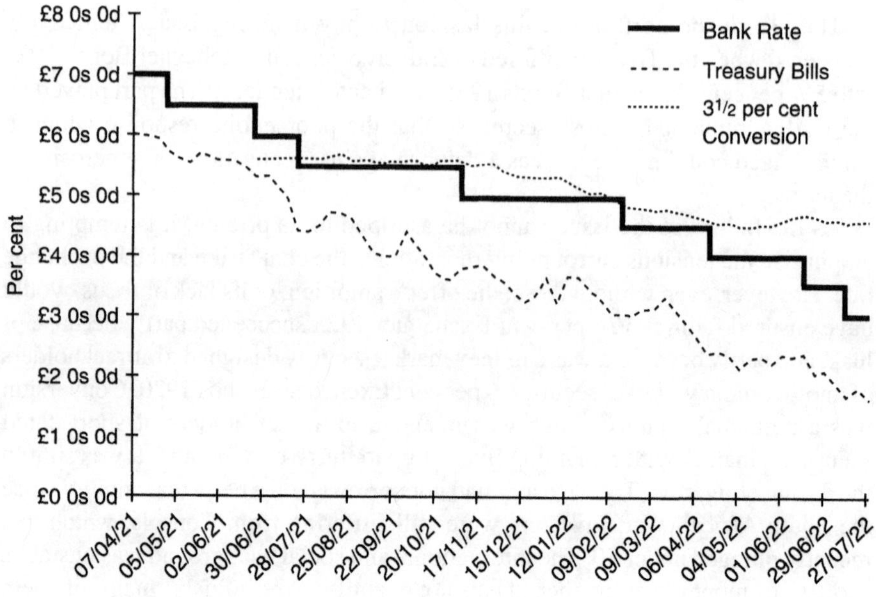

Figure 14.2 Bank rate, the discount rate on three-months' Treasury Bills and the running yield on 3$^1/_2$ per cent Conversion: April 1921 to July 1922. Source: *The Economist.*

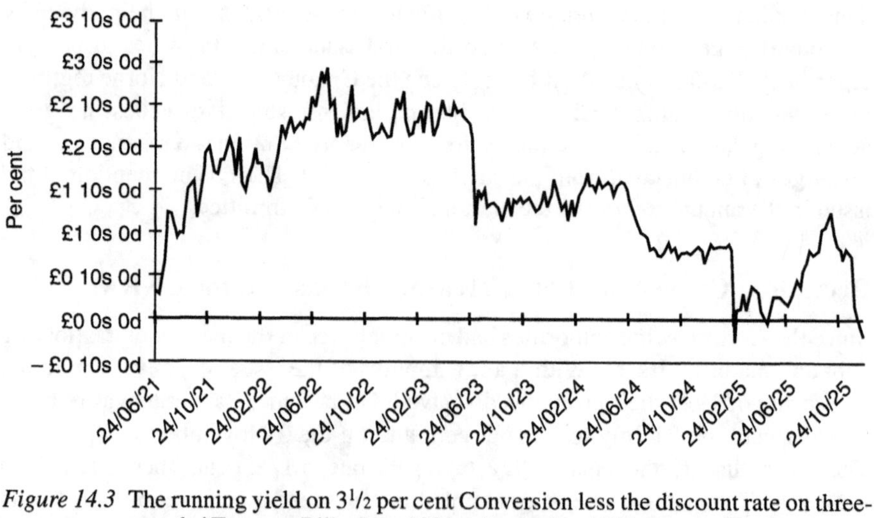

Figure 14.3 The running yield on 3$^1/_2$ per cent Conversion less the discount rate on three-months' Treasury Bills: June 1921 to December 1925. Source: *The Economist.*

almost doubling (Figure 14.3). Sterling improved steadily against the US dollar, rising from $3.565 at the end of July 1921 to $4.635 at the end of December 1922, where it remained until the summer of 1923.[79]

The authorities sold heavily into this powerful bull market. The floating debt had been £1,275.3m on 31 March 1921. Three years later, it was £774.5m. Within it, the Treasury Bill issue fell more sharply, from £1,120.8m to £588.3m. Bank Ways and Means disappeared, except for seasonal Deficiency Advances (Figure 14.1). During the same three years, the authorities repaid or converted £1,081.2m Exchequer Bonds, Treasury Bonds and War Bonds (Table 14.4).[80] In comparison with the years between 1914 and 1921, the process was humdrum; there was no spectacular offer and no furore. New issues were safely open-ended and the savings movement limited itself to selling Savings Certificates. Seeking to avoid the embarrassment of another dramatic failure and to reduce servicing costs, the authorities made no direct sales of long-dated or perpetual paper. Instead, they relied on short-dated Treasury Bonds, with options to convert into their funding vehicle – Conversion – at prices higher than those ruling when the option was

Table 14.4 Operations in 3½ per cent Conversion, 5 per cent War Loan, National War Bonds, Exchequer Bonds and Treasury Bonds: 1920–1 to 1923–4 (£m nominal)

	Increase	*Decrease*	*Net*
1920–1			
3½ per cent Conversion	–	–	–
5 per cent War Loan 1929–47	–	48	–48
National War Bonds	7	70	–63
Exchequer Bonds	–	29	–29
Treasury Bonds	23	–	+23
1921–2			
3½ per cent Conversion	266	–	+266
5 per cent War Loan 1929–47	–	42	–42
National War Bonds	12	224	–212
Exchequer Bonds	–	104	–104
Treasury Bonds	430	–	+430
1922–3			
3½ per cent Conversion	427	10	+417
5 per cent War Loan 1929–47	147	3	+144
National War Bonds	21	269	–248
Exchequer Bonds	–	35	–35
Treasury Bonds	173	215	–42
1923–4			
3½ per cent Conversion	–	17	–17
5 per cent War Loan 1929–47	74	4	+70
National War Bonds	3	136	–133
Exchequer Bonds	–	–	–
Treasury Bonds	46	–	+46

Source: *National Debt: annual returns.*

given. This technique was new to the gilt-edged market, although a variation involving a new security had been used when issuing British dollar obligations in New York (see pp. 153 and 234–5). It was underpinned by the CNRA portfolio, which in only a few months in the middle of 1921 became the central tool of debt management: it bought maturing issues; when an offer came, it converted its purchases into Treasury Bonds; it converted the Treasury Bonds into Conversion; and it sold the Conversion into the market as demand was felt.

5½ per cent Treasury Bonds due 1 April 1929 (11 July 1921)

On 23 June 1921, Bank rate was cut to 6 per cent in expectation that the coal strike would be broken. On 30 June, an agreement was reached which ended an industrial dispute in the engineering industry and on 4 July the mines reopened.[81] Taking advantage of the news, on 5 July the Chancellor announced an unlimited issue of 5½ per cent Treasury Bonds, due 1 April 1929, stressing that the 'sole purpose' was to refinance debt. More optimism followed; on 10 July, President Harding issued an invitation to a disarmament conference in Washington and the following day there was a truce in Ireland.[82] Presumably because the decision was opportunistic, printing had not been arranged and the prospectus was not published until 11 July (Table 14.1).

There were to be two series; the first was on tap from 12 July to 30 September, and the second, 'Series B', from 3 October to 30 November. They were issued at 97 (£6 0s 0d per cent if bought on 12 July) and at 98 (£5 16s 8d per cent if bought on 3 October). The only tax privilege was to formalise into the prospectus the exemption from Corporation Tax. Commissions to agents returned to ⅛ per cent on both cash and conversion applications.

There were conversion options both into, and out of, the Bonds; the first to help roll forward maturities, and the second to make the issue more attractive by providing an option on a long-dated security at a fixed price, albeit at a higher level than that currently available. Holders of 5 per cent Exchequer Bonds 5 October 1921 and the War Bonds of 1 October 1922, 1 April 1923, and 1 September 1923 were given the option to convert into the first series. Since the maturing Bonds were being surrendered at par to buy an issue at 97, a cash payment was made to those converting of £4 per cent in the case of the first two issues and £3 10s 0d per cent in the case of the others. This meant that there was a bonus of £1 per cent for those converting from the Exchequer Bonds, which were maturing in three months' time at par. The War Bonds, which were not an immediate problem, were redeemable at 102, so that the payment covered only part of the £5 per cent sacrificed by converting.

Holders of the new Bonds were given the option on 1 April and 1 October 1922 of converting into Conversion at the rate of £146 of Loan for £100 of the Bonds. This was simple to administer as the interest dates on the new Bonds were the same as those on Conversion and conversion took place on the interest dates. The implied price for Conversion was £68 9s 10d and the running yield £5 2s 2d per cent, or some ten to twelve shillings beneath those implied by the April offer. At the time of issue, the market price of Conversion was about 63.

It was poor design to make the option price the same on both dates, for it enabled investors to delay converting without incurring any penalty. Moreover, by waiting, they enjoyed the higher running yield on the shorter issue for six months. The lesson was noted and later in the decade the authorities gave options at deteriorating prices when issuing short-dated paper convertible into 4 per cent Consols.

There was a successful attack on 5 per cent Exchequer 1921, aided by a display of aggressive management by the CNRA; £52.9m were converted, leaving only £18m to be paid off at maturity on 5 October. Over one-quarter (£14.7m) of those converted had been bought in the market by the CNRA. The Banking Department bought and converted a further £1.1m, which it promptly sold. Perhaps reflecting the less generous bonuses, the offer to the holders of the War Bonds was less successful. It applied to £548.6m of the Bonds, and only £37.9m were converted, £1.1m by the CNRA. In 1922, the CNRA converted all the Bonds it had taken.[83]

Applications for cash started slowly, but in September £40m were sold, including £10m to Lloyds Bank. Sales for cash of the first series were £58.9m and of the second series £95.4m. With conversions of £90.8m, the total became £245.2m (Table 14.1).[84]

5½ per cent Treasury Bonds due 15 May 1930 (30 November 1921)

Despite the success of this issue, at the beginning of November the Treasury was still forecasting an increase in the floating debt during 1921–2.[85] Thus, when the 5½ per cent Treasury Bonds 1929 were withdrawn on 30 November, a replacement was announced simultaneously. This was an unlimited issue of 5½ per cent Treasury Bonds of 15 May 1930, which were similar in all respects, except as to date of maturity and coupon payments, to the previous issue. There were no conversion options. They were on tap from 1 December 1921 to 17 January 1922 at a price of 99 (£5 13s 8d per cent). By the beginning of January, the yield on 5 per cent War Bonds 1929 had reached £5 10s 4d, and on 6 January the rate of discount on Bills fell almost £0 10s 0d per cent to £3 5s 0d per cent. In such conditions demand was strong, and a total of £134.7m of the Bonds were sold without the CNRA or the Commissioners being involved, £56m in a single week as expectations grew that Bank rate would be cut and the price raised or the issue withdrawn (Table 14.1).[86]

5 per cent Treasury Bonds due 1 February 1927 (21 January 1922)

The Bank duly recommended moving to a lower yield. As the 5½ per cents of 1930 were withdrawn, they announced an unlimited issue by tap of 5 per cent Treasury Bonds 1927 at 99 (£5 4s 6d per cent). The shorter date was to minimise comparisons with 5 per cent War Loan and the longer War Bonds with the same coupons, at the same time allowing the market in the longer maturities to settle down after the recent sales. It was also a cheaper point on the yield curve.[87] Other than in coupon and date, the new Bonds were the same as the previous issue and had no conversion rights.

Conversion offer for 5 per cent Exchequer Bonds due 1 April 1922 (18 February 1922)

The 5 per cent Exchequer Bonds 1927 remained on tap from 23 January until 14 February 1922, when sales were suspended to avoid disrupting an offer to holders of 5 per cent Exchequer Bonds 1922, which matured on 1 April. This new form of conversion was rushed out on 18 February, taking advantage of what *The Economist* described as a 'vigorous upward movement' in the market.[88] Instead of an option to convert before maturity, holders were offered the opportunity on the due date of taking, in place of cash, £136 Conversion for each £100 of the Bonds; this was equivalent to a price of £73 10s 7d (£4 15s 2d per cent). Once again, the interest payment dates coincided, and the holder simply rolled over from one issue to another on 1 April. Holders of £14.5m of the Exchequer Bonds accepted the offer, leaving £20.6m to be paid off. The CNRA's tactics were by now predictable: it had been a steady buyer in the market and at maturity it rolled over £12.4m of the Exchequer Bonds into £16.8m Conversion, thus being responsible for 85 per cent of the result.

It can be surmised that there were two reasons for making the offer instead of refinancing the maturity by continuing to sell 5 per cent Treasury Bonds 1927. The market was very strong, and the authorities might have judged (wrongly, as it transpired) that holders would have an appetite for a funded issue. The manoeuvre could also have been intended to rebuild the CNRA's holdings of Conversion, which had been depleted by heavy sales over the previous six months. The Account had acquired £90.4m when the security was created in May. At first, sales had been slow; on 28 September 1921, its holding was still £82.5m, but on 28 December it had fallen to £39.6m, and on 29 March 1922 to £14.2m.[89] If this was the explanation, it was a further development in the management of the portfolio: an offer made with the primary purpose of replenishing the Account's holdings, rather than to camouflage a failure, with the later sale being incidental.

By converting its 5½ per cent Treasury 1929 the following spring and autumn, the CNRA was able to make further acquisitions. The rise in the market had made this option very attractive: by 1 October, Conversion had risen to 72, compared with the exercise price of just under 68½. On 1 April and 1 October 1922, holders converted £214.5m of the outstanding £245.2m Treasury Bonds into £313.2m Conversion (Table 14.1). The CNRA acquired £21.7m Conversion on 1 April (and a further £14.8m six months later), so that by 1 April 1922 its holding had recovered to £52.9m.[90]

Tenders for 5 per cent Treasury 1927 and Treasury Bills (10 March 1922)

With the settlement of Bond sales and revenue gathering, the market was feeling the shortage of Treasury Bills and it was being asked whether the reduction in the floating debt was being carried too far.[91] No record has been found of any decision, but about this time policy became less restrictive. Although all but seasonal Bank

Ways and Means disappeared at the end of March 1922, the Bank had been adding to bankers' balances by buying government securities; the Bank's holdings, less its Ways and Means, began rising as early as the final quarter of 1921.[92] The change was reflected in the market. Beginning on Friday, 17 March 1922, the Treasury began offering by tender a mixture of 5 per cent Treasury 1927 and Bills, making it clear that it did not intend to resume sales at a fixed price.[i]

This was another innovation, the first occasion on which a gilt-edged security had been sold by weekly tender. On the Bank's advice, the Treasury did not bind itself to sell every week, or to sell only the 5 per cents of 1927; it merely specified the total of Bonds and Bills it would sell on the selected day and, within this total, the maximum amount of Bonds. It did not bind itself to issue Bonds up to this maximum. The arrangement offered great flexibility; having seen the pattern of tenders, the Bank could respond to market demand, allotting Bills or Bonds as it thought fit, or refusing to sell any Bonds if the bids were too low. If the market was short of money market paper, the Bank could increase the allotment of Bills and reduce that of Bonds.[j]

Conversion of War Bonds into either 4½ per cent Treasury Bonds 1930–2 or 3½ Conversion Loan (21 April 1922)

On the day of the final tender, a conversion offer was made for the War Bonds due on 1 October 1922 and 1 April 1923. This was another innovation, combining in a single prospectus an offer to convert maturities into either a medium-dated Treasury Bond or Conversion. The Bonds, 4½ per cent Treasury Bonds 1930–2, were themselves a new departure, the first time a Treasury Bond or Exchequer Bond had been given a double-date.

Effective on 1 April 1922, the common interest payment date, holders could convert £100 of War Bonds into £134 of Conversion Loan, another improvement in terms and the equivalent of £74 12s 6d (£4 13s 10d per cent).

Alternatively, holders could convert £100 of War Bonds into £100 of the Treasury Bonds. The two War Bonds were large (£262.8m at 31 March 1922) and the first (£133.9m) was due in only six months. The authorities, therefore, gave a cash incentive to those accepting the offer, which was rolled up into a payment of

i The Treasury gave the market plenty of time to accustom itself to the new system. The Chancellor announced the tenders on 6 March, details of the first tender were given on 10 March, and the first tenders were received on 17 March. The Bonds were dated any working day the following week at the option of the tenderer. *Hansard* (Commons), 6 March 1922, col. 867; *The London Gazette*, 10 March 1922.

j There were six tenders, the last being held on 21 April. Accepted prices for the Bonds ranged from £99 13s 7d (£5 1s 6d per cent) in March to £101 17s 9d (£4 11s 6d per cent) in April; £69m were sold by tender, raising total sales of the issue to £110.1m (Table 14.1). *BGS*, p. 270; BoE, Loan Wallet 279, Harvey to Blackett, 4 March 1922; *Hansard* (Commons), 6 March 1922, col. 867. Loan Wallet 279 contains the results of the tenders for both 5 per cent Treasury 1927 and 4½ per cent Treasury 1930–2.

£4 per cent. Of this, £2 per cent was compensation for the loss of the premiums on redemption. A further amount was required to make good the loss of running yield incurred by switching before maturity from a 5 per cent to a 4 per cent Bond. In the case of the shorter War Bond (due on 1 October 1922), this absorbed 10s of the remaining £2, and, in the case of the longer (1 April 1923), £1. Thus, as would be expected, the incentive to convert was greater for the shorter issue.[k]

Conversion of War Bonds into 5 per cent War Loan 1929–47, the first War Bond maturity

The rise in the market had made profitable the option attached to the first three series of 5 per cent War Bonds to convert into the 5 per cent War Loan: holders of £26.4m of the 1 October maturity took advantage of this option, £3.8m being on account of the CNRA.[93] Thus, after two conversion offers, surrenders for taxes and conversions into 5 per cent War Loan, the first War Bond matured. On 31 March 1918, when it came off tap, £237.9m had been outstanding. At maturity, only £43.8m remained to be paid off. Even this problem was reduced by the CNRA, which, in a piece of market management that was unique in the years 1920–5, bought £10m during the summer and held them to redemption.[94]

The 1922 budget

Horne presented the 1922 budget on 1 May.[95] The recession and coal strike had taken their toll and the payments to the railways companies under the wartime agreements had been duly incurred. Both revenue and expenditure had fallen short of their estimates and the surplus was £45.7m, rather than the £80m for which the Chancellor had hoped. This, with £25m from the New Sinking Fund and other repayments treated as expenditure, had allowed £88.5m to be applied to debt reduction. The surplus, and the success of the conversion and refinancing operations, allowed the Chancellor to be optimistic about the Debt, in contrast to the previous year. The floating debt had been reduced from £1,275m to £1,030m, and other debt maturing within four years (excluding Savings Certificates and including premiums on War Bonds) from £887m to £627m.

> I have every hope that the year 1922–23 will bring a further improvement...Thanks to the improvement in the market price of British securities – although this is, in part, unfortunately due to trade depression – the taxpayer is securing a substantial alleviation of the burden of interest on

k The offer resulted in £70.5m, or 26.8 per cent, of the two War Bonds being converted into £94.5m Conversion Loan (Table 14.1). The CNRA was responsible for nearly 60 per cent: it converted £36.2m of the 1 October Bonds and £5.7m of the 1 April Bonds into £56.2m Conversion Loan, so that by 28 June its holding had risen to £63.8m, although it had made substantial sales in the meantime. The offer to convert into the 4½ per cent Treasury 1930–2 was less successful, mainly because the CNRA played no part: private holders converted £13.8m into £14.2m.

> floating debt, and there is reason to hope that before very long it may be possible to effect the conversion of early maturing debt into funded debt on terms which will further reduce the annual liability for interest.

After some minor changes, the Chancellor forecast a surplus of £38.2m for 1922–3. However, this was struck without the contractual and statutory debt repayments normally included in expenditure. These were estimated to cost between £30m and £35m – a level much reduced from previous years because the rise in prices had made it unattractive to use securities to pay taxes. Pointing to high taxes and the depressed state of the economy, the Chancellor said that he would find the money for the contractual debt payments from new borrowing and cut the standard rate by a shilling, at a cost of £32.5m in 1922–3 and £52m in a full year.

Sale of 4½ per cent Treasury Bonds 1930–2 by tender

Between 26 May 1922 and 16 March 1923, the Treasury sold a further £95.6m 4½ per cent Treasury Bonds 1930–2 by tender, using the same system as that for 5 per cent Treasury 1927 (Table 14.1).[1] Prices ranged from £98 0s 0d (£4 15s 0d per cent to 1932) in June to £100 16s 0d (£4 7s 7d per cent to 1930) in July. The authorities were less aggressive than when allotting 5 per cents of 1927. With the former, they generally allotted the maximum quantity, whereas with the new Bond they often allotted less than the maximum and for two months during the late summer they allotted none at all. Weekly sales ranged between £0.25m and £10m.[96]

The 1923 budget

During 1922, disagreements about Ireland and policy in the Near East, with distrust of Lloyd George's style of government, produced increasing strains between the Conservative backbenchers and their leaders. The Coalition broke up in October; the subsequent general election the following month brought the Conservatives to power under Bonar Law. With most senior Conservatives, including Horne, refusing to desert Lloyd George, there were few experienced politicians from whom to form a government. Bonar Law offered the Treasury to McKenna, but he was unwilling to give up his bank Chairmanship for a post in a government whose prospects seemed insecure and Bonar Law chose Baldwin in his stead.[97] In May 1923, Bonar Law resigned, fatally ill, and Baldwin became Prime Minister. Once more, the Treasury was offered to McKenna. With the agreement of his Board and doctor, he provisionally accepted, but wanted three months in which to recover his health and find a constituency. In the meantime, Baldwin ran the Treasury, where he stayed until it became clear in August that the City

1 There were two series: the final tender of the First Series was held on 14 October 1922, and the following week they were replaced by 'Series B'. The two series were consolidated after the first ex-dividend date.

Conservatives would not offer the Liberal McKenna a seat.[98] Neville Chamberlain then became Chancellor.

Baldwin delivered his first and only budget on 16 April 1923. The previous year had seen an improvement in trade and fall in unemployment.[99] Revenues, despite very disappointing EPD and Special Miscellaneous Receipts, were £3m higher than forecast. Expenditure was lower by £97.5m, so there was a surplus of £101.5m, instead of the bare balance forecast by Horne. Moreover, this was found after meeting £24.7m out of revenue for the contractual and statutory sinking funds, instead of from borrowing, as Horne had planned. In 1923–4, on existing policies, revenue would be £862.7m and expenditure £816.6m. Baldwin pointed out that special receipts had been some £770m since the Armistice and warned that they would cease after the £40m expected in 1923–4. In addition, after recent efforts, there was little potential for cutting expenditure. Nonetheless, he bowed to public pressure for lower taxation and used the forecast surplus of about £36m to cut the standard rate of income tax by a further 6d, at a cost of £19m in the current year and of £26m in a full year, and to reduce beer duty. After the changes, he forecast a surplus of £2m for 1923–4.

The Chancellor made optimistic comments about the Debt. The floating debt had been reduced by a further £220m. The problem of maturing issues had been much reduced; after repaying the 1 April War Bonds, there remained the rump of the 1 September 1923 and 1 February 1924 War Bonds amounting to only £84.5m. Stafford Northcote's Fixed Charge was to be replaced by the 'New Sinking Fund (1923)' of £40m in 1923–4, rising to £45m in 1924–5, and £50m in 1925–6 (see pp. 680–1).

Conversion offer for War Bonds due 1 April 1923 (22 February 1923)

4½ per cent Treasury Bonds 1930–2 were chosen as the vehicle for the next conversion offer, made on 22 February 1923 to holders of the 5 per cent War Bonds of 1 April 1923.[m] Following this, £11.5m War Bonds were converted into a similar amount to the new Bonds, so that with the £14.2m issued on account of the conversion offer made in April 1922 the total of the new Bonds created for conversions rose to £25.7m and the overall total of the issue to £121.3m (Table 14.1).

The official portfolios played an important part. The CNRA bought 1 April 1923 War Bonds during January and March 1922 and converted £5.2m at the time of the second offer, selling its new holding during the spring and summer. It is not clear whether other official transactions involved conversion or acquisition at

m The terms were £100 nominal for £100 nominal, together with a cash payment of £2 15s 0d per cent. The premiums on the War Bonds were £2, and the most recent tenders for the Treasury Bonds had been at discounts of 10s to 11s. Thus, a 'bonus' of between 4s and 5s was being offered to convert, a miserly incentive compared with those offered earlier, and evidence of the authorities' confidence.

tender. At the end of August 1922, the Banking Department had £8.3m, of which it sold half during the following eighteen months. The Commissioners became substantial, long-term, investors: their holding at the end of 1922–3 was £5.8m and £22.4m a year later. At the time of their 1927 accounts, they owned £41.8m, or over one-third of the issue, mainly on behalf of the POSB, the TSBs and the NHI Funds.[100]

4 per cent Treasury Bonds 1931–3 (23 March 1923)

On 23 March, the prospectus for the sale of £15m 4 per cent Treasury Bonds 1931–3 at £94½ (£4 13s 10d per cent) was published (Table 14.1). The terms were standard, except that £5 per cent was payable on application and commission was ¼ per cent. The issue closed two days early, almost three times oversubscribed. It had been intended that the offer would be a pathfinder, and at the end of the month it was announced that from 6 April the new Bonds would be the subject of a weekly tender in the manner of the 5 per cents of 1927 and the 4½ per cents of 1930–2.

The tenders were to continue for three years, often in parallel with other issues. It appears that the final series was withdrawn in front of the April 1926 dividend.[n]

The authorities were relaxed when no tenders were received and no Bonds allotted for long periods: £22.5m were sold in April and May 1923, immediately after their introduction, but in the second half of the year, after Bank rate was raised to 4 per cent on 5 July, Bonds were allotted on only two occasions. In 1924, it was not until April that the first Bonds were allotted and none were allotted for three months in the late summer and autumn. Looking forward, none were allotted for almost nine months of 1925. Altogether, there were allotments in only forty-one weeks in the three years. For such a long period, prices ranged narrowly: the lowest average tender price was £94 0s 0d (September 1925) and the highest £95 6s 11d (May 1923, shortly after they were introduced). The total sold, including the initial £15m, was only £49.6m.[o]

The end of the first refinancing phase

At the end of May 1923, Norman noted that McKenna, who had provisionally

n There were to be six series, designated ‘A’ to ‘F’, a new series being issued in front of a coupon date so that the series which had just been withdrawn could be amalgamated with all the previous series.

o In contrast to the records of other issues, those of this issue (BoE, Loan Wallet 294 and AC 19/657) are chaotic. There are only sporadic entries of the prices or amounts accepted at tender. Prices quoted here are from *The Economist*, although it sometimes disagrees with the fragmentary Bank records. There is no formal record of the issue being withdrawn, although there is a passing reference in 1932 to the Bonds having been on weekly tender until April 1926. *The Economist* provided space for the Bond allotment, alongside that for Bills, until 8 October 1926. From 10 April 1926, the magazine ceased recording that the Bonds were on offer. BoE, Loan Wallet 397, Lefeaux to Waterfield, 17 April 1932.

accepted the Chancellorship, did not 'quarrel with policy of last 2 years which he thinks was right *vis a vis* Exchequer, but traders need more consideration...He approves tender system for Bills + Bonds + will not alter it, but few Bonds, rather than many...'[101] It was McKenna who had spoken out most publicly against the policy of selling Treasury Bonds to deflate the floating debt, irrespective of economic conditions. In his annual address to shareholders the previous January, he had drawn attention to the contraction in bank deposits during the previous year which had been caused, he claimed, by using the proceeds of Bond sales to repay Bills. He argued that the initial sales had had little effect as the general public was merely exchanging Bills for Bonds. But, once the holdings of Bills had been run off, sales of Bonds were for cash and reduced bank deposits or, if made to the banks, reduced their ability to lend.[102]

The implication coincided with the conclusions, if not the reasoning, of a paper written the previous month by Hawtrey at the Treasury. He said that sales of Bonds had 'on balance' been contracting credit. The banks had been the buyers, but recently had been replaced by the general investor. The floating debt was no longer a threat to the control of credit because Bills were sold by tender, so that rates would move automatically to absorb the volume on offer: 'there would be no great harm in suspending for a time the attempt to reduce floating debt.'[103] To this the Bank added the more technical consideration mentioned by McKenna: unless there was an increase in the volume of commercial bills, the money market would not have a sufficient corpus of short paper for traders to maintain liquidity.[104]

Bonar Law, as so often, was sympathetic to a less restrictive policy, but a decision on whether to continue with tenders was delayed because the Chancellor and Norman were in the USA for the debt negotiations.[105] Predictably, Niemeyer was cautious. He argued that general investors held few Bonds, and that those sold by tender went 'almost invariably' to discount houses and foreign banks. There was no evidence that the banks lacked liquid resources or the ability to lend to credit-worthy customers. On the contrary, there had been 'great ease in the money market' and money had been 'frequently unlendable'. Policy should aim at protecting the Treasury when trade recovered and Bills became difficult to sell for, if Bills could not be renewed, increased Ways and Means would produce inflation, depressed exchanges and increased prices and wages. Interest rates would have to be raised. Maturities threatened, notably the War Bonds on 1 April, and these should be refinanced while the markets were favourable. Finally, US inflation was rising, the exchange rate was strong and, when it arrived at par, 'we shall get all the inflation we want here.'[106]

The discussions during January and February 1923 were not responsible for radical change, as allotments at the tenders for the 4½ per cent Treasury Bonds 1930–2 had been less generous for about a year. Niemeyer, who was not above ignoring the activities of the CNRA to make a point, claimed that £45m maturities were paid off and £44.5m raised from Treasury Bonds between 1 October 1922 and 31 March 1923. Between 1 April and 20 May, when War Bonds were maturing, £16.5m were paid off for cash and £24.5m Treasury Bonds sold.[107]

On 1 November 1923, Norman noted another conversation with McKenna:

> McKenna. half an hour on details of policy: I try to keep market adequately supplied with cash fr day to day: not largely to increase floating debt: I intend to sell T. Bonds to within £5 or £10 mil of Bonds maturing during this fin. year: to sell no T. Bonds in Feb or Mch + I hope to convert in Apl next £500mil 5% W Loan into 20–25 year – as a start to programme of dealing with mass of W. Loan. He agrees + will cooperate.[108]

The urgency of the post-war years had passed and, as the threat to monetary control posed by the floating debt receded, other aspects of debt management came into the foreground. The cost of servicing Bills had played its part, alongside a reluctance to deflate during the post-Armistice social tensions, in the Cabinet's unwillingness to raise rates during 1919 and 1920. In the second half of the decade, the cost moved from being an irritation, a reason for inertia out of which ministers had to be argued, to being the Chancellor's preoccupation. For this there were many reasons. Interest costs came into a fuller view as government revenue and expenditure settled down after the lurches of the war and immediate post-war years; steadier, more predictable, budgets drew attention to the large, and seemingly immovable, cost of the Debt. In part, it was that deflation increased the real cost of a fixed-interest debt, and increased the real incomes of holders. In part, it was an aspect of the decision to return to gold at pre-war par and the policies which were required to underpin it. More generally, it was the combination of inelastic revenues; other, persistent, demands on the Treasury's resources; Winston Churchill's penchant for dramatic fiscal gestures; and the temptation to reduce interest rates to stimulate growth.

Endnotes

1 BoE, G3/175, Governor to Chancellor, 10 July 1919.
2 Osborne (1926), I, pp. 482–3; BoE, G3/175, Governor to Chancellor, 10 July 1919. The Governor wanted to spread maturities by issuing twelve and, perhaps even, twenty-four months' Bills.
3 Cab. 27/71 (FC 1) Appendix, 24 July 1919; Howson (1975), p. 15.
4 CLCBm, 29 July and 31 July 1919.
5 The Treasury announcement is reproduced in the *Bankers' Magazine*, September 1919, pp. 262–3.
6 Osborne (1926), I, pp. 284–5
7 Howson (1975), p. 15.
8 Self (1995), Austen Chamberlain to Ida Chamberlain, 19 July 1919, p. 117.
9 Cab. 24/84, GT 7729, Chamberlain, 'The Financial Situation', 18 July 1919.
10 *Hansard* (Commons), 7 August 1919, cols 632–45; Cab. 27/71 (FC 3), 20 August 1919.
11 FRBNY, 1000.3, Strong Papers, Strong's Journal, 15 September 1919.
12 Clay (1957), p. 120; Howson (1975), pp. 15–16; FRBNY, 1000.3, Strong Papers, Strong's Journal, 15 September 1919. The letter from the Governor to the Chancellor is in Cab. 27/72 (FC 5).
13 Self (1995), p. 119, Chamberlain to Ida Chamberlain, 26 October 1919.

14 FRBNY, 1000.3, Strong Papers, Strong's Journal, 19 September 1919; MGP, B. Hist. 3, F. 22, no. 70166, MG to JPM (Copy handed to Governor), 22 October 1919, and no. 87956, JPM to MG (Copy to Blackett and Governor), 24 October 1919. The remainder of this paragraph is based on *Hansard* (Commons), 29 October 1919, cols 737–57, *Revised Statement of Revenue and Expenditure (1919–20) by the Chancellor of the Exchequer* (Cmd. 377) and *Memorandum by the Chancellor of the Exchequer on the Future Exchequer Balance Sheet* (Cmd. 376), both 23 October 1919.

15 *Hansard* (Commons), 29 October 1919, cols 737–57; *Revised Statement of Revenue and Expenditure (1919–20)* (Cmd. 377), 23 October 1919; *Future Exchequer Balance Sheet* (Cmd. 377), 23 October 1919; T 172/1384, Blackett, 'Dear Money', 19 February 1920, p. 21; Osborne (1926), I, p. 139.

16 Clay (1957), p. 120–3; Osborne (1926), I, p. 155–6; Howson (1975), pp. 16–17; *Hansard* (Commons), 15 December 1919, cols 43–4.

17 Osborne (1926), I, p. 451; *BGS*, pp. 207 and 285.

18 CNRA ledgers; *BGS*, p. 483; BoE, C98/6938.

19 *BGS*, p. 483; CNRA ledgers; T 172/1137, statement of Commissioners' holdings, enclosed with Heath to Gower, 9 February 1920.

20 CNRA ledgers; *BGS*, pp. 180–1, 188–9, 196–7 and 483–4; T 172/1137, statement of Commissioners' holdings, enclosed with Heath to Gower, 9 February 1920.

21 Cokayne to Chancellor, 24 December 1919, quoted in Osborne (1926), I, pp. 164–7 and 455–6 [underlining in the original].

22 Royal Commission on Income Tax, *Report* (Cmd. 615), 11 March 1920, p. 37.

23 BoE, Loan Wallet 254, '6% Exchequer Bonds due 16th February 1920', 20 December 1919.

24 CNRA ledgers; *BGS*, p. 483; T 172/1137, statement of Commissioners' holdings, enclosed with Heath to Gower, 9 February 1920, and Hamilton to Heath, 10 February 1920.

25 The data for the 5 per cent and 6 per cents are derived from the *National Debt: annual returns* and Osborne (1926), I, p. 456.

26 Osborne (1926), I, pp. 159 and 172. News of the refusal to authorise a rise in rates was contained in a letter from Strong.

27 Morgan (1952), p. 284. The data are for the Ministry of Labour Cost of Living Index, 'All Items'.

28 Morgan (1952), p. 77; *The Economist*, 3 January 1920, p. 22, 10 January 1920, p. 65, 17 January 1920, p. 109, and 24 January 1920, p. 147; Osborne (1926), I, p. 166. Osborne quotes Cokayne to Chancellor, 24 December 1919.

29 *The Morning Post*, 11 February 1920, p. 2. A collection of Press cuttings are in BoE, Loan Wallet 254. Also, see *The Economist*, 17 January 1920, p. 91.

30 Osborne (1926), I, pp. 169–71. He quotes Norman to Strong, 15 January 1920.

31 *The Economist*, market reports, various dates.

32 MND, 4 February 1920. This paragraph is based on Clay (1957), pp. 123–8; Howson (1975), pp. 18–23, and Osborne (1926), I, pp. 168–87.

33 T 172/1384, Blackett to Chancellor, 21 February 1920, and 4 March 1920.

34 Select Committee on Increase of Wealth (War), *Evidence*, Blackett, para. 1535, 11 March 1920. Also, see T 172/1384, f. 20, Blackett, 'Dear Money', 19 February 1920.

35 T 172/1384, Cokayne, 'Memorandum as to Money Rates', 10 February 1920, and Cokayne to Chancellor, 25 February 1920.

36 MND, 8 and 9 March 1920; T 172/1384, Conference with the Bankers, 9 March and 11 March 1920; Osborne (1926), I, p. 186.

37 *Hansard*, (Commons), col. 74; Osborne (1926), I, pp. 186–7.

38 The following three paragraphs are based on *Hansard* (Commons), 19 April 1920, cols 69–100; Mallet and George (1929), pp. 231–84; Hirst and Allen (1926), pp. 297–350.

39 This paragraph is based on Clay (1957), pp. 128–33; Osborne (1926), I, pp. 191–218 and 483–4; Sayers (1976), I, pp. 123–5; Howson (1975), pp. 25–7; BoE, CO/399, 'Treasury Bills', p. 9.

40 CTM, 11 August 1920.

41 *The London Gazette*, relevant dates.

42 *Hansard* (Commons), 28 April 1920, col. 1233.

43 Osborne (1926), I, p. 457.

44 BoE, Loan Wallet 259, Norman to Blackett, 21 April 1920. Norman used 'floating debt' in the nineteenth-century sense of debt with a due date.

45 T 172/1146, Blackett, 'Mr. Bevan's proposals for funding', 26 July 1920. For the importance of housing, see Chapter 20.

46 CTM, 27 October 1920; BoE, C40/397, Norman to Blackett, 8 September 1920; T 172/1146, Blackett, 'Mr. Bevan's proposals for funding', 26 July 1920; *Hansard* (Commons), 28 April 1920, cols 1231–3, and 16 August 1920, col. 592.

47 *The Times*, 4 May 1920, pp. 17–18.

48 *The Economist*, 8 May 1920, p. 955.

49 *The Economist*, 30 April 1921, p. 860; *The Statist*, 30 April 1921, pp. 711–12; *The Times*, 28 April 1921, p. 16; Hargreaves (1930), pp. 256–7; Morgan (1952), p. 118; Hirst and Allen (1926), pp. 357–8, 376; Howson (1975), p. 26. Norman described the reaction as 'bitter'. He pointed to the bankers as a source of the criticism and thought this reflected the uses they had for gilt-edged securities as they approached maturity. BoE, G35/2, Norman to Strong, 3 May and 14 May 1921.

50 *National Debt: annual returns;* Morgan (1952), p. 147. The data are for averages of weekly figures. The original data are in *The London Gazette*. . About one-quarter of the Bills were held within the government sector, the main holder being the CNRA: its holding was £186.7m at end-March 1920 and £197.7m at end-March 1921. CNRA Ledgers.

51 T 171/196, Blackett to Chancellor, 14 March 1921; *BGS*, pp. 190–5 and 399; Morgan (1952), p. 147.

52 This paragraph is based on *Hansard* (Commons), 25 April 1921, cols 67–88, and Hirst and Allen (1926), pp. 351–76.

53 Self (1995), p. 157, Chamberlain to Ida Chamberlain, 3 April 1921.

54 *Hansard* (Commons), 25 April 1925, cols 85–6.

55 T 171/196, Blackett to Chancellor, 14 March 1921.

56 Ibid.

57 *The Economist*, 17 September 1927, p. 465; T 175/15, Hopkins to Chancellor, 28 October 1929.

58 T 171/196, Blackett to Chancellor, 14 March 1921; T 160/1090/F16070/2, Niemeyer to Chancellor, 15 December 1924. The first mention of the advantage of breaking away 'from the high interest rates to which the war has accustomed the public' was in June 1921. It was a glancing reference. In his evidence to Colwyn in November 1925, Niemeyer did not emphasise that the low nominal rate had been chosen to lead expectations lower. On the same occasion, and again in 1927, at about the time that 4 per cent Consols were first issued, he argued that a large Debt demanded a range of issues with differing nominal payments to meet all tastes. Again, there is no contemporary evidence that this was an influence in the selection of a $3^1/_2$ per cent rate in 1921. T 172/1225, Niemeyer, 'Funding Operations', June 1921; Committee on National Debt and Taxation (Colwyn Committee), *Minutes of Evidence*, pp. 627–8; T 188/14, Finance Bill 1927, 'Note on New Clause (Exchange and Issues of Securities)', undated, but probably May 1927.

59 T 171/196, Blackett to Chancellor, 14 March 1921.

60 T 171/196, Blackett to Chancellor, 14 March 1921; BoE, Loan Wallet 272, Memorandum, 2 March 1921 and '$3^1/_2$ Conversion Loan', 9 March 1921.

61 T 172/1225, Niemeyer, 'Funding Operations', June 1921. It was a brief for the Chancellor following a critical speech by Sir Godfrey Collins. *Hansard* (Commons), 23 June 1921, cols 1674–6.
62 BoE, G35/2, Norman to Strong, 3 May 1921; T 172/1225, Niemeyer, 'Funding Operations', June 1921.
63 T 171/196, Blackett to Chancellor, 14 March 1921; T 172/1225, Niemeyer, 'Funding Operations', June 1921.
64 BoE, G 35/2, Norman to Strong, 3 May 1921.
65 T 160/1090/F16072/2, Niemeyer to Chancellor, 15 December 1924.
66 Sayers (1976), I, pp. 120 and 122–3.
67 Morgan (1952), pp. 70, 278–9, 284 and 286.
68 Osborne (1926), I, pp. 196–201; BoE, G35/2, Norman to Strong, 17 February 1921.
69 Morgan (1952), p. 77; Osborne (1926), I, 204–5. Osborne quotes Norman to Strong, 3 February 1921.
70 *Hansard* (Commons), 11 April 1921, cols 745–6; Osborne (1926), I, pp. 479 and 483–8; BoE, C40/399, 'Treasury Bills'.
71 Norman to Strong, 2 April 1921, quoted in Osborne (1926), I, p. 213; Morgan (1952), p. 209.
72 BoE, Loan Wallet 272, Norman, 'Funding', 2 March 1921.
73 Kent (1989), pp. 103–45; Middlemas (1969), I, pp. 155–6; Roskill (1970–4), pp. 219–22; Morgan (1952), p. 351; Leith-Ross (1968), pp. 78–80; *The Economist*, various dates.
74 Mitchell and Deane (1962), p. 72.
75 Middlemas (1969), pp. 131–53 and 158–61; Bullock (1960), pp. 167–79; Morgan (1979), Chapter 3; Morgan (1952), p. 70.
76 BoE, G35/2, Norman to Strong, 14 May 1921.
77 BoE, Loan Wallet 272, 'Memorandum: 3½% Conversion Loan', 19 October 1921.
78 Ibid., BoE, C40/871, 'Currency Notes'; CNRA ledgers; *BGS*, p. 486; CTM, 27 April 1921; BoE, ADM 19/11.
79 Morgan (1952), pp. 351–3 and 364.
80 *National Debt: annual returns*; Morgan (1952), p. 147; *BGS*, pp. 400, 402 and 404.
81 BoE, G35/2, Norman to Strong, 23 May and 22 June 1921.
82 *The Economist*, relevant dates; *Hansard* (Commons), 5 July 1921, cols 226–8.
83 CNRA ledgers; BoE, C40/871, 'Currency Notes', undated and unsigned, and ADM, 19/10 and 19/11; *BGS*, pp. 191, 485–6; *National Debt: annual returns*.
84 Osborne (1926), I, p. 464. The £0.1m disagreement with Table 14.1 is caused by rounding.
85 T 171/205, Niemeyer, 'Ways and Means Budget', 4 November 1921, and Blackett, 8 November 1921.
86 CNRA Ledgers; *BGS*, p. 277.
87 BoE, Loan Wallet 279, Bank to Treasury, 14 January 1922.
88 BoE, Loan Wallet 282, Harvey to Deverell, 15 February 1922; *The Economist*, 18 February 1922, p. 283.
89 CNRA ledgers; BoE, C40/871, 'Currency Notes', undated and unsigned.
90 CNRA ledgers; BoE, C40/871, 'Currency Notes'. The Banking Department was also active. Sometime between 31 August 1921 and 28 February 1922, it acquired a further £14.2m Conversion, probably by purchasing Bonds in the market and converting. This did not include a further £5m which it had transferred to the Issue Department at the end of February 1922. These were also, presumably, acquired by conversion. BoE, ADM 19/10, 19/11, 17/4 and 17/5.
91 For example, *The Economist*, 18 February 1922, pp. 263–4, and 8 April 1922, pp. 662–3; *The Times*, 15 February 1922, p. 17, and 13 March, p. 18.
92 Morgan (1952), pp. 208–10, especially Table 23; Howson (1975), pp. 27–8; Moggridge (1972), p. 26

93 *Hansard* (Commons), 1 May 1922, col. 1027; CNRA ledgers; BoE, C40/871, 'Currency Notes', undated and unsigned.
94 CNRA ledgers; *National Debt: annual returns*; BoE, C40/871, 'Currency Notes', undated and unsigned.
95 These paragraphs are based on *Hansard* (Commons), 1 May 1922, cols 1019–42 and Hirst and Allen (1926), pp. 377–414.
96 BoE, Loan Wallet 279.
97 Blake (1955), p. 462.
98 MND, 28 May 1923; Middlemas and Barnes (1969), pp. 175–7; Dilks (1984), pp. 332–3.
99 These two paragraphs are based on *Hansard* (Commons), 16 April 1923, cols 1721–41 and Hirst and Allen (1926), pp. 415–59.
100 *BGS*, pp. 487–91; CNRA ledgers; BoE, ADM 19/10 and 19/11, and C40/871, 'Currency Notes', undated and unsigned.
101 MND, 28 May 1923.
102 London Joint City & Midland Bank Limited, McKenna, address to the Ordinary General Meeting. The speech is reproduced in *The Economist*, 27 January 1923, pp. 158–62.
103 T 176/5, Hawtrey, 'Effect of Treasury Bonds on the Credit Situation', 18 December 1922.
104 FRBNY, Strong Papers, 1117.1, Trotter to Strong, 6 March 1923.
105 T 176/5, Niemeyer to Bonar Law, 17 January 1923.
106 T 176/5, Niemeyer to Chancellor, 'Treasury Bonds', 24 January 1923; ibid., Fisher to Chancellor, 29 January 1923; ibid., Niemeyer, 'The policy of funding debt', 6 June 1923.
107 T 176/5, Niemeyer, 'The policy of funding debt', 6 June 1923.
108 MND, 1 November 1923.

15 The external market and Canada

The Treasury's preoccupation with converting or paying off short-term debt extended to its foreign currency obligations, whether due to the markets, to banks, or to the governments of the Dominions, allies and neutral countries. Indeed, paying off overseas obligations had a greater priority than reducing the internal floating debt. In 1919–20, when there was a budget deficit, it meant converting external debt into internal floating debt or, alternatively, into longer-dated internal debt – War Bonds, Victory Bonds or Funding Loan – whose sale would otherwise have reduced the floating debt. Thereafter, when there were budget surpluses, it absorbed revenue which would have paid off internal floating debt. The repayment was dramatic. The three years ending 31 March 1922 saw a net £223.6m ($1,088.2m at par of exchange) paid off in cash, with a further £59.9m (C$291.6m) due to the Dominion of Canada cancelled by offsets.[a] The Morgan call loan, the dollar Treasury Bills, the Anglo-French Loan, the Notes and Bonds held by US industrialists, the loans from the Argentinian and Uruguayan governments, and the advances from European neutrals had disappeared, together with all but £3m of those taken from Japan. There remained £2.1m (C$10m) owed to the Canadian banks, which was due to be repaid on the first day of the new financial year; £25.4m (C$127.4m) owed to the Canadian government,[b] £7.7m (in sterling) due to the Straits Settlements; 8.1m rupees (£0.5m) due to Mauritius; £3.1m ($15m) owed to the Central Argentine Railway; three public issues in New York;[c] and, towering above all, the debts to the US Treasury, whose funding Blackett and Albert Rathbone, the US Treasury's representative in Europe, tried to negotiate between November 1919 and May 1920 (Table 15.1).[d]

a Net repayment. An additional C$110.4m due to the Canadian Finance Department was cancelled against new debt incurred by the Canadian government in 1919–20. See pp. 309 and 468 and *Canadian Government (Advances)* (Cmd. 651), TM, 29 March 1920.

b Shown as C$122.7m in *Canada, Public Accounts for the Fiscal Years ended March 31, 1920–24*.

c Strictly, there were four New York issues. An eccentric holder, or holders, of $13,850 (£3,000) of the Anglo-French Loan had taken up the option to convert into Bonds maturing in 1940.

d The data exclude British debts to France, Russia and Italy of £113.5m at 31 March 1919 and £128m at 31 March 1922, representing gold deposited in London as part of the wartime arrangements for British advances. As the British advances were many times greater than the gold deposited, the debt represented by the gold was ignored. *External Debt as on 31 March 1919, 31 March 1920, 31 March 1921 and 31 March 1922* (Cmd. 1648), 1922.

Table 15.1 Foreign currency debt outstanding: 31 March 1919, 1920, 1921 and 1922

	1919	*1920*	*1921*	*1922*
US dollars				
Anglo-French Loan	250.0	250.0	–	–
US Treasury Advances:				
Pittman Silver	122.0	122.0	122.0	91.5
Austrian Relief	–	16.0	–	–
Other	3,970.0	4,074.8	4,074.8	4,074.8
$5^1/_2$ per cent Notes 1/11/19	130.5	–	–	–
$5^1/_2$ per cent Notes 1/11/21	129.0	129.0	111.5	–
$5^1/_2$ per cent Notes 1/11/22	–	101.6	95.1	53.4
$5^1/_2$ per cent Bonds 1/8/29	–	148.4	125.9	116.4
$5^1/_2$ per cent Bonds 1/2/37	143.6	143.6	143.6	143.6
Treasury Bills	93.3	45.2	16.7	–
Morgan Call Loan	72.5	–	–	–
Asiatic Petroleum Co.	14.2	–	–	–
Rifle Notes, Marlin Arms, Bliss & Co., American Locomotive	32.8	–	–	–
Japan £/$ Treasury Bills	47.7	47.7	28.6	14.3
Central Argentine Railway	15.0	15.0	15.0	15.0
Danish Government [Virgin Islands]	25.0	–	–	–
5 per cent Argentinian Government Loan	95.1	95.1	–	–
5 per cent Uruguayan Government Loan	18.4	23.8	–	–
Canadian dollars				
Dominion Government	446.8*	181.5	132.3	127.4†
CPR (Bank of Montreal)	4.3	–	–	–
Bankers' Munitions Loan	100.0	100.0	100.0	10.0
Royal Wheat Loan	100.0	70.0	25.0	–
Japanese yen				
6 per cent Exchequer Bonds	100.0	–	–	–
Treasury Bills	85.8	70.0	–	–
Dutch guilders				
5 per cent Exchequer Bonds 7/11/20 (Java sugar)	13.8	8.9	–	–
Dutch government (PoW)	7.9	–	–	–
5 per cent Exchequer Bonds 31/12/23	17.7	–	–	–
Treasury Bills 20/9/19	0.7	–	–	–
Swiss francs				
Bills of Exchange	84.5			
Norwegian kroner				
Various bank facilities	208.2			
Swedish kronor				
6 per cent sterling one-year Notes	2.7	–	–	
Three-year krona Notes	31.3	12.5	12.5	
Spanish peseta				
Rio Tinto Zinc Peseta Loan	50.0			

Table 15.1 continued.

Loans from Colonies				
Fiji (£)	0.4	0.4	–	–
$5^1/_4$ per cent Straits Settlements 1928 and 5 per cent Straits Settlements 1929 (£)	8.3	7.7	7.7	7.7
6 per cent Mauritius 1922 (rupees)	8.0	8.1	8.1	8.1
Gold deposited by France, Italy and Russia (£)	113.5	113.5	126.5	128.0

Notes
*Shown as C$466.7m in *Canadian Government (Advances)* (Cmd. 583), TM, 1 January 1920. See Table 10.2, note (7).
†Shown as C$123.4m in the *National Debt: annual return*, 1922.

Sources: adapted from Tables 6,2, 6,3 and 6.4 and *External Debt as on 31 March 1919, 31 March 1920, 31 March 1921 and 31 March 1922* (Cmd. 1648), 1922.

From where did the foreign currency come? US advances provided only $185m (£38m) in the year beginning 31 March 1919 and the final $7m was drawn on 25 June.[1] These were absorbed by existing purchasing contracts, especially those for food, so that maturing capital liabilities had to be met from the UK's own resources. $257.9m (£53m) was raised from the sale of securities, mainly to repay the public issues for which they formed the collateral. In the autumn of 1919, with several large market debts maturing, the Treasury issued $250m Notes and Bonds in New York (Table 6.2). The current account of the balance of payments moved into surplus sometime in the second half of 1919 and in the following three calendar years was to show a balance of some £700m. The data are not unambiguous but, in the three financial years starting April 1919, the Treasury may have bought over $600m in the open market.[2]

This chapter chronicles the repayment of the British foreign currency debt to the markets, the governments of neutral and allied countries, and to the Canadians. Chapter 16 describes the attempt by Blackett and Albert Rathbone, the US Treasury's representative in Europe, to negotiate the funding[e] of the British debt to the US Treasury to the point, in May 1920, when the British broke off negotiations having decided that they were only prepared to fund as part of a general settlement of inter-allied indebtedness. Chapter 17 describes the relationship between reparations and the British debt to the US Treasury, before showing how the terms of the Bonds were agreed in the first six months of 1923.

Debt repayment in the winter of 1918–19

The second British public issue to mature in the USA was the two-year 5 per cent

e Henceforth, the book follows contemporaries in using 'funding' to describe 'conversion' of the US Treasury Debt into Bonds, even though they were dated. 'Funding' continues to be used in its strict sense when internal debt is being discussed.

Note sold on 1 September 1916. Originally $250m, purchases and cancellations had reduced it to $192.9m. There followed, on 18 September 1918, $6.3m Metropolitan Water Board Notes, whose dollar repayment was guaranteed by the UK Treasury (Tables 6.2 and 6.3). Arranging US Treasury advances to cover these was painless compared with the dramas of the previous January when the 1 February Notes were nearing maturity (see pp. 267–74). In the middle of June, Russell Leffingwell, Assistant Secretary for fiscal affairs since October 1917, told McAdoo that the US markets were too weak to absorb sales of the British collateral and that, if prices fell, the US Treasury's own 'tremendous issues of Certificates [of indebtedness]' would suffer. The dollars advanced to repay the British Notes would stay in the USA, provided the US Treasury did not reimburse the UK for its expenditure on behalf of France in the Empire and it shared with the USA the cost of French expenditure in neutral countries. In addition,

> borrowing on the part of the British Government on our markets on extortionate terms would be injurious to British credit, create an unfavourable impression as to the extent of the sympathy between the two governments, and impair our own position because of the discredit it would throw upon the credit of our largest debtor.

US troops were now actively and successfully engaged in France and the war was enjoying great popular enthusiasm. The Secretary should inform Congress that the situation had changed and advances should be used to repay allied debts incurred before April 1917.[3] That the US Treasury would, indeed, have to help became clear in July when Reading asked Morgans to sound the market about the terms on which the UK could raise $200m to meet the maturities. Jack Morgan reported that it was possible to form a syndicate, but only if the coupon was 6 per cent, the length just thirty months, the price to the public 97½ or 97¾ and commissions 3 per cent. At 94½, the price to the UK, the GRY would be 8.36 per cent. The reasons for the 'extremely onerous terms', wrote Jack Morgan, 'are not any doubt either of the sufficiency of the borrower or of the security', but of the small amount of money available for investment other than in Liberty Bonds. Perhaps aware that his letter would be passed to the US Treasury, he added that 'It is hardly necessary for me to say that I sincerely hope some other way may be found by the British Government in which the needed money may be obtained at a less cost.'[4] On 23 July, Leffingwell told Reading that the US Treasury would provide advances on the same terms as those made in February and, on 29 August, a credit was established for $400m to cover the repayments and the UK's October expenditure.[5]

After the Armistice, with advances limited by the Liberty Bond Acts to 'providing for the national security and defense and prosecuting the war', the US Treasury moved quickly to end its commitments to the allies and return the provision of credit to the private sector. On 14 December, the arrangements for allied purchasing were wound up and borrowing governments were instructed to apply directly to the US Treasury if they wanted to incur expenditure involving official credit.[6] Amid violent disapproval from sections of Congress, the US Treasury continued to make liberal advances to some allies, but the UK, believed to possess unused financial resources and expected to re-emerge as a major commercial and financial competitor, was the exception. The final wartime credit, for $200m, was established on 12 November and when a further advance was arranged on 18 December it came in the form of a 'special credit' of $250m to be liquidated by the payment of sterling in London for the use of the US government.[7] When the UK Treasury estimated its requirement for advances to the end of June to be a further $500m, the US Treasury refused, citing lack of authority and the hostility of Congress; it was, reported Lever, 'seriously alarmed about its ability to raise funds needful for its own outgoings during January.' The UK was told that it should rely on reimbursements, payments for the transport of American troops, sales of stores and securities, and replacing cash payments for imports with trade credit.[8]

There were also the UK's capital commitments. $14.2m Royal Dutch Petroleum Notes were due on 17 January 1919 and $37.3m Bethlehem Steel Co. Notes on 1 February. Also on 1 February, $142.9m 5¹/2 per cent two-year secured Notes, the twin of the $100m one-year Note which had matured in February 1918, would come due unless holders converted them, under the terms of the original prospectus, into 5¹/2 per cent unsecured Gold Bonds of 1 February 1937. Further ahead, in April and July, there were maturities of $6m Notes held by industrial firms (Tables 6.2 and 6.3).

McAdoo resigned as Secretary of the Treasury with effect from 15 December and was replaced by Carter Glass, who until his appointment was a Congressman for Virginia. Morgans confirmed that the Treasury's policy of returning allied financing to the private markets had not changed under the new Secretary and then, over Christmas, proposed a public issue to refinance the Bethlehem and Dutch Petroleum Notes, together with any of the 1 February maturity left unconverted. They judged that between $100m and $120m, perhaps even $150m, could be raised in the form of a 6 per cent five-year Note priced to cost about 6.5 per cent. It would be convertible into a 5 per cent twenty-year Bond and the cost over the full twenty years would be 5.45 per cent. The US Treasury encouraged the plan, hoping to demonstrate to Congress that no advances to repay British debts had been made after the Armistice. At the same time, the issue would test and develop the markets' appetite for foreign loans. The US Treasury's only concern was to ensure that the issue did not interfere with its own certificates of indebtedness and for this reason it wanted the yield to the investor to be no more than 6 per cent, even if it meant reducing the size so that the British had to make a further issue.

In London, the Treasury was unenthusiastic and told Crosby that the amount was too small and that it, too, feared that the issue might damage the US Treasury's own borrowing; it preferred to wait until the markets were free for a much larger issue which could cover the Morgan overdraft, dollar Treasury Bills, maturities and other short-dated liabilities. It also wanted to cease providing collateral on its loans, while paying no more than in London. If the yield had to be such that

British capital was attracted from sterling to dollar-denominated debt, special taxation would be imposed on UK resident holders.[9]

Until the end of December, both the US Treasury and Morgans thought that a large part of the British maturity would be converted. In the first ten days of the New Year, however, the price weakened to 100³/₈ as some holders, not wanting to convert, took advantage of the premium to take a profit. In response, Morgans suggested that the new issue be postponed and that they should form a syndicate to underwrite the conversion of any unconverted balance of the Notes in return for a commission of 1 per cent of the amount outstanding, which was $120m. The cost of the Bonds created in this way would be about 5.58 per cent for the eighteen years, or slightly more than Morgans' proposed Note-cum-twenty-year Bond.[10] The underwriting syndicate would stimulate market activity, perhaps improve the price, persuade holders to convert, buy any unconverted Notes, convert and sell the new Bonds.

After a short delay while Austen Chamberlain settled into his new appointment as Chancellor, the Treasury proposed that Morgans buy the outstanding unconverted Notes at 99, all subsequent conversions by investors being met by reducing the amount of Notes presented for conversion by the syndicate. The effect was the same as Morgan's proposition, the syndicate being paid the difference between 99 and 100 on the whole amount and being liable for the unconverted balance.[11] The advantage for the UK authorities was that they would appear to be issuing an eighteen-year Bond at 99, which would disappear at its nominal value into the anonymity of the annual returns under 'Other debt created under the War Loan Acts, 1914–18', instead of paying a commission, which would appear as expenditure in the budget.

The transaction did not go smoothly, despite Jack Morgan's presence in London and his personal negotiation with officials. The source of the difficulty was that every day which passed saw additional Notes being converted by their holders, so reducing the underwriting syndicate's liability. Thus, the Morgan partners in New York were happy with the Treasury's counter-proposition, but pointed out that since their proposition had been put to the Treasury the amount unconverted had fallen from $120m to $110m and that the one point spread on the price was posited on the syndicate dividing $1.2m, not $1.1m.[12] When the Chancellor finally accepted on Wednesday, 15 January, the amount unconverted had fallen to $95m and that was the amount which the Chancellor was prepared to sell: 'His point is that he cannot pay what amounts to 1% commission on Notes already converted, and cannot see his way to date the proposition back to the time you made it instead of the time he accepts it', cabled Jack Morgan.[13] The New York partners argued: it was embarrassing to go back to the members of the syndicate to divide only $0.95m; the residue represented holders less likely to convert; Morgans were waiving their management fee; the US Treasury were encouraging the operation; could the basis not be $100m? If it had to be $95m, could not the price be 98³/₄? Finally, they said, 'We await final word from you.'[14]

The transaction had never had the enthusiastic backing of British officials. Although Jack Morgan himself, isolated from his partners, told the Treasury that he was doubtful if he would have accepted the terms had he been Chancellor, there was a suspicion that Morgans, or other members of the syndicate, were behind the weakness in the price of the Notes, hoping to push the British into underwriting the conversion. Officials were aware that, inasmuch as members of the syndicate were themselves holders, the Treasury was paying a premium of 1 per cent to convert Notes which might be converted anyway. 'If we had more funds in hand we could be our own underwriters' had been Andrew McFadyean's comment and, when the Chancellor finally decided to refuse Morgan's proposition, Keynes made a note which foreshadowed the techniques used by the CNRA in the domestic market:

> I am glad we are not getting this underwritten…I suggest that we ourselves convert any unconverted balance and then sell on the market as opportunity offers. That is much better than giving Morgans 1¼%.[15]

On receiving Jack Morgan's cable, the partners in New York assumed their proposal had been accepted; the arguments in their subsequent cable, they said, had not been conditions of acceptance, but intended to persuade the Chancellor to improve his terms, and they had told the members of the syndicate that the transaction was in place and that they were committed. The New York partners had not appreciated the implication when they wrote 'We await final word from you'. Some of the arguments used to persuade London to accept the position were standard: the syndicate included those who had helped with the original issue at a difficult time; it had already rendered service by persuading clients to convert; and some conversions had taken place in expectation of the better market that would be created when the syndicate had absorbed the overhang of Notes. Another was redolent of the renegotiation of the rifle contracts in the autumn of 1916; the members of the syndicate were indispensable to future British borrowing and, if they were treated roughly, they would be unwilling to join in buying the unconverted rump on 1 February or of participating in a new issue later.[16] Bradbury was generous:

> Mr. Morgan came to me in great distress about this to-day. The American partners want to make out that their [cable] was an acceptance & your counter-offer under protest. Mr. Morgan fully realises that this is absurd, but says with great truth that they have put him 'in a hole' and frankly appeals to our good nature to get him out of it by…treating your offer of last Wednesday [15 January] as having been accepted.
>
> This is of course not business, but as Mr. Morgan himself has behaved so well in the matter I felt pretty sure that you would be willing to fall in with his wishes.

It was a *fait accompli* and an angry Chamberlain accepted it as such.[17]

Morgan's syndicate bought $94.5. of the Notes, the amount unconverted on the evening of 15 January. During the following sixteen days, holders presented

$50m for conversion, leaving $44.5m to be converted by the syndicate. Of this $44.5m, syndicate members retained $16.3m as an investment. The remaining $28.2m, together with $3.6m bought to support the price in the second half of January when the syndicate was seeking to encourage conversions by holders, were offered to the public on 13 February by the 417 members of a selling syndicate, who paid par and re-offered them at 101, two points above the price paid to the UK. The syndicate had difficulty finding buyers. By 19 February, about half had been sold, and the balance of $12.5m was bought at par by a group headed by First National Bank.[18] On 31 March 1920, $143.6m of the Bonds were outstanding.[19]

The end of the call loan

In the summer of 1917, the Treasury's response to Morgans' demand for the repayment of the call loan had been to sell the securities lying behind it at a pace which would not disturb the markets or damage US Treasury borrowing, to issue dollar Treasury Bills and to promise the US Shipping Board's compensation. The same policy was followed in 1917–18 when $222m was repaid from the sale of $66.5m of securities, $86m of Treasury Bills and just $0.5m of gold, while $69m (net) came from the Treasury Account, including the ship money (Table 15.2).

In the winter of 1917–18, sales of securities were stopped in response to the weak markets and the US Treasury's anxiety about its own financing; disposals, which had been $35m in October–December, fell to only $6m in January–March.[20] At the end of June 1918, when advising the Secretary that US Treasury funds should be made available to repay the 1 September maturity, Leffingwell also suggested that the British should be permitted to sell collateral, so reducing both the call loan and the Bill issue: the Bills, he said, issued at a discount rate of 6 per cent, had 'many attractions which interfere to a certain extent with our 4½% certificates'.[21] When he consulted Jack Morgan, he was told that the call loan was

Table 15.2 Sources of the funds used for repayment of the call loan: 1917–18 to 1919–20 ($m)

	1917–18	*1918–19*	*1919–20*
Sales of securities	66.5	47.0	16.5
Russian receipts	–	–	0.5
Gold	0.5	–	19.0
Dollar Treasury Bills	86.0	6.0	5.0
Treasury Account (net)	69.0*	10.0	13.5
Exchange purchased	–	–	18.0
Reduction	222.0	63.0	72.5

Note
*Includes payment by the US Shipping Board.

Source: T 170/134, Chadwick, 'British Government Transactions in America', 1922.

provided by the same banks as held the maturing Notes and, if the Notes were repaid from US advances and Morgans were given permission to sell collateral, 'the call loan need give us no further trouble'.[22] At the end of July, when the loan was $128m, sales of securities were resumed, 'very carefully with a view to avoiding any disturbance of quotations'.[23]

The following January (1919) the weekly offer of dollar Treasury Bills was increased, with the intention of raising the total volume to about $100m and applying the proceeds to the call loan (Tables 6.2 and 6.4).[24] This contributed to a further reduction of $63m in 1918–19 (Table 15.2).[25]

In the spring of 1919, funds for repayment came from two additional sources. In April or May, the British shipped between $25m and $30m of gold to the USA, $19m of which was applied to the call loan during June.[26] Also in April, an improvement in sterling's exchange rate led Grenfell to suggest that dollars be bought in the market. There was no depth: £100,000 could move the rate 1 or even 2 cents and Jack Morgan envisaged only limited purchases, perhaps as little as $5m each month. Bradbury did not want to influence the exchange rate and limited Morgans to 'occasional' purchases. The accounts show that dollar purchases contributed $18m to the repayment of the loan between 31 March 1919 and 25 July, when Jack Morgan cabled Grenfell that 'You will be very glad to hear that the Call Loan is no more.'[27]

5½ per cent Dollar Notes and Bonds convertible into War Bonds (23 November 1919)

Repayment of the call loan was followed by rapid accumulation of UK Treasury balances in New York. Late in July 1919, Blackett asked for instructions on their use; by 11 August, Morgan Grenfell described them as 'heavy'. At mid-September, deposits were $53m, with a further $27m to come within a few days and payments within sight of only $30m. To earn a higher rate, the Treasury was buying acceptances, with repurchase agreements timed to provide it with $50m cash for capital liabilities,[28] $27.1m Rifle Notes due 21 October, $130.5m three-year 5½ per cent UK Treasury Notes due 1 November, ¥100m ($49.8m) Exchequer Bonds due 15 December and ¥85.8m ($42.8m) due to the Japanese government on 18 January 1920 (Tables 6.2, 6.3 and 15.1).

When the obligations matured, the labour unrest and speculation accompanying the American post-war boom were at their height. At the beginning of October, Morgans described 'investment conditions here…[as] extremely unsatisfactory. There seems practically no money available for purely investment purposes, while at the same time there seems to be unlimited amount for speculative opportunities.' The Anglo-French Loan, with one year to run, was yielding 7.75 per cent, the secured UK 5½ per cents of 1921 were yielding 6.25 per cent, and the new unsecured UK 5½ per cent Bonds of 1937 were yielding 5.8 per cent.[29] Recent issues for foreign borrowers – Sweden, Switzerland and the City of Copenhagen – had left investors with losses, and Morgans were issuing $50m for Belgium at a level that would imply a cost to the British that, they said, could not be contemplated.[30] UK Treasury Bills were not selling well, and from the end of August Morgans had been supporting them in the secondary market; on 9 October, the rate was raised from 5½ per cent to 6 per cent.[31] Because the maturing Notes were, in effect, Treasury Bills, Morgans also supported their market, selling when the price improved, aiming to hold the yield at around 5½ per cent. In the middle of September, they bought $13.5m of the Rifle Notes before maturity.[32]

Morgans and the Treasury agreed that it was necessary to give a speculative flavour to the refinancing issue, their chosen method being to exploit American investors' new interest in foreign currencies by giving an option on the sterling exchange rate. The Treasury wanted to combine this with the conversion of the indebtedness from dollars into sterling. Designing the security proved difficult; the money could not be made available until after the maturity on 1 November and, as the market was over-full with short paper such as the British Treasury Bills, the call loan was reactivated to cover the $70m by which the maturity exceeded the balance on the Treasury Account.[33] Repayment was made on 7 November from the proceeds of the new issues.

An early suggestion from Blackett was for a straight sterling Exchequer Bond, a simple wager on the exchange rate but 'very expensive for the Treasury' should sterling return to par. It did not appeal to Morgans, who thought that the underlying security had to be denominated in dollars, whatever the frills, if American investors were to find it attractive. They proposed a dollar issue with National War Bonds as collateral. Holders would have the right to convert into the War Bonds at a fixed exchange rate, or the War Bonds could be sold and the sterling converted into dollars and used to repay the dollar Bonds, either by lot or by purchase in the market. In the latter case, there could be no fixed redemption price and it was envisaged that towards the end of the issue's life holders would benefit from being bought out at a premium with any surplus collateral – a tontine, said Morgans. They thought that they might be able to sell upwards of $150m to yield about 5¾ per cent.[34]

The Treasury judged the design too complex and asked for the terms for a straight dollar Note, an unsecured dollar Bond convertible into a sterling Bond at a fixed exchange rate, and a straight sterling Bond.[35] The last was once more dismissed and the cost of the first was prohibitive; an issue of only $50m to $100m for two or three years would have to yield 6½ per cent to the investor and, with 2½ per cent expenses, would cost the Treasury well over 7 per cent. A twenty-year Bond would have to carry a coupon of 6 per cent, be issued at par, with 3 per cent expenses, for only $50m. Morgans also warned that irrespective of the cost, the amounts were dangerously small: the Treasury might be more relaxed about its financial position and prepared to make a small issue, with another later, but investors would feel badly treated if a second issue followed closely on the first.[36]

These time-consuming discussions clarified the principles on which the Treasury wanted to work. The terms should be such that the holder would be able to convert into a sterling security throughout its life. An option on sterling at a fixed rate would tend to stabilise the exchanges because the dollar debt would only be converted when the rate was strong, 'the most natural and satisfactory means of gradually converting a foreign debt into an internal debt as and when such transactions can be absorbed in the Exchange market'. At one point the Treasury had greater ambitions, to leapfrog the intermediate stage of dated (temporary) sterling debt, and convert the dollar debt straight into permanent debt. It had always said that although being prepared to borrow for only three years it wanted as much as possible to be for ten. How, it asked, did Morgans react to an option into 2½ per cent Consols at a small premium over the current price?[37]

The yield on Consols was judged too low and War Bonds were selected.[38] Subscriptions were invited for either a 5½ per cent Note of 1 November 1922 at 98 (6.26 per cent) or a 1 August 1929 Bond at 96¼ (6.02 per cent). The prices paid by the underwriting syndicate were 96½ (6.83 per cent) and 94 (6.33 per cent). With sterling about $4.20, holders of the dollar Bonds had the option of converting into the Fourth Series of 5 per cent War Bonds due 1 February 1929 at $4.30, the equivalent of £232 12s 0d War Bonds for each $1,000 of the dollar Bonds. The amounts of each maturity to be allotted was at the discretion of the Treasury, only to be decided when the applications had been received, but the aggregate could not exceed $250m. The Notes could be converted at any time before maturity and the Bonds at any time before the maturity of the War Bonds in February 1929.

These terms offered the income on the Notes or Bonds plus 18.9 per cent if the exchange rate returned to par and the War Bond was held to its redemption price of 105, or 13.2 per cent if the exchange rate returned to par and the War Bond was sold at par (Table 15.3). Despite the attractions, Morgans found investors unenthusiastic. As the syndicate of over 800 underwriters was trying to interest investors, the Treasury in London warned that the Chancellor's financial statement, due on 29 October, would refer to a deficit, which, catching the eye of American journalists, could damage confidence. Morgans briefed the press, emphasising the willingness of British taxpayers to meet their debts, the resilience of the tax base, the money owed to the UK by the allies and the overseas investments still owned by British residents. This may or may not have been helpful in selling the issues, but it must have encouraged those in Congress determined to make the UK meet its debts to the US Treasury in full. There was also a flurry when rumours spread that Belgium was raising a large loan in London.

US exporters were found asking why they should lend to the UK so that it could sell on credit, winning business in competition with themselves. In addition, tight financial conditions were killing appetites. On 24 October, the day after the syndicate began to sell, Morgans reported themselves to be 'seriously disappointed' at the reception of the issues, the public to be 'lethargic in matter of all foreign credits' and enquiries being made about the possibility of cancelling the sale. Stressing the provision of credits to America's customers, Morgans pressed industrial companies such as Standard Oil, US Steel and Bethlehem Steel to subscribe.[39] Call rates closed at 19 per cent on 1 November, and on 3 and 6 November the Federal Reserve system raised administered rates.[40] The rise in the value of the exchange rate option as sterling fell to $4.1675 at the end of October and $4.0175 at the end of November should have increased appetites, but investors

Table 15.3 Potential profit on United Kingdom of Great Britain and Ireland three-year and ten-year 5½ per cent Convertible Gold Notes and Bonds issued on 1 November 1919

	Amount realised for each $100 of Notes or Bonds	
Rate of exchange US$/£	*If War Bonds sold at £100*	*If War Bonds held to maturity at £105*
4.30	$100.00	$105.00
4.40	102.34	107.46
4.50	104.67	109.90
4.60	106.99	112.34
4.70	109.32	114.79
4.80	111.64	117.22
4.8665	113.19	118.85

Source: prospectus.

being investors they probably thought more of what it said about the UK's credit rating.

At the end of October, with only $41.4m Notes and $81.9m Bonds sold, Morgans thought underwriters were failing to subscribe *qua* investors in expectation that they would be left with securities *qua* underwriters: the old problem. To inveigle them into subscribing, Morgans asked that the Bank of England follow the wartime procedure and join them in an application for $60m to make it appear that the whole issue had been subscribed.[41] Jack Morgan, in London, warned his partners that it would be difficult to persuade the Chancellor to pay any price higher than that paid by the underwriters and that to ask him was 'practically proposing that [he] should pay the Syndicate and do the Syndicate's work'.[42] Morgan was right. On 30 October, when it was first suggested, the Chancellor was unwilling to agree to any subscription at all. The previous day, when he had made his statement in the Commons, he had referred to the success of the issues in New York and had specifically mentioned the sum of $250m as having been raised. At best, he could be accused of misleading the Commons and, at worst, lying. When pressed, he agreed that the Treasury should subscribe for a maximum of one-half of the $60m, but on five conditions. The application would be for the Bonds, not the Notes; the price would be the 94 paid by the underwriters; Morgans would not charge their ½ per cent management fee on the amount subscribed by the Treasury; an earlier agreement to provide up to $20m for market support should be cancelled; and, if the amount subscribed did not cover the issue even after the Bank's contribution, the underwriters would take Bonds rather than Notes.[43]

That the Treasury, and not the Bank, would be the subscriber reflected changes in post-war budgeting. If the Bank subscribed and a loss was incurred, the compensation paid to the Bank under the Treasury guarantee could no longer be lost in the anonymity of the Votes of Credit. By the 'Treasury', Chamberlain almost certainly meant the equally anonymous CNRA.

Morgans could not agree to give the Treasury the same price as that paid by the underwriters. In allotting the $250m, they had, in effect, already distributed to over 800 banks and institutions the difference between the price to the underwriters and the price to the public. They could not expect those outside their own immediate New York issuing group to give this up, especially as the risk had already been taken. Moreover, these country underwriters would have to be told why they had to surrender part of their commitment and the reason would undoubtedly become public. Morgans were unable to provide the $30m from their share of the underwriting because some had been transferred to US Steel to persuade it to subscribe. If the full $30m was taken back from the New York Group's share, the loss of commission would make it unlikely that they would be prepared to join in a special application alongside Morgans and the Treasury. In any case, asking the favour would be difficult because the issuing group's subscription would relieve the country underwriters, leaving the issuing group with more securities than they would have been left with as underwriters had the issues been declared undersubscribed.[44]

In London, the Chancellor was struggling to persuade the Cabinet to raise interest rates: on 6 October, with much reluctance, it had agreed to increase Bill rates, but by the end of the month the Chancellor was seeking further restriction (see p. 410). This was to come on 6 November, but in the meantime he was unwilling to expose himself unnecessarily. So, when Morgans approached him again, he reacted as Jack Morgan had predicted. He could not see how he could defend himself if he had to explain to the Commons that he had paid a syndicate to underwrite and distribute the issues and that, when the time came for the underwriters to fulfil their commitments, he had subscribed for a large amount to save them from loss.[45]

Although there was no help from London, Morgans were

> so deeply persuaded that it would be calamitous to the whole European situation to announce that the American public has not taken the Loan and that therefore it has been thrown back upon the underwriters, that we propose to-morrow to attempt to organise a New York Group…to subscribe for the remainder.[46]

When books closed, subscriptions were $75.6m for the Notes and $99.2m for the Bonds. On 7 November, the New York Group subscribed for $40.2m Notes and $35m Bonds and the issue was declared fully subscribed. After various swaps and adjustments, $101.6m Notes and $148.4m Bonds were created.[47]

Sterling's return to pre-parity in 1925 ensured that the design successfully converted external into internal debt. The largest conversions, as would be expected, were in 1922 and 1923 as the option became profitable, but even when the exchange rate made it unprofitable the Treasury bought the issues in New York for conversion.[48] When the final conversions were made on 1 February 1929, $244.8m Notes and Bonds had already been converted into £56.9m War Bonds, and at maturity on 1 August 1929 only $2m (£0.4m) Bonds remained to be paid off.[49]

The Anglo-French Loan

The Treasury, at Morgans' instigation, originally authorised $20m to support the secondary market in the two issues of November 1919.[50] Later, the Chancellor volunteered an increase to soften his refusal to subscribe to the issues except at the underwriters' price. When Morgans took up his offer, they asked that $50m be made available.[51] In the event, only $30m was authorised, as support for the November 1919 issues had become entangled with finding the dollars with which to repay the British half of the $500m Anglo-French Loan (the 'Loan'), which came due on 15 October 1920.[52]

Shortly before Christmas 1919, the Loan was yielding 11.5 per cent and, said Morgans, deterring buyers of other foreign issues.[53] By 21 January, both of the November issues had fallen to 95, support had cost the Treasury $23.2m and the subscribing New York Group still held some $51m of its original $75.2m. Morgans feared that more of the new Bonds would come onto the market as investors anticipated a refinancing of the Loan.[54] During December, with funds being absorbed in support of the November issues and the purchase of yen and Swiss francs for capital repayments (Table 6.3), the Treasury was cautious in its buying of the Loan, securing paper only if it was cheap. It also tried to improve the price by keeping the market liquid, Morgans having advised that, although small purchases could not permanently raise the price, the Loan was widely held, treated by investors as one of their more liquid assets, and Treasury intervention – both as a buyer and a seller – would keep the market alive and make the Loan more attractive.[55]

Shortly before Christmas, the Treasury stopped this two-way trading and instead retained whatever it purchased. However, the size of the maturity required more radical action. The unabsorbed November issues were, Morgans claimed, 'stopping up the neck of the bottle', preventing confidence from growing to support a refinancing. Morgans made three suggestions, all with drawbacks: the Treasury could clear the market by buying and cancelling the New York Group's holding; another selling group could be formed and the New York Group's holding sold at a lower price in a further public offering; and the Treasury could buy the New York's Group's holding and refinance it, together with the securities already acquired in supporting the market, with a new short-dated issue. The first would involve using money which the British needed for the Anglo-French maturity; the second would admit that there had been a failure, with damage to British credit; the first and third would both be unacceptable to the Chancellor because they would be relieving the underwriters at the taxpayers' expense.[56]

A decision had to wait until Davison arrived from New York and Blackett returned from Paris, where he had been trying to sort out Anglo-French financial relations, including the Loan. Blackett came back prepared to support the market so that the French could make a new issue of, perhaps, $100m in April, followed by another in June.[57] However, French finances were in dire straits. Morgans, as the French Treasury's New York financial agent, were warning that its credit in the USA was exhausted, and in the middle of January Norman told Strong that French credit in London had 'gone to pieces'. It became clear that the French would not be able to make the proposed issues and that the British might have to meet the entire $500m.[58] With the possibility of having to find an additional $250m in October, the British refused to increase their support for the November issues beyond the $30m already sanctioned. By 12 February, the issues had fallen a further three points.[59]

On 17 February, Davison and Grenfell had what the former described as 'a very satisfactory and reassuring interview' in London with the Chancellor and the French Finance Minister, Frederic Francois-Marsal. A record of the conversation has not been found, but it can be assumed that the decision was taken to repay the Loan in cash, a move which Morgans could well describe as 'satisfactory' because it could be expected to raise the price of the November issues, as well as that of the Loan itself. The decision was not made public until 5 March, when the two governments announced that they were 'taking the necessary steps to provide for its [the Loan's] repayment.'[60] With less ambiguity, three days later, the Chancellor told the Commons that the British share would not be re-borrowed outside the UK, so that external debt would become internal debt. Any balance would be met from shipping gold.[61]

Between the decision and the announcement, the British, privileged with the knowledge of their own intentions, bought. At the 17 February meeting, instructions were given to Morgans to withdraw support for the November issues, but to continue purchasing the Loan, without raising its price, up to the $20m limit. Two weeks later, the authority was increased to $50m, and on 8 March to the full $250m. On 8 June, the Chancellor announced that 'well over' half of the British share had been bought and that funds in New York or in sight were sufficient to cover the remainder and, indeed, all British market obligations until the end of the year.[62]

When the Loan matured, $207.4m of the British share had been bought. The bulk of the purchases had been made in just three months: $53.9m in March (at an average price of 97½), $31.1m in April (98½) and $58m in June (99½). Including the balance of $42.6m paid off at par on maturity, the cost was $247.1m; $48.7m (£10m) of the Bank's gold was used, with a further $30.1m (£7.7m) bought from the Hong Kong and Shanghai Bank and shipped to New York.[f]

f The source of the Bank's gold is unclear. In March, the Treasury proposed a shipment of £27.2m ($132.4m), £5m ($24.3m) from the Bank and £22.2m ($108.5m) held by the Bank under agreements between the British and Italians, dated 8 July and 9 November 1915, whereby the British provided advances against the deposit of gold. On 14 August, it was recorded that £2.2m of the Bank's shipment was, in fact, Italian, and on 6 October that £4.5m of the Italian gold remained. However, 'Loans from certain Allied Governments' (deposited gold), did not fall in the year to end-March 1920, and rose in the years to end-March 1921 and 1922. Osborne (1926), I, p. 185; *External Debt as on 31 March 1919, 31 March 1920, 31 March 1921 and 31 March 1922* (Cmd. 1648), 1922; T 160/53/F1874, 'Gold realisations', 14 August 1920, and Niemeyer to Blackett, 6 October 1920. It is possible that the Far Eastern gold had an exotic source. Sir Charles Addis recorded on 30 March 1920 that the Hong Kong and Shanghai Bank had completed the sale of £10m gold. This may refer to the resale of what was known as 'Kolchak gold', after the White Russian leader, or as 'Omsk gold', after his capital. King, (1988), pp. 20–1. The reference made is to Sir Charles Addis's Diary (King, 1988) held in the School of Oriental and African Studies, PP. MS. 14/38.

The securities were held in the Treasury account with Morgans in New York and transferred to the CNRA, whose accounts reveal a puzzle. On 29 December 1920, a holding of $178m is recorded, although maturity of the Loan *qua* Notes was on 15 October. The holding had disappeared by the following March. The only explanation is that the Treasury first decided to convert part of the holding with a view to a later sale and then changed its mind, perhaps because its financial position was stronger than expected – an early example of the kind of transaction which the CNRA was later to carry out in the sterling market.[63]

The buying of the UK's $250m went smoothly, but the French kept the Treasury on tenterhooks. When Francois-Marsal returned to Paris, Chamberlain had no doubts that the French would meet their share.[64] His confidence did not last: when the French made their intention public, they deleted the reference to each country being responsible for its half. Blackett informed the Cabinet on 11 May that the French repayment was a 'continual nightmare'; four days later, Chamberlain took the opportunity of a meeting between the French and British Prime Ministers and Finance Ministers at Lympne to pin them down. Francois-Marsal explained that financial negotiations were taking place with the USA, and arrangements might be made which would make unnecessary the export of gold: there was no question of the British having to meet the French half.[65] He gave no details, but Morgan Grenfell were making available to the UK Treasury copies of cables between Morgans in New York and the Finance Ministry in Paris. The British knew that the Ministry had no gold of its own to ship and that the Banque de France was refusing to lend any of its holding. Francois-Marsal was trying to win Parliamentary consent to a tighter fiscal programme; he was prepared to legislate to make the Banque de France provide gold, but only as a final resort when his internal programme had been agreed, and then only at the last moment. It was not until the end of June – Francois-Marsal's tax reform became law on 25 June – that the first purchase was authorised, and then only $5m.[66] In September, *The New York Times* reported that the French Treasury had begun to ship gold and had accumulated dollars from market purchases; $100m came from a public issue, handled by Morgans, and another $35m from an increase in the Treasury Bill issue, $10m of which had to be taken by the British.[67]

The repayment of the dollar Treasury Bills

The increase in the dollar Treasury Bill issue authorised in January 1919 lasted until the end of October, when, as a response to the rise in the cost to 6 per cent, the weekly offering was reduced by $1m.[68] A larger reduction was made as part of the arrangements for the 1 November issues (Table 6.2). The reasons for this decision are not recorded, but it can be surmised that the market was overfull with short paper similar to the British Bills – we know that Morgans were having some difficulty with placing them. Morgans may also have been fearful of the Federal Reserve Board and the US Treasury, which were – as so often – anxious about long-term borrowing being carried as short-term paper constantly rolled over. A more commercial reason may have been that the banks were stretched by the boom and did not want to increase their lending to the UK; a bargain may have been struck whereby some members of the underwriting group, who were also members of the syndicate underwriting the weekly Bill issue, agreed to take new Notes or Bonds provided they were relieved of Treasury Bills.[69]

Morgans' original suggestion was to reduce the issue by $25m.[70] The Treasury gave no answer until it knew how much cash it was going to raise, but when this turned out to be $237m, some $100m more than the minimum it had indicated, it ordered a gradual reduction in the Bill issue to $50m, to be completed by 1 March 1920.[71] At the beginning of April 1920, with the rate on French Bills 6½ per cent, Morgans found difficulty in placing even the $50m, and the Treasury authorised a reduction to $40m.[72] With the money market continuing tight, at the end of April the Treasury sanctioned a further reduction to $25m, but, with continued buying of the Anglo-French Loan and the prospect of finding $50m for the arrangement with Argentina on 15 May, it wanted to retain the freedom to increase the issue once more (Table 6.3).[73] On 22 August, it renewed for one year the agreement with the underwriting syndicate, notifying Morgans that, provided the French met their half of the Anglo-French Loan, it intended to discontinue the issue within the year.[74]

Morgans took the authorisation to reduce the issue to $25m as permissive and by the end of September had increased it to $36m. The Bills were held in large blocks and there is more than a hint that Morgans were indulging their close friends. The Treasury's next, somewhat tart, instruction was to reduce the issue to $20m as 'an absolute maximum...the purpose...in continuing this form of borrowing at all being mainly to keep it open for the present as a possible means of expansion in case of need. It is not a form of borrowing on which the Treasury desire to rely for ordinary purposes.'[75]

At the end of December 1920, the issue was $16.7m and instructions were given for the underwriting syndicate to be wound up (Table 6.2).[76] In July 1921, with Treasury balances of $94m and another $55m expected during July and August on account of purchases in the foreign exchange market, the maximum issue was reduced to $10m.[77] In October 1921, Morgans were finding the Treasury balance uncomfortably large for the money market, and on 9 November London told them to discontinue issuing and run off the maturities.[78] The last Bills were repaid in January or February 1922.

The five-year 5½ per cent secured Notes 1921 and subrogation

In September 1920, as it became clear that the UK would not have to repay the French half of the Anglo-French Loan, the Treasury authorised the first purchases of the 5½ per cent Notes due on 1 November 1921. The initial $10m was increased to $30m in mid-October, but the pace was slow and on 9 November only $12.2m had been acquired.[79] At the end of the financial year, $17.6m were cancelled (Table 6.2).[80]

In addition to the utilisation of heavy balances and good debt management, there were two reasons for buying the secured Notes before maturity – both connected with releasing the collateral which lay behind them; some of the securities were Canadian Bonds, part of the Dominion's debt to the UK, which had to be surrendered to the Department of Finance before the Department's advances to the UK could be cancelled. Others had been borrowed under Scheme B and were due to be returned to their British owners by 31 March 1922. The Treasury had been seeking to terminate their use as collateral and return them to the UK since the autumn of 1919.[81]

The second reason was related to efforts to secure the release of the securities subrogated to the US Treasury which, in the summer of 1921, still amounted to $196.3m: C$28m Dominion of Canada, C$43.6m CPR, $20.7m US Bonds, $25m US ordinary shares and $79m Argentinians and Chileans.[82] In May of that year, the Cabinet refused a Treasury request for permission to ask the US Treasury to release them (see pp. 516–17). The appeal would probably have been refused: Andrew Mellon, the new Republican Secretary of the Treasury, was seeking wider powers to negotiate the settlement of allied war debts and it would have complicated his task if Congress had learnt that he had released the subrogated securities without first agreeing the funding of the debt.[83]

Unable to put a direct request to the US Treasury, the UK Treasury told the market on 6 July 1921 that it stood ready to purchase the 1 November Notes at par. By 22 July, it had bought another $25m.[84] This manoeuvre, with the release of collateral behind the Notes, was accompanied by a rearrangement of the subrogated securities. On 10 June, Blackett had asked Morgans to explore with the US Treasury the possibility of substitutions and, in the meantime, consider replacement purchases in the market.[85] At the end of the month, Morgans were authorised to buy up to $20m US equity and preferred stocks with the intention of either returning them to British investors in place of those subrogated or, in the case of securities for which the market was narrow or non-existent, swapping them for others subrogated. Five weeks later, the authorisation was raised to $25m, the full amount of US corporate equities subrogated.[86] On 9 July, the British asked Lamont to enquire unofficially whether the US Treasury would be prepared to substitute Colonial government and British railway issues for the non-American subrogated securities.[87] The US officials wanted to be helpful, but only within the limits of the trust agreements to which they had become heirs. In particular, they would only substitute one security for another as long as it did not disturb the various categories of pledged securities (Table 6.2).[88] With this in mind, Morgans negotiated swaps of securities which the UK Treasury owned outright with those subrogated, presenting the US Treasury with possible combinations of British railway sterling securities, Local Loans Stock, Canadian railways, and the Bonds of New Zealand, South Africa, Canada and Australia that represented their war debts to the UK. Finding securities of the same category to replace the Argentinians and Chileans proved particularly troublesome. The substitution package was finally agreed in the middle of October.[89] By then, the purchases of US corporates had reduced the amount the UK had wanted to swap to $183.8m. This was duly released in return for other securities, of which the largest categories were C$163.8m Dominion war debt and C$6.1m CPR.[90] By July 1922, only a 'comparatively small' part of the securities originally subrogated were still held to the order of the US Treasury, and all the borrowed securities had been returned.[91]

The Canadian Debt: the chartered banks

At the Armistice, the Imperial Treasury owed the Canadian chartered banks C$200m under three agreements.[92] The First Munitions Loan (C$76m), syndicated on 1 April 1916, was extended four times, as was the Second Munitions Loan (C$24m), which had been syndicated on 3 July 1916. The Royal Wheat Loan (C$100m) had been drawn in six tranches: C$50m on 1 November 1917 and the balance in tranches of C$10m on the first day of January through to May 1918. The C$50m was renewed twice, until November 1920. The five units of C$10m were repaid seriatim as they matured in the first half of 1920 with funds transferred from Morgans, a transaction which, it can be assumed, was facilitated, if not financed, by the US$250m Notes and Bonds sold by the Treasury in New York in November 1919.

In September 1920, as it became clear that the British would not be liable for the whole Anglo-French Loan, the Treasury 'semi-officially' proposed that the three debts should be amalgamated into a 'general scheme of repayment'. It was suggested that, as each of the three came up to maturity, it should be extended under a new agreement, with a new schedule of payments on account of capital and interest. Those on account of capital would be C$5m a month for the six months from 1 November 1920 to 1 April 1921 and C$10m a month for the twelve months from 1 May 1921 to 1 April 1922, when all would have been paid off.[93] The repayment of the Anglo-French out of the way, the new agreement was signed on 31 October 1920 (Table 10.1).[94]

The Canadian Debt: The Department of Finance

Between 31 March 1915 and 31 March 1919, the UK borrowed some C$829m from the Canadian Finance Department (but see pp. 309–11). In the same period, the Department of Finance borrowed C$714m from the UK in the form of sterling advances in London. Between 31 March 1919 and the end of the calendar year, the British made further advances of £22m (C$107.1m, or C$110.4m including interest), mainly it can be surmised to finance the repatriation of the Canadian Expeditionary Force, and the Canadians made advances for commercial purchases, such as C$25m for timber, which were drawn when the sterling rate was particularly weak.[95] In addition, the sums owed – on both sides – were adjusted from time to time as bills were presented or expenditure identified and its size determined.

There was, therefore, ample scope for cancelling offsetting advances, a measure which the Treasury in London was keen to use as a way of reducing its published debt without the necessity of parting with any cash. In April 1918, it proposed

Table 15.4 Identified cash repayments to the Canadian Department of Finance by the UK Treasury: 1920–1 to 1923–4

Years ending 31 March		
1921	£20m	'with other repayments, we have reduced…our debt in Canada by £20,000,000.'(1)
1922	£6.6m	'Net amount expended.'(2)
1923	(a) £13.8m or C$62m	'Net amount expended.' £8.8m 'direct Exchequer Debt' and £5m 'collateral loan'.(3) The implied exchange rate is C$4.475.
	(b) £12.7m	repayment, offset by an increase of £1.7m on account of 'exchange adjustment' and £23,000 on account of a 'cash adjustment'.(4)
	(c) C$62m	'We have repaid to Canada in the year $62m.'(5)
1924	(a) £2.4m	plus cancellation of £12.1m (C$58.9m at par of exchange) in bonds.(6)
	(b) C$8.7m	was paid in cash on 28 March 1924 as part of the final settlement.(7) The implied exchange rate is C$3.625. The market rate varied between C$4.4025 and C$4.7325 during the financial year, so it can be assumed that there was a cash payment before the final settlement.(8)

Notes
(1) *Hansard* (Commons), 25 April 1921, col. 71.
(2) T 171/205, 'Net amounts expended in 1921–2 in paying off external debt,' undated.
(3) T 171/214, 'Net amounts expended in 1922–3 in paying off external debt and the amount of debt paid off,' undated.
(4) *National Debt: annual returns*, 1923, p. 33.
(5) *Hansard* (Commons), 16 April 1923, col. 1727.
(6) *National Debt: annual returns*, 1924, p. 36. The exact figure is shown as £2.353m. *Hansard*, 29 April 1924, col. 1592, gives £2.543m. The figure in *Hansard* may be taken as a misprint.
(7) *Canadian Government (Advances)* (Cmd. 2181), TM, 27 May 1924.
(8) Morgan (1952), Table 54.

that the temporary debt of the Dominion government be cancelled inasmuch as the lesser size of British indebtedness allowed. Although the Canadians were immediately in agreement, they were slow to discuss the details. Pressed by the Treasury, anxious to include the arrangement in the debt returns for 31 March 1919, it was only in November that the cancellation was announced. It was made effective from 1 April 1918, the earliest date which would not disturb the previous year's accounts. Included were C$405.3m, C$384.5m capital and C$20.9m interest, representing nearly all the temporary advances the UK had extended to the Canadians. Of the British debt, the advances on account of cheese (C$34.3m), meat (C$5m) and interest (C$25.8m) were included, with the balance of C$340.2m being set off against the munitions debt.[96]

Four further cancellations, totalling C$403m (£82.8m), took place in 1919–20.[g] On 31 March 1919, the Treasury believed that the Canadians owed them C$252m (plus the Bond indebtedness) and they owed the Canadians C$466.7m. With effect from 1 April 1919, C$252m was cancelled, the British debt being set against the advances taken for cereals and other foodstuffs in the second half of 1918. The balance of C$100.5m was set off against the munitions debt, leaving it as C$214.7m.[97] The maturity of the British issue in New York on 1 November 1919 released some of the Canadian Bonds held as collateral. On 1 December, C$30m of the 4½ per cent Bonds were cancelled. An issue price of 99 had been used and C$29.7m of Canadian advances disappeared as an offset. On 1 March 1920, C$10.4m 3½ per cent Bonds were also cancelled. These had been issued at 95 and another C$9.9m of advances were cancelled. Earlier, on 31 December, the C$110.4m, or £22m, advanced by the British in the first nine months of the 1919–20 financial year was also cancelled.[98] At the time of the final adjustment on 28 March 1924, C$65.2m 4½ per cent War Loan 1925–45 and C$2m 3½ per cent War Loan 1925–8 were cancelled. In this transaction, the original issue price was ignored and their present value was determined by applying an interest rate of 5½ per cent to their par values in 1945 and 1928. This gave prices of 87.48 and 92.91, enabling a further C$58.9m of the British debt to the Dominion to be cancelled.[99]

The cancellations (taking the 1918 cancellation at the British value of C$405.3m) amounted to C$866.2m, or more than the British debt shown in Table 10.2. There may be additional reasons, but the most obvious is that the Table does not include the £22m borrowed by Canada after the Armistice or the post-Armistice commercial advances, of which only those for timber have been identified.[100]

This said, Table 15.4 shows the cash repayments recorded by the British debt returns, the Chancellor's Financial Statements and occasional Treasury papers. Only the data for 1922–3 and 1923–4 is unequivocal, but the total of £42.8m (C$208.3m) in the four years seems not unreasonable.

✣ ✣ ✣

The process of repaying the debts discussed in this chapter was accompanied by only a few adventures. Until the last moment, there was anxiety about whether the French would meet their share of the Anglo-French Loan. Morgans earned their fees during the British loan operations, but the problems were little more than the ordinary travails of an issuing House. The rearrangement of that liberal legacy – McKenna's system for mobilising securities – took diplomacy, care and some enterprise, but it was not fraught. Nor did the Treasury receive much

g The later cancellations are not shown separately in Table 10.2 because the Canadian accounts, from which it is derived, do not identify them. See pp. 309–11.

additional tuition in the management of its Debt, although it displayed wartime experience; it learnt more about conversions, and showed that it understood the advantages of taking a shorter issue into an official portfolio and selling it back into the market in its converted form. In buying in the Anglo-French Loan, it showed that it was prepared to exploit to its financial advantage the market's ignorance of official decisions already taken.

The comparative ease with which the debts were repaid had two effects on British policy: it helped convince the Treasury that the UK economy, given time to recover, could meet the much larger debt to the US Treasury without unacceptable strain; and it strengthened its view that repayment was not a matter of generating budget surpluses, but of converting external debt into internal debt, a foreign exchange problem. This belief was translated into concrete measures: with the November 1919 issues, which gave an option to convert dollar securities into sterling War Bonds; in the terms Blackett negotiated with Rathbone in the winter of 1919–20; and in the options incorporated into the final settlement with the US Treasury.

Endnotes

1 *ARSF*, 1920, pp. 334–6.

2 T 170/134, ff. 13, 16 and 19, Chadwick, 'British Government Transactions in America', 1922; Feinstein, T 38; *The Economist*, various dates. The data are unclear, in part, because dollars were sold to settle debts in other currencies. See, for example, the section on Canada (p. 468).

3 US National Archives, RG 39, Box 115, GB 132.5/17–4, Leffingwell, 'Memorandum for the Treasury', 20 June 1918, and Box 116, GB 132.5/19–1, Davis, 'Memorandum for the Secretary', 21 November 1919.

4 US National Archives, RG 39, Box 115, GB 132.5/17–11, Jack Morgan to Reading, 16 July 1918.

5 US National Archives, RG 39, Box 115, GB 132.5/17–11, Leffingwell to Reading, 23 July 1918, and McAdoo to Wilson, 26 August 1918; *ARSF*, 1920, p. 326.

6 Leffingwell Papers, Box 6 – LB 3, f. 374, Rathbone to Lever, 4 December 1918; MGP, B. Hist. 3, F. 19, no. 81973, JPM to Grenfell (shown to Governor and Treasury), 27 November 1918; *ARSF*, 1919, pp. 13 and 67.

7 Senate Document No. 86 (1921), *United States Foreign Loans During the War and Since the War*, pp. 20, Rathbone to Crosby, 18 December 1918, and 22–3, Memorandum from the Chancellor, 26 December 1918. Henceforth referred to as Senate Document No. 86 (1921).

8 T 172/447, Lever to Chancellor, 31 December 1918; Senate Document No. 86 (1921), pp. 23–4, Rathbone to Lever, 31 December 1918.

9 MGP, B. Hist. 3, F. 19, no. 81973, JPM to Grenfell (shown to Governor and Treasury), 27 November 1918, no. 83266, JPM to Grenfell (shown to Governor), 25/27 December 1918, and no. 83362, JPM to Grenfell, 7 January 1919; T 172/447, Lever to Chalmers, 27 December 1918, and Lever to Chancellor, 31 December 1918 and 2 January 1919; Thomas Lamont Papers, IVA, F 165–28, Jack Morgan to Lamont, 13 February 1919. Also, see T 172/447, f. 27–8, Chancellor to Lever, 23 December 1918, and US National Archives, RG 39, GB 132/19–1, Box 119, Crosby to Glass, 7 January 1919.

10 T 172/447, Rathbone for Chancellor, 3 January 1919; MGP, B. Hist. 3, F. 19, no. 83400, JPM to MG, 10 January 1919.

11 MGP, B. Hist. 3, F. 19, no. 83400, JPM to MG, 10 January 1919, no. 64450, Jack Morgan to JPM, 13 January 1919, and no. 83438, JPM to Jack Morgan, 15 January 1919.

12 MGP, B. Hist. 3, F. 19, no. 83438 JPM to Jack Morgan, 15 January 1919.

13 MGP, B. Hist. 3, F. 19, no. 64485, Jack Morgan to JPM, 15 January 1919.

14 MGP, B. Hist. 3, F. 19, no. 83455, JPM to Jack Morgan, 17 January 1919.

15 T 160/18/F557/015/2, Lever to Bradbury, 11 January 1919, Bradbury to Chancellor, 13 January 1919, and McFadyean to Keynes, 17 January 1919, with note by Keynes, 18 January 1919.

16 MGP, B. Hist. 3, F. 20, no. 83478, Lamont to Jack Morgan, 18 January 1919.

17 T 160/18/F557/015/2, Bradbury to Chancellor, 18 January 1919, and Chancellor to Bradbury, 19 January 1919.

18 PML, Syndicates No. 9, f. 147; MGP, B. Hist. 3, F. 21, no. 87743, JPM to MG (copy shown to Governor, Deputy-Governor and Blackett), 4 October 1919.

19 *External Debt as on 31 March 1919, 31 March 1920, 31 March 1921 and 31 March 1922* (Cmd. 1648), 1922. It will be noted that Table 6.2 gives the amount converted as $142.9m. That figure is taken from T 170/134, Chadwick, 'British Government Transactions in America', 1922. There is no explanation for the discrepancy.

20 T 170/134, Chadwick, 'British Government Transactions in America', 1922, ff. 26–7.

21 US National Archives, RG 39, GB 132.5/17–4, Box 115, Leffingwell, Memorandum for the Secretary, 20 June 1918.

22 US National Archives, RG 39, GB 132.5/17–11, Box 115, Leffingwell to Reading, 23 July 1918.

23 MGP, B. Hist. 3, F. 18, no. 79657, Jack Morgan to MG (to Chalmers), 31 July 1918.

24 MGP, B. Hist. 3, F. 20, nos 64539, 64555 and 64571, Jack Morgan to JPM, 20, 22 and 23 January 1919, and nos 83504 and 83519, JPM to Jack Morgan, 22 and 23 January 1919.

25 T 170/134, Chadwick, 'British Government Transactions in America', 1922, f. 27A.

26 Leffingwell Papers, Box 9, LB 3, ff. 337–8, Rathbone to Davis, 16 April 1919; T 170/134, Chadwick, 'British Government Transactions in America', 1922, f. 27A; T 172/452, f. 79, Lever to Bradbury, 3 June 1919.

27 T 170/134, Chadwick, 'British Government Transactions in America', 1922, f. 27A; MGP, B. Hist. 3, F. 20, no. 66212, Grenfell to Jack Morgan, 10 April 1919, and no. 85191, Jack Morgan to Grenfell, 12 April 1919; ibid., no. 87111, Jack Morgan to Grenfell, 25 July 1919; T 1172/450, f. 22, Blackett to Bradbury, 24 April 1919; T 172/451, f. 89, Bradbury to Blackett, 1 May 1919. The last cable provides a unique glimpse of the sources of the call loan: US Steel provided over half.

28 T 172/453, Blackett to Bradbury, 24 July 1919; MGP, B. Hist. 3, F. 21, no. 68324, MG to JPM, and no. 68722, Whigham to JPM (Copy to Blackett), both 13 September 1919; ibid., no. 87598, JPM to MG (Copies to Blackett and Governor), 18 September 1919.

29 MGP, B. Hist. 3, F. 21, no. 68722 (Copy to Blackett), Whigham to JPM, 13 September 1919, and no. 87743, JPM to MG (Copy to Governor and Blackett), 4 October 1919.

30 MGP, B. Hist. 3, F. 21, no. 87373, JPM to MG, and no. 87598, JPM to MG (Copies to Blackett and Governor), both 18 September 1919.

31 MGP, B. Hist. 3, F. 21, no. 87433, JPM to MG (Copy to McFadyean), 29 August 1919, and no. 87845, JPM to MG, 15 October 1919.

32 MGP, B. Hist. 3, F. 21, no. 87464, JPM to MG (to Bradbury), 3 September 1919, and no. 68623, MG to JPM, 5 September 1919; ibid., no. 87634, JPM to MG (copy to Blackett), 23 September 1919, and no. 68814, MG to JPM, 23 September 1919; ibid., no. 87664, JPM to MG (Copy to Blackett), 26 September 1919.

33 MGP, B. Hist. 3, F. 22, no. 70190, MG to JPM (Copies to Blackett and Governor), 23 October 1919.

34 MGP, B. Hist. 3, F. 21, nos 87598 (Copy to Blackett and Governor) and 87685 (Copy to Blackett and Governor), JPM to MG, 18 September 1919 and 27 September 1919.
35 MGP, B. Hist. 3, F. 21, no. 68914, MG to JPM (Copy to Governor and Blackett), 1 October 1919.
36 MGP, B. Hist. 3, F. 21, no. 87743, JPM to MG (Copy to Governor and Blackett), 4 October 1919.
37 MGP, B. Hist. 3, F. 21, nos. 70069 and 70070, MG to JPM (Copies to Blackett and Governor), 14 October 1919; *Hansard* (Commons), 29 October 1919, cols 752–3.
38 MGP, B. Hist. 3, F. 21, no. 87870, JPM to MG (Copy to Blackett), 17 October 1919.
39 MGP, B. Hist. 3, F. 22, no. 89000, JPM to MG (Copy to Blackett and Governor), 29 October 1929.
40 MGP, B. Hist. 3, F. 21, no. 70166, MG to JPM (Copy to Blackett and Governor), 22 October 1919; ibid., F. 22, no. 87956, JPM to MG (Copy to Blackett and Governor), 24 October 1919; ibid., no. 70231, MG to JPM (Copies to Blackett and Governor), 25 October 1919; ibid., nos 89001 and 89012, JPM to MG (Copy to Blackett), 29 October 1919 and 30 October 1919; ibid., no. 70303, Grenfell to JPM (Copies to Blackett and Governor), 30 October 1919.
41 MGP, B. Hist. 3, F. 22, no. 89012, JPM to MG (Copy to Blackett), 30 October 1919.
42 MGP, B. Hist. 3, F. 22, no. 70291, Jack Morgan to JPM, 30 October 1919.
43 *Hansard* (Commons), 29 October 1919, cols 752–3; MGP, B. Hist. 3, F. 22, no. 70305, MG to JPM (Copies to Blackett and Governor), 30 October 1919.
44 MGP, B. Hist. 3, F. 22, no. 89020, JPM to MG (Copy to Blackett), 31 October 1919, and no. 70321, MG to JPM (Copy to Blackett), 31 October 1919.
45 MGP, B. Hist. 3, F. 22, no. 70324, MG to JPM (Copy to Fisher and Blackett), 31 October 1919.
46 MGP, B. Hist. 3, F. 22, no. 89035, JPM to MG (Copy to Fisher and Blackett), 1 November 1919.
47 MGP, B. Hist. 3, F. 22, no. 89045, JPM to MG (Copies to Fisher and Blackett), 3 November 1919; PML Archives, Syndicates No. 9. There is a discrepancy between a cable to Morgan Grenfell in January, which states that $75.2m Notes and Bonds were taken by the Group, and the J. P. Morgan Syndicate Books, which say that it took $80.2m. The latter can be relied on to present the final position, so it has to be assumed that investor(s) for $5m had a change of mind. MGP, B. Hist. 3, F. 23, no. 20/2032, JPM to Grenfell, 21 January 1920.
48 For example, MGP, B. Hist. 3, F. 25, no. 88855, MG to JPM, 30 April 1921, and F. 26, no. 90306, MG to JPM, 23 July 1921.
49 *BGS*, p. 226; *National Debt: annual returns*, 1930.
50 MGP, B. Hist. 3, F. 21, no. 19/2168, JPM to MG, 16 October 1919, and no. 70118, MG to JPM (Copies to Governor and Blackett), 17 October 1919.
51 MGP, B. Hist. 3, F. 21, no. 70324, MG to JPM (Copy to Fisher and Blackett), 31 October 1919, and no. 89037, JPM to MG (Copy to Fisher and Blackett), 3 November 1919.
52 MGP, B. Hist. 3, F. 22, no. 70988, MG to JPM, 19 December 1919.
53 MGP, B. Hist. 3, F. 22, no. 89490, JPM to MG, 17 December 1919.
54 MGP, B. Hist. 3, F. 23, no. 20/2032, JPM to Grenfell, 21 January 1920.
55 MGP, B. Hist. 3, F. 22, no. 89441, JPM to MG, 12 December 1919; ibid., no. 70911, MG to JPM, and no. 89490, JPM to MG, 17 December 1919.
56 MGP, B. Hist. 3, F. 22, no. 20/2032, JPM to Grenfell, 21 January 1920, and no. 20/4546, Grenfell to JPM, 23 January 1920.
57 MGP, B. Hist. 3, no. 72819, Grenfell to Jack Morgan or Lamont, 5 February 1920.
58 MGP, B. Hist. 3, F. 23, no. 91063, JPM to MG, 7 February 1920; BoE, G35/1, Norman to Strong, 15 January 1920.
59 MGP, B. Hist. 3, F. 23, no. 20/2062, JPM to Davison, 12 February 1920.

60 MGP, B. Hist. 3, F. 23, no. 74027, MG to JPM, no. 74048, Davison to JPM, 17 February 1920, and no. 74293, Grenfell to Jack Morgan, 28 February 1920; ibid., no. 74704, MG to JPM, 6 March 1920.
61 *Hansard* (Commons), 9 March 1920, col. 910.
62 *Hansard* (Commons), 8 June 1920, col. 282; MGP, B. Hist. 3, F. 23, nos. 74027, 74292 and 74755, MG to JPM, 17 February, 28 February and 8 March 1920; ibid., F. 24, no. 78679, MG to JPM, 9 June 1920.
63 CNRA Ledgers; T 160/53/F1874, Blackett, 'Amount to be issued from the Exchequer in repayment of British share of Anglo-French Loan', 15 September 1920, and 'Anglo-French Loan: Purchases in market', undated.
64 T 160/365/F557/1, Chancellor to Secretary of the US Treasury, 12 March 1920.
65 Cab. 24/105, CP 1259, Blackett, 'British Government's Debt to the United States Government', 11 May 1920; US National Archives, RG 39, GB 132.9/19–7, Box 120, Rathbone to Treasury Department and Davis, 21 May 1920; *DBFP*, First Series, VIII, 'Proceedings of the First Conference of Hythe May 15–16, 1920', pp. 260–1.
66 MGP, B. Hist. 3, F. 22, no. 70961, MG to JPM, 18 December 1919; ibid., F. 24, no. 20/2158, JPM to MG, 22 June 1920, and no. 78783, MG to JPM, 24 June 1920; ibid., no. 93068, JPM to MG, 28 June 1920.
67 MGP, B. Hist. 3, F. 24, no. 20/2219, JPM to MG, 10 September 1920; ibid., no. 80822, MG to JPM, 14 September 1920, and no. 20/2235, JPM to MG, 29 September 1920. The French issue was very expensive. It was for twenty-five years at par. The coupon was 8 per cent and there was a most onerous sinking fund, which operated at 110. The cost to the French Treasury was said to have been 9.42 per cent. It was quickly oversubscribed. *The New York Times*, 8 September 1920, p. 18, 9 September 1920, p. 18, and 10 September 1920, p. 20.
68 MGP, B. Hist. 3, F. 21, no. 70085, MG to JPM, 15 October 1919.
69 MGP, B. Hist. 3, F. 21, no. 87598, JPM to MG (Copy to Blackett and Governor), 18 September 1919, and F. 22, no. 89090, JPM to MG (Copy to Blackett), 7 November 1919; Leffingwell Papers, Box 12, LB 3, ff. 44–5, Leffingwell to Lamont, 13 October 1919.
70 MGP, B. Hist. 3, F. 21, no. 87870, JPM to MG (Copy to Blackett), 17 October 1919.
71 MGP, B. Hist. 3, F. 21, no. 68989, MG to JPM, 8 October 1919 (Copy to Blackett); ibid., F. 22, no. 70358, MG to JPM, 3 November 1919, and no. 70597, MG to JPM (Copy to Blackett), 21 November 1919.
72 MGP, B. Hist. 3, F. 23, nos 76438 and 76611, MG to JPM, 30 March and 7 April 1920, and no. 91512, JPM to MG, 3 April 1920.
73 MGP, B. Hist. 3, F. 24, no. 91700, JPM to MG, 28 April 1920, and no. 78078, MG to JPM, 29 April 1920; ibid., no. 91728, JPM to MG, 1 May 1920, and MG to JPM, 4 May 1920.
74 MGP, B. Hist. 3, F. 24, no. 80421, MG to JPM, 19 August 1920.
75 MGP, B. Hist. 3, F. 24, nos 80874 and 80971, MG to JPM, 16 September and 22 September 1920, and no. 93571, JPM to MG, 20 September 1920.
76 MGP, B. Hist. 3, F. 25, no. 86607, MG to JPM, 10 December 1920.
77 MGP, B. Hist. 3, F. 26, no. 90180, MG to JPM, 5 July 1921.
78 MGP, B. Hist. 3, F. 26, no. 90782, MG to JPM, 9 November 1921.
79 T 160/71/F2361/03, Blackett, 11 November 1920; MGP, B. Hist. 3, F. 24, nos 80777 and 82749, MG to JPM, 11 September and 18 October 1920, and no. 93543, JPM to MG, 14 September 1920; ibid., F. 25, no. 86938, MG to JPM, 6 January 1921.
80 MGP, B. Hist. 3, F. 25, no. 88466, MG to JPM, 3 March 1921, and no. 95650, JPM to MG, 7 March 1921.
81 T 160/71/F2361/03, Blackett, 11 November 1920.
82 MGP, B. Hist. 3, no. 97423, JPM to MG, 4 August 1921. All values are at market prices.
83 MGP, B. Hist. 3, F. 26, no. 21/2105, Lamont to Grenfell, 25 June 1923.

84 MGP, B. Hist. 3, F. 26, no. 90180, MG to JPM, 5 July 1921, and no. 97340, JPM to MG, 22 July 1921. It will be recalled that the Treasury would have had to pay a premium of 1 per cent if it used its option to call the Notes. See Table 6.2.

85 MGP, B. Hist. 3, F. 26, no. 21/2105, Lamont to Grenfell, 25 June 1921.

86 MGP, B. Hist 3, F. 26, no. 90144, Grenfell to JPM, 28 June 1921, and no. 90409, MG to JPM, 5 August 1921.

87 MGP, B. Hist. 3, F. 26, no. 90223, Grenfell to JPM (shown to Governor), 9 July 1921.

88 MGP, B. Hist. 3, F. 26, no. 97423, JPM to MG, 4 August 1921, and no. 97440, JPM to MG, 6 August 1921.

89 MGP, B. Hist. 3, F. 26, no. 97753, JPM to MG, 14 October 1921.

90 MGP, B. Hist. 3, F. 26, no. 97743, JPM to MG, 10 October 1921.

91 US National Archives, RG 35, Box 116, GB 132.5/22–1, Memorandum for Parker Gilbert, 18 July 1922.

92 The following two paragraphs are based on NAC, RG19/595/155–35–3 to 5, RG19/596/155–35–13 and 16.

93 NAC, RG19/596/155–35–13, Griffiths to Deputy Minister of Finance, 23 September 1920, and Ross to Saunders, 11 October 1920, with 'Schedule of Payments'.

94 NAC, RG19/596/155–35–13, 'Memorandum of Agreement', 30 October 1920.

95 *Canadian Government (Advances)* (Cmd 651), TM, 29 March 1920 ; CO 42/1014, f. 495–6, Heath to High Commissioner, 25 March 1919. There is other correspondence on the timber advance in the same file. The credit was originally arranged for $50m.

96 CO 42/1009, f. 284, Chancellor to Acting Finance Minister, April 1918; ibid., ff. 293–6, Ramsay to the Under-Secretary of the CO, 29 June and 25 July 1918; ibid., ff. 315–16, Bradbury to the Under-Secretary of State of the CO, 15 November 1918; *Canadian Government (Advances)* (Cd. 9234), TM, 14 November 1918.

97 *Canadian Government (Advances)* (Cmd. 583), 1 January 1920; CO 42/1029, ff. 347–9, Blackett, April 1919.

98 *Canadian Government (Advances)* (Cmd. 616 and 651), TMs, 1 and 29 March 1920. A price of 99 for the $4^1/_2$ per cent Bonds was two or three shillings too high (see Chapter 4).

99 *Canadian Government (Advances)* (Cmd. 2181), TM, 27 May 1924.

100 *Canadian Government (Advances)* (Cmd. 651), TM, 29 March 1920.

16 The debt to the US Treasury and the Blackett–Rathbone talks

> there is undoubtedly in existence here a latent underlying feeling that the Allies have made the great and most vital sacrifices in the war, both of men and finance and in material damage suffered, that our sacrifices have been slight and our profits immense, and that the existence of this great debt due on demand is a sword of Damocles hanging over their heads.
>
> Strong to Leffingwell, 25 July 1919, Strong Papers, 1000.3 (2).

> Most of the really levelheaded able men that I met, like Cokayne and Norman in the Bank of England, Sir Charles Addis and the Chancellor, Mr. Austin [*sic*] Chamberlain, do not expect forgiveness of the debt…it is fair to say that Englishmen whom you and I would likely meet in our daily talks feel that England, both rich and poor, should work, economize and pay their debts.
>
> Strong to Leffingwell, 31 July 1919, Strong Papers, 1000.3 (2).

Neither the British nor the Americans believed that the autumn of 1919 was the right moment to negotiate the funding of their inter-governmental war debt, but there was no alternative: the UK wanted to postpone the payment of interest and the US Treasury did not have powers under the Second and subsequent Liberty Bond Acts to delay its collection unless it was incorporated into the 'form and terms' of new Bonds. Whatever might have been the views of individual officers, it was not a desire to contribute to the financial stability of Europe which initiated, drove and shaped negotiations, but the limitations placed by statute on the US Treasury.

The strait-jacket in which the US Treasury found itself is strikingly displayed in the cables which passed between Glass, David Houston (who replaced Glass as Secretary of the Treasury on 2 February 1920), Norman Davis (Assistant Secretary in charge of the Foreign Loan Bureau) and Leffingwell in Washington and Albert Rathbone, the US Treasury's representative in Europe. The President was incapacitated. Leadership was non-existent. In the elections held shortly before the Armistice, the Democrats lost control of both Houses. Policy was in a vacuum as isolationists in Congress successfully fought ratification of the Peace Treaty and membership of the League of Nations. To many in Congress, deferral of interest looked very like non-payment – cancellation – and the US Treasury had to step carefully if it was to show that it was necessary, politic and within the Treasury's competence to grant. After March 1921, matters were to change. With a Republican President and Congress, with recognition of the cost to American trade of the chaos in European finances, came greater flexibility. In 1919 and 1920, the US Treasury officers, tightly bound by the Liberty Bond Acts, had been frequently exasperated by the British failure to understand the limitations set by the Acts on their powers and their problems with Congress. In the background – sometimes in the foreground – was irritation that the indebted British took insufficient account of American interests and Congressional sensitivities, even in matters closely related to the funding negotiations, such as the repayment of the Anglo-French Loan and the arrangements to cover Argentinian and Japanese debts. The pressure under which the US Treasury officers were working was reflected in their instructions to Rathbone; harassed, edgy, long-winded, sometimes incoherent and frequently unclear. Until late in the negotiations, they were ambiguous on the issue that was to be crucial to the breakdown of the talks, the changes in British policy that the Administration would require before agreeing to exchange the obligations which Rathbone had negotiated.

The British regarded the Americans as legalistic, narrow, unable to grasp the 'larger' matters of policy necessary to stabilise European finances. This attitude exacerbated more fundamental differences. London favoured cancellation of all official war debts. It stressed the connection between its ability to pay the US Treasury and repayment of the advances to the continental allies, and to receipts from reparations. The Americans denied the connection, stressing that their advances were solely a matter between the UK and the USA. If repayment was impossible for the time being, the British should say so, and the US Treasury would judge the validity of the claim and whether it was able to delay collection and justify deferral to Congress. To use the later term, it would judge the 'capacity to pay'. Nor did the US accept that all its creditors had a right to equal treatment: the UK was their most solvent debtor, American taxpayers felt themselves overburdened, and commerce dictated realistic terms. Thus, while Blackett stressed that the negotiations were taking place in the context of the 'bigger picture' – a general settlement of war debts – Rathbone stressed that the agreement was purely bilateral.

From February 1920, Treasury officials in London, supported by the Foreign Office, argued that there was nothing to be gained but ill will and financial chaos from trying to collect debts from countries which did not accept the debts' legitimacy and, in any case, could not pay. The only realistic British policy was to cancel the debts owed to the UK, while paying the debts owed to the US. Some ministers, led by Lloyd George and Churchill, thought it impossible to tell electors that, burdened as they were by post-war taxation, they were to pay everything they owed, while eschewing all that was owed to them. Looking ahead, said two Presidents of the Board of Trade, one-sided cancellation could leave France relatively stronger. To these ministers, the only realistic policy was the cancellation of all war debts.

Many of the positions adopted by the two governments were unsound, in principle, or in logic. It was certainly possible to separate the debts owed by the British to the Americans from the debts owed by France and Italy to the Americans, and treat them differently. By May 1920, the British budget was under control: outside the USA, they were creditors of much of the world; the current account of their balance of payments was in surplus; they had signed the obligations and as net creditors and bankers, they had every reason to safeguard the sanctity of contract. They were repaying their non-sterling market debts, and those owed to neutral and allied governments, with speed and surprising ease. France and Italy had signed the obligations, but otherwise were in a different position on every count. On the other hand, it was not possible to separate the debts owed to the UK by France and Italy from those owed by the same debtors to the Americans, another point accepted later by Mellon. If the British demanded interest or principal from their allies, there would be defaults which would damage the obligations held by the USA. If either the British or the Americans cancelled the debts owed to them, it would enhance the value of the debts owed to the other, making possible payments to one creditor which would not have been possible to both. In the unlikely event that the British collected on their debts, the USA would expect to receive its share, pro rata. An agreement on the distribution and priority of repayments was needed. Although different debtors might receive different terms, it was necessary for the terms given by the USA and the UK to be the same for common debtors, otherwise priorities in collection would creep in by the back door; most obviously, the obligations held by one country might specify a higher interest rate or earlier repayment of principal than those held by the other.

Nor, in strict commerce, would the British be justified in claiming equal generosity with the US Treasury if all war debts were cancelled. The obligations of each debtor had a different value and the UK and US portfolios contained different amounts of each. The obligations held by the UK might have a nominal value of $8,606m (£1,769m), but $2,763m (£568m) were Russian and considered by both the USA and the UK to be worthless. In contrast, of the $9,416m (£1,935m) obligations held by the USA, only $188m (£39m) were Russian, but $4,277m (£879m) were British, which, judging by the prices of their issues on the open market in New York, had a value somewhere near par if they were given a current coupon.[1] In the absence of market prices for other nations' debt, it was impossible to put a value on the British and American portfolios, but it was clear both that there was room for disagreement and that it would be commercially foolish for the USA to swap British obligations for those of any other country, including reparation Bonds issued by Germany.

The Liberty Bond Acts and the nature of the securities

Between 24 April 1917 and 15 November 1920, under the Liberty Bond Acts, the US Treasury established credits of $9,711m in favour of eleven foreign governments, \$9,581m of which had been disbursed.[a] Of the latter sum, the largest takers had been the UK (\$4,277m), France (\$2,998m), Italy (\$1,631m), Belgium (\$349m) and Russia (\$188m).[2] After the Armistice, obligations were received for advances made for other purposes and under other Acts: surplus stores sold by the Secretary of War and the Secretary of the Navy, supplies furnished by the American Relief Administration and grain supplied by the United States Grain Corporation. On 15 November 1922, these debts amounted to \$715.8m. The British did not borrow under these schemes.[3]

It will be recalled that the Liberty Bond Acts authorised the Secretary of the Treasury, with the approval of the President, to establish credits in the USA for foreign governments 'engaged in war with the enemies of the United States' with 'the purpose of more effectually providing for the national security and defense and prosecuting the war' (p. 247). The authority ceased on the 'termination of the war between the United States and the Imperial German Government'. The first Act did not specify whether this meant an Armistice, the signature of a peace treaty, or ratification, but the second Act stipulated that the date was to be fixed by Presidential proclamation. The ambiguity was to be the opportunity for Congressional attack when the Treasury continued to make advances between the Armistice (11 November 1918) and the official end of the war (2 July 1921) to enable governments to meet commitments made in the USA 'in connection with the prosecution of the war.'[4]

Once a credit had been established, the Secretary of the Treasury could make disbursements to the borrower, up to the limit of the credit, for purposes of which he approved. The representatives of the borrowing governments on drawing the cash signed promissory notes, certificates of indebtedness, which were payable on demand. The certificates, bearing interest at a specified rate and payable in gold coin of the USA, contained the agreement of the borrower to convert them, at the request of the Secretary of the Treasury, into an equal nominal amount of Bonds conforming to the provisions of the Act under whose authority the money was advanced. Thus, the terms of the relevant Liberty Bond Act governed the terms of the obligation of the borrower.[5]

The machinery for making advances established under the First Act remained unchanged in subsequent Acts, but the Secretary's discretion to determine the terms of the obligations was altered. In common with those for British advances to its allies and Empire, the First Act aimed to hold the US Treasury harmless by ordering that the obligations be issued 'bearing the same rate of interest and containing in their essentials the same terms and conditions' as the securities sold to US investors under the Act.[6] The Second widened the Secretary's powers by

a The advances were made under powers granted by the four Acts approved by the President on 24 April and 24 September 1917 and on 4 April and 9 July 1918. No advances to foreign governments were made under a fifth Act, the Victory Liberty Loan Act, approved on 3 March 1919. The most important Acts determining the Treasury's powers were the First and Second, the Third and Fourth Acts being mainly concerned with increasing the size of the authorisations. The Acts authorised credits of up to \$10,000m.

authorising him to buy obligations 'containing such terms and conditions as...[he] may from time to time determine', but then added three restrictions: the interest rates could be no lower than the highest rate borne by any Liberty Bonds at the time the obligations were bought; the interest rate on the Bonds into which the demand obligations were converted could be no lower than the rate borne by the short-term obligations themselves; and the obligations had to mature 'at such date or dates, not later than the Bonds of the United States then last issued [under the First and Second Acts]'.[7] The last condition meant a final date of 15 June 1947 for advances made under the First Act and 15 October 1938 for the remainder. These dates were subsequently confirmed by the Victory Liberty Loan Act in 1919.[8] That borrowers should enjoy the longest date was never given statutory authority and it was not until 1920 that the Secretary said publicly that he thought that borrowing governments should be allowed the full periods.[9]

Following British precedent, the first two Acts gave holders of Liberty Bonds the option to convert into later wartime issues bearing higher interest rates: Bonds issued under the First Act could be converted into Bonds issued under the Second Act, and both could be converted into those issued under the Third.[b] Congress stipulated that the rate charged on advances should be raised to reflect any increase in the cost of servicing the Liberty Bonds which resulted from conversions; if half an issue was converted, half of the advances derived from that issue should likewise carry the higher rate.[10] This meant that \$1,155m advances to Britain (those made from the proceeds of securities issued under the First Act) carried a rate of 3½ per cent, but that this was reduced to \$774.6m once holders had used their conversion options.[11]

In the event, Congress unintentionally blurred both restrictions and calculations by attaching a string of tax privileges to the Liberty Bond Act securities. These differed from issue to issue, so that the cost to the US Treasury in revenue forgone changed every time a holder converted. Even when the war was over and the First and Second issues of Liberty Bonds no longer enjoyed the privilege of conversion into new issues, the cost of servicing the obligations would change whenever taxes changed. The margin to be added to the apparent yield was not, therefore, calculable, or even stable; in February 1919, market prices implied that investors valued the tax privileges as at least ¾ per cent per annum in the yield.[12]

Two other restrictions were to be central to the negotiations. While the First Act, by stipulating the 'same terms and conditions', required the US Treasury to convert demand obligations into longer securities which matched the maturity of the Liberty Bonds, the later Acts gave the Secretary discretion over the 'form and terms' of conversion, within the interest rate and maturity constraints already described:

> The Secretary of the Treasury is hereby authorised...to convert any short-time obligations of foreign governments which may have been purchased

b The result is dramatically shown by a list of tax-exemptions published in the *ARSF*, 1920, pp. 97–8.

> under the authority [of the Acts] into long-time obligations…in such form and terms as the Secretary of the Treasury may prescribe.

They also gave the Secretary the power

> under such terms and conditions as he may from time to time prescribe, to receive payment, on or before maturity…and, with the approval of the President, to sell any of such obligations (but not at less than the purchase price with accrued interest unless otherwise hereafter provided by law), and to apply the proceeds thereof, and any payments so received from foreign governments on account of the principal of such obligations, to the redemption and purchase, at not more than par and accrued interest, of any bonds of the United States [issued under authority of the First and Second Acts].[13]

Finally, in contrast to the detailed restrictions on the interest rates and the ordering of the application of monies repaid or raised from the sale of obligations, the Acts were silent on whether repayment of principal was to be demanded before maturity and in what manner. It was only in 1920, in its *Annual Report*, that the Secretary said that a 'moderate' sinking fund was desirable. It never received statutory authority.[14]

Negotiations between the summers of 1917 and 1919

Between 1917 and 1919, there were occasional skirmishes between the US and the UK Treasuries, but detailed negotiations about the conversion of the demand obligations and the design of the Bonds did not begin until autumn 1919. In August 1917, to satisfy the terms of the First Liberty Bond Act, which required the US Treasury to purchase obligations whose terms matched the securities it was selling, Oscar Crosby (the Assistant Secretary) raised with debtors the question of conversion and submitted the draft of a Bond. In London, the Chancellor found two of the proposed terms particularly objectionable: an exemption from UK, Dominion or colonial taxation, on principal and interest, irrespective of the country of residence of the holder; and a clause giving holders the option of payment in sterling over the entire life of the securities. Negotiations took place during the autumn, but wartime was no time for prolonged discussion of details and, in any case, the Second Act, approved in October, gave the Secretary discretion over whether to request conversion. Sometime in November, the matter was shelved.

In May 1918, Chalmers enquired whether the certificates of indebtedness were to be automatically converted into long-term Bonds and, if so, in what form. Leffingwell's reply drew attention to the US Secretary's discretion under the Second and Third Liberty Bond Acts to decide how to treat the certificates and was, according to one unpublished official history, the moment when the Treasury in London realised the discretion which the Secretary had been given to determine the form of the Bonds or, even, whether to call for Bonds at all.[15] In July 1918, an anxious Treasury asked Reading to clarify the US Treasury's intentions.

Leffingwell told him he had not had time to consider the details of the Bonds to be issued under the terms of the First Act and that he thought it best to keep advances made under the later Acts as demand obligations until after the war when 'the whole question of inter allied indebtedness will have to be considered broadly from a variety of standpoints.' The question was then dropped.[16]

In October 1918, Rathbone informed the British that the interest rate for the six months to 15 November would be 5 per cent, the margin over the rate on Liberty Bonds meeting the cost of printing, issuing and advertising, the tax privileges and the rate on certificates. The Treasury considered the rate to be justified, but only if the obligations were treated as if they were long-term. This, Rathbone vehemently denied. The Chancellor failed to understand that:

> the borrowings of your government, with the exception of the advance under the original act, remain in point of form of short period…the obligations in question are in form and in fact demand obligations and, as your government has long since been advised, as to such obligations the Secretary of the Treasury is under no commitment whatsoever to convert them into long-time obligations. The Secretary of the Treasury is entirely free to demand their payment at any time.[17]

The Chancellor's reply stressed that the legal position was of little importance. 'Of course' he was aware that the obligations were in demand form, but he understood that this was only wanted until the US Treasury had designed the permanent obligations. He understood that there was no intention to demand payment 'or to take any other advantage from the present form of the obligations except to retain a free hand as to the manner in which they shall be eventually funded', and added that this 'had, of course, always been the informal understanding between the responsible representatives of both Governments'.[18]

The Armistice signed, on 23 December 1918 the Chancellor instructed Lever to open funding discussions and by the middle of February 1919 an informal exchange of views had taken place which provided an outline of US and British attitudes.[19] Lever reported that the Americans, whatever they expected of other governments, assumed that the British would want to repay as soon as possible. Opening a line of argument that was often to be repeated, they expected the US and UK terms for common debtors to be similar, but there was no need for the terms given by the Americans to the British to be the same as those given to others. Negotiations should be between individual creditors and debtors and take account of reparations and the terms of settlements already made with other creditors. Thus, there could be no general settlement, although negotiations could take place simultaneously. Without further legislation, all terms had to be included in the Bonds and, therefore, within the powers already provided by the Liberty Bond Acts. This made the longest terms 15 October 1938 and 15 July 1947. The interest rate would be 5 per cent. At least some repayment should take place during the life of the Bonds, possibly by means of annuities or by issuing them in series maturing every few years. Some provision should be included enabling the Bonds to be used to support the dollar, perhaps by giving an option for repayment in sterling at pre-war par. 'Impressed by the inconveniences that arise from holding by one Government and [*sic*] of large amount of obligations of another Government', the Bonds should be suitable for resale to the general public. Finally, there should be special arrangements to cover subrogated securities and the advances made under the Pittman Act.

Although the British changed their minds in the autumn, they had at this stage no objection in principle to giving a Bond suitable for resale in the markets, provided the yield was not such as to draw capital from the UK. Nor did they object to an arrangement to protect the dollar, although they preferred an undertaking to sell sterling and use the dollars to repay the US Treasury, over giving the USA the right to sell sterling Bonds and apply the proceeds to the purchase of dollars. Repayment was another matter:

> it is clear…that we cannot at this stage contemplate entering into an engagement to redeem our debt on the annuity system or even to repay the principal at intervals of say 5 years. It will, I think, be obvious to the United States Treasury that we cannot enter into definite commitments as to the reduction of our capital indebtedness until the future becomes clearer. Our debt to the United States cannot be divorced from the debts of France and Italy to ourselves, and our power to pay the former is to a very considerable extent determined by the rate at which the latter can be repaid to us.

Moreover, the British should have precedence in collecting these debts. The USA recognised the British case for flexibility in repayment of principal, agreed that definite commitment should wait on the settlement of reparations, but did not accept that French and Italian debts to the British should have priority over those to the USA.[20]

The Blackett–Rathbone talks

The interest due on 15 April and 15 May 1919 was met from US advances. The last credit for the UK under the 'special' arrangement, for $80m, was established on 14 May 1919 and the last cash was taken on 25 June.[21] Towards the end of July, Strong, on a visit to Europe, cabled Leffingwell from London that financial circles considered the 'indefiniteness' of the terms of the US Treasury debt to be a 'latent menace.' The USA was no longer providing credits, sterling was weak and the time was approaching when dollars would have to be bought for the interest due in November. The City expected exchange rate difficulties to come to a head in the autumn. More relief would be given by defining the debt than 'anything else we can do'.[22] Leffingwell's reaction was brusque. The US Treasury was ready to discuss conversion at any time, but there had been no British Ambassador or High Commissioner in Washington for months. If British bankers were worried, they should press their government to act.[23] Almost as he wrote, policy was changing. On 8 August, Blackett reported that the US Treasury wanted to begin funding talks. Five days later, Leffingwell, in a briefing for the Secretary, warned of 'catastrophe, political, economic/and social' in Europe which would spread to the USA through trade and example. To make peace permanent, the Treaty of Versailles had to be ratified and the League established with US membership; business could only flourish where political boundaries and commercial risks were known. A few days later, the US Treasury informed the French and British that funding discussions should begin at 'the earliest opportunity', although as Leffingwell told Strong 'The truth is that our whole plan for financing Europe…must remain in abeyance pending the ratification of the treaty'.[24]

The political struggle over the Treaty delayed the US Treasury's next move on the debt for six weeks. In the middle of August, the Secretary drafted a letter outlining the terms on which he envisaged deferring interest for the reconstruction period and asserting that the Liberty Bond Acts gave him the necessary powers so long as it was part of a funding of the demand obligations. The Treasury sent the letter to Wilson with a view to publication, but the President was fighting for his League of Nations and the Treaty. On 3 September, he left Washington to take his case to the country. The letter was not published until 26 September, the day the President collapsed.[25]

At the end of August, the Chancellor had agreed that Blackett should resume informal discussions on the understanding that there was no commitment until the Treasury had had the opportunity of 'carefully considering the terms'.[26] Talks were to continue until May of the following year, first in Washington and then, when Blackett was appointed Controller of Finance in the reorganised Treasury and Rathbone went to Europe as the US Treasury's Representative, in London and Paris. They covered eight related topics: the terms for deferring interest payments, including the terms the British would offer their debtors; the terms for repayment of principal; the conditions under which the Bonds could be used by the USA to support the dollar; the interest rate; the release of the subrogated British securities; the terms for repaying the advances used to buy silver under the Pittman Act; reimbursement of the UK's expenditure in neutral countries on behalf of France, Italy and Belgium; and the repayment of US advances used to relieve famine in Austria. The results were contained in drafts of memoranda produced by Rathbone on 10 May, which Blackett saw, and another, dated 22 May, embodying points discussed between the two officials in the interval, which he never saw. As Mellon was careful to stress two years later, the two men had known each other for some years and the talks were

> most informal, and the drafts of memoranda and of forms of proposed obligation were merely a means of putting on paper, as a convenient basis of discussion, the suggestions of both. The papers cannot be said to have been in any sense the drafts or proposals of either, and the fact that any provision is contained in them does not indicate that either was prepared to agree to it.

Thus, even apart from the question whether the terms would have been acceptable to either government, we do not know whether they were acceptable to Blackett himself.[27]

Interest

The talks moved to Paris on 1 and 2 November 1919 and, after exchanges of letters on 8 and 18 November and 14 January, were resumed on 15 January 1920. In contrast to the negotiations between the Baldwin Mission and the USA in January 1923, the rate of interest on the new British Bonds was agreed without difficulty. Blackett was merely instructed 'to secure some evidence in support of the claim that...the rate is justified' by the cost of raising the money, before 'finally' agreeing to 5 per cent. Rathbone's opening proposal used 5 per cent throughout and Blackett did not even think it necessary to mention the rate in his Memorandum of the talks.[28] Instead, the negotiations centred on deferral of the interest. These went well at first. Blackett's instructions were to win a breathing space of at least three years and ensure no interest was paid on the postponed interest. On 1 November, on his own initiative, Rathbone proposed deferral, giving as an example Bonds for which the interest was postponed for three years and repaid between October 1922 and October 1934 at rates rising from 1/2 per cent a year to 1 1/2 per cent a year.[29] There was further discussion of postponement in January and, at the beginning of February, Blackett confirmed the Chancellor's understanding that three years' postponement would be agreed when the UK Treasury requested it.[30]

This was running well ahead of domestic US politics. The Secretary's assertion that he had the power to defer interest so long as it was part of a funding operation had provoked such an adverse reaction in Congress that on 18 December he had written to the Chairman of the House Ways and Means Committee, Joseph Fordney, and the Chairman of the Senate Finance Committee, Boies Penrose, telling them that, although he was advised that he already had the power to defer interest, he would introduce legislation should the Ways and Means Committee question it. His defence, tailored to an increasingly isolationist Congress, was pitched in terms of American self-interest. The European currencies were at massive discounts to their par values and payment of interest would drive them lower, damaging the demand for US produce without making any additional dollars available to the debtors. The Europeans could not use gold to settle the debts because their entire stock of gold would only cover two years' interest. Unless the debtors were given time to recover, they would never be able to pay either interest or principal.[31]

No doubt such arguments were the only way to approach Congress, but they meant that the US Treasury could only defend postponement on the grounds that it was necessary because payment was impossible and the alternative default. The implication was that any country able to pay should be made to pay, or the US Treasury would have misled the legislature. The UK was the largest debtor, the only country with which serious negotiations were being conducted, and subject to hostile lobbying from the usual groups. It was in a clearly healthier condition than its allies, with a narrowing deficit on both budgetary and external accounts. In the middle of January, the Chancellor touched this nerve when, in seeking to clarify US intentions, he said that he would rather pay the interest, irrespective of the effect on the exchange rate, than be liable for interest on interest. The admission of financial strength prompted Davis and Leffingwell to question whether they had been justified in asking Congress to remit the full three years' interest and to consider imposing a condition that the British give credits to France and Italy. They thought they should protect themselves by asking for a formal written request for postponement, couched in terms of necessity.[32]

Two difficulties grew out of this. First, the UK Treasury was not prepared to have its credit damaged by an admission of financial weakness sufficiently bald to satisfy the US Treasury that it could demonstrate to Congress that there was no alternative to deferral. As Blackett's draft request put it,

> The British Government is not prepared to say that it would be impossible for it to make payment...In such a matter there is a distinction between absolute inability to pay and the necessity of finding means of relieving what might prove an intolerable burden.

Second, the British draft request claimed it would be a 'simple matter' to pay the interest if it were possible to collect interest from its own debtors. To do this, Blackett said, would be contrary to the British and American view that it was undesirable to try to extract payments from continental Europe and inconsistent with the plans for a common approach to common debtors. The draft then proposed that both Treasuries offer deferral to their debtors for three years and convert obligations into Bonds bearing similar terms.[33]

This was irrelevant to a US Treasury which was attempting to tailor the British request to a Congress which would only sanction deferral for those able to show that it was a necessity and which could not accept that there was any connection between others' debts to the British and British debts to the USA. Undisguised irritation enters into the cables passing to Rathbone. Although agreeing that necessity existed, and sympathising with the British unwillingness to say unequivocally that they could not pay, Davis thought that the draft would not provide a defence against Congressional attack and would discredit his own evidence to the Ways and Means Committee: 'Do not...think Treasury should act on mere argumentative statement resting in substantial part upon claim that British necessity arises out of inability to collect interest from governments debtor to her.'[34]

The US Treasury officials thought there were three ways of dealing with Congress: they could press for legislation to enable them to postpone the interest; they could argue with the Ways and Means Committee about the extent of the US Treasury's powers; or they could, with the Committee's permission, continue negotiations and then present the result to Congress for statutory sanction.[35] They chose the second course, and spent three months negotiating with the Committee, which did not withdraw its objection until 2 April. Rathbone's discussions came to a standstill. It was not until 30 April that he presented the British with a new draft of the Bond, which was then refined in discussion with Blackett until 10 May.[36]

Repayment and the sterling option

The discussions about the terms on which the Bonds would be repaid fell into five related parts: final maturity, sinking funds, options to repay before the final maturity date, terms under which the USA could obtain sterling with which to support the dollar, and marketability. Final maturity was agreed without difficulty. Blackett returned to London in the autumn of 1919 believing that the US Treasury would propose the longest dates authorised by the Liberty Bond Acts and, on 1 November, Rathbone duly presented arrangements based on two series of Bonds, maturing on 15 October 1938 and 15 June 1947.[37] These were the dates specified in Blackett's instructions and the Chancellor duly accepted them.[38]

The sinking fund was only a little less easy. Rathbone's approach was thoroughly orthodox and would have been heartily endorsed by a Bradbury, a Blackett or a Niemeyer in a domestic context: the 'soundness' of sinking funds were 'universally recognised', they were 'important in principle' and they should be welcomed by the debtors as 'providing for a gradual and orderly extinguishment of debt', allowing budgets to be planned. However, the reasons cited earlier in the year for the UK not being bound to a rigid programme of repayment still stood.

Rathbone's first proposal, which seems to have been worked out on the back of an envelope, involved a partial sinking fund. For both series of Bonds it would start in 1928 at a rate of 1/2 per cent a year, rising to 2 1/2 per cent (over $100m a year) in 1934. Equal annual instalments for unequal periods produced very different results by the due dates, 17.8 per cent being paid off in the case of the shorter Bonds and 55.7 per cent in the case of the longer. Blackett was quick to point out that the latter was too high and as the rates were only illustrative Rathbone was happy to ask for alternatives.[39] He reacted positively when these were presented to him in mid-January; the postponed interest would be repaid by 1934 and a sinking fund on the main body of the debt would repay 11 per cent on the Bonds maturing in 1938 and 28.7 per cent on those maturing in 1947.[40] Because the sinking fund would make the Bonds less attractive to private investors, the US Treasury asked for an option to discontinue it when the large denomination Bonds were converted into saleable smaller sizes. This was included in both 10 and 22 May drafts.[41]

The right of early repayment, the terms on which the USA could have access to sterling with which to support its exchange rate and the right of sale of British obligations to private investors were the subject of prolonged negotiation, mainly because the objectives of the British were the mirror image of those of the Americans: the British wanted to be free to repay whenever it suited them and the USA wanted to be able to turn the British obligations into sterling cash whenever the dollar fell beneath pre-war par. Both threatened loss of national control over the money markets, which neither Treasury was prepared to grant. As Rathbone put it:

> All the arguments that you [Leffingwell and Davis] employ against granting the British the right at their option to repay obligations…prior to maturity

> apply with greater force to an objection on the part of the British to granting to the United States this unlimited right [to sell the British Bonds in the UK].[42]

Behind the US Treasury's demand for access to sterling lay a fear that the transfer of economic and financial power to the USA might only be temporary, brought about by war, and that the UK's industrial and financial capacity would soon be restored. 'We are convinced', cabled Davis in April 1920, 'that British position will under wise arrangements be rehabilitated quickly and British will ultimately be able to repay loans'.[43] In October 1919, in a philosophical vein, Leffingwell told Rathbone it was not possible

> to foretell the history of the world. Five years ago the occurrence of the events which turned Great Britain from a creditor to a debtor would have seemed impossible. While there is no reason to suppose that during the life of the Bonds the balance will again be reversed, it is equally impossible to be sure that it will not.

The US Treasury would look very foolish if it owned $10,000m of foreign government obligations and was unable to use them in an emergency.[44] This anxiety was aggravated by a specific, and immediate, worry that the USA might be drained of the gold it had accumulated during the war. Towards the end of 1919 and in the first half of 1920, as Blackett and Rathbone talked, the British balance of payments was moving into surplus and US gold stocks contracting as the metal was shipped to South America and the Far East. This was caused, the US Treasury believed, by other countries, including the UK, selling their dollar balances to buy gold to cover their bilateral payments deficits with those regions. Hence, the advice proffered to the British in January 1920 – that they should not buy gold in the USA and ship it to pay off their yen debts – and the anger in the US Treasury in May 1920 when the British took up a maturing Argentinian government loan in New York so that Argentina had no need to ship gold to the USA (Table 6.3).[45]

If the US attitude was based on an apprehension that fortune's wheel might turn again, the British view of the Bonds was based on a blend of a realisation of their own current weakness and confidence in the recovery of the UK economy and public finances. The Treasury saw four advantages in having the right to make early repayment. By matching repayments by the allies and German reparations with their own payments to the USA, they could ease the burden on their exchange rate and budget while making the US Treasury recognise a connection between the inflow to the UK and the outflow to the USA. If they could choose their own moment for repayment, they could convert foreign currency debt into sterling debt with the minimum pain and at times of sterling strength, in the manner of the dollar Notes and Bonds issued on 1 November 1919. With the option, they need not fear locking themselves into capital repayments, which subsequent events might make unduly burdensome. And, finally, by attaching to the Bonds repayments of principal of unknown amounts and date, they hoped to make the Bonds less attractive to potential purchasers in the private markets.

Rathbone tended to sympathise with the British insistence that they have the option of early repayment, provided that any deferred interest had been paid and there was no cost to the US Treasury. Davis was less understanding.[46] Disagreement came to a head in the middle of May, at a time when Washington was urging Rathbone to take a stronger line in the negotiations. Davis thought the British were gaining sufficient advantage by borrowing at 5 per cent when they were paying higher rates in sterling; perhaps Treasury Bills or $5^3/_4$ per cent Exchequer Bonds 1925, issued in January, had caught his eye, although both were a very different type of security:

> It is not customary for the borrower to have the right to pay off long-time obligations at his leisure without giving to the holder of the Bonds some similar right to call for redemption prior to maturity…England's right to pay off any or all of their Bonds at leisure irrespective of our convenience would give them a control over our money market which we are not prepared to grant.[47]

When the talks were broken off, Rathbone had successfully resisted the British demand for the right to repayment at any time. Blackett's most recent response had been a proposal well designed to provoke Davis's ire: a provision whereby the British had the option to repay on the same dates in 1928 and 1938 as the US Treasury's own wartime obligations matured.[48]

The US Treasury's 1917 draft of the Bond included both marketability and an option for the principal and interest to be paid in sterling at a fixed rate of $4.865. The UK resisted the latter because, at a given level of yields, it would make the British Government's dollar Bonds more attractive to British investors than its sterling debt and the price of an option extending for twenty or thirty years could not be calculated. During the negotiations at the end of 1918 and beginning of 1919, the UK had agreed that in principle the obligations should be available to safeguard the dollar, but proposed that the mechanism should not be redemption of the UK's Bonds, as the US Treasury had suggested, but an undertaking by the UK to buy dollars. The USA accepted this arrangement and, in September 1919, Blackett was instructed to agree to the UK buying sufficient dollars to stop the rate depreciating below pre-war par so long as the US Treasury held British debt.[49] The question of whether, or how many of, the dollars thus acquired could be retained by the British for general use and how much should be applied to repayment seems to have been ignored during November, but in January Rathbone proposed that all deferred interest should become payable as soon as sterling returned to par.[50]

Despite the protection provided by this, the US Treasury pressed for the right to sell the Bonds, both in the USA and the UK. To the desire to defend itself against an unknown future and the potential for misunderstanding of owning claims on another government was added the more pedantic consideration that the US Treasury should enjoy the full rights attaching to the ownership of the Bonds and the sense that it should not deny itself powers contained in the Liberty Bond Acts, even if the rights were only permissive.

Blackett's instructions were to persuade the USA that the Bonds should be unmarketable and, if he met resistance, to try to have the right to sell postponed for ten years, by which time, it was assumed, UK finances would have recovered. The instructions also drew attention to the possibility of drawing the terms so that although 'ostensibly saleable' the Bonds would be so unsuitable as an investment that private investors would never buy them.[51] The US Treasury was sympathetic to the UK's anxieties: it was only too aware that the restrictions placed by the Liberty Bond Acts on the price at which it could sell the obligations made disposal improbable. It wanted to encourage foreign government borrowing on its private markets and saw that the obvious course was not the sale of the US Treasury's British Bonds, but public borrowing by the UK, with the proceeds used to repay the American holdings. All the same, the US Treasury thought that it was unable to deny itself the formal right to sale.[52] Rathbone helpfully suggested the Bonds be issued for such high denominations that they would be difficult to market and only convertible into saleable sizes after an agreed interval: five years, said the Americans; ten years, said the British. This would still leave the British vulnerable to the sale of certificates of participation in the Bonds and the Chancellor pressed for complete protection: agreement that the Bonds would not be sold, hypothecated or dealt in for their entire lives. Rathbone would go no further in surrendering his rights of ownership. Once again stressing the need to protect their market operations in the USA, the British proposed that they have the right to redeem the Bonds before the US Treasury offered them for sale and a period of notice which would enable them to raise funds in the market should they decide to exercise the right.

The length of the protected period, and the size of the Bonds in the meantime, had been only tentatively agreed when negotiations were called off. The previous November, Blackett had proposed Bonds of $1,000m, a grotesque size, which six months later Davis was to call 'indefensible'. In May, Davis returned to the question, telling Rathbone that, unless he had committed himself to five years, he should try to have the fallow period eliminated or shortened. In any event, the Bonds should not be greater than $1m because the UK balance of trade might turn favourable within a few years.[53] Rathbone resisted: he felt bound by his earlier agreement, pointed out that certificates of participation could be sold at any time and refused to reopen the matter without specific instructions.[54]

Subrogation

Writing in February 1919, Lever warned that the US Treasury had on occasions 'shown an inclination' to regard the securities subrogated to it as available for sale. In resisting this, the British argued that the securities were not owned by the UK Treasury but only borrowed, and that the rights of the underlying holders should be protected. The USA, not concerned in the commitment to the owners, claimed that its rights were superior. It was probable, said Lever, that the UK would be pressed to release the securities by making an early public issue in the USA and using the proceeds to repay those advances applied to the maturities of 1 February and 1 November 1918.[55] When negotiations opened at the beginning of November 1919, Rathbone stressed that it was not the intention of Congress that advances should be used to repay debts incurred before the USA entered the war and suggested that they should be separated from the main body of the obligations and converted into five-year Bonds. Following his Instructions, Blackett pressed hard, threatening to open negotiations for parallel repayment from the continental allies, emphasising the importance of the securities' release and pointing to the arrangement made between the USA and the French in December 1918 and January 1919, which provided for the repayment of part of France's pre-April 1917 debt without subrogation having been demanded.

Blackett saw flexibility in the US position when Rathbone suggested that the advances might be liquidated by the gradual sale of the collateral or that other securities, such as Belgian government post-Armistice Bonds, might be substituted for those borrowed.[56] He was right, for during November and December the American attitude changed. It originated with Leffingwell, who had not sympathised with McAdoo's original demand for subrogation and who now argued that its continuation would damage US interests. When introduced in February 1918, subrogation had been designed to put the advances onto a different basis from other credits in case Congress learnt of the transaction. This was no longer necessary, McAdoo having told Congress about the advances when the Fourth Liberty Loan Bill was being considered. Also, with the end of the Armistice, it was no longer necessary for the USA to have access to British securities for borrowing in neutral countries. The legal position helped the British case. The agreement gave the US Treasury the right to call for the securities to be subrogated to it, but it had never exercised the right and they remained deposited with Morgans. Its officers agreed that, whereas the US Treasury would have required Congressional authority to return the securities, had they been pledged, it did not need authority to refrain from exercising the right. The securities to which the right of subrogation applied were constantly changing and, with US Treasury permission, substitutions were made when sinking funds operated or Bonds matured. The right of subrogation was not attached to any particular British obligations and the securities withdrawn when the British made repayments were not identified. There were also the practical and commercial aspects. Neither Congress nor the American and British public had been told about the arrangement. The proportion of the total advances covered by the subrogated securities was small and the existence of a few secured obligations reduced the value of the unsecured balance. The US Treasury believed that its claim was an embarrassment to British finance, contributing to the weakness of sterling and thus reducing the demand for US exports. It accepted that the British government had grounds to fear the political consequences if its public learnt of the arrangement when security had never been demanded when the British made advances.

The arguments, developed by Leffingwell, were accepted by Davis and, in the middle of December, Rathbone was told that the right of subrogation was undesirable and should be surrendered. Blackett was not told of the change in policy, which Davis described as 'a very unimportant concession' for the USA, although of considerable value to the British. Instead, surrender of the right was to be used as a lever with which to settle other matters.[57] In May, the British tried unsuccessfully to detach the release of the securities from the general settlement of the debt. The US attitude was hardening: Davis thought that the US Treasury should show that its patience was exhausted, and he suspected that the British were in a weak position as the securities might be needed to help with the French half of the Anglo-French Loan.[58]

The 'larger' question

Throughout the negotiations the more general question of inter-allied indebtedness kept intruding itself. British policy was formally spelt out in September 1919 in Blackett's Instructions. After stressing that the British debt to the USA came 'largely if not entirely' from British lending to the allies, both before and after April 1917, they repeated the statement made the previous February:

> Similarly [to the origins of the debt] the power of the British Treasury to pay interest and eventually to repay principal to the United States Treasury depends largely if not entirely upon the arrangements made for the payment of interest and repayment of principal by the other Allied Governments upon their obligations held by the British Treasury.

It followed that until the UK Treasury knew the views of the US Treasury regarding the obligations (including those of the UK) held by it, the Chancellor could make proposals neither to his debtors nor to his own creditor, the US Treasury. That said, he was 'so seriously concerned at the political and diplomatic dangers which may arise…from the existence of a large body of debts due to one Allied and Associated Government to another that he would be glad, as part of a general arrangement between Governments for dealing with Inter-Allied indebtedness' to recommend to Parliament the cancellation of the obligations represented by British advances to its allies. The Chancellor was also ready, provided it was part of a general arrangement, to agree to a less radical solution, such as a complete or partial deferral of interest, reduction in the principal of the British-held obligations or the conversion of whole or part into German Reparation Bonds.[59]

The negotiations which followed had been carried out on the decks of a steamer. Blackett made clear that agreement on the terms of conversion was without prejudice to the 'larger' and more 'general question' of inter-allied debts, making reference to allied repayments as one of the determinants of Britain's ability to repay the USA. Rathbone refused to recognise any connection and emphasised that their agreements were always tentative and subject to the Secretary's final word. Such was the lack of common ground on the strategic issues that it is not surprising that, when the participants looked up from their deckchairs, the negotiations faltered and, finally, collapsed. Three episodes give the flavour. After the first talks at the beginning of November, Blackett emphasised that the Chancellor was agreeing the terms for conversion provided they did not 'in any way prejudice the general question of Inter-Allied Indebtedness, to the ultimate settlement of which along broad lines he attaches great importance'. Rathbone replied that he did not know what Blackett meant, but the US Treasury had not changed its view or modified its position and regarded 'the obligations of the various allied Governments held by the Government of the United States as representing the debt of each' to the USA.[60] The talks continued. On 22 January 1920, as the discussion moved to the period for which interest should be postponed, Rathbone reported that the British 'constantly refer to payment to them of their loans as a means by which they can pay moneys borrowed from us'. Davis, temporarily acting as Secretary of State, retorted that:

> Blackett's contention that British cannot postpone payment of interest to its [*sic*] debtors unless United States postpones payment of interest to Great Britain [*sic*] is not sound…The British could not collect interest from the Allies now if they wanted to do so, whether or not we extend their interest, and they have no intention whatever of attempting it. This contention is merely a continuing attempt to give a relation between the respective debts which as you have explained does not exist…if we postpone collection of interest from British…it will be because the British Government requires such assistance and not because they forgo or fail in collecting interest from the other Allied Governments.[61]

At the end of March, Davis asked Rathbone for his views on deferring British interest for two years and that of the other European debtors for three. Two reasons for different treatment were reasonable: the condition of UK finances made it less necessary for the British interest to be deferred and they had announced their intention of repaying their moiety of the Anglo-French Loan in cash, thus demonstrating that they were in less need of help; the other could only have come from irritation, the British had 'endeavoured to make their payment of interest to us conditional upon collecting from her debtors'.[62]

Disagreement about the 'larger' issues surfaced in February. On 26 January, Rathbone told the Treasury in Washington that he sensed that the British believed that the burden of inter-allied debts could not be sustained and that some adjustment or cancellation was inevitable. They would not make the request, but they would be happy to cancel their advances to the allies, provided the US Treasury cancelled its advances to them. He added that the USA must be careful not to play into their hands: if the USA demanded interest, the other allies would default, the British would pay and then exploit the situation to produce a general readjustment of debt from which they would benefit.[63]

The same day, Leffingwell told Ronald Lindsay, British Counsellor in Washington, that he saw the Continent of Europe as 'irretrievably lost' and the UK as being 'gravely imperilled by the danger so created'. He asked whether the Chancellor saw grounds for optimism and for his assessment of the outlook.[64] This enquiry coincided with the furore in Congress over the deferral of interest and came just after the meeting between Rathbone and Blackett in the middle of January, when it had become clear that the British had failed to win several of the more important arguments: there was to be a sinking fund, a sterling option at pre-war par, marketability after five years, with no protection against sales by means of participation certificates in the meantime. UK officials and, in particular, Blackett were increasingly frustrated that the talks were being limited to the terms for the postponement of interest and funding the obligations. There were strong and, they believed, compelling reasons for general cancellation, which they had placed before US officials and, most recently, before Rathbone. These approaches had been informal and the Americans had brushed them aside; cancellation had never been officially tabled.

The UK Treasury took advantage of Leffingwell's request to bring its policy into the open. On 4 February, Blackett, writing on behalf of the Chancellor, formally drew Rathbone's attention to the dangers posed by the inter-governmental debt and warned that interest deferral and funding might not bring sufficient relief. The British government had 'more than once' suggested informally that the two governments in concert should find 'some large solution of this problem', and the Chancellor had said that he was ready 'to take any steps toward relieving the governments which are debtors to the British Government of the burden of their debts which the United States Treasury might feel able to propose in regard to the obligations of the governments which it holds.'[65] Three days later, the Chancellor replied direct to Leffingwell, giving an optimistic account of the UK's own financial position, but describing the Continent as a prey to bankruptcy and, possibly, to anarchy, and a USA unable to provide credits because of financial 'difficulties' (a misinterpretation by Lindsay of an observation made to him by Leffingwell): it was 'largely because of these dangers that we should welcome a general cancellation of Inter-Governmental war debt.'[66]

On 6 February, the Chancellor circulated to the Cabinet a memorandum, written by Blackett, advocating that the British should unilaterally cancel the debts owed to them, while continuing to recognise their own to the USA. In places it is obscure and, in others, bitter. Blackett had been British Treasury Representative in the USA for over two, very active, years, liaising and negotiating with the heart of the US Administration and chiefly with the US Treasury itself. Yet the paper shows a lack of understanding of the workings of the US government machine in general, and the political situation in particular, which amounted to the wilful. Blackett's role was not to condemn the US Treasury for a failure to accept British policy, but to understand the reasons why it behaved as it did, with a view to more effectively shaping the approach of his government to influencing it. Nothing came of the paper, but it is an important waymark in the deterioration in Anglo-American financial relations.

British efforts to co-operate with the USA, wrote Blackett, 'have almost invariably meant that we have had to abandon without even putting on formal record the policies which we have favoured whether in great matters [cancellation] or in small [the terms of the Bonds]'. British policies had never penetrated beyond the individual US officers with whom they were discussed. Moreover,

> ...our attitude is almost invariably misrepresented...because the United States Treasury's sole preoccupation is usually to persuade an unwilling congress [*sic*] to take a small step forward in the direction desired by the United States Treasury, and it frequently does the persuading by putting forward arguments which are from our point of view irrelevant and unfair.

From the first, British policy had been to deflate the world's balance sheet. The government believed that the allies would never be able to repay their debts to the USA and the UK, and that they 'lay like a dead weight upon the credit of continental Europe and made reconstruction even slower and more painful than it need be'. The 'statesmanlike thing' was to wipe out the debts with a stroke of the pen. The British had put this informally to US officials, saying that they would like to propose it formally, but that this was difficult when the USA was their creditor; the USA was the only country which could make the proposal without being open to misinterpretation. The US Treasury had

> from the first been horrified with even the mention of such a plan. A few individuals outside the United States Treasury may have some inkling of the truth that these paper debts must ultimately be cancelled...but the United States Treasury itself seems incapable of appreciating the position and congress [*sic*] as usual is entirely ignorant of and untouched by the realities of the case.

During the negotiations on the terms of the Bonds and, especially, the deferment of interest, the US Treasury had 'abused its position as our creditor and [shown] its inability or unwillingness to tell Congress the truth for the purpose of making us accept whatever the [US Treasury] wants'. It often went further (as when asking that the UK request deferment on grounds of necessity) and demanded that 'we shall put forward its views as if they were being pressed on it by us':

> In order that we may secure postponement of all interest on inter-allied debts including interest on our debt to the United States of America, the United States Treasury demands that we should officially appear as the authors of this policy (which seems to us only a pis-aller) and should appear in the somewhat undignified attitude of supplicants...for relief.
>
> It is quite beyond the United States Treasury's vision to see that a handsome offer of postponement of interest originating in appearance at least from the generous creditor would be a far finer method of approach. Unfortunately even if the United States Treasury realised this fact, it would be far too much afraid of Congress to act on it.[67]

Chamberlain did not endorse Blackett's paper, but he agreed with the tone. In an angry moment the day before Blackett's paper was signed off, he privately described the American mind as 'so ignorant' of European conditions and so 'suspicious of English intentions' and so afraid of the electorate that 'they complicate every problem & give no help in settling any of them.' They were an impossible people in their foreign relations and there was no action the British could take which was right in their eyes.[68]

Had they seen these comments, the officers of the US Treasury would have thought that they showed a complete lack of understanding of the relationship between themselves and Congress. Their only powers were those provided under the Liberty Bond Acts, adjusted at the edges, after lengthy wrangles, by such matters of interpretation as the deferral of interest:

> Europe seems to overlook the fact that Congress alone has power to make any new financial arrangements and that no official who might even favour some composition could assume the moral responsibility of discussing such matters when knowing that in so far as we are concerned nothing else can come of it…

was to be Davis' comment, half-angry and half-despairing, at the end of April.[69] Indeed, Lindsay's report of Davis and Leffingwell's reaction to the British proposal was that they shared the British view that the debts were an 'extreme inconvenience' and that 'speaking abstractedly, both recognise desirability of writing them off.' The US Treasury was having difficulties with Congress over deferral because of its similarities to cancellation; they were a demonstration, if one were needed, that 'deflating the balance sheet' was not practical politics. A Presidential election was approaching – primaries were to be held between March and June – and politics and attitudes reflected the mood of a country wanting lower taxes and withdrawal from the complexities of a Europe which seemed unable, or unwilling, to help itself. Not only did the US Treasury believe that cancellation would be refused by Congress and the public, but it thought that the suggestion would make it more difficult for the Administration to play an active role in European diplomacy, while damaging the credit and reputation of any country making the proposal.[70]

Houston, who had replaced Glass as Secretary of the Treasury at the beginning of February, replied to Chamberlain's letter on 5 March. He stressed that cancellation would not be acceptable to either the American people or Congress and discussing it would raise hopes in the debtor countries 'of the efficacy and justice of such a plan', with damage when they were disappointed. He recognised general cancellation would be of advantage to the UK and involve her in no losses, but the USA had no debts and so cancellation would not 'involve mutual sacrifice…it simply involves a contribution mainly by the United States.' Europe's way forward was to return to work and to fiscal and monetary discipline. Chamberlain's reply was dignified; he appreciated the Secretary's attitude towards the war debts, but Leffingwell had asked for his views and he had wanted to answer him fully. The proposal would not be repeated.[71]

Breakdown: May and June 1920

In January, shortly after his second round of talks with Blackett, Rathbone cabled that he had made it plain that, while he knew the Secretary's general views, 'arrangement would have to go to him for his approval which would depend in part upon general European situation and manner in which program of general economic and financial readjustment was being dealt with.' He described the US Treasury's plan as the negotiation of the funding terms, which would include postponement of interest for a period which was to be at the Secretary's discretion. Exchange would not take place until the Secretary was satisfied that 'other matters requisite for the financial and economical rehabilitation of Europe had been provided for,' the most important of which was reparations. This would enable the Secretary to keep open the option of whether to defer the interest until the exchange took place.[72] The plan and the flexibility it gave to the US Treasury became crucial in February and March when the House Ways and Means Committee was deciding whether the Secretary had authority to defer interest, for, if the Committee decided to challenge him, he would have to delay the exchange until he had new powers. Indeed, cabled Houston on 20 April, political conditions were such that there was never 'immunity from sudden attack' and Congress could modify the Liberty Bond Acts and his right to postpone interest at any time until the obligations were exchanged.[73]

Although the British government knew that Rathbone's agreements were only provisional and final approval had to come from the Secretary of the Treasury, it was apparently unaware until May of the wide range of political, financial and economic matters that the Secretary wanted to see adjusted before the obligations were exchanged. Conditionality had become a real, rather than a theoretical, possibility. American officials were exercised by the British decision, taken without consultation, to take up the Argentinian maturity in New York. They also felt that their difficulties with Congress had been increased when the British decided to repay their half of the Anglo-French Loan in cash, a decision which was also announced without consultation. On 25 April, the San Remo oil agreement was confirmed by Lloyd George and Alexandre Millerand, and on 12 May the US Ambassador in London delivered a strong Note to the Foreign Office listing US grievances about British oil policy in the mandated territories.[c]

US officials must have become aware that the British might not have understood American intentions because, on 28 April, Davis asked Rathbone to confirm the extent to which the Secretary 'would be bound to put into effect the exchange of obligations' should he approve the terms Rathbone was negotiating. Was it clear to the British that, on approving the funding agreement, the Secretary was

c The agreement divided Mesopotamian oil between the UK and France. The Note delivered by the US Ambassador on 12 May listed grievances about British policy and discriminatory action by the British against American nationals in the mandated territories. Kent (1976), pp. 150–5 and 175–8; Shwadran (1955), pp. 203–8; US National Archives, RG 39, GB 132.9/19–7, Box 120, Davis to Rathbone, 12 May 1920; *Correspondence between His Majesty's Government and the United States Ambassador respecting Economic Rights in Mandated Territories* (Cmd. 1226), reproduces the correspondence between the UK and the USA.

approving the terms but reserving the right to put the agreement into effect until he was satisfied with the other conditions he had selected?

> I wish to be clear whether the British distinctly understand this so that if he [the Secretary] should later decide not to put the funding arrangement into effect, it would not be considered by them as a breach of faith.

Was it understood that pending agreement by the Secretary to exchange the obligations he was free to demand the interest on short notice? If the Secretary agreed to put the funding agreement into effect, would it be subject to 'legal details', such as authorisation by Parliament? The conditions would need to be decided soon. Should it be linked to settlement of the reparation problem? To increased British advances to France and Italy? To equal access for the USA to 'trade etc.' (by which he meant oil concessions) in mandated territories?

> I am afraid we are getting this [*sic*] into a difficult position if the negotiation [*sic*] is tentatively concluded by you subject to consummation if and when the Secretary shall determine. In such event, I fear Secretary would soon be faced with the necessity of concluding the arrangements without further conditions or of defining just what conditions shall be complied with as a prerequisite to his consummating agreement.[74]

When this unclear demand for clarity was translated into Rathbone's legal prose, it provoked an explosion from Chamberlain, who was already labouring under criticisms of his budget and worries about whether to introduce a capital levy. On 12 May, the day the US Ambassador delivered the Note on British oil policy, the Chancellor circulated to the Cabinet a short note, covering a memorandum written by Blackett, saying that he had changed his mind since February, mainly because of the 'intolerable pretensions of the United States Government.' He had told Rathbone privately that he 'would sooner pay if I could, and default if I could not, than sell my country into Bondage, by signing any document containing language like that quoted.' He was now in favour of cancelling allied and Dominion debts to the UK and paying the US deferred interest ($210m), current interest ($220m) and sinking fund ($100m) – sums which Blackett described as not 'unduly burdensome' when one considered the comparative ease with which $400m of dollar debt had been repaid to the markets in the first few months of 1920. Blackett's memorandum drew the Cabinet's attention to the difference between the British and American view of inter-allied debts:

> The British Government regard these debts, whether from its standpoint as creditor or from its standpoint as debtor, as an obstacle to good relations, and wish to reach a comprehensive settlement as soon as possible. The United States Government regard the fact that it now holds a large amount of demand obligations of the British and Allied Governments as a useful instrument for securing the acceptance of its point of view in any controversy which may arise out of the Peace Treaties or the general European situation.

Rathbone had agreed to modify the most discourteous parts of his draft but, according to Blackett, 'he is unwilling, and, indeed, unable, to commit the United States Government to make a final settlement without reserving its power to use its holding of Allied obligations in terrorem.' Blackett also drew attention to other areas of dispute. Postponement of interest was not guaranteed if the debtor accepted the terms, but would depend on the Secretary's judgement of each country's capacity to pay. All deferred interest, and current interest as it became due, would become payable when a debtor's currency reached par against the dollar, a condition which, it was assumed, was most relevant to sterling, so making the terms of the British obligations more onerous than those of the other allies. The US Treasury wanted the British to agree to impose the same terms on its debtors as the USA was imposing on them, which meant that the debts owed to the British could be used by the US Treasury to make the other allies accept American policies. Finally, it wanted the UK to mismatch its receipts and payments by accepting definite coupon and sinking fund dates on its Bonds, while those on its debtors' Bonds would be *pari passu* with those they agreed to make to the USA.[75]

The stiffening in the US Treasury's attitude was very noticeable by the time the Chancellor circulated Blackett's Memorandum, Davis being particularly irritated by the British attempts to win the right to early repayment and their resistance to the sterling option and marketability. There is also more than a hint that the officials in Washington felt that Rathbone was being insufficiently tough. Certainly, with garbled cables, Davis's rambling and imprecise language, the time difference and six months without personal contact, relations between the Treasury in Washington and Rathbone in Europe had become strained. It will be recalled that Rathbone left for Europe before Davis was appointed. On 11 May, Davis told Rathbone that 'Apparently British either do not desire to reach general settlement or have gathered impression we are so desirous of terminating all pending questions that we will continue to make concessions.' Davis, Houston and Leffingwell had agreed that the British should be told that the US Treasury had, in the face of great political difficulties, tried to make arrangements for the revival of Europe and that without immediate agreement Rathbone's return would mean that negotiations would have to be resumed in Washington.[76] The following day, he added that 'We are strongly of opinion that British are overplaying their position by reason of their belief that we will make large concession...the delivery of a practical ultimatum, with strong presentation of our views, is most likely to bring them round'.[77] The British were making constant demands for concessions and 'seem to have the impression that settlement is for our benefit rather than theirs. We do not share their apparent impression that they are doing us a favour by reaching a general settlement.'[78]

War debts and reparations: the Cabinet breaks off negotiations

Blackett's February proposal for one-sided cancellation had divided ministers in London. Comment concentrated on four aspects: the Administration's reaction to a move which its public opinion might interpret as an attempt to embarrass the

USA into cancelling the debts; the timing, given the US Presidential elections; the effect on the relative prosperity and power of the UK and France; and British electoral considerations. Lloyd George was hostile.[79] The Chancellor was in favour. In mid-April, support on general grounds of foreign policy came from Lord Curzon at the Foreign Office. He first restated Blackett's arguments. The USA would not agree to cancellation, while those nations in debt to the UK had made no plans to pay interest and were unlikely to be able to repay principal. The Treasury 'view is, I understand, that by renouncing our debt we stand to lose practically nothing except vexatious claims for money which we shall not get' and that a prosperous France and Italy was worth more than a claim for £800m, 'the justice of which was not fully accepted by the debtors.' Making comparison with the French indemnity paid to Germany after 1870, he warned that the increase in imports – or decrease in exports – necessary to enable continental debtors to make payment to the UK would dislocate British trade. The prerequisite for European recovery was the restoration of the financial system and, 'of all measures within the range of practical politics, cancellation of the allied debts owing to this country is the only measure comprehensive enough in scope to give the necessary impetus to the machine.'

Passing to his own responsibilities, Curzon said that it was certain that there would be bad feeling if the British, who were relatively rich, pressed for repayment from France and Italy, who were relatively poor. As long as the debts remained, Germany, although liable for reparations, was not much worse off, if at all, than France and Italy. The USA and the UK, through debt repayments, would become the sole beneficiaries of reparations. In such circumstances, if the UK insisted on payment of its debts, it would be seen as oppressive and unjust, and it would be unable to influence European policy. If the UK renounced its debts, it would clear 'the atmosphere at once. We obtain the moral leadership of the world at a stroke'. The French and Italians were 'bankrupt and sullen in victory'; they needed a practical earnest that better times were coming. The alternative to cancellation was bitter relations. The US government, and many citizens, would no doubt resent a move which they would regard as designed to force them to cancel their loans to the UK, but there would be a reaction because 'conscience does not die in so sentimental and idealistic people; it is only numb'. With the reaction, relations, not only with the UK, but also with Europe as a whole, would improve.[80]

Opposition came from Churchill at the War Office in a half page whose *obiter dicta* showed a magnificent ignorance of the facts and issues. His warnings were of lost bargaining power if the UK was to seek cancellation of its debts to the USA and of 'a violent outbreak of anger' when British public opinion learnt that, while the UK had forgiven French debts, taxes were to remain higher in Britain than in France. 'A simple and straightforward policy was open to us.' The UK should declare that it was prepared to wipe out its £1,600m claims against the Continent if the USA would wipe out its £800m claims against the UK.[81] From the Board of Trade came two papers, from Sir Auckland Geddes and then, after he went to Washington as British Ambassador, from his successor, Sir Robert Horne. Geddes also feared that the USA would see one-sided cancellation as an attempt to force its hand, be resentful, and, perhaps, retaliate by cancelling all debts but those owed by the UK. If the UK cancelled the debts owed by France, and the USA followed suit, in ten years' time France might be financially stronger than the UK. While the British would gain from an all-round cancellation, it could not be assumed that one-sided cancellation would produce that result; it was a gamble and the issues were too great to be settled in such a way.[82] Horne was more optimistic than either the Treasury or the Foreign Office about the prospects of reparations being paid and thought it premature to offer cancellation. If the USA cancelled all debts, which seemed unlikely, the UK would benefit. If the USA cancelled all debts except those owed by the UK, the British would become the most indebted of all the allies. If the UK cancelled all debts owing to it, but the USA insisted on repayment of all the debts owing to it, the UK's action might not benefit the continental allies, but merely enable them to pay the USA what they could not otherwise have paid.[83]

On 15 and 16 May, a meeting was held at Lympne (Hythe) between David Lloyd George, Austen Chamberlain, Millerand and Francois-Marsal with the purpose of mending 'an Alliance that has been nearly ruptured' and to prepare for a meeting with the Germans at Spa which would discuss their failure to fulfil the disarmament terms of the Peace Treaty, make coal deliveries and pay reparations. The greater part of the talks was about finance: determining Germany's bill, and deciding how the proceeds should be divided. When the French pressed for new arrangements for allocating payments so that devastated regions – France and Belgium – would be given greater priority, the British resisted, partly because it would mean reopening negotiations with the Dominions, and partly because British and Empire claims would be relegated.[84] The ministers sent the proposals to officials for further discussion, with guidance which, *inter alia*, linked inter-allied debts with reparations:

> in order to provide a solution for the economic difficulties which are gravely weighing upon the general situation of the world, and in order to mark a definite beginning of the era of peace, it is important to arrive at a settlement which will embrace the whole body of the international liabilities which have been left as a legacy of the War, and which will, at the same time, ensure a parallel liquidation of the Inter-Allied War Debts and of the Reparation Debts of the Central Empire.

The important departure in policy was, apparently, included at Millerand's suggestion as part of a compromise over the division of the German payments and after a private, and unminuted, conversation with Lloyd George.[85]

The Conclusions were circulated for a Cabinet meeting held on 19 May. After discussion, Churchill raised the subject of inter-allied indebtedness, without prior notice and prompted, thought Maurice Hankey, the Cabinet Secretary, by hints in the French press that the UK might make the payment of its French debts conditional on the French receiving reparations from the Germans. Churchill's concern was that nothing should be done, for the moment, to forgive the French debts. Instead, he proposed that the UK should make it clear that it would be glad to see France reduce the size of the reparations it was claiming from Germany. To secure this, it should say that it was prepared to release France from some of her debts, provided that the USA made a corresponding remission of the debts due to her from the UK. The idea, apparently, was to 'mobilise the whole sequence of debts in this order, so as to put America in an invidious position before the world if she refuses to take part.'

Provoked, the Chancellor told the Cabinet that the talks with Rathbone were pointing towards the UK paying the interest: that the Prime Minister (who was absent) did not approve of the policy of paying current interest, back interest and sinking fund and that the Treasury was proceeding with the funding talks as 'a number of other financial adjustments' hinged on them. There was, thought Hankey, a 'very general feeling…that any arrangement of this kind [paying interest, whether back or current is unclear] might prejudice the general question of Inter-Allied Indebtedness' and ministers had asked for a discussion. In the meanwhile, the Cabinet concluded that the talks with Rathbone should be interrupted.[86]

The requested Cabinet discussion took place, with Lloyd George present, two days later. The Chancellor provided a history of the negotiations, stressing the problem of the subrogated securities and the harsher treatment of the UK implied by the stipulation that the deferred interest would become payable when a currency returned to par. Even if the British were prepared to swallow the conditions envisaged by the US Treasury before obligations were exchanged, the Chancellor felt he could not be party to coercing the allies into accepting them: Rathbone's proposals, he said, left 'little doubt that the United States wanted to use this Agreement as a weapon to compel [the French to agree to] what they [the USA] considered proper conditions as regards the German indemnity.' This, apparently, was a power which only the British should be allowed, for he also described one of the advantages of settling inter-allied debts and reparations in parallel to be the 'checking' of the French (by the British) should they show themselves 'unreasonable' in their demands on the defeated Central Powers. If the USA insisted on retaining powers of coercion, the British would be justified in defaulting and the grounds would be so strong that it would not affect their credit.

Ministers made five points: once the Bonds were sold into the market, remission or cancellation under any general scheme for reducing inter-allied indebtedness would become impossible; the political situation in the USA, with the approach of the Presidential elections, made it an unfavourable moment for decisions; there was every advantage to be gained from the French and Italians participating in the negotiations; the Lympne conversations justified discontinuing the bilateral talks; and it was 'no more dishonourable' for the British to renege on the debt than the French or Italians. No minister is recorded as mentioning that the obligations were contracts, signed by representatives of the British government, nor was there any further word of the effect on future borrowing should the UK fail to fulfil its commitment. Nor, apparently, was there further consideration of the Treasury's wholly proper response to the problem, namely repaying the USA, leaving the UK free to treat French and Italian obligations as was thought best.

The decision was wholly political, based on short-term considerations and contrary to Treasury and Foreign Office advice. If a single date can be found on which the British government's attitude towards contractual financial obligations changed from that of the nineteenth to that of the twentieth century, it was surely 21 May 1920.

The Cabinet concluded that discussions should continue at ministerial level, the Prime Minister should write to the US President and the Chancellor should tell Rathbone of the decision.[87]

Austria, Pittman silver and reimbursement

During the summer of 1920, after the Blackett–Rathbone talks were called off, the repayment or funding was agreed of three debts – Chamberlain's 'other financial adjustments' – whose settlement was within the discretion of the British and American Treasuries. They had been negotiated by Blackett and Rathbone alongside the terms for conversion, implementation was expected to take place as part of the funding agreement, but it was not envisaged that the agreements would be incorporated into the British Bonds. A fourth item suggested by Blackett, the release of the subrogated securities, was regarded by the US Treasury as only negotiable as part of a comprehensive agreement and was taken no further.[88]

Advances by the US Treasury to the UK, France and Italy for the relief of famine in Austria originated in March 1919. The Liberty Bond Acts did not authorise the US Treasury to lend to enemy or ex-enemy states and the advances to the three European countries were a subterfuge. The three allies used the advances to buy surplus American foodstuffs, mainly held in Trieste, which they then sold on credit to the Austrian government, which pledged foreign securities requisitioned from its nationals, together with state-owned salt mines and forests. The agreement with the US Treasury stipulated that the proceeds of sales of the hypothecated securities should be applied to the repayment of the advances. On 14 April 1919, $10m was authorised for each country, followed by a further $5m in May and another $1m in June.[89]

The advances were secured by standard certificates of indebtedness, and at their meeting on 1 and 2 November Rathbone proposed to Blackett that they should be funded into 1938 Bonds similar in all respects to the Bonds into which the remainder of the British obligations were to be converted, except that, in accordance with the original terms for the advances, the British would undertake to repay principal if they realised any of the pledged securities. Blackett accepted this proposition.[90] By the summer of 1920, the British had decided that they wanted to be free to deal with the pledged securities as they wished.[91] Repayment was made on 19 August and a similar amount of British demand obligations were cancelled.[92]

In contrast to this settlement, the repayment of the advances made by the US Treasury to enable the British to buy the silver sold under the Pittman Act was the subject of lengthy negotiations. When the arrangement was made in the spring of 1918, the US Treasury had not overtly agreed to lend the British the dollars with which to buy the silver, and, instead, had turned a blind eye when its regular advances were used. Ever since, according to Blackett, it had lived in fear of Congressional attack. There was also ill-feeling because India, or the UK, believing that it was irrelevant after June 1919 when the USA lifted its gold export ban, failed to live up to its promise to ship $50m of gold when the metallic proportion in the Currency Reserve Account reached 40 per cent: the initial $10m had been sent, as promised, but no further shipment had been made, although the proportion had breached 40 per cent in August 1919. During the talks at the beginning of November 1919, Rathbone had suggested that the US Treasury could be protected from attack if India, instead of shipping gold, sold 7½m rupees each month in the USA and the proceeds were used to repay the $122m advances.[93] Blackett resisted on the general grounds that the advances were similar to all the others, while recognising that the $40m should be treated differently. Adapting Rathbone's proposal, he suggested that, provided the balance was treated like the other advances, India should sell $40m of rupees over eight or ten months and apply the proceeds to the British debt.[94]

The USA would not accept this. The Treasury officials and, especially, Leffingwell felt strongly that the advances came into a special category, a 'debt of honour', as well as a legal obligation. The US Treasury, said Rathbone, felt 'particularly proud' of its behaviour when it had first been informed by the British of the threat to the Indian currency system. Although the silver dispute of the previous century rumbled scarcely beneath the surface, it had prepared, and seen passed within a week, the Pittman legislation. It had made available 200m ounces from its currency reserve. It had made advances, outside the Act, to enable the British to buy additional silver on the open market for its own use. The market had been controlled, and other countries' demands curtailed, to clear the way. It had even waived the $1 price limit. What had happened? Despite Reading's promise to support the dollar against the rupee, a further fall had taken place, increasing costs to the US importer. The silver reserve of the USA had become demand obligations of the UK, instead of being used to settle US purchases in India. It was, said Leffingwell, 'our most Quixotic exploit'.[95]

At the end of March, after 'prolonged argument', the British accepted the US Treasury's 'insistent demand that scheme should be prepared for liquidating balance of sums due for silver'.[96] The agreement, set out in a draft dated 17 May, was a hybrid, drawing on Rathbone's proposal for the sale of rupees in New York and incorporating repayment of some of the demand obligations – no separate securities were issued – for the balance. The British would repay $18.3m and interest on 15 April 1921, 1922, 1923 and 1924, and $12.2m and interest on 15 May of the same years; a total of $122m, a small balance being paid in cash to round the debt down.[d] In addition, until the debt was cleared, the Government of India was to place rupees at the disposal of the FRBNY for sale to US nationals.

d In the event, the repayment due in 1924–5 was brought forward to 1923–4. *Hansard* (Commons), 29 April 1924, col. 1591; *National Debt: annual returns*, 1924, p. 36.

The FRBNY would credit the UK Treasury Account at Morgans with dollars and the UK Treasury would credit the Government of India account at the Bank of England with sterling. Sales were limited to 10m rupees (£1m or $4.9m, at par of exchange) in any one month and of 70m rupees (£7m or $34m) in any one year. The dollars from the sales would be applied to the payment of the fixed annual instalments to the US Treasury. There was to be no shipment of the $40m gold.[97]

This was a clear American victory: it won access to rupees for its nationals, providing a defence against attack; it also won the right to buy rupees up to the entire amount of the debt, and not just the $40m which should have been paid in gold; and, instead of any balance being funded, the British were to repay over four years. The British came away with a breathing space of less than one year, which arguably meant nothing because 15 April and 15 May 1920, which would have been the payment dates for interest and principal, had already passed.

The system of 'running accounts' was established to enable the British Treasury to be reimbursed by the US Treasury when the UK had spent dollars on behalf of the allies in the USA. The dollars were paid over without the expenditure having been finally vetted and agreed, so that the UK could be reimbursed as bills were presented, rather than when auditors and bureaucracy had signed them off. The running accounts were extended to cover the allies' expenditure in neutral countries, where the burden was to be shared by the two countries. The amounts to be contributed by each Treasury was never agreed, and by May 1920 they had not been audited, but the British claimed reimbursement of all French neutral expenditure and, although the USA objected, they were paid.[98]

The US Treasury's original claim on the UK for the reimbursement of monies paid into the running accounts to meet allied expenditure in neutral countries in excess of the amounts finally approved was $180m (£37m).[99] The negotiations were lengthy and detailed, but the USA finally agreed to meet two-thirds of the expenditure which had been incurred on behalf of France and pay $40m towards that of Italy: 'so clear a gain that we should clinch on this' commented a Treasury official in London. It was also agreed that the British were due $30.8m from the USA on account of under-reimbursement for Italy and Belgium and that the USA was due $37.2m from the UK on account of over-reimbursement for France. The matter was finally settled by the British paying the US Treasury $6.4m, together with the $30.8m received from the Italians and Belgians. It was also agreed that the British would make no further reimbursement claims and that, if a valid claim was made, the money would not be paid, but returned to the US Treasury to be applied to the debts of the relevant country.[100]

✤ ✤ ✤

In August 1919, when the Chancellor agreed that Blackett could resume informal discussions, the British balance of payments was scarcely in surplus, a demand from the US Treasury for interest on its debt more than a possibility, maturities for the following year daunting and the exchange rate weak. Domestically, the Chancellor was struggling to persuade ministers to retrench and the Bank was endeavouring to persuade the Cabinet to raise interest rates, reduce the floating debt and tame the booming economy. In May 1920, when the negotiations were broken off, the position had been transformed. The boom had been broken, there was a clear payments surplus, the previous month's budget had forecast debt repayment from revenue of £234m, there had been heavy repayment of foreign currency debt in the previous six months and there had been assurances from the French that they would meet their half of the Anglo-French Loan. The Chancellor, who four months previously had opposed Blackett's plan for the one-sided cancellation of war debts, told the Cabinet that he had changed his mind and now favoured paying some $530m to the USA in interest and sinking fund.

Although the British financial position had strengthened during the months of talking, it would be misleading to dismiss the negotiations as beginning when the British needed to defer interest payments and ending when their position had stabilised. Throughout, both parties called attention to the tentative nature of the talks. The US Treasury knew that the British favoured cancellation of all war debts, that they saw a connection between the debts owed to them and the debts they owed to the US government. Not so obviously, the British knew that the USA intended to impose conditions before the conversion that was being negotiated was implemented.

The discussions between Blackett and Rathbone were the only attempt to settle the British debt as a technical matter between Treasuries. The UK was seeking to rid itself of its short-term debt, both in sterling and in foreign currencies, including that owed to the governments of Japan, Sweden, Argentina, Uruguay and Holland. Except for the February 1919 conversion and the 1 November 1919 issues in New York, the foreign currency debt was being paid off in cash. There were only two differences between the debt owed to the US government and the other foreign currency debt: its size, which dictated conversion, and the connection with the debts owed by continental allies to the UK.

The Treasury in London was in no doubt that, if all-round cancellation proved unacceptable to the USA, its debt should be repaid within the terms of a funding agreement, with, or without, the cancellation of the debts owed to the UK by other governments. The Treasury also had no doubt of its ability to repay and had a clear view of the method; not to repay foreign currency debt from budget surpluses, but to convert it into sterling debt. As this made it a foreign exchange problem, and the UK's ability to generate current account surpluses could be assumed to fluctuate, the terms for repayment should be highly flexible. Hence the stress placed on the options for early repayment, a stress which was to be seen again in 1923, the next occasion when the debt was to become a technical matter between the two Treasuries.

Endnotes

1 *ARSF*, 1919, p. 65; Cab. 24/5, G 257, 'Memorandum by the Treasury on the Financial Position and Future Prospects of this Country', 18 July 1919. The data for the UK include $978m (£201m) obligations of India and the Dominions and are for 1 April 1919. Those for the USA are for 15 November 1919.

2 *ARSF*, 1920, pp. 326–36. The cash advanced is gross. On 15 November 1920, $31.5m had been repaid by the French and $80.2m by the British. The other borrowers were Cuba, Czechoslovakia, Greece, Liberia, Roumania and Serbia.
3 *ARSF*, 1922, p. 18.
4 *ARSF*, 1920, p. 53.
5 *Foreign Affairs*, April 1925, Rathbone, 'Making War Loans to the Allies', p. 371–5.
6 The First Liberty Bond Act, s. 2. The rates specified were maximums of 3½ per cent under the First Act, 4 per cent under the Second and 4¼ per cent under the Third and Fourth.
7 Second Liberty Bond Act, s. 2.
8 Victory Liberty Loan Act, s. 8.
9 *ARSF*, 1920, p. 61.
10 Second Liberty Bond Act, s. 3.
11 T 160/365/F557/1, f. 83, Lever, 'Sir H. Lever's Memorandum', February 1919. The British were inclined to discount the importance of the lower rate on advances made under the First Act because, if he were pressed, the Secretary had the discretion to raise the rate paid on advances under the Second and Third Acts so that the average interest rate was unchanged. Similarly, he could raise the rate to reflect the cost to the US Treasury of the tax privileges.
12 T 160/365/F557/1, f. 83, 'Sir H. Lever's Memorandum', February 1919; Leffingwell Papers, Box 14, LB 3, ff. 328–34, Davis to Rathbone, 27 March 1920.
13 Second Liberty Bond Act, s. 3.
14 *ARSF*, 1920, p. 61.
15 Baldwin Papers 233, 'History of the Anglo-American Debt', p. 46. A note pasted in the front of this volume reads [1923?], but a footnote on p. 50 refers to a book published in September 1932. The history was probably prepared as background to the British note of 1 December 1932, explaining its decision to renegotiate the Bonds.
16 Baldwin Papers 233, 'History of the Anglo-American Debt', pp. 42–6; T 160/365/F557/1, f. 106, 'Further Negotiations in the U.S.A. August 1917 to August 1919', and Lever, 'Sir H. Lever's Memorandum', February 1919, ff. 95–105: T 172/435, ff. 122–6, Lever to Chancellor, 31 August 1917.
17 Leffingwell Papers, Box 6, LB 2, ff. 335–6, Rathbone to Lever, 16 November 1918.
18 Senate Document No. 86 (1921), p. 16, Crosby to McAdoo, 30 November 1918; T 160/365/F557/1, ff. 106–7, 'Further Negotiations.'
19 T 172/447, Chancellor to Lever, 23 December 1918; T 160/365/F557/1, f. 107, 'Further Negotiations.'
20 T 172/447, f. 27, Lever to Chancellor, 17 January 1919, ff. 6–8, Chancellor to Lever, 6 February 1919, and ff. 2–3, Lever to Bradbury, 15 February 1919; T 160/365/F557/1, ff. 107–9, 'Further Negotiations.'
21 *ARSF*, 1920, pp. 328 and 336.
22 Strong Papers, 1000.3 (2), Strong to Leffingwell, 24 July and 25 July 1919.
23 Leffingwell Papers, Box 11, LB 3, f. 34, Leffingwell to Strong, 31 July 1919. Leffingwell was exaggerating. Reading left the USA in May and Ronald Lindsay, the Counsellor, assumed temporary charge until Lord Grey was appointed in August. Grey arrived in Washington on 27 September and left on 2 January 1920.
24 Leffingwell Papers, Box 11, LB 3, ff. 369–70, Leffingwell memorandum for Strong, 13 August 1919, and f. 455, Leffingwell to Strong, 16 August 1919.
25 Cab. 27/72 (FC1), 'Instructions to British Treasury Representative', 23 September 1919; T 160/365/F557/1, ff. 5–13, Blackett, 'Memorandum of Interview with Mr. Albert Rathbone', 3 November 1919; T 172/454, ff. 17–19, Blackett to Bradbury, 30 August 1919; Leffingwell Papers, Box 13, LB 2, ff. 270–5, Davis to Rathbone, 19 December 1919.
26 T 172/454, f. 34, Bradbury to Blackett, 26 August 1919.

27 T 160/365/F557/3, ff. 51–4, Mellon to Geddes, 11 May 1921. The memoranda are in the same file, ff. 55–81.

28 Cab. 27/72 (FC1), 'Interest Payments upon Demand Obligations of the British Government held by the United Sates Treasury and Question of their Conversion into Long-term Bonds', 23 September 1919; T 160/365/F557/1, ff., 14–17, 'Memorandum dated 1st November 1919 by Mr. Albert Rathbone', 1 November 1919, and ff. 5–13, Blackett, 'Memorandum of interview with Mr. Albert Rathbone', 3 November 1919.

29 T 160/365/F557/1, ff. 14–17, Rathbone, 'Memorandum dated 1st November by Mr. Albert Rathbone', and ff. 5–13, Blackett, 'Memorandum of Interview with Mr. Rathbone', 3 November 1919; US National Archives, RG 39, GB 132.9/19–7, Box 120, Chancellor to Rathbone, 11 December 1919.

30 US National Archives, RG 39, GB 132.9/19–7, Box 120, Rathbone to Leffingwell and Davis, 22 January 1920, and Blackett to Rathbone, 3 February 1920.

31 Leffingwell Papers, Box 13, LB 2, ff. 270–5, Davis to Rathbone, 19 December 1919; *Congressional Record*, 19 December 1919, p. 933.

32 Leffingwell Papers, Box 13, LB 3, ff. 447–50, Leffingwell and Davis to Rathbone, 17 January 1920, and ff. 458–9, 19 January 1920; US National Archives, RG 39, GB 132.9/19–7, Box 120, Davis and Leffingwell to Rathbone, 19 January 1920.

33 US National Archives, RG 39, GB 132. 9/19–7, Box 120, Rathbone to Leffingwell and Davis, 26 January 1920.

34 US National Archives, RG 339, GB 132/9/19–7, Box 120, Davis to Rathbone, 27 February 1920.

35 Leffingwell Papers, Box 13, LB 3, ff. 482–3, Davis and Leffingwell to Rathbone, 20 January 1920.

36 US National Archives, RG 39, GB 132. 9/19–7, Box 120, Rathbone to Davis, 24 February 1920, Davis to Rathbone, 27 February 1920, Houston to Rathbone, 2 April 1920, and Houston to Rathbone, 16 April 1920; Leffingwell Papers, Box 13, LB 3, ff. 462–3, Leffingwell and Davis to Rathbone, 20 January 1920.

37 T 160/365/F557/1, ff., 14–17, 'Memorandum dated 1st November 1919 by Mr. Albert Rathbone', 1 November 1919, and ff. 5–13, Blackett, 'Memorandum of interview with Mr. Albert Rathbone', 3 November 1919.

38 Cab. 27/72 (FC1), 'Interest Payments upon Demand Obligations of the British Government held by the United Sates Treasury and Question of their Conversion into Long-term Bonds', 23 September 1919; Blackett to Rathbone, 8 November 1919.

39 T 160/365/F557/1, ff. 5–13, Blackett, 'Memorandum of interview with Mr. Albert Rathbone', 3 November 1919; US National Archives, RG 39, GB 132.9/19–7, Box 120, Blackett to Rathbone, 8 November 1919, and Rathbone to Blackett, 18 November 1919.

40 US National Archives, RG 39, GB 132.9/20–6, Box 120, 'Negotiations Carried out by Mr. Rathbone', 6 May 1921.

41 T 160/365/F557/1, 'Further Negotiations', f. 121–2; T 160/365/F557/3, ff. 55–81, drafts of 10 and 22 May 1920.

42 US National Archives, RG 39, GB 132. 9/19–7, Box 120, Rathbone to Leffingwell and Davis, Section 3, 21 May 1920.

43 US National Archives, RG 39, GB 132. 9/19–7, Box 120, Davis to Rathbone, 28 April 1920.

44 Leffingwell Papers, Box 12, LB 3, ff. 351–3, Leffingwell to Rathbone, 31 October 1919.

45 Leffingwell Papers, Box 12, LB 3, ff. 351–3, Leffingwell to Rathbone, 31 October 1919, f. 372, Leffingwell, Memorandum for Secretary of Treasury, 15 January 1920, and ff. 447–50, Leffingwell and Davis to Rathbone, 17 January 1920; ibid., Box 13, LB 2, f. 465, Glass to Secretary of Commerce, 29 December 1919; ibid., Box 14, LB 3, ff. 458–9, Davis, Memorandum for Polk, 2 April 1920; ibid., Box 15, LB 43a, ff.

253–5 and 276, Davis to Rathbone, 20 April and 22 April 1920; ibid., Box 15, LB 42b, ff. 46–54, Leffingwell to Blackett, 2 March 1920; US National Archives, RG 39, GB 132.9/19–7, Box 120, Davis to Rathbone, 13 May 1920.

46 US National Archives, RG 39, GB 132.9/19–7, Box 120, Rathbone to Davis, 11 May 1920.

47 US National Archives, RG 39, GB 132.9/19–7, Box 120, Davis to Rathbone, 13 May 1920.

48 Baldwin Papers 233, 'History of the Anglo-American Debt', f. 107; T 160/365/F557/1, p. 122, 'Further Negotiations'; US National Archives, RG 39, GB 132.19–7, Box 120, Davis to Rathbone, 13 May 1920, and Rathbone to Davis, Section 3, 21 May 1920; ibid., GB 132.9/20–6, Box 120, 'Negotiations Carried out by Mr. Rathbone', 6 May 1921.

49 T 172/435, f. 122–6, Lever to Chancellor, 31 August 1917; T 160/365/F557/1, f. 89, 'Sir H. Lever's Memorandum', February 1919, and ff. 108–9, 'Further Negotiations'; Cab. 27/72 (FC1), 'Instructions to British Treasury Representative', 23 September 1919.

50 US National Archives, RG 39, GB 132.9–7, Box 120, Rathbone to Leffingwell and Davis, 26 January 1920.

51 Cab. 27/72 (FC1), 'Interest Payments upon Demand Obligations of the British Government held by the United Sates Treasury and Question of their Conversion into Long-term Bonds', 23 September 1919; T 172/454, f. 34, Bradbury to Blackett, 26 August 1919.

52 T 172/454, ff. 17–19, Blackett to Bradbury, 30 August 1919.

53 US National Archives, RG 39, GB 132.9/19–7, Box 120, Blackett to Rathbone, 8 November 1919, Rathbone to Blackett, 18 November 1919, Davis to Rathbone, 13 May 1920, and Rathbone to Davis, Leffingwell and Secretary of the Treasury, Section Three, 21 May 1920; Baldwin Papers 233, 'History of the Anglo-American Debt', pp. 93–4 and 107; T 160/365/F557/1, ff. 5–13, Blackett, 'Memorandum of interview with Mr. Albert Rathbone', 3 November 1919.

54 US National Archives, RG 39, GB 132.9/19–7, Box 120, Rathbone to Davis, Leffingwell and Secretary of the Treasury, Section Two, 21 May 1920.

55 T 160/365/F557/1, f. 92, 'Sir H. Lever's Memorandum', February 1919; Leffingwell Papers, Box 7, LB 3, f. 406, Rathbone to Lever, 22 January 1919.

56 T 160/365/F557/1, ff. 5–13, Blackett, 'Memorandum of interview with Mr. Albert Rathbone', 3 November 1919; US National Archives, RG 39, GB 132.9/19–7, Box 120, Blackett to Rathbone, 8 November 1919, and Rathbone to Blackett, 18 November 1919; ibid., GB 132.5/19–1, Box 116, Leffingwell to Secretary of the Treasury, 21 November 1919; Cab. 27/72 (FC1), 'Interest Payments upon Demand Obligations of the British Government held by the United Sates Treasury and Question of their Conversion into Long-term Bonds', 23 September 1919.

57 US National Archives, RG 39, GB 132.5/19–1, Box 116, Leffingwell to Glass, 21 November 1919, Glass to Rathbone, 15 December 1919, Davis to Rathbone, 17 December 1919, and Rathbone to Glass, 22 December 1919.

58 US National Archives, RG 39, GB 132.9/19–7, Box 120, Davis to Rathbone, 12 May 1920.

59 Cab. 27/72 (FC1), 'Instructions to British Treasury Representative', 23 September 1919.

60 US National Archives, RG 39, GB 132.9/19–7, Box 120, Blackett to Rathbone, 8 November 1919, and Rathbone to Blackett, 18 November 1919.

61 US National Archives, RG 39, GB 132.9/19–7, Box 120, Rathbone to Leffingwell and Davis, 22 January 1920, and Davis to Rathbone, 3 February 1920.

62 Leffingwell Papers, Box 14, LB3, ff. 328–34, Davis to Rathbone, 27 March 1920.

63 US National Archives, RG 39, GB 132.9/19–7, Box 120, Rathbone to Leffingwell and Davis, 26 January 1920.

64 Cab. 24/97, CP 597, Lindsay to FO, 27 January 1920.
65 US National Archives, RG 39, GB 132.9/19–7, Box 120, Rathbone to Leffingwell and Davis, 10 February 1920.
66 Cab. 24/97, CP 597, Chancellor to Lindsay, 9 February 1920.
67 Cab. 24/97, CP 584, Blackett, 'Inter-Allied Indebtedness', 2 February 1920.
68 Self (1995), p. 128, Chamberlain to Ida Chamberlain, 1 February 1920.
69 US National Archives, RG 39, GB 132.9/19–7, Box 120, Davis to Rathbone, 28 April 1920.
70 T 160/365/F557/1, ff. 40–4, Lindsay, 26 February 1920; US National Archives, RG 39, GB 132.9/19–7, Box 120, Davis to Rathbone, 28 April 1920; Leffingwell Papers, Box 15, LB 42b, ff. 46–54, Leffingwell to Blackett, 2 March 1920; ibid., LB 43a, ff. 351–2, Davis to Rathbone, 30 April 1920.
71 Cab. 24/100, CP 842, Houston to Chamberlain, 5 March 1920; T 160/365/F557/1, ff. 50–1, Chamberlain to Houston, 12 March 1920.
72 US National Archives, RG 39, GB 132. 9/19–7, Box 120, Rathbone to Leffingwell and Davis, 22 January 1920. Rathbone's description of the plan was confirmed by Houston, who added that there could be a 'considerable period of months' between final agreement on the terms of the Bonds and the Secretary agreeing that his conditions had been met. Ibid., Houston to Rathbone, 16 April 1920. Houston wrongly dates Rathbone's cable as 12 January.
73 US National Archives, RG 39, GB 132.9/19–7, Houston to Rathbone, 2 and 16 April 1920.
74 US National Archives, RG 39, GB 132.9/19–7, Box 120, Davis to Rathbone, 28 April 1920.
75 Cab. 24/105, CP 1259, Chamberlain, 'Inter-Allied and Anglo-American Debts', 12 May 1920, and Blackett, 'British Government's Debt to the United States Government', 11 May 1920.
76 US National Archives, RG 39, GB 132.9/19–7, Box 120, Davis to Rathbone, 11 May 1920.
77 US National Archives, RG 39, GB 132.9/19–7, Box 120, Davis to Rathbone, 12 May 1920.
78 US National Archives, RG 39, GB 132.9/19–7, Box 120, Davis to Rathbone, 13 May 1920 (second cable).
79 Cab. 23/21, Cabinet 29 (20), 19 May 1920, Conclusion 3.
80 Cab. 24/103, CP 1093, Curzon, 'Foreign Policy and Inter-Allied Debts', 17 April 1920.
81 Cab. 24/104, CP 1156, Churchill, 'Inter-Allied Debts', 23 April 1920.
82 Cab. 24/98, CP 621, Geddes, 'Inter-Allied Indebtedness', 12 February 1920.
83 Cab. 24/105, CP 1202, Horne, 'Proposed Remission of Debts Owing by European Allies'.
84 *DBFP*, First Series, VII, chapter II; Roskill (1970–4), II, pp. 166–8.
85 *DBFP*, First Series, VIII, pp. 277–9; Cab. 24/105, CP 1297, Hankey, 'The Conversations at Hythe', 17 May 1920; US National Archives, RG 39, GB 132.9/19–7, Box 120, Rathbone to Davis and Leffingwell, Section 3, 21 May 1920; Baldwin Papers 233, 'History of the Anglo-American Debt', p. 113n.
86 Cab. 23/21, 29 (30), Conclusion 4, 19 May 1920; LGP, F/24/2/36, Hankey to Lloyd George, 19 May 1920.
87 Cab. 23/21, 30 (20), Conclusion 2, 21 May 1920, and Appendix.
88 T 160/7/F220/1, ff. 69–71, Treasury to Geddes, 18 June 1920.
89 *FRUS*, *The Paris Peace Conference 1919*, X, pp. 33, 158, 179, 321–3 and 367–8; T 172/451, f. 39, Lever to Bradbury, 14 May 1919, and f. 20, Bradbury to Lever, 27 May 1919; T 172/453, Bradbury to Blackett, 30 July 1919. For the background to these loans, see Hemery (1988), chapter 9 (part 3).

90 T 160/365/F557/1, Blackett, 'Memorandum of interview with Mr. Albert Rathbone', ff. 5–13, 3 November 1919; US National Archives, RG 39, GB 132.9/19–7, Box 120, Blackett to Rathbone, 8 November 1919.
91 T 160/365/F557/1, Chancellor to Prime Minister and Bonar Law, 23 June 1920.
92 T 160/7/F220/1, Geddes, 17 August 1920; T 172/453, f. 2, Bradbury to Blackett, 30 July 1919; US National Archives, RG 39, GB 132.9/20–6, Box 120, Rathbone to Geddes, 14 July 1920. The cancelled certificates of indebtedness are in T 160/7/F220/1.
93 T 160/365/F557/1, Blackett, ff. 5–13, 'Memorandum of Interview with Mr. Albert Rathbone', 3 November 1919; IOL, L/F/5/35, p. 131, Secretary of State for India to Viceroy, 28 August 1919.
94 US National Archives, RG 39, GB 132.9/19–7, Box 120, Blackett to Rathbone, 8 November 1919.
95 US National Archives, RG 39, GB 132. 9/19–7, Box 120, Rathbone to Blackett, 18 November 1919; Leffingwell Papers, Box 15, LB 42b, ff. 46–54, Leffingwell to Blackett, 2 March 1920.
96 IOL, L/F/5/35, p. 259, Secretary of State for India to Viceroy, 31 March 1920.
97 T 160/21/F700, 'Pittman Silver Advances', Draft of 17 May 1920, and Blackett to US Treasury, 30 June 1920; IOL, L/F/5/35, pp. 247–8, India Office to Blackett, 27 February 1920, and pp. 259–60, Secretary of State to Viceroy, 31 March 1920.
98 US National Archives, RG 39, GB 132.9/19–7, Box 120, Davis to Rathbone, 11 May 1920, and Rathbone to Davis and Leffingwell, 21 May 1920, Section 2.
99 US National Archives, RG 39, GB 132.9/19–7, Box 120, Davis to Rathbone, 11 May 1920; T 160/365/F557/2 Part 1, Chancellor to Bonar Law and Lloyd George, 23 June 1920.
100 T 160/21/F700, 'Draft of May 18', Rowe-Dutton to Blackett, 23 July 1920, and Treasury to British Ambassador in Washington, 28 June 1920; Baldwin Papers 233, 'History of the Anglo-American Debt', p. 37.

17 The Balfour Note and the Baldwin Settlement

> I regard the obligations of France, Italy, Serbia and Greece held by the British Government as of little worth. In the state of exhaustion to which Europe has been reduced these debts cannot be paid.
>
> Austen Chamberlain, 3 December 1920, Cab. 24/116, CP 2214A.

> To talk at the present time about cancellation or reduction is a mere waste of time. The position of this Government has always been that question of debts is irrelevant to the question of German reparations. Germany cannot pay a mark more or less because of what France may owe and France cannot collect what Germany cannot pay.
>
> Charles Evan Hughes to the US Ambassador to France and Roland Boyden, 17 October 1922, Charles Evans Hughes Papers, Box 4B, File October 1922.

After the Blackett–Rathbone talks were called off, the problem of the inter-governmental war debt could have been resolved in three ways. The British could have refused to recognise either interest or principal: repudiation. They could have met the terms of the contracts signed by their representatives and converted ('funded') on such terms as the US Secretary of the Treasury selected: fulfilment. Or they could have done nothing, continuing to recognise the debt but refusing to place it on a basis whereby the interest and repayments of principal were fixed as the US Treasury wanted: inertia. The Cabinet's insistence that there was a connection between the British debt to the Americans and continental debts to the British gave shading to each possibility. Repudiation could have been consequential on Germany failing to pay reparations to France, and France refusing to pay its debt to Britain. Funding, the fixing of the payments of interest and repayments of principal on the British debt to the Americans, could have been made dependent on the fixing of the Continent's payments to the British. And the size and timing of the payments received from Britain's debtors could determine the terms on which Britain's debts to the USA were funded.

The official Treasury and Bank never contemplated repudiation. On the few occasions it was discussed in Cabinet, the term was used loosely and tended to become confused with non-fulfilment, a failure to fund the obligations when requested.[1] Repudiation, default, was simply not realistic. The whole ethos of the responsible officials, whether in Whitehall or the Bank, was to meet debts according to the terms of their prospectuses: in this case, the certificates of indebtedness and the Liberty Bond Acts. The UK was a creditor of the world outside the USA, drawing from overseas in 1922 a net £180m ($860m) in profits, interest and dividends, a sum which far exceeded the payments which would be made under any debt settlement.[2] The City of London, whatever the threat from New York, was a valuable source of employment and invisible income derived from the provision of financial services based on contract. The value of the continental war debts may have been open to debate, but some income and principal, sometime, might be expected. Britain was also a creditor of her Empire on account of war debts, which were regarded as good.

The most powerful argument for keeping the obligations in demand form was that it would leave the door open to cancellation or a lower rate of interest. Otherwise, the arguments against repudiation applied equally well to a refusal to fund when requested. The terms of the certificates were unequivocal, as those advocating fulfilment stressed. To the sanctity of contract were added more practical arguments. How could budgets be drawn up, fiscal policy planned, if a major item of expenditure was not known? How could a sustainable sterling rate be maintained with a huge demand liability hanging over the exchanges? If it was intended to face reality and fund at some stage in the future, why pay 5 per cent on the demand obligations in the meantime? What would happen to the funding arrangements already reached with the Empire if London refused to fund its own debts to the USA?

Fulfilment it had to be. The only questions of importance were the terms, whether it could be made part of a general arrangement covering all war debts and whether some room for renegotiating the terms, perhaps a most-favoured-nation clause, could be inserted. In the second half of 1922, three developments came together to force the Cabinet to change the policy of inertia into which it had drifted since May 1920. First, the new Republican Administration, which took power in March 1921, had asked for wider authority to handle the war debts. Legislation establishing a Funding Commission, deputed to negotiate the repayment of the debts, proved controversial and confirmation of the membership was delayed until April 1922. It immediately asked indebted governments to present proposals for settling or funding. Second, interest on the demand obligations came due in October and November 1922 after three years' tacit deferral. The Chancellor had reminded the Commons in April 1921 that the payment had to be made, it was included in the budget estimates, refusal would be tantamount to repudiation, but how much was required? Third, inflation was destroying Germany's capacity to pay reparations and the French were threatening to take by force what they could not obtain peacefully. The Balfour Note was a last, futile, attempt to use European instability as a weapon with which to force the USA to reduce its financial demands on Britain and, by the end of 1922, the Cabinet had accepted that the demands it implied were only pushing France into even greater intransigence.

Inertia: summer 1920 to spring 1921

Lloyd George was in no hurry to send Wilson the letter on which the Cabinet had decided when it called off the Blackett–Rathbone talks in May 1920. A second conference with the French was held at Lympne on 20 June 1920 at which ministers discussed at greater length, and explicitly, the connection between Germany's liability and inter-allied debts. Lloyd George said that he favoured the cancellation of all debts. If this was unacceptable to the USA, he would agree to cancel French and Italian debts to the extent that the USA cancelled British debts. However, the US elections made it a bad moment for negotiations and one-sided cancellation would mean the surrender of Britain's only bargaining counter. The two governments agreed that delay was the best course, with an understanding that they both favoured cancellation and the French should not be pressed for repayment.[3]

In the meantime, the US Treasury's response to the British decision to call off the Blackett–Rathbone talks was predictable, unambiguous, uncompromising, laced with the bitterness of disappointed efforts, conviction that agreement had been near, and suspicion that Rathbone had been treated with discourtesy. Geddes, now British Ambassador in Washington, was told sharply that his government had repeatedly been informed that there was no relation between its debts to the USA and advances made by the USA or the UK to other governments, or to German reparations. As it well knew, interest could only be deferred if the debts were funded. The British should send a representative to the USA to complete the negotiations.[4]

Lloyd George's letter to Wilson went through half a dozen drafts between the end of June and its despatch on 5 August, after the Spa Conference. At House's suggestion, the Cabinet's decision was just one of several subjects covered and it came at the end of a survey of European politics. It was also deliberately discursive. There is no evidence that the Treasury provided any advice.[5] Reporting on the talks with the French, Lloyd George wrote that the British believed that the German indemnity should be fixed at a reasonable sum so that loans could be raised on the security of defined payments. Millerand had had great difficulty persuading his own government of this, but had at length succeeded. It was, however, impossible for France 'to agree to accept anything less than it was entitled to under the Treaty unless its debts to its Allies and Associates in the war were treated in the same way.' Although the British thought this was fair, they did not think they could cancel sums owed by France except as part of a general settlement of inter-allied debts. 'British public opinion would never support a one-sided arrangement at its sole expense' and, if there were such, it would seriously embitter Anglo-American relations:

> Accordingly the British Government has informed the French Government that it will agree to any equitable arrangement for the reduction or cancellation of Inter-Allied indebtedness, but such an arrangement must be one which applies all round.[6]

The Americans were also in no hurry. The President, incapacitated by his stroke, could only sporadically attend to business. The election was imminent. It can be safely assumed that Treasury officers were responsible for drafting the part of his letter dealing with the debt, sent on 3 November, the day after the election. It was tough, insistent and threatening. Having outlined the legal position, it stated baldly that:

> It is highly improbable that either the Congress or popular opinion in this country will ever permit a cancellation of any part of the debt of the British Government…in order to induce the British Government to remit, in whole or in part, the debt to Great Britain of France or any other of the Allied Governments, or that it would consent to a cancellation or reduction in the debts of any of the Allied Governments as an inducement towards a practical settlement of the reparation claims.

Any arrangements the British might make with its allies should be settled in the light of this position and any arrangements that the USA might make with other debtors would be on the understanding that they would not affect the payment of the British debt to the USA. Funding the obligations would 'do more to strengthen the friendly relations' between the two countries than 'any other course of dealing with the same.' The long delay in funding was already embarrassing the US Treasury,

> which will find itself compelled to begin to collect back and current interest if speedy progress is not made with the funding. Unless arrangements are completed for funding such loans and in that connection for the deferring of interest, in the present state of opinion here, there is likely to develop an unfortunate misunderstanding.

A representative should be sent to Washington without delay 'to arrange to carry out the obligation of the British Government to convert its demand obligations held by our Treasury into long-time obligations.'[7]

The Chancellor was anxious even before he saw Wilson's letter.[8] When he did receive the letter, he renewed his plea for one-sided cancellation. He stressed that the continental debts were practically worthless; even interest was unlikely to be paid for some years, and then only at the cost of weak exchange rates and increased competition. As long as the debts were outstanding, there would be tensions and misunderstandings. Why keep the shadow, damaging relations and curtailing the demand for British goods, when there was no substance? The UK was bound by the obligations held by the US Treasury: the USA had insisted that they be funded, in accordance with their terms, and Britain had not complied. The British had proposed all-round cancellation and had been refused. It would be demeaning and pointless to repeat the suggestion. If the Cabinet continued to do nothing, the US Treasury would, 'for its own protection, in face of a hostile Congress,' have to call for payment of back interest of $314.6m (£89.9m at an exchange rate of $3.50). Unlike a demand for the repayment of principal, this was not 'a manifest absurdity', but it would entail heavy gold shipments and the suspension of convertibility, with unknown effects on credit. Moreover, to refuse would not be 'compatible with our honour' and would damage British credit. There was no alternative but to send a representative to resume negotiations, but with the proviso that the Bonds should be retained by the US Treasury and not sold, as Warren G. Harding the President-elect had proposed.[9]

On 17 December, the Cabinet thoroughly confused themselves (or the Cabinet Secretary) over whether a failure to negotiate was repudiation, before agreeing to send an official.[10] Chalmers, who had retired from the Treasury in March 1919, was asked to be the expert. He was told that the Cabinet was ready to fulfil the terms of the obligations, although still believing that all-round cancellation was the best policy. Nevertheless, the agreement should not take a form which precluded later reconsideration of the terms. There should be no conditions about the terms the UK should give its debtors, or the financial or commercial policy of the UK or Europe, as had been threatened in May. This said, the UK intended to give terms to its debtors which were at least as favourable as those it received from the USA.[11]

The Mission was announced on 2 January 1921 and Chalmers was expected to sail on 22 January. At Lloyd George's behest, his departure was postponed so that Geddes, who was to visit the UK, could be consulted. On 4 February, the Chancellor told the public for the first time that the UK had proposed all-round cancellation and that the USA had refused to consider it. This produced a furore in Congress, which knew nothing of the proposal, and in the Administration, which had not been warned that the statement was coming. Coincidentally, Houston told the Chairman of the Senate Foreign Affairs Committee that he would cease debt negotiations so that his successor might be free to pursue his own policy.[12] It was clearly pointless to send Chalmers before the new Administration was in place; his journey was once more postponed.

Using as a lever the approaching date for the return to their owners of the subrogated securities, the Chancellor urged during March that Chalmers should sail as soon as possible (see p. 467).[13] Nothing came of this, but, presenting the budget, Chamberlain, speaking on behalf of Horne, pushed policy into a corner by reminding the Commons that at least half of a whole year's interest had to be provided in 1922–3.[14] The Treasury thus made public a hitherto unspoken assumption: that whether the British agreed to convert the demand obligations or no they would start paying interest after the three-year deferral, which had been discussed, but never agreed, during the Blackett–Rathbone negotiations.

The Cabinet did not discuss the debt again until 10 May, when another paper from the Treasury drew attention to the cost should subrogated securities not be returned to their owners by 31 March 1922. The Chancellor suggested approaching the US Treasury with a request to release the securities 'independently of the general question of conversion', hoping that it would accept that 'our promise to pay will be equally binding without this specific security'. The question widened to whether negotiations should be resumed. Some in the Cabinet, led almost certainly by Austen Chamberlain (now Lord Privy Seal) and Horne, argued that the time was ripe, that the policy of the Republicans would be similar to that of the Democrats, that further delay was 'inconsistent with the national dignity', possibly damaging to British credit, and that relations with Washington might be poisoned. Others, probably led by Churchill, argued that delay had done no harm so far, that the new Administration seemed more conciliatory and that, given time, it might be 'guided' towards universal cancellation. The Cabinet finally refused to agree that the request be made and, Austen Chamberlain dissenting, it decided to continue its policy of inactivity.[15]

What did inactivity mean? In the middle of July, Blackett told the Chancellor that he did not think that there was any

> clearly defined policy except to postpone discussion of the subject in the hope that conditions...may be more favourable at a later date. H.M.G. certainly regards it as inequitable that it should be forced to pay interest & repay principal on the British debt to the U.S.A. unless simultaneously France, Italy, etc., begin to make corresponding payt. on their debts to the British Govt. On the other hand H.M.G. seems resigned to the necessity of beginning to pay interest on this debt in Oct. 1922, & does not exclude the possibility that France & Italy may not then begin paying on their debts to the British Govt.
>
> In fact, H.M.G.'s policy is, I think, to watch events & in due course to secure a round-table discussion of the whole problem on the broadest possible terms.[16]

Incoherent, unrealistic and divided, the Cabinet had stumbled on a policy. Although Andrew Mellon, the new US Treasury Secretary, initially believed that he could continue to negotiate funding of the British certificates at the point where Rathbone had left off, he later decided that he needed to ask Congress to grant him more flexible powers.[17]

The World War Foreign Debt Commission

A bill giving Mellon virtually unlimited authority to negotiate funding terms was sent to the Finance Committee of the Senate and the Ways and Means Committee of the House on 22 June 1921. Since the Armistice, there had been a recognition among a wide range of American industrial, financial and agricultural interests that US and European prosperity were connected. Translating this perception into policy advice had been hampered by the cost and unpopularity of cancellation – as in the UK, there was a widespread feeling that the taxpayer was unduly burdened

– and the sense that Europe's problems were inflicted on itself by reparations, armaments expenditure and fiscal and monetary indiscipline. It was, therefore, not complete cancellation or even interest deferment for more than a few years that these interests sought, but moderation in the US Treasury's demands which would help stabilise the European markets and enable private American capital to facilitate recovery.[18]

Mellon's letter to the President requesting him to transmit the bill to Congress showed how recession and a Republican Administration had allowed these views into the open air. It pointed out that the Liberty Bond legislation was complex and the Secretary had no power to extend maturities or defer interest on obligations financed under other Acts:[a] simplification would make it easier to negotiate terms which would make the obligations more attractive and better protect American interests.The reason for seeking flexibility was that:

> In some cases the debtor nations owe large amounts to other countries as well as to the United States, and it may be advisable, and in some cases indeed necessary, to consider comprehensively the entire debt of such countries, its financial condition and resources, so as to work out a refunding plan reasonably within the ability of such country to carry out.

Some countries might find it impossible to pay either interest or principal and insistence might be disastrous for them. In such circumstances, it was impossible for the Treasury to deal fairly with the debtors and simultaneously protect US interests when planning the funding of the obligations.

Congress was not prepared to surrender its authority over the war debt. Despite Republican control of both Senate and House, there was the traditional suspicion of the Executive. Some thought that the debts were an aspect of finance and fell into the budgetary process. Republicans thought a Democratic Treasury had lent to the allies without adequate safeguards and in contravention of the intentions of Congress, especially after the Armistice. Most Democrats wanted the Treasury to negotiate individual agreements, before submitting them for ratification. From the start there was violent opposition to the power, included in the draft bill, enabling the Secretary to substitute the obligations of one country for those of another: for taking, say, German or Austrian Bonds in place of British or French. This, some believed, could mean the USA becoming the owner of assets of a lesser quality, with a greater risk of default and loss to the tax payer.[19] The Democrats tried to appropriate war debt payments to a bonus for discharged soldiers, asserting that the Republicans cared more for Europe's Treasuries than for American veterans. Taxpayers, farmers and the unemployed all pressed for attention, and politicians of all persuasions had to move nimbly when the $10,000m debt was costing $450m in annual interest, some 10 per cent of Federal expenditure.

a These were held by the American Relief Administration ($84.1m), the War and Navy Departments on account of the sale of surplus stores ($565m) and the US Grain Corporation ($56.9m). US Secretary of the Treasury, *ARSF*, 1921, p. 40.

Apart from the substitution of the Bonds of one borrower for those of another, Congress feared three possibilities: the Secretary would not keep Congress informed – a disquiet which had been increased by Austen Chamberlain's admission that the British had mooted cancellation; the Secretary would negotiate very long maturities and low interest rates; and he might cancel debts. When Mellon gave evidence in June and July, he failed to convince and the bill was much amended. The Treasury accepted the changes and on 19 October introduced a new bill, which finally received Presidential approval on 9 February.[20]

Little was left of the proposal sent to Congress the previous summer. The 'Refunding Act' created a World War Foreign Debt Commission (the 'Commission' or 'Funding Commission'), with five members, to negotiate with foreign governments. The Chairman was the Secretary of the Treasury, the other four members being appointed by the President, in the usual form, 'by and with the advice and consent of the Senate.' By adding a string of restrictions, the Act left deferral of interest as the Commission's sole important authority. The longest maturity could be 15 June 1947 and the lowest interest rate 4¼ per cent; when obligations had been converted or refunded, the Commission's powers ceased; no debt could be cancelled; obligations of one government could not be exchanged for those of another; the authority provided by the Act lasted only three years; the report of the Commission was to be published annually; and copies of agreements were to be sent to Congress immediately. Thus, once again, Congress tied the Administration's hands and the only way the British could deflate Europe's balance sheet was to offer its debtors one-sided cancellation, as its Treasury had been urging since February 1920.

The Balfour Note

Harding nominated the members of the Commission in February. Hughes, the Secretary of State, and Herbert Hoover, the Secretary of Commerce, were expected. The other two nominees, Senator Reed Smoot and Representative Theodore Burton, meeting opposition on the grounds that they were members of the legislature, were not confirmed until 11 April, nearly ten months after Mellon had sent his bill to Congress. The Commission held its first meeting a week later and, without more ado, decided that debtors should be told that it wished to receive 'proposals or representations' for the 'settlement and refunding' of their obligations.

As the invitation was delivered in London, Geddes saw Hughes in Washington. There are two versions of the conversation, so different as to invite the suspicion that Geddes, like George Harvey, the US Ambassador in London, was trying to push his government into a settlement. According to Geddes, the Secretary urged the British to be the first government to respond and to send a mission at once. Hughes, Geddes said, had stressed that the Commission had no power to consider any matters wider than the funding terms and had suggested that the Americans might agree to a treaty or convention which would preclude them from giving any other borrower better terms without the consent of the British. The American record of the conversation does not mention pressing the British into sending delegates at an early date and shows that Geddes proposed the most-favoured-nation agreement, Hughes studiously refusing to be drawn, merely inviting the British to put the proposal in writing.[21]

The American version rings true. Most-favoured-nation treatment would have been an unrealistic promise, awarding the British such terms as were necessary to enable a Greece, a Cuba or a Liberia to meet their debts. It would have required legislation, which would never have passed Congress. It was the reverse of the policy which the Commission was to adopt, of writing funding terms which reflected each borrower's capacity to pay. 'Without the consent of the British' removed any weight from the proposal, promising only lengthy negotiation each time agreement had been reached with other governments. Moreover, as Blackett pointed out, it would have been superfluous because the British could always protect themselves by giving their debtors the same terms as the USA gave the British. Although Geddes gave it prominence and some ministers took it up when they debated the Balfour Note and the possibility of keeping the door open to a lower rate or cancellation, the UK Treasury expected no such agreement. It also warned that the USA would give better terms to other debtors and that these would not alter those negotiated by the UK (see p. 522). It followed that the Treasury's opposition to making the securities marketable was based on the damage to British credit if they were sold, rather than on the difficulties of renegotiating the terms once the Bonds passed out of the ownership of the US Treasury.[22]

The US Commission's invitation came when Germany's failure to meet its reparation liabilities was once more straining the Anglo-French relationship. In December 1921, Germany warned the Reparation Commission that she would be unable to pay the instalments due in January and February. In January, the Germans were asked to submit plans for 1922, together with proposals for fiscal and monetary reform which would ensure that the payments could be made. The plans were presented at the end of January, but Germany's financial condition was such that they did not include definite proposals for payment. On 21 March, the Commission imposed conditions designed to ensure that resources were available: the abolition of subsidies, controls on the export of capital, a more independent central bank and increased taxes. Performance was to be examined by the Commission on 31 May. If the Commission was satisfied, the moratorium would be confirmed; if not, the old schedule of payments would be resumed, payment would be demanded within two weeks and, in the event of failure (which was inevitable), default would be declared in the middle of June.

Germany rejected the demands at the beginning of April. At the beginning of May, the Commission asked a committee of bankers to assess Germany's capacity and advise on whether she could raise an external loan to help pay the reparations. The Germans made the April and May payments and, at the end of that month, promised reforms sufficient to pass the 31 May deadline. On 10 June, the bankers reported that a loan would be impossible if the reparations burden remained at its existing level.

These events, and the government's sales of paper marks for the foreign currencies needed to pay the reparations, produced a further depreciation of the German currency; on 1 January 1922, the rate against sterling was 771, on 1

March it was 1,007, and on 1 June 1,188. The fall accelerated as the Cabinet in London deliberated on the US Commission's invitation, so that by 1 July the rate was 1,750 and by 11 September 5,725.[23]

Despite the German collapse, British policy had changed little since May 1920, when the Cabinet broke off the inter-Treasury negotiations; only if the USA reduced British debts would Britain reduce those owed by France, so enabling Germany to be relieved. During 1922, this clear, if short-sighted, approach was found wanting. The German morass demanded lower, realistic, reparations; the French would only agree if their war debts were reduced or cancelled; and the USA was insistent that the British fund their debt. The Cabinet procrastinated. At the end of April, Blackett told the Chancellor that 'it remains to be decided whether we are really willing to enter into an early discussion of the narrow question of funding the British debt. We are of course ready and anxious to discuss with the U.S. Govt. the broad questions of Inter-Allied indebtedness and reparation'.[24] Three months later, the Cabinet decided on two courses: it would tell the Funding Commission that in accordance with the terms of its obligations it would discuss the 'narrow question'; and, with the Balfour Note, it tried to influence American opinion towards a more generous settlement by publicly linking the amount the UK would demand of Europe to the amount the USA demanded of the UK. The effect would have been to balance British external payments and receipts on account of war debts (other than those to and from the Empire) with the same result as all-round cancellation. The Note, despatched after lengthy Cabinet debates, set Austen Chamberlain, *quondam* Chancellor, and Horne, current Chancellor, against Lloyd George and Churchill.

The French reaction to Germany's failure to pay was unforgiving and relations with Britain deteriorated as she threatened independent military action in the Ruhr. On 23 May 1922, five months after Germany asked for a moratorium, the British Cabinet met with Bradbury (the British representative on the Reparation Commission), Lord D'Abernon (Ambassador to Berlin) and Blackett in attendance. Ministers agreed with Bradbury that the failure to find the resources with which to make payment was rooted in 'the gross mismanagement of Germany's public finances', rather than a weak balance of payments: the tax burden was 'ridiculously low' so that the government had to print money to buy foreign currencies. The Prime Minister, the Chancellor and Chamberlain agreed with D'Abernon that the measures needed to end inflation would produce such unemployment and social discontent that revolution might be expected. The Prime Minister warned that this would be a more attractive example to the British than that of Russia:

> He was anxious to press the Germans to pay but do not let us in so doing produce a disaster which would shake Europe. Russia is now more or less discounted but Germany was an essential part of the economic organism of Europe and a disaster to her would be immediately and directly reflected in all countries.

Bradbury reminded the Cabinet that avoidance of a violent French reaction depended on the Germans being able to issue an external loan and that the bankers might recommend that this be made dependent on a reduction in reparations to a realistic figure. The French would say that this was unacceptable and the question of modifying inter-allied debts would be raised. But, said Lloyd George, it was not possible for the government to face the electorate with a national debt of £8,000m and unemployment of two million and announce that it intended to forgive all those who owed the UK money, while paying everything it owed. The position would be different if the USA would cancel the UK's debts as the UK cancelled those of its debtors. He favoured proposing to the USA that the British should only collect their debts from Continental Europe to the extent that the USA collected from her.[25]

On 8 June, the Chancellor told the Cabinet that he thought that the Funding Commission's invitation should be accepted and a mission sent to Washington. When the paper came before the Cabinet, it decided that Balfour (the Acting Secretary of State for Foreign Affairs, Curzon being ill) should draft a letter, for despatch to the European debtors, referring to the American demand, recognising the obligation and explaining why the UK felt it had to make a similar demand. Emphasis was to be placed on giving the same terms to all the US Treasury's debtors; most-favoured-nation treatment. A second letter was to be prepared for the Funding Commission, acknowledging the debt but stating that the UK could not respond until it had consulted its debtors 'on the kindred question of her European debts'.[26] This was never sent. Instead, on 7 July, the Cabinet decided that the Commission should be told that a delegation would arrive in Washington early in September to discuss the funding of the debt and that in the meantime the British Government 'would make arrangements without prejudice for the payment of interest'. The letter was despatched on 14 July, but without the reference to the interest, which had to wait until the day after Balfour's Note was sent.[27]

The Note was discussed four more times during the following five weeks as the Cabinet reconsidered its policy in the light of the mark's collapse. The Chancellor's case for agreeing to fund was clear, realistic and persuasive. It started with a warning. The Commission's powers were limited to funding the obligations and the British mission would be unable to discuss inter-allied debts or reparations. Once the Bonds had been sold to the public, every cent would have to be paid without reference to reparations or the terms later received by France and Italy: 'A decision to send out a delegation will therefore be a decision to pay the British debt to the United States Government in full, whatever may happen in other directions.' There were no budgetary implications; the estimates already included the interest and any sinking fund could be refinanced in the sterling market,

b There was one unexplained departure from the standard Treasury line that repaying the US debt was not a tax problem, but an exchange rate problem. It comes on the page following : 'The problem is not how to find the dollars, but simply how to persuade our own people to pay the taxation involved in the transfer of the dollars to the Exchequer's control'. Cab. 24/137, CP 4020, Horne, 'British Debt to the United States Government', 8 June 1922. For a different interpretation, see Schuker, 'American Policy Towards Debts and Reconstruction', pp. 118–19, in Fink *et al.* (1991).

converting external into internal debt.[b] This would only change in the unlikely events of the USA demanding that back interest or capital be paid immediately or being prepared to take reparation Bonds in lieu of the British certificates. The Treasury acknowledged that the most powerful argument against funding was that it would mean surrendering the strongest weapon for forcing the USA to discuss all war debts, agreeing payments to the USA *pari passu* with payments by continental Europe to the UK. However, it was pointless to press France and Italy, for no cash could be forthcoming in the near future and it would merely 'drive European public finance deeper into the slough and increase unemployment in the British Isles.' The Cabinet must accept that if the debt was to be funded there would be no counterbalancing receipts from the Continent. Not only so, but it was clear that the USA would have to forgive much of the Continent's debts and the UK would be paying the USA without the benefit of the easier terms the USA would be giving its other debtors.

Notwithstanding this, the Chancellor used a host of arguments to support a recommendation that the UK should agree to convert the certificates. A contract was a contract. Even if it wished otherwise, for at least two or three years political constraints would ensure that US Administrations would be unable to remit, cancel or exchange obligations. Although no one really thought that the USA would demand immediate repayment, while the demand obligations were hanging over the market sterling could not stabilise. A failure to fund could lead to 'unpleasant incidents' during the approaching US elections, while funding might enable the UK to influence the course of American legislation, which was threatening to raise tariffs and subsidise American shipping. Finally, once the USA had settled with its only solvent debtor, there was a chance it would cancel or reduce the debts of the Continent and start to co-operate in European affairs. At the least, the UK would have regained the freedom to handle the debts owed to itself and reparations as it thought fit:

> The paramount necessity of employing our people makes it urgent that, since the United States Government will not take the initiative, we should cut the knot ourselves, even at the cost of giving up whatever hope there might otherwise be of escaping from part of the burden of the debt to the United States Government.[28]

The collapse of the mark gave the case immediacy. France, said Horne, would not accept lower reparations until she knew the size of her debts to the UK and the USA. How could one tell her that she had to reduce her demands on Germany and, simultaneously, tell her to pay the UK?

The rest of Horne and Chamberlain's case rested on judgements about the American reaction. While stressing that, irrespective of how the USA treated others, it would exact every cent from Britain, they thought that there might be a change in attitude in the longer term; Geddes had told the Cabinet that, although the US public still saw the debt as a commercial obligation, both Mellon and Hughes thought that, if properly handled, opinion would come round to cancellation. The

USA, said Horne, would be irritated to be held up as a 'Shylock', yet the terms of the obligations gave it the right to sell them and, without further legislation, the Funding Commission could only agree to the 'grievous burden' of 4¼ per cent repayable in twenty-five years. The Note would make matters 'infinitely worse'. While Chamberlain, prickly and proud as ever, called the US official attitude 'selfish' and 'almost insolent', he also thought that the effect of the proposed letter would be ruinous, undoing the good done by the Washington Naval Conference. The British had proposed cancellation on general grounds and been refused. How could they now ask for remission on narrow and selfish grounds?

Churchill put the case for sending the Note with his usual verve. He did not believe that cancellation at some future time was a realistic prospect. No US government would be prepared to court unpopularity by forgiving the debt once the Bonds were issued. If the USA was unhelpful when the UK was in financial straits, it would be less helpful when it had recovered. The British public had the right to be told the facts and know the government's policy. Equally, the American public was unaware of the strength of the British case. There would be no improvement in the funding terms if a mission was sent and it was 'a pious, illusory and vain hope, based on no reasonable foundation', to think otherwise. The UK's debtors would not be upset because they would know that the UK did not mean to ask them to pay, even though the UK intended to pay its debts to the USA:

> In view of the state of Europe this was a righteous and a proper document, enunciating a policy of wisdom, firmness and broad justice…It would be a cruel wrong to the British people to force them to give up all that was owing to them while at the same time compelling them to pay every farthing they owed.

The letter would cause 'momentary irritation', but it would then make the Americans search their consciences and question whether they were right.

The final Cabinet showed that it was the Prime Minister who had proposed the Notes and that his reasons were electoral, mixed with resentment at the growth of US power. Although the French and Italians would be 'a little angry…it was time we asserted ourselves and made clear that this whole trouble ought not to be settled at our expense.' France was a rich country. Taxation was higher in Britain than elsewhere, and yet it was suggested that she pay all her debts. He heavily discounted the importance of the American reaction and was unprepared to ask for favours. The USA had exploited British commercial weakness during the war and was now trying to capture the international shipping business and attain naval supremacy. It wanted commercial and financial supremacy. The advances had been taken to finance the allies and American businesses had made 'huge' profits from them. He carried the day and, with Horne and Chamberlain recording their dissent, the Cabinet concluded that after minor changes the Notes to the continental debtors should be sent.[29]

Although addressed to the representatives in London of France, Italy, Roumania, Portugal, Greece and the Serb–Croat–Slovene State, the Note that came out of these discussions reads exactly as had been intended: a powerfully written message to the US Administration and people. It began with a statement of policy – that the UK was prepared, as part of a satisfactory international settlement, 'to remit all the debts due to Great Britain by our allies in respect of loans, or by Germany in respect of reparations' – and then explained why this had become difficult to accomplish:

> With the most perfect courtesy, and in the exercise of their undoubted rights, the American Government have required this country to pay the interest accrued since 1919 on the Anglo-American debt, to convert it from an unfunded to a funded debt, and to repay it by a sinking fund in twenty-five years. Such a procedure is clearly in accordance with the original contract. His Majesty's Government make no complaint of it; they recognise their obligations and are prepared to fulfil them.

Funding and repayment of the British debt to the USA must, however, 'profoundly' modify the policy of cancellation:

> They [the British government] cannot treat the repayment of the Anglo-American loan as if it were an isolated incident in which only the United States of America and Great Britain had any concern. It is but one of a connected series of transactions, in which this country appears sometimes as debtor, sometimes as creditor, and, if our undoubted obligations as a debtor are to be enforced, our not less undoubted rights as a creditor cannot be left wholly in abeyance.

The British government was reluctant to change its policy and ask for repayment of the debts owed by its allies. It would have the clear advantage if all the debts were repaid, but the matter could not be looked at from such a narrow standpoint. The allies had been

> partners in the greatest international effort ever made in the cause of freedom; and they are still partners in dealing with some, at least, of its results. Their debts were incurred, their loans were made, not for the separate advantage of particular States, but for a great purpose common to them all…
>
> To generous minds it can never be agreeable, although for reasons of State, it may perhaps be necessary, to regard the monetary aspect of this great event as a thing apart, to be torn from its historical setting and treated as no more than an ordinary commercial dealing between traders who borrow and capitalists who lend.

The 'distaste' with which the British government adopted the new method of dealing with its allies' debts was increased by its awareness of the damage to the world economy – to credit, exchange, production and trade – wrought by the 'weight of international indebtedness'.

Withholding demands for repayment was only possible if it was mutual, for 'It cannot be right that one partner in the common enterprise should recover all that she has lent, and that another, while recovering nothing, should be required to pay all she has borrowed.' Such a course would be contrary to 'every principle of natural justice and cannot be expected to commend itself to the people of this country.' Suffering from unprecedented taxation and with much of their wealth destroyed, British taxpayers would ask why they had been singled out to bear a burden which, even if contractual, was 'obviously one-sided'. There was only one answer. The British government, abandoning its favoured policy, must ask its allies to pay such interest and principal as was necessary to enable it to pay the USA: 'the amount of interest and repayment for which they ask depends not so much on what France and the other Allies owe to Great Britain as on what Great Britain has to pay America.'[30]

This was powerful and elegant, unambiguous even after Cabinet adjustment, although including at least one statement of doubtful accuracy which subtracted from the general effect and was to give Mellon an easy target. The tone was reasonable, managing at the same time to be both courteous and provocative. The shafts were true, demonstrating that the author understood how the Americans viewed themselves and where they were most sensitive. It enunciated a generous policy, formally offering to sever the link between monies lent and the obligation to repay. £1,300m owed by the European allies, £650m owed by Russia and £1,450m owed by Germany would be cancelled in return for the USA cancelling £850m of British debt. Ignoring reparations, and assuming that the remaining £1,950m had been borrowed from the British investor on the 4¼ per cent allowed to the Funding Commission, the offer entailed writing off a net £1,100m, or £47m ($227m) a year in interest; some 6 per cent of the revenues forecast in the budget.

It was also maladroit, a gamble and impractical. Maladroit because it put British policy on reparations into a strait-jacket, precluding the flexible use of the cancellation weapon to inveigle France into reducing her demands on Germany. A gamble because the Cabinet had already decided to pay interest and send a mission to fund the obligations, a decision which had been confirmed by Horne in the Commons even as the Cabinet debate was in full swing. But the Cabinet had not decided to pay irrespective of the rate; the comment to Hughes by Geddes that 'so far as the financial question was concerned, in the light of the fact of payment, the note made no difference whatever' was misleading. The Note was only justified if the Cabinet had judged correctly that it would move American opinion towards a more generous settlement and that the possibility of obtaining a lower rate was worth the loss of goodwill and reputation it would cost.[31]

It was impractical because the financial demands on the allies implied by the Note were wholly beyond their resources. This had been stressed by the Chancellor when making his final attempt to stop the Note being sent, and was repeated by Blackett on 12 July when he made his last plea. Assuming that Britain's European debtors demanded from Germany everything that Britain demanded from them, Germany would have to find £57m a year for the British debt to the USA, in addition to the sums being demanded by France. Add a moderate amount for other claimants and Germany's liability would be £184m a year for twenty-five years, higher than the revised schedule of payments which was proving quite beyond her capacity. This would be increased further if the USA failed to cancel the debts owed by the Continental debtors:

> Is it really possible to pretend in face of these figures that we are sincere in our professed policy of paying the U.S.A. and making Europe pay us the equivalent?
>
> ...Our policy being to persuade France to agree to a big reduction in the total of Reparation in the interest of European civilisation, can we reasonably pretend that we expect Europe to provide what we pay to the U.S.A.?
>
> ...if we really mean to try and save Europe and are now merely venting our preliminary grumble before doing so, is it worth while to begin by pillorying American selfishness?[32]

The Note had immediate repercussions in Europe. Poincaré, finding the British threatening to demand repayment at a time when the French fiscal position was deteriorating further, became even more intransigent. At an Inter-Allied Conference held in London in the middle of August to discuss another German request for a moratorium, the French proposed that the allies seize German resources – mines, forests and customs dues – and, for the third time, asked for agreement to an occupation of the Ruhr. After the British resisted, and the Conference broke down, the problem was returned to the Reparation Commission. The German attitude hardened, the government refusing to countenance the surrender of productive resources and declaring that food imports would take precedence over reparations. Coercion was only avoided when Belgium agreed to take German Treasury Bills in payment for the remaining cash due in 1922, all of which fell to her. During this uncertainty, the mark fell to around 10,000 against sterling. By 1 September, it had rallied to 5,750, only to relapse to 7,125 by the beginning of October. On 1 November, the rate was 20,000.[33]

The turmoil ensured that the short-sightedness of the Note was made apparent in quick order. Ten days after its despatch, the Cabinet met to discuss how the government should react to the French demands for the seizure of German resources. What sort of bargain could be offered? The most obvious was to write off debt in return for a more reasonable attitude towards Germany. This had the advantage that it would appear that the UK was not just watching the situation on the Continent deteriorate without making an effort to help, but it had two drawbacks. It was thought that the French and Italians did not intend to meet their debts to the British and Americans, so the promise of cancellation might be of little value to them. And, as Lloyd George reminded his colleagues, forgiveness would affect negotiations with the USA:

> if we made it clear to the United States that the action of America was responsible for the continuance of the chaos in Europe, it would be a negotiating pawn when our representatives went to Washington. That, he believed, was the view which the Cabinet had taken.

Averting the risk that France and Germany would be relieved at the UK's sole expense and bringing home to the USA her responsibility for the problems of Europe was the purpose of the Note. Why 'fritter away' the policy?

The problem could have been side-stepped by adjourning the conference until the allied funding missions returned from the USA with the terms settled. When the French refused delay, the Cabinet started to dismantle its policy: first, although it had already been decided to make the first interest payment to the USA on 15 October, it gave its representatives discretion to postpone the collection of interest and principal from the allies until the missions had returned and, then, to cancel back interest and interest accruing during any moratorium. Not very generous, perhaps, but a distinct break with the principle of the Note.[34]

The American reaction

Although the US Administration had been pressing the British to send a mission and in July the French had sought diplomatic advantage by sending a representative to Washington, there was further delay. Hughes was to visit Brazil for her centenary celebration, while Mellon and Burton planned holidays in Europe.[35] This was convenient, for feelings in the USA were running high that summer. Chamberlain had warned the Cabinet that it was 'gibbeting' the USA before the world. The reaction bore him out. *The Times*, in London, immediately saw the resentment which would be felt.[36] Harvey, writing to the President from London, called the Note a 'blunder'.[37] Hoover, the member of the Commission who took the most stubborn line on cancellation, was reported to be 'incensed'.[38] Strong, the cool central banker, described it as 'most unfavourable to the prompt adjustment of the debt problem.'[39] In Congress, the Note provided ammunition for those trying to earmark debt repayments to veterans' bonuses, a proposal which would have reached the statute book had it not received the Presidential veto on 19 September. At the Treasury, on 24 August, Mellon issued a rebuttal, repeating that the British debt was a bilateral matter, unconnected to the debts between other countries or with reparations, and (justifiably) attacking the Note's suggestion that the USA had 'insisted, in substance, if not in form', that the UK should be the borrower, although the allies were the spenders.[40]

Hughes gave the State Department's reaction to Geddes on 14 August. The Note had had 'the effect of stiffening public opinion as it was regarded as placing the responsibility upon the United States'. The size of reparations was a question of Germany's capacity to pay and the maintenance of a stable government able to make the payments. It was confusing to make a link with debts owed to the USA by other nations because their repayment depended on each governments' capacity to pay 'in the light of all the circumstances'. The 'fundamental matter' was the size of reparations, for the French needed cash, which could only be satisfied by an international loan. This meant fixing Germany's liability at a level she could afford.[41]

Also on 14 August, ministers agreed that the Chancellor should be the chief delegate in Washington, with discretion to agree terms within the general lines indicated by the Cabinet's discussions; on 6 October, the Funding Commission was told that the delegates would be the Chancellor and Norman, who would sail on 28 October. However, the Coalition broke up on 19 October, after Conservative junior ministers and backbenchers had voted to fight the next election as an independent party. Bonar Law named his new government on 24 October and, at the election on 15 November, the Conservatives were returned with a large majority over all other parties combined. Lloyd George, Horne, Austen Chamberlain, Churchill and Balfour, the main protagonists since 1920 in the cancellation debate, left the government. Curzon, who had supported one-sided cancellation in 1920 and considered the Note 'extremely unwise', remained at the Foreign Office.[42] Baldwin, whose views on the policy are unidentified in the Cabinet conclusions but whose biographers believe had followed the Treasury's line, became Chancellor.[43]

The first interest payments

Although the Cabinet would not countenance one-sided cancellation and waited before putting the US debt on a permanent basis, there had been no real doubt that interest would be paid from October 1922, three years after the deferral which had been tacitly permitted by the US Treasury after the Blackett–Rathbone talks failed. By the summer of 1922, even Churchill believed that payment would be made.[44] It is unclear how the decision was reached, or whether a decision was needed. Nearly a decade later, in January 1931, Horne wrote that the question had been frequently discussed, but there is no contemporary record of Prime Ministerial or Cabinet decision. Indeed, there is only one reference to the resumption of payment, and that was in December 1921 during a general Cabinet discussion of the economic situation: a warning of the difficulty of stopping payments once they began and of the effect of taxation on British competitiveness.[45]

The reminder, given to the Commons in April 1921, that interest would have to be found in the 1922–3 budget was followed in February 1922 by the announcement that, although the exact amount required was not yet known, £25m would be provided in the estimates; the statement was an answer to a planted question and Horne felt no need to elaborate. A month later he reminded the Commons that the understanding had been that deferral would last for only three years and, accordingly, provision had now to be made: there was no possibility that the USA would 'let the UK off' and he was 'certainly not one to ask that it should be let off'.[46] By the time of the budget on 1 May, the ground was so well prepared that the Chancellor was able to make only a passing reference to the £25m.[47] The intention was not officially communicated to the USA, but the receipt was included in the Federal budget for the financial year to end-June 1923.[48]

In April 1922, Blackett had advised paying a sum on account, enabling the funding mission to be delayed until after the Congressional elections in November, while meeting the liability.[49] The Cabinet debate on the Balfour Note ensured that the proposal was never made, but the tactic was used in the autumn when the British mission was delayed by the election. The despatch sent on 2 August, formally telling the USA that interest would be paid in October and November, noted that the October payment would be too close to the negotiations to enable the remittance to be arranged and proposed that it be made independently of them. To this end, the British asked the US Treasury to calculate the exact amount of dollars due, adding artlessly that it was 'observed' that the minimum rate of interest permitted under the Funding Act was $4^1/_4$ per cent, while that on the demand obligations was 5 per cent. They therefore suggested that the autumn payments be calculated at $4^1/_4$ per cent, without prejudice to the ultimate settlement.[50] The Funding Commission agreed to payments, 'without prejudice', at a rate of $4^1/_4$ per cent, but calculated the principal by adding the unpaid interest at 5 per cent to the nominal value of the obligations. This was not only a higher rate than the British were anticipating, but was the interest on interest which the Treasury had resisted in 1919 and 1920 and which Rathbone had abandoned. It gave the debt a nominal value of $4,686m. Hardly surprisingly, Blackett judged the response 'very unsatisfactory' and, since there was no 'suitable lead', he proposed paying $50m on account on 15 October, while leaving the exact amount to be determined during the negotiations and adjusted in the November payment.[51]

The second payment was due on the day of the general election. The Treasury initially considered postponing it until the exact sum had been fixed in the funding negotiations, now envisaged for January.[52] This appalled Geddes, who thought that it would give the anti-British press an excuse to claim default. He suggested a sum should be paid on account, as in October. $50m was paid, leaving the distribution between interest and principal to be settled later.[53]

France, Germany, the USA: Britain in the middle, Christmas 1922

Baldwin and Norman travelled to Washington as the consequences of Germany's failure to pay reached their climax, forcing the Cabinet to depart further from the policy embodied in the Balfour Note. In November, the Germans notified the Reparation Commission that they could make no further payments until the mark was stabilised. The Commission had to respond by 15 January, when an Inter-Allied Conference was to be held in Brussels. A preparatory meeting of the British, French, Belgians and Italians was held in London in the middle of December. Once again, the French would not agree to a moratorium unless it was accompanied by measures to guarantee payment, including an occupation of the Ruhr. As in August, the policy of linking the war debts was so limiting that Bonar Law changed his ground at an early stage of the conversations. As France was not getting all it expected from Germany, the UK must reduce its claims:

> For that reason – and he thought this was an important statement – if he saw some chance of a complete settlement with a prospect of finality he would be willing to run the risk in the end of having to pay an indemnity, that is to say, of paying more to the United States of America than Great Britain would receive from the Allies and Germany.[54]

At the end of December, the Cabinet went further, agreeing in principle to surrender all British claims on her European debtors in return for the transfer to the UK of the debtors' share of new German Bonds: there would be a four-year reparations moratorium, with further reductions thereafter; the gold deposited with the UK by France and Italy as security for wartime advances would be surrendered; and the remaining new Bonds, representing deferred and contingent German liabilities, would be distributed to each ally in proportion to its American obligations and become a common fund for the discharge of European debts to the USA. All reparation claims, other than those represented by the plan, would be cancelled. On 2 January 1923, when the talks resumed in Paris, the French refused the scheme. To them, it meant changes to the Peace Treaty, requiring legislative sanction, and reduced powers for the Reparation Commission: there were no guarantees during the four years when Germany was paying little or nothing; Germany would be left at the end of fifteen years as the only country in Europe without external debts; and, because British debts to the USA were greater than those of France, the British would become the largest owners of the German Bonds and, therefore, the largest recipient of any reparations.[55]

Yet, Bonar Law hankered for the policy of Lloyd George and the Balfour Note. On 12 December, he acknowledged that there had been a change, but two days later stressed that British securities had been sold or pledged to pay for supplies for all the allies and that, if it had not been done, there would have been no need to borrow from the US Treasury: 'From the point of view of justice, it cannot be right that we alone should make payment as a result of this.' Then, in words that carry personal conviction, he said that those advocating one-sided cancellation did not realise what it entailed and he was convinced that paying without receiving payment from elsewhere would 'reduce the standard of living in this country for a generation, and would be a burden upon us which no one who talks of it now has any conception of. We cannot do it.'[56]

There was no change in the Administration's policy, although for at least a year there had been public recognition that the American economy would be strengthened by improved overseas demand. At the end of 1921, when explaining the need for the Funding Act, the Secretary of the Treasury had stressed that unstable exchange rates and recession were contributing to poor US trade and that the obligations held by the USA were adding to the uncertainties and limiting the credit which the American private sector would provide to Europe.[57] Diagnosis was another matter. For the Administration, it was not the debts to the USA, but reparations which were the cause of Europe's financial problems, and there could be no stability until they had been reduced to realistic levels. A solution could best be found by distancing the question from politics by appointing an investigating committee of businessmen, supported by their governments, and including some from the USA. The Committee would reduce the 'undefined reparation asset' to certainty and report on the state of French finances, after which Congress would be in a position to consider whether a change in the law governing the war debts was necessary. Hughes added little to this when Geddes pressed for American attendance at the Paris conversations in the New Year of 1923: if the

USA did attend the meeting, it would be unable to discuss its own debt, which was, in any case, not 'vital to the settlement of the reparation problem'; if the British wished to press their own view that reparations and debts were connected, the USA would be unable to join the discussions.[58]

This was, of course, the standard US position. But public opinion was changing as falling demand damaged American trade, and especially agricultural exports. A greater interest was being taken in inter-allied indebtedness and, said Lamont, the conviction was growing that 'moderation must be practised, or our foreign trade must end.' Of the members of the Funding Commission, Mellon was 'hard-boiled', Hoover was hypocritical and Burton's 'bark was somewhat worse than his bite'. Hughes was the most liberal, and was hoping that the Commission would be able to return to Congress for modifications to the Funding Act, a procedure which Morgans had been advocating.[59] At the end of December, the normally isolationist Senator William Borah, pressed by his agricultural lobby, called for the Administration to organise an international economic conference to discuss conditions in the 'war-torn nations of Europe'. In response, Hughes, in a wide-ranging review of foreign policy, pointed out that the Administration was trying to influence European affairs without the wide-ranging powers to negotiate debt settlements it had sought in June 1921. Harding, more bluntly, told the Senate it would be futile to call a conference until the European governments welcomed it 'within the limits of discussion which the expressed will of Congress compels the Government to impose.' Congress would not allow an American representative to sit on the Reparation Commission without its express authority, which had not been given. The Funding Commission was restricted in the terms it could offer debtors:

> If Congress really means to facilitate the task of the Government in dealing with the European situation, the first practical step would be to free the hands of the commission so that helpful negotiations may be undertaken.

Both Democratic and Republican Administrations had insisted that reparations and inter-allied debts were unconnected, but European governments held a contrary view and 'it is wholly inconsistent to invite a conference for the consideration of questions in dealing with which the Government is denied all authority by act of Congress.'[60]

On 8 January 1923, Baldwin delivered his opening address to the Funding Commission. The following day, the Reparation Commission – the British dissenting – voted the Germans in default on coal deliveries, and on 10 January the French and Belgians told the German government that they intended to use their powers under the Treaty to send engineers with military protection into the Ruhr to seize coal. In the midst of this, on 9 January in Washington, President Harding told journalists that it was not possible for any nation to settle within the terms of the Funding Act and neither he nor the members of the Commission expected the British so to do. Instead, he expected the Commission to negotiate an agreement and send him a recommendation. He would then ask Congress for new legislation.[61]

Funding negotiations in Washington, Cabinet crisis in London

In August and October 1922, Blackett, in preparation for Horne's and Norman's mission, had reviewed the UK's capacity to repay the debt. As in 1919, he was relaxed about the rate and had no doubt that the UK could afford to pay 4¼ per cent, with redemption in twenty-five years. The annual interest cost on a debt which he calculated to be $4,594m would be $195m and the sinking fund $107m: a total of $302m. Accepting the obligation to pay this sum every year would, he thought, be dangerous, although it would be 'quite safe' to accept an obligation of $195m a year, together with another to repay the principal within twenty-five years. His approach to amortisation had not changed since 1919: it was not a question of repayment from revenue, but of converting external into internal debt. The uncertainties were how much the exchange rate could bear – there would be years in which 'it will not be difficult to repatriate as much as £100,000,000' – and the cost of borrowing in the sterling markets. The object of the Mission should, therefore, be to secure the 'utmost possible freedom to redeem at any time'.[62] The limit of 1947 stipulated in the Funding Act was 'unduly short', but could be accepted provided the repayment schedule was flexible. Bonds should not be agreed because they would be marketable, hamper conversion of dollar debt into sterling debt, make later cancellation more difficult and, if sold, damage British credit: the ideal was an annuity, or series of annuities. Paying a higher rate would be justified if an option to make early repayment under discount at a good rate could be negotiated. Repaying debt with dollars bought to support the exchange rate should be limited, but would be useful if it enabled the UK to repay early with cheap dollars. Complete remission of back interest should be sought and, if this failed, the rate should not be higher than 4¼ per cent. Finally, the Pittman settlement should not be disturbed and the subrogated securities should be returned.

This was very different from Blackett's negotiating position, which would exploit the Administration's unconcealed view that the Funding Act was too rigid, while protecting British credit by leaving the impression on 'sober opinion throughout the world' that a reasonable proposal had been made. Selecting a suitable plan was a matter of personal judgement, but his own included: a non-negotiable security repayable over fifty years by half-yearly sinking fund; back interest payable at 1 per cent; 2 per cent interest for the five years to 1927; and 4 per cent thereafter.[63]

How the Treasury's assessment translated into the Mission's bargaining position is not known since, in contrast to the written instructions given to Blackett and Chalmers, Baldwin was provided with only broad guidelines. On the other side of the hill, the US Debt Commission did not wish to put anything in writing lest Congress called for papers, while its consultations with Senators and Congressmen, by their nature, went unrecorded.[64] Thus, the British Cabinet's directions and the course the horsetrading took have to be inferred from the cables passing between the Mission and London, and from statements made by Smoot and Burton.

The Chancellor negotiated the interest rate, the length, and the size and incidence of the annual repayment of principal, while the Governor and Eliot Wadsworth, the Assistant Secretary of the US Treasury and secretary of the Commission, discussed the details of the security on the assumption that the main talks would be successful. The Chancellor's first proposal was an annuity based on an interest rate of 2 per cent. It was rejected out of hand. Reporting to London, the Mission explained that some Senators would regard the whole payment on the annuity as interest and assume that the capital would never be received. It did not mention the Commission's reaction to the interest rate, although Smoot, reporting to Congress in February, laid emphasis on this. Nor, as he had already suffered attack about the marketability of the Bonds, did he say anything about the difficulties of selling an annuity to investors.[65]

It was the rate which almost broke the negotiations. Whatever Blackett's assessment of British capacity, Baldwin left London authorised by Bonar Law to settle for a maximum of £25m a year, or about 2½ per cent of the principal, if valued at par of exchange. This, which would have permitted 2 per cent interest and ½ per cent sinking fund, appears to have been born in the unauthorised activities of Ambassador Harvey in London. In July 1922, when the Balfour Note was under discussion, Lloyd George gave a lunch for the US Chief Justice (William Taft), Harvey, Bonar Law, Horne and some newspaper proprietors, at which Harvey made proposals for settling the debt. Taft later told Harding that he thought that Lloyd George and Horne did not understand Harvey's plan, but that Bonar Law was 'very quick to appreciate' it. The lack of understanding is borne out by the incoherence of the report made to the Cabinet. This said that Harvey had maintained that, once the debt had been funded, the backing of the British and American Treasuries would make the Bonds the 'finest security in the world, and would result in so great an appreciation that the real interest charge upon this country would fall to anything from 2 to 2½ per cent.' During January, the story was confirmed by Horne, who claimed that he had appreciated that Harvey was not speaking for his government, but that 2 per cent had become entrenched in Bonar Law's mind.[66]

The Commission unhesitatingly rejected a straight Bond with a 2 per cent coupon.[67] Then, after the first negotiating session, Geddes told Baldwin that he thought that the Commission would be prepared to submit to Congress a scheme costing £30m a year. Surprisingly, in the light of later events, Bonar Law scarcely hesitated before authorising the increase so long as the life was no more than fifty years.[68] After a further five days of discussion, the Commission offered to recommend 3½ per cent, with ½ per cent sinking fund, payable for sixty-one years. The deferred interest would be capitalised at 5 per cent, making the debt $4,686m and the annual payment $187m. Baldwin replied that his government would 'in no case' agree and that it could only afford $140m (the £30m already authorised at the existing market rate of $4.64) for fifty years.[69]

During the adjournment, Geddes again sounded the Commissioners and reported to Baldwin that they might recommend 3 per cent with ½ per cent sinking fund for sixty-six years. If the deferred interest was capitalised at 5 per cent, the cost would be $164m a year, or if capitalised at 3 per cent, $156m. Baldwin, Norman and Geddes agreed this should be accepted. Cabling Bonar Law, Baldwin stressed it was a far better settlement than the Treasury had thought possible only a few months earlier and a 'vast' improvement on the terms contained in the Funding Act. If the British made such an offer, and it was refused, he thought that it would be seen as fair and, if accepted, the less important matters of flexible repayment, subrogated securities, marketability and most-favoured-nation treatment would fall into place. His final word was to remind Bonar Law that they were required by the obligations to settle on the terms chosen by the Commission.[70]

Bonar Law's reaction to the Commission's 3½ per cent was 'impossible'. The reasons were visceral. The debt had been incurred in a cause for which both nations had fought and there would have been no debt if the UK had not lent to its allies or had only used its US securities for its own needs. The proposal was harsher than would have been expected from commercial bankers, who would give time for their customers to collect from their own debtors before they demanded settlement. Moreover, as the UK would not be able to pay unless it were solvent, the rate should reflect the joint security of the UK and the US governments over a long period, which would – shades of Harvey and pre-war Consols – 'in all probability not exceed 2½'. If the USA would not settle on terms which seemed reasonable, Baldwin would 'have no alternative but to ask for further time for consideration and to return.'[71] His reaction to 3 per cent was more measured. He still thought that the offer was 'most ungenerous' and 'that under the circumstances' the rate should not be more than 2½ per cent, but if the USA would remit the deferred interest, and Baldwin still advised acceptance, he would recommend the terms to the Cabinet.[72]

The Commission did not accept Baldwin's proposal, but countered with 3 per cent for ten years and 3½ per cent thereafter, together with a reduction in the rate on arrears from 5 per cent to 4¼ per cent and an option to delay interest for up to three years. With a sinking fund of ½ per cent, the debt would be extinguished in sixty-one years at a cost of $161m a year, rising to $184m after ten. Alongside this, Baldwin thought that he could obtain the right to prepay in US Treasury debt at par, so making the debt 'practically' unmarketable.

A month after the event, Norman reported that the settlement had been urged on Baldwin by Strong, Jack Morgan, Cravath, Polk, Leffingwell and Davis, as well as the members of the Commission.[73] It was passed to London with a recommendation from all the members of the Mission. The terms, Baldwin reiterated, showed a 'tremendous' advance in American opinion and, he believed, were the best available. They had to be accepted immediately or there would not be time to legislate before 4 March, when Congress adjourned. If they waited until December, when it met again, the parties would be more evenly balanced, more prone to debate the British debt in a partisan spirit, and less influenced by the reparations crisis and the French and Belgian action in the Ruhr. No reasonable settlement could be expected until after the next Presidential election, when the debt would be unhappily prominent:

> We feel very strongly that a settlement is well nigh essential and that without it we cannot expect improvement in general financial conditions...Issue then

> is whether settlement now proposed is so burdensome as to outweigh all these disadvantages. I have little doubt that Great Britain would not regard 33 million sterling yearly as being too high a price to pay to escape appearing as a defaulter...What is quite certain is that if we fail to settle now not only American opinion but world opinion will question our willingness to pay with serious damage to our prestige.
>
> All of us who are working here are convinced of necessity of settlement and I urge cabinet to accept.[74]

The seven ministers available that Monday (15 January) were unanimous in rejecting the recommendation. Because it was 'highly improbable' that interest rates over such a long period would be 3.42 per cent, the average over the sixty-one years, the settlement could be considered high for a commercial debt, and mean for one between allies: 'in view of all the circumstances' it would be 'intolerably unjust.' The Cabinet could not believe that American public opinion would 'permanently' regard the proposal as fair, but once the Bonds were signed they could not be changed. It was to be expected that the settlement would be attacked in Parliament, damaging relations with the USA. The ministers instructed Baldwin to tell the Commission that its offer was far above anything that he had contemplated before leaving the UK, that he had no power to accept, and that he must return for discussions. If the negotiations came to an end, he should make it clear that he had recommended that the Cabinet accept 3 per cent, although he thought it too high.[75]

In a private cable on the same day, Bonar Law told Baldwin that he had consulted McKenna, who had advised refusal despite the risks. 'Is it not possible', asked Bonar Law, 'that you are too much under the influence of Washington which is not even the New York atmosphere? What would you have thought of such proposals before you left?'[76] More persuasively, he pointed out that the occupation of the Ruhr had made it less likely that the Germans would pay reparations or France its debt to the UK: trade might be damaged and, if sterling depreciated, the cost of buying the dollars would rise.[77]

The Commission and the British team were careful to keep the door open, and the Mission's return to London was to be presented as an adjournment and not a breakdown. On 17 January, however, the Commission lost much of the freedom of manoeuvre which it had been trying to retain by not recording its proceedings. That morning, *The Times* in London carried details of the American offer and a well-informed description of the state of the negotiations, the Washington correspondent tilting his story strongly towards the advantages of acceptance. It was made to look as if Baldwin was returning to place a non-negotiable proposition in front of the Cabinet, while ensuring that, in future, any changes would be seen as one side or the other winning a point.[78] The newspapers put in their oars once more when Baldwin arrived at Southampton on Saturday, 27 January. Interviewing journalists, Baldwin admitted under forceful questioning that he believed that the terms were the best available and described the negotiations in such a way that it was clear that he believed that they should be accepted. He also drew attention to the differences in the USA between the East Coast and the west and mid-west, where many of the constituencies were rural and isolated, with limited understanding of international finance. Read today, his comments seem moderately pitched and perfectly reasonable. Crossing the Atlantic in 1923, and in the hands of sometimes hostile journalists seeking stark headlines, the words caused a furore, which was not designed to help the Administration obtain Congressional consent to the Commission's proposal, let alone acceptance of better terms. The Embassy in Washington had to limit the damage as best it might.[79]

The minutes of the Cabinet meetings at which the offer was discussed give no hint that the Prime Minister threatened to resign if the terms were accepted. At the first, on 30 January (Tuesday), the Chancellor gave a full account of the 'position in regard to the Anglo-American Debt'; after a 'preliminary discussion' the Cabinet agreed to adjourn until the following afternoon, when the Cabinet accepted the proposal in principle.[80]

Having arrived on a Saturday (27 January), Baldwin did not see Bonar Law for two days. On Monday evening, the Chancellor was accompanied by Harvey, whose trail of destruction had been lengthening. In Washington at the beginning of January for the negotiations, he had upset Baldwin and Geddes by offering to draft Baldwin's introductory speech to the Commission. The Chancellor said he felt able to write his own and Hughes had disowned his envoy, asking that the British treat the offer as a sign of Harvey's 'over-zealous interest in securing an agreement'.[81] At about the same time, Harvey had told the Chief American correspondent of the London *Morning Post* that there was a 'very agreeable surprise' coming, namely an offer which would cost only £15m per year.[82] Two weeks later, on 21 January, Hughes learnt from Geddes about Harvey's loose talk. With Geddes's enthusiasm for a settlement, it must have been satisfying for him to add that the Mission had been unable to understand Bonar Law's attitude or the replies it was receiving from London. All had now been made clear; Harvey's suggestion the previous summer had 'fixed itself in Bonar Law's mind which had held up the whole settlement' and 'immediate efforts must be made to dislodge this impression.' Hughes promised to instruct Harvey, who was on his way back to the UK, 'to take steps to remove this impression', and to stress that the terms were the best available and that they should be accepted immediately.[83]

At the end of January, on that Monday afternoon in London, Harvey had already had a long interview with Bonar Law and had pressed him to accept the Commission's offer. He had also told Bonar Law, or Bonar Law understood him to say, that the US authorities would allow the British to raise a loan in New York which would enjoy the same tax privileges as the US Treasury's own Liberty Bonds. The cost could be assumed to be well under 3 per cent and, presumably, Harvey had in mind easing Bonar Law's decision with the prospect of refinancing the debt at a lower cost. Bonar Law found this perplexing, as well he might, and asked Geddes to seek confirmation. Hughes, and then Mellon, denied that any such suggestion had been made. As in the UK, tax privileges were contrary to Treasury policy and they would require Congressional sanction, which would not be forthcoming.[84] 'The proposal is inadmissible,' Hughes cabled Harvey, and he had told Geddes as much:

> It is highly important that no alterations in terms of settlement proposed by American Commission and stated here should be entertained by you in London, as this involves possibilities of misunderstandings while time is short...It is desirable that you should emphasise the importance from an international standpoint of an adjustment of the debt and of the acceptance of the terms...You should not discuss any departure from these terms.[85]

Thus, Harvey had another reason to deliver an uncompromising message: the terms were final, no modification would be considered, and it would be futile or, even, disastrous to suggest changes; 'Bonar Law reluctantly and Baldwin unhesitantly agreed.'[86]

Even if Bonar Law agreed that Monday evening, he did not the next day. Baldwin opened the Cabinet discussion of 30 January by pointing out that the previous government had contemplated an annual payment of £50m ($243m at par of exchange), but that this was based on what it thought the budget could stand, rather than on what was owed.[87] Funding the debt would replace a variable with a fixed liability and ensure that the UK did not continue rolling up the interest, leaving the capital liability untouched. The terms were the best available and would not be improved by waiting. Austen Chamberlain's speech in February 1921 was still remembered, cancellation was out of the question, delay would arouse American ire, and the debt would become the subject of partisan debate. A failure to agree would arouse the suspicion that the UK never meant to pay and leave the country to be classed with the bankrupt states of the Continent. In reply to questions, Baldwin said that Norman considered that it was not possible to obtain a most-favoured-nation agreement, that it would be possible to have the right to tender US debt at par in payment and that the Bonds would have to be marketable, although the options attached to them would make sale impracticable.

Bonar Law's grounds for refusal were, once more, largely emotional. He repeated that he feared the effect on living standards, inflation and taxation of paying without receiving anything from the Continent. He felt the real problem was that public opinion wanted to settle, but in two or three years' time the same public opinion would castigate him for accepting. He had decided that the offer was unreasonable and, if the Cabinet wanted to settle, it could do so without him. Supported in a tepid fashion by only two other ministers, he was the clear loser in the subsequent debate, several times contradicting himself. He still hewed to the policy of the Balfour Note, being prepared to pay the USA only as much as the Continent paid the UK, and would not accept that this meant default; he would delay that by paying 3½ per cent for two or three years. As this was the rate on the Bonds after ten years, it would have increased the immediate burden, and left the cost uncertain, while the remaining 1½ per cent would roll up. It became plain that the other ministers neither wanted to reject the deal nor wanted the Prime Minister to resign just after an election with no replacement available from a weak and inexperienced team. Bonar Law adjourned the Cabinet until the following day.

The next morning ministers met without Bonar Law and, with only one dissenter, agreed that rejection would be the worst course.[c] Lord Derby, the Secretary of State for War, and William Bridgeman, the Home Secretary, were particularly strong in their views. What to do about Bonar Law? The Duke of Devonshire, Lord Cave and Baldwin were deputed to persuade him to stay. They found it surprisingly easy, whether because, on reflection, he realised he had been the loser in the debate or, as Hankey records, because he understood that there was no obvious successor and he could badly damage his party, is unclear. He may have been influenced by a meeting that morning with McKenna, who had earlier advised rejection because he thought that the interest rate should be such as to hold the USA harmless: 'If we pay less than that [the cost of the money to the USA], you are making us a present. If we pay more, you are making us a present.' He now advised that it was more important to settle, to get an irritant out of the way, than to 'haggle over the basis of settlement, or the little more or the little less.' When the Cabinet met that afternoon, it took only a few minutes to decide to accept the proposals.[88]

With the press in London already informed of the Cabinet's decision, Geddes was instructed to tell the Debt Commission without delay that its offer had been accepted in 'principle'. A more leisurely cable followed with instructions to ask the Commission to accept points which had been discussed by the Governor and Wadsworth: options to pay half the interest in Bonds for the first five years and to make payments in US Treasury securities, together with a 'definite arrangement' to ensure the Bonds were unmarketable. The first two requests were received favourably and were included in both the Commission's Report to the President and the Bill submitted to Congress. The third was refused, the Commission pleading political difficulties.[89]

The terms in Congress

The Commission sent its report to the President on 3 February. Four days later he addressed a joint session of Congress, endorsing the report's recommendations and asking for prompt legislation. In making his request, the President blended half a dozen aspects of the settlement to suit legislators' varying tastes. It was 'fair and just to both Governments', would make a 'most important contribution to international stability', but was 'a business settlement, fully preserving the integrity of the obligations.' It was a denial of the calls for cancellation and an acknowledgement of a debt in a world which was crying out for the validity of contracts. Playing to those who believed that debt forgiveness would merely enable some European governments to spend more on arms, he called it 'a plight against war and war expenditures...to that production and retrenchment which enhances stability precisely as it discharges obligations.' While the Commission had gone as far as the 'American sense of fair play would justify,' the interest rate reflected

c Baldwin's biographers used 'repudiation' when the context clearly shows that that they meant 'rejection.' Whether their muddle reflects the ministerial muddle is unclear. Middlemas and Barnes (1969), pp. 146–7.

'normal rates' paid by 'strong governments over a long term of years' with a 'temporary interest rate and suitable options adjusted to the tremendous problems of readjustment and recuperation.' Then, in a rapid change of tack, he asked for prompt passage of the Shipping Bill, which was causing the British such anxiety.[90]

The new Act took the form of an amendment to that of February 1922 which had established the Commission. A statement of the debt was followed by a recital of terms: the coupons and maturity; the payment dates; and repayment by instalments, subject to the options to pay in three-yearly periods, to pay early, to pay in US Treasury Bonds and to defer interest for five years. The membership of the Commission was increased to eight, not more than four of whom could be from the same party.

The Congressional debate centred on the rate of interest and the length of the Bonds. Ignoring the cost of the tax privileges (which, indeed, were ignored throughout), opponents argued that the US Treasury was paying $195.5m each year to service the debt incurred to make the advances and that, at their highest point, receipts of interest and principal combined would be only $186m. Thus, at no time would the payments cover the cost and, at the end of sixty-two years, the British would have repaid their debt and the US Treasury would still have its capital liability. Moreover, the options to pay half the interest in new British Bonds and to defer the annual repayments of principal for three years meant that the debt could rise by a further $395m in the first five years. This, some thought, had never been Congress's intention. The Liberty Bond Acts had envisaged rates and maturities which matched those on the US Treasury's own obligations and the Funding Act had not envisaged increased lending to the UK. The more extreme anti-British Senators from the south and west coupled the failure of the term to match those on the Liberty Bonds with the options, which they recognised as limiting the Bonds' marketability. Without this, the US Treasury would have to hold to maturity and 'for 62 years we shall be tied to the fortunes of the British Empire.'[91] The circumstances in which the loans were incurred were mulled over. On the one side were those, such as Carter Glass, who spoke eloquently of British military prowess and war losses, of partnerships in endeavour and of British loans to its allies. On the other were those who argued that the advances were a commercial transaction, that the USA had saved the British from defeat and the least they could do was to make full repayment. The British, it was said, had charged a full price for the transport of American troops, so why should they not pay the USA in full for supplies? They could afford to pay. They were creditors of all the world, except the USA. They, unlike America, had gained territories under the Treaty, and these were rich in oil. Reparations would, in time, yield them something. Who in their right minds would voluntarily exchange good obligations giving 4¼ per cent for others giving only 3 or 3½ per cent?[92]

A form of most-favoured-nation agreement was inserted – and deleted – during the Bill's passage. Burton, rejecting the version produced by the Senate's drafting bureau, wrote his own Bill. With the intention of providing a new benchmark for settlements with other debtors, he included a clause which, as amended by the Ways and Means Committee of the House, read 'settlements, similar and not more favourable in terms with other governments indebted to the United States...are hereby authorized to be made, subject to the approval of the President.'[93] When the Bill came before the Senate, the clause was opposed by Smoot, the Commission member sponsoring the measure for the Administration.[94] Although Geddes thought otherwise, the provision was emphatically not intended to give the British the benefit of any lower rate of interest agreed subsequently with other debtors.[95] Indeed, the possibility of the clause leading to a lower rate was scarcely mentioned, nor is such an interpretation easily to be found in its wording. Instead, Senators were anxious lest it constitute a commitment not to give more favourable terms to other debtors. Congress, of course, always had the power to approve easier terms but, if it did so and the clause was retained, it believed that the British would be justified in taking offence. Moreover, the British were the strongest debtors and it could be assumed that the terms of their settlement would be the harshest. The only effect of the provision would be to lower the expectations of other debtors from the 4¼ per cent and twenty-five years of the 1922 Act to the 3 and 3½ per cent and sixty-two years of the British settlement. Finally, the 1922 Act, after lengthy debate, had been based on the principle that Congress should retain the final say, unless the rate was 4¼ per cent or above, and many legislators felt that this should not be changed. The Senate's view prevailed and the clause in its final version read 'settlements with other governments indebted to the United States are hereby authorized to be made upon such terms as the commission...may believe to be just, subject to the approval of Congress by Act or joint resolution.'[96]

Designing the Bonds

It remained for officials to determine how the broad authorities should be reflected in the Bonds. When Baldwin's Mission left Washington, it was thought Norman might return, but by the beginning of February both the Treasury and the Commission believed that no questions of principle had been left outstanding and that, in any case, he could not arrive in time to help the Bill's passage through Congress.[97] The negotiations were entrusted to Ernest Rowe-Dutton, a junior Treasury official in the Mission who had remained in Washington after the other members went back to London. Until 20 February, his talks were mainly held with Wadsworth, who then went to Europe for discussions on the costs of the American Army of Occupation in Germany. Rowe-Dutton stayed on to brief Smoot and Burton while they defended the Bill in Congress and to continue negotiations with Seymour Parker Gilbert, Under-Secretary of the Treasury.[98] Rowe-Dutton left for London on 3 March to be on hand while Niemeyer negotiated further details with Wadsworth; only if points of principle were raised was it envisaged that discussions would be resumed in Washington. It was not until the end of April that the British discovered, to their annoyance, that there had been a misunderstanding, that Wadsworth had no powers, and that they should have been talking to the Commission in the USA. Geddes was then instructed to take over the negotiations.[99]

The Bonds went through three drafts. The first, a raw outline, was produced by

Rowe-Dutton on 9 February, before the Bill had been enacted. The second came from Parker Gilbert two weeks later, shortly after Wadsworth went to Europe. The third, a complete recasting, came from the US Treasury on 22 March.[100]

As finally agreed, the terms were embodied in the Bonds themselves and in a separate 'proposal' made by the British and accepted by the Commission.[101] A straight agreement, signed by each party, would have been equally effective in avoiding unnecessary recitals on the face of the Bonds and would have satisfied the Americans, but a proposal suited the British better. The UK Treasury had powers under the War Loan Act 1919 to issue securities, or exchange securities issued under the War Loan Acts 1914 to 1918, but it was doubtful whether it had power to agree to issue securities. Also, the power to charge the Consolidated Fund was contained in the authority to issue securities, not in an authority to agree to issue securities. A proposal solved the problem, leaving the Bonds as the effective security. As the Treasury saw it, the Cabinet had bound itself to a contract when it accepted the Commission's terms and it remained to 'fulfil this Agreement which is best done by fulfilling it, not by making another agreement to fulfil it.'[102]

The United Kingdom Sixty-Two-Year 3–3½ per cent Gold Bonds signed on 5 July 1923 by Henry Chilton, Counsellor of His Britannic Majesty's Embassy at Washington, were dated 15 December 1922 and matured on 15 December 1984. The Bonds, which were printed in black on four sides of unassuming buff paper, were each for $4.6m and numbered 0001 to 1,000. Since each Bond was for 0.1 per cent of the debt, the annual repayment on each was always a round number of tens of thousands of dollars.

The calculation of the debt, to the nearest cent, was laid out in both the proposal and the new Act:

Principal of the demand obligations	$4,074,818,358.44
Interest accrued and unpaid up to 15 December 1922, at the rate of 4¼ per cent	$629,836,106.99
Total	$4,704,654,465.43
Less payments made on 15 October and 15 December 1922	$100,000,000.00
Less interest from 15 October and 15 November 1922 to 15 December 1922 at 4¼ per cent	$526,379.69
Total	$4,604,128,095.74
Paid in cash on 15 March 1923	$4,128,085.74[d]
Total indebtedness to be funded	$4,600,000,000.00

d The Commission forgave the interest payable between 15 December 1922 and 15 March 1923 on the amount paid in cash. T 160/366/F557/8, f. 94, Geddes to Curzon, 7 February 1923.

In reciting the value of the securities to be issued, the proposal drew attention to the exclusion of the advances 'deemed' to have been made to cover purchases of silver under the Pittman Act and stressed that they were being repaid under a separate agreement 'already made between the parties.'

Payments on account of principal were to be made on 15 December each year. The coupons, 3 per cent until December 1932 and 3½ per cent thereafter, were payable on 15 June and 15 December.[e] They, and the principal, were payable in 'United States gold coin of the present standard of weight and fineness, or its equivalent in gold bullion,' the latter being added at the insistence of the British in case the US mint was closed against them by strikes or legislation. Alternatively, the British had the option, on giving thirty days notice, of paying in US Treasury Bonds. To avoid advantage being taken of low-coupon pre-war Bonds standing at heavy discounts, these were limited to those issued, or yet 'to be issued', since 6 April 1917.

The British had the option to pay half of the interest accruing in the five years ending 15 December 1927 in their own Bonds containing provision for repayment of their principal by annual instalments 'corresponding substantially' to the schedule of payments on those they were issuing. They also had the option to repay principal in three-year periods, with the proviso that the instalment due in the third year could not be deferred for more than one year unless the instalment due from the first year was paid on the date of the third instalment. The instalment due in the fourth year could not be deferred at all until, or unless, the instalment due in the second year had been paid. The effect was to allow only two deferred payments to be outstanding at any time. Unsurprisingly, the clause proved difficult to draft and, when the Americans succeeded, it received a rare accolade from the British, Rowe-Dutton admitting it was 'ingenious' and 'well dealt with.'[103]

The wording of the provision for repayment was designed to emphasise that a distinct payment was being made each year on account of principal. Thus, the US Act spoke of 'The principal of the Bonds' being paid in 'annual instalments on a fixed schedule' and the British proposal of 'the total principal of the debt before maturity' being repaid by means of a provision 'the effect of which shall be that Great Britain shall make to the United States payments on account of the original principal amount.' To drive the point home, the proposal listed the 'Annual instalments to be paid on account of principal', showing the amount of all sixty-two payments: $23m in 1923 and 1924, $24m in 1925, and $25m in 1926 and 1927. By 1932, they had risen to $30m and in 1984, when the principal was $175m, to $175m. The British had the option, on giving not less than ninety days' notice, of making additional payments on account of principal. Such payments were to be applied, first, to any Bonds issued in lieu of interest between 1922 and 1927 and, second, to the other Bonds.

e The coupons and principal were exempt from 'all British taxation, present or future, so long as they [were] in the beneficial ownership of the United States, or of a person, firm, association or corporation neither domiciled nor ordinarily resident in the United Kingdom.'

Bar the paragraph listing the sixty-two capital payments, the longest part of the proposal was that ordering the exchange into marketable obligations of the 1,000 Bonds to be issued to the US Treasury. In this, the British undertook, at the request of the Secretary of the Treasury, to convert any, or all, into new Bonds 'suitable for sale to the public.' The converted obligations would have the same terms as those about to be issued to the US Treasury, except that the terms for repayment would be 'as shall be agreed upon.' The lengthy negotiations this promised when the time came for marketable Bonds to be issued were kept within bounds by several, more specific, provisions; unless there was agreement to the contrary, the Bonds would be repaid 'substantially' at the same rate as those about to be issued, so that all the Bonds would be repaid by 15 December 1984 by annual drawings at par.

The British had the option to buy at par any Bonds which the US Treasury asked to be exchanged into a marketable form and the Americans were to offer marketable Bonds at par to the British government before offering them for sale in the UK.

Finally, there were two side-letters. The first, promising the release of the subrogated securities, was uncontentious from the start.[104] The second, giving the opinion of the US Attorney-General that 'Bonds' included Notes and certificates of indebtedness, was necessary because, by error, the Commission's Report to the President and the clause in the Act authorising interest and principal to be paid in securities omitted forms of debt other than Bonds. The point was of little importance to the British, who merely wanted to trade the mistake for other matters, but it was only settled after a lively debate in the Commission where Smoot and Burton, looking over their shoulders at their Congressional critics, argued for a strict interpretation.[105]

Only the call options and the terms for marketability need amplification. During February, it appeared possible that the Bonds would provide for early repayment in sterling in the event of dollar weakness. The principle had the support of the Commission, and was only rejected because of the difficulties of drafting clauses which were clear, comprehensible to Congress and defendable in debate. Stabilising the exchange rate had been discussed by Norman and Wadsworth in January. At the beginning of February, Rowe-Dutton suggested a balanced formula whereby sterling would be available to the USA when the sterling rate rose above the gold import point and British payments on the Bonds would be suspended when sterling fell to the gold export point. The scheme appealed neither to the British nor to the Commission. Rowe-Dutton himself pointed out that it would 'disturb the equilibrium of gold values in order to maintain the equilibrium of United States Exchange rates.'[106] Wadsworth was reluctant to give the British the right to defer interest, but wanted access to sterling if the USA became involved in 'serious difficulties such as a war or a prolonged strike.'[107] Without being clear what Norman had in mind, Phillips thought it 'entirely superfluous'. Niemeyer, aware that the Prime Minister had earlier attached importance to protecting the exchange rate, said that he was happy that it 'stand over for the present'. Most importantly, the Commission thought that there was no hope of obtaining Congressional approval for any but the 'most straightforward recommendations. [It] would assuredly view with the darkest distrust any complex scheme.'[108]

Parker Gilbert was keener, envisaging an agreement whereby either country could obtain the other's currency if the rate moved to an extreme, say twenty-five cents, from par. However, he saw the difficulties of including such a provision on the face of the Bond and, reported Rowe-Dutton, 'thinks we may not be able to get more in than a declaration of amity on the subject.'[109] Two of the drafts which resulted were merely statements of good intentions, while the third was specific and, thought Niemeyer, potentially damaging:

> What they [the US Treasury] have produced seems to me worthless, and indeed in the full version harmful because it makes you undertake to accelerate repayment of Exchange as against America without giving you any protection if exchange is the other way round...the only thing of any value to us would be a definite provision suspending interest and repayment if the dollar fell below a given point...I doubt if we could get anything of this nature from the Americans and on the whole I am inclined not to ask for it.[110]

It was best, he told Rowe-Dutton, for the matter to be settled between the Bank and the Federal Reserve, with the Bond confined to generalities and the agreement relegated to a supplemental letter.[111] The matter was finally put to rest by the Commission's draft Bond of 22 March, which left stability to be provided by the three British options already described: paying in three-yearly periods, deferring half the interest for five years, and paying in US Treasury debt.[112]

Conflict over the terms for making the Bonds marketable was presaged at the beginning of December when Wadsworth told members of the House Appropriations Committee that the Commission would be seeking negotiable Bonds.[113] The Commission was riding two horses. It admitted, and Senators knew, that the limitations on its own powers and the British options made the Bonds unsaleable. The Liberty Bond Acts only authorised sale at par or above and legislation would be required if it were to be otherwise (see pp. 481 and 490). There would be no demand for a security, half of whose interest could be paid during the first five years in the obligor's own Bonds taken at par, the market price of which need not be such as to make the interest worth the nominal value of the Bond; which could be paid before maturity on not less than ninety days' notice; and whose interest, sinking fund and early repayment could be made in the US Treasury's own securities at par when it was profitable for the British so to do. That is, when, and only when, those securities were worth less than par. Yet the Commission had to pretend that the US Treasury enjoyed all the rights of ownership, including the right of sale. It certainly could not allow inclusion of a clause which baldly precluded sale.[114] Despite the options, the British fought tooth and nail the American attempts to make the securities more marketable for, as in 1920, they foresaw their Bonds being sold to investors at yields which would interfere with their own refinancings. British savers might buy British government debt in the USA, straining the exchange rate. To these old concerns was added a new one: that negotiating a revised rate would be impossible once the Bonds had passed into the hands of investors. Any hope of cancellation or most-favoured-nation treatment would be dead.

The Debt Commission's first attempt to reconcile a marketable Bond with the British options came in mid-February after Smoot had been given a mauling in the Senate.[115] The Commission envisaged an indenture, whereby the US Treasury would become a trustee for the investor: it would issue the securities, receive payments on account of interest and principal and pass them – in a form of its own choosing – to the holders. It was akin to a participation certificate, such as had concerned Blackett in 1920. The British maintained that Baldwin's agreement was for the issue of Bonds and an indenture could not be substituted: the Bonds must remain the operative security. Hoping later negotiations would become bogged down in detail, they emulated the tactic used by Norman during his talks with Wadsworth: that it was best to leave matters vague and only consider them when a sale was being planned.[116]

Mellon's own choice appeared unheralded in the Debt Commission's draft in March. 'Serial Bonds' entailed breaking up the debt so that Bonds equivalent to each year's repayment of principal would come due each year. The US Treasury, with sixty-two maturities in its portfolio, would be able to sell whatever the market demanded: 'American investors might well take a yearling British Bond [*sic*] at $3^1/_2$ interest, when they would look askance at a Bond maturing in 1984.'[117] And every year that passed would see another, and ever bigger, yearling created.

In presenting Serial Bonds the Commission did not conceal its intention of enhancing marketability and avoiding later negotiations on amortisation. It admitted that, unless the maturities were fixed, the Bonds could not be sold. The discussions were long, 'hard driven and at times heated' with Geddes reporting that he had 'fought for the point with all my vigour', although he, personally, believed that the options made the Bonds unmarketable whatever the outcome of his talks.[118] He also warned that if the Cabinet decided to stand firm there would be a 'fairly savage' reaction from the American press. The British decided that they would service the Bonds as if agreement had been reached and made arrangements for announcing the breakdown.[119]

They also decided on compromise and firmness. Niemeyer advised that the UK had to protect itself against marketability, even at the price of 'some friction' with the USA: the credit position was too uncertain, the weight of American debt too heavy and sales of amounts such as those held by the US Treasury would depress British securities on both sides of the Atlantic. The refusal was accompanied by a powerful barrage of evidence, taken from the speeches and comments of the Commissioners themselves, showing that they had not contemplated Serial Bonds until the time of the US Treasury's draft in March. At the same time, the Treasury offered to tighten the repayment terms to be attached to marketable Bonds, with the result already described (p. 544).[120] It worked. Without admitting that it had been proposing any change from the original agreement, the Commission dropped its 'suggestion' of Serial Bonds. It had been, as Rowe-Dutton said, a 'try-on.'[121]

The result of the negotiations were Bonds which gave the British great flexibility and which were, in effect, unmarketable. Although nominally issued for sixty-two years, they could be called at short notice, so that they could run for anything between three months and sixty-two years at the option of the borrower. This gave an option on the rate: when interest rates fell, the British could borrow in the markets and repay the US Treasury. The securities could be justly described as 3–3½ per cent Bonds, or such lower rate as the market allowed at any time during the following sixty-two years.

✣ ✣ ✣

The British agreed to fund the demand certificates because they believed they had to meet the obligations their representatives had signed; because, as a creditor of much of the rest of the world, they had a vested interest in the sanctity of contract; and because the political and economic advantages of a prompt settlement were worth more than the far prospect of lower payments if the price was to be a breakdown of the negotiations, strained relations and US isolation from European affairs.

In the background there was the knowledge that the USA, unlike the French in the Ruhr, were not prepared to use coercion. As Mellon was to recognise in January 1926 when defending settlements with the Italians and Belgians, a national creditor would only pay what 'public opinion and the necessities of its own credit' compelled it to pay and that insisting on repayments 'in excess of the capacity of the nation…would justify it in refusing to make any settlement.' Unless a settlement was thought to be fair, the creditor would receive nothing.[122] This said, once the British had decided that it was in their interests to meet their liabilities, the settlement became a compromise between what the British were prepared to pay and what Congress could be persuaded to accept. European monetary chaos, the reparations tangle, the damage to US export markets and the invasion of the Ruhr helped change American attitudes, but in the end the terms were a straight horse-trade.

As the settlement itself became history, it was remembered differently. The cost of the money borrowed by the US Treasury to finance its advances to the allies could not be determined because no security ran for sixty-two years, the refinancing cost of the Liberty Bond maturities and the rolled over certificates of indebtedness were unknowable, and the value of the tax privileges would change every time tax rates changed. Despite this, contemporaries compared the amount of the principal written off by discounting the interest and sinking fund at a rate of 4¼, the rate borne by much of the US war debt and the minimum rate specified in the Funding Act. On this basis, the UK settlement was made at about 82 (18 per cent of the debt was cancelled), that of France at 47, that of Italy at 26 and that of Belgium at 51 or 54.[123]

The rationalisation for these departures from the terms laid out in the Liberty Bond Acts and the 1922 Funding Act was called 'capacity to pay' and the British terms became the standard against which later settlements were determined. In 1926, Mellon described the British settlement as:

> entirely based on our estimate of Great Britain's capacity to pay. It is a precedent for the recognition of the principle of capacity to pay and it is not a set formula to control other cases of substantially less capacity.

It was a rule, he said, that debtors had to treat all their creditors the same. It was also a rule that creditors could give whatever terms they wished to their debtors:

> It [the creditor] may insist on payment in full from one, give time to another, and cancel the indebtedness of a third, and no one of the three debtors has a right to complain of the treatment accorded the other.

The amount of debt the USA was prepared to cancel depended on the budgets (as a measure of the ability of governments to extract resources from their citizens), foreign trade (bearing on the capacity to make transfers) and national income (the 'ultimate source of a country's capacity to pay'). These were useful, but not exact, pointers to capacity to pay over long periods, which had ultimately to be a matter of opinion. In the opinion of the Commission, the settlements it had made were consistent with the British Funding Act. They were just.[124]

Endnotes

1 Cab. 23/23, Cabinet 72 (20), Conclusion 5, 17 December 1920; Middlemas and Barnes (1969), pp. 144–6.
2 Feinstein (1972), T. 84.
3 *DBFP*, 1919–39, VIII, Chapter IV, especially pp. 315–17.
4 Cab. 24/106, CP 1382, Rathbone to Chancellor, 24 May 1920; T 160/365/F557/2, Part 1, ff. 20–6, Geddes to FO (two cables), 18 June 1920, and ff. 7–8, Wiseman, 'Memorandum', June 1920.
5 Cab. 23/22, Cabinet 58 (20), Conclusion 2, 28 October 1920; T 160/365/F557/2, Part 1, f. 31, Chancellor to Geddes, 25 June 1920; Baldwin Papers 233, 'History of the Anglo-American Debt', p. 119. The drafts of the letter, corrected in Lloyd George's hand, are in LGP F/60/1/28.
6 T 160/365/F557/2, Part 1, ff. 43–5, 'Extract re Finance from President Wilson's Letter', 5 August 1920.
7 Ibid., Part 1, ff. 63–8, Wilson to Lloyd George, 3 November 1920.
8 ibid., Part 1, ff. 49–50, Geddes to FO, 23 October 1920, and f. 47, Chamberlain to Gower, 29 October 1920.
9 Cab. 24/116, CP 2214, Chamberlain, 'Our American Debt', 30 November 1920, and CP 2214A, 3 December 1920.
10 Cab. 23/23, Cabinet 72 (20), Conclusion 5, 17 December 1920.
11 Cab. 24/118, CP 2404, 'Anglo-American Debt – Instructions to Lord Chalmers', 3 January 1921; T 160/365/F557/1, ff. 143–74, 'Lord Chalmers Brief', January 1921.
12 *The Times*, 5 February 1921, p. 8, and 8 February 1921, p. 11; Self (1995), pp. 145–6, Chamberlain to Ida Chamberlain, 12 February 1921; T 160/365/F557/3, ff. 14–15, Craigie to FO, 9 February 1921, and ff. 24–7, Craigie to Curzon, 17 February 1921.
13 Cab. 24/120, CP 2705, 11 March 1921.
14 *Hansard* (Commons), 25 April 1921, cols 77–8.
15 Cab. 23/25, 37 (21), Conclusion 4, 10 May 1921; Cab. 24/122, CP 2875, Horne, 'Our American Debt and Subrogated Securities', 26 April 1921
16 T 160/365/F557/3, ff. 92–4, Blackett to Chancellor, 7 July 1921.

17 Ibid., ff. 41–3, Geddes to FO, 3 May 1921, and ff. 51–4, Mellon to Geddes, 11 May 1921.
18 Leffler (1972), pp. 586–91.
19 *Congressional Record*, 67th Congress, 1st Session, 24 June 1921, pp. 3021–8, 3139–44; T 160/365/F557/3, f. 84, Geddes to FO, 24 June 1921. The Treasury file contains a copy of the *Congressional Record* for 24 June 1921, pp. 3139–44.
20 Leffler (1972), pp. 591–601; Baldwin Papers 233, 'History of the Anglo-American Debt', pp. 134–8. The Treasury in London kept an anxious eye on the Bill's progress. The cables and copies of relevant Congressional publications sent to London are in T 160/365/F557/4.
21 T 160/365/F557/5, f. 65, Geddes to FO, 25 April 1922, and Harvey to Curzon, 25 April 1922; Charles Evans Hughes Papers, Box 175, File 76 (b) GB, 'Memorandum of Interview with the British Ambassador', 25 April 1922.
22 Cab. 24/137, CP 4020, Horne, 'British Debt to the United States Government', 8 June 1922; Cab. 23/30, Cabinet 38 (22), Conclusion 2, 7 July 1922; T 160/365/F557/5, Blackett to Chancellor, 'British Debt to the U.S. Govt.', April 1922.
23 Cab. 24/136, CP 3987, FO, 'German Reparations', 23 May 1922; Cab. 24/140, CP 4348, FO, 'Memorandum on the Reparation Position', 5 December 1922; Kent (1989), pp. 173–85.
24 T 160/365/F557/5, ff. 114–19, Blackett to Chancellor, 'British Debt to the U.S. Govt.', April 1922.
25 Cab. 23/30, Cabinet 29 (22), Conclusion 2, 23 May 1922.
26 Cab. 23/30, Cabinet 35 (22), Conclusion 6, 16 June 1922.
27 Cab. 23/30, Cabinet 38 (22), Conclusion 2, 7 July 1922; T 160/365/F557/6, f. 41, Crowe to Harvey, 14 July 1922, and ff. 53–4, Balfour to Harvey, 2 August 1922.
28 Cab. 24/137, CP 4020, Horne, 'British Debt to the United States Government', 8 June 1922.
29 Cab. 24/137, CP 4020, Horne, 'British Debt to the United States Government', 8 June 1922; Cab. 23/30, Cabinet 35 (22), Conclusion 6, 16 June 1922; ibid., Cabinet 36 (22), Conclusion 4, 30 June 1922; ibid., Cabinet 38 (22), Conclusion 2, 7 July 1922; ibid., Cabinet 40 (22), Conclusion 2, 20 July 1922; ibid., Cabinet 42 (22), Conclusion 3, 25 July 1922.
30 *Despatch to the Representatives of France, Italy, Serb–Croat–Slovene State, Roumania, Portugal and Greece at London respecting War Debts* (Cmd. 1737), 1 August 1922.
31 *Hansard* (Commons), 14 July 1922, col. 1675; Charles Evans Hughes Papers, Box 175, File 76 (b) GB, 'Memorandum of Interview with the British Ambassador', 14 August 1922. Two days after the Note was sent, Horne repeated that the Cabinet intended to send a mission and fund the debt. *Hansard* (Commons), 3 August 1922, col. 1744.
32 Cab. 23/30, Cabinet 42 (22), Conclusion 3, 25 July 1922; T 160/365/F557/2, ff. 34–6, Blackett, 'Inter-Governmental Debt', 12 July 1922.
33 Kent (1989), pp. 186–92; Cab. 24/140, CP 4348, FO, 'Memorandum on the Reparation Position', 5 December 1922; Cab. 23/30, Cabinet 44 (22), Conclusion 1, 10 August 1922; ibid., Cabinet 45 (22), Conclusion 2, 12 August 1922; ibid., Cabinet 46 (22), Conclusion 2, 14 August 1922.
34 Cab. 23/30, Cabinet 45 (22), Conclusion 2, 12 August 1922, and Cabinet 46 (22), Conclusion 1, 14 August 1922; *DBFP*, First Series, XX, Chapter II, especially p. 221.
35 T 160/365/F557/6, ff. 36, 37 and 45, Chilton to FO, 13, 15 and 21 July 1922.
36 *The Times*, 2 August 1922, p. 8.
37 Harding Papers, Roll 234, Harvey to Harding, 20 September 1922.

38 T 160/365/F557/6, f. 107–8, Geddes to FO, 6 October 1922; ibid., ff. 125–9, 'Address of Secretary Hoover at Toledo', 16 October 1922; ibid., ff. 157–63, British Embassy briefs on the members of the Funding Commission, December 1922.
39 Strong Papers, 1116.3, Strong to Norman, 18 October 1922.
40 *FRUS* (1922), I, pp. 413–14, 'Statement Issued to the Press by the Secretary of the Treasury, 24 August 1924.
41 Charles Evans Hughes Papers, Box 175, File 76 (b) GB, 'Memorandum of Interview with the British Ambassador', 14 August 1922.
42 Cab. 23/32, Cabinet 64 (22), Appendix IV, 'Foreign Affairs. Summary of Statement made to the Cabinet by the Secretary of State for Foreign Affairs on Wednesday November 1, 1922.'
43 Middlemas and Barnes (1969), pp. 132–3.
44 T 160/365/F557/6, f. 9, Churchill to Horne, 13 June 1922.
45 Cab. 23/27, Cabinet 93 (21), Conclusion 2, 16 December 1922; Baldwin Papers 233, 'History of the Anglo-American Debt', p. 143n; *The Times*, 20 January 1931, pp. 13–14.
46 *Hansard* (Commons), 20 February 1922, col. 1528, and 21 March 1922, cols 240–1.
47 *Hansard* (Commons), 1 May 1922, cols 1024–5 and 1029.
48 Cab. 24/137, CP 4020, Horne, 'British Debt to the United States Government', 8 June 1922.
49 T 160/365/F557/5, ff. 114–19, Blackett to Chancellor, 'British Debt to the U.S. Govt.', April 1922.
50 T 160/365/F557/6, ff. 53–4, Balfour to Harvey, 2 August 1922.
51 Ibid., ff. 69–70, Post Wheeler to Curzon, 21 August 1922; ibid., f. 71, Blackett, untitled memorandum, 25 August 1922; ibid., ff. 84–5, Secretary of State to Harvey, 7 September 1922.
52 Ibid., ff. 131–2, FO to Geddes, 30 October 1922.
53 Ibid., ff. 134–5, Geddes to FO, 3 November 1922, and ff. 139–40, FO to Geddes, 6 November 1922.
54 *Inter-Allied Conferences on Reparations and Inter-Allied Debts* (1923) (Cmd. 1812), p. 35.
55 Cab. 23/32, Cabinet 72 (22), Conclusion 1, 29 December 1922; Cab. 24/140, CP 4376, 'Plan for General Settlement of Reparation and European Inter Allied Debts', 29 December 1922; *Inter-Allied Conferences on Reparations and Inter-Allied Debts* (1923) (Cmd. 1812), pp. 112–19 and 120–32. The drafts of the plan, which was designed by Bradbury, are in the Davidson Papers, DAV 138.
56 *Hansard* (Commons), 12 December 1922, cols 2585–6, and 14 December 1922, col. 3233.
57 *ARSF*, 1921, pp. 40–3.
58 Kent (1989), pp. 198–9; Charles Evans Hughes Papers, Box 4B, File October 1922, Hughes to Herrick and Boyden, 17 October 1922, and Box 175, File 76 (b) GB, Hughes, 'Memorandum of Interview with the British Ambassador', 18 December 1922; T 160/365/F557/7, ff. 12–15, Geddes to FO, 18 December 1922.
59 Thomas Lamont Papers, Series II, F 111–14, Lamont to Grenfell, 19 October 1922, and Lamont to Grenfell, 24 October 1922.
60 *The New York Times*, 28 December 1922, pp. 1 and 2, 29 December 1922, p. 1, 30 December 1922, pp. 1 and 2; *Congressional Record*, 67th Congress, 4th Session, 28 December 1922, p. 982, Harding to Lodge, 28 December 1922.
61 T 160/365/F557/7, ff. 24–5, Geddes to FO, 10 January 1923; *The New York Times*, 10 January 1923, p. 3.
62 T 160/365/F557/1, ff. 179–86, Blackett, 'Points regarding Funding of British Debt to United States Government', 17 August 1922.
63 T 160/365/F557/1, ff. 179–86, Blackett, 'Points regarding Funding of British Debt to United States Government', 17 August 1922, and ff. 187–91, 'British Debt to the United States Government', 10 October 1922.

64 *Congressional Record*, 13 February 1923, p. 3547, copy of letter from Wadsworth to McCumber, 10 February 1923; *Refunding Foreign Obligations*, US House of Representatives, Hearings before the Committee on Ways and Means, on HR 14235, 8 February 1923, p. 10; *Refunding of Obligations of Foreign Governments*, US Senate, Hearings before the Committee on Finance, on HR 14254, 10 February 1923.

65 T 160/365/F557/7, f. 29, Chancellor to Prime Minister, 10 January 1923; Baldwin Papers 233, 'History of the Anglo-American Debt', pp. 312–13; T 160/366/F557/8, ff. 13–14, Rowe-Dutton to Niemeyer, 6 February 1923; Clay (1957), p. 178; *Congressional Record*, 15 February 1923, p. 3692; *Refunding of Obligations of Foreign Governments*, US Senate, Hearings before the Committee on Finance, on HR 14254, 10 February 1923.

66 Cab. 23/30, Cabinet 38 (22), 7 July 1922, Conclusion 3; Harding Papers, Roll 234, PPP – Hughes, Hughes to Harding, 26 July 1922; Charles Evans Hughes Papers, Box 175, Folder 77 (a) GB, 'Memorandum of Interview with the British Ambassador', 21 January 1923; ibid., by telephone, 26 January 1923; Grigg (1948), p. 99. The 7 July Cabinet also heard of a suggestion that, if the UK funded and her credit improved, she would be able to repay the Bonds early, using money borrowed more cheaply in the markets. There is no suggestion that this was in Harvey's mind, but Hankey's poor grasp of matters financial should, once again, be stressed.

67 *Congressional Record*, 15 February 1923, p. 3692; *Refunding of Obligations of Foreign Governments*, US Senate, Hearing before the Committee on Finance, on HR 14254, 10 February 1923, p. 6.

68 T 160/365/F557/7, ff. 20–1, Baldwin to Bonar Law, 8 January 1923, and f. 23, Bonar Law to Baldwin, 9 January 1923; *Refunding of Obligations of Foreign Governments*, US Senate, Hearings before the Committee on Finance, on HR 14254, 10 February 1923, p. 6.

69 T 160/365/F557/7, f. 113, Chancellor to Bonar Law, 13 January 1923; *Congressional Record*, 15 February 1923, p. 3692.

70 Cab. 24/158, ff. 114–15, Chancellor to Prime Minister, 13 January 1923.

71 T 160/365/F557/7, ff. 40–1, Prime Minister to Chancellor, 13 January 1923.

72 Ibid., f. 47, Prime Minister to Chancellor, 13 January 1923.

73 Norman to Blackett in Clay (1957), p. 179; Baldwin Papers 233, 'History of the Anglo-American Debt', pp. 267–8 and 270–1.

74 Cab. 24/158, ff. 119–22, Chancellor to Prime Minister, 14 January 1923 (Sunday).

75 Cab. 23/45, Cabinet 2 (23), Conclusion 3, 15 January 1923; T 160/365/F557/7, ff. 54–5, Prime Minister to Baldwin, 16 January 1923.

76 Middlemas (1969), p. 227.

77 Cab. 24/158, CP 16 (23), 'Anglo-American Debt', Bonar Law to Baldwin, 17 January 1923.

78 *The Times*, 17 January 1923, p. 10; *The New York Times*, 18 January 1923, pp. 1 and 3; Baldwin Papers 233, 'History of the Anglo-American Debt', p. 272; Grigg (1948), p. 101. *The New York Times* did not carry details of the offer until the end of the month. *The New York Times*, 28 January 1923, p. 3.

79 Middlemas and Barnes (1969), pp. 143–4; *The New York Times*, 28 January 1923, pp. 1 and 3; T 160/365/F557/7, ff. 75–6, Geddes to FO, 29 January 1923, and ff. 79–81, FO (marked 'PM approves') to Geddes, 31 January 1923; Charles Evans Hughes Papers, Box 175, File 77 (a) GB, 'Memorandum of Interview with the British Ambassador', 1 February 1923. *The New York Times* published much of the interview verbatim.

80 Cab. 23/45, Cabinet 4 (23), Conclusion 2, 30 January 1923, and Cabinet 5 (23), 31 January 1923.

81 Charles Evans Hughes Papers, Box 172, File 29, Beerits, 'Funding the Allied War Debts', undated.

82 Charles Evans Hughes Papers, Box 175, File 77 (a) GB, William Phillips to Hughes, 30 January 1923.

83 Charles Evans Hughes Papers, Box 175, Folder 77 (a) GB, 'Memorandum of Interview with the British Ambassador', 21 January 1923. Geddes did not see Hughes 'officially' and no record of the conversation has been found in the British archives.

84 Charles Evans Hughes Papers, Box 175, File 77 (a) GB, 'Memorandum of Interview with British Ambassador', 29 January 1923; ibid., Box 172, File 29, Beerits, 'Funding the Allied War Debts', undated; T 160/366/F557/8, ff. 87–8, Geddes to Curzon, 7 February 1923.

85 Charles Evans Hughes Papers, Box 4 B, File January–February 1923, Hughes to Harvey, 29 January 1923.

86 Charles Evans Hughes Papers, Box 172, File 28, Harvey to Hughes, 30 January 1923.

87 He was, presumably, referring to Blackett's papers of August and October, already discussed. Unless otherwise specified, the following three paragraphs are based on Middlemas and Barnes (1969), pp. 144–6, and Baldwin Papers 132, 'History of the Anglo-American Debt', pp. 281–4. Middlemas and Barnes cite an account in the 'Davidson Papers'. This has not been found.

88 Middlemas (1969), pp. 227–8; Roskill (1970–4), II, p. 334; Thomas Lamont Papers II, 96–13, McKenna to Lamont, 12 March 1923; Cab. 23/45, Cabinet 5 (23), 31 January 1923; Clay (1957), p. 179.

89 T 160/365/F557/7, ff. 77–8 and 86, FO to Geddes, 31 January 1923, and ff. 89–90, Geddes to FO, 1 February 1923; T 160/366/F557/8, ff. 88–90, Geddes to Curzon, 7 February 1923; *Refunding of Obligations of Foreign Governments*, US Senate, Hearing before the Committee on Finance on HR 14254, 10 February 1923, p. 8.

90 *Congressional Record*, 7 February 1923, pp. 3213–4.

91 *Congressional Record*, 14 February 1923, p. 3626.

92 *Congressional Record*, 9 February 1923, pp. 3301–6 and 3338–72, 13 February 1923, pp. 3542–61 and 3607–29, 15 February 1923, pp. 3669–74 and 3679–93, 16 February 1923, pp. 3741–87; *Refunding of Obligations of Foreign Governments*, US Senate, Hearings before the Committee on Finance, on HR 14254, 10 February 1923; *Refunding Foreign Obligations – British Debt*, US House of Representatives, Hearings before the Committee on Ways and Means, on HR 14235, 8 February 1923.

93 *Refunding Foreign Obligations – British Debt*, US House of Representatives, Hearings before the Committee on Ways and Means, on HR 14235, 8 February 1923, pp. 5–7.

94 *Congressional Record*, 9 February 1923, pp. 3339 and 3548–9.

95 T 160/366/F557/9, ff. 78–9, Geddes to Curzon, 15 February 1923.

96 *Congressional Record*, 9 February 1923, p. 3339, and 13 February 1923, pp. 3548–9 and 3554–7.

97 T 160/365/F557/7, f. 94, Geddes to FO, 1 February 1923.

98 T 160/366/F557/8, ff. 15–18, Rowe-Dutton to Niemeyer, 9 February 1923, and ff. 50–1, 18 February 1923.

99 T 160/366/F557/9, ff. 10–12, Rowe-Dutton to Niemeyer, and f. 12, Niemeyer to Rowe-Dutton, 1 March 1923; T 160/366/F557/10, f. 59, Baldwin to Geddes, 24 April 1923, and ff. 54–7, Niemeyer to Geddes, 25 April 1923.

100 T 160/366/F557/8, ff. 19–27, 9 February 1923, and ff. 100–7, Rowe-Dutton to Niemeyer, 24 February 1923; T 160/366/F557/10, ff. 39–48, 22 March 1923.

101 The British proposal, the American acceptance and a copy of the Bond were published as Cmd. 1912, *American Debt: Arrangements for the Funding of the British Debt to the United States of America*, 1923.

102 T 160/366/F557/8, ff. 108–9, Rowe-Dutton to Niemeyer, 24 February 1923; T 160/366/F557/10, ff. 54–7, Niemeyer to Geddes, 25 April 1923, and f. 60, 'American Debt Funding Proposal', late April 1923.

103 T 160/366/F557/10, f. 49, Rowe-Dutton to Phillips, 7 April 1923, and f. 64, Rowe-Dutton, 'American Debt Funding Proposal', end-April 1923.

104 T 160/366/F557/8, f. 92, Geddes to Curzon, 7 February 1923; T 160/366/F557/10, f. 38, Mellon to Geddes, 21 March 1923.
105 T 160/366/F557/10, f. 50, note by Phillips, 10 April 1923, and ff. 62–3, 'American Debt Funding Proposal', late-April 1923; ibid., f. 80, Geddes to Niemeyer, 5 May 1923.
106 T 160/366/F557/7, ff. 96–7, Rowe-Dutton to Niemeyer, 2 February 1923 (two cables).
107 T 160/366/F557/8, ff. 90–1, Geddes to Curzon, 7 February 1923.
108 T 160/366/F557/7, f. 104, Rowe-Dutton to Niemeyer, 3 February 1923; ibid., f. 96, Phillips to Niemeyer, 9 February 1923; ibid., f. 106, Chancellor to Niemeyer, 6 February 1923; T 160/366/F557/9, f. 16, Rowe-Dutton to Niemeyer, 3 February 1923; T 160/366/F557/8, f. 98, Niemeyer to Chancellor, 26 February 1923.
109 T 160/366/F557/8, ff. 44–5 and 52, Rowe-Dutton to Niemeyer, 18 February 1923 (one cable and one letter).
110 T 160/366/F557/8, ff. 68–70, Rowe-Dutton to Niemeyer, 22 February 1923, and f. 98, Niemeyer to Chancellor, 26 February 1923; T 160/366/F557/9, ff. 17–22, 'Exchange Protection, Alternative 1, 2 and 3', marked 'sent to Governor', end-February 1923.
111 T 160/366/F557/8, f. 99, Niemeyer to Rowe-Dutton, 26 February 1923.
112 T 160/366/F557/10, ff. 36–7, Mellon to Geddes, 20 March 1923.
113 T 160/366/F557/7, ff. 8 and 11, Geddes to FO, 8 and 15 December 1922, and f. 9, article from the *Washington Herald*, 7 December 1922.
114 T 160/366/F557/7, ff. 89–90, Geddes to FO, 1 February 1923; T 160/366/F557/8, f. 90, Geddes to Curzon, 7 February 1923.
115 *Congressional Record*, 14 February 1923, pp. 3621–8.
116 T 160/366/F557/8, ff. 44–5 (cable) and 50–1 (letter), Rowe-Dutton to Niemeyer, 18 February 1923; ibid., f. 66, Niemeyer to Rowe-Dutton, 21 February 1923.
117 T 160/366/F557/10, f. 49, Rowe-Dutton to Phillips, 7 April 1923, and ff. 85–6, Niemeyer to Chancellor, 10 May 1923.
118 T 160/366/F557/10, ff. 76–82, Geddes to FO, 5 May 1923.
119 T 160/366/F557/10, ff. 83–4, Geddes to FO, 5 May 1923, and ff. 92–3, Chancellor to Geddes, 14 May 1923.
120 T 160/366/F557/10, ff. 85–6, Niemeyer to Chancellor, 10 May 1923, and ff. 109–23, Geddes to Mellon, 16 May 1923.
121 T 160/366/F557/10, ff. 140–4, Mellon to Geddes, 23 May 1923, and ff. 146–8, Rowe-Dutton to Niemeyer, 6 June 1923.
122 *Foreign Debt Funding Legislation*, US House of Representatives, Hearings before the Committee on Ways and Means, on HR 4743 etc., 4 January 1926, p. 7.
123 T 160/365/F557/7, ff. 107–9, Bradbury to Niemeyer, 3 February 1923; *Foreign Debt Funding Legislation*, US House of Representatives, Hearings before the Committee on Ways and Means, on HR 4743 etc., 4 January 1926, p. 2; Thomas Lamont Papers, II, 111–21, 'Memorandum for Mr Leffingwell, 4 October 1929. The reductions given here are slightly different from those provided by Moulton and Pasvolsky (1932), p. 101. They show the settlements (also using $4^1/_4$ per cent) implied prices of 80.3 (UK), 47.2 (France), 24.6 (Italy) and 46.5 (Belgium). I am grateful to Professor Pressnell for drawing these alternatives to my attention.
124 *Foreign Debt Funding Legislation*, US House of Representatives, Hearings before the Committee on Ways and Means, on HR 4743 etc., 4 January 1926, pp. 1–7.

18 The price of indebtedness, 1924–31

These successive maturities, sweeping upon us one after another like ocean waves at a time when the ship was not in particularly seaworthy condition owing to the quarrelsome behaviour of those on board, have been a serious cause of preoccupation to my expert financial advisers.

Winston Churchill, *Hansard* (Commons), 24 April 1928, col. 826.

If I look back…I see that, running throughout the whole of that period, we have had to deal with certain special problems…There was, for instance, the troublesome question of perpetual maturities of Debt occurring practically from year to year and giving us no respite.

Montagu Norman, evidence to the Committee on Finance and Industry (Macmillan Committee), 26 March 1930, para. 3317.

In the middle 1920s, the turbulence of the post-war years gave way to a precarious stability. Experience had shown that falling exchanges and political tensions accompanied attempts to collect reparations; the most recent default had led, in January 1923, to a French and Belgian occupation of the Ruhr and economic breakdown in Germany. The occupation had yielded little and damaged the exchange rates of the French and Belgians, as well as contributing to the destruction of the German currency. Realising that they were driving themselves into a cul-de-sac, European governments accepted, in varying degrees, that the recovery of the victors was only possible if Germany was prosperous. German monetary stabilisation came with the replacement in November 1923 of the worthless Reichsmark with the Rentenmark and a new approach to reparations. The two Dawes Committees started their discussions in January 1924 and published their recommendations in April. The proposals were accepted after inter-governmental negotiations during July and August. The Plan, which protected Germany against transfers which would depreciate her currency and tailored payments to her capacity to pay, was underpinned by an external loan: the Dawes Loan, issued in October for 800m gold marks (£39m or \$191m). As a condition, the French and Belgians agreed to evacuate the Ruhr. The Locarno non-aggression pacts were initialled in October 1925, and declared effective in February 1926.

Confidence was further strengthened by a widespread return to the gold standard. For Sweden, this came in March 1924, with others making clear their intention to follow. The Anglo-American debt agreement had been ratified by the British in June 1923 and by 1925 there was experience of the payments being properly met. On 28 April, the Chancellor announced in his budget that the embargo on the export of gold would not be renewed when it ran out at the end of the year and that, in the meantime, licenses would be freely given. Eighteen other countries followed, with France stabilising her internal finances after July 1926, pegging the franc *de facto* in December 1926.[1]

The return to gold did nothing to ease the management of the UK government debt and, in particular, the refinancing of the War Bonds. The small stock of gold and foreign exchange held by the Bank, the accumulation of short-term foreign claims on sterling and the Chancellor's reluctance to raise Bank rate when unemployment was high made the currency vulnerable to financial and monetary developments elsewhere – especially in the USA, France and Germany. In the six years between Churchill's announcement and the abandonment of gold in September 1931, there was continuous conflict between those wanting to ease financial policy to relieve unemployment and those looking to impose the disciplines necessary to protect the fixed exchange rate.

The authorities' operations in the markets were a mixture of the humdrum and the anxious. After a pause in the middle of the decade, maturities came thick and fast, the single date on the War Bonds giving no freedom to pick the most advantageous moment for refinancings. Instead, flexibility came from the CNRA's portfolio: from buying up the maturities, offering conversion before the due date when conditions were propitious, converting, and then selling the converted issues as demand appeared. Operated without the knowledge of market participants, the effect was to blunt, if not wholly to neutralise, the disadvantages inherent in single-dated securities. It became standard practice, used in all the major operations in the second half of the decade and responsible for the absence of refinancing crises. Without it, the maturities and a fixed exchange rate would have been a lethal combination.

In principle, of course, there was no threat to monetary control; refinancing was a question of paying the necessary rate at the time. The activities of the CNRA, good debt management, were merely the alternative to more expensive borrowing. From this viewpoint, the techniques were reducing political strains – avoiding higher taxes or lower expenditure. Always in the background was the threat that if the pressure from servicing the debt became too severe the sinking fund would be raided, a danger made evident in the absurdity of Churchill's later budgets, which reduced assets so that liabilities might be equally reduced.

Cutting debt costs are a basic Treasury concern in any age, whether by repaying debt from revenue, or lowering the interest rate, or a combination of the two. In the late nineteenth century, once the benefits of Goschen's conversion had been felt, it had to be reduction from revenue. In the second half of the 1920s, the emphasis shifted from repayment from sinking funds and casual surpluses, whose effects are felt over the long-term, to relieving the costs of Churchill's fiscal adventures and optimistic forecasting. Disputes about the management of the Debt came to be rooted in cost: the value of deep discount issues, breaking up the mass of 5 per cent War Loan, replacing Baldwin's sinking fund with a Fixed Charge and the treatment of the accrued interest on Savings Certificates.

The refinancings were eased by information available only to officials. The relationship between Norman and Strong, Norman's knowledge of American developments and intentions, greatly strengthened the authorities' hands when planning their market moves, notably in 1927 when they broke the back of the refinancings of the second half of the 1920s. The information was of limited help in handling Treasury Bills, which had to be constantly rolled over, whatever the cost at the time, but in the gilt-edged market timing is all: once longer-dated or permanent debt is sold, its cost is fixed.

This chapter has two purposes. It shows how the maturing War Bonds were handled in the second half of the 1920s and it lays the foundations for understanding the conversion of 5 per cent War Loan in 1932. It shows how the CNRA operated, how new issues were selected, and how the timing and planning were affected by developments and information coming from overseas, especially from the USA.

5 per cent War Loan 1929–47 into 4½ per cent Conversion Loan 1940–4 (1 April 1924)

The election of 6 December 1923 left the Conservatives in an overall minority and Labour as the second largest party. The first Labour government, dependent on Liberal support and weak from the outset, lasted for just nine months, from the second half of January to the beginning of November 1924. The conversions and refinancings of the previous two and a half years and a pause in maturities meant that the Labour Chancellor, Philip Snowden, was responsible for only one issue. In comparison with those described in Chapter 14, this was a luxury: an operation to try to reduce the bulk of 5 per cent War Loan 1929–47, as had been foreshadowed in Norman's diary the previous November.

At the end of March 1924, £2,100m 5 per cent War Loan represented 27 per cent of the nominal Debt. At a time when tax revenues were expected to be about £720m, the interest was costing over £100m a year gross. The government need not repay until 1947, but the servicing cost dictated action as soon after 1929 as possible. The problem fell into two parts: making the size manageable, and reducing the interest rate. They were connected because investors would feel more vulnerable, and more prepared to accept an offer of conversion, if the size and, therefore, the risks to monetary stability of calling the Loan could be reduced.

The advantages of whittling the issue down to manageable proportions before full-scale conversion in 1929 was Niemeyer's starting point when he broached the subject with Snowden on 21 March 1924. He advised attacking the issue between 1924–5 and 1926–7, when maturities were light (Table 18.1). A start should be made at once because the offer would be the forerunner of others on more favourable terms, each benefiting from greater confidence as the size of the Loan was reduced. An early offer was also desirable because the new government,

Table 18.1 Internal debt maturing in the two financial years following the beginning of each financial year: 1924–29 (£m nominal)

	Ways and Means	*Treasury Bills*	*Securities*	*Total*
As at 31 March 1924				
1924–5	186	588	150	924
1925–6	186	588	44	818
As at 31 March 1925				
1925–6	167	576	36	779
1926–7	167	576	110	853
As at 31 March 1926				
1926–7	139	565	115	819
1927–8	139	565	301	1005
As at 31 March 1927				
1927–8	117	599	178	894
1928–9	117	599	443	1159
As at 31 March 1928				
1928–9	162	527	267	955
1929–30	162	527	46	735
As at 31 March 1929				
1929–30	37	700	60	798
1930–1	37	700	135	872

Source: *National Debt: annual returns.*

dependent on the support of the Liberals, could run into political trouble and because the demand for credit could rise with a recovery of trade, borrowing for housing (where the ambition and cost of the government's measures were not yet known) and for the reparations loan which were to be recommended by the Dawes Committees.[2]

Niemeyer originally suggested including an offer to convert the outstanding £134.6m $5^3/_4$ per cent Exchequer Bonds, due on 1 February 1925. Even as he made the suggestion, he had been doubtful of its chances and, as there was no such offer, he must have been persuaded that this was the case. In other respects, the terms published on 1 April were almost identical to those originally proposed. Investors were offered a new security, $4^1/_2$ per cent Conversion 1940–4, on the basis of £103 of $4^1/_2$ per cent Conversion for £100 of 5 per cent War Loan, the equivalent of offering $4^1/_2$ per cent Conversion at £97 1s 9d (£4 15s 11d per cent to 1940 and £4 14s 11d per cent to 1944). This increased the nominal value of the Debt but, said Niemeyer, it was of 'no importance' because the annual cost would fall; £5 0s 0d per cent was being replaced with £4 12s 8d per cent.[3] The offer was limited to £200m of the War Loan on the registers of the Banks of England and

Ireland and to £10m on that of the Post Office, on the basis of first come, first served.

The response depended on whether holders judged it profitable to surrender a yield of 1/4 per cent a year on War Loan for a period which might be as short as five years (1929) but could be as long as twenty-three (1947) for the certainty of a yield for a period which might be as long as twenty years (1944) but could be as short as sixteen (1940). Thus the decision rested squarely on the expected movement of interest rates throughout a quarter century. Few investors can make such a judgement and it is not surprising that applications were less than the full £200m, £148.4m War Loan being converted into £152.9m 4½ per cent Conversion (Table 14.1).[a]

The 1924 budget

Snowden delivered the first Labour budget on 29 April 1924.[4] Revenue in the previous year was £18.5m above estimate and expenditure £27.8m below, giving a surplus of £48.3m. On existing policies, a surplus of £38.1m was forecast for 1924–5. Snowden used this to reduce or abolish a range of taxes on imports, consumer goods and services and to end the life of an unloved Corporation Tax. After the changes the surplus was estimated to be £4m.

Once again, a Chancellor spoke optimistically about the Debt. With the surplus of £48.3m and the New Sinking Fund (1923) of £40m, some £88m had been available for repayment in the previous year. The £40m had been applied to the contractual sinking funds, the penultimate repayment on account of Pittman silver (£6.6m) and the sinking fund on the Baldwin Bonds ($23m, or £4.9m at an exchange rate of $4.70). The casual surplus had been spent on the War Bonds which had matured on 1 February (about £20m, with a further £1m provided by the balance of the New Sinking Fund), Bills (£15.8m) and Ways and Means (£3.3m). The remainder of the surplus went on the last payment on Pittman silver (£6.7m), which had been brought forward a year, and the final payment to the Canadian Department of Finance (£2.4m) (see Table 15.4 and pp. 469 and 504n).[5]

4½ per cent Conversion 1940–4 and 4½ per cent Treasury Bonds 1934 (15 November 1924)

At the election held at the end of October 1924, the Conservatives won a substantial majority over all other parties. Baldwin returned as Prime Minister, appointing Winston Churchill as Chancellor. In the six months between Churchill's taking office and his announcement of sterling's return to gold, there were three operations

a About 20 per cent may have been on behalf of the official portfolios and the Bank: it is certain that the CNRA converted £9.6m and the Banking Department £5m; it is probable that the Commissioners, pressed by Niemeyer, converted over £15m. CNRA ledgers; BoE, ADM 19/10 and 19/11, and C40/871, 'Currency Notes', undated and unsigned; *BGS*, pp. 488–9; T 160/198/F7548, Niemeyer to Heath, 9 April 1924.

in the gilt-edged market, undertaken as Norman and Strong co-ordinated monetary policy to facilitate sterling's rise to pre-war par.

On both sides of the Atlantic, the authorities were foreseeing restriction. The US economy reached the trough of a mild recession during the summer of 1924. The Federal Reserve began to ease monetary conditions during the winter of 1923–4, and became more aggressive in the spring and summer of 1924, the Federal Reserve Bank of New York (FRBNY) discount rate being cut by one-and-a-half points in three stages on 1 May, 12 June and 8 August. Meanwhile, although unemployment was beginning to rise, Norman maintained conditions in London. In July, unable to find reasons for raising Bank rate which ministers would accept, he pushed less sensitive market rates higher: Treasury Bill rates rose from £2 18s 4d per cent in June to about £3 15s 0d per cent in August, where they rested until Bank rate was raised in March 1925 (Figure 18.1). While in April 1924 New York money market rates were above those in London, by July they were 1½ per cent below.

US market rates began rising in August. The Open Market Investment Committee of the Federal Reserve (OMIC) moved to a neutral stance at the end of October and on 4 November Strong warned Norman that policy was changing. On 8 December, Norman told Strong that if the FRBNY rate was raised ½ per cent Bank rate would go up by a full 1 per cent. In the event, the New York rate was not increased until 27 February 1925, Bank rate in London being raised from 4 to 5 per cent on 5 March. Two days before the New York rate was increased, Norman warned that a further rise, to 6 per cent, would be required if the London gold market was freed in April.[6]

In May 1924, sterling had fluctuated in the $4.30s. By 1 December, it was $4.64; at the end of the year $4.74; and before the announcement $4.81.[7] The long end of the gilt-edged market was largely unmoved as short rates moved higher, flattening the yield curve (Figure 14.3). There was a short-lived rise in prices after the election, but otherwise the running yield on 3½ per cent Conversion stayed around £4 10s 0d per cent until the 1925 budget (Figure 18.1).

With earlier conversion offers the authorities had been uncomfortable if maturities had not been reduced to rumps by the time of repayment. It is not surprising that Niemeyer had considered dealing with the 5¾ per cent Exchequer Bonds in April 1924.[8] The issue had always been held by the money market and banks, so there was no danger that non-bank resources would be lost to other markets as the Bonds approached maturity, but repayment in cash would have expanded the floating debt; officials must have been waiting nervously through the summer for the lifting of the political uncertainty. Thus, although Strong had recently warned Norman that US policy could tighten at any time, the imminence of the maturity on 1 February compelled a move on 15 November 1924, only nine days after the new Chancellor was appointed.

The issue was large, originally £166.7m, but reduced by puts to £134.6m. Holders were offered two alternatives. First, £100 4½ per cent Conversion 1940–4, plus £2 5s 0d cash, for each £100 Exchequer Bonds. Those accepting received the full coupon on the Exchequer Bonds on 1 February and the full half-year

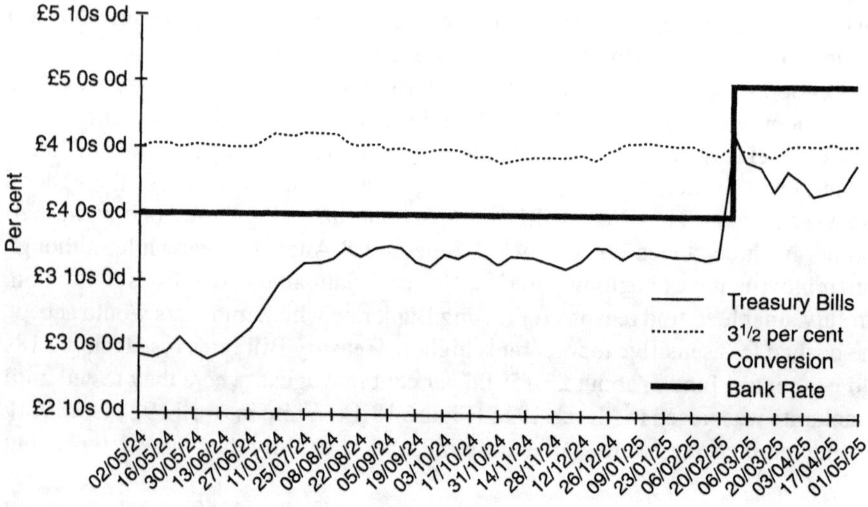

Figure 18.1 Bank rate, the discount rate on three-months' Treasury Bills and the running yield on 3½ per cent Conversion: May 1924 to May 1925. Source: *The Economist*.

interest payment on 4½ per cent Conversion on 1 July. The one month extra interest on 4½ per cent Conversion was worth £0 7s 8d per cent, so the price was £97 7s 4d (£4 15s 0d per cent to 1940 and £4 14s 2d per cent to 1944), comfortably above the £97 1s 9d of the previous April. Second, £100 of a new 4½ per cent Treasury Bond was offered for each £100 of the Exchequer Bonds. Thus, although officials knew that the maturing Bonds were held by the money market and banks, they offered a longer security in hopes that some holders might be inveigled longer, and a shorter security because they thought the hope futile. If investors did not take the longer, the Treasury would be happy to park some in the CNRA and wait.

The shorter security was given some of the characteristics of 5¾ per cent Exchequer Bonds, which had provided the holder, but not the Treasury, with the right to put the Bonds each year. On this occasion, the Treasury, showing that its hand had strengthened, took the right to call the issue: although the final date was 1 February 1934, the Bonds had a put and call effective on 1 February in any year between 1927 and 1933, triggered by giving notice in January of the previous year. As with the 5¾ per cent Exchequer Bonds in 1922, this was to cause embarrassment.

Holders of £82m Exchequer Bonds accepted the offer, leaving £52.6m to be repaid on 1 February 1925. £24.3m 4½ per cent Treasury Bonds 1934 and £57.7m 4½ per cent Conversion Loan were created (Table 14.1).[9] All the Treasury Bonds were on account of private sector conversions, but the success of 4½ per cent Conversion relied on the official portfolios. Just as the CNRA had bought issues which were to be converted into 3½ per cent Conversion, so it now bought 5¾ per cent Exchequer Bonds, converting £21.1m into 4½ per cent Conversion. The Commissioners converted a further £5m or so and the Banking Department just under £1m. In all, the three portfolios may have been responsible for nearly half.[10]

Sales of 3½ per cent Conversion Loan for cash (1 January 1925 and 25 March 1925)

There were two straight sales of 3½ per cent Conversion Loan before the 1925 budget, the first funded issues made for cash since the Boer War. Both were sold by tender and, with the minimum application £10,000, they were clearly aimed at the professional market – the predominant holder of the £52.6m 5¾ per cent Exchequer Bonds, £23.6m 5–15 year Treasury Bonds and some residual War Bonds, which were being refinanced. The variable rate Treasury Bonds, with their minimum coupon of 5 per cent, had become expensive borrowing and had been called at the first opportunity, the first and last occasion in the decade that the Treasury redeemed an issue before it was compulsory.

It can be inferred that when the authorities held the first tender they were uncertain whether a single operation could be made to cover both maturities and made their decision only when the results had been considered. In the middle of December, with the market temporarily weak, Strong warning that US rates were about to rise, and the conversions of the 5¾ per cents greater than expected, Niemeyer thought of limiting the offer to between £70m and £75m nominal, or around £55m cash, enough to refinance the Exchequer Bonds, but not the Treasury Bonds. There was also the possibility of using £12m lying in the New Sinking Fund (1923). The prospectus published on 1 January showed that a decision had been avoided: it specified neither the amount for which tenders were being invited nor whether the Treasury bound itself to accept all tenders at or above the minimum price. The authorities were thus able to see the level of the bids and their size before making allotments. The procedure was to be repeated on later occasions and, despite the problems it must have presented for investors, it did not excite comment either in the official records or in the press.

The minimum price at the tender was £77 10s 0d, but holders would receive a full interest payment on 1 April, so that it included over three months' income which had not been earned: allowing for this, the price was £76 14s 3d (£4 11s 3d per cent), which was marginally cheap to the market. Over 900 tenders, for £68.1m, were received and £59.7m, worth £46.3m cash, was allotted (Table 14.1). The average accepted price was £77 11s 0d, so those tendering at the minimum price received no allotment, ensuring that the authorities did not appear too eager and investors' appetites were whetted. Of the successful tenders, £10m came from the CNRA.[11] When the time came to pay off the Exchequer Bonds, the Treasury applied the £12m sinking fund monies so that, with the £46.3m raised from the tender, there was a small balance available to reduce the floating debt. The 5–15 year Treasury Bonds were to be repaid with a second operation.[12]

The day after the decision to return to gold was taken (20 March) Norman proposed that another tranche of Conversion should be offered in the five weeks remaining before the announcement.[13] On 2 April, £30m were sold, also by tender, to finance the £3.6m which remained of the 5 per cent War Bonds of 1 April 1925, the redemption of the 5–15 year Treasury Bonds and £8.9m War Bonds maturing on 1 September, although it was expected (correctly in the event) that the latter would be reduced by conversions into 5 per cent War Loan.[14] The minimum price at the tender, which on this occasion did specify the amount to be sold, was £76 15s 0d, and the average accepted price was £76 17s 0d (£4 11s 1d per cent). Interest was considerable and over twelve hundred applications were received for £83.6m. The CNRA took only £1.8m.[15]

When proposing the issue, Niemeyer envisaged that 'most' of the issue would be taken 'in the first place by the Bank and ourselves'. The comment is noteworthy as the first explicit record of the part being played by the CNRA.[16]

In April 1924, the offer to convert War Loan into 4½ per cent Conversion 1940–4 had been marred by the premature posting of some prospectuses.[17] A year later, both the tenders for 3½ per cent Conversion were accompanied by accusations that the operations had been leaked to the market. The first occasion did not evoke much comment, but the Bank had to rush out an announcement of the coming issue the day before the prospectus was published.[18] On the second, there were questions in the Commons and the Chancellor asked Warren Fisher, the Permanent Secretary to the Treasury, to investigate. After interviewing officials in the Bank and Treasury, Fisher concluded that there was no truth in the suggestions and that the price movements on the afternoon in question were not abnormal.[19]

Sale of 3½ per cent Conversion Loan for cash (23 September 1925)

The announcement of the return to gold was made at the beginning of the Chancellor's Financial Statement on 28 April 1925, being given equal place with the establishment of a contributory state pension scheme for the old, widows and orphans. The surplus in 1924–5 had turned out to be £3.7m, very close to the forecast. On existing policies, expenditure in 1925–6 would be £799m (including the full £50m New Sinking Fund (1923)), revenue £826m and the surplus £27m. Despite his devotion to free trade, Churchill reintroduced a range of import duties, thus allowing some Imperial preference. In the name of wealth creation, he balanced a reduction in taxes on incomes with an increase in death duties, cutting the standard rate by 6d in the £, at a cost of £24m in the first year and £32m in a full year. His comments on debt policy were as orthodox as Snowden's. The country had punctually paid off its liabilities and, if allowance was made for the interest on the US debt, which was now being paid, the reward had been a fall of about £70m in the annual servicing cost and a reduction in the rate on borrowing from 6½ to 4½ per cent. Profitable conversion operations had resulted, and this would continue:

> Much larger conversion operations impend within the lifetime of the present Parliament, and from these important savings may be realised by the taxpayer. But they will only be realised by strict adherence to the principles of sound financial policy…If those principles are maintained and this process of debt redemption continues, a speedy and a substantial reward will be reaped by the taxpayer and the benefit will come to hand even before the present Parliament has separated.[20]

During 1925–6, holders of £57.6m War Bonds converted into 5 per cent War Loan, of which about £4m was from the 1 September War Bond; £4.6m remained, maturing at 103. This would not itself have required a refinancing issue, except that a budget deficit was now expected, rather than the small surplus forecast in April: market Treasury Bills were rising; sterling was weak against the US dollar; and an early operation would pre-empt autumn industrial issues and the lifting of the embargo on public issues for overseas.[21]

There were also reasons for moving quickly. Attractive interest rates, the confidence which came from the return to the gold standard and chaos in France's finances drew short-term capital to London for several months after the budget. The ensuing rise in the gold stock was inconsistent with the tight policy required to help the economy adjust to the new fixed exchange rate. Norman, therefore, planned to lower money market rates and reverse the flow of gold, so that he would have an excuse to tighten once more. This manoeuvre was believed at the time to be a traditional response to monetary ease which was considered unjustified.[b] On 6 August, after a coal dispute had been temporarily settled, the Bank cut its rate to 4½ per cent and, on 1 October, to 4 per cent. With seasonal outflows, in September the Bank began to lose gold and substantial amounts went to New York in October and November. On 3 November, the embargo on foreign capital issues, which had been introduced the previous year, was lifted. US developments supported Norman's ploy. Strong had been concerned since late summer about securities speculation in New York and business expansion. Starting on 10 November in Boston, the Reserve Banks raised their rates; the FRBNY raised its rate on 8 January 1926. Policy in the UK could be tightened once more and, after some hesitation because Churchill was expected to resist higher rates when unemployment was high, on 3 December Bank rate returned to 5 per cent.[22]

The tender was held on 29 September (Tuesday), timed to catch the enthusiasm of those anticipating the Bank rate cut and the War Bond and Conversion Loan interest payments on 1 October (Thursday). It was for £40m 3½ per cent Conversion with a minimum price of £76 5s 0d (£4 11s 10d per cent). Once again, it was aimed at the professional market. The response was apathetic, for the authorities had mistimed their offer by a few weeks and had been caught by an unexpected rise in New York call rates;[c] sterling was at, or beneath, its gold export point and the market treated the cut in Bank rate with scepticism.[23]

The 1926 budget

The Chancellor had been warned that his 1925 budget was 'taking many risks'

b Since supporting sterling was one of the reasons for an issue given to the Chancellor, it is possible that Niemeyer did not know about Norman's 'ease-squeeze' plan. It is more likely that he thought it wiser not to tell Churchill that Norman was plotting higher rates.

c Four hundred and fifty tenders were received for £51.1m, of which £24.8m came from the CNRA and, perhaps, £3m from the Banking Department. The average accepted price was £76 6s 0d (£4 11s 9d per cent). BoE, Loan Wallet 324; CNRA Ledgers.

and 'leaving...practically no margin'; he was, said Tom Jones to his diary, 'gambling on the chance of a steady recovery in trade in the next twelve months'. Already, two months after Churchill spoke, Niemeyer was looking ahead to a deficit of £30m in 1926–7.[24] In the event, 1925–6 benefited from windfalls from Italian debt repayments and reparations: it would have shown a surplus of nearly £5m if it had not been decided at the beginning of August to avoid a coal strike by providing a subsidy. Originally estimated at £10m, the subsidy was £23m, £19m of which fell into 1925–6. As a result, the year showed a deficit of £14m.[25]

Protecting the appearance of debt repayment from the cost of the coal subsidy was the central feature of the 1926 budget. Although the 1926–7 estimates showed his advisers' warnings were well-founded, Churchill continued to ignore them. He accepted – indeed he stressed – the dangers of inelastic revenues and the reliance on exceptional miscellaneous receipts. He forecast expenditure of £812.6m and revenues of £804.7m on current policies. He introduced a new tax on betting and some minor changes in import duties. For the rest, he appropriated £7m of the accumulated surplus of the Road Fund, took £3.5m from taxes previously earmarked for the roads, and brought forward £5.5m of the duties collected by the brewers and £4m of a war debt repayment promised by the French, a total of £20.0m. Opining that subsidies, the reason for the deficit, were 'questionable', and certainly should not be met from borrowing, the Chancellor used one-half of the released assets to cover the forecast deficit of £10m for 1926–7 and the other half to increase the Sinking Fund from £50m to £60m. The increase in the Sinking Fund, together with the £4m 1924–5 casual surplus ('old sinking fund', which had already been appropriated to debt repayment), was notionally set against the previous year's deficit of £14m, so that he could claim to have had a balanced budget in the two years 1925–6 and 1926–7 combined. Revenue in 1926–7 would be £824.8m and expenditure, including the enhanced Sinking Fund, £820.6m.[26]

5 per cent Treasury Bonds 1927 into 4½ per cent Treasury Bonds 1934 (29 September 1926)

Deterioration in the budgetary position came as the Treasury began to plan for the heavy refinancings of the late 1920s. In the four financial years ending 31 March 1930, fourteen issues (including those which had already been put by 31 March 1926) were due. They had a nominal value of £1,064.0m and, because of the premiums on the War Bonds, a maturity value of £1,092.1m (Table 18.2). The Commissioners owned £68.0m and the CNRA just £6.4m.[27]

Through much of 1926, sterling was firm and interest rates steady. There was no change in Bank rate between December 1925 and April 1927. 3½ per cent Conversion was 75¼ at the end of December 1925, and 75½ a year later. Beneath this calm surface all was not well. The current account, damaged by the General Strike and the coal stoppage, moved into deficit, while long-term borrowing by foreigners increased. The effect on the exchange rate was masked by heavy, unidentified and potentially volatile inflows: commercial balances, US short-term capital and, most importantly, capital escaping from France.[28]

Table 18.2 Maturities of marketable domestic issues, 31 March 1926 to 31 March 1930, as at 31 March 1926

	£m nominal	*Maturity value*
5 per cent Treasury Bonds 1 February 1927	109.6	100
4$^1/_2$ per cent Treasury Bonds 1 February 1927	5.1	100
5 per cent War Bonds 1 October 1927	158.1	105
4 per cent War Bonds 1 October 1927	80.0	100
3$^1/_2$ per cent War Loan 1 March 1928	62.7	100
5 per cent War Bonds 1 April 1928	122.3	105
4 per cent War Bonds 1 April 1928	37.4	100
5 per cent War Bonds 1 September 1928	189.8	105
4 per cent War Bonds 1 September 1928	20.6	100
5 per cent War Bonds 1 February 1929	92.7	105
4 per cent War Bonds 1 February 1929	4.8	100
5$^1/_2$ per cent Treasury Bonds 1 April 1929	30.6	100
3 per cent Exchequer Bonds 28 January 1930	15.6	100
5$^1/_2$ per cent Treasury Bonds 15 May 1930	134.7	100
Total	1,064.0	

Source: *National Debt: annual return*, 1926.

As viewed from 31 March 1926, the maturities began on 1 February 1927 with £109.6m 5 per cent Treasury Bonds (the issue which helped bring the floating debt under control in the bull market of January and February 1922) and £5.1m 4$^1/_2$ per cent Treasury Bonds 1934, which had been put the previous January. There followed, on 1 October, £158.1m 5 per cent War Bonds and £80m 4 per cent tax-compounded War Bonds. The pace of maturities then continued unabated into 1929 when the 5 per cent War Loan option began (Tables 18.1 and 18.2).[29]

The first move was an offer to convert the 5 per cent Treasury Bonds 1927 into further amounts of 4$^1/_2$ per cent Treasury Bonds 1934, the issue with the put and call. The conversion was a simple nominal for nominal: the coupon dates coincided and those accepting the offer rolled over on 1 February 1927, when the new Bonds would be consolidated with the existing issue; £1 cash per cent was offered to those accepting. This was an odd incentive for an issue with an uncertain final maturity date: by reducing the price to 99, it raised the GRY by an amount that varied with the date at which a holding was to be put or called.[30]

The result broke the back of the 1 February maturity, with £83.8m (including £1.4m on the POR) accepting (Table 14.1).[d]

d Records of the transactions of the CNRA have not survived beyond the end of 1925 and we have to rely on end-quarter balance sheets. They show that in the first quarter of 1926 the Account began adding to its existing holding of 5 per cent Treasury Bonds and that by the end of September, some two weeks before the conversion became effective, it owned £14.4m. At the end of March 1927, it held about the same amount of 4$^1/_2$ per cent Treasury 1934. CNRA Ledgers.

4 per cent Consols, 1957 or after (29 December 1926)

In September 1925, at the time of the third cash sale of 3½ per cent Conversion, Niemeyer told Churchill the issue had become as large as was 'convenient to handle' and that a replacement would be required for 'bigger' operations. In the meantime, as it already had a market, the Loan could continue as a vehicle for small financings.[31] This needs explanation because the Treasury did not have to repay a perpetual annuity and there was no reason in principle why Conversion should not grow to represent as large a proportion of the Debt as had 2½ per cent Consols in 1900.

The problems lay in the sinking fund attached to Conversion – a contradiction in the design of a perpetual issue – and the low nominal rate with its corollary, a price well beneath par. The Colwyn Committee, whose Report[32] on the Debt was in the Treasury's hands during November in time to influence the design of the new issue, criticised the principle of attached sinking funds. The Committee made three points: as the sinking funds were mainly attached to longer issues, reborrowing or conversion of maturities had to be greater than if the whole of the sinking fund monies were available for general purposes; repaying one issue while reborrowing on another was 'probably' more disturbing to the market than straightforward borrowing on a single issue; and sinking funds might not be attached to the security which 'over a long period it is most desirable to support.' This, translated, meant that there would be the largest savings in debt costs if the sinking fund monies were available to buy the cheapest issue. For officials, there was an additional problem specific to Conversion; its sinking fund was a percentage of the nominal outstanding and rose as more was issued. The pre-emption of a growing part of the sinking fund monies by a single issue was reducing flexibility in debt management.[33]

The Colwyn Committee's criticism of deeply discounted issues was accepted by two Treasury officials, Hawtrey and Phillips. Thus, on 7 December, Phillips showed why Conversion's replacement should bear a nominal rate of 4½ per cent and be priced near par. Niemeyer, while reluctantly agreeing in principle with the Committee's criticisms, argued that they were invalid when a huge debt was being managed and a range of nominal rates was needed to attract investors with differing requirements. With the disagreement, 4 per cent Consols, redeemable on or after 1 February 1957, had a difficult birth: the prospectus went into six printed proofs before a price or interest rate was included and the Governor himself spent a day working on it. In the event, Niemeyer made a tactical withdrawal. A 4 per cent rate was not high enough to permit issue at par, but it was a restrained bow to the Committee's views; although not accepting that Conversion was an error, it was an acknowledgement that the Committee had a point; and it could be called for the defence in the event of attack in the future (for a discussion of issuing beneath par, see Chapter 22).[34]

Three other terms were tightened to reflect the experience with Conversion. The sinking fund was limited to ten years, it could not exceed £10m a year, irrespective of the size to which the issue grew, and the first optional date was ten years earlier than that on Conversion in 1921, when it was first issued.[35]

The offer, dated 29 December 1926, was for cash and conversion. That for cash was partly paid at 85 (a running yield of £4 14s 1d per cent), with the calls extending to May and earlier payments in full being accepted under discount at 3 per cent. The conversion offer, at first sight, gave discounts of up to half a point to the cash price, but these disappeared when adjustment – complex adjustments – were made for the value of broken interest payments and differences in the running yields between the time conversions took effect and the time when the converted issues would have matured.

£9.2m 5 per cent Treasury Bonds 1927, £65.3m 5 per cent War Bonds and £35.4m 4 per cent War Bonds were converted into £133.8m Consols. A further £32.6m nominal of Consols were issued for cash. The CNRA took £35m, 20 per cent of the total (Table 14.1).[36]

Niemeyer's report to Churchill, who was in Rome, was uncharacteristically euphoric: it had been, after all, his decision to issue at 4 per cent. Churchill was dissatisfied with the reduction in the servicing cost and in the nominal value of the Debt, and the success of the issue gave Niemeyer the opportunity to show how the stream of conversions could be managed. He emphasised that a success, entailing a small premium for the investor, could encourage the market and enable a long-term refinancing programme on steadily improving terms:

> As our most optimistic estimate was one hundred millions all told, the present result can only be called extremely satisfactory. It has been received as such by all the Press here, and the dealings to-day will shortly start at a slight premium. This is very much to our advantage, as it will tend to improve Government Stocks generally, and also enable us to sell gradually in the market the thirty five million 4% Consols which we took up. We shall then be in a position, perhaps by the summer, to make a further offer of 4% Consols on more favourable terms...This is precisely the object at which we ought to aim, and the method by which we must eat at our future debt maturities.[37]

On 1 February, the £5.1m 'put' 4½ per cent Treasury Bonds 1934 and the remaining £16.6m 5 per cent Treasury Bonds 1927 were paid off for cash, the latter absorbing £15m from the New Sinking Fund.[38]

The 1927 budget

The General Strike only lasted for a week (3–12 May 1926), but the stoppage in the coalfields continued for seven months.[39] This was convenient for, when presenting his third budget on 11 April 1927, Churchill could blame the unrest for the greater part of the £36.5m deficit he had to report: loss of tax revenue (£17.5m), relief of unemployment and distress (£4.3m), the emergency Vote (£0.4m), interest on the Bills issued to finance the deficit together with higher rates on all Bills (£6m), and the accrued interest on 'exceptional' encashments of Savings

Certificates caused by the pressure of 'civil strife' on savings (£3m).[e] On existing policies, there would also be a deficit the following year: revenue was forecast to be £796.9m and expenditure £818.4m.

The Chancellor continued his habit of saying one thing and doing another. Once again, he placed great emphasis on repaying debt; by 'strict and severe provision of Sinking Funds' and the maintenance of 'sound finance' lower interest charges could be won and the finances of future governments strengthened. Confidence in British credit was always vital, but it was particularly important at a time when the 'dominant fact in our finance' was the opportunity to refinance maturities at lower interest rates. He said that he had been advised by many to meet the deficit by a partial suspension of the Sinking Fund, but to 'shirk' the duty of raising taxes at the expense of 'our settled policy of debt repayment would be cowardly and wrong…deeply injurious to the national interest.' Having rolled out these Treasury sentiments, he repeated the previous year's exercise of raiding assets to maintain the appearance of debt repayment. £12m came from winding up the Road Fund and transferring the cost of road improvements to the Treasury, £5m from a further tightening of Brewers' credit and £14.8m from collecting the withholding tax on rents in one instalment in January instead of two instalments, one of which fell in the following financial year. With increased taxation of £5.9m and the minimum of political damage, a deficit of £21.5m was transformed into a surplus of £16.4m. This was used to increase the Sinking Fund from £50m to £65m, making good almost one-half of the previous year's deficit. Expenditure, including the Sinking Fund, became £833m and revenue £835m.

'*The Times* calls it ingenious, but most of the other papers speak of trickery' was Tom Jones's description of the press reaction. Baldwin thought that 'As a work of art…Winston's speech [was] as good as it could possibly be. There was a general sense of bewilderment at the end of it.' Churchill's comment to the Governor 'It was as good a get-out as we could get', received no reply.[40]

Sale by tender of 4½ per cent Treasury 1934 to finance the remaining 1 October 1927 War Bonds (6 September 1927)

In July 1926, after the franc had collapsed to nearly 210 against sterling, a new government successfully tackled France's fiscal problem. There was a return of confidence and from the autumn of 1926 capital started to flow back to Paris. In December, the franc was stabilised *de facto* and in June 1928 *de jure*. In April 1927, the Banque de France announced that it had repaid early in a single sum a £33m loan taken from the Bank of England in 1923. In mid-May 1927, seeking to

e The argument was concocted by Niemeyer. He argued that the increased expenditure on Bills was twofold: the interest on the Bills issued to cover the costs of the strike and the increase in the interest rate paid on all Bills. The latter was justified because the increased supply and disturbed money markets had held Bill rates at a higher level than had been expected. T 177/6, Niemeyer to Chancellor, 11 February 1927; *Hansard* (Commons), 11 April 1927, col. 61.

check the inflows into francs, the Banque de France began to use its newly acquired sterling to buy gold in the hope and expectation that it would compel the British to tighten credit, in its turn forcing similar restriction elsewhere in Europe. The purchases caused great alarm in the Bank of England, which, while refusing to raise its rate, during May squeezed money market rates higher: at the beginning of the month, the Treasury Bill rate was about £3 12s 0d per cent, and by the end of the month £4 7s 0d per cent, where it rested until the end of the year (Figure 18.2). The immediate problem was solved by a temporary deterioration in the French balance of payments and a reshuffling of gold and sterling between the French and the FRBNY. When their payments surplus reappeared in August, the French authorities handled it differently; by manipulating short-term interest rates and providing forward cover, they encouraged those wishing to hold francs to sell spot and buy forward. With this encouragement, the private sector accumulated foreign currencies, curtailing the rise in the Banque de France's reserves and in currency in circulation. The commitments reached their peak in June 1928, when $600m was outstanding, largely in sterling.

The British authorities may have been unaware of the extent of the support being provided for sterling by the Banque de France's swaps. The relief provided by two other sources was more obvious. At the beginning of July, at a meeting of central bankers on Long Island, the Reichsbank and the Banque de France agreed to buy gold in New York, rather than London, and the French agreed to sell some sterling to the FRBNY for dollars. Also, in late July and early August, the US authorities, believing that their economy was about to enter recession and aiming

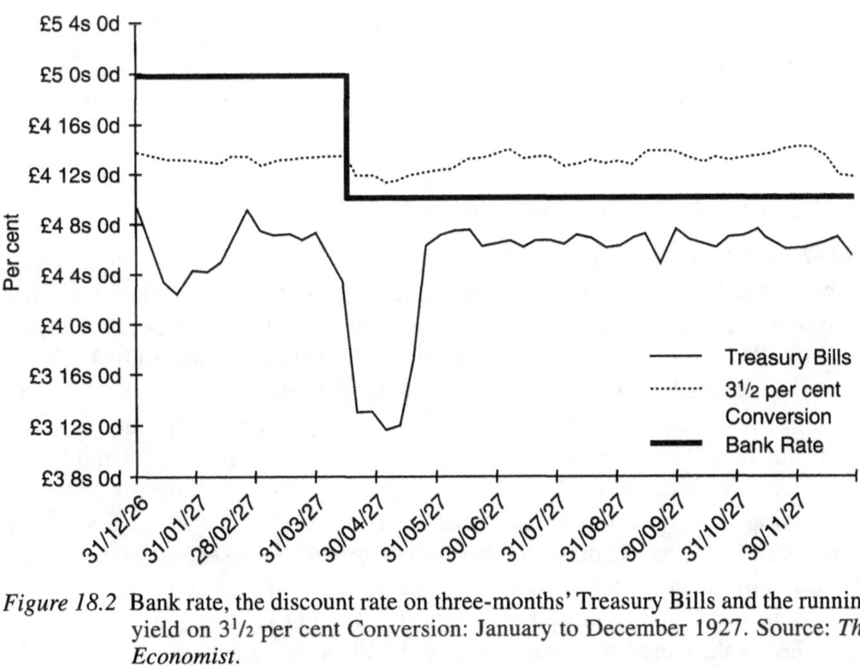

Figure 18.2 Bank rate, the discount rate on three-months' Treasury Bills and the running yield on 3½ per cent Conversion: January to December 1927. Source: *The Economist*.

to help sterling, eased monetary policy. With sterling rates held at the higher levels introduced in May, the margin in favour of London widened and the UK became one of the major beneficiaries of the US capital exports. The demand for long-term funds and trade finance shifted from London to New York. The Bank accumulated substantial amounts of dollars in the second half of the year and by the beginning of October the FRBNY had been able to sell the sterling it had bought from the French.[41]

Sterling's strength after mid-year may have been fragile, dependent as it was on the protection afforded by the Long Island agreements, the temporary easing in US policy and the Banque de France's swaps, but it provided a healthy market for the refinancing of maturities. Niemeyer had left the Treasury to join the Bank and Sir Richard Hopkins was now Controller of Finance, coming from the Board of Inland Revenue, where he had been chairman since 1922. He had never visited the Bank before his new appointment.[42] For a short time at the end of 1927, he was assisted by Frederick Leith-Ross, whose usual duties lay in overseas finance. Hopkins's first market operations are unusually well-documented for, as a novice, he exchanged notes with Leith-Ross and kept the Chancellor briefed in greater detail than had been Niemeyer's practice.

In the first half of June 1927, a further £38m 1 October War Bonds were converted into the 4 and 5 per cent War Loans so that, at maturity, only £43.4m of the 5 per cent War Bonds and £33.2m of the 4 per cents remained. With the New Sinking Fund contributing £12.1m, £66.7m of cash was required on 1 October.[43] This was secured from a further tranche of 4½ per cent Treasury 1934, the issue with the put and call. The sale was made by tender on 13 September, with a minimum price of £99 6s 0d. The issue was regarded as attractive to the professional short-term market and it was allotted aggressively.[44] There were over 600 applications for some £80m. Tenders for £65m were accepted at an average price of £99 7s 5d (£4 12s 6d per cent to 1934) and those applying at just 6d above the minimum received 50 per cent (Table 14.1).[45]

The last tranche of 3½ per cent Conversion (15 September 1927)

Nine days later came an offer to convert the maturities of the following spring. Since 1 March 1925, 3½ per cent War Loan 1925–8 had been callable, but had been protected by its low nominal rate. The issue had stood at about £63m since the cancellations of 1915. The 31 March 1927 accounts record £110.1m 5 per cent and £36.4m 4 per cent War Bonds of 1 April 1928.

For the last time, the vehicle was 3½ per cent Conversion. At the market prices on the day before the issue, the running yields were £4 13s 1d per cent and £4 14s 6d per cent. This would not have been enough to decide the choice in favour of Conversion, even if the first Consols had been absorbed: as it was, the CNRA still owned £27.7m at the end of September, and there were at least £5m in the Banking Department. In addition, Consols stood at a discount of between a quarter and a half point to their issue price and Hopkins, no doubt repeating a recent lesson from the Bank, feared the effect on 'the credit of the Stock and indeed to the credit of the Government' of issuing another tranche at a lower price; Consols was to be the mainstay of future large-scale conversions and 'we should not dissipate its possibilities.'[46]

Because of the issue's greater size, holders of the taxable War Bonds were offered the most generous terms; after adjusting for the value of broken interest payments, differences in the running yields between the time conversions took effect and the time when the converted issues would have matured, they received Conversion Loan at £73 18s 11d (£4 14s 8d per cent), whereas holders of War Loan received their new Stock at £74 17s 0d (£4 13s 6d per cent) and holders of the tax-compounded War Bonds received theirs at £74 15s 0d (£4 13s 8d per cent), after allowing for the value of the tax privilege for six months.

Forty-five per cent of the 5 per cent War Bonds (£49.2m), 28 per cent of the 4 per cents (£10.3m) and about one-third of the War Loan (£21.2m) were converted into £111.7m Conversion (Table 14.1).[47]

5 per cent Treasury Bonds 1933–5 convertible into 4 per cent Consols (22 December 1927)

Writing in November 1927, Hopkins divided the problem of the 1928 refinancings into three: converting the 1 September 1928 War Bond maturities; raising £90m in cash to pay off 3½ per cent War Loan on 1 March and the 4 and 5 per cent War Bonds on 1 April; and, later in the summer, raising the cash to repay any 1 September maturities which remained unconverted. He warned that the market was tired from the Treasury's continuous demands, but the end was in sight as, once they had dealt with the £100m 1 February 1929 maturities, they had only £519m of Treasury Bonds at various dates up to 1934, and it 'may well be hoped that the difficulty of dealing with them will be on an altogether lower plane.' Turning to the offer to convert the autumn maturities, he recommended including an offer for cash; the result would be small, but 'we can afford to miss no chance'.

Hopkins had considered delaying an offer until April or May, but:

> there is an obvious risk in this course. The hope which my uninstructed mind was at first inclined to harbour that things might be better in the Spring, is not shared by the Governor, and where such large issues are at stake, I do not feel it would be right to advise you to take a considerable risk in the hope of gaining a comparatively moderate advantage.

There was one other consideration, which must have been in officials' minds on earlier occasions, although it has left no record. An early offer prevented holders of the War Bonds from using their options to convert into the 5 and 4 per cent War Loans. In the case of the 5 per cent Loan, the option expired as late as 15 June and the conversion terms gave a running yield of £5 5s 3d per cent on the newly created securities, very expensive borrowing compared with, say, the £4⅝ or £4¾ per cent paid on 3½ per cent Conversion in September and the £4 12s 6d per cent paid on 4½ per cent Treasury 1934 in June.

Consideration was given to $3^1/_2$ per cent Conversion, and was rejected because of the effect on the nominal value. Consols, however, still stood at a discount to their issue price. The solution was to use Consols, but to 'mask' the price by issuing a short-dated security with an option to convert into them at a price above 85, the level at which they were sold the previous January. This was the first use of such a ploy by the British government in London, although it had been used in New York.[f] It was envisaged that the balance of the cash for the February and April maturities would be found by an issue of another short Bond in the New Year.[48]

Sterling was particularly strong against the dollar during December and gold flowed to London from New York. The terms, published on 22 December, were greeted enthusiastically. The issue was of an unlimited amount of 5 per cent Treasury Bonds 1933–5 at 101 (£4 16s 8d per cent to 1933). Each £100 nominal of the 5 per cent War Bonds (maturing at £105) could convert into £105 10s 0d of the new Bonds and each £100 nominal of the tax-compounded War Bonds into £99 10s 0d. In the former case, the extra half point was to ensure that the running yield matched that available from converting into 5 per cent War Loan: at a price of £94 15s 9d, a 5 per cent security yielded £5 5s 6d per cent.[49]

In their turn, the Bonds were convertible into Consols; if the price of issue is taken as £101 0s 0d, the price of Consols on the first occasion (July 1928) was £86 6s 8d (£4 12s 8d per cent) and on the second occasion (January 1929) £88 4s 2d (£4 10s 8d per cent).

The operation was such a success that the issue of short Bonds planned for February was unnecessary. It had originally been intended to keep the lists for the cash offer open for seven days, but with applications for £80m received by the second afternoon they were closed that evening. 'I am so glad yr first important activities in this sphere have been successful' was Churchill's comment, although he could not refrain from adding that he considered the terms 'liberal'.[50] Applications amounted to £86.1m (£87m cash), sufficient to cover $3^1/_2$ per cent War Loan on 1 March (£41.5m) and the 5 and 4 per cent War Bonds on 1 April (£26.3m and £19.6m). Of the applications, £10m were on behalf of the CNRA.[51] The conversion was equally successful: £112m of the 5 per cent War Bonds of 1 September 1928 were converted into £118.2m of the new issue, so that only some £45m remained. This was further reduced in June by conversions into 5 per cent War Loan, so that there were only £29.7m to be paid off at maturity; £13m 4 per cents were converted into the Treasury Bonds, and only £5.1m remained at maturity (Table 14.1).[52]

Hopkins, with only five months experience of the vagaries of the gilt-edged market, allowed himself to be pleased:

f The closest parallel was with the 1 November 1919 issues, which were convertible into an existing issue of War Bonds. The Anglo-French Loan in 1915 and the Notes and Bonds issued on 1 February 1917 were convertible into an issue which was not to be created until conversion took place. See Chapters 8 and 15.

> We still need to raise about £40 millions of cash to pay off the unconverted September maturities [he was writing before the conversions into the War Loans] and we have to handle roughly £100 millions of National War Bonds falling in on the 1st February 1929 and £30 millions of Treasury Bonds falling in two months later.
>
> This is not a very large commitment and it seems to me possible that when the time comes (say in the late summer) we may be able to deal with it in a single operation.
>
> We have got through better than I had hoped.[53]

The 4½ per cent Treasury 1934 option

Hopkins's optimism lasted just two weeks for, by the end of January, holders of £72.8m 4½ per cent Treasury 1934 had unexpectedly exercised their options and claimed repayment for 1 February, one year later. The Bank advised that as the Bonds were 'almost purely a bankers' security', there would be 'no special difficulty' in replacing them with further short borrowings. The size of the puts would have to be published, however, and this could make it more difficult, or at least more expensive, to refinance the £4.8m 4 per cent and £95.2m 5 per cent War Bonds, which were to mature on the same day, and the £30.6m 5½ per cent Treasury Bonds 1929, which were due two months later.[54]

Hopkins took the early claim for repayment of the 4½ per cent Treasury Bonds as a lesson in design. Few of the Bonds issued in November 1924 had been put and the claim came equally from the tranches sold in September 1926 and 1927.[55] This suggested that the terms on the latter occasions were at fault. The Bonds created in 1924 (at par) had given a GRY of 4½ per cent to all the option dates, whereas those created in September 1926 (at a discount) had yielded £5 0 8s per cent if put in 1929 and £4 13s 4d per cent if held to maturity in 1934: those sold for cash in September 1927 had yielded £4 19s 11d per cent and £4 12s 6d per cent.

In November 1927, Hopkins and Leith-Ross had criticised a plan conceived by the Governor for a similar Bond, with puts at such prices that the GRY was higher in the early years than in the later. The Governor argued that the money market would not take the Bonds unless it was offered a high yield for a short period and the Treasury men that yields should rise over the life of the Bond, so providing an incentive for holders to retain them. Norman thought that few would take advantage of the early puts because the price would improve as each date approached. The success of the December 1927 issue meant that the February 1928 operation was shelved, but the claims of the holders of the 4½ per cent Treasury 1934 argued that Hopkins and Leith-Ross had been right.[56]

The market price of 4 per cent Consols in the second half of July 1928 was just sufficient to make conversion from the 5 per cent Treasuries of 1933–5 profitable and about £134m, 62 per cent of the issue, were converted into £157m Consols.[57]

The 1928 budget

When Churchill delivered his fourth budget on 24 April 1928, the financial year 1927–8 showed a surplus of £4.3m and the estimate for 1928–9, on unchanged policies, was £5.5m.[58] He proposed that the New Sinking Fund (1923) should be replaced by a Fixed Charge and that the Currency and Bank of England Note issues be amalgamated, with the incidental effect of freeing the assets of the CNIRA for the Exchequer (see pp. 684–8). The centrepiece, however, was a partial exemption of industry from rates (local taxes), with the local authorities compensated by the central government for the loss of the revenue. The greater part of the cost was to be met from a tax on imported light oils, which was expected to raise £14m in 1928–9 and £17.8m in 1929–30. Lower rates for industry would come into effect in October 1929 and, in the meantime, the extra revenue, together with the previous year's Old Sinking Fund diverted from the repayment of debt, would accumulate in a Suspensory Account.

The pull of Wall Street: 1928 and 1929

The world-wide financial breakdown of the 1930s began in the summer of 1928 with the boom in equity prices on Wall Street. The effective US interest rate became the call rate on loans against securities, which was pulled higher by the potential for speculative profits; the FRBNY discount rate was raised by 1/2 per cent stages in February, May and July 1928 (from 3 1/2 per cent to 5 per cent), while the call rate doubled, reaching an average of 8.60 per cent in December. Gold was attracted to the USA so that, whereas in the year ended June 1928 the USA sold about $500m, in the sixteen months ending October 1929 it bought $300m. To this strain was added gold being absorbed by Paris. The French payments surplus was much reduced in 1929, but the Banque de France swaps matured in the second half of the year and the proceeds were used to purchase gold: the central bank's reserves rose by $434m in the same sixteen months to October 1929.

Of the major countries, Germany and the UK were the worst affected by the reversal of the capital flows. Sterling had been strong in the first half of 1928 and the Bank was able to buy both gold and dollars: in June, Bill rates fell from around £4 per cent to about £3 15s 0d per cent. The problems began with the July discount rate rise in New York. At first, the Bank sold dollars, but at the end of September it began shipping gold, a more public sign that a movement of capital was afoot. Pressed by Churchill not to aggravate the problems of industry by raising Bank rate, and knowing that such a move would merely provoke rises elsewhere in Europe, Norman pushed market rates higher; Bill rates rose from £3 15s 0d per cent in June to about £4 5s 0d per cent in August and £4 7s 6d per cent in October.[59] Such movements were ineffective when call rates in New York were 7 or 8 per cent, and by the end of the year the Bank's holdings of dollars had fallen by £25m and its gold by some £20m. With sales continuing in the new year and no sign of relief from New York, on 7 February 1929 the Bank raised its rate to 5 1/2 per cent.[60]

Second Tranche of 5 per cent Treasury 1933–5 (16 August 1928)

At the end of July 1928, Hopkins proposed a further issue of 5 per cent Treasury Bonds 1933–5 with a minimum price of 101½ to raise £36.3m cash to repay the remaining £34.8m nominal of the 1 September War Bonds.[61] By 10 August, with gold being lost to Germany, high rates in the USA weakening sterling to near the gold export point and Bill rates rising, Hopkins thought that even £101 might not be feasible. The Bank would try to avoid raising its rate, as Churchill wanted, but Hopkins warned that, if a further rise in the discount rate came in New York, the 'effects would be serious' in London. As the problem being addressed in the USA was financial speculation, not general excess, and a Presidential election was due in November, any rise would be short-lived, so it might be best to increase the floating debt until 'the present cloud has dispersed.'[62] The only encouragement was a large conversion of Consols out of 5 per cent Treasury Bonds 1933–5 during the second half of July. With a wary eye on New York, and intervention by the Bank to stop gold being shipped, the Treasury went ahead at £101 0s 0d, selling £35m of the Bonds on 23 August (Table 14.1).[63] Because the Bonds were to be amalgamated with the existing issue on the first ex-dividend date (2 January 1929), they would enjoy the right to convert into Consols at £88 4s 2d in the second half of the month (see p. 572).

4½ per cent Treasury Bonds 1932–4 (28 November 1928)

The next operation, planned, as so often, to coincide with the 1 December 5 per cent War Loan dividend, broke new ground by offering to convert the Treasury Bonds which were to mature on 1 February 1929 because their holders had used their options to claim repayment. Hitherto, it had been assumed that 'put' Bonds had no future but to be repaid in cash; now, they were to be treated like any other maturity. Due on the same day as these £72.8m put 4½ per cent Treasury Bonds were about £95.2m 5 per cent War Bonds and £4.8m 4 per cent War Bonds.[64] Including the premiums on the 5 per cents, the cash value of the three issues would be £177.6m. It was envisaged that the next maturity, £30.2m 5½ per cent Treasury due on 1 April 1929, would be refinanced from an issue for cash, either in the operation being proposed, if successful, or subsequently, if not.

The refinancing vehicle was a new security, 4½ per cent Treasury Bonds 1932–4, priced at 99 (£4 14s 6d per cent). As usual, the conversion terms gave a small inducement, on this occasion, 5s per cent. Following the precedent of the 5 per cents of 1933–5, the new Bonds enjoyed an option in the second half of July 1929 to convert into 4 per cent Consols, at £88 7s 10dxd. The price of Consols at the time of issue was about 86xd. By now, Hopkins knew his Chancellor and described the terms as 'stiff':

> they anticipate a considerable improvement in Government credit next year: if when the time comes they are exercised we shall have put away this money into long stock on terms much more favourable than those now obtaining: if

they are not exercised our opportunity will arise again on the maturity of the bonds in 1934.[65]

The Governor, judging the market in 4 per cent Consols to be tired after the recent issues, had originally suggested an option into 3½ per cent Conversion. This was opposed by the Treasury. Phillips calculated that the discount would make it so expensive that it would be difficult to justify, even if the conversion terms themselves were highly priced (see pp. 715–19). Hopkins warned of the political consequences – a general election was approaching – of issuing at a deep discount. He also reminded the Chancellor of his promise, when introducing the Fixed Charge, that the capital element would be sufficient to cover the contractual sinking funds and the accruing interest on Savings Certificates. More Conversion would mean a larger attached sinking fund, which could not be met from within the Charge. The pledge had become a sensitive issue because the Labour Party claimed that the sinking fund was being cut to the bone (see p. 687). Indeed, the reason for excluding the 1 April maturity from the conversion scheme and paying it off in cash was that conversion would have brought a £550,000 interest payment into the current financial year, reducing capital repayment by a similar amount.[66]

£104m of the Bonds were created on account of the conversion of £51m of the 5 per cent, £2.3m of the 4 per cent War Bonds and £46.8m of the 'put' 4½ per cent Treasury Bonds.[67] On 3 April, a further £46.2m of the Bonds were sold, with an £89 per cent call, to pay off the 1 April maturity (Table 14.1).

The result relied on the official portfolios. The amalgamation of the CNRA and the Issue Department became effective on 22 November; some records of the Issue Department's transactions and portfolio have survived.[68] They show that the Issue Department was responsible for £25.3m, or over half, of the cash subscriptions. The Department took a further £19.6m by conversion, mainly out of a holding of the put 4½ per cents. On 30 November, the Commissioners held £11.6m 5 per cent War Bonds, with a further £5.1m owned by other government accounts, mainly the Crown Agents. They also held £6.8m, and other Government accounts £3.6m, of the put Treasury Bonds. All the tax-compounded 4 per cents were held in the market.[69] Ignoring the 1 April maturity, and assuming that all the 1 February maturities were converted, the official portfolios were responsible for nearly half of the conversions and subscriptions. By 31 July 1929, 4 per cent Consols had fallen to 82⅝ and the option was clearly worthless. Despite this, £9.7m were converted into £10.9m. The Commissioners at this stage held some £25m of the issue and were responsible for £7.5m of the conversions. The reasons for this action are discussed on pages 711–12.

In January 1929, Hopkins advised the Chancellor to avoid further new borrowing. The November issue was still partly paid, the market was 'heavy', there was uncertainty in the USA, the exchanges were adverse and the Issue Department still had its large holding of 4½ per cent Treasury Bonds 1932–4. The cash needed on 1 February and 1 April should be found from Bills and Ways and Means, 'the course which has been followed on other similar occasions.'[70] On 20 February, two weeks after the rise in Bank rate, the Governor warned the

Committee of Treasury that a further increase in the New York discount rate was to be expected and that a move to 6½ per cent in London would follow. A fortnight later there was difficulty in covering the Bill tender.[71]

Hopkins's advice had to be taken. On 1 February, £45.2m of the 5 per cent War Bonds (£14.7m held in Issue), £2.5m of the 4 per cents (£0.3m) and £26m of the put 4½ per cent Treasury Bonds (£10.2m) were paid off for cash. On 1 April, £30.2m of the 5½ per cent Treasury Bonds (£6.9m held in Issue) were outstanding and paid off from the £89 per cent call on 4½ per cent Treasury Bond 1932–4.[72] It was the only occasion in the decade that the decision was made to pay off substantial maturities by increasing the floating debt.

5 per cent Conversion 1944–64 (2 November 1929)

The New York discount rate was not raised and the pressure eased until the summer. At home, Churchill delivered his last budget on 15 April 1929 under the shadow of an election which was to be held on 30 May and which was to return a second Labour government. In 1928–9, there had been a surplus of £18.4m, which was carried as planned to the Rating Relief Suspensory Account. With the rise in Bill rates, interest had taken £7.5m more than forecast, so that debt repayment within the Fixed Charge had been £57.5m instead of £65m. On unchanged policies, a surplus of £12m was forecast for 1929–30. This was reduced to £4.1m after abolition of the duty on tea and other minor changes.[73]

When Snowden became Chancellor on 7 June 1929, the tensions emanating from Wall Street were approaching their climax. The Bank was beginning to lose gold and, by the beginning of August, Norman was warning the Committee of Treasury that unless conditions changed in the USA and France some European countries, including the UK, might have to abandon the gold standard.[74] The Bank had been keeping market rates tight against its discount rate: Bill rates had been around £5 6s 0d per cent in March, but had been allowed to slip a trifle in April. Now, in June, they returned to £5 6s 0d per cent and in July and August to just under £5 10s 0d per cent.

To increasing restriction in the USA were added more local difficulties, such as the uncertain reaction of the financial markets to the Labour government. Another was a disagreement with the French about the distribution of reparation payments. Between July and October, the French used sterling to buy $129m of gold. The Bank would normally have responded by raising Bank rate, but, at a conference held at The Hague during August, Snowden brought Anglo-French relations to breaking point by refusing to accept a reduction in Britain's share of the German payments. If the Bank had caused a general rise in European rates, it would have made difficulties for British diplomacy, as well as increasing the financial threat to Germany, and hence sterling. It would also have been unpopular in the UK, where the reaction to the February rise in Bank rate had shown how sensitive opinion was to monetary restriction. Snowden would be sympathetic, but neither he nor the country would welcome a diversion when he was fighting such a public, and nationally acclaimed, battle for British interests.[75]

It was not until 26 September, after the ending of the Hague Conference and the Hatry collapse, that the Bank felt able to raise its rate to 6½ per cent.[g] By then, the Federal Reserve's assault was undermining Wall Street. The peak in equity prices was reached on 7 September and the crash started on 24 October. The central banks reacted immediately. The New York discount rate was reduced from 6 per cent to 5 per cent on 1 November, and to 4½ per cent on 15 November. Bank rate fell to 6 per cent on 31 October, to 5½ per cent on 21 November and to 5 per cent on 12 December.

In the improved conditions, on 2 November the authorities announced an unlimited issue of 5 per cent Conversion 1944–64 at par, the most controversial and clumsily handled sale of the second half of the 1920s. The immediate reason for the operation was about £30m maturities: £0.9m 3 per cent Exchequer Bonds, the rump of the issue made in 1912 and 1913 when the Post Office bought the National Telephone Co., were due on 1 January 1930. These were followed on 28 January by £15.6m of the 3 per cent Exchequer Bonds, which had been issued in 1918 in exchange for the Tsarist Treasury Bills and commercial bills, and on 1 February by £14.6m 4½ per cent Treasury Bonds, which had been put the previous January. Further ahead, on 15 May, £134.7m 5½ per cent Treasury Bonds 1930 matured. These were held overwhelmingly by large investors, especially the clearing banks (£61.5m) and the money market (£14.5m). The Commissioners owned only £1.5m, with a further £5m in the POSB, but the Issue Department had been buying in the market in its normal fashion: it held few of the January and February maturities, presumably because the market was narrow, but by the end of October it held £11.9m of the 5½ per cent Treasury and was to buy more.[76]

The Governor had advised that 'it was not safe, in present conditions', to issue without some part being pre-placed – an 'unusual' procedure – but one, he said, which would not have to be repeated. The proposal was probably made before Wall Street finally broke on 24 October and was certainly made before the first cuts in official rates on either side of the Atlantic. The decision was not altered as sterling strengthened, the prospect of a fall in short rates grew and the gilt-edged market improved. This is not surprising since it took the authorities some months to absorb the new situation; papers written in December show they did not appreciate how powerful were the deflationary forces being let loose in the USA. Although capital was returning to London from New York, gold exports to France were continuing. The first of the 1930 maturities were less than two months away, and the experience of the previous February had emphasised the advantages of dealing with them long before their due dates.[77] After adding to the floating debt on that occasion, there had been difficulties in renewing Bills in March and in August.[78] In the early summer, raw from the winter's experiences, Hopkins had noted that:

g Clarence Hatry (1888–1965) was a company promoter and financier. Fraud led to the collapse of his companies, with large losses to investors. He was convicted at the Old Bailey in January 1930.

> For some years past we have been occupied with recurrent maturities of National War Bonds. It has been difficult to keep pace, and at times we have tended to fall behind and increase the volume of Treasury Bills...
>
> So large a volume of Bills is not merely inconvenient; in times of pressure and high money rates it may at any time become difficult to secure that the market will take all that the Government need to offer. They may themselves become the cause of an increased bank rate.[79]

In October, he urged an issue sufficient to both cover the maturities and reduce the floating debt. That irresistible bait for any politician, the War Loan option, began on 1 June and was a powerful argument for selling longer securities: 'If we are ever going to tackle the conversion of the main body of 5% War Loan it will be an essential preliminary to reduce our floating debt to the lowest possible dimensions.'[80]

Fiscal weakness was also adding to the Bills held in the market, for some of Churchill's raids involved spending money hitherto lent by departments on Bills or Ways and Means; the budget might appear to balance, but the departments' funds had to be borrowed from elsewhere, in the first instance from the market, on Bills, or from the Bank, on Ways and Means.[81] The general budgetary position was scarcely mentioned during the discussions, perhaps because its deterioration was common knowledge to those responsible for market management. In October, shortly before Parliament reassembled, Snowden asked for a forecast of financial prospects. Even on optimistic assumptions, deficits were to be expected. Pitched to make ministers reconsider their programmes, the forecasts made alarming reading. Increased spending on social services, a rise in the Treasury contribution to the Unemployment Fund, increased benefits and the prospect of a repeal of taxes on food at a time of falling revenues threatened deficits of £45m in 1930–1, £60m in 1931–2 and over £68m in 1932–3.[82]

The Governor's first proposal had been to use 4 per cent Consols at about 81 (£4 18s 11d per cent), but this had been rejected by Snowden because of the heavy discount. Hopkins's brief showed that the Treasury now thoroughly understood the case against issuing below par. Even if it had not, it was sensitive ground for Snowden and Frederick Pethick-Lawrence, his Financial Secretary, who in opposition had criticised Churchill for making such issues.[83] The Chancellor asked for an alternative which could be priced near to par and be offered both for cash and for converting part of 5 per cent War Loan. The conversion would have two objects. It would, as in 1924, help split up the Loan's 'unwieldy mass', and it would produce a larger and more marketable new issue than would be possible if the operation were limited to cash subscriptions.

The Bank proposed a dated Loan with a twenty-year option and a 5 per cent nominal rate. These terms had the administrative advantage that £100 War Loan could be converted into £100 new Loan and the budgetary advantage that the interest cost would be unchanged. To protect capital repayment within the Fixed Charge, the payment dates were made only one month earlier than those on War Loan, so falling into the same financial years. Taking a leaf out of McKenna's book in 1915, holders of War Loan could only convert if they held a similar nominal value of the new issue.

1944–64 was chosen to provide an incentive to convert. 1929 had arrived and holders could lose their secure 5 per cent on War Loan at any time yields fell and would certainly lose it by 1947. By converting, they were securing 5 per cent until at least 1944 and possibly until 1964. The 5 per cent was only in jeopardy for the overlapping three years, a contrast to Snowden's earlier offer in 1924, in which converting could have meant a loss of income for as long as twenty-three years (see p. 558).

Hopkins was optimistic. Only £10 per cent would be required on cash applications, with the balance payable on 1 February, so creating a 'mildly speculative atmosphere' and helping to produce larger subscriptions than if long-term investors were the only subscribers.[h] There would be the £30m pre-placing, perhaps £20m from the general investor and £50m from the Issue Department. Conversions from 5½ per cent Treasury Bonds might produce a further £50m. If all the holders used their holdings to convert 5 per cent War Loan, a £300m issue would be created.[84]

The day after the prospectus was published, the Government Broker placed the £30m, enough to cover the January and February maturities. Although it was called commission, the remuneration took the form of a ½ per cent discount in the price, a more ostentatious and provocative method of making the payment. It was, perhaps, inevitable that the first issue by a new Labour government should be accompanied by questions about whether the proceeds were destined for public works and combating unemployment. This was easily answered by a directing finger at the maturities. Less easy to explain was the handling of disclosure, for the intention to place part had not been mentioned in the prospectus. As news of the placing leaked out from those who had been approached, there was an outcry, in Parliament, in the press and from those who had been excluded from a lucrative transaction. The government was criticised for issuing to a favoured few at a lower price than to the general public and of permitting them to make an immediate turn by selling at a price higher than they paid, but lower than that available to applicants. The failure to state that a part had been placed was described as inviting subscriptions under a false prospectus, a sensitive suggestion just after the Hatry fraud and a new Companies Act, which, although exempting the Treasury, had tightened the disclosure rules for the private sector.[i] The authorities claimed that they could not have advertised the placing in the prospectus as it was not carried out until the day after it was published and that making the placing known would have risked the terms becoming public.[85] They also sought precedents to use in the Chancellor's defence.[86]

h This is the first recorded instance of very low payments on cash applications being used deliberately to create speculative interest.

i The Companies Act 1928 received the Royal Assent on 3 August 1928 and the Companies Act 1929 on 10 May 1929.

The Treasury and Bank ran into further trouble. Although they never intended to offer conversion to the holders of the January and February maturities, they had intended to make an offer to the holders of the more substantial 5½ per cent Treasury Bonds of 15 May 1930. However, for reasons which go unrecorded and are difficult to understand, even with the benefit of hindsight, it had never been intended to include an offer in the prospectus for 5 per cent Conversion. Instead, it came four days later in a supplementary notice, and led to further allegations that information had been withheld or an error made.[87] The Chancellor explained, somewhat obscurely, that the offer

> was intended to secure a reduction in the amount of the Bonds without necessarily committing the Government to the conversion on these terms of the whole of the Bonds outstanding. As this was subsidiary to and not a primary object of the issue it was thought better to make the offer separately.[88]

The market had been strong in the last week of October and vulnerable to profit-taking; on the announcement of the issue 4 per cent, Consols fell two points and 3½ per cent Conversion 2⅝ points. Developments in the USA were too favourable for this to last and the market quickly recovered. Hopkins's optimism was justified: £323m of the new issue was created, £155.3m for cash, £79.4m for conversions from 5½ per cent Treasury Bonds and £88.3m for conversions from 5 per cent War Loan (Table 14.1).[89]

Cheap money: a further tranche of 4½ per cent Conversion 1940–4 (22 February 1930)

In the first half of 1930, short rates in London collapsed as speculative funds were withdrawn from the USA and the world moved into depression. While exports of long-term capital revived, short-term deposits returned to London, so that the Bank's gold and dollar holding rose by £8m. Bank rate was reduced to 4½ per cent on 6 February, 4 per cent on 6 March, 3½ per cent on 20 March and 3 per cent on 1 May, where it rested for over a year. Bill rates were £3 17s 3d per cent at the end of January and £2 1s 6d per cent at the beginning of May. By the end of March, 4 per cent Consols, which had been 82⅞xd (£4 16s 6d per cent), were over 89 (£4 10s 11d per cent) (Figure 18.3).

On the day Bank rate fell to 4½ per cent, Hopkins made proposals for dealing with the remaining £54.9m of the 5½ per cents of 1930, of which about £43m were held outside the government portfolios. He advised against a short-date on general principles: maturities should be refinanced with long-dated paper sold outside the banks and money market. This policy, pursued in the autumn, 'has had & is having good effects'. The Issue Department's holding of the intermediate 5 per cent Conversion 1944–64 had not yet been absorbed, so the natural choice became 4 per cent Consols, where the Issue Department's holding was only £5.1m. The discount would draw criticism and the price would need to be beneath that of the previous sale, but it would be a small tranche and would not affect the choice

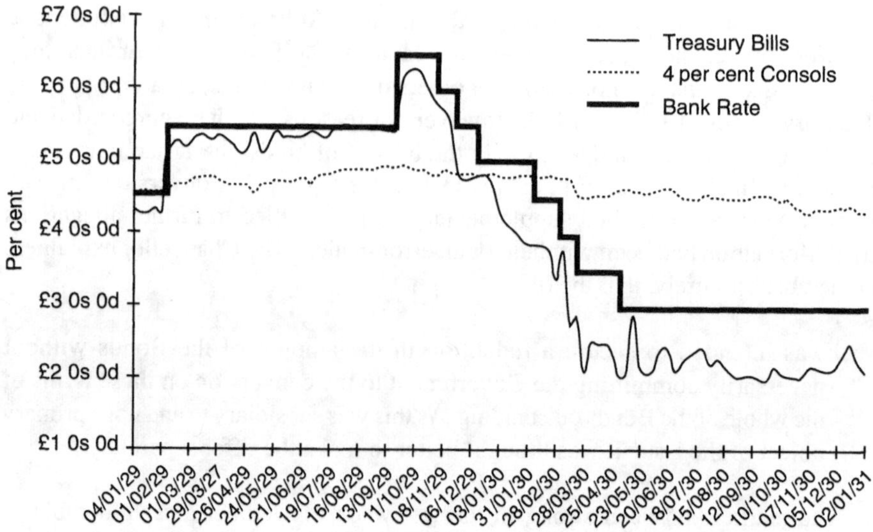

Figure 18.3 Bank rate, the discount rate on three-months' Treasury Bills and the running yield on 4 per cent Consols: January 1929 to December 1930. Source: *The Economist*.

when issuing on a larger scale in the future. Another tranche of 4½ per cent Conversion 1940–4 should be considered, but the date was inconvenient and 'for some reason' it was unpopular.[90] That it was the issue in fact selected was probably, once again, a decision taken by the Chancellor in the light of his earlier criticism of deep discount issues. The clean price in the market was about 95½ and the new tranche was made for cash at £95 0s 0d (£4 19s 9d per cent) and in exchange for 5½ per cent Treasury Bonds at the equivalent of £94 15s 9d. After adjustments for interest, this was a price of about £94 12s 1d.

£60.8m were sold for cash, with the proceeds spread over the end of the financial year, and a further £32m were created for those converting from £30.3m 5½ per cent Treasury Bonds (Table 14.1). There remained £24.6m, which were paid off on 15 May.[91]

The 1930 budget

On 14 April 1930, Snowden opened the first budget of the second Labour government with the comment 'The House of Commons and the country are already painfully aware of the main features of the financial problem with which I have been faced.'[92] Churchill's £4.1m surplus had turned into a £14.5m deficit, with expenditure exceeding the forecast by £6.7m and revenue falling short by £11.9m. Snowden forecast a deficit on existing policies of £47.7m for 1930–1. As intended, £16m would come from drawing on Churchill's Rating Relief Suspensory Account. To cover the remainder, the Chancellor raised the standard rate of income tax, surtax, death duties and beer duty to provide a surplus of £2.2m.

Refinancing of 4 per cent War Loan 1929–42 (2 October 1930)

A second operation in the period of relatively cheap money between the winter of 1929 and the 1931 financial crisis exploited the drop in short-term rates to refinance with Treasury Bonds the redemption of 4 per cent War Loan 1929–42, the tax-compounded twin of 5 per cent War Loan issued in 1917. The press pointed out that this operation reversed the policy of the previous autumn, when the object of 5 per cent Conversion 1944–64 was to use the proceeds of long-dated borrowing to repay the banks and money market,[93] but the argument failed to acknowledge that the drop in yields had pulled the redemption date forward from 1942 so that the Loan had become a short; double-dated issues, whose first option dates had already passed, would become Treasury Bills whenever the Treasury found it profitable to call them.

During the year to August 1930, the running yield on 4 per cent Consols fell by some eight shillings and the GRY on 4½ per cent Treasury 1934 by nearly 2 per cent, to about 3⅞ per cent. The drop in the yield on long-dated issues, wrote Phillips in September 1930,

> is good as far as it goes but it has not gone far enough yet and everyone, including of course the Governor, thinks it would be wrong to try any more nibbling at the 5% War Loan at present.
>
> If we do any conversion now all the circumstances point to an issue of short bonds. The price of such bonds has improved very greatly during the spell of cheap money and there is a very active demand from the banks for this type of security…It is a reasonable assumption that we could now raise quite substantial sums at 4 per cent on short bonds (say 4 to 6 years).[94]

The only maturity facing the Treasury was £11m 4½ per cent Treasury Bonds 1934 put by investors for 1 February 1931, but the fall in yields had made it profitable to call three other issues: £120.9m 4½ per cent Treasury 1930–2, callable since 15 April; the remaining £12.8m of McKenna's 4½ per cent War Loan 1925–45, callable since 1 December 1925; and Bonar Law's tax-compounded Loan, callable since 15 October 1929.[j]

Replacing the 4½ per cent Treasury Bonds 1930–2 with a 4 per cent coupon would save about £600,000 a year, a result Phillips described as 'good but not specially brilliant.' The tax-compounded Loan was cheap, yielding the equivalent of £5 3s 3d per cent, with tax at £0 4s 6d. If converted to a taxable 4 per cent, it would cost the same £3m a year in interest, but tax revenue would be increased by

j The tax-compounded Loan had originally been £52.4m. Changes in its price and, therefore, purchases by the Depreciation Fund had been much complicated by changes in income tax rates and, therefore, the value of the tax privilege. Since 1917, purchases and cancellations by the Depreciation Fund had reduced the issue by £21.9m and there had been £1.1m surrendered for death duties. £46.1m had been created on account of conversions from the tax-compounded War Bonds. By the end of 1930, the issue had grown to £75.4m. *BGS*, pp. 226 and 293.

£675,000. This Phillips described as 'pretty handsome' on £75m. However, the vital decision was choosing the best time for exercising the option. A further drop in the yield on short paper in the spring was 'a not unreasonable expectation' and one held by the Governor. It was a question of balancing the saving currently being offered against the saving which might become available. If rates fell a further ¼ per cent, there would be a reduction of £145,000 in the annual cost of the tax-compounded Loan and over £300,000 a year on the bigger 4½ per cent Treasury Bonds. This pointed to action on the Loan, and delay on the Bonds: 'It is much more reasonable to take the risk of postponement in the case of the 4½% Bonds than in that of the tax free loan.'

Phillips reported that the Governor wanted to issue £150m and apply the balance of £63m to the floating debt. He himself was not 'enthusiastic' about paying off a lot of Bills for several reasons – none of which he specified – and he would limit the sale to £100m.[95] On 30 September, the Governor wrote to Hopkins, pressing for a large issue:

> I wish…to draw your attention again to the Floating Debt as represented by the amount of Treasury Bills in the hands of the Public…It is most disturbing…to notice that in spite of the fact that the total volume of Bills outstanding at the present time is about £128m less than at the corresponding date a year ago, the reduction in the total held by the Public…is less than £19 millions and that this reduction is steadily diminishing…once again the total of Bills held publicly has reached a figure which experience has shown to be unmanageable.[96]

On 2 October, the tax-compounded Loan was called for 15 January 1931 and an unlimited issue by tender of 4 per cent Treasury Bonds 1934–6 announced at a minimum price of £100 10s 0d. There was no conversion offer. The new Bonds were £10 paid, with the balance due on the day on which the tax-compounded Loan was to be repaid. Applications were £116.3m, of which £105m were accepted at an average price of £100 11s 7d (£3 17s 8d per cent to 1934). The Issue Department was responsible for £70m of the accepted tenders. It immediately started to sell vigorously.[97]

✣ ✣ ✣

If the £12.8m rump of McKenna's 4½ per cent War Loan is ignored, exercising the option on the tax-compounded War Loan left only one wartime issue to be converted: Bonar Law's £2,085m 5 per cent War Loan. It was dealt with in 1932 (see Chapter 19). Calling the tax-compounded War Loan marked a turning point in other ways. Since 1919, the authorities had enjoyed little freedom in their handling of the market. First, as a means of reasserting their control over credit, they had to sell gilt-edged securities to reduce the floating debt. Later, they had to convert or refinance the mass of single-dated Exchequer Bonds and War Bonds issued during the war. In these operations they had had to accept whatever was the market price for the year or so before the maturity, a price set high by the wider considerations of breaking the post-war boom and of maintaining the gold standard. In 1930, in contrast, there was no necessity to exercise the option on the tax-compounded War Loan – the issue could have run for a further twelve years. This had happened only once before, with the small issue of 5–15 year Treasury Bonds. Moreover, unless the Treasury had been prepared to refinance the tax-compounded Loan with a short- or medium-dated issue, it would not have been a profitable operation: as it was, date had succumbed to cost. The problem did not present itself in these terms for long since the world-wide depression and the abandonment of the gold standard was soon to reduce the yields on long-dated and perpetual securities.

Endnotes

1 Clarke (1967), pp. 80, 105–6 and 110–11; Clay (1957), p. 154.
2 Clarke (1967), pp. 50–1.
3 T 160/198/F7548, 'Conversion of War Loan 1929–47', Niemeyer, 21 March 1924.
4 This paragraph is based on *Hansard* (Commons), 29 April 1924, cols 1587–1610 and Hirst and Allen (1926), pp. 460–90.
5 *Hansard* (Commons), 29 April 1924, col. 1591; *National Debt: annual returns*.
6 Clarke (1967), pp. 85–9; Sayers (1976), I, pp. 138–46; Morgan (1952), pp. 70–1.
7 *The Economist*, relevant dates. The newspaper, quoting Samuel Montagu & Co., identified the gold points as $4.8480 and $4.9067.
8 T 160/198/F7548, 'Conversion of War Loan 1929–47', Niemeyer, 21 March 1924.
9 *National Debt: annual returns*.
10 CNRA ledgers; BoE, ADM 19/10 and 19/11, and C40/871, 'Currency Notes', undated and unsigned; *BGS*, pp. 488–9.
11 CNRA ledgers; BoE, C40/871, 'Currency Notes', undated and unsigned; *BGS*, pp. 488–9.
12 BoE, Loan Wallet 314, Niemeyer to Norman, 16 December 1924; *National Debt: annual returns*.
13 T 160/226/F8469, Norman to Niemeyer, 21 March 1925.
14 *National Debt: annual returns*; T 160/226/F8469, Holmes to Niemeyer, '5/15 year Treasury Bonds', 23 March 1925.
15 BoE, Loan Wallet 320 and C90/871, 'Currency Notes', undated and unsigned.
16 T 160/226/F8469, Memorandum, Niemeyer for the Chancellor, 24 March 1925.
17 T 160/198/F7548, Niemeyer to Murray and Norman to Niemeyer, 1 April 1924, and Murray to Niemeyer, 4 April 1924; CTM, 2 April 1924.
18 A note of the rumours and a copy of the Bank's announcement are in BoE, Loan Wallet 314.
19 *The Evening Standard*, 26 March 1925; CTM, 1 April 1925; MND, 27 March 1925; *Hansard* (Commons), 30 March 1925, col. 940. The papers concerning the leak, and a record of Niemeyer's handling of the paperwork, are in T 160/226/F8469. The story was also carried by *The Times* and *The Daily Express*.
20 *Hansard* (Commons), 28 April 1925, col. 51.
21 T 160/239, Niemeyer to Chancellor, 17 September 1925.
22 Sayers (1976), I, pp. 214–16; Clarke (1967), pp. 99–102; Chandler (1958), pp. 325–30.
23 *The Economist*, 3 October 1925, pp. 523–4.

24 Middlemas (1969) p. 316; O'Halpin (1989), p. 143; Gilbert (1990), p. 110, quoting Niemeyer to Churchill, 6 April 1925; T 176/21, Niemeyer, memorandum, 26 June 1925. O'Halpin cites Chamberlain's Diary, 1 November 1925.
25 *Hansard* (Commons), 19 July 1926, col. 908.
26 *Hansard* (Commons), 26 April 1926, cols 1687–1721.
27 *BGS*, p. 490; CNRA Ledgers. The data exclude 3 per cent Exchequer Bonds 1 January 1930. This was the issue which financed the acquisition of the National Telephone Co. in 1911–13. Much had been cancelled and on 31 March 1926 it was £1.9m, of which the Commissioners held £0.6m.
28 Clarke (1967), pp. 103–5; Sayers (1976), I, p. 217, and III, pp. 308, 310, 312; Feinstein (1972), T 82.
29 *National Debt: annual returns*.
30 *The Economist*, 2 October 1926, p. 540.
31 T 160/239/F8970, Niemeyer to Chancellor, 17 September 1925.
32 Committee on National Debt and Taxation, *Report* (Cmd. 2800), 1927.
33 Ibid., paras 217 and 1008, and *Evidence*, para. 8814; T176/39, ff. 63–70, Hawtrey, Funding, 6 April 1926.
34 BoE, Loan Wallet 339; MND, 20 December 1926; T 160/551/F9973/1, Phillips, 'Four per cent,' 7 December 1926, and Niemeyer, untitled, 15 December 1926.
35 BoE, Loan Wallet 339.
36 *National Debt: annual returns*; T 160/551/F9973/1, Niemeyer to Churchill, 20 January 1927; *BGS*, p. 147. Other government accounts were pressed unusually hard to accept the offer; at the end of their 1926–7 years, the Commissioners held over £10m of the 5 per cent War Bonds and a year later they held over £13m Consols. Other conversions came from the Crown Agents. *BGS*, pp. 491–2. The correspondence between the departments and Niemeyer is in T 160/551/F9973/1.
37 T 160/551/F9973/1, Niemeyer to Churchill, 20 January 1927.
38 *National Debt: annual returns*.
39 These two paragraphs are based on *Hansard* (Commons), 11 April 1927, cols 59–99.
40 Middlemas (1969), p. 98.
41 Clarke (1967), pp. 108–43; Sayers (1976), I, pp. 211–21, and III, p. 351; Clay (1957), pp. 225–37.
42 MND, 9 September 1927.
43 *National Debt: annual returns*.
44 *The Economist*, 10 September 1927, p. 429, and 17 September 1927, pp. 464 and 486.
45 BoE, Loan Wallet 347. The official portfolios appear not to have applied. CNRA Ledgers.
46 CNRA Ledgers; BoE, ADM 19/10 and 19/11; T 175/15, Hopkins to Chancellor, 24 November 1927.
47 *National Debt: annual returns*.
48 T 175/15, Memorandum from Governor, 26 October 1927; Hopkins to Leith-Ross, 2 November 1927; Leith-Ross to Hopkins, 'Issue of Short-Term Bonds', 9 November 1927; 'Notes for Discussion', undated and unsigned; 'Conversion Programme', 17 November 1927, unsigned; Leith-Ross to Hopkins, 21 November 1927; '5% Exchequer Bonds 1933–35', 21 November 1927, unsigned; Hopkins to Chancellor, 24 November 1927.
49 T 175/15, working notes, unsigned and undated; *The Economist*, 24 December 1927, pp. 1130 and 1152, and 31 December 1927, pp. 1176–7.
50 T 175/15, marginal note on letter from Hopkins to Chancellor, 30 December 1927.
51 *National Debt: annual returns*; T 175/15, Hopkins to Chancellor, 31 December 1927.
52 T 175/15, Press Notice, 18 January 1928; *National Debt: annual returns*; BoE, Loan Wallet 357.
53 T 175/15, Hopkins to Chancellor, 13 January 1928.

54 T 160/419/F9083, various notes from Hopkins, Phillips and Holmes, 27 and 29 February, 1, 2 and 9 March 1928, and Hopkins to Chancellor, 15 March 1928; *National Debt: annual returns*. The data for the maturities are taken as at 31 March 1928.

55 T 160/419/F9683, Hopkins to Chancellor, 15 March 1928.

56 The papers covering the discussions with the Governor are in T 175/15 and the yields and the Bank estimates of the amount of each issue which were put are in T 160/419/F9083.

57 *The Times*, 17 August 1928, p. 17. The total for the two dates was £137.7m into £161m. *National Debt: annual returns*.

58 This paragraph is based on *Hansard* (Commons), 24 April 1928, cols 823–74.

59 T 175/15, Churchill to Hopkins, 14 August 1928; Sayers (1976), I, p 223.

60 Clarke (1967), pp. 144–68; Sayers (1976), I, pp. 222–6, and III, p. 352; Clay (1957), pp. 238–50.

61 T 175/15, Hopkins to Churchill, 30 July 1928.

62 Ibid., Hopkins to Chancellor, 10 August 1928, and Churchill to Hopkins, 14 August 1928.

63 T 175/15, Hopkins to Churchill, 13 August 1928; BoE, G1/424, Lubbock to Strong, 9 and 18 August 1928. The average tender price was £101 1s 0d (£4 16s 2d per cent).

64 T 175/15, Hopkins to Chancellor, 16 November 1928.

65 Ibid.

66 Ibid., Phillips, 'Conversion to 4½ Bonds', 9 November 1928, and Hopkins to Chancellor, 16 November 1928; *Hansard* (Commons), 24 April 1928, col. 829.

67 *National Debt: annual returns*.

68 BoE C40/579 and C40/580, 'Alterations Effected in the Securities Held in the Issue Department During the Month of…' The monthly balance sheets have disappeared, but Professor Moggridge has kindly provided me with his notes. Both records will henceforth be referred to as 'Issue Department Ledgers'.

69 T 175/25, Phillips, 'Approaching Maturities', 3 January 1929; BoE, Loan Wallet 358, 'Holdings of £250 and over', Chief Cashier's Office, 27 November 1928; Issue Department Ledgers; CTM, 5 December 1928.

70 T 175/25, Phillips, 'Approaching Maturities', 3 January 1929, and Hopkins to Chancellor, 10 January 1929; Issue Department Ledgers.

71 Sayers (1976), I, pp. 225–6; Clay (1957), pp. 245–50; CTM, 20 February 1929.

72 Issue Department Ledgers; *National Debt: annual returns*.

73 *Hansard* (Commons), 15 April 1929, cols 27–68; *Financial Statement 1929–30* (HCP 84), 15 April 1929.

74 CTM, 7 August 1929.

75 Clarke (1967), pp. 159–68; Clay (1957), 266–71; Sayers (1976), I, 226–8, and III, pp. 352–3; Snowden (1934), II, pp. 778–830; T 176/13 Part 2, ff. 69–72, Hopkins to Grigg, 19 August 1929; ibid., ff. 61–5, rough drafts by Phillips and Hopkins, undated.

76 Issue Department Ledgers; BoE, AC 30/491, '5½% Treasury Bonds 1930', 30 October 1929.

77 T 175/15, Hopkins to Chancellor, 28 October 1929; Sayers (1976), I, pp. 230–1; BoE, G1/466, Hopkins, 'Money Rates in the Early Future', undated, and Stewart, 'Note on Hopkins: Money Rates in the Early Future', 19 December 1929.

78 Sayers (1976), I, pp. 226–8; Clay (1957), p. 252. The CTM to which Clay refers are 5 and 12 June and 14 August 1929. Clay speaks of the problem of the floating debt as having been exercising the Committee 'for months.' The most recent prior reference was at the beginning of 1927, so he must have been drawing on additional sources. CTM, 29 December 1926 and 5 January 1927.

79 T 175/26, Hopkins, 'Notes for Evidence. Conversion Loan and paying-off Treasury Bills', quoted in Howson (1975), p. 40.

80 T 175/15, Hopkins to Chancellor, 28 October 1929.

81 The process is described in T 171/287, Hopkins, with covering letter from Fisher to Chancellor, 5 January 1930.

82 T 172/1684, 'The Growth of Expenditure', 18 October 1929, together with preparatory memoranda; T 171/287, Hopkins to Snowden, 10 October 1930; Snowden (1934), II, pp. 843–5; Williamson (1992), p. 77.

83 *Hansard* (Commons), 12 April 1927, cols 234 and 267, 15 November 1927, col. 827, 16 February 1928, col. 1042, 25 April 1928, cols 931–2, 6 December 1928, cols 1393–4, and 13 December 1928, col. 2328.

84 T 175/15, Hopkins to Chancellor, 28 October 1929.

85 *Hansard* (Commons), 7 November 1929, cols 1247–51, and 12 November 1929, cols 1719–26; T 175/15, Phillips to Hopkins, 7 November 1929. BoE, Loan Wallet 366, contains a selection of newspaper cuttings and C40/418 contains a précis of press criticisms.

86 The investigations failed to find the placing of the 3 per cent Exchequer Bonds 1903 in August 1900 and Edward Hamilton's comment that prospectuses should give notice of a pre-placing 'boldly'. They found Morgans' role in the issues of Consols in 1901 and 1902, but failed to note that they were parts of larger transactions, which were divulged in the prospectuses. It was not recalled that the prospectus for Lloyd George's Loan in 1914 had stated that £100m had been placed. The 'special subscription' of the banks in 1915 was ignored. They did discover, and cite, the issues in New York during 1916. *Hansard* (Commons), 12 November 1929, col. 1723. The briefing papers are in T 175/15, BoE, AC 30/491 and Loan Wallet 366.

87 A copy of the supplementary notice is in BoE, Loan Wallet 366.

88 *Hansard* (Commons), 12 November, col. 1723.

89 *National Debt: annual returns*. The Issue Department was responsible for over a quarter of the cash subscriptions (£40m), £10m less than Hopkins had assumed, and 17 per cent of the conversions from $5^1/_2$ per cent Treasury Bonds (£13.5m). It had no War Loan to convert. There was a further £1.4m cash subscription by the Departments, most from the Crown Agents, and they acquired a further £2.5m by conversion from the $5^1/_2$ per cents. BoE, Loan Wallet 366, Phillips to Hopkins, 22 November 1929; Issue Department Ledgers.

90 T 160/429, Hopkins to Chancellor, 6 February 1930; Issue Department Ledgers.

91 *National Debt: annual returns*; *BGS*, pp. 156, 277 and 493–5. The Issue Department played its usual role: after converting its $5^1/_2$ per cent Treasury Bonds into 5 per cent Conversion the previous year, it rebuilt its holding of the Bonds and converted £18.2m into £19.2m. Subscribing also for a further £25m, it was responsible for nearly half of the tranche. Issue Department Ledgers.

92 This paragraph is based on *Hansard* (Commons), 14 April 1930, cols 2659–82.

93 There is a selection of press clippings in Loan Wallet 377.

94 T 188/14, Phillips to Grigg, 15 September 1930. Underlining in the original.

95 Ibid., Phillips to Grigg, 15 September 1930.

96 BoE, G 14/158, Governor to Hopkins, 30 September 1930; CTM, 1 October 1930.

97 Issue Department Ledgers.

19 The great conversion

> The continued existence of this great block of 5 per cent stock has a depressing effect on all our affairs. It is very costly. It prevents our credit rising to a satisfactory level. It is a great obstacle to all proposals for economy and it is becoming more and more difficult to justify drastic cuts in other directions while no effort is made to reduce this wasteful burden on our resources.
>
> Frederick Phillips, '5 per cent War Loan Conversion', 6 June 1932, T 212/2.

Individual gilt-edged issues have rarely caught the public eye or enjoyed the attention of politicians outside the Treasury. This had happened to 5 per cent War Loan. To the general public, it had come to represent the *rentier* enjoying a fixed and safe income at a time of falling prices and high unemployment. To politicians, it had become the focus of the debate over the cost of the Debt and its importance in determining the level of taxation. For the leadership of the TUC, an attack on the incomes of its holders should be a part of the fair distribution of the cuts in living standards made necessary by the Depression. Even officials felt its influence, although accustomed to handling a stream of maturities and conversions and to considering the Debt in the aggregate. An individual item of expenditure of this size would have drawn the attention of a careful Exchequer at any time, and these times were far from normal. It was a period of unusual social and political tensions, of unemployment and depression. Exchequer revenues and expenditure were under extreme strain, which culminated in a fiscal crisis and Cabinet split. By 1932, after thirteen years of struggling to roll back spending after wartime extravagances, officials thought that other items had already been cut to the bone, and if it were necessary to cut into the bone, a reduction in such a notorious item of expenditure would ease the pain. When the suspension of the gold standard freed monetary policy to counter the Depression, the rate on War Loan gained new importance as an obstacle to the cheapening of money.

While all this argued for an early conversion, a host of inconvenient features gave officials pause. The size of the Loan would mean a massive increase in the floating debt if the whole were called and an offer to convert proved unsuccessful. If there were a compulsory conversion, the Loan had to be called in its entirety, increasing the risks of failure. The large number of individual holders made it impossible to apply the market management techniques developed during the 1920s. And the large overseas holding made sterling a possible casualty.

This chapter describes the conversion preparations made during 1931 in the context of the politicians' need to cut expenditure and attack the *rentier* living on fixed incomes. It shows that by the end of May the major features of the offer had been decided, before the financial chaos in Continental Europe spilled over into sterling, producing political crisis and a new government. It then describes how the markets were groomed and the conversion administered in 1932.

War Loan, the personification of the Debt: myth and reality

On 31 March 1932, 5 per cent War Loan had a nominal value of £2,085m, equivalent to 32.9 per cent of the internal Debt and 28.2 per cent of the whole Debt.[a] In 1931–2, the interest had taken £104.3m, the equivalent of 36 per cent of the monies spent on interest, management and expenses or 13.6 per cent of the £767m revenue that Neville Chamberlain was to forecast when presenting his 1932–3 budget.[1] Although this made its service a major item of expenditure, the public much exaggerated the issue's significance. The nominal rate of 5 per cent, which was widely considered to be both high and a relic of the exigencies of war, was not as anomalous as often believed. Although it was the highest rate on the gilt-edged list, it was shared by two other issues which did not catch the public's attention – 5 per cent Conversion 1944–64 (£323m outstanding) and the 5 per cent Treasury Bonds of 1933–5 (£114.6m, although £252.3m had been created). Nor was the rate exceptional compared with the market as a whole: on 31 March 1932, the lowest rate on any dated issue was 4 per cent. Five per cent only seemed exceptional because it was attached to a large block of Debt with a large number of holders.

Although holders had come to personify the *rentier*, the Loan was widely held by the small investor. In May 1931, the Bank estimated that its register contained about 1,500,000 accounts, with a further 1,000,000 holding £90m at the Post Office. Of those registered at the Bank, about 625,000 were in joint names, so that the total number of holders was over three million. At the Bank, 460,000 accounts were of £105 or less and 265,000 were of between £105 and £210. In November 1931, there was only £178m of inscribed and registered Stock held in amounts of £0.5m and more. In addition to these holders, there were those of about £40m on the Dublin register, £20m in Belfast and £215m Bonds.[2]

The public was correct in believing that the Loan was distinguished by the size of the overseas stake but, again, it was much exaggerated; one circular produced by a member of the London Stock Exchange in 1930 referred to foreign ownership as being 'possibly one-quarter of the whole'.[3] By 1932, the only Loans whose interest was exempt from withholding tax if it could be shown that the holder was

a The Debt is taken to exclude both the 4 per cent Funding Loan and Victory Bonds tendered for death duties held by the Commissioners and the wartime gold deposits from France, Italy and Russia.

non-resident were 4 per cent Funding Loan and the 4 per cent Victory Bonds, in which the drawings complicated the yield and made them of doubtful attraction to foreigners. Only War Loan paid interest, without deduction of tax, automatically, to all holders. The estimates need to be treated with caution, but between £130m and £140m of the Loan may have been held overseas, including the Empire and Irish Free State.[b]

No analysis had been made of the country of residence of the holders of inscribed and registered War Stock, but an analysis of Bonds was carried out by the Inland Revenue at the end of 1930. At that stage, £88m was thought to be held overseas: Egypt was the largest single holder (£16m, nearly all in three holdings), followed by Holland, Spain with Portugal, France (all £7m), Japan and India (£5m).[4]

Analysis of changes was very tentative and, again, only possible for Bonds. Data for coupons paid without withholding tax being deducted for reasons of non-residency were collated by the Bank in January 1932; surprisingly, they showed that there had been a rise in the holdings of War Loan, Victory Bonds and Funding Loan during the period leading to the suspension of the gold standard, a drop from £84m to £80m in the holdings of War Loan being accompanied by a rise of £11m in holdings of Funding Loan.[5]

That the high nominal rate was stopping or, at least, retarding the fall in long-dated yields was stressed by the Chancellor when announcing the conversion scheme to the Commons:

b Measurement required identification of holdings of bearer Bonds, registered Stock and Stock registered in Dublin. Tradition and ease of settlement meant that overseas investors favoured Bonds. There was a discrepancy between the data for coupons paid without deduction of tax by reason of non-residency supplied by the Dividend Pay Office in the Bank and the Inland Revenue, but it seems that in the second half of 1931 between £130m and £140m Funding Loan, Victory Bonds and War Loan were held overseas: between £70m and £80m was War Loan. This can be checked against Bonds held by banks on behalf of overseas customers and Stock held in their nominee companies. No enquiry was made of the banks until the beginning of 1932, when the returns showed £155m of Bonds and Stock so held: one Bank estimate made at the beginning of July 1932 suggested that about £70m of this might be War Loan, all but £5m being Bonds, divided equally between Empire and foreign holders.

Identifying holdings of inscribed and registered Stock was more difficult. The large number of individual accounts made the extraction of the data from the Bank's books unrealistic and sampling was used. In 1926, an analysis was conducted for the Inland Revenue by the Accountant's Department at the Bank. This took actual data for all accounts of more than £100,000 and a 10 per cent sample of smaller holdings. It covered over 80 per cent of the gilt-edged market by value. It showed that 1.65 per cent of inscribed and registered Stock was held overseas. This result, applied to the War Stock outstanding in 1932, gave an overseas holding of about £30m.

To these data for Bonds and Stock needed to be added £40m registered in Dublin, of which an unknown proportion was held by residents of the Irish Free State.

BoE, EID 14/94, various papers and memoranda, and T 212/2, Leith-Ross to Niemeyer, 10 May 1927.

The uncertainty was recognised by the Treasury. In July 1932, a minister told the Commons that 'from such indications as exist it seems that the total foreign holdings (excluding holdings in the British Empire) do not exceed £100 millions and may be as low as in the neighbourhood of £50 millions only'. *Hansard* (Commons), 7 July 1932, col. 603.

> There is a great consensus of opinion that the continued existence of a vast body of British Government stock *yielding* a 5 per cent. return is an artificial obstacle to a fall in interest rates to a lower level at which [*sic*] they would otherwise naturally stand.[6]

He did not elaborate on how the obstacle was thought to work and in this reflected a striking failure in contemporary analysis, both inside and outside official circles.[7] This is unfortunate for, to the historian, the effect of a high nominal rate on an individual single-dated issue at a time of falling yields would be to push the price above par so that the GRY remained in line with comparable securities. Alignment might not be perfect; there would be uncertainties about the yields at which the interest payments could be reinvested and the tax treatment of the loss as the price moved back to par, but this would be the general effect. The belief that War Loan's high nominal rate supported yields may have grown out of the obsession with the annual servicing cost of the Loan, which diverted attention from both the return to the investor and the difference between the running yield and the GRY. It is noticeable how often politicians, as in Chamberlain's announcement, and journalists assumed that investors were receiving a 5 per cent return on their money even when the Loan was standing above par. Officials, who certainly knew better, slipped into the same error. Hopkins, when briefing Baldwin before he met the bankers on 5 July 1932, compared the 5 per cent available on unassented Loan with the ¾ per cent available on Treasury Bills, although the Loan was at a premium and the yields were broadly in line. Phillips, drafting the Chancellor's letter to stockholders in the middle of June, wrote of all securities being depressed because investors could earn 5 per cent on the Loan.[8]

It was not the nominal rate, but the nominal rate in combination with the long optional redemption period, which destabilised the market and supported yields. From 1 June 1929, the government had the right to call the Loan at any time on three months' notice, but it would only do so if it could reborrow at less than 5 per cent. This meant that investors did not know if they owned a three-months' Treasury Bill or a security with a life of up to eighteen years. As Phillips put it in 1931:

> If it were clear to everybody that the Govt. could repay the loan in full at once the market price would be 100; if it were clear to everybody that the Govt. could not repay the loan before 1947 its market price would stand at about 107 under present conditions. The actual market price is 103 ex-dividend showing that the public expect neither immediate repayment nor the postponement of repayment to 1947.[9]

Such instability in the length of an asset would have demanded a higher yield even in an age when institutions with measurable long-dated liabilities were less important than they were to become later.

There was another uncertainty. There was not just one refinancing cost. The possibility of the Loan being called depended on the cost of refinancing, not at a single point, but at various points on the yield curve. In principle, a drop in Treasury Bill rates, unaccompanied by a drop in longer yields, should not have affected the

Loan because the government would not have been able to find new longer-dated finance at a lower cost. On the other hand, a drop in short yields might be accompanied by a drop in medium-dated yields, which would allow cheaper refinancing, albeit of a length that the Treasury might find less than ideal. Holders, therefore, needed to watch the cost of replacing the Loan with new borrowing at any point, or combination of points, on the yield curve and not just in the very longs. Investors had been reminded of this at the beginning of 1931 when the 4 per cent tax-compounded War Loan, with nearly twelve years of the government option still to run, was refinanced with 4 per cent Treasury Bonds 1934–6 (see pp. 583–4).

The uncertainty about the length of the Loan limited the Government's freedom to make a partial conversion. If a compulsory conversion was being offered, the price of the Loan would move to par – the price at which it would be taken against the new issue. If voluntary conversion was being offered, and the Loan stood above par, the price of the new issue would need to reflect the premium, or there would be little incentive for investors to accept. Thus, as officials pointed out at the beginning of 1931, if the investor could sell the Loan in the market at 103 to buy £113½ 4 per cent Consols to yield £4 7s 10d per cent, a partial offer would need to give terms at least as good.[10] In addition, natural investor caution and inertia made partial conversion a difficult proposition: officials appreciated that success would come from making investors feel exposed if they refused the terms. An offer for even £500m, such as was being contemplated at the beginning of 1931, could merely leave investors believing that a huge amount remained, that further offers would need to be made, possibly on better terms, and that they should do nothing.

The Loan since 1917[c]

Although the Treasury chipped pieces off the Loan between 1917 and 1932, it failed to reduce its size. As we have seen, Snowden converted £148.4m into 4½ per cent Conversion 1940–4 in April 1924 and another £88.3m into 5 per cent Conversion 1944–64 in November 1929. The Depreciation Fund, active in the first five years of the Loan's life when interest rates were high, bought and cancelled £158.2m. Also in the early years, when the price stood beneath par, £29.0m were tendered for taxes. A further £45.3m were cancelled by the Commissioners with various gifts and Indian and colonial war contributions. Yet, on 31 March 1917,

c The main files in the PRO covering War Loan conversion are T 212/1, T 212/2 and T 172/1796B. Sayers did not see them before his history of the Bank was published. When he saw the new evidence in 1976, he redrafted parts of pp. 438–9 and left a copy in BoE, M 124.27.

d Sayers gives the size of the original issue as £2,553m. This is correct for all the Loan created, throughout its life, on account of cash subscriptions and conversions. He mistakenly assumes that all the Loan created on account of conversions was created in 1917, before any Loan had been bought in, cancelled or converted into other issues. Sayers (1976), II, p. 431n, and *BGS*, p. 297.

Table 19.1 Creations and cancellations of 5 per cent War Loan 1929–47: years ending 31 March (£m nominal)

	Created for cash	*Created for Conversions*	*Transferred/ cancelled*	*Surrendered for taxes*	*Purchased by Depreciation Fund for cancellation*
1917	836.5	1,230.8	0.2	–	–
1918	8.3	0.2	0.8	2.9	34.0
1919	–	1.6	0.9	3.9	23.3
1920	–	4.1	3.5	4.5	30.8
1921	–	0.1	2.2	8.4	37.5
1922	–	–	1.7	8.9	31.3
1923	–	147.0	3.1	0.3	–
1924	–	74.2	4.3	–	–
1925	–	40.4	5.3	–	–
1926	–	60.6	3.6	–	–
1927	–	48.0	3.8	–	–
1928	–	89.1	5.0	–	–
1929	–	12.9	0.7	–	–
1930	–	–	0.2	–	–
1931	–	–	9.0	–	–
1932	–	–	0.4	0.1	1.5
1933	–	–	0.4	–	–
Total	844.8	1,709.0	45.3	29.0	158.2

– denotes no transaction or less than £50,000.

Source: *BGS*, p. 297.

the issue was £2,067m, and fifteen years later it had grown to £2,085m (Table 19.1).[d]

The increases came from holders of the first three series of War Bonds finding it profitable to convert into the Loan, a use of the options which the Treasury found convenient when it was having difficulty with maturities and irritatingly expensive at other times. In all, £454.1m 5 per cent War Bonds were converted into £478.3m of the Loan. The Loan was the recipient of over one-third of all converted War Bonds, more War Bonds were converted into it than were paid off for cash, and more War Bonds were converted into it than into 3½ per cent Conversion and 4 per cent Consols combined.[11]

During the 1920s, the Loan's size and cost made its conversion a common topic in financial circles. As well as the natural focus of debate about the Debt, it was the target for those seeking easy, easier or even painless methods of repayment – voluntary or compulsory. The Treasury opposed dramatic and wholesale moves. To officials, with memories of Bank Ways and Means and the inflationary boom of 1919–20 still fresh, it was the Loan's size which distinguished it from all other issues; if an offer was a failure, and a large number of holders took cash, there could be an uncontrollable increase in the floating debt. This was threatened, in any case, by the constant stream of War Bond maturities; calling a huge issue –

deliberately increasing the size and number of refinancings – would have been a foolhardy increase in risk.

Instead, the Treasury favoured breaking the Loan up with 'nibbles' at the lower rates that it expected to be the norm after the high levels of wartime borrowing. Niemeyer was the most powerful advocate of continuity, whether he was considering the maturity of War Bonds or the redemption of the Loan: a gradual improvement in financial conditions allowing reductions of the Loan to 'manageable proportions' on improving terms, steady, unspectacular sapping, taking the minimum of risk, but with each operation contributing to a large cumulative result. The issues in the early 1920s had been the 'ground bait for the catch that is coming,' he told the Colwyn Committee in November 1925; an extensive programme of conversion must involve worse terms at the beginning and better terms as you proceed. A few days later, writing to Norman, he insisted that the alternative to proposals for a scheme for conversion of debt into tax-free annuities under threat of a penal income tax was not

> a single big issue of vast dimensions – a project I believe to be wholly unrealisable – but...a series of issues starting in the year 1926...and culminating round the preponderatingly important 5% War Loan maturity [*sic*] in 1929–30.
>
> This would be in continuation of the process on which we have been steadily working for the last three years, and might be expected to produce the minimum of disturbance and friction.

There were two conditions, both useful for bringing wayward Chancellors to heel: a 'steadily balanced budget' and a 'steadily maintained sinking fund.'[12]

In 1927, Churchill was restless at the meagre reductions in the size and cost of the Debt being produced by his officials. In January, Niemeyer successfully warded off a scheme to reduce the Debt's nominal value by buying and cancelling 2½ per cent Consols, but it was immediately followed by a suggestion for a special income tax to repay debt.[13] The following month, Sir Frederick Wise, a stockbroker and MP, made a range of suggestions for a conversion issue, with a reducing interest rate, such as that originally attached to 2½ per cent Consols.[14] No design features could avoid the problem that long yields were around 4¾ per cent and the conversion of maturities pressing, but Wise's suggestions focused attention on two possibilities: making conversion compulsory unless the investor actively dissented and reducing the risks by taking powers to repay dissentients by stages.[15] In the autumn, officials, prompted by Churchill and with Hopkins having replaced the unyielding Niemeyer, re-examined a scheme submitted the previous April by John Hanson-Lawson, a partner in stockbrokers Pember & Boyle. It was also found wanting, but notice was taken of two of Lawson's concerns – the size of the issue and the 'lethargy' of holders.

The two outsiders were pointing in the same direction; the threat posed by the Loan's size could be reduced if the Treasury was able to pay off dissentients in batches and the amount to be paid off could be reduced if the lethargic who did not reply to an offer could be deemed to have accepted. In March, when examining Wise's proposals, Phillips had written a short report on earlier conversions, including that of Goschen. He now looked at the precedents more closely and advised that the case of War Loan was 'exactly on all fours' with the New Three per cent Annuities: dissentients, he argued, could be repaid in any order, at any time or times after the required notice had been given. War Loan need not be repaid in a block on a single date, so vastly reducing the risks of calling it.[16] However, the Treasury Solicitor disagreed, and in October gave the tentative opinion that legislation to pay off dissentients by instalments 'might be challenged as interference with vested rights of the public creditor'.[17]

The Treasury was in no hurry to confirm this advice with the Law Officers. Yields in the long end were still $4\frac{3}{4}$ per cent and June 1929 was some way off. The subject was not reopened until September 1928, when Phillips advised delay until yields fell further:

> as a matter of arithmetic it would pay us better to postpone conversion for even 10 years from 1929, if by doing so we could finally convert on a 4 per cent basis. Similarly it is worth waiting even 5 years to convert on a $4\frac{1}{4}\%$ basis. Conversion on a $4\frac{1}{4}\%$ basis at any time before 1934 or on a 4% basis at any time before 1939 would be much better than conversion at $4\frac{1}{2}\%$ now.[18]

It followed that any offer should be only of a small part, to reduce the bulk, merely acting as a warning that the whole Loan was soon to be attacked. However, plans were being made for converting the 1929 maturities and the Governor felt that it would be easier if the immediate policy for the Loan was settled. This, he thought, required taking the Law Officers' views on paying off dissentients by stages.[19] Their opinion, delivered shortly before Christmas, considerably increased the risks. Once called, the Loan must be repaid at the end of three months, 'as a whole and without discrimination between individuals.'[20]

Prelude: winter 1930–1

During January and February 1931, a partial conversion offer was prepared. The motivation was political for, although Bill rates had been under $2\frac{1}{2}$ per cent for seven months, the yield on 4 per cent Consols was only just under $4\frac{1}{2}$ per cent, implying terms which would scarcely justify an offer (Figure 19.1). The high yield on Consols reflected ominous events. There were defaults on foreign Bonds, devaluation of the currencies of primary producing countries, *coups d'etat* in Eastern Europe and South America, a rise in American tariffs, and banking failures in France and the USA. Reichstag elections in September increased the representation of both National Socialists and Communists, shaking confidence in Germany, Europe's largest short-term debtor. As elsewhere, depression had deepened in the UK, raising unemployment and the cost of benefits, while reducing tax revenue. Nominal wages had held up as prices fell and the UK's free trade policy sustained imports as the overseas markets for her exports contracted: with

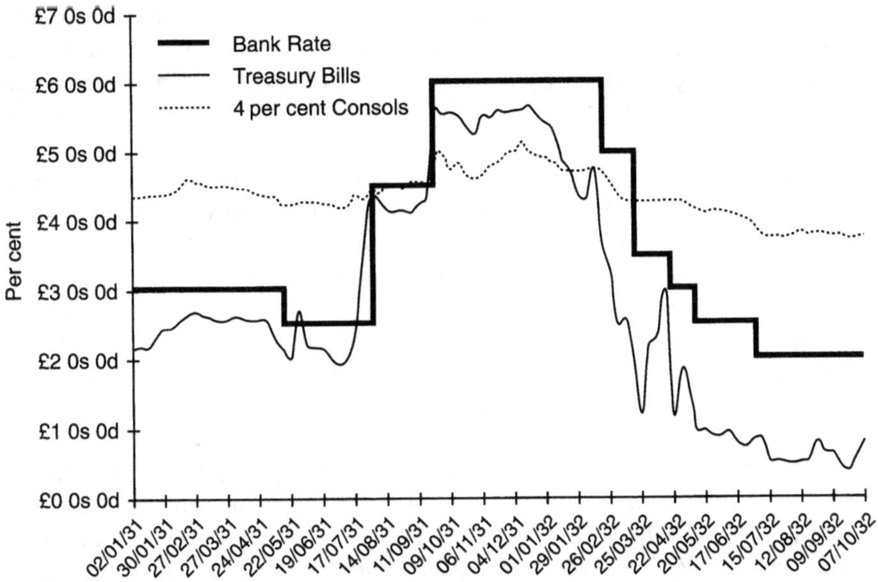

Figure 19.1 Bank rate, the discount rate on three-months' Treasury Bills and the running yield on 4 per cent Consols: January 1931 to October 1932. Source: *The Economist*.

invisible earnings falling, the balance of payments on current account deteriorated.[21] Confidence in sterling was waning, with the finger being pointed at wage costs, the balance of payments, the budget and borrowing by the Unemployment Fund. There was growing pressure for retrenchment from industrialists, the City and officials.

On 7 January, Snowden put his name to a paper which described the fiscal prospect for 1931–2 as 'grim', while defending debt repayment with orthodox Treasury arguments: reducing the sinking fund would be a breach of contract with holders of securities with attached repayment arrangements; there was extra-budgetary expenditure which meant that the sinking fund was not all it seemed; and suspension would raise yields on all government securities and entail delay in the conversion of War Loan:

> The falling off of revenue coupled with the constant increase of expenditure and the great demands for new capital resources occasioned by borrowing, particularly for the Unemployment Fund, are swiftly bringing back our floating debt to the dangerous high level at which it stood a year ago. The improvement in the short term position effected by the new issues of the autumn of 1929 and the spring of 1930 will be worse than lost, and next year further borrowing will be required...If in these conditions the public look upon the budget as unsound, it will become a question whether they can be induced to subscribe for the short term accommodation which is vital to finance and whether they can be induced to subscribe to any necessary long term loans...Failure to

> secure the necessary short term accommodation will prejudice the continuance of cheap money...Failure to obtain necessary long term money at reasonable rates will not merely postpone all prospects of successful conversion of the war debt, but will jeopardise the whole improvement in the long term rate of interest...
>
> This is not scare-mongering; in present conditions of gloom and anxiety these would be the necessary consequences of unsound state finance: nor is the probability of other graver consequences – a breakdown of our financial organisation and the removal of great sums abroad – lightly to be dismissed. There are disquieting indications that the national finance, and especially the continuously increasing load of debt upon the Unemployment Fund, are being watched and criticised abroad. There are already signs that London is losing the confidence of foreign markets.[22]

At the beginning of February, the Cabinet refused to agree emergency action to reduce the cost of benefits. Then, needing Liberal support for an increase in the Unemployment Fund's borrowing, on 11 February Snowden accepted a Liberal amendment to a Conservative retrenchment motion.[24] With the Cabinet's authority, he agreed to the appointment of a committee of businessmen (the 'May Committee') to examine economies, at the same time emphasising the principle of general and balanced sacrifice.[23]

The Cabinet accepted the necessity of reducing borrowing and recognised that retrenchment could only come from policy changes; on 14 January, Snowden met no opposition to his presentation of the budget problem and its effect on national credit, or to his view that the sinking fund was sacrosanct and raising taxation necessary. Where the Cabinet differed was on how the effects should be distributed.[25] Reducing the cost of War Loan, whether by a general tax on incomes from fixed-interest securities or by conversion, contributed to social justice, as well as reducing expenditure *per se*. A note scribbled by Snowden during a meeting of a Cabinet Committee appointed on 14 January to discuss retrenchment reads 'Alexander. Conversion. Rentier as part of all round Cut...Thomas. 10% Cut all round. 10% Tariff. Would have to deal with the rentier.'[26]

To the Treasury, conversion was the more attractive option since it reduced the *rentier's* income in a manner sanctioned by contract, by the terms of the prospectus. The problem was that the politicians' need for savings was immediate, but the terms for conversion unprofitable. A stream of refinancings, a steady improvement in financial conditions and a gradual reduction in debt costs *à la* Niemeyer was neither sufficiently fast in producing savings nor sufficiently dramatic to satisfy the Cabinet. Later in the year, with the demand for cuts even more immediate, this shifted attention more emphatically from conversion to taxing the *rentier* and raiding the sinking fund.

On 15 January, the repayment and refinancing of the tax-compounded 4 per cent War Loan was completed. Although on 24 January Phillips described the conditions for a conversion offer for the 5 per cent Loan as 'not too brilliant', sometime in the second half of the month the Chancellor requested the Bank to prepare a prospectus.[27] By the beginning of February, the Bank had proofs for a partial and voluntary offer to convert up to £500m of the Loan into a new issue, 4 per cent First Refunding Loan 1956 or after. It was clearly only to placate Snowden's critics: War Loan was standing in the market at about 103 and 4 per cent Consols gave £4 7s 10d per cent at 91⅛. Of the new 4 per cent conversion issue, £113½ would need to be offered to give a comparable yield, increasing the nominal capital of the Debt and saving less than £2m per year.[28]

The appointment of the May Committee postponed discussion of retrenchment; Snowden could wait in the confident expectation of strong recommendations and those opposed to cuts could bide their time until action was needed. There were grumbles at a special meeting of the Parliamentary Labour Party on 17 February and an unofficial meeting on 25 February blamed the deterioration on world events and declared that the policy of deflation had already gone too far: its chosen remedies were cuts in defence, a suspension of the sinking fund, a special tax on those with fixed incomes who had benefited from deflation and a moratorium on war debts and reparations. Ministers ignored both meetings.[29] Not only was there a political stand-off, but the market had forestalled an offer; the threat of increased taxation, talk of a development loan for public works, an attack by Lloyd George on the City and the increase in Unemployment Fund borrowing, coming on top of nervousness about fiscal policy and sterling, had done its work. By 17 February, after 4 per cent Consols had fallen nearly four points, the scheme had been postponed.[30]

The first 1931 budget

At the end of April, Snowden presented a budget which reflected his judgement that the political climate would be more receptive to unpopular measures in the autumn after May had reported.[31] Depression or no, the previous year's debt repayment was still large, although insufficient to satisfy the orthodox. Thanks to the reduction in short rates and cheaper Bill finance, £66.8m – fully £11.4m more than forecast – had been available within the Fixed Charge for repayment.[32] In addition, a windfall of £9m had come from the British share of the proceeds of the Young Loan, so that £52.5m was applied, despite a deficit of £23.3m. In some countries, Snowden pointed out, the budget would have been regarded as being in surplus.

Merely drawing attention to this showed that he was about to fall short of his usual austere standards. The 1929–30 budget had shown a deficit of £14.5m, which it had been intended to pay off, in accordance with the 1930 Finance Act, by increasing the Fixed Charge by £5m in 1930–1 and 1931–2 and by £4.5m in 1932–3 (see p. 690). In 1930–1, £5m had been duly provided and was included in that year's expenditure and deficit. Snowden now proposed that the reparation windfall be set-off against the rest of the 1929–30 deficit, and that there be no further charge in 1931–2 or 1932–3.

Nor did he increase the 1931–2 Charge to repay the 1930–1 deficit. The previous year had seen a larger repayment than forecast and he had included a liberal estimate for Bills and Savings Certificates for the coming year, which made it 'not improbable' that, once again, debt repayment within the Fixed Charge would be higher than forecast. In addition, 'Conditions might...be favourable for considerable Debt conversion operations.' The rationale was that, although he had

> always favoured every possible effort at Debt reduction, I have always agreed with Mr. Gladstone's view that, in times of industrial depression and unemployment, it is better to use our resources to stimulate trade than to make undue sacrifices for the reduction of Debt. It is in times of prosperity and abounding revenue and of budget surpluses that we can afford to lessen the intolerable burden of debt...

Without the contribution to the earlier deficit, and on unchanged policies, the deficit for 1931–2 was estimated to be £37.4m. Once more seeking justification in the prospect of radical change after May had reported, he proposed to find most of this, in the manner of Churchill, by raids and forestalments: £20m would come from reducing the capital of the Exchange Account,[e] £3m from the Account's accumulated reserve, £10m from bringing forward into 1931–2 one half of the income tax due in July 1932 under schedules B, D and E;[f] £7.5m in 1931–2 was to come from an increase in oil duties.

Conversion: spring 1931

Harvey, long after the event, remembered the conversion story as beginning in the spring of 1931, probably in April.[33] This is consistent with the records, which show that the Bank had prepared the main features of the scheme by the second half of May. On 4 May, the Governor had seen Lord Glendyne, Edward Gosling (the senior Government Broker) and Hugh Priestley, who had advised against conversion until there was a change of government. If an offer was necessary, they advised trying to convert £500m into a 4½ per cent 20–25 year issue at 97½; another nibble.[34] This advice was taken, or coincided with the Governor's own views, and work on the prospectuses restarted, with a date of 1952–62. The

e The Account held money borrowed during the war and placed in reserve. After the war, it had been used for purchasing and holding dollars with which to make payments on the US debt. By 1931, about £10m was still required for a short period each year. Of the remaining £23m, some was invested in US securities. These could be transferred to the Issue Department. The balance was no longer needed because the dollars paid to the UK on account of reparations and French and Italian war debts could be deposited in the newly created BIS until they were needed to pay the USA. T 171/287, Hopkins for Chancellor, 4 December 1930; *The Economist*, 2 May 1931, p. 936.

f Schedule B was tax charged on the profits, or assumed profits, of farmers. Schedule D covered the main sources of income tax revenue – income or profits from trade, the professions or other employment, interest not taxed at source (including that on 5 per cent War Loan) and income from overseas securities or other property. It also included any income or profits not falling into the other Schedules. Schedule E was the tax charged on the incomes from public offices and pensions. Royal Commission on Income Tax (Cmd. 288–1), *First Instalment of the Minutes of Evidence*, Appendix 2.

prospectuses went through many forms: differences in names (Conversion, War Loan, Reduced War Loan), rates (4 per cent and 4½ per cent) and maturities (1951 or after, and 1947–52, 1947–60). The conventional prospectus was abandoned and the offer became a notice that holders could agree to 'continue' their old holdings, subject to changes in the terms. The Depreciation Fund and the option to use the Loan to pay death duties disappeared.[35]

The problem with a partial offer, as Phillips pointed out in the middle of May, was to persuade investors that it was the final voluntary conversion:

> I think your press friends will very likely take the line that this is too timid and the offer should be wider.
>
> Not for a moment must we offer a 4½ with a due date without limit. The £500 million restriction on that stock is necessary. It does however introduce an element of doubt, because holders may reflect that anyhow there will be £1500 million left, that the Try cannot swallow £1,500m at a gulp, and that they had better keep their 5's and see what happens next.[36]

The suggestion that, as previous offers had met little success, consideration should be given to dealing with the whole Loan came from Harvey on 20 May in a memorandum containing many of the features which were to be incorporated in 1932. The date for repayment should be five or six months after notice had been given, so that the authorities would know for two or three months how much cash would be required at redemption, be able to make their plans and complete the administration of the conversion. If there was no response within three months, the holder would be deemed to have accepted. If a dissented holding was sold during the three months, the dissent would become void and the new owner could assent or dissent, thus ensuring that dissented holdings had a second opportunity of being assented. If large amounts of cash needed to be paid out, it could be reborrowed from the banking system by the Bank and be advanced as Ways and Means to the Treasury. Foreign holders might receive the same tax privileges as those on the existing Loan, but they would cease if ownership changed. Finally, there was the insight which was to become the central, adventurous, feature of the offer; the reinvestment of the cash would raise the prices of other securities, so enabling the following issue to be on improved terms.[37] The Bank adjusted and filled out this view of the market's reaction a week later: when the Loan was called, long-dated yields would fall to 4 per cent; short-dated 4½ per cent double-dated issues would move to a basis which reflected the probability of redemption at the earliest option date; the addition of the Loan to the supply of short-dated paper might raise Bill rates; and repatriation of funds by overseas holders, either on redemption or in anticipation of redemption, might strain sterling.[38]

The Bank's judgement that it would need a yield of 4 per cent if notice were given to pay off the whole Loan, but 4½ per cent if there was a voluntary offer, pointed the Treasury firmly towards the bolder course; and an even more emphatic need for a long period of stability. At the beginning of June, Phillips summed up the arguments. They could do nothing, they could have another nibble, or they could give notice to pay off the whole issue and, simultaneously, offer conversion.

The argument for the first was that interest rates had further to fall. The second was more expensive than calling the entire issue, previous partial offers had been a failure and holders would think £1,500m 'hardly less formidable' than £2,000m, and respond accordingly. The arguments against doing nothing were 'fairly weighty': the present opportunity was 'at least fairly good'; '£2,000m' of 5 per cent Stock was precluding government credit from reaching 'a really satisfactory level'; and conversion, reducing the income of the *rentier*, would ease the passage of economy measures. The risk of calling the whole issue was:

> essentially an exchange risk. So far as dissentients keep their money in this country methods could be devised to surmount such difficulties as would be presented by a substantial volume of dissent. But dissent by foreign holders (who including the Irish Free State may hold £200 million) may be a serious matter leading to withdrawal of gold, and an attempt by English dissentients to invest their redemption money abroad would increase the difficulty.[39]

The exchange risk was growing. Financial tremors had been coming out of Central Europe even before 12 May, when the Governor had signalled the renewal of preparations by sending for a copy of the February prospectus. The previous day, the executives of the Credit-Anstalt had told their government that losses had cost the bank its entire capital. Although the Austrian authorities came to the bank's aid, withdrawals of Austrian and overseas deposits and a run on the schilling followed. Money fleeing continental Europe tended to pass to London, at least in the first instance, and the Bank's reserves had recovered from their losses at the end of 1930. Although such capital was volatile, on 14 May the Bank followed a move by the FRBNY and cut its rate from 3 to 2½ per cent, hoping to ease the Depression and reduce the cost of the Debt.[40] The following day, a run on banks in Hungary began and by the end of the month the infection had reached Germany. London's liquidity was damaged: banks on the Continent called on their balances; short-term claims (reported to be some $300m, or £60m, for Germany alone), were frozen under a standstill agreement;[41] and the Bank of England made advances to the central banks of Hungary, Austria and Germany, which also became frozen. It was not only the UK which was affected, for Germany's largest creditor was the USA and the authorities were fearing for some of New York's banks, already weakened by their domestic problems. By 13 June, the Treasury and Foreign Office in London were discussing the postponement of reparations and, on 20 June, Hoover proposed a one-year moratorium on payments of interest and principal on inter-governmental debts and reparations – a proposal welcomed in London, although it cost the budget £11m.

At the beginning of July, Nordwolle, a large German textile producer, failed, followed on 13 July by the Darmstadter-und-Nationalbank (the Danat Bank), Nordwolle's largest source of credit. Thereafter, the upheaval could no longer be regarded as a limited continental crisis with side-effects elsewhere as the demand for liquidity increased. For, also on 13 July, in London, the *Report* of the Macmillan Committee on Finance and Industry disclosed the extent of the UK's short-term liabilities to a market already made nervous by the rumours of the losses in Germany.[42] There was a break in sterling and on 15 July the rate reached $4.84¼, well beneath the gold export point to New York.[43] The Bank's reserves were insufficient to hold the level for more than a few days, and Bank rate was raised to 3½ per cent on 23 July, and to 4½ per cent on 30 July.

Conversion: summer 1931

The prospect of lower expenditure on the Debt when other items were being cut or threatened kept conversion alive, even when market prices made it unprofitable: on 30 July, after Bank rate had been raised two weeks running, Snowden was still brandishing the weapon, telling the Commons that he had prepared a scheme which would effect 'a very large saving in interest' and that it would have been launched already if the markets had not been so weak.[44] The decision to delay was made in the Bank in the middle of June, although the Treasury – further from the Continent and nearer to the political jungle – continued to believe until the beginning of July that an operation might be possible that year.[45] On 10 June, the Governor told the Committee of Treasury that:

> He proposed to advise the Chancellor that while the proposals are financially attractive, there would be a grave risk in taking such a step at the present time in view of the unsatisfactory conditions, both political and financial, now obtaining at home and abroad…

and a week later Harvey said that the Chancellor was still considering, but that a decision was some days away.[46] Seven draft prospectuses were produced during June; the last was dated 11 June, the day after Norman expressed his doubts. The final draft of the press release was dated 18 June and, in view of the speed with which the crisis in Central Europe developed after the middle of the month, this can be assumed to have been the moment when the Bank finally decided that an offer was impracticable. The date is consistent with movements in the gilt-edged market, which was late in demanding delay, the long end remaining steady well into the Central European crisis. The running yield on 4 per cent Consols had been just under 4½ per cent for most of April, when a rally during May took it to 4¼ per cent. It remained at around that level until the selling of sterling started in mid-July, but even then the yield did not rise above 4½ per cent. It was not until September, as sterling left the gold standard and Bank rate was raised to 6 per cent, that a sharp deterioration set in, the yield rising to £5 0s 0d per cent (Figure 19.1).[g]

g A briefing paper for the new Chancellor written in September 1931 described the level of interest rates during June and July as having been 'favourable' for an offer. The other condition, a calm background for at least four or five months, was not assured and the Chancellor was stopped by events in Austria and Germany. T 171/293, 'Notes on 5 per cent War Loan'. It is unsigned, but Howson (1975), p. 192, note 58, ascribes it to Phillips.

Technical and legal preparations continued through the summer and autumn. From the middle of May, it was envisaged that some of the terms would have to be authorised by statute, the National Debt (War Loan Conversion and Redemption) Bill.[47] The Bill was a casualty of the summer's events, but the opportunity was taken to include its provisions in the Finance (No. 2) Act 1931 in the autumn.[48] To meet Hopkins's concern that the Treasury should not be tied to the procedure should conversion prove impossible until circumstances had changed, the Treasury was given discretion whether to use the powers.[49] Otherwise, the provisions grew straight out of the discussions of the previous years. Holders would be entitled to continue their holdings beyond the redemption date on such terms as would be specified in the notice of redemption. If neither a continuance nor a repayment application was in force at the end of the three-month notice period, the Act would have effect as if a continuance application had been received. Unless the Treasury directed otherwise, a repayment application could be revoked within the three-month notice period, a privilege which was to cause trouble later. The Treasury were given the power to make cash bonuses and to borrow to pay for them. Trustees were indemnified. A long-running question of whether dealers in securities (in particular, the banks) were liable to income tax on any profits on the original holding when they converted was settled by leaving it to dealers themselves to decide how they wished to be treated.

Crisis and recovery: the authorities await their moment

There was no possibility of a conversion for the remainder of that summer and autumn, although it would have been greatly welcomed by ministers as a painless method, sanctioned by contract, of distributing lower living standards over a wider area. By the time the Labour Cabinet split over the fiscal measures necessary to restore confidence to sterling, it had taken no radical steps. The institutional arrangements surrounding the gilt-edged market had survived, questioned, debated, but unscathed; there was no special tax on *rentier* or fixed-interest incomes, no compulsory conversion, no levy on capital and no suspended sinking fund. It was the fear of what might be done as ministers struggled for survival, the political uncertainty, pressure on sterling, fears of higher short rates and the eventual departure from the gold standard (on 21 September) which had destabilised the debt markets.

When Snowden, Chancellor in the new National Government, announced measures to balance the 1931–2 and 1932–3 budgets on 10 September, he estimated a deficit of £74.7m for 1931–2, instead of the nominal surplus he had forecast in April.[50] £34m of the change came from taking the Road and Unemployment Insurance Funds into current spending and £29m from reductions in the estimates for tax revenue. Another £11m was the difference between the £30.3m of war debt repayments from Europe and the Empire forgone under the terms of the Hoover Moratorium and the £13.5m in interest and £5.8m in capital which the UK would not be paying to the USA. The prospect for the following year, 1932–3, including the full £50m debt repayment within the Fixed Charge, was for a deficit of £170m. Tax revenue was expected to be £46m lower than estimated in April 1931 and the £37m from raids and forestalments would not be available. There were increases in expenditure of £17m (of which an increase in Transitional Benefit accounted for £10m) and the Road and Unemployment Insurance Funds, again charged on the Votes, would cost £70m. Reductions in expenditure, to be announced the following day, were planned to contribute £22m to balancing the budget in 1931–2 and £70m in 1932–3. The rest of the deficits were met by increases in income tax, surtax and the duties on beer, tobacco, entertainments and petrol.

Labour was heavily defeated at the general election held on 27 October 1931 and a National Government was formed by MacDonald with Neville Chamberlain as Chancellor in place of Snowden. With the prospect of political stability, talk of a dollar devaluation and a wave of American banking failures, short positions in sterling were closed. By the end of October, two-fifths of the central bank credits extended during August had been repaid. The rate held at between $3.75 and $3.95, and then weakened in mid-November when some central banks cut their losses and importers anticipated the introduction of tariffs. On 30 November, it fell through $3.40, and on 2 December touched $3.24. Amid fears of inflation in the USA, it recovered over the following two weeks, reached $3.40, and steadied. In the New Year, the current account showed seasonal improvement and Indian gold arrived in greater quantities while , in the USA, bank failures continued and Congress moved to mitigate the pain of depression (Figure 19.2).

In the UK, the Depression pointed to easier money, but the Governor was cautious until sterling had experienced a period of stability and gold or foreign exchange had been accumulated with which to repay the rest of the central bank credits. It was not until 18 February that Bank rate was reduced to 5 per cent. Sterling continued in demand, the Bank withdrawing from the market to allow it

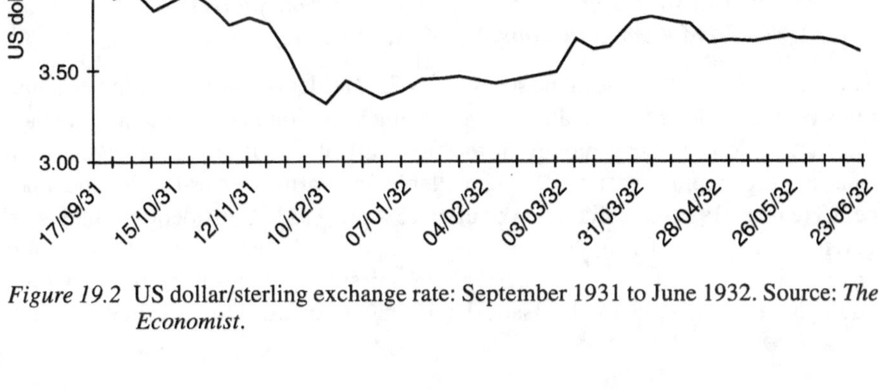

Figure 19.2 US dollar/sterling exchange rate: September 1931 to June 1932. Source: *The Economist*.

to move up to $3.82 by the end of March; Bank rate was successively cut – to 4 per cent (10 March), 3½ per cent (17 March) and 3 per cent (21 April). A further cut to 2½ per cent was made on 12 May as confidence in the dollar ebbed further. On 4 March, $150m of a Morgan credit was repaid, and the balance cleared by 5 April.[51] Bill rates followed Bank rate. Having been over £5 12s 0d per cent in the first three weeks of December, they fell under £5 0s 0d per cent in the middle of January and then collapsed.

The long end of the market also found November and December uncomfortable. The running yield on 4 per cent Consols was 5 per cent at the end of September and 5¼ per cent in the middle of December. Recovery was as rapid: the yield was under 5 per cent by the end of the year and under 4½ per cent by the beginning of March. It then stayed in the range 4 per cent to 4¼ per cent until the middle of June (Figure 19.1).

The 1932 budget

Neville Chamberlain presented his first budget on 19 April 1932.[52] In September, Snowden had forecast a surplus of £1.5m and a repayment of debt within the Fixed Charge of about £32.5m. In the event, there had been a surplus of £0.4m, although only £12.8m had been appropriated from the Exchange Account, instead of the £23m that had been envisaged. Allowing for this, the surplus was some £9m larger than the September forecast. The improvement had come from a reduction in spending on supply services, which was over £13m less than forecast, partly because of lower unemployment. The forecasts for the coming year assumed that there would be neither receipts nor payments on account of reparations and war debts, with the effect of reducing Miscellaneous Revenue by £10m and the Fixed Charge by £13.5m. Although reductions in unemployment benefit and other savings were to be greater than previously expected, receipts from income tax and surtax were forecast to be weak. The result, on unchanged policies, would have been a deficit of £34.7m. The situation was almost saved by the revenue from new tariffs, tentatively forecast to be £33m. The rest of the shortfall was covered by the reintroduction of the duty on tea, which was expected to raise £3.6m in the coming year.

4½ per cent Treasury Bonds 1930–2 into 4½ per cent Conversion Loan 1940–4 and 4 per cent Consols (16 March 1932)

There were two operations in the spring of 1932. Holders of issues bearing nominal rates of over 4 per cent and an early government option had been exposed since the first period of cheap money in the first half of 1930. There were two such issues: 4½ per cent Treasury 1930–2, callable on or after 15 April 1930, and 4 per cent Treasury 1931–3, callable on or after 15 April 1931. Consideration had been given in the spring of 1931 to exercising the options. Although conversion would have had the advantage of giving the Commissioners long-dated paper, which could have been sold to the Issue Department to provide Advances for the

Unemployment Fund, the opportunity was allowed to pass, probably because of the fall in borrowing costs which was expected once the plan to convert War Loan had been announced. On 15 April, $4^1/_2$ per cent Treasury 1930–2 was allowed to come due.[53]

On 16 March, holders were offered conversion into $4^1/_2$ per cent Conversion Loan 1940–4 at the rate of £97 12 6d of Conversion Loan for each £100 nominal of the maturing Bonds (a price of £102 8s 8d) or 4 per cent Consols at the rate of £107 of Consols for each £100 nominal of the Bonds (a price of £93 9s 2d). As a result, £68.5m were converted into £73m Consols and a further £42.7m into £41.7m $4^1/_2$ per cent Conversion Loan (Table 14.1). Only £4.9m of the £116.1m Treasury Bonds to which the offer applied remained to be paid off on 15 April.[54] Eighty per cent of the conversions came from the Issue Department, which had been buying very short Bonds from the savings banks to enable them to make advances to the Unemployment Fund.[h] The offer fitted neatly, enabling the Department to convert these Bonds and replenish its holdings of longer-dated paper (see pp. 653–4).

3 per cent Treasury Bonds 1933–42 (29 April 1932)

The second transaction involved the first short-dated issue with an attached sinking fund operated by means of drawings since Austen Chamberlain sold $2^3/_4$ per cent Exchequer Bonds 1906–15 in 1905. On 29 April, the Treasury called £64.6m of the 4 per cent Treasury Bonds 1931–3 for 15 August and announced the offer by tender of an unlimited amount of 3 per cent Treasury Bonds 1933–42 at a minimum price of £97 15s 0d (£3 8s 8d per cent).[i] The drawings were to be annual, each being of not less than 10 per cent of the original nominal issued.

With no recent experience of such an issue and with short rates plummeting, the authorities had difficulty selecting a minimum price. Using 4 per cent Treasury 1934–6 (yielding $3^3/_4$ per cent) as a guide, Phillips, seven days before the prospectus was published, envisaged a price of at least 97 (calculated to give a GRY of £3 12s 1d per cent over an average life of about $5^1/_2$ years). Three days later, Leslie Lefeaux thought the price might be as high as 98 (£3 8s 0d per cent) and at one time the Governor agreed $97^1/_2$ (£3 10s 0d per cent). The $97^3/_4$ finally selected was calculated to give £3 9s 0d per cent.[55]

Tenders for £120.1m were received, of which £110m were accepted (Table 14.1).[j]

h The Department had also been buying in the market. At the end of March 1931, it had held £30.9m, and at the end of December £72.4m. By March, it had £88.7m, which it converted into £55.4m 4 per cent Consols and £37m $4^1/_2$ Conversion. It sold vigorously as prices rose in April and May. Issue Department Ledgers.

i An additional, but unspecified, sum was sought to help reduce the floating debt. The issue was partly paid, with a 30 per cent instalment due on the day the 4 per cents were to be paid off.

j Those at the minimum price were allotted 58.5 per cent and the average price was £97 16s 2d (£3 8s 8d per cent), only just above the minimum. The Issue Department took £65.9m and the Commissioners another £7m. T 160/527/F12995, Waterfield to Phillips, with marginal notes by Phillips, 26 April 1932, and Bank to Ismay, 2 May 1932.

The last-minute decision to raise the minimum price and the large participation by the Issue Department may have been designed to underline the fall that had taken place in yields and rattle investors. Whether it was the intention or not, the coupling of the repayment of a Bond bearing a 4 per cent coupon with the sale of another with 3 per cent emphasised the change in the cost of borrowing and served to remind investors of the risks of War Loan being called.

The calling of War Loan

In October 1931, as the election was being held, the Governor reminded the Committee of Treasury of the importance of an early conversion of War Loan and reduction of the floating debt, even if it meant a 'voluntary-forced' conversion. He proposed sending papers to May, who had recently retired from the Prudential Assurance Co., for his views.[56] Nothing came of this; as has been indicated, after a short hiatus, the financial position improved rapidly, making possible a voluntary, market-driven conversion; the control of the floating debt became a question of reconciling the monetary conditions which would facilitate economic recovery with the lengthening which the Treasury traditionally sought when private credit demand was slack; and the Governor's advisers were the Government Brokers, Gosling and Edward Cripps, together with Glendyne.

There was delay in November and December as sterling weakened and long yields rose. When the turn came in the New Year, the rebound was so fast that it would have been impossible to select terms, even if it had been thought wise to make an offer when conditions were moving so rapidly in the authorities' favour. It was only when the long end of the market had settled down in April that Percival Waterfield once again brought the matter to Hopkins's attention.[57]

Preliminary discussions with the Bank and POSB were completed on 27 May.[58] On the morning of 3 June (Friday), Norman, having previously given the subject little attention, saw Glendyne and Cripps. In the afternoon, he saw Hopkins and Phillips and told them that they faced a period of uncertainty, with threats of default from many countries as the end of the Hoover Moratorium approached. He expected investors to hoard any cash they received and believed that yields had further to fall: if they waited, they might see them down to 3½ per cent. As soon as the two officials had left the Bank, Harvey persuaded the Governor to consult his advisers again. On the following Monday (6 June), he saw Glendyne, Cripps and Gosling and immediately decided that conversion was a possibility. It was after this meeting that Norman recorded in his diary the rate of 3½ per cent, the critical importance of the conferences at Lausanne and Ottawa and Glendyne's advice that assessment of the political risks should be left to the Chancellor.[59]

Bank and Treasury officials had already agreed several recommendations by the time Norman became involved. The easiest decision was that they should offer one security. In May, *The Economist* had suggested that there should be three issues, a short, a medium and a long. This would have provided fare for all appetites, and alternatives for those institutions treating War Loan as a short.[60] However, the scheme worked out the previous year had relied on simplicity, namely continuing into a single issue, with holders who failed to act being deemed to have agreed. This would not be possible if investors were required to make a choice.

It took longer to conclude, even provisionally, that the preferable redemption date was 1 December 1932, that is, the existing Loan should be called by the middle of July. It was feared that, if further economies in public spending were necessary in the autumn, the demand from the press and public for conversion, even 'by means of repudiation' (that is, compulsion), might become overwhelming. Interest rates had further to fall, but the four to five months that must elapse between calling the Loan and redemption meant that conversion had to be carried out as this happened and the timing could not be too precise. Onto this picture was superimposed the Lausanne Conference on Reparations and Inter-Allied War Debts, which, opening on 16 June and closing on 9 July, coincided with the decision on whether to proceed with the scheme. Officials considered the Conference so crucial that they were prepared to cancel the offer if it failed. The diplomatic challenge was how to find a bridge between the French and the absent Americans, who wanted payments to continue, and the British and the Germans, who wanted cancellation. After tense negotiations, a formula was found whereby the Germans made a token payment in the form of a deposit of £150m of Bonds with the Bank for International Settlements (BIS). However, ratification depended on a later agreement with the Americans on war debts. Because the USA rejected cancellation, both reparations and war debts remained unsettled, although from this point revival of the Versailles impositions on Germany was unlikely.

Uncertainty at the time when the Treasury was deciding whether to make the offer came from a decision by the French Cabinet on the weekend of 25–26 June to move towards political reconciliation on a basis suggested by the Germans the previous Friday. On returning to Lausanne on Monday 27 June, Édouard Herriot, the French Premier, found that the German Chancellor had had to toughen his position. The crisis was resolved when the British, assisted by American pressure on the Germans, pointed the way to the Bond issue and deposit formula. The success of the plan waited on a session of the delegates held on 29 June (Wednesday). The first week of July was taken up largely by negotiations on the amount of Bonds to be deposited.[61]

Contemporaries took it for granted that settlement of the debt problem was a precondition for the return of financial and economic stability and a recovery in world trade. During May, officials had discussed the Conference's effect on the prospects for conversion, and they seem to have accepted Waterfield's advice that a decision would not be easier even if they had known the outcome. Success would signal an industrial revival, but failure might undermine the gilt-edged market. Without economic recovery, confidence might ebb by the time of the 1933 budget, but with recovery the gilt-edged market would lose its attraction. If the Conference ended without a rupture, but with no final settlement of reparations and war debts, existing conditions in the market might continue for the rest of the year, or longer.[62]

With this range of possibilities, officials could only ignore the larger picture and focus on the immediate danger that disagreement between France and the UK would lead to a break in relations. The Conference's influence on the timing of the scheme increased at the beginning of June when it became clear that, although the Bank and the POSB preferred a dividend day and broken dividends would have to be absorbed messily into the bonus, they could handle any first day of a month. This greater flexibility meant that, depending on events at Lausanne, the Loan could be called on 1 September for 1 February or on 1 October for 1 March.

There were both political and market arguments for reducing the risk with a preliminary offer, but the decision really followed from the recommendation to call the whole Loan in July, Lausanne permitting. At first, officials had found the idea of a partial offer attractive, but by the beginning of June they had changed their minds. There was no reason for believing that it would succeed where the earlier offers had failed. It would be difficult to work up momentum for £400m or £500m: investors would tarry, knowing that another offer was on the way, £1,500m seemed scarcely easier to handle than £2,000m and the powers taken the previous September to harness investor inertia could not be used. A failed preliminary offer would embarrass the government and make the main offer more difficult or, even, impossible. Critics would claim that it did not match expectations or lift public morale. It would do nothing to facilitate the campaign to curb government spending. Most important, it would have pushed the main offer back into the autumn and officials judged conditions to be so propitious that a full conversion should be tackled immediately:

> Every alternative use to which dissentients might be tempted to put their money, whether to finance industry, to buy industrial stocks, or to invest in foreign or Dominion securities, is for the time being under a cloud. The money paid out must in the opinion of the Treasury come back into the British gilt edged market and they think that we shall never be better placed for this type of operation than we are now…stock held by residents abroad may be put roughly at £150 millions. If a substantial proportion…were to dissent from conversion, one would in normal circumstances dread an adverse effect on the exchanges of a magnitude sufficient to force a country [*sic*] off the gold standard. But here again we are in the Treasury view ideally placed. Not only are alternative investments abroad under a cloud but everyone will want to leave his money here and the exchange value of the pound is inconveniently strong rather than inconveniently weak.[63]

On 6 June, after his meeting with the brokers, the Governor called on the Chancellor and told him that he thought the scheme was practicable. According to Hopkins, by that evening the Chancellor had agreed in principle that it should go ahead. The next major decision was taken a week later. Writing on the day the Chancellor gave his agreement, Phillips suggested a 4 per cent of 1947–60 or a $3^1/_2$ per cent of 1957–70 at a discount.[64] The latter was favoured and, until 13 June, the Treasury was contemplating a GRY of $3^3/_4$ per cent, $^1/_4$ per cent lower than the running yield on $3^1/_2$ per cent Conversion, which at 88 yielded nearly 4 per cent.[k] The recommendation that the new issue should be 3½ per cent at par came from the Bank and surprised Phillips, although it was in accord with the previous year's advice that yields would fall ½ per cent once a scheme had been announced:

> The Bank of England...recommend 3½ per cent stock at par on the ground that holders have no real option but to take the offer. If the holders of very great amounts of stock dissent, they will in their efforts to find a fresh investment raise the level of gilt edged stock to a figure high enough to enable us to borrow the necessary cash to pay off dissentients at not more than 3½. This is at first sight a somewhat radical view to emanate from the Bank since it implies that by merely offering certain conversion terms we can make the price of 3½ per cent stock jump from 88 to 100.
>
> On the other hand there is no doubt that it is simply the existence of this large body of 5 per cent stock which has kept the interest in [*sic*] British Government stocks at so high a level...Their [the Bank's] view that the stockholder is really helpless is probably correct.[65]

The Chancellor was at Lausanne and the Prime Minister in Geneva for the General Disarmament Conference during the second half of June. Baldwin, the Lord President of the Council, was the senior minister in London and made decisions that could not be taken at long range by a Chancellor busy with other matters. The telephone and telegraph were considered insecure and used only briefly with a time-consuming code. Letters were the main means of communication and, as a result, the decisions, and who made them, are well documented. The correspondence shows that important aspects of the scheme remained open until the final week of June, that the Governor's guidance, once he had taken a grip on the arrangements, was accepted on all important matters and that the terms tightened as he gathered confidence.

On 22 June (Wednesday), Norman and Harvey, having consulted the brokers (Glendyne and Cripps, this time joined by Gosling), gave the Treasury strong advice that the scheme be announced on the evening of Thursday, 30 June:

> although the newspapers were talking of 1st September as the likely date for the scheme, the City was on tiptoe for the scheme, and markets were toning themselves up in the hope of one, and that, if the turn of the month, i.e. 1st July, came without an announcement their hopes would fade and the present extremely favourable conditions would deteriorate.

Their advice was subject to the 'overriding' importance of Lausanne and, if there

k 4 per cent Consols were ignored because the heavy sales by the Issue Department during April and May had kept the yield artificially high. T 212/2, Waterfield, 12 May 1932; Issue Department Ledgers.

was a danger of a break between France and Britain, the Chancellor would have to make the decision in the light of the effect he expected on confidence in the City, on the markets and on the general public influenced by the press. Baldwin was inclined to accept this.[66] On Friday (24 June), the Germans put their new proposals to the French and the British believed that their Bond deposit recipe gave a way out should a breakdown threaten. The same day, the Chancellor, judging that a complete rupture was unlikely and no decision imminent, said that the scheme should go ahead unless there was some serious unanticipated development: the times were so uncertain, he was reported as saying, that risks had to be taken and there was as much risk in delaying the launch as in embarking on it.[67]

The maturity was only decided after a series of last-minute discussions. On 22 June, the Treasury, believing that investors would 'look askance' at an issue with no final date, was recommending 1952–72. The Governor had become anxious about the liability, once again, to repay a large issue on a single date, and the following day told the Treasury that he preferred a perpetual annuity. Hopkins feared that this would appreciably increase redemptions and that the risk was not worth taking for a benefit which would accrue in the far and distant future:

> We in the Treasury should not by any means have come to the Governor's conclusion. An irredeemable loan…is often criticised in the financial papers as an unsatisfactory form of loan. We should have expected that at any rate large holders and trustee holders of War Loan, when asked to accept a reduction of the interest rate to $3^1/_2$%, would regard it as a quite serious additional detriment…and we should have said that this would jeopardise the success of the undertaking. This is especially the case as the majority of gilt edged investments have a fixed redemption date…
>
> The Governor however, after taking advice, is extremely emphatic that it would be quite unnecessary and quite unwise to give a fixed final date for redemption. He says that a redeemable loan is not expected, – that the disfavour which recently attached to irredeemable loans no longer exists, – that people do not trouble about what happens to a loan after a generation, – and that he is entirely satisfied that by inserting no fixed date for redemption we shall not jeopardise the venture at all.[68]

Once again, Baldwin was inclined to accept this advice, while wanting to leave the final decision to the Chancellor. He made no comment and the issue became a perpetual.[69]

The decision on the date was linked to that of whether the bonus should be £1 0s 0d or £1 10s 0d. Hopkins favoured a large bonus: it would enable the Treasury to placate assentors, should markets so move that the dissentients gained, and $1^1/_2$ per cent, added to the $3^1/_2$ per cent, would enable it to be said that 5 per cent was still being paid for the first year after conversion.[70] Writing on 13 June, the Chancellor had favoured a rate of $3^1/_2$ per cent, a simple exchange of £100 into £100 and a £1 10s 0d bonus. He liked the former because:

> We may have to do various things which will be difficult and unpopular both by way of economy and possibly later in the way of reduction of taxation. These things will be made easier if it appears that the rentier (who is always supposed to live exclusively on War Loan) has been made to suffer a substantial cut…

and the latter because:

> It has the advantage of tempering the wind [providing some compensation to the investor] and also increasing the attraction of acceptance. At the same time it is less ostentatious than a premium on the exchange and would tend to fall out of sight.[71]

On 22 June, the Governor advised that £1 0s 0d per cent would be sufficient. Two days later, Baldwin, influenced by Fisher and Hopkins, provisionally agreed to £1 10s 0d per cent. In the meantime, the Chancellor had minuted that he favoured the smaller amount. The two officials went back to Baldwin on 26 June (Sunday) and again argued strongly for £1 10s 0d per cent on the grounds that there were considerations, especially in regard to the Loan being perpetual, which had not been placed before the Chancellor. However, Baldwin, after consulting Harvey, now considered that 'this was not the time nor the occasion for trying to sweeten the pill, it is rather the time for asking the loanholders to take their gruel with as good a grace as they may' and that he had decided in favour of £1 0s 0d per cent.[72]

Initially, there was disagreement between the Governor and the Treasury about retaining the Depreciation Fund. This, and the privilege of tendering the Loan in payment of death duties, had been of no recent value to holders and the Treasury felt justified in abolishing them. There was no argument about the latter, but at first the Governor felt that it would be 'very strong medicine' to dispense with the Depreciation Fund at the same time as the nominal rate of interest was reduced and the possibility of a fall in price increased. A compromise was suggested by which the Fund would continue for five years and then be abolished, but the Governor changed his mind at the same time as he was advising that other aspects of the offer should be tightened. As the Treasury had reluctantly agreed to retention, it happily agreed to abolition.[73]

Continuing to pay interest without deduction of withholding tax was agreed at an early stage. Although there was a widespread belief in the City that the privilege was expensive, the Inland Revenue advised that the loss of revenue was, in fact, negligible.[74] With sterling floating, it had become less important to encourage non-residents to continue their holdings, and it was the large number of small holders on low incomes who would have to reclaim the tax if it were withheld, which determined the decision. The only consideration which made officials pause was the potential for wealthy individuals to form companies overseas to draw tax-free income. At one time, the Treasury considered reserving power in the prospectus to propose to Parliament that the privilege could be removed from holdings should it be abused in a manner prescribed by the Act. The Inland Revenue had insufficient time to consider this and both the Governor and officials thought it would be open to misinterpretation, creating suspicion and uncertainty.[75]

One other complication cropped up during the final week of preparations. Section II (2) of the September 1931 Finance Act, under which the scheme was being conducted, permitted repayment applications to be revoked any time up to 1 December by a later continuation application. This had been considered a great advantage; Loan which had been continued remained continued and Loan which was to be redeemed could become continued. Belatedly, the Bank realised that investors had been given an option; by forfeiting the bonus and lodging a redemption application, holders had an option running for five months either to take cash on 1 December or to relodge their application and continue. The Treasury's only defence lay in the same section, which gave powers 'in any particular case' to refuse an application for continuance if it had previously been a redemption application, but the lawyers advised that a provision expressed in such terms could not be used in every instance.

The Bank felt the option to be a threat to the success of the scheme. Legislation was considered impossible and the Treasury had recourse to reinterpretation. It let it be known that it felt it to be unreasonable that applications could be altered once plans were being prepared to meet the redemptions and that after 30 September it would refuse to allow redemption applications to be revoked without good reason. If there was any argument, it would say that Parliament could not have meant to allow repayment applications to be cancelled after preparations had been made to meet them and, if necessary, it would legislate.[76]

Terms and mechanics

The notice that the Loan would be redeemed on 1 December 1932 was published in a supplement to *The London Gazette* on 30 June. The offer by the Banks of England and Ireland ('the Banks') was not a standard prospectus with the terms of the contract between borrower and lender, but an announcement that holders could continue their holdings in accordance with the existing prospectus for 5 per cent War Loan with five modifications: the rate of interest was to be 3½ per cent; redemption was to be at par any time after 1 December 1952, on three months' notice, either in one operation or by successive operations;[1] the right to tender the issue in satisfaction of death duties was to lapse; the Depreciation Fund was to cease; and the name of the issue was to become 3½ per cent War Loan.

Investors were given three months, until 30 September, to notify the two Banks if they wished to continue their holdings. If they gave notification before 31 July, they would receive a bonus of £1 0s 0d per cent, which was not liable to UK income tax, except in the case of dealers in securities. Commission of 5s per cent would be paid to agents (banks, stockbrokers, solicitors and Scottish Law Agents)

1 This predictable change was approved by the Law Officers, but with the proviso that it might require statutory authority if partial redemption were effected other than by a proportionate redemption of all holdings. BoE, Loan Wallet 400B, Lefeaux, 28 June 1932.

if requests for continuation bearing their stamp were lodged before 31 July: this dropped to 2s 6d per cent during the remaining two months. Because no notices could be sent to the owners of bearer Bonds, those wishing to continue their holdings could either lodge their Bonds with the Bank of England, who would then send the owners the forms for completion, or collect the forms at any bank in the UK or Irish Free State.

Holders had until 30 September to tell the Banks if they wished to have their holdings redeemed in cash on 1 December. If they were silent, they would be assumed to have accepted the offer, and they would not receive a bonus. As we have seen, there was a further bias in the arrangements for revoking repayment applications (see p. 614). If a holding for which a redemption form had been lodged was sold, the request for redemption became void and the holding would be continued as new Loan after 1 December unless another redemption form was completed by the new owner before 30 September. On the other hand, if a holding for which a continuance request had been made and recorded by the Banks was subsequently sold, it remained assented.[m]

The simplicity of the offer is striking. Swapping nominal for nominal and the same dividend dates eliminated the complications of broken dividends and odd amounts of Stock. The nominal value of a holding in the Banks' books remained unchanged, but with a new designation and a reduced semi-annual interest payment. It was not even necessary to issue replacement certificates. However, there was little in the actual terms that was new, most of the procedures having been used before or having recognisable antecedents. Retaining the same nominal values and dividend dates had been first suggested by Bradbury in 1916 when conversion of McKenna's War Loan was under discussion. The provision that those who had not lodged a form by the 30 September could be deemed to have accepted came from Goschen's conversion. Commission of as much as 5s per cent and payment

m Holdings of inscribed and registered Stock for which redemption had been requested could not be transferred after 30 September. The last dividend on the old Loan of $2^1/2$ per cent was to be paid on 1 December and dividends of $1^3/4$ per cent on the new Loan would then be paid on the standard 1 June/1 December. All stockholders, whether on sole or joint account, who were inscribed or registered in the books of the Banks on 30 June were sent a letter from the Chancellor, a copy of the announcement made to holders and an explanatory leaflet. Sole holders, and first-named holders in the case of joint accounts, were also sent a form of request for continuance, in the case of the Bank of England (the Bank of Ireland operated a different system) a red slip with their holding's folio number, a redemption form and a stamped addressed envelope. It was simple for those on the Bank of England's books to make a request to continue a holding. The holder, or the first-named where there were more than one holder, attached the red slip with the holding's folio number to the form for request for continuance. The holder (or, if it was a joint account, both holders, or, if there were more than two, a majority of the holders) signed, and either returned the forms to the Bank in the stamped addressed envelope or handed them to an agent. In the case of registered holdings, it was not necessary to surrender the stock certificate. Unsurprisingly, redemption was made more difficult. The redemption form had to be completed with the full details of the account and then signed. If there were more than one holder, all had to sign. The form was then to be sent to the Banks or handed to an agent together with the stock certificate, if the holding was registered.

to agents handling conversion forms was common from the early 1920s. Paying a higher commission on earlier than on later applications had been introduced in 1921 with the first issue of 3½ per cent Conversion. Goschen was the precedent for the inclusion of solicitors as agents. The payment of bonuses to those converting was normal during the 1920s.[n] In short, the operation was another example of continuity in Debt management.

Guiding the market

The first indication of the government's intentions was given on 28 June (Tuesday) when the London Stock Exchange, at the request of the Governor, announced that it was to open on 2 July, a Saturday. Over the previous two months, the Bank's open market operations had made money easier. It had bought securities, so that bankers' deposits at the Bank and the public's deposits with the clearing banks expanded; conditions in the Discount Market had become so easy that, for the first time since 1919, the half-year window-dressing passed without help from the Bank's Discount Office.[77] When Bank rate was reduced to 2½ per cent on 12 May, Bill rates had dropped to just under £1 0s 0d per cent. At the tender on 24 June, the average of accepted bids was £0 15s 0d per cent. The change in the longer end was not so dramatic, the major improvement having already taken place in January and February; the running yield on 4 per cent Consols was £4 3s 1d per cent at the beginning of June and £3 19s 3d on the eve of the offer (Figure 19.1).

On the Thursday before the announcement, Bank rate was reduced to 2 per cent, where it was to stay until August 1939. This, and the news of the Saturday opening, gave the markets a strong scent. They reacted enthusiastically to the Chancellor's speech, with sharp rises in industrial prior charges, overseas Bonds and UK ordinary shares, as well as in the gilt-edged market itself. Yields in the long end reached towards 3⅝ per cent, with 4 per cent Consols at one stage rising almost eight points, before the inevitable reaction. By the end of the first week of trading, long-dated yields had fallen by four or five shillings.

Once the scheme was launched, the Bank used its influence to keep prices at levels which would encourage conversion and ensure that holders received only encouraging news. The guidance of the discount market, banks and press can be explained by the financial and political importance of the offer. But even if it had been otherwise, the size and wide ownership of the issue would have required a different approach from that adopted for the many conversions of the previous decade. The Loan dwarfed the Issue Department's portfolio. Even if it had been

n This detail was made possible by the way the bonus was paid. Those in earlier conversion offers had taken the form of a cash payment, a discount to the market price, the overlapping of interest, or some combination of the three. The size of the 5 per cent Loan and the large number of holdings in the hands of the general investor meant that the bonus had to be made overt, while the simplicity of swapping £100 nominal for £100 nominal and a new security would have made a discount to the market price or the overlapping of dividends an unnecessary complication, rather than an administratively simple way of sweetening the terms.

otherwise, there would have been difficulty controlling and disguising the cash being released into the money markets. The large number of individual holders were unlikely to have been receptive to the Department's manoeuvres. The need to keep up the momentum, limit the uncertainty and complete the conversion before the investment climate changed made purchase by Issue, followed by steady sale, unsuitable.

In the first half of July, there were rumours that the government departments controlled an improbable one-third of the Loan. This was denied by the Treasury, which had found only £36.5m, all but £1m of which was in the hands of departments acting as trustees,[o] such as the Charity Commissioners and the Accountant-General of the Supreme Court, who had to refer to the ultimate holders before acting and had not found it possible to respond to the earlier offers.[78] In fact, officials had assumed from an early stage that the Departments would play a minor role.[p] The Commissioners could provide little help as they had already accepted the earlier 'nibbles'. Issue's transactions and holdings of War Loan had always been small and, although its intervention increased after the announcement, it was still light in comparison with previous conversions. As might be expected, it dealt mainly in non-assented Loan, and was primarily a buyer.[q]

So the authorities had to rely on persuasion. Two measures to reduce competition from other investments were included in the Chancellor's announcement: a voluntary embargo on new capital issues, relying on the co-operation of the issuing houses and Stock Exchanges, strengthened by the Governor's frowns; and the suspension of sales of Savings Certificates. The latter was necessary because, unlike the targets of earlier conversions, the Loan was widely held by small investors and Certificates would have been an attractive alternative to War Loan with its reduced rate (see pp. 642–3).[79]

As soon as the offer was announced, the Governor sought the co-operation of the banks. The handling of the senior officers began badly when they were allowed to feel that the Chancellor had ignored them. Some quick diplomacy by the Governor and a fake message from the Chancellor, pointing to an unexpected

o This is consistent with the accounts of the Commissioners' funds for the end of 1931 and March 1932, which show holdings of £1.2m. *BGS*, pp. 495 and 496.

p Although intervention was not planned to play an important role, the Treasury did muster its resources. Thus, the Depreciation Fund Regulations were widened to permit the balance of the Fund to be used to purchase securities approved by the Treasury, including long-dated securities other than War Loan. T 160/425/F10701, Waterfield to Lefeaux, 19 July 1932, and Lefeaux to Waterfield, 20 July 1932; BoE, C40/427, Chief Cashier's Office, '5% War Loan Continued as $3^1/2$ % War Loan', 7 May 1936.

q At the end of December 1931, the Issue Department owned £19.2m, all but £1m bought in two sudden and unexplained bursts in 1930, the first in March and the second in August. The holding was almost halved by a single sale in March 1932, after which there were no transactions until June, when another £4.5m were sold. In July 1932, it bought £36.5m non-assented (of which £25m came from McKenna), less than a million assented, and assented a further £3m after purchase. It sold £23.6m non-assented and £3.6m assented. Its transactions totalled less than £20m over the remaining four months and it redeemed £7.1m for cash on 1 December. Issue Department Ledgers.

return to Lausanne, soothed their feelings and on 5 July (Tuesday) they had a meeting with Baldwin.[80] The banks had already agreed at a meeting of General Managers held at the Bank the previous Friday to give free advice to any holder who called at one of their branches. This, however, could not be described as philanthropic, since the banks were to be paid commission on forms bearing their stamp.[81] Baldwin now appealed to them to continue their own holdings, permit their action to be publicised, and co-operate in making non-assented Loan unattractive. The banks had recently bought large amounts of short-dated Treasury Bonds and the authorities were anxious about how they would react to a request to replace 5 per cent War Loan, which they were treating as very short-dated, with $3^1/_2$ per cent War Loan, a perpetual annuity. It seems that officials had in mind coming to an arrangement, similar to that made during the war, to relieve them of their Loan in return for a shorter security. They may even have canvassed the idea already, for the following day Goodenough of Barclays said that he was prepared to see such an arrangement to relieve the recalcitrant Midland of its holding. Although Harvey thought that they were taken aback at Baldwin's requests, the banks were helpful.[82] Barclays led the way, telling the Treasury on the evening of the meeting (Monday, 4 July) that it was converting £25.5m held by itself and its colonial subsidiary.[83] Only Lloyds, the National Bank, the Midland and Williams Deacon's hesitated, before falling into line.[84] The Midland caused the Governor trouble.

The story is well-known. McKenna told Baldwin that he had been buying large amounts of both shorts and longs and that if he converted his War Loan, which was being treated as cash as of 1 December, he would become illiquid. His comments were partially echoed by Lloyds.[85] The Governor tried to persuade him to change his mind: 'I urge. he jibs', as his diary records.[86] Norman saw him again the following day:

> I appeal to him to convert (along with all other Bks) He refuses: says he has £30 War Loan + £40 Govt. Secs. too: Regards former as necessy cash Dec 1. Obviously untrue + and misleading. After discussion he declares he will only convert if we buy £25. at today's price for cash – leaving him £5.[87]

The Governor's reply was 'I'll buy the lot'.[r] McKenna was left with the £5m, which he converted, and the decision of the clearing bankers to convert all their holdings was duly given publicity.[88]

r The transaction took place on 14 July. On that day, the Issue Department bought £26.25m of the Loan at $101^1/_{32}$. Its balance sheet for 20 July shows a single holding acquired during the previous week of £24,997,802. The Midland's records show a sale of exactly £25m on 14 July. The proceeds in the Midland Bank's books do not exactly match $101^1/_{32}$ and the difference must have represented commission paid to the Government Broker and a turn for putting the transaction through a jobber. It is described as assented, but it is not clear whether it was assented by the Department after purchase or the arrangement was that the Midland should assent and then sell it at a pre-arranged price. The long interval between the conversation with the Governor and the date of the transaction makes the latter more likely. BoE, C81/36 and ADM 18/37, relevant dates; MBa, 220/54.

The Bank also took measures to taint non-assented Loan in the money market. From the start, the Bank feared that the discount market would treat non-assented Loan as an attractive alternative to Treasury Bills maturing on 1 December, and that the increased supply of short paper would push up rates.[s] The Bank told the discount market to avoid non-assented Loan and that the Discount Office would not accept it as security for advances. The Bank could not be so direct with the bankers, but when Baldwin met them on 5 July he urged them to co-operate by withholding accommodation which would normally be granted on the non-assented security.

Alongside this, the Bank tried to make non-assented Loan illiquid by limiting transactions. Almost at once the Bank relaxed a little, in part because it feared that the money market would sell its holdings if the securities became unmarketable and of little value as collateral. It let it be known that 'reasonable' dealing in the non-assented Loan was acceptable and that, although the Bank itself would not lend against it, the banks would be asked to lend normally to the bill market on existing holdings, and to the jobbers. The following day, the Governor urged the discount market to convert their holdings and promised not to penalise houses for holding such a long-dated security.[89]

The Bank also modified its policy to protect dealing in the gilt-edged market. The rise in prices on the first day of trading was accompanied by greatly increased turnover. This was caused, in part, by sales by small holders, who wanted neither to continue nor to redeem, and purchases of this non-assented paper by professional investors, who were prepared to continue it before the end of July, so earning the £1 bonus and the 5s commission. A rise in turnover had been foreseen, with fears that it might strain the Bank's Transfer Office, which normally guaranteed to post new ownership in its books on the business day after the transaction. At the Bank's request, on the first day of dealing, the London Stock Exchange ruled that settlement could be delayed for seven days.[t] However, this meant that the jobbers were uncertain when they would receive title to the War Loan they had bought and when they would be able to pass it onto the buyers and receive payment.[u] As the Bank's activities in tainting non-assented Loan was damaging its value to the money market, which was threatening to become a seller, and the banks were unwilling to lend against the jobbers' holdings, the market became reluctant buyers and appealed to the Bank to help keep a free market. In response, the Bank not

s The anxiety was justified; although Bank rate was reduced on 30 June, Bill rates did not start falling until the third week in July.

t For a different interpretation, see Sayers (1976), II, pp. 442–3. The need for seven days' settlement was part of the plan outlined in 'Suggested Modus Operandi' in T 212/2, 23 June 1932. The decision was announced to the London Stock Exchange on the Friday morning after the Chancellor's speech, before the rise in turnover had taken place.

u The problem was not that the jobbers could not keep their books balanced, in the sense that their long positions matched their short positions, but that they could not deliver Loan they had bought and receive payment. It was, therefore, a financing problem. Even some in the Bank failed to appreciate this. See, for example, BoE, C40/736, 'Bank Borrowings against Loans of Stock', 1 October 1932.

only said it would buy unwanted non-assented Loan but it arranged to lend the jobbers non-assented Loan from its own portfolio, enabling them to pass title to their buyers although they had not yet received settlement from their many small sellers.[90]

Publicity

The cost of the Debt, the supposed happy position of the *rentier*, and the financial shocks of the previous year had made the public unusually aware of War Loan and the possibility of conversion by the time the conference at Lausanne drew the headlines and focused public attention on reparations and war debts. The ground was, therefore, well prepared when the Chancellor returned to London from Switzerland on 30 June to make his announcement to the Commons. This was appreciated by Geoffrey Dawson, editor of *The Times*, when he advised the Treasury on the handling of the press in the initial stages of the campaign. The newspapers had been demanding a conversion for so long, he said, that their first instinct would be to give support: if they were given prior warning they would have time to pick holes and think of ways of taking a different approach from their competitors. Instead, a letter signed by the Chancellor should be sent to the editors of the 200 London and provincial newspapers, together with a transcript of his speech and copies of the material which was being sent to holders. The newspapers would carry the public and advertising would not be important, except perhaps towards the end of the campaign.[91] Dawson was right, Hopkins reporting to Fergusson on 4 July:

> Everything continues to go extraordinarily well. The acceptance by the popular press has been rapturous, and the more sober newspapers give us plenty of space and speak almost exclusively in very favourable terms.[92]

Great care had been taken. The announcement had been timed to begin at 9.30 p.m., so that the North American markets would be closed, but it could catch the deadline for the morning newspapers in the UK. Hence the need for an elaborate organisation to ensure the press received the Chancellor's letter as he rose to speak, with Bank and Treasury officials available late into the night to answer journalists' questions. In addition, the Chancellor sent a personal letter to the Lords Beaverbrook, Camrose and Rothermere asking for the support and sympathy of their newspapers – the answer to be in writing.[v] Prince George, delivering a broadcast speech between 9.35 p.m. and 9.50 p.m. that evening on behalf of the Prince of Wales, referred to the offer as he concluded.

v T 212/5 contains copies of the Chancellor's letters and Beaverbrook's enthusiastic reply. There are no replies from Rothermere or Camrose.

General Seely, the chairman of the National Savings Committee since May 1926, was put in charge of general propaganda and George Steward, a Treasury Press Officer, was summoned from Lausanne to look after the principal newspapers. As well as organising advertising, a War Loan Conversion Publicity Bureau helped guide the press and persuade any newspaper which might be going astray, or losing interest, to return to a more virtuous path. A team of writers was recruited to produce draft articles. The Bank and POSB supplied daily progress reports and interesting correspondence which could be worked up into articles, as well as questions from holders with the answers. In the first twenty-four hours, there was the printing of fifteen million forms at HMSO in Harrow, their loading into fourteen lorries marked 'Urgent – War Loan Conversion Forms', which were given the right of way by the police at crossroads, and their despatch in three million pre-addressed envelopes. Good copy was found in the recruitment of temporary labour and in the two aeroplanes, chartered from Imperial Airways, bringing the envelopes which had been addressed to holders on the Bank of Ireland register from Dublin and Belfast to London. Space was given to talks on the radio by the Prime Minister, Baldwin, Chamberlain and George Lansbury. There were statements of support from leaders of industry and commerce. Following the precedent of the Great War, the names of prominent holders who had converted were circulated by the Press Bureau and, if all else failed, became the centrepiece for the daily story: the clearing banks had all converted (amount unspecified), as had the Prudential (£12m), Eagle Star Assurance (£1m) and banks, prominent individuals and official bodies in Egypt (£23m, plus a further £4.5m, bought in its non-assented form and assented).[93] Not that all else failed very often. Car stickers could be obtained by stopping AA and RAC scouts. The Prince of Wales had asked the Duchy of Cornwall to convert. Seventy thousand pillar boxes carried advertisements (partly designed by the Prince), as did government and private offices, post offices and shop windows. Hundreds of bonus warrants had been returned as gifts to the nation and, towards the end of July, there were stories of letters being received at both the Bank and POSB asking that their requests for redemption be ignored.[94]

Results

'As events have turned out a month's delay might have been fatal', *The Economist* commented in the middle of August.[95] A rise in US ordinary shares had started towards the end of July and had been accompanied by a transfer of funds from London; weakness in sterling produced its inevitable effect on gilt-edged prices. At the end of the month, the Bank felt that the market would have been expecting a rise in Bank rate if the conversion had been unsuccessful, and a fortnight later the Governor told the Discount Market that the sky was clear except for the Wall Street revival, 'which is always a threat to cheap money'.[96] Assented War Loan, which had been above par in July, fell to 97¼ on 9 August. It all came too late to stop the momentum of the campaign from carrying the offer to success. In the middle of August, the Bank announced that about £1,850m of the Loan had been continued with the benefit of the cash bonus and that only £48m had been non-assented.[97] By the end of September, when the offer closed, £1,920.8m of the Loan had been assented and a similar amount of 3½ per cent War Loan had been created. On 1 December, £163.5m was repaid at par, 7.8 per cent of the Loan to which the offer was made.[98] Amazingly, despite all the anxiety about investor inertia, no record has been found of the amount which was deemed to have been assented in accordance with the September 1931 Finance Act.[w]

✣ ✣ ✣

The reduction in interest rates when departure from the gold standard enabled monetary policy to play its part in mitigating the Depression transformed the budgetary importance of the Debt. Between 1929–30 and 1933–4, the gross cost of interest and management fell by £91m, or from £307.3m to £216.3m (Table 21.1).[x] The reduction came from just three items. The most important was the conversion of War Loan, which in its 5 per cent form had cost £109.2m a year and in its 3½ per cent form £67.2m, a saving of £42m. The interest on Treasury Bills fell from £28.7m to £4.1m, a saving of £24.6m. The decision to make only a nominal payment on the US Treasury debt gave a reduction from £27.5m to £3.3m, a saving of £24.2m.

War Loan's double-date and size made the exercise of the government's option and its conversion very different from that of the single-dated War Bonds in the 1920s. The option placed a heavy responsibility on those in the Treasury and Bank advising the Chancellor on the outlook for interest rates. None of the previous operations depended on the exercise of their judgement in this manner, or on this scale; the tension, heightened by the Loan's fiscal, social and political importance, can still be felt in the correspondence between London and Lausanne in June

w The borrowing needed to pay off dissenters merged into a larger programme, which exploited the drop in yields to call double-dated issues. On 30 August, the Treasury gave notice of its intention to redeem on 1 December £139.8m 4½ per cent Treasury 1932–4 and the remaining £12.8m of McKenna's 4½ per cent War Loan 1925–45. Two months later, it called £114.6m 5 per cent Treasury 1933–5 for 1 February 1933, the same day as investors were due to be paid £14.1m for the 4½ per cent Treasury 1934 put the previous January. These transactions, and the unassented War Loan, demanded £431.7m. The amount was increased to £450m because the Governor wanted to reduce a Bill issue swollen by sales of sterling by the EEA. To give an opportunity for assented War Loan to settle down and to satisfy the reinvestment needs of those who had been holding non-assented Loan as a short, the requirement for 1 December was met from the issue on 10 October of 2 per cent Treasury 1935–8 at par: £76.8m were sold for cash and £73.2m for conversion from the 4½ per cent Treasury Bonds 1932–4, ostensibly meeting most of the 1 December needs except that the Issue Department was responsible for £61.9m of the conversions and £20m of the cash applications. To meet the 1 February payments, on 3 November the Treasury sold £301.8m 3 per cent Conversion 1948–53 at 97½ (£3 4s 3d per cent to 1948 and £3 3s 5d per cent to 1953). T 160/496, Waterfield, 26 September 1932, Hopkins to Chancellor, 27 October 1932, and Fisher, 'New Government Borrowings', August 1932.

x Excluding the interest on that part of Savings Certificates cashed that was borrowed. See p. 694.

1932. Moreover, the risks could not be reduced by a judicious adjustment of the Issue Department's portfolio. If something had gone wrong, the cash released by the repayment would have swamped the banking system, increased the floating debt – with constant renewal of Treasury Bills and more volatile short-term interest rates – and threatened monetary control. Since the Loan was not only exceptional in size, but also widely held by non-professional holders, the big drum had to be rolled out for the first time since 1919.

The operation was made necessary by a mixture of short-sighted debt management (allowing a single issue to grow to such proportions) and good design (giving the Loan a double-date). Debt policy in the Great War may be criticised in many respects, but the wisdom of issuing War Loans with a government option to repay or refinance over a range of years is beyond dispute. Seen in the long perspectives of debt management, the option attached to 5 per cent War Loan enabled the Treasury to take advantage of the first post-war drop in rates of any seriousness. In January 1917, as in November 1914 and June 1915, the Treasury was working on first principles and it can hardly have been expected to have seen the precise political and social conditions in which the option would be used. The double-date turned out to be a powerful weapon, all that Bradbury could have hoped for, in protecting government credit from interference and damage as the Cabinet thrashed around in 1930 and 1931. It is not difficult to imagine the extra dimension which would have been added to the problems of debt management if War Loan could not have been called until, say, 1947.

Endnotes

1 *National Debt: annual returns*; *Hansard* (Commons), 19 April 1932, col. 1438.
2 BoE, C40/427, 'Estimated Holdings in £5% War Stock 1929–47', 22 May 1931, and 'Memorandum', 6 November 1931; T 172/1796B, Hopkins to Fergusson, 27 June 1932.
3 Sayers (1976), II, p. 434n.
4 BoE, EID 14/94, various letters and memoranda.
5 Ibid., Osborne to Walker, 27 January 1932.
6 *Hansard* (Commons), 30 June 1932, col. 2122. Italics added.
7 See, for example, T 188/14, Niemeyer, 'Sir F. Wise's Suggested Conversion Scheme for 5 per cent War Loan', 23 March 1927; T 160/F13047/449/1, Phillips, '5 per cent War Loan', June 1931; *The Economist*, 14 February 1931, p. 353, 2 May 1931, p. 930, and 21 May 1932, pp. 1120–1; Clay (1957), p. 457; Sayers (1976), II, p. 432; Howson and Winch (1977), pp. 82 and 104.
8 T 177/4, Hopkins to Baldwin, 4 July 1932; T 212/3, Phillips, draft of the Chancellor's letter, mid-June 1932.
9 T 160/F13047/449/1, Phillips, February 1931. Also see Sayers (1976), II, pp. 431–2.
10 T 160/F13047/449/1, Fraser, 'Notes on Suggested 4% First Refunding Loan', 3 February 1931, and Phillips, 'Debt Schemes (24 January 1931)', 24 January 1931.
11 *BGS*, pp. 156–7, 158–9, 226–7 and 296–7.
12 Committee on National Debt and Taxation, *Minutes of Evidence*, Niemeyer para. 8648; BoE, C40/427, Niemeyer, 'Conversion', covering letter dated 11 November 1925.
13 Gilbert (1979), p. 919, Grigg to Churchill, 22 January 1927, and pp. 924–6, Churchill to Niemeyer, 26 January 1927; T 188/14, Niemeyer to Chancellor, 5 February 1927.

14 T 212/1, Wise, 'Suggestions for the Conversion of the 5 per cent War Loan (or other stocks)', 22 February 1927.
15 T 188/14, Phillips, 'Suggested Conversion Scheme for 5 per cent War Loan' and 'Previous Conversion Schemes of the Type Suggested', 5 March 1927, Niemeyer, 'Sir F. Wise's Suggested Conversion Scheme for 5 per cent. War Loan', 23 March 1927, and Niemeyer to Chancellor, 27 April 1927; Howson (1975), p. 71.
16 T 188/14, Phillips, 'Previous Conversion Operations of the type suggested', 5 March 1927, and '5% War Loan', 30 September 1927; ibid., Leith-Ross to Hopkins, 3 October 1927; Howson (1975), pp. 71–2. Hanson Lawson's suggestions are in T 212/1.
17 T 188/14, Gwyer to Hopkins, 14 October 1927.
18 T 175/15, Phillips to Leith-Ross, 29 September 1928. Underlining in the original.
19 T 212/1, Governor to Fisher, 11 September 1928; T 175/15, Phillips to Leith-Ross, 29 September 1928, and Hopkins to Chancellor, 8 October 1928.
20 BoE, G1/466, 'Opinion of the Law Officers of the Crown', 13 December 1928; Sayers (1976), II, p. 433; T 212/1, 'Opinion of the Law Officers.'
21 Clarke (1967), pp. 172–7.
22 T 171/287, CP 3(31), Snowden, 'The Financial Situation', 7 January 1931.
23 Cab. 23/66, Cabinet 11 (31), 4 February 1931, and Cabinet 13 (31), 11 February 1931.
24 *Hansard* (Commons), 11 February 1931, cols 427–542; Snowden (1934), II, p. 892; Cab. 23/66, Cabinet 13 (31), Conclusion 4, 11 February 1931.
25 Cab. 23/66, Cabinet 6 (31), Conclusion 4, 14 January 1931; Williamson (1992), pp. 218–19.
26 Williamson (1992), pp. 192–222; Clay (1957), pp. 369–72; Sayers (1976), I, pp. 233–4, and II, p. 433; T 171/287, note in Snowden's hand, second half of January 1931.
27 T 160/449/F13047/1, Phillips, 'Debt Schemes (24 January 1931)'; BoE, C40/427, note in the Governor's hand, undated.
28 T 160/449/F13047/1, Phillips, 'Debt Schemes (24 January 1931)' and Fraser, 'Notes on Suggested "4% First Refunding Loan"', 3 February 1931. The drafts of the prospectuses are in BoE, C40/427. A copy of the fourth proof is in T 160/449/F13047/1. The date on the copy in the BoE is corrected in the Governor's hand to 1952–62, but it is not clear whether this was added in February or May. The latter is most likely because it is marked 'copy to Governor. 12/5/31' and there is no mention of a due date in the records until May, when Phillips minuted that 'Not for a moment must we offer a $4^1/_2$% with a due date without limit'.
29 Williamson (1992), p. 224; T 171/287, Lindsay to Snowden, 3 March 1931, with 'Memorandum for consideration of Cabinet', 26 February 1931.
30 Williamson (1992), pp. 222–3; *The Economist*, 14 February 1931, pp. 331–2, 338–9 and 352–3, and 21 February 1931, pp. 383–6; BoE, C40/427, Note in the Governor's hand, 17 February 1931.
31 Snowden (1934), II, p. 904; Middlemas and Barnes (1969), p. 608; *Hansard* (Commons), 27 April 1931, col. 1397.
32 The rest of this paragraph is based on *Hansard* (Commons), 27 April 1931, cols 1391–1413.
33 BoE, G15/572, Harvey to Clapham, 12 October 1944.
34 MND, 4 May 1931.
35 The draft prospectuses are in BoE, C40/427.
36 T 160/449/F13047/1, Phillips to Hopkins, 12 May and 16 May 1931.
37 Clay (1957), p. 457. The memorandum, 'War Loan', is in BoE, C40/427. It is dated 20 May, but is unsigned. Sayers says that the paper was written by Harvey. Sayers (1976), II, p. 434 and footnote. Also see BoE, G15/572, Harvey to Clapham, 12 October 1944.

38 BoE, C40/427, Lefeaux, 'Possible Effects of Conversion', 27 May 1931, and, unsigned, 'Suggested Basis', 30 May 1931.
39 T 160/449/F13047/1, Phillips, '5 per cent War Loan', about 4 June 1931. Howson (1975), p. 73, dates the memoranda as May, but the paper quotes a 3 June price for 4 per cent Consols.
40 Sayers (1976), II, pp. 390–1.
41 Clarke (1967), p. 202. He cites *Report of the Committee appointed on the Recommendation of the London Conference, Annex V, August 18, 1931* and *Hansard* (Commons), 21 September 1931, col. 1294. The latter, a statement by Snowden, gives the amount of British 'assets locked up' in Germany as £70m, but does not specify whether these were only the banking assets. Sayers (1976), II, p. 504, says 'Almost all the London claims were acceptance credits' and that they totalled £54m.
42 Committee on Finance and Industry (Macmillan Committee), *Report*, para. 260; Clarke (1967), p. 202.
43 Clarke (1967), p. 202.
44 *Hansard* (Commons), 30 July 1931, col. 2513.
45 Sayers (1976), II, p. 435.
46 CTM, 10 June and 17 June 1931; Sayers (1976), II, p. 435.
47 T 160/F13047/449/1, Hopkins to Harvey, 15 May 1931, Phillips, 'Powers to be Obtained', mid-May 1931, and '£5 per cent War 1929–47. Post Office Issue', first half of June 1931, and Fraser to Phillips, '5% War Loan 1929–47', about 3 June 1931.
48 T 160/449/F13047/1, Hopkins, 9 July 1931.
49 ibid., Phillips to Rowlatt, 10 July 1931.
50 This paragraph is based on *Hansard* (Commons), 10 September 1932, cols 297–312, and *Revised Financial Statement, 1931–2 and 1932–3* (HCP 145), 10 September 1931.
51 Sayers (1976), II, pp. 416–30; Clay (1957), 399–409; *The Economist*, various issues; PML, Archives, Syndicates 12, f. 127–8.
52 This paragraph is based on *Hansard* (Commons), 19 April 1932, cols 1411–39, and *Financial Statement (1932–3)* (HCP 63), 19 April 1932.
53 T 160/F13047/449/1, Phillips, 'Debt Schemes (24 January 1931)', and BoE, C40/27, Lefeaux, 'Further Suggestions', 30 May 1931.
54 *National Debt: annual returns*; *BGS*, pp. 146–7,156–7, 264–5.
55 T 160/527/F12995, Phillips, 23 April 1932, and Waterfield to Phillips, with marginal notes by Phillips, 26 April 1932. BoE, Loan Wallet 397, contains press clippings and working papers.
56 CTM, 21 and 28 October 1931; BoE, C40/427, Harvey to May, 10 November 1932; Sayers (1976), II, pp. 437–8. A Copy of the dossier sent to May is in BoE, C40/427. May's views are outlined in MND, 16 March 1932.
57 T 212/2, Hopkins, 'War Loan Conversion', January 1933.
58 The four paragraphs covering events to 13 June are based documents in T 212/2. Waterfield, 12 May 1932, 'Notes on War Loan Conversion', 27 May 1932, and 'Note of Discussion' with Catterns, Lefeaux and Banks, 27 May 1932; Hopkins, draft for introduction to Phillips's '5 per cent War Loan Conversion', beginning of June 1932; Phillips, '5 per cent War Loan Conversion', 1 June 1932 (revised) and 6 June 1932; Hopkins and Fisher to Chancellor (with Chancellor's comments in the margin), 13 June 1932; Phillips, '5 per cent War Loan', 13 June 1932, and Hopkins, 'War Loan Conversion', January 1933. Also see MND, relevant dates.
59 T 212/2, Hopkins, 'War Loan Conversion', January 1933, and Phillips, '5 per cent War Loan Conversion', 6 June 1932; MND, 3 and 6 June 1932.
60 *The Economist*, 21 May 1932, pp. 1120–1.
61 *The Times*, various dates; Roskill (1970–4), III, pp. 44–51; Kent (1989), pp. 366–72. There are letters tracing the development of the plan in T 172/1796B.

62 T 212/2, Waterfield, 12 May 1932.
63 Ibid., Phillips, '5 per cent War Loan Conversion', 1 June 1932.
64 Ibid., Phillips, 'War Loan Conversion', 6 June 1932.
65 Ibid., Phillips, '5 per cent War Loan', 13 June 1932.
66 T 172/1796B, Hopkins to Fergusson, 22 and 23 June 1932 (two letters).
67 Ibid., Fergusson to Hopkins, 24 June 1932, Leith-Ross to Hopkins, 24 June 1932, and Hopkins to Leith-Ross, 27 June 1932.
68 T 212/2, Hopkins to Baldwin, 23 June 1932.
69 BoE, M 124.27, Sayers, redraft of *Bank of England 1891–1944*, II, pp. 438–9; T 212/2, Phillips, '5 per cent War Loan Conversion', 6 June 1932, 'Term of the Loan', 21 June 1932, Hopkins, 'Length of the Loan', 22 June 1932, Hopkins to Fergusson, 24 June 1932, Hopkins, Memorandum, 24 June 1932, and Hopkins to Fergusson, 27 June 1932.
70 T 212/2, Hopkins to Chancellor and Fisher, 13 June 1932. A £2 0s 0d per cent bonus was also mentioned in this paper.
71 Ibid., Chancellor's comment in the margin of Hopkins to Chancellor and Fisher, 13 June 1932.
72 Ibid., Hopkins to Fergusson, 24 June 1932, Hopkins, note of meeting with Baldwin, 24 June 1932, Hopkins, 'Today's Decision of the Lord President', 24 June 1932, Chamberlain, scribble on bottom of Hopkins, 'Cash Bonus', 24 June 1932, and Hopkins to Fergusson, 27 June 1932.
73 Ibid., Phillips, '5 per cent War Loan Conversion', 6 June 1932, 'Depreciation Fund', 21 June 1932, and Hopkins to Baldwin, 23 June 1932.
74 Ibid., Phillips, '5 per cent War Loan Conversion', 1 June 1932.
75 Ibid., Phillips, '5 per cent War Loan Conversion', 6 June 1932, and 'Income Tax', 21 June 1932; Sayers (1976), II, p. 434.
76 T 212/2, Hopkins to Baldwin, 23 June 1932; T 172/1796B, Hopkins to Fergusson, 24 June 1932; *The Economist*, 30 July 1932, p. 235.
77 PDO, 30 June 1932; Sayers (1976), II, pp. 436–7.
78 *The Economist*, 9 July 1932, p. 81, and 16 July 1932, p. 133; *Hansard* (Commons), 13 July 1932, cols 1303–4. A letter from the Commissioners to Waterfield, dated 25 July 1932, says that the Commissioners owned £1.8m, all but £71,500 of which had been converted. T 160/449/F13047/03, 25 July 1932.
79 *Hansard* (Commons), 30 June 1932, col. 2125; Sayers (1976), II, p. 440.
80 T 172/1796B, Baldwin to Goschen and Hopkins to Fergusson, 4 July 1932.
81 BoE, Loan Wallet 400, Neville Chamberlain to Goschen, 30 June 1932; T 177/4, Hopkins to Baldwin, 4 July 1932.
82 T 212/2, Phillips, '5 per cent War Loan Conversion', 1 June 1932; T 172/1796B, Hopkins, note of bankers' meeting with Baldwin, 5 July 1932; BoE, Loan Wallet 400B, Lefeaux, 'Meeting at the Bankers Clearing House', 6 July 1932, and C40/427, Hopkins to Harvey, 16 June 1932; Sayers (1976), II, p. 443.
83 T 212/5, Goodenough to Chancellor, 4 July 1932; T 172/1796B, Hopkins to PPS, 4 July 1932.
84 BoE, Loan Wallet 400B, Lefeaux, 'Meeting at the Bankers Clearing House', 6 July 1932, and Norman to Chancellor, 7 July 1932. Williams Deacon's had recently been bought by the Royal Bank of Scotland after incurring large losses on its lending to the Lancashire cotton industry. The take-over had been at the instigation of the Bank and after it had injected £1.5m. The reason for the take-over and the part the Bank had played were secret. It can be assumed that Williams Deacon's could not give an answer to the Bank's request until it had consulted both the Royal Bank and, privily, with the Bank itself. Sayers (1976), I, pp. 253–9.
85 T 172/1796B, Hopkins, note of bankers' meeting with Baldwin, and Hopkins to Fergusson, 5 July 1932.
86 MND, 6 July 1932.

87 MND, 7 July 1932. It is unclear why the Governor thought it 'untrue' and 'misleading.' McKenna's story is confirmed by the Midland's end-June accounts, which show £71.7m of investments. MBa, General Ledgers of the Midland Bank.

88 Sayers (1976), II, pp. 443–4; Clay (1957), p. 458. By the end of December, McKenna had sold half of the £5m. MBa, General Ledgers of the Midland Bank.

89 T 177/4, Hopkins to Baldwin, 4 July 1932; T 172/1796B, Hopkins, note of bankers' meeting with Baldwin, 5 July 1932; BoE, Loan Wallet 400B, Lefeaux, 'Meeting at the Bankers Clearing House' and 'Meeting with the Discount Market', 6 July 1932; MND, 7 and 19 July 1932; PDO, 4, 5, 6 and 7 July 1932; Sayers (1976), II, pp. 441–2. A note from the Governor with instructions on lending against the Loan as a short is pinned into PDO, 4 July 1932.

90 BoE, C40/736, 'Bank Borrowings against Loans of Stock', 1 October 1932; Loan Wallet 400B, Lefeaux, 'Conclusions reached at the Meeting with Representatives of the Stock Market', 5 July 1932, 'Meeting in the Stock Exchange Committee Room', 14 July 1932, and C40/427, '5% War Loan continued as 3½% War Loan', 7 May 1936.

91 *Hansard* (Commons), 30 June 1932, cols 2121–6; T 172/1796B, Hopkins to Fergusson, 22 June 1932.

92 T 172/1796B, Hopkins to Fergusson, 4 July 1932.

93 T 212/5, Hopkins, 'Meeting with City Editors', 11 July 1932.

94 Ibid.,section on the press; *The Times*, relevant dates.

95 *The Economist*, 13 August 1932, p. 321.

96 PDO, 28 July and 11 August 1932.

97 BoE, Loan Wallet 400, 15 August 1932.

98 *National Debt: annual returns*.

20 Savings Certificates, savings banks and capital advances

In the years between the Armistice and the Depression, the Treasury found small savings a much needed source of finance, an irritant and a convenience. Irritation came from Certificates; from an arrangement whereby local authorities could borrow some of the proceeds of the securities sold in their areas; in the budgetary problem caused by the system of accounting for accrued interest; and in their unpredictable annual cash cost. Convenience came from the savings banks. The wartime growth in the Debt had reduced the relative importance of their portfolios and the CNRA had grown to provide the authorities with a new *masse de manoeuvre*, but the Funds continued to facilitate the Treasury's operations by accepting conversion offers, absorbing Local Loans and Irish Land issues and providing capital advances.

Four threads run through the Treasury's small savings policy. Most obviously, it sought to minimise the cost of Certificates, reducing their yield as market rates fell, while limiting the cost of the tax exemption by keeping restrictions on the size of holdings. Less obviously, it sought to protect the savings banks' profits, in which it shared, by holding down the rate paid to depositors. Safeguarding the Exchequer's income had to be balanced against maintaining the volume of deposits, so that the banks could contribute to the reduction in the floating debt and increase their capital advances without selling marketable securities and disturbing the stream of conversions. With the same object, and scarred by its experiences with the Special Investment Departments during the war, the Treasury opposed the extension of municipal savings banks beyond Birmingham. Alongside these fiscal and regulatory concerns, it kept a wary eye on the size of the call liabilities represented by the savings banks' deposits and Certificates, a precaution which became of real moment in 1931.

This chapter describes the conflict over the application of Certificate money to housing, the terms of the Certificates introduced over the following thirteen years, the operations designed to convert or prolong maturing Certificates and the consequences of the accounting treatment of accruing interest. It then traces the development of the savings banks, the Treasury's successful campaign to protect them from municipal banks, the switches of the savings banks' assets from marketable securities into capital advances and the part this played in the financial problems of the summer of 1931.

Savings Certificates

The Treasury never really liked Certificates. They were protected against depreciation, repayable on demand, expensive to service and administratively cumbersome. Although not treated as such in the annual accounts, they could be considered part of the floating debt, albeit with features that gave them greater stability than, say, Treasury Bills. Because they were intended for savers who paid little or no income tax, they had to be priced to give a gross yield comparable to that on taxable debt so that, when held by investors paying the standard rate, they were an expensive form of borrowing. They also gave the Treasury a disproportionate amount of trouble: in the early 1920s, it found itself surrendering half of the gross proceeds to the Local Loans Fund; the distribution and age of the First Series was poorly recorded; there was an unexpected rise in encashments in 1926 and 1927, with damage to the budget when it was anyway proving difficult to balance; and there was the consequent need to reshape the system of debt repayment. After 1925–6, there was not even the consolation that the Certificates provided much of a contribution to refinancing other debt. In 1930–1, there was an exceptional £13.2m of purchases in excess of repayments but, generally, until 1932–3 receipts from new sales matched the repayments of principal (Table 20.1).

Table 20.1 Savings Certificates: volume outstanding, created and repaid: 1916–33 (£m)

Years ending	*Amount outstanding*		*Created for*		*Repaid*	
31 March	*Principal*	*Interest**	*Cash*	*Conversion*	*Principal*	*Interest*
1916	1	–	1	–	–	–
1917	74	–	73	–	–	–
1918	138	–	63	–	–	–
1919	227	12	89	–	–	†
1920	274	24	72	–	25	1
1921	285	35	41	–	30	3
1922	342	45	93	–	36	7
1923	354	65	40	–	28	5
1924	366	80	45	–	33	7
1925	369	90	32	–	30	7
1926	376	100	35	–	28	7
1927	372	121	32	‡	35	12
1928	362	121	36	2	39	15
1929	361	122	41	1	41	18
1930	358	121	41	1	44	20
1931	372	125	49	1	36	16
1932	379	98	48	38	48	24
1933	384	91	43	10	40	18

Notes
*Estimated.
†£111,204.
‡£181,619.

Sources: *BGS*, p. 317; *National Debt: annual returns; Annual Finance Accounts*.

Table 20.2 Conversions of Savings Certificates: 1927–33 (£)

Years ending 31 March	*Conversions into* $4\frac{1}{2}$ *per cent Conversion 1940–4*	*4 per cent Savings Bonds*	*Savings Certificates*
1927	322,659	53,584	111,289
1928	6,050,249	341,190	951,782
1929	1,317,309	110,161	653,505
1930	317,876	38,896	573,535
1931	217,347	50,585	823,485
1932	7,944,854	1,544,269	21,169,225
1933	1,420,921	529,998	5,842,252
Total	17,591,215	2,668,683	30,125,073

Note
£30,416,852 $4\frac{1}{2}$ per cent Conversion 1940–4 and £4,657,550 4 per cent Savings Bonds were created to satisfy the Certificates and the accrued interest being converted.

Sources: *BGS*, pp. 156, 315 and 317; *National Debt: annual returns.*

The conversion offers were a failure until the Savings Certificates (Conversion Issue) in 1931–2 (Table 20.2).

The First Series

The 15s 6d War Savings Certificate introduced on 19 February 1916 remained on sale until 31 March 1922. The original terms, whereby interest accumulated to give the Certificates a value of £1 at the end of five years, were modified twice. The Finance Act 1918 gave the Treasury power to extend the currency of a holding by five years from the maturity date of the latest dated Certificate held by an investor and the War Loan Act 1919 authorised it to extend the currency of any Certificate to ten years.[a] The powers were used in October 1918 and May 1920, when the Treasury ordered that any Certificates not cashed at the end of five years would accumulate by 1d each month, and enjoy a bonus of 1s if held to maturity.[b] The new name, National Savings Certificate, was recognised in the Savings Banks Act 1920.

a Nothing has been found to show why it was decided to prolong the life of Certificates by allowing investors to hold them for a further period from the date of the most recently purchased of the same series, but it was probably to allow all the Certificates held by one individual to mature at the same time and thus reduce administration.

b This accumulated to a value of 26s 0d, a yield of £5 6s 2d per cent over ten years, compared with £5 4s 7d per cent over the original five years.

Savings Certificates and Housing Bonds

During the early summer of 1920, the Certificates were at the centre of a heated disagreement between the National Savings Committee, which wanted some of the proceeds made available to local authorities for building houses, and Treasury officials, who wanted the money to continue to be available to the central government. Housing was the responsibility of the Ministry of Health, whose minister was Christopher Addison, a Coalition Liberal. He was a social reformer, an enthusiastic supporter of state intervention and of the 'Homes Fit for Heroes' so lightly promised at the 1918 election. His ministerial career had been one of central direction: he had been Minister of Munitions, and then of Reconstruction and, when the former was abolished in January 1919, President of the Local Government Board. In June that year, he became the first Minister of Health.

An important contribution to the social and industrial discontent of the spring and summer of 1919 came from the poor availability and quality of working-class houses. On 31 July, the Housing, Town Planning, &c. Act 1919 became law. This placed on local authorities the duty of providing houses, if they were needed, and introduced the principle of Treasury subsidy for building. In view of the Treasury's own debt problems, it left local authorities to raise the capital themselves on their own credit and from their traditional sources. At the end of November, a Housing Finance Committee recommended that local authorities should be given powers to borrow on local Bonds, or 'Housing Bonds', to fulfil their responsibilities under the earlier Act. These recommendations, with provision for issues at $5^1/_2$ per cent or any other rate selected by the Treasury, were incorporated in the Housing (Additional Powers) Act 1919. The timing was unfortunate; despite efforts by Lloyd George and Bonar Law to retain cheap money, the Treasury was curbing the post-war boom with high interest rates, Austen Chamberlain was about to raise taxes to create a larger budget surplus with which to repay floating debt and, in the spring, the new 5–15 year Treasury Bonds were to be issued. The Treasury, concerned at the effect on the market for its own issues and the prospects for funding the floating debt, successfully stopped a National Housing Loan.[1]

The Housing Bonds were not a success and the building programme remained bogged down in supply shortages and labour disputes. On 3 May 1920, Bonar Law launched a campaign to sell the Bonds, either by public offer or over the counter in small amounts.[2] The Savings Committee, now under the Chairmanship of Lord Islington, saw the opportunity to give its movement a sense of purpose, which had been lacking since the end of the war. In July 1918, Kindersley had suggested to the Ministry of Reconstruction's Housing Committee that, since the kind of security used for funding the floating debt was unlikely to attract the small investor, 'Housing Savings Certificates' should be put on sale. These would be guaranteed by the Treasury, but the proceeds would be paid into a central housing fund and used for building. The Housing Committee considered the proposal to be sound and recommended it for consideration.[3] Now, two years later, the Savings Committee reverted to the idea. It was finding that, since the Armistice, voluntary workers had lost their enthusiasm, while the local authorities were giving little support, or even showing an active hostility, as they competed to sell their own Housing Bonds. After experiencing the bitterness of small investors who had bought securities other than Certificates and taken losses as interest rates rose, the Committee did not feel that it could properly encourage them to buy any security unless it was encashable at short notice and did not fluctuate in price. It suggested that part of the proceeds from the sale of Certificates should be lent to local authorities for housing in proportion to the value of the sales made in their areas. The local authorities would have an incentive to help the savings movement, and the movement could sell Certificates to the small investor and Housing Bonds to the large. The danger of the small investor being inveigled into Housing Bonds by the local authorities, or suffering if a local authority ran into financial difficulties, would be reduced.[4]

From the start, Islington was opposed by Blackett and Niemeyer, although the Chancellor kept an open mind.[5] While accepting that the scheme would provide some help to the savings movement and protect small savers from the repayment and default risk of lending to individual local authorities, the officials argued the greater priority of using the Certificate money to reduce the floating debt. Moreover, repayments of Certificates were increasing. It was too early to say that Housing Bonds had been unsuccessful and the Local Loans Fund (which only lent to the smaller local authorities) was a simpler way of providing finance.[c] In any case, it was risky to finance housing with money borrowed for only five years; assets and liabilities would be mismatched and it would be contrary to the policy of lengthening the Debt. They should wait. Ultimately, Certificate money might be used for Local Loans in the manner of the savings bank deposits, but not until the Treasury's post-war debt problems had subsided and a balance between purchases and maturities had been found, so that it was known how much could be prudently locked up for a long period.[6]

In May 1920, Addison confirmed the Savings Committee's fear that he intended to establish a rival organisation when he requested the Chancellor to second officials to his ministry from the Savings Committee .[7] In time-honoured fashion, the Chancellor sent the dispute to a committee of officials – from the Treasury, the Ministry of Health and the Savings Committee – with Niemeyer in the chair. Almost immediately, at Islington's instigation, Niemeyer was replaced by Baldwin, the Joint Financial Secretary. Around the same time, the Treasury officials, while still disliking the Savings Committee's scheme, accepted that it was necessary if they were to avoid Islington's resignation and a drying up of Certificate sales.[8] It was not easy to design the machinery. A scheme was wanted that, in the same breath, would neutralise those pressing for the new tax-free local authority savings certificate, provide the investor with a Treasury guarantee, curb those local authorities borrowing on short-dated securities to invest in housing, include large

c The Local Loans Fund was established by the National Debt and Local Loans Act 1887 to provide loans to local bodies. It was under the control of the National Debt Commissioners. The Public Works Loan Commissioners were an independent body charged with investigating applications and granting loans from the Local Loans Fund.

authorities who had not hitherto had access to the Local Loans Fund and avoid duplicating the Local Loans Fund.

The officials' starting point was that the investor should have a Treasury guarantee, but that the connection between the purchase of the Certificates and the availability of the funds to the local authorities need not be real, only apparent. They suggested that Certificates should continue to be sold as hitherto, the Treasury retaining responsibility for repayment, but that 50 per cent of the gross proceeds should be paid to the Commissioners for investment in Local Loans Stock and thus contribute to the resources of the Local Loans Fund. All local authorities, not just the smaller, would have access to the Fund up to the value of one-half of the Certificates sold in their areas. There would, therefore, be no duplication of administrative machinery.

While the inter-departmental Committee was sitting, there was a reminder from the Scottish Savings Committee that, in his recent budget, the Chancellor had emphasised the necessity of reducing the floating debt and had pointed to the part played by Certificates in its contraction the previous year. He had proposed that the savings movement should adopt as its target for 1920–1 the sale of £50m Certificates, which would be earmarked to redeem the British share of the Anglo-French Loan, which matured on 15 October 1920.[9] This target had been adopted with enthusiasm by the Scottish Committee, which now saw the ground being cut from under its feet.[10] To mollify Scotland, and save the Chancellor from embarrassment, officials suggested that the scheme should start at the beginning of the following financial year, enabling all the Certificates sold in 1920–21 to be earmarked for repaying the Loan. However, housing carried greater influence than the Scottish Committee and the proposal made by the Chancellor in his budget, and the starting date was made 30 September 1920. The rest of the scheme was adopted, and powers to divert half of the new money raised from Certificates from the repayment of debt to the Local Loans Fund were included in the Finance Act 1920.[11]

Applications for Advances did not keep pace with sales of Certificates, mainly because the larger local authorities could borrow more cheaply through their traditional channels. In the summer of 1920, the political climate became more hostile to state expenditure and the Cabinet agreed to restore some measure of Treasury control over departmental spending: Addison and his policies were a symbol of profligate government and were a target for those seeking retrenchment. In November 1920, Chamberlain asked for cuts in the spending of all departments, including a limit on the number of houses for which the Treasury was responsible.[12] At the end of June the following year, the Cabinet Finance Committee decided that building contracts should be cancelled and that the government had no alternative but to decide housing questions 'not on merits, but on financial considerations only'.[13]

The local authorities' reduced requirement for housing finance was the occasion for extending the purposes for which Advances under the scheme could be used. Since December 1920, Islington and local authority treasurers had been pressing the Chancellor to widen the scope, reduce the rate of interest and introduce a break clause, so that repayment could be made after ten, instead of after sixty, years.[14] The Treasury were willing to see the scheme extended to Advances for local authority investment other than housing but resisted the latter change because Local Loans Stock was perpetual and the assets had to be matched if the Fund was not to suffer losses if interest rates fell. Moreover, said Niemeyer, local authorities were already borrowing excessive amounts repayable within five or ten years and should not be encouraged in the habit of borrowing for short periods to invest in housing.[15]

The increase in the scope of the scheme still left demand well short of one-half of Certificate sales; earmarked Advances in two and a half years represented only £2.4m of the Local Loans Fund's total of £73.2m. Gross sales of Certificates were £153.5m, the Treasury's half share £76.7m and repayments to surrendering holders £77m. The Treasury had found itself advancing only a fraction of the money due to the Local Loans Fund, being repaid unused Advances and reborrowing as Ways and Means further sums which had been advanced but not used. This could not be defended when every penny was required to meet debt maturities.[16]

In November 1922, a committee was appointed, with Montagu as chairman, to consider the arrangement. Reporting the following March, it recommended that the Treasury should be relieved of the obligation to pay the Local Loans Fund half of the proceeds of sales, but that the arrangement whereby local authorities could borrow in accordance with sales should continue. It also supported the Treasury in its refusal to offer break clauses and in the discouragement it was giving to local authorities which were borrowing short at a time when the Treasury was trying to reduce the volume of floating and short-dated debt.[17] The recommendations were accepted and incorporated in the Finance Act 1923. The last Advances to the Local Loans Fund were made in 1922–3, by which time the balance held by the Commissioners had risen to £21.9m. The Commissioners repaid the remaining balance of £15.2m to the Treasury in 1925–6. The local authorities continued to make only minor use of the facility: on 31 March 1932, Advances for housing had grown to £11.5m and those for other purposes to £13.2m.[18]

The Second and Third Series

As interest rates fell through the second half of 1921 and the first half of 1922, the Treasury sold gilt-edged securities heavily (see pp. 433–6). With the floating debt at a more comfortable level and maturities under control, officials could afford to worry about the cost of the Certificates held by higher-rate taxpayers and the dangers of the early encashment option. At the beginning of August 1921, Blackett warned the Chancellor that the time was approaching when the £5 4s 7d per cent yield free of tax on Certificates would have to be reduced. It was not just the cost. Their hurried introduction in 1916 had been accompanied by poor record keeping, which could not be rectified without a new issue, and the size of the Series was becoming unwieldy. By 31 March 1922, £446.1m (575.6m Certificates) of the

Table 20.3 Cash value (yield per cent if cashed) of Savings Certificates: First, Second and Third Series

At the end of year	*First Series*	*Second Series*	*Third Series*
1	£0 15s 9d (£1 12s 3d)	£0 16s 0d None	£0 16s 3d (£1 11s 3d)
2	£0 16s 9d (£3 19s 1d)	£0 17s 0d (£3 1s 7d)	£0 17s 0d (£3 1s 7d)
3	£0 17s 9d (£4 12s 5d)	£0 18s 0d (£4 0s 1d)	£0 17s 9d (£3 10s 5d)
4	£0 18s 9d (£4 17s 6d)	£0 19s 0d (£4 7s 9d)	£0 18s 6d (£3 13s 11d)
5	£1 0s 0d (£5 4s 7d)	£1 0s 0d (£4 11s 3d)	£0 19s 3d (£3 15s 4d)
6	£1 1s 0d (£5 3s 10d)	£1 1s 0d (£4 12s 9d)	£1 0s 0d (£3 15s 9d)
7	£1 2s 0d (£5 2s 7d)	£1 2s 0d (£4 13s 1d)	£1 0s 9d (£3 15s 8d)
8	£1 3s 0d (£5 1s 2d)	£1 3s 0d (£4 12s 10d)	£1 1s 6d (£3 15s 3d)
9	£1 4s 0d (£4 19s 6d)	£1 4s 0d (£4 12s 2d)	£1 2s 3d (£3 14s 8d)
10	£1 6s 0d (£5 6s 2d)	£1 6s 0d (£4 19s 6d)	£1 4s 0d (£4 2s 9d)

Sources: T 160/107/F4035/1, 'National Savings Certificates' and Margerison to Niemeyer, 22 June 1923.

First Series would have been sold; £104m of these would have been repaid, to leave £342.1m of principal and an estimated £45m of interest. In November, the Savings Committee agreed that an increased price was necessary.[19]

The terms of the new series reflected the Treasury's stronger position. The yield over five years was reduced from £5 4s 7d per cent to £4 11s 3d per cent by raising the price from 15s 6d to 16s. The interest accrued to give a value of exactly £1 at the end of five years and £1 6s 0d at the end of ten years, but no interest accrued in the first year and the holder had to wait for ten years before becoming eligible for a 1s bonus (Table 20.3).[d]

The Second Series remained on sale from 1 April 1922 to 30 September 1923. In April of that year, the Treasury began to sell 4 per cent Treasury 1931–3 by tender, attaining prices which gave a yield of around $4\frac{5}{8}$ per cent. The yield on Certificates of £4 11s 3d per cent tax free over five years was clearly too high.[20] In June, the Treasury sent three suggestions for a new series to the Savings Committee. These incorporated a rise in the purchase price, retaining the value after five years

d The limit of 500 Certificates was to apply to an investor's holding of both series combined. The right to hold earlier purchased Certificates until the most recently acquired Certificate matured was to apply to the Second Series, but holdings of the new series could not be used to prolong the life of the old.

at £1 and, once again, no accrual of interest during the first year; justification for the latter had been provided by POSB officials, who had been anxious when they found deposits being attracted to Certificates.[21]

The Committee advised that the suggested purchase prices would make it awkward to calculate the value of Certificates and that if the price could be kept at 16s savings associations would not have to change their methods of bookkeeping. An alternative design was suggested by William Schooling, one of the Vice-Chairmen, and accepted by the Treasury. The purchase price remained 16s, with the life being increased to provide the lower yield; £1 was attained after six years and £1 4s 0d after ten. The Certificate accrued by 3d in the first year and 9d a year thereafter, with rests every four months. As with the Second Series, the 1s bonus only accrued after ten years. The yield was £3 15s 4d per cent after five years, a reduction from £4 11s 3d per cent, and £4 2s 9d per cent after ten years (Table 20.3). The increase in value of 50 per cent over ten years and the uniform rate of accrual gave the movement a 'simple and direct' story, said the Committee.[22]

The maximum holding of Certificates of all series remained 500 and the provision that a holding could be continued for ten years from the date of the most recently purchased of the same series was left unchanged. A further improvement in administration was introduced: for the first time, all purchases, irrespective of size, were to be completed over the counter by the seller handing the investor a combination of different value Certificates equal to the investment.[e]

The Treasury tried to save about £20,000 a year by stopping the payment of commission to joint stock banks and TSBs which handled purchases. This met violent opposition from the Savings Committee who, in addition to fearing lower sales, foresaw the loss of voluntary support from branch bank staff. The change was held responsible for a sharp reduction in sales and in February 1924 Niemeyer, who had stoutly supported the change, recommended that commissions should be reinstated.[23] Although the decision was reversed, many in the savings movement believed that the episode caused lasting damage.

Conversion of the First Series into 4½ per cent Conversion 1940–4 and 4 per cent Savings Bonds (25 June 1926)

As matters stood in February 1926, investors who had bought the First Series in February 1916, and had made no further purchases, were due to see their Certificates mature in February 1926. Certificates purchased in March 1922, together with other Certificates bought earlier by the same holder, were to mature

e Until the Third Series, units for £1, £12 and £25 were kept in stock. Higher value Certificates were prepared individually by the Accountant-General's Department. With the Third Series, the £12 Certificate was withdrawn and new denominations of £10 and £50 introduced. All purchases were settled by the issue over the counter of a combination of the four denominations. A £5 Certificate was added in February 1925. T 160/107/F4035/1, Sydney-Turner to A.K. Wright, July 1923; National Savings Committee, *Ninth Annual Report*, 1925.

in March 1932 (see p. 373). Between these extremes lay all the maturities of the Series. An inter-departmental committee, chaired by Cecil Lubbock, a director of the Bank, with members from the National and Scottish Savings Committees, was appointed in April 1925 to consider how best to handle the maturities.[24] Their *Interim Report* was delivered in November. It recommended that all Certificates of the First Series should be extended to March 1932 with interest accruing by 1d a month, giving a yield of £3 16s 11d per cent in the first year and dropping steadily to £3 4s 6d per cent in the sixth year. This was similar to £1 11s 3d per cent in the first year rising to £3 15s 4d per cent over five years on the Third Series, which was then on sale (Table 20.3).[f] Thus, those wishing to retain their holding were able to earn a comparable rate without having to go to the trouble of reinvesting. Such terms, with normal investor inertia, were expected to retain a large proportion of the maturities.[25]

Lubbock's *Final Report* was published in February 1926 with recommendations, accepted by the Treasury, which would meet the needs of holders wishing to convert, rather than retain, their Certificates. It suggested that holders should be able to convert into the current series without first cashing their holdings. However, the First Series could be worth up to £650 (500 Certificates at £1 6s 0d apiece), but the maximum investment in the Third Series was limited to £400 (500 Certificates at £0 16s 0d apiece). There was also the problem that many skilled workers had accumulated the maximum 500 Certificates. Despite this, the Committee was unanimous in recommending the retention of the limit: they thought that the security should continue to be available to everyone, including those paying high rates of income tax, which made them an expensive form of borrowing that was also repayable on demand.

An alternative offer was necessary if some of the proceeds from the larger holdings were not to leak out of government securities. First, to tempt the higher-rate taxpayer for whom the Certificates were not designed and from whom it was expensive to borrow tax-free, holders were given the option of converting, free of charge, into newly created 4½ per cent Conversion 1940–4 on the Post Office Register at the market price of the day. To deter the smallest holders, who needed to be protected from depreciation, the minimum value which could be converted at any one time was £50. Like 5 per cent War Loan, interest was paid gross, but was liable to income tax.

Second, there was a new security (designed by Schooling) to meet the needs of those who disliked fluctuations in the value of their capital: 4 per cent Savings

f Because holders came from all incomes, there was uncertainty about the average tax rate which would have been payable had the Certificates been subject to income tax. A small sample, made by the Inland Revenue in the middle 1920s, suggested that the rate varied between 9d and 2s 11d. In 1932, after tax rates had been raised, it advised that the average was 3s, with an error of 6d either way. When analysing Lubbock's proposals, Phillips calculated the equivalent yields on a taxed security to be £4 16s 2d and £4 0s 7d per cent. T 160/261/F10367/03, Phillips, 'Savings Certificates of the First Series: Extension of Term', 12 November 1925; T 160/1063/F10367/4, Phillips to Hopkins, 13 November 1931; T 160/532/F13096, Waterfield to Phillips and Hopkins, 'National Savings Certificates: New Fourth Series', 25 May 1932.

Bonds, redeemable at a premium of 103 after ten years. Again, interest was paid gross, but was liable to income tax. The minimum amount which could be converted was Certificates to the value of £20 and the maximum holding was £500. Savings Bonds were not marketable, but were redeemable at par on six months' notice, with the premium only payable at maturity. In private emergencies, application could be made to the POSB for repayment at 98 (plus accrued interest), but this was a privilege and not a right and was at the discretion of the Postmaster-General.[26]

The Bonds resembled Certificates in being non-transferable, being protected against depreciation and giving an incentive to hold for the full life. Although they were to be a failure, the Treasury considered them very attractive. Phillips urged caution:

> The issue of a new series of Government Bonds safeguarded against depreciation and bearing interest at 4% is of course an innovation to be carefully watched. It is admissible as a conversion scheme applicable to money already invested in Savings Certificates. The National Savings people are not without hopes of some day persuading the Treasury to let them make such an issue for the purpose of attracting new money. This would get us into grave trouble with the Trustee Savings Banks who can pay only 3½% even in their special investment Department and with our own Post Office Savings Bank depositors. It is most important therefore that no undertaking to develop the system in that direction be given.

'Certainly', scribbled Niemeyer.[27]

The accrual of interest on Certificates

For the Treasury, the conversion offer in the summer of 1926 had two advantages. Over the remainder of the decade, it had to refinance or convert further heavy War Bond maturities and then, from 1929, it had the option of calling 5 per cent War Loan. Clearly, it wanted to avoid other demands on the market, such as refinancing Certificates. As important, conversion on these terms would capitalise the interest which had accrued on the Certificates.

Because there was no way of knowing when they would be surrendered and, therefore, no way of calculating the accruing interest, Certificates were shown in the annual returns at their original sale value of 15s 6d. In the early 1920s, Chancellors made a point in their budget statements of referring to the accruing interest and, from 1919, footnotes in both the annual returns and the Finance Accounts gave estimates of the interest which had accrued on Certificates, although the data for the Debt in the main accounts continued to refer only to the original sales value. Until 1928, Treasury budgeting ignored the interest accruing on the corpus of the securities and estimated only for the accrued interest on the Certificates which it expected to mature, or be encashed, in the course of the year. Because the accrual of interest on the corpus of Certificates was greater than that on the maturing and encashed Certificates, Debt interest, the Debt's size and the sinking fund were being systematically understated.

The Treasury gave two reasons for the treatment of the accrued interest. Lack of manpower, the speed with which the securities were introduced at the beginning of 1916 and, by implication, their unexpected success, meant that the system for issuance and registration was rudimentary. The records of the Money Order Department of the Post Office showed the total value of Certificates issued and paid off each month. They did not show how many issued in a particular year had matured or been encashed in a particular year. Thus, the Post Office did not know the age of the outstanding Certificates or the amount of interest which had accrued, although this had to be calculated for Certificates as they were paid off.[28] The Treasury also argued that because the budget was primarily an estimate of cash income and expenditure there were difficulties in accounting for interest due, but not paid, and in parking the monies destined for interest as they awaited payment.

Two other kinds of security were issued in a form in which the interest was paid by means of discount. The practice for Treasury Bills, and War Expenditure Certificates during their short life, was to pay the interest at the time the securities were issued; the Treasury issued to the Bank the amount of the discount, charging it to debt interest, and the Bank paid to the Treasury the full nominal value of the Bill, which was entered in its books as principal borrowed. This had the convenience that the interest always fell into the year in which the Bill was issued.[29] It was argued that a parallel system could not be used for Certificates because, although they were initially issued for five years, they were encashable on demand, of unknown maturity and the amount of the 'discount' which would need to be paid was unknowable. If a fund was set up to receive monies to the value of the difference between the Certificates encashed or matured and the estimated accrual on the Certificates outstanding, it would be merely a suspense account until it became payable, temporarily investing in other government securities. In effect, therefore, it would fall into old sinking fund, have been used for the redemption of debt and be unavailable to meet the liability on Certificates when they matured or were encashed. Equally, if the sinking fund was increased, it would be used to buy other securities for cancellation and would not be available to pay Certificate interest when it was needed.

Provoked by a costly underestimation of repayments in 1926–7, the Treasury asked the Government Actuary to carry out a sample of the records and provide harder data. The instruction was twofold: to determine the age of existing Certificates, and thus the amount of accrued interest outstanding; and to identify the number of Certificates which had been repaid each year and thus find evidence of how the pattern of repayments were affected by age. These data provided an indication of the future pattern of repayments, the interest accruing each year, the extent to which Certificates were held to maturity, with the consequent liability to pay the bonus, and, of particular importance at the time, the extent to which holders would run on their holdings of the First Series on similar terms to those being currently offered.[30] The Actuary's report was the foundation of the conversion and continuation terms subsequently offered for Certificates and his estimate that interest was accruing at an average rate of about £20m a year was a necessary precondition for the establishment of Churchill's Fixed Debt Charge.

Repayments of Certificates in the three years before 1926–7 had been running at a level which required a charge for accrued interest of a little over £7m a year (Table 20.1). In 1926–7, the Treasury's forecast was for the same sum. In fact, to Churchill's outrage, it turned out to be £12.3m.[31] Officials offered two reasons for the unexpected rise: encashments by those squeezed by the General Strike in May 1926, whose effect could be assumed to be temporary, and encashments of purchases made in bunches ten years earlier. Such a concentration had taken place in February 1917, when the 5 per cent War Loan campaign was in full swing, and had appeared as heavy repayments at the end of 1926–7 and the beginning of 1927–8. Officials had hoped that the conversion offer launched in June 1926 would prevent this, but the results had been disappointing. They now faced a similar rise in encashments from a hump in sales in March 1918.[32] Forewarned, and with Churchill under budgetary pressure, during the summer of 1927 officials prepared a campaign to minimise the damage. In the autumn, Hopkins described the position:

> the amount falling due for payment though difficult to forecast is not entirely outside our control. So far as we can persuade holders to convert Savings Certificates into long Stocks the interest is capitalised (in defiance, it may be, of pure principle but not, I think, of present expediency) and does not come in for payment as interest at all...[There is] a scheme already matured for a conversion campaign this autumn...Too much cannot be hoped from this action for the inertia of the small holder in a matter of this kind is hard to overcome, but I can see no other means for evading our just bill on this part of the National Debt.[33]

The scheme had been prepared before Hopkins had moved to the Treasury and just before Niemeyer went to the Bank. It was considered of such importance that the officials who were normally responsible for small savings were brushed aside as both Niemeyer and Phillips became involved. After all, it would, as Phillips commented, 'be an infernal nuisance' if surrenders 'landed us in a deficit'.[34] The Savings Committee was told that the campaign was more important than selling new Certificates and was given extra funds for an intensive advertising campaign to run between 10 October 1927 and 31 March the following year, coinciding with the 1918 hump. Post Offices displayed posters and 700,000 prospectuses and application forms were sent to large holders. The Treasury, which had hitherto refused to sanction such profligacy, allowed joint stock banks and TSBs commission on the conversion applications they handled. The terms were also improved. The minimum which could be converted into 4½ per cent Conversion was reduced from £50 to £20 and Conversion was to be offered at a 10s per cent discount to the market price.[g] Phillip's concerns about a call liability protected

g Until the last moment, 3½ per cent Conversion was to be one of the options. It was dropped on the usual grounds that the discount would be criticised.

from depreciation ensured that little was done to revive the 4 per cent Savings Bonds – 'Schooling's corpse', as he described it. The £500 limit and the condition that at least one Certificate should have been held for at least ten years were dropped.[35]

Conversion into Savings Bonds remained open on the same terms after the campaign closed on 31 March, but the provision for converting into 4½ per cent Conversion did not include the discount of 10s per cent. Little was expected, for it was clear that the offer had been a failure, with Certificates to the value of only £12.4m converted during the period from 1 July 1926. It had already been decided that the unpredictability of the cost of Certificates and Bills should be resolved by introducing a Fixed Debt Charge (see pp. 684–7).[36]

The Conversion of the First Series (29 December 1931)

By the time the last Certificates of the First Series were due to mature in March 1932, about £84m of principal and £69m of accrued interest were estimated to be outstanding (Table 20.4). The maximum value that any individual could hold had grown to £800. Repayment was out of the question and, as Hopkins admitted, the records were in such bad order that it would have been difficult, even if the money could have been reborrowed. Early in 1931, Snowden authorised discussions with the Savings Committee and these continued through that summer of financial and political troubles. In the meantime, the Treasury took powers in the Finance Act 1931 to extend the Series until March 1940.

Much of the conversion scheme, dated 29 December 1931, followed that of 1926 and 1927. First, holders who took no action would have 1d a month added to the value of their Certificates until 31 March 1940. Second, there was a new issue of Savings Certificates (Conversion Issue). This was a departure. The low yields in the early years, designed to encourage investors to hold for the full period and to protect the savings banks' deposits, was thought unsuitable for a conversion. Instead, a more even accumulation was provided (from 16s to £1 in six years, and to 24s in ten years) and the yields over the two periods were made exactly the

Table 20.4 Estimated amounts of principal and accrued interest outstanding on Savings Certificates: 31 March 1932 (£m)

	Principal	*Accrued interest*
First Series in issue from 19 February 1916 to 31 March 1922	84	69
Second Series in issue from 1 April 1922 to 30 September 1923	39	20
Third Series in issue from 1 October 1923 [to 30 June 1932]	247	31
Total of three series	370	120

Source: T 160/1063/F10367/4, Hopkins to Chancellor, 26 November 1931.

same as those on the Third Series, £3 15s 9d per cent and £4 2s 9d per cent. The issue was limited to 500 Certificates, which at the issue price of 16s meant only £400 could be invested.[h] Third, 4 per cent Savings Bonds and 4½ per cent Conversion were made available to mop up balances of over £400.[i] This part of the earlier offer had remained open on unchanged terms since April 1928. Now, once again, for a short period, the Treasury offered a discount to the market price of the 4½ per cent Conversion: 10s per cent was considered, as in 1927 and 1928, but this was reduced to 5s per cent when yields rose on marketable issues in the final two months of the year. The terms for the Savings Bonds were modified to improve their liquidity.[j] Making changes to the existing Savings Bonds would have required issuing a notice to all the holders, so a new series was created, designated 'B'.[37]

The offer, which remained open from 18 January to 30 April 1932 during the collapse in short rates, showed the sensitivity of the small saver to relative yields: £66.7m were converted, £16.2m into 4½ per cent Conversion, £3.6m into Savings Bonds and £46.8m into Certificates (Conversion Issue); £9.7m was paid off for cash and £0.8m placed in savings bank deposits. There were further redemptions during the remainder of 1932, so that by the end of the year it was estimated that only £60m of the £446.1m originally invested in the Series was outstanding.[38]

Prolonging the lives of the Second and Third Series

The Second Series had always been small, having been on sale for only eighteen months, and by the end of March 1932 it was thought that only £39m of principal and £20m of interest remained (Table 20.4). Few Certificates had been bought during the first months that the issue had been on sale, ten years earlier, when the POSB was busy with the closure of the First Series. In 1932, with interest rates falling and the success of the conversion offer for the First series, the Treasury was only too aware that the terms judged suitable in March might be too generous by the time the bulk of the Second Series began to mature. It, therefore, confined the offer to prolonging the Certificates' lives until 31 March 1941, with the addition of 1d a month, to give a yield of £3 11s 8d per cent over five years.[39]

The Third Series had been on sale since October 1923 and the amount outstanding was approaching £250m. It was becoming unwieldy and there had been plans the previous autumn to replace it with another issue yielding about 2s 6d per cent less. This fell foul of the weakness in the gilt-edged market in November

h Holders continued to be limited to 500 Certificates of all the series combined.

i The possibility was considered of using 4 per cent Consols or 3½ per cent Conversion. It was felt that using Consols might be criticised if the fixed £10m sinking fund was not raised as the size of the issue increased. As usual, 3½ per cent Conversion was rejected because of its discount. BoE, C40/408, unsigned, 23 November 1931.

j The notice for repayment being reduced from six months to fourteen days, but with interest forfeited for the broken period since the previous coupon date. The minimum value of Certificates which could be converted into either security was reduced to £10.

and December 1931. The rally in the first half of 1932 took yields on both short- and long-dated securities to slightly over 4 per cent, and during May and June another replacement was designed. Over the previous four years, investment in Certificates had averaged about £45m a year; by the spring this had increased to an annual rate of about £65m. The Treasury was in a hurry and intended to announce the new series early in July; by now it was borrowing expensively and it wanted to encourage the building societies to reduce their rates. After some debate, the Savings Committee agreed to a yield of £3 11s 1d per cent over eleven years. The offer was cancelled when the decision to launch the conversion of 5 per cent War Loan became irreversible at the end of June and, instead, the Chancellor announced the suspension of the Third Series when he announced the conversion of War Loan.[40]

Details of the replacement had already been agreed with the Savings Committee, who had advised that the terms should be made known immediately the old series was withdrawn, and they were duly announced the following day. There was a month's delay before they went on sale but, to preserve momentum, savings associations were able to continue to collect contributions for temporary deposit in the POSB. The earlier terms had taken account of the fall in yields to 4 per cent and the 3½ per cent rate on the new War Loan required a further reduction. The price remained 16s, with the maturity value reduced from 24s at the end of ten years to 23s (£3 7s 1d per cent) at the end of eleven years.[41]

The savings banks

The deposits of the POSB and the ordinary departments of the TSBs were similar to Certificates in that they were call liabilities of the Treasury and free from the risk of depreciation. They differed in two respects. There was a lengthy history which showed the aggregate to be stable, so that the Treasury felt justified in treating them as a source of long-term finance, and they were invested in government and government-guaranteed securities and in capital advances made under a range of acts which allowed the Treasury to borrow to meet some categories of departmental expenditure. The deposits also differed from Savings Certificates in that they were a cheap form of borrowing. This was not because the savings banks lent to the Treasury at low rates: they paid market rates for capital advances and the Commissioners' transactions on the savings banks' behalf, whether in the market or with the CNRA and the Issue Department, were at market prices. The benefit came indirectly from the Treasury's share of the profits, or surpluses, of the savings banks, which were taken into miscellaneous revenue (Table 20.5). Starting in 1926–7, the Treasury's share of the profits of the POSB was raised from 50 per cent to 80 per cent, its share of those of the TSBs remaining at 50 per cent. For these purposes, profits depended on expenses and the difference between the 2½ per cent paid on deposits and the yield on investments.[k] This would have

k In practice, because interest was not paid on fractions of a pound or broken parts of a month, the rate paid was about £2 8s 0d per cent. Committee on Municipal Savings Banks (Bradbury Committee), *Report* (Cmd. 3014), 1928, para. 45.

Table 20.5 Exchequer receipts from the POSB and the TSBs (£m)

*Year ending**	*POSB*	*TSBs*	*Total*
1920	0.382	0.077	0.458
1921	0.614	0.196	0.809
1922	1.977	0.278	2.255
1923	1.156	0.316	1.472
1924	1.339	0.327	1.666
1925	1.546	0.362	1.909
1926	1.579	0.366	1.945
1927	2.812	0.416	3.228
1928	2.922	0.445	3.367
1929	2.990	0.458	3.448
1930	3.144	0.481	3.625
1931	3.341	0.487	3.828
1932	3.270	0.467	3.737
1933	3.506	0.490	3.996

Notes
*The POSB's year end was 31 December and the TSBs' 20 November. The accounts took some months to prepare, so the sum received by the Exchequer in its financial year related to the savings banks' accounting period ending in the previous calendar year.

Source: *Finance Accounts of the United Kingdom.*

made them very comfortable had the savings banks not been holders of 2½ per cent Consols and long-dated securities as they depreciated.

Deposits grew slowly between 1919 and 1931. Those at the POSB were £266.3m at the end of 1919 and £289.4m at the end of 1931. They showed declines in 1921, 1926, 1929 and 1931. Deposits at the ordinary departments of the TSBs grew from £71.9m to £77.9m over the same twelve years, showing declines in the same years as the POSB, as well as in 1927. Some of the responsibility for this lay with industrial distress, unemployment and competition from the building societies and the savings departments of the joint stock banks. However, the rapid growth of the special investment departments of the TSBs, which were able to offer higher rates than the ordinary departments, and the success of the POSB and the ordinary departments during the years of high unemployment and cheap money in the 1930s, is evidence that the responsibility lay largely with uncompetitive interest rates (Figure 1.1; Table 20.6).

Growth was not helped by poor co-operation among the POSB, the TSBs and the National and Scottish Savings Committees. Many savings associations saw their role primarily as sellers of Certificates. The TSBs resented the competition from these tax-free securities, which they considered so attractive that they could sell themselves without the help of the savings movement.[42] At times, even the POSB felt driven to protest, in 1923 pointing out that during the previous year £3m of its deposits had been switched into Certificates and, as a result, the Treasury had lost the profit on the deposits, was paying out more in interest and losing the income tax revenue on the interest.[43] The same year, the Montagu Committee,

Table 20.6 POSB and TSBs (Ordinary Departments): deposits, 1919–33 (£m)

Years ending 20 November (TSBs) 31 December (POSB)	*TSBs*	*POSB*
1919	71.9	266.3
1920	75.1	266.5
1921	73.1	264.2
1922	75.8	268.1
1923	79.6	273.1
1924	82.3	280.4
1925	83.4	285.5
1926	82.0	283.7
1927	81.4	284.6
1928	81.7	288.6
1929	79.3	285.0
1930	79.1	290.2
1931	77.9	289.4
1932	80.0	305.7
1933	88.8	326.7

Source: Horne (1947), Appendices II and III.

reviewing the relationship between the savings banks and the savings movement, tried to mend the rift, suggesting that the savings committees and the savings banks were 'complementary rather than competitive':

> We have thus three bodies: one with machinery for thrift and localised propaganda [the TSBs]; one with machinery for thrift and no propaganda [the POSB]; and one whose primary object is propaganda [the National and Scottish Savings Committees].

Montagu stressed that the yield on Certificates was not competitive with the savings banks' deposit rates until the Certificates had been held for two years and that deposits were the most suitable investment for money required at short notice. The TSBs and local savings committees should co-operate; the committees should be responsible for the general encouragement of thrift and the POSB should be the collecting point.[44] Discussions were held between the institutions after publication of the report and then broke down. Suspicion was too strong. The Bradbury Committee, sitting in 1926 and 1927 to consider the future of municipal savings banks, briefly considered the TSBs and recommended that the co-operation between them and the local committees advocated by Montagu should be extended to a national level. In 1929, talks reopened between the savings committees and the TSBs and the following year a committee was set up with the POSB to work out joint savings schemes.[45] By 1939, the success of the co-operation would be such that a Treasury committee on small savings could report that only 12 per cent of National Savings groups dealt solely with Certificates and 88 per cent were mainly interested in savings bank deposits.[46]

Although welcoming the revenue and capital provided by the savings banks, the Treasury retained its traditional concern about the liquidity of the deposits and continued to impose limits on their size. At the end of 1915, the Treasury had suspended both the annual and the total limits (see pp. 127–8). As it might look odd if the limits were reimposed at a time when the government was encouraging saving, the Savings Banks Act 1920 abolished the limits until six months after the official end of the war, while giving the Treasury the power to reimpose them.[47] Limits were considered as short rates dropped towards the savings banks' deposit rate in the first half of 1922. At first, no action was taken, it being felt that the conditions governing deposit and withdrawal were sufficient to make the savings banks unattractive unless rates dropped well under 2½ per cent.[1] Later, in March 1923, the Treasury was forced to act when several banks, including Lloyds, attempted to deposit several million pounds in the POSB. An annual limit of £500 was imposed on both the POSB and the TSBs' ordinary departments, with the same exceptions for Friendly Societies, charities and so forth which existed before 1915.[48] With minor changes in 1929, the limits remained unaltered until 1940.

The Treasury had standard arguments whenever a rise in the deposit rate from 2½ per cent was proposed. It pointed to the contribution to revenue represented by the surpluses and warned that any reduction would have to be made good by increasing taxation. Over a long period, the assets had not earned 2½ per cent if capital losses were taken into account. Since the Treasury was guarantor of the deposits, the large capital deficiency could be ignored, but because it had borne the loss on capital account it should enjoy the surplus on income account. The 1915 Montagu Committee had pointed out that the small saver wanted security of capital and ease of access rather than a high interest rate, and that 2½ per cent for money on deposit was not low, taking one year with another. Those advocating a higher rate were confusing a deposit rate with a long-term investment rate, which should carry with it the risk of capital depreciation. Bradbury had called attention to the danger that a higher return would attract rate-sensitive money and that it was the low rate which made the deposits inert. If small savers wanted a higher yield, they could buy Certificates or other government securities. Once the rate had been raised, it would be difficult to reduce it once again. Finally, as long as depositors were happy to lend the money on these terms, there was no reason for the Treasury to pay more.[49]

In 1929, the level of the deposit rate became entangled in politics, in part because of the general rise in short interest rates which, as in 1921, exposed the savings

1 Interest ran from the first day of the month after deposit and ceased on the last day of the month preceding withdrawal. The formalities were cumbersome for a professional investor and, unless the account was closed, interest was only paid at the end of the year. T 160/1387/F3779/01/1, Joy to Niemeyer, 18 February 1922, Heath to Niemeyer, 25 February 1922, and Niemeyer to Blackett, 27 February 1922.

banks' 2½ per cent, and in part because the Labour Party had come to see the rate as unfair to the small saver. The Savings Banks Bill of 1929 was designed to make some minor improvements to the law on savings banks, but was the occasion for Frederick Pethick-Lawrence, who was to become Financial Secretary to the Treasury in June, to press for a rise in the rate to 3 per cent.[50] Lord Arnold, a stockbroker who was to become Paymaster-General, showed indignation and surprise, although the Treasury had been appropriating the profits of the POSB for nearly seventy years:

> The Labour Party has urged throughout the debates on this Bill that the deposit rate of interest of 2½ per cent…is too low; and two days ago we learnt that because of this low rate the Government is making a profit…we regard this as a wrong and indefensible state of things. It means that the Government is making a very large profit at the expense of, broadly speaking, the poorest members of the community and mostly women and children…if we are returned to power this is a matter which the Labour Government will immediately go into, with a view to remedying the injustice and giving better and fairer terms.[51]

Labour Party propaganda at the 1929 election promised a rise in the rate, and when it was duly returned Treasury ministers were repeatedly pressed for a change.[52]

In fact, the subject had never been dropped. The TSBs had asked for a change in 1921 and they returned to the attack in the middle of 1926.[53] This, evidence taken by the Bradbury Committee, and the stagnation of deposits, lay behind inter-departmental discussions in 1928 and 1929. They centred on the policy towards thrift in general, protecting the Treasury's capital and income and selecting changes which would be administratively feasible. A scheme was wanted which would simultaneously produce an impact on the saver, satisfy the politicians, produce more deposits and cost little or nothing. A flat increase covering all deposits would have been expensive: ½ per cent would have reduced the profits received from the POSB in 1928 by nearly £1.5m, offset by any profits earned on the expansion of deposits over and above the growth to be expected had rates not risen. This pointed to allowing higher rates on marginal deposits, but keeping the rates on the existing corpus unchanged. Minds turned to a special investment department for the POSB, open to those who already had a minimum deposit in the ordinary department.[54] A scheme was suggested to the Chancellor in July 1929, with a request that he should indicate the amount of revenue he was prepared to sacrifice. The pressure from the TSBs for a rise in the rate intensified at the end of 1929, but during the summer the Chancellor had decided not to deal with it until the budget and by then interest rates had begun to drop.[55] It was not until 1971 that the rate was changed, to 3½ per cent.

Municipal savings banks

The capital resources provided to the Treasury by the savings banks were also threatened by local authorities' attempts to follow Birmingham's example and establish municipal banks. At the beginning of 1919, the Ministry of Reconstruction's Housing Committee had recommended that they should be encouraged as a 'supplement to existing facilities'.[56] As the 1916 Act had stipulated that banks should be wound up within three months of the end of the war, later in 1919 the Birmingham Corporation included in a private Bill authority to establish a savings bank without most of the restrictions of the 1916 Act. In June, the Local Legislation Committee of the Commons concluded that wider powers could be granted to such a large and important city and the legislation went through the Commons without Treasury intervention.[57] By this time, Bradbury distrusted municipal banks for the reasons which had led the CLCB to oppose them during the war. In 1916, he had been concerned about the effect on the maturity structure of local authority debt if they borrowed money at call from local savings banks. Now, he pointed to the same problem, but for the banks themselves: taking deposits and advancing them for housing and other municipal works – borrowing short and lending long – was from the point of view of sound banking 'the sin against the Holy Ghost'. The danger was the greater in that municipal banks would draw their deposits from a limited area and, if there was local industrial distress, both they and their sponsoring local authority would be affected simultaneously. Even the POSB, which could offset withdrawals in one part of the country with new deposits from another, might need help. No doubt the hostility of the joint stock banks came from fear of competition, but it was justified if municipal banks were not properly supervised, kept insufficient liquidity and became 'parasitic' on the commercial banking system. He suggested that the Treasury should take wide powers to regulate the bank in Birmingham.[58] When the Bill came before the Lords, the Chancellor (Austen Chamberlain), with the agreement of the Lord Mayor (Neville Chamberlain), had a clause inserted providing that the bank should conduct its business in accordance with regulations agreed with the Treasury. These would cover the deposit rate and use of funds.[59]

Between 1920 and 1929, proposals to establish other banks were repeatedly brought forward in private bills and there were four attempts to enact general powers. All were defeated or withdrawn at the Treasury's behest. It helped that the Tories were in power for much of the decade. Although the Birmingham precedent was impeccably conservative, the pressure for municipal banks came primarily from the Labour Party, which, valuing them as state-owned institutions, a source of cheap finance and a method of bringing banking to a wider public, gave them a place in its 1928 programme. When, after the publication of the Bradbury Report, a motion encouraging the extension of municipal banks was debated, Pethick-Lawrence spoke in favour.[60]

The Bradbury Committee on Municipal Savings Banks had been appointed by the Treasury in September 1926. The moving spirit was Niemeyer, hoping to stamp out expansion of the banks once and for all. In this, he failed. Despite hostile evidence from the POSB, the Debt Commissioners and the Bank, the Committee was inclined at one time to recommend encouragement of the banks' expansion and enabling legislation. It was not until Niemeyer was called for the second time, and spoke strongly and adversely, that the Committee accepted official advice.[61] Niemeyer stressed two aspects. The danger to the banking system echoed the arguments of Bradbury himself in 1919. New was the emphasis on the POSB and TSBs' ordinary departments as the source of capital advances and a support for the gilt-edged market when short-dated debt needed converting and War Loan was approaching its first option date. For the foreseeable future, the demand for capital advances was so heavy that the savings bank funds would not only be unable to support the market, but would actually need to be sellers. The Birmingham bank had had a powerful effect on sales of Certificates and deposits with the local branches of the POSB and the TSB. Irrespective of views on municipal banks themselves, 'I do not think a more unfortunate time for extending this experiment could possibly have been chosen than in the next five or six years.'[62]

The Committee reported against an extension of municipal banks on four grounds: the additional incentive to thrift would be small 'in relation to the whole'; they would tend to increase municipal expenditure; they would be a potential source of banking instability; and they would seriously embarrass the national finances at a critical time.[63]

Only in 1930, under a Labour government, was official advice disregarded. Snowden cited lack of parliamentary time when refusing general legislation, but allowed Cardiff and Birkenhead, in private Bills, to acquire enabling powers.[64] However, the regulations which the Treasury envisaged were so restrictive that the banks were never established.[65] Later in the decade, there were several other attempts to acquire powers, notably by Glasgow in 1934 and 1935. They all failed. After the second war, the Local Authorities Loans Act 1945 centralised local authority borrowing in the Local Loans Fund with lending rates practically the same as those in the gilt-edged market. This, together with the low rates generally prevailing, gave Hugh Dalton, then Chancellor, the justification to discourage further moves.[66]

Annuities and capital advances

The structure of the Treasury's debt to the savings banks underwent major changes between the end of the Great War and the conversion of War Loan in 1932. Least important, because the capital had already been much reduced, were the departmental annuities, the last of which were repaid in the middle 1920s. It will be recalled that they had been set up in 1899 to expire in 1923, but had been suspended for two years during the Boer War, although maintained throughout the Great War. The first had been in lieu of £15m cancelled 2½ per cent Consols and the second in lieu of £13m Book Debt (see pp. 25–6). By the end of March 1923, only £0.8m was required to replace the cancelled Consols, which stood at 59 5/16. The Treasury expected Consols' price to rise, increasing the amount it would need to pay the savings banks, and the year was ending with an unexpectedly large budget surplus. It was decided to use part of this, relieving the following year, which was forecast to be much tighter, to pay off the annuities two years early. As was customary, it was not envisaged that the Commissioners would actually replace the Consols, but that they would use the money elsewhere. Because the Book Debt annuities were a fixed sum of money, a rise in security prices would not affect the cost of repayment. They, therefore, were allowed to run to their natural deaths in 1924–5.[67]

Capital advances – 'other capital liabilities' – grew from £46.1m at the end of March 1919 to £215.9m at the end of March 1933. Advances under the pre-war acts – military works, the acquisition of sites for public buildings and their construction, the purchase of enterprises, colonial development and imperial telephone links – shrank as the advances were repaid and not replaced by new borrowing. The only pre-war borrower to increase its demands was the Post Office, which was investing heavily in the telephone system. Its debt grew by £85.4m. The only major new borrower was the Unemployment Fund. It started taking Advances in July 1921, and by 1933 they had grown to £115m. So important

Table 20.7 Other capital liabilities: 1919 to 1933 (£m)

Year ending 31 March	*Telephones**	*Unemployment†*	*Other‡*	*Total*
1919	11.4	–	34.7	46.1
1920	12.8	–	34.1	46.9
1921	17.4	–	33.3	48.7
1922	24.0	14.0	28.3	66.2
1923	29.4	16.8	24.1	70.3
1924	35.2	10.5	20.9	66.5
1925	42.8	7.4	17.8	68.0
1926	52.4	7.5	15.2	75.1
1927	60.8	24.9	12.4	98.1
1928	67.7	24.6	11.0	103.2
1929	74.9	36.0	9.7	120.5
1930	81.7	39.0	6.5	127.2
1931	88.8	75.4	5.4	169.6
1932	94.3	115.0	4.8	214.0
1933	96.9	115.0	4.1	215.9

Notes

*Telegraph Acts 1892 to 1925 and Post Office and Telegraph (Money) Acts 1928 and 1931.

†Unemployment Insurance Acts, 1920 to 1931.

‡Uganda Railways Acts 1896 to 1902; Public Offices (Acquisition of Site) Act 1895; Public Offices (Whitehall) Site Act 1897; Royal Niger Company Act 1899; Naval Works Acts 1895 to 1905; Military Works Acts 1897 to 1903; Land Registry (New Buildings) Act 1900; Pacific Cable Act 1901; Public Offices Site (Dublin) Act 1903; Public Expenses Act 1903; Cunard Agreement (Money) Act 1904; Telephone Transfer Act 1911; Post Office (London) Railway Act 1913; Housing Act 1914; Anglo-Persian Oil Co. (Acquisition of Capital) Acts 1914 and 1919; and (Payment of Calls) Act 1922; West Indian Islands (Telegraph) Act 1924.

Rows may not sum because of rounding.

Source: *BGS*, pp. 343-51.

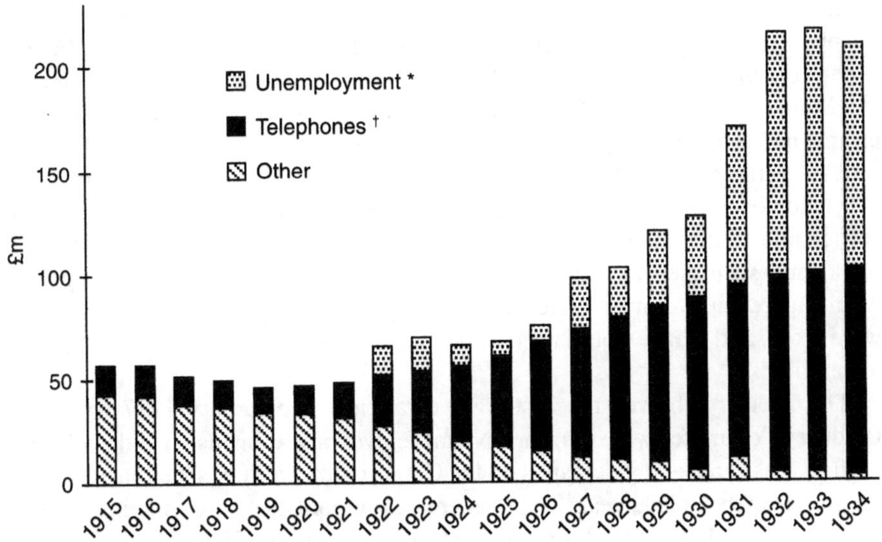

Figure 20.1 Other capital liabilities: 31 March 1915 to 1934.
*Advances under the Unemployment Insurance Acts 1920–31.
† Advances under the Telegraph Acts 1892–1925.

Source: *BGS*, pp. 343, 345 and 351.

were telephones and unemployment that if they had been excluded other capital liabilities would have fallen from £34.7m at end-March 1919 to £4.1m at end-March 1933 (Table 20.7; Figure 20.1).[m]

The system of advance and repayment worked quietly, rarely catching the public eye. An exception was 1931, when the savings banks had difficulty finding the money for Advances to the Unemployment Fund and played a minor role in that year's political crisis. Savings banks' ability to lend to the Treasury depended on the growth in deposits, cash balances, repayments of earlier Advances, receipts from their annuities and sales of marketable securities. The machinery for Local Loans and Irish land purchase differed from that for capital advances. When the Local Loans Fund borrowed from the savings banks (or from other funds under the Commissioners' management), they were issued with newly created 3 per cent Local Loans Stock. If the market permitted, this could be sold to the public, freeing the savings banks to acquire further securities or make further Advances. Thus, between 1919 and 1933, funds managed by the Commissioners increased their holdings of Local Loans Stock by only £54.7m, although they were issued with £272.1m.[68] The system for Irish land purchase was similar, the security created

m These data exclude advances made under the Telephone Transfer Act 1911 for the purchase of the National Telephone Co., which was financed with 3 per cent Exchequer Bonds 1930. *BGS*, pp. 345–51.

being 3 per cent Guaranteed Stock.[n] When the savings banks made Advances for telephones, they received a Terminable Annuity charged on the Post Office Votes. When Advances were made to the Unemployment Fund, they were a charge on the Ministry of Labour Vote and evidenced by a certificate of indebtedness, promising repayment in five years. These, unlike Local Loans and Guaranteed Stocks, were unmarketable. In the second half of the 1920s and until support for the unemployed was put on the Votes in September 1931, deposits were not growing sufficiently to meet the Treasury's demands and the Commissioners had to sell marketable securities. In so doing, they were selling liquid securities, whose prices would appreciate as interest rates fell, and acquiring illiquid claims, whose prices were fixed, and which would need to be reinvested on maturity at, it was feared, lower yields.

The Treasury showed the first signs of anxiety in February 1927 when the Bradbury Committee was sitting and Niemeyer was preparing his second evidence. Phillips was forecasting demands on the Commissioners' funds well in excess of the growth in their resources.[69] The smaller local authorities were borrowing heavily from the Local Loans Fund for housing,[o] Advances to the Unemployment Fund were rising, savings bank deposits had suffered during the previous year of industrial unrest and the savings bank funds had been selling gilt-edged securities (Tables 20.6 and 20.7).The National Health Insurance Fund, which had been accumulating assets, was turning seller. The only source of new money was the Widows Pension Fund, but this was to run down from the beginning of 1928. Although the Treasury had completed a successful conversion offer at the beginning of the year, it did not want to make a public issue of Local Loans Stock as the market had not yet absorbed the paper acquired by the CNRA and it faced further maturities in the autumn. Phillips's comment to Niemeyer was:

> If we are to go on without a public local loans issue, I think our policy of selling securities may perhaps need to be looked out [*sic*]. It is better in general to sell long term stuff than short but this ruthless slaughter of all our best securities, £1,000,000 a week last year, is having a specially depressing effect on conversion prospects. It may be well to consider if we should not at any rate sell <u>some</u> Bonds (of which National Debt Commissioners have an unlimited supply) particularly those that are close to or over redemption price.[70]

Although demand from the local authorities fell back after 1928 and the

n The Commissioners made no sales of 3 per cent Guaranteed Stock after the war because the market was very thin and it was assumed that it would have to be repurchased for the Irish Land Purchase Fund (the sinking fund) at a higher price. In the event, the sinking fund was invested in other securities. *BGS*, pp. 210–11; T 160/403/F13113, Phillips to Hopkins, 28 February 1930, and Headlam to Chancellor, 20 February 1931.

o The funds managed by the Commissioners were issued with £2.4m Local Loans Stock in 1923–4, £28.6m in 1924–5, £40.4m in 1925–6, £57.5m in 1926–7, £31.1m in 1927–8, £25.1m in 1928–9, £18m in 1929–30, and £8.7m in 1930–1.

Commissioners were able to sell Local Loans to the market, Advances for telephones and unemployment continued to grow. By October 1930, Phillips described himself as 'becoming panic stricken about the position of the N.D.O.' His worry was the deteriorating liquidity of the assets. From this point of view, he described £157m as 'complete washouts' (Advances), £141m as 'duds' ($2^1/_2$ per cent Consols and the Irish Land Stocks), £79m as 'dubious' (Local Loans, saleable in driblets, and very short Treasury Bonds, which ought not to be sold to the public at all) and only £20m as 'good stuff'. Of a portfolio of £397m, 'good stuff' was only 5 per cent, or the 'amount we make Municipal Banks keep in cash'.

> The policy of financing these Govt. operations *sub silentio* through N.D.O. has definitely reached the breaking point after many years. Short of some operation which would replace old Consols by a readily marketable security, we absolutely must have a public long term loan not later than the Spring for Local Loans/or telephones.

In the meantime, as an emergency measure, the Issue Department should take Local Loans and short Bonds from the savings banks and sell them or, if necessary, hold them.[71] Starting that month, Issue bought Local Loans (£5.4m in December alone) from the Commissioners, while selling them heavily into the market.[72]

Phillips's panic had been occasioned by the prospect of a formal letter from Maurice Headlam, Comptroller-General of the NDO, which drew attention to the low level of readily saleable securities in the savings bank funds.[73] When the position continued to deteriorate, he sent a further protest in February 1931, requesting specific authority from the Chancellor, in his capacity as a Commissioner, to continue selling and asking for new instructions.[74] Phillips agreed the situation was parlous:

> It is an immense convenience that the Funds exist because they enable the government to obtain the capital sums that it needs for such domestic purposes week by week and year by year without ever resorting to a public issue and without any publicity. But obviously this must stop when the available money has all been borrowed and we are now getting very near that state of affairs.

He estimated that the savings bank holdings of quoted securities would be only £88m by the end of March and £36m a year later. Of these, £30m were illiquid $2^1/_2$ per cent Consols and £44m were maturing short Bonds, purchased to aid conversion operations, which should remain in official hands. By the end of the following financial year, the Treasury would be forced to seek external funds. In the meantime, Issue could take the few marketable securities remaining, although this would involve a rise in the floating debt as it sold Treasury Bills to pay for them. Phillips warned that the drying up of the savings bank funds and increased borrowing in the open market would be 'exceedingly inconvenient to Government financial operations', but there was no 'real remedy however except in a reduction of Unemployment Fund borrowing.'[75]

'Inconvenient' meant politically embarrassing. The Treasury had no power itself to borrow and onlend to the Post Office or the Unemployment Fund. Borrowing would need to be in the name of the borrowers themselves, albeit with a Treasury guarantee. There would be issues of, say, Treasury Bills (Unemployment) or Treasury Bonds (Telephones). Although a unified issue combining telephones and unemployment was envisaged, the largest element would be for unemployment. The Treasury feared damage to government credit, and Snowden the political repercussions of 'dole' Bonds.

Another warning was sent by the NDO at the beginning of May 1931. The cash value of the savings banks' marketable long-dated and perpetual issues had been reduced to £3.3m, or the equivalent of three weeks' Advances to the Unemployment Fund. In addition, they held £15.1m Local Loans, worth £10.3m. The Chancellor was warned that any further sales would endanger the normal day-to-day running of the NDO and it was recommended that the Treasury should start raising money for the Unemployment Fund from the public.[76] In the middle of May, Headlam saw the Governor who agreed, as a stopgap, to take more Local Loans for a week and then, unwillingly, to take some short Bonds. He refused to touch 2½ per cent Consols.[77] Writing three days later, Phillips concluded that the Commissioners would have to sell sufficient Local Loans, whether to the Bank or in the market, to make the Local Loans Fund self-supporting. The 2½ per cent Consols would have to go, despite their poor marketability, the establishment of a loss and their potential to rise in capital value if yields fell. The Bank might take short Bonds, although it was inconvenient for market management and would increase the floating debt in the hands of the public. If the Bank refused, the securities would have to be sold in the market. Finally, he agreed that these measures might be supplemented in the autumn by a public issue of Bonds for unemployment. [78] The Bank took the shorts: from June 1931 until February the following year, after which the Issue Department ledgers cease distinguishing between purchases from the market and those from the Commissioners, the Department was a continuous buyer of 4½ per cent Treasury 1930–2 and, from September, 4½ per cent Treasury 1932–4.[79] It was still only an expedient, with Phillips estimating that Advances would reach £300m by the end of March 1932 and that just £35m of other assets would remain to meet deposit liabilities.[80]

The savings bank funds: autumn 1931

At the beginning of August 1931, as selling of sterling continued, Phillips told Hopkins that, with the help of the sale of short Bonds, he 'thought they would get through until November certainly and quite likely to well after Xmas.' In the meantime, the Chancellor should be warned, so that the problem could be included in the Cabinet economy committee's discussions about the financing of the Unemployment Fund and the level of benefit.[81] On 8 August, Hopkins handed a memorandum to the Chancellor:

The May Committee strongly recommend that borrowing for the

> Unemployment Fund should cease after the present year and that any deficit, whatever it may be, should be provided out of Revenue…
>
> In the present note I am leaving on one side the merits of this recommendation. My purpose is to call attention to the fact that, if the May recommendation is not adopted and borrowing continues, the present methods of borrowing cannot continue. Indeed an important and difficult change may be forced upon us within a few months from now.[82]

Four days later, on 12 August, the economy committee began its discussions. A background paper, designed by Snowden to nudge opinion towards expenditure cuts, had been circulated two days earlier. As well as revising the budget deficits for 1931–2 and 1932–3 and warning that the limits of direct taxation of higher incomes had been reached, it advocated putting all unemployment benefit on the Votes. One reason for doing this was the shortage of marketable paper in the savings bank portfolios:

> Hitherto borrowing for the Unemployment Fund has been managed in an unobtrusive and practically secret way. Every week as the fund [*sic*] has required money, the National Debt Office has found it…But within a few months from now this resource will have come to an end, the National Debt Office having run dry. All money required for the Unemployment fund [*sic*] must then be borrowed direct from the public. 'Dole Bonds' as they would inevitably be called, however carefully they may be dressed up, would quite obviously be difficult to place and their issue would still further depress Government credit.[83]

The decision to meet the cost of supporting the unemployed from revenue came in the nick of time, but the problem which had been faced that summer was loosely related to a spat between the National Government and the Labour party in the final days of the election campaign in October. Henderson, the leader of the Labour Party between the time it split and the election, used the POSB's deposits as an example of the safety of small savings in a state-owned credit system. This provoked Walter Runciman, who was to become President of the Board of Trade in the new government, into claiming that in both April and August the Labour government had become anxious about the deposits:

> A substantial part of the assets of the Post Office Savings Bank had already been lent to the Insurance Fund. That brought home to the Cabinet the difficulties with which they would be faced if serious distrust of British credit set in.

Snowden said that he had warned the Labour leaders of the threat to savings deposits and MacDonald was reported as admitting that the government had, at one time, been 'concerned at the position'. In his turn, Henderson pointed to the government guarantee and accused the National Government of striking 'a dangerous and treacherous blow at British credit both at home and abroad' by questioning the ability of the British government to meet its obligations. The subject was taken up with vigour by the *Daily Mail*, which gave the danger to small savers in the POSB and the extravagance of the Labour government some colourful and unbalanced coverage on its main news pages.[84]

It was reopened in November, when George Lansbury (the leader of the Labour Party in the Commons after Henderson lost his seat at the election) claimed that it was a 'low trick' to use such a suggestion to beat the Labour Party and demanded that Runciman should clarify his statement. If memory invoked during a Commons exchange can be relied on, the problem was not understood by at least one member of the Labour Cabinet, Jim Thomas recalling that they had 'received an official intimation that not another copper could be borrowed for the Unemployment Fund'.[85]

In briefing the new Chancellor, Neville Chamberlain, to meet the same attack, Hopkins adjusted his emphasis:

> The real danger to the Savings Bank depositor was, I think, the fear of a run due to panic: in any first class crisis a run on Savings Banks is one of the things a Government most fears. The danger was aggravated by the fact, – which might at any moment receive publicity, – that a large part of the assets were frozen, – and this would have increased the panic because depositors would not stop to think that the Government guarantee was their primary safeguard.[86]

Dalton says that the threat of a run was mentioned by MacDonald when explaining the collapse of the government to junior ministers on 24 August, but how much weight was actually placed on the possibility is unclear.[87] There is no evidence that this concern played a part in the Treasury's treatment of the problem in 1930 and 1931. It was the limit to the finance of the Advances *sub silentio*, the rise in the floating debt in market hands as the Issue Department sold Treasury Bills to buy the savings banks' securities and the threat to government credit if the Unemployment Fund had been forced to borrow in the markets that exercised officials.

In one sense, there was no problem. Savings bank deposits enjoyed the guarantee of the Consolidated Fund and the assets could be viewed as part of the machinery for using the deposits. The immediate monetary effects of a run on the savings banks, whether financed by loans from the Treasury or by sales of marketable assets to the Issue Department, were the same – an increase in the floating debt in the hands of the public and the implied need to increase sales of gilt-edged securities to the market at the next opportunity. Inasmuch as there was a problem, it was self-inflicted. The savings banks' funds were a great convenience to governments wanting to finance expenditure outside the budget without exposing themselves to public scrutiny at inconvenient moments. Snowden could have chosen to raise the money for Unemployment Advances by making a public issue, leaving the savings banks' assets undisturbed. The decision to continue selling marketable securities until holdings were almost dry and normal market management threatened, was partly politics – the avoidance of critical fire as 'dole Bonds' were offered to the public – and partly the desire to avoid presenting government credit as an easy target. It was only in November that Hopkins pointed to the real threat. The savings banks would not have been able to meet a major run because their Advances were unmarketable. Publicity would have accompanied Treasury help, attention would have been drawn to the existing method of financing the Unemployment Fund, and any run on deposits could have fed on itself.

Endnotes

1 Cab. 27/66, Interim Report of the Treasury Committee on Housing Finance, 27 November 1919, and Draft Conclusions of the Finance Sub-Committee of the Housing Committee, 17 November 1919; Morgan and Morgan (1980), pp. 100–1 and 109–10.
2 *The Economist*, 8 May 1920, p. 955.
3 Housing (Financial Assistance) Committee, *Final Report*, (Ministry of Reconstruction) (Cd. 9238), 5 February 1919.
4 T 160/41/F1356, Islington to Chamberlain, 4, 11 and 14 May 1920, and Islington, 'The National Savings Organisation and the Housing Bond Campaign', 4 May 1920.
5 Ibid., Chancellor to Blackett and Niemeyer, 4 May 1920.
6 Ibid., Niemeyer to Blackett, 6 May 1920, with note by Blackett, Niemeyer to Blackett, 'Lord Islington's letter on Housing', 17 May 1920, and Blackett to Chancellor, 18 May 1920.
7 Ibid., Islington to Chamberlain, 11 May 1920, and Annex, Grigg to Islington, 12 May 1920.
8 Ibid., Niemeyer, 'Lord Islington's letter on Housing', 17 May 1920.
9 *Hansard* (Commons), 19 April 1920, cols 76–7; T 160/41/F1356, Blackett to Chancellor, 18 May 1920.
10 T 160/41/F1356, JEH Findlay to Niemeyer, 14 May 1920, and Blackett to Baldwin, 31 May 1920.
11 Ibid., Niemeyer to Baldwin, 20 May 1920, Blackett to Baldwin, 31 May 1920, Niemeyer, 'Alternative', 15 June 1920, and Niemeyer to Heath, 16 June 1920.
12 Cab. 27/71, FC 28 (2) and (7), 29 November 1920; Cab. 27/72, FC 66, 'Memorandum by the Minister of Health', 25 January 1921.
13 Morgan and Morgan (1980), pp. 128–9; Cab. 27/71, FC 35 (1), 30 June 1921.
14 T 160/894/F1753/1, Margerison to Treasury, 25 April 1921, Niemeyer to Strohmenger, 21 June 1921, Strohmenger to Niemeyer, 23 June 1921, Niemeyer to Blackett, 25 June 1921, Islington to Chancellor, 13 July 1921, Chancellor to Islington, 14 September 1921.
15 Ibid., Niemeyer to Blackett, 'Savings Certificates Deputation', 28 July 1921.
16 Committee of Enquiry into Savings Certificates and Local Loans, etc. (Second Montagu Committee), *Report* (Cmd. 1865), 1923, pp. 7 and 9–10.
17 Ibid.,pp. 19–20; T 160/158/F6178, Niemeyer to the Commissioners, 12 May 1923.
18 *BGS*, p. 556; National Savings Committee, *Sixteenth Annual Report*.
19 T 160/894/F1753/1, Blackett to Chancellor, 1 August 1921; T 160/107/F4035/1, Niemeyer to Blackett, 24 November 1921; Committee on the Maturity of Savings Certificates of the First Issue (Lubbock Committee), *Report* (Cmd. 2610), 1926, p. 7; *National Debt: annual returns*, 1922; National Savings Committee, *Sixth Annual Report*.
20 T 160/107/F4035/1, Sydney-Turner, 'Savings Certificates', 5 June 1923.

21 Ibid., Joy, 'Memorandum', June 1923, Sydney-Turner, 'Savings Certificates', 5 June 1923, Sydney-Turner to A.K. Wright, July 1923, and unsigned to Bunbury, 12 July 1923.
22 Ibid., Margerison to Niemeyer, 22 June 1923.
23 T 160/107/F4035/2, Ismay, 'Savings Certificates: Commission to Banks', 12 October 1923, Niemeyer to Islington, 23 October 1923, Martin-Holland to Fass, 28 October 1923, Islington to Chancellor, 29 October 1923, Circular from Martin-Holland to banks, October 1923, Schooling to Niemeyer, 29 January 1924, and Niemeyer to Financial Secretary, 1 February 1924; National Savings Committee, *Eighth Annual Report*.
24 Committee on the Maturity of Savings Certificates of the First Issue, *Interim and Final Reports* (Cmd. 2610), 1926,
25 T 160/261/F10367/03, Phillips, 'Savings Certificates of the First Series: Extension of Term', 12 November 1925.
26 Committee on the Maturity of Savings Certificates of the First Issue, paras 10, 11–16.
27 T 160/261/F10367/03, Phillips, 'Final Report of the Committee on Savings Certificates', 27 February 1926. Underlining in the original.
28 T 176/18, Holmes, 'National Savings Certificates', 30 October 1925; Committee on National Debt and Taxation, *Minutes of Evidence*, Niemeyer, para. 8726.
29 BoE, C40/399, 'Treasury Bills', p. 14, and TM, 31 May 1889.
30 T 160/1025/F13866/1, 'National Savings Certificates: Report by the Government Actuary', 16 March 1928.
31 T 177/6, Churchill to Fisher and Hopkins, 27 September 1927.
32 Ibid., Niemeyer to Chancellor, 'The Year 1926', 18 February 1927, Phillips, 'Savings Certificates', October 1927, and Holmes, 10 March 1927; T 160/1062/F1037/1, Phillips to Niemeyer, 29 June 1927.
33 T 177/6, Hopkins to Chancellor via Fisher, October 1927.
34 T 160/1062/F1037/1, Phillips to Niemeyer, 14 June 1927.
35 Ibid., Phillips to Niemeyer, 14 and 29 June 1927, Ismay to Margerison, 1 July 1927, Ismay to Bond, 11 August 1927; T 160/1062/F10367/2, Ismay to Leith-Ross, 8 August 1927.
36 T 160/1062/F10367/2, Hopkins to Chancellor, 24 March 1928.
37 T 160/1063/F10367/4, Waterfield, 'Savings Certificates', 10 November 1931, Phillips to Hopkins, 13 November 1931, Hopkins to Chancellor, 26 November 1931; T 160/1063/F10367/5, Waterfield to Hopkins, 'National Savings Certificates', 9 December 1931; T 175/59, Hopkins to Seely, 30 November 1931; BoE, C40/408, 'Savings Bonds', 20 July 1931; BoE, C40/408, unsigned, 23 November 1931, and Lefeaux to Waterfield, 25 November 1931.
38 National Savings Committee, *Sixteenth Annual Report*.
39 T 160/1063/F10367/5, Ismay to Waterfield, 21 March 1932, and Press Notice, 31 March 1932.
40 T 160/532/F13096, Ismay to Waterfield, 'Savings Certificates – New Series', 15 May 1932, Phillips to Waterfield, 23 May 1932, Waterfield to Phillips and Hopkins, 'National Savings Certificates: New Fourth Series', 25 May 1932, with notes by Phillips and Elliot, Elliot to Chancellor, 2 June 1932, with note by Chancellor, Elliot to Seely, 6 June 1932, and Seely to Elliot, 8 June 1932; *Hansard* (Commons), 30 June 1932, col. 2135.
41 T 160/532/F13096, Waterfield to Phillips and Hopkins, 'Savings Certificates', 16 June 1932, and Hopkins to Baldwin, 29 June 1932; National Savings Committee, *Seventeenth Annual Report*.
42 Committee of Enquiry into Savings Certificates and Local Loans, etc. *Report*, Report of Sub-committee, paras 8–21; Horne (1947), 336–7.
43 T 160/107/F4035/1, Joy, 5 June 1923.

44 Committee of Enquiry into Savings Certificates and Local Loans, etc. *Report*, paras 22–36. This recommendation did not apply to TSBs because the Committee considered that the independence and local nature of the TSBs made it 'less easy to secure' their co-operation.
45 Horne (1947), pp. 338 and 343–4; Committee on Municipal Savings Banks, *Report*, paras 144–6; *The Economist*, 10 January 1931, p. 74; T 160/532/F13096, Ismay to Waterfield, 10 May 1932.
46 T 160/1090/F16070/2, Committee on Small Savings, Report, 10 August 1939.
47 T 160/1387/F3779/01/1, Joy, Memorandum, 21 July 1919; BoE, G3/175, Cokayne to Blackett, 20 October 1919.
48 T 160/1387/F3779/01/1, Sydney-Turner to Niemeyer, undated, Sydney-Turner, 'Savings Banks Limits', 14 August 1922, with comment by Blackett, 15 August 1922; Horne (1947), p. 327. The regulation was the 'Savings Banks (Limits of Annual Deposit) Order, 1923', 23 March 1923.
49 T 160/1305/F3756/1, Gatliff, 'Post Office Savings Bank Rate of Interest', 2 March 1928; T 160/1305, Phillips, 'Savings Bank Finance', 10 July 1929, and Hopkins to Chancellor, 16 July 1929; Committee on War Loans for the Small Investor (First Montagu Committee), *Report*, para. 11; Committee on Municipal Savings Banks, *Report*, para. 98.
50 *Hansard* (Commons), 26 March 1929, cols 2368–74.
51 *Hansard* (Lords), 2 May 1931, cols 397–8. See also 23 April 1931, cols 115–18, and 30 April 1931, cols 244–8.
52 For example, see Labour Party leaflet 256. A copy is in T 160/1305/F3756/2. T 160/1305/F3756/2, McKenzie to Pethick-Lawrence, 18 September 1929; *Hansard* (Commons), 11 July 1929, col. 1090, 18 July 1929, col. 664, 23 July 1929, col. 1077, 24 December 1929, col. 2103, 23 January 1930, col. 357, 4 March 1930, col. 258, and 6 May 1930, cols 759–60.
53 The papers and correspondence are in T 160/1305/F3756/1.
54 T 160/1305/F3756/2, Ismay, 'Savings Banks Rate of Interest', 1929, Headlam, 'Notes on Mr. Ismay's Suggestions as to Interest Concessions', undated, and Gatliff to Ismay, 24 March and 10 June 1929.
55 Ibid., Phillips, 'Savings Bank Finance', 10 July 1929, Hopkins to Chancellor, 16 July 1929, Hopkins to Phillips, 23 July 1929, 'Resolution by the Scottish Area of the Trustee Banks Association', 31 October 1929, Headlam to Treasury, 27 November 1929, Gatliff to Sydney-Turner, 4 December 1929, and Phillips to Hopkins, 21 December 1929.
56 Housing (Financial Assistance) Committee, *Final Report*, (Ministry of Reconstruction) (Cd. 9238), 5 February 1919.
57 T 160/1170/F4850/2, Niemeyer to Bradbury, 3 July 1919; Committee on Municipal Savings Banks *Report*, para. 8; Horne (1947), p. 322.
58 T 160/1170/F4850/2, Bradbury to Chancellor, 10 July 1919.
59 ibid., Gower to Bradbury and Niemeyer, 14 July 1919.
60 T 160/1410/F9615/2, Niemeyer, 2 and 10 February 1926; Horne (1947), p. 340; *Labour and the Nation*, p. 26; *The Citizen*, February 1929; T 160/1411/F9615/5, Hopkins to Fisher, Financial Secretary and Chancellor, 5 February 1930; *Hansard* (Commons), 22 February 1928, cols 1679–1736.
61 T 160/250/F9615/019, Gatliff, 'Municipal Savings Bank Committee', briefing for Niemeyer, undated, and Niemeyer, second evidence to Bradbury, undated, probably March 1927; T 160/1410/F9615/4, Note for Chancellor and Fisher, 8 December 1927, and Note for Ismay, December 1927. The evidence is in T 160/247/F9615/01/1–5.
62 T 160/250/F9615/019, Niemeyer, second evidence to Bradbury, undated, probably March 1927; Committee on Municipal Savings Banks, *Report*, Appendix 2.
63 Committee on Municipal Savings Banks, *Report*, para. 149.

64 T 160/1411/F9615/5, Pethick-Lawrence, 'Cardiff and Birkenhead applications for Municipal Banks', 13 February 1930, with comments by Snowden. When the cases first came up to the Chancellor, Snowden gave consent to both. On further consideration, he decided that Birkenhead should be refused since it already had a branch of the Liverpool TSB and the town was too small. Birkenhead protested that its population had grown from 147,000 at the 1921 census to over 159,000. It seems that, when Pethick-Lawrence was preparing his statement on the restrictions which the Treasury would apply to the banks, he slipped in a minimum size of 150,000, instead of the 200,000 agreed with Snowden, and Birkenhead had to be authorised. See the papers in T 160/1411/F9615/6 and T 160/1411/F9615/6, Compton to Ismay, 8 May 1934.

65 T 160/1411/F9615/5, Phillips to Hopkins, 27 January 1930, Headlam to Chancellor, January 1930, Hopkins to Fisher, Financial Secretary, 5 February 1930, Pethick-Lawrence, 'Cardiff and Birkenhead applications for Municipal Banks', 13 February 1930, with comments by Snowden; T 160/1411/F9615/6, Ismay to JJ Wills, 7 June 1934; T 160/1411/F9615/7, Waterfield, 'Municipal Savings Banks', 19 January 1935; *Hansard* (Commons), 20 February 1930, cols 1569–70, and 30 April 1930, cols 317–21.

66 The papers are in T 160/1411/F9615/8. For Dalton's statement see *Hansard* (Commons), 16 July 1946, cols 1049–50.

67 *National Debt: annual returns*; T 160/158/F6165, Holmes, 28 March 1923 (two memoranda), Fass to Niemeyer, 29 March 1923, Heath to Treasury, 29 March 1923, and TM, 29 March 1923.

68 *BGS*, pp. 212, 483 and 497. The figures are not strictly comparable as the issues are for the years ending 31 March and the funds managed by the Commissioners had other year-ends.

69 T 160/1410/F9615/3, Phillips, 'Capital Expenditure', 18 February 1927.

70 T 160/248/F9615/03, Phillips to Niemeyer, 18 February 1927. Underlining in the original.

71 T 160/403/F13113, Phillips to Hopkins, 2 October 1930. The paper is marked '[19]30' overwritten with '[19]31'. Internal evidence places the year as 1930.

72 Issue Department Ledgers.

73 T 160/403/F13113, Headlam to Treasury, 3 October 1930.

74 Ibid., Headlam to Phillips, 16 February 1931, and Headlam to Chancellor, 20 February 1931.

75 Ibid., Phillips to Hopkins, 'Mr. Headlam's Memorandum to the Chancellor', 28 February 1931.

76 Ibid.,Headlam to Chancellor, 1 May 1931.

77 Ibid., Headlam to Phillips, 13 May 1931.

78 Ibid., Phillips, 15 May 1931.

79 Issue Department Ledgers.

80 T 160/403/F13113, Phillips, 15 May 1931.

81 Ibid., Phillips to Hopkins, with draft of brief for the Chancellor, first week in August 1931, and Hopkins to Harvey, 6 August 1931.

82 Ibid., Hopkins to Chancellor, 8 August 1931. Underlining in the original.

83 T 171/288, N.E. 31(2), 'Cabinet Committee on the Report of the Committee on National Expenditure: Note by the Chancellor of the Exchequer', about 10 August 1931; Williamson (1992), p. 295.

84 *Daily Mail*, 26 October 1931, pp. 10 and 11, and 27 October 1931, p. 11; *The Times*, 24 October 1931, p. 15, and 26 October 1931, p. 8. Dalton (1953), pp. 295 and 297; Middlemas and Barnes (1969), p. 651; Pethick-Lawrence (1943), pp. 168–9. There is a cutting of the 26 October article from *The Times* in T 172/1752.

85 *Hansard* (Commons), 10 November 1931, col. 56, and 16 November 1931, cols 537–40. Also, see 11 November 1931, cols 120–1, 13 November 1931, col. 448, 16 November 1931, col. 528, 17 November 1931, cols 668–9, and 18 November 1931, cols 853–4.
86 T 172/1752, Hopkins to Fergusson, 11 November 1931.
87 Dalton (1953), p. 272.

21 Debt repayment and the sinking funds

> So long as we have a national debt of £6,000,000,000 to £8,000,000,000 with an annual debt charge of £300,000,000 to £400,000,000 the rentier will be the subject of perpetual jealousy and perpetual attack: the owners of other forms of capital wealth whose property could, at any rate in the opinion of a large section of the public, be appropriated to meet the rentier's claims will be in a position scarcely less vulnerable. The slower the restoration of general prosperity, the heavier will become the pressure of taxation and the greater the popular discontent.
>
> John Bradbury, 'Conscription of Wealth',
> 29 January 1918, T 171/167.

For the pre-war Treasury, debt repayment in time of peace had been an unquestioned policy. Only thus could taxes be reduced in peacetime and, it was thought, damage to government credit minimised in wartime. This assumption was not far from the surface when, in June 1925, Niemeyer described the goals of the Treasury's financial policy since the Armistice to have been to balance the budget out of revenue, to reduce the Debt and to cut public expenditure, so remitting taxation.[1] As so often, he was simplifying to make a case. Since the Armistice, the Debt's size and structure had been a monetary, budgetary and, above all, a political question. In the immediate aftermath of the war, a large floating debt had hampered the disciplining of the boom. Advised that funding would be impossible, a Conservative Chancellor raised taxes to help repay floating debt and came near to imposing a radical solution, a levy on wealth accumulated during the war. A conservative fiscal policy – high taxes, controlled expenditure and revenue surpluses – helped set the tone for refinancing or converting the constant stream of maturities, a threat to monetary control if they ran off into cash, and to the budget if they were refinanced clumsily. A sinking fund, the Treasury advised, was a pre-condition for a reduction in debt costs. It was a 'good thing to redeem your debt,' Niemeyer told the Colwyn Committee, but it was not the main purpose of a sinking fund, which was to improve 'our credit' and 'enable us to deal on more favourable terms with the opportunity' that the heavy maturities presented.[2] The great prize, and the most immediate incentive for Chancellors to keep to virtuous paths, was the prospect of converting 5 per cent War Loan. Other arguments were used – repayments would not be spent by recipients, but passed straight through as increased finance for industry, financial preparations had to be made in case of another war – but prospective budgetary savings were always at the forefront.

Before the South African War, officials had sought to hide the sinking funds, 'wrapping' them in legislation and obfuscation, to deter importunate Chancellors. In 1905, Hamilton advised that annuities should not be renewed as they fell, in part because it would reassure creditors if the effort involved in maintaining repayment was more visible.[3] After 1919, the necessity for advertising the size of the sinking fund was even greater. Hence, in part, the contrast between the advertised sinking fund and its reality. Early in the post-war decade, receipts from sales of war stores, departmental balances and allied and colonial debt repayments were used as revenue on a scale which dwarfed the debt ostensibly repaid. In 1923, three years' interest on the US Treasury debt was capitalised. In the second half of the decade, Churchill appropriated assets to protect the sinking fund, a habit followed on a lesser scale by the orthodox Snowden. Throughout, there were major counterweights to the published repayment: borrowing outside the budget for unemployment and telephones and capitalisation of interest on Savings Certificates. Thus, to the traditional suspicion of politicians' weakness was added present delinquency to make officials fear for the sinking funds.

If repayment was to be advertised, protective devices were ever more necessary. A statutory sinking fund treated as budgetary expenditure was retained. Contractual or statutory sinking funds attached to individual issues, introduced during the war to reassure investors that the price of their holdings would not depreciate, were later presented as reasons for maintaining repayment from revenue. Both were evidence of officials' commitment to the tradition of debt repayment and their suspicion of politicians. However, Baldwin's sinking fund was weaker than Northcote's since the interest saved was not added to the fund and rises in interest costs fed directly into the budget. Its replacement, Churchill's Fixed Charge, was scarcely expected to cover the interest accruing on Savings Certificates.

The protection afforded by attached sinking funds was bought at the price of the flexibility built into the pre-war system. Savings bank annuities wrapped in a Fixed Charge involved no contract with the public holder of securities; the arrangements were internal to the Treasury and the Commissioners, albeit sanctioned by statute. Although designed to make tampering difficult or, at least, public, the Treasury was left with the freedom to prolong or terminate the annuities. This was regarded by Hamilton as one of the great advantages of the machinery (see pp. 8 and 10). It was a most basic distinction, but was never mentioned by post-war officials, perhaps because it undermined their case for an invulnerable sinking fund.

This chapter describes the debate over a capital levy and Austen Chamberlain's flirtation with a tax on war accumulations as a means of bringing the floating debt under control. It explains the role of repayment from revenue in the Treasury's debt management plans, before showing how the Baldwin sinking fund was introduced. The frailty of that mechanism was so great that it was soon replaced by a Fixed Charge, whose design was stronger, but whose size was inadequate.

Finally, the chapter describes Snowden's moves to strengthen repayment, before priorities changed in the first half of the 1930s.

A general levy on capital

A tax assessed on the value of individuals' assets, a 'levy on capital', was initially used to describe a small annual payment to help defray the cost of the war. Later, it described a tax, levied only once, whose proceeds would be used to repay part, or all, of the National Debt. With this meaning, it was at the centre of a debate between 1917 and 1923 about the affect of the Debt on economic growth and the part its cancellation might play in redistributing wealth. It also came to be applied to a tax on increases in the value of wealth, loosely called war profits, which had accrued since 1914. This would have been more limited in its incidence and came near to being implemented, partly to satisfy the widespread demand for action against 'war profiteers' but mainly as a measure to reduce the floating debt.

A levy on capital had been mooted after Marlborough's Wars by the MP Archibald Hutcheson, and after the Napoleonic Wars by David Ricardo, but its modern origins lay in the radical wing of the Liberal Party and with liberal economists, who were mainly responsible for elaborating its details. The proposals were not fully developed until 1918, but the increased scope of conscription in 1916 had provoked the Labour Party and the trade union leadership to join radical liberals in questioning why people had been coerced and wealth had not. By 1921 or 1922, the levy had become the property of the labour movement, but between 1916 and 1921 it enjoyed broad cross-party support.[4] Liberal economists, and those seeking to exploit the potential of the levy for redistributing wealth, gave it the most consistent backing, but at one time or another, and in one form or another, contingent on practicability and equity, figures as diverse as Asquith, Bonar Law, Austen Chamberlain, Churchill, Beaverbrook, Montagu, Addison, Cassel, Pigou, Keynes, Bradbury, Blackett and Niemeyer were sympathetic to the proposal.

As long as the war continued, the Treasury could not countenance any form of capital levy. A tax assumed to be paid from capital would not release current production for war purposes, so officials accepted from the start that the proceeds could only be used to pay off debt. It would have taken a year to pass legislation, set up the administrative machinery and then conduct a census of wealth; in the interval, the uncertainty would have disturbed the war savings campaign and checked the sale of securities. Even when the revenue started to flow, the levy would have been insufficient to cover war expenditure unless it were repeated annually, so that new borrowing would have continued alongside it.[5] However, 1917 found both Bonar Law and Bradbury receptive to a levy once the war was over. In September 1916, the TUC passed a resolution demanding increased direct taxation, including a levy.[a] When, in February 1917, a deputation delivered the resolution to the Chancellor, he pointed to the high rates already being paid in

a It was symptomatic of its confusion that the resolution failed to make it clear whether the TUC had in mind the finance of expenditure or the cancellation of debt.

EPD, income tax and supertax: he thought it would be 'folly' to have a levy while the war continued, but when peace came it would simply be a question of whether it was best for the country to have a levy and reduce the Debt immediately, or repay it from traditional taxes over a long period.[6] The comment was not reported in the press until the following October, shortly before the Chancellor received another deputation representing several factions from within the labour movement. This drew from him the same sentiments, stated more freely and with greater emphasis. He also offered his own opinion, which he later claimed to have been unconsidered, that:

> ...it would be better, both for the wealthy classes and the country, to have this Levy on capital and reduce the burden of the National Debt; that is my own feeling.[7]

The reaction when the remarks became public a week later provoked articles, comment and letters in the press, the start of a general controversy which continued until well into the following decade. It also showed that the Chancellor's views were not shared by many of his own party, industrialists, bankers or the Conservative press and he had to extricate himself as best he could.[8]

In two papers prepared for the Chancellor that winter, Bradbury used many of the arguments which would later be at the centre of the public debate. The Debt was a mortgage on wealth and the income derived from it. The income tax could be regarded as a 'rent charge' on the income-producing power of wealth. If the state took a proportion of all assets, the income could be used to pay the interest on the Debt. In this way, existing wealth would be attacked and the fruits of future exertion and new saving would be left free from the burden of interest and sinking fund. However, he warned that the immediate cash yield would be small and it was 'therefore an engine of post-war readjustment, not a machine for raising "money" for expenditure.' Action should be postponed to enable war fortunes to be included, and because the insecurity would threaten current saving and subscriptions to War Bonds. He agreed that there would be a collapse in asset prices if a levy was demanded in cash and used for current spending, but buyers would equal sellers provided the proceeds were used to buy government debt for cancellation, thus returning cash to debt holders for reinvestment as fast as it was taken from the levy payers. Other securities would be held by the state until buyers could be found, landowners might surrender a proportion of their estates or a charge over them and owners of private businesses provide a mortgage or annuity. As the Treasury liquidated the assets, the proceeds would be applied to the purchase of debt for cancellation. The belief that a levy would destroy the incentive to save was 'far-fetched' since, although the gross income derived from savings would fall, the net income would remain the same, the income tax having been reduced in the same proportion as the capital. The argument that it would restrict the capital available to industry was a fallacy because the community *qua* tax payers would be richer by the same amount as individuals *qua* levy payers would be poorer. A levy would not be repudiation as it applied to all property, and not just to the government's own securities. Finally, if there were greater prosperity, it could be argued that even the levy payers would benefit because the assets retained would rise in value and they would be more secure in them; the rich would have to bear most of the burden of the Debt after the war and accepting this openly at the outset would help relieve social tensions.[9] He omitted only two arguments of importance: a levy, promptly imposed after the war, would enable debt to be repaid when prices were still inflated; and the difficulty of persuading levy payers that the impost would not be repeated and that income tax would, indeed, be reduced by the amount by which the interest charge was reduced.

The public debate was vigorous in the first half of 1918 and the subject gathered a considerable literature. For economists, a common starting point was that, once abnormal war revenue, such as EPD, had ceased, the payment of interest on the Debt would require such a rise in income tax that enterprise, investment and economic recovery would be hampered. A levy, as Bradbury had suggested, seemed an attractive way of ensuring that the charge for the Debt fell on 'old wealth', leaving new accumulations free. It would also have the moral advantage of being paid mainly by those who were too old to have fought, thus going some way towards equalising the cost of the war in its widest sense. Depending on political persuasion, emphasis was placed on the redistribution of wealth and the potential for using freed resources for social spending. Those on the left tended to see the surrender of non-government securities as a step towards state ownership.

An airing in the *Economic Journal* during the summer and autumn showed that a levy had collected support among some academics, including Pigou. In one article, Joseph Stamp grounded some of the wilder estimates of the potential yield[b] by adapting the estimates he had made of the value of wealth in 1914 to arrive at the capital which could be subject to a levy on individuals in 1918. With a warning for the need for caution, he estimated the total to be £16,000m, or £5,250m more than four years previously.[10] Among politicians, two stand out for the early strength of their views. Pethick-Lawrence was not in the Commons, having failed to win a seat as a peace candidate in April 1917. In March 1918, he wrote a short article for *The Contemporary Review* and in April published the first full study of the tax. At the end of 1919, he was responsible for the Labour Party's official pamphlet on the subject.[11] Arnold was an Independent Liberal until 1922, when he joined the Labour Party. In April, he presented the outlines of a scheme to the Commons, pitching it as a business proposition. Like Bradbury, he assumed that only the better off – the income tax payers – had shoulders broad enough to bear the burden of the Debt and that a levy was merely an alternative, but prompter, way of meeting an obligation which they would have to meet anyway. Unlike Bradbury, he emphasised the importance of debt repayment while prices were still at wartime levels.[c]

b For example Arnold, in April 1918, suggested that the capital liable to a levy would be £24,000m. *Hansard* (Commons), 23 April 1918, col. 895.

Austen Chamberlain – a levy on war wealth

Austen Chamberlain had been hostile to a general levy long before he became Chancellor in January 1919.[12] In his budget statement at the end of April that year, he described the tax as 'hazardous' and 'disastrous'. The income tax was the best method of making a small annual charge. If a 'large slice was to be taken out of accumulated capital', it would be an attack on those who had heeded the call to save and buy war securities. Valuations for death duties were evenly distributed over time, but it would be impossible to make a fair and accurate valuation of all property at the same moment. Sales of securities would upset prices. If the state took the securities in lieu of cash, it would become the owner of a mass of small holdings in enterprises and land, which would be difficult to sell. If there were anxiety that a levy would be repeated, it would encourage waste and deter saving and enterprise.[13] This hostility mirrored that of the Board of Inland Revenue, which, while accepting that the task was 'not absolutely unsurmountable', had advised in March that the difficulties were such that it should not be adopted until all else had failed.[14] Shortly after the budget, in preparation for a debate on the levy, it provided an analysis of the difficulties presented by trusts and settlements, in which the capital value depended on the beneficiaries' life expectancy: these amounted to between 12 and 15 per cent of potentially chargeable wealth and were considered by the Board to be one of the major obstacles to an equitable tax.[15] It also provided a briefing on an alternative, a tax on increases in wealth accumulated during the war. While advising that any levy would excite fears of repetition, it said that, if applied only to increases in wealth, the shock to confidence and the disincentive to save and invest would be reduced since the levy payers would consider another great inflation unlikely. It would be paid by fewer people than a general levy, an important consideration when determining its practicability. The major drawback was that it would apply to the difference between two valuations and the revenue would be heavily affected by small changes in either. Most importantly for the ministerial assessment of risk and reward, it advised that as EPD, income tax and supertax had already been paid on the accumulations the maximum rate could not be higher than 60 per cent, and the average 30 per cent. The yield would, therefore, be much beneath those being suggested for a general levy and it would not be safe to rely on more than £600m to £800m.[16]

When the Chancellor reviewed the financial position in the Commons at the end of October, he made clear that he would resign rather than be responsible for a general levy. However, he thought that a levy on increases in war wealth would

c Arnold distinguished four methods of payment. No sales of assets would be necessary when government debt was surrendered and cancelled; other securities could be surrendered and the Treasury would then exchange them for government securities; and credit could be provided when assets were illiquid. He expected little would be paid in cash. *Hansard* (Commons), 23 April 1918, cols 890–912. Arnold repeated his suggestions in the debate on the second reading of the 1919 Finance Bill; ibid., 1 May 1919, cols 436–57.

be fair in principle, but warned that it would have to be decided whether the problems of administration, enforcement and equity outweighed the benefits. He had already asked the Inland Revenue to prepare a scheme, propose the best rates and estimate the yield, and suggested that the House should appoint a Select Committee to investigate.[17] The statement provoked a rise in the circulation of high denomination Bank notes, which the Chancellor countered by promising that the valuation date would be at some point in the past, so that there was no reason to hide assets.[18]

The Chancellor must have been filled with doubts for the Committee was not appointed until 16 February 1920 and the *Report* was not published until 13 May. It added little to the debate. It found that a levy was a practical proposition, although opposed by industrial, commercial and banking interests, but the members could not report unanimously unless there was a generous scale of tax-free allowances so that the levy would not fall on the small saver or on gains which only reflected inflation. The recommended rate would raise £500m (£350m in the first year and £150m over the following ten years), and should not be imposed unless there was an emergency and the money could not be obtained elsewhere. It left it to ministers to decide whether it was desirable or expedient.[19] The estimated proceeds were vastly smaller than those which had been mooted[d] and, although it was not appreciated at once, it weakened the case since it had become increasingly common ground, at least outside the labour movement, that only a very large yield would justify the dislocation, insecurity and risk of a steep fall in the financial markets.

The Chancellor confessed to the Cabinet in June 1920 that he had hoped that the Committee would provide a convincing case against the tax so that it might be decently dropped. His attitude had changed during March as the levy presented itself as an attractive way of freeing policy from the monetary and political difficulties being encountered in controlling the post-war boom.[20] It will be recalled that interest rates had been rising since the previous October and, although there was no sign of growth and inflation receding, in February the Chancellor had found himself being urged by some of his colleagues to ease his policy to help the sale of Housing Bonds and cut the cost of the floating debt. The Governor, meanwhile, was pressing the opposite case. The banks, facing a squeeze on their cash, were running off Treasury Bills. At the beginning of the month, Keynes had advised a rise in Bank rate, possibly as high as 10 per cent, and acceptance of a financial crisis.[21] To avoid a further rise in rates, the Chancellor had sought a voluntary reduction in advances, and on 11 March the bankers had refused. Five days later, on 16 March, the Governor's request for higher Bill rates was turned down. These finally came in the middle of April (see pp. 419–20).

d The Inland Revenue's estimate for the increase in individually held wealth was lower than that of Stamp. It calculated the increase during the war to have been £4,180m, which was reduced to £2,850m in the hands of 340,000 persons when the first £5,000 of post-war capital held by each individual was exempted. It originally presented two graduated scales of duty applicable to the smaller sum, which would have yielded £900m and £1,000m respectively. Select Committee on Increase of Wealth (War), *Report*, para. 8.

Also on 11 March, Blackett, who had become Controller of Finance in the reorganisation of the Treasury five months before, drew the Committee's attention to the part a levy might play in re-establishing monetary control. Without revealing his own view, he insisted that it was not so much the overall debt that was the problem as the size of the floating debt. In theory, it could be repaid from ordinary revenue, but its size made this impracticable and, anyway, surpluses had to be applied to the attached sinking funds before the floating debt could be touched. The sinking funds would pay off the Debt eventually, but the problem of the floating debt was immediate. Funding was impossible 'almost at any figure': investors would not buy a funding loan until the floating debt had been reduced and the floating debt could not be reduced without a funding loan or a revenue surplus in excess of the specific sinking funds.[22] A few days later, shortly before the request for higher Bill rates was refused, the Chairman of the Select Committee saw the Chancellor. While discussing an increase in the exemption limit to reduce both the opposition and the administrative problems, the Chancellor does not seem to have drawn attention to the floating debt.[23] However, when the Chancellor saw the Chairman again on 24 March he pointed out the

> enormous sums of money that he [the Chancellor] will have to provide for sinking fund and floating debt…There does not seem any reasonable opportunity of getting this reduction of the floating debt out of the ordinary taxation of the country…I understand that he [the Chancellor] is rather looking to us to help him to provide us with a sum of money which may prevent him putting really crushing taxation on to the trade and industry of the country.

With this purpose in mind, the Inland Revenue had been instructed to draw up the scheme to tax capital.[24] In further written evidence in April, it described the 'main purpose of the Levy' to be the reduction of the floating debt.[25]

In his budget later that month, the Chancellor raised taxes to increase the surplus, explicitly to allow a contribution to be made to reducing the floating debt. Among the measures was a rise in EPD, accompanied by a promise that it would be reversed if a levy was imposed. The Select Committee stressed that this had helped change the financial position, coupling it (most curiously) with the effect on the floating debt of the issue of the 5–15 Year Treasury Bonds, which had been put on tap on 3 May. The Cabinet discussed the *Report* twice at the beginning of June. The Chancellor drew attention to three objectives:

> (a) To make some approach to equalisation of War sacrifice in the field of finance;
> (b) To reduce the war debt as soon as possible and at a time when money values had a close relationship to the values prevailing when the debt was contracted;
> (c) To reduce the floating debt.[26]

He had changed his mind about the third objective. He now thought that he could not 'argue the case for the war levy very strongly on the grounds of its help with the floating debt' because the tax would be paid 'largely' in war securities.[e] He accepted that large fortunes accumulated during the war were causing resentment in all sections of the community and that this was fanning the flames of the discontent with the capitalist system. It was not possible to distinguish legal accumulations from the proceeds of profiteering:

> A tax is the wise policy but for one thing – the panic. The City always has cold feet but this time they have frightened me. If there were a series of failures they would be attributed to us. It is monstrous that a sum like 500 millions should produce panic but there it is.[27]

The Cabinet agreed that there was widespread discontent centring on war profiteers and that there were good arguments for making them pay more tax. To fail to act, when a Select Committee had said that a levy was feasible, would make the government look like a friend of the rich and put a weapon in the hands of extremists. Asquith, it was said, was in favour, as were some 'sound financiers' and Treasury officials. On the other hand, few would believe that it would not be repeated, there was the possibility of a panic and of all increases in wealth being taxed, irrespective of their origin: the efficient would be taxed as heavily as the inefficient, the virtuous saver as heavily as the vicious profiteer. When EPD was introduced, it was intended to encourage efficiency by allowing some profit to be retained; it was now proposed to tax that profit. EPD would produce over £300m each year when the April increase was felt and would be phased out over three years if a levy was imposed. Business, the Coalition's natural constituency, preferred it to a levy. Yet the levy, as proposed by the Select Committee, would raise only £500m over a period, and perhaps less if business was dislocated. Lloyd George, calling it 'one of the most difficult and important questions which the Cabinet had been called upon to decide', summed up against. The Cabinet split

e The problem of the floating debt was producing support for higher, earmarked, taxes from unlikely places. On 12 April 1920, the Governor and nine other senior figures from the City sent the Chancellor a memorandum advocating a rise in income and supertax, the proceeds to be earmarked to the redemption of the floating debt. The Chancellor's reply, pointing to the small revenue which would be produced in comparison with the floating debt, is in the same file. The signatories included Gaspard Farrer, May, Martin-Holland, Vassar-Smith, Leaf and Goodenough. In Cabinet on 2 June, the Chancellor said that the Governor, although opposed to the levy, did not think that there would be an 'actual panic though other bankers thought there would be.' The Chancellor advised that a forced loan 'would play havoc with the loans now pending'. It can be assumed that this referred to housing loans, about which the Cabinet were sensitive, and the 5–15 year Treasury Bonds, which were on tap. The following day, the Governor saw the Chancellor, who he described as 'at his worst from worry and pressure', to press his views further. BoE, G30/5, 'Memorandum for the information of the Chancellor of the Exchequer', 12 April 1920; AC 25/4/24, Notes of Cabinet 31 (20) Conclusion 5, 2 June 1920; MND, 3 June 1920; CTM, 31 March and 9 June 1920. For views within the Bank, see Sayers (1976), I, pp. 113–14.

on party lines, the Liberal Churchill asking that his dissent be recorded.[28] In private, Chamberlain considered the strongest argument in favour was that it would divert the attacks being made on capital by those angered by war profits, while being an insurance against a different government attacking capital more vigorously. He was afraid of a 'catastrophe' when trade was slackening, thought the credit position to be 'none too secure' and judged financial and commercial opinion to be 'frightened'. Those whose views he respected on financial questions, such as Lord Milner, Bonar Law, Horne, Worthington-Evans and the Prime Minister, were opposed. Those in favour spoke as politicians and were ignorant of finance – Lord Curzon, Churchill, Montagu, Edward Shortt and Thomas Macnamara. He was 'greatly relieved' when the Cabinet decided against the tax – he thought the decision was right and it would have been a great labour and administrative responsibility for him personally.[29]

The capital levy in the 1920s

A levy remained part of the Labour Party's programme until 1924, but both MacDonald and Snowden increasingly felt it to be an electoral liability and gave it only lukewarm support. In the elections of 1922 and 1923, they sought to present it as an alternative to other forms of taxation, although it was given prominence by some of their supporters and in 1922, when it appeared in the guise of a 'War Debt Redemption Fund', it was attacked vigorously by the Conservatives. Within a month of taking office in January 1924, the Committee on National Debt and Taxation was appointed in expectation that it would bury it and MacDonald, with a minority government, announced that no measure would be enacted in that Parliament: the levy was, he said, merely a technique for easing the tax burden on industry, rather than a 'stage to socialism'.[30] The wish was duly fulfilled, although the Committee did not report until 1927 after the Conservatives had been in power for two years. The *Majority Report* eschewed all the unorthodox tax and repayment schemes put before it, including the levy.

Three considerations finally killed the tax. Two had been mainstays of the Inland Revenue's case since 1917. It had argued that in the income tax there was already a simple, effective and generally accepted method of charging wealth. In effect, a proportion of capital was owned by the state as it enjoyed the income that flowed from it. Income was easily identified and measured, whereas the valuation of capital was filled with pitfalls. The Inland Revenue had a mass of information on income tax payers and its officials had experience of assessment and collection. Evasion was difficult. A levy was feasible, but it had few advantages in comparison. Second, the Board had advised that, in view of the difficulties of assessment, the levy would need to be felt to be fair by those paying it. Taxpayers in the UK expected assessment to be precise and were accustomed to dealing with the tax collector with the help of professional advisers who, in the absence of goodwill, could clog the process as they had the Land Values Duties. In addition, if it was badly received, financial panic and deflation could threaten. In this context, both the majority and minority Colwyn *Reports* commented, as had witnesses and other contemporaries, that a general levy would have been more acceptable immediately after the war, when there was a widespread feeling that unique circumstances made a 'sacrifice' by wealth to those who had fought appropriate.[31]

The third consideration was of more recent origin. The debate after the war was pitched almost exclusively in terms of the gross saving in interest; expenditure was assumed to fall by, say, 4½ per cent of the nominal sum written off the Debt. Contributing to this emphasis were very low estimates for the loss of tax revenue on the income from cancelled war securities provided to the Committee on Wealth by the Inland Revenue in April 1920.[32] In 1923, Dalton, a strong advocate of a levy, calculated that the annual loss in revenue from income tax, supertax and death duties on a reduction of £3,000m in the Debt would cut the gross budgetary saving by about one-half. The Inland Revenue's evidence to Colwyn confirmed this, the loss being estimated at between 50 and 60 per cent of the gross yield, depending on the scale of duty selected. It was this realisation, said the *Report*, which had led both Keynes and Pigou, who had once supported the levy, to change their minds.[33] The main *Report* concluded that 'even if there were a prospect of a Capital Levy being well received, the relief from debt which it offers would be insufficient to justify an experiment so large, difficult and full of hazard.'[34] The *Minority Report* concluded lamely that if the levy were understood and the tax accepted 'the nation may yet turn to the Capital Levy as a wise and practicable measure offering the best road out of its difficulties'.[35] Both, therefore, recommended increases in the traditional sinking fund, the *Minority Report* wanting the money to come from an increase in taxes on investment income and death duties.[36]

The repayment machinery after the war

If unorthodox measures were eschewed, repayment could only come from the traditional source: an excess of ordinary revenue over expenditure. By the beginning of 1920, when the Treasury was able to contemplate the possibility of its first post-war surplus, the arrangements for debt repayment from revenue were chaotic. Northcote's Fixed Debt Charge was still in existence, but the New Sinking Fund had been suspended by a clause in the Finance Act each year since 1914, while the annuities paid to the public and the savings banks continued. The Fixed Charge remained responsible for the interest on 2½ per cent and 2¾ per cent Annuities, 2½ per cent Consols, the debts to the Banks of England and Ireland, deficiency advances, Bills for Supply and Terminable Annuities. The National Debt Act 1887 excluded from the Fixed Charge interest on new debt unless the Act authorising the debt expressly stated that it was to be included. The interest on the war debt had not been so included, except for that on Ways and Means Advances. Included in the budget as expenditure was the interest on all war debt (other than Ways and Means), the sinking funds for 4 per cent Victory Bonds and 4 per cent Funding Loan and the balance of the monies payable to the Commissioners to enable them to buy from the Inland Revenue those two securities tendered in settlement of death duties. Excluded from the budget and met from

Exchequer balances (revenue surplus or new borrowing) were payments to the Inland Revenue to enable it to buy other securities tendered for death duties (4 and 5 per cent War Loans, some Exchequer Bonds and all War Bonds) and EPD (some Exchequer Bonds and all War Bonds), together with the Depreciation Fund for the 4 and 5 per cent War Loans. Finally, included in the Debt Charge were the expenses of management payable to the Banks of England and Ireland (that is, for the cost of all internal debt, including the war debt), but the budget met the expenses of management of the overseas debt and new issues. It was, as Niemeyer commented in February 1921, 'extremely difficult to set out in any intelligent [*sic*] form to the public'.[37]

The complications had grown from the retention of the Fixed Charge as the interest on war debt grew and from the terms offered to make individual issues more attractive. The latter arrangements came to be called 'contractual and specific sinking funds', a term used to describe repayment of debt which was part of the contract between the government and creditors holding specific obligations. These were contrasted with repayment of the Debt in general. The term was used carelessly. Indeed, it included privileges which were not sinking funds at all. It embraced three routes to repayment: the purchase of securities with funds supplied by the Treasury; the privilege of tendering securities at the issue price in settlement of certain taxes; and annuities.[f] As a complication, the first group included official purchases from the market whose intention was stated to be price stabilisation, albeit that this involved the repayment of debt. Nor was 'contractual' sufficiently precise, since some provisions were embodied in the prospectuses, under general statutory powers, and others were included in prospectuses and later given statutory authority. With the exception of 4 per cent Consols in 1926, the terms of the mechanism attached to long-dated loans were initially contained in the prospectuses and later confirmed by statute. The privileges attached to some Exchequer Bonds and all War Bonds relating to their use in payment of EPD, Munitions Exchequer Payments and death duties were granted under general statutory powers granted to the Treasury by the Finance Acts 1916 and 1917. The machinery whereby the Commissioners purchased 4 per cent Victory Bonds and Funding Loan surrendered for death duties were not incorporated in any contract, being an internal Treasury arrangement. Life annuities, Terminable Annuities and Savings Bank annuities were a charge on the Consolidated Fund under a range of nineteenth century Acts (see pp. 4–6).

Besides the annuities, on 31 March 1920 the securities with attached mechanisms for repayment comprised three groups.

The terms of issue of 4 per cent War Loan 1929–42 and 5 per cent War Loan 1929–47 required the Treasury to provide each month a sum equivalent to 1/8 per cent of the original nominal value to be used for purchases in the market whenever

f There were also capital repayments within the departmental annuities owed to the savings banks – 'other capital liabilities'. However, these payments were a charge on the departmental Votes and the Treasury did not include them when speaking of 'sinking funds'.

the Loans' prices fell beneath their issue levels. The monthly payments were to cease if the unexpended balance reached £10m. The Finance Act 1917 gave the Treasury the power to borrow for the Depreciation Fund, and it did so until 1922–3. In addition, the two War Loans were accepted at their issue prices in settlement of death duties.[g] The funds with which the Inland Revenue bought the securities were provided by the Exchequer. Under the 1917 Finance Act, securities surrendered in payment of death duties (and Munitions Exchequer Payments and EPD) were deemed to have matured on the day they were transferred to the Inland Revenue. Thus, the funds advanced by the Exchequer logically had to come from new borrowing or revenue surplus, as did those for repayment of debt maturing in the normal fashion. Consistent with this, until 1922–3, the Treasury drew on Exchequer balances.[h]

The terms of issue of 4 per cent Victory Bonds and 4 per cent Funding Loan 1960–90, confirmed in the War Loan Act 1919, required the Treasury to set aside at the close of each half-year a sum equal to 2¼ per cent of the original nominal value of the securities. After deducting the interest, the balance was to be issued to the Commissioners to be applied as sinking fund. In the case of Victory Bonds, the money was to be applied to annual drawings at par. In the case of Funding Loan, it was to be applied to purchases in the market when the price was below par, and invested in Funding Loan or other securities when the price was above par. From the start, the funds were included in the budget as expenditure.

Also accepted at par by the Inland Revenue in settlement of death duties were 4 per cent Victory Bonds. The Bonds were purchased by the Debt Commissioners from the Inland Revenue and held by them until drawn. Interest and repayments of principal received by the Commissioners on these holdings were applied to meeting the payments to the Inland Revenue, with any further sums required being met from the Treasury. Surpluses, which started to accrue from 1936–7, were to be paid to the Treasury. Under the War Loan Act 1919, the Treasury had the power to direct that the provision that surrendered securities were to be treated as maturing debt and met from new borrowing should not apply to the issue. It had so directed, and the funds paid to the Inland Revenue were included in the budget as expenditure. The machinery was purely internal and was not a contract with the holder.

A similar provision applied to 4 per cent Funding Loan, but at the issue price of 80. The prospectuses for both Victory Bonds and Funding Loan were later confirmed in the War Loan Act 1919.

g The Treasury had no power to offer this privilege at the time of the issues. The prospectus promised legislation, which was duly provided in the 1917 Finance Act.

h At first sight, this procedure may appear strange. The intention was to ensure that the Inland Revenue could pay into the Consolidated Fund as cash the full amount collected as duty and that the securities could be cancelled. In order to provide the cash, the Treasury increased its other borrowing. As Blackett described the process, 'If the machinery complications are left out of account what has really happened is that £x of Revenue from Excess Profits Duty has been used to meet a maturity of an equivalent amount of Government securities.' T 171/235, Blackett, 'Sinking Funds', 8 March 1920.

Under general powers contained in the Finance Acts 1916 and 1917, the later Exchequer Bonds (at their issue price) and all four series of War Bonds (at their nominal value) could be tendered at par in settlement of death duties, EPD and Munitions Exchequer Payments. Under the Finance Act 1917, the Bonds were deemed to have matured and, as with the 4 and 5 per cent War Loans' Depreciation Fund, the monies came from Exchequer balances.

Two other domestic issues and one overseas debt were to be added to these in the course of the decade. The terms of 3½ per cent Conversion Loan first issued in 1921 required that the Treasury set aside for purchases in the market for cancellation in the succeeding half-year a sum equal to 1 per cent of the nominal value of the Loan outstanding at the end of any half-year when the average daily price during the half-year, as certified by the Bank, had been less than 90. The terms were confirmed in the Finance Act 1921.

Under the terms of the prospectus for 4 per cent Consols, the Treasury undertook, for ten years from 1 May 1927, to apply monies at the rate of £2½m each quarter to purchases in the market for cancellation when the price was at or below par. By an oversight, the payments were not given statutory authority at the time of issue. Powers were later included in the Finance Act 1932.[38]

Under the terms of the agreement for funding the war debt to the US Treasury, the UK issued Bonds with annual payments on account of capital to extinguish them in 62 years (see pp. 542–4).[39]

Re-establishing a Fixed Charge: 1920 to 1923

In February 1920, Niemeyer proposed rolling all the specific sinking funds into a new Fixed Charge, which would be included in the budget as expenditure. He thought it particularly desirable that borrowing should cease for the Depreciation Fund and death duty surrenders as the process was replacing long-dated debt with floating debt – 'unfunding' with a vengeance. The only sinking funds outside the Charge should be those involving the tender of securities in payment of EPD, which was a temporary tax and only attached to short-dated securities. The privilege merely pointed to a 'heavy' sinking fund.[40] Blackett, although agreeing that a Fixed Charge should be re-established, did not believe that the time was ripe. As he was to point out to the Select Committee on Wealth a few days later, the specific sinking funds were either a prior call on revenue surpluses or had to be met by borrowing elsewhere – a funding loan, about whose prospects he was pessimistic, or an increase in the floating debt. About £113m would be required in 1920–1 for specific sinking funds, £25m for the maturity of 5 per cent Exchequer Bonds of 1 December 1920 and about £80m for foreign currency debt. Savings Certificates might refinance about £50m. If the remainder were met from revenue, the floating debt would be unchanged in a year's time. What was needed was a surplus, over and above the money provided to the Commissioners for the contractual repayments, which could be retained in Exchequer balances and reduce borrowing on Bills and Ways and Means.[41]

In the 1920 budget, the Chancellor restored the Fixed Charge to £24.5m, where it had stood in 1913–14. It was a gesture, merely earmarking a small part of the revenue surplus to purposes for which it would have been used in any case. His ambition climbed higher. When he stood up, there was £164m available from revenue for the reduction of debt:

> But is that surplus sufficient? In the opinion of His Majesty's Government it is not. It is true that it represents more than 2 per cent. on the total debt, and a Sinking Fund of 2 per cent. would redeem the debt in 26 years – just a generation. This, in ordinary circumstances, would be, not merely an ample, but an extravagant, Sinking Fund. But the circumstances are not ordinary, and…I am going to call upon the Committee and the country for a further generous effort to improve our credit, and, by present sacrifice, to lighten our future burden and establish securely our national credit…Last year we actually added to our debt; this year we must begin to reduce it, and the beginning must be substantial.[42]

Taxes were raised to produce £77m in 1920–1 and £198m in a full year. In 1920–1, this would enable £70m to be applied to the floating debt after meeting 'all maturing liabilities, without reborrowing, except by the continued sale of Savings Certificates':

> We were told on Saturday that two such budgets might destroy the Empire. I will not stop to retort that twenty such budgets would redeem the whole of our debt. I am content to say that after such a war as that in which we have been engaged, and after such gigantic financial sacrifices, this is a position of unexampled and unequalled strength…we are obliged to impose fresh taxes and to call for further sacrifices. That may not bring popularity to the Government or to the Minister. I am proud to say that we have not sought it…Our object has been …[to] leave to our successors an ample revenue and to our country a national credit second to none.[43]

The measures were startling in their scale. The increases were additional to a level of taxation which had been thought sufficient for a great war. They were raised explicitly to pay off a floating debt which was roughly equal to annual government revenues. When the Chancellor rose to speak, the sum available for debt repayment already amounted to 12.2 per cent of estimated revenue. When he sat down, it was 16.5 per cent. A further 24.3 per cent of estimated revenue was destined to pay interest. 'Interest and sinking fund' were therefore intended to be equal to 40.8 per cent of estimated revenues.

During the summer, the strong fiscal position was reflected in a diversion of colonial war contributions to debt repayment. Under a Treasury Minute of 31 December 1917, all gifts from colonies and protectorates had been treated as revenue, being taken into the Exchequer as Miscellaneous Revenue like India's £100m. This was reasonable, as the gifts enabled borrowing by the UK Treasury to be reduced. Some of these gifts took the form of instalments, payable over extended periods. In August 1920, the Treasury ordered that the monies should be paid direct to the Commissioners and applied to the purchase and cancellation of war debt, without first passing through the budget. The contributions, from Bermuda, Ceylon, the Gold Coast, the Falkland Islands, the Straits Settlements, Sarawak and Jamaica, became part of the 'hidden sinking funds', which Churchill absorbed into the Fixed Debt Charge in 1928.[44]

The following year, Blackett, with Niemeyer once more dissenting, still thought it was too early to revert to a realistic Fixed Charge. With the economy in recession, he placed less emphasis on the floating debt, and instead pointed to the uncertain size of the contractual repayments. Surrenders for death duties would continue for many years, but those for EPD, although being important in the coming year and having some effect in 1922–3, would matter little thereafter. £25m a year might have to be earmarked for capital repayments to the US Treasury and a new funding loan might well carry its own sinking fund. A recession was an unsuitable time to ask Parliament to fix a heavy charge for many years ahead; 1921–2 was the last year, until 1925–6, when maturities were few and the opportunity should be taken to reduce the floating debt. Not that the rest from refinancing was very great: some £300m, including about £80m for foreign currency debt, would have to be raised from revenue or refinanced if the floating debt were to be unchanged at the end of the year, with another £35m 5 per cent Exchequer Bonds 1922 maturing on the first day of the 1922–3 financial year (see pp. 425–6). There was no new Permanent Charge but, after quoting Blackett's figures, in April the Chancellor announced the issue of 3½ per cent Conversion.[45]

The funding of war pensions and the budget of 1922

The debt repayment problem receded or, at least, changed shape, as the boom gave way to recession and money was diverted into the gilt-edged market. The floating debt was reduced, monetary control reasserted, and the rise in prices made it less attractive for holders to surrender securities against taxes. In 1920–1, £84.2m was required to meet surrenders for EPD and death duties, £43.1m in 1921–2, but only £8.8m in 1922–3. The cost of the Depreciation Fund fell from £31.9m in 1920–1, to £29.3m in 1921–2, and £1.2m in 1922–3.[46] The relief felt by officials was tempered by increasingly strident demands for lower taxation.[47]

One possibility, which particularly agitated the Treasury, was to 'fund' war pensions. This would have involved the Treasury paying an even annual sum to a new off-budget fund, which would borrow in its early years when the pensions liability was heavy and repay in later years when it became lighter. The saving to the Treasury in 1922–3 would have been broadly the same as the estimated cost of the contractual sinking funds for that year, or about £35m. In December, the Government Actuary sent calculations of the present capital value and annual payment pattern of war pensions to the Geddes Committee, which was investigating the scope for cutting government spending.[48] Blackett urged that the pensions continue to be met from revenue as, if the monies were borrowed, it would be a reduction in the provision for debt repayment from revenue. Geddes rejected the funding proposal, but the Treasury had to accept a suspension of debt repayment; according to Niemeyer a year later, it feared that elaborate statutory arrangements would be required if pensions were to be funded and that the step would be irreversible, whereas a suspension of the sinking funds could be limited to a single year.[49]

In the 1922 budget, Horne suspended the New Sinking Fund and gave himself powers to borrow to meet the sinking funds other than Terminable Annuities:

> Unemployment is widespread...The unparalleled depression which beset us throughout the whole of the course of last year is still with us...The burdens of taxation...are now felt to be so oppressive as to check enterprise and deepen despondency. Is it essential that we should maintain this pressure? Is it not possible by slackening it to give some much needed stimulus to trade, thereby lessening our expenditure and next year at least, if not this, gain some revenue as a result of the augmented profits of revived industry?...[the repayment of debt] enhanced our credit, and it put back into the hands of industry considerable sums which were unprofitably in the hands of the State...It is possible by making too great exactions on the taxpayer to defeat the very object at which you aim.[50]

With the £30m to £35m released, he cut the standard rate of income tax by a shilling.

Until that winter, debt repayment had not been seriously questioned and there had been little need for Treasury officials to marshal their arguments: whatever the differences of opinion displayed during the debate over the capital levy, it was common ground that the Debt should be reduced. So great was the concern about the floating debt that even Treasury officials and the Governor had supported unorthodox measures to tax capital. In 1922 and 1923, officials found themselves defending debt redemption, first as Horne moved to reduce taxes and then, the following year, as they sought to establish a fixed debt repayment. Inevitably, the arguments were tailored to suit the occasion and the attitudes of different Chancellors, but the main outlines remained the same even after 1929 when the question of debt repayment was being debated alongside the desirability of borrowing to increase public works spending.

As in so much, immediately after the Armistice the yearning for pre-war conditions was powerful. Debt repayment in times of peace had been the norm. Since 1875, it had taken the form of Northcote's Fixed Charge, and it was this that officials expected to see revived. Behind it lay a deeply held conviction that both current and capital expenditure should be met from taxation, deficits in time of peace were unjustified and that debts should be discharged in full, even if it involved heavy taxation. This, in all its austerity, was spelled out by Blackett in March 1922 as Horne moved towards suspending the contractual sinking funds:

> The British financial system has for generations been held up to the admiration of the world as a model, and it owes its pre-eminence largely to the stern

> observance of the rule that expenditure must be covered by revenue and must include a reasonable provision for amortisation of debt...The credit of the British Government and of British finance generally owes much to the Government's record of steady debt reduction out of revenue over the century since Waterloo, and it was mainly through its policy of debt reduction that Britain was able to make such a gigantic financial effort during the war.

The defences were strengthened with more contemporary arguments. It was not difficult to roll over floating debt while trade was poor, but in normal times it involved competing with whatever rate the private sector offered or else inflating credit. The floating debt was still a danger, and if it became the basis for a new rise in prices a check to activity and employment more severe than in 1920 would need to be applied: hopes of a return to the gold standard would have to be abandoned. In addition, there was maturing debt to refinance. A sinking fund, even if small, would:

> pro tanto reduce the amount of reborrowing necessary, but there is a large class of lenders, not usually very vocal, whose faith in British Government credit has been greatly strengthened by the reduction of debt out of revenue since the Armistice...In my opinion it will be quite impossible to avoid some inflation and considerable additions to Floating Debt between now and April 1925 unless a regular sinking fund is provided out of revenue.

Finally, there came the argument which Bradbury had used in 1919 and which was to recur in Treasury memoranda, notably in 1928 and 1929 when the Treasury opposed Lloyd George's plans to borrow for public works spending:

> Government expenditure met by pure creations of credit increases the money available to be spent simply because it creates spending power out of nothing. But, unless resort is had to paper creations of credit, the whole of the money which the Government spends has to be withdrawn from the sums otherwise available for spending by private individuals. Taxation and borrowing both draw from the same source, that is from the spending power of the individual...trade stands to gain most by the application out of surplus revenue of a reasonable sum towards debt reduction. Every penny devoted by Government to reducing debt goes straight back to help trade, and as a general rule it is safe to assume that trade employs it at more profitable rates than is represented by the yield on the government debt paid off. Moreover, the taxation imposed to raise the surplus for debt reduction will certainly have resulted in some enforced saving.[51]

A year later, Niemeyer (whose phraseology is unmistakable in Blackett's paper) put this more strongly, describing sinking funds as, perhaps, 'one of the most potent means of mobilising – under the compulsion of the tax gatherer – capital for industrial investment'. Every issuing house tried to bring out new issues when the government was paying interest or repaying debt. Always penetrating and vigorous, especially when defending the orthodox, Niemeyer produced a string of reasons for reintroducing a substantial sinking fund from revenue. Most were to resurface over the years whenever a Chancellor, especially Churchill, showed signs of backsliding. A sinking fund of 1/2 per cent (say £35m) was less than the pre-war level, when the size of the Debt gave little cause for concern. The Treasury was not a free agent because there were many issues with contractual sinking funds attached. How could a budget be said to balance if it did not provide for 'normal and unavoidable' annual charges, such as these payments? There was a procession of maturities, culminating with 5 per cent War Loan, which made the Debt one of the largest fields for savings: 'Nothing will so much assist this as a steady statutory sinking fund provided from revenue'; a second year's suspension would be seen as 'much more serious' than the first. Reduction of interest costs would relieve the pressure from those wanting drastic measures, such as a capital levy, to repay debt. Other countries had already worked off their war debts, by repayment, depreciation or inflation: as sterling appreciated, the real value of repayment would increase. If interest rates rose, the contractual sinking funds would absorb more repayment resources so that the Treasury would be unable to take advantage of market opportunities and buy back the cheapest issues.[52]

The Baldwin Sinking Fund

In his 1923 budget, Baldwin announced a replacement for Northcote's Fixed Charge. Selecting from the menu of arguments provided by his officials, he told the King that he had been persuaded by the size of the Debt, the prospect of heavy maturities and the need for conversions to relieve the taxpayer when the potential for reducing other items of expenditure was narrowing.[53] In future, there would be a single charge against the budget to include interest and management on both the war and pre-war debts, together with a separate fixed sum to be applied to capital repayment. The latter, the 'New Sinking Fund (1923)', was set at £40m in 1923–4, £45m in 1924–5, and £50m thereafter.[54] Reversing its defeat of the previous year, the Treasury had diverted to debt repayment year-by-year the monies released by the contraction in war pensions.[55]

The fixed annual repayment may have provided Niemeyer with the certainty which he argued would give investors confidence, but it could not be called traditional. Nor was it strong. Northcote's Fixed Charge covered interest and management, with the balance being used for repayment; more was applied to capital repayment as debt was repaid and the amount spent on interest fell. Baldwin's sinking fund was only applied to capital, with the interest saved by conversions and repayment falling into the general budget to be spent elsewhere or returned to the taxpayer. Baldwin's mechanism also entailed Chancellors legislating each time they wanted to increase debt redemption, whereas, with the Fixed Charge, they had to legislate to prevent an increase in repayment. Well after the event, in November 1925 when giving evidence to the Colwyn Committee, Niemeyer defended the form of sinking fund on three grounds: the temper of the taxpayer was such that the discipline of ever higher repayments of capital would not have long survived; the need was to buttress confidence by making the size of debt repayment obvious to all; and the specific sinking funds already provided protection.[56]

Events began to show the system's frailty shortly after Niemeyer spoke. Putting on the budget a fixed sum for debt repayment and a separate variable charge for interest, management and expenses was no threat so long as the servicing charge was stable or falling. However, if interest rates rose, the extra cost would pass straight through into expenditure. In contrast, the sinking fund within Northcote's Fixed Charge provided a cushion, which automatically contracted if debt costs rose; repayment was protected because Chancellors were not subjected to the temptation of interfering with the Fixed Charge in years of high interest rates. The shortcomings of the 1923 Sinking Fund were driven home in 1926–7 and 1927–8.

Snowden and Churchill

Three weeks after taking power, MacDonald described his attitude towards the Debt in unforgiving terms. Although it was increasing the costs of production, damaging competitiveness and reducing living standards, it could only be reduced by 'honest means'. These did not include either inflation or repudiation.[57] Since at the same time he ruled out a capital levy during that Parliament, reductions could only come from the application of traditional revenues, repayment of war debts and savings from conversions. This chimed with his Chancellor's orthodoxy. Snowden was reputed to be the Treasury's favourite Chancellor. He gave clear instructions and, having made up his mind, defended his policy with determination. His comments on repayment in the sole budget of the first Labour government must have warmed Niemeyer's heart:

> the burden of the Debt is a very heavy one, and I am afraid it must be for some years to come...It is clear that we must take every opportunity and devote as much of our resources as possible to the redemption of Debt. Some people seem to think that Debt reduction is something which confers no public advantage. I know a reduction of 1s. in Income Tax is much more spectacular than paying off £50,000,000 of Debt. In the first case the relief is obvious, in the second it is indirect, but none the less real, and is in fact more widespread and penetrating in its benefits. Improvement in national credit in its turn regulates the rates at which money can be borrowed for industrial purposes. Moreover, in view of the great conversion schemes which we shall have to carry out in a not far distant future, the maintenance and improvement of British trade [*sic*] is a matter of the most vital importance.[58]

Snowden believed in honest finance, balanced budgets and debt repayment. 'The difference between us does not lie in a nice calculation of figures...A well balanced budget is not a luxury which is to be avoided: it is a necessity which must be provided for', he wrote to Churchill in January 1930. In his autobiography, he described himself as having to follow a Chancellor who 'had played "ducks and drakes" with the national finances', and had been living from hand to mouth, using capital to meet current expenditure, and 'robbing every hen roost' on which he could lay his hands.'[59] The comment was no doubt political, but it was fair. Churchill's public pronouncements may have been as orthodox as Snowden's, but his budgets were balanced by sleight of hand. There was optimistic estimating of revenues anyway weakened by industrial unrest and slow economic growth. He was prone to expensive gestures, whose costs were left to be met by later Chancellors. He had reformist sympathies, which led him to the extension of state pensions and expensive changes to the rating system. His undisciplined mind was accompanied by just enough command of the arguments to be dangerous. His imagination needed drama and grand solutions. He relished living dangerously, a characteristic alien to those normally responsible for national finances. Steady application of monies having their effect over many decades, the essence of a sinking fund, was completely alien to his temperament. It is not surprising that Treasury officials found him difficult.[60]

Churchill had long been sceptical of the benefits of repayment. In October 1919, when he was at the War Office, he had told the Cabinet Finance Committee that a 1/2 per cent sinking fund would have 'no effect on the enormous debt' and that a levy or forced loan would eventually be adopted: he continued to advocate a levy into 1920 and regret the Cabinet's decision into 1921.[61] As Chancellor, his general discontent with debt policy came to a head in 1927. It had been inflexible, dead to the wider implications for the nation and favoured the bankers, the City and the *rentier*:

> We have assumed since the war, largely under the guidance of the Bank of England, a policy of deflation, debt repayment, high taxation, large sinking funds and Gold Standard. This has raised our credit, restored our exchange and lowered the cost of living. On the other hand it has produced bad trade, hard times, an immense increase in unemployment involving costly and unwise remedial measures, attempts to reduce wages in conformity with the cost of living and so increase the competitive power, fierce labour disputes arising therefrom, with expense to the State and community measured by hundreds of millions.

Debt and taxation lay 'like a vast wet blanket across the whole process of creating new wealth by new enterprise'. He feared that, at some stage, the electorate would compare the apparently beneficial results of repudiation and inflation in Germany with those of repayment and orthodoxy in Britain and draw 'most misleading deductions'.[62]

Churchill's general scepticism was inflamed by the specific failures to reduce either the size or the cost of the Debt. Issues made at a deep discount, increasing the nominal value of the Debt even as sinking funds reduced it, provided particular ground for attack. In one skirmish, Niemeyer described the effect on the Debt of an issue of 4 per cent Consols at a price of 85 as 'an imaginary evil'. Churchill responded:

> After all £37 millions [increase in the nominal value] will have to be paid by our children and raised by taxation from them. Moreover, the dead hand of the debt will continue to rest for a longer period and with greater weight upon the productive energies of the country.[63]

When Niemeyer persuaded him otherwise, Churchill shifted his ground and pointed to the minimal savings in interest which had been attained, the difficulty of explaining to a disappointed public the difference between cash applied and nominal cancelled, and the increase in the real value of the 'Bondholders' claim' as prices fell.[64] On other occasions, he bombarded his officials with unorthodox and unrealistic ideas for reducing both the Debt and the annual cost: buying and cancelling 2½ per cent Consols to reduce the nominal value outstanding with the minimum of cash outlay; a forced loan based on the income tax at a submarket interest rate; a conversion of 5 per cent War Loan into a tax-free 4 per cent dated 'Liberation Loan' by means of an 'immense campaign' of propaganda and a period of artificially cheap money; compulsory conversions into Terminable Annuities; and the various schemes aimed specifically at 5 per cent War Loan (see p. 595). True to his temperament, at the end of 1927 he admitted that he could see advantages in a strikingly increased sinking fund, such as Snowden (and both Colwyn Committee Reports) supported, but no means of escape in adding merely '£10 or £15 or £20 millions a year'; he had tried 'the proper and orthodox' and it had failed.[65]

Niemeyer's standard defence of deeply discounted perpetual issues – that the nominal was irrelevant as long as the annual cost to the taxpayer was reduced – was effective in the first year of Churchill's tenure. It was coupled with the argument that the process of refinancing and conversion was continuous, aiming at an accumulation of lower debt costs from many operations:

> Every time we reiterate our sinking fund policy it has increased effect: every time we *increase* the sinking fund it has a cumulative push. We pushed the market a lot by the 4% Loan [4 per cent Consols]: we should change the spirit still more by an increased sinking fund.[66]

The case for heavy debt repayment was strengthened by the Colwyn Committee's recommendation in its *Majority Report* that Baldwin's £50m sinking fund was too weak and that it should be increased to £75m a year. The Committee hoped that this would be possible over, perhaps, five years, from additional war debt repayments, conversions and the savings on debt repaid. If the budgetary outlook did not justify this, then taxation should be increased. The repayment should be raised further, to £100m, over seven to ten years from the application of interest savings. The application of 'hidden sinking funds' outside the budget and the Old Sinking Fund should continue to be additional to the fixed repayment.

Other expenditure, 'of whatever nature', should not be increased unless the sinking fund was able to reach this target. The *Minority Report* went further, recommending that, if there were no levy on capital, an additional tax on investment income for the purpose of increasing debt repayment by £100m a year should be introduced, and at once. Hardly surprisingly, the *Report* was welcomed by Niemeyer, although some of his pets, such as deeply discounted issues, were criticised. Equally unsurprising was Churchill's reaction:

> I am startled at all this folly you have been shoving in Colwyn's mouth. It may be all right to teach Socialists to pay off the National Debt. So far as I am concerned I think a £50 million sinking fund is already excessive.

Removal of overtaxation, which artificially checked consumption, would do more for the country's economic strength than 'comparatively small increases which are recommended in the speed of amortisation'.[67]

Churchill's Fixed Charge

The cost of debt service, having reached a low point in 1922–3, rose to a peak in 1926–7 (Table 21.1 and Appendix VII). Some of the damage came from borrowing to pay the premiums on War Bonds and the replacement of Departmental Ways and Means Advances, taken at artificially low interest rates, with market borrowing. Using sinking fund monies to repay US Treasury debt (costing 3 per cent) rather than sterling debt (costing 1 or 2 per cent more) meant that the full advantage of repayment was not being felt. Conversions were failing to provide the promised benefits.[68] More of the damage, the greater part, came from rising Bill rates and the encashments of Savings Certificates.

The Treasury did not see the Certificate problem until it had arrived (see p. 640). It did see the vulnerability of the Budget to variable and unpredictable short rates; that was, after all, one of the first principles of debt management. It had been stressed by Niemeyer when giving evidence to the Colwyn Committee in November 1925:

> obviously the cost of Treasury Bills is a varying item. At the moment it costs us slightly over 3¾ per cent., but it has been as low as 2 per cent.; it has been, within the last five years, as high as 6 per cent.; that is to say, that our interest charge for Treasury Bills has varied from about £20,000,000 to something like £60,000,000 a year. Clearly the possibility of variations of that size is not desirable in an ordinary budget…they introduce into the budget a more or less incalculable element of a very varying character.[69]

The Treasury had underestimated Bills in 1924–5, when they cost £20.8m, instead of £18m. The year Niemeyer made his comments they cost £25.3m (£21m) and in 1926–7 £28.0m (£22.2m). In the second half of May 1927, gold was drawn to Paris, with the inevitable effect on the money market and, in the autumn, Churchill

Table 21.1 Interest, management and expenses of the National Debt met from revenue: 1920 to 1934 (£m)

Year ending 31 March	*1*	*2*	*3*	*4*	*5*	*6*
1919	265.2	2.8	260.0	–	268.0	*38.1*
1920	322.5	4.1	326.6	–	326.6	*44.8*
1921	326.1	2.3	328.3	–	328.3	*69.0*
1922	302.2	5.1	307.3	–	307.3	*49.3*
1923	297.3	2.0	299.3	–	299.3	*16.2*
1924	305.8	1.5	307.3	–	307.3	*17.4*
1925	309.2	2.9	312.2	–	312.2	*20.8*
1926	307.0	1.2	308.2	–	308.2	*25.3*
1927	316.4	2.2	318.6	–	318.6	*28.0*
1928	312.0	1.8	313.8	–	313.8	*25.3*
1929	310.1	1.4	311.5	–	311.5	*26.2*
1930	305.0	2.3	307.3	4.8	312.1	*28.7*
1931	291.9	1.3	293.2	–	293.2	*12.5*
1932	287.6	1.9	289.5	8.4	297.9	*20.7*
1933	280.1	2.1	282.2	2.7	284.8	*5.9*
1934	215.2	1.1	216.3	–	216.3	*4.1*

Notes
Column headings:
1 Interest met from revenue.
2 Management and expenses.
3 Total interest, management and expenses met from revenue.
4 Interest borrowed (Savings Certificates).
5 Total interest, management and expenses.
6 Of which interest on Treasury Bills.
Rows may not sum because of rounding.
Excluding charges connected with other capital liabilities.

Source: *National Debt: annual returns*.

drew attention to the 'hideous' rise in rates since the return to the gold standard.[70] The estimate for that year had been £23.8m. The out-turn was to be £25.3m (Table 21.1).[i]

In his 1928 budget, Churchill replaced Baldwin's Sinking Fund with a Fixed Debt Charge. Not only would overruns in the interest on Bills and Certificates no longer fall into increased current spending, but he was able to draw forward into the public eye the 'hidden sinking funds' (the 'other miscellaneous revenue' in Table 21.4) and add them to the New Sinking Fund so, in effect, freeing revenue for other purposes. Interest on all securities (with the conditional exception of Certificates), management costs, specific sinking funds and general debt repayment

i Average Bill rates were £4 15s 0d per cent in 1919–20; £6 9s 0d per cent in 1920–1; £4 6s 10d per cent in 1921–2; £2 6s 6d per cent in 1922–3; £2 18s 0d per cent in 1923–4; £3 11s 11d per cent in 1924–5; £4 4s 11d per cent in 1925–6; and £4 10s 8d in 1926–7.

were rolled up into an annual Charge of £355m. In the first year of Churchill's six-year forecast (1928–9), there was expected to be £78.5m available for sinking fund and the interest on Certificates, falling to £66.5m in 1929–30 and then £69m, £72m, £73.5m and £71m; an average of £71.8m. Specific sinking funds were forecast to absorb £50.3m a year, general repayment £1.2m and the accruing interest on Certificates £20.3m, the amount calculated by the Government Actuary. In principle, if the interest paid fell short of this, the cash available for general debt repayment would be greater. The system of budgeting only for the interest on expected encashments of Certificates ceased.

The average took account of a fall in the cost of interest as the repayments compounded and the rise in the interest rate on the US Treasury debt, from 3 per cent to 3½ per cent in 1933. The large repayment of £78.5m forecast for the first year was provided by a temporary increase in the Fixed Charge to £369m made possible by the amalgamation of the Currency Note and Bank of England issues, which freed the assets of the CNRIA for the Exchequer. They amounted to £13.2m, and by adding £0.8m from general resources, the £14m was found. This was accompanied by a raid on the £4.2m Old Sinking Fund of 1927–8, which (together with that expected for 1928–9) was diverted from debt repayment to the Suspensory Account, which would contribute to the partial derating scheme (Table 21.3).

Making no acknowledgement of the real reason for the introduction of the Fixed Charge, the Chancellor stated his policy to be:

> The interest saved by the annual repayments of Debt and any economies which may be effected in the administration of the Debt will each year be automatically added to the Sinking Fund. I propose, as far as I have anything to say to it, that the Income Tax payer shall look forward to any relief which may be yielded by conversion of the Debt or any large portion of the Debt to a lower rate of interest ...All the rest of the annual sum will continue to roll up until, or unless, the day dawns when some unholy hand is laid upon it.[71]

The 'accumulator', at 4½ per cent for gilt-edged issues and 4 per cent for Bills, would repay the Debt in 'exactly' fifty years.[72]

It was a weak sinking fund, reflecting the tight fiscal position and Churchill's predilections. Losing the benefits of conversions to the general budget made the sinking fund less powerful than that of Northcote, although it followed Hamilton's advice in the tighter fiscal conditions of 1897 that 'The taxpayers have an unanswerable claim to the relief (or greater part of it) afforded by the reduction of interest on Consols'.[73] Minimal resources were expected to be available for general repayment: the average of £1.3m a year over the first six years was tiny in comparison with the forecasting errors. Moreover, it was struck after two rearrangements: revealing the hidden sinking funds reduced debt repayment by £5m or £6m a year (see p. 694) and the interest no longer paid on the 4 per cent Victory Bonds and 4 per cent Funding Loan surrendered in payment of death duties and held by the Commissioners was to rise rapidly from the £3.3m it would have been worth in 1927–8 had the arrangement then been in force (Table 21.4).

Table 21.2 Repayment (–) of debt from specific (contractual and statutory) sinking funds: 1919 to 1934 (£m)

Years ending 31 March	*1*	*2*	*3*	*4*	*5*	*6*	*7*	*8*	*9*
1919	–2.0	–	–	–	–	–	–	–	–2.0
1920	–2.0	–0.9	–	–2.5	–	–	–	–	–5.4
1921	–2.1	–1.8	–2.1	–7.9	–	–	–	–	–13.9
1922	–2.1	–1.9	–2.2	–9.7	–	–	–	–	–15.9
1923	–3.0§	–2.0	–2.3	–7.5	–7.4	–1.3	–1.2	–	–24.7
1924	–1.8	–2.1	–2.4	–7.3	–13.6	0	–	–	–27.2
1925	–1.8	–2.1	–2.5	–7.8	–13.2	0	–	–	–27.4
1926	–1.1	–2.2	–2.6	–7.0	–14.4	–0.2	–7.5	–	–35.1
1927	–1.0	–2.3	–2.8	–8.4	–15.1	–0.2	–2.7	–	–32.5
1928	–1.0	–2.4	–2.9	–12.3	–14.7	–0.2	–1.7	–9.2	–44.4
1929	–1.0	–2.5	–3.0	–11.5	–16.5	0	–1.7	–10.0	–46.3
1930	–1.0	–2.6	–3.2	–9.3	–16.1	–	–	–10.0	–42.2
1931	–0.9	–2.7	–3.3	–12.1	–15.7	0	–	–10.0	–44.7
1932	–0.9	–2.8	–3.5	–	–15.3	–	–	–10.0	–32.5
1933	–0.9	–2.9	–3.6	–	–7.5	–	–	–2.3	–17.2
1934	–0.9	–3.1	–3.7	–	–	–	–	–	–7.7

Notes

Column headings:

1 Annuities*.
2 4 per cent Victory Bonds.
3 4 per cent Funding Loan.
4 Deficiency on death duties surrenders account†.
5 3½ per cent Conversion Loan.
6 For purchase of securities surrendered in settlement of death duties and EPD‡.
7 4 per cent and 5 per cent War Loans Depreciation Fund.
8 4 per cent Consols.
9 Total specific, attached sinking funds.

* Annuities for Life and Terms of Years and Savings Banks and Book Debt Annuities.

†Issues to the Commissioners to meet the deficiency in the sum available from the interest and principal repayments on their holdings of 4 per cent Victory Bonds and 4 per cent Funding Loan to pay the Inland Revenue for those two issues surrendered in settlement of death duties.

‡Issues in respect of Exchequer Bonds, National War Bonds and 4 per cent and 5 per cent War Loans of 1929–42 and 1929–47 surrendered in payment of EPD, Munitions Exchequer Payments and death duties.

§Includes a special issue of £840,460 to extinguish the Savings Banks' Annuities set up in 1899.

0 signifies less than £50,000.

– signifies that there was no transaction.

Rows may not sum because of rounding.

Source: *National Debt: annual returns.*

That the Treasury acknowledged that the Fixed Charge was tightly drawn was shown by a procedure which ordered how the New Sinking Fund was to be applied to the attached sinking funds. Money remaining after meeting interest and management was to be spent in a hierarchy: such part of Terminable Annuities as represented capital, the 4 per cent Victory Bonds and Funding Loan sinking funds, the 3½ per cent Conversion Loan sinking fund, the 4 per cent Consols sinking

Table 21.3 Repayment (–) of debt from revenue: 1919 to 1934 (£m)

Year ending 31 March	*1*	*2*	*3*	*4*	*5*	*6*	*7*	*8*
1919	–2.0	–	*	–	–	–2.0	+1690.3	+1688.3
1920	–5.4	–	*	–	–	–5.4	+326.2	+320.8
1921	–13.9	–	–7.3	–	–	–21.3	–230.6	–251.8
1922	–15.9	–	–9.1	–	–	–25.0	–45.7	–70.7
1923	–24.7	–	*	–	–	–24.7	–101.5	–126.2
1924	–27.2	–11.5	–	–1.4	–	–40.0	–48.3	–88.3
1925	–27.4	–5.2	–	–12.2	–	–45.0	–3.7	–48.7
1926	–35.1	–5.0	–	–10.0	–	–50.0	+14.0	–36.0
1927	–32.5	–5.1	–	–22.3	–	–60.0	+36.7	–23.3
1928	–44.4	–5.1	–	–15.5	–	–65.0	(–4.2)†	-65.0
1929	–46.3	–5.5	–	–	–5.6	–57.5	(–18.4)†	-57.5
1930	–42.2	–5.5	–	–	None	–47.7	+14.5	–33.2
1931	–44.7	–5.8	–	–	–16.3	–66.8	+23.3	–43.6
1932	–32.5	–	–	–	None	–32.5	–0.4	–32.8
1933	–17.2	–9.1	–	–	None	–26.3	+32.3	+5.9
1934	–7.7	–	–	–	–0.1	–7.8	–31.1	–38.9

Notes
Column headings:
1 Total specific sinking funds (internal).
2 Total specific sinking funds (US).
3 Balance of New Sinking Fund of 1875.
4 Balance of New Sinking Fund of 1923.
5 Balance of New Sinking Fund of 1928.
6 Total repayment (–) from sinking funds.
7 Surplus (–) revenue (Old Sinking Fund) applied to debt redemption.
8 Total repayment (–) from revenue.
*Sinking fund suspended.
†The surpluses (Old Sinking Fund) for 1927–8 and 1928–9 were appropriated to the Rating Relief Suspensory Account.
The data are for issues from the Consolidated Fund. In some cases, the cash was not applied until the following year.
– signifies that there was no transaction.
Rows may not sum because of rounding.

Source: *National Debt: annual returns.*

fund, the capital repayments on the Bonds held by the US Treasury, the funds for the purchase of 4 per cent Victory Bonds and Funding Loan surrendered for death duties, the interest in respect of Certificates, the 4 and 5 per cent War Loans Depreciation Fund and other debt (except Ways and Means Advances). In the event, resources did not stretch as far as the interest on Certificates in 1929–30, 1931–2 and 1932–3 and the money had to be borrowed (Tables 21.3 and 21.4).

Snowden: the last of orthodoxy

'It can hardly be disputed that too little was provided for debt redemption' Phillips told Hopkins in June 1929, after the election. Churchill had not increased the sinking fund as Colwyn had recommended. Instead, he had introduced the Fixed

Table 21.4 Adjusted repayment (–) of debt from revenue: 1919 to 1934 (£m)

Year ending 31 March	*1*	*2*	*3*	*4*	*5*	*6*	*7*	*8*	*9*
1919	–	n/a*	–	–	–	–0.1	–3.1	–3.2	+1685.1
1920	+33.1†	+12.5	–	–0.1	–	–0.8	+0.8	+45.5	+366.3
1921	+35.6†	+11.0	–	–0.4	0	–1.7	+1.9	+46.4	–205.4
1922	+35.6†	+10.0	–	–0.9	–0.1	–1.5	+17.5	+60.6	–10.1
1923	+4.6†	+15.0	–	–1.2	–0.1	–3.3	+4.1	+19.1	–107.1
1924	–	+15.0	–	–1.6	–0.2	–4.3	–3.8	+5.2	–83.1
1925	–	+15.0	–	–1.9	-0.3	–7.9	+1.5	+6.4	–42.3
1926	–	+15.0	–	–2.3	-0.3	–5.2	+7.0	+14.2	–21.8
1927	–	+16.3‡	–	–2.7	–0.4	–5.8	+23.0	+30.4	+7.1
1928	–	+4.6‡	–	–3.3	–0.5	–8.1	+5.1	–2.2	–67.2
1929	–	+2.4‡	–	0	–0.7	–1.4	+17.4	+17.6	–39.9
1930	–	+0.1‡	+4.8	–	–0.7	–0.6	+6.7	+10.3	–22.9
1931	–	+3.9‡	–	–	–0.9	-9.6	+42.4	+35.9	–7.7
1932	+19.3§	-2.1‡	+8.4	–	–1.0	–0.5	+44.4	+68.6	+35.8
1933	+13.6§	-1.4‡	+2.7	–	–1.1	–0.3	+1.9	+15.3	+21.2
1934	+36.2§	+8.0	–	–	–1.1	–0.8	–7.9	+34.4	–4.5

Notes

Column headings:

1 Accrued interest on US advances.
2 Accrued interest on Savings Certificates.
3 Interest on Savings Certificates borrowed.
4 4 per cent Victory Bonds and 4 per cent Funding Loan held by the Commissioners (interest).
5 4 per cent Victory Bonds and 4 per cent Funding Loan held by the Commissioners (principal).
6 Other miscellaneous revenue applied to debt repayment.
7 Other capital liabilities (net).
8 Total adjustments.
9 Adjusted repayment (–) of debt from revenue.

*Data for the accrued interest were not published before 31 March 1919, when the total was estimated to be £11.5m.

†The US Treasury calculated that $629.8m (£108.9m at par of exchange) had accrued up to 15 December 1922. The UK had paid $100m on 15 October and 15 November, so that the interest outstanding was $529.8m. The interest was $122.9m in 1922–3, so that $22.9m (£4.6m) of interest was unpaid in that year. There is a difference of $0.5m (£0.1m), which was the interest which should not have been paid on the $100m between the dates of British payment and 15 December. The $4.6m was paid in cash on 15 March 1923 to round the debt down to exactly $4,600m, the value of British Bonds issued. The amount of the accrued interest, therefore, depends on whether that $4.6m was regarded as having been paid on account of interest or of principal. This Table treats it as a payment on account of principal.

‡Adjusted for the accrued interest capitalised by conversions into 4 per cent Savings Bonds, $4^1/2$ per cent Conversion Loan 1940–4 and other issues of Savings Certificates.

§Under the terms of the Hoover Moratorium, $93.9m of the interest and principal of the British Bonds held by the US Treasury were capitalised on 15 December 1931, and a further $66.2m of interest on 15 June 1932. Repayments were by means of a $9.7m annuity. The full amount of interest and principal ($95.6m) was paid on 15 December 1932. Only $10m was paid on 15 June 1933 and the remaining $65.9m interest was capitalised. Only $7.5m was paid on 15 December 1933, when $110.2m was capitalised: the $68.5m of interest, the annuity of $9.7m and $32m of principal. (Source: *Papers Relating to British War Debt* (Cmd. 5189), May/June 1936. The dollar values are translated into sterling at $4.86.

0 signifies less than £50,000.

– signifies that there was no transaction.

Rows may not sum because of rounding.

Sources: *National Debt: annual returns*; *BGS*, p. 343; *Congressional Record*, 13 February 1923, p. 3559.

Charge, implying a repayment of only £50m a year. The Baldwin Sinking Fund had its weaknesses, but that was no reason to replace it with another weak arrangement. It was no doubt true that the taxpayer would be unwilling to continue spending large sums on repayment for the full fifty years, but that was no reason to start by relaxing efforts. The failure was even greater if it was recalled that the deficits of 1925–6 and 1926–7 had not been made good and that the hidden sinking funds had been incorporated into the advertised repayment; '1928 is done with and 1929 is past praying for' but, for the future, he proposed a permanent addition of £5m per year to the existing £355m Debt Charge, a 'far from heroic policy…[but] the minimum that can be done to make the thing sound'. Four months later, this became the basis of a recommendation Hopkins made to the new Chancellor.[74]

The collapse in Bill rates after the Wall Street Crash gave Snowden reason to avoid such a permanent addition to the Charge in his 1930 budget.[75] When it had been introduced in 1928, Snowden had thought the £355m represented, in its early stages, a 'distinct slackening' in the efforts to repay the Debt. Events, he said, had proved him right; in the recent year, the Charge had been expected to provide £50.4m for repayment after £304.6m had been spent on interest and management. The increased cost of the floating debt had actually taken interest and management to £312.1m, so that although the contractual sinking funds cost less than expected the Charge failed to cover £4.8m of the interest on Certificates (Tables 21.1 and 21.4). Thus:

> The Committee will…see that a budget deficit of £14.523m is not quite the full story of last year. £14,500,000 was the sum by which the budget failed to provide a total of £355,000,000 for Debt services free of fresh borrowing. Even if the budget had provided that sum, it would have been insufficient to meet the actual Debt charge by nearly £5,000,000 [the interest on Certificates borrowed]. In these circumstances, I have had to consider two questions, first, whether I should make any permanent change in the Fixed Debt provision; and, second, how the budget deficit of 1929 is to be dealt with…I could not persuade myself to leave the provision at £355,000,000 if I thought there was a serious risk that it would, for the third time, fail to cover our debt obligations.

Without assuming that Bills could continue to be sold at a rate as low as 2½ per cent, he did feel able to estimate for only £17.3m of interest on the floating debt, compared with the £28.8m of the previous year. This enabled him to estimate that £23m of Certificate interest and the full £50.4m of contractual sinking funds would be met from an unchanged £355m Fixed Charge. The deficit of the previous year was a different matter, and could not be allowed to stand:

> Whether we rely on a fixed Sinking Fund or a Fixed Debt Charge, there is one certain method by which all efforts to reduce Debt can be rendered futile, and that is by leaving budget deficits uncovered. I will not labour this truth, which is appreciated widely and has been recognised ever since the days of William Pitt.

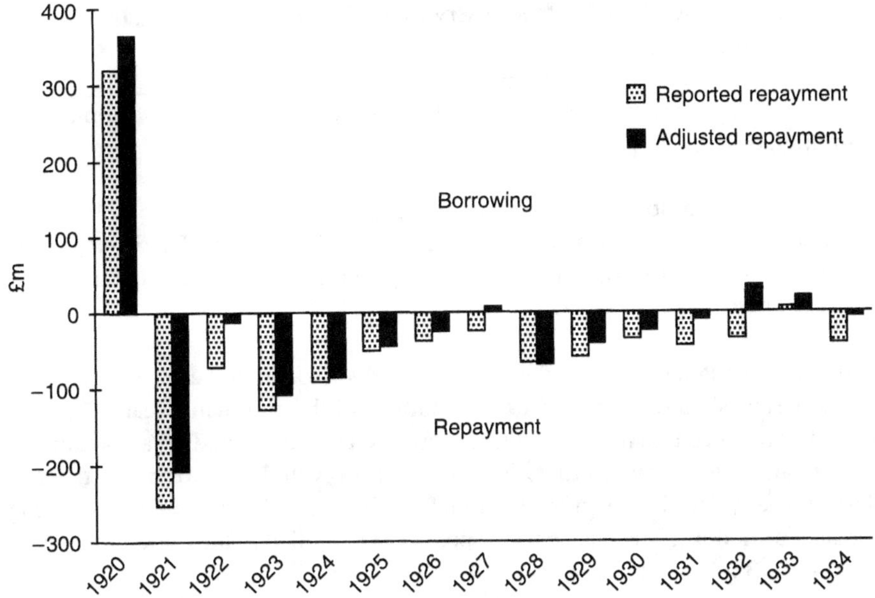

Figure 21.1 Debt repayment from revenue: 1920–1 to 1933–4. Source: Tables 21.3 and 21.4.

He proposed making special payments out of revenue to wipe out the deficit, adding £5m to the sum available for debt redemption in 1930–1 and 1931–2 and £4.5m in 1932–3.

The special payments were an aspect of a measure redolent of the late nineteenth century. Before the war, a Chancellor facing a deficit could borrow during the year on Ways and Means. These could run on for three months into the following year, by which time, it was assumed, he would have raised the money from taxation or requested Parliament – in the full glare of publicity – to authorise the issue of securities. The War Loan Act 1919 gave the Treasury sweeping powers to borrow to replace war debt, Bills, and Ways and Means, with new securities. These enabled the authorities to respond flexibly and speedily to opportunities to refinance maturities and replace floating debt with longer-dated paper. Although not intended, it also had the effect of weakening Parliamentary control because, in the first instance, a deficit was met by borrowing on Bills or Ways and Means. The 1919 Act then allowed these to be refinanced with longer-dated paper without further statutory authority (see p. 395). Thus, the deficit of one year could be added to the Debt and nothing more need be done. Moreover, there was a bias, which the nineteenth-century Treasury would not have accepted. If the Chancellor did nothing, the deficit was automatically added to the Debt:

> If the Chancellor wants to pay off the deficit he cannot do it without a special clause in the Finance Bill. It is urged that this is all wrong, that the ordinary law should require the deficit to be paid off in the next year, and it is departures

> from that principle and not the observance of it which ought to require specific legislative sanction.[76]

The words were written by Phillips, but they could equally well have come from Hamilton, or from Hopkins:

> Although the doctrine may seem a little rigorous, I think the only sound practice is one under which surpluses go to swell the Sinking Fund, but deficits go in diminution of the Sinking Fund without specific Parliamentary authority.[77]

Snowden accepted the case and a clause was added to the Finance Bill providing that a deficit should be treated as expenditure in the following year, that is, it should be repaid out of revenue. In future, a deficit was to be paid off automatically unless Parliament decided otherwise: a Chancellor would need to change the law, defending any decision to ignore a deficit already incurred. Events were too strong for such orthodoxy. The clause was repealed as it applied to the deficits shown in 1930–1, 1932–3 and 1936–7.

It could be argued that the pre-war habit of incurring debt outside the budget in parallel with repaying debt from a sinking fund inside the budget was acceptable, albeit odd, as long as fiscal policy as a whole was under control. Capital liabilities could have been regarded as one of the other contingent Treasury liabilities to which Niemeyer referred in his evidence to Colwyn: pensions, the accrued interest on Certificates, guarantees, or the premiums on War Bonds, which did not appear in published expenditure or the balance sheet against which the sinking fund provided a general offset.[78] By the early 1930s, borrowing outside the budget exceeded the sinking fund (Figure 21.1; Table 21.4). If there was confidence in the overall stance of policy, it would be justifiable to expect attitudes to change, even if the sinking fund was reduced or suspended. The two years after 1931 made the point. The priority that had been placed on debt redemption over the previous decade was put into reverse, the monies for the contractual sinking funds were borrowed and the whole of the relief from conversions appropriated. With the budgets broadly balancing and the exchange rate at levels which the markets saw as realistic, there were few adverse consequences.

✣ ✣ ✣

Sinking fund policy between 1920 and 1932 was where tradition, the desire for pre-war normality, the legacy of the war, slow growth in revenue and the newly expanded electorate's demand for greater social spending met. Tradition was the winner in the early years, as was dramatically shown by Austen Chamberlain's budget in April 1920. Politics were the clear winner once Churchill became Chancellor and Niemeyer left the Treasury for the Bank. Optimistic forecasting, expensive policy initiatives, the cost of support for the unemployed and sluggish revenue unbalanced his budgets. But even then, feckless as he was, Churchill bowed to tradition – or the need to protect the British government's credit, paving the way for War Loan conversion – and dressed up his Budgets to show surpluses, after including sinking fund as expenditure. The oddest aspect of this was the flexible attitude of officials, who did not press Chancellors about the growth of other capital liabilities until they reached extreme levels in the early 1930s, the problem of finding saleable securities in the savings bank portfolios became acute and the gold standard was threatened. Likewise, the accruing interest on Savings Certificates was tucked away into footnotes and out of expenditure until the volume of maturities forced action to be taken.

At each stage, the Treasury offered persuasive reasons for the treatment accorded each item. The result, however, was that over the fourteen financial years 1920–1 and 1933–4 there was a marked difference between the ostensible and actual volume of repayment. A total of £910.1m was applied to repayment from revenue: £569.6m via the New Sinking Funds of 1875, 1923 and 1928, and £340.5m (net) from Old Sinking Fund. Of the latter, £230.6m came in the single year 1920–1 (Table 21.3). When adjustment is made for 'hidden sinking funds', interest on debt capitalised and increases in other capital liabilities, the sum spent on debt repayment falls to only £547.9m, of which two-fifths came in Austen Chamberlain's year of austerity (Tables 21.3 and 21.4; Figure 21.1). If further adjustment is made for raids on the Road and Exchange Funds and the changes in the timing of the payment of beer duty and income tax, repayments fall by a further £63m.[79] The total adjusted repayment may be regarded as £483.8m, or nearly one-half of that published. If about £800m of Vote of Credit assets sold and spent outside the budget are deducted, the Treasury was actually a substantial borrower.[80]

A note on Tables 21.2 to 21.4

Tables 21.2 and 21.3 trace the payments for the contractual sinking funds and from the Old and New Sinking Funds as they were presented in government accounts and the Chancellor's Financial Statements. Table 21.4 adapts this conventional presentation to provide for hidden sinking funds, capitalisation of interest, other capital liabilities and so forth.

Column 1 of Table 21.2 shows Annuities for Life and Terms of years and the Savings Banks' and Book Debt Annuities. Columns 2 and 3 show the monies paid to the sinking funds attached to 4 per cent Funding Loan and the 4 per cent Victory Bonds. Column 4 shows the monies paid to the Commissioners from the Consolidated Fund to enable them to purchase from the Inland Revenue the 4 per cent Funding Loan and Victory Bonds tendered in settlement of death duties. Until 1928, this was the balance required after both the interest and principal from their accumulated holdings of the securities had already been applied; after 1928, it was the amount required after the repayments of principal had been applied. Column 5 is the sinking fund for 3½ per cent Conversion Loan. Column 6 is the payment made to enable securities tendered for death duties, EPD and Munitions Exchequer Payments to be purchased from the Inland Revenue and cancelled. They are excluded until 1922–3 because they were met from borrowing and a small item thereafter as the 4 and 5 per cent War Loans stood above their issue price for most of the period and the volume of Exchequer Bonds and National War Bonds in issue fell until the last matured in 1929. Column 7 shows the monies issued for the Depreciation Fund attached to the 4 and 5 per cent War Loans. Like the previous item, until 1922–3 it was met from borrowing. The payments made in 1929–30 and 1931–2 do not appear since they could not be met from the Fixed Charge and the money was borrowed. Column 8 is the sinking fund attached to 4 per cent Consols. Column 9 brings the previous eight columns together and is the total of contractual sinking funds, other than for the British Bonds held by the US Treasury.

Table 21.3 shows debt repayment from revenue, that is, without adjustment for hidden sinking funds. Column 1 is carried over from the final column of Table 21.2. Column 2 shows the capital repayment made each year to the US Treasury under the 1923 agreement. The 1924 data include the final payment on account of Pittman silver. Columns 3–5 show the balance of the Sinking Funds of 1875, 1923 and 1928 available for general debt repayment after meeting the priority capital repayments shown in Table 21.2 and to the US Treasury. Until 1923–4, and from 1928–9, they are struck after meeting management expenses, which are not shown. Column 6 brings together the previous five columns to show the total payments made each year from sinking funds. Column 7 shows any surplus of revenue over expenditure (Old Sinking Fund) applied to debt redemption. Column 8 shows the total applied to debt redemption from revenue.

Table 21.4 adjusts for hidden sinking funds, other capital liabilities and interest accrued, but not paid. Column 1 shows the interest accrued on the war debt to the US Treasury, which was met from further advances up to and including those due in April and May 1919 and then capitalised until 1922–3. Column 2 shows the interest accrued, but not paid, on Savings Certificates. Between 1926–7 and 1932–3, it is adjusted for the accrued interest estimated to have been capitalised as a result of conversions of Certificates into 4 per cent Savings Bonds, 4½ per cent Conversion 1940–4 and later issues of Certificates. Column 3 shows the interest on matured and surrendered Certificates which was borrowed in the years when the Fixed Charge of 1928 was unable to meet the payments. Columns 4 and 5 show the interest and principal repayments on the 4 per cent Victory Bonds and Funding loan tendered for death duties and held by the Commissioners. Until 1927–8, both interest and principal were available to buy newly surrendered securities from the Inland Revenue and were outside the budget. The balance of funds was provided from the published sinking fund. Interest on these holdings was no longer paid after 1927–8, but the principal repayments continued to be available before the sinking fund was called on. Column 6 shows miscellaneous revenue, which was applied to debt redemption without having first passed through the budget: it includes the capital element of some colonial and allied debt repayments, gifts and some small sums payable under a range of acts direct to the Commissioners for debt redemption.[j] Column 7 shows the net change in other capital liabilities, including loans to the Unemployment Fund and the Post Office for telephones. Column 8 brings together all these adjustments and the final column presents an adjusted total for debt repayment from revenue.

Endnotes

1 T 176/21, Niemeyer to Prime Minister, 26 June 1925.
2 Committee on National Debt and Taxation (Colwyn Committee), *Minutes of Evidence*, Niemeyer, para. 68.
3 T 168/94, Hamilton, 'Sinking Fund', 25 September 1905.
4 Cline (1963), pp. 59–65.
5 These points are put most succinctly by Niemeyer in a note to Bradbury in T 171/167, 10 November 1917. Also see T 171/167, Nott-Bower and Fisher to Chancellor, 9 February 1917, and IR 63/86, 'Proposed Capital Taxation in France', 15 March 1919.
6 T 171/167, TUC, Birmingham, Resolutions, September 1916, and Deputation from the TUC to the Chancellor, Transcript, 15 February 1917.
7 T 171/167, TUC, Blackpool, Resolutions, September 1917, and 'Conscription of Wealth, etc.', Deputation from the TUC Parliamentary Committee, The War Emergency Workers' National Committee, The Executive of the Labour Party and the Executive of the Miners' Federation, Transcript, 14 November 1917.
8 *Hansard* (Commons), 29 January 1918, cols 1500–3; *The Times*, report of a speech at Leeds by Bonar Law, 6 November 1922, p. 9; Chairman's statements at AGMs of Barclays Bank, *The Economist*, 26 January 1918, p. 126, and of the Union of London and Smiths Bank, p. 176; *The Daily Telegraph*, 31 January 1918, p. 4. Correspondence with Sutton, journalists and the public is in T 172/670.
9 T 171/167, Bradbury, 'Conscription of Wealth', 12 November 1917, and 'Conscription of Wealth', covering note 14 January 1918.
10 *EJ*, June and September 1918. Contributors included Pigou, Arnold, W.R. Scott and Stamp. Stamp, 'Estimate of the Capital Wealth of the United Kingdom in Private Hands', *EJ*, September 1918, and Stamp (1916). The Inland Revenue described the estimates as 'admittedly problematical' and 'perhaps over-liberal'. IR 63/86, Board of Inland Revenue, 19 May 1919.
11 Pethick-Lawrence (1918a; 1918b; 1920).
12 *Hansard* (Commons), 29 October 1919, cols 754–5.
13 Ibid., 30 April 1919, cols 207–9.
14 IR 63/86, Board of Inland Revenue to Chancellor, 15 March 1919.
15 Ibid., 'General Capital Levy', 19 May 1919.
16 Ibid., Board of Inland Revenue, 'Capital Taxation', 19 May 1919.
17 *Hansard* (Commons), 29 October 1919, cols 754–5; Cab. 27/72, FC 22 (2), 29 October 1919.

j Examples were Land Tax Redemption and Surplus Land Tax and the Composition of Stamp Duty. Another minor account was the Victory Bonds Redemption Account. Sinking fund monies were issued half-yearly, but the drawings were annual. The account held the monies while they were waiting to be applied. The interest from the securities in which these balances were temporarily invested was used to buy and cancel other securities. *BGS*, p. 543, and the *National Debt: annual returns* from 1930.

18 Cab. 27/72, FC 31, copy of letter from Governor to Chancellor, 29 November 1919; Cab. 27/71, FC 15 (1), 6 November 1919.
19 Select Committee on Increase of Wealth (War), *Report*; AC 25/4/11, Chamberlain to Anderson, 15 March 1920; Short (1985), p. 72.
20 AC 25/4/24, Notes of Cabinet 31 (20), Conclusion 5, 2 June 1920.
21 Keynes (1971–89), XVII, pp. 180–1.
22 Select Committee on Increase of Wealth (War), *Evidence*, Blackett, 11 March 1920, paras 1533–45 and 1657–9. For the context in forming the budget, see T 171/235, 'Sinking Funds', Blackett, 8 March 1920.
23 AC 25/4/11, Chamberlain to Anderson, 15 March 1920; Short (1985), p. 72.
24 Select Committee on Increase of Wealth (War), *Evidence*, Sir William Pearce, paras 2701 and 2704.
25 Ibid., Board of Inland Revenue, p. 283.
26 Cab. 23/21, Cabinet 31 (20), Conclusion 5, 2 June 1920.
27 AC 25/4/24, Notes of Cabinet 31 (20), Conclusion 5, 2 June 1920.
28 Middlemas (1969), pp. 114–15; Cab. 23/21, Cabinet 31 (20), Conclusion 5, 2 June 1920, and Cab. 23/21, Cabinet 32 (20), Conclusion 1, 4 June 1920; AC 25/4/24, Notes of Cabinet 31 (20), Conclusion 5, 2 June 1920, and AC 25/4/25, Notes of Cabinet 32 (20), Conclusion 1, 4 June 1920; Short (1985), pp. 80–3.
29 Self (1995), Austen Chamberlain to Ida Chamberlain, 27 May 1920, and to Hilda Chamberlain, 6 June 1920.
30 Dalton (1953), pp. 122, 138, 140 and 143–4; Pimlott (1985), pp. 142–4; Whiting (1987), pp. 142–4; Snowden (1934), II, p. 595; Cline (1963), pp. 59–65; *Hansard* (Commons), 12 February 1924, col. 761, and 14 February 1924, cols 1095–7; Daunton (1996), p. 896; Short (1985), pp. 86–8 and 248–9. Short cites Stamp to McGowan, 24 February 1924.
31 T 171/167, Nott-Bower and Fisher to Chancellor, 6 November 1917; IR 63/86, Fisher and Hamilton to Chancellor and 'Proposed Capital Tax in France', 15 March 1919; IR 75/108, 'The Proposal of a Capital Tax (mainly with reference to its practical aspects)', undated with comments by Stamp; 'Memorandum by the Board of Inland Revenue on the Practicability of Levying a Duty on War-time Wealth', in Memoranda submitted to the Committee on Increase of Wealth (War), para. 116 and p. 233; Committee on National Debt and Taxation, *Report*, paras 709–710, 769, 859, 866 and 873–6, and Appendix XXII, and *Minority Report*, para. 232.
32 Select Committee on Increase of Wealth (War), pp. 282–6, 'Memorandum by the Board of Inland Revenue', April 1920; Short (1985), pp. 73–4.
33 Dalton (1923), pp. 80–4; Committee on National Debt and Taxation, *Report*, paras 731–3 and Appendix XXIII; Daunton (1996), p. 895. Keynes's E. in C. did not stress this as much as he did under cross-examination. Keynes (1971–89), XIX, Part II, pp. 840 and 842–3.
34 Committee on National Debt and Taxation, *Report*, para. 876.
35 Committee on National Debt and Taxation, *Minority Report*, para. 234.
36 Ibid., paras 245–7.
37 T 171/196, Niemeyer, 'Permanent Annual Charge', 11 February 1921; *National Debt: annual returns*.
38 T 171/296, Hopkins to Chancellor, 22 March 1932.
39 *National Debt: annual returns*; 'Arrangements for the Funding of American Debt' (Cmd. 1912), 1923.
40 T 171/235, Niemeyer, 'Sinking Funds', 26 February 1920.
41 Ibid., Blackett, 'Sinking Funds', 8 March 1920.
42 *Hansard* (Commons), 19 April 1920, cols 79–80.
43 Ibid., 19 April 1920, cols 99–100.
44 *Colonies and Protectorates (War Contributions)*, 1920 (Cmd. 798) and (897), TMs of 31 May and 4 August 1920.

45 T 171/196, Niemeyer, 'Permanent Debt Charge', 11 February 1921, and Blackett, same title, 27 February 1921; *Hansard* (Commons), 25 April 1921, col. 84.

46 T 171/205, '1921–2, Exchequer Issues to redeem Deadweight Debt'; T 171/214, 'Amounts issued from Exchequer in Respect of Bonds &c. Surrendered for Duties', undated; *National Debt: annual returns*.

47 Cab. 24/132, CP 3649, Inland Revenue and Board of Trade, 'Industry and the Weight of Taxation', 24 January 1922, describes how the Board of Inland Revenue saw the demands for lower taxes and contains its analyses of the justification.

48 T 171/202, Watson to Beharrell, 9 December 1921, and statement prepared for Geddes by the Government Actuary, 9 December 1921.

49 T 171/202, Blackett, 'Liquidation of Post-War Liabilities', January 1922; T 171/205, Niemeyer to Chancellor, 22 April 1922; T 171/214, Niemeyer, 'Funding Pensions', 9 February 1923.

50 *Hansard* (Commons), 1 May 1922, cols 1039–40.

51 T 172/1272, Blackett, 'Budgeting for a Deficit', 24 March 1922. Also see Howson (1975), pp. 12–13, 37–8 and 42, and Clarke (1988), p. 29. Similar arguments are to be found in the Treasury's papers on funding war pensions in T 171/202 and in T 171/214.

52 T 171/214, Niemeyer, 'Sinking Funds', 23 January 1923; T 176/38, 'Clause 18', April 1923.

53 T 171/214, Chancellor to Stamfordham, 12 April 1923.

54 *Hansard* (Commons), 16 April 1923, cols 1729–31. The Chancellor emphasised that the £40m for 1923–4 was, in any case, required for contractual repayments and US Treasury debt. In the event, the contractual funds took £27.2m, the regular repayment to the US Treasury was £4.9m and the last instalment of Pittman silver £6.6m.

55 T 171/214, Niemeyer, 'Sinking Funds', 23 January 1923, and 'Funding Pensions', 9 February 1923.

56 T 175/40, Phillips, 'Sinking Fund Policy', 22 June 1929; Committee on National Debt and Taxation, *Evidence*, Niemeyer, para. 8792.

57 *Hansard* (Commons), 14 February 1924, col. 1096.

58 Ibid., 29 April 1924, cols 1592–3.

59 T 175/40, Snowden to Churchill, 23 January 1930; Snowden (1934), II, p. 853.

60 Middlemas (1969), I, pp 315–16, and II, p. 98; O'Halpin (1989), pp. 142–7; Newman (1972), pp. 71–5; Rhodes James (1969), pp. 207–9; Short (1985) pp. 206–8; Cannadine (1994), pp. 130–62. Grigg's kinder comments in *Prejudice and Judgement* (Grigg, 1948), pp. 175–80, were written some twenty years later, after Churchill had become a venerated war leader.

61 Cab. 27/71, Finance Committee, 22 October 1919; LGP, F/10/1/10, Churchill to Lloyd George, 8 October 1921.

62 Gilbert (1979), pp. 997–8, Churchill to Niemeyer, 20 May 1927 .

63 Ibid., pp. 924–5, Churchill to Niemeyer, 26 January 1927.

64 Ibid., pp. 996–7, Churchill to Niemeyer, 20 May 1927.

65 Ibid., Churchill to Niemeyer, pp. 924–6 and 989–90, 26 January 1927 and 16 April 1927, and Churchill to Fisher and Hopkins, 17 December 1927; T 160/551/F9973/1, Niemeyer to Chancellor, January 1927; T 176/39, Niemeyer to Chancellor, 11 February 1927; T 212/1, Niemeyer, May 1927.

66 T 177/6, Pt. 1, Niemeyer, February 1927. Underlining in the original.

67 Committee on National Debt and Taxation, *Report*, paras 1000–1005, and *Minority Report*, paras 235–46 and p. 429; T 160/257/F9893, Niemeyer to Churchill, 22 November 1926; Gilbert (1979), p. 861, Churchill to Niemeyer, 28 October 1926, .

68 Gilbert (1979), pp. 1079–80, Churchill to Hopkins, 30 October 1927; T 175/15, Phillips to Hopkins, 7 November 1927; *National Debt: annual returns*.

69 Committee on National Debt and Taxation, *Evidence*, Niemeyer, para. 8689. Niemeyer's figures do not match the data in the annual returns. He was probably excluding the interest on Bills held by the Departments.
70 T 177/6, Churchill, 'Treasury Bill Rates', September or October 1927.
71 *Hansard* (Commons), 24 April 1928, col. 829.
72 T 175/40, Phillips, 'Sinking Fund Policy', 22 June 1929. The statement was conservative: repayment, according to Phillips, would be 'within' fifty years.
73 T 168/86, Hamilton, 'The Sinking Fund', 30 September 1897.
74 T 175/40, Phillips to Hopkins, 22 June 1929, and Hopkins to Chancellor, 21 October 1929.
75 This paragraph is based on *Hansard* (Commons), 14 April 1930, cols 2659–82.
76 T 175/40, Phillips, 'Treatment of Budget Deficits', 3 January 1930. Underlining in the original.
77 T 175/40, Hopkins to Chancellor and Fisher, 24 January 1930.
78 Committee on National Debt and Taxation, *Evidence*, Niemeyer, para. 8730.
79 *Hansard* (Commons), 11 April 1927, cols 94–5 and 98, 24 April 1928, col. 830, and 19 April 1932, col. 1411; *Finance Accounts, 1928–9*. The gain from the first raid on the Brewers' Credit in 1926–7 and the appropriations of the Road Fund in 1927–8, of the surplus of the CNIRA in 1928–9 and of the balance in the Exchange Account in 1931–2 are the outcomes as reported in the *Finance Accounts*. The data for the second raid on Brewers' Credit and the change in Schedule A are the forecasts made in the budget statements.
80 A footnote to the estimated assets published in *National Debt: annual returns* records 'estimated value of other Vote of Credit Assets (Surplus Stores, Ships, &c),' to be £800m at 31 March 1919 and £700m a year later. The footnote continued until 31 March 1929, but without an estimate. See also *Hansard* (Commons), 30 April 1919, cols 182–3, and 1 May 1922, cols 1046–7.

22 The development of market management

The size of the Debt, and the conversion and refinancing challenges it presented between 1919 and 1932, posed new questions about the terms the Treasury should be offering on its securities and how they could be sold at the best price. Securities sold between 1914 and 1919 had been either short- or medium-dated Bonds, with a single maturity date, or longer Loans, with double-dates. When the resumption of borrowing on funded debt came in 1921, it was controversial: a low interest rate was chosen, with a price well beneath par, adding substantially to the Debt's nominal value. The Treasury continued its preference for permanent debt until 1932, when it converted 5 per cent War Loan: at the end of March 1920, funded debt was only 4 per cent of the nominal total, by 1932 it was 19 per cent and a year later it was 42 per cent (Appendix IV).[1] In this, the Treasury felt it was returning to a pre-war normality, although it never felt sufficiently confident to forgo specific sinking funds until that great conversion into the falling interest rates of the Depression.

Before 1914, the mismatch between the continuous flow of savings and the occasional sale of new securities was circumvented in two ways: by paying intermediaries, most often merchant banks, to buy and hold the paper until it had been absorbed by investors; and by issuing the securities with calls stretching over long periods. After the end of 1915, there were open-ended taps, with securities created and sold 'day-by-day' as savings accrued: once 3 per cent Exchequer Bonds 1920 had been issued in the spring of 1915, only the conversion and partly paid offers of the $4^1/_2$ per cent, 4 per cent and 5 per cent War Loans closed at dates named in their prospectuses.

The last open-ended taps were the Fourth Series of War Bonds. The Victory Bonds and Funding Loan which followed were sold for cash partly paid in a limited period, like the War Loans. Thereafter, investors were required to respond to conversion and refinancing offers by dates specified in the prospectuses. It is unclear whether the authorities had a fully developed plan when the decision was made in 1921 to buy maturing War Bonds for the CNRA and convert them into $3^1/_2$ per cent Conversion Loan; their intention may have the camouflaging of a failure. The potential was promptly recognised and the system became the accepted method of bridging the gap between investors' responses and offers restricted in time.

The need to attract capital, from home and overseas, led to a range of tax privileges being attached to individual issues between 1915 and 1920. Officials particularly disliked non-deduction of income tax at source, the right of overseas residents to receive interest free of income tax and the use of securities to settle EPD bills. These concessions were dropped at the first opportunity. Officials also calculated that the Treasury did not receive a sufficiently high price for the death duty privilege to justify its continuance. In 1925, an analysis of the cost of the option forgone by issuing under par led some officials to advocate an end to the practice, at least as far as market conditions would permit, and this view was confirmed by the Colwyn Committee in 1927.

This chapter looks more closely at some of the methods of managing the market and pricing new issues which have appeared in earlier chapters: the role of the CNRA, and the relationship between the Treasury and the other Departmental portfolios; the amalgamation of the Issue Department and the CNRA portfolios; tax privileges; and the pricing of new issues at deep discounts.

Official portfolios and market management before 1919

The use of official portfolios to ease the Treasury's conversions originated in the nineteenth century and involved the savings bank funds managed by the Commissioners. The episodes were as sporadic as the conversions themselves but, when they occurred, they had been controversial. The TSBs had urged that the Commissioners were trustees for the funds and should invest those funds solely for the benefit of the depositors. The Treasury had claimed savers could not lose because the deposits enjoyed the guarantee of the Consolidated Fund and the holdings of government securities were but machinery (see pp. 13–14). This was put somewhat dramatically by Gladstone in 1859:

> There cannot be a more gross delusion than to think that the funds in the hands of the Commissioners of the National Debt are the funds of the depositors in the savings banks…they have no interest in the employment of the money: it does not signify to them if you fling it to the bottom of the sea…if he [the Chancellor] invests it well, they are no richer; and if he plays the tricks of the mountebank, or disposes of it with the artifices of the swindler, they are none the poorer.[2]

In 1900, Hamilton had warned that selling securities direct to depositors might draw attention to the use to which their money was being put when 'All they know and have the right to know is that for every pound deposited they will get 20/- on demand.' On that occasion, the Treasury had considered and rejected a scheme for avoiding an increase in the funded debt by selling savings bank Consols to the market and replacing them with newly issued shorter securities.[3] Two years later, Hamilton, anticipating the events of 1931, suggested that the publication of the savings banks' balance sheets should be discontinued: over a few years, they had moved from surplus to deficit because of a change in the price of Consols; 'Such an account may at any moment be used by mischievous people to create a panic, and give 'busy-bodies' ...an excuse for expatiating on the solvency of the funds'.[4]

The tension between the 'banker's' view and the 'trustee's' view of the funds was to reappear at intervals, but it may be assumed that the former enabled the Treasury to slip easily into the decision to use the CNRA to take up the block of 3 per cent Exchequer Bonds 1920 in the spring of 1915 (see pp. 96–7). Other uses are only to be glimpsed. The CNRA lent £25.7m in cash to the savings banks funds in 1915 to enable them to pay the calls on their applications for 4$^{1}/_{2}$ per cent War Loan, holdings which, in their turn, enabled the Funds to convert Consols and Annuities. The liability was then liquidated by the sale of a similar amount of War Loan to the CNRA (see p. 117).[5] During 1915, the Treasury was reluctant to become involved in the problems of the TSB Special Investment Departments and the Bank of England was left to provide support, although it was both limited and expensive. At the beginning of February 1916, Blackett minuted that as a result of mismatching assets and liabilities 'both banks [the TSBs' Special Investment Departments] & municipalities are now in trouble...& need Exchequer Assistance in some cases.'[6] Advances directly to the TSBs from the Treasury would have been subject to Parliamentary scrutiny, although they did not require legislation. Depositors might panic, and a general run might be triggered. If confidence in the banking system were shaken, sterling could be affected. The Central Powers would have been handed an easy target for propaganda. Under a Treasury Minute of 29 February 1916, the CNRA was authorised to make advances to those TSB Special Investment Departments which had become insolvent because of the depreciation of their investments. There was at least one such advance, of £530,000 to the Glasgow bank, at the end of 1917, and as late as 31 March 1920 a stray record of the CNRA's assets show advances to TSBs of £190,000.[7]

The CNRA and market management in the 1920s

The steps by which official operations in the gilt-edged market developed after the war have left scarcely a trace in the records: officials, and especially Bank officials, reacting to swiftly developing market challenges were not prone to write carefully argued memoranda. A readiness to document change was likely to be particularly scarce when it involved financial, monetary and political sensitivities, not to mention the potential for embarrassing criticism from those in the markets believing themselves damaged by official activities. The operations of the CNRA were known to very few officials, new Chancellors were enjoined to secrecy and the few records of its transactions are studded with reminders of the need for security.[a] We are left with surmise.

a Even the formal side-letter from the Bank undertaking to act in consultation with the Treasury in the management of the Issue Department portfolio after the amalgamation of the Note issues emphasised the need for 'strict secrecy at all times regarding the nature of the Securities held in the Issue Department and of the operations which may take place from time to time.' Copies are in BoE, C40/872 and T 175/125.

The gilt-edged and money markets had changed in five ways since 1914. As the 1920s unfolded, it became clear that, even apart from debt charges, the flows of money through the banking system on account of government revenue and expenditure were not going to return to their 1914 levels. Second, the war had bequeathed a float of Treasury Bills, which not only presented the challenge to monetary control that has been emphasised until now but had the potential for development into an instrument for influencing the money market. Third, there was the growth of a fiduciary note issue, whose backing of government securities gave the authorities a *masse de manoeuvre* which could be exploited in market operations. Fourth, the war left a vastly increased corpus of dated government securities of varying maturities, many requiring early refinancing. Finally, there was immediate cause for adaptation in the withdrawal of the various *ad hoc* measures for draining the banking system of the cash injected by government war spending and for setting a floor to money market rates. The special deposit scheme ended in the summer of 1919, the Treasury Bill tap was replaced by a fixed volume on weekly tender in the spring of 1921, and by the end of 1921 the Treasury had ceased using Bank Ways and Means (other than Deficiency Advances), so making necessary greater precision in the selection of the volume of Bills to be sold at tender.

The origins of the tap system, in the sense of subscription by a portfolio under the control of the authorities with the intention of later sale to the secondary market, was post-war. The Victorian and Edwardian Debt was overwhelmingly funded and the number and size of maturities was too small to demand innovation. The Bank's subscription for the Exchequer Bonds in 1891 and the later sales of newly created Bonds as demand appeared may have been the first recorded taps, but they had the limited aim of obtaining better prices than those available at the time of issue (see pp. 19–20). During the war, 'tap' was used to describe the issues of Treasury Bills, Exchequer Bonds and War Bonds when they were continuously on sale; the 5 per cent Exchequer Bonds 1920 issued on 16 December 1915 are often designated the first tap. These issues are to be distinguished from taps as they were known after 1921. During the war, securities were created as investors subscribed and the paper was sold in the primary market. After 1919 – with only a few exceptions – securities were issued in a size specified in a prospectus or as a result of a conversion offer, which closed on a planned day and resulted in the creation of securities whose size was announced and could not be increased later to suit the official portfolios in changed circumstances. Part of these finite issues were taken by the CNRA, which peddled the securities into the secondary market as demand was felt.

It is surmise, but the experience with the Treasury's public issues in New York was probably the stimulus to continuous activity in the secondary market in the 1920s. Morgans used five techniques, all of which became known to both the Treasury and Bank or, indeed, involved the Bank as principal and the Treasury as guarantor. First, to ensure that issues could be described as fully subscribed or oversubscribed, Morgans applied on behalf of themselves or the Bank, later selling the securities in the secondary market. Second, they stood ready to intervene in the secondary market immediately after issue, again either on their own account or on that of the Bank. Third, in the case of the Anglo-French Loan, they continually intervened, initially as a buyer, later as both buyer and seller, for the British and French Treasuries. This was intended to ensure that a small break did not cause alarm and thus a larger drop.[8] These three procedures were kept secret from the market, for they would have been less effective if published: although legal, the intention was to mislead investors. The other two ploys were known to the public. The sale of collateral to raise money with which to buy issues was permitted under the terms of the prospectuses. It had no relevance to post-war domestic borrowing except to show the Treasury that, with imagination and aggression, markets could be massaged. The purchase of maturing Notes in January 1919, and their conversion into Bonds, was a foretaste of what was to become a well-tried technique in the gilt-edged market.

For six years after the war, the CNRA's activities in the gilt-edged market can only be inferred from the transactions recorded in its accounts, which have survived from March 1919. Besides these, the first records of the CNRA's post-war role are the discussions in the Bank before the amalgamation of the Issue Department's Notes with the Treasury's Currency Notes, that is, some four or five years after the accounts show the existence of active market management. The portfolio was described as being used to buy up maturing issues with a view to converting them for later sale or with the intention of 'easing the position on redemption'. The ability to exchange the assets held in the portfolio was, wrote Phillips, 'really the only power we have to carry on <u>continuous</u> conversion operations', which would become more important as the start of the 5 per cent War Loan option approached. There was agreement that such a block of securities was vital: in the absence of an alternative, the new Issue Department would have to continue where the CNRA had left off.[9]

Since at least 1916, the Account had acted as a counterparty to other government departments, such as the India Office, the Northern Ireland government, the Clearing Office for Enemy Debts and, especially, the National Debt Commissioners. It had three roles. First, the market might not be sufficiently liquid to handle the large block that a Department might want to buy or sell: the Account would take or supply the paper and reverse the transaction in the market in small amounts when conditions permitted. Second, the holding might be a short date which the authorities wanted to keep under their own control for conversion or redemption. Third, if the Commissioners were exchanging marketable securities for, say, capital advances, the Account could take the Commissioners' paper, which might have a less ready market, and sell some other security which was in greater demand (see pp. 651–4).[10]

The CNRA invested in the early post-war maturities, but both the issues themselves and the Account's holdings were small. Most important, the Account purchased little as the issues approached maturity. In March 1919, it had a small holding of 5 per cent Exchequer Bonds of 1 December 1919, and made no further purchases. It appears to have taken cash on 1 December. It had a small investment in the next maturity, 6 per cent Exchequer Bonds of 16 February 1920, of which half were bought in the final quarter of 1919, but it was only £2m and was most likely a chance acquisition. Although the issue of the 6 per cents was large, and the Treasury and Bank nervous, it was left to the innate attractions of the new 5¾ per cent Exchequer Bonds to ensure success; the Account merely accepted the offer and converted such of the 1920 maturities as it happened to own. It also had a small holding of 5 per cent Exchequer Bonds of 1 December 1920. This was never enlarged.[11]

In contrast, there was continuous intervention in New York during 1920, when Morgans bought so much of the Anglo-French Loan as agents for the Treasury that at maturity on 15 October only $42.6m of the British share remained in the hands of the public.[12] In 1921, Morgans' techniques were introduced wholesale into London: buying maturing issues in the market, accepting the conversion offers and then dribbling out the newly acquired holdings were combined in the handling of the offer to convert into 3½ per cent Conversion (see pp. 432–3). By 1925, subscriptions for longer-dated securities, which had begun as a way of ensuring sales in an unenthusiastic market, had grown to the point where the decision whether to make a particular issue might be determined by whether the Account's operations could make use of the particular security.

The Account also became the means of influencing the size of the overall floating debt and that part held in the private sector. At the end of the war, the Bank, assuming that the large issue of Treasury Bills was temporary, confined its operations to helping the market to absorb new Bills, minimising the volume of its Ways and Means Advances. On occasion, it bought Bills when money was particularly tight, sometimes on the understanding that the proceeds would be used to apply for new Bills. The small size of the Bank's Bill portfolio limited its ability to use Bill sales and purchases to maintain a desired level of rates. From May 1923, the Bank reverted to its pre-war practice of borrowing directly from those with large deposits with whom it had a close relationship, such as, at different times, Barings, Schroders, the National Bank of Egypt, the National Bank of Hungary and the Commonwealth Bank of Australia.[13]

Although the part played by the CNRA is not clear in the immediate post-war years, by 1925 officials were at ease with several procedures. The floating debt could be reduced by the Account applying for a new issue and paying by running off its Bills or Ways and Means. For a more immediate impact, the application would be fully paid. If it was desired to reduce the volume of Bills held in the private sector, the Account's securities, preferably long-dated, could be sold in the market. Again, the authorities could massage the timing of the effects by selecting either fully paid or partly paid issues. The Account's Bill portfolio was in constant use facilitating the Exchequer's transactions with the market. Subscriptions for longer-dated securities were influenced by whether they would fit in with the desired size and maturity of the Account's Bill holdings. Whenever the CNRA subscribed for a new issue, it was exchanging either Ways and Means or Bills for longer-dated securities, the Bills being sold or run off – depending on the maturities of the Bills already held in the market – and the proceeds applied to paying the calls as they became due. If the dates of the Bills did not coincide with the calls, they would still be run off, and the proceeds lent to the Treasury for a few days as Ways and Means.[14] Inevitably, seasonal fluctuations in revenue and expenditure produced volatility in the Exchequer's residual financing needs. If this had been met by changing the size of the Bill tender, it would have produced volatility in rates. To some extent, it was smoothed by taking Deficiency Advances from the Banking Department, a standard practice around heavy dividend dates, such as the £50m required half-yearly for 5 per cent War Loan.[15] But this was occasional, and the Exchequer's activities were continuous.

Switching between Bills of different maturities, and between Ways and Means Advances and Bills, limited the impact on the banking system of the Exchequer's transactions. The CNRA became, in Phillips's words, 'a source of daily cash when it is needed and a sink for cash when it is not needed.'[16] The Account could sell Bills in the market and lend the money to the Treasury on Ways and Means when money was needed, or buy Bills, reducing Ways and Means, when the Treasury was in surplus. It could switch the portfolio so that it held more Bills maturing in heavy weeks than in light, smoothing the volume in the market. The Treasury could also issue more Bills in light weeks than it needed to meet its deficit. It would then use the extra funds to repay the Account's Ways and Means Advances, the Account using the money to buy Bills maturing in heavy weeks. An alternative, used only occasionally, was to keep the volume sold at tender below the Treasury's needs, at the same time running off the Account's Bills as they matured, or selling them in the market. The Account then lent the money which had been freed to the Treasury as Ways and Means. Although none of these manoeuvres changed either the total volume of the floating debt or the volume in the hands of the market, which were set by the Treasury's residual financing needs, they did alter the maturities of the Bills held by the market.[17]

The way in which these operations worked is illustrated by transactions in the first quarter of 1929, shortly after the amalgamation of the Note issues. The Treasury had to pay off some £74m maturities on 1 February, with a further £30.2m on 1 April. It had sold £46.2m 4½ per cent Treasury Bonds 1932–4 for cash at the end of the previous year, on which a call of £89 per cent was payable on 3 April. The Issue Department had subscribed for £25m. The Chancellor having been advised that there should be no further new issues for the time being and that he should rely on Bills and Ways and Means (see pp. 576–7), a solution was needed which would either bring forward into February the proceeds of the call on the 4½ per cent Treasury Bonds due on 3 April or, if extra Bills had to be sold to meet the February maturities, minimise the effect on the market. Three courses were adopted. During January and February, the Issue Department sold 4½ per cent Treasury Bonds, both partly and fully paid, with the call on the initial sales of the latter paid by running off the Issue Department's Bills and the proceeds being used to pay up the call on the next batch of Bonds destined for sale. The Treasury started to issue Bills in excess of its needs, putting the Issue Department in funds by repaying Ways and Means; the Department then used the funds to buy the February Bill maturities. At the same time, the Bank offered to buy the 1 February gilt-edged maturities early, at a discount.[18]

The amalgamation of the Note issues

The amalgamation of the Note issues on 22 November 1928 was important to the development of market management in two ways: the replacement of most of the Ways and Means Advances previously provided by the CNRA with Treasury Bills; and the powers given to the Bank to hold securities of any nature in the Issue Department portfolio. Until the amalgamation, the Bank was constrained in its market operations by the lack of assets under its direct control. The Banking Department had bought perpetual issues to secure the income for a stable dividend, with the result that in the first half of the 1920s only £10m to £15m was available for investment in Bills and short-dated gilt-edged issues. The Issue Department held £19m against the fiduciary issue, of which £11m was the historic debt. The two Departments together could, therefore, hold only £20m Bills and other short debt, a portfolio which could not provide the wide spread of Bill maturities needed to manage the market. The Bank had to rely on the CNRA. However, while the Bank was kept informed of the Account's activities, and made suggestions and gave advice, the operations were conducted on the Treasury's initiative and on the Treasury's account. It may have been prepared to adjust to suit the Bank's needs, but control is different from advice, even if the advice is normally accepted.[19] The Bank looked forward to controlling a bigger portfolio.

A large part of the CNRA's assets were Ways and Means, which Bank and Treasury officials agreed should cease. Hitherto they had been concealed in the weekly Exchequer Returns by inclusion within Advances made by government departments as a whole. If they were to be made by the Issue Department, they would need to be separately identified as coming from the Bank. Because Advances from the Banking Department were sporadic, this would, in effect, show the size of Advances from Issue. There was also the danger that they would be confused in the public mind with those from the Banking Department, which were still a sensitive memory after five or six years.[20] The replacement of Ways and Means with Bills was the obvious answer except that, in accordance with the 1915 Treasury Minute, the Account's Ways and Means paid no interest. Paying the market rate for Bills would not alter the balance of the budget: the profits of the Issue Department were to be paid to the Treasury, which would merely pay out more in interest and receive it back as miscellaneous revenue. It would affect the Fixed Charge: the proportion absorbed by interest would rise, that devoted to debt repayment would fall. This had to be avoided; in his Financial Statement on 24 April, the Chancellor was to present firm plans for the debt repayment to be expected within the Charge. An alternative was to replace the Ways and Means with unmarketable non-interest-bearing Book Debt. This would have been cumbersome and, more importantly, because the size of the fiduciary issue had to be stipulated in the Act, it would have reduced the volume of assets available for market management. There would need to be good reasons for limiting the Bank's room for manoeuvre in this way. The argument was strengthened by the Governor, who pointed out that the Bank already had wide discretion over the assets held in the existing Issue Department and that the 1844 Bank Act merely prescribed 'securities'. He persuaded the Treasury of his views and the 1928 Act followed that of 1844.[21]

The solution came to the Treasury shortly before the budget. The £260m securities held by the new Issue Department would have earned about £11m a year at a commercial rate, but £4.75m a year would be ample to meet expenses and possible depreciation of a portfolio of £60m longer securities. If these provided an income of, say, £2.75m a year, the remaining £200m assets should be designed to produce £2m a year. The Treasury had power to issue Bills in place of Ways and Means. The Treasury Minute of 1889, already published, authorised the issue of Bills to the Commissioners or other persons at a fixed rate of discount selected by the Treasury and with any maturity not exceeding twelve months. There was nothing to prevent the Treasury issuing £200m Bills to the Issue Department at an arbitrary discount rate. There would be no need for a clause in the legislation and no publicity as the weekly Exchequer Return would merely show a composite figure. If the Bills were resold, they would be indistinguishable from those bought at tender by the market. The Issue Department would make a loss when selling the Bills to the market at the higher commercial rate, but a profit on those it bought. If the Department was selling longer paper, it would invest the proceeds in these 'tap' Bills or run off its existing holdings.

The Bank greeted the idea with enthusiasm.[22] By a Treasury Minute of 22 November 1928, the rate for Bills was fixed at 1 per cent for the Issue Department only, Ways and Means remaining interest free.[b] The Treasury had already begun issuing Bills in excess of its needs, repaying Ways and Means as the CNRA tendered: on the eve of the amalgamation, the Account's Bill holdings had risen to £185m and Advances had fallen to £15.3m; of the latter, £13.2m were to be utilised in the repayment of the CNRIA's surplus to the Treasury.[23]

The Bank had freedom to switch the securities held in the existing Issue Department portfolio and wanted this to be extended to the assets taken over from the CNRA. In October 1927, Niemeyer had suggested an exchange of letters in which the Bank would promise to continue to manage the assets as the Treasury had managed those of the CNRA, but as late as April the draft bill included a clause requiring close consultation with the Treasury and compliance with its directions.[24] At about this time the Treasury came to accept the case for giving the Bank discretion, apparently fearing overseas opinion might think that the Notes were not a central bank issue if the Department were controlled by the Treasury.[25] The Treasury also thought it should have the final say on which securities were held, but was not confident of winning Parliamentary sanction for retaining control. In short, it was ready to accept an amendment, if the Bank strongly pressed the point. The result was that a side-letter said:

b This continued until 1 July 1932 when, in view of the drop in short rates, the rate of discount on Bills was made the same rate as that on 'Additional Bills', with a maximum of 1 per cent. TM, 1 July 1932.

> the Bank recognise that the Government are entitled to ask that the Treasury shall be kept fully and constantly informed regarding all operations affecting the securities held from time to time in the Issue Department.
>
> ...in their future management of the securities in the Issue Department the Bank will act in personal consultation with the Treasury on lines similar to those hitherto followed in connection with operations affecting the Securities of the Currency Note Account,[26]

while the Act stipulated: 'The Bank shall from time to time give to the Treasury such information as the Treasury may require with respect to the securities held in the issue department'.

There are only occasional glimpses of the change in the running of the portfolio brought about by the amalgamation. The position before November 1928 is shown by the tone of a letter from the Governor to Hopkins in September 1927. The context was the maturity of War Bonds, a tender for Treasury Bonds and an exchange of securities with the savings banks' portfolios:

> I make the following suggestions in a letter in order that we may discuss them at your convenience...I suggest a tender should...be lodged next Tuesday for not less than £15,000,000 of the 4½ Bonds, and you could well afford to make the price £99: 8: –. This will enable me to sell a long stock to the public while you keep a short stock in hand with a view to its conversion on some future occasion.[27]

This can be compared with the deference paid to the Bank's independence in 1930 and 1931 when the question of which securities the Issue Department would be prepared to buy from the Commissioners was under discussion. Having sold their most marketable holdings, the Commissioners still held 2½ per cent Consols, which the Governor refused to 'touch' (see p. 654).[28] The Bank could be 'requested' to buy the short-dated Bonds being held by the Commissioners to assist conversion and:

> it may be that the Bank would be willing to adopt this course, although the Bank have the last word in the matter...We should ascertain whether the Bank is willing to take over short Bonds...though...it may not be in accordance with the Bank's views. If the Bank is not willing to take the short Bonds to keep, they must be sold to the market.[29]

The Governor took the short Bonds, but not Consols, even in the emergency of 1931.[30]

Official operations – the Commissioners

With the exception of the CNRA (the Issue Department being part of the Bank), the National Debt Office had more continuous contact with the markets than any other government department. The Commissioners were responsible for administering Northcote's sinking fund and the sterling operations of the sinking funds of 1923 and 1928, as well as various public funds. As before 1914, by far the most important were those of the POSB and the TSBs, which, in 1925, represented nearly three-quarters of the total.[31] The Treasury's relationship with the Commissioners lay in an intermediate position between the direct control it exercised over the portfolio of the CNRA and its influence over the post-1928 Issue Department. The Chancellor, the Governor and the Deputy-Governor were only three of seven Commissioners, but they formed a quorum and the Comptroller of the Debt Office accepted their decisions as final.[c] Not that it often came to this for, except *in extremis*, the Comptroller administered the funds in accordance with the Treasury's explicit or implicit needs. They were handled sympathetically to aid the Treasury's operations in the gilt-edged market, absorbing maturing issues and, in general, accepting offers to convert or sell securities to the CNRA or Issue Department. The funds supported market prices. Transactions were carried out with a view to their effect on the floating debt and that part held in the private sector. Content to provide the volume of capital advances ordained by the Treasury on wider grounds of policy, even if it did not suit their portfolios, the Comptroller became restless only when the marketable holdings had been shredded by the Advances to the Unemployment Fund in 1930. Even then, his protests may have been made with the connivance (or, even, at the initiative) of Treasury officials (see pp. 653–4). Finally, the Treasury had an interest in the profits of the savings banks.

While paying lip-service to the funds' quasi-independent status, the Treasury often treated the funds in a cavalier fashion. This was, perhaps, an inevitable consequence of the guarantee and the Treasury's ultimate responsibility for the portfolios. The tradition was a long one. In 1905, the Chancellor had baldly described the simplest method of funding as the Commissioners buying up Bills and Exchequer Bonds with savings bank money and converting them into newly issued Consols. The tone of a further memorandum from Hamilton six months later, describing the working of the sinking funds and savings bank annuities, led to a protest from Turpin which probably reflects the nuance of the pre-war relationship:

> you will scarcely expect me to be in harmony with the keynote which runs all through it [the memorandum], namely that the Savings Banks funds are to be exploited for the benefit of the Exchequer. But beyond putting on record my protest against such a heretical doctrine...I do not propose to say more.[32]

c In 1948, the Financial Secretary confirmed that for many years the Chancellor, Governor and Deputy Governor formed a quorum: 'day-to-day decisions by the National Debt Commissioners are taken in the office of the National Debt Commissioners and under the guidance and control of the Comptroller-General. It is only in matters of policy and where decisions are slightly out of the day-to-day running of the department are concerned [*sic*], that they go to the National Debt Commissioners themselves for advice, guidance and decision.' *Hansard* (Commons), 19 July 1948, cols 177–9.

It can be assumed that the availability of the portfolios of the CNRA and the Issue Department for the more adventurous Treasury transactions removed the most serious tensions felt by the Debt Office personnel acting simultaneously as civil servants and trustees, but the Treasury's treatment remained ambiguous. This was most noticeable in its attitude towards the capital position of the savings banks. The profits were calculated without allowing for capital shortfall, which was considerable in the 1920s and early 1930s when yields were high. Because of the guarantee, the Treasury felt able to ignore this, but it still contended that, as the assets had not given a sufficient return once capital losses were taken into account, the rate paid to depositors should not be raised (see p. 646). In 1930 and 1931, it paused over selling 2½ per cent Consols because of the potential loss to the State of selling a low interest rate security at such a discount.[33]The capital advances made at its behest had the effect of freezing the value of assets, insulating values when yields were rising but depriving the funds of appreciation when yields fell. In 1922–3, the Treasury decided to repay a savings bank annuity early because it believed that gilt-edged prices were about to rise, so that it would have cost more if it waited (see pp. 649–50).

In the mid-thirties, the Debt Office regarded its conventional policy as the retention of 'satisfactory' holdings, even when there were profits to be taken or a higher yield to be obtained. It had always been considered 'undesirable for a Government Department to do anything in the nature of speculation'. 'Speculation' was drawn very widely, and included exchanging a dated for a perpetual issue with a view to minimising depreciation when yields were expected to rise. The Debt Office also feared the effect of large transactions, although less than before 1914, when £½m in the gilt-edged market could move prices. It needed to be sensitive about other holdings where the market was very thin: the 2¾ per cent and 3 per cent Guaranteed Stocks and, to a lesser extent, Local Loans. It had to avoid 'reckless' transactions and, more politically, avoid any transaction which might look to be a 'blunder' if the expectations on which it was based proved false: in Hawtrey's words, 'there should be no very wide departure from the principles of puritanical finance.'[34]

One example of the relationship was provided in April 1924, when holders of 5 per cent War Loan were being offered conversion into 4½ per cent Conversion Loan 1940–4. Niemeyer called for details of all departmental holdings on the Bank's register and wrote to the administrators of each, including the Debt Office.

> From my point of view it is of considerable importance that as much of these holdings as possible should be converted and I should have thought that from your point of view it was good policy also, at any rate as regards sums that you are likely to be holding up to and beyond 1929. Perhaps you would let me know how much you think you can do?[35]

Niemeyer pressed the Commissioners again at the end of 1926, when it was a question of converting maturing War Bonds into 4 per cent Consols:

> I hope you are taking active steps ..I don't think you need be unduly obsessed about liquidity. The new 4%'s should be pretty readily saleable: and in any case you enjoy special facilities for liquefying, if necessary, via the Currency Note Account.[36]

In these cases, there was an eminent Treasury Knight, responsible for policy, putting officials in a less august administrative department on the spot; the pressure was expected to be taken seriously, and the reaction showed that it was. However, in both examples, a commercial case could have been made (see pp. 558 and 567). This was not so in July 1929, when the question was whether to convert part of the savings banks' holding of 4½ per cent Treasury 1932–4 into 4 per cent Consols. The savings banks held £25m of the Bonds, which had been issued late the previous year. When the option was priced, 4 per cent Consols were 85⅜; by 26 July, they had fallen to 82⅝, but the 4½ per cent Treasury Bonds had also fallen, to reach 95¹⁵⁄₁₆. The option had to be taken up by 31 July (see p. 576). By selling the Treasury Bonds and reinvesting in 4 per cent Consols in the market, the funds could have bought £1m more Consols than by converting. Despite this, the Debt Office converted £7.5m of their Bonds, a quarter of their holding.

Phillips had already written to Hopkins on 24 July:

> It seems to me very much in our general interests that he [Headlam, the Comptroller] should convert since we want to lighten our future conversions in every way possible. I have arranged for Bank [*sic*] to report to Ismay Saturday morning whether Headlam has converted. If he hasn't acted by then perhaps you would have a word with him. I should much prefer that he converted on his own initiative without suggestions from here, but if he doesn't do so we must try to persuade him.[37]

The staff of the Debt Office were also urging the Comptroller to convert, but the loss was such that he did not feel justified in doing so without the authority of the Chancellor, acting in his capacity as a Commissioner. The Comptroller said that there were three possibilities. First, to accept the option and take the loss. This would help the government's conversion efforts at no risk to the depositors, who had their guarantee, and there would be the hope that a rise in the market would make the transaction profitable compared with taking cash at maturity in 1932 or 1934 and reinvesting in 4 per cent Consols. Second, to use the market to sell the Bonds and reinvest, as would a private trustee. The Government Broker believed that this was feasible, provided the transaction was carried out slowly. However,

> while the National Debt Commissioners are also Trustees of these Funds, they could not, in my view, take the risk of injuring Government credit, while, as a Government Department, it would mean acting in a sense contrary to the Government's intention.

Third, to hold the Bonds to maturity and receive either cash or convert into whatever was then offered.

The Comptroller's own view was that the first alternative, with its 'apparent loss', would be difficult for the Commissioners to justify. The second alternative was 'out of the question'.[38] Hopkins agreed that making an exchange in the market would be unacceptable, emphasised that conversion would not affect the depositors, whose interest was 'secured by government guarantee', and that conversion would leave the interest income unchanged but fixed for longer. The financial position was so fragile that it would be 'unreasonable' to convert the complete holding and, when the results were published, a large response would excite public comment in view of the loss involved. Thus, £10m 'looks rather too high', but Headlam should 'be encouraged' to convert a quarter of the holding. The Chancellor accepted the recommendation.[39]

Official operations – other departments

The deference paid by other departments to the Treasury's requests varied with their responsibilities, the administrative complexity of complying and the extent to which they could call upon support from other centres of power or influence. The records show that their defences, when properly deployed, could hold the Treasury at bay. In April 1924, the Official Trustees of Charitable Funds effortlessly countered Niemeyer's suggestion that they convert 5 per cent War Loan by pointing out that they held the paper on behalf of some five thousand separate charities and that they could not make the applications on their own initiative.[40] A different argument protected the Paymaster-General for and on behalf of the Supreme Court of Judicature, the holder of £9.5m War Loan. In his case, most of the funds were held on behalf of many different individuals, each with different requirements, with conflicts between tenants for life and annuitants. Every holding would have to be considered on its merits, in consultation with the beneficiaries. Niemeyer accepted that it would be 'quite impossible for the Supreme Court to convert en masse after the manner of Charlemagne baptising the Saxons', but asked that the Paymaster circularise those with an interest advocating conversion.[41]

The Crown Agents saw themselves as trustees for the colonies on whose behalf they invested. At the beginning of January 1927, they refused to convert War Bonds held on behalf of the Malay States into 4 per cent Consols because they feared depreciation; the securities were being held, for gradual sale, as the Colonies' contribution to the construction of the Singapore Naval Base. The Agents proposed that, if they converted and the securities depreciated, the Treasury should guarantee to buy the Consols at the issue price. This was refused, but they were persuaded to switch into 1928 War Bonds through the Bank: 'We are always glad to help the Treasury in such matters so far as we can do so with due regard to our position as trustees', the agents wrote. 'Not they', scribbled Niemeyer.[42]

Pricing issues: tax privileges

Between 1915 and 1920, five tax privileges had been attached to new issues of government securities:

1 Exemption of the interest from liability to assessment to UK income tax, but not supertax. This privilege was carried by the tax-compounded securities[d] and Savings Certificates.

2 Payment of interest in full, without deduction of income tax at source, but with liability to assessment in the hands of the recipients. This privilege was first given (retrospectively) to the issue of 5 per cent Exchequer Bonds 1920 in December 1915 and was attached to all subsequent issues (with the exception of tax-compounded issues, where it was irrelevant) up to and including the Fourth Series of War Bonds in January 1919.

3 Exemption of interest from income tax and supertax, so long as it was shown in the manner directed by the Treasury that the securities were in the beneficial ownership of persons who were not ordinarily resident in the UK.

4 Exemption from all taxation, present or future, including death duties, so long as it was shown in the manner directed by the Treasury that the securities were in the beneficial ownership of persons who were neither domiciled nor ordinarily resident in the UK.

(3) and (4) were first given (in this case, not retrospectively) on the 5 per cent Exchequer Bonds 1920 in December 1915. They were attached to all subsequent issues (other than tax-compounded issues) up to and including that of 5¾ per cent Exchequer Bonds 1925 issued in January 1920.[e]

5 The right to tender securities to the Inland Revenue in settlement of death duties, EPD and Munitions Exchequer Payments. This was introduced for death duties with the issue of 6 per cent Exchequer Bonds 1920 in September 1916 and for EPD and Munitions Exchequer Payments with the 5 per cent Exchequer Bonds 1922 in April 1917. The privilege was attached to all subsequent issues up to and including the Fourth Series of War Bonds.

d There was no statutory definition of 'tax-compounded'. The principle was that no income tax would be levied on the interest, but the tax not paid would be added back for the purpose of calculating allowances and the liability to supertax. Thus, the interest was to be treated 'as if the amount received represented the net income after deduction of income-tax at the full normal rate.' That is, if the normal (basic) rate of income tax were 5s (as it was in 1916–17 and 1917–18), a net dividend of £400 was to be returned as a gross income of £533 6s 8d. *Hansard* (Commons), 5 May 1917, col. 1291.

e Committee on National Debt and Taxation, Appendix V, p. 20, says that the privilege of non-deduction and freedom from tax for non-residents was given first to 3 per cent Exchequer Bonds 1920 issued in March 1915. There is no record of this. In accordance with a statement in the prospectus for 5 per cent Exchequer Bonds 1919 and 1921 issued on 27 May 1916 and using powers contained in the Finance Act 1916, the privilege was given retrospectively in July 1916 to the 5 per cent Exchequer Bonds 1920 issued on 16 December 1915. There was no mention of extending the privilege to the March 1915 issue. The privilege relating to non-residents first appeared in the prospectus for 5 per cent Exchequer Bonds 1920 on 16 December 1915.

The draft prospectuses for the abortive January 1919 funding Loan show that the privilege relating to EPD and Munitions Exchequer Payments would have ended with that issue, had it proceeded. Instead, it was maintained with the Fourth Series of War Bonds issued at the end of that month and was not discontinued until the issue of the 4 per cent Victory Bonds and Funding Loan in June 1919.[43] The argument was one of cost, rather than their attraction to industrial and commercial capital awaiting surrender to the Inland Revenue. The abortive Loan would have had a running yield of £5 4s 0d per cent, compared with £5 0s 0d per cent on the 5 per cent War Bonds (if the premium on maturity was ignored), and would have been valued at the equivalent of par if used to pay taxes. Holdings destined for the payment of EPD would thus have received an extra 4s per cent interest, although there would have been no advantage to the Treasury as both the War Bonds and the envisaged Loan were, in effect, Treasury Bills maturing on the date they were tendered for tax. If £100m was held by those intending to tender them in settlement of EPD, the Treasury would be paying an extra £200,000 a year in interest and £250,000 (¹/₄ per cent) in commission 'for the mere appearance' of funding that much short debt.[44]

The last issues to include the death duties privilege were 4 per cent Victory Bonds and Funding Loan. When 5 per cent War Loan was converted in 1932, the concession was dropped, leaving Victory and Funding as the only issues carrying the clause.

In March 1920, the Royal Commission on Income Tax recommended that income tax should be deducted at source from the interest on British government securities and that, as the income arose in the UK, non-residents should be liable to assessment to the tax, as had been the standard practice before 1915.[45] The two recommendations were linked inasmuch as it would have been pointless to withdraw the non-resident privileges unless deduction at source was reimposed: there was no mechanism for taxing non-residents once the gross interest had been paid. The Treasury had never liked non-deduction, had accepted it with great reluctance, and was quick to reimpose it. In December 1918, Bradbury advised that 'It would be very unwise to continue the exemption in favour of the non resident for an indefinite period'. However, such was the need at the time to persuade both domestic and foreign holders to switch longer into the envisaged funding loan that he compromised and suggested that non-deduction should be maintained with the new Loan, but for a period limited to ten years.[46] Taxation at source was reintroduced in June 1919 for the 4 per cent Victory Bonds and Funding Loan, the non-resident privileges being retained. The latter were also retained for the 5³/₄ per cent Exchequer Bonds 1925, issued in January 1920, and were then withdrawn for issues subsequent to the Royal Commission's Report.

The Treasury fleshed out its dislike of tax privileges in its evidence to the Colwyn Committee. Exemptions were objectionable because they enabled some people to be free of general tax liabilities, they were complicated to administer and it was doubtful if the State received an adequate price for them. They were meant to make an issue attractive, presumably as an alternative to a lower price:

> Their radical defect from this point of view is the necessary uncertainty of their value to the recipient. He does not know what his future income will be, or (in the case of death duties) how soon and under what market conditions he will enjoy the privilege of tendering his securities at par...He naturally tends to estimate the advantages of a tax concession with a very safe margin in his own favour. In these circumstances it is hardly doubtful that the State does not in fact obtain in improved loan conditions anything approaching the real value of the tax concessions it gives. At best it is entering on a doubtful speculation instead of, as in the alternative of e.g. a lower issue price, facing a certainty, the financial effect of which is known to both parties...The only defence for such privileges is that in moments of emergency they may be unavoidable and that in dealing with a National Debt of £7,000 millions it may be impossible to avoid second-rate financial expedients.

The draft, of course, came from Niemeyer.[47]

Pricing issues: heavy discounts

The Colwyn Report was 'in entire agreement' with the Treasury that investors would not pay, in the form of a higher price, the equivalent of the tax concessions attached to government securities.[48] By 1926, this was of no practical importance: the terms of existing issues could not be changed and the Treasury had not made issues with tax privileges since 1920 and had no intention of resuming. However, the Committee's attack on issues at a heavy discount, described by Phillips as 'one of the more controversial parts of the Report,' was highly relevant to current policy for the Treasury was still issuing 3½ per cent Conversion and was considering its replacement.[49] The practice had been hotly disputed since 1921, the grounds for criticism usually being those stated by Churchill: that the increase in the nominal value meant an increase in the burden of the capital on future generations (see pp. 682–3). Niemeyer had not participated in the original decision to issue Conversion but he had become its principal defender, continually stressing that the nominal value of the Debt was irrelevant and that the cost of issues should be judged by their annual servicing costs.

Officials' realisation that they were selling expensive paper came slowly in 1925 and 1926, coinciding with the discussions which were drawing attention to the value of the long option on 5 per cent War Loan and the sensitivity of the budget to differences in the new, lower, nominal rates, which might become feasible. In February 1925, Phillips pointed out that a comparison of the yields in the long end of the market showed that the investor did not mind whether the coupon was '3, 3½ or 4' and, in the case of double-dated issues, placed no value on the last date, provided it was sufficiently distant; the GRYs and Net Redemption Yields (NRYs) on Local Loans (callable at any time), Conversion (callable after 1961), 4 per cent Victory Bonds and 4 per cent Funding (callable between 1960 and 1990) were all within a penny or two of each other. In contrast, the yield on 4½ per cent Conversion 1940–4 was some £0 5s 0d per cent above that on perpetual and longer-dated paper. It followed, he said, that the Treasury did not get a better price by promising repayment by 1944, but paid heavily for the right to repay in 1940, and that 'the possibility of redemption after 15 years is treated very seriously, while redemption after 35 years is treated as a matter of indifference.'[50] Phillips had not pursued the line of thought, but the value of a distant option was Hawtrey's starting point in April 1926 when he sought, successfully, to demonstrate that the original sale of Conversion had been an expensive mistake and that, in future, issues should be made at or near par with a current nominal rate. He pointed out that, although it might not matter to investors whether they were repaid £7,700 or £10,000 in forty years' time, it did matter to the government, whose debt policy

> must be based on long views. Sinking fund policy is framed for a generation ahead. An option which may be worth hundreds of millions to the Government in 1961 must be regarded as very valuable.

The nominal value of a funded issue was the amount the government had to pay to redeem the capital; a larger nominal capital meant a less favourable option. The higher the interest rate on an issue, the more yields had to fall to make it profitable for the government to call it. Calling a 4½ per cent issue in 1961 and converting it to 3½ per cent would save £1m a year for each £100m of nominal debt, with a capital value of nearly £30m and a present value (at 4 per cent) of about £7m, or seven points in the price. Moreover, rates had been so high in 1921 that it was likely that they would fall. What would investors pay, in the form of a lower nominal rate, for greater protection against being called in 1961? Would they pay anything at all? 'It is doubtful.' Investors were certainly deterred by a very early option, but not by an event forty or fifty years hence. In short, funded issues should be priced near par.[51]

Six months later, in his second evidence to the Colwyn Committee, Niemeyer acknowledged that 'a great deal' of the criticism of the original issue of Conversion was justified. He agreed that, as a general proposition, it was preferable to issue at or near par. But conversions and refinancings did not always come at convenient moments and 'you have to make the best arrangements you can in the light of the then position of the market.' He emphasised the size of the Debt, with the necessity of offering a range of nominal rates to vary the diet, and the long-term plan of leading yields lower as conversion followed conversion, with the low coupon providing the carrot of a capital gain: 'to make your stocks popular, you have to make people think, each time, that they never will get them on such favourable terms again.' He offered two other defences: the attached sinking fund meant that a 'good deal' of the Stock would be paid off beneath par before 1961, after which the government had the right to call the issue; and that there was no liability to repay at all 'unless the State thinks it is desirable or thinks that it is in their [*sic*] interest to pay it off.' It would be foolish to issue a perpetual Stock with a high nominal rate of interest, such as 6 or 7 per cent, but a rate such as 3½ per cent had been reached 'even in pre-war days, which at any rate for many years ahead is not so expensive that it need cause us anxiety.' He then declared that 'actuarially'

4^1/2 per cent at par was the same as 3^1/2 per cent at 73.[52] The members did not pursue this uncharacteristically muddled evidence and, instead, focused their questions on the preference of holders for tax-free capital gain over taxable current interest.[53]

When the Treasury received the Colwyn Report in November 1926, Niemeyer established an internal committee, chaired by Phillips, to consider it.[54] Hawtrey's analysis was developed further. Phillips treated the question as an aspect of the debate about attaching tax privileges to specific securities. To take his example, the Treasury could issue £101m nominal of 4^1/2 per cent debt at 99 to raise £100m, at an annual charge of £4.545m for 35 years. Alternatively, it could issue £121m nominal of 3^1/2 per cent debt at 82^1/2 to raise the same sum, at an annual charge of £4.242m. By choosing the 3^1/2s, the Treasury would save £300,000 a year in interest for 35 years, but would increase the capital cost of redemption by £20m. If tax was ignored, the interest saving balanced the extra cost of redemption. But, assuming income tax was paid at 20 per cent, the £300,000 interest saving on the 3^1/2s dropped to £240,000. The capital gain, represented by the difference between the issue price and par, was free of tax. Allowing for this, the saving in interest and the increased cost of redemption did not balance. The Treasury, therefore, had to obtain a price higher than 82^1/2 for the 3^1/2s if it was not to be the loser. It had decided in the case of tax privileges that the investor would not pay a sufficiently high price to compensate it for the loss of revenue involved in giving the advantage and there was, wrote Phillips, no reason to think differently in this case.

Perpetual issues were different. 3^1/2 per cent at 77 was the same as 4^1/2 per cent at 99 in that each raised £99m and cost £4.545m a year to service. In neither case was there an obligation on the Treasury to redeem. In both cases, there was an option to redeem after, say, 1961. That option, agreed the Colwyn Committee, Hawtrey and Phillips, had a value. If the Treasury issued at 4^1/2 per cent, and yields fell to 3^1/2 per cent, the Treasury could convert in 1961 and save £1m a year. If it had borrowed at 3^1/2 per cent, the issue would have risen to par, the holder would have benefited, but the Treasury option would be worthless. Phillips's calculation of the value of the option mirrored Hawtrey's. A saving of £1m a year from 1961 was worth £28.571m of capital with a present value of about £7m – seven points in the price – when discounted at 4 per cent. If it was assumed that there was an even chance of yields falling to 3^1/2 per cent in 1961, the difference between issuing at 3^1/2 per cent and 4^1/2 per cent was three and a half points in the price. If it was assumed that yields would fall to some intermediate point, the option would be worth less, but would still have a value. The question thus became, again, a part of the argument about how much investors would pay for a privilege, in this case protection from conversion after 1961. The Colwyn Committee had no doubts. Private investors looked to their own needs, as individuals with a single life, and paid little attention to the yield at which they would be able to reinvest sometime after 1961. Only the first date was important as guaranteeing an income for a period which was within investors' horizons. Investors would not pay a higher price sufficient to compensate the Treasury for issuing at 3^1/2 per cent.

Coupled with this was the question, addressed by Phillips but not by the Colwyn Committee, of whether to issue funded debt or debt with two dates, the second being in the far distance like 4 per cent Funding 1960–90. A perpetual annuity, for instance 3½ per cent Conversion, would need to be issued at £77 15s 7d to yield 4½ per cent. The present value of £22 4s 5d due in 1990 was only £1 4s 0d. Would the investor pay that amount extra for the certainty of the holding being worth par in 1990? Phillips thought not.

Phillips considered the argument 'unassailable in logic.' The only question was whether the Committee had rightly judged the unwillingness of the investor to pay for the option. Surely, the different ways that issues with different nominal interest rates would behave as yields moved was 'obvious to the intelligent investor'; the private investor might behave as the Colwyn Committee suggested, but it was difficult to believe that banks and insurance companies did not make precise calculations of yields on different assumptions, and of the value of options. Also, the Debt was large and the diet might need to be varied to suit different tastes. The Committee's recommendation did not amount to a demonstration that 'in no circumstances' should issues be at a heavy discount. If issues near par did not appeal to the investor, it might be necessary to offer something different:

> Nevertheless as a guide to future action rather than a criticism of the past, there is much to be said for the Committee's recommendation. We ought always to prefer to issue stock near par if we can. Though the private investor holds only one third of our total debt, he holds a far higher proportion of our funded debt and in the long run he is the factor we shall be most concerned with.[55]

A lower coupon might attract more money, but the decision was just a matter of price.[56]

The debate was in danger of delaying market operations. In the middle of December, Niemeyer repeated the defence of Conversion which he had used in his evidence to the Colwyn Committee, adding that the Committee had misjudged the willingness of the investor to pay for the option implicit in issues beneath par:

> As a theoretical proposition, I should not wish to dissent from the idea that, as a general rule, and if you can, it is better to issue stock near par; but such a general proposition does not help us very much in the practical problem with which we have to deal. We have got to sell what we can and, as in other things, to compromise with necessity where we cannot avoid doing so.

The Debt was large, you had to cater for different needs and for 'every kind of assumption investors may make.' The market was full of 3½, 4½ and 5 per cent issues; 'the investor is fed up with these stocks and as a practical proposition can't be made to take any more.' Flooding the market with a type of paper which it could not absorb could easily lead to losses greater than the theoretical losses produced by paper issued at a deep discount.[57] Thus were 4 per cent Consols born.

During December, Phillips had argued that they be issued with a 4½ per cent coupon at par. In February 1927, in fine Treasury fashion, and with Niemeyer destined for the Bank, Phillips provided a defence of the decision in favour of 4 per cent at a discount. It was, he said, a move in the direction of the Colwyn recommendation: it was a coupon for which there was no existing competition from similar securities; the difference in the price between a 4½ per cent issue at par and the 4 per cent at 85 was only two points, and less if it was accepted that the investor would pay something for the option; and the offer was the first of a series in a programme, with the next, perhaps, at 90. This would imply a price above par for the first issue, if it had borne a 4½ nominal rate. This said, 'It must be realised…that it will be a very different matter to defend, against the Committee's arguments, any future issue of stock at a price in the 60's or 70's.'[58]

The records of the issue of 5 per cent Conversion 1944–64 show that in November 1929 officials thoroughly understood the costs involved in Niemeyer's reliance on Conversion. In opposition, Snowden had been hostile to issues at a deep discount and refused to countenance another tranche of Consols, probably at about 81. Hopkins took the opportunity to tell him why he had recommended an issue with a high nominal rate. Consols could not be redeemed with 'profit for the State' until yields had dropped beneath 4 per cent. If that happened, the Loan would not have cost the running yield of £4 18s 9d per cent, but the redemption yield of 6 per cent to 1957. If the issue ran for forty or fifty years, it would cost 'little more than 5 per cent', but many conversion opportunities would have been missed.[59]

Endnotes

1 *BGS*, pp. 397, 421 and 423.
2 Quoted in Horne (1947), pp. 146–7.
3 T 170/31, Hamilton, 'Methods of Borrowing', 12 January 1900.
4 GRO/HBP/PC/PP/69, Hamilton to Chancellor, 11 January 1902. Mowatt did not accept the case in full and, instead, recommended that the market values should no longer be published: 'The more we say about a balance sheet and the more detail we supply in it, the more support we shall give to the idea that the invested funds are the security to which the depositor has to look.' Ibid., Mowatt, 'The Post Office Savings Bank', 7 January 1902.
5 NDO 15/9, ff. 117, Turpin to Ramsay, 27 October 1915; T 133/1, Ramsay to Commissioners, 22 November 1915.
6 NDO 15/9, ff. 112 and 114, Turpin to Stewart (Savings Bank, Manchester), 14 July 1915, and Turpin to Rollit, 19 August 1915; T 160/1170/F4850/1, Blackett for McKenna and Montagu, 7 February 1916.
7 NDO 15/9, f. 125, Turpin to Munro, 5 November 1917; T 133/1, Ramsay to Commissioners, 7 November 1917; T 171/235, f. 14, 'Investments held on behalf of the Currency Note Redemption Account on 31st March 1920.'
8 MGP, B. Hist. 1, F. 8, no. 11199, JPM to Grenfell (Copy to Governor), 1 December 1915.

9 BoE, C40/870, Mahon, 'Amalgamation of Currency and Bank Note Issues', 9 November 1925; BoE, G15/150, Lefeaux, Report on Amalgamation, 16 July 1926; BoE, C40/871, Phillips to Niemeyer, October 1927. T 160/795/F8759/1, Memorandum for Chancellor, covering note from Hopkins, 21 January 1928. Also see CTM, 5 December 1928. Underlining in the original.
10 T 177/1 Pt. I, Phillips to Niemeyer, 7 October 1925; T 177/6, Pt. I, Holmes to Niemeyer, 4 January 1927; T 133/1, Ramsay to Commissioners, 26 May 1916; BoE, C40/615, Memorandum on Capital Liabilities and Local Loans in 1926–7, undated; CNRA Ledgers.
11 CNRA Ledgers.
12 T 160/53/F1874, 'Anglo French 5 Year Bonds,' undated. Between December 1919 and October 1920, $207.4m was purchased in the market.
13 Sayers (1976), I, pp. 298–309.
14 T 175/15, 'Tender of Treasury Bills', 1925.
15 Committee on National Debt and Taxation (Colwyn Committee), *Evidence*, Niemeyer, paras 8709–11.
16 T 160/795/F8759/2, Phillips to Hopkins, 13 October 1928.
17 BoE, C40/870, Mahon, 'Amalgamation of Currency and Bank Note Issues', 9 November 1925, and C40/871, Mahon, 'Amalgamation of Note Issues', 29 June 1927.
18 Issue Department Ledgers; T 175/25, Phillips, 'Approaching Maturities', 3 January 1929, Leith-Ross to Phillips and Hopkins, 4 January 1929, Note by Hopkins, 9 January 1929, and Draft Notice from Bank, 9 January 1929.
19 Sayers (1976), I, p. 306–7; BoE, C40/870, Mahon, 'Amalgamation of Currency and Bank Note Issues', 9 November 1925, and ADM 19/10 and 19/11.
20 T 175/125, Phillips to Hopkins, 11 April 1928, and Phillips to Graham-Harrison, 11 April 1928.
21 *Hansard* (Commons), 24 April 1928, cols 829–32; BoE, C40/872, Niemeyer, 'First Thoughts', 4 April 1928; BoE, G15/150, Lefeaux, Report on Amalgamation, 16 July 1926; ibid., 'Report of the Committee appointed in March 1927 on the Amalgamation of the Note Issues, December 1927; BoE, C40/871, Niemeyer to Leith-Ross, 25 October 1927; ibid., Phillips to Niemeyer, October 1927; ibid., Leith-Ross to Niemeyer, 3 November 1927; ibid., Note of discussion between Hopkins, the Governor and the Deputy Governor, 3 February 1928; T 160/795/F8759/1, Memorandum for Chancellor, covering note from Hopkins, 21 January 1928; Sayers (1976), I, p. 295; BoE, C40/871. Also see CTM, 5 December 1928.
22 BoE, C40/872, Phillips to Niemeyer, 17 April 1928, and Niemeyer to Phillips, 18 April 1928.
23 CNRA Ledgers.
24 BoE, C40/871, Niemeyer to Leith-Ross, 25 October 1927.
25 T 171/275, 'Notes on Clauses', 10 May 1928; BoE, C40/871, Notes of Discussions between Hopkins, the Governor and the Deputy Governor, 3 and 8 February 1928.
26 T 175/125, Draft Letter Approved by the Treasury, 17 April 1928. The letter was formally acknowledged on 3 August 1928. Ibid., Hopkins to Governor and Deputy Governor, 3 August 1928.
27 BoE, G1/464, Governor to Hopkins, 8 September 1927.
28 T 160/403/F13113, Headlam to Phillips, 13 May 1931.
29 Ibid., Phillips, 15 May 1931.
30 Issue Department Ledgers.
31 *BGS*, p. 489.
32 T 168/94, Chamberlain, 'The Unfunded Debt', 14 February 1905, Hamilton, 'Sinking Fund', 25 September 1905, and Turpin to Hamilton, 10 November 1905.
33 T 160/403/F13113, Phillips, 15 May 1931.

34 T 160/948/F13487/1, Headlam to Waterfield, 12 July and 11 August 1933, Headlam, 10 November 1934, Hawtrey, 'Investment Policy', 15 January 1935. This file contains correspondence and memoranda from 1933 and 1935 on the desirability of switching between dated and undated issues.
35 T 160/198/F7548, Niemeyer to Heath, 9 April 1924.
36 The correspondence is in T 160/551/F9973/1.
37 T 160/551/F9973/1, Phillips to Hopkins, 24 July 1929.
38 T 160/551/F9973/1, Headlam to Chancellor, 26 July 1929.
39 Ibid., Hopkins to Chancellor, 27 July 1929, and Chancellor to Headlam, 29 July 1929.
40 T 160/198/F7548, Niemeyer to C. F. Ritchie (Charity Commission), 8 April 1924, and Ritchie to Niemeyer, 9 April 1924.
41 T 160/198/F7548, Claude Schuster to Niemeyer, with enclosures, 11 April 1924, and Niemeyer to Claude Schuster, 12 April 1924.
42 T 160/551/F9973/1, Ezechiel to Niemeyer, 31 December 1926, and Leith-Ross to Holmes and Niemeyer, 14 January 1927.
43 The draft prospectuses are in BoE, C40/397.
44 BoE, C40/397, 'The Funding Loan and Income Tax', Bradbury's comments on the 'abortive January 1919' Funding Loan, December 1918.
45 Royal Commission on Income Tax, *Report*, paras 45 and 159.
46 BoE, C40/397, 'The Funding Loan and Income Tax', Bradbury's comments on the 'abortive January 1919' Funding Loan, December 1918. Aspects of the argument is repeated in Committee on National Debt and Taxation, *Report*, para. 176.
47 Committee on National Debt and Taxation, *Report*, para. 172; T 160/194/F7380/01/2, Niemeyer to Hopkins, 23 October 1925. Niemeyer reiterated his comments in his evidence, paras 8674–85.
48 Committee on National Debt and Taxation, *Report*, para. 173.
49 T 160/551/F9973/1, Phillips, 'The issue of loans at a heavy discount,' 30 November 1926.
50 T 172/1471, Phillips to Niemeyer, 9 February 1925; T 160/1090/F16070/2, Phillips to Niemeyer, 28 October 1925; *The Athenaeum*, 7 February 1925, p. 662. A copy of the article is in T 172/1471.
51 T 176/39, ff. 63–70, Hawtrey, 'Funding', 6 April 1926.
52 Committee on National Debt and Taxation, *Evidence*, Niemeyer para. 8759.
53 Ibid., paras 8760–76.
54 T 160/257/F9893, Niemeyer to Chancellor, 22 November 1926.
55 T 160/551/F9973/1, Phillips, 'The issue of loans at a heavy discount', 30 November 1926; Committee on National Debt and Taxation, *Report*, cols 155–70. Underlining in the original.
56 T 160/551/F9973/1, Phillips, 'Four per cent', 7 December 1926.
57 T 188/14, Niemeyer to Chancellor, 15 December 1926.
58 T 176/39, ff. 104–10, Phillips, 'The Issue of Loans at Heavy Discount,' 3 February 1927.
59 T 175/15, Hopkins to Chancellor, 28 October 1929.

Conclusion

In any age, five features of a National Debt will be at the centre of its managers' attention: cost, stability (or, at least, the predictability) of cost, maturity structure, the flexibility of the securities' repayment terms, and the currency in which the obligations are denominated. Two episodes in the history of British government borrowing between 1900 and 1932 illustrate the part that these features can play in ensuring that a Debt continues to be recognised and properly serviced. Without the double-date on 5 per cent War Loan, the Treasury would have been unable to select the moment after 1929 to reduce the Loan's nominal interest rate and relieve the strains that the Debt was putting on the political and social consensus. Second, irrespective of their size and the circumstances in which they had been incurred, the advances taken from the US Treasury in 1917 and 1918 were on such unrealistic terms that friction between borrower and lender, leading to a questioning of the debt's legitimacy, was all but inevitable.

The Edwardian Debt approached the ideal. It was wholly denominated in sterling and its chief constituents – Consols and the two marketable Annuities – bore a low, fixed nominal interest rate, and were repayable only at the Treasury's option. In addition, since the application of most of the New Sinking Fund was not part of a contract with the holder of the securities, sinking fund monies could be diverted to the payment of interest, enabling more money to be borrowed without the cost of the Debt increasing.

Treasury Bills were the extreme of marketable due-dated debt, exemplifying both its advantages and disadvantages: price stability for the holder, combined with the opportunity for the Treasury to borrow at lower interest rates, uncertain cost and the potential for loss of monetary control if the Bills ran off into cash. The longer single-dated securities – Exchequer Bonds and National War Bonds – issued between December 1915 and May 1919 were a compromise between stability and flexibility, providing the Treasury with a fixed cost for between three and ten years, followed by the opportunity to escape from the high interest rates which officials believed were only temporary. Moreover, selling the Bonds by tap enabled the issues to be closed off whenever the Treasury chose, so giving it control over the maturity structure being created. In contrast, the Treasury had no control over the size of the great war loans and their effect on the Debt's maturity structure: the options attached to McKenna's War Loan, the Exchequer Bonds and National War Bonds meant that existing securities rolled up into the 1917 Loans, while the method of sale meant that the Treasury could not close the issues when new-money applications threatened to make the Loans unwieldy.

The advantages of the Exchequer Bonds and War Bonds were more apparent than real. Although the Bonds secured money for the government at an annual cost fixed for the periods specified in their prospectuses, the conversion options meant that the cost would rise whenever a new long-dated issue was produced. The same options meant that the Bonds' contribution to the maturity structure was not that of the original issue, but that of the life of the longer-dated security into which they were converted. Thus, both the cost and the maturity were unknown when the Bonds were issued: those Exchequer and War Bonds with the options could best be described as having the maturity and interest rate specified in their prospectuses, or such longer lives and interest rates as might be borne by future wartime issues.

From the adoption of due-dated borrowing in 1914 flowed the internal debt management challenges of the 1920s: the stream of maturities, conversions and refinancings with the ever-present anxiety that conditions might become such that maturities would be run off into cash. In response, there was the exploitation of the CNRA's portfolio as a means of avoiding the selection of the suitable size and moment for offers, and the emphasis on the appearance of debt repayment to bolster confidence and improve government credit. Inasmuch as the refinancings and conversions involved issuing short- and medium-dated securities, they were consistent with ostensible wartime policy: nominal interest rates were judged to be high, so the Treasury should not lock them in for longer than necessary. The borrowing on perpetual debt after 1921 during a period of historically high nominal rates was, however, a departure: a subordination of cost to maturity structure and the surrender for many years of the opportunity to reduce the cost. The issue of Conversion at a deep discount, implying that a heavy fall in interest rates was necessary before it could be profitably called, underscored officials' concern to lengthen the Debt and was, perhaps, the greatest error in inter-war debt management. The Treasury could not have foreseen when, and in what circumstances, a fall in interest rates would provide the opportunity to place the Debt on a permanent cheaper basis, but in the long perspectives of debt management it should have been preparing for the opportunity presented in the early 1930s.

Between the autumn of 1915 and April 1917, British borrowing in the USA was cautious, although neither the Treasury nor Morgans considered it so. Prudence did not come from any policy decision – the British would have been only too happy to expose their credit to greater risks – but from the American custom of lending against acceptable and marketable securities. Thus, with the exception of the Anglo-French Loan, all borrowing was fully secured, with ample margin. The implications were twofold. First, access to US credit for British war purposes was limited to those securities owned by UK residents which American lenders were prepared to accept as collateral. Second, *in extremis* (again with the exception of the Anglo-French Loan), the Treasury could have ignored McKenna's promises, sold the collateralised securities, and repaid the obligations, so there was little risk to Morgans, the members of their banking syndicate, or the holders of British debt in the wider American investing community.

After the USA became a belligerent in 1917, the terms of British borrowing weakened dramatically. With the exception of those advances made under the authority of the First Liberty Bond Act, the obligations the US Treasury sold were repayable on demand, bearing interest rates which could be changed, and were changed, whenever the USA so decided: the cost to the borrower was neither fixed nor predictable. The obligations were convertible into long-term Bonds bearing coupons and provisions for repayment which, at the time the Debt was incurred, were unknown. The obligations were denominated in a foreign currency whose sterling equivalent could, and did, fluctuate unpredictably. There were political, military and strategic reasons to borrow thus, but, in debt management terms, the provisions committed every sin. Moreover, they reflected neither the canons of prudent borrowing and lending nor the realities of relations between states.

The amount borrowed, then as now, should have been related to the resources the debtor could be expected to make available to debt service. Yet those two determinants of the annual cost – the interest rate and the period over which the capital was to be repaid – were unknown when the British representatives in Washington signed the certificates and the money changed hands. To lend and borrow thus was to make the transaction political: loans made and taken in a size, for a purpose, and with risks, which were not commercial. Until 1921, the US Administration, as was its right, treated the advances as both commercial and political; that is, commercial terms with political conditions selected by the USA for implementing their conversion into longer obligations. The 1923 funding agreement was a compromise, rationalised by 'capacity to pay': a writing down of loans whose size had been determined by the needs of a wartime alliance to a size which the borrower could be expected to service without intolerable strain. Denominated in a foreign currency, their legitimacy questioned even as they were created, their real value increased by a world depression and sterling's depreciation, the British recognised their Bonds for just ten years.

Appendix I

Settlement and registration

Exchequer Bonds were bearer instruments to which were attached coupons. Interest was paid when the coupons were presented to the paying agent on or after their due date: the principal was repaid when the bonds were presented to the paying agent on or after their maturity date. 'Registered Bonds', a contradiction in terms, were issued for the first time during the First War (see p. 193). Treasury Bills were bearer instruments without coupons, the interest taking the form of a difference between the issue price and the repayment price. Transfer of both Bonds and Bills was by physical delivery – handing the piece of paper to the buyer.

Until 1912, the registration and transfer of Consols and Annuities was governed by the National Debt Act 1870 and regulations subsequently introduced by the Bank.[1] The system, as *The Economist* commented in 1912, was 'archaic'.[2] Ownership was evidenced by entries in books held by the Bank. No document of title was issued, although a 'Certificate of Inscription' was produced by the Bank when ownership was written into its books. The Certificate was of no value and there was no need to produce the document when the securities were transferred. When holdings were sold, sellers had to make personal appearances at the Bank and, if known to officials, sign the book, recording the transfer of the holding. If sellers were not known to the Bank, they had to be accompanied by someone whom officials did know and were prepared to accept as competent to vouch for their identity. This was generally the seller's broker or a representative of a commercial bank. If sellers were unable to attend in person, they had to execute a Power of Attorney so that an agent, known to officials, could sign the book on the seller's behalf. Until the issue of 5 per cent War Loan 1929–47 in 1917, there was a £0 10s 0d stamp duty chargeable on the Power of Attorney, which was much resented by holders outside London.

The process of writing ownership into the Banks' books was known as 'inscription' and the Stock (always with a capital letter) was known as 'inscribed Stock': only when ownership had been inscribed was the holding known as 'Stock'. Inscribed stock was also known as 'Book Stock'.[3]

Instead of being inscribed, Consols could be held in the form of 'Stock Certificates to bearer' in denominations of £100, £200, £500 and £1,000. These differed very little from bearer bonds: coupons were attached and, provided no name had been filled in, the Stock was transferable by physical delivery. It was said that this form was commonly used by overseas holders. 'Loan' was introduced in 1900 with National War Loan, which was the first issue that could be held as either Bonds or inscribed Stock.

During the second half of the nineteenth century, transfer by 'Deed' (again, always with a capital letter), or written instrument, signed by both buyer and seller and involving the issue of a certificate of title to be held by the owner, became the preferred method of transferring the ownership of the securities issued by companies and public bodies. After the South African War, and the wider ownership of government securities which accompanied its financing, demands grew for a method of transfer familiar to a wider investing public.

Provincial holders found inscription slow and cumbersome. Their London agent had to apply to the Bank for a Power of Attorney, made out in their favour. This was issued by the Bank the same day and sent to the seller in the provinces by the agent. The seller executed the document and returned it to the London agent for lodgement at the Bank. As a further check, when the London agent applied for the Power of Attorney, the Bank wrote to the holders to notify them of the intended change and to give them the opportunity to object.

After raising the matter with the Bank in 1904, in 1905 the Council of Associated Stock Exchanges approached the Chancellor and suggested the introduction of either transfer by Deed or transfer at the Bank's branches, with emphasis on the latter. In May 1906, the Council urged the Chancellor to introduce the transfer of Consols by Deed. When asked for its reaction, the Bank said that inscription provided 'unequalled' security of title and simplicity of transfer, but accepted that transfer by Deed could be operated alongside it. Otherwise, there would be opposition from London banks, brokers and large holders of Consols who, under the system of inscription, could obtain cash within an hour of a sale. If Deed became the sole method of transfer, there would be delay as the Bank sent a notice to the holder that a Deed had been lodged, and a period allowed while the holder was able to lodge an objection.

The Chancellor tarried while provincial business groups continued to press their case. It was not the principle which caused delay, but disagreements about the nature of the legislation required, the additional fee the Treasury would have to pay the Bank for running the facility and the question of whether the Bank or Treasury would be responsible for the increased risk of fraud. Political pressure coincided with further weakness in Consols. At a bankers' dinner on 10 May 1911, the Governor discussed the question of wider facilities for the transfer of Consols, and said that the Bank would be happy to operate transfer by Deed. The Finance Act 1911 provided for the issue of Certificates and the transfer by Deed of Consols, Annuities, Local Loans Stock and Irish Guaranteed Land Stocks.[4]

In accordance with the regulations, published in 1912, the Bank established separate 'Transfer by Deed' registers for holdings of 'Deed Stock'.[5] The investor could request that all or part of a holding could be transferred to these registers, where it became known as 'Stock transferable by Deed'. The Bank issued a 'register certificate', which was taken as prima facie evidence that the person named on the Certificate was the owner of the Stock. When the Stock was sold, the Certificate was surrendered to the Bank, together with the signed and witnessed transfer Deed, and the Bank issued a new Certificate to the new holder.

It seems that the new system was little used at first. Inscription had advantages for the London markets and those institutions administered from London. As the Bank had said in 1906, a seller, if known to the Bank or accompanied by someone known to it, could attend the Bank, sign the Book and be in funds. The buyer could resell the holding the next day – a great convenience for those trading the securities or using them as collateral.

In expectation of an increase in the volume of war securities, a Treasury Minute of 7 January 1915 provided for Stocks issued under the War Loan Act 1914 to be transferable by Deed.

In the autumn of 1916, the Associated Stock Exchanges urged that, in the interests of a free market, all fees should be abolished, and on 26 January 1917 it was announced that fees would no longer be charged on transfers of inscribed into Registered Stock and for the registration of Bonds or Transfer Deeds from the date when dealings began in the new War Loans.

The Bank did not publicise Transfer by Deed.[6] Until the summer of 1915, allotment letters (scrip) had to be inscribed before they could be transferred to the Deed register and, until 1917, a fee was payable. Until 1917, only inscribed Stock and bearer bonds were mentioned in Loan prospectuses. The Government Broker refused to accept Deed Stock when making purchases for official portfolios or sinking funds. The Certificates were slow in being issued, while the London market refused to pay for Stock until it had been reinscribed in the buyer's name. Preferring the convenience of inscribed Stock, the Government Broker made sales to investors in this form unless requested to do otherwise. In 1915, the Council of Associated Stock Exchanges described the new system as 'a dead letter'.[7]

In 1922, when the provincial stock exchanges were still pressing for measures to allow greater use of Deed Stock, the Bank denied that the new system was preferred by investors:

> This statement is not borne out by the actual figures as both in numbers of holders and amounts held (in the latter case overwhelmingly so) the balance is very much in favour of 'Book Stock'. In pre-war stocks the amount held as Deed Stock is negligible.[8]

An analysis of holdings made by the Bank in 1931 confirms this. Of 2½ per cent Consols, 87.9 per cent were Book. Of inscribed Stock, 5 per cent War Loan 1929–47 had the lowest proportion: 50.8 per cent was Book, 37.1 per cent Deed and 12.1 per cent Bearer. More typical was 4 per cent Consols (58.6 per cent Book, 32.5 per cent Deed and 8.9 per cent bearer) and 3½ per cent Conversion (61.4 per cent, 31.3 per cent and 7.3 per cent). Some of the short-dated Treasury Bond issues were three-quarters inscribed. This reflected the government's practice of holding departmental portfolios in Book form.[9]

At the outbreak of the Second World War, the Registrar's Department was evacuated and personal attendance by sellers became impossible. The Government and other Stocks (Emergency Provisions) Act 1939 was passed in September 1939, requiring that all government securities be transferred by Deed for the duration of the war, although it was still required that new issues be set up in both inscribed and Deed form. During 1940 and 1941, Norman pressed for the complete abolition of inscription, but the work that this would involve for Parliamentary Counsel investigating its ramifications through seventy years of statute and regulation was considered by the Treasury to be so heavy and Parliamentary time so precious that his request was resisted. Instead, inscription for all future war issues was abolished by the Treasury under powers given by the National Loans Act 1941.[10] With Norman maintaining the pressure, inscription was finally abolished using powers given in the Finance Act 1942.[11] The first government security to be transferable by written transfer, and no other method, was 2½ per cent War Bonds 1949–51, issued on 9 October 1941.[12]

Endnotes

1 The Banks of England and Ireland kept separate books. For simplicity, 'Bank' is used in this Appendix.
2 *The Economist*, 16 March 1912, p. 581.
3 BoE, AC 19/129 contains papers relating to the regulations introduced in 1912 and descriptions of the existing system.
4 BoE, AC4/1, pp. 1–6, G. Blunden, 'A Short History of the Development of the System of Transfer of British Government Stocks by Instrument in Writing', November 1952.
5 *The Transfer of Government Stocks by Deed* (Cd. 6127), 15 February 1912.
6 During the Great War, the Bank published guides to the methods of holding gilt-edged securities. Those circulated at the time of the first two war loans in 1914 and 1915 make no mention of transfers by Deed. A copy of the first is in BoE, Loan Wallet 226, and of the second in T 172/247.
7 T 172/247, President of the Council of Associated Stock Exchanges to Chancellor, 20 October 1915. Also see *The Economist*, 5 June 1915. p. 1161.
8 T 160/900, Bank to Niemeyer, 23 February 1922.
9 BoE, C40/427, 'British Government Stocks' at 30 September 1931, Chief Accountant's Office, 3 November 1931.
10 The Government Stock (Transfer) Regulations, 1941 (8 October 1941).
11 The Government Stock Regulations, 1943 (1 January 1943). The papers covering the abolition of inscription are in T 160/1097. Especially see 'Memorandum by the Financial Secretary to the Treasury', undated, but probably summer 1940, 'Abolition of Inscription of Stocks', Wilson Smith, 28 March 1941, Hopkins to Governor, 31 March 1941, and 'Inscribed Stock', Wilson Smith, 13 May 1941. Also see Governor to Hopkins, 21 December 1939, in BoE, G14/158.
12 BoE, AC4/1, p. 92, Blunden, 'A Short History of the Development of the System of Transfer of British Government Stocks by Instrument in Writing', November 1952.

Appendix II

New issue procedures before 1914

Before 1914, prospectuses for government issues were published in the newspapers, but without an application form. These, together with prospectuses, were always available from the Banks of England and Ireland and the Government Broker: they were sometimes available at the Banks' branches. Because it was hoped that they would have a popular appeal, prospectuses for the Consols and National War Loan issued during the Boer War were also made available at the principal stockbrokers and London banks.

Applications had to be accompanied by a deposit, usually of a few pounds per cent. Generally, issues were partly paid, with provision for early payment of instalments under discount.

If the issue was oversubscribed, and there was 'partial allotment', the balance of the sum paid as a deposit was either returned to the applicant or applied to the payment of the first instalment. In the latter case, and if there was a surplus after making the first payment, the balance was returned to the applicant. If the applicant failed to pay any instalment on the specified date, the instalments previously paid were liable to forfeiture.

The administrative process went through three stages:

(1) If the application was successful, a 'provisional receipt' was issued.

(2) If the issue was partly paid, the provisional receipt was exchanged for a 'scrip certificate', or 'allotment letter', which was a bearer document with coupons attached for the dividends payable during the period that the issue was partly paid. As each call was paid, it was recorded on the 'scrip'. If the issue was fully paid, or the applicant had selected to apply fully paid, the scrip was inscribed at once.

(3) When the instalments had been paid in full, the scrip certificate was 'inscribed' in the Banks' books, that is, it was converted into Stock. In the case of new issues of Consols, the scrip could also be exchanged for 'Stock Certificates to bearer'. If the issue could be held in bearer form (such as National War Loan 1910), those selecting bearer could exchange the scrip for the 'definitive bonds', once they had been prepared.

Inscribed Stock could be converted into Bonds at any time after a specified date, without charge. Bearer bonds could be inscribed at any time after a specified date on payment of a fee of 1s per Bond. In the case of Consols, inscribed Stock could be converted into Stock Certificates to bearer on payment of a fee of 2s per cent and Stock Certificates to bearer could be inscribed on payment of a fee of 1s per cent.

Exchequer Bonds, as the name implies, were available only in bearer form (see p. 193, note b). The minimum Bond was £100. The issues of Consols and National War Loan 1910 during the Boer War were also in minimum units of £100, but thereafter the inscribed Stock was transferable in multiples of 1d.

The First War found the Bank unprepared for the expansion in the number of issues or holders. There were particular problems presented by the lack of premises and trained managers, overworked and unhealthy staff and the lack of warning of new issues.[1] Additional strain came from the exercise of conversion options:

> Previous to 1914 the Bank of England had never handled a Loan for more than £60,000,000, the amount of a Consols issue made in April 1901...Half of this, moreover, was allotted before issue...The system which had grown up was quite adequate for Loans of the dimensions hitherto experienced, but required considerable modifications in respect of the enormous issues now to be made. The huge increase in the volume of the work was first felt, moreover, at a time when the Bank staff was beginning to be depleted.

The first two loans, 3½ per cent War Loan 1925–8 and 4½ per cent War Loan 1925–45, were issued with little change in the machinery. The volume of applications and conversions strained the Bank and the opportunity was taken with the issue of 5 per cent Exchequer Bonds 1920, on tap from December 1915, to make changes (see Chapter VII).[2]

Endnotes

1 Osborne (1926), I, pp. 380–1.
2 Ibid., pp. 401–4.

Appendix III

The National Debt: size and composition (£m), year ending end-March (1892–1934)

Notes to table overleaf
Rows may not sum because of rounding.
Column headings:

1 Ways and Means Advances.
2 Treasury Bills.
3 Unfunded marketable securities.
4 Savings Certificates.
5 Other capital liabilities.
6 Estimated capital value of Terminable Annuities.
7 Debts to the Banks of England and Ireland.
8 Funded marketable securities.
9 Book debt.
10 Foreign currency debt, including securities issued to overseas lenders payable in sterling.
11 Total National Debt (gross).
12 *Less* Funding Loan 1960–90 and Victory Bonds tendered in settlement of death duties and held by the National Debt Commissioners
13 Total National Debt (net).

Foreign currency debt is translated into sterling at pre-1914 par of exchange.
War Expenditure Certificates are included in unfunded marketable debt.
Accrued interest on Savings Certificates is excluded.
From 1920 data exclude loans from France, Italy and Russia in the form of gold deposited against British advances.
Savings Bonds are included in unfunded marketable debt.
The Exchequer Bonds issued under the Capital Expenditure (Money) Act, 1904, for the purpose of the Naval and Military Works Acts, under the Cunard Agreement (Money) Act, 1904, and under the Telephone Transfer Act, 1911, are not included in unfunded marketable debt, but are included in other capital liabilities.

Source: *National Debt: annual returns.*

Year	*Floating debt* 1	2	3	4	5	6
1892	0	12.4	22.9		2.9	64.4
1893	0	11.3	9.4		2.6	60.8
1894	0.8	11.8	8.9		2.9	57.1
1895	0	12.4	5		3.2	53.6
1896	0	6.5	3.5		4.1	49.4
1897	0	8.1	0		4.1	44.9
1898	0	8.1	0		3.8	40.5
1899	0	8.1	0		7.5	36.2
1900	0	16.1	0		10.2	60.2
1901	3	21.1	54		14.7	61.7
1902	0	21.1	54		20.5	63.2
1903	0	21.1	54		27.6	55.6
1904	2	21.1	50.5		31.9	51.4
1905	0	21.1	50.5		41.7	47.8
1906	0	19.2	46.5		45.8	43.5
1907	0	10.7	41		49.7	40.9
1908	0	12	32		50.9	39.4
1909	0	14.5	28.3		51.4	38
1910	4	31.5	27		49.2	35.9
1911	0	14.5	26		47.8	34.4
1912	0	8.1	25		50.1	33
1913	0	9.5	22		54.8	31.5
1914	0	13	20.5		56.4	29.6
1915	0	77.2	416.5		57	28
1916	19.9	566.8	1139.8	1.4	56.7	26.2
1917	217.5	463.7	2546	74.5	52.2	24
1918	192.3	973.4	3233.3	137.7	49.2	21.9
1919	455	957.2	4164.7	227	46.1	20.6
1920	204.9	1107.3	4679.4	273.5	46.9	19.3
1921	154.5	1120.8	4560.5	285	48.7	17.7
1922	147.3	877.2	4625.9	342	66.2	16.2
1923	193.9	616	4439.7	353.8	70.3	13.7
1924	186.2	588.3	4418.7	366.1	66.5	13.5
1925	166.6	575.6	4376.2	368.8	68	13.1
1926	139.4	564.9	4337.4	375.6	75.1	12.6
1927	116.6	599.2	4200.1	371.8	98.1	12.2
1928	161.9	526.9	4100.2	362.4	103.2	12.6
1929	37.1	700.3	3919.7	361.2	120.5	12.5
1930	48.5	588.9	4033.9	358	127.2	12.2
1931	24.5	569.8	4058.3	371.6	169.6	12
1932	7.5	604.5	3995.2	378.9	214	11.7
1933	34.6	775.9	2123.3	383.7	215.9	11.9
1934	44.9	799.8	2286.5	389.3	208.1	12.1

Marketable funded debt				*Total debt*		
7	*8*	*9*	*10*	*11*	*12*	*Net total*
13.6	564.3	0	0	680.5	0	680.5
13.6	562.9	13	0	673.6	0	673.6
13.6	561	13	0	669.1	0	669.1
13.6	559.4	13	0	660.2	0	660.2
13.6	562.5	13	0	652.5	0	652.5
13.6	561.1	13	0	644.9	0	644.9
13.6	559.1	13	0	638.3	0	638.3
13.6	556.5	13	0	635	0	635
13.6	539	0	0	639.2	0	639.2
13.6	537.5	0	0	705.7	0	705.7
13.6	595.9	0	0	768.4	0	768.4
13.6	626.4	0	0	798.3	0	798.3
13.6	624	0	0	794.5	0	794.5
13.6	622	0	0	796.7	0	796.7
13.6	620.4	0	0	789	0	789
13.6	618.3	0	0	774.2	0	774.2
13.6	612	0	0	759.8	0	759.8
13.6	608.2	0	0	754.1	0	754.1
13.6	601.2	0	0	762.5	0	762.5
13.6	596.7	0	0	733.1	0	733.1
13.6	588.6	0	0	718.4	0	718.4
13.6	579.8	0	0	711.3	0	711.3
13.6	573.1	0	0	706.2	0	706.2
13.6	569.6	0	0	1162	0	1162
13.6	304.8	0	60.6	2189.8	0	2189.8
13.6	304.1	0	367.9	4063.6	0	4063.6
13.6	304.1	0	995.5	5921.1	0	5921.1
13.6	304	0	1292.8	7481.1	0	7481.1
13.6	301.3	0	1118.9	7765.1	3	7762.1
13.6	301.2	0	1005.5	7507.6	11	7496.6
13.6	567	0	959.2	7614.5	22	7592.5
13.6	984.2	0	1029.4	7714.7	30.2	7684.6
13.6	966.6	0	995.6	7615.1	39.6	7575.5
13.6	1009	0	987.7	7578.7	48.5	7530.2
13.6	1059.9	0	976.8	7555.3	57.3	7498
13.6	1206.1	0	967.5	7585.3	68.3	7517
13.6	1336.3	0	961.3	7578.4	83.1	7495.3
13.6	1464.6	0	951	7580.6	95.2	7485.4
13.6	1442.4	0	940.7	7565.4	104.4	7461
13.6	1411.4	0	933.5	7564.3	116.4	7447.9
13.6	1453.4	0	957.7	7636.5	123.5	7513.1
13.6	3362.7	0	927.3	7848.9	124	7724.8
13.6	3360.7	0	903.4	8018.4	122.9	7895.5

Appendix IV

The maturity structure of the internal marketable debt (including Ways and Means Advances) as a percentage of the National Debt: 1900–34

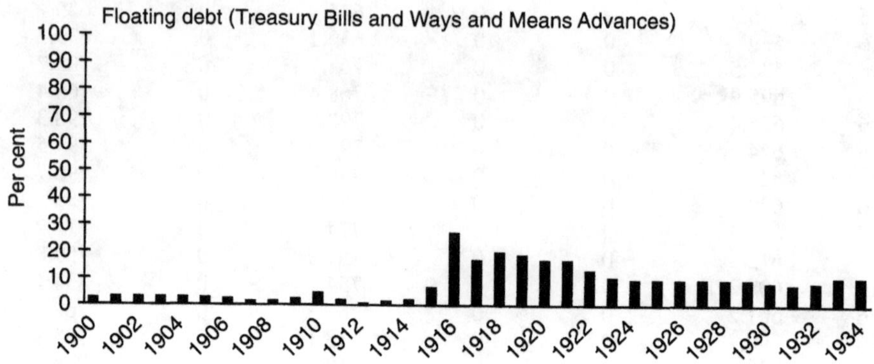

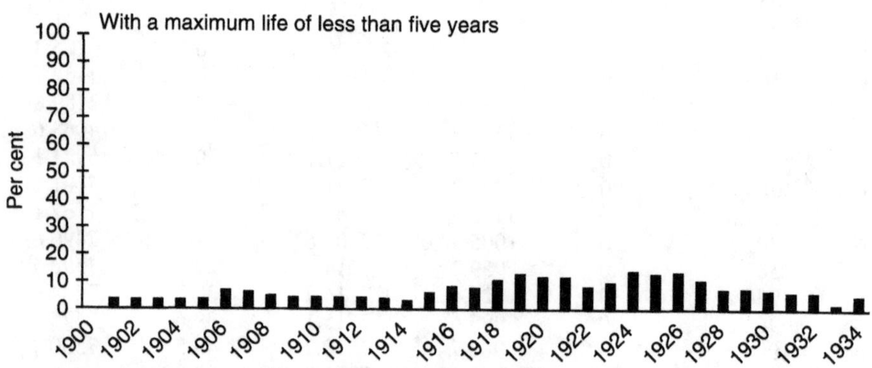

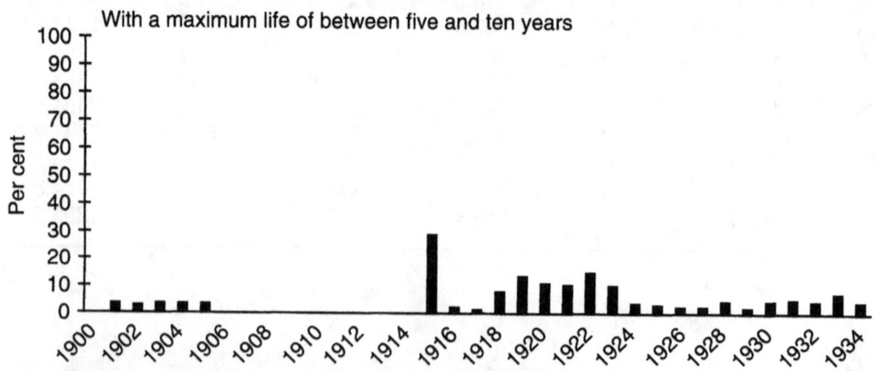

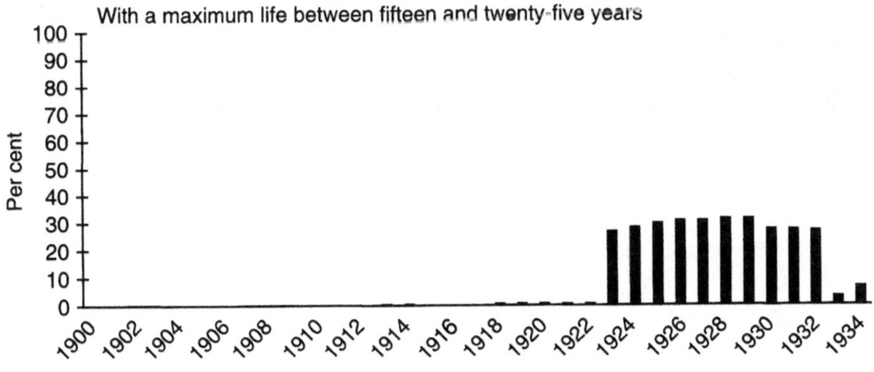

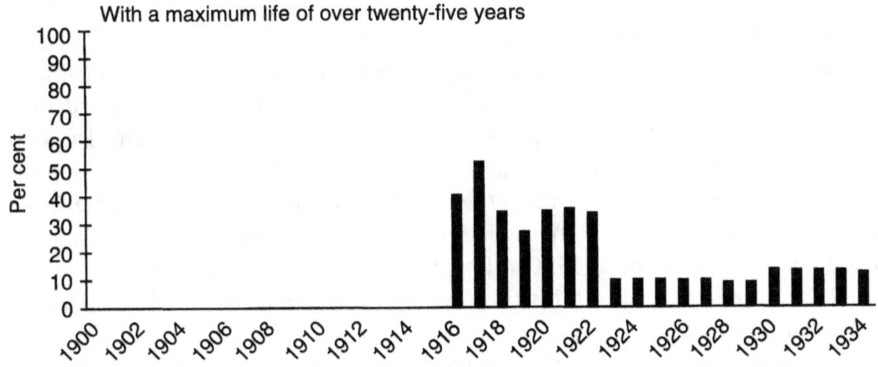

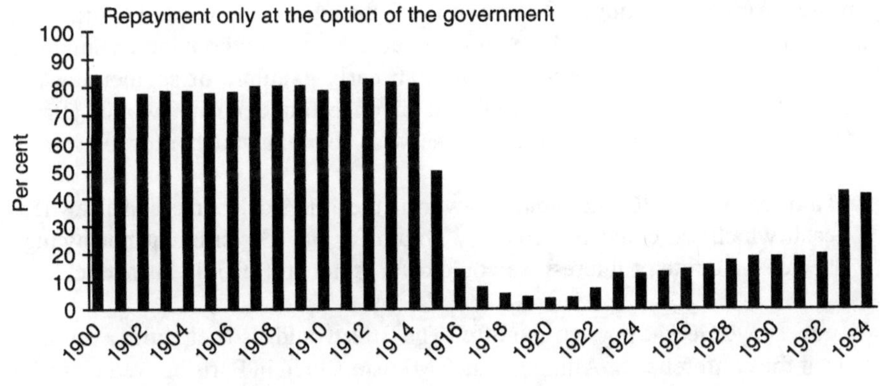

In the case of double-dated issues, the first date is taken when the price is above par (clean) and the second date when the price is below par (clean). Source: *BGS*, pp. 357–425.

Appendix V

The Tsarist debts: 3 per cent Exchequer Bonds 1930 (28 January 1918)[1]

The tremor in British government credit at the time of the Soviets' repudiation of Tsarist debts, the partial cause of the stumble in the War Bond campaign in November 1917, was the most important ingredient in a Cabinet decision to compensate with 3 per cent long-dated Exchequer Bonds holders of pre-Revolutionary Russian sterling Treasury Bills and acceptances. The Russian obligations were two of the three issues made for allied (as opposed to Empire) governments in the London market during the war, the other being a sterling–French franc tranche of a domestic French Republic perpetual National Defence Loan sold in December 1915. On the latter occasion, the intermediary was the Bank of England, acting with the 'consent and approval of His Majesty's Government.'[2]

For the British, facilitating the sale of the Russian Treasury Bills had several purposes. At the beginning, in February 1915, the authorities wanted to drain the money market and put upward pressure on interest rates, without increasing their own borrowing costs. Their method was an early example of segmenting the market. The Bills, with a high rate and of uncertain security, would attract speculative money which would have otherwise been unavailable for the war:

> I am anxious that Russia should draw from the joint stock banks and elsewhere cash which we could not possibly obtain for our Government borrowings because the rate of interest we could offer is not sufficiently attractive...

was how Lloyd George put it to Cunliffe.[3] The Bills would also help fulfil a promise made at the conference of Allied Finance Ministers held in Paris between 2 and 5 February that Russia should be allowed to raise £50m on each of the London and Paris markets. That agreement specified that the Bank of England would be prepared to undertake 'the business of issuing (but not guaranteeing or underwriting) public loans sold under the accord'.[4] At a time when British government yearlings were being issued at a discount of about 2 7/8 per cent, £10m one-year Russian Bills were issued at a discount of 5 per cent with, as the prospectus said, the 'approval' of the British government. The issue was oversubscribed.

As part of a bargain which included supervision of the Russian use of British advances and restrictions on the use of British credits for general support of the rouble exchange rate, Clause IV of the Anglo-Russian Financial Agreement signed on 30 September 1915 bound the Bank to use its good offices to ensure the renewal of the Bills.[5] When the Bills matured in February 1916, there was insufficient demand to cover their renewal and the Bank took £0.45m, with the Treasury providing a guarantee against loss and receiving the difference between the 6 per cent discount and ½ per cent beneath Bank rate. At renewal in February 1917, again at 6 per cent, the Bank was left with £1.4m.

The acceptance facility for Russian banks was established in October 1915 to provide support for the rouble exchange rate after the Treasury had increased the restrictions on the use of its advances.[6] The proposition was put to the CLCB by the Governor and Peter Bark, the Russian Finance Minister. The Committee was not attracted on 'business' grounds, while recognising that there might be political reasons for agreeing, and said that its members would provide only £6m unless the British government provided a guarantee. This, the Governor made clear, 'was out of the question'.[7] After considerable delay and with contributions from the Scottish and colonial banks and the acceptance houses, £7½m was provided.[8]

The Treasury had made the elementary error of not making the extent of its responsibility absolutely clear. It had allowed language to be used in the prospectus that was ambiguous. It had encouraged the banks to provide funds that it was not prepared to provide itself. It had permitted, or encouraged, the Governor to organise the subscriptions. The errors matured at an unfortunate moment.

Although Bonar Law recognised that the Treasury bore some responsibility for the Russian debts, he did not agree that it should take all the losses. After rehearsing the origins of the acceptance facility, he told the Cabinet that:

> It was now contended, and undoubtedly with truth, that this money was provided not in the ordinary way of business, but in order to meet the wishes of the Government, and that therefore the Government should bear the liability. Although [he was] unable to admit that we had any legal liability, he did not consider that the whole of whatever loss had eventually been incurred should fall upon the Government [*sic*], and he proposed, therefore, to make the best arrangements he could with the firms which had accepted these bills – subject to the avoidance of any appearance of treating them meanly.

The Treasury Bills, with their statement that they were issued with the approval of the government, would be treated in the same way.[9]

Compensation took the form of £15.6m 3 per cent Exchequer Bonds 1930, judged to have a market value of 82¼ (£4 19s 5d per cent), in return for the surrender to the Treasury of all rights in the Tsarist paper.

Would the Treasury have been so generous if there had been no threat to its own credit? The incident stood at the frontier between implied contract, financial confidence, politics and budgetary prudence. By issuing the Bonds, the Treasury admitted some responsibility for pushing the markets and the banks into extending the credits. In its selection of the coupon, it decided its contribution should be some 80 per cent of the cost of the default. A different coupon could have been selected, and a different distribution of the losses imposed. As so often in such matters, it was not contract which determined the outcome, but a judgement of the terms which would give the government the best protection against conflicting interests.

Endnotes

1 No prospectus for this issue has been found in either the PRO or the Bank of England archives. There are drafts in T 111/2, together with the TM and Warrants.
2 *Bankers' Magazine*, January 1916, pp. 37–8, and February 1916, p. 292, and *The Economist*, 4 December 1915, p. 967. The Loan was perpetual, with an option to call it after 1931.
3 T 171/107, Keynes, 'Russia', 30 January 1915, reproduced in Keynes (1971–89), XVI, pp. 67–71; T 172/260, Lloyd George to Cunliffe, 8 February 1915, and Keynes, 'Paraphrase and Notes on the Discussions of the Paris Conference', early February 1915.
4 T 172/260, British draft of the agreement following the Paris Conference, February 1915; Neilson (1984), p. 67.
5 T 171/149, 'Financial agreement between the British and Russian Ministers of Finance at London', 30 September 1915; Keynes (1971–89), XVI, pp. 128–34; Neilson (1984), pp. 112–13.
6 Cab. 24/39, Memorandum, 14 January 1918; Neilson (1984), pp. 182–3.
7 CLCBm, 30 September 1915; MGP, Grenfell Letter Books, Grenfell to Jack Morgan, 17 January 1918.
8 Cab. 23/5, WC 322 (17), 15 January 1918, and Memorandum, GT 3339, 14 January 1917.
9 Cab. 23/5/322, 15 January 1918.

Appendix VI

India's £100m of 5 per cent War Loan 1929–47

When Indian troops were first employed outside India, it was arranged that the Government of India would pay the ordinary costs and the Imperial Exchequer any extraordinary war charges. A contribution by India to general war costs was first suggested to the Secretary of State for India, Austen Chamberlain, by the Aga Khan at the time of the issue of the 4½ per cent Loan in 1915. This came to nothing because British policy was to encourage investors in the Dominions and colonies to support their own government's loans, rather than contribute to those of the Imperial Government, and the Indian economy and budget had been dislocated by the outbreak of war.[1] In 1916, growing Indian prosperity, the world-wide demand for rupees and increased British need weakened these arguments. A contribution was discussed by the Cabinet at the beginning of 1916, but the Government of India wanted to meet the cost by a rise in the customs, but not the excise, duty on cotton goods. The Cabinet were concerned that this would reignite protectionist controversy in the UK, threatening the delicate balance of the Coalition, and the proposal was shelved at London's request.[2] In the autumn, the Viceroy suggested a contribution of £50m, but this was refused since the:

> Prime Minister and Chancellor of the Exchequer fear that offer of 50 million as total contribution would be ill received here. Chancellor names 100 millions as sum which from his enquiries he thinks would be expected, say an annual charge of 5 millions or 5½ millions with sinking fund.

It was suggested that the most valuable help would be to float Indian securities in the USA to raise dollars.[3] Having taken Morgans' advice, at the end of December the Treasury shelved the idea.[4] In January 1917, Austen Chamberlain, who remained the Secretary of State in the new Coalition, asked the Viceroy whether India could contribute the £100m mooted by the previous Chancellor.[5] This was agreed by the Government of India but, once again, only if the import duties on cotton goods were increased. The condition was accepted by the Cabinet subject to testing of opinion in Japan, which had just provided a timely US dollar loan, and in the Lancashire industry.[6] Announcement of the contribution was delayed until the beginning of March when Lancashire's reaction produced a heated row, which culminated in a Commons debate on 14 March and talk of a government defeat.[7]

The contribution did not affect the size of the Loans. Instead, it took the form of the Government of India raising a rupee loan and giving the proceeds outright to the Imperial government. In addition, India assumed responsibility for paying the interest and sinking fund on the 5 per cent War Loan to the extent of the difference between the proceeds of the rupee loan and £100m. It was expected that the rupee loan would make a minor contribution to the £100m but, in the event, it amounted to some £34m. The receipt was treated as miscellaneous revenue in the British Finance Accounts.[8] As planned, India assumed financial responsibility for the remaining £66m.

Endnotes

1 AC 21/1/8, Chamberlain, Memorandum, 6 July 1915. A copy is in T 172/238, together with a covering letter from Chamberlain to McKenna, dated 7 July.

2 AC 21/1/14, Chamberlain to Viceroy, 26 January 1916; AC 21/1/11, Chamberlain, 'India's Financial Contribution to the War', undated. The file contains several papers by officials examining how the size of the contribution should be determined.

3 AC 21/1/38, Chamberlain to Viceroy, 29 November 1916. The Chancellor's agreement to the telegram is in AC 21/1/37, Hamilton to Lucas, 28 November 1916.

4 AC 21/1/41, Chamberlain to Viceroy, 23 December 1916; MGP, B. Hist. 2, F. 13, Jack Morgan to Grenfell, 21 December 1916.

5 Cab. 23/1, WC 24(13), 1 January 1917; AC 21/1/42, Chamberlain to Viceroy, 5 January 1917.

6 AC 21/1/45, Chamberlain to Hardinge, 10 January 1917, and AC 21/1/60, Bonar Law, Memorandum, 27 January 1917; Cab. 23/1, Cabinet 31 (17), Conclusion 15, 10 January 1917; Cab. 23/1, Cabinet 48 (17), Conclusion 10, 30 January 1917, and Appendices II and A.

7 *Hansard* (Commons), 5 March 1917, cols 3–5, and 14 March 1917, cols 1137–1238; Self (1995), p. 42, and Austen Chamberlain to Hilda Chamberlain, 6 and 17 March 1917; Turner (1992), pp. 188–91. The newspapers had the story earlier. See *The Economist*, 3 March 1917, pp. 426–7, 10 March 1917, pp. 463–4, and 17 March 1917 pp. 503–4.

8 *Hansard* (Commons), 22 April 1918, col. 693.

Appendix VII

Expenditure on interest and management: 1900–34

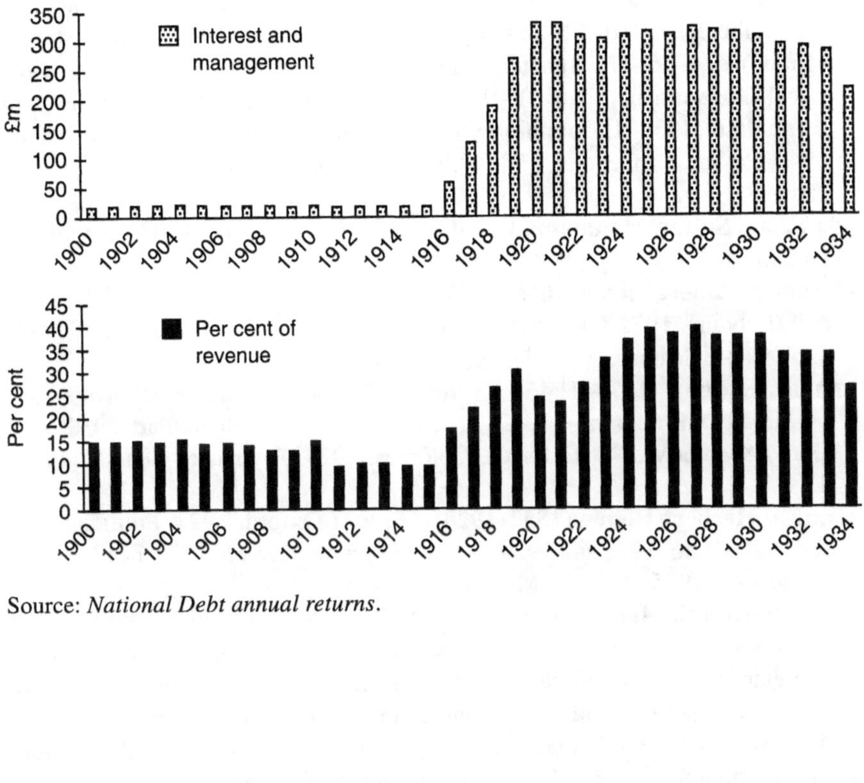

Source: *National Debt annual returns*.

Biographies

Addison, Christopher (1869–1951) Baron, 1937. Viscount, 1945. KG, 1947. MP (Liberal), 1910–22, and (Labour) 1929–31 and 1934–5. Minister of Munitions, 1916–17. Minister of Reconstruction, 1917–19. President of the Local Government Board, 1919. Minister of Health, 1919–21. Minister of Agriculture, 1930–1. Dominion Secretary, 1945–7. Commonwealth Secretary, 1947. Paymaster-General, 1948–9. Leader of the Labour Party in the Lords, 1940–51.

Aga Khan, Sultan Mohammad Shah (1877–1957) KCIE, 1907. Head of the Ismaili Muslims.

Alexander, Albert Victor (1885–1965) Viscount, 1950. Earl, 1963. KG, 1965. MP (Labour), 1922–31 and 1935–50. First Lord of the Admiralty, 1929–31 and 1940–6. Minister of Defence, 1946–50.

Arnold, Sydney (1878–1945) Baron, 1924. Manchester stockbroker and politician. MP (Liberal), 1912–21. Member of the Labour Party, 1922–38. Under-Secretary of State for the Colonies, 1924. Paymaster-General, 1929–31.

Asquith, Herbert Henry (1852–1928) Earl of Oxford, 1924. Politician. MP (Liberal), 1886–1918 and 1920–4. Home Secretary, 1892–5. Chancellor of the Exchequer, 1905–8. Prime Minister, 1908–16.

Babington Smith, Henry (1863–1923) KCB, 1908. Principal Private Secretary to Goschen, 1891. Represented Treasury at many international conferences. Secretary of the Post Office, 1903–9. Chairman, the Royal Commission on the Civil Service, 1915, and the Committee on Indian Currency, 1919. President, the National Bank of Turkey, 1909. Member of the Anglo-French Financial Mission to USA, 1915. Director of the Bank of England, 1920–3.

Bagehot, Walter (1826–77) Economist and journalist. Editor of *The Economist*, 1860–77.

Baldwin, Stanley (1867–1947) Earl, 1937. MP (Unionist), 1908–37. Joint Financial Secretary to the Treasury (with Lever), 1917–21. President of the Board of Trade, 1921–2. Chancellor of the Exchequer, 1922–3. Lord Privy Seal, 1932–4. Prime Minister, 1923–4, 1924–9 and 1935–7.

Balfour, Arthur James (1848–1930) Earl, 1922. MP (Conservative and Unionist), 1874–1922. Chief Secretary for Ireland, 1887–91. Leader of the

Commons, 1891–2. Leader of the Opposition, 1892–5. Leader of the House of Commons, 1895–1906. Prime Minister, 1902–5. First Lord of the Admiralty, 1915–16. Foreign Secretary, 1916–19. President of the Council, 1919–22 and 1925–9. Head of British Mission to USA, 1917, and British Mission to Washington Naval Conference, 1922.

Banbury, Frederick George (1850–1936) Bt., 1902. Baron, 1924. Stockbroker, 1873–1906. MP (Conservative), 1892–1924. Chairman of the Great Northern Railway. Director of the London and Provincial Bank, 1906–17. Member of the CLCB, 1916–18.

Banks, Thomas Macdonald (1891–1975) KCB, 1935. Exchequer and Audit Department, 1909. Private secretary to the Secretary of the General Post Office and to Postmasters-General, 1920–3. Deputy Controller of the Post Office, 1924, and Controller, 1931. Director-General of the Post Office, 1934–6. Member of the National Savings Committee, 1931–9.

Bark, Peter (1869–1937) Kt., 1935. Russian banker. Vice-Governor of the Imperial Bank of Russia, 1906. Under-Secretary of State of the Ministry of Commerce, 1911. Finance Minister, 1914–17.

Barlow, (Clement) Anderson (1868–1951) KBE, 1918. Bt., 1924. Lawyer, philanthropist and politician. MP (Conservative), 1910–23. Parliamentary Secretary to the Ministry of Labour, 1920–2. Minister of Labour, 1922–4. Adopted name of Montague-Barlow, 1946.

Barnes, George Nicholl (1859–1940) Politician. MP (Labour), 1906–22. General-Secretary of the Amalgamated Society of Engineers, 1896–1908. Minister of Pensions, 1916–18. Minister without Portfolio, 1919. Member of the War Cabinet, 1917. Chairman of the National Organising Committee for War Savings, 1916. Member of the National War Savings Committee and the National Savings Committee, 1916–25.

Beaverbrook, William Maxwell Aitken (1879–1964) Kt., 1911. Bt., 1917. Baron, 1917. Newspaper proprietor and politician. MP (Unionist), 1910–17. Minister of Information, 1918. Various ministerial appointments, 1940–45. Proprietor of the *Daily Express* and *Evening Standard*.

Bell, Henry (1858–1935) Banker. General Manager of Lloyds Bank, 1912–23, and Director, 1916–35. Director of Lloyds and National Provincial Foreign Bank, Phoenix Assurance. Member of the Committee on War Loans for the Small Investor and the Committee on National Debt and Taxation. British delegate to the International Financial Conference at Brussels, 1920, and the International Economic Conference at Genoa, 1922.

Benson, Robert Henry (1850–1929) Senior partner of Robert Benson & Co., merchant bankers.

Berry, William Ewert (1879–1954) Baron Camrose, 1929. Viscount, 1941. Newspaper proprietor. Joint proprietor of the *Daily Telegraph* and director of other newspaper companies.

Blackett, Basil Phillott (1882–1935) KCB, 1921. Treasury, 1904. Secretary, Royal Commission on Indian Finance and Currency, 1913–14. Member of Anglo-French Financial Mission to USA, 1915. Member of National War

Savings Committee, 1916. Treasury representative in USA, 1917–19. Controller of Finance, Treasury, 1919–22. Finance Member, Executive Council of the Viceroy of India, 1922–8. Director of the Bank of England, 1929–35.

Bonar Law, see Law

Borah, William Edgar (1865–1940) US lawyer and Senator (Republican) for Idaho, 1907–40. Chairman, Senate Committee on Foreign Relations, 1924–40. Particularist, opposing US involvement in international organisations with political powers, especially the League of Nations and the World Court. Supported Washington Naval Conference.

Borden, Robert Laird (1854–1937) GCMG, 1914. Canadian lawyer and politician. MP (Conservative), 1896–1904, 1905–21. Leader of the Conservative Party in Commons, 1901. Prime Minister, 1911–20. Formed Unionist Government, 1917. Canadian Representative at Imperial War Cabinet and Imperial Conferences, 1917 and 1918. Canadian Delegate, Paris Peace Conference, 1919.

Boyden, Roland William (1863–1931) US lawyer and statesman. Unofficial US Representative on the Reparation Commission, 1920–3.

Bradbury, John Swanwick (1872–1950) KCB 1913. Baron, 1925. Treasury official. Private secretary to Asquith, 1905–8. An Insurance Commissioner and a member of the National Health Insurance Joint Committee, 1911–13. Joint Permanent Secretary to the Treasury (with Heath until 1916, and then with Heath and Chalmers), 1913–19. Member of the Committee on War Loans for the Small Investor, 1915–16. Principal British Representative on the Reparation Commission, 1919–25. Member of the Macmillan Committee, 1929–31.

Briand, Aristide (1862–1932) French lawyer and politician. Minister twenty-five times and Prime Minister eleven times, 1906–32, including January 1921 to January 1922.

Bridgeman, William Clive (1864–1935) Viscount, 1929. MP (Unionist), 1906–29. Minor ministerial posts, 1915–22. Home Secretary, 1922–4. First Lord of the Admiralty, 1924–9.

Burn, Joseph (1871–1950) KBE, 1920. Fellow and Past-President of the Institute of Actuaries. Actuary, 1912–20, Actuary and General Manager, 1920–5, and General Manager, 1925–41, of the Prudential Assurance Co. Member of the National War Savings Committee and the National Savings Committee, 1916.

Burton, Theodore Elija (1851–1929) US politician (Republican). Congressman, 1889–91, 1895–1909 and 1921–8. Senator, 1909–15 and 1928–9. Member, National Monetary Commission, 1908–12. Member, World War Foreign Debt Commission, 1922–7.

Camrose, see Berry.

Cargill, Alexander (?–?) Actuary of the Edinburgh Savings Bank, 1906–21.

Carnegie, Andrew (1835–1919) Industrialist and philanthropist. Born in Scotland, emigrated to USA, 1848. Co-founder, the Woodruff Sleeping Car Co. Principal owner of several steel businesses, including Homestead and Edgar

Thompson Steel Works. Interests consolidated into Carnegie Steel Co., 1889. Merged into US Steel Co., 1901.

Cassel, Ernest (1852–1921) GCMG, 1905. GCB, 1909. Financier. Arrived in London in 1869 from Cologne. Joined Bischoffsheim & Goldschmidt, loan contractors. Associated with Schiff at Kuhn, Loeb & Co., New York. Active in financing governments.

Catterns, Basil Gage (1886–1969) Entered Bank of England, 1908. Deputy Principal, Discount Office, 1923–5. Deputy Chief Cashier, 1925–9. Chief Cashier, 1929–34. Executive Director, 1934–6. Deputy Governor, 1936–45.

Cave, George (1856–1928) Kt., 1915. Viscount, 1918. Lawyer and politician. MP (Unionist), 1906–18. Home Secretary, 1916–19. Lord Chancellor, 1922–4 and 1924–8.

Chalmers, Robert (1858–1938) KCB, 1908. Baron, 1919. Treasury official. Principal Clerk, 1899–1903. Assistant-Secretary, 1903–7. Chairman of the Board of Inland Revenue, 1907–11. Permanent Secretary to the Treasury and Auditor of the Civil List, 1911–13. Governor of Ceylon, 1913–16. Joint-Permanent Secretary to the Treasury (joining Bradbury and Heath), 1916–19. Under-Secretary for Ireland, 1916. Master of Peterhouse, Cambridge, 1924–31.

Chamberlain, Arthur Neville (1869–1940) Politician. Lord Mayor of Birmingham, 1915–16. Director-General of National Service, 1916–17. Postmaster-General, 1922–3. Paymaster-General, 1923. Minister of Health, 1923, 1924–9 and 1931. Chancellor of the Exchequer, 1923–4 and 1931–7. Prime Minister, 1937–40.

Chamberlain, Joseph (1836–1914) Politician. MP (Liberal and then Liberal Unionist), 1876–1914. President of the Board of Trade, 1880–5. President of the Local Government Board, 1886. Colonial Secretary, 1895–1903.

Chamberlain, (Joseph) Austen (1863–1937) KG, 1925. Politician. MP (Conservative), 1892–1937. Financial Secretary to the Treasury, 1900–2. Postmaster-General, 1902–3. Chancellor of the Exchequer, 1903–5. Chairman of the Royal Commission on Indian Finance and Currency, 1913. Secretary of State for India, 1915–17. Member of the War Cabinet, 1918. Chancellor of the Exchequer, 1919–21. Leader of the House of Commons, 1921–2. Foreign Secretary, 1924–9. First Lord of the Admiralty, 1931.

Childers, Hugh Culling Eardley (1827–96) Politician. MP (Liberal), 1860–85. First Lord of the Admiralty, 1868–71. Chancellor of the Duchy of Lancaster, 1872–3. Secretary for War, 1880–2. Chancellor of the Exchequer, 1882–5. Home Secretary, 1886.

Chilton, Henry Getty (1877–1954) KCMG, 1930. Diplomatic service, 1902. Counsellor, 1921–4, and Envoy Extraordinary and Minister Plenipotentiary, 1924–8, of Embassy in Washington. Signed the Bonds into which the British debt to the US Treasury was funded, 1923.

Chisholm, Hugh (1866–1924) Assistant editor (1892–7) and editor (1897–1900) of the *St. James's Gazette*; leader writer of the *Standard* (1900) and *The Times*; Editor of the 10th, 11th and 12th editions of the *Encyclopaedia Britannica*;

Director of Times Publishing, 1913–16; Financial Editor of *The Times*, 1913–20.

Churchill, Winston Leonard Spencer (1874–1965) KG, 1953. Politician, journalist and writer. Under-Secretary of State for the Colonies, 1906–8. President of the Board of Trade, 1908–10. Home Secretary, 1910–11. First Lord of the Admiralty, 1911–15. Chancellor of the Duchy of Lancaster, 1915. Minister of Munitions, 1917. Secretary of State for War and Air, 1919–21. Secretary of State for Air and the Colonies, 1921, and for the Colonies, 1921–2. Chancellor of the Exchequer, 1924–9. First Lord of the Admiralty, 1939–40. Prime Minister, 1940–45.

Clemenceau, Georges (1841–1929) French journalist and politician. Prime Minister and Minister of the Interior, 1906–9. Prime Minister, 1917–20.

Cokayne, Brien (1864–1932) KBE, 1917. Baron Cullen of Ashbourne, 1920. Banker. Director of the Bank of England, 1902–32, Deputy Governor, 1915–18, Governor, 1918–20.

Colwyn, Frederick Henry Smith (1859–1946) Bt., 1912. Baron, 1917. Indian rubber and cotton manufacturer. Chairman, Royal Commission on Income Tax, 1919, and the Committee on National Debt and Taxation, 1924–6.

Cravath, Paul D. (1861–1940) US lawyer. Advisory Counsel to IAC.

Crawford, Richard Frederick (1863–1919) KCMG, 1911. KBE, 1917. Minister Plenipotentiary in HM's diplomatic service. A Commissioner of Customs, 1904–11. Adviser to Turkish Ministry of Finance, 1911. Commercial Adviser to British Embassy, Washington, January 1915-December 1918.

Cripps, Edward Stewart (1885–1955) Kt, 1946. Partner in stockbrokers Mullens, Marshall, Steer, Lawford & Co. Deputy Government Broker, 1932–7. Senior Government Broker, 1937–50.

Crosby, Oscar Terry (1861–1947) US businessman and government official. US Army, 1882–7. Director, Belgian Relief Commission, 1915. Assistant Secretary of the Treasury, 1917. President of IAC, 1917–19.

Cunliffe, Walter (1855–1920) Baron, 1914. Banker. Director of the Bank of England, 1895, Deputy Governor, 1911–13, Governor, 1913–18. Chairman, the Committee on Currency and Foreign Exchanges after the War.

Curzon, George Nathaniel (1859–1925) Baron, 1898. Earl, 1911, and Marquess of Kedleston, 1921. MP (Conservative), 1886–98. Viceroy of India, 1898–1905. Lord Privy Seal, 1915–16. Lord President, 1916–19 and 1924–5. Foreign Secretary, 1919–24.

D'Abernon, Edgar Vincent (1857–1941) Kt., 1887. Baron, 1914. Viscount, 1926. Diplomat and public servant. Financial Adviser to Egyptian government, 1883–9. Governor, Imperial Ottoman Bank, Constantinople, 1889–97. MP (Conservative), 1899–1906. Ambassador to Berlin, 1920–6.

Dalton, Edward Hugh John Neale (1887–1962) Baron, 1960. Economist and politician. MP (Labour), 1924–31 and 1935–59. Sir Ernest Cassel Reader in Commerce, 1920–35, and Reader in Economics, University of London, 1925–36. Under-Secretary of State for Foreign Affairs, 1929–31. Minister for

Economic Warfare, 1940–2. President of the Board of Trade, 1942–5. Chancellor of the Exchequer, 1945–7.

Davies, Henry (1856–1936) Kt., 1917. Controller of the Savings Bank Department of the Post Office, 1906–19.

Davis, Norman Hezekiah (1878–1944) US banker and diplomat. Organised Trust Company of Cuba, 1905. Adviser to Secretary of Treasury on Foreign Loans, 1917–18. Special US Delegate to Spain and Representative of US Treasury in London and Paris, 1918. Financial Adviser to US Commission at the Peace Conference, 1919. Assistant Secretary of the US Treasury in charge of Foreign Loans Bureau, November 1919 to June 1920. Under-Secretary of State, June 1920 to March 1921. US Delegate to Geneva Economic Conference, 1927. Member, League of Nations Finance Committee, 1931. Member, US Delegation to Geneva Disarmament Conference, 1932, and Chairman of US Delegation, 1933. Head of US Delegation to London Naval Conference, 1935–6. Head of US delegation to Nine-Power Treaty Conference, Brussels, 1937.

Davison, Henry Pomeroy (1867–1922) Banker. Co-Founder, Bankers Trust, 1903. Vice-President, First National Bank, 1902. Partner, J. P. Morgan, 1909. Adviser to the National Monetary Commission, 1908. Chairman of the six-power Chinese Loan Conference. Chairman of the American Red Cross War Council, 1917–19.

Dawson, Geoffrey (1874–1944) Editor of *The Times*, 1912–19 and 1923–41. Colonial Office, 1898–1901. Private Secretary to Milner in South Africa, 1901–5. Editor of *Johannesburg Star*, 1905–10. Changed name from Robinson, 1917.

Derby, Edward George Villiers Stanley (1865–1948) 17th Earl. MP (Conservative), 1892–1906. Secretary of State for War, 1916–18 and 1922–4. Ambassador to France, 1918–20.

Devonshire, Victor Christian William Cavendish (1868–1938) 9th Duke. MP (Liberal Unionist), 1891–1908. Governor-General of Canada, 1916–21. Colonial Secretary, 1922–4.

Dodge, Marcellus Hartley (1881–1963) US manufacturer. Grandson of Marcellus Hartley, founder of the Union Metallic Cartridge Co. and President and owner of Remington Arms Co. Chairman, Remington Arms Co. Sometime director, Equitable Life. Married to daughter of William Rockefeller.

Ellerman, John Reeves (1862–1933) Bt., 1905. Shipowner. Controlling owner of Ellerman, City, Hall and Bucknall Lines.

Farrer, Gaspard (c. 1861–1946) Second Senior Partner, Baring Brothers & Co., 1902–35. Member of the LEC, 1916–19, the Cunliffe Committee, 1918–19, and of the Committee on Currency and Bank of England Note Issues, 1924–5.

Fisher, Norman Fenwick Warren (1879–1948) KCB, 1919. Inland Revenue, 1903; Deputy Chairman, 1914–18; Chairman, 1918–19. Permanent Secretary of the Treasury, 1919–39. Member of the Royal Commission on Income Tax, 1919.

Ford, Henry (1863–1947) US motor manufacturer. Helped found the Ford Motor Co., 1903. Introduced Model T motor car, 1908. Issued militant pacifist denunciations of war, summer 1915. Chartered liner to take peace delegates to a proposed 'Neutral Conference for Continuous Mediation' in Europe, December 1915. Attacked war profiteers, 1916.

Fordney, Joseph Warren (1853–1932) US politician and lumberman. Congressman, 1899–1923. Member, 1907–23, and Chairman, 1919–23, House Ways and Means Committee. Protectionist, giving his name to the Fordney–McCumber Act.

Foxwell, Herbert Somerton (1849–1936) Economist and bibliophile. Fellow of St. John's College, Cambridge. Professor of Political Economy, University College, London, 1881–1928.

François-Marsal, Frederic (1874–1958) French soldier, banker and politician. Finance minister, 1920 and 1924. Prime Minister, 1924.

Fraser, Drummond Drummond (1867–1929) KBE, 1920. Banker. Manager, London, City and Midland Bank, Manchester. Later, Managing Director of the Manchester, Liverpool and District Bank. Fellow and Member of the Council of the Royal Statistical Society. Vice-President of the Institute of Bankers. President of the Manchester Statistical Society and Manchester Bankers' Institute. Lecturer (1903–9), and Hon. Lecturer (1909–29) in Banking at Manchester University and co-founder of the Faculty of Commerce. Organiser of International Credits, League of Nations, 1921–2.

Fraser, William Robert (1891–1985) CB, 1939. KBE, 1944. KCB, 1952. Treasury, 1914. Principal, 1919. Assistant-Secretary, 1932. Principal Assistant Secretary, 1934–9. Various other government appointments, 1939–62.

Frick, Henry Clay (1849–1919) US coal owner, steel manufacturer, art collector and philanthropist.

Geddes, Auckland Campbell (1879–1954) Baron, 1942. Politician, diplomat and teacher of medicine. MP (Unionist), 1917–20. President of the Local Government Board, 1918–19. Minister of National Service and Reconstruction, 1919. President of the Board of Trade, 1919–20. Ambassador to Washington, 1920–3.

George, David Lloyd (1863–1945) Earl of Dwyfor, 1945. Politician. MP (Liberal), 1890–45. President of the Board of Trade, 1905–8. Chancellor of the Exchequer, 1908–15. Minister of Munitions, 1915–16. Secretary of State for War, 1916. Prime Minister, 1916–22. Leader of the Liberal Party, 1926–31, and of the Independent Liberal Group, 1931–5.

Gibson, Alfred H. (1880–1949) Northern District Manager of the Anglo-South American Bank, Bradford. Fellow of the Institute of Bankers and the Royal Statistical Society.

Gilbert, Seymour Parker (1892–1938) US banker. Counsel on War Loan matters, Office of the Secretary of the Treasury, 1918–20. Assistant Secretary of the Treasury, 1920–1, and Under-Secretary, 1921–3, in charge of fiscal affairs. Partner, Cravath, Henderson & de Gersdorff, 1923–4. Agent-General for Reparation Payments, 1924–30. Partner, J. P. Morgan, 1931–8. Director, Bankers Trust.

Gillett, George Masterman (1870–1939) Kt., 1931. MP (Labour), 1923–31, and (National Labour), 1931–5. Local government politician, 1900–24. Secretary of the Overseas Trade Department, 1929–31. Parliamentary Secretary, Ministry of Transport, 1931.

Gladstone, William Ewart (1809–98) Politician. Chancellor of the Exchequer, 1852–5, 1859–66, 1873–4, 1880–2. Prime Minister, 1868–74, 1880–5, 1886, 1892–4. Introduced Post Office Savings Bank Bill, 1861.

Gladstone, Samuel Steuart (1837–1909) Banker. Director of Peninsular and Oriental Steamship Co. Deputy Governor of the Bank England, 1897–9: Governor, 1899–1901.

Glass, Carter (1858–1946) US politician (Democrat) and newspaper publisher. Representative for Virginia, 1902–19. Chairman, House Committee on Banking and Currency. Floor Manager of the Federal Reserve Act 1913. Secretary of the Treasury, December 1918 to February 1920. Senator, 1920–46. Co-sponsor, the Glass–Steagal Act, 1933.

Glendyne, John Nivison (1878–1967) 2nd Baron, s. father 1930. Senior partner of R. Nivison & Co., stockbrokers.

Glendyne, Robert Nivison (1849–1930) Bt, 1914. Baron, 1922. Senior partner of R. Nivison & Co., stockbrokers.

Goldstone, Frank Walter (1870–1955) Kt., 1931. MP (Labour), 1910–18. General Secretary of the National Union of Teachers, 1924–31.

Goodenough, Frederick Crawfurd (1866–1934) General Manager, 1903, Director, 1913, and Chairman, 1917–34, Barclays Bank.

Goschen, George Joachim (1831–1907) Viscount, 1900. Politician, banker and writer. Partner in Fruhling & Goschen, bankers. MP (Liberal and Unionist), 1863–1900. Chancellor of the Duchy of Lancaster, 1866. President of the Poor Law Board, 1868–70. First Lord of the Admiralty, 1871–4. Chancellor of the Exchequer, 1887–92. First Lord of the Admiralty, 1895–1900.

Goschen, Sir Harry (William Henry Neville) (1865–1945) KBE, 1920. Bt., 1927. Partner, Cunliffe & Goschen, bankers. Director, 1901–1933, and Chairman, 1929–33, National Provincial Bank. Chairman, CLCB, 1917–18.

Gosling, Edward Lambert (? –1960) Partner in stockbrokers Mullens, Marshall, Steer, Lawford & Co. from 1897. Senior Government Broker, 1929–37.

Goulburn, Henry (1784–1856) Politician. Chief Secretary for Ireland, 1821–7. Home Secretary, 1834–5. Chancellor of the Exchequer, 1841–6.

Graham, William (1887–1932) Labour Member, Edinburgh Town Council, 1913–19. MP (Labour), 1918 to October 1931. Financial Secretary to the Treasury, January–November 1924. President of the Board of Trade, June 1929 to August 1931.

Grenfell, Edward Charles (1870–1941) Baron St. Just, 1935. Banker. Partner, Morgan Grenfell, 1904. Senior Resident Partner, 1905. MP (Conservative), 1922–35. Director of the Bank of England, 1905–40.

Guggenheim, Daniel (1856–1930) US financier and philanthropist. Entered family copper business, 1884. Helped form American Smelting & Refining

Co., 1901. Established many mining businesses overseas, including Chile, Canada, Bolivia, Belgian Congo and Angola.

Hamilton, Edward Walter (1847–1908) KCB, 1894. GCB, 1906. Treasury official. Private secretary to Lowe, 1872–3, and Gladstone, 1873–4 and 1882–5. Principal Clerk Finance Division, 1885. Assistant Financial Secretary, 1892. Joint Permanent Secretary (with George Murray), 1902–7.

Hamilton, Horace Perkins (1880–1971) KCB, 1921. Civil servant. Private secretary to the Chancellor of the Exchequer, 1912–18. Deputy Chairman of the Board of Inland Revenue, 1918–19. Chairman of the Board of Customs and Excise, 1919–27. Permanent Secretary of the Board of Trade, 1927–37. Permanent Under-Secretary of State for Scotland, 1936–7.

Hanson-Lawson, John. (?–1955) Member of the London Stock Exchange, 1919–55. Partner of stockbrokers, Pember & Boyle.

Harcourt, William George Granville Venables Vernon (1827–1904) Kt., 1873. Politician. MP (Liberal), 1868–1904. Home Secretary, 1880–5. Chancellor of the Exchequer, 1886 and 1892–5.

Harding, Warren Gamaliel (1865–1923) US President (Republican). Senator for Ohio, 1915–21. President, 1921 to August 1923.

Harding, William Procter Gould (1864–1930) US banker. Southern member of the Federal Reserve Board, 1914–22, and Governor, 1916–22. Managing Director, War Finance Corporation, 1918–19. Governor of the Federal Reserve Bank of Boston, 1923–30.

Harmsworth, Cecil Bisshopp (1869–1948) Baron, 1939. MP (Liberal), 1906–10 and 1911–22. Parliamentary Under-Secretary to the Home Office, February–May 1915. Parliamentary Private Secretary to McKenna and Runciman, 1915–17. Member of Lloyd George's Secretariat, 1917–19. Under-Secretary for Foreign Affairs, 1919–22.

Harrison, George Leslie (1887–1958) Deputy Governor, FRBNY, 1920–8. Governor, 1928–36. President, 1936–40.

Harvey, Ernest Musgrave (1867–1955) KBE, 1920. Bt., 1933. Entered Bank of England, 1885. Comptroller, 1925–8. Deputy Governor, 1929–36.

Harvey, George Brinton McClellan (1864–1928) US journalist, newspaper proprietor and diplomat. Broke with Wilson, 1911. Supported Harding's nomination, 1920. US Ambassador in London, 1921–3.

Harvey, (Henry) Paul (1869–1948) KCMG, 1911. Private Secretary to Secretary of State for War, 1895–1900. British Delegate to International Commission on Greek Finance, 1903. British Representative on International Commission for Control of Macedonian Finance, 1905. Financial Adviser to the Egyptian Government, 1907–12 and 1919–20. Chief Auditor of NHI, 1912. Secretary of the Air Board, 1916–18. Compiled and edited *The Oxford Companion to English Literature*, 1932, and *The Oxford Companion to Classical Literature*, 1937.

Hawtrey, George Ralph (1879–1975) Kt., 1956. Civil servant, economist and publicist. Treasury, 1904–45. Director of Financial Enquiries, 1919–45.

Headlam, Maurice Francis (1873–1956) Entered civil service, 1897. Treasury,

1899. Assistant Secretary, 1920–6. Comptroller-General of the NDO, 1927–38.

Hearst, William Randolph (1863–1951) Editor and proprietor of US newspapers and magazines. Founder of Yellow Journalism. US Congressman, Democrat, 1903–7. Bid for Presidential Democratic nomination, 1904. His newspapers were mildly pro-German and bitterly anti-British, 1914–17. Opposed US membership of League of Nations and participation in World Court.

Henderson, Arthur (1863–1935) Labour leader and politician. MP (Labour), 1903–18, 1919–22, 1923, 1924–31, 1933–5. Chairman of the Parliamentary Labour Party, 1908–10 and 1914–17. Secretary of the National Executive of the Labour Party, 1912–35. President of the Board of Education, 1915–16. Member of the War Cabinet, 1916–17. Secretary of State for Home Affairs, 1924. Secretary of State for Foreign Affairs, 1929–31. Leader of the Labour Party and of the Opposition, August–October 1931.

Herriot, Édouard (1872–1957) French Prime Minister, 1924–5, 1926 and 1932.

Hervey, George William (1845–1915) CB, 1898. KCB, 1906. Comptroller-General of the NDO, 1894–1910.

Hicks-Beach, Michael Edward (1837–1916) Bt., 1854. Viscount, 1906. Earl St. Aldwyn, 1914. Politician and banker. MP (Conservative), 1864–1906. Chief Secretary for Ireland, 1874–8 and 1886–7. Colonial Secretary, 1878–80. President of the Board of Trade, 1888–92. Chancellor of the Exchequer, 1885–6 and 1895–1902. Director, London Joint Stock Bank, 1905–16, and the Yorkshire Penny Bank, 1911–16. Chairman, CLCB, 1915–16.

Holden, Edward Hopkinson (1848–1919) Bt., 1909. Banker. MP (Liberal), 1906–10. Joint General Manager, 1891–7, managing director, 1898–1919, and Chairman, 1908–19, London City and Midland Bank.

Holland R. M. and Martin-Holland R., see Martin.

Homberg, Octave Marie Joseph (1876–1941) French diplomat and banker. Chairman or Director of many colonial banks and utilities. Member of Anglo-French Financial Mission to US, 1915.

Hoover, Herbert (1874–1964) US President (1929–33) (Republican). Mining engineer, 1895–1913. Chairman, Commission for Relief in Belgium, 1915–19. US Food Administrator, June 1917 to July 1919. Economic Director, Supreme Economic Council. Director General, American Relief Administration, 1919. Secretary of Commerce, 1921. Member, World War Foreign Debt Commission, 1922–7 .

Hopkins, Richard Valentine Nind (1880–1955) KCB, 1920. Board of Inland Revenue, 1916. Chairman, 1922. Controller of Finance and Supply Services of the Treasury, 1927–32. Second Secretary, 1932–42, Permanent Secretary, 1942–5.

Horne, Robert Stevenson (1871–1940) KBE, 1918. Viscount, 1937. Lawyer, politician and businessman. MP (Unionist), 1918–37. Minister of Labour, 1919–20. President of the Board of Trade, 1920–1. Chancellor of the Exchequer, 1921–2. Later was director of many public companies.

House, Edward Mandell (1858–1938) US presidential adviser. Democratic Party organiser, but never candidate for office. Personal representative of Wilson to Europe, 1914, 1915 and 1916. Chief agent in relations with the Allies, 1917–19. Appointed to represent US in Supreme War Council, 1917, and to negotiate Armistice, 1918. Member American Commission to negotiate peace, 1918–19.

Houston, David Franklin (1866–1940) US academic and politician. Secretary of Agriculture, 1913–20. Secretary of the Treasury, February 1920 to March 1921.

Hughes, Charles Evans (1862–1948) US lawyer and politician. Governor, New York State, 1907–10. Associate of the Supreme Court, 1910–16. Republican Presidential candidate, 1916. Secretary of State, 1921–5. Member World War Foreign Debt Commission, 1922–5. Chief Justice of the Supreme Court, 1930–41.

Hutcheson, Archibald (c. 1659–1740) Lawyer and economist. MP (Whig), 1713–27.

Inchcape, James Lyle Mackay (1852–1932) Baron Inchcape, 1911. Viscount Inchcape, 1924. Earl, 1929. Merchant, shipowner and public servant. Chairman, P & O and British India Steam Navigation Companies. Member of the Legislative Council of the Viceroy of India, 1897–1911. Member of the War Risks Advisory Committee. Chairman of the Blue Book Committee. Member of the Imperial Defence Committee, 1917. Member of the Committee on Currency and Foreign Exchanges after the War. Chairman of the Committee of Enquiry into Banking Amalgamations, 1918. Chairman of the Committee to control Banking Amalgamations, 1918–23.

Isaacs, Rufus Daniel (1860–1935) Baron Reading, 1914. Viscount, 1916. Earl, 1917. Marquess, 1926. Barrister and politician. MP (Liberal), 1904–13. Solicitor-General, 1910. Attorney-General, 1910–13. Lord Chief Justice, 1913–21. President of Anglo-French Financial Mission to US, 1915. Special envoy to the US, 1917. High Commissioner and Special Ambassador to the US, 1918. Viceroy and Governor-General of India, 1921–6. Secretary of State for Foreign Affairs in the first National Government, 1931.

Islington, John Poynder Dickson-Poynder (1866–1936) Baron, 1910. MP (Conservative), 1892–1910. Governor of New Zealand, 1910–12. Chairman, Royal Commission on Indian Public Services, 1912–14. Under-Secretary of State for the Colonies, 1914–15. Parliamentary Under-Secretary for India, 1915–18. Chairman of the National Savings Committee, 1920–6.

Johnson, Hiram Warren (1866–1945) US politician. A founder of the Progressive Party, 1912, and Progressive Governor of California, 1911–17. Senator, 1917–45. Opposed Treaty of Versailles, membership of the League of Nations and of the World Court, Hoover's moratorium on war debts. Violent enemy of British Empire. Sponsored Johnson Act, prohibiting loans to foreign governments in default on war debts, 1934.

Jones, William Kennedy (1865–1921) Journalist and newspaper proprietor. MP (Unionist), 1916–21. Joint founder of the *Daily Mail* and *Daily Mirror*.

News editor of the *Evening News*, 1894–1900. Responsible for the Publicity Department of the National War Savings Committee during the 1917 War Loan campaign. Director-General of Food Economy, the Ministry of Food, 1917–19.

Kent, Fred. I., (1869–1954) US banker. Bankers Trust, 1909. Deputy Governor, FRBNY, 1917–18. Director, Division of Foreign Exchange of Federal Reserve Board, until after the Armistice. A US representative on Organising Committee of Reparation Commission.

Keynes, John Maynard (1883–1946) Baron, 1942. Economist, journalist and civil servant. Treasury official, 1915–19. Member of the Royal Commission on Indian Finance and Currency, 1913–14, and of the Macmillan Committee, 1929–31. Principal Representative of the Treasury at the Paris Peace Conference, 1919. Treasury adviser, 1940–6. Director of the Bank of England, 1941–6.

Kiddy, Arthur William (1868–1950) Assistant City Editor of *Daily News*, 1891–9. City Editor of the *Standard*, 1899–1914. City Editor of the *Morning Post*, 1915–37. City Editor of the *Spectator*, 1917–37. London Financial Correspondent of the *New York Evening Post*, 1895–1933. Associate City Editor of the *Daily Telegraph* and the *Morning Post*, 1937–46; Editor of the *Bankers' Magazine*, 1895–1946.

Kindersley, Robert Molesworth (1871–1954) KBE, 1917. Baron, 1941. Banker. Member of The London Stock Exchange, 1901. Lazards, 1906; Chairman, 1919–53. Director of the Bank of England, 1914–46. Governor of the Hudson's Bay Company, 1916–25. Chairman of the War Savings Committee, 1916–20. President of the National Savings Committee, 1920–46.

Kitchin, Claude (1869–1923) US congressman (Democrat), 1911–23. Chairman of House Ways and Means Committee and Majority Leader, 1915–20. Ceased active politics, 1920.

Kylsant, Owen Cosby Philipps (1863–1937) KCMG, 1909. Baron, 1923. Shipowner. Chairman of the Royal Mail Steam Packet Company and the Union Castle Line. MP (Liberal) 1906–10, and (Conservative) 1916–22. Served as President of the London Chamber of Commerce and the Chamber of Shipping of the United Kingdom. Purchased the Oceanic Steam Navigation Company (the White Star Line), 1927. In 1931, charged with falsifying the accounts of the Royal Mail Line, and with circulating a false prospectus for which he received a year's imprisonment.

Lamont, Thomas William (1870–1948) US banker and philanthropist. Secretary, Treasurer and Vice-President, Bankers Trust, 1903–9. First National Bank, 1909–11. Partner, J. P. Morgan, 1911–33. Director, J. P. Morgan & Co. Inc., 1933–48, and Chairman, 1943–8. US Treasury Representative at Peace Conference, 1919.

Lansbury, George (1859–1940) Politician. MP (Labour), 1910–12 and 1922–40. Editor of the *Daily Herald*, 1913–22. First Commissioner of Works, 1929–31. Leader of the Labour Party and Leader of the Opposition, October 1931 to 1935.

Lansing, Robert (1864–1928) US politician and lawyer. Appeared as US counsel or agent in front of many international arbitration tribunals, 1892–1914. Counselor of the State Department, 1914–15. US Secretary of State, 1915–20.

Law, Andrew Bonar (1858–1923) Businessman and politician. MP (Conservative), 1900–10 and 1911–23. Parliamentary Secretary to the Board of Trade, 1902–6. Secretary of State for the Colonies and member of the War Committee, 1915–16. Chancellor of the Exchequer and Leader of the Commons, 1916–19. Member of the War Cabinet, 1916–19. Lord Privy Seal and Leader of the Commons 1919–21. Prime Minister, 1922–3. Unionist leader, 1911–21 and 1922–3.

Leaf, Walter (1852–1927) Banker and classicist. Director, London and Westminster Bank, London County and Westminster Bank, London County Westminster and Parr's, and Westminster Bank, 1891–1927. Chairman, London County Westminster and Parr's, later Westminster Bank, 1918–27. Chairman, CLCB, 1918–19. London County councillor, 1901–4. President, Institute of Bankers, 1919–21.

Le Bas, Hedley Francis (1868–1926) Kt., 1916. Businessman. Enlisted man in 15th Hussars *c.* 1886–93. Founded Caxton Publishing Co., 1899. Joint Hon. Secretary The Prince of Wales Fund. Member of the National War Savings Committee, 1916–25. According to Northcliffe, invented 'Your Country Needs You' when responsible for publicity for the War Office recruitment campaign, 1915. Responsible for the 1915 War Loan publicity and, initially, that for the 1917 loans.

Lefeaux, Leslie (1866–1962) Entered Bank of England, 1904. Assistant Principal, Discount Office, 1922–3. Auditor, 1923–1930. Deputy Chief Cashier, 1930–2. Assistant to the Governor, 1932–4. Governor of the Reserve Bank of New Zealand, 1934–40.

Leffingwell, Russell Cornell (1878–1960) US banker, lawyer and government official. Partner, Cravath & Henderson, 1907–17. Special counsel in charge of the first Liberty Loan, 1917. Assistant Secretary of the US Treasury for fiscal affairs, October 1917 to May 1920. Partner, Cravath, Henderson, Leffingwell & de Gersdorff, 1920–3. Partner J. P. Morgan, 1923–40. On incorporation in 1940 became Vice-Chairman and, in 1943, Chairman, of the Executive Committee. Chairman of the Board, 1948–50, and Vice-Chairman, 1950–5.

Leith-Ross, Frederick William (1887–1968) KCMG, 1930. Treasury official and banker. Treasury, 1909. Private Secretary to Asquith, 1911–13. British Representative on Finance Board of Reparation Commission, 1920–5. Deputy Controller of Finance, 1925–32. Chief Economic Adviser to HMG, 1932–46. Director of various banks, 1946–66.

Lever, Samuel (Hardman) (1869–1947) KCB, 1917. Bt., 1920. Chartered Accountant. Assistant Financial Secretary, Ministry of Munitions, 1915–16. Financial Secretary to the Treasury, 1916–17, and Joint Financial Secretary (with Baldwin), 1917–21. Head of Treasury Mission in US, 1917–18.

Lloyd George, see George.

Lubbock, Cecil (1872–1956) Director of the Bank of England, 1909–1942.

Deputy Governor, 1923–5 and 1927–9. Chairman of the Committee on the Maturity of Savings Certificates of the First Issue, 1925–6. Member of the Macmillan Committee, 1929–31.

McAdoo, William Gibbs (1863–1941) US politician and lawyer. Promoted Hudson River crossings, 1901–9. Wilson's campaign manager, 1912. Secretary of the Treasury, 1913–19. Contender for the Democratic nomination, 1924. US Senator, 1933–9. He was Wilson's son-in-law.

MacDonald, James Ramsay (1866–1937) Politician. MP (Labour), 1906–18, 1922–35 and 1936–7. Leader of the Labour Party, 1922–31, and of the National Labour Party, 1931–7. Prime Minister and Foreign Secretary, January–November 1924. Prime Minister, 1929–35.

McFadyean, Andrew (1887–1974) Kt., 1925. Entered Treasury, 1910. With Lever in USA, 1917. Treasury representative, Paris, 1919–20. Secretary to British Delegation to the Reparation Commission, 1920–22. General Secretary to Reparation Commission, 1922–4. Secretary to Dawes Committee, 1924.

McKellar, Kenneth Douglas (1869–1957) US politician (Democrat). Congressman (Tennessee), 1911–17. Senator, 1917–52.

McKenna, Reginald (1863–1943) Politician and barrister. MP (Liberal), 1895–1918. Financial Secretary to the Treasury, 1905. President, Board of Education, 1907–8. First Lord of the Admiralty, 1908–11. Home Secretary, 1911–15. Chancellor of the Exchequer, 1915–16. Chairman, London Joint City and Midland Bank, after 1923, the Midland Bank, 1919–43. Member of the Macmillan Committee, 1929–31.

Mackinder, Halford John (1861–47) Kt., 1920. MP (Unionist), 1910–22. Geographer and politician. Reader in Geography in University of London, 1900–23, and Professor, 1923–5. Director of the London School of Economics, 1903–8. Member of the National War Savings Committee, 1916. Member of the Royal Commission on Income Tax, 1919.

Macnamara, Thomas James (1861–1931) MP (Liberal), 1900–18, and (Coalition Liberal), 1918–24. Minister of Labour, 1920–2.

Mahon, Cyril Patrick (1882–1945) Entered Bank of England, 1901. Assistant Principal, Discount Office, 1916. Chief Cashier, 1926–9. Comptroller, 1929–32.

Mallet, Ernest (1863–1956) French banker. Regent of the Banque de France, 1906–36. Member of Anglo-French Financial Mission to US, 1915.

Martin-Holland, Robert (1872–1944) Banker. Director of Martins Bank and other companies. Hon. Secretary of the Bankers' Clearing House, 1905–35.

May, George Ernest (1871–1946) KBE, 1918. Bt., 1931. Baron, 1935. Actuary and officer of the Prudential Assurance Co. Manager of the American Dollar Securities Committee, 1915–18. Chairman of Committee on National Expenditure, 1931.

Mellon, Andrew William (1855–1937) US industrialist, banker and art collector. Secretary of the Treasury, 1921–32. Chairman, World War Foreign Debt Commission, 1922–7. US Ambassador in London, 1932–3.

Midleton, William St. John Fremantle Brodrick (1856–1942) Succeeded to

Viscountcy, 1907. Earl, 1920. Politician. MP (Conservative), 1880–1906. Various Under-Secretaryships, 1886–92, 1895–8 and 1898–1900. Secretary of State for War, 1900–3, and for India, 1903–5.

Millerand, Étienne Alexandre (1859–43) French lawyer and politician. Deputy (Socialist), 1885–1920. Various ministerial posts, 1899–1915. President of the Council and Foreign Minister, January 1920. President, 1920–4.

Milner, Alfred (1854–1925) KCB, 1895. Baron, 1901. Viscount, 1902. KG, 1921. High Commissioner for South Africa, 1897–1905. Member of the War Cabinet, 1916–18. Secretary for War, 1918–19. Colonial Secretary, 1919–21.

Money, Chiozza (1870–1944) Kt., 1915. Politician, economist and journalist. MP (Liberal), 1906–18. Defeated as a Labour candidate, 1918. Parliamentary-Secretary to Lloyd George, 1915–16. Parliamentary-Secretary to several other Ministers, 1916–17. Member of many Government advisory bodies, 1907–24.

Montagu, Edwin Samuel (1879–1924) Politician. MP (Liberal), 1906–22. Parliamentary Private Secretary to Asquith, 1906–10. Parliamentary Under-Secretary of State for India, 1910–14. Chancellor of the Duchy of Lancaster, February to May 1915 and January to July 1916. Financial Secretary to the Treasury, February 1914 to February 1915 and May 1915 to July 1916. Minister of Munitions, July to December 1916. Secretary of State for India, 1917–22. Chairman, Committee on War Loans for the Small Investor, 1915–16, and Committee of Enquiry into Savings Certificates and Local Loans, 1923.

Morgan, John ('Jack') Pierpont Jr. (1867–1943) US Banker. Partner, J. P. Morgan & Co., 1892. Senior partner, 1913–33. Chairman of J. P. Morgan & Co. Inc., 1933–43. Member of the Advisory Council of the Federal Reserve, 1914.

Mowatt, Francis (1837–1919) KCB, 1893. Treasury official, 1856–1903. Permanent Secretary, 1894–1903.

Murray, George Herbert (1849–1936) KCB, 1899. Civil servant. Foreign Office, 1873. Treasury, 1880. Chairman, Inland Revenue, 1897–9. Secretary, Post Office, 1899–1903. Joint Permanent Secretary to the Treasury (with William Hamilton until 1907), 1903–11.

Niemeyer, Otto Ernst (1883–1972) KCB, 1924. Treasury, 1906. Controller of Finance, 1922–7. Member of the Financial Committee of the League of Nations, 1922–37. Bank of England, 1927; Director, 1938–52.

Norman, Montagu Collet (1871–1950) Baron, 1944. Director of the Bank of England, 1907–44. Deputy-Governor, 1918–20. Governor, 1920–44.

Northcliffe, Alfred Charles William Harmsworth (1865–1922) Bt., 1904. Baron, 1905. Viscount, 1917. Newspaper proprietor. Owner of *The Times*, *Daily Mail*, *Evening News*, *Daily Mirror*. Chairman of the British War Mission to US, 1917. Director of Propaganda in Enemy Countries, 1917.

Northcote, Stafford Henry (1818–87) Earl of Iddesleigh, 1885. MP (Conservative), 1855–7 and 1858–85. President of the Board of Trade, 1866–7. Secretary of State for India, 1867–8. Chancellor of the Exchequer, 1874–80. Foreign Secretary, 1886–7.

Nott-Bower, Edmund Ernest (1853–1933) KCB, 1914. Barrister. Assistant

Secretary to the Board of Inland Revenue, 1895–1902. A Commissioner 1902–8. Deputy Chairman 1908–14. Chairman 1914–18.

Page, Walter Hines (1855–1918) US journalist, publisher and diplomat. US Ambassador to London, 1913–18.

Paish, George (1867–1957) Kt., 1912. Assistant Editor, 1894–1900, and Joint Editor, 1900–16, of *The Statist*. Special adviser to the Chancellor of the Exchequer, 1914–16.

Penrose, Boies (1860–1921) US politician. Senator, 1897–1921. Protectionist. Member, 19??-21, and Chairman, 1911–21, Senate Finance Committee.

Peppiatt, Kenneth Oswald (1893–1983) KBE, 1941. Bank of England, 1911. Norman's secretary, 1924. Principal of the Discount Office, 1928–34. Chief Cashier, 1934–49. Executive Director, 1949–57.

Pethick-Lawrence, Frederick William (1871–1961) Baron, 1945. Journalist and politician. MP (Labour), 1923–31 and 1935–45. Imprisoned as militant suffragette, 1912. Financial Secretary to the Treasury, 1929–31. Secretary of State for India and Burma, 1945–7.

Phillips, Frederick (1884–1943) KCMG, 1933. Treasury official. Assistant Secretary, 1919–27. Principal Assistant Secretary, 1927–31. Deputy Controller, 1931. Under-Secretary, 1932–9. Head of Treasury mission in US, 1940–3.

Pigou, Arthur Cecil (1877–1959) Professor of Political Economy in the University of Cambridge, 1908–43.

Pittman, Key (1872–1940) US Senator (Nevada), 1913–40. Lawyer, miner and minor politician, 1892–1913. Secretary, Senate Democratic caucus, 1913–17. US delegate to World Economic Conference, London, 1933. Chairman of Senate Foreign Relations Committee, 1933–40.

Plender, William Plender (1861–1946) Kt., 1911. Bt., 1923. Baron, 1931. Senior partner, Deloitte, Plender, Griffiths & Co., chartered accountants, 1904. Member of many public enquiries and government committees. Chairman of the City of London War Savings Association, 1916–41.

Poincaré, Raymond (1860–1934) French politician. Prime Minister, 1911–13. President, 1913–20. Prime Minister and Minister for Foreign Affairs, 1922–4. Minister of Finance, 1926–8. Prime Minister, 1926–9.

Polk, Frank Lyon (1871–1943) Lawyer, municipal reformer and diplomat. Counselor of the State Department, 1915–19. Under-Secretary of State, 1919–20. Directed US Peace Delegation, Paris, July–December 1919.

Priestley, Hugh W. (1890–1932) Partner in jobbers Wedd Jefferson. At the instigation of the Bank, moved in 1929 to become a partner in Mullens, Marshall, Steer, Lawford & Co. Deputy Government Broker, 1929–32.

Rathbone, Albert (1868–1943) US lawyer. New York bar, 1890. Assistant Secretary, US Treasury, in charge foreign loans, 1918–19. Financial Adviser to American Peace Commission and unofficial American representative on Reparation Commission, 1919–20.

Reading, see Isaacs.

Revelstoke, John Baring (1863–1929) Banker. Baron, 1897. Director of the Bank of England, 1898–1929, and a partner in Baring Brothers & Co.

Ricardo, David (1772–1823) Stockbroker, speculator and economist. MP (Independent), 1819–23.

Ritchie, Charles Thompson (1838–1906) Baron, 1905. Politician. MP (Conservative), 1874–92 and 1895–1905. President of the Local Government Board, 1886–92. President of the Board of Trade, 1895–1900. Home Secretary, 1900–2. Chancellor of the Exchequer, 1902–3.

Rockefeller, John Davison (1839–1937) US industrialist and philanthropist. Entered oil business, 1863. Helped found the Standard Oil Company of Ohio, 1870. By 1878, the Standard Alliance dominated the oil industry. Established University of Chicago, 1889, and Rockefeller Foundation, 1913.

Rockefeller, William (1841–1922) Industrialist and financier. Brother of John D. Rockefeller. Audacious promoter, especially of gas and railway companies. President, Standard Oil of New Jersey until 1911. Director of many companies, including Anaconda Copper Mining. Director, National City Bank, 1895–1922.

Rothermere, Harold Sidney Harmsworth (1868–1940) Bt., 1910. Baron, 1914. Viscount, 1919. Air Minister, 1917–18. Chief proprietor of the *Daily Mail*, *Daily Mirror*, *London Evening News*, *Weekly Dispatch* etc.

Rothschild, Nathanial Mayer (1840–1914) Bt., 1876. Baron, 1885. Banker, partner in N. M. Rothschild, London.

Rowe-Dutton, Ernest (1891–1965) KCMG, 1949. Treasury official. Entered Inland Revenue, 1914. Treasury, 1919. British Funding Mission to US, 1923. Financial Adviser to British Embassy in Berlin, 1928–32, and in Paris, 1934–9. Third Secretary of Treasury, 1947.

Runciman, Walter (1870–1949) Bt., 1906. Viscount, 1937. MP (Liberal), 1899–1900, 1902–18 and 1924–37. Financial Secretary to the Treasury, 1907–8. President of the Board of Education, 1908–11, and Agriculture, 1911–14, and Trade, 1914–16 and 1931–7.

Ryan, Gerald Hemmington (1861–1937) Kt., 1911. Bt., 1919. Chief General Manager, 1908–19, Director, 1920–37, and Chairman, 1920–31, Phoenix Assurance Co. President of the Institute of Actuaries, 1910–11. Chairman of the Treasury Committee on the working of the National Insurance Act 1916.

Schiff, Jacob Henry (1847–1920) US banker and philanthropist. Born Frankfurt. Emigrated to USA, 1865. Naturalised, 1870. Partner, Kuhn, Loeb & Co., 1875. Senior partner, 1885. Active in railway finance. Director of many companies, including Equitable Life, Western Union Telegraph and Wells Fargo.

Schooling, William (1860–1936) KBE, 1920. Author and journalist. Hon. Secretary Advisory Committee for War Savings, 1916. Member of the War Savings Committee and the National Savings Committee, 1916–33. Vice-Chairman of the National Savings Committee, 1920–33. Member of the Lubbock and Bradbury Committees.

Schuster, Felix (1854–1936) Bt., 1906. Banker and public servant. Governor of the Union Bank of London, afterwards the Union of London and Smith's Bank, 1895–1918. Director of the National Provincial Bank. Member of various government committees of enquiry and banking associations. Deputy Chairman of the CLCB, 1904–13 and 1924; Chairman, 1913–15 and 1925. Member of the LEC, 1915–19. Member of the Council of India, 1906–16.

Seely, John Edward Bernard (1868–47) Baron Mottistone, 1933. Soldier and politician. MP (Liberal), 1900–22 and 1923–4. Various minor ministerial posts, 1908–19. Secretary of State for War, 1912–14. Chairman of the National Savings Committee, 1926–43.

Shortt, Edward (1862–1935) Barrister. MP (Liberal), 1912–22. Chief Secretary for Ireland, 1918–19. Home Secretary, 1919–22.

Smoot, Reed (1862–1941) Businessman. Apostle of the Mormon Church, 1890. US Senator for Utah (Republican), 1903–33. Chairman, Finance Committee of the Senate, 1923. Opposed League of Nations. Protectionist, sponsoring 'Smoot–Hawley' Tariff. Member, World War Foreign Debt Commission, 1922–7.

Snowden, Philip (1864–1937) Viscount, 1931. Chairman of the Independent Labour Party, 1903–6 and 1917–20. MP (Labour), 1906–18 and 1922–31. Chancellor of the Exchequer, 1924 and 1929–31.

Spring-Rice, Cecil Arthur (1859–1918) KCMG, 1906. Diplomat. Chargé d'Affaires, Tehran, 1900. British Commissioner of Public Debt, Cairo, 1901. First Secretary, Petrograd, 1903–5. Minister to Persia, 1906–8. Minister to Sweden, 1908–12. Ambassador at Washington, 1912–18.

Steward, George Frederick (1884–1952) Journalist and public relations adviser. Employed by Ministry of Information and the Foreign Office from 1915. Attended many inter-war conferences as Press Officer. Treasury and 10 Downing Street, 1931. Chief Press Liaison Officer of HMG, 1937.

Strong, Benjamin (1872–1928) US banker. President, Bankers Trust, 1914. Governor, FRBNY, 1914–28.

Sutton, George (1869–1947) Bt., 1919. Joined *Answers*, 1889. Director, 1902, Vice-Chairman, 1913, and Chairman, 1915–26, Amalgamated Press. Managing Director Associated Newspapers, 1927, and Vice-Chairman, 1934–7. Director of Publicity, National War Bond campaign, 1917–19.

Taft, William Howard (1857–1930) US President and Chief Justice. Secretary of War, 1904. President (Republican), 1909–13. Defeated by Wilson, 1912. Kent Professor of Law, Yale, 1913–21. Chief Justice of the Supreme Court, 1921–30.

Thomas, James Henry (1874–1949) MP (Labour), 1910–31, and (National Labour), 1931–6. General Secretary of the National Union of Railwaymen, 1918–24 and 1925–31. Secretary of State for the Colonies, 1924. Lord Privy Seal, 1929–30. Secretary of State for the Dominions, 1930–1, and for the Dominions and Colonies in first National Government, and for the Dominions, 1931–5, and for the Colonies, 1935–6.

Tritton, Herbert Leslie Melville (1870–1940) Banker. Director, Barclays Bank, 1914–40. Chairman, Barclays DCO, 1934–7.

Turpin, William Gibbs (1854–1940) KCB, 1916. Civil servant. NDO, 1873. Assistant-Comptroller, 1904. Comptroller-General, 1910. Chairman of the American Dollar Securities Committee.

Vanderlip, Frank Arthur (1864–1937) US banker and government official. Journalist, 1889–97. Assistant-Secretary of the Treasury, 1897–1901. Vice-President, 1901–9, and President, 1909–19, National City Bank. Chairman of National War Savings Committee (US), 1917–18.

Vassar-Smith, Richard (1843–1922) Bt., 1917. Chairman of Lloyds Bank, 1909–22, and director of many other companies. Chairman of CLCB, 1916–17.

Wadsworth, Eliot (1876–1959) US businessman and public servant. Assistant Secretary to the Treasury, 1921–5. Secretary to the World War Foreign Debt Commission, 1922–5.

Walton, Sydney (1882–1964) Journalist. Attached to Ministry of Munitions and Ministry of Food during the Great War. Director of Publicity, Victory Loan Campaign, 1919.

Warburg, Paul Moritz (1868–1932) Banker. Partner, M. M. Warburg & Co., Hamburg, 1895–1914. Partner, Kuhn, Loeb & Co., 1902–14. US citizen, 1911. New York Member of the Federal Reserve Board, 1914–18. Member, Advisory Council, Federal Reserve Board, 1921–6.

Waterfield, (Alexander) Percival (1888–1965) Kt., 1944. Treasury, 1911. Principal Assistant Secretary, 1934–9. Various other government appointments, 1939–58.

Welby, Reginald Earle (1832–1915) Baron, 1894. Treasury official. Assistant Financial Secretary, 1880. Permanent Secretary, 1885–94. Chairman of the LCC, 1900.

White, William Thomas (1866–1955) KCMG, January 1916. Canadian lawyer, financier and politician. Vice-President and General Manager, National Trust Co. Minister of Finance, 1911–19.

Wilson, Woodrow (1856–1924) US politician. President of Princeton, 1902–10. Governor of New Jersey, 1911–13. President of US, 1913–21.

Wilson Smith, Henry (1904–78) KBE, 1945. Civil servant and industrialist. General Post Office, 1927–9. Treasury, 1930. Assistant Private Secretary to Chancellor of the Exchequer, 1932. Principal Private Secretary, 1940–2. Under-Secretary, Treasury, 1942–6. Permanent Secretary, Ministry of Defence, 1947–8.

Wise, Frederick (1871–1928) Kt., 1924. Stockbroker. MP (Unionist), 1920–8.

Wiseman, William George Eden (1885–1962) 10th Bt., 1893. Lived in North America, 1909–14. British army, 1914–16. Head of British Intelligence (MI6) in Washington, 1916–17. Met House 17 December 1916. Partner, Kuhn, Loeb & Co., 1929–62. Member, International Committee of Bankers on Mexico.

Withers, Hartley (1867–1950) Journalist. City Editor of *The Times*, 1905–10. City Editor of the *Morning Post*, 1910–11. Seligman Brothers, 1911. Director of Financial Enquiries, the Treasury, 1915–16. Editor of *The Economist*, 1916–21.

Wood, Thomas McKinnon, (1855–1927) MP (Liberal), 1906–18. Under-Secretary for Foreign Affairs, 1908–11. Secretary for Scotland, 1912–16. Financial Secretary to the Treasury, 1911–12, and July–December 1916.

Worthington-Evans, Laming (1868–1931) Bt., 1916. MP (Conservative), 1910–31. Minister of Blockade, 1918–19. Minister of Pensions, 1919–20. Minister without Portfolio, 1920–1. Secretary for War, 1921–2 and 1924–9. Postmaster-General, 1923–4. Assumed additional surname of Worthington, 1916.

Zimmerman, Artur (1864–1940) German diplomat. Entered Foreign Office, 1902 or 1903. Under-Secretary of State for Foreign Affairs, 1911–16. Secretary of State, November 1916 to August 1917.

Works consulted and the full references for material cited

Archives and unpublished sources held in the Public Record Office, Kew, Surrey, UK

Cabinet Office Records.
Colonial Office Records.
Foreign Office Records.
Inland Revenue Records.
National Debt Office Records.
Treasury Records.

Archives and unpublished sources held elsewhere

Asquith Manuscripts, Bodleian Library, Oxford, UK.
The Association of British Insurers: Minutes of the Life Offices Association, London, UK.
Baldwin Papers, Cambridge University Library, UK.
Bank of England Archives, London, UK.
Bonar Law Papers, House of Lords Record Office, London, UK.
Austen Chamberlain Papers, Birmingham University Library, UK.
Neville Chamberlain Papers, Birmingham University Library, UK.
Charles S. Hamlin Papers, Library of Congress, Washington DC, USA.
Committee of London Clearing Banks, Minutes, London, UK.
Davidson Papers, House of Lords Record Office, London, UK.
Hicks-Beach Papers, Gloucestershire Record Office, Gloucester, UK.
India Office Library, London, UK.
Lloyd George Papers, House of Lords Record Office, London, UK.
Lloyds TSB Group Archives, London, UK.
Edward M. House Papers, Yale University Library, CT, USA.
HSBC Group Archives (including Midland Bank Archives), London, UK.
Harding Papers, Library of Congress, Washington DC, USA.
Charles Evans Hughes Papers, Library of Congress, Washington DC, USA.
Thomas Lamont Papers, Harvard University Library, MA, USA.
Leffingwell Papers, Library of Congress, Washington DC, USA.
McKenna Papers, Churchill College, Cambridge, UK.
Edwin Montagu Papers, Trinity College, Cambridge, UK.
Milner Papers, Bodleian Library, Oxford, UK.

Montagu Norman Diaries, held in Bank of England Archives, London, UK.
Morgan Grenfell Papers, Deutsche Morgan Grenfell, London, UK.
Morgan Grenfell Papers, Guildhall, London, UK.
US National Archives, Department of the Treasury Records, Washington DC, USA.
National Archives of Canada, Ottawa, ON, Canada.
Northcliffe Papers, British Library, London, UK.
Pierpont Morgan Library, archives, New York, NY, USA.
Post Office Archives, London, UK.
The Rothschild Archive, London, UK.
Strong Papers, Federal Reserve Bank of New York, NY, USA.

UK government publications

Canadian Government Advances (Cd. 9234), TM, 14 November 1918.
Canadian Government Advances (Cmd. 583), TM, 1 January 1920.
Canadian Government Advances (Cmd. 616), TM, 1 March 1920 .
Canadian Government Advances (Cmd. 651), TM, 29 March 1920 .
Canadian Government Advances (Cmd. 2181), TM, 27 May 1924 .
Colonies and Protectorates (War Contributions) (Cmd. 798 and 897), TMs, 31 May and 4 August 1920.
Committee on Currency and Foreign Exchanges after the War ('Cunliffe Committee'), *First Interim Report* (Cd. 9182), 1918. *Final Report* (Cmd. 464), 1919.
Committee of Enquiry into Savings Certificates and Local Loans, etc. ('Second Montagu Committee'), *Report* (Cmd. 1865), 1923.
Committee on Finance and Industry ('Macmillan Committee'), *Report* (Cmd. 3897), 23 June 1931.
Committee on the Maturity of Savings Certificates of the First Issue ('Lubbock Committee'), *Interim and Final Reports* (Cmd. 2610), 1926.
Committee on Municipal Savings Banks ('Bradbury Committee'), *Report* (Cmd. 3014), 1928.
Committee on National Debt and Taxation ('Colwyn Committee'), *Report* (Cmd. 2800), 1927. *Appendices*, 1927. *Minutes of Evidence*, 1927.
Committee on National Expenditure ('May Committee'), *Report* (Cmd. 3920), 31 July 1931.
Committee on War Loans for the Small Investor ('First Montagu Committee'), *Interim Report* (Cd. 8146), 28 December 1915. *Report* (Cd. 8179), 26 January 1916.
Correspondence between His Majesty's Government and the United States Ambassador respecting Economic Rights in Mandated Territories (Cmd. 1226), 1921.
Exchequer Bills Forgery: Report of the Commissioners, British Parliamentary Papers, 1842, XVII (IV).
External Debt as on 31 March 1919, 31 March 1920, 31 March 1921 and 31 March 1922 (Cmd. 1648), 1922.
Finance Accounts of the United Kingdom, annual.
Financial Statements, annual.
Further Note Addressed by Her Majesty's Government in the United Kingdom to the United States Government relating to the British War Debt (Cmd. 4215), 1932.
Government Department(s) Securities, HCP, annual, 1879–1915.
Housing (Financial Assistance) Committee, *Final Report* (Ministry of Reconstruction) (Cd. 9238), 1919.

Inter-Allied Conferences on Reparations and Inter-Allied Debts held in London and Paris, December 1922 and January 1923 (Cmd. 1812), 1923.

Memorandum submitted by the Board of Inland Revenue to the Select Committee of the House of Commons on Increase of Wealth (War) (Cmd. 594), 1920.

National Debt: annual returns: Return showing the Aggregate Gross Liabilities of the State as represented by the nominal Funded Debt, Estimated Capital Value of Terminable Annuities, Unfunded Debt...at the close of each financial year, 1892–1934.

National Debt, annual return of debt repayment 1908–29. That to 1914 is HCP 219, 29 April 1915.

National Debt (Conversion and Redemption Operations) (HCP 153), 29 April 1890.

National Debt: History of the Earlier Years of the Funded Debt, from 1694 to 1786 (C. 9010), 1898.

National Debt: Report by the Secretary and Comptroller General of the Proceedings of the Commissioners for the Reduction of the National Debt from 1786 to 1890 (C. 6539), 1891.

National Savings Committee, *Annual Reports*, 1920–33.

National War Savings Committee, *Annual Reports*, 1917–19.

Papers relating to The Payment due from His Majesty's Government in the United Kingdom to the United States Government (Cmd. 4353), 1933.

Royal Commission on Unemployment Insurance, *First Report* (Cmd. 3872), 1 June 1931, and *Final Report*, Cmd. 4185, 27 October 1932.

Royal Commission on Income Tax, *Report* (Cd. 615), 1920. *Evidence, with Appendices and Index* (Cmd. 288), 1919.

Scottish War Savings Committee, *Annual Reports*, 1917 and 1918.

Select Committee on Increase of Wealth (War), *Report, Minutes and Appendices* (HCP 102), 13 May 1920.

Select Committee on Premium Bonds, *Report, Minutes and Appendices* (HCP 168), 16 January 1918.

Sinking Funds [annual accounts], 1904–14.

US government publications

Department of State (1926) *Papers relating to the Foreign Relations of the United States, 1917*. Washington DC: Government Printing Office.

Department of State (1932) *Papers Relating to the Foreign Relations of the United States, 1917*, Supplement 2, The World War, Volumes I and II. Washington DC: Government Printing Office.

Department of State (1933) *Papers Relating to the Foreign Relations of the United States, 1918*, Supplement 1, The World War, Volume II. Washington DC: Government Printing Office.

Department of State (1933) *Papers Relating to the Foreign Relations of the United States, 1918*, Supplement 2, The World War, Volume II. Washington DC: Government Printing Office.

Department of State (1938) *Papers Relating to the Foreign Relations of the United States, 1922*. Washington DC: Government Printing Office.

Department of State (1947) *Papers Relating to the Foreign Relations of the United States, 1919*, The Paris Peace Conference, Volume X. Washington DC: Government Printing Office.

Department of the Treasury, *Annual Reports of the Secretary of the Treasury on the State of the Finances, 1917–22*. Washington DC: Government Printing Office.
US House of Representatives, *Hearings before the Committee on Ways and Means*.
US Senate, *Hearings before the Committee on Finance*.
US Senate (1922) 67th Congress, 2nd Session, *United States Foreign Loans During the War and Since the War*. Senate Document No. 86.
US Senate (1937) 74th Congress, 2nd Session, *Special Committee on Investigation of the Munitions Industry, Hearings*, Vols. XXV–XXX. Washington DC: Government Printing Office.

Dominion of Canada publications

Canada, Public Accounts for the Fiscal years ending 1915–1921 (1916–22). Ottawa: King's Printer.

Books and articles

Adler, C. (1929) *Jacob H. Schiff: His Life and Letters,* 2 vols. London: Heinemann.
Anonymous (1920) *The State Debt and the National Capital*. London: Methuen.
Ashton, R. (1960) *The Crown and the Money Market 1603–1640*. Oxford: Clarendon Press.
Bagehot, W. (1965–86) *Collected Works*, Vols. I–XV. St. John-Stevas, N. (ed.). London: *The Economist*.
Bahlman, D.W.R. (ed.) (1993) *The Diary of Sir Edward Hamilton, 1885–1906*. Hull: University of Hull Press.
Barnett, L.M. (1985) *British Food Policy During the First World War*. London: Allen & Unwin.
Barnstaple, C.F. (1892) *Public Finance*. London: Macmillan.
Beaverbrook, M. (1928) *Politicians and the War 1914–16*, 2 vols. London: The Lane Publications.
Bell, A.C. (1961) *The Blockade of Germany, 1914–1918*, London: HMSO.
Beveridge, W.H. (1928) *British Food Control*. London: Oxford University Press.
Blake, R. (1955) *The Unknown Prime Minister: the Life and Times of Andrew Bonar Law 1858–1923*. London: Eyre & Spottiswoode.
Bliss, M., (1992) *A Canadian Millionaire: The Life and Business Times of Sir Joseph Flavelle, Bart. 1858–1939*. Toronto: Toronto University Press.
Boyle, A. (1967) *Montagu Norman: a Biography*. London: Cassell.
Brock, M. and Brock, E. (1982) *H. H. Asquith: Letters to Venetia Stanley*. Oxford: Oxford University Press.
Brown, W.A. (1940) *The International Gold Standard Re-interpreted*. New York: National Bureau of Economic Research.
Bullock, A. (1960) *The Life and Times of Ernest Bevin: Trade Union Leader 1881–1940*. London: Heinemann.
Burk, K. (ed.) (1982) *War and the State*. London: Allen & Unwin.
—— (1985) *Britain, America and the Sinews of War*. London: Allen & Unwin.
—— (1989) *Morgan Grenfell 1838–1938*. Oxford: Oxford University Press.
Buxton, S.C. (1888) *Finance and Politics: An Historical Study, 1783–1885*. London: Murray.

Cannadine, D. (1994) *Aspects of Aristocracy*. New Haven: Yale University Press.

Capie, F. and Webber, A. (1985) *A Monetary History of the United Kingdom, 1870–1982*, vol. I. London: Allen & Unwin.

Carnegie, D. (1925) *The History of Munitions Supply in Canada, 1914-1918*. London: Longmans, Green & Co.

Carosso, V.P. (1970) *Investment Banking in America: a History*. Cambridge, MA: Harvard University Press.

—— (1987) *The Morgans: Private International Bankers 1854–1913*. Cambridge, MA: Harvard University Press.

Chandler, A.D. and Salsbury, S. (1971) *Pierre S. du Pont and the Making of the Modern Corporation*. New York: Harper & Row.

Chandler, L.V. (1958) *Benjamin Strong: central banker*. Washington: Brookings Institution.

Clapham, J. (1944) *The Bank of England: A History*, 2 vols. Cambridge: Cambridge University Press.

Clarke, P. (1988) *The Keynesian Revolution in the Making 1924–36*. Oxford: Clarendon Press.

Clarke, S.V.O. (1967) *Central Bank Cooperation 1924–31*. New York: Federal Reserve Bank of New York.

Clay, H. (1957) *Lord Norman*. London: Macmillan.

Cline, C.A. (1963) *Recruits to Labour: The British Labour Party 1914–31*. Syracuse: Syracuse University Press.

Dalton, H. (1923) *The Capital Levy Explained*. London: Labour Publishing Co.

—— (1953) *Call Back Yesterday*. London: Frederick Muller.

Daunton, M.J. (1996) 'How to Pay for the War: State, Society and Taxation, 1917–24.' *English Historical Review*, September.

Day, J.E. (1912) *Stockbroker's Office Organisation, Management and Accounts*. London: Pitman.

Day, J.G. and Jamieson, A.T. (1980) *Institutional Investment*, Vol. II. London: The Institute Of Actuaries and the Faculty of Actuaries.

Documents on British Foreign Policy, 1919–39 (1947–55) First, Second and Third Series. London: HMSO.

Dickson, P.G.M. (1967) *The Financial Revolution in England: a study in the development of public credit, 1688–1756*. London: Macmillan.

Dictionary of American Biography (1928–) New York.

Dictionary of National Biography (1885–) Oxford: Oxford University Press.

Dilks, D. (1984) *Neville Chamberlain: 1869–1929*, vol. I. Cambridge: Cambridge University Press.

Easton, H.T. (1912) *Tate's Modern Cambist*. London: Effingham, Wilson.

Eichengreen, B. (1992) *Golden Fetters*. New York: Oxford University Press.

Feinstein, C.H. (1972) *National Income Expenditure and Output of the United Kingdom, 1855–1965*. Cambridge: Cambridge University Press.

Ferguson, N. (1995) *Paper & Iron*. Cambridge: Cambridge University Press.

Fink, C., Frohn, A. and Heideking, J. (eds) (1991) *Genoa, Rapallo, and European Reconstruction in 1922*. Cambridge: Cambridge University Press.

Fowler, W.B. (1969) *British–American Relations, 1917–18*. Princeton: Princeton University Press.

Foxwell, H.S. (1919) *Papers on Current Finance*. London: Macmillan.

Fraser, D.D. (1917) *Day-By-Day Government Borrowing in War-Time*. Manchester: Hebalo & Walker.

French, D. (1995) *The Strategy of the Lloyd George Coalition 1916–1918*. Oxford: Clarendon Press.
Garside, W.R. (1990) *British Unemployment, 1939–39: A Study in Public Policy*. Cambridge: Cambridge University Press.
George, D.L. (1933–6) *War Memoirs*, 6 vols. London: Nicolson & Watson.
Gilbert, C. (1970) *American Financing of World War I*. Connecticut: Greenwood Press.
Gilbert, M. (1979) *Winston S. Churchill, The Exchequer Years: 1922–29*, Companion. V. Part 1. London: Heinemann.
—— (1990) *Prophet of Truth*. London: Minerva.
Gillett Brothers Discount Company Ltd. (1976) *The Bill on London: or, the Finance of Trade by Bills of Exchange*. London: Methuen.
Goodhart, C.A.E. (1972) *The Business of Banking, 1891–1914*. London: The London School of Economics and Political Science.
Gregory, T.E. (1936) *The Westminster Bank Through a Century*, 2 vols. London: Westminster Bank.
Grigg, P.J. (1948) *Prejudice and Judgement*. London: Jonathan Cape.
Haig, R.M. (1929) *The Public Finances of Post-war France*. New York: Columbia University Press.
Hamilton, E.W. (1889) *An Account of the Operations under the National Debt Conversion Act, 1888, and the National Debt Redemption Act, 1889*. London: Eyre and Spottiswood.
Hamilton, H.P. (1951) 'Sir Warren Fisherand the Public Service'. *Public Administration*, XXLX, Spring.
Harding, W.P.G. (1925) *The Formative Period of the Federal Reserve System*. London: Constable.
Harley, C.K. (1976) 'Goschen's Conversion of the National Debt and the Yield on Consols'. *Economic History Review*, February.
Hargreaves, E.L. (1930) *The National Debt*. London: Arnold.
Heath, T.L. (1927) *The Treasury*. London: Putnam.
Hemery, J. A. (1988) 'The Emergence of Treasury Influence in British Foreign Policy 1914–21'. Unpublished Ph.D. thesis, Cambridge.
Higgs, H. (1914) *The Financial System of the United Kingdom*. London: Macmillan.
Hilton, J.P. (1927) *Britain's First Municipal Savings Bank: The Romance of a Great Achievement*. London: Blackfriars Press.
Hirst, F.W. and Allen, J.E. (1926) *British War Budgets*. London: Humphrey Milford.
Hobson, J.A. (1919) *Taxation in the New State*. London: Methuen.
Holmes, A.R. and Green, E. (1986) *Midland: 150 Years of Banking Business*. London: Batsford.
Horne, H.O. (1947) *A History of Savings Banks*. Oxford: Oxford University Press.
Howson, S.K. (1974) 'The Origins of Dear Money, 1919–20'. *Economic History Review*, February.
—— (1975) *Domestic Monetary Management in Britain 1919–38*. Cambridge: Cambridge University Press.
Howson, S.K. and Winch, D. (1977) *The Economic Advisory Council 1930–1939*. Cambridge: Cambridge University Press.
Imlah, A.H. (1958) *Economic Elements in the Pax Britannica*. Cambridge, MA: Harvard University Press.
James, H. (1986) *The German Slump: Politics and Economics 1924–1936*. Oxford: Clarendon Press.

Johnson, P.B. (1968) *Land Fit for Heroes: The Planning of British Reconstruction 1916–1919*. Chicago: University of Chicago Press.

Kent, B. (1989) *The Spoils of War: The Politics, Economics, and Diplomacy of Reparations 1918–1932*. Oxford: Clarendon Press.

Kent, M. (1976) *Oil and Empire: British Policy and Mesopotamian Oil 1900–20*. London: Clarendon Press.

Keynes, J.M. (1971–89) *The Collected Writings of John Maynard Keynes*, 30 vols. London: Macmillan.

King, F.H.H. (1988) *The Hongkong Bank between the Wars and the Bank Interned, 1919–1945: Return from Grandeur*. Cambridge: Cambridge University Press.

King, W.T.C. (1936) *History of the London Discount Market*. London: Routledge.

Kirkaldy, A.W. (ed.) (1915) *Credit, Industry, and the War*. London: Pitman.

Kirkaldy, A.W. (ed.) and Gibson A.H. (co-ordinator) (1921) *British Finance 1914–21*. London: Pitman.

Knox, F.A. (1940) 'Canadian War Finance'. *The Canadian Journal of Economics and Political Science*, May.

Labour Party (1927?) *Labour and the Nation*. London: The Labour Party.

Lamont, T.W. (1933) *Henry P. Davison: The Record of a Useful Life*. New York: Harper.

Leffler, M. (1972) 'The Origins of Republican War Debt Policy, 1921–23: A Case Study in the Applicability of the Open Door Interpretation'. *The Journal of American History*, December.

Leith-Ross, F.W. (1968) *Money Talks: Fifty Years of International Finance*. London: Hutchison.

Liddell Hart, B. (1970) *History of the First World War*. London: Cassell.

Livermore, S.W. (1966) *Woodrow Wilson and the War Congress, 1916–18*. Seattle: Washington Press.

Lloyd George, see George.

Mallet, B. (1913) *British Budgets 1887–88 to 1912–13*. London: Macmillan.

Mallet, B. and George C.O. (1929) *British Budgets 1913–14 to 1920–21*. London: Macmillan.

McEwen, J.M. (ed.) (1986) *The Riddell Diaries*. London: Athlone Press.

McFadyean, A. (1964) *Recollected in Tranquillity*. London: Pall Mall Press.

Michie, R.C. (1987) *The London and New York Stock Exchanges, 1850–1914*. London: Allen & Unwin.

Middlemas, K. (ed.) (1969) *Thomas Jones: Whitehall Diary*. I. 1916–1925. II. 1926–30. Oxford: Oxford University Press.

Middlemas, K. and Barnes, J. (1969) *Baldwin: a Biography*. London: Weidenfeld & Nicolson.

Ministry of Munitions (1921) *History of the Ministry of Munitions*, vol. II. London: HMSO.

Mitchell, B.R. and Deane, P. (1962) *Abstract of British Historical Statistics*. Cambridge: Cambridge University Press.

Moggridge, D.E. (1972) *British Monetary Policy 1924–1931: The Norman Conquest of $4.86*. Cambridge: Cambridge University Press.

Morgan, E.V. (1943) *The Theory and Practice of Central Banking, 1797–1913*. Cambridge: Cambridge University Press.

—— (1952) *Studies in British Financial Policy, 1914–25*. London: Macmillan.

Morgan, K.O. (1979) *Consensus and Disunity. The Lloyd George Coalition Government 1918–1922*. Oxford: Clarendon Press.

Morgan, K.O. and Morgan, J. (1980) *Portrait of a Progressive: The Political Career of Christopher, Viscount Addison*. Oxford: Clarendon Press.
Morley, J. (1903) *The Life of William Ewart Gladstone*, 3 vols. London: Macmillan.
Moulton, H.G. and Pasvolsky, L. (1932) *War Debts and World Prosperity*. Washington: Brookings Institution.
Myers, M.G. (1931) *The New York Money Market: Origins and Development*. I. Beckhart, B.H. (ed.). New York: Columbia University Press.
Neilson, K. (1984) *Strategy and Supply: The Anglo-Russian Alliance, 1914–17*. London: Allen & Unwin.
Newman, N. (1972) 'The Role of the Treasury in the Formation of British Economic Policy 1918–25'. Unpublished Ph.D. thesis, Durham.
Northcote, S.H. (1862) *Twenty Years of Financial Policy*. London: Saunders, Otley & Co.
O'Halpin, E. (1989) *Head of the Civil Service: A Study of Sir Warren Fisher*. London: Routledge.
Osborne, J.A.C. (1926) 'The Bank of England 1914–21'. I and II. Typed manuscript. London: Bank of England archives, ADM 2/1–2.
Palgrave, R.H.I. (ed.) (1894) *Dictionary of Political Economy*. London: Macmillan.
Pember & Boyle (1950) *British Government Securities in the Twentieth Century*, 2nd edn. London: privately published.
Pethick-Lawrence, F.W. (1918a) 'A Levy on Capital after the War'. *Contemporary Review*, March.
—— (1918b) *A Levy on Capital*. London: Allen & Unwin.
—— (1920) *The Capital Levy: How the Labour Party would Settle the War Debt*. London: The Labour Party.
—— (1943) *Fate Has Been Kind*. London: Hutchison.
Pigou, A.C. (1916) *The Economy & the Finance of the War*. London: Dent.
Pimlott, B. (1985) *Hugh Dalton*. London: Jonathan Caps.
Poley, A.P. and Carruthers Gould, F.H. (1907) *The History, Law, and Practice of the Stock Exchange*. London: Pitman.
Rhodes James, R.V. (1969) *Memoirs of a Conservative: J. C. C. Davison's Memoirs and Papers, 1910–37*. London: Weidenfeld & Nicolson.
Rignano, E. (1925) *The Social Significance of Death Duties*. London: Noel Douglas.
Roseveare, H. (1969) *The Treasury: The Evolution of a British Institution*. London: Allen Lane.
Roskill, S. (1970–4) *Hankey: Man of Secrets*, 3 vols. London: Collins.
Sabine, B.E.V. (1970) *British Budgets in Peace and War 1932–45*. London: Allen & Unwin.
Sayers, R.S. (1957) *Lloyds Bank in the History of English Ban*king. Oxford: Clarendon Press.
—— (1976) *The Bank of England 1891–1944*, 3 vols. Cambridge: Cambridge University Press.
Self, R.C. (ed.) (1995) *The Austen Chamberlain Diary Letters: the Correspondence of Sir Austen Chamberlain with his Sisters Hilda and Ida 1916–1937*. Camden, Fifth Series, V, Cambridge University Press for the Historical Society.
Short, M.E. (1985) 'The Politics of Personal Taxation: Budget-making in Britain, 1917–31'. Unpublished Ph.D. thesis, Cambridge.
Shwadran, B. (1955) *The Middle East, Oil and the Great Powers*. New York: Praeger.
Snowden, P. (1934) *An Autobiography*, 2 vols. London: Iver, Nicolson and Watson.
Spalding, W.F. (1924) *Eastern Exchange Currency and Finance*. London: Pitman.

Stamp, J.C. (1916) *British Incomes and Property: the application of official statistics to economic problems*. London: P. S. King.

Sykes, E. (1905) *Banking and Currency*. London: Butterworth.

Tansill, C.C. (1932) *The Purchase of the Danish West Indies*. Baltimore: Johns Hopkins Press.

Turner, J. (1992) *British Politics and the Great War: Coalition and Conflict 1915–18*. London: Yale University Press.

Vale, V. (1984) *The American Peril: Challenge to Britain on the North Atlantic 1901–4*. Manchester: Manchester University Press.

Van Cleveland, B.H. and Huertas, T.F. (1985) *Citibank 1812–1970*. Cambridge, MA: Harvard University Press.

Wainwright, D. (1990) *Government Broker: the story of an office and of Mullens & Co*. East Molesey, Surrey: Matham.

We Can Conquer Unemployment: Mr Lloyd George's Pledge (1929). London: Cassell.

Weems, F.C. (1923) *America and Munitions: The work of Messrs. J. P. Morgan & Co. in the World War*. New York: privately printed.

Whiting, R.C. (1987) 'The Labour Party, Capitalism and the National Debt', in Waller, P.J. (ed.) *Politics and Social Change in Modern Britain*. Brighton: Harvester.

Williamson, H.F. (1961) *Winchester: The Gun that Won the West*. New York: A. S. Barnes.

Williamson, P. (1992) *National Crisis and National Government: British Politics, the economy and Empire, 1926–1932*. Cambridge: Cambridge University Press.

Withers, H. (1915)*War and Lombard Street*. London: Smith, Elder & Co.

Who was Who (1897–) London: Black.

Who was Who in America (1943–) Chicago: Macmillan.

Newspapers and periodicals

Bankers' Magazine
The Citizen
Congressional Record
Contemporary Review
Daily Telegraph
The Economic Journal
The Economist
The Financial News
Foreign Affairs
Hansard
Evening Standard
The London Gazette
Manchester Guardian
The New York Times
The Old Lady
The Silver Bullet
The Statist
The Stock Exchange Official Year Book
The Times
The War Savings Journal

Contents of the documentary volumes *National Debt in Britain 1850–1930*[1]

National Debt: Report by the Secretary and Comptroller General of the Proceedings of the Commissioners for the Reduction of the National Debt, From 1786 to 31st March 1890, C. 6539, 1891.

Hargreaves, E.L., *The National Debt*, (London, Arnold, 1930).

Extracts from 'The Bank of England 1914–21,' Osborne, J.A.C. Vol. I, pp. 242–502, and Vol. II, pp. 1–87. Bank of England Archives, ADM 1 and 2.

Committee on National Debt and Taxation, *Report*, Cmd. 2800, 1927, and part of *Appendices*. Appendices XXII, XXIII and XXIV.

Return showing the Aggregate Gross Liabilities of the State as represented by the nominal Funded Debt, Estimated Capital Value of Terminable Annuities, Unfunded Debt...at the close of each financial year, ['National Debt: annual returns']. 1892 (HCP 332, 1892), 1914 (Cd. 7426), 1919 (Cmd. 429) and 1933 (Cmd. 4415).

Extracts from Pember & Boyle, *British Government Securities in the Twentieth Century*, (privately printed, London, second edition, 1950). Pp. 316–7, 325, 333, 343, 345–51.

'The Financing of Naval and Military Operations', John Bradbury, 12 February 1900. T170/31.

'Wars in South Africa and China (Cost and Expenditure)', (HCP 130, 1903).

'Memorandum by the Treasury as to the Financial Effort of Great Britain and the Cost of the War', Malcolm Ramsay, 2 December 1918. T171/149.

Hamilton, E. W., *Conversion and Redemption: An account of the Operations under the National Debt Conversion Act, 1888, and the National Debt Redemption Act, 1889*, (London, Eyre and Spottiswoode, 1889).

Extract from W. E. Gladstone's speech introducing Exchequer Bonds. *Hansard* (Commons), 8 April 1853, Cols 821–5.

'Floating Debt of the United Kingdom: Memorandum drawn up to give information requested by the Netherlands Government', 23 January 1878. Reginald Welby. T168/5.

Treasury and Exchequer Bills Act, 1877.

'Treasury Bills', anonymous Bank of England official, about 1930. Bank of England Archives, C40/399.

'Ways and Means Advances', Edward Hamilton, 30 August 1893. Bank of England Archives, G15/103.

1 *National Debt in Britain 1850–1930*, ed. by Jeremy Wormell. Nine volumes (London, Routledge/Thoemmes Press, 1999). ISBN 0-415-19578-0.

Documents relating to the decision to issue 2³/4 per cent National War Loan in 1900.
Murray to Eddie [Hamilton], 10 January 1900.
Hamilton to Chancellor, 12 January 1900.
'Opinion of Mr. Schuster', 20 January 1900.
'Further opinion of Mr. Schuster', 25 January 1900.
'Opinion of Mr. Andrew Hichins', 25 January 1900.
Note by Edward Hamilton, 27 January 1900.
'The Opinion of Rothschilds', 7 February 1900.
'Opinion of Sir E. Cassel', 7 February 1900.
'Note of Further Talk with Sir E. Cassel', 12 February 1900.
'Crimean War Loans', Edward Hamilton, 15 February 1900.
Edward Hamilton to Chancellor, 21 February 1900.
'Points for Discussion with Lord Rothschild' and Note of Interview on 27 February 1900.
Edward Hamilton to Chancellor, 3 March 1900.
Note of Edward Hamilton's meeting with Cassel, 5 March 1900.
'Memod. of position of affairs after the Budget', 7 March 1900. Edward Hamilton, 7 March 1900.
Edward Hamilton, Note made on Thursday 8 March 1900.
Ditto, 9 March 1900.
Ditto, 15 March 1900.
T168/87.
Extract from Higgs, H., *The Financial System of the United Kingdom* (London, Macmillan, 1914), Chapter VIII.
'War Loans', William Turpin, 31 August 1914. T170/31.
Extract from R.S. Sayers, *The Bank of England 1891–1944* (Cambridge, 1976), Vol. II, pp. 430–47.
Sayers's redraft of pp. 438–9 of the above. Bank of England Archives, M 124.27.
'War Loan Conversion', Richard Hopkins, January 1933. T212/2.
Prospectuses.
'National Debt (Conversion) Act, 1888', March 1888.
2³/4 per cent National War Loan, 1910, 9 March 1900.
2³/4 per cent Exchequer Bonds 1906/15, 12 April 1905.
4¹/2 per cent War Loan 1925/45, 21 June 1915.
5 per cent War Loan 1929/47 and 4 per cent War Loan 1929/42, 11 January 1917.
Continuation Notice for the above, 30 June 1932.
National War Bonds, First Series, 1 October 1917.
4 per cent Funding Loan, 1960–90, 12 June 1919.
4 per cent Victory Bonds, 12 June 1919.
5–15 Year Treasury Bonds, 1925–35, 30 April 1920.
War Loans for Small Investors: Copy of an Interim Report of the Committee on War Loans for the Small Investor, and of a Treasury Minute therein, dated 28 December 1915 (Cd. 8146), 1915.
War Loans for Small Investors, Cd. 8179, 1916.
National War Savings Committee, *First Annual Report*, 1 March 1917 (Cd. 8516); *Second Annual Report*, 1 June 1918, Cd. 9112; *Third Annual Report*, 2 June 1919 (Cmd. 194).
Extract from 'A Short History of the Development of the System of Transfer of British Government Stocks by Instrument in Writing', George Blunden, November 1952, pp. 1 to 6. Bank of England Archives, AC4/1.

Extract from Morgan, E. V., *Studies in British Financial Policy 1914–25* (London, Macmillan, 1952), pp. 122–137,

Extracts from *British Government Securities in the Twentieth Century* (privately printed, London, second edition, 1950), pp. 334 and 335.

'British Transactions in America', Thomas Chadwick, 1922. T170/134.

Extract from Burk, K., *Britain, America and the Sinews of War 1914–1918* (Allen & Unwin, London, 1985., pp. 67–75.

Documents relating to the Anglo-French Loan.

Prospectus for '$500,000,000 Anglo-French Five Year External Loan', 1 November 1915.

'From Recognised Authorities Figures have been Compiled Showing Some of the Essential facts About Great Britain and France'.

'$500,000,000 Anglo-French Loan', letter from J. P. Morgan, Agents for Syndicate Managers.

Syndicate Agreement for the above, 5 October 1915.

Pierpont Morgan Library Archives, Syndicate Books.

Jack Morgan to Edward Grenfell, 16 November 1915. Pierpont Morgan Library Archives, Box 12.

Thomas Lamont, 'Memo. of Chicago Trip', November 1915. Harvard University Library, Lamont papers, II, 81–15.

'Report of the American Dollar Securities Committee', letter to the Chancellor, 4 June 1919. T170/130.

Prospectuses for public issues in New York, 1916–1919.

$250m. United Kingdom of Great Britain and Ireland Two-Year 5% Secured Loan Gold Notes, 22 August 1916.

$300m. United Kingdom of Great Britain and Ireland 5½% Secured Loan Gold Notes, 30 October 1916.

$300m. United Kingdom of Great Britain and Ireland One-Year and Two-Year 5½% Secured Loan Gold Notes, 22 January 1917.

$250m. United Kingdom of Great Britain and Ireland, Ten-Year 5½% Convertible Gold Bonds 1 August 1929 and Three-Year Convertible Gold Notes due 1 November 1922, 23 November 1919.

The First Liberty Bond Act, approved 24 April 1917.

The Second Liberty Bond Act, approved 24 September 1917.

The Third Liberty Bond Act, approved 4 April 1918.

A copy of a 'certificate of indebtedness'. T160/7/F220/1.

'An Act to Create a commission authorized under certain conditions to refund or convert obligations of foreign Governments held by the United States of America…', commonly known as 'The World War Foreign Debt Commission'. Approved 9 February 1922.

An Act to amend the above, commonly known as 'The British Loan Agreement'. Approved 28 February 1923.

Despatch to the Representatives of France, Italy, Serb-Croat State, Roumania, Portugal and Greece at London respecting War Debts, commonly known as 'The Balfour Note', Cmd. 1737, 1922.

American Debt: Arrangements for the Funding of the British Debt to the United States of America (Cmd. 1912), 1923.

Extract from Middlemas, K. and Barnes, J., *Baldwin* (London, Weidenfeld & Nicholson, 1969), pp. 136–48.

Extract from *Congressional Record*, 7 February 1923, pp. 3212–4.

Ditto, 9 February 1923, pp. 3302–4.

Government Department[s] Securities, Return of Classified Amounts of various Government Securities held by Several Government Accountants and Departments on 31st day of March 1879, HCP 376, 1879.

Ditto, 1899, HCP 147, 1899.

Ditto, 1915, HCP 247, 1915.

Extract from Stafford Northcote's speech introducing his sinking fund. *Hansard* (Commons), 15 April 1875, Cols 1037–42.

Sinking Fund Act, 1875.

'Memorandum on the Sinking Funds', Edward Hamilton, 16 October 1896. T168/11.

'The Sinking Fund', Edward Hamilton, 30 September 1897. T168/86.

National Debt Charges, Treasury Minute, 11 April 1899. T168/86.

'The Financial Outlook vis à vis the City', Edward Hamilton, 9 October 1903. T168/61.

'The Unfunded Debt', Austen Chamberlain, 14 February 1905. T168/94.

'Sinking Fund', Edward Hamilton, 25 September 1905. T168/94.

'The National Debt and Sinking Fund', Edward Hamilton, 1 January 1906. T168/94.

Extract from H. H. Asquith's budget speech introducing a new approach to the repayment of Debt. *Hansard*, 30 April 1906, Cols 288–95.

'Permanent Debt Charge,' Otto Niemeyer, 11 February 1921. T171/196.

Extracts from *British Government Securities in the Twentieth Century* (privately printed, London, second edition, 1950), pp. 522, 523, 524, 525, 533, 534, 535, 536, 537, 540, 541, 542, 543, 544, 545, 546 and 547.

Extract from Stanley Baldwin's budget speech introducing his sinking fund. *Hansard* (Commons), 16 April 1923, Cols 1729–31.

Extract from Winston Churchill's budget speech introducing his Fixed Debt Charge. *Hansard* (Commons), 24 April 1928, Cols 825–30.

Finance Act, 1928, sections 23 and 26.

Trades Union Congress, Birmingham, September 1916. 'Resolutions to be Submitted to the Chancellor of the Exchequer.' T171/167.

Deputation from the Trades Union Congress – Birmingham to the Chancellor of the Exchequer, 15 February 1917. T171/167, ff. 11–16.

Two memoranda, both called 'Conscription of Wealth.' (1) 12 November 1917, (2) 14 January 1918, John Bradbury. T171/167.

Articles in *The Economic Journal*.

Pigou, A. C., June 1918, 'A Special Levy to Discharge War Debt,' pp. 135–56.

Arnold, S., ditto, 'A Capital Levy: The Problems of Realisation and Valuation', pp. 157–66.

Scott, W. R., September 1918, 'Some Aspects of the Proposed Capital Levy', pp. 247–67.

Stamp, J., ditto, 'An Estimate of the Capital Wealth of the United Kingdom in Private Hands,' pp. 276–86.

The Labour Party, F. W. Pethick Lawrence, *The Capital Levy (How the Labour Party would Settle the War Debt)*, 1919.

'Proposed Capital Tax in France', Board of Inland Revenue, 15 March 1919. IR/63/86, ff. 297–303.

'Capital Taxation,' Board of Inland Revenue, 19 May 1919. IR/63/86, ff. 280–5.

Select Committee on Wealth (War) together with the Proceedings of the Committee, Minutes of Evidence and Appendices, *Report*, HCP 102, 1920.

Minutes of the Cabinet discussion on the Levy on War Wealth, 2 June 1920. Cab. 23/21, Cabinet 31(20), (Conclusion 5), ff. 168–176.

Keynes' Evidence-in-Chief and extract from his evidence to the Committee on National Debt and Taxation. Evidence, II, pp. 534–5.

Index

For Product Safety Concerns and Information please contact our EU representative GPSR@taylorandfrancis.com
Taylor & Francis Verlag GmbH, Kaufingerstraße 24, 80331 München, Germany

www.ingramcontent.com/pod-product-compliance
Lightning Source LLC
LaVergne TN
LVHW021040011026
849160LV00007BA/207
9781138995550